Collins EURO
ESSENTIAL ROAD ATLAS

Published by Collins
An imprint of HarperCollins Publishers
Westerhill Road
Bishopbriggs
Glasgow G64 2QT
www.harpercollins.co.uk

First published 2004

New edition 2020

A catalogue record for this book is available from the British Library

ISBN 978-0-00-837433-4

10 9 8 7 6 5 4 3 2 1

Printed and bound by Imago Malaysia

All mapping in this atlas is generated from Collins Bartholomew digital databases. Collins Bartholomew, the UK's leading independent geographical information supplier, can provide a digital, custom, and premium mapping service to a variety of markets.
For further information:
e-mail: collinsbartholomew@harpercollins.co.uk
or visit our website at: www.collinsbartholomew.com

If you would like to comment on any aspect of this book, please contact us at the above address or online.
e-mail: collinsmaps@harpercollins.co.uk

facebook.com/collinsref @collins_ref

Contents

Distance map and chart
ii – iii Map symbols
iii Map symbols and country identifiers
iv International road signs and travel web links
v Key to map pages
vi – xvii Route planning maps 1:4 654 000
2 – 181 Road maps 1:1 000 000
182 – 187 Road maps 1:750 000
188 – 191 Index to place names 1:750 000
192 – 207 City through-route maps
192 Amsterdam, Athina, Barcelona, Belfast
193 Beograd, Berlin, Bern, Birmingham
194 Bonn, Bordeaux, Bratislava, Brussel/Bruxelles
195 București, Budapest, Cardiff, Chișinau
196 Dublin, Edinburgh, Firenze, Frankfurt
197 Glasgow, Göteborg, Den Haag, Hamburg
198 Helsinki, İstanbul, København, Köln
199 Leipzig, Lisboa, Ljubljana, London
200 Lyon, Madrid, Manchester, Marseille
201 Milano, München, Napoli, Oslo
202 Palermo, Paris, Podgorica, Praha
203 Rīga, Roma, Rotterdam, Sankt Peterburg
204 Sarajevo, Sevilla, Skopje, Sofia
205 Stockholm, Strasbourg, Tallinn, Torino
206 Toulouse, Valencia, Venezia, Vilnius
207 Warszawa, Wien, Zagreb, Zürich
208 – 211 City street plans
208 Amsterdam, Athina, Berlin, Bern
209 Brussel/Bruxelles, Dublin, Helsinki, København
210 Lisboa, London, Madrid, Oslo
211 Paris, Roma, Stockholm, Wien
212 – 272 Index to place names 1:1 000 000
Driving information and web links

Map symbols

	Road maps	Carte routière	Strassenkarten
E55	Euro route number	Route européenne	Europastrasse
A13	Motorway	Autoroute	Autobahn
	Motorway – toll	Autoroute à péage	Gebührenpflichtige Autobahn
	Motorway – toll (vignette)	Autoroute à péage (vignette)	Gebührenpflichtige Autobahn (Vignette)
37	Motorway junction – full access	Echangeur d'autoroute avec accès libre	Autobahnauffahrt mit vollem Zugang
12	Motorway junction – restricted access	Echangeur d'autoroute avec accès limité	Autobahnauffahrt mit beschränktem Zugang
	Motorway services	Aire de service sur autoroute	Autobahnservicestelle
309	Main road – dual carriageway	Route principale à chaussées séparées	Hauptstrasse – Zweispurig
	Main road – single carriageway	Route principale à une seule chaussée	Hauptstrasse – Einspurig
516	Secondary road – dual carriageway	Route secondaire à chaussées séparées	Zweispurige Nebenstrasse
	Secondary road – single carriageway	Route secondaire à seule chaussée	Einspurige Nebenstrasse
	Other road	Autre route	Andere Strasse
	Motorway tunnel	Autoroute tunnel	Autobahntunnel
	Main road tunnel	Route principale tunnel	Hauptstrassetunnel
	Motorway/road under construction	Autoroute/route en construction	Autobahn/Strasse im Bau
	Road toll	Route à péage	Gebührenpflichtige Strasse
16 / 10	Distance marker Distances in kilometres Distances in miles (UK only)	Marquage des distances Distances en kilomètres Distances en miles (GB)	Distanz-Markierung Distanzen in Kilometern Distanzen in Meilen (GB)
	Steep hill	Colline abrupte	Steile Strasse
2587	Mountain pass (height in metres)	Col (Altitude en mètres)	Pass (Höhe in Metern)
	Scenic route	Parcours pittoresque	Landschaftlich schöne Strecke
	International airport	Aéroport international	Internationaler Flughafen
	Car transport by rail	Transport des autos par voie ferrée	Autotransport per Bahn
	Railway	Chemin de fer	Eisenbahn
	Tunnel	Tunnel	Tunnel
	Funicular railway	Funiculaire	Seilbahn
Rotterdam	Car ferry	Bac pour autos	Autofähre
2587	Summit (height in metres)	Sommet (Altitude en mètres)	Berg (Höhe in Metern)
	Volcano	Volcan	Vulkan
	Canal	Canal	Kanal
	International boundary	Frontière d'Etat	Landesgrenze
	Disputed International boundary	Frontière litigieuse	Umstrittene Staatsgrenze
	Disputed Territory boundary	Frontière territoriale contestée	Umstrittene Gebietsgrenze
GB	Country abbreviation	Abréviation du pays	Regionsgrenze
	Urban area	Zone urbaine	Stadtgebiet
28	Adjoining page indicator	Indication de la page contigüe	Randhinweis auf Folgekarte
	National Park	Parc national	Nationalpark

1:1 000 000

1 centimetre to 10 kilometres — 0, 10, 20, 30, 40, 50, 60, 70, 80 km

1 inch to 16 miles — 0, 10, 20, 30, 40, 50 miles

	City maps and plans	Plans de ville	Stadtpläne
★	Place of interest	Site d'interêt	Sehenswerter Ort
	Railway station	Gare	Bahnhof
	Parkland	Espace vert	Parkland
	Woodland	Espace boisé	Waldland
	General place of interest	Site d'interêt général	Sehenswerter Ort
	Academic/Municipal building	Établissement scolaire/installations municipales	Akademisches/Öffentliches Gebäude
	Place of worship	Lieu de culte	Andachtsstätte
	Transport location	Infrastructure de transport	Verkehrsanbindung

Places of interest

Museum and Art Gallery	Musée / Gallerie d'art	Museum / Kunstgalerie
Castle	Château	Burg / Schloss
Historic building	Monument historique	historisches Gebäude
Historic site	Site historique	historische Stätte
Monument	Monument	Denkmal
Religious site	Site religieux	religiöse Stätte
Aquarium / Sea life centre	Aquarium / Parc Marin	Aquarium
Arboretum	Arboretum	Arboretum, Baumschule
Botanic garden (National)	Jardin botanique national	botanischer Garten
Natural place of interest (other site)	Réserve naturelle	landschaftlich interessanter Ort
Zoo / Safari park / Wildlife park	Parc Safari / Réserve sauvage / Zoo	Safaripark / Wildreservat / Zoo
Other site	Autres sites	Touristenattraktion
Theme park	Parc à thème	Freizeitpark
World Heritage site	Patrimoine Mondial	Weltkulturerbe
Athletics stadium (International)	Stade international d'athlétisme	internationales Leichtathletik Stadion
Football stadium (Major)	Stade de football	Fußballstadion
Golf course (International)	Parcours de golf international	internationaler Golfplatz
Grand Prix circuit (Formula 1) / Motor racing venue / MotoGP circuit	Circuit auto-moto	Autodrom
Rugby ground (International - Six Nations)	Stade de rugby	internationales Rugbystadion
International sports venue	Autre manifestation sportive	internationale Sportanlage
Tennis venue	Court de tennis	Tennis
Valcotos Winter sports resort	Sports d'hiver	Wintersport

Country identifiers

A	Austria	Autriche	Österreich		I	Italy	Italie	Italien	
AL	Albania	Albanie	Albanien		IRL	Ireland	Irlande	Irland	
AND	Andorra	Andorre	Andorra		IS	Iceland	Islande	Island	
B	Belgium	Belgique	Belgien		L	Luxembourg	Luxembourg	Luxemburg	
BG	Bulgaria	Bulgarie	Bulgarien		LT	Lithuania	Lituanie	Litauen	
BIH	Bosnia and Herzegovina	Bosnie-et-Herzégovine	Bosnien und Herzegowina		LV	Latvia	Lettonie	Lettland	
BY	Belarus	Bélarus	Belarus		M	Malta	Malte	Malta	
CH	Switzerland	Suisse	Schweiz		MA	Morocco	Maroc	Marokko	
CY	Cyprus	Chypre	Zypern		MC	Monaco	Monaco	Monaco	
CZ	Czechia (Czech Republic)	République tchèque	Tschechische Republik		MD	Moldova	Moldavie	Moldawien	
D	Germany	Allemagne	Deutschland		MNE	Montenegro	Monténégro	Montenegro	
DK	Denmark	Danemark	Dänemark		N	Norway	Norvège	Norwegen	
DZ	Algeria	Algérie	Algerien		NL	Netherlands	Pays-Bas	Niederlande	
E	Spain	Espagne	Spanien		NMK	North Macedonia	Macédoine du Nord	Nordmazedonien	
EST	Estonia	Estonie	Estland		P	Portugal	Portugal	Portugal	
F	France	France	Frankreich		PL	Poland	Pologne	Polen	
FIN	Finland	Finlande	Finnland		RKS	Kosovo	Kosovo	Kosovo	
FL	Liechtenstein	Liechtenstein	Liechtenstein		RO	Romania	Roumanie	Rumänien	
FO	Faroe Islands	Iles Féroé	Färöer-Inseln		RSM	San Marino	Saint-Marin	San Marino	
GB	United Kingdom GB & NI	Grande-Bretagne	Grossbritannien		RUS	Russia	Russie	Russland	
GBA	Alderney	Alderney	Alderney		S	Sweden	Suède	Schweden	
GBG	Guernsey	Guernsey	Guernsey		SK	Slovakia	République slovaque	Slowakei	
GBJ	Jersey	Jersey	Jersey		SLO	Slovenia	Slovénie	Slowenien	
GBM	Isle of Man	île de Man	Insel Man		SRB	Serbia	Sérbie	Serbien	
GBZ	Gibraltar	Gibraltar	Gibraltar		TN	Tunisia	Tunisie	Tunisien	
GR	Greece	Grèce	Griechenland		TR	Turkey	Turquie	Türkei	
H	Hungary	Hongrie	Ungarn		UA	Ukraine	Ukraine	Ukraine	
HR	Croatia	Croatie	Kroatien

International road signs and travel web links

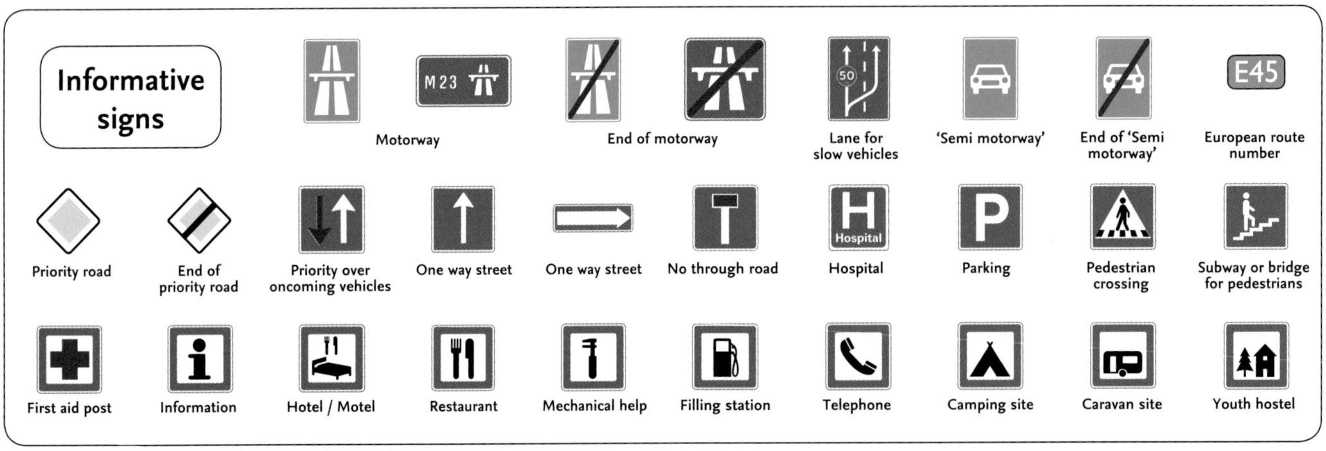

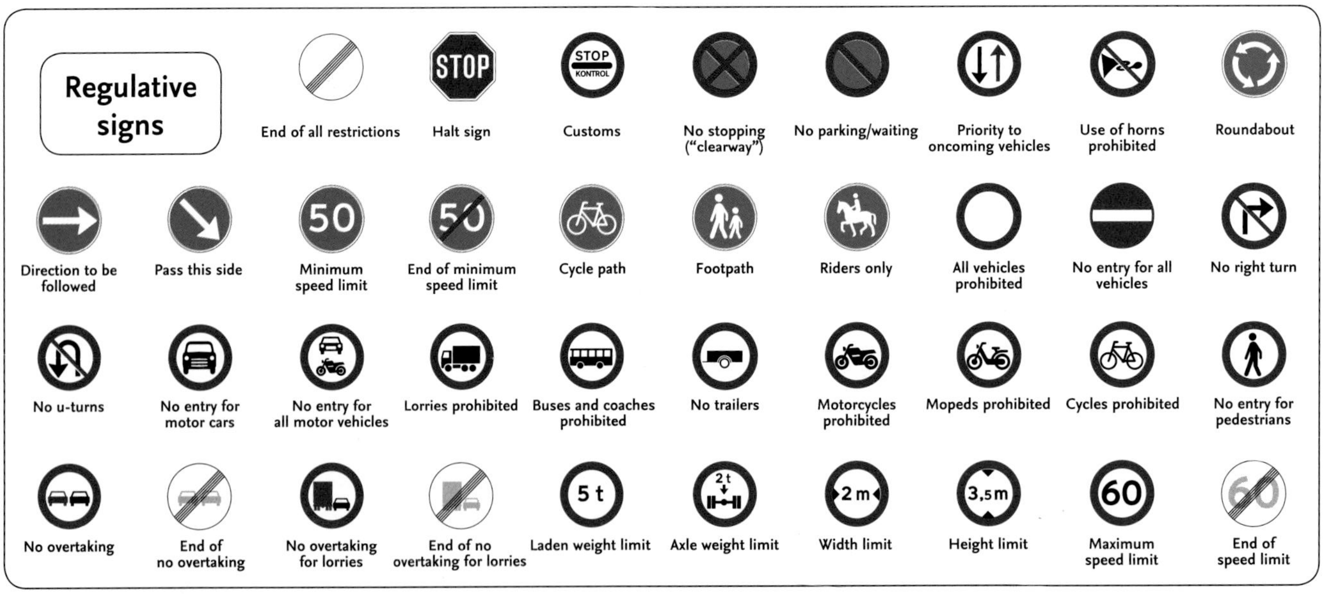

Travel & route planning

Driving information	www.drive-alive.co.uk
The AA	www.theaa.com
The RAC	www.rac.co.uk
ViaMichelin	www.viamichelin.com
Bing Maps	www.bing.com/mapspreview
Motorail information	www.seat61.com/Motorail
Ferry information	www.aferry.com
Eurotunnel information	www.eurotunnel.com/uk/home/

General information

UK Foreign & Commonwealth Office	www.gov.uk/government/organisations/foreign-commonwealth-office
Country profiles	www.cia.gov/library/publications/resources/the-world-factbook/index.html
World Heritage sites	whc.unesco.org/en/list
World time	wwp.greenwichmeantime.com
Weather information	www.metoffice.gov.uk

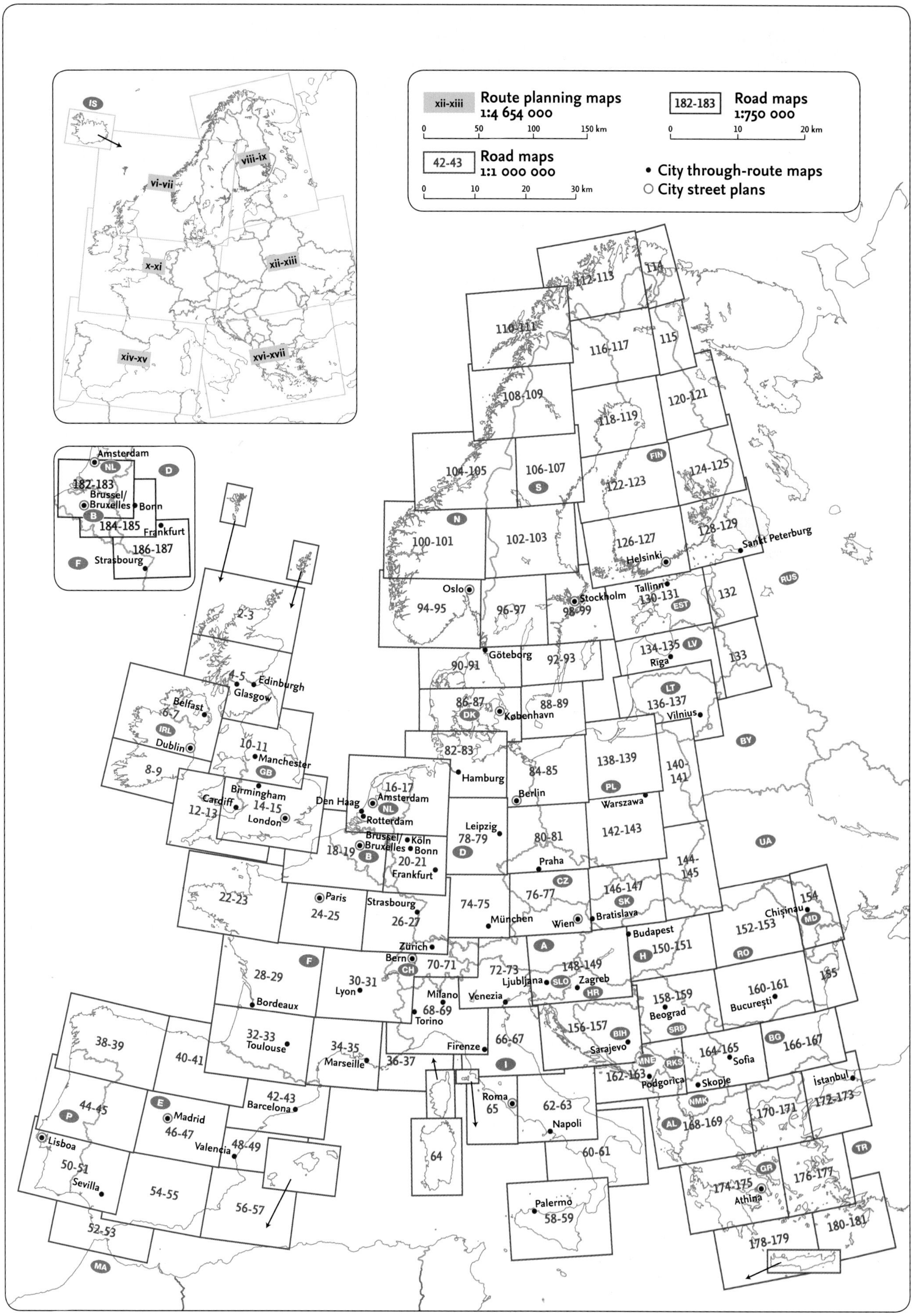
xii-xiii Route planning maps
1:4 654 000
0 50 100 150 km
182-183 Road maps
1:750 000
0 10 20 km
42-43 Road maps
1:1 000 000
0 10 20 30 km
• City through-route maps
○ City street plans
IS
vi-vii
viii-ix
x-xi
xii-xiii
xiv-xv
xvi-xvii
Amsterdam
NL
D
182-183
Brussel/
Bruxelles
Bonn
B
184-185
Frankfurt
186-187
F
Strasbourg
112-113
114
110-111
115
116-117
108-109
120-121
118-119
104-105
106-107
S
FIN
124-125
122-123
N
100-101
102-103
126-127
128-129
Sankt Peterburg
Helsinki
Oslo
94-95
96-97
Stockholm
98-99
Tallinn
130-131
EST
132
RUS
2-3
90-91
Göteborg
92-93
134-135
LV
Riga
133
4-5
Edinburgh
Glasgow
Belfast
6-7
IRL
Dublin
8-9
86-87
DK
København
88-89
LT
136-137
Vilnius
BY
10-11
Manchester
GB
82-83
Hamburg
84-85
Berlin
138-139
PL
Warszawa
140-141
Birmingham
Cardiff
12-13
14-15
London
Den Haag
16-17
Amsterdam
NL
Rotterdam
Leipzig
78-79
D
80-81
142-143
UA
18-19
Brussel/
Bruxelles
B
Köln
Bonn
20-21
Frankfurt
Praha
144-145
22-23
Paris
24-25
Strasbourg
26-27
74-75
CZ
76-77
146-147
SK
München
Wien
Bratislava
152-153
Chişinau
154
MD
Zürich
Bern
CH
70-71
A
Budapest
H
150-151
RO
28-29
F
30-31
Lyon
72-73
Ljubljana
SLO
148-149
Zagreb
HR
155
Bordeaux
Milano
68-69
Torino
Venezia
158-159
Beograd
SRB
160-161
Bucureşti
38-39
40-41
32-33
Toulouse
34-35
Marseille
36-37
Firenze
66-67
156-157
BIH
Sarajevo
MNE
RKS
164-165
Sofia
BG
166-167
I
162-163
Podgorica
Skopje
İstanbul
44-45
E
Madrid
46-47
42-43
Barcelona
Roma
65
62-63
Napoli
NMK
AL
168-169
170-171
172-173
P
Lisboa
Valencia
48-49
64
60-61
TR
50-51
Sevilla
54-55
56-57
Palermo
58-59
GR
174-175
Athina
176-177
52-53
178-179
180-181
MA

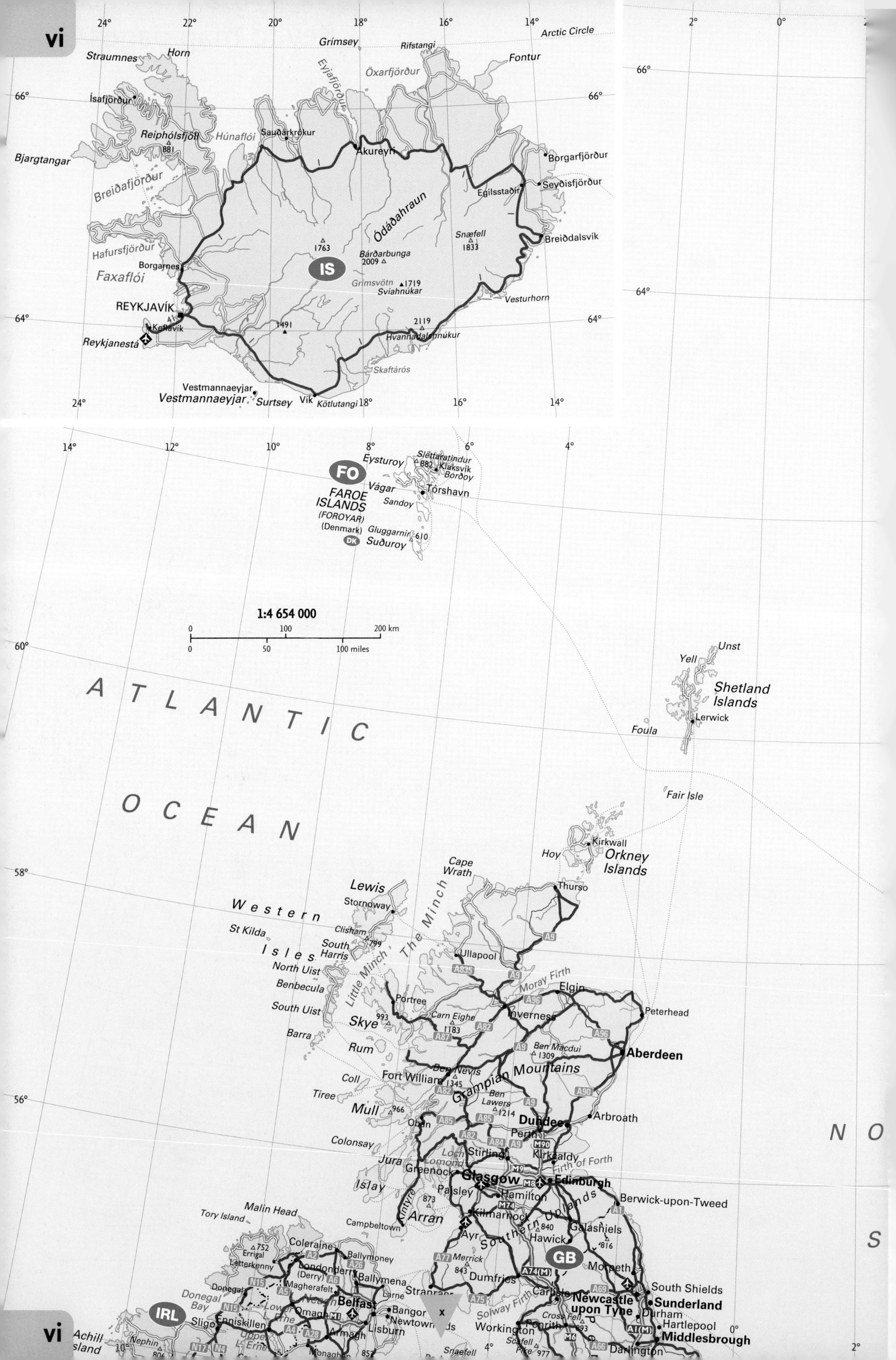
Arctic Circle
Grímsey
Rifstangi
Straumnes
Horn
Fontur
Eyjafjörður
Öxarfjörður
Ísafjörður
Reiphólsfjöll
881
Húnaflói
Sauðárkrókur
Akureyri
Bjargtangar
Borgarfjörður
Breiðafjörður
Seyðisfjörður
Egilsstaðir
Ódáðahraun
Breiðdalsvík
Snæfell
1833
1763
Hafursfjörður
Bárðarbunga
2009
Borgarnes
IS
Faxaflói
Grímsvötn
1719
Svíahnúkar
Vesturhorn
REYKJAVÍK
Keflavík
2119
1491
Reykjanestá
Hvannadalshnúkur
Skaftárós
Vestmannaeyjar
Vestmannaeyjar
Surtsey
Vík
Kötlutangi
Eysturoy
Slættaratindur
882
Klaksvík
Borðoy
FO
Vágar
Tórshavn
FAROE
ISLANDS
(FOROYAR)
(Denmark)
Sandoy
Gluggarnir
610
DK
Suðuroy
1:4 654 000
0
100
200 km
0
50
100 miles
ATLANTIC
OCEAN
Unst
Yell
Shetland
Islands
Lerwick
Foula
Fair Isle
Kirkwall
Hoy
Orkney
Islands
Cape
Wrath
Thurso
Lewis
Stornoway
Western
Isles
The Minch
Little Minch
St Kilda
Clisham
799
South
Harris
Ullapool
North Uist
Benbecula
South Uist
Moray Firth
Elgin
Portree
Peterhead
Carn Eighe
1183
Inverness
993
Skye
Barra
Ben Macdui
1309
Aberdeen
Rum
Ben Nevis
1345
Grampian Mountains
Coll
Fort William
Tiree
Ben
Lawers
1214
Mull
966
Dundee
Arbroath
Oban
Perth
Colonsay
Stirling
Kirkcaldy
Loch
Lomond
Firth of Forth
Jura
Greenock
Glasgow
Edinburgh
Islay
Paisley
Hamilton
Berwick-upon-Tweed
873
Kilmarnock
Southern Uplands
Malin Head
Tory Island
Kintyre
Arran
Campbeltown
840
Galashiels
Ayr
Hawick
816
752
Errigal
Coleraine
Ballymoney
Letterkenny
Merrick
843
GB
Londonderry
(Derry)
Ballymena
Dumfries
Morpeth
Donegal
Magherafelt
Larne
Stranraer
South Shields
Donegal
Bay
Belfast
Bangor
Solway Firth
Newcastle
upon Tyne
Sunderland
IRL
Omagh
Newtownards
Carlisle
Durham
Sligo
Enniskillen
Lough Erne
Cross Fell
893
Hartlepool
Achill
Island
Nephin
806
Armagh
Lisburn
Workington
Penrith
Scafell
Pike
977
Middlesbrough
Monaghan
852
Snaefell
Darlington
NO
S
x
A1
A2
A5
A6
A9
A26
A28
A66
A69
A74(M)
A75
A77
A82
A84
A85
A87
A90
A96
A835
M1
M6
M8
M9
M74
M90
N4
N15
N17
24°
22°
20°
18°
16°
14°
66°
64°
2°
0°
14°
12°
10°
8°
6°
4°
60°
58°
56°

Arctic Circle
Sandnessjøen
viii
Vega
Brønnøysund
Vikna
Namsos
Namdalen
Steinkjer
Verdalsøra
Hellesvik
Frøya
Hitra
Trondheim
Stjørdalshalsen
Smøla
Kristiansund
Løkken
Støren
Molde
Åndalsnes
Ålesund
Stranda
Storskrymten
Røros
Tynset
Volda
Måløy
Sandane
Galdhøpiggen
Gudbrandsdalen
Østerdalen
Otta
Florø
Førde
Hoyanger
N
Lillehammer
Rena
Elverum
Hamar
Gjøvik
Valdres
Sula
Bergen
Hardangervidda
Harteigan
Hønefoss
Lillestrom
OSLO
Sandvika
Asker
Ski
Drammen
Kongsberg
Numedal
Vestfjorddalen
Møsvatnet
Gausta
Bømlo
Haugesund
Karmøy
Stavanger
Sandnes
Setesdal
Horten
Tønsberg
Skien
Porsgrunn
Sandefjord
Larvik
Moss
Askim
Sarpsborg
Fredrikstad
Halden
Arvika
Kongsvinger
Egersund
Arendal
Kristiansand
Lindesnes
SKAGERRAK
Øksskolten
Norra Storfjället
Uddjaure
Sorsele
Storavan
Arvidsjaur
Älvsbyn
Rossvatnet
Storuman
Marsfjället
Jörn
Skellefteå
Lycksele
Malgomaj
Vilhelmina
Limingen
Tunnsjøen
Dorotea
Åsele
Robertsfors
Umeå
Vännäs
Holmsund
Strömsund
Hammerdal
S
Järpen
Storsjön
Östersund
Brunflo
Sollefteå
Kramfors
Örnsköldsvik
Härnösand
Bräcke
Ånge
Timrå
Sundsvall
Brämön
Sylarna
Hede
Sveg
Femunden
Ljusdal
Hudiksvall
Hornslandet
Iggesund
Särna
Bollnäs
Söderhamn
Älvdalen
Mora
Siljan
Rättvik
Falun
Sandviken
Gävle
Borlänge
Ludvika
Avesta
Fagersta
Sala
Uppsala
Enköping
Västerås
Märsta
Täby
STOCKHOLM
Köping
Eskilstuna
Tumba
Södertälje
Arboga
Hjälmaren
Karlskoga
Örebro
Karlstad
Kristinehamn
Säffle
Åmål
Kumla
Katrineholm
Nynäshamn
Nyköping
Oxelösund
Norrköping
Finspång
Motala
VÄNERN
Mariestad
Lidköping
Skövde
Skara
Linköping
Mjölby
Tranås
Vättern
Vänersborg
Uddevalla
Trollhättan
Lilla Edet
Falköping
Alingsås
Jönköping
Västervik
Visby
Kungälv
Lerum
Borås
Nässjö
Eksjö
Göteborg
Mölnlycke
Kungsbacka
Kinna
Oskarshamn
Värnamo
Växjö
Nybro
Kalmar
Öland
Varberg
Falkenberg
Ljungby
Halmstad
Ronneby
Karlskrona
Karlshamn
Kristianstad
Ängelholm
Hässleholm
Hanöbukten
Helsingør
Helsingborg
Landskrona
Lund
Malmö
KØBENHAVN
Ystad
Trelleborg
Bornholm (Denmark)
Rønne
Skagen
Grenen
Hirtshals
Hjørring
Frederikshavn
Læsø
KATTEGAT
Anholt
Brønderslev
Hanstholm
Thisted
Aalborg
Aalborg Bugt
Hobro
Skive
Randers
Grenaa
Struer
Viborg
Holstebro
Herning
Silkeborg
Aarhus
Ikast
Skanderborg
Ringkøbing
DK
Horsens
Vejle
Frederikssværk
Hillerød
Holbæk
Kalundborg
SJÆLLAND
Ringsted
Køge
Varde
Fredericia
Esbjerg
Kolding
Middelfart
Fyn
Odense
Nyborg
Slagelse
Korsør
Næstved
Store Bælt
Ribe
Haderslev
Svendborg
Langeland
Lolland
Møn
Falster
Nykøbing
Nakskov
Rømø
Aabenraa
Sønderborg
Lille Bælt
Sylt
Flensburg
Nordfriesische Inseln
Schleswig
Eckernförde
Husum
Rendsburg
Kiel
Kieler Bucht
Fehmarn
Mecklenburger Bucht
Ribnitz-Damgarten
Stralsund
Rügen
Kap Arkona
Bergen
Greifswald
Wolgast
Zatoka Pomorska
Kołobrzeg
Koszalin
Gryfice
Ustka
Słupsk
Jezioro Łebsko
xi
ix
NORTH SEA
GULF OF BOTHNIA
Södra Kvarken
Kalmarsund
BAL

1:4 654 000
0 50 100 200 km
0 100 miles
Nordkynhalvøya
Varangerhalvøya
Vardø
Vadsø
Kirkenes
Nikel'
Zapolyarnyy
Polyarnyy
Severomorsk
Murmansk
Kola
Tumannyy
Murmanskiy Bereg
Gremikha
Vozvyshennost' Keyvy
Terskiy Bereg
Arctic Circle
Kuzomen'
Lovozero
Olenegorsk
Monchegorsk
Kirovsk
Apatity
Polyarnye Zori
Kandalaksha
Umba
Kandalakshskiy Zaliv
Kovdor
Alakurtti
Loukhi
Kesten'ga
Karelskiy Bereg
Kem'
Belomorsk
Rabocheostrovsk
Solovetskiye Ostrova
Onezhskaya Guba
Pomorskiy Bereg
Onega
Severodvinsk
Dvinskaya Guba
Yushkozero
Kalevala
Kostomuksha
Vøynitsa
Kuhmo
Salla
Kemijärvi
Kuusamo
Taivalkoski
Ammänsaari
Hyrynsalmi
Kajaani
Muhos
Oulu
Oulainen
Ylivieska
Raahe
Kalajoki
Kokkola
Rovaniemi
Saarenkylä
Sodankylä
Ivalo
Inarijärvi
Kittilä
Tornio
Kemi
Haparanda
Ylitornio
Pello
Muonio
Övertorneå
Luleå
Piteå
Boden
Vuollerim
Gällivare
Kiruna
Jokkmokk
Älvsbyn
Arvidsjaur
Skellefteå
Robertsfors
Umeå
Holmsund
Vännäs
Lycksele
Åsele
Vilhelmina
Dorotea
Storuman
Sorsele
Strömsund
Hammerdal
Järpen
Nordkapp
Magerøya
Porsangerhalvøya
Hammerfest
Sørøya
Seiland
Jiesjávri
Tromsø
Kvaløya
Ringvassøy
Senja
Harstad
Andøya
Vesterålen
Lofoten
Narvik
Kebnekaise 2114
Akkajaure
Sarektjåkkå 2090
Hornavan
Uddjaure
Bodø
Saltfjorden
Glomfjord
Snøtinden 1594
Mo i Rana
Norra Storfjället 1792
Oksskolten 1915
Mosjøen
Sandnessjøen
Vega
Moskenesøy
Værøy
Vestfjorden
Røssvatnet
N
FIN
S
vii

STOCKHOLM
HELSINKI
TALLINN
RIGA
Sankt-Peterburg
MOSKVA
RUS
EST
LT
BY
GULF OF BOTHNIA
Gulf of Finland
Gulf of Riga
BALTIC SEA
ÅLAND
Gotland
Öland
Saaremaa
Hiiumaa
Ladozhskoye Ozero
Onezhskoye Ozero
Ozero Beloye
Lake Peipus
Valdayskaya Vozvyshennost'
Tikhvinskaya Gryada
Uppsala
Västerås
Örebro
Norrköping
Linköping
Gävle
Sundsvall
Härnösand
Örnsköldsvik
Falun
Borlänge
Mora
Turku
Tampere
Espoo
Vantaa
Lahti
Jyväskylä
Kuopio
Joensuu
Vaasa
Pori
Rauma
Kotka
Hamina
Vyborg
Petrozavodsk
Medvezh'yegorsk
Novgorod
Pskov
Tartu
Pärnu
Narva
Kuressaare
Haapsalu
Daugavpils
Liepāja
Ventspils
Jelgava
Jūrmala
Klaipėda
Panevėžys
Šiauliai
Tver'
Rzhev
Velikiye Luki
Cherepovets
Mariehamn
Visby
Kalmar
Karlskrona
Västervik

ix

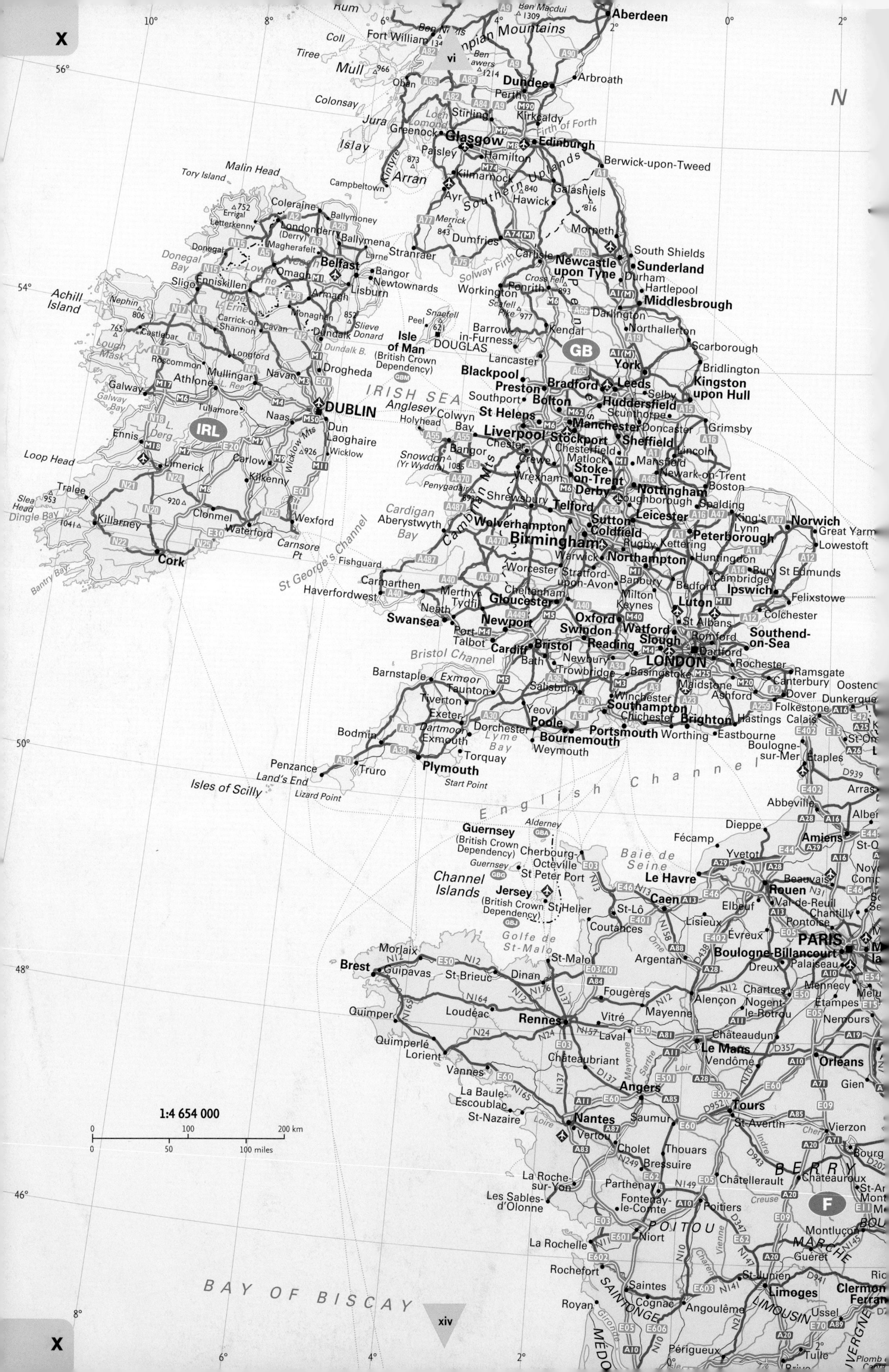

vi
xiv
GB
IRL
F
N
10°
8°
6°
4°
2°
0°
56°
54°
50°
48°
46°
Aberdeen
Ben Macdui
Grampian Mountains
Fort William
Ben Nevis
Coll
Tiree
Mull
Oban
Dundee
Arbroath
Perth
Colonsay
Jura
Stirling
Kirkcaldy
Firth of Forth
Greenock
Glasgow
Edinburgh
Islay
Paisley
Hamilton
Kintyre
Arran
Berwick-upon-Tweed
Malin Head
Tory Island
Campbeltown
Kilmarnock
Southern Uplands
Galashiels
Ayr
Hawick
Coleraine
Errigal
Letterkenny
Ballymoney
Londonderry (Derry)
Ballymena
Magherafelt
Merrick
Dumfries
Morpeth
Donegal
Larne
Stranraer
Carlisle
Newcastle upon Tyne
South Shields
Sunderland
Donegal Bay
Belfast
Omagh
Bangor
Newtownards
Solway Firth
Durham
Sligo
Enniskillen
Lisburn
Workington
Penrith
Hartlepool
Achill Island
Nephin
Armagh
Cross Fell
Middlesbrough
Lower Lough Erne
Scafell Pike
Darlington
Monaghan
Slieve Donard
Snaefell
Peel
Carrick-on-Shannon
Cavan
Castlebar
Lough Mask
Dundalk
Barrow-in-Furness
Kendal
Northallerton
Isle of Man
DOUGLAS
Scarborough
(British Crown Dependency)
Longford
Roscommon
Dundalk B.
Lancaster
Mullingar
Drogheda
Bridlington
Athlone
Navan
Blackpool
York
Galway
Galway Bay
Preston
Bradford
Leeds
Kingston upon Hull
IRISH SEA
Southport
Bolton
Selby
Huddersfield
Tullamore
DUBLIN
Anglesey
Colwyn Bay
St Helens
Scunthorpe
Naas
Dun Laoghaire
Holyhead
Liverpool
Manchester
Doncaster
Grimsby
Ennis
L. Derg
Wicklow Mts
Wicklow
Bangor
Chester
Stockport
Sheffield
Loop Head
Limerick
Carlow
Snowdon (Yr Wyddfa)
Crewe
Chesterfield
Matlock
Lincoln
Mansfield
Kilkenny
Wrexham
Stoke-on-Trent
Newark-on-Trent
Pen-y-gadair
Cambrian Mts
Tralee
Shrewsbury
Derby
Nottingham
Boston
Slea Head
Dingle Bay
Clonmel
Loughborough
Spalding
Cardigan Bay
Telford
Leicester
King's Lynn
Norwich
Great Yarmouth
Killarney
Waterford
Wexford
Aberystwyth
Wolverhampton
Sutton Coldfield
Peterborough
Lowestoft
Birmingham
Carnsore Pt
Cork
Rugby
Kettering
Huntingdon
Bantry Bay
Fishguard
Warwick
Northampton
St George's Channel
Worcester
Stratford-upon-Avon
Banbury
Cambridge
Bury St Edmunds
Carmarthen
Haverfordwest
Merthyr Tydfil
Cheltenham
Milton Keynes
Bedford
Ipswich
Felixstowe
Gloucester
Luton
Colchester
Neath
Oxford
St Albans
Swansea
Newport
Swindon
Watford
Southend-on-Sea
Port Talbot
Reading
Romford
Cardiff
Bristol
Slough
Dartford
Bristol Channel
Bath
Newbury
LONDON
Rochester
Barnstaple
Exmoor
Trowbridge
Basingstoke
Ramsgate
Taunton
Canterbury
Salisbury
Maidstone
Dover
Oostende
Tiverton
Winchester
Ashford
Dunkerque
Southampton
Folkestone
Exeter
Yeovil
Chichester
Brighton
Hastings
Calais
Bodmin
Dartmoor
Dorchester
Poole
Portsmouth
Worthing
Eastbourne
Exmouth
Lyme Bay
Bournemouth
Boulogne-sur-Mer
Torquay
Weymouth
Étaples
Penzance
Truro
Plymouth
Land's End
Start Point
Isles of Scilly
Lizard Point
English Channel
Arras
Abbeville
Alderney
Dieppe
Guernsey (British Crown Dependency)
Fécamp
Amiens
Cherbourg-Octeville
Baie de Seine
Yvetot
Guernsey
St Peter Port
Le Havre
Beauvais
Channel Islands
Rouen
Jersey (British Crown Dependency)
Caen
Val-de-Reuil
St Helier
St-Lô
Elbeuf
Chantilly
Lisieux
Pontoise
Coutances
Évreux
PARIS
Golfe de St-Malo
Morlaix
Argentan
Boulogne-Billancourt
Brest
Guipavas
St-Brieuc
St-Malo
Dreux
Palaiseau
Dinan
Fougères
Chartres
Mennecy
Alençon
Nogent-le-Rotrou
Étampes
Quimper
Loudéac
Rennes
Vitré
Mayenne
Nemours
Laval
Quimperlé
Lorient
Châteaudun
Le Mans
Châteaubriant
Vendôme
Orleans
Vannes
Gien
Angers
La Baule-Escoublac
Saumur
Tours
St-Nazaire
Nantes
St-Avertin
Vierzon
Vertou
Cholet
Thouars
Bressuire
BERRY
La Roche-sur-Yon
Parthenay
Châtellerault
Châteauroux
Les Sables-d'Olonne
Fontenay-le-Comte
Poitiers
Niort
POITOU
Montluçon
La Rochelle
MARCHE
Guéret
Rochefort
Saintes
St-Junien
Limoges
Clermont-Ferrand
SAINTONGE
BAY OF BISCAY
Royan
Cognac
Angoulême
LIMOUSIN
Ussel
Périgueux
Tulle
1:4 654 000
0
100
200 km
50
100 miles

KATTEGAT
Aalborg
Thisted
Hanstholm
Hobro
Skive
Randers
Struer
Viborg
Grenaa
Holstebro
Herning
Silkeborg
Aarhus
Ikast
Skanderborg
Ringkøbing
DK
Horsens
Vejle
Varde
Esbjerg
Fredericia
Middelfart
Kolding
Odense
Nyborg
Svendborg
Haderslev
Rømø
Aabenraa
Sønderborg
Sylt
Flensburg
Nordfriesische Inseln
Schleswig
Kieler Bucht
Fehmarn
Husum
Eckernförde
Rendsburg
Kiel
Heide
Neumünster
Bad Segeberg
Bad Schwartau
Helgoland
Helgoländer Bucht
Itzehoe
Lübeck
Ostfriesische Inseln
Cuxhaven
Elmshorn
Norderstedt
Stade
Hamburg
Reinbek
Norden
Bremerhaven
Wilhelmshaven
Aurich
Emden
Waddeneilanden
Groningen
Oldenburg
Bremen
Lüneburg
Leeuwarden
Drachten
Harlingen
Assen
Delmenhorst
Verden (Aller)
Uelzen
Den Helder
Sneek
NL
Stadskanaal
Celle
Meppen
Nienburg (Weser)
Alkmaar
Hoorn
Hoogeveen
Lingen (Ems)
Garbsen
Hannover
Wolfsburg
Zaandam
Lelystad
Zwolle
Almelo
Haarlem
AMSTERDAM
Amstelveen
Deventer
Rheine
Minden
Braunschweig
Hildesheim
Salzgitter
Hilversum
Utrecht
Apeldoorn
Enschede
Osnabrück
Herford
Bielefeld
Hameln
Detmold
Leiden
Amersfoort
Gravenhage
Gouda
Arnhem
Münster
Warendorf
Gütersloh
Höxter
Paderborn
Delft
Rotterdam
Nijmegen
Bocholt
Vlaardingen
Spijkenisse
Dordrecht
's-Hertogenbosch
Wesel
Hamm
Recklinghausen
Breda
Tilburg
Bottrop
Dortmund
Roosendaal
Essen
Hagen
Arnsberg
Göttingen
Eindhoven
Duisburg
Krefeld
Düsseldorf
Kassel
Antwerpen
Mönchengladbach
Remscheid
Eschwege
Gent
Mechelen
Genk
Leverkusen
Siegen
Eisenach
Aalst
Hasselt
Leuven
Maastricht
Köln
Troisdorf
Marburg
Bad Hersfeld
Anderlecht
BRUSSEL/ BRUXELLES
Liège
Aachen
Bonn
Gießen
Fulda
Mouscron
Roubaix
Verviers
Neuwied
Wetzlar
Mons
Namur
Andenne
Malmédy
Koblenz
Frankfurt am Main
Charleroi
Dinant
Wiesbaden
Mainz
Offenbach am Main
Cambrai
B
Bastogne
Wittlich
Bingen am Rhein
Groß-Gerau
Darmstadt
Würzburg
Hirson
Charleville-Mézières
Bitburg
L
Idar-Oberstein
Tauberbischofsheim
Sedan
Arlon
Trier
Ludwigshafen am Rhein
Mannheim
Heidelberg
Laon
LUXEMBOURG
Merzig
Kaiserslautern
Speyer
Ansbach
Thionville
Saarlouis
Saarbrücken
Heilbronn
Reims
Verdun
Châlons-en-Champagne
Metz
Freyming-Merlebach
Karlsruhe
Ludwigsburg
Château-Thierry
Pforzheim
Sindelfingen
Stuttgart
Aalen
Bar-le-Duc
Pont-à-Mousson
Sarrebourg
Vitry-le-François
Nancy
St-Nicolas-de-Port
Schwarzwald
Reutlingen
Ulm
Lunéville
Toul
St-Dizier
Strasbourg
Romilly-sur-Seine
Montereau
Troyes
Épinal
St-Dié
Vosges
Colmar
Rottweil
Villingen
Chaumont
Freiburg im Breisgau
Tuttlingen
Langres
Mulhouse
Schaffhausen
Konstanz
Vesoul
Belfort
Basel
Frauenfeld
Dijon
Delémont
Baden
Zürich
Olten
Solothurn
Zug
Besançon
Dole
Biel
Emmen
Luzern
CH
Neuchâtel
BERN
Beaune
Autun
Pontarlier
Yverdon
Fribourg
Thun
Sarnen
Schwyz
Altdorf
Le Creusot
Chalon-sur-Saône
Lons-le-Saunier
Lausanne
Spiez
Montceau-les-Mines
Morges
Vevey
Montreux
Berner Alpen
Digoin
Paray-le-Monial
Mâcon
Bourg-en-Bresse
Genève
Nyon
Monthey
Sion
Brig
Vichy
Villefranche-sur-Saône
Bonneville
Martigny
Roanne
Ambérieu-en-Bugey
Annecy
Cluses
Villeurbanne
Lyon
Aix-les-Bains
Mt Blanc
Albertville
Aosta
Vienne
Chambéry
Gran Paradiso
Ivrea
St-Étienne
Voiron
Massif de la Vanoise
Grenoble
Torino
Vercelli
Novara
Milano
Monza
Bergamo
Brescia
Como
Lecco
Varese
Lugano
Bellinzona
Domodossola
Omegna
Arona
Busto Arsizio
Piacenza
Cremona
Stradella
Voghera
Alessandria
Mantova
Manerbio
Verona
Vicenza
Padova
Rovigo
Legnago
Ferrara
Chioggia
Venezia
Mestre
Treviso
Conegliano
Vittorio Veneto
Belluno
Feltre
Rovereto
Riva del Garda
Trento
Bolzano
Merano
Sondrio
Morbegno
Bressanone
Brunico
Lienz
I
Tolmezzo
Gemona del Friuli
Udine
Gorizia
Monfalcone
Trieste
Koper
Portogruaro
Golfo di Venezia
Istra
Pula
Rijeka
Krk
Chur
VADUZ
Feldkirch
Bregenz
St Gallen
Herisau
Friedrichshafen
Kempten (Allgäu)
Memmingen
Biberach an der Riß
Marktoberdorf
Garmisch-Partenkirchen
Innsbruck
Schwaz
Kufstein
Rosenheim
Hohe Tauern
Großglockner
Spittal an der Drau
Villach
Klagenfurt
St Veit an der Glan
Judenburg
Knittelfeld
Niedere Tauern
Bad Ischl
Hallein
Salzburg
Bad Reichenhall
Traunstein
Gmunden
Vöcklabruck
Wels
Linz
Amstetten
St Pölten
A
Mürzzuschlag
Braunau am Inn
Waldkraiburg
Passau
München
Augsburg
Freising
Landshut
Günzburg
Donauwörth
Ingolstadt
Straubing
Regensburg
Schwandorf
Cham
Deggendorf
Regen
Amberg
Erlangen
Fürth
Nürnberg
Roth
Weißenburg in Bayern
Crailsheim
Forchheim
Bamberg
Schweinfurt
Coburg
Bayreuth
Weiden in der Oberpfalz
Plzeň
Domažlice
Klatovy
Šumava
Böhmerwald
Strakonice
Písek
Tábor
České Budějovice
Jindřichův Hradec
Benešov
Beroun
PRAHA
Kladno
Karlovy Vary
Chomutov
Most
Teplice
Ústí nad Labem
Litoměřice
Děčín
Liberec
Mladá Boleslav
Erzgebirge
Plauen
Hof
Zwickau
Chemnitz
Gera
Jena
Erfurt
Gotha
Saalfeld
Suhl
Meiningen
D
Mühlhausen (Thüringen)
Sonderhausen
Nordhausen
Leipzig
Halle
Hettstedt
Dessau
Torgau
Riesa
Meißen
Dresden
Bautzen
Görlitz
Jelenia Góra
Senftenberg
Cottbus
Lutherstadt Wittenberg
Magdeburg
Schönebeck
Halberstadt
Wolfenbüttel
Helmstedt
Haldensleben
Stendal
Brandenburg
Potsdam
BERLIN
Luckenwalde
Frankfurt an der Oder
Fürstenwalde
Zielona Góra
Rathenow
Neuruppin
Wittenberge
Perleberg
Wittstock
Eberswalde-Finow
Kostrzyn
Gorzów Wielkopolski
Poznań
Prenzlau
Pasewalk
Szczecin
Stargard Szczeciński
Pyrzyce
Choszczno
Piła
PL
Neustrelitz
Neubrandenburg
Waren
Ludwigslust
Parchim
Schwerin
Wismar
Güstrow
Teterow
Malchin
Demmin
Rostock
Greifswald
Wolgast
Świnoujście
Nowogard
Szczecinek
Świdwin
Białogard
Kołobrzeg
Koszalin
Sławno
Słupsk
Ustka
Lębork
Bytów
Gryfice
Ribnitz-Damgarten
Stralsund
Bergen
Rügen
Kap Arkona
Falster
Nykøbing
Møn
Lolland
Langeland
Nakskov
Næstved
Køge
Slagelse
Korsør
Ringsted
SJÆLLAND
Holbæk
Kalundborg
KØBENHAVN
Hillerød
Frederiksværk
Helsingør
Helsingborg
Landskrona
Malmö
Lund
Trelleborg
Ystad
Bornholm (Denmark)
Rønne
Hanöbukten
Kristianstad
Karlshamn
Ronneby
Karlskrona
Hässleholm
Ängelholm
Halmstad
Falkenberg
Ljungby
Anholt
S
BALT

BALTIC
Karlshamn
Karlskrona
Kristianstad
Hanöbukten
Ystad
Trelleborg
Bornholm (Denmark)
Rønne
Møn
Rügen
Bergen
Stralsund
Wolgast
Świnoujście
Neustrelitz
Prenzlau
Pasewalk
Szczecin
Gryfino
Eberswalde-Finow
BERLIN
Fürstenwalde
Frankfurt an der Oder
Cottbus
Senftenberg
Bautzen
Dresden
Görlitz
Děčín
Liberec
Ústí nad Labem
Litoměřice
Mladá Boleslav
PRAHA
Hradec Králové
Pardubice
Havlíčkův Brod
Tábor
Písek
Jihlava
Třebíč
Jindřichův Hradec
České Budějovice
Znojmo
Brno
Olomouc
Ostrava
Opava
Šumperk
Nový Jičín
Přerov
Vyškov
Uherské Hradiště
Břeclav
Stockerau
St Pölten
WIEN
Baden
Neunkirchen
Mürzzuschlag
Bruck an der Mur
Graz
Wolfsberg
Maribor
Celje
Trbovlje
Ptuj
Čakovec
Varaždin
Koprivnica
Bjelovar
ZAGREB
Karlovac
Sisak
Bihać
Prijedor
Banja Luka
Bosanska Gradiška
Doboj
Tuzla
Zvornik
Zenica
Jajce
Ustka
Słupsk
Koszalin
Kołobrzeg
Sławno
Białogard
Szczecinek
Wejherowo
Lębork
Gdynia
Sopot
Gdańsk
Tczew
Starogard Gdański
Malbork
Elbląg
Chojnice
Wałcz
Piła
Stargard Szczeciński
Pyrzyce
Choszczno
Gorzów Wielkopolski
Kostrzyn
Bydgoszcz
Grudziądz
Świecie
Chełmno
Toruń
Inowrocław
Gniezno
Poznań
Świebodzin
Zielona Góra
Głogów
Leszno
Kościan
Rawicz
Polkowice
Lubin
Legnica
Jawor
Wałbrzych
Świdnica
Wrocław
Oława
Brzeg
Opole
Kłodzko
Kluczbork
Kalisz
Ostrów Wielkopolski
Jarocin
Września
Konin
Włocławek
Płock
Kutno
Łowicz
Łódź
Zgierz
Pabianice
Sieradz
Bełchatów
Wieluń
Piotrków Trybunalski
Radomsko
Częstochowa
Tarnowskie Góry
Bytom
Gliwice
Katowice
Sosnowiec
Dąbrowa Górnicza
Rybnik
Żory
Bielsko-Biała
Frýdek-Místek
Čadca
Kraków
Skawina
Bochnia
Tarnów
Nowy Sącz
Nowy Targ
Gorlice
Jasło
Krosno
Rzeszów
Mielec
Sanok
Przemyśl
Jarosław
Kielce
Ostrowiec Świętokrzyski
Sandomierz
Stalowa Wola
Tarnobrzeg
Radom
Skarżysko-Kamienna
Starachowice
Tomaszów Mazowiecki
Skierniewice
Pruszków
WARSZAWA
Mińsk Mazowiecki
Siedlce
Łuków
Lublin
Lubartów
Chełm
Zamość
Biłgoraj
Biała Podlaska
Ostrów Mazowiecka
Wyszków
Ciechanów
Mława
Działdowo
Nidzica
Ostróda
Iława
Brodnica
Olsztyn
Szczytno
Łomża
Białystok
Ełk
Suwałki
Gołdap
Węgorzewo
Bartoszyce
Braniewo
Kaliningrad
Baltiysk
Svetlogorsk
Zelenogradsk
Gur'yevsk
Gvardeysk
Chernyakhovsk
Gusev
Sovetsk
Neman
Klaipėda
Kretinga
Palanga
Plungė
Gargždai
Šilutė
Šilalė
Tauragė
Jurbarkas
Raseiniai
Kelmė
Šiauliai
Telšiai
Mažeikiai
Skuodas
Radviliškis
Panevėžys
Pakruojis
Pasvalys
Biržai
Rokiškis
Kupiškis
Zarasai
Utena
Ukmergė
Kėdainiai
Kaunas
Jonava
Širvintos
Molėtai
Ignalina
Švenčionys
Visaginas
Daugavpils
Jēkabpils
Aizkraukle
Bauska
Jelgava
Dobele
Saldus
Liepāja
Šakiai
Vilkaviškis
Marijampolė
Prienai
Alytus
Trakai
VILNIUS
Varėna
Druskininkai
Šalčininkai
Ashmyany
Smarhon'
Valozhyn
Lida
Hrodna
Shchuchyn
Masty
Dzyarzhynsk
Stowbtsy
Baranavichy
Slonim
Vawkavysk
Lyakhavichy
Nyasvizh
Klyetsk
Ivatsevichy
Hantsavichy
Byaroza
Kobryn
Zhabinka
Brest
Drahichyn
Ivanava
Pinsk
Luninyets
Mikashevichy
Dubrovytsya
Varash
Sarny
Kovel
Volodymyr-Volyns'kyy
Novovolyns'k
Luts'k
Kostopil'
Rivne
Korets'
Zdolbuniv
Dubno
Slavuta
Shepetivka
Izyaslav
Radyvyliv
Brody
Sokal'
Chervonohrad
Tomaszów Lubelski
Lubaczów
Kam''yanka-Buz'ka
Yavoriv
L'viv
Horodok
Zolochiv
Ternopil'
Krasyliv
Volochys'k
Peremyshlyany
Berezhany
Terebovlya
Sambir
Drohobych
Stryy
Zhydachiv
Kalush
Dolyna
Ivano-Frankivs'k
Chortkiv
Borshchiv
Horodenka
Dunayivtsi
Kam''yanets'-Podil's'kyy
Kolomyya
Nadvirna
Chernivtsi
Sokyryany
Mukacheve
Berehove
Khust
Rakhiv
Uzhhorod
Vynohradiv
CARPATHIAN MTS
Žilina
Považská Bystrica
Martin
Prievidza
Žiar nad Hronom
Zvolen
Banská Bystrica
Poprad
Kežmarok
Spišská Nová Ves
Prešov
Humenné
Michalovce
Košice
Trebišov
Rimavská Sobota
Lučenec
Levice
Nitra
Trnava
Pezinok
BRATISLAVA
Galanta
Nové Zámky
Komárno
Győr
Mosonmagyaróvár
Sopron
Kapuvár
Tatabánya
Szombathely
Sárvár
Veszprém
Várpalota
Székesfehérvár
Körmend
Zalaegerszeg
Keszthely
Nagykanizsa
Siófok
Balatonfüred
Kaposvár
Dombóvár
Szigetvár
Pécs
Mohács
Barcs
Virovitica
Osijek
Đakovo
Vukovar
Slavonski Brod
Županja
Vinkovci
Dunaújváros
Paks
Kiskunfélegyháza
Kecskemét
Kiskunhalas
Szekszárd
Baja
Szeged
Subotica
Hódmezővásárhely
Makó
Orosháza
Békéscsaba
Gyula
Szolnok
Cegléd
Mezőtúr
Karcag
BUDAPEST
Érd
Vác
Dunakeszi
Gyöngyös
Eger
Salgótarján
Miskolc
Kazincbarcika
Nyíregyháza
Debrecen
Oradea
Satu Mare
Carei
Baia Mare
Sighetu Marmației
Șimleu Silvaniei
Zalău
Dej
Gherla
Bistrița
Cluj-Napoca
Turda
Aiud
Târgu Mureș
Reghin
Gheorgheni
Târnăveni
Mediaș
Sighișoara
Alba Iulia
Sebeș
Deva
Orăștie
Hunedoara
Sibiu
Făgăraș
Brașov
Codlea
Săcele
Sfântu Gheorghe
Miercurea-Ciuc
Comănești
Onești
Adjud
Focșani
Râmnicu Sărat
Buzău
Ploiești
Câmpina
Târgoviște
Pitești
Găești
Titu
Costești
Urziceni
Slobozia
Râmnicu Vâlcea
Drăgășani
Târgu Jiu
Motru
Strehaia
Drobeta-Turnu Severin
Petroșani
Caransebeș
Reșița
Lugoj
Timișoara
Arad
Lipova
Vršac
Zrenjanin
Kikinda
Senta
Sombor
Vrbas
Bečej
Bačka Palanka
Novi Sad
Inđija
Ruma
BEOGRAD
Pančevo
Smederevo
Požarevac
Mladenovac
Velika Plana
Lazarevac
Loznica
Suceava
Botoșani
Fălticeni
Vatra Dornei
Câmpulung Moldovenesc
Borșa
Piatra Neamț
Buhuși
Bacău
Rîșnov
SLAVONIJA
CZ
PL
SK
H
HR
BIH
SRB
RO
LT
LV
RUS
D
A
S
DK
Courland Lagoon
Gulf of Danzig
Jezioro Łebsko
Zatoka Pomorska

Velikiye Luki
Toropets
Rzhev
Novosokol'niki
Zapadnaya Dvina
Nelidovo
Solnechnogorsk
Zelenograd
Sergiyev Posad
Mytishchi
Khimki
MOSKVA
Noginsk
Orekhovo-Zuyevo
Balashikha
Zhukovskiy
Kirzhach
Petushki
Lakinsk
Sobinka
Kosterevo
Roshal'
Shatura
Vyksa
Melenki
Egor'yevsk
Voskresensk
Oz Velikoye
Nevel'
Ruza
Mozhaysk
Odintsovo
Podol'sk
Gagarin
Naro-Fominsk
Klimovsk
Kolomna
Lukhovitsy
Kasimov
Polatsk
Haradok
Vyaz'ma
Obninsk
Maloyaroslavets
Serpukhov
Stupino
Ozery
Zaraysk
Rybnoye
Ryazan'
Sasovo
Vitsyebsk
Yartsevo
Safonovo
Protvino
Kashira
Ozherel'ye
RUS
Shilovo
Rudnya
Dorogobuzh
Kondrovo
Yasnogorsk
Venev
Mikhaylov
Lyepyel'
Smolensk
Kaluga
Aleksin
Leninskiy
Tula
Novomoskovsk
Novomichurinsk
Novalukoml'
Smolenskaya Vozvyshennost'
Korablino
Orsha
Pochinok
Suvorov
Bolokhovo
Shchekino
Kimovsk
Donskoy
Skopin
Talachyn
Horki
Kirov
Sukhinichi
Uzlovaya
Bogoroditsk
Ryazhsk
Morshansk
Shklow
Mstsislaw
Desnogorsk
Kozel'sk
Sosnovka
Smalyavichy
Roslavl'
Lyudinovo
Belev
Plavsk
Chaplygin
Pervomayskiy
Mahilyow
Byerazino
Chavusy
Krychaw
Dyat'kovo
Chervyen'
Klimavichy
Zhukovka
Sel'tso
Bolkhov
Mtsensk
Dankov
Lebedyan'
BY
Bykhaw
Kastsyukovichy
Kletnya
Bryansk
Karachev
Orel
Yefremov
Michurinsk
Tambov
Asipovichy
Babruysk
Rahachow
Surazh
Pochep
Navlya
Yelets
Lipetsk
Kotovsk
Gryazi
Syrskiy
Klintsy
Unecha
Lokot'
Livny
Zadonsk
Dobrinka
Usman'
Zhlobin
Svyetlahorsk
Novozybkov
Pogar
Zheleznogorsk
Zherdevka
Ertil'
Homyel'
Dobrush
Klimovo
Rechytsa
Semenivka
Novhorod-Sivers'kyy
Dmitriyev-L'govskiy
Shchigry
Semiluki
Voronezh
Zhytkavichy
Kalinkavichy
Mazyr
Shostka
Kursk
Kurchatov
Anna
Snovs'k
Hlukhiv
Krolevets'
L'gov
Gubkin
Staryy Oskol
Bobrov
Liski
Mena
Slavutych
Chernihiv
Oboyan'
Ostrogozhsk
Chernyanka
Borzna
Konotop
Buryn'
Bilopillya
Ovruch
Polis'ke
Bakhmach
Nizhyn
Nosivka
Sumy
Novyy Oskol
Alekseyevka
Pavlovsk
Olevs'k
Korosten'
Kozelets'
Ichnya
Romny
Borisovka
Belgorod
Volokonovka
Bobrovytsya
Shebekino
Rossosh'
Malyn
Novohrad-Volyns'kyy
Borodyanka
Vyshhorod
Brovary
Pryluky
Hadyach
Okhtyrka
Zolochiv
Valuyki
Chernyakhiv
Irpin
KYIV
Boryspil'
Pyryatyn
Bohodukhiv
Kharkiv
Chuhuyiv
Kantemirovka
Korostyshiv
Zhytomyr
Vasyl'kiv
Hrebinka
Myrhorod
Lyubotyn
Valky
Kup"yans'k
Polonne
Fastiv
Obukhiv
Pereyaslav-Khmel'nyts'kyy
Lubny
Merefa
Svatove
Berdychiv
Kaharlyk
Khorol
Zmiyiv
Bila Tserkva
Uzyn
Zolotonosha
Poltava
Karlivka
Starobil's'k
Bilovods'k
Skvyra
Myronivka
Balakliya
Pervomays'kyy
Izyum
Kozyatyn
Korsun'
Cherkasy
Hlobyne
Krasnohrad
Kreminna
Rubizhne
Syeverodonets'k
Lysychans'k
Pohrebyshche
Shevchenkivs'kyy
Kremenchuts'ke Vdskh.
Lyman
Barvinkove
Slov"yans'k
Kadiyivka
Vinnytsya
Tetiyiv
Zhashkiv
Smila
Kremenchuk
Lozova
Bakhmut
Luhans'k
Shpola
Dniprodzerzhyns'ke Vdskh.
Kramators'k
Alchevs'k
Nemyriv
Tal'ne
Novomyrhorod
Oleksandriya
Novomoskovs'k
Pavlohrad
Kostyantynivka
Debal'tseve
Khrystynivka
Haysyn
Uman'
Znam"yanka
Verkhn'odniprovs'k
Kam"yans'ke
Myrnohrad
Yenakiyeve
Horlivka
Khrustal'nyy
Rovenky
Tul'chyn
Kirovohrad
Dnipro
(Dnipropetrovs'k)
Synel'nykove
Pokrovs'k
Makiyivka
Novoshakhtinsk
Mohyliv-Podil's'kyy
Novoukrayinka
UA
Donets'k
Yampil'
Bobrynets'
Vil'nyans'k
Amvrosiyivka
Soroca
Kodyma
Pervomays'k
Kryvyy Rih
Zaporizhzhya
Volnovakha
Novocherkassk
Yuzhnoukrayinsk
Marhanets'
Orikhiv
Taganrog
Podil's'k
Enerhodar
Polohy
Rozivka
Bălţi
MD
Voznesens'k
Nikopol'
Dniprorudne
Tokmak
Novoazovs'k
Taganrogskiy Zaliv
Azov
Bashtanka
Kakhovs'ke Vdskh.
Vesele
Mariupol'
(Zhdanov)
Yeysk
Ungheni
Berezivka
Nova Odesa
Snihurivka
Melitopol'
Berdyans'k
Starominskaya
CHIŞINĂU
Mykolayiv
Beryslav
Kakhovka
Yakymivka
Prymors'k
Rozdil'na
Tighina
Tiraspol
Kherson
Nova Kakhovka
Oleshky
Kanevskaya
Hînceşti
Cimişlia
Odesa
Novotroyits'ke
Sea of Azov
Primorsko-Akhtarsk
Comrat
Chornomors'k
Kalanchak
Armyans'k
Bryukhovetskaya
Timashevsk
Ciadâr-Lunga
Bilhorod-Dnistrovs'kyy
Skadovs'k
Krasnoperekops'k
Kalininskaya
Karkinits'ka Zatoka
Artsyz
Dzhankoy
Temryuk
Krasnoarmeyskaya
Tecuci
Cahul
Tatarbunary
CRIMEA
Nyzhn'ohirs'kyy
Kerch
Slavyansk-na-Kubani
Bolhrad
Krasnohvardiys'ke
(RESPUBLIKA KRYM)
Krasnodar
Galaţi
Kiliya
Krymsk
Saky
Bilohirs'k
Feodosiya
Anapa
Abinsk
Il'skiy
Brăila
Reni
Izmayil
Yevpatoriya
Goryachiy Klyuch
Tulcea
Măcin
Simferopol'
Sudak
Novorossiysk
Khadyzhensk
Delta Dunării
CRIMEA: ADMINISTERED BY RUSSIA
Bakhchysaray
Gelendzhik
Babadag
Alushta
Hârşova
DOBRUJA
Sevastopol'
Yalta
Novomikhaylovskiy
Ţăndărei
30°
32°
34°
36°
38°
40°
46°
50°
52°
54°

ix
xvii

1:4 654 000
0
100
200 km
0
50
100 miles
BAY OF BISCAY
Gulf of Gascony
La Roche-sur-Yon
Les Sables-d'Olonne
Fontenay-le-Comte
Niort
La Rochelle
Rochefort
Saintes
SAINTONGE
Cognac
Royan
Gironde
MÉDOC
Mérignac
Pessac
Bordeaux
Arcachon
La Teste
Mont-de-Marsan
Adour
Dax
Bayonne
Biarritz
Orthez
Oloron-Ste-Marie
Pau
Ferrol
A Coruña
Cabo Fisterra
Santiago
A Estrada
Lalín
Vilagarcía de Arousa
Pontevedra
Vigo
Lugo
Monforte de Lemos
Ourense
Avilés
Gijón/Xixón
Costa Verde
Oviedo
Cangas del Narcea
Mieres
Pola de Siero
Picos de Europa
2450
Santander
Torrelavega
Bilbao
Algorta
Laudio/Llodio
Irun
Donostia/San Sebastián
Vitoria-Gasteiz
Miranda de Ebro
Pamplona/Iruña
Logroño
CORDILLERA CANTÁBRICA
Catoute
2117
Ponferrada
El Teleno
2188
Sa de la Cabrera
León
Burgos
Sierra de la Demanda
Tudela
Huesca
Palencia
Valladolid
Aranda de Duero
Soria
Alto del Moncayo
2313
Zaragoza
Calatayud
Viana do Castelo
Póvoa de Varzim
Braga
Guimarães
Chaves
Bragança
Sierra de la Culebra
Zamora
Matosinhos
Vila Real
Porto
Douro
Duero
Embalse de Almendra
Ovar
São João da Madeira
Ria de Aveiro
Aveiro
Viseu
Salamanca
Segovia
Sierra de Guadarrama
Colmenar Viejo
Guadalajara
Alcalá de Henares
MADRID
Fuenlabrada
Arganda del Rey
Embalse de Buendía
Serranía de Cuenca
Teruel
Ávila
San Sebastián de los Reyes
Almanzor
2592
Valle de Tiétar
Sierra de Gredos
Coimbra
Serra da Estrela
Torre
1993
Covilhã
Guarda
Figueira da Foz
Leiria
Marinha Grande
Plasencia
Castelo Branco
Tomar
Torres Novas
Peniche
Caldas da Rainha
Torres Vedras
Santarém
Talavera de la Reina
Aranjuez
Toledo
Montes de Toledo
Corral de Cantos
1410
Cuenca
Cáceres
Sierra de San Pedro
Las Villuercas
1601
Sierra de Guadalupe
Embalse de Cijara
Portalegre
Amadora
Cascais
Almada
LISBOA
Vila Franca de Xira
Elvas
Badajoz
Mérida
Don Benito
Villanueva de la Serena
Almendralejo
Alcázar de San Juan
LA MANCHA
Tomelloso
La Roda
Albacete
Ciudad Real
Valdepeñas
Puertollano
La Vall d'Uixó
Sagunt
Requena
Torrent
València
Algemesí
Sueca
Cullera
Gandia
Catarroja
Carcaixent
Almansa
Oliva
Alcoy/Alcoi
Villena
Jumilla
Elda
Novelda
Alicante
Elche/Elx
Molatón
1242
Hellín
Setúbal
Baia de Setúbal
Évora
Barragem de Alqueva
Beja
Barragem de Andévalo
Peñarroya-Pueblonuevo
SIERRA MORENA
Linares
Andújar
Úbeda
Jaén
Caravaca de la Cruz
Cieza
Orihuela
Murcia
Córdoba
Guadalquivir
Martos
Montilla
Lucena
Alcalá la Real
ALGARVE
Lagos
Portimão
Cabo de São Vicente
Faro
Olhão
Huelva
Las Marismas
Costa de la Luz
Sevilla
Carmona
Écija
Utrera
Puente-Genil
Loja
Granada
Guadix
Lorca
Cartagena
Águilas
Cabo de Palos
Costa Blanca
GULF OF CÁDIZ
Lebrija
Morón de la Frontera
Antequera
Vélez-Málaga
Mulhacén
Sierra Nevada
3482
Almería
El Ejido
Motril
Golfo de Almería
Sanlúcar de Barrameda
Jeréz de la Frontera
El Puerto de Santa María
Ronda
Coín
Málaga
Cádiz
San Fernando
Chiclana de la Frontera
Marbella
Estepona
Costa del Sol
Barbate de Franco
Cabo Trafalgar
Algeciras
La Línea de la Concepción
Gibraltar (U.K.)
Strait of Gibraltar
Tanger
Ceuta (Spain)
Islas Canarias
Isla de Alborán (Spain)
Tétouan
Larache
Ksar el Kebir
Al Hoceima
Baie d'Al Hoceima
Chaouèn
Melilla (Spain)
Nador
Ghazaouet
Beni-Saf
Aïn Temouchent
Oran
Arzew
Aïn Tédélès
Mostaganem
Nédroma
Sidi Bel Abbès
Souk el Arbaâ du Rharb
Berkane
Maghnia
Tlemcen
Oujda
Télagh
Sebdou
Taounate
Kénitra
E
P
MA
x
46°
10°
8°
6°
4°
2°
0°
44°
42°
40°
38°
36°

Montrond
Moulins
Digoin
Montluçon
BOURBONNAIS
Paray-le-Monial
Mâcon
Bourg-en-Bresse
Genève
Nyon
Morges
Vevey
Montreux
Sion
Martigny
Brig
Sondrio
Morbegno
Trento
Riva del Garda
Rovereto
MARCHE
Guéret
Monts du Beaujolais
Villefranche-sur-Saône
Ambérieu-en-Bugey
Bonneville
Cluses
Annecy
Mt Blanc
Aosta
Domodossola
Bellinzona
Lugano
Lecco
Bergamo
Como
Varese
Omegna
Arona
Busto Arsizio
Monza
Milano
Brescia
Vicenza
Verona
Padova
Mestre
St-Junien
Limoges
LIMOUSIN
Clermont-Ferrand
Riom
Thiers
Vichy
Roanne
Villeurbanne
Lyon
Vénissieux
Aix-les-Bains
Chambéry
Albertville
Gran Paradiso
Ivrea
Novara
Rho
Manerbio
Monselice
Legnago
Rovigo
Ussel
Issoire
St-Étienne
Givors
Vienne
Voiron
Massif de la Vanoise
Vercelli
Pavia
Cremona
Mantova
Ferrara
AUVERGNE
MASSIF
Annonay
Grenoble
Torino
Stradella
Piacenza
Mirandola
Carpi
Modena
Argenta
Tulle
Brive-la-Gaillarde
Plomb du Cantal
Aurillac
Le-Puy-en-Velay
Tournon-sur-Rhône
Mont Mezenc
Romans-sur-Isère
Valence
Alpes du Dauphiné
Mt Pelvoux
Briançon
Moncalieri
Alessandria
Asti
Carmagnola
Voghera
Tortona
Novi Ligure
Parma
Reggio nell' Emilia
Bologna
Imola
Forlì
Bergerac
Dordogne
CENTRAL
Aubenas
Mende
Montélimar
Gap
Mte Viso
Acqui Terme
Ovada
Genova
Alpi di Succiso
Mte Cimone
Figeac
Cahors
Pierrelatte
Bollène
Orange
Fossano
Borgo San Dalmazzo
Cuneo
Mondovì
Savona
Rapallo
Sestri Levante
Carrara
Pistoia
Prato
Firenze
Rodez
Millau
Alès
Cévennes
Digne-les-Bains
Alpes Maritimes
Cima dell'Argentera
Albenga
Golfo di Genova
La Spezia
Massa
Viareggio
Lucca
Empoli
Moissac
Montauban
Carmaux
Gaillac
Albi
Avignon
Cavaillon
Manosque
Nice
Imperia
San Remo
MONTE CARLO
Pisa
Livorno
Poggibonsi
Nîmes
Arles
Verdon
Antibes
Cannes
Siena
Toulouse
Montpellier
Salon-de-Provence
Grasse
Aix-en-Provence
Rosignano Marittimo
Cecina
Colomiers
Muret
Mazamet
LANGUEDOC
CAMARGUE
Marignane
Brignoles
St-Raphaël
Côte d'Azur
LIGURIAN SEA
Arcipelago Toscano
Montepulciano
Béziers
Sète
Agde
Marseille
Aubagne
Toulon
La Ciotat
Îles d'Hyères
Cap Corse
Isola d'Elba
Portoferraio
Follonica
Grosseto
Carcassonne
Narbonne
Golfe du Lion
Monte Stello
Bastia
Orbetello
Monte Argentario
Pamiers
St-Gaudens
Foix
Durban-Corbières
Étang de Leucate ou de Salses
Tarquinia
PYRENEES
Pic d'Estats
Perpignan
Monte Padro
Monte Rotondo
CORSE (CORSICA)
Civitavecchia
ANDORRA LA VELLA
Puigmal
Port-Vendres
Figueres
Golfe de Sagone
Olot
Ajaccio
Pnte d'Ovace
Porto-Vecchio
Costa Brava
Vic
Girona
Segre
Manresa
Blanes
Capo Pertusato
Strait of Bonifacio
la Maddalena
Igualada
Sabadell
Mataró
Barcelona
Golfo dell'Asinara
Olbia
El Prat de Llobregat
Reus
Vilanova i la Geltrú
Porto Torres
Tempio Pausania
Tarragona
Sassari
Ozieri
Siniscola
Golf de Sant Jordi
Alghero
Nuoro
Golfo di Orosei
SARDEGNA (SARDINIA)
Macomer
Arbatax
Menorca (Minorca)
Oristano
MALLORCA (MAJORCA)
Cap de Formentor
Ciutadella
Maó (Mahón)
Terralba
Puig Major
Inca
Guspini
San Gavino Monreale
Villacidro
Palma de Mallorca
Manacor
Iglesias
Quartu Sant' Elena
Carbonia
Cagliari
Golfo di Cagliari
Sant' Antioco
Eivissa (Ibiza)
Illa de Cabrera
ILLES BALEARS (BALEARIC ISLANDS)
Formentera
MEDITERRANEAN SEA
Bizerte
Mateur
Menzel Bourguiba
Tébourba
L'Ariana
Collo
Skikda
Annaba
El Hadjar
El Tarf
El Kala
Béja
Aïn Taya
Dellys
Bejaïa
Jijel
El Milia
Azzaba
Dréan
Jendouba
Zaghouan
ALGER
Koléa
Boumerdes
Blida
Tizi Ouzou
El Arrouch
Guelma
Tipasa
Gouraya
Ténès
Cherchell
Larba
Akbou
Bougaa
Chelghoum el Aïd
Mila
Constantine
Oued Zénati
Souk Ahras
Le Kef
Siliana
Kebira
Kerba
Aïn Defla
Miliana
Médéa
Bouira
Sour el Ghozlane
Tazmalt
Sétif
El Eulma
Sédrata
M'Daourouch
Ouled Farès
Ech Chélif
Berrouaghia
Bordj Bou Arreridj
Aïn Oulmene
Aïn M'Lila
El Aouinet
Aïn Azel
Oum el Bouaghi
Aïn Beïda
Morsott
Relizane
Ksar el Boukhari
Theniet El Had
Sidi Aïssa
M'Sila
Aïn el Hadjel
Batna
Tébessa
Jebel Chambi
Kasserine
Tissemsilt
Zemmora
Chahbounia
Mahdia
Aïn Oussera
Zenzach
Chott el Hodna
Barika
Khenchela
Chéria
Sidi Bouzid
Tiaret
Atlas Tellien
Bou Saâda
Takhemaret
Sougueur
Ksar Chellala
Zahrez Chergui
Frenda
Zahrez Rharbi
Aïn Deheb
Biskra
Sidi Okba
Gafsa
Djelfa
Ouled Djellal
Metlaoui
Charef
Chott Melrhir
F
I
E
DZ
TN
xi
xvi

Villach
Klagenfurt
Völkermarkt
Zalaegerszeg
Siófok
Kecskemét
Keszthely
Balaton
Kiskunfélegyháza
Paks
H
Orosháza
Békéscsaba
Gyula
Kiskunhalas
Dombóvár
Szekszárd
Hódmezővásárhely
Szeged
Makó
Baja
Subotica
Pécs
Mohács
Szigetvár
Barcs
Tolmezzo
Belluno
Feltre
Vittorio Veneto
Conegliano
Gemona del Friuli
Udine
Jesenice
Kranj
Maribor
Ptuj
Čakovec
Celje
Varaždin
Trbovlje
LJUBLJANA
Gorizia
Monfalcone
Trieste
Koper
SLO
Trebnje
Koprivnica
Bjelovar
ZAGREB
HR
Virovitica
Osijek
Vukovar
Đakovo
SLAVONIJA
Slavonski Brod
Županja
Novi Sad
Zrenjanin
Bečej
Kikinda
Senta
Sombor
Vrbas
Bačka Palanka
Ruma
Inđija
Vršac
Timișoara
Bergamo
Brescia
Vicenza
Verona
Padova
Treviso
Mestre
Venezia
Golfo di Venezia
Portogruaro
Manerbio
Mantova
Monselice
Legnago
Rovigo
Chioggia
Mirandola
Carpi
Ferrara
Porto Tolle
Codigoro
Modena
Argenta
Comacchio
Valli di Comacchio
Bologna
Imola
Ravenna
Faenza
Forlì
Cesena
Rimini
SAN MARINO
RSM
Pistoia
Prato
Lucca
Firenze
Empoli
Poggibonsi
Siena
Pesaro
Fano
Urbino
Senigallia
Ancona
Osimo
Jesi
Fabriano
Arezzo
Cortona
Gubbio
Perugia
Assisi
Montepulciano
Civitanova Marche
Macerata
Fermo
Foligno
Spoleto
Todi
Orvieto
Grosseto
Lago di Bolsena
Narni
Terni
Rieti
Ascoli Piceno
San Benedetto del Tronto
Giulianova
Roseto degli Abruzzi
Teramo
Montesilvano
Pescara
Chieti
Ortona
Lanciano
Vasto
L'Aquila
Sulmona
Atessa
Termoli
Viterbo
Tarquinia
Civitavecchia
ROMA
Tivoli
Avezzano
Frascati
Pomezia
Aprilia
Latina
Anzio
Sabaudia
Sora
Frosinone
Cassino
Isernia
Campobasso
Fondi
Gaeta
Mondragone
Golfo di Gaeta
Sessa Aurunca
Benevento
Caserta
Napoli
Torre del Greco
Castellammare di Stabia
Vesuvio
Avellino
Salerno
Battipaglia
Eboli
Golfo di Salerno
Agropoli
Ariano Irpino
Foggia
Lucera
San Severo
Sannicandro Garganico
Vieste
Monte Sant'Angelo
Manfredonia
Golfo di Manfredonia
Cerignola
Barletta
Andria
Molfetta
Bari
Bitonto
Le Murge
Melfi
Minervino Murge
Gravina in Puglia
Altamura
Monopoli
Fasano
Brindisi
Mesagne
Francavilla Fontana
Lecce
Matera
Potenza
Avigliano
Ginosa
Massafra
Taranto
Manduria
Pisticci
Policoro
Nardò
Copertino
Galatina
Gallipoli
Casarano
Tricase
Capo Sta Maria di Leuca
Golfo di Taranto
Sala Consilina
Lauria
Monte Pollino
Castrovillari
Corigliano Calabro
Rossano
Cetraro
Montalto Uffugo
Acri
Paola
Cosenza
Amantea
LA SILA
Cirò Marina
San Giovanni in Fiore
Petilia Policastro
Crotone
Isola di Capo Rizzuto
Nicastro
Golfo di Sta Eufemia
Catanzaro
Golfo di Squillace
Soverato
Vibo Valentia
Rosarno
Palmi
Taurianova
Villa San Giovanni
Reggio di Calabria
Messina
Milazzo
Capo d'Orlando
Lipari
Isole Lipari
Isola Stromboli
Isola di Ustica
Capo San Vito
Palermo
Trapani
Alcamo
Marsala
Valdi Mazara
Mazara del Vallo
Castelvetrano
Corleone
Termini Imerese
Cefalù
Castelvetrano
Casteltermini
Sciacca
Agrigento
Enna
Caltanissetta
Canicattì
Caltagirone
Paternò
Adrano
Monte Etna
Taormina
Giarre
Acireale
Catania
Lentini
Augusta
Siracusa
Avola
Golfo di Noto
Pachino
Ragusa
Vittoria
Gela
Licata
Niscemi
SICILIA
(SICILY)
Isola di Pantelleria
Gozo
Birkirkara
VALLETTA
Malta
Isole Pelagie
TYRRHENIAN SEA
IONIAN SEA
MEDITERRANEAN SEA
ADRIATIC SEA
Istra
Pula
Rijeka
Krk
Cres
Lošinj
Pag
Kočevje
Karlovac
Sisak
Velebit
Gospić
Zadar
Dugi Otok
Šibenik
Split
Šolta
Brač
Hvar
Vis
Korčula
Lastovo
Dubrovnik
DALMACIJA
Bihać
Bosanska Krupa
Bosanski Novi
Prijedor
Bosanska Dubica
Bosanska Gradiška
Banja Luka
Doboj
Tuzla
Lukavac
Zvornik
Ključ
Titov Drvar
Mrkonjić-Grad
Jajce
Travnik
Zenica
Vitez
Bugojno
Visoko
SARAJEVO
BIH
Livno
Gornji Vakuf
Jablanica
Konjic
Mostar
Nevesinje
Čapljina
Stolac
Trebinje
Goražde
Foča
Pljevlja
Priboj
Prijepolje
Sjenica
MNE
Nikšić
Bijelo Polje
Berane
PODGORICA
Cetinje
Bar
BEOGRAD
Pančevo
Smederevo
Požarevac
Loznica
Valjevo
Mladenovac
Velika Plana
Lazarevac
Gornji Milanovac
Kragujevac
Užice
Požega
Čačak
Paraćin
Trstenik
Kruševac
Aleksinac
Novi Pazar
Leskovac
Mitrovicë
Vushtrri
Podujevë
PRISHTINË
RKS
Gjilan
Rahovec
Gjakovë
Ferizaj
Prizren
Preševo
Shkodër
Kukës
Tetovo
SKOPJE
Gostivar
Veles
Lezhë
Peshkopi
Debar
Kičevo
Negotino
Burrel
Krujë
Durrës
TIRANË
AL
NMK
Prilep
Struga
Ohrid
Bitola
Elbasan
Lushnjë
Pogradec
Fier
Berat
Kuçovë
Korçë
Florina
Kastoria
Ptolemaida
Kozani
Vlorë
Çorovodë
Ersekë
Tepelenë
Gjirokastër
Sarandë
Kerkyra
Kerkyra (Corfu)
Ioannina
Trikala
Igoumenitsa
Karditsa
Arta
Preveza
Lefkada
Agrinio
Mesolongi
Patra
Kefallonia (Cephalonia)
Ionia Nisia (Ionian Islands)
Zakynthos (Zante)
Zakynthos
Pyrgos
Kalamata
1:4 654 000
0 100 200 km
0 50 100 miles
14°
16°
18°
20°
36°
38°
40°
42°
xii
xv

Cluj-Napoca
Reghin
Gheorgheni
Târgu Mureș
Bacău
Roman
Vaslui
Huși
Cimișlia
Odesa
Chornomors'k
Kalanchak
Skadovs'k
Turda
Aiud
Târnăveni
Comănești
Miercurea-Ciuc
Onești
Bârlad
Comrat
Ciadâr-Lunga
Bilhorod-Dnistrovs'kyy
Karkinits'ka Zatoka
Mediaș
Sighișoara
Târgu Secuiesc
Adjud
Artsyz
Alba Iulia
Sebeș
Deva
Orăștie
Sibiu
Făgăraș
Sfântu Gheorghe
Focșani
Tecuci
Cahul
Bolhrad
Tatarbunary
Chornomors'ke
Krasnohvardiys'ke
Codlea
Brașov
Râmnicu Sărat
Galați
Reni
Izmayil
Kiliya
Yevpatoriya
Crimea: administered by Russia
Bakhchysaray
Sevastopol'
Petroșani
Câmpulung
Brăila
Tulcea
Măcin
Caransebeș
Râmnicu Vâlcea
Câmpina
Buzău
Ianca
Delta Dunării
Târgu Jiu
Târgoviște
Ploiești
Babadag
Motru
Pitești
Găești
Titu
Urziceni
Slobozia
Hârșova
Țăndărei
Strehaia
Drăgășani
Costești
Dobruja
București
Călărași
Constanța
Craiova
Bals
Slatina
Bolintin Vale
Videle
Drăgănești-Olt
Roșiorii de Vede
Dunav (Danube)
Silistra
Basarabi
Calafat
Băilești
Caracal
Alexandria
Giurgiu
Ruse
Dulovo
Mangalia
Corabia
Turnu Măgurele
Zimnicea
Ludogorie
Dobrich
Lom
Svishtov
Razgrad
Kavarna
Balchik
Black Sea
Knjaževac
Montana
Pleven
Byala
Shumen
Novi Pazar
Devnya
Varna
Provadiya
Vratsa
Lukovit
Lovech
Pavlikeni
Tŭrgovishte
Mezdra
Veliko Tŭrnovo
Kamchiya
Botevgrad
Troyan
Sevlievo
Dryanovo
Gabrovo
BG
Kostinbrod
Novi Iskŭr
Stara Planina
Sofia
Pernik
Radomir
Zlatitsa
Karlovo
Kazanlŭk
Sliven
Karnobat
Aytos
Pomorie
Burgas
Sredna Gora
Ikhtiman
Samokov
Panagyurishte
Stara Zagora
Nova Zagora
Yambol
Grudovo
Kostenets
Pazardzhik
Radnevo
Elkhovo
Dupnitsa
Plovdiv
Dimitrovgrad
Rila
Blagoevgrad
Asenovgrad
Haskovo
Kharmanli
Svilengrad
Kırklareli
Razlog
Rodopi
Edirne
Vize
Saray
Pınarhisar
Gotse Delchev
Smolyan
Kŭrdzhali
Momchilgrad
Babaeski
Lüleburgaz
Sandanski
Madan
Uzunköprü
Çorlu
Sarıyer
Beykoz
Kandıra
Karasu
Zonguldak
Ereğli
Alaplı
Devrek
Çaycuma
Bartın
Akçakoca
Düzce
Hendek
Adapazarı
Akyazı
Strumica
Petrich
Xanthi
Komotini
Hayrabolu
Muratlı
İstanbul
Kadıköy
Bakırköy
Kartal
İzmit
Serres
Drama
Kilkis
Malkara
Tekirdağ
Marmara Denizi (Sea of Marmara)
Karamürsel
Gölcük
Sapanca
Geyve
Bolu
Gerede
Köroğlu Tepesi
Giannitsa
Kavala
Alexandroupoli
Keşan
Yalova
Orhangazi
İznik
Thessaloniki
Kalamaria
Thasos
Samothraki
Fengari
Saros Körfezi
Gelibolu
Şarköy
Erdek
Bandırma
Gemlik
Mudanya
Yenişehir
Nallıhan
Beypazarı
Karacabey
Bursa
Bilecik
Bozüyük
Etimesgut
Athos
Gökçeada
Çanakkale
Biga
Çan
Gönen
Mustafakemalpaşa
Uludağ
Sarıyar Barajı
Sündiken Dağları
Thermaïkos Kolpos
Olympos
Mysia
Eskişehir
Polatlı
Susurluk
Ezine
Tavşanlı
Sivrihisar
Limnos
Balıkesir
Edremit
Dursunbey
Kütahya
Türkmen D.
TR
Larisa
Kaz Dağı
Burhaniye
Bigadiç
Emet
Edremit Körfezi
Madra Dağı
Savaştepe
Akdağ
Simav
Emirdağ
Volos
Voreies Sporades
Ayvalık
Bergama
Soma
Simav Dağları
Demirci
Gediz
Bolvadin
Yunak
Cihanbeyli
Alonnisos
Skiathos
Pagasitikos Kolpos
Lesvos (Lesbos)
Mytilini
Dikili
Kırkağaç
Akhisar
Uşak
Banaz
Afyon
Çay
Şuhut
Akşehir Gölü
Skopelos
Skyros
Aegean Sea
Aliağa
Foça
Manisa
Kula
Eşme
Sandıklı
Yalvaç
Akşehir
Ilgın
Kadınhanı
Psara
Menemen
Turgutlu
Salihli
Çivril
Uluborlu
Eğirdir Gölü
Şarkikaraağaç
Liakoura
Chalkida
Evvoia (Euboea)
Chios
Çeşme
İzmir
Bornova
Urla
Kemalpaşa
Boz Dağları
Alaşehir
Sarıgöl
Dinar
Beyşehir Gölü
Livadeia
Bayındır
Ödemiş
Buldan
Eğirdir
Beyşehir
Seferihisar
Torbalı
Tire
Aydın Dağları
Sarayköy
Söğüt Dağı
Isparta
Nea Liosia
Kifisia
Athina
Peiraias
Aigios
Kuşadası Körfezi
Samos
Kuşadası
Aydın
Nazilli
Denizli
Tavas
Burdur
Seydişehir
Korinthos
Saronikos Kolpos
Andros
Ikaria
Söke
Batı Menteşe Dağları
Çine
Doğu Menteşe Dağları
Bucak
Dimitrios
Tzia
Tinos
Fournoi
Yatağan
Akseki
Nafplio
Aigina
Mykonos
Patmos
Milas
Korkuteli
Ermoupoli
Syros
Güllük Körfezi
Muğla
Kythnos
Kyklades
Leros
Serik
Myrtoo Pelagos
Serifos
Paros
Naxos
Kalymnos
Bodrum
Antalya (Adalia)
Manavgat
Sparti
Sifnos
Kos
Marmaris
Elmalı
Antalya Körfezi
Alanya
Dodekanisa (Dodecanese)
Dalaman
Fethiye
(Cyclades)
Amorgos
Pelagos
Ios
Hisarönü Körfezi
Symi
Tilos
Rodos
Gytheio
Milos
Astypalaia
Lakonikos Kolpos
Steno Elafonisou
Santorini
Finike Körfezi
Atavyros
Kythira
Rodos (Rhodes)
Steno Karpathou
Administered as Northern Cyprus
Steno Antikythiro
Kritiko Pelagos
Morfou (Güzelyurt)
Lefkosia (Lefkoşa)
Ammochostos (Gazimağusa)
C. Arnaoutis
Kriti (Crete)
Chania
Ormos Almyrou
Kolpos Irakleiou
Karpathos (Scarpanto)
CY
Larnaka
Rethymno
Irakleio
Siteia
Agios Nikolaos
Pafos
Lemesos
Kolpos Messaras
Alexandria
RO
MD
UA
xiii

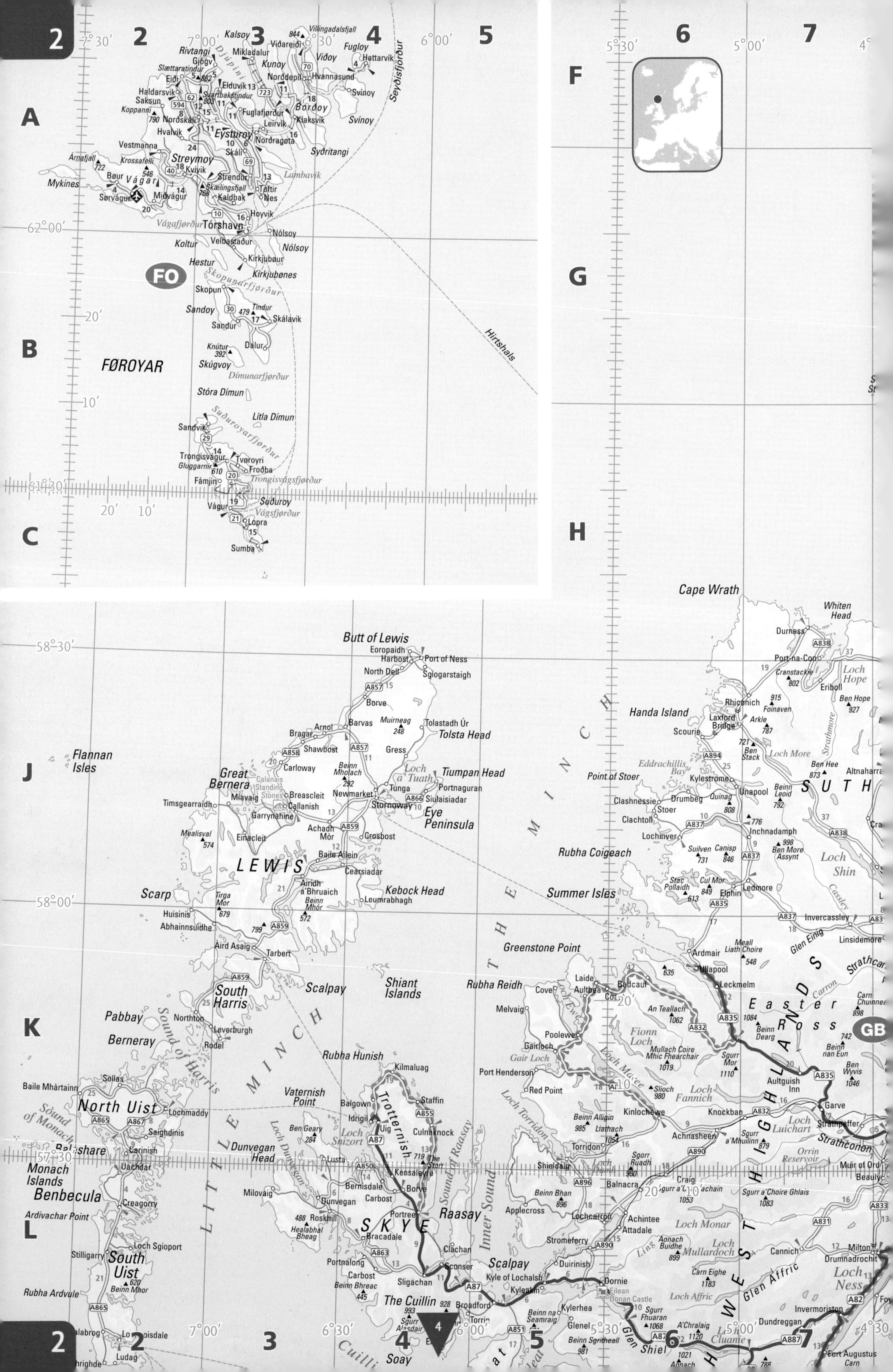
FØROYAR
FO
Kalsoy
Viðoy
Fugloy
Borðoy
Svínoy
Eysturoy
Streymoy
Vágar
Mykines
Tórshavn
Nólsoy
Koltur
Hestur
Kirkjubøur
Kirkjubønes
Skopun
Sandoy
Sandur
Skálavík
Dalur
Skúgvoy
Stóra Dímun
Lítla Dímun
Sandvík
Trongisvágur
Tvøroyri
Froðba
Fámjin
Suðuroy
Vágur
Lopra
Sumba
Hirtshals
Cape Wrath
Butt of Lewis
Port of Ness
Flannan Isles
Great Bernera
Callanish
Stornoway
Tolsta Head
Tiumpan Head
Eye Peninsula
LEWIS
Scarp
Tarbert
Scalpay
Shiant Islands
South Harris
Leverburgh
Pabbay
Berneray
Sound of Harris
LITTLE MINCH
THE MINCH
North Uist
Lochmaddy
Benbecula
Monach Islands
South Uist
Rubha Hunish
Vaternish Point
Trotternish
Staffin
Uig
Dunvegan
Dunvegan Head
Portree
Raasay
SKYE
Inner Sound
Sound of Raasay
The Cuillin
Sligachan
Broadford
Kyle of Lochalsh
Kyleakin
Soay
Handa Island
Scourie
Laxford Bridge
Durness
Whiten Head
Loch Hope
Point of Stoer
Lochinver
Rubha Coigeach
Summer Isles
Ullapool
Greenstone Point
Rubha Reidh
Gairloch
Poolewe
Loch Maree
Kinlochewe
Torridon
Shieldaig
Applecross
Lochcarron
Dornie
Eilean Donan Castle
Garve
Strathpeffer
Loch Ness
Glen Affric
Loch Mullardoch
Loch Monar
Cannich
Drumnadrochit
Invermoriston
Fort Augustus
Glen Shiel
Loch Shin
Lairg
Easter Ross
NORTH WEST HIGHLANDS
GB
A835
A832
A87
A890
A82
A887
A838
A837
A894
A857
A859
A865
A850
A855
A863

Fair Isle
Stonybreck
Papa Westray
The North Sound
North Ronaldsay
North Ronaldsay Firth
Noup Head
Pierowall
Skelwick
Westray
Midbea
Burness
Broughtown
Overbister
Westray Firth
Calfsound
Kettletoft
Sanday
Sanday Sound
Rousay
Wasbister
Eday
Loth
Backaland
Westness
Whitehall
Stronsay
Brough Head
Birsay
Brinian
Stronsay Firth
Aith
Twatt
Tingwall
Rothiesholm
A966
A986
Shapinsay
Mainland
Bimbister
Balfour
Sandgarth
Neolithic Orkney
A965
Stromness
Greenigo
Kirkwall
Scapa
ORKNEY ISLANDS
Skaill
A964
Orphir
A960
Gritley
Ward Hill 479
Houton
Linksness
Scapa Flow
St Mary's
Aberdeen
Hoy
Flotta
Burray
Lyness
Bow
St Margaret's Hope
Longhope
Herston
A961
Cleat
South Ronaldsay
Burwick
Pentland Firth
Brough Ness
Island of Stroma
Pentland Skerries
Dunnet Head
Brough
John o'Groats
Duncansby Head
Strathy Point
A836
Mey
Scrabster
Thurso Bay
Strathy
Dounreay
Thurso
Castletown
Freswick
Melvich
Buldoo
Reay
A9
A99
Keiss
Bettyhill
Strath Halladale
Loch Calder
Roadside
Sinclair's Bay
Halkirk
A882
Reiss
Noss Head
Olgrinmore
Spittal
Watten
Westerdale
Mybster
Wick
Beinn Stumanadh 527
Strathnaver
CAITHNESS
Syre
Forsinard
Thrumster
Loch Loyal
A897
Thurso
Achavanich
Ulbster
Loch Naver
Latheron
Lybster
Kinbrace
Morven 706
Scaraben 626
Latheronwheel
Loch Choire
Strath of Kildonan
Dunbeath
Kildonan Lodge
Berriedale
Newport
Helmsdale
Lothmore
Brora
Loch Brora
Ben Horn 521
A839
Pittentrail
Golspie
Bonar Bridge
A949
Dornoch
Tarbat Ness
Dornoch Firth
A836
Portmahomack
Edderton
Tarrel
Beinn Tharsuinn 692
Cnoc an t-Sabhail 379
Tain
Hill of Fearn
Balintore
Barbaraville
Alness
Invergordon
Balnapaling
Cromarty
Cromarty Firth
Moray Firth
Black Isle
A832
Rosemarkie
Fortrose
Ardersier
Nairn
A96
Burghead Bay
Hopeman
Lossiemouth
Burghead
Findhorn
Kinloss
Forres
Elgin
Dyke
A941
Rafford
Kellas
Longmorn
Fochabers
A939
Littlemill
Mill Buie 371
Dallas
Lossie
Rothes
Cawdor
Croy
Ben Aigan 471
Spey
A95
Ferness
A940
Upper Knockando
Aberlour
Craigellachie
Inverness
A862
Daviot
Findhorn
Marypark
Dufftown
Lochend
Moy
Lochindorb
Dava
Carn na Loine 549
Ben Rinnes 840
Dores
Farr
Loch Ashie
A939
Grantown-on-Spey
Strathspey
Hills of Cromdale
Tomatin
659
Tomnavoulin
Errogie
Carrbridge
Dulnain Bridge
Lynemore
Strath Dearn
Nethy Bridge
Boat of Garten
Tomintoul
Carn Mor 804
Carn Odhar 802
Dulnain
Aviemore
Geal Charn 821
Carn Ealasaid 792
Lecht
Coylumbridge
Cairngorm
Cairngorms National Park
Cairn Gorm
Alvie
Kincraig
Avon
Kingston
Buckie
Findochty
Portknockie
Cullen
Portsoy
Whitehills
Macduff
Banff
Spey Bay
A98
Kirktown of Deskford
Durn Hill 199
Forgie
Newmill
Knock Hill 430
Keith
Aberchirder
Finnygaud
Deveron
Bogniebrae
A97
Kirktown of Auchterless
Huntly
A920
Strathbogie
Cook's Cairn 755
A941
Culdrain
Tap o' Noth 563
Correen Hills
Mossat
A944
Alford
Don
Kemnay
Monymusk
Troup Head
Rosehearty
Fraserburgh
Inverallochy
St Combs
Gardenstown
New Aberdour
Memsie
Loch of Strathbeg
Ladysford
A981
Crimond
Rattray Head
A947
New Pitsligo
Strichen
A90
St Fergus
Turriff
A950
Mintlaw
Peterhead
Darra
Cuminestown
New Deer
Maud
A952
Boddam
Badenscoth
Auchnagatt
Hill of Dudwick 174
Hatton
Fyvie
Methlick
Ythan
A948
Cruden Bay
Bay of Cruden
Tarves
Ellon
A975
Collieston
Oldmeldrum
Newburgh
Inverurie
A96
Balmedie
Kintore
Dyce
Blackburn
Bridge of Don
Dunecht
Kirkton of Skene
Echt
Aberdeen
A956
Lumphanan
Morven
Herma Ness
Valsgarth
Burrafirth
Haroldswick
Unst
Baltasound
A968
Cullivoe
Uyeasound
Belmont
Yell
Yell Sound
Gutcher
Point of Fethaland
Oddsta
Fetlar
Mid Yell
West Sandwick
Houbie
Funzie
North Roe
Aywick
Colgrave Sound
The Faither
Ronas Hill 450
A970
Otterswick
Hamnavoe
Ulsta
Burravoe
Esha Ness
Urafirth
Ollaberry
Toft
Out Skerries
Stenness
Hillswick
Mossbank
St Magnus Bay
Lunna
Brae
Muckle Roe
Vidlin
Papa Stour
Laxo
Symbister
Voe
Whalsay
Melby
Setter
Aith
Weisdale
South Nesting Bay
A971
Bixter
Walls
Garderhouse
Whiteness
Veensgarth
Bressay
Culswick
Skeld
Lerwick
Scalloway
Isle of Noss
Ham
SHETLAND ISLANDS
Hamnavoe
Foula
West Burra
Cunningsburgh
GB
Sandwick
Hoswick
Bigton
Mousa
Levenwick
Scousburgh
Boddam
Sumburgh
Toab
Sumburgh Head
Kirkwall
Lerwick
Mainland
59°30′
60°30′
60°00′
58°00′
57°30′
4°00′
3°30′
3°00′
2°30′
2°00′
1°30′
1°00′

Sea of the Hebrides
Cuillin Sound
Soay
Canna
Rum
Eigg
Muck
Sleat
Knoydart
Arisaig
Moidart
Ardnamurchan
Coll
Tiree
Treshnish Isles
Mull
Iona
Ross of Mull
Morvern
Loch Linnhe
Lismore
Kerrera
Oban
Seil
Luing
Scarba
Firth of Lorn
Colonsay
Oronsay
Jura
Sound of Jura
Islay
Gigha
Knapdale
Kintyre
Arran
Kilbrannan Sound
Firth of Clyde
Ailsa Craig
North Channel
Rathlin Island
Inishowen
Lough Foyle
Inishtrahull Sound
Malin Head
Giant's Causeway
Antrim Hills
Sperrin Mountains
Londonderry (Derry)
Coleraine
Ballymena
Larne
Antrim
Carrickfergus
Newtownabbey
Bangor
The Rhins of Galloway
Stranraer
Fort William
Ben Nevis
Glen Coe
Rannoch Moor
Loch Awe
Loch Fyne
Inveraray
Greenock
Helensburgh
Campbeltown
Mull of Kintyre
Mull of Galloway
Barra
Vatersay
Sandray
Pabbay
Mingulay
Berneray
IRL
GB

8
9
10
11
12
13
A
B
C
D
E
F
57°00′
56°30′
56°00′
55°30′
55°00′
4°00′
3°30′
3°00′
2°30′
2°00′
1°30′
3
10
11
Aberdeen
Aviemore
Coylumbridge
Cairngorm
CAIRNGORMS NATIONAL PARK
Cairngorm Mountains
Kingussie
Newtonmore
Laggan
Dalwhinnie
Badenoch
Forest of Atholl
Braemar
Balmoral Castle
Ballater
Crathie
Banchory
Aboyne
Stonehaven
Glenshee
Lochnagar
Glen Esk
Glen Clova
GRAMPIAN MOUNTAINS
Pitlochry
Blair Atholl
Killiecrankie
Kinloch Rannoch
Loch Rannoch
Aberfeldy
Dunkeld
Blairgowrie
Kirriemuir
Forfar
Brechin
Montrose
Arbroath
Carnoustie
Dundee
Perth
Crieff
Comrie
St Fillans
Loch Earn
Strath Earn
GB
Callander
Dunblane
Stirling
Alloa
Falkirk
Grangemouth
Dunfermline
Kirkcaldy
Glenrothes
St Andrews
Cupar
Leuchars
Fife Ness
Isle of May
Firth of Forth
Firth of Tay
Sidlaw Hills
Ochil Hills
North Berwick
Bass Rock
Dunbar
Edinburgh
Musselburgh
Dalkeith
Livingston
Bathgate
Linlithgow
Bo'ness
Cumbernauld
Kilsyth
Kirkintilloch
Milngavie
Bearsden
Clydebank
Renfrew
Glasgow
Coatbridge
Airdrie
Motherwell
Hamilton
East Kilbride
Wishaw
Lanark
Biggar
Peebles
Penicuik
Galashiels
Melrose
Selkirk
Kelso
Jedburgh
Hawick
Lauder
Duns
Eyemouth
Coldstream
St Abb's Head
Berwick-upon-Tweed
Holy Island (Lindisfarne)
Bamburgh
Seahouses
Alnwick
Amble
Rothbury
Morpeth
Ashington
Blyth
Whitley Bay
Cramlington
Newcastle upon Tyne
Gateshead
Jarrow
Hexham
Haltwhistle
Consett
Durham
Bishop Auckland
Pentland Hills
Moorfoot Hills
Lammermuir Hills
Tweeddale
Teviotdale
Cheviot Hills
Ettrick Forest
Kielder Water
NORTHUMBERLAND NATIONAL PARK
Redesdale
Liddesdale
SOUTHERN UPLANDS
Moffat
Annandale
Lockerbie
Langholm
Nithsdale
Dumfries
Lowther Hills
Carlisle
Gretna
Annan
Solway Firth
Wigtown Bay
Kirkcudbright
Castle Douglas
Newton Stewart
Cumnock
Sanquhar
Muirkirk
Kilmarnock
Maryport
Workington
Cockermouth
Penrith
Inglewood Forest
Wigton
Aspatria
A1
A9
A68
A74(M)
M6
M8
M9
M74
M80
M90
A90

1
2
3
4
5
6
10°30′
10°00′
9°30′
9°00′
8°30′
B
C
D
E
F
55°00′
54°30′
54°00′
53°30′
20′
10′
Tory Island
Tory Sound
Bloody Foreland
Mín na Claodaí (Meenacladdy)
Bun na Leaca (Brinlack)
Gort an Chiorce (Gortahork)
An Bun Beag (Bunbeg)
Gaoth Dobhair
Anagaire (Annagry)
Rosses Bay
Croithlí
Errigal 752
An Leadhb Gharbh
Arranmore Island
Ailt an Chorráin (Burtonport)
An Clochán Liath (Dungloe)
Derryveagh Mts
Slieve Snaght
An Dúchoraidh (Doochary)
Crohy Head
Gweebarra Bay
Croaghgheheen 383
Leitir Mhic an Bhaird
Aghla Mountain 598
Dawros Head
Maas
Narin
Glenties
Loughros More Bay
Kilrean
Tangaveane
Slievetooey 444
Ardara
353
Blue Stack Mts
Glen Bay
Rossan Point
Gleann Cholm Cille (Glencolumbkille)
Málainn Mhóir
Malin Bay
Mín na bhfiann
504
494
Málainn Beag
601
Slieve League
An Charraig
Cill
Killybegs
Inver
Mountcharles
Charthaigh
Shalwy
Muckross Head
Fintragh Bay
Inver Bay
Doorin Point
St John's Point
Rossnowlagh
Coolmore
Ballintra
Donegal Bay
Ballure
Ballyshannon
Mullaghmore Head
Bundoran
Tullaghan
Kinlough
Cliffoney
Castlegal
Streedagh Point
Buckode
522
Garrison
Benbulben 525
Darty Mts
643
Truskmore
Glenade
Roskeeragh Point
Sligo Bay
Sranea
Dough Mt 461
Shanvus
Aughris Head
Rosses Point
Sligo (Sligeach)
Manorhamilton
Leckaun
Kilargue
Gubaveeny
Lough Gill
Templeboy
Knockalongy 542
Beltra
Dowra
Corry
Slieve Gamph (Ox Mountains)
Collooney
Drumkeeran
Coola
Lough Allen
Caisleán Bhaile an Mhóta
Ballymote
Lough Arrow
Ballyfarnan
Bunnanadden
Keadue
Tubbercurry
Kesh
Ballinafad
Lough Key
Mullany's Cross
Curry
Gorteen
Mullaghroe
Leitrim
Bellahy
Charlestown
Lough Gara
Boyle
Carrick
Carracastle
Edmondstown
Killukin
Ballaghaderreen
Kingsland
125
Croghan
Lough Boderg
Ballyglass
Lurgan
Frenchpark
Elphin
Lisacul
Loughglinn
Kilglass
Strokestown
Tulsk
Castlerea
Ballyhaunis
Castleplunket
Ballinlough
Derrywode
Curraghroe
Lanesborough
Roscommon
Emmoo
Ballymurry
Knockcroghery
Athleague
Ballygar
Lough Ree
Creggs
Kilsallagh
Glenamaddy
Curragh West
Cashel
Dunmore
Gorteen
Clonbern
Kilkerrin
Kiltoom
Ballyforan
Brideswell
Athlone (Baile Átha Luain)
Mountbellew
Moylough
Barnaderg
Horseleap
Castleblakeney
Caltra
Ahascragh
Ballinasloe (Béal Átha na Sluaighe)
Newtown
Kilconnell
Monivea
Cloonfad
Grand Canal
Laurencetown
Eyrecourt
Killimor
Shannon
Benwee Head
Erris Head
Broad Haven
Béal Deirg
Downpatrick Head
Lenadoon Point
Easky
Dromore West
Killala Bay
Bunalty
Maumakeogh 380
Ballycastle
Rathlee
Béal an Mhuirthead (Belmullet)
Barr na Trá (Barnatra)
Gleann na Muaidhe (Glenamoy)
An Geata Mór (Binghamstown)
Bun na hAbhna
Creevagh
Killala
Inniscrone
The Mullet
Carrowmore Lake
Inishkea North
Attavalley
Belville
Corbally
Bangor Erris
Inishkea South
An Eachléim (Aghleam)
Owenmore
Bellacorick
Crockets Town
Ballycroy National Park
Ballina (Béal an Átha)
Largan
Moylaw
Blacksod Bay
Slieve Car 772
Nephin Beg
629
Castlehill
Slieve More 672
Ballycroy
Nephin Beg Range
Lough Conn
Croaghaun 668
Dooagh
Bun an Churraigh
Derreen
806 Nephin
Achill Head
Birreencorragh 700
Gob an Choire (Achill Sound)
714
Cushcamcarragh
Lough Feeagh
Pontoon
Foxford
Beltra
Lough Cullin
Swinford
Achill Island
Corraun Peninsula
Mulrany
Rosturk
Newport
Bellavary
Bohola
Kilkelly
Kiltimagh
Castlebar (Caisleán an Bharraigh)
Manulla
Clare Island
Clew Bay
Westport Quay
Westport
Cloonkeen
Balla
Knock
Scrín Chnoc Mhuire
Croagh Patrick 764
Ballyhean
Ballintober
Barnеycarroll
Murrisk
Inishturk
Liscarney
Lough Carra
Claremorris
Carrowkennedy
Partry
Cregganbaun
Kilnock
Cloonfad
Inishbofin
Benbury 795
Bengorm 702
Ballindine
Irishtown
Inishark
Killary Harbour
Mweelrea 819
Aasleagh
Benwee 682
Partry Mts
Lough Mask
Ballinrobe
Milltown
Ballynakill Bay
650
Kilmaine
Moyard
Connemara National Park
Maumturk Mts
An Fhairche (Clonbur)
Neale
Benbaun 730
667
Joyce Country
Clifden
The Twelve Pins
Bencorr 712
Lough Inagh
An Mám (Maum)
Cong
Cross
Shrule
Belclare
Tuam
Beagh
Mannin Bay
Connemara
Corr na Móna
Ballinaboy
Sraith Salach
613
Lough Corrib
Headford
Moylough
Ballyconneely
Toombeola
Cashel
Oughterard
Moneen
Slyne Head
Roundstone
Doire Iorrais
Ballyconneely Bay
Screeb
Ros Cathail
Cloonboo
Glinsce (Glinsk)
Iar Connaught
Bertraghboy Bay
Cill Chiaráin (Kilkieran)
Cinn Mhara (Kinvarra)
Maigh Cuilinn (Moycullen)
Leacht Seoirse
Baile an Dúlaigh
Cashla
An Aird Mhóir (Ardmore)
Casla (Costelloe)
Galway (Gaillimh)
Athenry
New Inn
Kiltullagh
Gorumna Island
An Cheathrú Rua (Carraroe)
Salthill
Oranmore
Bullaun
Golam Head
Indreabhán (Inverin)
An Spidéal (Spiddal)
Bearna (Barna)
North Sound
Galway Bay
Kilreekill
Ballydavid
Loughrea
Drumatober
Kilcolgan
Ardrahan
Cill Rónáin (Kilronan)
Black Head
Murroogh
Fanore
Burren
Ballyvaughan
Bealaclugga
Kinvara
Peterswell
Inishmore
Aran Islands
Slieve Elva 345
Kiltartan
Daly stown
Knockmoyle
Abbey
Portumna
Portland
Inishmaan
Slieve Aughty Mts
Bunnaglass
Power's Cross
Woodford
Terryglass
Inisheer
Burren
Gort
Lisdoonvarna
Gorteeny
Lough Derg
Kilshanny
Aughrim
Scalp 327
Cliffs of Moher
Kilfenora
Kilnaboy
Derrandoora
Coolbaun
Borrisokane
Rivers
N3
N4
N5
N15
N16
N17
N26
N56
N58
N59
N60
N61
N63
N65
N66
N67
N83
N84
M6
M17
M18
A46
8

7
8
9
10
11
12
B
C
D
E
F
Inishtrahull Sound
Malin Head
Inishowen
Lough Foyle
Lough Swilly
Londonderry (Derry)
Letterkenny
Strabane
Sperrin Mountains
Omagh
Coleraine
Giant's Causeway
Ballymena
Antrim Hills
Larne
Antrim
Lough Neagh
Newtownabbey
Belfast
Belfast Lough
Carrickfergus
Bangor
Newtownards
Lisburn
Ards Peninsula
Portadown
Craigavon
Lurgan
Armagh
Dungannon
Cookstown
Enniskillen
Lough Erne
Monaghan
Newry
Mourne Mountains
Dundrum Bay
Dundalk (Dún Dealgan)
Dundalk Bay
Carlingford Lough
Cavan
Drogheda (Droichead Átha)
Navan (An Uaimh)
Mullingar (An Muileann gCearr)
Lough Ennell
Lough Sheelin
Longford
Tullamore (Tulach Mhór)
Swords
DUBLIN (BAILE ÁTHA CLIATH)
Dún Laoghaire
Bray (Bré)
Lambay Island
Naas (An Nás)
Newbridge (Droichead Nua)
The Curragh
Wicklow (Cill Mhantáin)
Wicklow Head
Blessington Lakes
Slieve Bloom Mts
Bog of Allen
North Channel
IRISH SEA
Mull of Kintyre
Campbeltown
Kintyre
Arran
Firth of Clyde
Ailsa Craig
Stranraer
The Rhins of Galloway
Liverpool (Birkenhead)
Douglas
Liverpool
Holyhead
Cherbourg
GB
IRL
7°30′
7°00′
6°30′
6°00′
5°30′
55°00′
54°30′
54°00′
53°30′

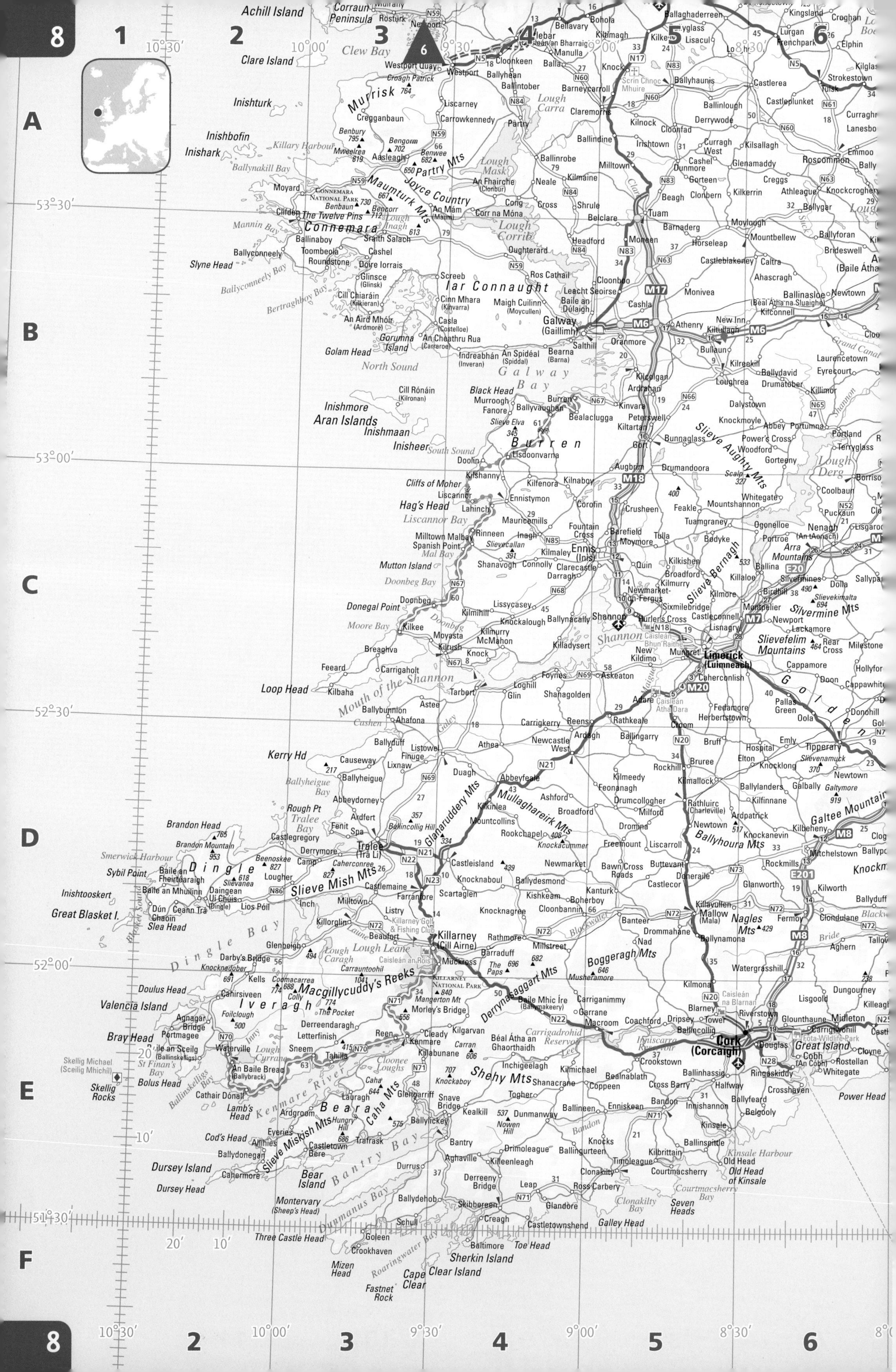
1
2
3
4
5
6
A
B
C
D
E
F
10°30′
10°00′
9°30′
9°00′
8°30′
53°30′
53°00′
52°30′
52°00′
51°30′
Achill Island
Corraun Peninsula
Rosturk
Newport
N59
Clew Bay
Westport Quay
Westport
Clare Island
Croagh Patrick 764
Murrisk
Inishturk
Inishbofin
Inishark
Killary Harbour
Ballynakill Bay
Cregganbaun
Liscarney
Carrowkennedy
Partry Mts
Maumturk Mts
Joyce Country
Connemara
Connemara National Park
Benbaun 730
Twelve Pins
Clifden
Ballinaboy
Ballyconneely
Slyne Head
Roundstone
Mannin Bay
Ballyconneely Bay
Bertraghboy Bay
Toombeola
Cashel
Glinsce (Glinsk)
Cill Chiaráin (Kilkieran)
An Aird Mhóir (Ardmore)
Gorumna Island
Golam Head
North Sound
Screeb
Iar Connaught
Cinn Mhara (Kinvarra)
Casla (Costelloe)
An Cheathrú Rua (Carraroe)
Indreabhán (Inveran)
An Spidéal (Spiddal)
Bearna (Barna)
Maigh Cuilinn (Moycullen)
Oughterard
Ros Cathail
Galway (Gaillimh)
Salthill
Oranmore
Galway Bay
Lough Corrib
Lough Mask
Lough Carra
Cong
Cross
Headford
Tuam
Athenry
Loughrea
Ballinasloe
Castlerea
Roscommon
Strokestown
Ballyhaunis
Claremorris
Ballinrobe
Knock
Kilkelly
Charlestown
Ballaghaderreen
M6
M17
M18
Kinvara
Gort
Slieve Aughty Mts
Lough Derg
Portumna
Black Head
Burren
Ballyvaughan
Lisdoonvarna
Doolin
Cliffs of Moher
Hag's Head
Liscannor Bay
Lahinch
Ennistymon
Inishmore
Aran Islands
Inishmaan
Inisheer
Cill Rónáin (Kilronan)
South Sound
Milltown Malbay
Spanish Point
Mal Bay
Mutton Island
Doonbeg Bay
Ennis (Inis)
Corofin
Tulla
Slieve Bernagh
Killaloe
Shannon
Limerick (Luimneach)
Kilrush
Kilkee
Moore Bay
Donegal Point
Loop Head
Carrigaholt
Mouth of the Shannon
Tarbert
Foynes
Askeaton
Adare
Newcastle West
Abbeyfeale
Listowel
Ballybunnion
Kerry Hd
Ballyheigue Bay
Tralee Bay
Rough Pt
Tralee (Trá Li)
Brandon Head
Brandon Mountain 953
Smerwick Harbour
Sybil Point
Dingle
Slieve Mish Mts
Inishtooskert
Great Blasket I.
Slea Head
Dingle Bay
Castlemaine
Killorglin
Killarney (Cill Airne)
Lough Leane
Muckross
Macgillycuddy's Reeks
Carrauntoohil 1041
Iveragh
Kells
Cahirsiveen
Valencia Island
Doulus Head
Bray Head
Portmagee
Waterville
Skellig Michael (Sceilig Mhichíl)
Skellig Rocks
Bolus Head
Ballinskelligs Bay
Kenmare
Kenmare River
Sneem
Lamb's Head
Beara
Caha Mts
Glengarriff
Slieve Miskish Mts
Castletown Bere
Bear Island
Dursey Island
Dursey Head
Cod's Head
Bantry
Bantry Bay
Durrus
Dunmanus Bay
Sheep's Head
Three Castle Head
Mizen Head
Crookhaven
Goleen
Schull
Roaringwater Bay
Cape Clear
Clear Island
Fastnet Rock
Sherkin Island
Baltimore
Skibbereen
Toe Head
Glandore
Ross Carbery
Clonakilty Bay
Galley Head
Seven Heads
Courtmacsherry Bay
Old Head of Kinsale
Kinsale
Bandon
Cork (Corcaigh)
Blarney
Ballincollig
Macroom
Shehy Mts
Derrynasaggart Mts
Boggeragh Mts
Millstreet
Mallow (Mala)
Nagles Mts
Fermoy
Mitchelstown
Galtee Mountains
Ballyhoura Mts
Charleville
Mullaghareirk Mts
Glanaruddery Mts
Kanturk
Cobh (An Cobh)
Great Island
Midleton
Crosshaven
Power Head
Tipperary
Golden
Silvermine Mts
Slievefelim Mountains
Nenagh
M7
M8
M20
N20
N21
N22
N69
N70
N71
N72
N28
E20
E201

7
8
9
10
11
12
A
B
C
D
E
F
IRISH SEA
Douglas
Liverpool
10
Holyhead
Fishguard
12
Pembroke Dock
Cherbourg
Cherbourg, Roscoff
Roscoff
St George's Channel
53°30′
53°00′
52°30′
52°00′
51°30′
7°30′
7°00′
6°30′
6°00′
5°30′
IRL
GB
Mullingar (An Muileann gCearr)
Navan (An Uaimh)
Drogheda (Droichead Átha)
Swords
DUBLIN (BAILE ÁTHA CLIATH)
Dún Laoghaire
Bray (Bré)
Greystones
Wicklow (Cill Mhantáin)
Wicklow Head
Arklow (An tInbhear Mór)
Wicklow Mountains
Naas (An Nás)
Newbridge (Droichead Nua)
The Curragh
Kildare
Tullamore (Tulach Mhór)
Portlaoise
Athy
Carlow (Ceatharlach)
Kilkenny (Cill Chainnigh)
Thurles (Durlas)
Cashel
Clonmel (Cluain Meala)
Carrick-on-Suir (Carraig na Siúire)
Waterford (Port Láirge)
New Ross
Wexford (Loch Garman)
Wexford Harbour
Rosslare Point
Rosslare Harbour
Enniscorthy (Inis Córthaidh)
Gorey
Dungarvan (Dún Garbhán)
Youghal (Eochaill)
Youghal Bay
Tramore (Trá Mhór)
Hook Head
Saltee Islands
Carnsore Point
Greenore Point
Ballyteige Bay
Blackstairs Mountains
Slieve Bloom Mts
Slieveardagh Hills
Comeragh Mts
Monavullagh Mts
Booley Hills
Bog of Allen
Lough Sheelin
Lough Owel
Lough Ennell
Lambay Island
Ireland's Eye
Howth
Dublin Bay
Brittas Bay
Mizen Head
Kilmichael Point
Cahore Point
Helvick Head
Mine Head
Knockadoon Head
St David's Head
St David's
Ramsey Island
St Bride's Bay
Pembrokeshire Coast National Park
Skomer Island
Milford Haven
St Ann's Head
Strumble Head
Haverford

Isle of Man
Isle of Man (British Crown Dependency)
Ramsey
Peel
DOUGLAS
Castletown
Port Erin
Calf of Man
Point of Ayre
IRISH SEA
Dublin
Belfast
Ards Peninsula
Mull of Galloway
Burrow Head
The Machars
Luce Bay
Wigtown Bay
Solway Firth
Dumfries
Annan
Gretna
Carlisle
Wigton
Maryport
Workington
Whitehaven
St Bees Head
Cockermouth
Keswick
Penrith
LAKE DISTRICT
NATIONAL PARK
Ambleside
Windermere
Coniston
Kendal
Ulverston
Barrow-in-Furness
Isle of Walney
Morecambe Bay
Morecambe
Lancaster
Forest of Bowland
Fleetwood
Blackpool
Lytham St Anne's
Preston
Southport
Formby
Crosby
Bootle
Wallasey
Liverpool
Birkenhead
St Helens
Warrington
Widnes
Runcorn
Wigan
Chester
Wrexham
Holyhead
Holy Island
Anglesey (Môn)
Bangor
Caernarfon
Caernarfon Bay
Llandudno
Colwyn Bay
Rhyl
Prestatyn
Conwy
Clwydian Range
SNOWDONIA
NATIONAL PARK
Snowdon 1085
Betws-y-Coed
Blaenau Ffestiniog
Bala
Llangollen
Lleyn Peninsula
Pwllheli
Porthmadog
Tremadog Bay
Harlech
Bardsey Island
Dolgellau
Cadair Idris
Barmouth
Cardigan Bay
Machynlleth
Welshpool
Oswestry
Shrewsbury
Telford
Whitchurch
Nantwich
Berwyn
Long Mynd

7
8
9
10
11
12
B
C
D
E
F
55°00′
54°30′
54°00′
53°30′
53°00′
2°00′
1°00′
0°30′
0°00′
IJmuiden
Rotterdam, Zeebrugge
GB
Morpeth
Ashington
Bedlington
Blyth
Whalton
Ponteland
Whitley Bay
Tynemouth
Killingworth
Gosforth
North Shields
South Shields
Newcastle upon Tyne
Hexham
Corbridge
Prudhoe
Gateshead
Jarrow
Sunderland
Angel of the North
Birtley
Washington
Houghton le Spring
Consett
Stanley
Chester-le-Street
Seaham
Allenheads
Lanchester
Durham
Easington
Horden
Peterlee
Stanhope
Wolsingham
Crook
Spennymoor
Ferryhill
Wingate
Trimdon
Hartlepool
Tees Bay
Bishop Auckland
Shildon
Sedgefield
Newton Aycliffe
Billingham
Redcar
Saltburn-by-the-Sea
Teesdale
Middleton in Teesdale
Barnard Castle
Staindrop
Aycliffe
Middlesbrough
Stockton-on-Tees
South Bank
Thornaby-on-Tees
Brotton
Skelton
Loftus
Hinderwell
Guisborough
Sandsend
Darlington
Yarm
Whitby
Brough
Bowes
Kirkby Stephen
Nateby
Stokesley
High Hawsker
Robin Hood's Bay
Scotch Corner
Richmond
Catterick
Cleveland Hills
Round Hill
454
North York Moors
NORTH YORK MOORS NATIONAL PARK
Staintondale
Hambleton Hills
Northallerton
Cloughton
Burniston
Hawes
Bainbridge
Aysgarth
Leyburn
Wensleydale
Middleham
Bedale
Lockton
Scalby
Scarborough
YORKSHIRE DALES NATIONAL PARK
Langstrothdale Chase
Thirsk
Kirkbymoorside
Helmsley
Wrelton
Pickering
Snainton
Seamer
Eastfield
Filey
Masham
Vale of Pickering
Buckden
Great Whernside
Nidderdale
Vale of York
Topcliffe
Malton
Norton
Yorkshire Wolds
Bempton
Flamborough
Flamborough Head
Horton in Ribblesdale
Kettlewell
Ripon
Easingwold
Hovingham
Stillington
West Knapton
Rudston
Bridlington
Pateley Bridge
Studley Park
Boroughbridge
Sutton-on-the-Forest
North Grimston
Sledmere
Langtoft
Hilderthorpe
Bridlington Bay
Grassington
Settle
Long Preston
Hetton
Summer Bridge
Ripley
Knaresborough
Haxby
Fridaythorpe
Fimber
Nafferton
Driffield
Skipsea
Skipton
Harrogate
National Railway Museum
York
York Minster
Stamford Bridge
Pocklington
Eastburn
Beeford
Bainton
Ilkley
Otley
Spofforth
Wetherby
Boston Spa
Osbaldwick
Fulford
Elvington
Hayton
Brandesburton
Hornsea
Leven
Sigglesthorne
Keighley
Yeadon
Horsforth
Tadcaster
Market Weighton
Molescroft
Skirlaugh
Aldbrough
Nelson
Colne
Bingley
Shipley
Leeds
Aberford
Ulleskelf
Cawood
Sherburn in Elmet
North Duffield
Bubwith
Holme-on-Spalding-Moor
North Cave
Beverley
Sproatley
Padiham
Burnley
Bradford
Pudsey
Garforth
Selby
South Cave
Anlaby
Bilton
Holderness
Withernsea
Kingston upon Hull
Rothwell
Castleford
Knottingley
Howden
Hook
Goole
Elloughton
North Ferriby
Barton-upon-Humber
Patrington
Easington
Rawtenstall
Todmorden
Halifax
Batley
Morley
Dewsbury
Wakefield
Pontefract
Snaith
Goxhill
Mouth of the Humber
Elland
Huddersfield
Askern
Eastoft
Moorends
Thorne
Crowle
Scunthorpe
Winterton
Immingham
Spurn Head
Rochdale
Littleborough
Heywood
Honley
Darton
Barnsley
South Kirkby
Stainforth
Hatfield
Bottesford
Brigg
Grimsby
Cleethorpes
Humberston
Bury
Middleton
Royton
Oldham
Holmfirth
Bentley
Doncaster
Epworth
Caistor
Laceby
Tetney
Mossley
Ashton-under-Lyne
Penistone
Wombwell
Mexborough
Bessacarr
Rossington
Kirton in Lindsey
South Kelsey
North Somercotes
Manchester
Stretford
Hollingworth
Glossop
Chapeltown
Rawmarsh
Rotherham
Blyton
Misterton
Beckingham
Binbrook
Fotherby
Stockport
Kinder Scout
High Peak
Sheffield
Maltby
Gainsborough
Lincolnshire Wolds
Market Rasen
Grimoldby
Louth
Marple
PEAK DISTRICT NATIONAL PARK
Aughton
South Anston
Ranskill
Mablethorpe
Castleton
Mosborough
Retford (East Retford)
Maltby le Marsh
Wilmslow
Alderley Edge
Chapel-en-le-Frith
Dronfield
Eckington
Staveley
Worksop
Saxilby
Dunholme
Wragby
Huttoft
Alford
Macclesfield
Buxton
Baslow
Brimington
Bolsover
Creswell
Tuxford
Lincoln Castle
Lincoln
Lincoln Cathedral
Chesterfield
Clay Cross
Market Warsop
Ollerton
North Hykeham
Branston
Bardney
Horncastle
Partney
Ingoldmells
Mansfield Woodhouse
Waddington
Woodhall Spa
Spilsby
Burgh le Marsh
Skegness
Congleton
Matlock
Mansfield
Sutton in Ashfield
Newark-on-Trent
Harmston
Metheringham
Tattershall
Coningsby
Wainfleet All Saints
Stickney
Biddulph
Leek
Warslow
Alfreton
Coddington
Billinghay
East Fen
Kidsgrove
Wirksworth
Somercotes
Kirkby in Ashfield
Hucknall
Southwell
Leadenham
West Fen
Boston Deeps
Audley
Ipstones
Ambergate
Belper
Ripley
Vale of Belvoir
Balderton
Leasingham
Holland Fen
Sibsey
Wrangle
Newcastle-under-Lyme
Stoke-on-Trent
Alton Towers
Ashbourne
Derwent Mills
Heanor
Eastwood
Arnold
Long Bennington
Sleaford
Old Leake
Lynn Deeps
Cheadle
Brailsford
Nottingham
Carlton
Heckington
Swineshead
Boston
Frampton
Hunstanton
Heacham
The Wash
Ilkeston
Derby
Beeston
Bingham
West Bridgford
Barkston
Great Gonerby
Helpringham
Stone
Uttoxeter
Barrowby
Grantham
Sutterton
Snettisham
Long Eaton
Folkingham
Gosberton
Surfleet
Holbeach Marsh
Gedney Drove End
Eccleshall
Tutbury
Hilton
Repton
Kegworth
Waltham on the Wolds
Great Ponton
Dowsby
Pinchbeck
Holbeach
Long Sutton
Terrington Marsh
Stafford
Great Haywood
Burton upon Trent
Ticknall
Morton
Spalding
Cowbit
Sutton Bridge
King's Lynn
Gnosall
Newport
Rugeley
Swadlincote
Ashby de la Zouch
Shepshed
Loughborough
Melton Mowbray
Colsterworth
Bourne
Thurlby
The Fens
West Winch
Penkridge
Burntwood
Measham
Coalville
Mountsorrel
Rothley
Cottesmore
Market Deeping
Crowland
Walsoken
Wisbech
Cannock
Green
Lichfield
Appleby Magna
Ibstock
Syston
Langham
Oakham
Rutland Water
Ryhall
Stamford
Northborough
Newborough
Thorney
Glinton
Outwell
Stradset
Downham Market
Denver
Brownhills
Tamworth
Twycross Zoo
Kirby Muxloe
Glenfield
Birstall
Leicester
Eye
Bedford Level (North Level)
Aldridge
Fazeley
Wigston
Uppingham
Wolverhampton
Walsall
West Bromwich
Sutton Coldfield
Atherstone
Earl Shilton
Hinckley
Nuneaton
Oadby
Great Glen
Husbands Bosworth
Harcourt
Cottingham
Rockingham
Rockingham Forest
Peterborough
Yaxley
Ramsey
Whittlesey
Elton
Wimblington
Bedford Level
March
Welney
Cosby
Wednesbury
Dudley

1
2
3
4
5
6
A
B
C
D
E
10
9
6°00′
5°30′
5°00′
4°30′
4°00′
52°00′
51°30′
51°00′
50°30′
50°00′
20′
10′
Cardigan Bay
Aberdovey
Borth
Enniscorthy
(Inis Córthaidh)
Kilnamanagh
Ballagkeen
Castleellis
Ballyvaldon
Blackwater
New Ross
Adamstown
N25
N11
Newbawn
IRL
Wellington
Carrick
Duncormick
Fethard
Ballyteige Bay
Kilmore
Kilmore Quay
Hook Head
Saltee Islands
Wexford Bay
Curracloe
Wexford (Loch Garman)
Rosslare Point
Wexford Harbour
Rosslare
Rosslare Harbour
Greenore Point
Carnsore Point
St George's Channel
CELTIC SEA
Aberystwyth
Llanbadarn Fawr
Llanrhystud
Llan-non
Cross Inn
Aberaeron
A487
New Quay
Llanarth
Temple Bar
Synod Inn
Talgarreg
A482
Aberporth
Plwmp
Ffostrasol
A486
Penrhiw-pâl
A475
Llanwenog
Llanybydder
Cardigan
Horeb
Llandysul
A484
Newcastle Emlyn
Llangeler
Llanfihangel-ar-arth
Rhos
Pencader
Llansawel
Newport Bay
Fishguard Bay
Strumble Head
Goodwick
Newport
Fishguard
(Abergwaun)
Eglwyswrw
Crymych
Mynydd Preseli
Trelech
Cynwyl Elfed
A485
Brechfa
St David's Head
St David's
A478
Greenway
Letterston
Maenclochog
Solva
Carmarthen
(Caerfyrddin)
National Botanic Garden of Wales
Llanegwad
Llanarthne
Ramsey Island
St Bride's Bay
Camrose
Llandissilio
Meidrim
A40
Haverfordwest
(Hwlffordd)
Clynderwen
Whitland
St Clears
A48
Ammanford
(Rhydaman)
Pembrokeshire Coast National Park
Broad Haven
A4076
Narberth
Tavernspite
Pontyberem
Skomer Island
Johnston
Templeton
Pendine
A4066
Kidwelly
(Cydweli)
Llannon
Milford Haven
A477
Neyland
A4075
Kilgetty
Carmarthen Bay
A476
Dale
Saundersfoot
A484
Trimsaran
Llanelli
St Ann's Head
Angle
Pembroke Dock
Pembroke
Tenby
Pembrey
Burry Port
Gorseinon
Castlemartin
Manorbier
Caldey Island
Whitford Point
Crofty
Cockett
Linney Head
Llanrhidian
Dunvant
St Govan's Head
Gower
Rhossili
Worms Head
A4118
Mumbles
Port Eynon
Lundy Island
Ilfracombe
A399
A3123
Morte Bay
Baggy Point
A361
Croyde
Braunton
Bideford Bay
Fremington
Barnstaple
Appledore
Westward Ho!
A39
Northam
A377
Hartland Point
Clovelly
Bideford
Hartland
Atherington
Great Torrington
Stibb Cross
Kilkhampton
A388
Torridge
A386
Winkleigh
Bude
Stratton
A3072
Hatherleigh
Holsworthy
Highampton
A3079
Folly Gate
Okehampton
Tamar
Wainhouse Corner
Boscastle
Yes Tor
619
Ottery
A30
Tintagel
Tintagel Castle
Hallworthy
Lifton
Lydford
Delabole
A395
Port Isaac Bay
Launceston
St Teath
Camelford
Congdon's Shop
Pentire Point
St Endellion
A39
A30
Bolventor
Tavistock
Trevose Head
Padstow
Bodmin Moor
Mining Landscape
Princetown
St Merryn
Wadebridge
A389
Callington
A390
Bere Alston
Horrabridge
Trenance
Watergate Bay
Bodmin
Lanivet
St Columb Major
A38
St Ive
Liskeard
Newquay
A392
A390
Roche
Lostwithiel
Saltash
Plympton
St Dennis
A387
St Germans
Plymouth
Perranporth
A3075
St Enoder
A391
Pelynt
Sandplace
Torpoint
Goonhavern
A3058
West Looe
East Looe
Millbrook
Plymstock
Yealm
St Agnes
St Austell
Polperro
Whitsand Bay
Rame Head
Newton Ferrers
Probus
St Austell Bay
Portreath
Tregony
Mevagissey
Bigbury
Truro
St Day
A3078
St Ives
St Ives Bay
Redruth
Zennor
Gwithian
Camborne
Dodman Point
Hayle
A393
St Just in Roseland
Pendeen
St Erth
Leedstown
Penryn
St Mawes
St Just
A3071
Falmouth
Penzance
Marazion
A394
Falmouth Bay
Sennen
Mount's Bay
Helston
Land's End
St Buryan
Porthleven
St Keverne
A3083
Mullion
Isles of Scilly
Black Head
Tresco
St Martin's
Lizard
St Mary's
Lizard Point
Hugh Town
St Agnes
Cherbourg, Roscoff
Santander
Roscoff

7
8
9
10
11
12
14
15
A
B
C
D
E
Birmingham
Dudley
Stourbridge
Kidderminster
Coventry
Solihull
Nuneaton
Bedworth
Rugby
Royal Leamington Spa
Warwick
Kenilworth
Redditch
Bromsgrove
Droitwich Spa
Worcester
Stratford-upon-Avon
Evesham
Vale of Evesham
Pershore
Great Malvern
Ledbury
Hereford
Leominster
Ludlow
Bridgnorth
Wenlock Edge
Corve Dale
Stourport-on-Severn
Tewkesbury
Cheltenham
Gloucester
Ross-on-Wye
Monmouth (Trefynwy)
Abergavenny (Y Fenni)
Brecon
Brecon Beacons National Park
Black Mountains
Black Mountain
Golden Valley
Hay-on-Wye
Builth Wells
Llandrindod Wells
Rhayader
Llanidloes
Newtown (Y Drenewydd)
Plynlimon
Cambrian Mountains
Mynydd Eppynt
Merthyr Tydfil
Tredegar
Ebbw Vale
Abertillery
Pontypool
Aberdare
Neath (Castell-y-Nedd)
Port Talbot
Bridgend
Porthcawl
Pontypridd
Caerphilly
Cardiff (Caerdydd)
Penarth
Barry
Newport (Casnewydd)
Cwmbrân
Caldicot
Chepstow
Thornbury
Bristol
Kingswood
Keynsham
Bath
Clevedon
Portishead
Weston-super-Mare
Bristol Channel
Flat Holm
Mendip Hills
Wells
Glastonbury
Street
Shepton Mallet
Frome
Trowbridge
Melksham
Chippenham
Corsham
Swindon
Cirencester
Stroud
Cotswold Hills
Oxford
Abingdon
Didcot
Witney
Banbury
Bicester
Kidlington
Vale of White Horse
Lambourn Downs
Marlborough Downs
Marlborough
Devizes
Hungerford
Newbury
Thatcham
Basingstoke
Andover
Salisbury Plain
Salisbury
Amesbury
Warminster
Winchester
Southampton
Eastleigh
Romsey
New Forest
Lymington
Christchurch
Bournemouth
Poole
Wimborne Minster
Ringwood
Cranborne Chase
Shaftesbury
Gillingham
Wincanton
Sherborne
Yeovil
Blandford Forum
Dorchester
Weymouth
Isle of Portland
Bill of Portland
Chesil Beach
Lyme Bay
Bridport
Lyme Regis
Isle of Purbeck
Swanage
St Alban's Head
The Needles
St Catherine's Point
Newport
Cowes
Gosport
Portchester
Fareham
Bridgwater
Taunton
Quantock Hills
Brendon Hills
Exmoor Forest
Exmoor National Park
Minehead
Wellington
Tiverton
Black Down Hills
Chard
Crewkerne
Honiton
Axminster
Sidmouth
Exmouth
Exeter
Dawlish
Teignmouth
Newton Abbot
Torquay
Paignton
Brixham
Dartmouth
Totnes
Kingsbridge
Salcombe
Start Point
Bolt Head
Prawle Point
Berry Head
Bridgwater Bay
Burnham-on-Sea
Somerton
Ilminster
GB
Cherbourg, Guernsey, Jersey, St Malo
50°00′
50°30′
51°00′
51°30′
52°00′
3°30′
3°00′
2°30′
2°00′
1°30′

Cambrian Mountains
Black Mountains
Black Mountain
Brecon Beacons National Park
Mynydd Eppynt
Bristol Channel
Exmoor National Park
Exmoor Forest
Brendon Hills
Quantock Hills
Black Down Hills
Mendip Hills
Cotswold Hills
Vale of Evesham
Vale of White Horse
Salisbury Plain
Lambourn Downs
Marlborough Downs
Hampshire Downs
North Downs
Cranborne Chase
New Forest
North Dorset Downs
South Dorset Downs
Isle of Purbeck
Isle of Portland
Bill of Portland
Chesil Beach
Lyme Bay
Poole Bay
The Solent
The Needles
St Catherine's Point
St Alban's Head
Wenlock Edge
The Long Mynd
Corve Dale
Golden Valley
Stoke-on-Trent
Newcastle-under-Lyme
Crewe
Wrexham (Wrecsam)
Shrewsbury
Telford
Wolverhampton
Walsall
West Bromwich
Sutton Coldfield
Dudley
Birmingham
Coventry
Nuneaton
Derby
Nottingham
Leicester
Burton upon Trent
Stafford
Lichfield
Tamworth
Kidderminster
Worcester
Hereford
Gloucester
Cheltenham
Stratford-upon-Avon
Royal Leamington Spa
Warwick
Rugby
Banbury
Oxford
Swindon
Newport (Casnewydd)
Cardiff (Caerdydd)
Bristol
Bath
Weston-super-Mare
Taunton
Exeter
Torquay
Paignton
Yeovil
Dorchester
Weymouth
Poole
Bournemouth
Salisbury
Southampton
Portsmouth
Winchester
Basingstoke
Newbury
Reading
Abergavenny
Merthyr Tydfil
Swansea
Port Talbot
Neath
Bridgend
Barry
GB
Cherbourg, Guernsey, Jersey, St Malo
Bilbao, St Malo, Guernsey, Jersey, Cherbourg & Santander
Caen, Le Havre

7
8
9
10
11
12
0°30′
0°00′
0°30′
1°00′
1°30′
52°30′
52°00′
51°30′
51°00′
B
C
D
E
F
11
18
The Wash
Boston Deeps
Lynn Deeps
Blakeney Point
Boston
Grantham
Melton Mowbray
Stamford
Spalding
The Fens
King's Lynn
Wisbech
Hunstanton
Sheringham
Cromer
Fakenham
North Walsham
Dereham
Norwich
Great Yarmouth
Lowestoft
The Broads
Peterborough
Rockingham Forest
Bedford Level (North Level)
Bedford Level (Middle Level)
Bedford Level
March
Downham Market
Swaffham
Thetford
Breckland
Isle of Ely
Ely
Huntingdon
St Ives
Mildenhall
Newmarket
Bury St Edmunds
Stowmarket
Diss
Beccles
Halesworth
Southwold
Aldeburgh
Orford Ness
Woodbridge
Ipswich
Felixstowe
Harwich
Landguard Point
Hoek van Holland
The Naze
Clacton-on-Sea
Frinton-on-Sea
Colchester
Sudbury
Haverhill
Saffron Walden
Cambridge
Kettering
Corby
Bedford
Milton Keynes
St Neots
Biggleswade
Royston
Letchworth Garden City
Hitchin
Stevenage
Luton
Dunstable
Bishop's Stortford
Braintree
Witham
Chelmsford
Maldon
Harlow
Hertford
St Albans
Hemel Hempstead
Watford
High Wycombe
Chiltern Hills
Brentwood
Basildon
Billericay
Southend-on-Sea
Canvey Island
Foulness Point
Romford
Ilford
Hendon
LONDON
Fulham
Uxbridge
Slough
Windsor
Maidenhead
Bracknell
Staines-upon-Thames
Thames
Dartford
Gravesend
Isle of Grain
Isle of Sheppey
Rochester
Gillingham
Chatham
Sittingbourne
Faversham
Whitstable
Herne Bay
Margate
North Foreland
Broadstairs
Ramsgate
Pegwell Bay
Canterbury
Sandwich
Deal
South Foreland
Dover
Folkestone
Hythe
Channel Tunnel
Romney Marsh
Dungeness
Rye Bay
Hastings
Bexhill
Eastbourne
Beachy Head
Seaford
Newhaven
Brighton
Hove
Worthing
Shoreham-by-Sea
Littlehampton
Bognor Regis
Chichester
Selsey Bill
South Downs National Park
Horsham
Crawley
Haywards Heath
Ashdown Forest
Crowborough
The Weald
Royal Tunbridge Wells
Tonbridge
Sevenoaks
Maidstone
Ashford
North Downs
Guildford
Woking
Epsom
Croydon
Reigate
Dorking
Aldershot
Farnham
Haslemere
Strait of Dover (Pas de Calais)
ENGLISH CHANNEL
LA MANCHE
Dieppe
Dunkerque
Calais
Cap Blanc Nez
Cap Gris Nez
Wimereux
Boulogne-sur-Mer
Le Portel
Hardelot-Plage
Étaples
Le Touquet-Paris-Plage
F

NORDSEE
Waddeneilanden
Waddenzee
IJsselmeer
Markermeer
Noordoost Polder
NL
Texel
Vlieland
Terschelling
Ameland
Schiermonnikoog
Den Helder
Alkmaar
Hoorn
Enkhuizen
Lelystad
Zaandam
Haarlem
AMSTERDAM
Amstelveen
Hilversum
Leiden
'S-GRAVENHAGE (DEN HAAG)
Zoetermeer
Delft
Rotterdam
Schiedam
Vlaardingen
Dordrecht
Gouda
Utrecht
Amersfoort
Apeldoorn
Deventer
Zwolle
Kampen
Meppel
Emmeloord
Harlingen
Leeuwarden
Franeker
Sneek
Heerenveen
Drachten
Ede
Arnhem
Nijmegen
Oss
's-Hertogenbosch
Tilburg
Breda
Roosendaal
Eindhoven
Helmond
Venlo
Antwerpen
B
Europoort
Newcastle upon Tyne
Kingston upon Hull
Harwich
Afsluitdijk
Westerschelde
Oosterschelde
4°00′
4°30′
5°00′
5°30′
6°00′
53°30′
53°00′
52°30′
52°00′
51°30′
1
2
3
4
5
6
A
B
C
D
E
F
20

7
8
9
10
11
12
82
Ostfriesische Inseln
Borkum
Juist
Norderney
Baltrum
Langeoog
Spiekeroog
Wangerooge
Mellum
Scharhörn
Neuwerk
Cuxhaven
Nationalpark Niedersächsisches Wattenmeer
Norden
Aurich
Wittmund
Jever
Wilhelmshaven
Bremerhaven
Emden
Leer
Oldenburg
Bremen
Delmenhorst
Groningen
Assen
Emmen
Meppen
Lingen
Nordhorn
Cloppenburg
Vechta
Osnabrück
Rheine
Enschede
Hengelo
Almelo
Münster
Bielefeld
Herford
Minden
Detmold
Paderborn
Gütersloh
Hamm
Lippstadt
Dortmund
Recklinghausen
Gelsenkirchen
Bochum
Essen
Oberhausen
Duisburg
Mülheim an der Ruhr
Moers
Hagen
Wuppertal
Arnsberg
Soest
Unna
Iserlohn
Nienburg
Verden
Zeven
OSTFRIESLAND
AMMERLAND
NORDERLAND
HARLINGERLAND
LAND HADELN
LAND WURSTEN
BUTJADINGEN
TEUFELS MOOR
EMSLAND
TECKLENBURGER LAND
MÜNSTERLAND
HONDSRUG
BOURTANGER MOOR
Wiehengebirge
Teutoburger Wald
SENNE
HOCHFLÄCHE
Haarstrang
OBERWÄLDER LAND
Egge
D
A
B
C
E
F
78
21

1
2
3
4
5
6
A
B
C
D
E
F
Braintree
Colchester
Clacton-on-Sea
Frinton-on-Sea
Walton on the Naze
Harlow
Epping
Chipping Ongar
Maldon
Witham
Tiptree
Tollesbury
West Mersea
St Osyth
Bradwell Waterside
Southminster
Burnham-on-Crouch
Foulness Point
Romford
Basildon
Rochford
Great Wakering
Southend-on-Sea
Canvey Island
Thames
Tilbury
Grays
Gravesend
Isle of Grain
Sheerness
Isle of Sheppey
Queenborough
Swanley
Rochester
Chatham
Gillingham
Sittingbourne
Whitstable
Herne Bay
Faversham
Margate
Birchington
North Foreland
Broadstairs
Ramsgate
Pegwell Bay
Royal St George's Golf Club
Sandwich
Canterbury
Deal
Walmer
South Foreland
Dover
Dover Castle
Folkestone
Hythe
Maidstone
West Malling
Sevenoaks
Tonbridge
Royal Tunbridge Wells
The Weald
Ashford
GB
Headcorn
Staplehurst
Biddenden
High Halden
Tenterden
Hawkhurst
Bedgebury National Pinetum
Bodiam Castle
Appledore
Romney Marsh
Dymchurch
Littlestone-on-Sea
New Romney
Lydd
Dungeness
Rye
Rye Bay
Winchelsea
Icklesham
Battle
Hastings
Bexhill
Pevensey
Pevensey Levels
Polegate
Willingdon
Eastbourne
Beachy Head
Isle of Oxney
Channel Tunnel
Strait of Dover (Pas de Calais)
ENGLISH CHANNEL
LA MANCHE
Newhaven
Kingston upon Hull
Calais
Sangatte
Cap Blanc Nez
Coquelles
Marck
Wissant
Cap Gris Nez
Audresselles
Ambleteuse
Wimereux
Marquise
Guînes
Ardres
Audruicq
Licques
St-Martin-Boulogne
Boulogne-sur-Mer
Le Portel
Outreau
Desvres
Hardelot-Plage
Neufchâtel-Hardelot
Samer
Étaples
Le Touquet-Paris-Plage
Montreuil
Berck
Gravelines
Grand-Fort-Philippe
St-Pol-sur-Mer
Grande-Synthe
Dunkerque
Coudekerque-Branche
Bourbourg
Bergues
Hondschoote
Watten
St-Omer
Arques
Longuenesse
Wizernes
Lumbres
Cassel
Hazebrouck
Aire-sur-la-Lys
Isbergues
Lillers
Béthune
Bruay-la-Buissière
Noeux-les-Mines
Bully-les-Mines
Lens
Avion
Arras
Bapaume
Albert
Doullens
St-Pol-sur-Ternoise
Hesdin
Fruges
Crécy-en-Ponthieu
Abbeville
Le Crotoy
St-Valery-sur-Somme
Cayeux-sur-Mer
Baie de la Somme
Pte du Hourdel
Fort-Mahon-Plage
Quend
Rue
Le Tréport
Mers-les-Bains
Eu
Criel-sur-Mer
Dieppe
Neuville-lès-Dieppe
Varengeville-sur-Mer
St-Valery-en-Caux
Veulettes-sur-Mer
Fécamp
Yvetot
Bolbec
Lillebonne
Barentin
Rouen
Le Petit-Quevilly
Le Grand-Quevilly
Sotteville-lès-Rouen
St-Étienne-du-Rouvray
Oissel
Elbeuf
Pont-Audemer
Mont-St-Aignan
Maromme
Neufchâtel-en-Bray
Forges-les-Eaux
Gournay-en-Bray
Gisors
Les Andelys
Aumale
Poix-de-Picardie
Amiens
Corbie
Villers-Bretonneux
Moreuil
Montdidier
Roye
Breteuil
Crèvecœur-le-Grand
Grandvilliers
Beauvais
Clermont
Liancourt
St-Just-en-Chaussée
Compiègne
Noyon
Creil
Montataire
Pont-Ste-Maxence
Nogent-sur-Oise
Verberie
Crépy-en-Valois
Estrées-St-Denis
Oostende (Ostend)
Middelkerke
Nieuwpoort
Koksijde
De Panne
Veurne
Diksmuide
Poperinge
Ieper
Armentières
Bailleul
F
PONTHIEU
TERNOIS
VIMEU
PICARDIE
SANTERRE
PAYS DE CAUX
VEXIN NORMAND
FLANDRE
Collines de l'Artois
15
23
24
51°30′
51°00′
50°30′
50°00′
49°30′
1°30′
2°00′
2°30′

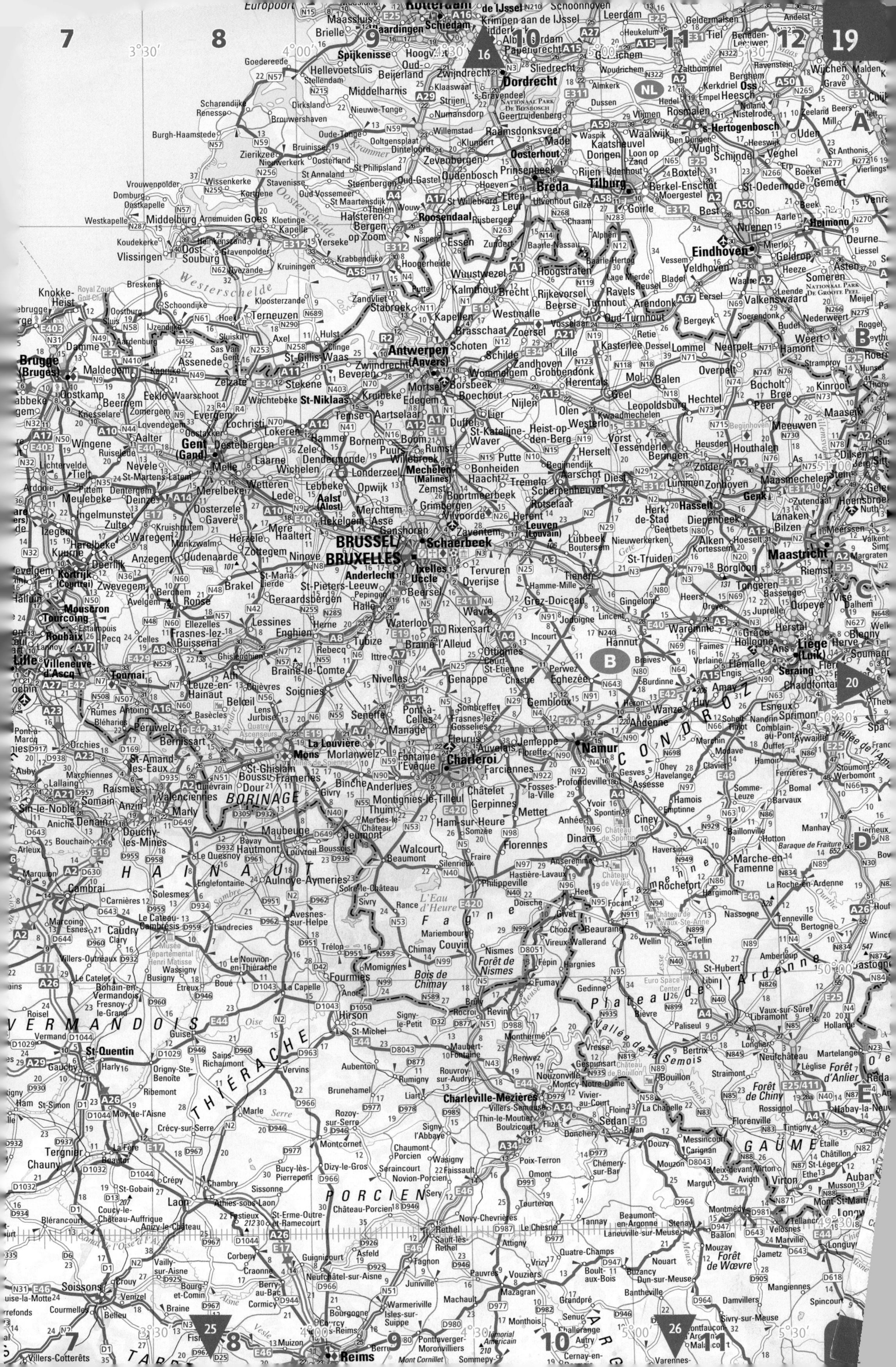
7
8
9
10
11
12
A
B
C
D
E
16
20
25
26
NL
B
Rotterdam
Schiedam
Dordrecht
Breda
Tilburg
's-Hertogenbosch
Eindhoven
Helmond
Middelburg
Vlissingen
Goes
Bergen op Zoom
Roosendaal
Oss
Brugge (Bruges)
Gent (Gand)
Antwerpen (Anvers)
St-Niklaas
Mechelen (Malines)
Aalst (Alost)
BRUSSEL BRUXELLES
Schaerbeek
Anderlecht
Ixelles
Uccle
Leuven (Louvain)
Hasselt
Genk
Maastricht
Liège (Luik)
Seraing
Namur
Charleroi
Mons
La Louvière
Tournai
Kortrijk (Courtrai)
Mouscron
Tourcoing
Roubaix
Lille
Villeneuve-d'Ascq
Valenciennes
Cambrai
St-Quentin
Charleville-Mézières
Sedan
Reims
Soissons
Laon
HAINAUT
BORINAGE
THIÉRACHE
VERMANDOIS
PORCIEN
CONDROZ
Famenne
Fagne
Plateau de l'Ardenne
GAUME
Vallée de la Semois
Oosterschelde
Westerschelde
Forêt de Nismes
Bois de Chimay
L'Eau d'Heure

NL
B
L
F
Dordrecht
Breda
Tilburg
Roosendaal
's-Hertogenbosch
Eindhoven
Nijmegen
Helmond
Venlo
Antwerpen (Anvers)
Mechelen (Malines)
BRUSSEL/BRUXELLES
Schaerbeek
Anderlecht
Leuven (Louvain)
Hasselt
Genk
Maastricht
Aachen
Mönchengladbach
Liège (Luik)
Verviers
Namur
Charleroi
Mons
La Louvière
Maubeuge
Charleville-Mézières
Sedan
Reims
LUXEMBOURG
Arlon
Bastogne
Thionville
Longwy
Esch-sur-Alzette
C O N D R O Z
Famenne
Fagne
Plateau de l'Ardenne
GAUME
PORCIEN
THIÉRACHE
BORINAGE

Dülmen
Hamm
Lippstadt
Paderborn
Bad Driburg
Recklinghausen
Gelsenkirchen
Bottrop
Herne
Dortmund
Unna
Soest
Duisburg
Oberhausen
Essen
Bochum
Witten
Hagen
Schwerte
Menden
Iserlohn
Arnsberg
Meschede
Brilon
Warburg
Marsberg
Wuppertal
Ratingen
Düsseldorf
Neuss
Remscheid
Solingen
Lüdenscheid
Leverkusen
Bergisch Gladbach
Köln
Gummersbach
Olpe
Siegen
Winterberg
Korbach
Frankenberg
Bad Berleburg
Marburg an der Lahn
Troisdorf
Siegburg
Bonn
St Augustin
Königswinter
Euskirchen
Neuwied
Koblenz
Limburg an der Lahn
Wetzlar
Gießen
Bad Homburg vor der Höhe
Frankfurt am Main
Offenbach am Main
Wiesbaden
Mainz
Darmstadt
Trier
Kaiserslautern
Mannheim
Ludwigshafen am Rhein
Heidelberg
Worms
Saarbrücken
Neustadt an der Weinstraße
Bad Kreuznach
HOCHFLÄCHE
OBERWÄLDER LAND
SAUERLAND
Rothaargebirge
BERGISCHES LAND
Westerwald
Eifel
Hunsrück
Taunus
Vogelsberg
ODENWALD
NORDPFÄLZER BERGLAND
SENNE
Haarstrang
E35
E34
E37
E41
E331
E40
E44
E45
E451
E42
E50
E31
E29
E422
17
78
74
27

2
3
4
5
6
A
B
C
D
E
F
4°30′
4°00′
3°30′
3°00′
2°30′
49°30′
49°00′
48°30′
48°00′
47°30′
20′
10′
ENGLISH CHANNEL
LA MANCHE
CHANNEL ISLANDS
Guernsey
GBG
Vale
St Peter in the Wood
Torteval
Plymouth
Cork, Rosslare
Sillon de Talbert
Pte du Château
Île de Bréhat
Plougrescant
Pleubian
Pte de l'Arcouest
Perros-Guirec
Penvénan
Trégastel
Louannec
Plouguiel
Ploubazlanec
Paimpol
Pleumeur-Bodou
Tréguier
Île de Batz
Trébeurden
Lannion
La Roche-Derrien
Plouézec
Roscoff
Pte de Primel
Baie de Lannion
TRÉGORROIS
Lanloup
Baie de Morlaix
Plougasnou
Locquirec
Ploubezre
Pontrieux
Brignogan-Plage
St-Pol-de-Léon
Lanmeur
Ploumilliau
Plouha
Kerlouan
Plouescat
Cléder
Carantec
Plestin-les-Grèves
Pluzunet
Bégard
Étables-sur-Mer
Erquy
Guissény
Plouguerneau
PAYS DE LÉON
Plouzévédé
Taulé
St-Martin-des-Champs
Plouaret
Lanvollon
Pléneuf-Val-André
Île d'Ouessant
Ploudalmézeau
Lannilis
Plouvorn
Morlaix
Pabu
Binic
Baie de St-Brieuc
Plouguin
Lesneven
Plounévez-Moëdec
Guingamp
Plélo
Porspoder
Le Folgoët
Plouigneau
Plougonven
Grâces
Châtelaudren
St-Alban
Lampaul
Landivisiau
St-Thégonnec
Belle-Isle-en-Terre
Ploumagoar
Plouagat
Plérin
St-Brieuc
Langueux
Brélès
Plabennec
Pleyber-Christ
Moustéru
Ploufragan
Lampaul-Plouarzel
Milizac
Gouesnou
Landerneau
Lampaul-Guimiliau
Trégueux
Lamballe
Passage du Fromveur
Plouarzel
St-Renan
Bohars
Guipavas
Plougonver
Bourbriac
Plouzané
Guilers
Le Relecq-Kerhuon
Ploudiry
St-Sauveur
Quessoy
Maroué
Locmaria-Plouzané
Brest
Sizun
Le Conquet
Goulet de Brest
Plougastel-Daoulas
Daoulas
Roch Trévezel
Monts d'Arrée
Berrien
Callac
Quintin
Plaintel
PENTHIÈVRE
Plénée-Jugon
Pte de St-Mathieu
Huelgoat
Roscanvel
Camaret-sur-Mer
Hanvec
Le Faou
Montagne St-Michel
Poullaouen
St-Nicolas-du-Pélem
Moncontour
Landes du Mené
Pte de Penhir
Presqu'île de Crozon
Plouyé
Maël-Carhaix
Corlay
Plœuc-sur-Lié
Collinée
Mer d'Iroise
Morgat
Crozon
Menez Hom
Pont-de-Buis-lès-Quimerch
Plonévez-du-Faou
Carhaix-Plouguer
Plounévez-Quintin
Uzel
Plouguenast
Pleyben
Landeleau
Rostrenen
Plouguernével
Gouarec
Cap de la Chèvre
Baie de Douarnenez
Châteaulin
Roc de Toullaëron
Trévé
Loudéac
Plémet
Merdrignac
Plomodiern
Châteauneuf-du-Faou
Mûr-de-Bretagne
Montagnes Noires
Gourin
Plouray
BRETAGNE
Plonévez-Porzay
Locronan
Briec
Silfiac
Cléguérec
La Chèze
Douarnenez
Séglien
La Trinité-Porhoët
Île de Sein
Le Cap
Ploaré
Coray
Noyal-Pontivy
Pte du Raz
Audierne
Pont-Croix
Plouhinec
CORNOUAILLE
Quimper
Guémené-sur-Scorff
Pontivy
Rohan
Bréhan
Le Faouët
Tourch
Scaër
Kernascléden
Landudec
Ergué-Gabéric
Plozévet
Pouldreuzic
Rosporden
St-Thurien
Inguiniel
Naizin
Josselin
Baie d'Audierne
St-Yvi
Bannalec
Tréméven
Bubry
Melrand
Pluméliau
Moréac
Guégon
Plonéour-Lanvern
Pleuven
Fouesnant
Melgven
Mellac
Plouay
Remungol
Pont-l'Abbé
Bénodet
Concarneau
Quimperlé
Baud
Locminé
Bignan
St-Jean-Brévelay
Plomeur
Anse de Bénodet
Trégunc
Riec-sur-Bélon
Inzinzac-Lochrist
Camors
Plumelec
St-Guénolé
Loctudy
Pont-Aven
Languidic
Landes de Lanvaux
Penmarch
Plobannalec
Névez
Moëlan-sur-Mer
Caudan
Hennebont
Pte de Penmarch
Guilvinec
Lesconil
Clohars-Carnoët
Guidel
Lanester
Pluvigner
Grand-Champ
Monterblanc
Le Pouldu
Lorient
Landévant
Elven
Anse de Pouldu
Ploemeur
Merlevenez
Plumergat
Brech
Larmor-Plage
Riantec
Port-Louis
Plouhinec
Plescop
St-Avé
Rochefort-en-Terre
Pluneret
Sulniac
Belz
Auray
Ploeren
Vannes
Questembert
Île de Groix
Groix
Erdeven
Bono
Arradon
Theix
Plouharnel
Crach
Baden
Noyalo
Noyal-Muzillac
Carnac
La Trinité-sur-Mer
Surzur
Ambon
Muzillac
Presqu'île de Quiberon
Locmariaquer
Port-Navalo
Sarzeau
St-Pierre-Quiberon
Baie de Quiberon
St-Gildas-de-Rhuys
Damgan
La Roche-Bernard
Pénestin
Quiberon
Presqu'île de Rhuys
Passage de la Teignouse
Île d'Houat
Herbignac
Assérac
Mesquer
Piriac-sur-Mer
Sauzon
Île de Hœdic
La Turballe
Guérande
Le Palais
Belle-Île
Le Croisic
Pte de Croisic
Batz-sur-Mer
Le Pouliguen
F
E50
E60
N12
N164
N165
N24
D786
D767
D790
D700
D768
D887
D785

7
8
9
10
11
Cap de la Hague
Pte de Barfleur
Cherbourg-Octeville
Valognes
COTENTIN
BAIE DE SEINE
Le Havre
Honfleur
Jersey
Guernsey
St Helier
Les Minquiers
Îles Chausey
Golfe de St-Malo
BESSIN
Bayeux
Caen
Lisieux
St-Lô
Coutances
Granville
Avranches
BOCAGE NORMAND
Vire
Flers
Falaise
Argentan
SUISSE NORMANDE
Collines de Normandie
Baie du Mont-St-Michel
St-Malo
Dinard
Dinan
Fougères
Rennes
Vitré
Laval
Mayenne
Alençon
Le Mans
MAINE
Château-Gontier
Sablé-sur-Sarthe
La Flèche
Châteaubriant
SEGRÉEN
ANJOU
Angers
BAUGEOIS
Saumur
SAUMUROIS
LES MAUGES
Nantes
St-Nazaire
GRANDE BRIÈRE
Redon
24
28

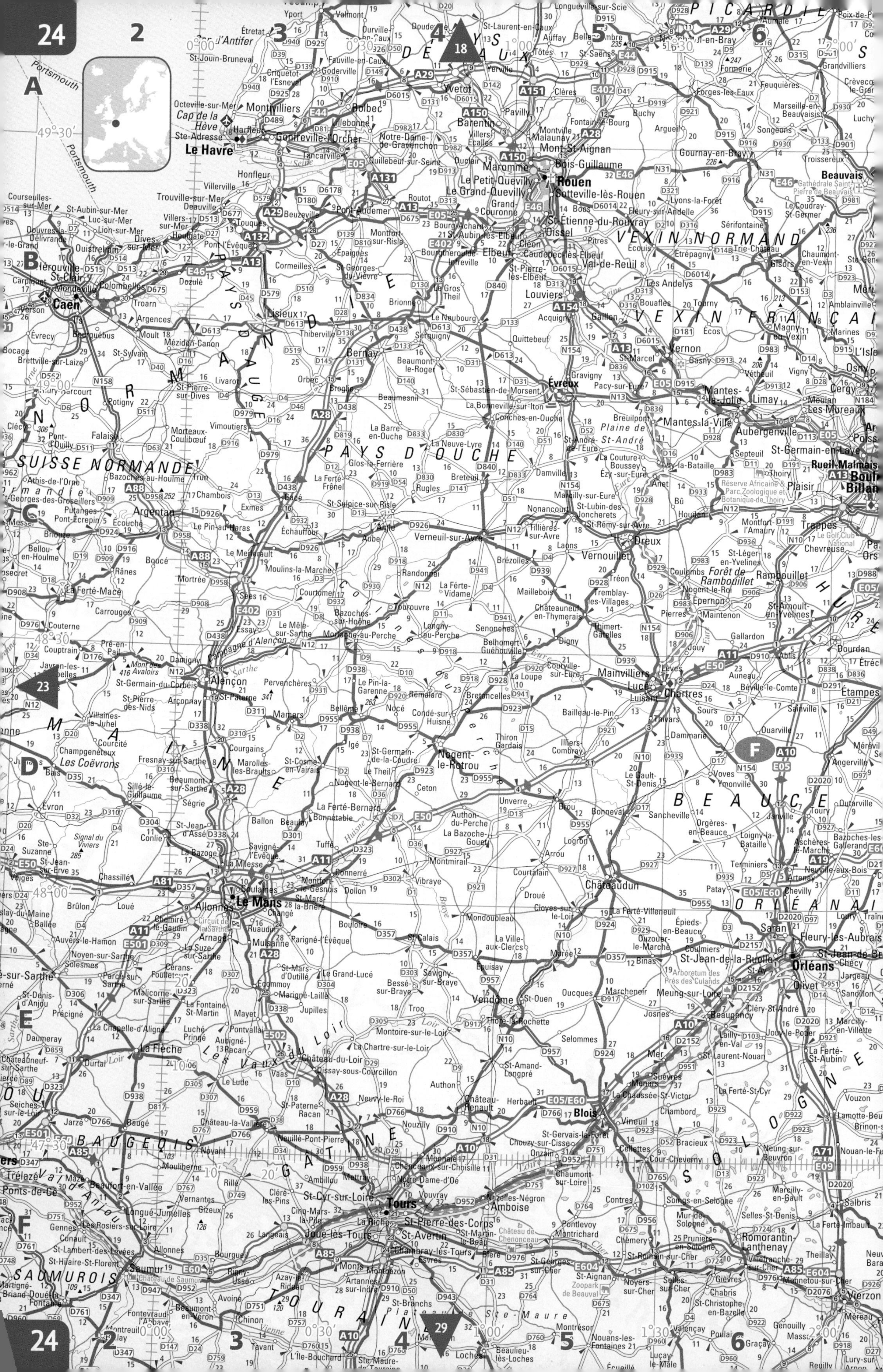

PICARDIE
PAYS DE CAUX
NORMANDIE
PAYS D'AUGE
VEXIN NORMAND
VEXIN FRANÇAIS
PAYS D'OUCHE
SUISSE NORMANDE
COLLINES DU PERCHE
MAINE
BEAUCE
ORLÉANAIS
SOLOGNE
GÂTINE
TOURAINE
BAUGEOIS
SAUMUROIS
Le Havre
Rouen
Caen
Évreux
Lisieux
Beauvais
Alençon
Le Mans
Chartres
Dreux
Orléans
Blois
Tours
Saumur
Vendôme
Châteaudun
Nogent-le-Rotrou
Mantes-la-Jolie
Vernon
Argentan
La Flèche
Amboise
Chinon
Vierzon
Romorantin-Lanthenay
Rambouillet
Étampes
Cap de la Hève
Honfleur
Deauville
Bernay
L'Aigle
Verneuil-sur-Avre
Évreux
Gisors
Les Andelys
Louviers
Elbeuf
Yvetot
Bolbec
Fécamp
Forêt de Rambouillet
Plaine de St-André
Campagne d'Alençon
Les Vaux du Loir
Les Coëvrons
Portsmouth

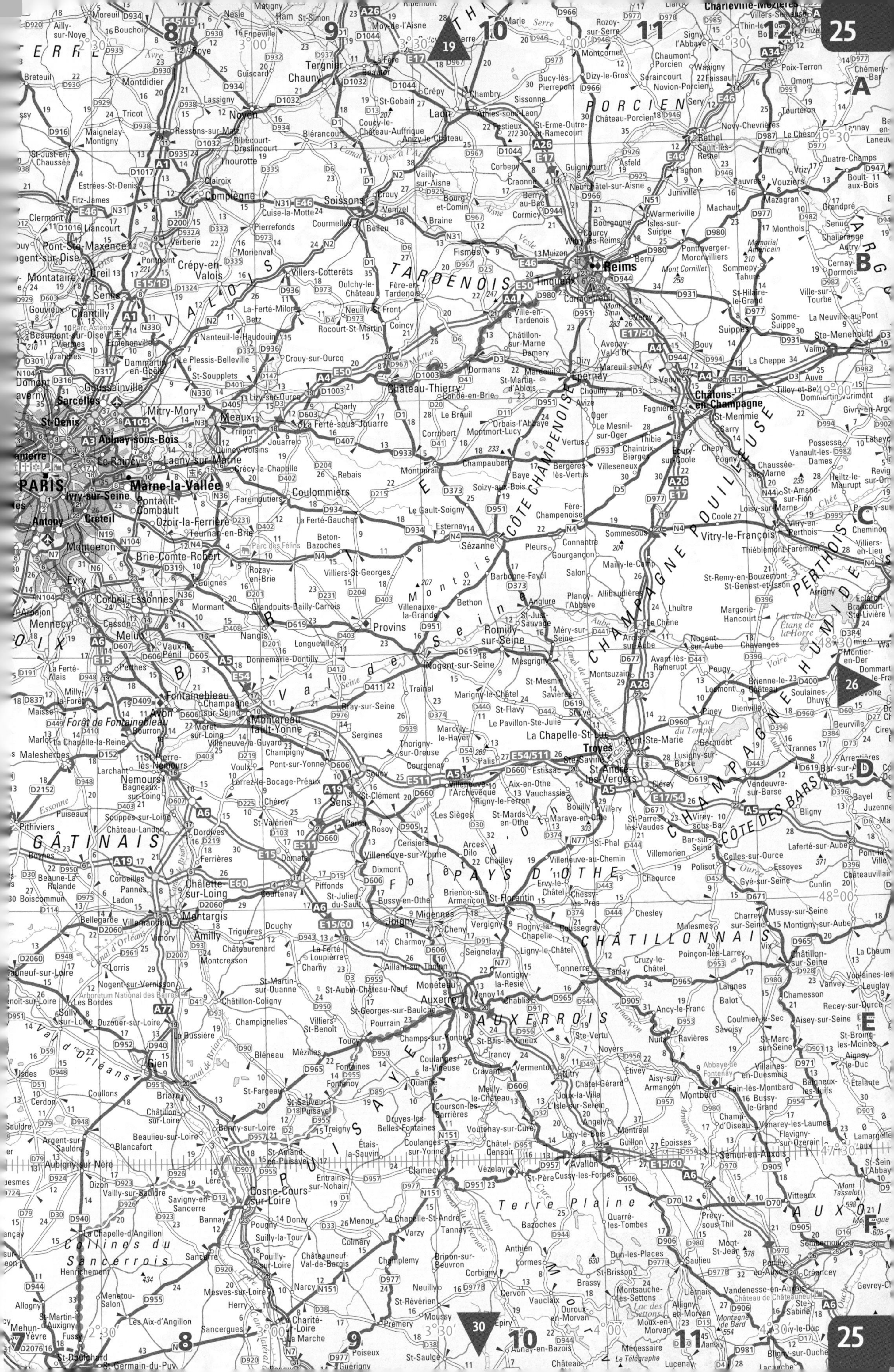

8
9
10
11
12
19
PARIS
St-Denis
Sarcelles
Aulnay-sous-Bois
Le Raincy
Ivry-sur-Seine
Marne-la-Vallée
Antony
Créteil
Montgeron
Évry
Corbeil-Essonnes
Melun
Fontainebleau
Forêt de Fontainebleau
Nemours
Montargis
Gien
Briare
Cosne-Cours-sur-Loire
La Charité-sur-Loire
Sancerre
Collines du Sancerrois
GÂTINAIS
Pithiviers
Malesherbes
Senlis
Chantilly
Creil
Compiègne
Noyon
Soissons
Laon
Chauny
Tergnier
Roye
Crépy-en-Valois
Villers-Cotterêts
VALOIS
TARDENOIS
Château-Thierry
Meaux
Coulommiers
Provins
Sézanne
Épernay
Reims
Châlons-en-Champagne
Vitry-le-François
CHAMPAGNE POUILLEUSE
CÔTE CHAMPENOISE
CHAMPAGNE HUMIDE
PERTHOIS
PORCIEN
Rethel
Charleville-Mézières
Vouziers
Ste-Menehould
Troyes
Romilly-sur-Seine
Nogent-sur-Seine
Montereau-Fault-Yonne
Sens
Joigny
Auxerre
AUXERROIS
PAYS D'OTHE
Forêt d'Othe
Tonnerre
CHÂTILLONNAIS
Châtillon-sur-Seine
Bar-sur-Aube
Bar-sur-Seine
CÔTE DES BARS
Avallon
Vézelay
Clamecy
Terre Plaine
PUISAYE
AUXOIS
Semur-en-Auxois
Montbard
Saulieu
Morvan
Pouilly-en-Auxois
Dommartin-le-Franc
26
30
A
B
C
D
E
F

Reims
Sedan
Arlon
LUXEMBOURG
Thionville
Metz
Verdun
Châlons-en-Champagne
Épernay
Ste-Menehould
Bar-le-Duc
St-Dizier
Vitry-le-François
Pont-à-Mousson
Nancy
Toul
Lunéville
Commercy
Neufchâteau
Chaumont
Bar-sur-Aube
Langres
Vittel
Épinal
Mirecourt
Châtillon-sur-Seine
Vesoul
Dijon
Besançon
Dole
Gray
Montbard
Lure
ARGONNE
LORRAINE
Plateau Lorrain
SAULNOIS
XAINTOIS
CHAMPAGNE POUILLEUSE
CHAMPAGNE HUMIDE
PERTHOIS
VALLAGE
BASSIGNY
CÔTE DES BARS
CHÂTILLONNAIS
AUXOIS
Plateau de Haute-Saône
La Vôge
Plaine Lorraine
Côtes de Meuse
GAUME
Forêt de Chaux
Forêt de Wœvre
Plaine de la Woëvre
A
B
C
D
E
F
1
2
3
4
5
6
20
25
31

NORDPFÄLZER BERGLAND
Worms
Mannheim
Ludwigshafen am Rhein
Heidelberg
Kaiserslautern
Neustadt an der Weinstraße
Saarbrücken
Neunkirchen
Zweibrücken
Pirmasens
Homburg
St Wendel
Landau in der Pfalz
Speyer
Germersheim
Karlsruhe
Bruchsal
Heilbronn
Pforzheim
Ludwigsburg
Stuttgart
Sindelfingen
Böblingen
Tübingen
Reutlingen
Baden-Baden
Rastatt
Strasbourg
Kehl
Offenburg
Freudenstadt
Haguenau
Saverne
Sarrebourg
Sarreguemines
Obernai
Sélestat
Colmar
Mulhouse
Belfort
Freiburg im Breisgau
Lahr
Emmendingen
Villingen
Schwenningen
Rottweil
Tuttlingen
Donaueschingen
Singen
Konstanz
Radolfzell am Bodensee
Schaffhausen
Waldshut
Lörrach
Basel
Liestal
Aarau
Olten
Solothurn
Biel
Delémont
Baden
Winterthur
Zürich
Frauenfeld
St Gallen
La Chaux-de-Fonds
Einsiedeln
D
CH
ODENWALD
KRAICHGAU
SCHÖNBUCH
HOTZENWALD
SUNDGAU
BREISGAU
HEGAU
VOSGES
ALSACE
21
70
74
7
8
9
10
11
A
B
C
D
E
F

1
2
3
4
5
23
A
B
C
D
E
F
47°00′
46°30′
46°00′
45°30′
45°00′
20′
10′
2°00′
1°30′
1°00′
0°30′
PAYS DE RETZ
LES MAUGES
SAUMUROIS
BOCAGE VENDÉEN
AUNIS
SAINTONGE
MÉDOC
POITOU
ENTRE-DEUX-MERS
Nantes
Savenay
Donges
Trignac
St-Nazaire
Pornichet
Cordemais
St-Étienne-de-Montluc
Sautron
Orvault
La Chapelle-sur-Erdre
Thouaré-sur-Loire
St-Herblain
Couëron
Le Pellerin
Rezé
Bouguenais
St-Sébastien-sur-Loire
Basse-Goulaine
St-Julien-de-Concelles
Vertou
Les Sorinières
Vallet
Le Pallet
Aigrefeuille-sur-Maine
Clisson
Gétigné
Montfaucon
Port-St-Père
Planète Sauvage
Ste-Pazanne
Arthon-en-Retz
St-Père-en-Retz
Rouans
Bourgneuf-en-Retz
Bourgneuf
Pte de l'Herbaudière
Noirmoutier-en-l'Île
Île de Noirmoutier
Barbâtre
Passage du Gois
Machecoul
Bouin
Beauvoir-sur-Mer
Fromentine
La Barre-de-Monts
Notre-Dame-de-Monts
St-Gervais
Marais Breton
Challans
La Garnache
Falleron
Legé
Paulx
Touvois
St-Philbert-de-Grand-Lieu
St-Philbert-de-Bouaine
Rocheservière
Montaigu
Cugand
La Bruffière
Les Lucs-sur-Boulogne
Palluau
Soullans
St-Jean-de-Monts
Commequiers
Le Fenouiller
Port-Joinville
Île d'Yeu
St-Hilaire-de-Riez
Pte de Grosse Terre
St-Gilles-Croix-de-Vie
Coëx
Aizenay
Le Poiré-sur-Vie
Belleville-sur-Vie
Les Essarts
Dompierre-sur-Yon
La Ferrière
Venansault
La Roche-sur-Yon
La Chaize-le-Vicomte
Brétignolles-sur-Mer
Brem-sur-Mer
La Mothe-Achard
Aubigny
St-Mathurin
Olonne-sur-Mer
Les Sables-d'Olonne
Château-d'Olonne
Pte de l'Aiguille
Talmont-St-Hilaire
Longeville-sur-Mer
Jard-sur-Mer
Avrillé
Moutiers-les-Mauxfaits
Mareuil-sur-Lay-Dissais
Luçon
Nalliers
St-Florent-des-Bois
Bournezeau
Chantonnay
Ste-Hermine
St-Fulgent
Les Landes-Genusson
La Gaubretière
La Verrie
Mortagne-sur-Sèvre
Mont des Alouettes
Les Herbiers
Mouchamps
Pouzauges
Puy Crapaud
Le Boupère
Les Épesses
Cholet
La Séguinière
St-Macaire-en-Mauges
Villedieu-la-Blouère
Beaupréau
Gesté
Chemillé
Jallais
Le May-sur-Èvre
Trémentines
Vezins
Coron
Chalonnes-sur-Loire
La Pommeraye
St-Florent-le-Vieil
Montrevault
St-Pierre-Montlimart
Bourgneuf-en-Mauges
Oudon
Ancenis
Liré
St-Mars-du-Désert
Melay
Vihiers
Thouarcé
Valanjou
La Jumellière
Brissac-Quincé
Martigné-Briand
Doué-la-Fontaine
Saumur
Les Rosiers-sur-Loire
St-Lambert-des-Levées
St-Hilaire-St-Florent
Gennes
Fontevraud-l'Abbaye
Montreuil-Bellay
Le Puy-Notre-Dame
Cersay
Thouars
Argenton-les-Vallées
Maulévrier
St-Pierre-des-Échaubrognes
St-Laurent-sur-Sèvre
Mauléon
Nueil-les-Aubiers
Les Aubiers
Ste-Radegonde
Oiron
St-Jouin-de-Marnes
St-Varent
Bressuire
Terves
Chiché
Courlay
Cerizay
La Forêt-sur-Sèvre
Montournais
Moncoutant
St-Pierre-du-Chemin
La Chapelle-St-Laurent
Airvault
St-Loup-Lamairé
Thénezay
Châtillon-sur-Thouet
Parthenay
Pompaire
Terrier de St-Martin
Vasles
Secondigny
Mazières-en-Gâtine
La Châtaigneraie
L'Absie
La Caillère-St-Hilaire
Vouvant
Mervent
L'Hermenault
Fontenay-le-Comte
Fenioux
Champdeniers-St-Denis
Coulonges-sur-l'Autize
St-Hilaire-des-Loges
Villiers-en-Plaine
Benet
Maillezais
Le Langon
Chaillé-les-Marais
Vix
Marans
Sèvre Niortaise
Niort
Échiré
La Crèche
St-Maixent-l'École
Pamproux
La Mothe-St-Héray
Ménigoute
Magné
Aiffres
Vouillé
Prahecq
Celles-sur-Belle
Melle
Frontenay-Rohan-Rohan
Mauzé-sur-le-Mignon
Beauvoir-sur-Niort
Chizé
Brioux-sur-Boutonne
Chef-Boutonne
Surgères
Loulay
Aulnay
Néré
Longré
St-Jean-d'Angély
Matha
La Tranche-sur-Mer
La Faute-sur-Mer
L'Aiguillon-sur-Mer
St-Michel-en-l'Herm
Triaize
Anse de l'Aiguillon
Pertuis Breton
Pte des Baleines
Pte de l'Aiguillon
St-Martin-de-Ré
Ars-en-Ré
La Couarde-sur-Mer
Le Bois-Plage-en-Ré
La Flotte
Île de Ré
Rivedoux-Plage
St-Xandre
Lagord
La Rochelle
Dompierre-sur-Mer
Nuaillé-d'Aunis
Courçon
Aigrefeuille-d'Aunis
Aytré
Angoulins
La Jarrie
Châtelaillon-Plage
Pertuis d'Antioche
Pte de Chassiron
St-Denis-d'Oléron
Île d'Aix
Fouras
Port-des-Barques
Muron
Breuil-Magné
Tonnay-Boutonne
St-Georges-d'Oléron
St-Pierre-d'Oléron
Dolus-d'Oléron
Île d'Oléron
Le Château-d'Oléron
Rochefort
Tonnay-Charente
St-Savinien
Bourcefranc-le-Chapus
St-Agnant
St-Trojan-les-Bains
Marennes
St-Just-Luzac
St-Porchaire
Ronce-les-Bains
La Tremblade
Étaules
Saintes
Burie
Cherves-Richemont
St-Hilaire-de-Villefranche
Cognac
Jarnac
Chérac
Châteaubernard
Segonzac
Salles-d'Angles
Pte de la Coubre
Zoo de la Palmyre
Vaux-sur-Mer
St-Palais-sur-Mer
Royan
Saujon
Médis
Semussac
St-Georges-de-Didonne
Pte de Grave
Le Verdon-sur-Mer
Meschers-sur-Gironde
Cozes
Arces
Gémozac
Talmont
Tesson
Pons
Soulac-sur-Mer
Talais
Mortagne-sur-Gironde
St-Genis-de-Saintonge
Archiac
Jonzac
Barbezieux-St-Hilaire
Lorignac
St-Fort-sur-Gironde
Grayan-et-l'Hôpital
St-Vivien-de-Médoc
Vensac
Montalivet-les-Bains
Vendays-Montalivet
Queyrac
Bégadan
Gaillan-en-Médoc
St-Christoly-Médoc
Mirambeau
St-Bonnet-sur-Gironde
Baignes-Ste-Radegonde
Lesparre-Médoc
St-Germain-d'Esteuil
St-Ciers-sur-Gironde
Naujac-sur-Mer
Vertheuil
St-Estèphe
Braud-et-St-Louis
St-Aubin-de-Blaye
Marcillac
Reignac
Montendre
Chevanceaux
Brossac
Hourtin-Plage
Hourtin
Pauillac
St-Julien-Beychevelle
Anglade
Eyrans
Étauliers
Cartelègue
Montlieu-la-Garde
Montguyon
Étang d'Hourtin et de Carcans
St-Laurent-Médoc
Blaye
Cars
St-Savin
Cavignac
Laruscade
Carcans-Plage
Maubuisson
Carcans
Listrac-Médoc
Lamarque
Moulis-en-Médoc
Castelnau-de-Médoc
Brach
Bourg
Peujard
Marcenais
Les Églisottes-et-Chalaures
Lagorce
Coutras
Les Peintures
Le Pizou
Lacanau-Océan
Lacanau
Étang de Lacanau
Ste-Hélène
Salaunes
Le Pian-Médoc
Cantenac
Ambès
St-André-de-Cubzac
Cubzac-les-Ponts
Prignac-et-Marcamps
Galgon
Fronsac
St-Denis-de-Pile
Lussac
Puisseguin
Montagne
Libourne
St-Émilion
St-Magne-de-Castillon
Castillon-la-Bataille
Le Porge-Océan
Le Porge
Saumos
St-Médard-en-Jalles
Le Temple
Blanquefort
Parempuyre
Bassens
St-Loubès
Arveyres
Génissac
Branne
Pujols
Bordeaux
Pessac
Floirac
Talence
St-Jean-d'Illac
Lège-Cap-Ferret
Andernos-les-Bains
Bassin d'Arcachon
Marcheprime
Cestas
Léognan
Cambes
Langoiran
Créon
Sauveterre
Rauzan
Blasimon
Lanton
Audenge
La Brède
Île aux Oiseaux
32
A87
A83
A10
E62
E03
E05
E601
E602
E603
E606
E70
E72
A837
A89
N249
N149
N11
N137
N141
N150
N10
N89

6
7
8
9
10
24
A
B
C
D
E
F
30
33
TOURAINE
CHAMPAGNE BERRICHONNE
BERRY
BRENNE
BRANDES
MARCHE
Plateaux de la Marche
COMBRAILLE
CONFOLENTAIS
LIMOUSIN
Plateaux du Limousin
Plateau de Millevaches
Plateau de Gentioux
PÉRIGORD BLANC
PÉRIGORD
PÉRIGORD NOIR
SÉGALA DU QUERCY
CHÂTAIGNERAIE
Massif du Cantal
Tours
Joué-lès-Tours
St-Avertin
Chinon
Loches
Châtellerault
Poitiers
Vierzon
Bourges
Issoudun
Châteauroux
St-Amand-Montrond
Le Blanc
Argenton-sur-Creuse
La Souterraine
Guéret
Aubusson
Montluçon
Bellac
Confolens
St-Junien
Limoges
Ussel
Tulle
Égletons
Brive-la-Gaillarde
Périgueux
Bergerac
Sarlat-la-Canéda
Aurillac
Montrond
Montmorillon
Chauvigny
Ruffec
Civray
Nontron
Brantôme
Uzerche
Eymoutiers
Bourganeuf
Cusset
F

Bourges
Nevers
La Charité-sur-Loire
Varennes-Vauzelles
Decize
Autun
Beaune
Le Creusot
Montceau-les-Mines
Paray-le-Monial
Digoin
Moulins
Yzeure
Montluçon
St-Amand-Montrond
Vichy
Cusset
Roanne
Riom
Châtelguyon
Chamalières
Clermont-Ferrand
Thiers
Issoire
Ambert
Montbrison
St-Étienne
Lyon
Villefranche-sur-Saône
Mâcon
Le Puy-en-Velay
Brioude
St-Flour
Aurillac
Tournon-sur-Rhône
Givors
Rive-de-Gier
St-Chamond
Firminy
Annonay
Vienne
BOURBONNAIS
BRIONNAIS
CHAROLLAIS
MÂCONNAIS
AUTUNOIS
Roannais
Monts du Beaujolais
Monts du Lyonnais
LIMAGNE
MASSIF CENTRAL
VELAY
PLANÈZE
Monts du Forez
Monts de la Madeleine
Monts du Livradois
Monts du Vivarais
Monts de la Margeride
Monts Dore
Massif du Cantal
Plaines de la Loire et de l'Allier
Forêt de Tronçais
Mont Mézenc 1753
Gerbier de Jonc 1551
Puy de Sancy 1885
Puy de Dôme 1464
Le Lioran
Super Besse

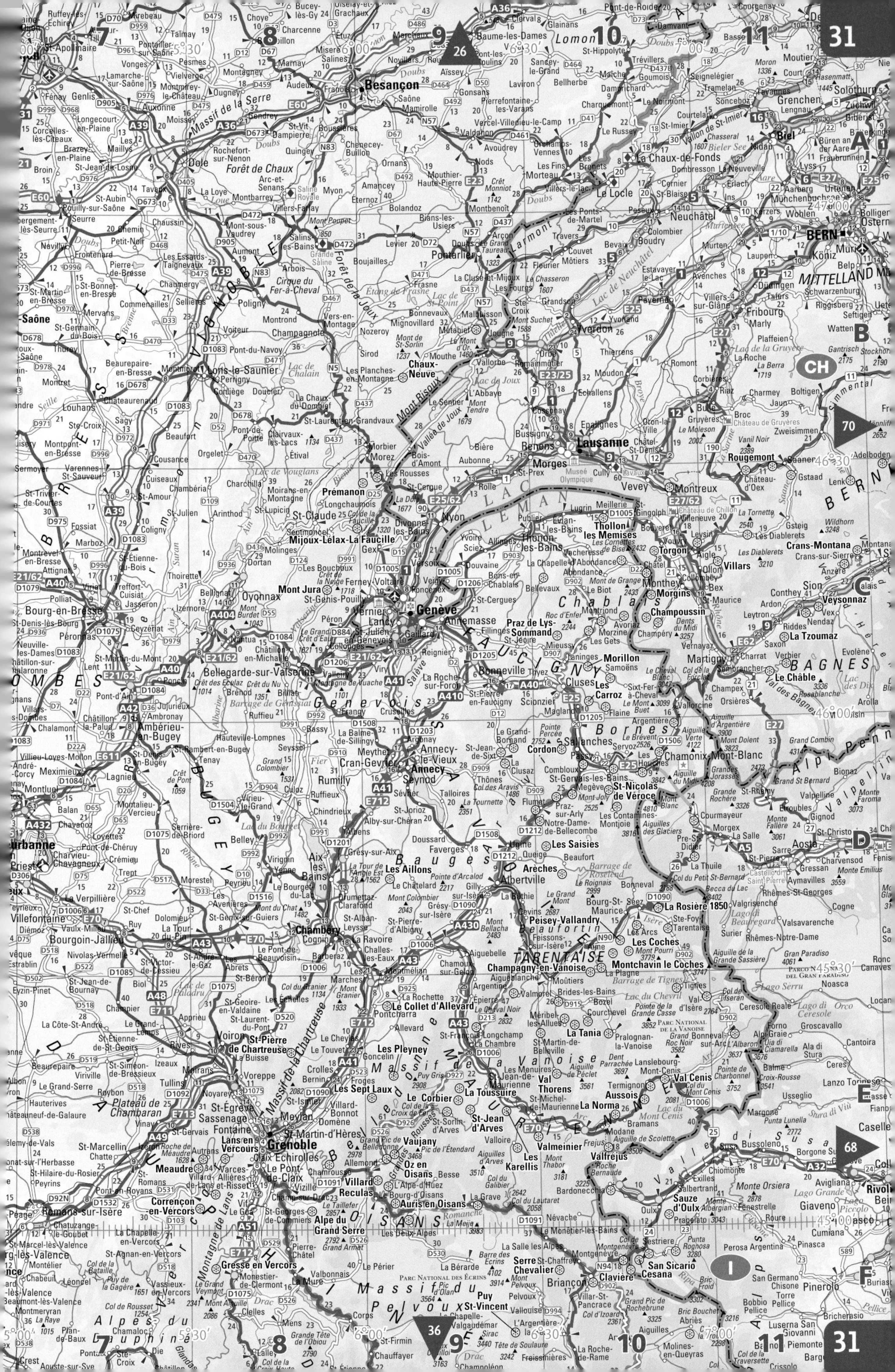
Besançon
Dole
Forêt de Chaux
Pontarlier
Lons-le-Saunier
Bourg-en-Bresse
Oyonnax
Genève
Lausanne
Neuchâtel
BERN
Fribourg
Montreux
Vevey
Morges
Nyon
LAC LEMAN
Thonon-les-Bains
Annemasse
Annecy
Chambéry
Aix-les-Bains
Grenoble
Albertville
Chamonix-Mont-Blanc
Martigny
Sion
Aosta
Bourg-St-Maurice
Val d'Isère
Briançon
Sestriere
Pinerolo
Massif de la Chartreuse
Massif du Pelvoux
Alpes du Dauphiné
TARENTAISE
Chablais
Faucigny
Genevois
Bauges
Bugey
Bresse
Dombes
Vignoble
MITTELLAND
BERN
CH
I
26
70
68
36

1
2
3
4
5
A
B
C
D
E
F
28
41
42
2°00′
1°30′
1°00′
0°30′
0°00′
44°30′
44°00′
43°30′
43°00′
42°30′
Bordeaux
Pessac
Talence
Floirac
Blanquefort
St-Médard-en-Jalles
Libourne
St-Émilion
Lège-Cap-Ferret
Andernos-les-Bains
Bassin d'Arcachon
Île aux Oiseaux
Arcachon
Cap Ferret
La Teste-de-Buch
Gujan-Mestras
Biganos
Le Teich
Audenge
Marcheprime
Cestas
Léognan
La Brède
Podensac
Cadillac
Langon
Bazas
Dune du Pilat
Étang de Cazaux et de Sanguinet
Sanguinet
Biscarrosse-Plage
Biscarrosse
Étang de Biscarrosse et de Parentis
Parentis-en-Born
Ychoux
Liposthey
Pissos
Belin-Béliet
Salles
Mios
Le Barp
Hostens
St-Symphorien
Villandraut
Captieux
Roquefort
Sore
Luxey
Mimizan-Plage
Mimizan
Ste-Eulalie-en-Born
Pontenx-les-Forges
Labouheyre
Commensacq
Trensacq
Escource
Solférino
Sabres
Contis-Plage
St-Julien-en-Born
Lit-et-Mixe
GRANDE LANDE
PAYS DE BORN
LANDES DE GASCOGNE
GRAVES
ENTRE
Morcenx
Arengosse
Labrit
Brocas
St-Girons-Plage
Vielle-St-Girons
Linxe
Castets
Léon
Moliets-et-Maa
Golf de Moliets
Messanges
Vieux-Boucau-les-Bains
Soustons
Magescq
Rion-des-Landes
Tartas
Mont-de-Marsan
St-Pierre-du-Mont
Villeneuve-de-Marsan
Aire-sur-l'Adour
Grenade-sur-l'Adour
St-Sever
Hagetmau
Dax
St-Paul-lès-Dax
St-Vincent-de-Paul
Tosse
Golf de Seignosse
Soorts-Hossegor
Capbreton
Bénesse-Maremne
Labenne
Ondres
Tarnos
Boucau
Golfe de Gascogne
Golfo de Gascuña
Côte d'Argent
Bayonne
Biarritz
Anglet
Bidart
St-Jean-de-Luz
Ciboure
Urrugne
Hendaye
Hondarribia
Irun
Donostia/San Sebastián
Pasai Donibane
Errenteria
Hernani
Orthez
Pau
Lescar
Oloron-Ste-Marie
Salies-de-Béarn
Sauveterre-de-Béarn
Navarrenx
Mourenx
Peyrehorade
Hasparren
Cambo-les-Bains
Espelette
Ascain
Sare
St-Pée-sur-Nivelle
Ustaritz
Bidache
St-Palais
Mauléon-Licharre
St-Jean-Pied-de-Port
St-Étienne-de-Baïgorry
Arnéguy
Irissarry
PAYS BASQUE
BÉARN
Zumaia
Getaria
Zarautz
Ondarroa
Mutriku
Deba
Elgoibar
Azpeitia
Azkoitia
Tolosa
Zumarraga
Legazpi
Beasain
Andoain
Elizondo
Doneztebe
Lesaka
Urdax-Urdazuli
Leitza
Lekunberri
Pamplona/Iruña
Burlada
Huarte
Villava
Barañáin
Noáin
Estella
Puente la Reina
Tafalla
Olite
Sangüesa
Lumbier
Jaca
Sabiñánigo
Canfranc
El Formigal
Astún
Candanchú
Col du Somport
Col du Pourtalet
Sallent de Gállego
Panticosa
Biescas
Broto
Torla
Gavarnie
Cauterets
Argelès-Gazost
Lourdes
Arette
Lescun
Urdos
Bedous
Laruns
Sierra de Aralar
Sierra de Urbasa
Sierra de Andía
Sierra de Lóquiz
Sierra de Abodi
Sierra de Leyre
Sierra de Izco
Sierra de Santo Domingo
Sierra de San Juan de la Peña
Puerto de Ibañeta
Puerto de Velate
Embalse de Yesa
Yesa
Santa Cilia de Jaca
Hecho
Ansó
Roncal
Isaba
Ochagavía
Orbara
Aribe
Garralda
Auritz
Orreaga
Zubiri
RIBERA NAVARRA
Palacio Real de Olite
Lerín
Falces
Calahorra
Logroño
Los Arcos
Viana
Sesma
Lodosa
Andosilla
Azagra
Caparroso
Carcastillo
Santacara
Murillo el Fruto
Sos del Rey Católico
Navardún
Uncastillo
Luesia
Biel
Ayerbe
Loarre
Castillo de Loarre
Caldearenas
Parc National des Pyrénées Occidentales
Mont Perdu (Monte Perdido)
Grande Cascade de Gavarnie
A63
A64
A65
A62
E70
E80
E05/E70
E07
AP15
A15
A1
A8
A10
A12
A21
A23
N134
E

PÉRIGORD NOIR
HAUT QUERCY
QUERCY
CAUSSE DE GRAMAT
Causse de Limogne
ROUERGUE
SÉGALA
CHÂTAIGNERAIE
Agenais
BAS QUERCY
LOMAGNE
ALBIGEOIS
ARMAGNAC
LAURAGAIS
Montagne Noire
NÉBOUZAN
Massif de l'Arize
Montagnes du Plantaurel
Forêt de la Grésigne
Pays de Sault
CORBIÈRES
CONFLENT
Montes Malditos
Toulouse
Montauban
Cahors
Agen
Auch
Albi
Castres
Carcassonne
Figeac
Villeneuve-sur-Lot
Moissac
Castelsarrasin
Gaillac
Foix
Pamiers
St-Gaudens
Tarbes
Lannemezan
Limoux
Castelnaudary
Mazamet
Rodez
Villefranche-de-Rouergue
Carmaux
Colomiers
Blagnac
Muret
Andorra la Vella
Ordino
Puigcerdà
Superbagneres
Val Louron
Guzet-Neige
Baqueria/Beret
Boi Taull
Super Espot
Port Aine
Pas de la Casa/Grau Roig
Masella
Val de Nuria
Vallter 2000
La Molina
Cerler (Huesca)
A62
A20
A64
A61
A66
A68
A680
E09
E80
E72
N124
N21
N125
N20
N88
N122
AND
F
6
7
8
9
10
A
B
C
D
E
F
29
34
43
33

1
2
3
4
5
29
30
33
43
A
B
C
D
E
F
AND
QUERCY
BAS QUERCY
SÉGALA DU QUERCY
CHÂTAIGNERAIE
ROUERGUE
SÉGALA
ALBIGEOIS
LAURAGAIS
MINERVOIS
LANGUEDOC
CORBIÈRES
CONFLENT
ROUSSILLON
Causse de Gramat
Causse de Limogne
Causse Comtal
Causse Noir
Causse de Sauveterre
Causse du Larzac
Forêt de la Grésigne
Monts de Lacaune
Monts de l'Espinouse
Montagne Noire
Sidobre
Massif de l'Arize
Montagnes du Plantaurel
Pays de Sault
Plateau de Lecamp
Côte Vermeille
Cahors
Montauban
Toulouse
Albi
Castres
Carcassonne
Narbonne
Béziers
Perpignan
Rodez
Millau
Figeac
Aurillac
Villefranche-de-Rouergue
Castelnaudary
Foix
Pamiers
Limoux
Mazamet
Lodève
Andorra la Vella
Ordino
Encamp
Les Escaldes
Pas de la Casa
Puigcerdà
Colomiers
Blagnac
Muret
Gaillac
Graulhet
Lavaur
Carmaux
Decazeville
Moissac
Castelsarrasin
Espalion
Marvejols
Clermont-l'Hérault
Bédarieux
Pézenas
Agde
Leucate
Port-Vendres
Banyuls-sur-Mer
Cerbère
Argelès-sur-Mer
Prades
Mont-Louis
Ax-les-Thermes
Saint-Girons
La Jonquera
Portbou
Le Perthus
Céret
Amélie-les-Bains-Palalda
Port Aine
Guzet-Neige
Super Espot
Masella
La Molina
Val de Nuria
Le Seu d'Urgell
44°30'
44°00'
43°30'
43°00'
42°30'
1°30'
2°00'
2°30'
3°00'
3°30'

6
7
8
9
10
A
B
C
D
E
F
4°00′
4°30′
5°00′
5°30′
44°30′
44°00′
43°30′
43°00′
42°30′
31
36
Valence
Privas
Aubenas
Montélimar
Pierrelatte
Bollène
Orange
Carpentras
Avignon
Nîmes
Alès
Uzès
Bagnols-sur-Cèze
Beaucaire
Tarascon
Arles
Montpellier
Sète
Frontignan
Lunel
Salon-de-Provence
Aix-en-Provence
Marseille
Aubagne
La Ciotat
Toulon
Martigues
Istres
Manosque
Pertuis
Cavaillon
Apt
Nyons
Sisteron
Vaison-la-Romaine
Valréas
Die
Crest
Gresse en Vercors
La Joue du Loup
CAMARGUE
PETITE CAMARGUE
CRAU
GARRIGUES
BARONNIES
BOCHAINE
Alpes du Dauphiné
Massif du Diois
Monts du Vivarais
Montagne du Lubéron
Monts de Vaucluse
Montagne de Lure
Alpilles
Golfe du Lion
Golfe de Fos
Golfe d'Aigues-Mortes
Étang de Vaccarès
Bastia, Calvi, L'Île-Rousse
Ajaccio, Propriano
Porto Torres, Porto Vecchio
Alger, Annaba, Bejaïa, Skikda, Tunis
Nador, Tanger, Palma de Mallorca
Oran

Massif du Pelvoux
Alpes du Dauphiné
Massif du Diois
BOCHAINE
Dévoluy
BARONNIES
Chabre
Montagne de Lure
Monts de Vaucluse
Montagne du Lubéron
Alpilles
CRAU
Plateau de Valensole
PROVENCE
Esterel
Massif des Maures
Parc National des Écrins
Parc National de Port-Cros
Îles d'Hyères
Grenoble
Gap
Briançon
Digne-les-Bains
Sisteron
Manosque
Montélimar
Orange
Avignon
Carpentras
Cavaillon
Apt
Aix-en-Provence
Marseille
Toulon
Hyères
Fréjus
St-Raphaël
Cannes
Grasse
Draguignan
Brignoles
Arles
Istres
Martigues
La Ciotat
Golfe de Fos
Golfe de St-Tropez
Golfe de Fréjus
Cap Sicié
Cap Camarat
Île de Porquerolles
Île de Port-Cros
Île du Levant
Ajaccio, Porto Vecchio, Porto Torres, Propriano
Alger, Annaba, Bejaïa, Skikda, Tunis
Tunis
Ajaccio
Oran
31
35
F
43°30′
43°00′
42°30′
5°00′
5°30′
6°00′
6°30′
7°00′
1
2
3
4
5
B
C
D
E
F
G

6
7
8
9
10
B
C
F
G
H
68
69
64
I
F
MC
7°30′
8°00′
8°30′
9°00′
44°30′
43°00′
42°30′
42°00′
41°30′
Piossasco
Orbassano
Moncalieri
Chieri
Cumiana
Pinerolo
Carignano
Carmagnola
Racconigi
Savigliano
Saluzzo
Fossano
Cuneo
Mondovì
Borgo San Dalmazzo
Bra
Alba
Asti
Cherasco
Canelli
Nizza Monferrato
Acqui Terme
Alessandria
Tortona
Voghera
Novi Ligure
Ovada
Genova
Savona
Albisola Superiore
Varazze
Arenzano
Cairo Montenotte
Ceva
Finale Ligure
Loano
Albenga
Alassio
Imperia
Taggia
San Remo
Ventimiglia
Bordighera
Menton
Roquebrune-Cap-Martin
Beausoleil
Monte-Carlo
Nice
Villefranche-sur-Mer
St-Laurent-du-Var
Antibes
Rapallo
Chiavari
Lavagna
Sestri Levante
Recco
Camogli
Portofino
Sta Margherita Ligure
Moneglia
Deiva Marina
Levanto
Bobbio
Ottone
Torriglia
Busalla
Limone Piemonte
Col de Tende
Tende
Saorge
Breil-sur-Roya
Sospel
St-Martin-Vésubie
Lantosque
San Grée di Viola
Artesina
Prato Nevoso
Golfo di Genova
Riviera di Ponente
Riviera di Levante
Côte d'Azur
Baie des Anges
Cap d'Antibes
CORSE
Cap Corse
Île de la Giraglia
Bastia
St-Florent
Golfe de St-Florent
Désert des Agriates
L'Île-Rousse
Calvi
Galéria
Golfe de Porto
Porto
Piana
Cargèse
Sagone
Golfe de Sagone
Ajaccio
Golfe d'Ajaccio
Îles Sanguinaires
Propriano
Golfe de Valinco
Sartène
Bonifacio
Capo Pertusato
Îles Lavezzi
Porto-Vecchio
Golfe de Porto-Vecchio
Îles Cerbicale
Solenzara
Aléria
Étang de Diane
Étang d'Urbino
Ghisonaccia
Corte
Venaco
Vivario
Bocognano
Monte Cinto 2706
Monte Rotondo 2622
Monte d'Oro 2389
Monte Rénoso 2352
Monte Padro 2393
Monte Incudine 2134
Col de Bavella
Forêt de l'Ospédale
CASTAGNICCIA
NEBBIO
Golfe de Santa-Manza
Golfe de Ventilegne
Livorno
Civitavecchia
Marseille
Nice, Marseille, Toulon
Bastia, Calvi, L'Île Rousse
Barcelona, Porto Torres
Marseille, Nice, Toulon, Genova, Savona

1
2
3
4
5
A
B
C
D
E
F
9°00′
8°30′
8°00′
7°30′
43°30′
43°00′
42°30′
42°00′
41°30′
Pta da Estaca de Bares
Cabo Ortegal
Cariño
Porto do Barqueiro
O Vicedo
Ría de Viveiro
Pta Candelaria
Ortigueira
Viveiro
Xove
Cervo
Cabo Burela
Cedeira
A Vila da Igrexa
Serra da Faladoira
Serra do Xistral
Cabo Prior
Pereiro
Ourol
Foz
San Cosme
A Gándara de Altea
Avenida do Marqués de Figueroa
Lago das Pontes
Ferreira
Castro de Ouro
Cabo Prioriño Grande
Ferrol
Neda
Fene
Muras
Vilanova
Mugardos
Ares
As Pontes de García Rodríguez
Mondoñedo
Trabada
A Coruña (La Coruna)
Ría de Betanzos
As Neves
Porto da Xesta
Abadín
El Llan
Illas Sisargas
Aquarium Finisterrae
Torre de Hércules
Pontedeume
O Chao
Pta Langosteira
O Real
Sada
A Armada
Xermade
As Rodrigas
A Baiuca
A Carreira
Rebordelo
Malpica
Caión
Carrio
A Pontenova
Pta Roncudo
Corme Porto
BERGANTIÑOS
Tarrío
Cambre
Betanzos
O Pazo de Irixoa
Vilalba
Pastoriza
Ponteceso
Laracha
San Marcos
AS MARIÑAS
Serpe
Laxe
A Carballa
Carballo
Oza
Ponte Aranga
A Feira do Monte
Carral
Meira
Camariñas
O Campo da Feira
Baio
San Roque
Guitiriz
Castro de Rei
Serra de Meira
O Mesón do Vento
Teixeiro
Begonte
Muxía
Vimianzo
Zas
Cesuras
Rábade
Mosteiro
A Fonsagrada
Cabo Touriñán
A Pontepedra
Ordes
Xanceda
Ru
Outeiro de Rei
Santa Catalina de Armada
Dumbria
Bembibre
Viaño Pequeno
Sobrado
Friol
Castroverde
A Gándara
Serra da Cova da Serpe
Lugo
O Cádavo
Corcubión
Cee
San Vicenzo
Tambre
Sigüeiro
Paradela
A Picota
Arzúa
Souto
O Corgo
Cabo Fisterra
Fisterra
Negreira
Santiago de Compostela
O Pedrouzo
Melide
Carreteira
Ría de Corcubión
Embalse de Portodemouros
Palas de Rei
Baralla
Carnota
A Serra de Outes
Pedrouzos
Bertamirans
Fonte Díaz
A Pobra de San Xiao
Becerreá
Treboll e
Muros
Noia
O Forte
Vila de Cruces
Portomarín
Sarria
As Nogais
Punta Carreiro
Os Dices
A Ramallosa
Antas de Ulla
Monterroso
Triacastela
Ría de Muros e Noia
Portobravo
Padrón
Vedra
Ulla
Agolada
Samos
Pedrafita do Cebre
Porto do Son
Taragoña
Enfesta
Taboada
Ponte Valga
Embalse de Belesar
Boiro de Arriba
Rianxo
A Estrada
Silleda
Lalín
Catoira
Cuntis
Alto de Nespereira
Rodeiro
A Pobra do Caramiñal
Vilagarcía de Arousa
Caldas de Reis
Santa Lucía de Moraña
O Castro de Ferreira
Chantada
Serra do Faro
Bóveda
A Cruz do Incio
Ribeira (Santa Uxía)
Vilanova de Arousa
Forcarei
Escairón
Folgoso de Courel
Cabo Falcoeira
Ría de Arousa
Currás
A Lagoa
A Barrela
Monforte de Lemos
A Pobla de Brollón
Serra do Courel
Cambados
A Escusa
O Mosteiro
Santo Antoniño
Cerdedo
Montes do Testeiro
O Irixo
Piñor
O Castro de Ferreira
O Grove
A Chan
Beariz
Cea
Embalse dos Peares
Quiroga
Illa de Salvora
O Convento
As Covas
Pontevedra
Serra do Suido
Boborás
O Carballiño
A Peroxa
Vilarchao
San Clodio
Vilamartín
Sanxenxo
Marín
Ría de Pontevedra
Ponte Caldelas
A Pedreira
O Igrexario
O RIBEIRO
Maside
Amoeiro
Luintra
Sil
A Teixeira
Embalse de San Estevan
A Rúa
Illa de Ons
O Toural
Leiro
San Amaro
Embalse de Velle
Parada de Sil
Castro-Caldelas
Petín
Bueu
O Rial
A Igrexa
Carballeda de Avia
A Forxa
Ourense (Orense)
Pereiro de Aguiar
Esgos
A Pobra de Trives
Moaña
Pazos
Redondela
Barral
Ribadavia
Toén
Barbadás
Alto de Couso
Alto do Rodicio
Manzaneda
O Bolo
Cangas
Ría de Vigo
Mondariz-Balneario
Santiago de Covelo
Melón
San Cibrao das Viñas
Paderne de Allariz
Maceda
Montederramo
Illas Cíes
Vigo
Reguengo
Mondariz
Cortegada
A Merca
Outomuro
Baños de Molgas
Serra do San Mamede
Embalse de Chandrexa de Queixa
Parque Nacional de las Islas Atlánticas de Galicia
A Cañiza
Taboadela
Xunqueira de Ambía
Embalse de Vao
Nigrán
Ponteareas
Crecente
Sobrado
Ramirás
Allariz
Cabo Silleiro
O Porriño
O Pazo
San Roque
Celanova
Sandiás
Vilar de Barrio
Embalse das Portas
Vilariño de Conso
Baiona
Gondomar
A Esfarrapada
As Neves
Melgaço
Paderne
Leirado
Carballo
Vilar de Santos
O Castelo
Monção
Valadares
Longos Vales
Cubalhão
Castro Laboreiro
Serra da Peneda
Xinzo de Limia
A LIMIA
Sarreaus
Trasmiras
Laza
A Gudiña
Alto do Canizo
Tui
Ganfei
Valença
Gandra
Riba de Mouro
Bande
A Forxa
Os Blancos
Porto de Estivadas
O Arrabal (Ola)
O Seixo (Tomiño)
Extremo
Serra da Peneda
Vila
Embalse das Conchas
Cualedro
Castrelo do Val
Serra do Larouco
Calvos
Baltar
Verín
Ríos
A Guarda
Candemil
Paredes de Coura
Pedrada
Soajo
Monte do Quinxo
Muiños
Embalse de Salas
Monterrei
Alto de Fumaces
Santalha
Punta dos Picos
Caminha
Coura
Arcos de Valdevez
Fondevila
Oimbra
Vilardevós
Moledo
Serra de Arga
Britelo
Lindoso
Serra do Gerês
Mauros
Serra
Vila Praia de Âncora
Orbacém
Cabração
Bárrio
Jolda
Parque Nacional da Peneda Gerês
Montalegre
Vilarelho da Raia
Vila Verde da Raia
São Vicente
Afife
Arcozelo
Ribeira
Ponte da Barca
Homem
Sarraquinhos
Outeiro Seco
Amonde
Outeiro
Ponte de Lima
Serra Amarela
Paradela
Chã
Barragem do Alto Rabagão
Tronco
Carreço
Meadela
Boalhosa
Vilar
Chaves
Águas Frias
Lebução
Rebordelo
Aresosa
Viana do Castelo
Darque
Seara
Souto
MINHO
Vilar da Veiga
Redondelo
Sonim
Anha
Barroselas
Freixo
Caldelas
Rio Caldo
Ruivães
Vila da Ponte
Boticas
Vilarandelo
Barragem de Venda Nova
Castelo do Neiva
Vila Verde
Amares
Venda Nova
Salto
Campos
Dornelas
Vidago
Loivos
Lagarelhos
Torre de Dona
Antas
Forjães
Vieira do Minho
Serra da Cabreira
Tâmega
Mar
Marinhas
Esposende
Arcozelo
Barcelos
Barcelinhos
Ucha
Prado
Palmeira
Adaúfe
Póvoa de Lanhoso
Gulhofrei
Monteiros
TRÁS-OS-MONTES
Carrazedo de Montenegro
Valpaços
Alto Douro
Vale de Salgueiro
Mascarenh
Braga
Aveleda
Celeiros
Este
Taíde
Arosa
Cabeceiras de Basto
Ribeira de Pena
Bornes de Aguiar
Rio Torto
Fão
Alvelos
Vila Nova
Caldelas
Taipas
Gandarela
Arco de Baúlhe
Vila Pouca de Aguiar
Mirandela
Vila Cova
Estela
Viatodos
Joane
Guimarães
Fafe
Cerva
Telões
Jou
Cedães
Vila Nova de Famalicão
Calendário
Molares
Franco
Murça
Frechas
Póvoa de Varzim
Caldas de Vizela
Serzedo de Basto
Celorico de Basto
Vila Verde
Populo
Trindade
Vila do Conde
Trofa
Santo Tirso
Campo
Ermelo
Adoufe
Parada de Pinhão
Abreiro
Muro
Pacos de Ferreira
Carvalhos
Amarante
Campeã
Cumieira
Vila Real
Constantim
Sabrosa
São Martinho de Anta
Alijó
Pombal
Carvalho de Egas
Vila Flor
Maia
Lousada
Alfena
Real
Tinhela
Corgo
Mente
Tuela
Rabaçal
Miño
Douro
P
44

6
7
8
9
10
A
B
C
D
E
F
6°30′
6°00′
5°30′
5°00′
43°30′
43°00′
42°30′
42°00′
41°30′
Costa Verde
Cabo de Peñas
Cabo Vidio
Cabo Lastres
Ría de Villaviciosa
Luanco
Candás
Piedras Blancas
Salinas
Avilés
Gijón/Xixón
Cudillero
Navia
Luarca
La Caridad
Coaña
Canero
Soto
Nubledo
Muros
Pravia
Tazones
Venta las Ranas
Villaviciosa
Colunga
Ribadesella
Nueva
Llanes
Colombres
Villayón
Boal
Sierra de Rañadoiro
Grullos
Posada
Lugones
Noreña
Pola de Siero
La Vega
Santa Eulalia
Arriondas
Cangas de Onís
Benia de Onís
Carreña
Las Arenas
Salas
La Espina
Cornellana
Santullano
Grado
Oviedo
Trubia
Nava
Infiesto
Tineo
Bárcena del Monasterio
Pola de Allande
Puerto del Palo
Casares
Soto de Ribera
Langreo
Martinporra
Bimea
Pola de Laviana
Sames
Parque Nacional de los Picos de Europa
Picos de Europa
Sotres
Tama
Grandas
Berducedo
Belmonte
Proaza
Santa Eulalia
Sotrondio
Mieres
Caranga
La Vega
Pola de Lena
Campo de Caso
Cabañaquinta
Oseja de Sajambre
Posada de Valdeón
Camaleño
Espinama
Potes
Cangas del Narcea
La Plaza
Bárzana
Moreda
Collanzo
Puerto de Tarna
Puerto del Pontón
Portilla de la Reina
Puerto de San Glorio
La Vega
Embalse de Salime
Venta Nueva
Genestoso
Pola de Somiedo
Valgrande-Pajares
Puerto de Pajares
Puerto de San Isidro
San Isidro
Puebla de Lillo
Burón
Riaño
San Antolín
Puerto de Somiedo
Puerto de Rañadoiro
Puerto de Leitariegos
Degaña
Piedrafita de Babia
Cabrillanes
Villaseca de Laciana
Villablino
San Emiliano
Cármenes
Embalse de Porma
Embalse de Riaño
Sierra de Alba
Triollo
Besande
Serra dos Ancares
Palacios del Sil
Sierra de Gistredo
Embalse de Barrios de Luna
Ciñera
Vegacervera
Crémenes
Boñar
La Pola de Gordón
La Vecilla
Los Barrios de Luna
Robles de la Valcueva
Vegaquemada
La Colilla
Sabero
Cistierna
Prado de la Guzpeña
Guardo
Santibáñez de la Peña
Cervera de Pisuerga
Candín
Murias de Paredes
Las Omañas
Vegarienza
La Magdalena
La Robla
La Ercina
Páramo del Sil
Fabero
Riello
Soto y Amío
Rioseco de Tapia
Santa Colomba de Curueño
Respenda de la Peña
Igüeña
Toreno
Boeza
Cuadros
Garrafe de Torio
Ambasaguas
Vegas del Condado
Villalba de Guardo
La Puebla de Valdavia
Vega de Espinareda
Bierzo
Quintana del Castillo
Sariegos
Villaquilambre
Gradefes
Almanza
Pino del Río
Arganza
Cabañas Raras
Congosto
Folgoso de la Ribera
Llamas de la Ribera
Cimanes del Tejar
San Andrés del Rabanedo
León
Villafranca del Bierzo
Cacabelos
Bembibre
Torre del Bierzo
Manzanal del Puerto
Carrizo de la Ribera
Quintana de Rueda
Villazanzo de Valderaduey
Saldaña
Corullón
Carracedelo
Camponaraya
Castropodame
Puerto del Manzanal
Valverde de la Virgen
Armunia
Onzonilla
Villarente
Villaturiel
Santervás de la Vega
Toral de los Vados
Ponferrada
Molinaseca
Villamejil
Turcia
Priaranza del Bierzo
Villar de los Barrios
Santa Marina del Rey
Benavides de Órbigo
Chozas de Abajo
Mansilla de las Mulas
Saelices del Río
Carucedo
Las Médulas
San Justo de la Vega
Astorga
Villarejo de Órbigo
Bustillo del Páramo
Valdevimbre
El Burgo Ranero
Renedo de la Vega
O Barco
Sobradelo
Puente de Domingo Flórez
Santa Colomba de Somoza
Montes de León
Riego de la Vega
Santas Martas
Cea
Lucillo de Somoza
Santiagomillas
Bercianos del Páramo
Sahagún
Ledigos
San Mamés de Campos
Luyego de Somoza
Soto de la Vega
Santa María del Páramo
Matallana de Valmadrigal
Gordaliza del Pino
Serra do Eixe
Destriana
La Bañeza
Laguna Dalga
Villamañán
Valencia de Don Juan
Grajal de Campos
Cervatos de la Cueza
Truchas
Melgar de Arriba
Villada
San Román de la Cuba
Encinedo
Roperuelos del Páramo
Toral de los Guzmanes
Albires
Cisneros
Sierra de la Cabrera
Santa Elena de Jamuz
Laguna de Negrillos
Saelices de Mayorga
Boadilla de Rioseco
Villaumbrosa
Paredes de Nava
Bolo
Porto
Castrocontrigo
Castrocalbón
Alija del Infantado
Villamandos
Mayorga
Frechilla
Sanabria
Espadañedo
Ayoo de Vidriales
Pozuelo del Páramo
Villaquejida
Becilla de Valderaduey
Becerril de Campos
Ribadelago
Galende
Uña de Quintana
Arrabalde
Pobladura del Valle
Villalón de Campos
Villaumbrales
Puebla de Sanabria
Peque
Santibáñez de Vidriales
Manganeses de la Polvorosa
San Cristóbal de Entreviñas
Valderas
Fuentes de Nava
Lubián
Requejo
Palacios de Sanabria
San Pedro de Ceque
Quiruelas de Vidriales
Valdunquillo
Cuenca de Campos
Villamartín de Campos
Portilla del Padornelo
Pedralba de la Pradería
Embalse de Cernadilla
Mombuey
Camarzana de Tera
Benavente
Fuentes de Ropel
Ceinos de Campos
Villarramiel
Castromocho
Hermisende
Manzanal de Arriba
Rionegro del Puente
Melgar de Tera
Santibáñez de Tera
Santa Cristina de la Polvorosa
Castrogonzalo
Villanueva del Campo
Castroverde de Campos
Villerías
Ampudia
Rio de Onor
Peña Mira
Embalse de Valparaíso
Burganes de Valverde
San Esteban del Molar
Villalobos
Tierra de Campos
Mofreita
Parâmo
Serra de Montezinho
Aveleda
Villardeciervos
Ferreras de Abajo
Ferreras de Arriba
Otero de Bodas
Morales de Valverde
Villamayor de Campos
Villafrechós
Medina de Rioseco
Trigueros del Valle
Sierra de la Culebra
Santovenia
Morales de Campos
Villalba de los Alcores
Mahíde
Figueruela de Arriba
Tábara
Bretocino
Villafáfila
Villalpando
Tordehumos
Montes de Torozos
Bragança
Deilão
Moreruela de Tábara
Granja de Moreruela
Villabrágima
La Mudarra
Cigales
Castelo de Bragança
Riofrío de Aliste
San Vitero
Ferreruela de Tábara
Villarrín de Campos
Villagarcía de Campos
Castromonte
Mucientes
Edrosa
Samil
Milhão
Rabanales
Manganeses de la Lampreana
Cañizo
San Pedro de Latarce
Urueña
Villanubla
Castillo de Fuensaldaña
Failde
Trabazos
Perilla de Castro
Castronuevo
Villardefrades
Peñaflor de Hornija
Wamba
Zaratán
Valladolid
Grochão
Outeiro
Alcañices
Samir de los Caños
Embalse de Ricobayo
San Cebrián de Castro
Pajares de la Lampreana
Belver de los Montes
Mota del Marqués
Torrelobatón
Serra de Nogueira
Santa Comba de Rossas
Pinela
São Martinho de Angueira
Losacino
Carbajales de Alba
Montamarta
Malva
Tiedra
Vega de Valdetronco
Simancas
Fonfría
Benegiles
Vezdemarbán
Casasola de Arión
Laguna de Duero
Edroso
Carção
Constantim
Andavías
Torres del Carrizal
Pinilla de Toro
Pozoantiguo
Bercero
Viana de Cega
Izeda
Vimioso
Embalse de Castro
Pino
La Hiniesta
Tierra del Pan
Coreses
Fresno de la Ribera
Morales de Toro
Villalar de los Comuneros
Vinhas
Macedo de Cavaleiros
Caçarelhos
Malhadas
Villadepera
Villalcampo
Moralina
Muelas del Pan
Zamora
Toro
Tordesillas
Morais
Miranda do Douro
Villaseco del Pan
Villaralbo
Peleagonzalo
Serrada
Valdestillas
Chacim
Algoso
Duas Igrejas
Torregamones
Luelmo
Embalse de Villalcampo
Morales del Vino
Moraleja del Vino
Sanzoles
Pollos
Matapozuelos
Peredo
Lagoa
Fariza
Pereruela
El Perdigón
Villabuena del Puente
Castronuño
Rueda
La Seca
Sayago
Venialbo
Siete Iglesias de Trabancos
Pozaldez
Azinhoso
Sendim
Muga de Sayago
Alfândega da Fé
Mogadouro
Villar del Buey
Bermillo de Sayago
Fresno de Sayago
El Piñero
Arguijillo
La Bóveda de Toro
Nava del Rey
Alaejos
Medina del Campo
Castelo Branco
Bemposta
Fermoselle
Embalse de Almendra
Tierra del Vino
Fuentelapeña
40
45
39

Santander
Torrelavega
Bilbao (Bilbo)
Barakaldo
Santurtzi
Portugalete
Algorta
Sestao
Leioa
Llanes
Ribadesella
Santoña
Laredo
Castro-Urdiales
Reinosa
Aguilar de Campóo
Burgos
Palencia
Valladolid
Aranda de Duero
Lerma
Miranda de Ebro
Briviesca
Medina de Pomar
Villarcayo
Santo Domingo de la Calzada
Haro
Peñafiel
Cuéllar
Picos de Europa
Parque Nacional de los Picos de Europa
Sierra de Peña Sagra
Sierra de Peña Labra
Sierra de Alba
LA LORA
LA BUREBA
LOSA
TIERRA DE CAMPOS
VALLES DE CERRATO
MONTES DE TOROZOS
Sierra de la Demanda
Sierra de Neila
Picos de Urbión
Sierra de Ayllón
MARQUESADO DE BERLANGA
Montes Obarenes
Montes de Ordunte
Sierra Sálvada
Embalse del Ebro
Embalse de Aguilar de Campóo
Embalse de Sobrón
Alto Campoo
Lunada
Valdezcaray
Bahía de Santander
Cabo Mayor
Cabo de Ajo
Plymouth, Portsmouth
Portsmouth
Monasterio de Santo Domingo de Silos
Castillo de Peñafiel
Castillo de Fuensaldaña
Castillo de la Mota
Altamira
Guggenheim Bilbao
Atapuerca
Catedral
Monasterios de San Millán
E70
E80
E05
E804
A8
A67
A62
A1
A11
A231
A73
A601
AP1
AP68
E05/80
43°30′
43°00′
42°30′
42°00′
41°30′
4°30′
4°00′
3°30′
3°00′

39

46

7
8
9
10
32
2°30′
2°00′
1°30′
1°00′
0°30′
Golfe de Gascogne
Golfo de Gascuña
Côte d'Argent
GASCOGNE
BÉARN
PAYS BASQUE
PAÍS VASCO
TREVIÑO
Mont-de-Marsan
Dax
Bayonne
Biarritz
Anglet
St-Jean-de-Luz
Hendaye
Irun
Hondarribia
Donostia/ San Sebastián
Orthez
Pau
Lescar
Oloron-Ste-Marie
St-Jean-Pied-de-Port
Vitoria-Gasteiz
Pamplona/Iruña
Logroño
Estella
Tafalla
Tudela
Calahorra
Jaca
Huesca
Zaragoza
Soria
Tarazona
Calatayud
Almazán
RIBERA NAVARRA
BÁRDENAS REALES
CINCO VILLAS
EL CASTELLAR
LOS MONEGROS
LLANO DE PLASENCIA
CAMPO DE GÓMARA
CAMPO DE CARIÑENA
Sierra de Aralar
Sierra de Urbasa
Sierra de Andía
Sierra de Abodi
Sierra de San Juan de la Peña
Sierra de Santo Domingo
Sierra del Moncayo
Sierra de la Virgen
Sierra del Madero
Sierra de Alcubierre
Embalse de Yesa
Embalse de Ullíbarri-Gamboa
A
B
C
D
E
F
42
47
48

B O R D E A U X
Lourdes
Argelès-Gazost
Bagnères-de-Bigorre
Lannemezan
St-Gaudens
Tarbes
B I G O R R E
PARC NATIONAL DES PYRÉNÉES OCCIDENTALES
Cauterets
Luz-Ardiden
Luz-St-Sauveur
Barèges
Col du Tourmalet
La Mongie
Gèdre
Gavarnie
Piau-Engaly
Aragnouet
St-Lary-Soulan
Val Louron
Bagnères-de-Luchon
Superbagnères
Astún
Candanchu
El Formigal
Sallent de Gállego
Panticosa
Balneario de Panticosa Huesca
Mont Perdu (Monte Perdido)
Grande Cascade de Gavarnie
PARQUE NACIONAL ORDESA - MONTE PERDIDO
Torla
Broto
Bielsa
Benasque
Cerler (Huesca)
Montes Malditos
Vielha
Baqueria/ Beret
Salardu
Boi Taull
PARC NACIONAL D'AIGÜES TORTES I ESTANY DE SANT MAURICI
Super Espot
Jaca
Sabiñánigo
Biescas
Canfranc
Hecho
Ansó
Berdún
Embalse de Yesa
Sierra de San Juan de la Peña
S O B R A R B E
Boltaña
Ainsa
Campo
C O N D A D O
Embalse de Mediano
Pont de Suert
Sierra de Guara
Huesca
Barbastro
Monzón
Graus
Benabarre
Tremp
La Pobla de Segur
Sort
Serra del Boumort
Serra del Montsec
S O M O N T A N O
L A L I T E R A
Binéfar
Fraga
Lleida (Lérida)
Balaguer
S E G R I À
U R G E L L
Tàrrega
Cervera
Les Borges Blanques
Zaragoza
Ejea de los Caballeros
C I N C O V I L L A S
Tauste
L O S M O N E G R O S
Sierra de Alcubierre
LLANOS DE CARDIEL
Caspe
Embalse de Mequinenza
Mequinenza
Alcañiz
DESIERTO DE CALANDA
Belchite
Híjar
Andorra
Alcorisa
Calanda
Valderrobres
Morella
Tortosa
B A I X E B R E
Amposta
Deltebre
Sant Carles de la Ràpita
Golf de Sant Jordi
L'Ametlla de Mar
Cambrils
Salou
Reus
Valls
Montblanc
Mora d'Ebre
Gandesa
Serra de la Fatarrella
Vinaròs
Montalbán
Utrillas
Aliaga
Cantavieja
Sierra de San Just
Sierra de la Garrucha
Castellote
Zorita del Maestrazgo

7
8
9
10
34
35
49
B
C
D
E
F
F
AND
1°30′
2°00′
2°30′
3°00′
3°30′
43°00′
42°30′
42°00′
41°30′
41°00′
Pamiers
Mirepoix
Limoux
Foix
Montagnes du Plantaurel
Quillan
CORBIÈRES
Pays de Sault
Tarascon-sur-Ariège
Ax-les-Thermes
Perpignan
Rivesaltes
Canet-en-Roussillon
Argelès-sur-Mer
Collioure
Port-Vendres
Banyuls-sur-Mer
Côte Vermeille
Cap Leucate
Golfe du Lion
Prades
CONFLENT
ROUSSILLON
Céret
Le Perthus
Cap Cerbère
Portbou
ANDORRA LA VELLA
Les Escaldes
Encamp
Ordino
Pas de la Casa/ Grau Roig
Sant Julià de Lòria
Puigcerdà
Llívia
Masella
La Molina
Val de Nuria
Vallter 2000
La Seu d'Urgell
Serra del Cadí
RIPOLLÈS
Ripoll
Camprodon
Olot
Figueres
Roses
Cap de Creus
Cadaqués
Golf de Roses
L'Escala
Banyoles
Girona (Gerona)
Torroella de Montgrí
Cap de Begur
Palafrugell
Palamós
Sant Feliu de Guíxols
Costa Brava
Lloret de Mar
Blanes
Malgrat de Mar
Pineda de Mar
Calella
Arenys de Mar
Mataró
Vic
Manlleu
Berga
BERGEDÀ
Solsona
Cardona
Manresa
Igualada
Terrassa
Sabadell
Granollers
Montmeló
Mollet del Vallès
Cerdanyola del Vallès
Sant Cugat del Vallès
Badalona
Barcelona
L'Hospitalet de Llobregat
Cornellà de Llobregat
Sant Boi de Llobregat
El Prat de Llobregat
Castelldefels
Sitges
Vilanova i la Geltrú
Vilafranca del Penedès
El Vendrell
Calafell
Torredembarra
Costa Daurada
Civitavecchia, Genova
Bejaïa
Alcúdia, Ciutadella de Menorca, Mahón
Eivissa, Palma de Mallorca

MINHO
TRÁS-OS-MONTES
DOURO
BEIRA ALTA
BEIRA LITORAL
BEIRA BAIXA
ESTREMADURA
RIBATEJO
Viana do Castelo
Braga
Guimarães
Póvoa de Varzim
Vila do Conde
Porto
Vila Nova de Gaia
Matosinhos
Vila Real
Peso da Régua
Lamego
Espinho
São João da Madeira
Ovar
Aveiro
Viseu
Figueira da Foz
Coimbra
Covilhã
Serra da Estrela
Castelo Branco
Leiria
Marinha Grande
Nazaré
Alcobaça
Caldas da Rainha
Peniche
Óbidos
Torres Vedras
Fátima
Tomar
Torres Novas
Entroncamento
Abrantes
Santarém
Portalegre
Cabo Carvoeiro
Cabo Mondego
Berlenga
Farilhões
Serra da Lousã
Serra do Caramulo
Serra de Montemuro
Serra do Marão
Serra da Cabreira
Serra de Aire
Serra de Guardunha
Rio Maior
41°30′
41°00′
40°30′
40°00′
39°30′
9°30′
9°00′
8°30′
8°00′
7°30′
A
B
C
D
E
F
2
3
4
5
38
50

MONTES
Serra de Nogueira
Mirandela
Macedo de Cavaleiros
Mogadouro
Vila Flor
Torre de Moncorvo
Barragem do Baixo Sabor
Serra de Bornes
Serra de Mogadouro
Douro
Embalse de Castro
Miranda do Douro
Alcañices
Samir de los Caños
Zamora
TIERRA DEL PAN
Embalse de Ricobayo
Toro
Tordesillas
SAYAGO
Bermillo de Sayago
Fermoselle
Embalse de Almendra
Embalse de Villalcampo
TIERRA DEL VINO
Fuentesaúco
Alaejos
Nava del Rey
Aldeadávila de la Ribera
Vilvestre
Embalse de Saucelle
Arte Rupestre do Vale do Côa
Vila Nova de Foz Côa
Freixo de Espada à Cinta
Barca de Alva
Vitigudino
Ledesma
Salamanca
LA ARMUÑA
Peñaranda de Bracamonte
Alba de Tormes
Embalse de Villagonzalo
ABADENGO
Lumbrales
Figueira de Castelo Rodrigo
Almeida
Pinhel
Guarda
Fuentes de Oñoro
Ciudad Rodrigo
Sierra de la Peña de Francia
Peña de Francia 1732
La Alberca
Embalse de Santa Teresa
Guijuelo
Béjar
Sierra de Gata
Las Hurdes
Embalse de Gabriel y Galán
Sierra de Candelario
Sierra de Gredos
Almanzor 2592
El Barco de Ávila
Piedrahita
Sierra de Malcata
Sabugal
Penamacor
Idanha-a-Nova
Barragem da Idanha
Monfortinho
Moraleja
Coria
Plasencia
LA VERA
Jarandilla de la Vera
CAMPO ARAÑUELO
Navalmoral de la Mata
Embalse de Valdecañas
Embalse de Borbollón
Embalse de Alcántara
Embalse de Alcántara II
Alcántara
Garrovillas
Puerto de Miravete
Embalse de Torrejón-Tajo
Sierra de las Villuercas
Embalse de Cedillo
Cáceres
Embalse de Cáceres
Trujillo
Castillo de Trujillo
Malpartida de Cáceres
Arroyo de la Luz
Valencia de Alcántara
Sierra de San Pedro
Sierra de Guadalupe
Santa María de Guadalupe
Embalse de Salor
Sierra de Montánchez
Montánchez
Embalse de la Peña del Águila
Alburquerque
Miajadas
Logrosán
Castilblanco
E82
E80
E90
E803
A66
A62
A5
A58
EX-A1
A50
A11
A25-IP5
IP2
E802
6
7
8
9
10
A
B
C
D
E
F
39
46
51
7°00'
6°30'
6°00'
5°30'
41°30'
41°00'
40°30'
40°00'
39°30'

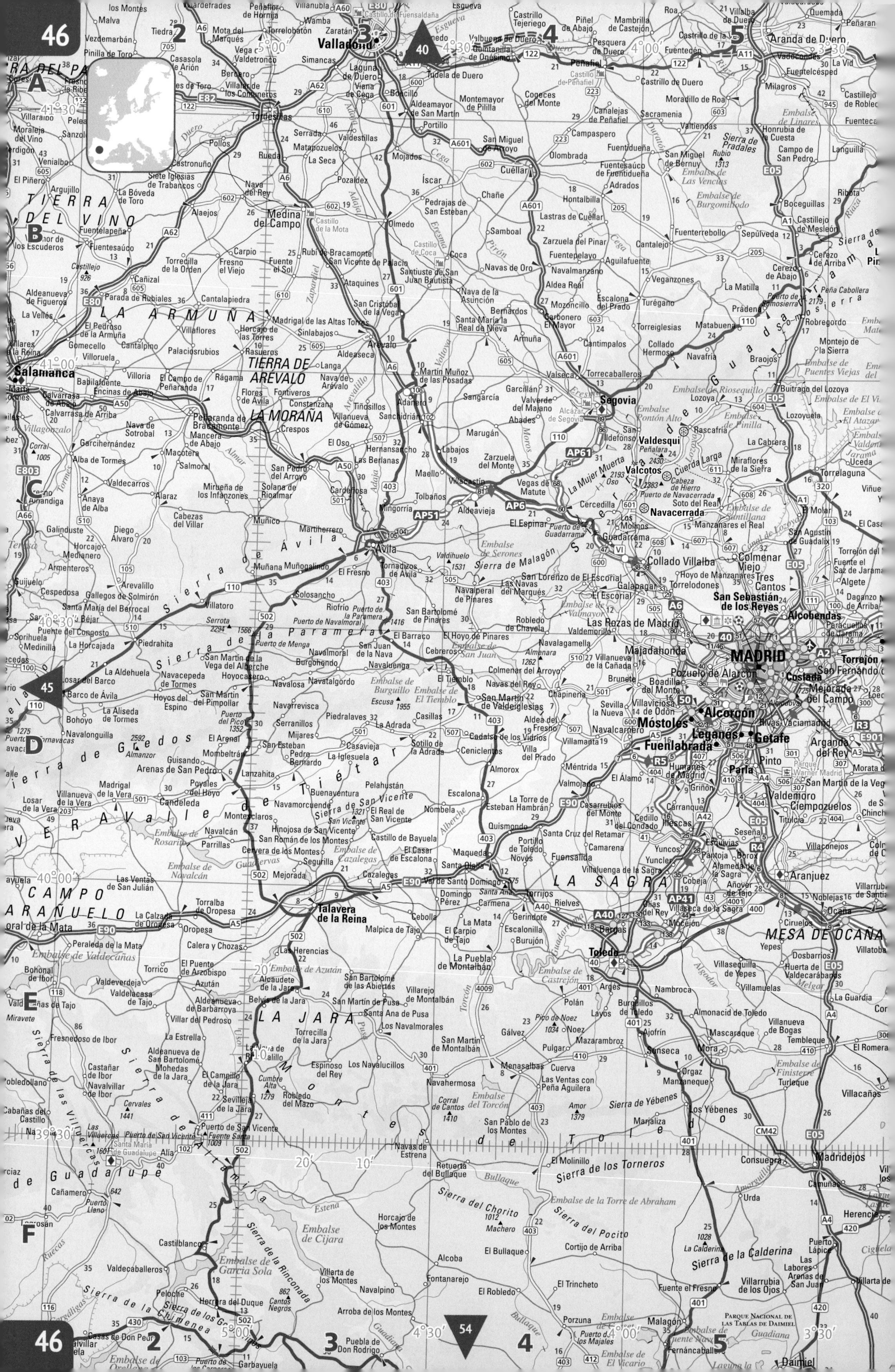
Valladolid
Tordesillas
Medina del Campo
Peñafiel
Aranda de Duero
Cuéllar
Segovia
Salamanca
Ávila
Arévalo
Madrigal de las Altas Torres
Peñaranda de Bracamonte
Alba de Tormes
Béjar
Piedrahita
Barco de Ávila
TIERRA DEL VINO
LA ARMUÑA
TIERRA DE ARÉVALO
LA MORAÑA
Sierra de Ávila
Sierra de la Paramera
Sierra de Gredos
Valle del Tiétar
VERA
CAMPO ARAÑUELO
Sierra de Guadarrama
Sierra de Malagón
Somosierra
Collado Villalba
El Escorial
San Lorenzo de El Escorial
Colmenar Viejo
Alcobendas
San Sebastián de los Reyes
Las Rozas de Madrid
Majadahonda
Pozuelo de Alarcón
MADRID
Torrejón
Coslada
San Fernando
Alcorcón
Móstoles
Leganés
Getafe
Fuenlabrada
Parla
Pinto
Aranjuez
LA SAGRA
MESA DE OCAÑA
Ocaña
Toledo
Talavera de la Reina
Oropesa
LA JARA
Montes de Toledo
Sierra de Altamira
Sierra de Guadalupe
Sierra de las Villuercas
Sierra de los Torneros
Sierra del Chorito
Sierra del Pocito
Sierra de la Calderina
Sierra de Yébenes
Sierra de la Rinconada
Sierra de la Chimenea
Sierra de los Gredos
Embalse de Valdecañas
Embalse de Azután
Embalse de Rosarito
Embalse de Navalcán
Embalse de Cijara
Embalse de García Sola
Embalse de la Torre de Abraham
Embalse de Castrejón
Embalse del Torcón
Embalse de Burguillo
Embalse de El Tiemblo
Embalse de San Juan
Embalse de Cazalegas
Embalse de Finisterre
Embalse de Puentes Viejas
Embalse de Riosequillo
Embalse de Pinilla
Embalse de Santillana
Embalse de Linares
Embalse de Las Vencías
Embalse de Burgomillodo
Madridejos
Consuegra
Mora
Orgaz
Los Yébenes
Puerto Lápice
Malagón
Fernáncaballero
Daimiel
Parque Nacional de las Tablas de Daimiel
Herencia
Villacañas
Tembleque
Guadalupe
Alía
Castilblanco
Herrera del Duque
Puebla de Don Rodrigo
Navas de Estena
Retuerta del Bullaque
El Bullaque
Navahermosa
Los Navalmorales
Valdesquí
Valcotos
Navacerrada
Guadarrama
Rascafría
Buitrago del Lozoya
Sepúlveda
Riaza
Torrelaguna
Villacastín
Sierra de Pradales
40
45
54
2
3
4
5
A
B
C
D
E
F
41°30′
41°00′
40°30′
40°00′
39°30′
5°00′
4°30′
4°00′
3°30′

7
8
9
10
A
B
C
D
E
F
41
48
55
CAMPO DE GÓMARA
MARQUESADO DE BERLANGA
CAMPO DE CARIÑENA
LA ALCARRIA
Serranía de Cuenca
Montes Universales
RINCÓN DE ADEMUZ
Altos de Cabrejas
LA OBISPALÍA
MANCHA
Sierra de la Virgen
Sierra de Armantes
Sierra de Vicort
Sierra de Algairén
Sierra de Pela
Sierra Ministra
Sierra de Solorio
Sierra de Santa Cruz
Sierra de Pardos
Sierra Cucalón
Sierra de Caldereros
Sierra Menera
Sierra Palomera
Sierra de Albarracín
Sierra de Valdemeca
Sierra del Tremedal
Sierra de Bascuñana
Sierra de Altomira
Sierra de las Cuerdas
Sierra del Monje
Sierra de Mira
Sierra de Rubial
Cerro Moro
Meseta de la Muela
Burgo de Osma
San Esteban de Gormaz
Almazán
Medinaceli
Sigüenza
Atienza
Calatayud
Daroca
Cariñena
La Almunia de Doña Godina
Molina de Aragón
Monreal del Campo
Albarracín
Guadalajara
Azuqueca de Henares
Brihuega
Cifuentes
Sacedón
Pastrana
Huete
Tarancón
Cuenca
Utiel
Motilla del Palancar
San Clemente
Quintanar de la Orden
Mota del Cuervo
Belmonte
Alcázar de San Juan
Campo de Criptana
Socuéllamos
Villarrobledo
La Roda
Tarazona de la Mancha
Madrigueras
Casas-Ibáñez
Requena
Ademuz
Embalse de Entrepeñas
Embalse de Buendía
Embalse de Bolarque
Embalse de Alarcón
Embalse de Contreras
Laguna de Gallocanta
Laguna del Hito
A2
A3
A15
A23
A31
A40
A43
E90
E901
AP36
3°00′
2°30′
2°00′
1°30′
41°30′
41°00′
40°30′
40°00′
39°30′

1
2
3
4
5
A
B
C
D
E
F
41
42
47
56
Zaragoza
CAMPO DE CARIÑENA
MONEGROS
LLANOS DE CARDIEL
DESIERTO DE CALANDA
BAIX EBRE
EL MAESTRAZGO
RINCÓN DE ADEMUZ
Meseta de la Muela
Sierra de Alcubierre
Sierra de Vicort
Sierra de Algairén
Sierra de Santa Cruz
Sierra de Pardos
Sierra Cucalón
Sierra de San Just
Sierra de la Garrucha
Sierra Palomera
Sierra de Albarracín
Montes Universales
Sierra de Javalambre
Sierra de Gudar
Sierra del Rayo
Sierra Menera
Sierra de Mequinenza
Serra de la Fatarrella
Sierra del Monte Turmell
Ports de Beseit
Serra d'Irta
Serra d'Espadà
Sierra de Mira
Sierra de Rubial
Serra Martés
Calatayud
Daroca
Calamocha
Monreal del Campo
Teruel
Alcañiz
Caspe
Fraga
Mequinenza
Morella
Vinaròs
Benicarló
Peñíscola
Castellón de la Plana/
Castelló de la Plana
Almazora (Almassora)
Vila-real
Burriana
Nules
La Vall d'Uixó
Segorbe
Sagunto
Puçol
Massamagrell
Lliria
Moncada
Burjassot
Paterna
Manises
Valencia
Torrent
Alfafar
Catarroja
Picassent
Silla
Almussafes
Sueca
Cullera
Algemesí
Alzira
Carlet
Requena
Utiel
Chiva
Cheste
Buñol
Golfo de Valencia
Costa del Azahar
Elvissa, Palma de Mallorca
Cabo de Oropesa
Punta de Capicorp
L'Albufera
Embalse de Mequinenza
Embalse de Caspe
Embalse de Calanda
Embalse de Santolea
Embalse de Arenós
Embalse de Sichar
Embalse del Regajo
Embalse de Loriguilla
Embalse de Benagéber
Embalse de Contreras
Embalse de Buseo
Embalse de Forata
Embalse de Tous
Embalse de Alarcón
Embalse de Mezalocha
Embalse de las Torcas
Embalse de Moneva
Embalse del Arquillo de San Blás
Laguna de Gallocanta
Laguna de Zaida
Ebro
Turia
Júcar
Cabriel
Mijares
Guadalope
Jiloca
Huerva
Martín
Alfambra
Palancia
AP2
AP7
A23
A2
A3
A7
E15
E90
E901
41°30'
41°00'
40°30'
40°00'
39°30'
1°30'
1°00'
0°30'
0°00'

6
7
8
9
10
A
B
C
D
E
F
URGELL
SEGARRA
Lleida
Tàrrega
Cervera
Igualada
Manresa
Terrassa
Sabadell
Granollers
Mataró
Badalona
Barcelona
L'Hospitalet de Llobregat
Cornellà de Llobregat
Sant Boi de Llobregat
El Prat de Llobregat
Castelldefels
Sitges
Vilanova i la Geltrú
Vilafranca del Penedès
El Vendrell
Calafell
Torredembarra
Tarragona
Reus
Valls
Cambrils
Salou
Cap de Salou
Vila-seca de Solcina
PortAventura Park
Les Borges Blanques
Montblanc
L'Hospitalet de l'Infant
Cap de Terme
L'Ametlla de Mar
Golf de Sant Jordi
Punta del Fangar
Deltebre
Illa de Buda
Sant Jaume d'Enveja
Sant Carles de la Ràpita
Platja del Trabucador
Calella
Pineda de Mar
Canet de Mar
Arenys de Mar
Vilassar de Mar
Premià de Mar
Mollet del Vallès
Cerdanyola del Vallès
Rubí
Sant Cugat del Vallès
Martorell
Gavà
Viladecans
Esplugues de Llobregat
Sant Vicenç dels Horts
Molins de Rei
Costa Dorada
Azahar
Islas Columbretes
ILLES BALEARS
MALLORCA
Sóller
Port de Sóller
Morro de sa Vaca
Valldemossa
Deià
Bunyola
Banyalbufar
Esporles
Estellencs
Puigpunyent
Sa Dragonera
Sant Elm
Andratx
Port d'Andratx
Cap de sa Mola
Peguera
Palmanova
Magaluf
Portals Vells
Cap de Cala Figuera
Es Cap Enderrocat
Badia de Palma
Palma de Mallorca
Can Pastilla
Cap Blanc
Civitavecchia, Genova
Sète
Alcúdia, Ciutadella de Menorca, Mahón
Mahón, Livorno
Salerno
Eivissa
EIVISSA
Pta Xarracó
Cap des Mossons
Sant Joan de Labritja
1°00′
1°30′
2°00′
2°30′
41°30′
41°00′
40°30′
40°00′
39°30′
43
57

1
2
3
4
A
B
C
D
E
F
R I B A T E J O
A L E N T E J O
A L G A R V E
LISBOA
Setúbal
Santarém
Évora
Beja
Faro
Sines
Portimão
Lagos
Caldas da Rainha
Torres Vedras
Sintra
Amadora
Cascais
Costa do Estoril
Cabo da Roca
Cabo Espichel
Baía de Setúbal
Costa Bela
Costa da Galé
Costa do Sol
Cabo de Sines
Cabo Sardão
Cabo de São Vicente (Cape St Vincent)
Pta de Sagres
Cabo de Santa Maria
Serra de Monchique
Serra do Cercal
Serra de Grândola
Serra de Monfurado
Serra do Caldeirão
Serra de Ossa
Barragem do Pego do Altar
Barragem de Montargil
Barragem do Alqueva
Alcácer do Sal
Grândola
Santiago do Cacém
Odemira
Montemor-o-Novo
Vendas Novas
Estremoz
Reguengos de Monsaraz
Moura
Serpa
Mértola
Ourique
Aljustrel
Almodôvar
Loulé
Olhão
Tavira
Albufeira
Silves
EL ANDÉVALO
Funchal, Islas Canarias
39°00′
38°30′
38°00′
37°30′
37°00′
9°00′
8°30′
8°00′
7°30′

Sierra de San Pedro
Valencia de Alcántara
San Vicente de Alcántara
Alburquerque
Malpartida de Cáceres
Sierra de Guadalupe
Madroñera
Garciaz
Logrosán
Castilblanco
Valdecaballeros
Sierra de la Chimenea
Sierra de Montánchez
Montánchez
Torremocha
Salvatierra de Santiago
Valdefuentes
Torre de Santa María
Alcuéscar
Almoharín
Miajadas
Escurial
Zorita
Santa Cruz de la Sierra
Villamesías
Abertura
Alcollarín
Campo Lugar
Madrigalejo
Navalvillar de Pela
Casas de Don Pedro
Embalse de Orellana
Talarrubias
Orellana la Vieja
Orellana de la Sierra
Acedera
Gargáligas
Villar de Rena
Rena
Santa Amalia
Medellín
Mengabril
Villanueva de la Serena
Don Benito
La Haba
Magacela
Campanario
La Coronada
La Guarda
Quintana de la Serena
LA SERENA
Castuera
Benquerencia de la Serena
Cabeza del Buey
Almorchón
Helechal
Embalse de la Serena
Peñalsordo
Zarza Capilla
Esparragosa
Puebla de Alcocer
Campo Maior
Elvas
Badajoz
Talavera la Real
Montijo
Puebla de Obando
La Roca de la Sierra
La Nava de Santiago
Cordobilla de Lácara
Carmonita
Aldea del Cano
Mirandilla
Aljucén
Trujillanos
Esparragalejo
La Garrovilla
Torremayor
Mérida
Valverde de Mérida
Don Álvaro
Villagonzalo
Zarza de Alange
Alange
Embalse de Alange
Oliva de Mérida
Guareña
Manchita
Valdetorres
Lobón
Puebla de la Calzada
Calamonte
Arroyo de San Serván
Torremegía
Olivenza
LLANOS DE OLIVENZA
Almendralejo
Solana de los Barros
Corte de Peleas
La Albuera
Valverde de Leganés
Torre de Miguel Sesmero
Santa Marta
Aceuchal
Villalba de los Barros
Villafranca de los Barros
TIERRA DE BARROS
Puebla de la Reina
Palomas
Hornachos
Ribera del Fresno
Puebla del Prior
Fuente del Maestre
Nogales
La Morera
La Parra
Feria
Salvaleón
Barcarrota
Alconchel
Táliga
Cheles
Valle de la Serena
Malpartida de la Serena
Zalamea de la Serena
Higuera de la Serena
Esparragosa de la Serena
Monterrubio de la Serena
Retamal
Campillo de Llerena
Peraleda del Zaucejo
Sierra de los Argallanes
Belalcázar
Hinojosa del Duque
Salvatierra de los Barros
Los Santos de Maimona
Zafra
Sierra de Feria
Hinojosa del Valle
Llera
Valencia de las Torres
Higuera de Llerena
Usagre
Puebla de Sancho Pérez
Medina de las Torres
Calzadilla de los Barros
Valverde de Burguillos
Burguillos del Cerro
Jerez de los Caballeros
Valle de Santa Ana
Valle de Matamoros
Higuera de Vargas
Villanueva del Fresno
Zahínos
Oliva de la Frontera
Valencia del Mombuey
Maguilla
Berlanga
Azuaga
Granja de Torrehermosa
Peñarroya-Pueblonuevo
Fuente Obejuna
La Coronada
Blázquez
Valsequillo
La Granjuela
Bienvenida
Villagarcía de la Torre
Llerena
Ahillones
Fuente de Cantos
Valencia del Ventoso
Montemolín
Casas de Reina
Reina
Fuente del Arco
Valverde de Llerena
Fregenal de la Sierra
Higuera la Real
Encinasola
Bodonal de la Sierra
Segura de León
Cabeza la Vaca
Calera de León
Fuentes de León
Monesterio
Pallarés
Puebla del Maestre
Guadalcanal
Sierra del Agua
Malcocinado
Alanís
San Nicolás del Puerto
Argallón
Cumbres de San Bartolomé
Cumbres Mayores
Cañaveral de León
Hinojales
Arroyomolinos de León
Embalse El Pintado
Sierra de Hinojales
Sierra de Aracena
Sierra de Aroche
Rosal de la Frontera
Vila Verde de Ficalho
Cortegana
Jabugo
Galaroza
Alájar
Aracena
Santa Ana la Real
Almonaster la Real
Santa Ollala del Cala
Corteconcepción
Cala
El Real de la Jara
Almadén de la Plata
Cazalla de la Sierra
Constantina
Las Navas de la Concepción
Hornachuelos
Sierra Pelada
Higuera de la Sierra
Zufre
Embalse de Zufre
Campofrío
La Granada de Riotinto
Minas de Riotinto
Nerva
El Castillo de las Guardas
El Ronquillo
El Garrobo
Zalamea la Real
El Campillo
Calañas
Valdelamusa
El Cerro de Andévalo
Cabezas Rubias
Santa Bárbara de Casa
Paymogo
Puebla de Guzmán
Tharsis
Villanueva de las Cruces
Alosno
Sotiel Coronada
Valverde del Camino
El Pedroso
Castilblanco de los Arroyos
Villaverde del Río
Cantillana
Alcolea del Río
Villanueva del Río y Minas
Lora del Río
Palma del Río
Peñaflor
La Campana
Guadajoz
Burguillos
Guillena
Gerena
Brenes
Alcalá del Río
La Rinconada
Aznalcóllar
EL ALJARAFE
La Algaba
Santiponce
Camas
Sevilla
Carmona
El Viso del Alcor
Mairena del Alcor
Marchena
Paradas
El Arahal
Alcalá de Guadaira
Dos Hermanas
CONDADO DE NIEBLA
Villalba del Alcor
Paterna del Campo
Manzanilla
La Palma del Condado
Niebla
Villarrasa
Trigueros
Gibraleón
Beas
El Almendro
Villanueva de los Castillejos
San Bartolomé de la Torre
San Silvestre de Guzmán
Villablanca
Cartaya
Lepe
Aljaraque
Huelva
San Juan del Puerto
Moguer
Palos de la Frontera
Punta Umbría
Isla Cristina
El Rompido
Mazagón
Bollullos Par del Condado
Rociana del Condado
Lucena del Puerto
Almonte
Hinojos
Pilas
Villamanrique de la Condesa
Aznalcázar
Sanlúcar la Mayor
Olivares
Castilleja de la Cuesta
San Juan de Aznalfarache
Palomares del Río
La Puebla del Río
Coria del Río
El Rocío
Los Palacios y Villafranca
Villafranco del Guadalquivir
Isla Menor
Isla Mayor
Marismas
Utrera
El Coronil
Montellano
Morón de la Frontera
La Puebla de Cazalla
Las Cabezas de San Juan
Lebrija
El Cuervo
Trebujena
Matalascañas
Playa de Castilla
Llanos de Huelva
Parque Nacional de Doñana
Sierra de Espartero
Santa Cruz de Tenerife, Las Palmas, Arrecife
5
6
7
8
9
A
B
C
D
E
45
52
54
7°00′
6°30′
6°00′
5°30′
39°00′
38°30′
38°00′
37°30′
37°00′

1
2
3
4
5
A
B
C
D
E
51
50
Serpa
Brinches
Pias
Sobral da Adiça
Sierra da Adiça
Vila Nova de São Bento
Vila Verde de Ficalho
Rosal de la Frontera
Cortegana
Jabugo
Aracena
Cala
El Real de la Jara
Cazalla de la Sierra
Constantina
El Pedroso
Almadén de la Plata
Cabeça Gorda
Mosteiro
Algodor
Alcaria Ruiva
Mértola
Santana de Cambas
Mina de São Domingos
Moreanes
EL ANDÉVALO
Paymogo
Santa Bárbara de Casa
Cabezas Rubias
Sierra de Aracena
Sierra Pelada
Almonaster la Real
Santa Ana la Real
Alájar
Valdelamusa
San Telmo
El Cerro de Andévalo
Campofrío
Minas de Riotinto
Nerva
Zalamea la Real
El Campillo
Higuera de la Sierra
Zufre
Santa Olalla del Cala
Corteconcepción
La Granada de Riotinto
El Castillo de las Guardas
El Ronquillo
Embalse de Aracena
Embalse de Zufre
Embalse de Cala
Embalse de Huezna
Castilblanco de los Arroyos
Villaverde del Río
Cantillana
Burguillos
Guillena
Brenes
Alcalá del Río
La Rinconada
El Garrobo
Gerena
Aznalcóllar
EL ALJARAFE
Embalse de Agrio
Embalse El Esparragal
Calañas
Villanueva de las Cruces
Sotiel Coronada
Valverde del Camino
Tharsis
Alosno
Puebla de Guzmán
São Sebastião dos Carros
Pomarão
São Miguel do Pinheiro
Espírito Santo
Granado
El Granado
El Almendro
Villanueva de los Castillejos
Alcoutim
Sanlúcar de Guadiana
Martim Longo
Giões
Pereiro
Vaqueiros
Embalse de Andévalo
San Bartolomé de la Torre
Embalse del Sancho
Embalse de Piedras
San Silvestre de Guzmán
Odeleite
Villablanca
Azinhal
Junqueira
Castro Marim
Ayamonte
Vila Real de Santo António
Isla Cristina
Lepe
La Antilla
Cartaya
El Rompido
Aljaraque
Gibraleón
Trigueros
Beas
El Tumbalejo
CONDADO DE NIEBLA
Niebla
Villarrasa
La Palma del Condado
Villalba del Alcor
Paterna del Campo
Manzanilla
Bonares
Rociana del Condado
Bollullos Par del Condado
Almonte
Lucena del Puerto
San Juan del Puerto
Huelva
Moguer
Palos de la Frontera
Punta Umbría
Mazagón
Hinojos
Villamanrique de la Condesa
Pilas
Aznalcázar
Carrión
Huévar
Sanlúcar
Olivares
Salteras
La Algaba
Santiponce
Camas
Castilleja de la Cuesta
San Juan de Aznalfarache
Tomares
Benacazón
Palomares del Río
Coria del Río
La Puebla del Río
Sevilla
Mairena del Alcor
Alcalá de Guadaira
Bellavista
Dos Hermanas
Utrera
Los Palacios y Villafranca
Villafranco del Guadalquivir
Isla Menor
Isla Mayor
Marismas
El Rocío
Matalascañas
Doñana
PARQUE NACIONAL DE DOÑANA
Playa de Castilla
Costa de Huelva
Costa de la Luz
GOLFO DE CÁDIZ
Santa Cruz de Tenerife, Las Palmas, Arrecife
Islas Canarias
Peralva
Alcaria do Cume
Alportel
Santa Catarina da Fonte do Bispo
Vila Nova de Cacela
Conceição
Tavira
Santo Estêvão
Moncarapacho
Ilha de Tavira
Olhão
Monte Gordo
Las Cabezas de San Juan
Lebrija
Trebujena
El Cuervo
Espera
Villamartín
Bornos
Gibalbín
Bonanza
Pta de Malandar
Pta del Perro
Sanlúcar de Barrameda
Chipiona
Nueva Jarilla
Arcos de la Frontera
Jédula
Jerez de la Frontera
Circuito de Jerez
Algar
San José del Valle
Embalse de Guadalcacín
Sierra de las Cabras
Pta Candor
Rota
El Puerto de Santa María
Bahía de Cádiz
Cádiz
Puerto Real
Paterna de Rivera
San Fernando
Isla de León
Chiclana de la Frontera
Isla Sancti Petri
Campano
Medina-Sidonia
Alcalá de los Gazules
San José de Malcocinado
Benalup de Sidonia
Conil de la Frontera
Cabo Roche
Vejer de la Frontera
Embalse de Celemín
Sierra Blanquilla
Sierra del Almodóvar
Barbate de Franco
Cabo Trafalgar
Zahara de los Atunes
Sierra de Retín
Sierra de la Plata
Facinas
Pta Camarinal
Pta Palomas
Tarifa
Strait
Cap Spartel
Tanger
Oued Mharhar
Dar Chaoui
Souk el Had el Rharbia
Asilah
37°30′
37°00′
36°30′
36°00′
7°30′
7°00′
6°30′
6°00′
20′
10′

6
7
8
9
54
55
A
B
C
D
E
5°30′
5°00′
4°30′
4°00′
37°30′
37°00′
36°30′
36°00′
Córdoba
Mezquita-Catedral de Córdoba
Montoro
Villafranca de Córdoba
Alcolea
El Carpio
Villa del Río
Bujalance
Cañete de las Torres
Porcuna
Arjonilla
Lopera
Arjona
Villanueva de la Reina
Higuera de Arjona
Mengíbar
Jabalquinto
Villargordo
Fuerte del Rey
Escañuela
Villardompardo
Torredonjimeno
Torre del Campo
Jaén
Jamilena
Martos
Los Villares
La Guardia de Jaén
Pegalajar
Mancha Real
Jimena
Bedmar
Cambil
Huelma
Cárchelejo
Sierra Mágina
Valdepeñas de Jaén
Fuensanta de Martos
Embalse de Quiebrajano
Campillo de Arenas
Noalejo
Castillo de Locubín
Alcalá la Real
Frailes
Montillana
Campotéjar
Benalúa de las Villas
Iznalloz
Piñar
Sierra Arana
Montejícar
Embalse de Colomera
Colomera
Moclín
Illora
Pinos-Puente
Atarfe
Albolote
Granada
Deifontes
Cogollos Vega
Alfacar
Santa Fe
Armilla
Gabia la Grande
Huétor Vega
Monachil
Zubia
Sierra Nevada
Alhendín
Dílar
Padul
Dúrcal
Lecrín
Nigüelas
Malá
Escúzar
Suspiro del Moro
Ventas de Huelma
Chimeneas
Cacín
Moraleda de Zafayona
Lachar
Chauchina
Fuente Vaqueros
Hornachuelos
La Puebla de los Infantes
Posadas
Almodóvar del Río
Guadalcázar
Palma del Río
Fuente Palmera
Peñaflor
Lora del Río
CAMPIÑA
La Carlota
San Sebastián de los Ballesteros
La Victoria
Fernán Núñez
Montemayor
Espejo
Castro del Río
Baena
Doña Mencía
Nueva-Carteya
Zuheros
Luque
Alcaudete
Montilla
Montalbán de Córdoba
La Rambla
Santaella
Aguilar de la Frontera
Cabra
Priego de Córdoba
Almedinilla
Fuente-Tójar
Carcabuey
Lucena
Moriles
Puente-Genil
La Campana
La Luisiana
Écija
Fuentes de Andalucía
A N D A L U C Í A
Marchena
Marinaleda
El Rubio
Herrera
Estepa
La Lantejuela
Osuna
Aguadulce
Gilena
Pedrera
Badolatosa
Casariche
Embalse de Cordobilla
Embalse de Malpasillo
Benamejí
Encinas Reales
Cuevas de San Marcos
Rute
Iznájar
Algarinejo
Montefrío
Zagra
Villanueva Mesía
Huétor-Tájar
Loja
Salar
El Arahal
La Puebla de Cazalla
Morón de la Frontera
Sierra de Esparteros
El Saucejo
Los Corrales
Martín de la Jara
Villanueva de San Juan
Algámitas
Almargen
Campillos
Sierra de Yeguas
La Roda de Andalucía
Humilladero
Laguna de Fuente de Piedra
Fuente de Piedra
Alameda
Palenciana
Cuevas Bajas
Villanueva de Algaidas
Villanueva de Tapia
Archidona
Antequera
Bobadilla
Alcazaba de Antequera
Villanueva del Trabuco
Villanueva del Rosario
Alhama de Granada
Zafarraya
Ventas de Zafarraya
Arenas del Rey
Jatar
Jayena
Embalse de los Bermejales
Montellano
Coripe
Pruna
Teba
Cañete la Real
Olvera
Puerto Serrano
Algodonales
Torre-Alháquime
Alcalá del Valle
Embalse del Conde de Guadalhorce
Ardales
Carratraca
Álora
Valle de Abdalajís
Villanueva de la Concepción
Casabermeja
Colmenar
Periana
Riogordo
Comares
Benamargosa
Almáchar
Vélez-Málaga
Canillas de Aceituno
Alcaucín
Cómpeta
Sierra de Almijara
Sayalonga
Torrox
Frigiliana
Nerja
Almuñécar
Salobreña
Motril
Vélez de Benaudalla
Órgiva
Lanjarón
Albuñuelas
Embalse de Béznar
Guájar-Faraguit
Ítrabo
Molvízar
Cabo Sacratif
Zahara
Setenil
Cuevas del Becerro
Embalse de Zahara-El Gastor
Arriate
Sierra Margarita
Grazalema
Montejaque
Benaoján
Ronda
Benaocaz
Ubrique
Sierra de Ubrique
El Burgo
Casarabonela
Pizarra
Almogía
Montes de Málaga
Yunquera
Alozaina
Tolox
Sierra de Tolox
Guaro
Coín
Alhaurín el Grande
Cártama
Alhaurín de la Torre
Málaga
El Palo
Rincón de la Victoria
Moclinejo
Torre del Mar
Algarrobo
Punta de Torrox
Punta de la Mona
Real Club de Campo de Málaga
Torremolinos
Benalmádena
Mijas
Monda
Ojén
Istán
Fuengirola
Punta de Calaburra
Marbella
San Pedro de Alcántara
Ensenada de Marbella
Benahavís
Estepona
Sierra Bermeja
Igualeja
Jubrique
Cortes de la Frontera
Algatocín
Gaucín
Casares
Jimena de la Frontera
Manilva
Pta de la Chullera
Club de Golf Valderrama
Castellar de la Frontera
San Roque
Pta Mala
La Línea de la Concepción
Los Barrios
Gibraltar (U.K.)
Moorish Castle
Europa Point
Algeciras
Pta del Carnero
Costa del Sol
Tanger
Melilla
Sète
Gibraltar
Pta Almina
Ceuta (Spain)
Souk Tleta Taghramet
Restinga
Cabo Negro
Mdiq
Jebel el Haouz
Martil
Tétouan
El Fendek
Cap Mazari
Dar Ben Karricha el Behri
Oued Laou
E
GBZ
MA
A4
A44
A45
A92
A92M
A7
AP7
AP46
E05
E15
E902
E15/902
N13
N16
A316

1
2
3
4
5
A
B
C
D
E
F
46
51
53
Navalpino
El Robledo
El Trincheto
Fuente el Fresno
Peloche
Herrera del Duque
Cantos Negros
Sierra de la Chimenea
Sierra de los Golondrinos
Arroba de los Montes
Porzuna
Malagón
Parque Nacional Las Tablas de Daimiel
Madrigalejo
Casas de Don Pedro
Valvillar
Puebla de Don Rodrigo
Puerto de los Majales
Embalse de Puerto Navarro
Fernáncaballero
Gargáligas
Embalse de Orellana
Puerto de los Carneros
Garbayuela
Embalse de El Vicario
Laguna la Albuera
Talarrubias
Tamurejo
Valronquillo
Piedrabuena
Picón
Carrión de Calatrava
Villanueva de la Serena
Esparragosa
Puebla de Alcocer
Siruela
Agudo
Valdemanco del Esteras
Saceruela
Luciana
Alcolea de Calatrava
Poblete
Ciudad Real
Torralba de Calatrava
La Haba
Motilla
Baterno
Miguelturra
Magacela
Sancti-Spíritus
Garlitos
Puerto del Rayo
Abenójar
Pozuelos de Calatrava
Corral de Calatrava
Los Pozuelos de Calatrava
Almagro
Campanario
Embalse de la Serena
Duranes
Cabezarados
El Collado
Caracuel de Calatrava
Valenzuela de Calatrava
Peñalsordo
Zarza Capilla
Capilla
Chillón
Villamayor de Calatrava
Ballesteros de Calatrava
Granátula de Calatrava
La Guarda
LA SERENA
Sierra de la Moraleja
Almadén
Fontanosas
Tirteafuera
CAMPO DE CALATRAVA
Serena
Castuera
Guadalmez
Cabeza del Buey
Almadenejos
Almodóvar del Campo
Argamasilla de Calatrava
Aldea del Rey
Embalse Vega del Jabalón
Malpartida de la Serena
Benquerencia de la Serena
Tiro
Almorchón
Alamillo
Alcudia
Valdeazogues
Puertollano
Calzada de Calatrava
Esparragosa de la Serena
Helechal
VALLE DE ALCUDIA
Puerto Pulido
Brazatortas
Mojina
Higuera de la Serena
Zalamea de la Serena
Horcón
Cabezarrubias del Puerto
Puerto de Mestanza
Villanueva de San Carlos
Monterrubio de la Serena
Belalcázar
Santa Eufemia
Sierra de Alcudia
Plaza del Judío
Hinojasas de Calatrava
Mestanza
San Benito
Tablillas
Puerto de Niefla
Embalse de Montoro
Encinas
Campillo de Llerena
Sierra de los Argallanes
Los Pedroches
Peraleda del Zaucejo
Hinojosa del Duque
El Viso
Dos Torres
Torrecampo
Puerto de Valderrepiso
Sierra Madrona
Solana del Pino
San Lorenzo de Calatrava
Sierra de San Andrés
Matachel
Blázquez
Valsequillo
Villaralto
Añora
Pedroche
Conquista
Rebollera
La Granjuela
Villanueva del Duque
Alcaracejos
Pozoblanco
Fuencaliente
Maguilla
Granja de Torrehermosa
Peñarroya-Pueblonuevo
Villanueva de Córdoba
Azuel
Valmayor
El Centenillo
Berlanga
Fuente Obejuna
Sierra Chimorra
MORENA
Cardeña
Embalse del Jándula
La Carolina
Azuaga
La Coronada
Calaveruela
Bélmez
Puerto Calatraveño
Chimorra
Venta del Charco
Embalse del Rumblar
Argallón
Villanueva del Rey
Espiel
Cuzna
Gato
Arenoso
Yeguas
Baños de la Encina
Sierra de los Santos
Erillas
Villaharta
Obejo
Embalse de Puente Nuevo
Embalse de Guadalmellato
Embalse del Encinarejo
Guarromán
Malcocinado
Bembézar
Benajarafe
Linares
Alanís
Villaviciosa de Córdoba
Embalse del Yeguas
Bailén
San Nicolás del Puerto
Névalo
Adamuz
Embalse de Arenoso
Marmolejo
Andújar
Montoro
Villanueva de la Reina
Cazalilla
Jabalquinto
Tiesa
Las Navas de la Concepción
Embalse del Bembézar
Villafranca de Córdoba
Pedro Abad
Villa del Río
Arjonilla
Torreblascopedro
Sierra de Córdoba
Embalse de S. Rafael Navallana
Alcolea
El Carpio
Embalse de Villafranca
Lopera
Higuera de Arjona
Mengíbar
Embalse de Mengíbar
Embalse de Retortillo
Embalse de la Breña
Mezquita-Catedral de Córdoba
Bujalance
Arjona
Villargordo
Gibarrayo
Córdoba
Porcuna
Fuerte del Rey
Hornachuelos
Cañete de las Torres
Escañuela
Villardompardo
La Puebla de los Infantes
Posadas
Almodóvar del Río
Guadalquivir
Embalse de José Torán
Guadalcázar
Valenzuela
Torredonjimeno
Torre del Campo
Jaén
Palma del Río
Fuente Palmera
Torreparedones
Santiago de Calatrava
Jamilena
Peñaflor
Espejo
Castro del Río
Martos
La Guardia de Jaén
Villanueva del Río y Minas
Lora del Río
CAMPIÑA
La Carlota
La Victoria
Fernán Núñez
Montemayor
Albendín
Los Villares
Embalse de Quiebrajano
Canal del Bajo Guadalquivir
San Sebastián de los Ballesteros
Alcolea del Río
La Rambla
Montalbán de Córdoba
Baena
Alcaudete
Fuensanta de Martos
Valdepeñas de Jaén
Guadajoz
La Campana
Santaella
Montilla
Nueva-Carteya
Doña Mencía
Luque
Víboras
Campillo de Arenas
La Luisiana
Écija
Aguilar de la Frontera
Zuheros
Castillo de Locubín
Noalejo
Carmona
Fuentes de Andalucía
Cabra
Lobatejo
Fuente-Tójar
Frailes
Montillana
ANDALUCÍA
Priego de Córdoba
Alcalá la Real
Campotéjar
El Viso del Alcor
Moriles
Lucena
Carcabuey
Almedinilla
Benalúa de las Villas
Marinaleda
El Rubio
Herrera
Puente-Genil
Tiñosa
Embalse de Colomera
La Lantejuela
Embalse de Cordobilla
Rute
Javerero
Montefrío
Sierra de Parapanda
Moclín
Paradas
Estepa
Badolatosa
Casariche
Embalse de Malpasillo
Encinas Reales
Cuevas de San Marcos
Algarinejo
Iznájar
Parapanda
Íllora
Pinos-Puente
El Arahal
Maestre
Osuna
Aguadulce
Becerrero
Gilena
Benamejí
Cuevas Altas
Cuevas Bajas
Zagra
Villanueva Mesía
Tocón
Fuente Vaqueros
Atarfe
Utrera
La Puebla de Cazalla
Pedrera
Palenciana
Alameda
Embalse de Iznájar
Huétor-Tájar
Lachar
Chauchina
Morón de la Frontera
La Roda de Andalucía
Fuente de Piedra
Villanueva de Algaidas
Villanueva de Tapia
Loja
Santa Fé
Armilla
Sierra de Yeguas
Humilladero
Moraleda de Zafayona
Chimeneas
Gabia la Grande
El Coronil
Los Corrales
Martín de la Jara
Laguna de Fuente de Piedra
Salar
Sierra de Esparteros
El Saucejo
Villanueva de San Juan
Archidona
Sierra Gorda
Cabras
Cerro de la Gallina
Cacín
Ventas de Huelma
Malá
Montellano
Sierra de San Juan
Algámitas
Almargen
Campillos
Bobadilla
Antequera
Alcazaba de Antequera
Gibalto
Cerro de Santa Lucía
Escúzar
Puerto del Suspiro del Moro
de San Juan
Coripe
Pruna
Teba
Cañete la Real
Embalse de Guadalhorce
Camorro Alto
Villanueva del Trabuco
Villanueva del Rosario
Alhama de Granada
Zafarraya
Puerto Serrano
Olvera
Sierra de Líjar
Embalse de Guadalteba
Valle de Abdalajís
Villanueva de la Concepción
Ventas de Zafarraya
Arenas del Rey
Embalse de los Bermejales
Jayena
Villamartín
Algodonales
Torre-Alháquime
Alcalá del Valle
Embalse del Conde de Guadalhorce
Periana
Riogordo
Alcaucín
Jatar
Albuñuelas
Ardales
Carratraca
Casabermeja
Colmenar
Embalse de la Viñuela
Sierra de Almijara
Setenil
Cuevas del Becerro
Canillas de Aceituno
Güájar-Faraguit
Embalse de Bornos
Zahara
Embalse de Zahara El Gastor
Álora
Almogía
Comares
Benamargosa
Cómpeta
Navachica
Sierra Margarita
Pinar
Arriate
Puerto del Viento
El Burgo
Puerto del León
Santopitar
Vélez-Málaga
Sayalonga
Prado del Rey
El Bosque
Grazalema
Montejaque
Puerto de las Abejas
Casarabonela
Montes de Málaga
Benamocarra
Frigiliana
Molvízar
Salobreña
Embalse de los Hurones
Benaojan
Ronda
Sierra Prieta
Yunquera
Pizarra
Moclinejo
E15/902
Algarrobo
Torrox
Benaocaz
Alozaina
El Palo
Torre del Mar
Nerja
Almuñécar
Ubrique
Sierra de Ubrique
Torrecilla
Tolox
Sierra de Tolox
Cártama
Málaga
Rincón de la Victoria
Punta de Torrox
Punta de la Mona
Coín
Alhaurín el Grande
Alhaurín de la Torre
Real Club de Campo de Málaga
Melilla
Guaro
Monda
Cortes de la Frontera
Igualeja
Istán
Mijas
Torremolinos
Sierra de Aznar
E05
E90
E902
A4
A41
A43
A44
A45
A92
A92M
A7
AP46
5°30′
5°00′
4°30′
4°00′
39°00′
38°30′
38°00′
37°30′
37°00′

LA MANCHA
Argamasilla de Alba
Tomelloso
Manzanares
Membrilla
La Solana
Ruidera
Ossa de Montiel
Sotuélamos
Munera
La Roda
Santa Marta
La Gineta
Motilleja
Mahora
Valdeganga
Jorquera
Juan Núñez
Barrax
Albacete
La Felipa
Alatoz
Pozo-Lorente
Hoya Gonzalo
Higueruela
Chinchilla de Monte Aragón
Villar de Chinchilla
Bonete
Altos de Chinchilla
Laguna Salada de Pétrola
Pétrola
Corral-Rubio
La Higuera
El Bonillo
Laguna de Navalcudia
Lezuza
Tiriez
Balazote
Laguna del Salobral
El Salobral
San Pedro
Argamasón
Pozuelo
Santa Ana
Pozo Cañada
Alhambra
Carrizosa
Sierra de Alhambra
San Carlos del Valle
Valdepeñas
Alcubillas
CAMPO DE MONTIEL
Villahermosa
Villanueva de los Infantes
Embalse de la Cabezuela
Montiel
Villanueva de la Fuente
Santa Cruz de los Cáñamos
Albaladejo
Terrinches
Almedina
Cózar
Torrenueva
Santa Cruz de Mudela
Torre de Juan Abad
Puebla del Príncipe
Villamanrique
Castellar de Santiago
Almuradiel
Viveros
Robledo
El Ballestero
Povedilla
Peñascosa
Alcaraz
Vianos
Salobre
Villapalacios
Bienservida
Villarrodrigo
Sierra de Alcaraz
Paterna del Madera
Bogarra
Masegoso
Casas de Lázaro
Ayna
Peñas de San Pedro
Pozohondo
Laguna de Ontalafia
Alcadozo
Liétor
Embalse de Talave
Tobarra
Hellín
Isso
Minateda
Ontur
Albatana
Fuente-Álamo
Sierra de las Cabras
Jumilla
Fábricas de San Juan de Alcaraz
Calar del Mundo
Molinicos
Peñarrubia
Elche de la Sierra
Agramón
Embalse del Cenajo
Cancarix
Villaverde de Guadalimar
Torres de Albánchez
Génave
Siles
Benatae
Orcera
Segura de la Sierra
Puente de Génave
La Puerta de Segura
Yeste
Letur
Embalse de la Fuensanta
Férez
Socovos
Moharque
Embalse de Camarillas
Embalse del Judío
Arguellite
Sierra de Lagos
Tragoncillo
Embalse de Taibilla
Benizar y la Tercia
Calasparra
Cieza
Abarán
Blanca
Moratalla
El Sabinar
Embalse de Argos
Archena
Aldeaquemada
Desfiladero de Despeñaperros
Santa Elena
Venta de los Santos
Montizón
LOMA DE CHICLANA
Arroyo del Ojanco
Chiclana de Segura
Beas de Segura
Castellar de Santisteban
Sorihuela del Guadalimar
Santisteban del Puerto
Cortijos Nuevos
Hornos
Embalse del Tranco de Beas
Sierra de Segura
Navas de San Juan
Vilches
Arquillos
Villanueva del Arzobispo
Villacarrillo
LOMA DE ÚBEDA
Embalse de Giribaile
Sabiote
Torreperogil
Úbeda
Baeza
Rus
Mogón
Santo Tomé
Pontones
Santiago de la Espada
Sierra de Cazorla
Embalse de la Novia
Nerpio
Sierra de Taibilla
Revolcadores
Caravaca de la Cruz
Cehegín
Archivel
Barranda
Bullas
Mula
Las Torres de Cotillas
Almudema
El Moral
Puerto de Almaciles
Puebla de Don Fadrique
Chilluévar
La Iruela
Cazorla
Sierra del Pozo
Peal de Becerro
Embalse de Pedro Marín
Embalse de Doña Aldonza
Sagra
Empanadas
Tornajuelos
Embalse de San Clemente
Los Royos
Topares
Zarcilla de Ramos
La Paca
Zarzadilla de Totana
Sierra de Espuña
Alhama de Murcia
Las Terreras
Totana
Embalse de Valdeinfierno
Jódar
Jimena
Bedmar
Quesada
Puerto de Tíscar
Huesa
Larva
Embalse de la Bolera
Castril
Huéscar
Galera
Orce
Castillejar
María
Vélez-Blanco
Vélez-Rubio
El Gabar
Gigante
Fuensanta
Embalse de Puentes
Lorca
Aledo
La Manilla
Sierra Mágina
Bélmez de la Moraleda
Cabra del Santo Cristo
Peña Cambrón
Hinojares
Pozo Alcón
Cortes de Baza
Embalse de Negratín
Sierra de Orce
Sierra de María
Chirivel
Puerto de Santa María de Nieva
Puerto Lumbreras
Almenara
Sierra de la Almenara
Mazarrón
Huelma
Alicún de Ortega
Cuevas del Campo
Benamaurel
Cúllar
Cúllar-Baza
Puerto de El Contador
Sierra de las Estancias
Alamedilla
Dehesas de Guadix
Villanueva de las Torres
Guadahortuna
Montejícar
Torre-Cardela
Zújar
Freila
Baza
Oria
Taberno
Santa María de Nieva
El Cabildo y la Campana
Pedro Martínez
Moreda
Huélago
Gorafe
Fonelas
Caniles
Sierra de Lúcar
Lúcar
Partaloa
Albox
Huércal-Overa
Almendricos
Pulpí
Águilas
Cabo Cope
Calabardina
Píñar
Iznalloz
Darro
Benalúa de Guadix
Diezma
Purullena
Sierra Arana
Guadix
Gor
Sierra de Baza
Santa Bárbara
Somontín
Olula del Río
Tíjola
Purchena
Cantoria
Arboleas
Zúrgena
Sierra de Almagro
Serón
Bayarque
Alcóntar
Sierro
Macael
Lijar
Cuevas de Almanzora
Vera
La Peza
Graena
Alcudia de Guadix
Lugros
Beas de Granada
Embalse de Quentar
Granada
Güéjar-Sierra
Jerez del Marquesado
Alquife
Lacalahorra
Fiñana
Abla
Abrucena
Las Menas
Bacares
Tetica de Bacares
Alcudia de Monteagud
Albánchez
Puerto de la Virgen
Benizalón
Tahal
Lubrín
Antas
Bédar
Los Gallardos
Garrucha
Sierra de los Filabres
Senés
Velefique
Uleila del Campo
Turre
Mojácar
Sierra Nevada
Embalse de Canales
Mulhacén
Pico Veleta
Alto de San Juan
Puerto de la Ragua
Chullo
Bayárcal
Gérgal
Alboloduy
Ohanes
Tabernas
Lucainena de las Torres
Sorbas
Sierra Cabrera
Trevélez
Mecina-Bombarón
Paterna del Río
Válor
Laujar de Andarax
Canjáyar
Instinción
Alhabia
Laroles
Alcolea
Fondón
Nigüelas
Capileira
Bérchules
Ugíjar
Huécija
Illar
Gádor
Rioja
Sierra Alhamilla
Níjar
Carboneras
Punta de la Media Naranja
Lecrín
Lanjarón
Pitres
Cádiar
Órgiva
Murtas
Embalse de Benínar
Punta del Sabinar
Alhama de Almería
Benahadux
Pechina
Torvizcón
Albondón
Sierra de Gádor
Huércal de Almería
Viator
El Alquián
Las Negras
Embalse de Rules
Vélez de Benaudalla
Sierra de Contraviesa
Cerrón
Berja
Dalías
Félix
Vícar
Enix
Almería
La Cañada de San Urbano
Punta de la Polacra
Sierra del Cabo de Gata
Punta de Loma Pelada
Albuñol
Sorvilán
El Ejido
Aguadulce
Roquetas de Mar
Punta del Río
El Cabo de Gata
San José
Motril
Conjuros
La Rábita
Adra
Castell de Ferro
Punta Negra
Balerma
Guardias Viejas
La Mojonera
CAMPO DE DALÍAS
Golfo de Almería
Cabo de Gata
Melilla, Nador
Salobreña
Calahonda
Punta Culo de Perro
Almerimar
Punta de las Entinas
Punta Sabinar
Sacratif
47
56

48
55
E
Albacete
Almansa
Yecla
Villena
Hellín
Jumilla
Cieza
Calasparra
Cehegín
Bullas
Mula
Archena
Molina de Segura
Murcia
Alcantarilla
Alhama de Murcia
Totana
Lorca
Águilas
Mazarrón
Cartagena
La Unión
Torre-Pacheco
San Javier
San Pedro del Pinatar
Torrevieja
Orihuela
Callosa de Segura
Almoradí
Guardamar del Segura
Santa Pola
Elche/Elx
Crevillente
Novelda
Aspe
Elda
Petrer
Monóvar
Pinoso
Alicante/Alacant
San Vicente del Raspeig
San Juan de Alicante
El Campello
La Vila Joiosa
Benidorm
Altea
Calpe
Jávea-Xàbia
Dénia
Oliva
Gandía
Tavernes de la Valldigna
Cullera
Sueca
Alzira
Carcaixent
Xàtiva
Ontinyent
Alcoy/Alcoi
Cocentaina
Ibi
Castalla
Jijona-Xixona
Caudete
Ayora
Mar Menor
Golfo de Mazarrón
Costa Blanca
Cabo de Palos
Cabo de la Nao
Bahía de Alicante
EIVISSA
Formentera
Eivissa
Sant Antoni de Portmany
Santa Eulalia del Río
Sant Josep de sa Talaia
Sant Joan de Labritja
Ibiza (Eivissa) Biodiversity and Culture
La Savina
San Francisco Javier
Es Caló
Pilar de la Mola
Cap de Barbaria
Valencia, Denia
Barcelona
Alger
Oran

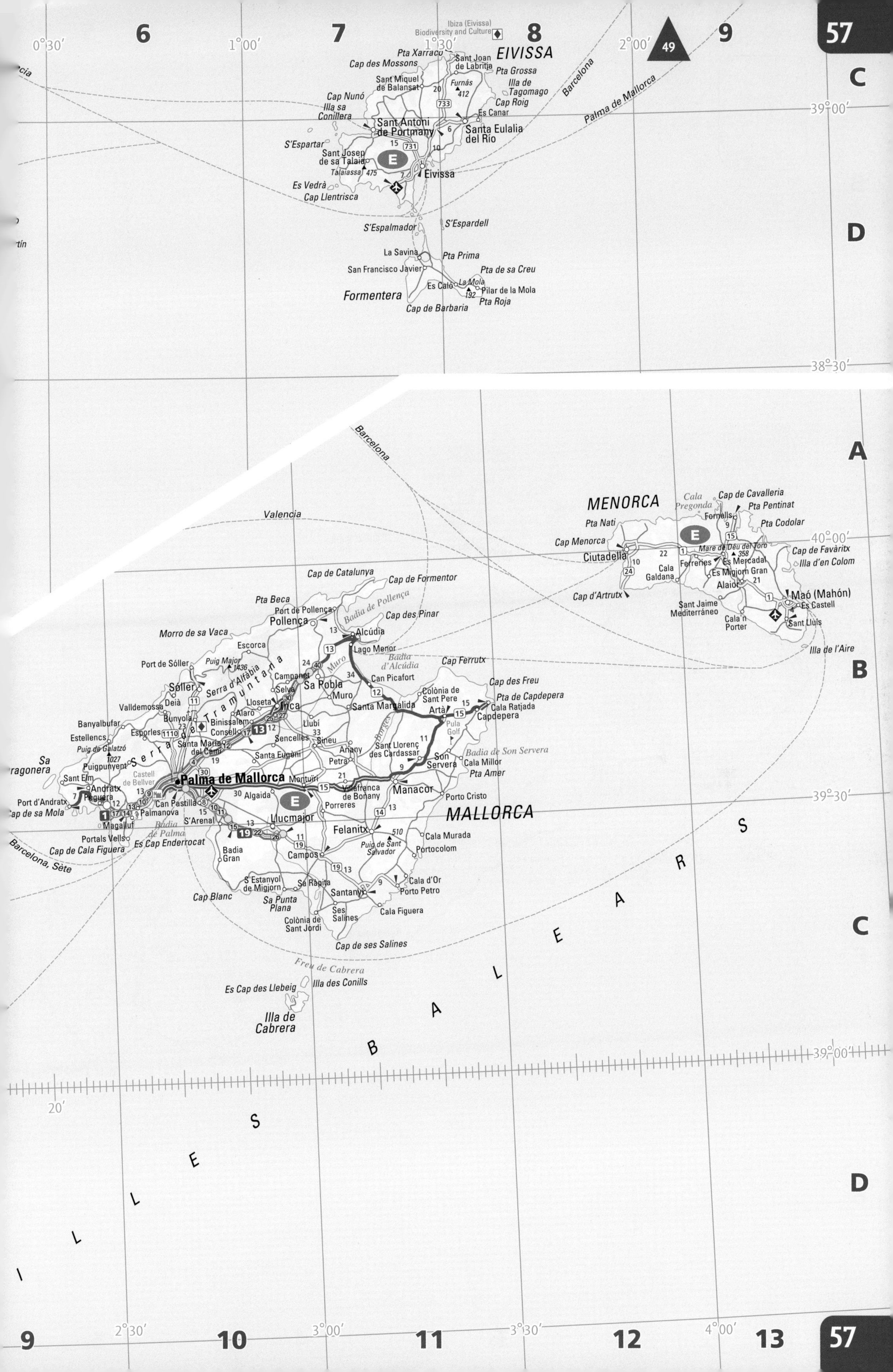
EIVISSA
Ibiza (Eivissa) Biodiversity and Culture
Pta Xarraco
Cap des Mossons
Sant Joan de Labritja
Pta Grossa
Sant Miquel de Balansat
Furnás 412
Illa de Tagomago
Cap Nunó
Illa sa Conillera
Cap Roig
Es Canar
Sant Antoni de Portmany
Santa Eulalia del Río
S'Espartar
Sant Josep de sa Talaia
Talaiassa 475
Eivissa
Es Vedrà
Cap Llentrisca
S'Espalmador
S'Espardell
La Savina
Pta Prima
San Francisco Javier
Pta de sa Creu
Es Caló
La Mola 192
Pilar de la Mola
Formentera
Pta Roja
Cap de Barbaria
Barcelona
Palma de Mallorca
Valencia
MENORCA
Cala Pregonda
Cap de Cavalleria
Pta Pentinat
Fornells
Pta Nati
Pta Codolar
Cap Menorca
Ciutadella
Mare de Déu del Toro 358
Cap de Favàritx
Illa d'en Colom
Cala Galdana
Ferreries
Es Mercadal
Es Migjorn Gran
Alaior
Cap d'Artrutx
Maó (Mahón)
Es Castell
Sant Jaime Mediterráneo
Cala'n Porter
Sant Lluís
Illa de l'Aire
Cap de Catalunya
Cap de Formentor
Pta Beca
Port de Pollença
Badia de Pollença
Cap des Pinar
Pollença
Morro de sa Vaca
Alcúdia
Lago Menor
Escorca
Badia d'Alcúdia
Cap Ferrutx
Port de Sóller
Puig Major 1436
Serra d'Alfàbia
Campanet
Muro
Sa Pobla
Can Picafort
Cap des Freu
Sóller
Selva
Colònia de Sant Pere
Pta de Capdepera
Deià
Valldemossa
Lloseta
Inca
Santa Margalida
Artà
Cala Ratjada
Capdepera
Bunyola
Alaró
Binissalem
Serra de Tramuntana
Banyalbufar
Esporles
Consell
Pula Golf
Estellencs
Llubí
Sencelles
Sineu
Santa Maria del Camí
Puig de Galatzó 1027
Sant Llorenç des Cardassar
Badia de Son Servera
Ariany
Santa Eugènia
Petra
Son Servera
Cala Millor
Puigpunyent
Castell de Bellver
Pta Amer
Sa Dragonera
Sant Elm
Andratx
Palma de Mallorca
Montuïri
Manacor
Port d'Andratx
Peguera
Algaida
Vilafranca de Bonany
Porto Cristo
Cap de sa Mola
Can Pastilla
Magalluf
Palmanova
Porreres
MALLORCA
S'Arenal
Llucmajor
Portals Vells
Badia de Palma
Felanitx
Cala Murada
Cap de Cala Figuera
Es Cap Enderrocat
Puig de Sant Salvador 510
Barcelona, Sète
Badia Gran
Campos
Portocolom
S'Estanyol de Migjorn
Sa Ràpita
Cala d'Or
Cap Blanc
Santanyí
Porto Petro
Sa Punta Plana
Ses Salines
Cala Figuera
Colònia de Sant Jordi
Cap de ses Salines
Freu de Cabrera
Es Cap des Llebeig
Illa des Conills
Illa de Cabrera
ILLES BALEARS
0°30′
1°00′
1°30′
2°00′
39°00′
38°30′
40°00′
39°30′
20′
2°30′
3°00′
3°30′
4°00′
6
7
8
9
10
11
12
13
A
B
C
D
49

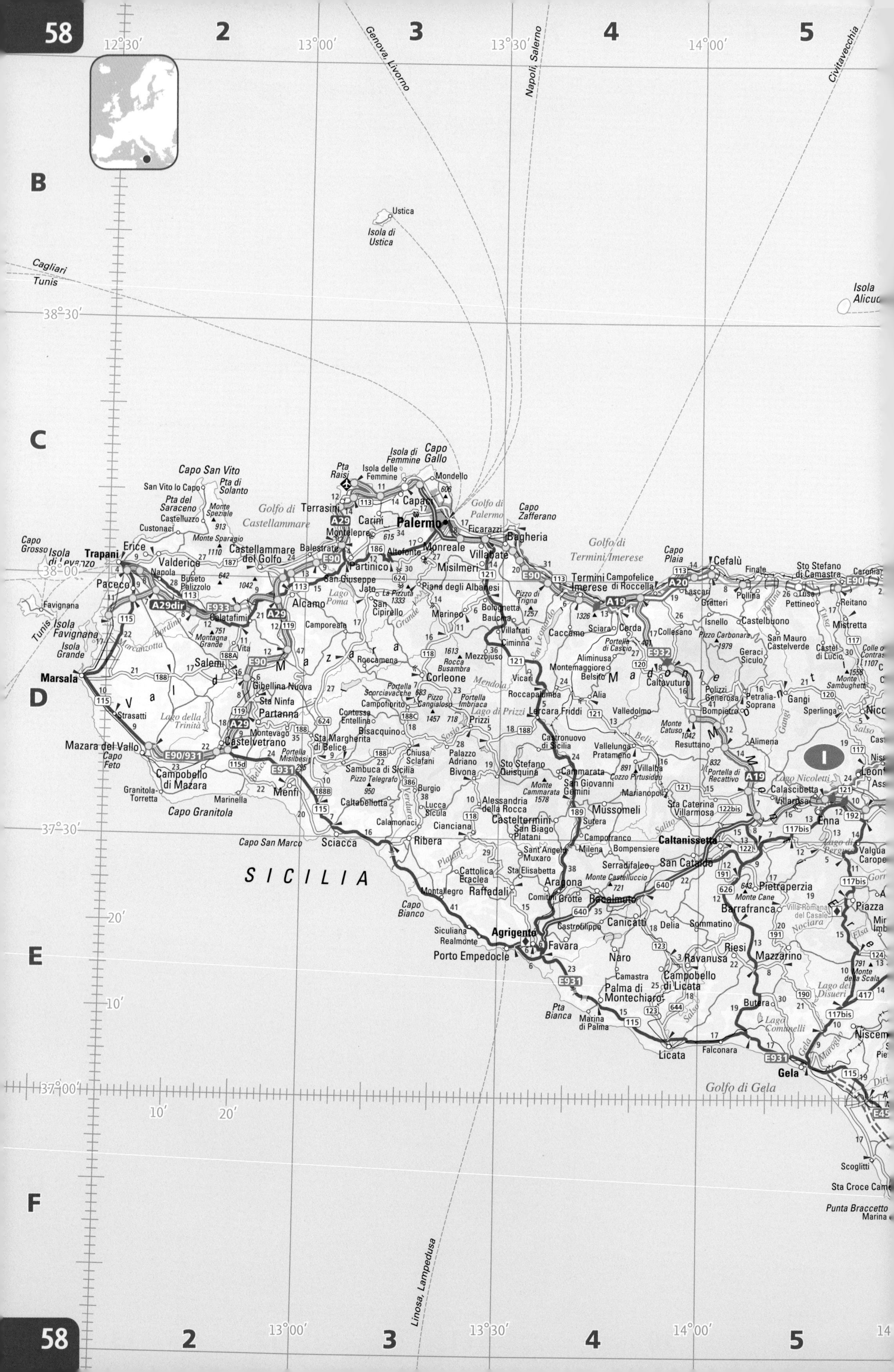
2
3
4
5
B
C
D
E
F
12°30′
13°00′
13°30′
14°00′
38°30′
38°00′
37°30′
37°00′
20′
10′
Genova, Livorno
Napoli, Salerno
Civitavecchia
Cagliari
Tunis
Ustica
Isola di Ustica
Isola Alicudi
Linosa, Lampedusa
SICILIA
Capo San Vito
San Vito lo Capo
Pta di Solanto
Pta del Saraceno
Monte Speziale
Castelluzzo
Custonaci
Monte Sparagio
Capo Grosso
Isola di Levanzo
Trapani
Erice
Valderice
Paceco
Napola
Buseto Palizzolo
Favignana
Isola Favignana
Isola Grande
Marsala
Strasatti
Mazara del Vallo
Capo Feto
Campobello di Mazara
Granitola-Torretta
Capo Granitola
Marinella
Menfi
Castelvetrano
Partanna
Sta Ninfa
Gibellina Nuova
Salemi
Calatafimi
Montagna Grande
Vita
Lago della Trinità
Val di Mazara
Golfo di Castellammare
Castellammare del Golfo
Balestrate
Alcamo
Terrasini
Carini
Capaci
Isola delle Femmine
Isola di Femmine
Capo Gallo
Pta Raisi
Mondello
Palermo
Golfo di Palermo
Montelepre
Partinico
San Giuseppe Jato
San Cipirello
Altofonte
Monreale
Ficarazzi
Bagheria
Capo Zafferano
Villabate
Misilmeri
Piana degli Albanesi
Marineo
Bolognetta
Baucina
Villafrati
Ciminna
Pizzo di Trigna
Camporeale
Roccamena
Corleone
Rocca Busambra
Mezzojuso
Contessa Entellina
Campofiorito
Bisacquino
Sta Margherita di Belice
Sambuca di Sicilia
Chiusa Sclafani
Pizzo Telegrafo
Caltabellotta
Burgio
Lucca Sicula
Calamonaci
Ribera
Sciacca
Capo San Marco
Palazzo Adriano
Bivona
Prizzi
Lago di Prizzi
Alessandria della Rocca
Cianciana
Cattolica Eraclea
Montallegro
Capo Bianco
Siculiana
Realmonte
Porto Empedocle
Agrigento
Raffadali
Favara
Aragona
Casteltermini
San Biagio Platani
Sant'Angelo Muxaro
Sta Elisabetta
Sto Stefano Quisquina
Cammarata
San Giovanni Gemini
Monte Cammarata
Lercara Friddi
Roccapalumba
Vicari
Castronuovo di Sicilia
Vallelunga Pratameno
Villalba
Mussomeli
Sutera
Campofranco
Milena
Bompensiere
Serradifalco
Montedoro
Grotte
Comitini
Racalmuto
Castrofilippo
Canicattì
Naro
Camastra
Palma di Montechiaro
Pta Bianca
Marina di Palma
Licata
Campobello di Licata
Ravanusa
Delia
Sommatino
Riesi
Butera
Falconara
Gela
Golfo di Gela
Niscemi
Mazzarino
Barrafranca
Pietraperzia
Piazza Armerina
Villa Romana del Casale
Lago di Disueri
Lago Comunelli
Caltanissetta
San Cataldo
Marianopoli
Sta Caterina Villarmosa
Resuttano
Alimena
Enna
Calascibetta
Villarosa
Lago Nicoletti
Leonforte
Valguarnera Caropepe
Golfo di Termini Imerese
Termini Imerese
Caccamo
Sciara
Cerda
Campofelice di Roccella
Capo Plaia
Cefalù
Lascari
Gratteri
Collesano
Isnello
Pizzo Carbonara
Castelbuono
Pollina
Finale
Geraci Siculo
Polizzi Generosa
Petralia-Soprana
Bompietro
Gangi
Sperlinga
San Mauro Castelverde
Castel di Lucio
Mistretta
Reitano
Tusa
Pettineo
Sto Stefano di Camastra
Caronia
Monte Sambughetti
Aliminusa
Montemaggiore Belsito
Alia
Valledolmo
Caltavuturo
Sclafani
Madonie
Monte Catuso
Monte Castelluccio
Scoglitti
Sta Croce Camerina
Punta Braccetto
Marina
A29
A29dir
A19
A20
E90
E931
E932
E933
E90/931

6
7
8
9
B
C
D
E
F
15°00′
15°30′
16°00′
16°30′
38°30′
38°00′
37°30′
37°00′
Napoli, Salerno
Civitavecchia, Genova
Isola Strombolicchio
Ginostra
San Vincenzo
Isola Stromboli
Isola Basiluzzo
San Pietro
Isola Lisca Bianca
Isola Panarea
Isole Eolie
Isola Salina
Malfa
Sta Marina Salina
Filicudi Porto
Rinella
Acquacalda
Isola Lipari
Canneto
Lipari
Porto Levante
Isola Vulcano
Scolaticci
Golfo di Milazzo
Capo di Milazzo
Capo Calavà
Capo d'Orlando
Gioiosa Marea
Milazzo
Villafranca Tirrena
Spadafora
Rometta
San Filippo del Mela
Sta Lucia del Mela
Barcellona Pozzo di Gotto
Castroreale
Patti
Oliveri
Falcone
Sant'Angelo di Brolo
Brolo
Naso
Piraino
Capri Leone
Castell'Umberto
Tortorici
Galati Mamertino
Alcara li Fusi
San Fratello
Floresta
Montalbano Elicona
Novara di Sicilia
Monti Peloritani
Monti Nebrodi
Messina
Stretta di Messina
Reggio di Calabria
Villa San Giovanni
Capo Peloro
Divieto
Spartà
Mortelle
Scilla
Bagnara Calabra
Palmi
Gioia Tauro
Rosarno
San Ferdinando
Golfo di Gioia
Nicotera
Joppolo
Capo Vaticano
Ricadi
Tropea
Parghelia
Zungri
Spilinga
Rombiolo
Limbadi
Vibo Valentia
Mileto
Pizzo
Golfo di Sta Eufemia
Lamezia
Capo Suvero
Nicastro
Gizzeria
Sambiase
Feroleto Antico
Catanzaro
Catanzaro Marina
Maida
Cortale
Curinga
Girifalco
Borgia
Filadelfia
Polia
Amaroni
Squillace
Copanello
Gasperina
Soverato
Davoli
Monterosso Calabro
San Vito sullo Ionio
Chiaravalle Centrale
Maierato
Stefanaconi
Simbario
Soriano Calabro
Serra San Bruno
Acquaro
Dinami
Badolato
Sant'Andrea Apostolo dello Ionio
Cardinale
Ferdinandea
Guardavalle
Sta Caterina dello Ionio
Stilo
Monasterace
Monte Crocco
Fabrizia
Laureana di Borrello
Melicucco
Rizziconi
Cinquefrondi
Polistena
Cittanova
Taurianova
Varapodio
Oppido Mamertina
Cosoleto
Seminara
Sinopoli
Delianuova
Stignano
Caulonia
Riace
Grotteria
Mammola
Gioiosa Ionica
Roccella Ionica
Marina di Gioiosa Ionica
Siderno
Locri
Ardore
Gerace
Passo di Cancello
Platì
Benestare
San Luca
Bovalino
Monte Scorda
Montalto
Parco Nazionale dell'Aspromonte
Gambarie
Calanna
Cerasi
Cardeto
Roghudi
St'Agata del Bianco
Bianco
Capo Bruzzano
Motta San Giovanni
Bagaladi
Condofuri
Bova
Staiti
Palizzi
Pellaro
Montebello Ionico
Capo dell'Armi
San Lorenzo
Melito di Porto Salvo
Bova Marina
Brancaleone
Capo Spartivento
San Gregorio
MARE IONIO
Scaletta Zanclea
Alì Terme
Nizza di Sicilia
Roccalumera
Furci Siculo
Sta Teresa di Riva
Francavilla di Sicilia
Letojanni
Taormina
Giardini-Naxos
Gaggi
Castiglione di Sicilia
Randazzo
Linguaglossa
Piedimonte Etneo
Fiumefreddo di Sicilia
Mascali
Riposto
Giarre
Monte Etna
Milo
Zafferana Etnea
Sta Venerina
Aci St Antonio
Acireale
Aci Catena
Aci Trezza
Aci Castello
Nicolosi
Trecastagni
Mascalucia
Gravina di Catania
Catania
Misterbianco
Paternò
Belpasso
Biancavilla
Adrano
Bronte
Maletto
Maniace
Cesarò
Monte Salici
Lago di Pozzillo
Regalbuto
Centuripe
Catenanuova
Castèl di Iudica
Lago di Ogliastro
Piana di Catania
Ramacca
La Montagna
Golfo di Catania
Capo Campolato
Palagonia
Lentini
Lago di Lentini
Scordia
Carlentini
Militello in Val di Catania
Mineo
Francofonte
Villasmundo
Augusta
Capo Sta Croce
Golfo di Augusta
Grammichele
Melilli
Sortino
Priolo Gargallo
Penisola Magnisi
Capo Sta Panagia
Siracusa
Floridia
Solarino
Canicattini Bagni
Cassaro
Buscemi
Palazzolo Acreide
Necropoli Rupestre
Buccheri
Vizzini
Licodia Eubea
Monterosso Almo
Giarratana
Chiaramonte Gulfi
Mazzarrone
Comiso
Ragusa
Modica
Scicli
Ispica
Rosolini
Noto
Avola
Testa dell'Acqua
Cassibile
Penisola della Maddalena
Golfo di Noto
Isola Vendicari
Marzamemi
Pachino
Isola Capo Passero
Portopalo di Capo Passero
Pozzallo
Sampieri
Punta Religione
Donnalucata
Punta della Formiche
Valletta
SIRACUSA
A2
A18
A19
A20
E45
E90
E848
E932

2
3
4
5
A
B
C
D
E
F
63
62
59
I
14°30′
15°00′
15°30′
16°00′
41°00′
40°30′
40°00′
39°30′
39°00′
20′
10′
Pratella
Lago del Matese
Sepino
Sta Croce del Sannio
San Bartolomeo in Galdo
Piedimonte Matese
Monte Mutria 1823
Vairano Patenora
Pietravairano
Roccamonfina
Teano
Sparanise
Monte Massico 813
Morcone
Cusano Mutri
Gioia Sannitica
Faicchio
Cerreto Sannita
Pontelandolfo
Colle Sannita
Circello
Baselice
Lago di Campolattaro
Monte Cornacchia 1151
Troia
Castelluccio Valmaggiore
Castelluccio dei Sauri
Ordona
Orta Nova
Carapelle
Stornarella
Stornara
Cerignola
San Ferdinando di Puglia
Margherita di Savoia
Saline
Montefalcone di Val Fortore
San Marco dei Cavoti
Molinara
San Giorgio la Molara
Castelfranco in Miscano
Orsara di Puglia
Greci
Guardia Sanframondi
San Salvatore Telesino
Telese
Solopaca
Vitulano
Foglianise
Torrecuso
Ponte
Pesco Sannita
Paduli
Buonalbergo
Casalbore
Montecalvo Irpino
Savignano Irpino
Panni
Bovino
Deliceto
Monteleone di Puglia
Accadia
Ascoli Satriano
Canosa di Puglia
Caiazzo
Frasso Telesino
Limatola
St Agata de' Goti
Monte Taburno 1394
Cautano
Benevento
Apice
Ariano Irpino
Villanova del Battista
Anzano di Puglia
Sant'Agata di Puglia
Candela
Rocchetta Sant'Antonio
Lago di Capaccioti
Posta Piana
Grazzanise
Casagiove
Caserta
Sta Maria Capua Vetere
Marcianise
Maddaloni
Airola
Montesarchio
Ceppaloni
Pannarano
San Giorgio del Sannio
Montemiletto
Mirabella Eclano
Grottaminarda
Flumeri
Carife
Vallata
Lacedonia
Bisaccia
Monteverde
Aquilonia
Minervino Murge
Lavello
Montemilone
Spinazzola
Castel Volturno
Villa Literno
Casal di Principe
Aversa
Lucciano
San Felice a Cancello
Cervinara
Cicciano
Avella
Baiano
Mercogliano
Avellino
Atripalda
Monti d'Avella 1598
Altavilla Irpina
Taurasi
Gesualdo
Frigento
Paternopoli
Castelfranci
Nusco
Guardia Lombardi
St'Angelo dei Lombardi
Andretta
Calitri
Rionero in Vulture
Monte Vulture 1326
Castello di Melfi
Melfi
Rapolla
Barile
Venosa
Palazzo San Gervasio
Maschito
Ripacandida
Atella
Forenza
Banzi
Genzano di Lucania
Poggiorsini
Lago del Rendina
Giugliano in Campania
Campania
St Antimo
Caivano
Acerra
Afragola
Casoria
Marigliano
Palma Campania
Sant' Anastasia
Ottaviano
San Giuseppe Vesuviano
Sarno
Mercato San Severino
Solofra
Serino
Volturara Irpina
Montella
Bagnoli Irpino
Teora
Conza della Campania
Lioni
Caposele
Calabritto
Laviano
San Fele
Ruvo del Monte
Filiano
Lago Pesole
Bradano
Acerenza
Monte Torretta
Pietragalla
Oppido Lucano
Marano di Napoli
Qualiano
Pozzuoli
Napoli
Portici
Bacoli
Monte di Procida
Procida
Isola di Procida
Capo Nisida
Miseno
Ischia
Barano d'Ischia
Torre del Greco
Torre Annunziata
Parco Nazionale del Vesuvio 1281 Vesuvio
Boscotrecase
Pompei
Angri
Pagani
Nocera Inferiore
Baronissi
Monte Mai 1607
Monti Picentini
Passo le Croci di Acerno 1809
Monte Cervialto
Acerno
Oliveto Citra
Colliano
Muro Lucano
Castelgrande
Monte San Croce 1407
Bella
Avigliano
Ruoti
Baragiano
Cancellara
Tolve
San Chirico Nuovo
Castellammare di Stabia
Gragnano
St'Antonio Abate
Cava de' Tirreni
Vico Equense
Meta
Monti Lattari 1131
Sorrento
Positano
Praiano
Amalfi
Vietri sul Mare
Salerno
Montecorvino Rovella
Pontecagnano Faiano
Bellizzi
Battipaglia
Eboli
Campagna
Palomonte
Contursi Terme
Buccino
San Gregorio Magno
Balvano
Picerno
Potenza
Vaglio Basilicata
Brindisi Montagna
Albano di Lucania
Tricarico
Golfo di Napoli
Massa Lubrense
Punta Campanella
Li Galli
Anacapri
Capri
Isola di Capri
Cagliari
Serre
Postiglione
Monte Alburno 1742
Auletta
Vietri di Potenza
Caggiano
Satriano di Lucania
Tito
Pignola
Passo Croce dello Scrivano 1143
Trivigno
Abriola
Anzi
Oliveto Lucano
Lago di Ponte Fontanelle
Accettura
Golfo di Salerno
Altavilla Silentina
Controne
Castelcivita
Albanella
Polla
St'Arsenio
Brienza
Atena Lucana
Sala Consilina
Marsico Nuovo
Calvello
Laurenzana
Monte Volturino 1836
St'Angelo a Fasanella
Capaccio
Roccadaspide
San Rufo
Roscigno
Monte Motola 1700
Teggiano
Sassano
Padula
Paterno
Marsico Vetere
Corleto Perticara
Guardia Perticara
Gorgoglione
Cirigliano
Viggiano
Armento
Aliano
Missanello
Castel San Lorenzo
Felitto
Laurino
Cilento
Parco Nazionale del Cilento e del Vallo di Diano
Tunis
Palermo
Valencia
Agropoli
Ogliastro Cilento
Cicerale
Torchiara
Rutino
Stio
Gioi
Sta Maria di Castellabate
Castellabate
Isola Licosa
Perdifumo
Oligastro Marina
Montecorice
Acciaroli
Pollica
Monte della Stella
Sessa Cilento
Casal Velino
Vallo della Lucania 1705
Monte Sacro
Montano Antilia
Monte Cervati 1898
Buonabitacolo
Tramutola
Montesano sulla Marcellana
Sarconi
Moliterno
Monte Sella Cessula 1040
Montemurro
Lago di Pietra del Pertusillo
San Chirico Raparo
St Arcangelo
Ceraso
Ascea
Rofrano
Sanza
Casalbuono
Laurito
Torre Orsaia
Caselle in Pittari
Casaletto Spartano
Lagonegro
Monte del Papa 2005
Castelsaraceno
Castronuovo di St'Andrea
Chiaromonte
Roccagloriosa
Vibonati
Sta. Marina
Rivello
Latronico
Fardella
Pisciotta
Centola
Monte Bulgheria 1225
Camerota
Scario
San Giovanni a Piro
Sapri
Monte Coccovello 1505
Trecchina
Lauria
Monte la Spina 1652
Episcopia
Francavilla in Sinni
San Severino Lucano
Palinuro
Capo Palinuro
Marina di Camerota
Punta degli Infreschi
Maratea
Castelluccio Inferiore
Laino Borgo
Viggianello
Rotonda
Parco Nazionale del Pollino
Monte Pollino 2248
Golfo di Policastro
Tortora
Aieta
Monte Ciagola 1462
Praia a Mare
Isola di Dino
Capo Scalea
Scalea
Mormanno
Papasidero
Sta Domenica Talao
Orsomarso
Morano Calabro
Castrovillari
Verbicaro
Cozzo del Pellegrino 1987
Saracena
Lungro
Sta Maria del Cedro
Grisolia
Buonvicino
San Donato di Ninea
Altomonte
Firmo
Diamante
Belvedere Marittimo
Monte Montea 1785
San Sosti
St Agata di Esaro
Roggiano Gravina
Bonifati
Fagnano Castello
San Marco Argentano
Cittadella del Capo
Cetraro
Acquappesa
Terme Luigiane
Cerzeto
Torano Castello
Guardia Piemontese
Rota Greca
Lattarico
Fuscaldo
Montalto Uffugo
Paola
San Fili
Rende
San Lucido
Cerisano
Falconara Albanese
Carolei
Fiumefreddo Bruzio
Monte Cocuzzo 1541
Dipignano
Longobardi
Lago
Belmonte Calabro
Amantea
Monte Pellegrino 644
Grimaldi
Aiello Calabro
Campora San Giovanni
Nocera Terinese
Falerna
Gizzeria
Sambiase
Capo Suvero
Lamezia
Golfo di Sta Eufemia
Catania, Messina, Valletta
Isola Stromboli
Isola Strombolicchio
Ginostra
San Vincenzo
A1
A2
A3
A14
A16
A30
E45
E55
E841
E842
E847
RA5

7
8
9
10
16°30′
17°00′
17°30′
18°00′
41°00′
40°30′
40°00′
39°30′
39°00′
A
B
C
D
E
F
Dubrovnik
Bar, Durrës, Kotor
Kerkyra, Paxoi, Igoumenitsa
Kerkyra, Paxoi, Igoumenitsa
Kefallonia, Patra, Sami, Zakynthos, Çesme
Kerkyra
Trani
Bisceglie
Molfetta
Giovinazzo
San Spirito
Castello Normanno-Svevo
Bari
Corato
Terlizzi
Bitonto
Palo del Colle
Modugno
Valenzano
Triggiano
Mola di Bari
Capurso
Noicattaro
Rutigliano
Polignano a Mare
Monopoli
Grumo Appula
Toritto
Sannicandro di Bari
Adelfia
Conversano
Casamassima
Acquaviva delle Fonti
Turi
Castellana Grotte
Cassano delle Murge
Sammichele di Bari
Putignano
Zoosafari e Fasanolandia
Fasano
Torre Canne
Altamura
Gioia del Colle
Noci
Selva
Trulli di Alberobello
Villanova
Santeramo in Colle
Alberobello
Cisternino
Locorotondo
Ostuni
Carovigno
Punta Penne
Isole Pedagne
Masseria Risana
Martina Franca
San Vito dei Normanni
Brindisi
Capo di Torre Cavallo
Murgia Sant'Elia
Sassi di Matera
Matera
Lago di San Giuliano
Laterza
Castellaneta
Mottola
Palagianello
Ceglie Messapica
San Michele Salentino
Villa Castelli
Ginosa
Crispiano
Massafra
Palagiano
Montemesola
Grottaglie
Monteiasi
Canale Reale
Mesagne
Latiano
Capo San Gennaro
Miglionica
Montescaglioso
Pomarico
Case Perrone
Francavilla Fontana
Oria
Torre Sta Susanna
San Pietro Vernotico
Casa l'Abate
Torchiarolo
Borgo Grappa
Ferrandina
Bradano
Isole Cheradi
Taranto
Mar Piccolo
Mare Grande
Carosino
San Giorgio Ionico
Talsano
Fragagnano
Erchie
San Pancrazio Salentino
San Donaci
Squinzano
Trepuzzi
San Cataldo
Surbo
Bernalda
Monte Finese
Capo San Vito
Leporano
Pulsano
Lizzano
Torricella
Sava
Manduria
Campi Salentina
Lecce
Carmiano
Murge Tarantine
Salice Salentino
Veglie
Avetrano
Craco
Pisticci
Basento
Lido di Metaponto
Marina di Pulsano
Maruggio
Monteroni di Lecce
Lizzanello
Roca Vecchia
Cavone
Montalbano Jonico
Leverano
Lequile
Vernole
Punta dell'Ovo
Campomarino
Copertino
San Donato di Lecce
Melendugno
Porto Cesareo
Tursi
Agri
Scanzano Jonico
Calimera
Policoro
Soleto
Martano
Carpignano Salentino
Nardò
Cursi
Otranto
Golfo di Taranto
Valsinni
Rotondella
Sinni
Lago di Monte Cotugna
Nova Siri
Galatone
Galatina
Cutrofiano
Maglie
Uggiano la Chiesa
San Giorgio Lucano
Nova Siri Scalo
Aradeo
Neviano
Sannicola
Rocca Imperiale
Canna
Isola Sant'Andrea
Gallipoli
Alezio
Collepasso
Scorrano
Poggiardo
Oriolo
Montegiordano
Parabita
Matino
Nociglia
Sta Cesarea Terme
Supersano
Torre del Pizzo
Taviano
Casarano
Castro
Roseto Capo Spulico
Capo Spulico
Andrano
Melissano
Ruffano
Montesano Salentino
Alessandria del Carretto
Amendolara
Racale
Alliste
Taurisano
Specchia
Tricase
Albidona
Ugento
Presicce
Corsano
Marina di Amendolara
Torre San Giovanni
Salve
Alessano
Villapiana
Morciano di Leuca
Marina di Novaglie
Trebisacce
Castrignano del Capo
Gagliano del Capo
Villapiana Lido
Marina di Leuca
Capo Sta Maria di Leuca
Sibari
Coscile
Marina Schiavonea
Capo Trionto
Corigliano Calabro
Mirto Crosia
San Demetrio Corone
Vaccarizzo Albanese
Rossano
Crosia
Trionfo
Sta Crista d'Acri
Paludi
Pta Fiume Nicà
Acri
Cropalati
Mandatoriccio
Cariati
Terravecchia
Longobucco
Bocchigliero
Mucone
Punta Alice
Parco Nazionale della Calabria
Monte Pettinascura
Campana
Crucoli
Cirò
Lago di Cecita
Camigliatello Silano
Cirò Marina
Lago di Ariamacina
Umbriatico
Monte Botte Donato
Savelli
Verzino
Pallagorio
Melissa
LA SILA
San Nicola dell'Alto
Strongoli
Aprigliano
San Giovanni in Fiore
Casabona
Colle d'Ascione
Lago Arvo
Caccuri
Rocca di Neto
Rogliano
Parenti
Lago Ampollino
Neto
Cotronei
Sta Severina
Monte Femminamorta
Petilia Policastro
Scandale
Soveria Mannelli
Carlopoli
Villaggio Mancuso
Mesoraca
San Mauro Marchesato
Crotone
Decollatura
Capo Colonna
Taverna
Magisano
Petronà
Cutro
Serrastretta
Zagarise
Sersale
Nicastro
Gimigliano
Pentone
Cropani
Isola di Capo Rizzuto
Feroleto Antico
Tiriolo
Simeri-Crichi
Steccato
Botricello
Capo Rizzuto
Catanzaro
Sellia Marina
Maida
Cortale
Borgia
Golfo di Squillace
Curinga
Girifalco
Catanzaro Marina

1
2
3
4
5
B
C
D
E
F
2
3
4
5
66
65
12°00′
12°30′
13°00′
13°30′
14°00′
42°30′
42°00′
41°30′
41°00′
20′
10′
Montepulciano
Chiusi
Panicale
Torgiano
Assisi
Bastia
Cannara
Spello
Foligno
Deruta
Bevagna
Gualdo Cattaneo
Marsciano
Collazzone
Montefalco
Trevi
Fratta Todina
Bastardo
Castèl Ritaldi
San Venanzo
Monte Castello di Vibio
Giano dell'Umbria
Campello sul Clitunno
Massa Martana
Todi
Orvieto
Castèl Giorgio
Lago di Corbara
Spoleto
Acquasparta
Avigliano Umbro
Baschi
Castiglione in Teverina
Guardea
Montecastrilli
Lago di Alviano
Alviano
Bagnoregio
Graffignano
Lugnano in Teverina
Amelia
Montefiascone
Attigliano
Penna in Teverina
Narni
Terni
Stroncone
Cascata delle Marmore
Lago di Piediluco
Montefranco
Ferentillo
Arrone
Bolsena
Lago di Bolsena
Gradoli
Valentano
Capodimonte
Marta
Ischia di Castro
Cellere
Canino
Arlena di Castro
Tuscania
Viterbo
Vitorchiano
Orte
Monte Soriano nel Cimino
Vignanello
Vasanello
Gallese
Canepina
Fabrica di Roma
Corchiano
Caprarola
Civita Castellana
Ronciglione
Lago di Vico
Vetralla
Blera
Monte Romano
Necropoli Etrusche
Tarquinia
Capranica
Sutri
Nepi
Bassano Romano
Vejano
Oriolo Romano
Tolfa
Allumiere
Manziana
Trevignano Romano
Lago di Bracciano
Bracciano
Anguillara Sabazia
Campagnano di Roma
Castelnuovo di Porto
Formello
Mazzano Romano
Faleria
Rignano Flaminio
Fiano Romano
Civitavecchia
Santa Marinella
San Severa
Cerveteri
Ladispoli
Fregene
Fiumicino
Ostia
Lido di Ostia
Vatican City
ROMA
Ciampino
Marino
Castèl Gandolfo
Albano Laziale
Genzano di Roma
Ariccia
Grottaferrata
Rocca di Papa
Frascati
Pomezia
Zoomarine
Tor Vaianica
Ardea
Aprilia
Lanuvio
Velletri
Lariano
Rocca Massima
Artena
Colleferro
Valmontone
Palestrina
Gallicano nel Lazio
Tivoli
Guidonia-Montecelio
Castèl Madama
Mentana
Monterotondo
Palombara Sabina
Moricone
Montelibretti
Fara in Sabina
Montopoli di Sabina
Poggio Mirteto
Poggio Catino
Forano
Casperia
Magliano Sabina
Tarano
Calvi dell'Umbria
Otricoli
Cottanello
Contigliano
Greccio
Rieti
Poggio Bustone
Rivodutri
Cantalice
Lago Lungo
Castèl Sant'Angelo
Borgo Velino
Antrodoco
Leonessa
Monte Terminillo
Belmonte in Sabina
Rocca Sinibalda
Torricella in Sabina
Poggio Moiano
Scandriglia
Orvinio
Lago di Turano
Lago del Salto
Petrella Salto
Fiamignano
Licenza
Vicovaro
Roviano
Arsoli
Carsoli
Subiaco
San Vito Romano
Olevano Romano
Genazzano
Paliano
Piglio
Acuto
Fiuggi
Guarcino
Anagni
Alatri
Ferentino
Frosinone
Veroli
Collepardo
Vico nel Lazio
Segni
Sgurgola
Montelanico
Carpineto Romano
Cori
Norma
Sermoneta
Bassiano
Sezze
Priverno
Roccagorga
Maenza
Prossedi
Ceccano
Patrica
Supino
Morolo
Torrice
Ripi
Pofi
Ceprano
Boville Ernica
Monte San Giovanni Campano
Strangolagalli
Arce
Isola del Liri
Arpino
Sora
Castelliri
Balsorano
Cisterna di Latina
Latina
Nettuno
Anzio
Lavinio-Lido di Enea
Torre Astura
Lido di Foce Verde
Lago di Fogliano
Lago di Caprolace
Pontinia
Sabaudia
Lago di Sabaudia
Parco Nazionale del Circeo
Monte Circeo
San Felice Circeo
Terracina
Golfo di Terracina
Sonnino
Monte San Biagio
Monte delle Fate
Monti Ausoni
Roccasecca dei Volsci
Amaseno
Vallecorsa
Lenola
Campodimele
Fondi
Lago di Fondi
Sperlonga
Torre Sant'Agostino
Gaeta
Torre d'Orlando
Formia
Itri
Monti Aurunci
Spigno Saturnia
Monte Petrella
Minturno
Torre Gianola
Esperia
Ausonia
San Giorgio a Liri
Pontecorvo
Pico
Castro dei Volsci
San Giovanni Incarico
Giuliano di Roma
Aquino
Cassino
Roccasecca
Monte Cairo
Abbazia di Montecassino
Sant'Elia Fiumerapido
Cervaro
Vallerotonda
Villa Latina
Atina
Alvito
San Donato Val di Comino
Campoli Appennino
Picinisco
Pescasseroli
Opi
Villetta Barrea
Lago di Barrea
Alfedena
Scanno
Villalago
Parco Nazionale d'Abruzzo
San Vincenzo Valle Roveto
Civita d'Antino
Collelongo
Villavallelonga
Morino
Filettino
Civitella Roveto
Capistrello
Luco dei Marsi
Trasacco
San Benedetto dei Marsi
Gioia dei Marsi
Pescina
Avezzano
Piana del Fucino
Celano
Cerchio
Collarmele
Magliano de'Marsi
Scurcola Marsicana
Tagliacozzo
Cappadocia
Monte Fontecellese
Monti Simbruini
Pescorocchiano
Borgorose
Rocca di Mezzo
Rocca di Cambio
Campo Felice
Ovindoli
Monte Sirente
Monte Velino
L'Aquila
Scoppito
Pizzoli
Forte Spagnolo
Paganica
Assergi
Poggio Picenze
San Demetrio ne'Vestini
Fontecchio
Barisciano
Capestrano
Navelli
Castèl del Monte
Ofena
Calascio
Gran Sasso d'Italia
Isola del Gran Sasso d'Italia
Monte Corno
Monte Camicia
Campotosto
Lago di Campotosto
Montereale
Amatrice
Cittareale
Posta
Accumoli
Lago di Scandarello
Arquata del Tronto
Monte Vettore
Norcia
Cascia
Preci
Visso
Castelsantangelo sul Nera
Monti Sibillini
Parco Nazionale dei Monti Sibillini
Parco Nazionale del Gran Sasso e Monti della Laga
Montemonaco
Montefortino
Amandola
Comunanza
Sarnano
San Ginesio
Sellano
Cerreto di Spoleto
Scheggino
Vallo di Nera
Sant'Anatolia di Narco
Monteleone di Spoleto
Poggiodomo
Monte Coscerno
Monte Fionchi
Rocca Albornoziana
Serravalle di Chienti
Pievе Torina
Muccia
Bolognola
Monte Fema
Appennino Umbro-Marchigiano
Acquasanta Terme
Ascoli Piceno
Castèl di Lama
Folignano
Sant'Egidio alla Vibrata
Civitella del Tronto
Montagna dei Fiori
Sant'Omero
Valle Castellana
Campli
Teramo
Torricella Sicura
Montorio al Vomano
Crognaleto
Tossicia
Basciano
Colledara
Castellalto
Notaresco
Cermignano
Cellino Attanasio
Bisenti
Atri
Penne
Elice
Loreto Aprutino
Civitella Casanova
Catignano
Cepagatti
Civitaquana
Torre de'Passeri
Bussi sul Tirino
Popoli
Corvara
Tocco da Casauria
Scafa
Acciano
Molina Aterno
Corfinio
Raiano
Pratola Peligna
Sulmona
Bugnara
Cansano
Pettorano sul Gizio
Rocca Pia
Monte Morrone
Monte Argatone
Monte Greco
Monte Meta
Abruzzo
Appennino
Servigliano
Petritoli
Monterubbiano
Pedaso
Cupra Marittima
Montefiore dell'Aso
Ripatransone
Grottammare
San Benedetto
Monteprandone
Porto d'Ascoli
Acquaviva Picena
Offida
Force
Castignano
Montalto delle Marche
Monsampolo del Tronto
Spinetoli
Venarotta
Colonnella
Martinsicuro
Nereto
Tortoreto
Alba Adriatica
Corropoli
Mosciano Sant'Angelo
Giulianova
Bellante
Roseto
Colle Corvino
Montesilvano
Sessa Aurunca
Roccamonfina
Teano
Carinola
Monte Massico
Cellole
Mondragone
Castèl Volturno
Cancello ed Arnone
Grazzanise
Villa Literno
San Cipriano d'Aversa
Giugliano in Campania
Lago di Patria
Pozzuoli
Monte di Procida
Isola di Procida
Procida
Lacco Ameno
Forio
Monte Epomeo
Ischia
Barano d'Ischia
Isola d'Ischia
Golfo di Gaeta
Isola Palmarola
Isole Ponziane
Isola Zannone
Parco Nazionale del Circeo
Isola di Gavi
Isola di Ponza
Ponza
Isola Ventotene
Fiumicino
Venafro
Mignano Monte Lungo
Rocca d'Evandro
Galluccio
Interamna
Pignataro
Sesto Campano
Cagliari
Palermo
Tevere
Nera
Velino
Salto
Liri
Sacco
Garigliano
Volturno
Tronto
Vomano
Melfa
Sangro
Amaseno
Mignone
Marta
Arrone
Tirreno
Cardito
Montaquila
Rionero Sannitico
I

MARE ADRIATICO
HR
156
Sveta Andrija
Rt Stupišće
Biševo
Komiža
Vis
Rt Stončica
Sušac
Palagruža
Isole Tremiti
Isole Capraia
Isole San Domino
Isole San Nicola
Pescara
Francavilla al Mare
San Giovanni Teatino
Punta di Ferruccio
Ortona
San Vito Chietino
Punta Cavalluccio
Rocca San Giovanni
Fossacesia
Lanciano
Punta della Penna
Paglieta
Casalbordino
Vasto
San Salvo
Atessa
Termoli
Campomarino
Guglionesi
Marina di Chieuti
Lago di Lesina
Lesina
Lago di Varano
Rodi Garganico
Peschici
Vieste
Testa del Gargano
Pugnochiuso
Baia della Zagare
Mattinata
Promontorio del Gargano
Parco Nazionale del Gargano
San Marco in Lamis
San Giovanni Rotondo
Monte Sant'Angelo
Manfredonia
Golfo di Manfredonia
Lido di Siponto
Sannicandro Garganico
Apricena
San Severo
Torremaggiore
Tavoliere
Lucera
Foggia
Zapponeta
Margherita di Savoia
Trinitapoli
Barletta
Trani
San Ferdinando di Puglia
Cerignola
Orta Nova
Canosa di Puglia
Andria
Corato
Ruvo di Puglia
Castel del Monte
Minervino Murge
Lavello
Melfi
Rionero in Vulture
Venosa
Spinazzola
Gravina in Puglia
61
Genzano di Lucania
Acerenza
Avigliano
Potenza
Tricarico
Grassano
Campobasso
Monti del Frentani
Monti del Sannio
Monti del Matese
Bojano
Isernia
Piedimonte Matese
Benevento
Ariano Irpino
Avellino
Atripalda
Caserta
Capua
Aversa
Napoli
Portici
Torre del Greco
Torre Annunziata
Castellammare di Stabia
Pompei
Sorrento
Capri
Punta Campanella
Amalfi
Positano
Golfo di Salerno
Salerno
Cava de' Tirreni
Nocera Inferiore
Battipaglia
Eboli
Monti Picentini
Campagna
Muro Lucano
Bella
Picerno
60
Tunis, Valencia
Messina, Valletta
A14
A16
A30
A3
A1
A2
E55
E45
E842
E847
14°30′
15°00′
15°30′
16°00′
42°30′
42°00′
41°30′
41°00′
B
C
D
E
F
6
7
8
9
10

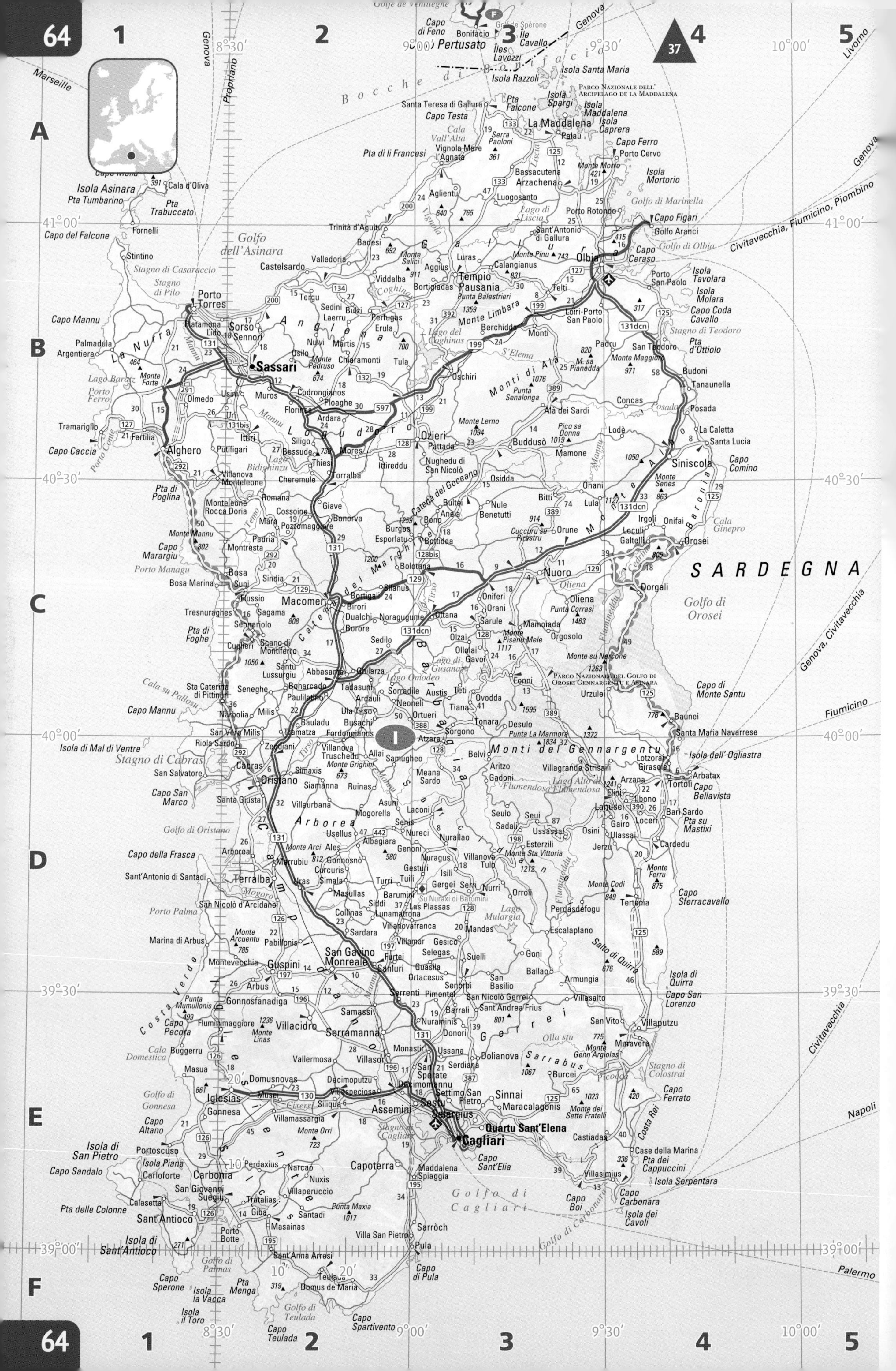

SARDEGNA
Bocche di Bonifacio
Bonifacio
Capo di Feno
Capo Pertusato
Capo di Spérone
Île Cavallo
Îles Lavezzi
Isola Razzoli
Isola Santa Maria
Isola Spargi
Isola Maddalena
Isola Caprera
La Maddalena
Palau
Parco Nazionale dell' Arcipelago de la Maddalena
Santa Teresa di Gallura
Capo Testa
Pta Falcone
Capo Ferro
Porto Cervo
Isola Mortorio
Golfo di Marinella
Porto Rotondo
Capo Figari
Golfo Aranci
Golfo di Olbia
Capo Ceraso
Olbia
Isola Tavolara
Isola Molara
Porto San Paolo
Capo Coda Cavallo
Stagno di Teodoro
San Teodoro
Pta d'Ottiolo
Budoni
Tanaunella
Posada
La Caletta
Santa Lucia
Siniscola
Capo Comino
Monte Albo
Baronia
Cala Ginepro
Orosei
Golfo di Orosei
Dorgali
Cala Gonone
Nuoro
Oliena
Orgosolo
Mamoiada
Fonni
Parco Nazionale del Golfo di Orosei Gennargentu e Asinara
Monte su Nercone
Urzulei
Capo di Monte Santu
Baunei
Santa Maria Navarrese
Isola dell'Ogliastra
Lotzorai
Girasole
Tortolì
Arbatax
Capo Bellavista
Lanusei
Bari Sardo
Pta su Mastixi
Cardedu
Tertenia
Capo Sferracavallo
Monte Ferru
Salto di Quirra
Isola di Quirra
Capo San Lorenzo
Villaputzu
Muravera
Stagno di Colostrai
Capo Ferrato
Costa Rei
Castiadas
Villasimius
Capo Carbonara
Isola Serpentara
Isola dei Cavoli
Capo Boi
Golfo di Cagliari
Cagliari
Quartu Sant'Elena
Capo Sant'Elia
Sinnai
Maracalagonis
Monte dei Sette Fratelli
Sarrabus
Gerrei
Capoterra
Maddalena Spiaggia
Sarròch
Villa San Pietro
Pula
Capo di Pula
Capo Spartivento
Teulada
Golfo di Teulada
Capo Teulada
Domus de Maria
Sant'Anna Arresi
Porto Botte
Golfo di Palmas
Isola di Sant'Antioco
Sant'Antioco
Calasetta
Pta delle Colonne
Carloforte
Isola di San Pietro
Capo Sandalo
Isola Piana
Portoscuso
Carbonia
Iglesias
Gonnesa
Golfo di Gonnesa
Capo Altano
Capo Sperone
Isola la Vacca
Isola il Toro
Pta Menga
Domusnovas
Musei
Siliqua
Villamassargia
Decimomannu
Assemini
Sestu
Selargius
Monastir
Villacidro
Serramanna
Sanluri
San Gavino Monreale
Guspini
Arbus
Gonnosfanadiga
Fluminimaggiore
Capo Pecora
Costa Verde
Buggerru
Cala Domestica
Masua
Marina di Arbus
Montevecchia
Campidano
Iglesiente
Sulcis
Terralba
Marrubiu
Uras
Arborea
Golfo di Oristano
Capo della Frasca
Sant'Antonio di Santadi
Porto Palma
Oristano
Santa Giusta
Cabras
Stagno di Cabras
Capo San Marco
San Salvatore
Riola Sardo
San Vero Milis
Isola di Mal di Ventre
Capo Mannu
Cala su Pallosu
Sta Caterina di Pittinuri
Cuglieri
Santu Lussurgiu
Pta di Foghe
Tresnuraghes
Bosa
Bosa Marina
Capo Marargiu
Porto Managu
Macomer
Ghilarza
Abbasanta
Lago Omodeo
Sorgono
Atzara
Tonara
Desulo
Monti del Gennargentu
Punta La Marmora 1834
Aritzo
Belvì
Villagrande Strisaili
Lago Alto di Flumendosa
Barbagia
Marmilla
Barumini
Su Nuraxi di Barumini
Laconi
Mandas
Isili
Escalaplano
Perdasdefogu
Lago Mulargia
Ballao
Armungia
Villasalto
Dolianova
Serdiana
Ussana
Donori
Senorbì
Nurri
Orroli
Sadali
Seui
Ozieri
Pattada
Buddusò
Alà dei Sardi
Monti di Alà
Oschiri
Berchidda
Monte Limbara
Tempio Pausania
Calangianus
Luras
Arzachena
Luogosanto
Gallura
Lago del Coghinas
Perfugas
Valledoria
Castelsardo
Anglona
Logudoro
Sassari
Porto Torres
Sorso
Sennori
Stintino
Stagno di Casaraccio
Golfo dell'Asinara
Isola Asinara
Pta Tumbarino
Pta Trabuccato
Cala d'Oliva
Capo del Falcone
Fornelli
Capo Mannu
Palmadula
Argentiera
La Nurra
Lago Baratz
Porto Ferro
Tramariglio
Capo Caccia
Porto Conte
Fertilia
Alghero
Pta di Poglina
Villanova Monteleone
Thiesi
Torralba
Bonorva
Ittireddu
Mores
Ploaghe
Codrongianos
Muros
Olmedo
Uri
Ittiri
Chiaramonti
Osilo
Sedini
Nulvi
Martis
Tula
Erula
Bortigiadas
Aggius
Viddalba
Badesi
Trinità d'Agultu
Aglientu
Vignola Mare
Pta di li Francesi
Nughedu di San Nicolò
Bultei
Anela
Bono
Bottidda
Burgos
Esporlatu
Catena del Goceano
Benetutti
Nule
Osidda
Bitti
Orune
Lula
Onani
Lodè
Mamone
Irgoli
Onifai
Loculi
Galtellì
Ottana
Orani
Sarule
Gavoi
Ollolai
Olzai
Teti
Austis
Tiana
Ovodda
Sedilo
Noragugume
Dualchi
Birori
Bortigali
Silanus
Bolotana
Orotelli
Oniferi
Sardara
Villanovafranca
Genoni
Nuragus
Gesturi
Villamar
Furtei
Samassi
Serrenti
Nuraminis
Golfo di Marinella
Genova
Livorno
Marseille
Propriano
Civitavecchia, Fiumicino, Piombino
Genova, Civitavecchia
Fiumicino
Civitavecchia
Napoli
Palermo
8°30'
9°00'
9°30'
10°00'
41°00'
40°30'
40°00'
39°30'
39°00'
1
2
3
4
5
A
B
C
D
E
F
37

Campiglia Marittima
Massa Marittima
Roccastrada
Montalcino
San Quirico d'Orcia
Montepulciano
Pienza
Chianciano Terme
Panicale
Torgiano
Bastia
Piombino
Golfo di Follonica
Follonica
Scarlino
Gavorrano
Paganico
Cinigiano
Campagnatico
Castel del Piano
Arcidosso
Monte Amiata 1738
Abbadia San Salvatore
Radicofani
Sarteano
Cetona
Città della Pieve
Monteleone d'Orvieto
Piegaro
Tavernelle
Paciano
Fabro
San Casciano dei Bagni
Allerona
Ficulle
Portoferraio
Rio Marina
Porto Azzurro
Capoliveri
Isola Palmaiola
Isola Cerboli
Scoglio dello Sparviero
Punta Ala
Castiglione della Pescaia
Grosseto
Marina di Grosseto
Marina di Alberese
Formiche di Grosseto
Talamone
Punta dei Ripalti
Pianosa
Parco Nazionale dell' Arcipelago Toscano
Roccalbegna
Monte Faete 770
Semproniano
Scansano
Castell'Azzara
Monte Civitella 1107
Santa Fiora
Piancastagnaio
Proceno
Acquapendente
Orvieto
Castel Viscardo
Lago di Corbara
Todi
San Lorenzo Nuovo
Onano
Sorano
Grotte di Castro
Castel Giorgio
Bolsena
Lago di Bolsena
Gradoli
Pitigliano
Manciano
Magliano in Toscana
Saturnia
Capodimonte
Valentano
Farnese
Ischia di Castro
Montefiascone
Marta
Piansano
Cellere
Canino
Arlena di Castro
Tuscania
Viterbo
Capalbio
Orbetello
Porto Santo Stefano
Monte Argentario
Porto Ercole
Ansedonia
l'Isolotto
Laguna di Orbetello
Punta Lividonia
Isola del Giglio
Giglio Castello
Punta del Fenaio
Poggio della Pagana 498
Punta del Capel Rosso
Isola di Giannutri
Barcelona, Toulon
Montalto di Castro
Montalto Marina
Necropoli Etrusche
Tarquinia
Tarquinia Lido
Vetralla
Monte Romano
Blera
Tolfa
Allumiere
Civitavecchia
Santa Marinella
Santa Severa
Cerveteri
Ladispoli
Fregene
Fiumicino
Ostia
Lido di Ostia
Roma
Vatican City
Ciampino
Pomezia
Zoomarine
Tor Vaianica
Ardea
Lavinio-Lido di Enea
Anzio
Nettuno
Bracciano
Lago di Bracciano
Anguillara Sabazia
Lago di Martignano
Trevignano Romano
Manziana
Oriolo Romano
Vejano
Bassano Romano
Sutri
Capranica
Ronciglione
Caprarola
Civita Castellana
Nepi
Lago di Vico
Canepina
Vignanello
Fabrica di Roma
Vasanello
Gallese
Corchiano
Soriano nel Cimino
Monte Cimino 1053
Vitorchiano
Orte
Bagnoregio
Castiglione in Teverina
Lubriano in Teverina
Graffignano
Attigliano
Amelia
Penna in Teverina
Otricoli
Magliano Sabina
Narni
Terni
Alviano
Lago di Alviano
Guardea
Montecastrilli
Avigliano Umbro
Acquasparta
Baschi
Monte Croce di Serra 994
Foligno
Bevagna
Gualdo Cattaneo
Montefalco
Giano dell'Umbria
Monte Martano 1094
Massa Martana
Calvi dell'Umbria
Tarano
Cottanello
Forano
Rignano Flaminio
Fiano Romano
Faleria
Mazzano Romano
Campagnano di Roma
Castelnuovo di Porto
Formello
Riano
Monterotondo
Mentana
Olbia
Olbia, Porto-Vecchio
Arbatax
Cagliari, Tunis, Catania, Valletta
MARE TIRRENO
Isola di Capraia
Capraia Isola
Livorno
San Vincenzo
Suvereto
Populonia
Monte Massoncello
Canale di Piombino
Isola d'Elba
Capo Vita
Rio nell'Elba
Marciana Marina
Marciana
Monte Capanne 1018
Marina di Campo
Punta di Fetovaia
Cima del Monte 516
Poggio Peroni 349
Poggio Ballone 630
Poggio Lecci 415
Poggio del Leccio 353
Monte Leoni 614
Punta del Marchese
Isola Pianosa
Monte della Fortezza 645
Isola di Montecristo
Arcipelago Toscano
Isola diutri
Ombrone
Bruna
Orcia
Fiora
Albegna
Paglia
Chiani
Tevere
Marta
Arrone
Mignone
Nera
Cornia
Merse
A1
A12
A1dir
A90
E35
E45
E78
E80
MAREMMA
MONTI VOLSINI
I
66
62
B
C
D
E
F
1
2
3
4
5
6

Verona
Vicenza
Padova
Venezia
Mantova
Parma
Reggio nell'Emilia
Modena
Bologna
Ferrara
Rovigo
Chioggia
Ravenna
Forlì
Cesena
Imola
Faenza
Lugo
Prato
Pistoia
Firenze
Lucca
Pisa
Livorno
Siena
Arezzo
Perugia
Cortona
Montepulciano
Chiusi
Cecina
Piombino
Rimini
San Marino
RSM
Urbino
Città di Castello
Gubbio
Sansepolcro
Poggibonsi
San Gimignano
Volterra
Empoli
Carpi
Sassuolo
Vignola
Comacchio
Adria
Legnago
Este
Monselice
Desenzano del Garda
Peschiera del Garda
Sirmione
Bardolino
Sona
Villafranca di Verona
Soave
San Bonifacio
Lonigo
Abano Terme
Piove di Sacco
Cavarzere
Porto Tolle
Codigoro
Copparo
Cento
San Giovanni in Persiceto
Castel Maggiore
Casalecchio di Reno
San Lazzaro di Savena
Castel San Pietro Terme
Medicina
Argenta
Portomaggiore
Bagnacavallo
Russi
Cervia
Cesenatico
Bellaria
Santarcangelo di Romagna
Savignano sul Rubicone
Montecatini Terme
Pescia
Viareggio
Massa
Pietrasanta
Seravezza
Castelnuovo di Garfagnana
Barga
Bagni di Lucca
Abetone
Monte Cimone
Pavullo nel Frignano
Sesto Fiorentino
Scandicci
Fiesole
Bagno a Ripoli
Pontassieve
Borgo San Lorenzo
Scarperia
Figline Valdarno
Montevarchi
San Giovanni Valdarno
Greve in Chianti
Castellina in Chianti
Colle di Val d'Elsa
Monteriggioni
Montalcino
San Quirico d'Orcia
Pienza
Castiglione del Lago
Lago Trasimeno
Magione
Corciano
Marsciano
Bastia
Assisi
Massa Marittima
Follonica
Golfo di Follonica
Rosignano Marittimo
Castagneto Carducci
San Vincenzo
Campiglia Marittima
Populonia
MONTEFELTRO
FRIGNANO
POLESINE
MAREMMA
Appennino Tosco-Emiliano
Colline Metallifere
Parco Nazionale del Monte Falterona, Campigna e delle Foreste Casentinesi
Autodromo Enzo e Dino Ferrari, Imola
Mirabilandia
Valli di Comacchio
A1
A4
A13
A14
A22
A31
E35
E45
E55
E70
E76
E78
E80
44°30′
44°00′
43°30′
43°00′
45°00′
10°30′
11°00′
11°30′
12°00′
12°30′
1
2
3
4
5
B
C
D
E
F
72
69
65

MARE ADRIATICO
Istra (Istria)
Kvarner
Kvarnerić
Gorski Kotar
Velika Kapela
Velebit
HR
SLO
73
156
62
Trieste
Piran
Izola
Koper
Portorož
Lucija
Umag
Buje
Buzet
Novigrad
Poreč
Eufrazijeva Bazilika
Vrsar
Rovinj
Pazin
Motovun
Karojba
Labin
Rabac
Plomin
Opatija
Rijeka
Bakar
Kraljevica
Crikvenica
Novi Vinodolski
Senj
Pula
Medulin
Premantura
Rt Kamenjak
Vodnjan
Fažana
Brijuni
Krk
Cres
Lošin
Mali Lošinj
Veli Lošinj
Unije
Susak
Ilovik
Rab
Lopar
Pag
Novalja
Silba
Olib
Premuda
Ist
Molat
Škarda
Sestrunj
Rivanj
Ugljan
Dugi Otok
Zadar
Ogulin
Brinje
Delnice
Platak
Jablanac
Starigrad
Karlobag
Rt Savudrija
Rt Zub
Rt Kriz
Rt Barbariga
Rt Kumpare
Rt Marlera
Rt Ubac
Rt Crna Pta
Rt Pernat
Rt Jablanac
Rt Pelova
Rt Sokol
Rt Kijac
Rt Osor
Rt Sveti Damjan
Rt Lun
Rt Vrulja
Vele Srakane
Durrës, Patra, Igoumenitsa
Split, Bar
Antalya, Izmir, Marmaris, Igoumenitsa, Istanbul, Çeşme, Kerkyra, Patra
Igoumenitsa, Çeşme, Kerkyra, Patra
Eraclea Mare
Riccione
Misano Adriatico
Cattolica
Gabicce Mare
Pesaro
Fano
Senigallia
Mondolfo
Fossombrone
Falconara Marittima
Ancona
Monte Conero
Sirolo
Numana
Jesi
Chiaravalle
Osimo
Castelfidardo
Loreto
Porto Recanati
Recanati
Potenza Picena
Civitanova Marche
Porto Sant'Elpidio
Sant'Elpidio a Mare
Macerata
Morrovalle
Corridonia
Tolentino
Montegranaro
San Severino Marche
Fermo
Porto San Giorgio
Marina Palmense
Pedaso
Cupra Marittima
Grottammare
San Benedetto del Tronto
Martinsicuro
Fabriano
Matelica
Camerino
Cingoli
Sassoferrato
Arcevia
Pergola
Gualdo Tadino
Nocera Umbra
Umbro-Marchigiano
13°00′
13°30′
14°00′
14°30′
45°00′
44°30′
44°00′
43°30′
43°00′
6
7
8
9
10
B
C
D
E
F

CH
F
Torino
Alessandria
Novara
Vercelli
Asti
Cuneo
Savona
Nice
San Remo
Imperia
Aosta
Ivrea
Biella
Chamonix-Mont-Blanc
Briançon
Sion
Martigny
Domodossola
Verbania
Alpi Pennine
Monte Rosa
Valle di Susa
Canavese
Alpes Maritimes
Riviera di Ponente
Côte d'Azur
Tarentaise
Val Dossola
Lago Maggiore
Bastia, Calvi, L'Ile Rousse
Barcelona, Porto Torres

7
8
9
10
11
A
B
C
D
E
F
9°00′
9°30′
10°00′
10°30′
11°00′
45°30′
45°00′
44°30′
44°00′
71
72
66
I
CH
Milano
Bergamo
Brescia
Verona
Trento
Mantova
Cremona
Piacenza
Parma
Reggio nell'Emilia
Modena
Genova
La Spezia
Massa
Carrara
Lucca
Pistoia
Prato
Firenze
Viareggio
Monza
Como
Lecco
Lodi
Pavia
Sondrio
Alpi Orobie
Lago di Garda
Lago di Como
Riviera di Levante
Golfo di Genova
Alpi Apuane
Appennino
Frignano
Olbia, Palau, Tunis, Bastia
Palermo, Catania

Sélestat
Colmar
Mulhouse
Freiburg im Breisgau
Basel
Belfort
Montbéliard
Vesoul
Besançon
Pontarlier
Biel
Solothurn
Bern
Neuchâtel
La Chaux-de-Fonds
Fribourg
Thun
Lausanne
Genève
Annecy
Chamonix-Mont-Blanc
Aosta
Sion
Sierre
Brig
Martigny
Montreux
Vevey
Yverdon
Olten
Aarau
Delémont
Lörrach
Rheinfelden
Bad Säckingen
Waldshut
Albertville
Annemasse
Thonon-les-Bains
Évian-les-Bains
Lure
Remiremont
Gérardmer
Épinal
Zermatt
Saas Fee
Grindelwald
Interlaken
Spiez
Gstaad
Crans-Montana
Verbier
Domodossola
SUNDGAU
HOTZENWALD
EMMENTAL
MITTELLAND
BERNER ALPEN
BAGNES
Chablais
Faucigny
Genevois
Bauges
Bornes
Lac Léman
Lac de Neuchâtel
Bieler See
Thuner See
Brienzer See
Mont Blanc
Monte Rosa
Alpi Pennine
Jungfrau
Eiger
Mönch
Finsteraarhorn
Matterhorn
Dufourspitze

74
75
72
69
D
CH
FL
A
I
Balingen
Burladingen
Sigmaringen
Tuttlingen
Saulgau
Biberach an der Riß
Memmingen
Mindelheim
Landsberg am Lech
Kaufbeuren
Schongau
Kempten
Füssen
Ravensburg
Weingarten
Friedrichshafen
Konstanz
Kreuzlingen
Singen
Radolfzell am Bodensee
Überlingen
Lindau
Bregenz
Dornbirn
Feldkirch
VADUZ
Bludenz
Schaffhausen
Winterthur
Zürich
St Gallen
Chur
Davos
Klosters
St Moritz
Landeck
Imst
Reutte
Oberstdorf
Lech
Zürs
St Christoph am Arlberg
St Anton
Samnaun
Scuol
Zernez
S-Chanf
Livigno
Bormio
Tirano
Sondrio
Chiavenna
Maloja
Sils-Maria
Bellinzona
Locarno
Lugano
Como
Lecco
Bergamo
Varese
Monza
Saronno
Malnate
BAAR
HEGAU
LINZGAU
ALLGÄU
TOGGENBURG
SURSELVA
UNTER ENGADIN
OBER ENGADIN
Rhätikon
Silvretta Gruppe
Samnaungruppe
Verwallgruppe
Lechtaler Alpen
Allgäuer Alpen
Alpi Orobie
Bodensee
Lago di Como
Lago Maggiore
Lago di Lugano
Valle Leventina
Passo del San Gottardo
Passo dello Spluga
Passo del Bernina
Passo dello Stelvio
Passo del Tonale
Rhaetian Railway
Parc Nazional Svizzer
Parco Nazionale dello Stelvio

75
71
66
D
CH
I
A
B
C
D
E
F
1
2
3
4
5
10°30′
11°00′
11°30′
12°00′
12°30′
47°30′
47°00′
46°30′
46°00′
45°30′
UNTER ENGADIN
OSTTIROL
Allgäuer Alpen
Lechtaler Alpen
Ammergauer Alpen
Estergebirge
Mangfallgebirge
Kaisergebirge
Karwendelgebirge
Stubaier Alpen
Ötztaler Alpen
Zillertaler Alpen
Tuxer Gebirge
Kitzbüheler Alpen
Hohe Tauern
Samnaungruppe
Verwallgruppe
Silvretta Gruppe
Chiemgauer
Dolomiti
Alpi
Giudicarie
Val Venosta
Pusteria
Lago di Garda
Kempten
Marktoberdorf
Schongau
Weilheim in Oberbayern
Wolfratshausen
Holzkirchen
Rosenheim
Bad Aibling
Miesbach
Bad Tölz
Penzberg
Murnau am Staffelsee
Oberammergau
Füssen
Schwangau
Immenstadt im Allgäu
Sonthofen
Oberstdorf
Garmisch-Partenkirchen
Mittenwald
Ehrwald
Reutte
Kufstein
Wörgl
Kitzbühel
Schwaz
Innsbruck
Hall in Tirol
Telfs
Imst
Landeck
St Anton
St Christoph am Arlberg
Zürs
Kleinwalsertal
Sölden
Obergurgl
Vent
Axamer Lizum
Kühtai
Igls
Mutters
Fulpmes
Mieders
Stubai Glacier
Brenner
Hintertux
Finkenberg
Mayrhofen
Ellmau
Scheffau
Going
Kirchberg in Tirol
Samnaun
Nauders
S-Chanf
Watles
Trafoi
Merano
Bolzano
Brixen/Plose
Bressanone
Brunico
Kronplatz/S. Vigilio
Toblach
Cortina d'Ampezzo
San Cassiano
Arabba
Campitello di Fassa
Vigo di Fassa
Moena
Obereggen
Kastelruth/Castelrotto
Alpe di Siusi/Seiser Alm
St Ulrich
Santa Cristina
Sarntal-Reinswald
Bellamonte
Chiesa
Belluno
Piancavallo
Vittorio Veneto
Conegliano
Treviso
Venezia
Mestre
Padova
Vicenza
Verona
Trento
Rovereto
Riva del Garda
Arco
Folgarida
Marilleva
Passo Tonale
Santa Caterina
Bormio
Tirano
Brescia
Desenzano del Garda
Malga San Giorgio
Schio
Bassano del Grappa
Castelfranco Veneto
Montebelluna
Feltre
Appiano sulla Strada del Vino
Monte Pora
E45
E60
E533
A12
A13
A22
A4
A27
A31

Salzburg
Berchtesgadener Land
Bad Reichenhall
Freilassing
Gmunden
Bad Ischl
SALZKAMMERGUT
Hallstatt
Bad Aussee
Liezen
Schladming
Ramsau am Dachstein
Bischofshofen
Zell am See
Saalfelden am Steinernen Meer
Maria Alm
Mühlbach am Hochkönig
Obertauern
Zauchensee
Niedere Tauern
Hohe Tauern
Heiligenblut
Badgastein
Bad Hofgastein
Lienz
Spittal an der Drau
Millstatt
Villach
Feldkirchen in Kärnten
St Veit an der Glan
Klagenfurt
Völkermarkt
Wolfsberg
St Andrä
Judenburg
Knittelfeld
Leoben
Trofaiach
Kapfenberg
Köflach
Voitsberg
Eisenerz
Admont
Rottenmann
Murau
Tamsweg
Karnische Alpen
Hermagor
Kötschach
Tarvisio
Pontebba
Tolmezzo
Sella Nevea
Gemona del Friuli
Udine
Cividale del Friuli
Pordenone
Codroipo
Palmanova
Gorizia
Nova Gorica
Monfalcone
Trieste
Muggia
Koper
Izola
Piran
Portorož
Latisana
Lignano Sabbiadoro
Grado
Caorle
Julijske Alpe
Kamniške in Savinjske Alpe
Karawanken
Jesenice
Bled
Kranj
Škofja Loka
LJUBLJANA
Domžale
Kamnik
Velenje
Trbovlje
Vogel
Kobla
Tolmin
Bovec
Idrija
Postojna
Logatec
Vrhnika
Ribnica
Kočevje
Novo Mesto
SUHA KRAJINA
GORSKI KOTAR
Rijeka
Opatija
SLO
HR
Golfo di Venezia
Ancona, Durrës, Patra, Igoumenitsa
Poreč, Pula, Rovinj
Zadar
76
77
67
148

78
21
27
70
71
NORDPFÄLZER BERGLAND
ODENWALD
BAULAND
TAUBERGR
KRAICHGAU
SCHÖNBUCH
Frankfurt am Main
Offenbach am Main
Wiesbaden
Mainz
Rüsselsheim
Darmstadt
Aschaffenburg
Mannheim
Ludwigshafen am Rhein
Heidelberg
Kaiserslautern
Neustadt an der Weinstraße
Worms
Karlsruhe
Pforzheim
Heilbronn
Ludwigsburg
Stuttgart
Esslingen am Neckar
Sindelfingen
Tübingen
Reutlingen
Göppingen
Schwäbisch Gmünd
Heidenheim
Ulm
Baden-Baden
Strasbourg
Offenburg
Freiburg im Breisgau
Bad Homburg vor der Höhe
Limburg an der Lahn
Bad Kreuznach
Fulda
Würzburg
Speyer
Landau in der Pfalz
Pirmasens
Zweibrücken
Homburg
Bad Mergentheim
Schwäbisch Hall
Rottweil
Villingen
Schwenningen
Sigmaringen
Balingen
Hechingen
Freudenstadt
Calw
Böblingen
Nürtingen
Biberach an der Riß
Sélestat
Haguenau
Wissembourg
F

7
8
9
10
11
79
Meiningen
Hildburghausen
Coburg
Sonneberg
Neustadt bei Coburg
Kronach
Lichtenfels
Kulmbach
Bayreuth
Helmbrechts
Münchberg
Hof
Plauen
Oelsnitz
VOGTLAND
Auerbach
Klingenthal
Aš
Selb
Cheb
Marktredwitz
Wunsiedel
Fichtelgebirge
Bad Kissingen
Bad Neustadt
Schweinfurt
Haßfurt
Bamberg
Staffelstein
Forchheim
Erlangen
Fürth
Nürnberg
Schwabach
Ansbach
Kitzingen
Neustadt an der Aisch
Bad Windsheim
Höchstadt an der Aisch
Herzogenaurach
Fränkische Schweiz
Pegnitz
Hersbruck
Lauf an der Pegnitz
Sulzbach-Rosenberg
Amberg
Weiden in der Oberpfalz
Neustadt an der Waldnaab
Tirschenreuth
Mitterteich
Mariánské Lázně
Tachov
CZ
D
Altdorf bei Nürnberg
Neumarkt in der Oberpfalz
Schwandorf
Cham
76
Regensburg
Straubing
Kelheim
Ingolstadt
Eichstätt
Weißenburg in Bayern
Treuchtlingen
Gunzenhausen
Dinkelsbühl
Feuchtwangen
Nördlingen
Aalen
Donauwörth
Neuburg an der Donau
Schrobenhausen
Pfaffenhofen an der Ilm
Freising
Landshut
Moosburg an der Isar
Dingolfing
Vilsbiburg
Erding
Dachau
München
Augsburg
Aichach
Friedberg
Landsberg am Lech
Starnberg
Mindelheim
Memmingen
Günzburg
Dillingen an der Donau
Neu-Ulm
Kaufbeuren
Rosenheim
Wasserburg am Inn
Mühldorf am Inn
Altötting
Traunreut
Trostberg
Holzkirchen
Wolfratshausen
DONAUMOOS
HALLERTAU
FIRNGRUND
Steigerwald
Haßberge
72
E45
E48
E49
E50
E51
E52
E53
E54
E56
3
6
9
70
71
73
92
93
94
96
99
995

1
2
3
4
5
6
B
C
D
E
F
80
75
72
73
Plauen
Oelsnitz
VOGTLAND
Klingenthal
Aš
Selb
Cheb
Fichtelgebirge
Wunsiedel
Marktredwitz
Karlovy Vary
Sokolov
Ostrov
Chodov
Mariánské Lázně
Chomutov
Kadaň
Klášterec nad Ohří
Žatec
Louny
Most
Doupovské Hory
Podbořany
Rakovník
Kladno
Slaný
Kralupy nad Vltavou
Beroun
Plzeň
Rokycany
Příbram
Dobříš
Tachov
Stříbro
Domažlice
Klatovy
Sušice
Strakonice
Písek
Vimperk
Prachatice
Český Krumlov
Šumava
Weiden in der Oberpfalz
Amberg
Schwandorf
Regensburg
Cham
Straubing
Deggendorf
Passau
Landshut
Vilshofen
Bayerischer Wald
Zwiesel
Regen
Sankt Englmar
Kelheim
Dingolfing
Landau an der Isar
Plattling
Eggenfelden
Pfarrkirchen
Mühldorf am Inn
Altötting
Burghausen
Braunau am Inn
Ried im Innkreis
Schärding
Mühlviertel
Linz
Wels
Traun
Ansfelden
Vöcklabruck
Gmunden
Rosenheim
Traunstein
Freilassing
Erding
Freising
München
Waldkraiburg
Dorfen
Vilsbiburg
Innviertel
Rottal
Hallertau
Böhmerwald
Oberpfälzer Wald
Tepelská Vrchovina
Rakovnická Pahorkatina
Křivoklátská Vrchovina
Brdy
Dunaugau
Neustadt an der Waldnaab
Sulzbach-Rosenberg
Burglengenfeld
Regenstauf
Neutraubling
Abensberg
Neustadt an der Donau
Mainburg
Moosburg an der Isar
Bad Griesbach im Rottal
Pocking
Bad Füssing
Grieskirchen
Marchtrenk
Leonding
D

Mladá Boleslav
Mělník
Neratovice
Brandýs nad Labem-Stará Boleslav
Čelákovice
Nymburk
Poděbrady
Jičín
Hradec Králové
Jaroměř
Náchod
Nové Město nad Metují
Kłodzko
Bystrzyca Kłodzka
Jeseník
Rychnov nad Kněžnou
Kolín
Pardubice
Chrudim
Kutná Hora
Čáslav
Říčany
Benešov
Vlašim
Ústí nad Orlicí
Vysoké Mýto
Litomyšl
Lanškroun
Zábřeh
Šumperk
Svitavy
Moravská Třebová
Polička
Hlinsko
Havlíčkův Brod
Humpolec
Pelhřimov
Tábor
Jihlava
Žďár nad Sázavou
Nové Město na Moravě
Boskovice
Prostějov
Olomouc
Blansko
Brno
Vyškov
Velké Meziříčí
Třebíč
Telč
Jindřichův Hradec
Třeboň
České Budějovice
Znojmo
Mikulov
Břeclav
Hodonín
Hustopeče
ČESKOMORAVSKÁ VYSOČINA
Železné Hory
Žďárské Vrchy
CZ
PL
SK
A
WALDVIERTEL
WACHAU
Zwettl
Horn
Hollabrunn
Mistelbach
Krems an der Donau
Tulln
Stockerau
Korneuburg
Klosterneuburg
WIEN
Schwechat
Mödling
Baden
St. Pölten
Melk
Amstetten
Freistadt
Enns
BRATISLAVA
Malacky
Waidhofen an der Ybbs
Wiener Neustadt
Eisenstadt
81
146
148
149
7
8
9
10
11
B
C
D
E
F

Lingen
Nordhorn
Rheine
TECKLENBURGER LAND
Osnabrück
Ibbenbüren
Bramsche
Wiehengebirge
Minden
Lübbecke
Rahden
Nienburg
Neustadt am Rübenberge
Hannover
Garbsen
Wunstorf
Stadthagen
Bückeburg
Rinteln
Bad Oeynhausen
Herford
Bielefeld
Bad Salzuflen
Lemgo
Detmold
Hameln
Bad Pyrmont
Gütersloh
Münster
MÜNSTERLAND
Teutoburger Wald
SENNE
Paderborn
Lippstadt
HOCHFLÄCHE
OBERWÄLDER LAND
Höxter
Holzminden
Warburg
Hofgeismar
Kassel
Hann. Münden
Recklinghausen
Gelsenkirchen
Herne
Dortmund
Essen
Bochum
Witten
Hagen
Hamm
Unna
Soest
Werl
Haarstrang
Arnsberg
Meschede
SAUERLAND
Iserlohn
Lüdenscheid
Wuppertal
Winterberg
Rothaargebirge
Olpe
Siegen
BERGISCHES LAND
Marsberg
Korbach
Bad Wildungen
Frankenberg
Marburg an der Lahn
Gießen
Wetzlar
Limburg an der Lahn
Koblenz
Neuwied
Bonn
Westerwald
Taunus
Bad Homburg vor der Höhe
Wiesbaden
Mainz
Frankfurt am Main
Offenbach am Main
Hanau
Fulda
Vogelsberg
Bad Hersfeld
Alsfeld
Spessart
Aschaffenburg
Bingen am Rhein
Rüsselsheim

Wolfsburg
Braunschweig
Salzgitter
Wolfenbüttel
Helmstedt
Magdeburg
Stendal
Tangermünde
Brandenburg
Burg bei Magdeburg
Schönebeck
Zerbst
Dessau
Lutherstadt Wittenberg
Halberstadt
Quedlinburg
Wernigerode
Goslar
Bad Harzburg
Aschersleben
Bernburg
Köthen
Bitterfeld
Halle
Leipzig
Merseburg
Weißenfels
Naumburg
Lutherstadt Eisleben
Sangerhausen
Nordhausen
Sondershausen
Mühlhausen
Bad Langensalza
Eisenach
Gotha
Erfurt
Weimar
Jena
Apolda
Gera
Zeitz
Altenburg
Zwickau
Plauen
Hof
Suhl
Ilmenau
Meiningen
Coburg
Kronach
Kulmbach
Schweinfurt
Saalfeld
Rudolstadt
Pößneck
Hildburghausen
Sonneberg
Selb
Cheb
CZ
COLBITZ-LETZLINGER HEIDE
DRÖMLING
ALTMARK
EICHSFELD
GOLDENE AUE
Thüringer Becken
Thüringer Wald
VOGTLAND
Fichtelgebirge
Hainich
Haßberge
Grabfeld
ZAUCHE
FLÄMING
A 9
A 14
A 38
A 71
A 73
A 4
A 2
A 36
E 30
E 40
E 49
E 51
83
80
75
7
8
9
10
11
12
B
C
D
E
F

BERLIN
Potsdam
Brandenburg
Magdeburg
Dessau
Lutherstadt Wittenberg
Halle
Leipzig
Dresden
Chemnitz
Zwickau
Gera
Jena
Plauen
Hof
Cottbus
Meißen
Riesa
Torgau
Luckenwalde
Jüterbog
Lübben
Lübbenau
Finsterwalde
Hoyerswerda
Bautzen
Freiberg
Pirna
Děčín
Ústí nad Labem
Teplice
Most
Chomutov
Karlovy Vary
Cheb
Kladno
Rakovník
Louny
Litoměřice
Z A U C H E
F L Ä M I N G
S P R E E W A L D
N I E D E R L A U S I T Z
V O G T L A N D
Fichtelgebirge
SÄCHSISCHE SCHWEIZ
Doupovské Hory
84
79
76

85
POJEZIERZE LUBUSKIE
POJEZIERZE WIELKOPOLSKIE
Poznań
Swarzędz
Luboń
Kórnik
Środa Wielkopolska
Mosina
Słubice
Kostrzyn
Międzyrzecz
Świebodzin
Sulechów
Zielona Góra
Nowa Sól
Eisenhüttenstadt
Krosno Odrzańskie
Gubin
Guben
Lubsko
Forst
Żary
Żagań
Szprotawa
Głogów
Leszno
Wschowa
Kościan
Grodzisk Wielkopolski
Nowy Tomyśl
Wolsztyn
Rawicz
Gostyń
Milicz
Lubin
Polkowice
Legnica
Chojnów
Bolesławiec
Wrocław
Oborniki Śląskie
Trzebnica
Wołów
Brzeg Dolny
Środa Śląska
142
PL
Görlitz
Zgorzelec
Niesky
Bad Muskau
Lubań
Zittau
Bogatynia
Jelenia Góra
Wałbrzych
Świdnica
Jawor
Strzegom
Dzierżoniów
Bielawa
Kłodzko
Nowa Ruda
Ząbkowice Śląskie
Strzelin
Kamienna Góra
Karpacz
Szklarska Poręba
Liberec
Jablonec nad Nisou
Jizerské Hory
Krkonoše
Pec Pod Snezkou
Janske Lazne
Trutnov
Náchod
Dvůr Králové
Jičín
Mladá Boleslav
Turnov
CZ
Hradec Králové
Pardubice
Kolín
Nymburk
Poděbrady
Mělník
PRAHA
Rychnov nad Kněžnou
Jeseník
Rychlebské Hory
Orlické Hory
Góry Bystrzyckie
77

N O R D S E E
Nordfriesische Inseln
Halligen
Helgoländer Bucht
Helgoland
Ostfriesische Inseln
Juist
Norderney
Baltrum
Langeoog
Spiekeroog
Wangerooge
Mellum
Scharhörn
Neuwerk
Trischen
Amrum
Föhr
Pellworm
Nordstrand
Süderoog
Nationalpark Schleswig-Holsteinisches Wattenmeer
Nationalpark Hamburgisches Wattenmeer
Nationalpark Niedersächsisches Wattenmeer
Flensburg
Schleswig
Husum
Rendsburg
Heide
Itzehoe
Brunsbüttel
Cuxhaven
Glückstadt
Stade
Bremerhaven
Wilhelmshaven
Nordenham
Aurich
Emden
Leer
Papenburg
Oldenburg
Delmenhorst
Bremen
Verden
Rotenburg
Buxtehude
Zeven
Bremervörde
Walsrode
Nienburg
Cloppenburg
Vechta
Meppen
Lingen
Nordhorn
Rheine
Osnabrück
Minden
Diepholz
Sulingen
Wildeshausen
Syke
Neustadt am Rübenberge
Wunstorf
Garbsen
Hannover
Bückeburg
Lübbecke
Bad Essen
Ibbenbüren
Delfzijl
Appingedam
Winschoten
Emmen
NORDERLAND
HARLINGER LAND
BUTJADINGEN
OSTFRIESLAND
AMMERLAND
LAND HADELN
LAND WURSTEN
KEHDINGEN
TEUFELS MOOR
BOURTANGER MOOR
EMSLAND
TECKLENBURGER LAND
Wiehengebirge
Jadebusen
Nord-Ostsee-Kanal
Küstenkanal
Mittellandkanal
Dümmer
Zwischenahner Meer
Weser
Elbe
Ems
Hunte
Aller
Leine
Wümme
Oste
Eider
Hase
NL
17
86
78
7°00′
7°30′
8°00′
8°30′
9°00′
9°30′
54°30′
54°00′
53°30′
53°00′
52°30′
A
B
C
D
E
F
1
2
3
4
5
6
7

82

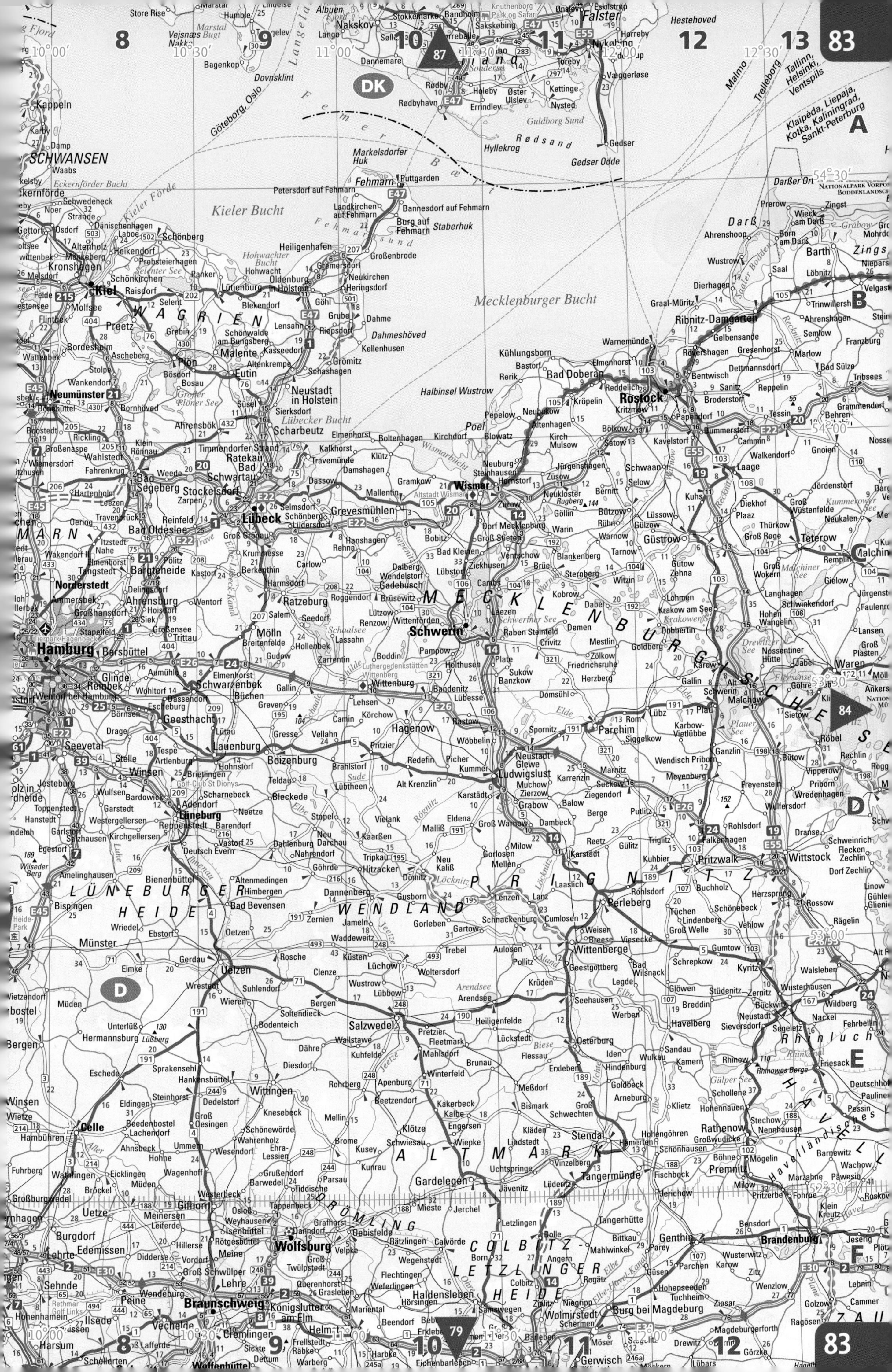

8
9
10
11
12
13
87
84
79
A
B
C
D
E
F
DK
D
10°00′
10°30′
11°00′
11°30′
12°00′
12°30′
54°30′
54°00′
53°30′
53°00′
52°30′
Nakskov
Falster
Nykøbing
Rødby
Rødbyhavn
Gedser
Gedser Odde
Femer Bælt
Fehmarn
Puttgarden
Burg auf Fehmarn
Kieler Bucht
Mecklenburger Bucht
Lübecker Bucht
Kappeln
SCHWANSEN
Eckernförde
Kiel
Kronshagen
Preetz
WAGRIEN
Plön
Eutin
Malente
Oldenburg in Holstein
Heiligenhafen
Großenbrode
Neustadt in Holstein
Scharbeutz
Neumünster
Bad Segeberg
Bad Oldesloe
Lübeck
Travemünde
Bad Schwartau
Ratzeburg
Mölln
Norderstedt
Ahrensburg
Bargteheide
Hamburg
Reinbek
Glinde
Schwarzenbek
Geesthacht
Lauenburg
Seevetal
Winsen
Lüneburg
LÜNEBURGER HEIDE
Bad Bevensen
Uelzen
Munster
Celle
Gifhorn
Wolfsburg
Braunschweig
Peine
Lehrte
Burgdorf
Sehnde
Wolfenbüttel
Helmstedt
Königslutter am Elm
Haldensleben
Wolmirstedt
Burg bei Magdeburg
Brandenburg
Rathenow
Genthin
Tangermünde
Stendal
Gardelegen
ALTMARK
DRÖMLING
COLBITZ-LETZLINGER HEIDE
Salzwedel
Wittingen
Dannenberg
WENDLAND
Lüchow
Wittenberge
Perleberg
Pritzwalk
Wittstock
Kyritz
Havelberg
PRIGNITZ
Ludwigslust
Hagenow
Boizenburg
Schwerin
Wismar
Gadebusch
Grevesmühlen
MECKLENBURGISCHE SEENPLATTE
Parchim
Lübz
Plau
Malchow
Waren
Güstrow
Bützow
Sternberg
Teterow
Rostock
Warnemünde
Bad Doberan
Kühlungsborn
Ribnitz-Damgarten
Barth
Darß
Zingst
Wustrow
Graal-Müritz
Laage
Malchin
Neuruppin
Rhinluch
HAVELLAND
Friesack
Premnitz
Falkenhagen
Meyenburg
Crivitz
Zarrentin
Wittenburg
Büchen
Boltenhagen
Poel
Halbinsel Wustrow
Dahme
Grömitz
Kellenhusen
Dahmeshöved

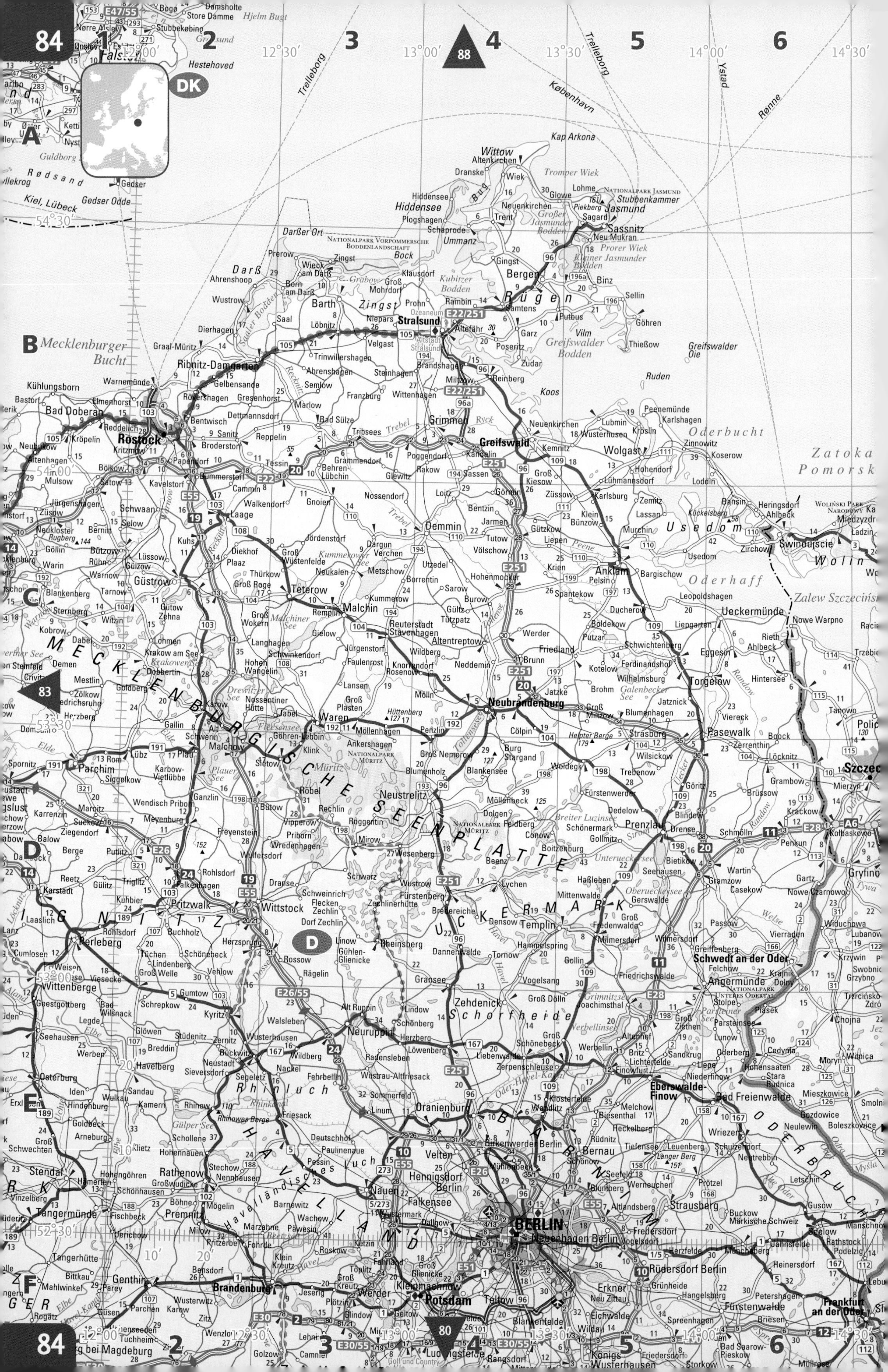
DK
88
83
80
Mecklenburger Bucht
Kap Arkona
Tromper Wiek
Nationalpark Jasmund
Stubbenkammer
Jasmund
Sassnitz
Hiddensee
Darßer Ort
Nationalpark Vorpommersche Boddenlandschaft
Darß
Zingst
Rügen
Bergen
Binz
Putbus
Göhren
Greifswalder Bodden
Greifswalder Oie
Ruden
Stralsund
Barth
Ribnitz-Damgarten
Warnemünde
Kühlungsborn
Bad Doberan
Rostock
Greifswald
Wolgast
Oderbucht
Zatoka Pomorska
Usedom
Świnoujście
Wolin
Oderhaff
Zalew Szczeciński
Anklam
Ueckermünde
Grimmen
Demmin
Teterow
Malchin
Güstrow
Bützow
Schwaan
Laage
Tessin
Gnoien
Mecklenburgische Seenplatte
Waren
Müritz
Nationalpark Müritz
Neubrandenburg
Friedland
Pasewalk
Torgelow
Strasburg
Prenzlau
Neustrelitz
Templin
Uckermark
Schwedt an der Oder
Angermünde
Nationalpark Unteres Odertal
Eberswalde-Finow
Bad Freienwalde
Oderbruch
Prignitz
Parchim
Lübz
Plau
Malchow
Pritzwalk
Wittstock
Perleberg
Wittenberge
Kyritz
Neuruppin
Rheinsberg
Zehdenick
Schorfheide
Oranienburg
Rhinluch
Havelland
Havelländisches Luch
Barnim
Stendal
Tangermünde
Rathenow
Nauen
Hennigsdorf
Bernau
Strausberg
BERLIN
Potsdam
Werder
Brandenburg
Genthin
Erkner
Fürstenwalde
Frankfurt an der Oder
Szczecin
Gryfino
Chojna
Rüdersdorf Berlin
Königs Wusterhausen
Ludwigsfelde
Seelow
Kiel, Lübeck
Gedser
Trelleborg
København
Ystad
Rønne
12°00′
12°30′
13°00′
13°30′
14°00′
14°30′
54°30′
54°00′
53°30′
53°00′
52°30′

7
8
9
10
11
12
15°00′
15°30′
16°00′
16°30′
17°00′
17°30′
89
Tallinn, Helsinki, Kaliningrad, Sankt-Peterburg,
Liepaja, Ventspils, Klaipėda, Kotka
A
B
C
D
E
F
138
81
PL
Łeba
Jezioro Sarbsko
Słowiński Park Narodowy
Wicko
Jezioro Gardno
Smołdzino
Główczyce
Ustka
Objazda
Jarosławiec
Jezioro Wicko
Duninowo
Jezioro Kopań
Postomino
Słupsk
Redzikowo
Kobylnica
Dębnica Kaszubska
Łupawa
Damnica
Potęgowo
Darłówko
Darłowo
Dąbki
Jezioro Bukowo
Sławno
Warszkowo
Sycewice
Malechowo
Kruszyna
Jezioro Jamno
Mielno
Ustronie Morskie
Tymień
Będzino
Mścice
Koszalin
Sianów
Kołobrzeg
Dźwirzyno
Zieleniewo
Dygowo
Biesiekierz
Bonin
Manowo
Świeszyno
Rosnowo
Kłanino
Polanów
Bytów
Miastko
Trzebielino
Tuchomie
Kołczygłowy
Niechorze
Rewal
Pobierowo
Trzebiatów
Karnice
Gościno
Karlino
Białogard
Gryfice
Płoty
Resko
Świdwin
Połczyn Zdrój
Barwice
Bobolice
Biały Bór
Szczecinek
Czarne
Człuchów
Chojnice
Nowogard
Łobez
Drawsko Pomorskie
Złocieniec
Czaplinek
Okonek
Jastrowie
Złotów
Krajenka
Goleniów
Stargard Szczeciński
Ińsko
Kalisz Pomorski
Mirosławiec
Wałcz
Piła
Wyrzysk
Nakło nad Notecią
Pyrzyce
Choszczno
Recz
Tuczno
Trzcianka
Chodzież
Wągrowiec
Barlinek
Myślibórz
Strzelce Krajeńskie
Drezdenko
Wieleń
Czarnków
Gorzów Wielkopolski
Skwierzyna
Międzychód
Sieraków
Wronki
Szamotuły
Oborniki
Rogoźno
Pniewy
Międzyrzecz
Świebodzin
Poznań
Swarzędz
Kostrzyn
Luboń
Sulęcin
Słońsk
Rzepin
Opalenica
Nowy Tomyśl
Drawieński Park Narodowy
Puszcza Notecka
POBRZEŻE KOSZALIŃSKIE
POJEZIERZE POMORSKIE
POJEZIERZE KRAJEŃSKIE
POJEZIERZE WIELKOPOLSKIE
POJEZIERZE LUBUSKIE
E28
E65
E30
E261
A2
S3
S5
S6
S10
S11

1
2
3
4
5
6
8°00′
8°30′
9°00′
9°30′
10°00′
10°30′
90
A
B
C
D
E
F
57°00′
56°30′
56°00′
55°30′
55°00′
VENDSYSSEL
Jammerbugten
Vigsø Bugt
Hanstholm
Thisted
THY
MORS
SALLING
Limfjorden
Nissum Bredning
Thyholm
Nykøbing Mors
Skive
Aalborg
Nørresundby
HIMMERLAND
Hobro
Mariager Fjord
Randers
Randers Fjord
Viborg
DJURSLAND
Aalborg Bugt
Lemvig
Struer
Holstebro
HARSYSSEL
JYLLAND
Herning
Ikast
Silkeborg
Aarhus
Århus Bugt
Ringkøbing
Ringkøbing Fjord
Holmsland Klit
Skanderborg
Samsø
Skjern
Horsens
DK
Billund
Legoland Billund
Vejle
Varde
Blåvands Huk
Fredericia
Esbjerg
Fanø
Fanø Bugt
Kolding
Middelfart
Odense
Fyn
Ribe
Mandø
Haderslev
Rømø
Aabenraa
Als
Sønderborg
Faaborg
Ærø
Tønder
Sylt
Westerland
D
Flensburg
Flensburg Fjord
Föhr
Nordfriesische
86
82

KATTEGAT
SJÆLLAND
KØBENHAVN
Frederiksberg
Malmö
Lund
Helsingborg
Helsingør
Landskrona
Halmstad
Falkenberg
Varberg
Ängelholm
Höganäs
Laholm
Hillerød
Roskilde
Køge
Næstved
Slagelse
Korsør
Kalundborg
Holbæk
Ringsted
Vordingborg
Nykøbing
Falster
Lolland
Nakskov
Maribo
Møn
Langeland
Nyborg
Grenaa
Anholt
Hesselø
Læsø
Amager
Trelleborg
Eslöv
Klippan
Hässleholm
Markaryd
Hallandsåsen
Söderåsen
Laholmsbukten
Køge Bugt
Fakse Bugt
Smålandsfarvandet
Store Bælt
Øresund
Kiel, Lübeck, Travemünde
Rostock, Travemünde
Sassnitz
Rønne
Oslo
E6/E20
E20
E47/55
E55
E65
E4
S
D

KATTEGAT
HANÖBU
SJÆLLAND
S
DK
D
Varberg
Falkenberg
Halmstad
Laholmsbukten
Ängelholm
Höganäs
Helsingborg
Helsingør
Hillerød
Frederikssund
Roskilde
KØBENHAVN
Frederiksberg
Amager
Malmö
Lund
Landskrona
Trelleborg
Ystad
Simrishamn
Kristianstad
Hässleholm
Ljungby
Värnamo
Gislaved
Osby
Älmhult
Köge
Køge Bugt
Stevns Klint
Fakse Bugt
Næstved
Møn
Møns Klint
Falster
Nykøbing
Anholt
Hesselø
Kullen
Hallandsåsen
Söderåsen
Linderödsåsen
Bolmen
Bornholmsg
Rønne
Kap Arkona
Wittow
Sassnitz
Świnoujście
Kiel, Lübeck, Travemünde
Rostock, Travemünde
E6/E20
E4
E22
E20
E47/55
E65
91
92
87
84
12°00′
12°30′
13°00′
13°30′
14°00′
14°30′
57°00′
56°30′
56°00′
55°30′
55°00′
1
2
3
4
5
6
A
B
C
D
E
F

ÖLAND
BALTIC SEA
Bornholm
Christiansø
Kalmar
Karlskrona
Karlshamn
Ronneby
Växjö
Nybro
Emmaboda
Lessebo
Tingsryd
Mönsterås
Borgholm
Färjestaden
Mörbylånga
Torsås
Bergkvara
Söderåkra
Brömsebro
Jämjö
Torhamn
Sturkö
Hasslö
Utlängan
Tärnö
Hanö
Hällaryd
Åryd
Listerby
Nättraby
Rödeby
Fridlevstad
Johannishus
Kallinge
Backaryd
Hallabro
Eringsboda
Holmsjö
Nävragöl
Spjutsbygd
Tving
Vissefjärda
Långasjö
Ljungbyholm
Rinkabyholm
Smedby
Trekanten
Lindsdal
Läckeby
Rockneby
Kristvallabrunn
Orrefors
Flerohopp
Boda glasbruk
Eriksmåla
Johansfors
Skruv
Kosta
Åseda
Fagerhult
Fågelfors
Högsby
Ruda
Blomstermåla
Ålem
Timmernabben
Alsterbro
Bäckebo
Pataholm
Påskallavik
Emsfors
Fliseryd
Virserum
Lenhovda
Älghult
Kråksmåla
Alstermo
Fröseke
Måleràs
Hovmantorp
Furuby
Ingelstad
Nöbbele
Linneryd
Väckelsång
Konga
Dångebo
Rävemåla
Gullabo
Påryd
Halltorp
Vassmolösa
Hagby
Tvärskog
Oskar
Örsjö
Böda
Löttorp
Källa
Persnäs
Djupvik
Köpingsvik
Löt
Egby
Bredsätra
Räpplinge
Gärdslösa
Rälla
Långlöt
Lerkaka
Runsten
Algutsrum
Skogsby
Gårdby
Världsarvet Södra Öland
Stenåsa
Alby
Hulterstad
Kastlösa
Segerstad
Degerhamn
Gräsgård
Grönhögen
Ottenby
Näsby
Stora Alvaret
Tejn
Gudhjem
Rø
Østerlars
Klemensker
Nyker
Østermarie
Listed
Svaneke
Årsdale
Rytterknægten
Lobbæk
Aakirkeby
Nexø
Pedersker
Snogebæk
Klaipėda
Gdynia
PL
Łeba
Choczewo
Wicko
Smołdzino
15°00′
15°30′
16°00′
16°30′
17°00′
17°30′
57°00′
56°30′
56°00′
55°30′
55°00′
A
B
C
D
E
F
7
8
9
10
11
12
13
85
93

SKAGERRAK
Jammerbugten
Jomfruland
Tannis Bugt
Ålbæk Bugt
Aalborg Bugt
Limfjorden
VENDSYSSEL
HIMMERLAND
THY
MORS
SALLING
Stavanger
Bergen
Tórshavn,
Seyðisfjörður
Skien
Porsgrunn
Sandefjord
Larvik
Langesund
Kragerø
Risør
Tvedestrand
Arendal
Grimstad
Lillesand
Kristiansand
Kristiansand Dyrepark
Flekkerøy
Mandal
Vennesla
Evje
Bygland
Byglandsfjord
Hirtshals
Hjørring
Frederikshavn
Løkken
Brønderslev
Sæby
Aalborg
Nørresundby
Thisted
Hanstholm
Nykøbing Mors
Hobro
Nordsøen Oceanarium
A
B
C
D
E
F
2
3
4
5
6
7
94
95
86
N
DK
E18
E39
E45
58°30′
58°00′
57°30′
57°00′
8°00′
8°30′
9°00′
9°30′
10°00′
10°30′

9
10
11
12
13
14
96
97
92
87
N
S
A
B
C
D
E
F
VÄNERN
DALBOSJÖN
KATTEGAT
Västergötland
Småland
Fredrikstad
Halden
Strömstad
Tanumshede
Grebbestad
Fjällbacka
Hamburgsund
Bovallstrand
Hunnebostrand
Kungshamn
Smögen
Lysekil
Fiskebäckskil
Grundsund
Ellös
Hällevikstrand
Mollösund
Tjörn
Skärhamn
Marstrand
Kynnefjäll
Dingle
Munkedal
Uddevalla
Vänersborg
Trollhättan
Vargön
Dals Långed
Bengtsfors
Billingsfors
Åmål
Säffle
Mellerud
Dala Rostock
Färgelanda
Stigen
Brålanda
Frändefors
Stenungsund
Ljungskile
Lilla Edet
Kungälv
Göteborg
Mölnlycke
Lerum
Alingsås
Vårgårda
Herrljunga
Borås
Ulricehamn
Kinna
Lindome
Kungsbacka
Varberg
Falkenberg
Halmstad
Lidköping
Skara
Götene
Mariestad
Skövde
Falköping
Tidaholm
Vara
Grästorp
Kållandsö
Läckö slott
Gislaved
Anderstorp
Värnamo
Tranemo
Svenljunga
Hyltebruk
Smålandsstenar
Skeppshult
Halmstad
Anholt
Læsø
Byrum
Nordre Rønner
Hornfiskrøn
Helsingborg, København
Kiel
Grenaa
Store Mosse Nationalpark
Djurö Nationalpark
11°00′
11°30′
12°00′
12°30′
13°00′
13°30′
59°00′
58°30′
58°00′
57°30′
57°00′

VÄNERN
DALBOSJÖN
Hjälmaren
Vättern
Västergötland
Småland
Östergötland
Tiveden Nationalpark
Djurö Nationalpark
Store Mosse Nationalpark
Norra Kvill Nationalpark
Läckö slott
Vadstena slott
Ekenäs slott
Åmål
Säffle
Lidköping
Götene
Skara
Mariestad
Hova
Töreboda
Skövde
Tidaholm
Falköping
Hjo
Karlsborg
Askersund
Laxå
Hallsberg
Örebro
Motala
Vadstena
Mjölby
Linköping
Finspång
Åtvidaberg
Tranås
Gränna
Jönköping
Huskvarna
Nässjö
Eksjö
Vimmerby
Hultsfred
Vetlanda
Sävsjö
Värnamo
Gislaved
Ulricehamn
Borås
Herrljunga
Vara
Alvesta
Växjö
Ljungby
Lessebo
Nybro
Emmaboda
Tingsryd
Markaryd
Vaggeryd
Eneryda
Hjältevad
Kisa
Boxholm
Ödeshög
Habo
Mullsjö
Tranemo
Svenljunga
Hyltebruk
Torup
Simlångsdalen
Kosta
Orrefors
Boda glasbruk
E4
E20
E45
13°00′
13°30′
14°00′
14°30′
15°00′
15°30′
16°00′
59°00′
58°30′
58°00′
57°30′
57°00′
91
97
98
88

99
Södertälje
Tumba
Västerhaninge
Nämdö
Tyresta Nationalpark
Villinge
Fjärdlång
Brevik
Ornö
Katrineholm
Flen
Malmköping
Gnesta
Järna
Mölnbo
Hölö
Sorunda
Mörkö
Ösmo
Muskö
Mysingen
Utö
Nynäshamn
Trosa
Vagnhärad
Västerljung
Nåttarö
Danziger gatt
Järflotta
Torö
Askö
Krabbfjärden
Studsvik
Nyköping
Arnö
Oxelösund
Örsbacken
Kolmårdens djurpark
Kolmården
Bråviken
Krokek
Nävekvarn
Buskhyttan
Norrköping
Östra Husby
Haradshammar
Tingstad
Jonsberg
Gransö
Arkösund
Söderköping
Aspöja
Östra Ryd
Mogata
Skallvik
St Anna
Yxnö
Ringarum
Börrum
Finnö
Yxnerum
Gusum
Yxningen
Valdemarsvik
Gryt
Fångö
Falerum
Hannäs
Tryserum
Vindommen
Stora Ålö
Östra Ed
Edsbruk
Kaggebo
Stora Askö
Överum
Gamleby
Tjust
Loftahammar
Björkö
Almvik
Hasselö
Södra Malmö
Piperskärr
Jenny
Västervik
Gunnebo
Ankarsrum
Hjorted
Hökhallen
Eknö
Getterum
Blankaholm
Stenbo
Misterhult
Kristdala
Fårbo
Figeholm
Björnhult
Århult
Oskarshamn
Blå Jungfrun Nationalpark
Skorpetorp
Påskallavik
Finsjö
Emsfors
Fliseryd
Vållö
Mönsterås
Oknö
Blomstermåla
Ålem
Timmernabben
Byxelkrok
Bödabukten
Böda
Löttorp
Källa
ÖLAND
Persnäs
Djupvik
Löt
Köpingsvik
Borgholm
Egby
Bredsätra
Räpplinge
Rälla
Gärdslösa
Långlöt
Lerkaka
Runsten
Algutsrum
Skogsby
Gårdby
Vassmolösa
Läckeby
Lindsdal
Trekanten
Rockneby
Fredriksskans (Kalmar FF)
Kalmar
Kalmar slott
Gotska Sandön
Gotska Sandön Nationalpark
Ventspils
Fårö
Holmudden
Fårösund
Hall
Fleringe
Bunge
Rute
Hangvar
Lärbro
Hellvi
Furilden
Lummelunda
Stenkyrka
Othem
Tingstäde
Slite
Väskinde
Lokrume
Boge
Visby
Hansestaden Visby
Bro
Fole
Bäl
GOTLAND
Vibble
Västerhejde
Endre
Vallstena
Follingbo
Gothem
Barlingbo
Dalhem
Stenkumla
Roma
Burs
Tofta
Björke
Anga
Gnisvärd
Eskelhem
Kräklingbo
Vänge
Östergarn
Sanda
Väte
Ala
Herrvik
Klintehamn
Klinte
Buttle
Ardre
Gammelgarn
Etelhem
Ljugarn
Fröjel
Garde
Karlsöarna
Ekstа
Stånga
Sproge
Fardhem
När
Hemse
Silte
Rone
Hablingbo
Alva
Ronehamn
Gansviken
Havdhem
Grötlingbo
Näs
Fide
Näsudden
Burgsviken
Burgsvik
Öja
Vamlingbo
Hamra
Sundre
Hoburg
Hoburgen
Gdańsk
89
16°30′
17°00′
17°30′
18°00′
18°30′
19°00′
59°00′
58°30′
58°00′
57°30′
57°00′
8
9
10
11
12
13
14
A
B
C
D
E
F

Bergen
Askøy
Hardangervidda
Hardanger
Folgefonna
Odda
Tyssedal
Eidfjord
Kinsarvik
Lofthus
Norheimsund
Jondal
Rosendal
Tysnesøy
Stord
Bømlo
Leirvik
Halsnøy
Sunnhordland
Haugesund
Karmøy
Utsira
Kopervik
Skudeneshavn
RYFYLKE
Ryfylke
Rennesøy
Finnøy
Ombo
Sauda
Røldal
Haukeligrend
Hovden
Bykleheiane
Bykle
Setesdal
Valle
Rjuven
Stavanger
Sandnes
Jæren
Egersund
Eigerøya
Dalane
Flekkefjord
Hidra
Lista
Farsund
Lyngdal
Mandal
Lindesnes
Kristiansand
Vennesla
Evje
Bygland
Sirdalen
Tonstad
Lysefjorden
Boknafjorden
Hirtshals
E39
E134

Geilo
Rødungen
Tunnhovd
Pålsbufjorden
Tunnhovd-fjorden
Fjellbunutun 1340
Bjørkeflåta
Uvdal
Rødberg
Uvdal Alpinsenter
Synhovd 1438
Sønstevatn
Borgsjåbrotet 1484
Lafsjå
Skrive-eggene 1381
Tinden 1399
Reksjåeggi 1478
Skarfjellet 1485
Tinn
Bakko
Tinnsjø
Mæl
Rjukan
Gaustablikk
Gausta 1883
Vestfjorddalen
Rudsgrendi
Lonin
Vindsjåen
Brattefjell 1541
Tinnoset
Austbø
Åmot
Sauland
Øvrella
Notodden
Mælefjell 1415
Nutheim
Ofte
Morgedal
Seljord
Seljordsvatnet
Lifjell 1288
Brunkeberg
Kviteseid
Bandak
Brokefjell 1074
Vrådal
Vråvatnet
Stor-Roan 1192
Kilen
Strengen
Flåvatnet
Fagerliheii 911
Bergstod
Steane
Nisser
Grova
Ruglefjell 847
Singusdal
Søftestad
Skornetten 883
Fjone
Kronfjell 925
Fyresvatn
Åmli
Sundsli
Nesvatn
Treungen
Tjønnefoss
Kjørull
Heiland
Dansevalheia 825
Dale
Oland
Raudåna
Gjerstad
Vegar
Vegarshei
Åmli
Dølemo
Hovdefjell 524
Hovde
Nelaug
Risdal
Svenes
Nidelva
Nesgrenda
Tvedestrand
Bøylefoss
Våje
Engesland
Langemyr
Froland
Blakstad
Arendal
Eydehavn
Saltrød
Kilsund
Rykene
Fevik
Vik
Grimstad
Beisland
Birkeland
Ogge
Rore
Tveit
Lillesand
Ryen
Brekkestø
Kristiansand Dyrepark
Bliksund
Skålevik
Hirtshals
Flå
Gulsvik
Åmot
Gråfjell 1466
Krøderen
Ørgenvika
Norefjell
Søland
Sølandsfjellet 1045
Eggedøla
Noresund
Sokna
Grønknuten 681
Krøderen
Båsheim
Prestfoss
Rollag
Numedal
Lågen
Gragalten 735
Bjørkeseet
Gerthus
Vikersund
Drolsum
Tyrifjorden
Breidliflaka 702
Åmot
Skotselv
Myrehogget 707
Lampeland
Flesberg
Svene
Bletoppen 1341
Lifjell 820
Follsjå
Hokksund
Vestfossen
Kongsberg
Skollenborg
Heistadmoen
Skrimfjell 871
Eikeren
Sirikjerka 635
Mjøndalen
Drammen
Krokstadelva
Heddalsvatnet
Hvittingfoss
Godal
Bø
Gvarv
Nordagutu
Akkerhaugen
Grorud
Svarstad
Såta 642
Steinsholt
Siljan
Lunde
Ulefoss
Heggland
Norsjø
Skotfoss
Skien
Bøfjell 503
Høydal
Åfoss
Porsgrunn
Nås
Herre
Langangen
Bostrak
Drangedal
Dalen
Hennseid
Sandnes
Brevik
Stathelle
Langesund
Nedre Tokke
Neslandsvatn
Dørdal
Valle
Fossing
Helle
Kil
Vad Foss
Kragerø
Kjølebrønn
Portør
Gjærnes
Jomfruland
Søndeled
Risør
Songe
Helgeroa
Nevlunghavn
Stavern
Larvik
Kvelde
Farris
Verningen
Lauve
Tjøme
Sandefjord
Stokke
Borgheim
Arøysund
Tønsberg
Sem
Andebu
Ramnes
Barkåker
Åsgårstrand
Borre
Horten
Våle
Skalhogg 424
Holmestrand
Bretangen
Tofte
Hof
Eidsfoss
Galleberg
Sande
Svelvik
Berger
Skoger
Røyken
Åros
Sætre
Drøbak
Klokkarstua
Stikkvasskollen 361
Slemmestad
Lierbyen
Asker
Sylling
Holsfjorden
Sandvika
Bærums Verk
Sollihøgda
Telenor Arena (Stabæk Fotball)
Bislett Stadion
OSLO
Nesoddtangen
Oppegård
Tusenfryd
Kolbotn
Siggerud
Langhus
Ski
Kråkstad
Vestby
Hølen
Son
Moss
Dilling
Rygge
Vansjø
Rade
Larkollen
Spetalen
Rolvsøy
Gressvik
Fredrikstad
Slevik
Øyenkilen
Kråkerøy
Revholmen
Skjærhalden
Sarpsborg
Greåker
Grålum
Varteig
Halden
Svinesund
Iddefjorden
Etholmen
Kebal
Strömstad
Skee
Tanumshede
Grebbestad
Fjällbacka
Rabbalshede
Bohus
Hamburgsund
Bovallstrand
Hunnebostrand
Kungshamn
Smögen
Fiskebäck
Grundsund
Hällevikss
Lys
Oslofjorden
Helsingborg, København, Kiel
Frederikshavn
Hønefoss
Ringerike
Hallingby
Ringen
Samsjøberga 527
Tyristrand
Nakkerud
Røyse
Åsa
Sundvollen
Jevnaker
Randsfjorden
Tangen
Lygna
Høgkorset 757
Jaren
Brandbu
Gran
Roa
Oppkuven 704
Harestua
Hakadal
Nittedal
Gullenhaugen 759
Rustad
Hurdalssjøen
Hurdalsverk
Minnesund
Langset
Gullverket
Eidsvoll
Eidsvoll Verk
Råholt
Dal
Maura
Gardermoen
Nannestad
Romerike
Jessheim
Nordkisa
Vormsund
Årnes
Gjerdrum
Ask
Kløfta
Åneby
Skedsmokorset
Lillestrøm
Strømmen
Slattum
Lørenskog
Rånåsfoss
Sorumsand
Fetsund
Aurskog
Elgheia 385
Fosser
Øyeren
Løken
Enebakk
Bråte
Trøgstad
Spydeberg
Askim
Mysen
Hobølvarde 202
Hobøl
Skiptvet
Våler
Bakkestad
Glomma
Sagstua
Storsjøen
Vardehøgda 411
Sperillen
Sørbo
Hallingdalselva
Kjølen
Ås

1
2
3
4
5
6
7
101
B
C
D
95
E
F
91
9°30′
10°00′
10°30′
11°00′
11°30′
12°00′
60°00′
59°30′
59°00′
58°30′
58°00′
Hadeland
Ringerike
Romerike
Numedal
N
OSLO
Sandvika
Asker
Drammen
Hønefoss
Jevnaker
Roa
Gran
Brandbu
Hurdal
Eidsvoll
Jessheim
Gardermoen
Lillestrøm
Strømmen
Lørenskog
Nessodtangen
Kolbotn
Ski
Drøbak
Moss
Horten
Tønsberg
Sandefjord
Larvik
Porsgrunn
Skien
Brevik
Langesund
Kragerø
Risør
Kongsberg
Hokksund
Notodden
Flesberg
Lampeland
Svene
Mjøndalen
Holmestrand
Askim
Mysen
Spydeberg
Sarpsborg
Fredrikstad
Halden
Rakkestad
Ørje
Kongsvinger
Skarnes
Årnes
Rånåsfoss
Fetsund
Bjørkelangen
Aurskog
Strömstad
Tanumshede
Grebbestad
Fjällbacka
Hamburgsund
Kungshamn
Smögen
Lysekil
Uddevalla
Munkedal
Vänersborg
Trollhättan
Lilla Edet
Stenungsund
Tjörn
Åmot
Vikersund
Sokna
Sundvollen
Tyrifjorden
Øyeren
Glomma
Oslofjorden
Jomfruland
Bohuslän
Dalsland
Kynnefjäll
Kroppefjäll
Charlottenberg
Töcksfors
Årjäng
Bengtsfors
Ed
Dals Långed
Färgelanda
Hirtshals
Frederikshavn
Helsingborg, København, Kiel

Hovfjället
Torsby
Sunne
Rottneros
Kil
Karlstad
Skoghall
Hammarön
Forshaga
Deje
Munkfors
Hagfors
Ekshärad
Råda
Uddeholm
Filipstad
Storfors
Kristinehamn
Karlskoga
Degerfors
Nora
Lindesberg
Kopparberg
Ludvika
Smedjebacken
Grängesberg
Hällefors
Grythyttan
Örebro
Kumla
Hallsberg
Askersund
Laxå
Arboga
Köping
Fagersta
Norberg
Avesta
Hedemora
Säter
Mora
Falun
Säffle
Åmål
Grums
Lidköping
Götene
Mariestad
Töreboda
Skövde
Skara
Hjo
Tibro
Karlsborg
Falköping
Vara
Vårgårda
Herrljunga
Motala
Vadstena
Mjölby
Linköping
Finspång
Tranås
Gränna
Åtvidaberg
Kisa
VÄNERN
DALBOSJÖN
Vättern
Bergslagen
Svealand
Kinnekulle
Kållandsö
Läckö slott
Djurö nationalpark
Tiveden nationalpark
Garphyttans nationalpark
Engelsbergs bruk
Narke
Hjälmaren
Glan
Roxen
Boren
Sommen
E18
E20
E45
E16
E4
8
9
10
11
12
13
14
102
103
92
98

Borlänge
Ludvika
Avesta
Hedemora
Fagersta
Sala
Bergslagen
Filipstad
Kristinehamn
Karlskoga
Lindesberg
Nora
Köping
Västerås
Hallstahammar
Enköping
Kungsör
Arboga
Eskilstuna
Strängnäs
Örebro
Hjälmaren
Kumla
Hallsberg
Laxå
Askersund
Katrineholm
Flen
Nyköping
Norrköping
Finspång
Motala
Linköping
Mjölby
Vadstena
Tranås
Åtvidaberg
Söderköping
Mariestad
Hjo
Karlsborg
Vättern
Sommen
Oxelösund
Valdemarsvik
103
102
97
92
S

9
10
11
12
13
14
17°30′
18°00′
18°30′
19°00′
19°30′
20°00′
20°30′
B
C
D
E
F
126
130
93
Södra Kvarken
Märket
Signilskär
Eckerö
Åland
Mariehamn
FIN
Geta
Ödkarby
Näs
Saltvik
Bergö
Finström
Sund
Godby
Kastelholman linna
Finby
Vårdö
Hammarland
Storby
Gölby
Jomala
Lumparn
Torp
Önningby
Lumparland
Lemland
Flaka
Degerby
Föglö
Delet
Teili
Enklinge
Kumlinge
Seglinge
Sottunga
Överö
Kökarsfjärd
Naantali, Turku
Helsinki, Tallinn
Ålands Hav
Paldiski
Riga
Ventspils
Gdańsk
Visby
Gotska Sandön
Gotska Sandön Nationalpark
Fårö
Holmudden
Fleringe
59°30′
59°00′
58°30′
58°00′
60°00′
Uppland
Uppsala
Uppsala domkyrka
Tierp
Skärplinge
Karlholmsbruk
Storfjärden
Gudinge
Böle
Örskär
Norrboda
Söderboda
Åkerby
Strömsberg
Lövstabruk
Hillebola
Forsmark
Johannisfors
Stenskär
Västerbyn
Öregrund
Snesslinge
Norrskedika
Långalma
Östhammar
Sixarby
Andersbo
Tobo
Örbyhus
Upplanda
Dannemora
Österbybruk
Rovsättra
Hökhuvud
Gimo
Harg
Hargshamn
Singöfjärden
Singö
Ellan
Herräng
Sjösäter
Grisslehamn
Tuthka
Norrby
Kvarnsand
Hallstavik
Havsskogen
Husby
Skyttorp
Läby
Kilby
Alunda
Vattholma
Björklinge
Skoby
Ortala
Älmsta
Väddö
Lövstalöt
Bälinge
Storvreta
Gåvsta
Solvalla
Knutby
Skebobruk
Broby
Salnö
Björkö
Söderby-Karl
Edsbro
Almunge
Länna
Roslagen
Marum
Svanberga
Erken
Nysättra
Havssvalget
Rånäs
Norrtälje
Vätö
Gräddö
Gisslingö
Södersvik
Baltora
Kapellskär
Sävja
Alsike
Mörby
Rimbo
Knivsta
Ekoln
Slottsskogen
Österlisa
Spillersboda
Furusund
Kårsta
Bergshamra
Köpmanholm
Oxhalsö
Vidinge
Ängsö Nationalpark
Svartlögafjärden
Eriksund
Sigtuna
Märsta
Eskogen
Rosersberg
Lindholmen
Spersboda
Yxlan
Blidö
Vagnsunda
Svartlöga
Karby
Brottby
Bålsta
Upplands-Väsby
Vallentuna
Brunna
Bro
Tibble
Ljusterö
Husarö
Kungsängen
Sollentuna
Åkersberga
Härjäro
Lennartsnäs
Täby
Svinninge
Tranvik
Möja
Nassafjärden
Resarö
Lökaön
Munsö
Adelsö
Färingsö
Vaxholm
Oskar-Fredriksberg
Vindö
Sollenkroka
Lidingö
Björkö
Stenhamra
STOCKHOLM
Brevik
Kopparmora
Hovgården
Drottningholms slott
Boo
Gustavsberg
Djurö
Södra Björkfjärden
Ekerö
Fisksätra
Stavsnäs
Ekeby
Alta
Saltsjöbaden
Runmarö
Tyresö
Nämdöfjärden
Södertälje
Tumba
Tyresta Nationalpark
Nämdö
Vårsta
Handen
Nykvarn
Pershagen
Uringe
Jordbro
Dalarö
Järna
Västerhaninge
Villinge
Gröddby
Brevik
Mölnbo
Fullbro
Ornö
Fjärdlång
Hölö
Segersäng
Sorunda
Muskö
Mörkö
Ösmo
Mysingen
Utö
Vagnhärad
Stora Vika
Trosa
Nynäshamn
Himmerfjärden
Nåttarö
Danziger gatt
Torö
Järflotta
Askö
Studsvik
Krabbfjärden
E4
E18
E20
E4/E20

1
2
3
4
5
6
7
A
B
C
D
E
F
104
94
Molde
Ålesund
Gossen
Harøya
Otrøy
Nordøyane
Vigra
Sunnmøre
Gurskøy
Stadlandet
Vagsøy
Bremangerlandet
Nordfjord
Sunnfjord
Atløy
Sula
Skorpa
Florø
Førde
Stryn
Hornindal
Hellesylt
Geiranger
Stranda
Sykkylven
Ørsta
Volda
Måløy
Nordfjordeid
Sandane
Skei
Jostedalsbreen
Jostedalsbreen Nasjonalpark
Lustrafjorden
Sogndalsfjøra
Kaupanger
Lærdalsøyri
Balestrand
Vangsnes
Hermansverk
Leikanger
Høyanger
Vadheim
Sognefjorden
Flåm
Aurland
Gudvangen
Nærøyfjorden
Voss
Vangsvatnet
Ulvik
Granvin
Brimnes
Eidfjord
Finse
Haugastøl
Osterfjorden
Nordhordland
Radøy
Holsnøy
Askøy
Bergen
Norheimsund
Hardangervidda
Åndalsnes
Romsdalsfjorden
Rauma
Valldal
Tafjord
Storfjorden
Otta
Grotli
Jostedalen
Luster
Urnes Stavkirke
Hurtigruten
Statthavet
E39
E136
E16
E39/E136
5°00′
5°30′
6°00′
6°30′
7°00′
7°30′
8°00′
62°30′
62°00′
61°30′
61°00′
60°30′

9
10
11
12
13
14
15
105
Sunndalsøra
Sunndalen
Gjøra
Oppdal
Ulsberg
Nerskogen
Berkåk
Fagerhaug
Nåverdal
Yset
Røros
Os
Dalsbygda
Tolga
Glåmos
Aursunden
Brekken
Jensvoll
Vika
Myrmoen
A
Dovrefjell
Dovrefjell Nasjonalpark
Snøhetta
2286
Hjerkinn
Vålåsjø
Drivstua
Driva
Engan
Lora
Lesja
Dombås
Dovre
Folldal
Dalholen
Grimsbu
Moskaret
Tynset
Fåset
Alvdal
Tron
Telneset
Storrøsta
Hodalen
Narbuvoll
Femunden
B
Gudbrandsdalen
Østerdalen
Rondane
Rondane Nasjonalpark
Vågåmo
Vågåvatn
Lom
Randen
Otta
Sjoa
Kvam
Vinstra
Harpefoss
Hundorp
Ringebu
Kvitfjell
Fåvang
Tretten
Atna
Barkald
Hanestad
Koppang
Stai
Evenstad
Rendal
Øvre Rendal
Unset
Elvål
Otnes
Åkerstrømmen
Femundsundet
Engerdal
Snerta
C
102
Jotunheimen
Jotunheimen Nasjonalpark
N
Beitostølen
Bygdin
Gausdal
Vestre Gausdal
Lillehammer
Maihaugen
Øyer
Hafjell (Øyer)
Nordsetter
Sjusjøen
Fåberg
Mjøsa
Gjøvik
Hamar
Brumunddal
Moelv
Biri
Vingrom
Elverum
Rena
Løten
D
Rustad
Vang
Grindaheim
Filefjell Skiheiser
Slidre
Fagernes
Valdres
Aurdal
Bagn
Dokka
Etna
Fluberg
Nordsinni
Hemsedal
Gol
Ål
Hallingdal
Torpo
Hol
Nesbyen
Hadeland
Raufoss
Reinsvoll
Eina
Kolbu
Skreia
Tangen
Espa
Stange
E
Flå
Gulsvik
Bromma
Tunnhovd
Nes
Sørum
Bjoneroa
Horn
Tangen
Lygna
Brandbu
Jaren
Gran
Hurdal
Minnesund
Eidsvoll
Hallingby
Randsfjorden
Hurdalssjøen
Sand
F
95
8°30′
9°00′
9°30′
10°00′
10°30′
11°00′
11°30′
62°30′
62°00′
61°30′
61°00′
60°30′
E6
E16
E136

Røros
Os
Vauldalen
Jensvoll
Glåmos
Alen
Unsholtet
Hodalen
Narbuvoll
Femunden
Femundsmarka Nasjonalpark
Elgå
Røstvollen
Gutulia Nasjonalpark
Femundsenden
Drevsjø
Lillebo
Flötningen
Storbo
Grötholen
Idre
Idre Fjäll
Drosbacken
Engerdalssetra
Engerdal
Snerta
Hylleråsen
Rømonysæter
Engerneset
Granberget
Jordet
Trysil
Nybergsund
Strand
Sandvik
Valmen
Vestby
Gjeveldshaugen
Midtskogberget
Kjemmoen
Rena
Elverum
Løten
Jømna
Solberg
Braskereidfoss
Våler
Holtet
Åsnes
Flisa
Gravberget
Finnskog
Ljordalen
Fulufjällets National Park
Gördalen
Mörkret
Storbäcken
Särna
Heden
Örebäcken
Foskvallen
Fjätervålen
Lillfjäten
Storfjäten
Foskros
Vassbo
Höstsätern
Grundagssätern
Störsätern
Björnliden
Grövelsjön
Töfsingdalens Nationalpark
Hävlingen
Högvålen
Brändåsen
Rannsundet
Käringsjön
Tännäs
Torbygget
Ljusnedal
Funäsdalen
Tänndalen
Fjällnäs
Bruksvallarna
Ramundberget
Mittådalen
Messlingen
Ljungdalen
Skarkdalen
Osvallen
Storsjö
Sårvsjön
Nysätern
Lunnäset
Sätervallen
Västerhållan
Kållberget
Börtnan
Galåbodarna
Torsborg
Arådalen
Tossåsen
Medskogsbygget
Långå
Hede
Husberget
Vemdalen
Hedeviken
Vemdalsskalet
Björnrike
Kölvallen
Skärsjövålen
Rånddalen
Sånfjället Nationalpark
Ortholmen
Härjedalen
Lofsdalen
Glöte
Dravagen
Sörvattnet
Slagavallen
Kölosen
Klutsjön
Linsell
Randsjö
Glissjöberg
Remmet
Mosätt
Överberg
Sveg
Byvallen
Älvros
Ytterberg
Duvberg
Herrö
Härjåsjön
Lillhärdal
Olingdal
Orrmo
Åsen
Kölsvallen
Lövnäsvallen
Ulvsjön
Kräckelbäcken
Myggsjö
Älvho
Unntorp
Bössbod
Ribbåsen
Näckådalen
Klitten
Brunnsberg
Älvdalen
Västermyckeläng
Blyberg
Våmhus
Evertsberg
Oxberg
Orsa
Slättberg
Bonäs
Mora
Färnäs
Nusnäs
Sollerön
Vinäs
Stenis
Gesunda
Mångberg
Siljan
Rullbo
Kattbo
Öje
Landbobyn
Finngruvan
Finnbodarna
Malung
Vallerås
Malungsfors
Gärdås
Lidsälen
Yttermalung
Vansbro
Järna
Nås
Floda
Björbo
Sälen
Tandådalen
Hemfjällstangen
Transtrand
Fiskarheden
Mångsbodarna
Risberg
Tiberget
Hammarsbyn
Lima
Ärnäs
Limedsforsen
Tandö
Venjan
Särnstugan
Rånäs
Nornäs
Sörsjön
Bunkris
Trängslet
Lövnäs
Fulunäs
Grundforsen
Stöa
Östby
Galåsen
Plassen
Flermoen
Rundfloen
Lutnes
Rådelsbråten
Uggelheden
Höljes
Kärrbackstrand
Gjuvberget
Brattmon
Sysslebäck
Vingäng
Bograngen
Kindsjön
Branäs
Likenäs
Transtrand
Backa
Falltorp
Bjurberget
Rotberget
Mamäs
Ambjörby
Lisskogsbrändan
Äppelbo
Opsaheden
Råforsen
Stöllet
Värnäs
Digerberget
Kristinefors
Röjdåfors
Aspe
Brunnberg
Backa
Vakern
Eldforsen
Skansbacken
Uppsälje
Skålö
Sveg
Rätan
Åsarna
Klövsjö
Storhågna
Sångbäcken
Röjan
Böle
Ratansbyn
Nederhögen
Bryngelhögen
Vemhån
Håkansvallen
Knätten
Bäckvallen
Överhogdal
Remmen
Kolsätter
Siksjön
Fågelsjö
Tandsjöborg
Lillhamra
Kvarnberg
Ämådalen
Skattungbyn
Fryksås
Bergkarlås
E45
E16
E16/45
101
106
96
97
N
S
61°00′
61°30′
62°00′
62°30′
60°30′

9
10
11
12
13
14
15
107
A
B
C
D
E
15°30′
16°00′
16°30′
17°00′
17°30′
18°00′
62°30′
62°00′
61°30′
61°00′
60°30′
Mellgård
Nyhem
Rotsjö
Storåsen
Vallsjön
Boda
Västana
Atervänningen
Kramfors
Härnösand
Hucksjöåsen
Gimdalen
Öretjändalen
Stavre
Grötingen
Bräcke
Sösjö
Albacken
Hemsjön
Sörbygden
Ljungå
Järkvissle
Sillre
Klärke
Liden
Skälgården
Slättmon
Bredsjön
Kväcklingen
Vike
Holm
Sunnås
Lagfors
Östloning
Ljustorp
Indal
Östanskär
Viksjö
Nordanå
Uland
Ålandsbro
Brunne
Sunne
Stigsjö
Lillroten
Bondsjö
Gånsvik
Härnön
Solumshamn
Svartvik
Antjärn
Hässjö
Hussjö
Häggdånger
Stavreviken
Bergeforsen
Timrå
Söråker
Tynderö
Åvikebukten
Skeppshamn
Åstholmsudde
Klingerfjärden
Sundsvallsbukten
Bensjö
Västra Stugusjö
Östra Stugusjö
Hemsjöarna
Brehungen
Marktjärn
Getterån
Holmsjön
Leringen
Indalsälven
Nordanede
Hullsjön
Stor-Hullsjön
Navarn
Medelpad
Koberget
Ånge
Tälje
Borgsjö
Parteboda
Erikslund
Fränsta
Grönsta
Viken
Torpshammar
Ljungaverk
Byberget
Alby
Östavall
Krog
Kölsillre
Viskan
Stöde
Kälen
Munkbyn
Västansjö
Nora
Gåltjärn
Kovland
Lillström
Huljen
Nedansjö
Sundsvall
Laggarberg
Bergsåker
Selånger
Hovid
Sundsbruk
Alvik
Tunadal
Alnön
Ankarsvik
Stockvik
Essvik
Juniskär
Skottsund
Njurundabommen
Lörudden
Brämön
Björkön
Skatan
Björköfjärden
Galtström
Julåsen
Råsjö
Lillmörtsjö
Jättensjö
Grundsjön
Hångstaörn
Gransjön
Fanbyklacken
Vigge
Lucksta
Lindsjö
Sörfors
Vattjom
Matfors
Rännö
Svartvik
Kvissleby
Ångom
Öjen
Sörböle
Västanå
Armsjön
Mellansjö
Naggen
Ulvsjön
Västansjö
Stensån
Minne
Fåssjodal
Flor
Kånne
Gassjö
Ramsjö
Valsjön
Geasjön
Skån
Norrbäck
Kölsjön
Långskog
Torringen
Malungen
Hassela
Hassela kyrkby
Ässjö
Årskogen
Knoppe
Ede
Gnarp
Norrfjärden
Sörfjärden
Gran
Sund
Tevansjö
Gåda
Hennan
Storsjön
Finneby
Öjeforsen
Brändbo
Brännås
Björsarv
Alsjö
Furuberg
Hasselasjön
Lennsjö
Älgered
Grängsjö
Jättendal
Hårte
Vitörarna
Mellanfjärden
Jättholmarna
Kårböle
Enskogen
Skålvallen
Backesjön
Sandvik
Ängebo
Västertråsjö
Moviken
Strömbacka
Fönebo
Bergsjö
Storsjön
Högen
Vattrång
Harmånger
Stocka
Strömsbruk
Laforsen
Letsbo
Gunnarsbo
Norra Dellen
Svedjebo
Friggesund
Järnblasten
Björsbo
Vattlång
Ilsbo
Härva
Korskrogen
Tallåsen
Föne
Nore
Ljusdal
Venås
Bjuråker
Norrbo
Hälsjö
Välsta
Rogsta
Bergön
Näsberg
Färila
Hybo
Delsbo
Södra Dellen
Överbyn
Näsviken
Storsand
Bålsön
Karlsfors
Fagerroskölen
Åbo
Rödmyra
Skästra
Järvsöklacken
Svedja
Uppsjö
Sörforsa
Hudiksvall
Idenor
Arnöviken
Kuggören
Hornslandet
Los
Dåasen
Lillskog
Risarven
Järvsö
Nor
Långsjön
Blacksås
Saltvik
Iggesund
Tunaolmen
Mössön
Hölick
Karlsberg
Hamra
Björkberg
Lörstrand
Tevsjön
Stavsätra
Harsa
Sidskogen
Öjung
Öratjärn
Nybyn
Nianfors
Näcksjö
Njutånger
Innerstön
Agön
Stora Öjungen
Orsjön
Simeå
Nordsjö
Stor-Nien
Boda bruk
Enånger
Våtnas
Lobonäs
Håven
Långbo
Fluren
Orbaden
Vallsta
Hälsingland
Bölan
Enhammarsfjärden
Norra Blommaberg
Mattsmyra
Ryggesbro
Långrösten
Galven
Arbrå
Storsjön
Långvinds bruk
Fäbodön
Storejen
Kyan
Röstabo
Galvsjön
Flästa
Lottefors
Växbo
Trönö
Skärså
Prästgrundet
Edsbyn
Roteberg
Knåda
Långhed
Äsbacka
Röste
Växsjön
Bollnäs
Rengsjö
Kungsgården
Svartvik
Humlegärdsstrand
Voxna
Homna
Ovanåker
Viksjöfors
Alfta
Söräng
Freluga
Glössbo
Mo
Stålnäset
Finnshögst
Sörbo
Mossbo
Varpen
Mohed
Söderhamn
Skatön
Mållångsbo
Hertsjö
Segersta
Ackstjära
Söderala
Marmen
Sandarne
Gullberg
Annefors
Flugen
Kilafors
Hanebo
Bergvik
Lynäs
Sandskär
Furudals bruk
Näset
Dalfors
Täningen
Skräddrabo
Hällbo
Sibo
Bergviken
Ljusne
Vallvik
Furudal
Östanvik
Amungen
Svartbo
Rickebo
Skog
Järvsjön
Maråker
Storjungfrun
Oresjön
Halgonberget
Getryggen
Skålsjön
Mållången
Rimsbo
Tönsen
Holmsveden
Stugubacken
Mårakersbotten
Granön
Dalbyn
Norrboda
Gruvberget
Långbo
Älgnäs
Noran
Kalvhararna
Gulleråsen
Finnbacka
Hälsingeskogen
Ödmården
Axmarsbruk
Gäshällan
Gåsholma
Katrineberg
Lingan
Dalstuga
Svabensverk
Mosjön
Lövtjärn
Grönviken
Högbacka
Axmar
Dödmansskär
Boda
Bingsjö
Hedsjön
Mörtebo
Viksjön
Östbjörka
Lamborn
Källsjön
Åmot
Bergby
Totra
Norrsundet
Ljugaren
Dådran
Balungen
Nerde Gärdsjö
Vallsbo
Mo
Hagsta
Rättvik
Kurbergets fab
Rönnbacken
Ockelbo
Hamrångefjärden
Iggön
Katrineholm
Tallås
Jädraås
Kolforsen
Norrtjärn
Trödje
Söderås
Ärtled
Övertänger
Hyn
Storsjön
Jädraån
Brattfors
Eskön
Mårtanberg
Marnäs
Vintjärn
Gammelboning
Hillevik
Vitgrundet
Enviken
Ågsjön
Gästrikland
Medskog
Oslättfors
Testeboån
Oppala
Björke
Utvalnäs
Falun
Linghed
Kungsberg
Kungsfors
Åbyggeby
Bönan
Lövgrund
Rogsjön
Svärdsjö
Svärdsjön
Hille
Leksand
Bjursås
Järbo
Skönvik
Strömsbro
Hagaström
Gävle
Gävlebukten
Sågmyra
Kvarntäkt
Bengtsheden
Lumsheden
Jäderfors
Sveriges Järnvägsmuseum
Furuvik
Insjön
Grycksbo
Tolfan
Hinsen
Högbo
Valbo
Järvsta
Skutskär
Lövstabukten
Bergsgården
Sundborn
Åshammar
Backberg
Sandviken
Forsbacka
Mårtsbo
Gårdskär
Fågelsundet
Hållen
Rexbo
Valshed
Danholn
Korsgården
Falun
Logärden
Hyn
Kungsgården
Storvik
Västerberg
Rörberg
Älvkarleby
Klungsten
Gagnef
Stora Kopparberget
Hofors
Barkhyttan
Storsjön
Hästbo
Älvkarleö
Fagerviken
Örskär
Djurås
Sifferbo
Ornäs
Torsång
Edsken
Tjärnäs
Långnäs
Årsunda
Verkebro
Karlholmsbruk
Gudinge
Djurmo
Båsna
Repbäcken
Fullen
Grycken
Torsåker
Ottnaren
Främlingshem
Hyttön
Storfjärden
Marma
Skärplinge
Böle
Norrboda
Gräsö
Mockfjärd
Borlänge
Framtidsmuseet
Vika
Långshyttan
Gammelstilla
Trösken
Finnböle
Mehedeby
Söderboda
Naglarby
Vikarbyn
Flinsen
Kratte masugn
Bodåsgruvan
Hedesunda
Åkerby
Lövstabruk
Forsmark
Halvarsgårdarna
Husby
Basttallet
Ålbo
Tierp
Johannisfors
Idkerberget
Tuna-Hästberg
Stålbo
Snesslinge
Finnsjön
98
99
E4
E14
E16

1
2
3
4
5
6
7
8
A
B
C
D
E
F
7°00′
7°30′
8°00′
8°30′
9°00′
9°30′
10°00′
65°00′
64°30′
64°00′
63°30′
63°00′
20′
10′
Frohavet
Frøyhavet
Frøyfjorden
Tarva
Frøya
Hitra
Havmyran
345
Smøla
Tustna
Averøya
NORDMØRE
Gossen
Kristiansund
Hurtigruten
Hustadvika
Trondheimsleia
Ramsøyfjorden
Edøyfjorden
Tingvoll
Molde
Bud
Orten
Aukra
Elnesvågen
Tornes
Aureosen
Hjelset
Eide
Kårvåg
Vevang
Bruhagen
Kvalvåg
Reinsvik
Sveggesundet
Hasløya
Mork
Høgset
Torvikbukt
Bøtnfjordsøra
Kleive
Steinløysa
Eidsøra
Eidsvåg
Angvik
Tjelle
Mittet
Sølsnes
Hesjestranda
Nesjegjerde
Seternes
Nauste
Åndalsnes
Rakkum
Ålvund
Kvanne
Svinvik Arboretum
Surnadalsøra
Todalsfjellet
Tingvoll
Aksnes
Hoems
Kvisvik
Øydegarden
Kanestraum
Heggem
Åsskard
Bøverfjord
Harang
Rindal
Sætra
Storås
Meldal
Løkken
Svorkmo
Vormstad
Hoston
Orkanger
Fannrem
Gjølme
Børsa
Buvika
Melhus
Lundamo
Hovin
Støren
Soknedal
Berkåk
Ulsberg
Grindal
Gåsbakken
Korsveggen
Søvassli
Vinjeøra
Todal
Ervik
Renndal
Betna
Halsa
Fjørvikan
Hennset
Aure
Ålmo
Arasvika
Vinsternes
Aukan
Leira
Solskjela
Korsvoll
Rossvoll
Straumen
Austsmøla
Frostadheia
Dyrnes
Nordvika
Veidholmen
Kvenvær
Forsnes
Titran
Norddyrøy
Sula
Svellingen
Hellesvik
Tuvnes
Sistranda
Hammarvika
Flatval
Storhallaren
Kjerringvåg
Hestnes
Straum
Fillan
Sandstad
Knarrlagsund
Selvåg
Hestvika
Kongsvoll
Sunde
Flesvik
Gjengstø
Helland
Heim
Storodden
Vikan
Vihalsen
Fonna
Årvågen
Kyrksæterøra
Krokstadøra
Skorild
Berdal
Åstan
Øyangen
Lensvik
Selbekken
Stadsbygd
Grønningen
Selva
Garten
Munken
Grandefjæra
Brekstad
Uthaug
Austrått
Opphaug
Botngård
Bjugn
Oksvoll
Vallersund
Gjølja
Teksdal
Lysøysund
Selnes
Tårnes
Ratvika
Harsvik
Tørrvika
Harbak
Kiran
Nordskjør
Utro
Roan
Bessaker
Vingsa
Brandsfjorden
Skråfjorden
Åfjord
Eide
Mørrevatnet
Fevåg
Rissa
Reinskloster
Hindrem
Vannvikan
Olsøy
Storvatnet
Flakk
Nidarosdomen
Byneset
Trond
Heim
Flakkfjorden
Orkdalsfjorden
Gulosen
Trondheimsfjorden
Stjørnfjorden
Tarvefjorden
Kråkvågfjorden
Fillfjorden
Hemnfjorden
Rovatnet
Søya
Surna
Follsjøen
Gråsjøen
Orkla
Sunndalsfjorden
Stangvikfjorden
Halsafjorden
Vinjefjorden
Tingvollfjorden
Kvernesfjorden
Hostadvatnet
Ila
Sokna
Gauna
Gjevilvatnet
Gjevilvasskamman
1627
Nerskogen
Storli
Nerdal
Sunndalsøra
Skålten
692
Urfjellet
979
Reinsfjellet
994
Høgfjellet
689
Hjelmen
978
Valsøybotn
Brattset
Drystolan
929
Gråfjellet
1040
Omnsfjellet
847
Todalsfjellet
821
Stabblandet
908
Smisetnebba
1175
Virumkjerringa
1374
Honnstadknyken
1071
Tindfjellet
1167
Rognnebba
1497
Snota
1668
Resfjellet
1162
Ilfjellet
1218
Kjerringheia
540
656
566
609
Øyangen
E39
E6
70
65
64
62
660
662
663
664
665
666
670
680
682
700
701
704
707
708
709
710
713
714
715
716
717
718
721
723
755
100
101
Enmo
Svardal
Økdal
Sandfjellet
Ler

9
10
11
12
13
14
15
16
108
106
102
A
B
C
D
E
F
N
S
BØRGEFJELL NASJONALPARK
GRESSÅMOEN NASJONALPARK
N a m d a l e n
I N N H E R A D
Hurtigruten
Rossvik
Kløsvika
Lande
Sefrivatn
Vennesund
Roytvollen
Holm
Bindalseit
Bindalsfjorden
Majavatn
Øyre Fiplingvatnet
Otervik
Gutuvikfjellet
Kveinsjøen
Helstad
Store Majavatnet
Smalåsen
Hortafjorden
Leka
Skei
Bogen
Terråk
Årset
Årsandøy
Solsem
Blåfjell
Åbjørvatnet
Store Namsvatnet
Fuglstad
Skatollet
Naustbukta
Eiternes
Haltussen
Foldereid
Fuglstadfjellet
Drottendalsfjellet
Bjørnstad
Namsvatn
Nursfjellet
Søre Steinfjellet
Lyngsnes
Austafjord
Ramstadlandet
Drag
Eidshaug
Rødseidet
Årfor
Skjolden
Heinsnes
Namsskogan
Mealhkoe
Vallervatnet
Valøy
Løddingen
Vikna
Rørvik
Ottersøy
Kjøringvassfjellet
Kongsmoen
Brekkvasseiv
Gjersvik
Røyrvik
Ornes
Jååvma
Stor-Blåsjön
Ankarvattnet
Ankarede Kapell
Mittilidén
Bergsnov
Kolvereid
Hofles
Geisnes
Mjøsundvatnet
Storvatnet
Strandval
Salsbruket
Tromsfjellet
Tunnsjø
Røyrvika
Mariafjellet
Trones
Stora Blåsjön
Jormvattnet
Lund
Abelvær
Foldfjorden
Salsvatnet
Øie
Øyevatnet
Salfjella
Gudfjelløya
Tunnsjøen
Furutangvikja
Limingen
Lassemoen
Mellanskogsfjället
Lilljorm
Blåsjöfallet
Fosnesvågen
Hestvik
Faksdal
Seierstad
Aglen
Flått
Skorva
Høylandet
Skarlandsfjellet
Aunfoss
Heimdalshaugen
Skorovatn
Ingulsvatn
Austnes
Storjorm
Jerikklumpen
Kycklingvattnet
Tommervikfjellet
Breksillan
Duna
Utvorda
Skorstad
Vikan
Leirvik
Åsan
Harran
Gartland
Nesåpiggen
Portfjellet
Leirlia
Kveli
Kvarnbergsvattnet
Gäddede
Hamnes
Vemundvik
Overhalla
Skogmo
Sanddøla
Skjellbreid
Kvesjøen
Murumoen
Gussvattnet
Lauvsnes
Statland
Namsos
Spillum
Grong
Nyneset
Vestre Brandsfjellet
Nordli
Eidet
Laksjøen
Sandsjøen
Håkafot
Fjelle
Tøttdal
Hemnafjellet
Geitfjellet
Sandnes
Formofoss
Häggnäset
Fågelsjön
Bangsund
Reinsjøfjellet
Heia
Lura
Kveaune
Jossund
Romstad
Lurudal
Grassåmoen
Sjøåsen
Langnesfjellet
Bangsjøen
Vegset
Agle
Stordselva
Lenglingen
Berglia
Murfjället
Årgård
Finnhuva
Tvärån
Snåsa
Hammer
Namdalseid
Deråsbrenna
Sørli
Jule
Skåle
Snåsavatnet
Imsa
Megardssætra
Langvatnet
Blåfjellshatten
Eidet
Gunnarvattnet
Tørring
Vesterås
Imsdalsfjellet
Austborg
Valsjöbyn
Sprova
Beitstad
Valøy
Brannheiklumpen
Grønningen
Finnvollheia
Malm
Sunnan
Bartnes
Holden
Hollås
Lustad
Gjevsjøen
Mahkene
Stor-Stensjön
Valsjön
Rötviken
Rörvattnet
Steinkjer
Skansen
Storfjellet
Follafoss
Vist
Bodom
Gaulstad
Løysmundhatten
Torrön
Burvattnet
Stuore-Tjåure
Långvattnet
Häggsjövik
Selavatnet
Tua
Beitstadfjorden
Kjerknesvågen
Mære
Sparbu
Veimo
Lågsjön
Mjölkvattsfjället
Korsvattnet
Ansätten
Bakvattnet
Verran
Straumen
Norem
Sakshaug
Leksdalsvatn
Åkran
Sandfjället
Jänsmässholmen
Skärvången
Vangshylla
Helgåa
Verrabotn
Mosvik
Veravatnet
Överäng
Ångsfjärden
Högrun
Akersjön
Meltingvatnet
Verdalsøra
Moen
Skäckerfjällen
Äcklingen
Ytteräng
Frankrike
Kolåsen
Olden
Åkersjön
Levanger
Vuku
Steine
Vaterholmsbru
Anjan
Kallsedet
Juvuln
Finnsäter
Vallrun
Slipra
Buran
Skarfjället
Sundet
Tångeln
Enarsvedjan
Tronvik
Falstad
Skogn
Sandvika
Böle
Sulviken
Rönnöfors
Landögssjön
Sul
Storrensjön
Kallsjön
Lien
Härskallen
Skalstugan
Övre-Konäs
Landön
Frosta
Åsen
Saxvallen
Vassnäs
Gärde
Tångeråsen
Kjølhaugen
Berge
Aggsjön
Feren
Getsjön
Almåsaberget
Långan
Kaxås
Åsenfjorden
Steinvikholmen Slott
Skjelstad
Medstugan
Häggsjön
Vigdenes
Medstugusjön
Husa
Kall
Offerdal
Tulleråsen
Funnsjø
Meråkervollen
Västra Middagsfjället
Tännforsen
Nordhallen
Krok
Åreskutan
Änge
Auran
Stjørdalshalsen
Hell
Hegra
Sona
Kjerringfjellet
Fjergen
Bodsjön
Åre-Duved
Kougsta
Stavre
Nordannälden
Hommelvik
Jonsvatn
Meråker
Brennmo
Koppera
Gevsjön
Ståa
Duved
Åre
Järpbyn
Bleckåsen
Alsen
Nälden
Södra Renssjön
Tångböle
Björnänge
Järpen
Mörsil
Trångsviken
Vaplan
Ytterån
Sonvatna
Skarvan
Storlien
Ånn
Hensjön
Indalsälven
Alsensjön
Mattmar
Hällbacken
Undersåker
Hålland
Ocke
Arvesund
Rödön
Bjørklia
Gilså
Visjövalen
Enafors
Trillevallen
Sällsjö
Brasta
Storsjön
Garberg
Enan
Snasahögarna
Handöl
Ånnsjön
Kosjön
Ottsjö
Hammarnäs
Selbustrand
Selbusjøen
Selbu
Ottsjön
Aumen
Håckrenmagasinet
Böle
Hallen
Norderö
Finnsjøen
Fongen
Vålådalen
Vallbo
Bäck
Marby
Slindvatn
Nea
Sørungen
Västra Bunnerstöten
Handölan
Stor-Anahögen
Hallbodarna
Bydalen
Hosjöbottnarna
Höglekardalen
Kråklivollen
Nesjøen
Vålån
Tuset
Bringen
Tydal
Ås
Øyfjell
Sylarna
Anarisfjällen
Glensjön
Gräftåvallen
Häggsåsen
Månsåsen
Granåsfjellet
Oviksfjällen
Lunndörsfjällen
Dörrsjön
Billsåsen
Kotsøy
Movollen
Glen
Arådalen
Hundshögen
Tossåsen
Hallom
Kövra
Gåre
Aunegrenda
Gaula
Nedalssjøen
Persåsen
Dalå
Helagsfjället
Stugusjøen
Grønfjellet
Kjølifjell
Tågåfjellet
Fora
Storfjellet
Ljungdalen
Torsborg
Galåbodarna
Myrhaug
Ålen
Nyhaugen
Morsetvollen
Unsholtet
Reitan
Riasten
Skarsfjället
Skarkdalen
Osvallen
Storsjö
Storsjön
Flåsjön
Börtnan
Kållberget
Bua
Berghøgda
Mittådalen
Mittån
Bamundberget
Murmoen
Hetenjaure
Gausta
Fiskåvattnet
E6
E14
11°00′
11°30′
12°00′
12°30′
13°00′
13°30′
14°00′
65°00′
64°30′
64°00′
63°30′
63°00′

108
105
102
Børgefjell Nasjonalpark
Gressåmoen Nasjonalpark
Namdalen
Snåsavatnet
Nordherad
Storsjön
Marsfjällen
Skäckerfjällen
Anarisfjällen
Lunndörsfjällen
Oviksfjällen
Kjøsvika
Lande
Toymskardlia
Simskardet
Kvanntli
Majavatn
Smalåsen
Store Majavatnet
Store Namsvatnet
Ljusfjället
Fättjarn
Grönfjället
Fjällfjällen
Rissjön
Grundfors
Fatmomakke
Marsfjället
Klimpfjäll
Lovberg
Saxån
Stornäs
Gryt
Autjoklimpen
Saxnäs
Satsfjället
Kultsjön
Bijelite
Jengegietje
Leka
Skei
Årset
Helstad
Terråk
Fuglstad
Åbjørvatnet
Skatollet
Haltussen
Foldereid
Heinsnes
Årfor
Skjolden
Fuglstadfjellet
Drottendalsfjellet
Bjørnstad
Søre Steinfjellet
Namsvatn
Nursfjellet
Hetenjaure
Raukasjön
Namsskogan
Mealhkoe
Røyrvik
Vallervatnet
Ornes
Jåavma
Stor-Blåsjön
Ankarvattnet
Storjola
Borgafjäll
Båtas
Råfatjårro
Kolvereid
Geisnes
Mjøsundvatnet
Salsbruket
Kongsmoen
Kjøringvassfjellet
Storvatnet
Brekkvasseiv
Gjersvik
Tromsfjellet
Tunnsjø
Røyrvika
Mariafjellet
Limingen
Mittiliden
Ankarede Kapell
Värjaren
Buorkantjakke
Øie
Øyevatnet
Trones
Tunnsjøelva
Gudfjelløya
Tunnsjøen
Furutangvikja
Stora Blåsjön
Sielkentjakke
Lövsjö
Salfjella
Lassemoen
Limingen
Jormvattnet
Lilljorm
Mellanskogsfjället
Bastunäsfjället
Tvärsele
Flått
Høylandet
Skarlandsfjellet
Skorovatn
Ingulsvatn
Austnes
Blåsjöfjället
Storjorm
Skorva
Duna
Leirvik
Aunfoss
Heimdalshaugen
Harran
Åsan
Gartland
Portfjellet
Leirlia
Kveli
Kvarnbergsvattnet
Jerikklumpen
Kycklingvattnet
Sjoutnäset
Inviken
Storsjouten
Storjoudan
Norrsjön
Skogmo
Nesåpiggen
Sanddøla
Skjellbreid
Gäddede
Murumoen
Gussvattnet
Fiskåfjället
Svanselet
Tjärmyrberget
Grong
Søndnes
Nyneset
Vestre Brandsfjellet
Nordli
Kvesjøen
Laksjøen
Eidet
Sandsjøen
Geitfjellet
Formofoss
Reinsjøfjellet
Heia
Lurudal
Lura
Håkafot
Västra Fiskåvattnet
Västra Fagelberget
Häggnäset
Fågelsjön
Sjulsåsen
Bunkfjället
Rotnäset
Risede
Skansnäset
Svedje
Grassåmoen
Kveaune
Hallingsån
Munsfjället
Dunnervattnet
Langnesfjellet
Bangsjøen
Vegset
Hammer
Agle
Snåsa
Stordselva
Finnhuva
Lenglingen
Berglia
Murfjället
Tvärån
Svaningen
Svaningssjön
Lidsjöberg
Fånån
Sørli
Jule
Skåle
Stora Ringsjön
Gubbhögen
Ringvattnet
Gärdnäs
Megardssætra
Imsa
Vesterås
Valøy
Langvatnet
Blåfjellshatten
Imsdalsfjellet
Brannheiklumpen
Fälpfjället
Storfulvurn
Stor-Byvattnet
Eidet
Gunnarvattnet
Austborg
Valsjöbyn
Hillsand
Dragan
Vedjeön
Höstoppen
Alavattnet
Grønningen
Hollås
Lustad
Gjevsjøen
Mahkene
Stor-Stensjön
Valsjön
Skalfjället
Storån
Renån
Gaulstad
Løysmundhatten
Torrön
Burvattnet
Stuore-Tjåure
Rötviken
Rörvattnet
Stora Foskvattnet
Öjarssjön
Renålandet
Öjarn
Bonäset
Skjækra
Lågsjön
Långvattnet
Häggsjövik
Storåbränna
Strand
Åkran
Helgåa
Veravatnet
Mjölksvattsfjället
Korsvattnet
Ansätten
Häggsjön
Tuvattnett
Ålåsen
Hotagen
Flykälen
Henningskälen
Oxsjön
Sandfjället
Bakvattnet
Laxsjö
Bredkälen
Näsviken
Russfjärden
Moen
Äcklingen
Överäng
Ångsfjärden
Jänsmässholmen
Norra Skärvången
Laxviken
Yxskaftkälen
Vaterholmsbru
Anjan
Kolåsen
Ytteräng
Frankrike
Högrun
Skärvången
Akersjön
Mörtsjön
Stångviken
Ottsjön
Hall-Håxåsen
Hallviken
Skarfjellet
Kallsedet
Juvuln
Olden
Finnsäter
Åkersjön
Östra Lövsjön
Föllinge
Storåsen
Gaxsjön
Sandvika
Sundet
Böle
Trången
Vallrun
Gysen
Forsåsen
Gäxsjö
Sikås
Sul
Storrensjøen
Skalstugan
Saxvallen
Kallsjön
Sulviken
Rönnöfors
Enarsvedjan
Landögssjön
Lillholmsjö
Sandviksjön
Klumpen
Fagerdal
Grenås
Övre-Konäs
Vassnäs
Lien
Gravbränna
Knutbränna
Raftsjöhöjden
Kjølhaugen
Medstugan
Äggsjön
Berge
Gärde
Tångeråsen
Getsjön
Landön
Långan
Munkflohögen
Hammerdal
Meråkervollen
Medstugusjön
Häggsjön
Almåsaberget
Lundsjön
Storbränna
Västra Middagsfjället
Kjerringfjellet
Fjergen
Tännforsen
Nordhallen
Huså
Kall
Krok
Kaxås
Offerdal
Änge
Tulleråsen
Loräs
Fyrås
Fyrsjön
Areskutan
Bodsjön
Indalsälven
Kougsta
Stavre
Nordannälden
Husås
Norderåsen
Ollsta
Skyttmon
Koppera
Södra Rensjön
Gevsjön
Sta
Åre-Duved
Åre
Duved
Järpbyn
Bleckåsen
Alsen
Ringsta
Häggenås
Korsmyrbränna
Halasjön
Storlien
Tångböle
Ann
Hensjön
Björnänge
Järpen
Alsensjön
Näldsjön
Nälden
Aspås
Storhogen
Öravattnet
Gilsåsen
Visjövalen
Enafors
Undersåker
Hålland
Mörsil
Mattmar
Trångsviken
Vaplan
Ytterån
Krokom
Lit
Handog
Nyby
Norra Greningen
Indalsälven
Enan
Snasahögarna
Handöl
Ånnsjön
Kosjön
Trillevallen
Ocke
Hällbacken
Arvesund
Rödön
Dvärsätt
Bye
Fjäl
Åsen
Nåverede
Sällsjö
Brasta
Storsjön
Ås
Lugnvik
Kyrkås
Ottsjön
Ottsjö
Hammarnäs
Frösö
Östersund
Brynje
Stugun
Nesjøen
Våldalen
Vallbo
Aumen
Håckrenmagasinet
Böle
Hallen
Norderö
Målsta
Opé
Lillsjöhögen
Västra Bunnerstöten
Stor-Anahögen
Hosjöbottnarna
Hallbodarna
Bydalen
Bäck
Marby
Sunne
Marieby
Grytan
Brunflo
Singsjön
Ismunden
Vålån
Handölan
Höglekardallen
Månsåsen
Orrviken
Ismundsundet
Boggsjö
Rissna
Sylarna
Anarisfjällen
Glensjön
Gräftåvallen
Häggsåsen
Hara
Lockne
Rossbol
Dörrsjön
Oviksfjällen
Myrviken
Oviken
Fåker
Tandsbyn
Hosjö
Nedalssjön
Helagsfjället
Tossåsen
Glen
Arådalen
Hundshögen
Billsåsen
Näs
Locknesjön
Berge
Pilgrimstad
Sundsjö
Hävdsjön
Hallom
Kövra
Hackås
Myssjö
Nåkten
Gällö
Persåsen
Skylnäs
Revsund
Mellgård
Ljungdalen
Dalåsen
Tunvågen
Grötingen
Rogsta
Bodsjö
Björnön
Idsjön
Skarsfjället
Torsborg
Galåbodarna
Skarkdalen
Osvallen
Storsjön
Vigge
Berg
Bodsjöbyn
Stavre
Skanderåsen
Svenstavik
Ösjö
Stor-Hogen
Mittådalen
Ortnan
Brynje
Österskucku
Sandnäset
Hunge
Våle
Grönå
Sösjö
Bräcke

107
10
11
12
13
14
15
16
A
B
C
D
E
F
16°00′
16°30′
17°00′
17°30′
18°00′
18°30′
19°00′
65°00′
64°30′
64°00′
63°30′
63°00′
109
118
122
103
S
Skansnäs
Grannäs
Bäckmark
Sandsele
Gargnäs
Sappetsele
Tjärnberg
Springliden
Södra Gardträsk
Fnöskberget
Järvträsk
Dikanäs
Daikanberg
Ersmark
Storuman
E12
Färingberg
Malåvännäs
Malå
Långträsk
Bergland
Gaskeluokt
Laisbäck
Stor-Boktjön
Gubbträsk
Sandsjön
Juktån
Vindelälven
Grundträsk
Västansjö
Brattåker
Långvattnet
Svärtträsk
Tväråträsk
Slappträsk
Hornträsket
Näsliden
Kalvberget
Daikanvik
Långsjöby
Lankasjön
Vindelgransele
Rentjärn
Malån
Storuman
Stensele
Barsele
Kristineberg
Röka
Gransjö
Lillholmträsk
Umeälven
Lycksaberg
Björksele
Fatsjön
Vojmsjön
Lubbträsket
Gunnarn
Kovallberget
Dobbmanberget
Bjurträsk
Dorris
Storberget
Skarvsjöby
Grundfors
Norsjö
Stor Dainan
Bergsäter
Vormsele
Vormträsk
Arnberg
Heligfjället
Blåviken
Norrbyberg
Åskilje
Södra Tresund
Ruskele
Lidträsket
Ruselè
Pauträsk
Ajaursjön
Risliden
Björnberget
Storsjöleby
Blåviksjön
Medelås
Falträsk
Rusktråsk
Vindelälven
Forsholm
Lövnäs
Siksjönäs
Nästansjö
Kattisavan
Hemmingsmark
Hedmark
Umeälven
Husbondliden
Strömnäs
Rönnäs
Malgomaj
Volgsele
Risträsk
Manjaur
Granträsket
Mark
Stalonäs
Umgransele
Sikselè
Kalvträsk
Bäsksjö
Norrbäck
Mårdsele
Vitberget
Skansholm
Björkberg
Lycksele
Vojmån
Betsele
Holmträsk
Loviden
Latikberg
Järvsjö
Vinliden
Örävan
Ytter-Busjö
Stutvattenberget
Malgovik
Laxbäcken
Vilhelmina
Bäsksele
Norrvik
Fäbodliden
Stora Arasjön
Tuvträsk
Arvån
Åmsele
Svannäs
Karonsbo
Hedlunda
Högland
Dalasjö
Siksjö
Hacksjö
Gransjön
Norrån
Bratten
Ekorrträsk
Statsås
Råberg
Kroksjö
Vägsele
Knaften
Gideåkroken
Tallsjöberget
Granån
Rodingträsk
Meselefors
Idvattnet
Västra Ormsjö
Svartklippen
Stor-Amselberget
Åttonträsk
Gäddträsk
Lillsele
Stryksele
Storsandsjö
Råsele
Västansjö
Hornmyr
Vänjaurbäck
Avanäs
Lövstrand
Östra Ormsjö
Fjällån
Häggås
Torvsjö
Lillögda
Långbäcken
Hällnäs
Ormsjön
Avaträsk
Ångermanälven
Siksjö
Byssträsk
Långsele
Almsele
Nordanås
Granträsk
Mossavattenberget
Vänjaurträsk
Granö
Tegnäset
Brattbäcken
Bellvik
Mårdsjö
Dorotea
Avasjö
Avasjön
Sängsjön
Yxsjö
Lögdån
Flakaträsk
Skarda
Tåsjö
Varpsjö
Storbergkullen
Norrfors
Skurträsk
Laiksjö
Lavsjö
Borgsjö
Vargträsk
Stor-Svartliden
Örträsk
Bjurfors
Lomsjö
Åsele
Tallsjö
Lögda
Lögdasjön
Vargån
Röström
Hoting
Grynberget
Sämsjön
Östernoret
Fårberget
Skivsjön
Flåsjön
Svanabyn
Sörnoret
Vispsjön
Klippen
Fredrika
Stora Sandsjön
Ramsele
Stornäset
Stora Skyrsjön
Bosundet
Grundsjö
Överissjö
Öreström
Storarmsjö
Gafsele
Granåsen
Ångermanbalen
Björksele
Långvattnet
Mesjöliden
Björnlandets Nationalpark
Stor-Holmsjön
Balsjö
Björnholm
Pengfors
Bodumsjön
Solberg
Övra
Hälla
Flärkån
Tegelträsk
Stora Tällvattnet
Vitvattnet
Brännland
Rossön
Hällbymagasinet
Åkerbränna
Stennäs
Gåxsjön
Nagasjön
Bleka
Jansjö
Brattsele
Tjärn
Gammtratten
Remmam
Bredträsk
Karlsbäck
Pengsjö
Hossjön
Käl
Lägsta
Aspele
Mjösjöby
Angnäs
Rudsjön
Fjällsjö
Backe
Vallen
Gulsele
Trattberget
Solberg
Rödvattnet
Studsviken
Brattsbacka
Hörnsjö
Malmsjön
Degersjö
Önskasjön
Kärrsjö
Norrfors
Nyåker
Hörnefors
Betarsjön
Nyåker
Åbosjö
Storsele
Nyliden
Djuptjärn
Trehörningsjö
Torrböle
Silsjönäs
Sil
Sunnersta
Innertällmo
Storbogaren
Lögdeälven
Örsbäck
Vängelälven
Vängel
Långvattnet
Tägsjöberg
Junsele
Kläppsjö
Östby
Pengsjö
Utterån
Gålberget
Mesjön
Hemling
Inre Lemelsjön
Klöse
Ledusjö
Brattfors
Nordsjö
Mo
Eden
Holmsjö
Järvberget
Yttre Lemelsjön
Långviksmon
Flyggsjö
Byviken
Nordankäl
Nässjön
Stora Tägsjön
Salberg
Olofsfors
Flyn
Tarsele
Västanbäck
Myckelgensjö
Hadanberg
Uttersjö
Flärke
Nyland
Lögdeå
Sörviken
Nässjö
Imnäs
Gårelehöjden
Juvanådammet
Saltjäm
Hemsjö
Kubbe
Björna
Svedje
Kroksjö
Rullnäs
Rönnholm
Storsjön
Kilforsen
Grundtjärn
Gissjön
Gideå
Skademark
Lafssjön
Ramsele
Fängsjön
Ångermanland
Skalmsjö
Norrflärke
Björnsjö
Gideälven
Gideå bruk
Ovanmo
Norr-Moflo
Sel
Hällvattnet
Sörflärke
Bureåborg
Bredbyn
Gottne
Västerlandsjö
Västanå
Husån
Degerfjärden
Lungsjön
Adalsliden
Näsåker
Mellansel
Fors
Törsbole
Björkhöjden
Edsele
Aspeå
Holm
Galasjö
Moliden
Klingre
Täftea
Grundsunda
Fanbyn
Ås
Skorped
Mosjö
Bärmsjön
Degersjön
Djupsjö
Nybyn
Västerhus
Gimåt
Arnäsvall
Husum
Boberg
Storkälen
Köttsjön
Meåstrand
Tängstamon
Resele
Basksjön
Nätraån
Billsta
Banafjäl
Ärtrik
Selsjön
Åkvisslan
Grätnäs
Sidensjö
Överhörnäs
Örnsköldsvik
Ulträ
Hälsjön
Berg
Stensjö
Faxälven
Björkån
Björksjön
Brynge
Alfredshem
Bonäset
Skagshamn
Ällön
Skeppsmalen
Hälan
Mo
Forsmo
Ed
Hinnsjön
Drömme
Sunnansjö
Bergom
Norrvåge
Överammer
Färsån
Runaberg
Rådom
Österås
Gålsjö bruk
Åbodarna
Fjällåkern
Bjästa
Sörvåge
Björkå
Sånga
Överlännäs
Stor Degersjön
Ämmnet
Köpmanholmen
Vågön
Strömsnäs
Höglunda
Gesunden
Ragunda
Hammarstrand
Långsele
Forsse
Helgum
Höga Kusten
Graninge
Sollefteå
Österforse
Boteå
Fålasjö
Östmarkum
Gålsjön
Skule
Skuleskogen
Skuleskogens Nationalpark
Norra Ulvön
Trysunda
Älgön
Sicksjön
Ragunda
Lien
Fångsjöbacken
Viksmon
Hällsjö
Tunsjön
Styrnäs
Dal
Almsjönäs
Utanskog
Käxed
Sandviken
Ulvöhamn
Bleckberget
Övsjöbyn
Östsrede
Bispgården
Valla
Malmån
Graningesjön
Västansjö
Sel
Sandslån
Dämsta
Dockstad
Skoved
Sund
Ullångerfjärden
Ullånger
Håsjö
Kälarne
Ansjö
Fors
Björnberget
Västeråsen
Utanede
Björknäset
Östergraninge
Bollstabruk
Dynäs
Sandviken
Köja
Bjärtrå
Grössjö
Salsåker
Mjällom
Norrfällsviken
Omnefjärden
Omne
Nordingrå
Hälle sjö
Rotsjö
Storåsen
Vallsjön
Korsåmon
Västana
Boda
Björnbaljen
Mjövattnet
Kramfors
Frånö
Lunde
Sprängsviken
Lugnvik
Herrskog
Klockestrand
Mädan
Gavik
Allsta
Bönhamn
Barsta
Fällsvikhamnen
Rävsön
Lungsjön
Hemsjön
Sörbygden
Käckelbäcksmon
Återvänningen
Visåsen
Ramvik
Högsjö
Hornön
Nordvik
Lövvik
Berghamn
Storön
Ljungå
Sillre
Klärke
Gråssjö
Viksjö
Nordanå
Laxsjön
Slättmon
Veda
Vålånger
Hemsö
Botsle
Hemsön
E45
E4
E12
90
92
87
86
323
331
335
344
345
346
348
352
353
360
363
365
370

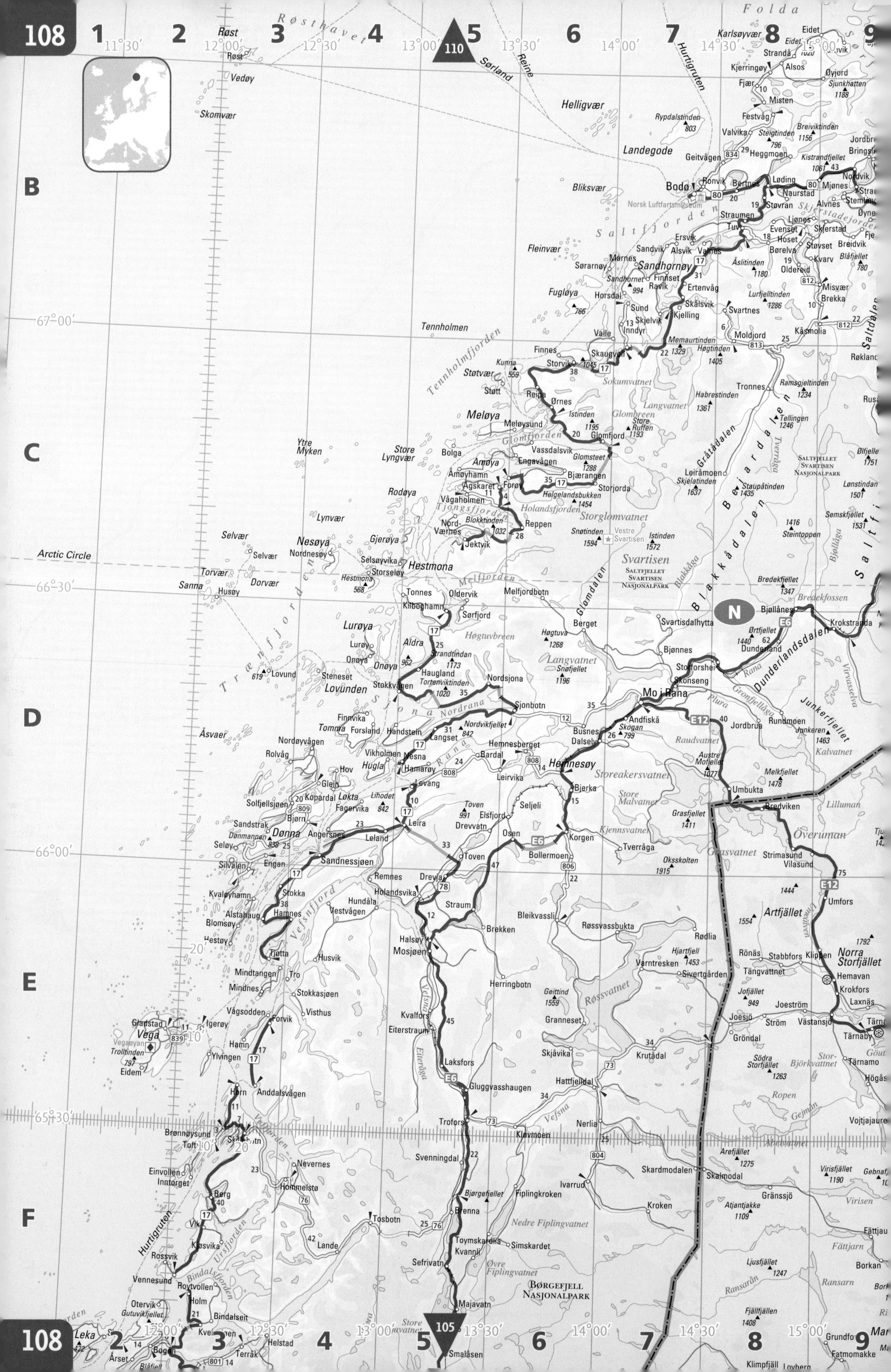
110
105
1
2
3
4
5
6
7
8
9
B
C
D
E
F
11°30′
12°00′
12°30′
13°00′
13°30′
14°00′
14°30′
15°00′
67°00′
66°30′
66°00′
65°30′
Arctic Circle
Folda
Røsthavet
Sørland
Reine
Hurtigruten
Røst
Vedøy
Skomvær
Helligvær
Landegode
Bliksvær
Bodø
Norsk Luftfartsmuseum
Rønvik
Bertnes
Løding
Nordvik
Mjønes
Naurstad
Støvran
Straumen
Tuv
Saltfjorden
Skjerstadfjorden
Karlsøyvær
Strandå
Eidet
Alsos
Øyjord
Kjerringøy
Fjær
Misten
Festvåg
Valvika
Geitvågen
Heggmoen
Rypdalstinden
803
Steigtinden
796
Breiviktinden
1156
Kistrandfjellet
1061
Sjunkhatten
1188
Fleinvær
Sørarnøy
Marnes
Sandvik
Alsvik
Ervik
Valnes
Sandhornøy
Sandhornet
994
Finnset
Ravik
Ertenvåg
Horsdal
Sund
Skålsvik
Skjelvik
Kjelling
Inndyr
Fugløya
766
Tennholmen
Tennholmfjorden
Valle
Finnes
Storvik
Skaugvoll
Memaurtinden
1329
Høgtinden
1405
Moldjord
Kåsmolia
Svartnes
Brekka
Misvær
Lurfjelltinden
1286
Åslitinden
1180
Oldereid
Børelva
Hoset
Evenset
Ljønes
Skjerstad
Støvset
Breidvik
Kvarv
Bláfjellet
780
Saltdalen
Røkland
Kunna
559
Støtvær
Støtt
Reipå
Ørnes
Sokumvatnet
Langvatnet
Glombreen
Istinden
1195
Store Ruffen
1193
Glomfjord
Meløysund
Meløya
Glomfjorden
Tronnes
Ramsgjeltinden
1234
Habrestinden
1361
Tellingen
1246
Ytre Myken
Store Lyngvær
Bolga
Vassdalsvik
Amøya
Engavågen
Glomsteet
1288
Bjærangen
Amøyhamn
Agskaret
Forøy
Storjorda
Vågaholmen
Helgelandsbukken
1454
Rodøya
Tjongsfjorden
Holandsfjorden
Storglomvatnet
Blokktinden
1032
Reppen
Nord-Værnes
Jektvik
Snøtinden
1594
Vestre Svartisen
Istinden
1572
Lynvær
Selvær
Nesøya
Nordnesøy
Gjerøya
Selsøyvika
Storseløy
Hestmona
568
Torvær
Dorvær
Sanna
Husøy
Melfjorden
Melfjordbotn
Svartisen
SALTFJELLET SVARTISEN NASJONALPARK
Leiråmoen
Gråtådalen
Skjelatinden
1637
Staupåtinden
1435
Beiardalen
Tverråga
Blakkådalen
1416
Steintoppen
Bjøllåga
Bredekfjellet
1347
Bredekfossen
Ølfjelle
1751
Lønstindan
1501
Semskfjellet
1531
Tonnes
Oldervik
Kilboghamn
Sørfjord
Glomdalen
Berget
Svartisdalhytta
Bjøllånes
Krokstranda
Ørtfjellet
1440
Dunderland
Dunderlandsdalen
Lurøya
Lurøy
Onøya
Aldra
962
Strandtinden
1173
Høgtuvbreen
Høgtuva
1268
Langvatnet
Snøfjellet
1196
Bjønnes
Storforshei
Skonseng
Trænfjorden
Lovund
619
Stenese
Lovunden
Haugland
Stokkvågen
Tortenviktinden
1020
Nordsjona
Sjona
Nordrana
Sjonbotn
Mo i Rana
Andfiskå
Skogan
799
Busnes
Dalsely
Rana
Gronfjelldåga
Plura
Jordbrua
Rundmoen
Junkerfjellet
Junkeren
1463
Kalvatnet
Virvasselva
Åsvaer
Finnvika
Tomma
Forsland
Handstein
Langset
Nordvikfjellet
842
Nordøyvågen
Rolvåg
Vikholmen
Nesna
Hugla
Hamarøy
Hov
Hemnesberget
Bardal
Leirvika
Hemnesøy
Storeakersvatnet
Raudvatnet
Austre Mofjellet
1077
Umbukta
Melkfjellet
1478
Glein
Solfjellsjøen
Kopardal
Løkta
Lihodet
842
Fagervika
Løvang
Store Malvatnet
Bjerka
Seljeli
Bredviken
Lilluman
Sandstrak
Dønnamannen
858
Dønna
Bjørn
Angersnes
Leland
Leira
Toven
991
Elsfjord
Drevvatn
Osen
Korgen
Kjennsvatnet
Grasfjellet
1411
Överuman
Seløy
Silvalen
Engan
Sandnessjøen
Toven
Bollermoen
Tverråga
Oksskolten
1915
Grasvatnet
Strimasund
Vilasund
Remnes
Drevja
Holandsvika
Hundåla
Vestvågen
Straum
Kvaløyhamn
Stokka
Alstahaug
Hamnes
Blomsøy
Hestøy
Vefsnfjord
Brekken
Bleikvassli
Røssvassbukta
Rødlia
Artfjället
1554
1444
Umfors
1792
Tjøtta
Halsøy
Mosjøen
Husvik
Hjartfjell
1453
Varntresken
Sivertgården
Rönäs
Stabbfors
Klippen
Norra Storfjället
Tängvattnet
Hemavan
Krokfors
Mindtangen
Tro
Mindnes
Herringbotn
Gettind
1559
Røssvatnet
Jofjället
949
Stokkasjøen
Vågsodden
Forvik
Visthus
Kvalfors
Eiterstraum
Vefsna
Granneset
Joesjö
Joeström
Laxnäs
Gladstad
Vega
Vegaøyan
Trolltinden
797
Eidem
Igerøy
Hamn
Ylvingen
Skjåvika
Krutådal
Ström
Västansjö
Gröndal
Tärnaby
Södra Storfjället
1263
Stor-Björkvattnet
Tärnamo
Högås
Eiteråga
Laksfors
Hattfjelldal
Ropen
Horn
Anddalsvågen
Gluggvasshaugen
Gejmån
Trofors
Nerlia
Klovmoen
Vojtjajaure
Brønnøysund
Toft
Skarsbotn
Velfjorden
Svenningdal
Arefjället
1275
Nevernes
Skardmodalen
Skalmodal
Virisfjället
1190
Einvollen
Inntorget
Hommelstø
Ivarrud
Gränssjö
Berg
Bjørgefjellet
Fiplingkroken
Kroken
Atjantjakke
1109
Virisen
Vik
Tosbotn
Brenna
Nedre Fiplingvatnet
Fättjau
Hurtigruten
Kløsvika
Ursfjorden
Lande
Toymskardet
Kvannli
Simskardet
Fättjarn
Rossvik
Sefrivatn
Øvre Fiplingvatnet
Ljusfjället
1247
Borkan
Vennesund
Bindalsfjorden
Roytvollen
Holm
BØRGEFJELL NASJONALPARK
Ransarån
Ransarn
Otervik
Gutuvikfjellet
Bindalseit
Majavatn
Fjällfjällen
1408
Leka
422
Kveingen
Store Majavatnet
Grundfors
Årset
Bogen
Terråk
Helstad
Smalåsen
Fatmomakke
Bláfjell
Klimpfjäll
Lovbern
E6
E12
17
12
78
76
73
34
25
804
806
808
809
812
813
834
839
801
80
N

10
11
12
13
14
15
16
17
16°00′
16°30′
17°00′
17°30′
18°00′
18°30′
19°00′
111
Horndal
Korken 1190
Gaskacokka 1512
Sommarset
Kalvik
Langvatnet
Kvarv
Kuoutelistjåkkå 1327
RAGO NASJONALPARK
Litlverivatnet
E6
Sildasjiegna 1128
Straumen
Gieddoavejiekna 1153
Sisovatnet
Blåmannen 1571
Øvrevatnet
Blåmannsisen
1664
Tverråmo
Hellarmo
830
Kokedaltinden 1707
Sulitjelma
Loamejavre
Suliskongen 1907
Sulitjelmabreen
Fagerli
Jakobsbakken
Skuortačohkka 1063
Vassavarre 1261
Storfjellet 1187
Nuort Saulo 1773
Balvatnet
Evenesdal
Årjep Saulo 1715
Ikesjaure
Aivotjåkkå 1427
Junkerdal
Tausafjellet 1709
24
77
dalen
95
Merkenes
Sieldutjåkkå
Tjaktjaure
Straitastjåkkå 1569
Lillviken
Norra Fierras 1606
Södra Fierras 1600
76
Sädvajaure
Sädvaluspen
PADJELANTA NATIONALPARK
Vastenjaure
Kutjaure
Vuojatädno
Akka 2015
Kisuris 1664
Allak 1348
Virihaure
Alatjåkkå 1572
Jeknaffo 1836
Rávvejaure
Tsäkkok 1565
Vaimok
Vuopmekietjtjåkkå 1436
Staika 1799
Pieskehaure
Mavasjaure
Kattsaj 1406
Kaskaure
Kaisetjåkkå 1627
1386
Bartaure
Barturte
Tjidtjakgaise 1587
Riebnes
Vuoktan 1008
Riebneskaise 1136
Tsatsa 1852
Tarrekaise 1828
Riepentjåkkå 1552
Kuoddujaure
Skanatjåkkå 1767
Sarektjåkkå 2090
Sarek 1217
Akkatjåkkå 1974
Äpar 1900
Skárki 1842
SAREKS NATIONALPARK
1934
Pårte 2005
Vaikantjåkkå 1308
Rapaälven
Kvikkjokk
Kassavare 957
Årrenjarka
Njavve
Saggat
Peuraure
Kaisatj 1046
Tjeggelvas
Stenudden
Skierfajaure
Rappen
Övernäs
Riebnesluspen
Labbas
Sundnäs
Lövnäs 825
Jäkkvik
PIELJEKAISE NATIONALPARK
Pieljekaise 1133
95
Laisälven
Tsangatjåkkå 1641
Svaipa 1431
Tjålmejaure
Adolfsström
Gauto
Hällbacken
Jutis
Hornavan
S
Aivotjåkkå 1365
Räker 1381
63
Laisvall
Laisvalls by
Niepsurt 912
Båtsjaur
Aisjaure
Akkelis 779
Vindelälven
Dellikälven
Slierogaise 1612
1133
Björkfjället
Racksund
Arjeplog
Fluka
Laisan
Hällvik
Galtis-buouda 800
Kakel
Stensund
Svannäs
Ammarnäs
Tärnasjön
704
Uljabuouda 780
Laisälven
Kurrokvejk
Uddjaure
Äivisåive 1249
363
Suttsknösen 909
Innervik
Maskaur
Myrås
Ånge
Giertsjaure
Djupfors
Kraddsele
Björkheden
Varåive 856
Bergnäs
Guvertfjället
Hemfjäll
Hällnäs
90
Kronlund
Mellanström
Nyhem
Skansnäs
Ängonåive 1052
Norra Fjällnäs
Stångfjället 1102
Överst-Juktan
Juksjaur
Boksjön
Sjuktevuoletjakke 1035
Storvindeln
Grannäs
Granselet
Nalovardo 770
Ryivegaise 1410
Övre Boksjön
Storskog
Yttervik
Bränaberg
Nedre Boksjön 1128
Fjällsjönäs
Fjosoken
Lars-Ersblaiken 858
Forsnäs
Laisheden
Örnäsudden
363
Lösträsket
Danasjö
Järvsjön
Ajaure
E12
55
Ajaureforsen
Jiltjaur
Sörberget 407
Sorsele
Forsmark
Nordanäs
Umnäs
Gardsjönäs
Slussfors
Forsbacken
Akkan
Abborrberg
Flakaträsk
Stensund
Olsberget 717
363
Gardfjället 1308
Gardsjöbäcken
Storjuktan
Nedre Saxnäs
30
Kanan
Gransjön
Umeälven
Ankarsund
Matsdal
730
Grönfjället 1375
Skansnäs
Grannäs
Strömsund
70
Bäckmark
Lillblaiken 789
Harrvik
Ullisjaur
Stornäs
Kittelfjäll
Dikanäs
Daikanberg
Långbäck
Ersmark
E12
Gaskeluokt
Storuman
Bergland
Laisbäck
Krutsjön
Västansjö
Långvattnet
Girisjön
Ajaure
Juobmotjåkkå 1160
Vietas
Stora Sjöfallet
Satihaure
Pietsaure
Kuotektjåkkå 1515
Njallatjåkkå 1141
Langas
Sitojaure
Laponia
Laitaure
Tjaktjajaure
Kabla 1188
Kiblos 795
Harrejaure
Tjåmotis
Njavve
Harrevarto 949
Vuoskonjaure
Maivesjaure
Karatj
Karats
Arvespakte 965
Arvesjaure
Jarre 931
Luvos
Piertinjaure
Akapuouta 812
Tjavelkjaure
Vuolvojaure
Bergviken
Bergnäsviken
Gallabuouda 783
Hällnäs
Gittun
Bårgå 856
Båtsa
Eggelats
Forsnäs
Stor-Stäkke 787
Piteälven
Jäknajaure
Abraur
Gublijaure
Abraur
Radnejaur
Östansjö
Jerfojaur
Luleb 783
85
Bellunåive 673
Långviken
Fälloheden
Nordanäs
Tallås
Kallön
Östra Mullejaure
Tjäkkjokk
Dvärjan
Bergnäsudden
Tjipko 741
Öv Långträsk
95
Gargaure
Gargovare 669
Strömholm
Storavan
Gullön
Avaviken
Naustajaure
Slagnäs
82
E45
Månsträsk
Buresjön
Ledvattsfjällen 733
Skellefteälven
Kåtaliden
Ledvattsfors
Nya Bastuselet
Aha
Gränsgård
Abmoträsket
Bockträsk
Ljungby
Verboberget 656
Abmoberget 667
Högbränna
Västra Verbosjön
Södra Johannisberg
Hundberg
Blattniksele
E45
Gargnäs
24
Sandsele
363
Sappetsele
Sappetavan
Käringberg
Sandsjönäs
Sandberget 552
Råstrand
Sandsjön
Holmsjö
370
Fnöskberget 620
34
Norra Malånäs
Malåvännäs
Vindelälven
Juktån
Stor-Boktjon 566
44
Gubbträsk
Tväråträsk
Slappträsk
Bjärnotjåkkå 1007
Nu
Sjaunjaätno
Kussåive 814
Juovvatjåkka 857
Saivatuottar 898
Karmas
B
Kaltesvare 853
Tjuolma 995
Stora Lulevatten
Ålloluokta
Appakis 784
Luspebryggan
67°00′
590
Nautijaur
Naustajåkkå
Tapmuk 661
Björkholmen
Randijaur
C
116
Randijaure
580
Pielnejaure
Purkijaur
Tjalmejaure
Sarmekåbbå 552
66°30′
Tårrajaur
Majtum
Naustajaure
D
Palja 697
Varto 682
Kuollejaure
Varjisån
Lulep 630
Varjisträsk
Trollforsen
Norrstrand
66°00′
Åberget
Malmesjaure
Åsen
Suddesjaur
118
Harrejaurelide 647
Tjappsåive
Strittjomvare
E
Auktsjaur
Västra Kikkejaure
44
Rönnberg
E45
Akkavare
Bäcklund
Deppis
95
Arvidsjaur
94
Stenträsket
95
Storberg
65°30′
Guorbabuouda
Aspliden
Abborrträsk
Mausjaure
Hedberg
Krutbergen 631
Bäcknäs
Grundträsk
Björkland
Adak
Kokträsk
Baktsjaur
24
Rönnliden
Utterliden
F
Tjärnberg
Springliden
Västra Lainejaure
Storliden 507
Södra Sandträsk
Järvträsk
Malå
Långträsk
Skellefteälven
Grundträsk
107
15°30′
16°00′
16°30′
17°00′
17°30′
18°00′
18°30′
19°00′
10
11
12
13
14
15
16
35
43

1
2
3
4
5
6
7
8
9
A
B
C
D
E
11°30′
12°00′
12°30′
13°00′
13°30′
14°00′
14°30′
15°00′
69°30′
69°00′
68°30′
20′
10′
68°00′
67°30′
Vesterålen
Norskehavet
Lofoten
Vesterålsfjorden
Vestfjorden
Folda
Røsthavet
Moskenestraumen
Napstraumen
Hurtigruten
Langøya
Skogsøy
Hadseløy
Austvågøy
Vestvågøy
Moskenesøy
Værøy
Røst
Engeløya
Store Molla
Lille Molla
Skrova
Litløy Fyr
Langenes
Nyksund
Vottestad 671
Strengelvåg
Gisløy
Myre
Sommarøy
Øksnes
Alsvåg
Hjellsand
Sminnes
Steinland
Snøkolla 760
Holm
Bremnes
Hovden
Utskor
Nykvåg
Skoltenes
Storvik
Neverness
Kråkberget
Rugge
Frøskeland
Malnes
Kjeipen 691
Kjerringvik
Straume
Søberg
Fore
Klakksjorda
Straumfjord
Sortland
Guvåg
Eidsfjord
Uvåg
Straumsnes
Hansatind 742
Jerstad
Kleiva
Bø
Steine
Sandes
Bitterstad
Breidvik
Stokmarknes
Hadsel
Ånstad
Melbu
Hennes
Kalljord
Helgenes
Lonkan
Fiskebøl
Strona 907
Hanøy
Myrland
Sløvra
Kongselva
Svartsundtindan 1054
Raften
Straumnes
Laukvik
Morrfjord
Grunnførfjord
Laupstad
Higravstind 1161
Tennstrand
Kvalnes
Brenna
Digermulen
Flovika
Eggum
Nesje
Haveren 811
Vik
Gimsøy
Eidet
Vestpollen
Slåttholmen
Holand
Rundfjellet 569
Unstad
Bostad
Alstad
Smødvik
Haugen
Sundklakk
Sydalen
Kleppstad
Slettjellet 763
Himmel 934
Utakleiv
Liland
Rørvik
Svolvær
Kabelvåg
Våje
Valberg
Kalle
Myrland
Vikten
Napp
Møkkevik
Henningsvær
Sund
Lekoes
Stamsund
Gravdal
Ure
Mortsund
Ballstad
Sand
Krystad
Ramberg
Selfjord
Finnbyen
Mjølnarodden
Sund
Nusfjord
Nesland
Hermansdaltinden 1034
Hamnøy
Reine
Sørvågen
Å
Lofotodden
Mosken
Nordland
Nordlandsnubben 456
Sørland
Bodø
Helligvær
Buvåg
Vagsfjellet 953
Skutvik
Lundøya
Mjelde
Steigen
Grønning
Alstad
Bogøy
Holkestad
Kvalnes
Nordskot
Hestdaltuva 857
Hatten 1031
Lund
Saursfjord
Myklebostad
Botn
Løiranger
Nordfold
Kråktinden 1048
Breidvik
Stamsvik
Laukvik
Muletinden 1037
Karlsøyvær
Eidet
Eidetinden 1020
Tårnvik
Bjørnsvikfjellet 955
Strandå
Alsos
Kjerringøy
Fjær
Misten
Røsvik
Ånsvik
E10
820
821
816
815
818
835
82
822
108

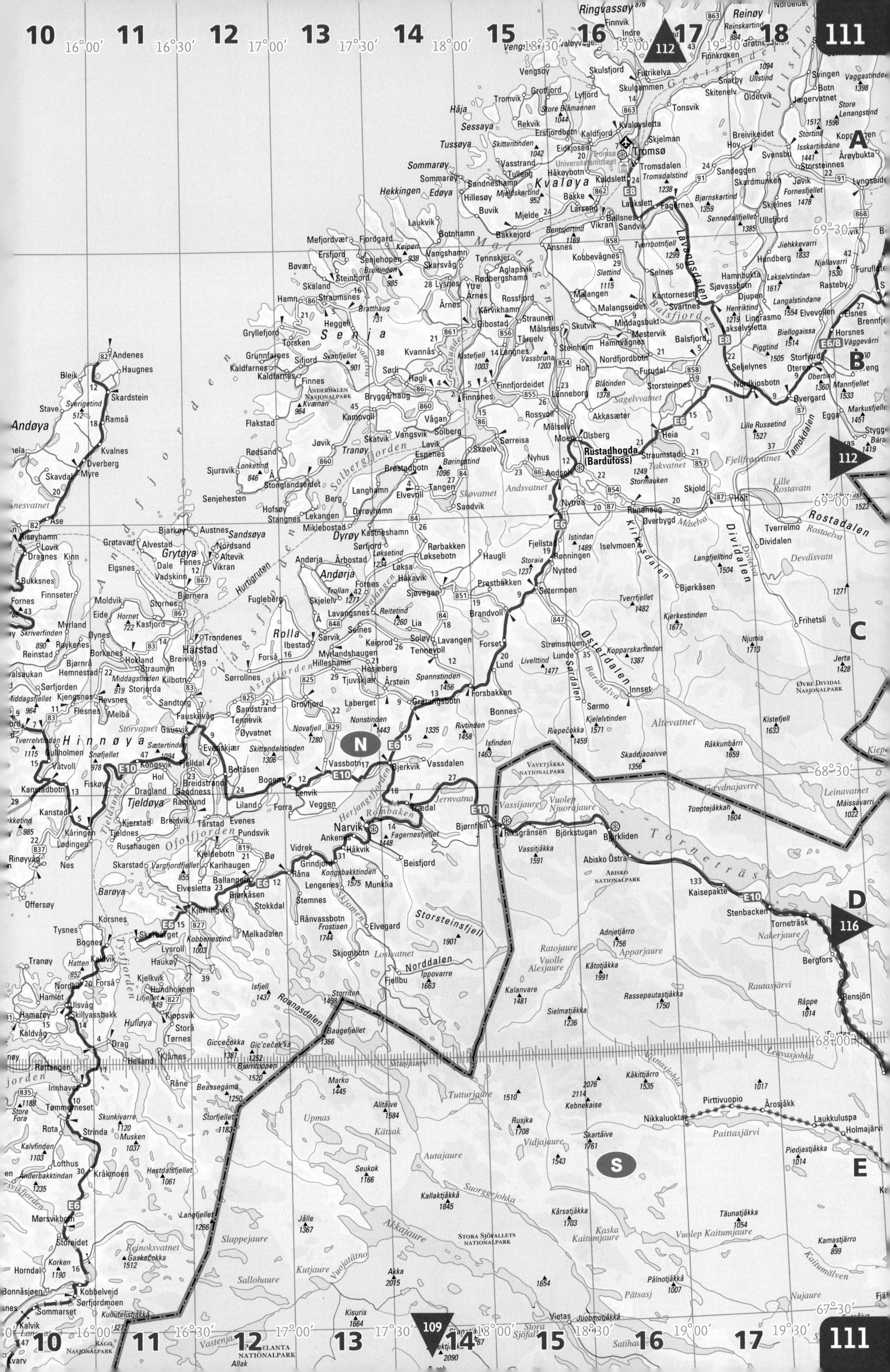
10
11
12
13
14
15
16
17
18
16°00′
16°30′
17°00′
17°30′
18°00′
18°30′
19°00′
19°30′
112
A
B
C
D
E
69°30′
69°00′
68°30′
68°00′
67°30′
Ringvassøy
Reinøy
Finnvik
Vengsøy
Skulsfjord
Futrikelva
Skulgammen
Tonsvik
Tromvik
Grøtfjord
Lyfjord
Håja
Sessaya
Rekvik
Store Blåmannen
1044
Ersfjordbotn
Kaldfjord
Kvaløysletta
Tussøya
Skittentinden
1042
Eidkjosen
Tromsø
Skjelman
Universitetsmuseet
Sommarøy
Vasstrand
Tulleng
Håkøybotn
Kaldslett
Tromsdalen
Tromsdalstind
Hekkingen
Edøya
Sandneshamn
Hillesøy
Kvaløya
Mjelde
Bakke
Larseng
Buvik
Bakkejord
Ballsnes
Sandvik
Vikran
Laukslett
Fagernes
Lavangsdalen
Laukvik
Botnhamn
Mefjordvær
Fjordgard
Keipen
Ersfjord
Senjehopen
Vangshamn
Skarsvåg
Bøvær
Steinfjord
Breitinden
985
Skaland
Lysnes
Ytre Årnes
Tennskjer
Aglapsvik
Rødbergshamn
Malangen
Kobbevågnes
Selnes
Hamn
Straumsnes
Heggeli
Bratthaug
731
Årnes
Rossfjord
Kårvikhamn
Gibostad
Strauen
Målsnes
Skutvik
Malangseidet
Middagsbukt
Mestervik
Balsfjorden
Balsfjord
Gryllefjord
Torsken
Senja
Tårnelv
Steinheim
Hamnvågnes
Nordfjordbotn
Furudal
Storsteinnes
Nordkjosbotn
Andenes
Haugnes
Grunnfarnes
Kaldfarnes
Sifjord
Svanfjellet
901
Kvannås
Kistefjell
1003
Langnes
Vassbruna
1203
Holt
Finnes
Sørli
Høgli
Finnsnes
Finnfjordeidet
Lenneborg
Blåtinden
1378
Sagelvvatnet
Bleik
Skardstein
Ånderdalen Nasjonalpark
Kvænan
964
Bryggerhaug
Rossvoll
Akkasæter
Andøya
Stave
Sverigetind
512
Ramså
Flakstad
Kampvoll
Vågan
Solberg
Målselv
Olsberg
Moen
Rustadhogda (Bardufoss)
Heia
Kvalnes
Dverberg
Myre
Skatvik
Vangsvik
Tranøy
Rødsand
Jøvik
Lavik
Espenes
Skoelv
Sørreisa
Straumstad
Takvatnet
Skavdal
Sjursvik
Lonketind
846
Stonglandseidet
Solbergfjorden
Brøstadbotn
Tangen
Børingstind
1096
Andsely
Andsvatnet
Nyhus
Fjellfrøsvatnet
Stormauken
Skjold
Holt
Lille Rostavatn
Senjehesten
Langhamn
Elvevoll
Skøvatnet
Sandvik
Nytrøa
Rundhaug
Øverbygd
Måselva
Dividalen
Rostadalen
Hofsøy
Stangnes
Berg
Lekangen
Dyrøyhamn
Miklebostad
Åse
Bjarkøy
Austnes
Sandsøya
Dyrøy
Kastneshamn
Rørbakken
Løksebotn
Haugli
Fjellstad
Istindan
1489
Iselvmoen
Kirkesdalen
Tverrelmo
Dividalen
Devdisvatn
Andørja
Årbostad
Grøtavær
Alvestad
Grytøya
Nordsand
Altevik
Vikran
Sørfjord
Løksetind
1234
Storaia
1237
Rønningen
Nysted
Løvik
Dragnes
Kinn
Elgsnes
Dale
Vadskinn
Fenes
Løksa
Håkavik
Langfjelltind
1504
Bjørkåsen
Bukksnes
Finnseter
Bjørnera
Hurtigruten
Fugleberg
Fornes
Trollan
Sjøvegan
Prestbakken
Setermoen
Moldvik
Stornes
Skjelelv
Lavangsnes
Reitetind
1260
Lia
Brandvoll
Tverrfjellet
1482
Fornes
Eide
Hornet
722
Kasfjord
Rolla
Sørvik
Ibestad
Keiprod
Salangen
Lavangen
Kjerkestinden
1677
Frihetsli
Myrland
Skriverfinden
890
Øynes
Trondenes
Harstad
Forså
Solvoll
Tennevoll
Forset
Strømsmoen
Kopparskartinden
1387
Njunis
1713
Reinstad
Røykenes
Borkenes
Hokland
Breivik
Myrlandshaugen
Hilleshamn
Hesjeberg
Lund
Lunde
Sørdalen
Østerdalen
Barduelva
Jerta
1428
Øvre Dividal Nasjonalpark
Hemnestad
Bjørnrå
Middagstinden
919
Straumen
Kilbotn
Storjorda
Sørrollnes
Astafjorden
Tjuvskjær
Årstein
Spannstinden
1456
Livelttind
1477
Innset
Sørfjorden
Kjengsnes
Revsnes
Sandtorg
Sandstrand
Grovfjord
Laberget
Gratangsbotn
Forsbakken
Bonnes
Sørmo
Altevatnet
Kistefjell
1633
Flesnes
Melbå
Storvatnet
Gausvik
Fauskevåg
Tennevik
Øyvatnet
Novafjell
1280
Nonstinden
1443
Rivtinden
1458
Isfinden
1463
Riepečokka
1459
Kjelelvtinden
1571
Råkkunbårri
1659
Hinnøya
Tverrelvtinden
1115
Gullholmen
Sætertinden
1094
Evenskjær
Skittendalstinden
1306
N
Skaddjaoaivve
1356
Vassdalen
Vavetjåkka Nationalpark
Våtvoll
Snøfjellet
978
Kongsvik
Fjelldal
Boltåsen
Vassbotn
Bjerkvik
Bogen
Gævdnajavrre
Leinavatnet
Kanstadbotn
Hol
Dragland
Breidstrand
Sandnes
Lenvik
Jernvatna
Vassijaure
Vuolep Njuorajaure
Tjeldøya
Ramsund
Liland
Forra
Veggen
Trædal
Tuoptejåkkah
1604
Máissávarri
1022
Kanstad
Tjeldsundet
Kjerstad
Breidvik
Tårstad
Evenes
Rombaken
Herjangsfjorden
Bjørnfjell
Riksgränsen
Bjørkstugan
Bjørkliden
Torneträsk
Kåringen
Tjeldnes
Pundsvik
Narvik
Ankenes
Fagernesfjellet
1448
Lødingen
Russhaugen
Ofotfjorden
Kjeldebotn
Håkvik
Vassitjåkka
1591
Abisko Östra
Abisko Nationalpark
Rinøyvåg
Nes
Skarstad
Vargfjordfjellet
855
Karihaugen
Bø
Vidrek
Grindjord
Beisfjord
Kaisepakte
Elvesletta
Ballangen
Råna
Kongsbakktinden
1575
Lengenes
Munkelia
Stenbacken
Barøya
Bjørkåsen
Stemnes
Storsteinsfjell
Torneträsk
Offersøy
Stokkdal
Skjomen
Nakerjaure
Korsnes
Kjerringvik
Rånvassbotn
Frostisen
1744
Elvegard
Adnjetjårro
1756
Tysnes
Skarberget
Melkadalen
Apparjaure
Bergfors
Bogen
Kobbenestind
1003
Lysroll
Ratojaure
Tranøy
Hatten
852
Kalvik
Haukøy
Skjombotn
Losvatnet
1901
Vuolle Alesjaure
Kåtotjåkka
1991
Rautasjärvi
Nordkil
Forså
Kjelkvik
Hundholmen
Norddalen
Fjellbu
Ippovarre
1663
Hamløt
Tysfjorden
Lifjellet
849
Isfjell
1437
Roanasdalen
Storriten
1498
Kalanvarre
1481
Rassepautastjåkka
1750
Råppe
1014
Rensjön
Hamarøy
Ulsvåg
Skillvassbakk
Kjøpsvik
Hulløya
Storå
Baugefjellet
1366
Sielmatjåkka
1236
Kaldvåg
Drag
Tørnes
Giccečokka
1387
Gic'cečok'ka
1252
Røttangen
Helland
Kjøpes
Bjørntoppen
1520
Sitasjaure
Leavasjokka
Innhavet
Råne
Beassegáma
1250
Marko
1445
Tutturjaure
1510
2076
2114
Kebnekaise
Kåkittjårro
1535
Pirttivuopio
1017
Årosjåkk
Tømmerneset
Store Fora
Storfjellet
1183
Alitáive
1584
Upmas
Rusjka
1708
Nikkaluokta
Laukkuluspa
Holmajärvi
Paittasjärvi
Rota
Strinda
Skunkivarre
1120
Musken
1037
Kätsak
Vidjajaure
Skartåive
1761
Kalvfinden
1103
Lofthus
1543
S
Piedjastjåkka
1014
Ånderbakktindan
1235
Kråkmoen
Hestdalsfjellet
1061
Autajaure
Seukok
1166
Sørfjorden
Suorggejohka
Kallaktjåkkå
1845
Mørsvikbotn
Langfjellet
1266
Jålle
1367
Akkajaure
Kårsatjåkka
1703
Stora Sjöfallets Nationalpark
Kaska Kaitumjaure
Täunatjåkka
1054
Vuolep Kaitumjaure
Storeidet
Slappejaure
Reinoksvatnet
Gaskačokka
1512
Kamastjårro
899
Horndal
Korken
1190
Vuojatätno
Kutjaure
Akka
2015
Kaitumälven
Bonnåsjøen
Kobbelvejd
Sørfjordmoen
Sallohaure
1654
Pålnotjåkkå
1007
Sommarset
Kuboutelistjåkkå
Kisuris
1664
Pätsasj
Vietas
Juobmotjåkkå
Kalvik
Rago Nasjonalpark
Vastenjaure
Padjelanta Nationalpark
Allak
109
Stora Sjöfall
Satihaure
2090
E6
E8
E10
E6/8
116

2 3 4 5 6 7 8 9 10
A B C D E F
19°00′ 19°30′ 20°00′ 20°30′ 21°00′ 21°30′ 22°00′ 22°30′ 23°00′
71°00′
70°30′
70°00′
69°30′
69°00′
N O R D I S H A V E T
L o p p h a v e t
Kamøya
Sandøyfjorden
Gattefjorden
Åfjorden
Storelv
Sørvær
Breivikbotn
Breivik
Haraldseng
Sørøya
Vatnafjellet
656
882
18
Hasvik
S ø r ø y s u n d e t
Seilandsjø
Loppa
Silda
Eliassen
939
949
Stjernøya
Bergkunsten i Alta
Fugløya
Fugløykallen
753
Nord-Kvaløy
Burøy
Torsvåg
Burøysund
Grøtøy
Vannareid
Alangen
737
Store Skorøya
Årviksand
Andsnes
Neset
Skavnakk
Øra
628
Sandland
Svartfjelljøkulen
1066
Nuvsvåg
Myrnes
Sletta
Øksfjord
Stjernsundet
Seglvik
Middagsfjellet
1071
Sør-Tverrfjord
Øksfjordjøkulen
Arnøya
Nymoen
1168
924
Helgøy
Hamre
Vanna
Vanntindan
1033
Vannavalen
Rebbenesøy
Bromnes
Rebbenesbotn
Mikkelvik
Davøya
Kammen
Kvitnes
Vannvåg
Skåningen
Lanesøyra
Karlsøy
Lauksletta
Hellnes
Laukøya
Rødøy
Langfjordjøkulen
1162
Nevernesfjellet
1181
1304
Gamvik
Storvik
Liv'luvarri
958
Fjelltindnasen
1041
Akkarvik
Arnoyhamn
Haugnes
Nikkeby
Haukøya
Jøkelfjordeidet
Tappeluft
Kjerringdal
Eidsnes
Langfjordbotn
Bognelv
Talvik
Sandøy
Engvik
Måsvik
Skarsfjord
Skogsfjord
Grunnfjord
Dåfjord
Both
Karlsøy
Skjervøy
Spildra
Hamnbukt
Alteidet
Lassefjellet
1166
Melsvik
Svartevasstind
876
Skogsfjordvatnet
Hessfjorden
Hansnes
Stakkvik
Reinskard
Nordeidet
Hurtigruten
Vorterøy
Kågen
Russelv
1098
Flåten
Storenga
Laukeng
Kviteberg
Burfjord
Stuora Hal'di
1149
Kåfjord
Ringvassøy
Finnvik
Indre Kårvik
Istind
953
Reinøy
Reinskartind
884
Nordlenangen
Straumen
Uloya
Klauvnes
Hamneidet
Sandelva
Mettevoll
Reisafjorden
Kvænangen
Dorras
Undereidet
Gierdoidvarri
810
Kvaløyvågen
Vengsøy
Skulsfjord
Finnkroken
Grøtnesdalen
Grøtsundet
Eidstranda
Tverrbakktind
1390
Styrmanstø
Sørlenangen
Uløybukta
1142
Bakkeby
Blåtind
Storslett
Lyngen
Storvik
Stornespamn
Sørstraumen
Gåsnes
Navit
Badderen
Sekkemo
Kjækan
Grotfjord
Lyfjord
Blåmannen
1044
Futrikelva
Skulgammen
Tonsvik
Ullstind
1094
Snarby
Skitenelv
Oldervik
Svingen
Botn
Vaggastinden
1398
Hamnes
Rotsundelva
Rotsund
Langslett
Sørkjosen
Vaddas gruver
Ersfjordbotn
Kaldfjord
Kvaløysletta
Eidkjosen
Skjelman
Tromsø
Tromsø Universitetsmuseet
Tromsdalen
Tromsdalstind
1238
Kvaløya
Kaldslett
Breivikeidet
Hov
Ullsfjorden
Jægervatnet
Store Lenangstind
Stortind
1596
1512
Isskartindane
1441
Storsteinnes
Djupvik
Nordmannvik
Lyngmoen
Nordmannviktind
1336
Olderdalen
Bæssetindan
1312
Rieppesgai'sa
1337
Haugset
Øvre Kildal
Bergmo
Nordbotn
Nubivarri
841
Badajokka
Mattiselva
Sandeggen
Svensby
Koppangen
Årøybukta
Fagernes
Ballsnes
Lauksletta
Vikran
Bentsjordtind
Bjørnskartind
1359
Sennedalfjellet
1385
Skardmunken
Skjelnes
Jøvik
Fornesfjellet
1478
Lyngseidet
Odden
1301
Abojávri
Sandvik
Tverrbotnfjell
1299
Ullsfjord
Kvalvik
Samuelsberg
Løkvoll
Trollvik
Fossheim
Birtavarre
Sappen
Bæccæhal'di
1326
Čuonjaoai'vi
1089
Kobbevågnes
Slettind
1115
Selnes
Hamnbukta
Hundberg
Jiehkkevarri
1833
Brennes
Manndalen
Isfjellet
1375
Kåfjorddalen
Bilto
Malangen
Malangseidet
Kantorneset
Lavangsdalen
Sjøvassbotn
Djupen
Lakselvtindan
1617
Njallavarri
1530
Rasteby
Furuflaten
Elvelund
Abmelaseter
Čiččenvárri
1312
Ankerlia
Sieima
Reisaelva
Mållejus
975
Cárajávri
Balsfjorden
Skutvik
Middagsbukt
Mestervik
Henriktind
1219
Lakselvsletta
Langalstindane
1554
Elvevollen
Skibotn
Skibotndalen
Čaravárri
887
Steinheim
Hamnvågnes
Balsfjord
Nordfjordbotn
Biellogaissa
1514
Elsnes
Brennfjell
Horsnes
Piggtind
1505
Storfjord
Våggevárri
1560
Oteren
Skibotnelva
Rássanibba
1252
Halti
1365
1328
Bidjovagge
Furudal
Storsteinnes
Blåtinden
1378
Seljelynes
Søreng
Obertind
1360
Mannfjellet
1533
Helligskogen
Somasjärvi
Pihtsosjärvi
Reisa Nasjonalpark
Lunneborg
Sagelvvatnet
Akkasæter
Nordkjosbotn
Øvergard
Egga
Goahteråšša
1371
Markusfjellet
1451
Heia
Olsberg
Rustadhogda (Bardufoss)
Straumstad
Lille Russetind
1527
Tamokdalen
Paras
Styggedalen
Báras
1419
Kahperusvaarat
1144
Porojärvi
Poroeno
Stuorajávri
Takvatnet
Stormauken
1249
Fjellfrøsvatnet
Rundhaug
Skjold
Holt
Lille Rostavatn
Kilpisjärvi
Saana
1029
Mosskkugáisi
1523
Jollanoaivi
1029
Rommajärvi
Stuorajavrre
Nytrøa
Øverbygd
Istindan
1489
Iselvmoen
Kirkesdalen
Tverrelmo
Rostadalen
Rostaelva
Dividalen
Kilpisjärvi
Tierbmesjärvi
Rommaeno
Kautokeino
FIN
Bas'tevarri
658
Langfjelltind
1504
Devdisvatn
Dividalen
Ailakkajärvi
Peeravaara
933
Bjørkåsen
S
Kiellijärvi
Tverrfjellet
Kjerkestinden
1677
Frihetsli
116
111
Kivijärvi
Saarikoski
Rostojaure
Gálaniitu
E6
E8
E6/8

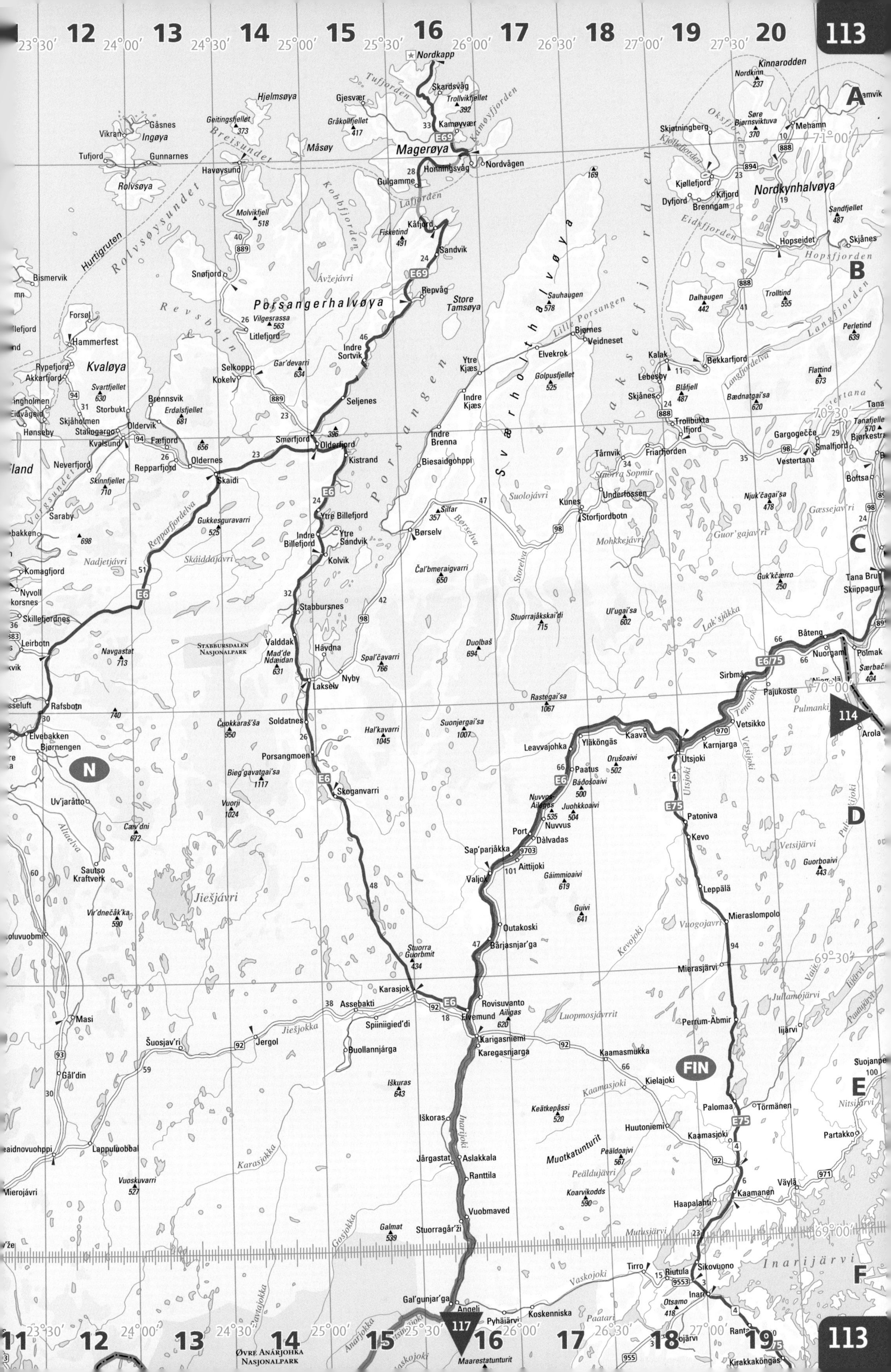

Nordkapp
Skarsvåg
Trollvikfjellet
Gjesvær
Tufjorden
Kamøyfjorden
Hjelmsøya
Gåsnes
Vikran
Ingøya
Geitingsfjellet 373
Gråkollfjellet 417
Kamøyvær
Måsøy
Magerøya
Honningsvåg
Nordvågen
Gunnarnes
Tufjord
Havøysund
Breisundet
Rolvsøya
Rolvsøysundet
Gulgamme
Kobbfjorden
Lafjorden
Hurtigruten
Molvikfjell 518
Kåfjord
Fisketind 491
Sandvik
Bismervik
Snøfjord
Åvžejávri
Repvåg
Porsangerhalvøya
Store Tamsøya
Revsbotn
Vilgesrassa 563
Litlefjord
Forsøl
Hammerfest
Kvaløya
Rypefjord
Akkarfjord
Svartfjellet 630
Selkopp
Kokelv
Gar'devarri 634
Indre Sortvik
Seljenes
Brennsvik
Erdalsfjellet 681
Storbukt
Skjåholmen
Stallogargo
Oldervik
Kvalsund
Hønseby
Fæfjord
Repparfjord
Oldernes
Smørfjord
Olderfjord
Kistrand
Neverfjord
Skinnfjellet 710
Skaidi
Porsangen
Saraby
Gukkesguravarri 525
Ytre Billefjord
Indre Billefjord
Ytre Sandvik
Kolvik
Komagfjord
Nyvoll
Skillefjordnes
Nadjetjávri
Skáiddajávri
Repparfjordelva
Stabbursnes
Leirbotn
Stabbursdalen Nasjonalpark
Navgastat 713
Valddak
Mad'de Ndæidan 631
Hávdna
Nyby
Lakselv
Spal'čavarri 766
Rafsbotn
Elvebakken
Bjørnengen
Soldatnes
Čuokkarašša 950
Porsangmoen
Hal'kavarri 1045
Bieg'gavatgai'sa 1117
Skoganvarri
Vuorji 1024
Uv'jarätto
Cæv'dni 672
Altaelva
Sautso Kraftverk
Jiešjávri
Vir'dnečåk'ka 590
Stuorra Guorbmit 434
Karasjok
Assebakti
Spiiniigied'di
Masi
Jergol
Šuosjav'ri
Buollannjárga
Jiešjokka
Gål'din
Lappuluobbal
Vuoskuvarri 527
Mierojávri
Karasjokka
Galmat 539
Iškuras 643
Gosjokka
Gal'gunjar'ga
Angeli
Øvre Anárjohka Nasjonalpark
Anarjokka
Ytre Kjæs
Indre Kjæs
Indre Brenna
Biesaidgohppi
Børselv
Silfar 357
Čal'bmeraigvarri 650
Duolbaš 694
Børselva
Storelva
Stuorrajåkskai'di 715
Rastegai'sa 1067
Suonjergai'sa 1007
Sværholthalvøya
Sauhaugen 578
Lille Porsangen
Bjørnes
Veidneset
Elvekrok
Golpusfjellet 525
Laksefjorden
Suolojávri
Kunes
Storfjordbotn
Mohkkejávri
Undørfossen
Tårnvik
Friarfjorden
Snorra Sopmir
Ul'ugai'sa 602
Leavvajohka
Yläköngäs
Kaava
Paatus
Orušoaivi 502
Bádosoaivi 500
Nuvvos-Ailegas 535
Juohkkoaivi 504
Nuvvus
Port
Dàlvadas
Sap'parjåkka
Aittijoki
Valjok
Gáimmioaivi 619
Guivi 641
Outakoski
Bårjasnjar'ga
Rovisuvanto
Ailigas 620
Elvemund
Karigasniemi
Karegasnjarga
Kaamasmukka
Luopmosjávrrit
Kaamasjoki
Kielajoki
Keätkepåssi 520
Iškoras
Inarijoki
Jårgastat
Aslakkala
Muotkatunturit
Ranttila
Peäldoajvi 567
Peäldujávri
Koarvikodds 590
Vuobmaved
Stuorragår'ži
Mutusjärvi
Vaskojoki
Tirro
Riutula
Koskenniska
Pyhäjärvi
Paatari
Otsamo 418
Maarestatunturit
Kinnarodden
Nordkinn 237
Mehamn
Søre Bjørnsviktuva 370
Skjøtningberg
Oksfjorden
Kjøllefjorden
Kjøllefjord
Kifjord
Dyfjord
Brenngam
Nordkynhalvøya
Sandfjellet 487
Eidsfjorden
Hopseidet
Skjånes
Hopsfjorden
Dalhaugen 442
Trolltind 555
Perletind 639
Langfjorden
Kalak
Bekkarfjord
Lebesby
Blåfjell 487
Flattind 673
Langfjordelva
Skjånes
Bædnatgai'sa 620
Trollbukta
Ifjord
Vestertana
Gargogečče
Smalfjord
Bjørkestrand
Tana
Tanafjellet 570
Boftsa
Njuk'čagai'sa 478
Gæssejav'ri
Guor'gajav'ri
Guk'kčærro 250
Tana Bru
Skiippagurra
Lak'sjåkka
Båteng
Nuorgam
Polmak
Særbač 404
Sirbmá
Pajukoste
Tenojoki
Pulmanki
Vetsikko
Karnjarga
Utsjoki
Arola
Vetsijoki
Patoniva
Kevo
Vetsijärvi
Guorboaivi 443
Leppälä
Mieraslompolo
Vuogojavri
Kevojoki
Mierasjärvi
Jullamojärvi
Iijärvi
Perrum-Äbmir
Suojanperä
Palomaa
Törmänen
Nitsijärvi
Huutoniemi
Kaamasjoki
Partakko
Väylä
Haapalahti
Kaamanen
Inarijärvi
Sikovuono
Inari
Ranta
Kirakkaköngäs
N
FIN
114
117

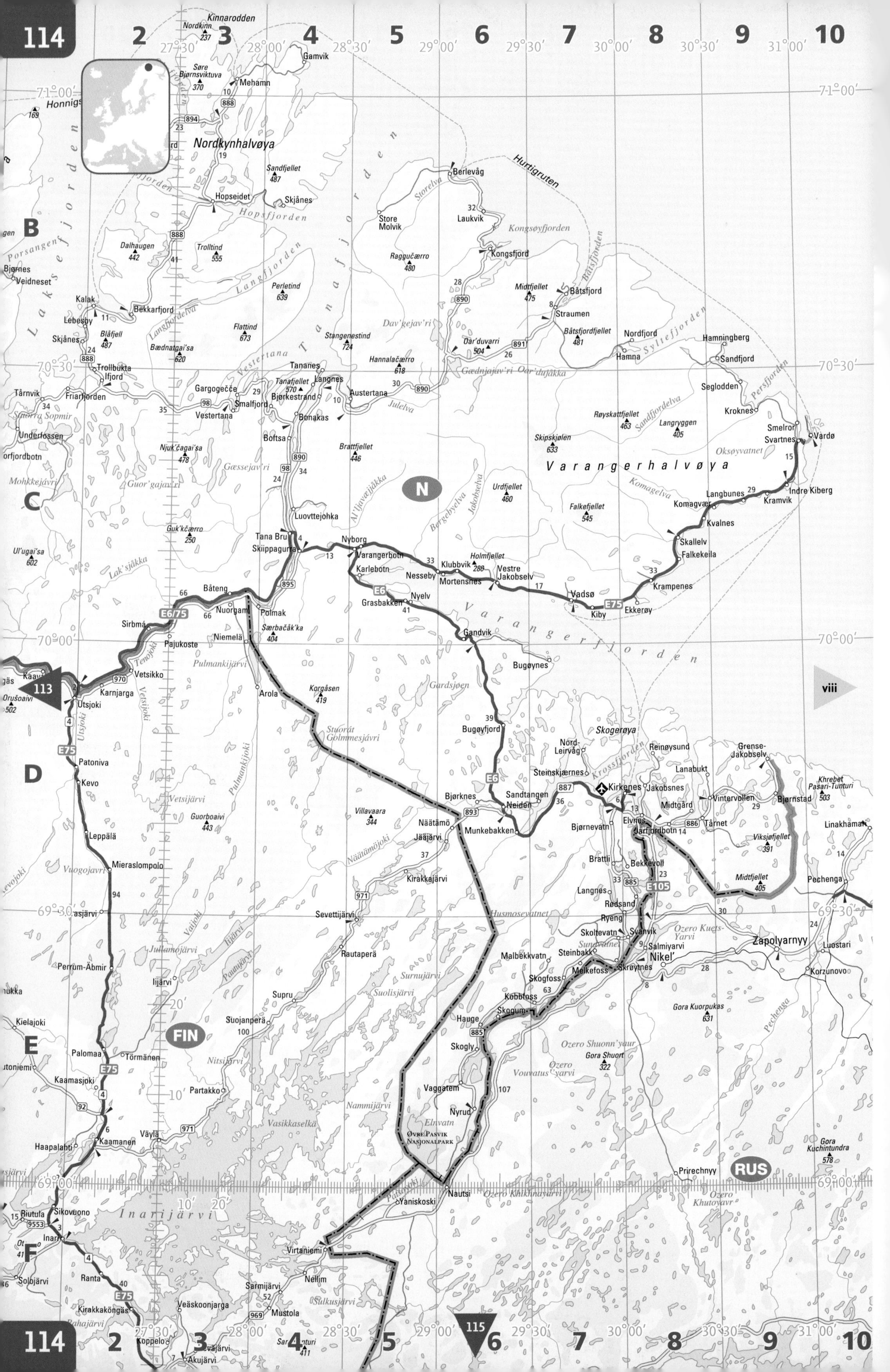
2
3
4
5
6
7
8
9
10
27°30′
28°00′
28°30′
29°00′
29°30′
30°00′
30°30′
31°00′
71°00′
70°30′
70°00′
69°30′
69°00′
B
C
D
E
F
Kinnarodden
Nordkinn
237
Gamvik
Søre
Bjørnsviktuva
370
Mehamn
Honnigs
169
Nordkynhalvøya
Sandfjellet
487
Hopseidet
Skjånes
Hopsfjorden
Dalhaugen
442
Trolltind
555
Porsangen
Bjørnes
Veidneset
Laksefjorden
Langfjorden
Perletind
639
Kalak
Bekkarfjord
Lebesby
Skjånes
Blåfjell
487
Flattind
673
Bædnatgai'sa
620
Vestertana
Tanafjorden
Stangenestind
724
Trollbukta
Ifjord
Tårnvik
Friarfjorden
Gargogečče
Smalfjord
Vestertana
Tananes
Tanafjellet
570
Langnes
Bjørkestrand
Austertana
Bonakas
Boftsa
Julelva
Underfossen
Orfjordbotn
Mohkkejávri
Njuk'čagai'sa
478
Gæssejav'ri
Guor'gajav'ri
Brattfjellet
446
Luovttejohka
Al'ljavæijåkka
Guk'kæærro
250
Ul'ugai'sa
602
Lak'sjåkka
Tana Bru
Skiippagurra
Nyborg
Varangerbotn
Karlebotn
Grasbakken
Nyelv
Nesseby
Klubbvik
Holmfjellet
286
Mortensnes
Vestre Jakobselv
Vadsø
Kiby
Ekkerøy
Krampenes
Båteng
Nuorgam
Polmak
Sirbmá
Pajukoste
Niemelä
Særbačåk'ka
404
Pulmankijärvi
Kaava
113
Vetsikko
Karnjarga
Utsjoki
Orušoaivi
502
Arola
Korgåsen
419
Gandvik
Bugøynes
Varangerfjorden
Gardsjøen
Stuorát Golmmesjávri
Bugøyfjord
Skogerøya
Nord-Leirvåg
Reinøysund
Grense-Jakobselv
Krossfjorden
Steinskjærnes
Lanabukt
Kirkenes
Jakobsnes
Khrebet Pasari-Tunturi
503
Sandtangen
Neiden
Bjørnstad
Vintervollen
Midtgård
Tårnet
Linakhamari
Bjørknes
Näätämö
Jääjärvi
Munkebakken
Bjørnevatn
Elvenes
Jarfjordbotn
Viksjøfjellet
391
Villavaara
344
Näätämöjoki
Kirakkajärvi
Brattli
Bekkevoll
Midtfjellet
405
Pechenga
Langnes
Rødsand
Ryeng
Skoltevatn
Svanvik
Salmiyarvi
Ozero Kuets-Yarvi
Zapolyarnyy
Luostari
Sevettijärvi
Husmosevatnet
Rautaperä
Malbekkvatn
Steinbakk
Melkefoss
Skrøytnes
Nikel'
Korzunovo
Skogfoss
Kobbfoss
Skogum
Gora Kuorpukas
631
Pechenga
Surnujärvi
Suolisjärvi
Supru
Suojanperä
Hauge
Skogly
Ozero Shuonn'yaur
Gora Shuort
322
Ozero Vouvatus'yarvi
Vaggatem
Nyrud
Elnvatn
Øvre Pasvik Nasjonalpark
Nammijärvi
Vasikkaselkä
Gora Kuchintundra
578
Prirechnyy
RUS
Nautsi
Ozero Khikhnayarvi
Yaniskoski
Ozero Khutoyavr
Virtaniemi
Nellim
Sarmijärvi
Mustola
Sulkusjärvi
Sarmituri
411
Kemi
115
Berlevåg
Hurtigruten
Storelva
Laukvik
Store Molvik
Kongsøyfjorden
Kongsfjord
Raggučærro
480
Båtsfjorden
Midtfjellet
475
Båtsfjord
Straumen
Dav'gejav'ri
Oar'duvarri
504
Båtsfjordfjellet
481
Nordfjord
Hamna
Syltefjorden
Hamningberg
Sandfjord
Hannalačærro
618
Gædnjajav'ri
Oar'dujåkka
Persfjorden
Seglodden
Kroknes
Røyskattfjellet
463
Sandfjordelva
Langryggen
405
Skipskjølen
633
Oksøyvatnet
Smelror
Svartnes
Vardø
Varangerhalvøya
N
Urdfjellet
460
Børgebyelva
Jakobselva
Komagelva
Falkefjellet
545
Langbunes
Komagvær
Kramvik
Indre Kiberg
Kvalnes
Skallelv
Falkekeila
viii
Patoniva
Kevo
Leppälä
Mieraslompolo
Vuogojavri
Vetsijärvi
Guorboaivi
443
Pulmankijoki
Rasjärvi
Vetsijoki
Perrum-Äbmir
Jullamojärvi
Iijärvi
Paatsjärvi
Kielajoki
FIN
Palomaa
Törmänen
Nitsijärvi
Kaamasjoki
Partakko
Haapalahti
Kaamanen
Väylä
Riutula
Sikovuono
Inarijärvi
Inari
Solojärvi
Ranta
Kirakkaköngäs
Veäskoonjarga
Rahajärvi
Koppelo
Akujärvi
Kaamasjärvi
E6/75
E6
E75
E105
888
894
890
891
98
895
970
893
887
885
886
971
92
969
9553

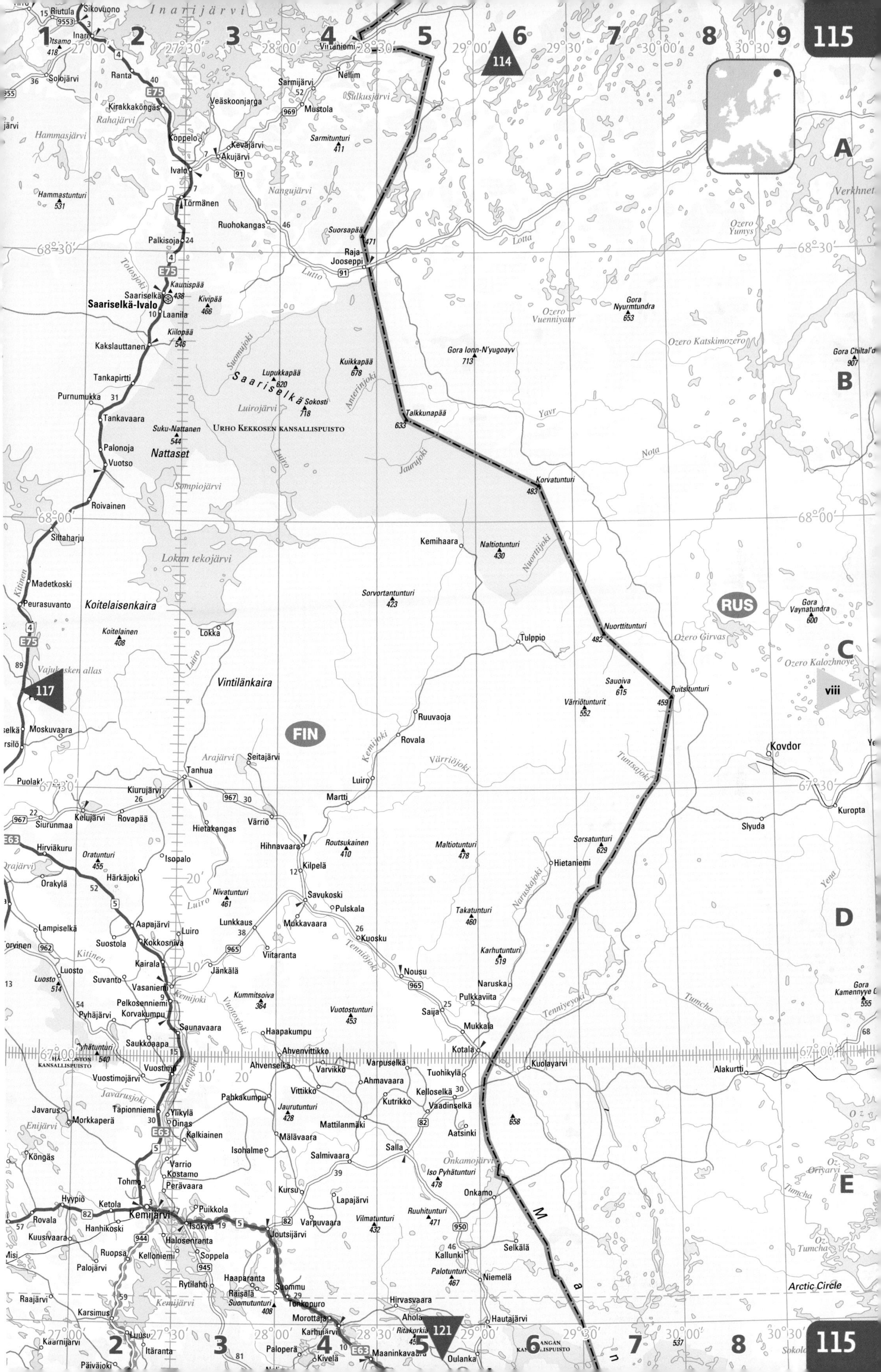
1
2
3
4
5
6
7
8
9
A
B
C
D
E
Inarijärvi
Riutula
Sikovuono
Inari
Otsamo
418
Ranta
Solojärvi
E75
Kirakkaköngäs
Rahajärvi
Hammasjärvi
Koppelo
Ivalo
Törmänen
Hammastunturi
531
Palkisoja
Veäskoonjarga
Kevajärvi
Akujärvi
Nangujärvi
Ruohokangas
Virtaniemi
Nellim
Sarmijärvi
Sulkusjärvi
Mustola
Sarmitunturi
411
Suorsapää
471
Raja-Jooseppi
Lutto
Lotta
114
Ozero Yumys
Verkhnet
Tolosjoki
Kaunispää
438
Saariselkä
Saariselkä-Ivalo
Kivipää
466
Laanila
Kiilopää
546
Kakslauttanen
Tankapirtti
Purnumukka
Tankavaara
Palonoja
Vuotso
Suku-Nattanen
544
Nattaset
Suomujoki
Lupukkapää
620
Saariselkä
Sokosti
718
Luirojärvi
Kuikkapää
678
Anterinjoki
Talkkunapää
633
URHO KEKKOSEN KANSALLISPUISTO
Luiro
Jaurujoki
Sompiojärvi
Roivainen
Ozero Vuenniyaur
Gora Nyurmtundra
653
Ozero Katskimozero
Gora Ionn-N'yugoayv
713
Gora Chiltal'o
907
Yavr
Nota
Korvatunturi
483
68°30′
68°00′
Siltaharju
Lokan tekojärvi
Kitinen
Madetkoski
Peurasuvanto
Koitelaisenkaira
Koitelainen
408
Lokka
Kemihaara
Naltiotunturi
430
Nuorttijoki
Sorvortantunturi
423
RUS
Gora Vaynatundra
600
Tulppio
Nuorttitunturi
482
Ozero Girvas
Ozero Kalozhnoye
Vajukosken allas
117
Vintilänkaira
Sauoiva
615
Puitsitunturi
459
Värriötunturit
552
viii
Moskuvaara
FIN
Ruuvaoja
Rovala
Kovdor
Arajärvi
Seitajärvi
Tanhua
Kemijoki
Luiro
Värriöjoki
Tuntsajoki
Puolakl
67°30′
Kiurujärvi
26
967
30
Martti
Kuropta
Kelujärvi
Rovapää
Siurunmaa
Hietakangas
Värriö
Hihnavaara
Slyuda
E63
Hirviäkuru
Oratunturi
455
Isopalo
Routsukainen
410
Maltiotunturi
478
Sorsatunturi
629
Hietaniemi
Orajärvi
Härkäjoki
Kilpelä
Orakylä
Nivatunturi
461
Savukoski
Pulskala
Naruskajoki
Yena
Lampiselkä
Aapajärvi
Luiro
Lunkkaus
Mukkavaara
Kuosku
Takatunturi
460
Suostola
Kokkosniva
Torvinen
962
965
Viitaranta
Tenniöjoki
Karhutunturi
519
Kitinen
Kairala
Jänkälä
Luosto
514
Suvanto
Vasaniemi
Nousu
Naruska
Gora Kamennyye
555
Pelkosenniemi
Kemijoki
Kummitsoiva
364
Pulkkaviita
Pyhäjärvi
Korvakumpu
Vuotosjoki
Vuotostunturi
453
Saija
Tenniyeyoki
Tumcha
Saunavaara
Haapakumpu
Mukkala
Pyhätunturi
540
Saukkoaapa
Ahvenvittikko
Kotala
67°00′
Vuostimo
Ahvenselkä
Varvikko
Varpuselkä
Ahmavaara
Tuohikylä
Kuolayarvi
Alakurtti
Vuostimojärvi
Vittikko
Kelloselkä
Javarusjoki
Pahkakumpu
Kutrikko
Vaadinselkä
Javarus
Tapionniemi
Ylikylä
Jaurutunturi
428
Enijärvi
Morkkaperä
Oinas
Mattilanmäki
Aatsinki
658
Kalkiainen
Mälävaara
Köngäs
Isohalme
Salla
Varrio
Salmivaara
Onkamojärvi
Oz. Orryarvi
Kostamo
Tohmo
Peräväara
Iso Pyhätunturi
478
Kursu
Onkamo
Lapajärvi
Hyypiö
Ketola
Puikkola
Rovala
Kemijärvi
Isokylä
Hanhikoski
Joutsijärvi
Varpuvaara
Vilmatunturi
432
Ruuhitunturi
471
Kuusivaara
Halosenranta
Misi
Ruopsa
Kelloniemi
Soppela
Kallunki
Selkälä
Palojärvi
Rytilahti
Haaparanta
Palotunturi
467
Niemelä
Räisälä
Suommu
Arctic Circle
Raajärvi
Suomutunturi
408
Tonkopuro
Hirvasvaara
Kemijärvi
Karsimus
Morottaja
Ahola
Hautajärvi
Luusua
Itäranta
Karhujärvi
Ritakorkia
121
Kaarnijärvi
Paloperä
Maaninkavaara
Päiväjoki
Kivelä
Oulanka
537
Sokolo
27°00′
27°30′
28°00′
28°30′
29°00′
29°30′
30°00′
30°30′

2
3
4
5
6
7
8
9
112
111
109
118
A
B
C
D
E
N
S
19°00′
19°30′
20°00′
20°30′
21°00′
21°30′
22°00′
22°30′
23°00′
68°30′
68°00′
67°30′
67°00′
Øverbygd
Tverrfjell
1482
Kopparskarfin
1387
Østerdalen
Innset
Sørmo
Altevatnet
Skaddjaoaivve
1356
Råkkunbårri
1659
Gævdnajavrre
Kistefjell
1633
Njumis
1713
Frihetsli
Devdisvatn
Dividalen
Rostadalen
Jerta
1428
Øvre Dividal Nasjonalpark
1271
1523
Moskkugáisi
Kilpisjärvi
1029
Rommajärvi
Tierniesjavri
Ailakkajärvi
Peeravaara
933
Kiellijärvi
Peera
Kivijärvi
Saarikoski
Rastojaure
Könkämäälven
E8
Iitto
112
Röpinsalmi
Naimakka
Ruutusoive
842
Pättikkä
Rostonsölkä
Ropi
945
Tarju
735
Torisen
Paltåive
915
Råstäno
Kautokeino
Gálaniitu
Urtivaara
633
Tarvantovaara
591
Tarvantojoki
Jietajoki
Läteäseno
Kelottijärvi
Luspa
Mauna
Maunu
Markkina
Kaaresuvanto
Karesuando
Kultima
Jatuni
Kuttanen
Kuttainen
Vähäniva
Palojoensuu
Suijavaara
Saivomuotka
E45
99
21
38
80
Mertajärvi
Idivuoma
Idijärvi
Keukiskero
Luongastunturi
Tornetråsk
Björkliden
Abisko Östra
Abisko Nationalpark
Tuoptejåkkah
1604
Leinavatnet
Máissávarri
1022
Kiepanjaure
Tavvaätno
Tsåktso
1119
Roopi
799
Lainioälven
Pulsujärvi
Järämä
Vassijärvi
Kaisepakte
E10
Stenbacken
Torneträsk
Adnjetjårro
1756
Nakerjaure
133
Bergfors
Rassepautastjåkka
1750
Rautasjärvi
Råppe
1014
Rensjön
Rautas
Rakisvare
985
Stalojaure
Puollanåive
796
Lulep-Patsajäkel
782
Alep Vuolusjaure
Vittangivaara
836
Övre Soppero
108
Nedre Soppero
Lannavaara
Nunasvaara
580
Jokujärvi
Nuulankivuoma
612
Käkittjårro
1535
Leavasjohka
1017
Lulep Vuolusjaure
Krovik
Kurravaara
Paanikielinen
Halju
551
Pessinki
Saankijoki
Lainioälven
Nikkaluokta
Pirttivuopio
Årosjåkk
Laukkuluspa
Holmajärvi
Paittasjärvi
Piedjastjåkka
1014
Kiruna
Tuolluvaara
Alttajärvi
Jukkasjärvi
Paksuniemi
Sautusjärvi
Esrange
Rautusakara
637
Vittangiälven
Sappisaasi
Temminkijärvi
Pasmajärvi
Olosjoki
Kitkiöjärvi
Lainio
Parkalompolo
Kalixforsen
48
Täunatjåkka
1054
Vuolep Kaitumjaure
Kamastjårro
899
Sjisjka
717
Svappavaara
27
Vittangi
395
Kuoksu
Öksajärvi
Kerantöjärvi
Pålnotjåkkå
1007
Kaitumälven
Kalixälven
660
Naankitunturi
515
Torneälven
Nujaure
Kaitum
Fjällåsen
Killinge
Piilijärvi
Merasjärvi
55
Nuuksujärvi
Lumivaara
449
Kussåive
814
Sjaunjaätno
Parakka
Kangos
Masugnsbyn
Neitsuanto
Paukitunturi
Puoltikasvaara
Skaulo
62
Vettasjärvi
Junosuando
Tervavuoma
Saivatuottar
898
Juovvatjåkka
Sjaunjaape
Tjårrokieble
820
Kääntöjärvi
Käymäjä
Karmas
Håmpjåkk
Tjautas
Mettajärvi
Saittarova
Lovikka
Lina älv
E10/45
Loukasvuoma
Männikkö
Anttis
Kaltesvare
853
Nilivaara
Tärendöälven
Kalixälven
Koskullskulle
Malmberget
Kuossakåbba
Stora Lulevatten
Ålloluokta
Nya Dundret
Gällivare
13
4
Markitta
Jertta
555
Peräjävuoma
Suorsapakka
324
Tärendö
Appakis
784
Nietsak
Dundret
821
Sakajärvi
Liikavaara
Purnuvaara
Granhult
Kompelusvaara
Luspebryggan
Jutsajaure
50
Dokkas
Leipojärvi
394
Äihämäjärvi
Stuor-Tålput
590
Ullatti
64
Kainulasjärvi
Nautijaur
611
Muddus Nationalpark
Råneträsket
Sammakko
Nuoksujärvi
Harsprånget
Muddusjaure
Palohuornas
Satter
Selkäjärvi
Narken
Tapmuk
661
Purnu
Hakkas
Yrttivaara
Pempelijärvi
Lahenpää
Björkholmen
Rutnajaure
Linaälven
Rapasvaarat
Lahnajärvi
Korpilombolo
Randijaur
Aspudden
Kilvo
Ainavarto
525
Mäntyvaara
Paharova
Limingoån
40
Urtimjaur
Nattavaara
Nattavaara by
Sarvisvaara
Skröven
Dirivaara
Teurajärvi
Stora Luleälven
Ängesån
Lahnasuando
Njetjavare
Luvos
580
Purkijaur
Vaikijaur
Miessaure
Högträsk
326
Svartberget
417
Vinsa
Piertinjaure
Harauddèn
Fatjas
Tjekartunturi
468
113
Lansjärv
Jockfall
Jokkmokk
Pielnejaure
Tjalmejaure
Arctic Circle
Mattisudden
Yttre Lansjärv
Ertsjärv
Muukajärv
Sarmekåbba
Kuouka
474
Neitas
Fiakaberg
Lillsaivis
Jutsavare
571
Vajmat
Muriek
43
97
Lilla Luleälven
Vallsjärv
Skiövån
Lansjärv
Kalixälven
Lillselet
392
116
29
Juh
14
12
E10

11
12
13
14
15
16
17
18
113
N
Øvre Anárjohka Nasjonalpark
Lemmenjoen kansallispuisto
Repokaira
Pomokaira
FIN
Pallas-Yllästunturin kansallispuisto
Pyhä-Luoston kansallispuisto
Koitelaisenkaira
Nattaset
Lokan tekojärvi
Porttipahdan tekojärvi
Vajukosken allas
Urho Ke
A
B
C
D
E
115
119
Inari
Ivalo
Akujärvi
Koppelo
Törmänen
Ruohokangas
Palkisoja
Saariselkä
Saariselkä-Ivalo
Laanila
Kaunispää
Kiilopää
Kakslauttanen
Tankapirtti
Purnumukka
Tankavaara
Palonoja
Vuotso
Roivainen
Sompiojärvi
Siltaharju
Madetkoski
Peurasuvanto
Lokka
Petkula
Mataraselkä
Moskuvaara
Kersilö
Sattanen
Puolakkovaara
Tanhua
Kiuru
Sodankylä
Siurunmaa
Rovapää
Isopalo
Hirviäkuru
Orakylä
Härkäjoki
Tähtelä
Aska
Aapajärvi
Luiro
Kokkosniva
Suostola
Lampiselkä
Torvinen
Kairala
Luosto
Suvanto
Vasaniemi
Pelkosenniemi
Korvakumpu
Pyhäjärvi
Saunavaara
Saukkoaapa
Pyhätunturi
Vuostimo
Vuostimojärvi
Tapionniemi
Ylikylä
Dinas
Javarus
Morkkaperä
Köngäs
Tohmo
Värrio
Kemijärvi
Hyypiö
Ketola
Hanhikoski
Rovala
Kalliosalmi
Kuusivaara
Ruopsa
Kelloniemi
Paloјärvi
Misi
Vika
Karsimus
Rovaniemi
Vikajärvi
Olkkajärvi
Nivankylä
Norvasalmi
Poikajärvi
Ala-Nampa
Yli-Nampa
Ristilampi
Korvala
Käyrämö
Raudanjoki
Vuojärvi
Lehtovaara
Seipäjärvi
Lismanaapa
Ristonmännikkö
Riipi
Palsselkä
Vaalajärvi
Länsiranta
Mikkola
Jeesiö
Välitalo
Rajala
Koskenkylä
Tepsa
Rovanpää
Suvantokumpu
Kelontekemä
Koskama
Kelontekemäjärvi
Hormakumpu
Kuusajärvi
Kuusajoki
Kittilä
Jeesiöjärvi
Nilivaara
Rasti
Kiistala
Lintula
Rouravaara
Hanhimaa
Köngäs
Rautuskylä
Sirkka
Levi-Sirkka
Levi
Kätkätunturi
Rikonkumpu
Tepasto
Korpela
Lompolo
Särkijärvi
Salanki
Pulju
Pokka
Kitinen
Kuttura
Repojoki
Ivalon Matti
Lisma
Menesjärvi
Lemmenjoki
Solojärvi
Otsamo
Ranta
Kirakkaköngäs
Veäskoonjarga
Angeli
Pyhäjärvi
Koskenniska
Gal'gunjar'ga
Maarestatunturit
Landjoivi
Morgam-Viibus
Hammastunturi
Uurrekarkia
Korsatunturi
Puljutunturi
Nunnanen
Peltovuoma
Vuontisjärvi
Enontekiö
Ounasjärvi
Pyhäkero
Ketomella
Outtakka
Yli-Kyrö
Raattama
Keräs-Sieppi
Kajanki
Kätkäsuvanto
Liepimäjärvi
Taivaskero
Pallasjärvi
Toras-Sieppi
Keimiötunturi
Jerisjärvi
Muonio
Olostunturi
Muonionalusta
Särkijärvi
Pöntsö
Rauhala
Veitservasa
Karsikkoniemi
Muotkavaara
Olos-Muonio
Äkäsjärvi
Kangosjärvi
Järvenpää
Tiurajärvi
Moloslaki
Lainiotunturi
Äkäslompolo
Ylläs
Hannukainen
Luosu
Ylläsjärvi
Kihlanki
Vanha-Kihlanki
Tapojärvi
Äkäsjokisuu
Niesa
Huuki
Saaripudas
Kaunisvaara
Kolari
Kaunisjoensuu
Teurajärvi
Kurtakko
Kallo
Palonselkä
Kaukonen
Tiukuvaara
Alakylä
Kokkovaara
Tuuliharju
Molkojärvi
Maunujärvi
Hinganmaa
Syväjärvi
Sassali
Kierinki
Unari
Kukasjärvi
Käärmelehto
Osma
Perttaus
Niesi
Saittanulkki
Venejärvi
Pohjasenvaara
Vaattojärvi
Kelloniemi
Kengis
Lappea
Sieppijärvi
Järvirova
Ruokojärvi
Juustovaara
Lohiniva
Kinisjärvi
Helppi
Pasmajärvi
Taapajärvi
Nuottavaara
Ruonajärvi
Maijanen
Jääskö
Tolonen
Meltaus
Marrasjärvi
Alajärvi
Suopajärvi
Törmänki
Patokoski
Marraskoski
Tapionkylä
Kuoksajärvi
Perunkajärvi
Sinettä
Sonka
Mäntyjärvi
Typpyrä
Nuasjärvi
Rattosjärvi
Ruuhijärvi
Konttajärvi
Rovanpää
Korpilompolo
Saukkoripi
Pello
Nivanpää
Matinlompolo
Lankojärvi
Sirkkakoski
Lampsijärvi
Romakkajärvi
Raanujärvi
Kaaraneskoski
Jolanki
Koutus
Alposjärvi
Ajankijärvi
Turtola
Svanstein
Ylinenjärvi
Lehmivaara
Valkeakoski
Rantajärvi
Penttäjä
Mettäjärvi
Aapua
Taka-Aapua
Teikosuvanto
Orajärvi
Naamijoki
Jarhoinen
Jarhois
Kardis
Väylänpää
Kassa
Hietanen
Aitamännikkö
Vittikkovuoma
Juoksengi
Ratasjärvi
Pakisjärvi
Meltosjärvi
Paloјärvi
Ylikylä
Saarenkylä
Arktikum-keskus
E8
E75
E63

1
2
3
4
5
6
7
8
116
109
107
122
S
B
C
D
E
F
19°00′
19°30′
20°00′
20°30′
21°00′
21°30′
22°00′
22°30′
66°30′
66°00′
65°30′
65°00′
64°30′
Purkijaur
Piertinjaure
Haraudden
Jokkmokk
Mattisudden
Fatjas
Miessaure
Högträsk
Kuouka
Tjekartunturi
468
Svartberget
417
Lansjärv
Yttre Lansjärv
Neitaskaite
Ertsjärv
E10
Polcirkeln
Vuottarauto
474
Akapuouta
Sarmekåbbå
552
Tjalmejaure
Lilla Luleälven
Vajmat
Jutsavare
571
Kåskats
Murjek
Porsi
Vuollerim
Kirtik
Flakaberg
Lillsaivis
Lansån
Marsjärv
Vuolvojaure
Tårrajaur
Tjapuouta
636
Majtum
Naustajaure
Luottåive
603
Kåpponis
Kårkul
Rimjokk
Költräsket
Råneälven
Vuottas
Pålkem
Stenträsk
Kerkejaure
Sudok
Randaträsk
Mårdudden
Lillåfors
Lakaträsk
Blåkölen
Forsnäs
E45
Storsand
Luleälven
Tallberg
Talljärv
Kesasjärv
Kälvjärv
Palja
697
Stor-Stákke
787
Varto
682
Piteälven
Stor-Sarkasvare
607
Lillå
Edefors
Holmsvattensel
Grundträsk
Klingersel
Aspliden
Långsel
Kuollejaure
Kittajaur
Puottaure
Krokfors
Forsnäs
Gullträsk
Degervattnet
Lappträsket
Kåbdalis
Varjisån
Snesudden
Kroktjärn
Spikberg
Grundsanden
Sandträsk
Övre Flåsjön
Valvträsk
Forshed
Tjäruträsk
Västannäs
Joknajaure
Lulep
630
Tellejåkk
Bodträskfors
Harads
391
Åträsk
Överstbyn
Forsträskhed
Hovlössjön
Abraur
Trollforsen
Varjisträsk
Svanisträsket
Gunnarsbyn
Morjärv
Norrstrand
374
Hapträsk
Södra Harads
97
Svartlä
Sörbyn
Niemisel
Bjurå
Avafors
356
Vitberget
594
Åberget
Ångesträsk
Åsen
Malmesjaure
Ljuså
Hundsjön
Vitåfors
Östansjö
Suddesjaur
Piteälven
Vitberget
Övre Bredåker
Årbyn
Bellunåive
673
Harrejaureliden
647
Moskosel
Junkerkölen
348
Norra Bredåker
Åskogen
Norra Prästholm
Vitå
Tabmokåive
556
Bredsel
Åkerholmen
Skogså
Skatamark
Böle
Tjappsåive
Vidsel
Björkberg
Vittjärv
Vibbyn
Råneå
Jämtön
Färholmen
Ljusträsk
Degerbäcken
Heden
Boden
Smedsbyn
Strittjomvare
Sleng
Grundvattnet
Enstakaberget
440
Brännberg
Lomträsk
Pilträsk
Vändträsk
Sävast
Borjelslandet
Sundom
Västra Kikkejaure
Auktsjaur
Stora Tallberg
Rättsel
Östra Granberg
Övre Tväråsel
Persön
Bocköfjärden
Rönnberg
Nystrand
Mockträsk
Krokträsk
Bergön
Öv Långträsk
Storberget
562
Nattberget
458
Vistheden
Unbyn
Södra Sunderbyn
Rutvik
Brändön
Vuotner
Grundsel
Vistbäcken
Avan
Selet
Avaviken
Akkavare
Bäcklund
Lauker
Vistån
Korsträsk
Älvsbyn
Pålsträsk
Klöverträsk
Gammelstaden
Bensbyn
Fjuskön
Arvidsjaur
Deppis
Guortesliden
557
Södra Bränntråsk
247
Bälinge
Notviken
Luleå
Månsträsk
Stenträsket
Norra Holmnäs
591
Storsund
Gammelstads kyrkstad
Storberg
Dartsel
Bänkerträsket
Tvärån
Backträsk
Bergnäset
Svartöstaden
Pjesker
330
Arvidsträsk
Alvik
Antnäs
Långträsk
Måttsund
Långön
Guorbabuouda
Byskeälven
Sikfors
Sjulsmark
Ersnäs
Kallax
Sandön
Mausjaure
Gråträsk
Manjärvträsk
Koler
Arnemark
E4
Hedberg
Huvåsen
Långsund
Storbrändön
Krutbergen
631
Aspliden
Abborrträsk
Strömnäs
Nybyn
Junkön
Bäcknäs
Grundträsk
Åträsk
Rönnberget
Norrfjärden
Rosvik
Björkland
Rissnabben
Stor-Flötuberget
426
Yttersta
Lillpite
Alhamn
Germandön
Adak
Kokträsk
Hålberg
Baktsjaur
Kåtaselet
Nördberget
469
Långträsk
Flötuträsk
Böle
Kopparnäs
Mannön
Kallfjärden
Tjärnberg
Rönnliden
Utterliden
Svanträsk
Roknäs
Trundön
Myrheden
Holmfors
Svensbyn
Öjebyn
Piteå
Baggen
Springliden
Moräng
Laisejaure
Granberg
Bergsviken
Vargön
Rödkallen
Södra Sandträsk
Glommersträsk
Ullbergsträsk
Granträskmark
Blåsmark
Munksund
Hortlax
Storliden
507
Järvträsk
Missenträsk
Stenstråsk
Åselet
Malå
Hemmingsmark
Pitsund
Mellerstön
Långträsk
Petikån
Klubbfors
Grönbo
Kälen
Bondön
370
Grundträsk
Skellefteälven
Storklinten
516
Åbyälven
Stor-Rebben
Jävre
Näsliden
Granbergsträsk
Ålund
Stenskäret
Rentjärn
Degerträsk
Fällfors
Gagsmark
Jävrefjärden
Malån
Röka
Östra Aliden
Finnträsk
Källbomark
Jävre Sandön
550
Jörn
Österjörn
Stavaträsk
Kinnbäcksfjärden
Lillholmträsk
Norrlångträsk
Åbyn
Rönnskär
Stora Kvammarn
Svansele
Nyträsk
Lillkågeträsk
Renholmen
Bjurträsk
Bjurselet
Tåme
Tåmfjärden
Ruskele
Norsjö
Kusfors
Häbberstiden
Byske
Byskefjärden
Renström
Södra Drängsmark
Arnberg
Sandfors
Furuögrund
Ajaursjön
Strömfors
Kusmark
Ostvik
Vindelälven
Boliden
Ersmark
Romelsön
Risliden
Bastumarks by
Svanström
Kåge
Forsholm
Basturäsk
Kågeälven
Varuträsk
Hemmingen
Boviken
Finnfors
Manjaur
Kattisträsk
Medle
Myckle
Skellefteå
Krångfors
Bergsbyn
Granträsket
Bjurfors
Ursviken
Siksele
Långvattnet
Buréälven
Gummark
Skelleftehamn
Mårdsele
Kalvträsk
Stor-Blåbergsliden
374
Östra Skråmträsk
Örviken
Vitberget
486
Bureå
Ytter-Busjö
Holmträsk
Sörbyn
Järvtjärn
364
Skelleftebukten
Västra Hjäggböle
Sjöbotten
Lycksele
Petisträsk
Karonsbo
Arvån
Villvattnet
Skötgrönnan
Södra Åbyn
Ljusvattnet
Ekorrträsk
Åmsele
Storbrännan
Burträsk
Mjövattnet
Vånören
Risån
Burträsket
Ekträsk
Bjuröfjärden
Amträsk
Storsavarträsk
Rotsjön
Kvarnbyn
Vallen
Bjuröklubb
Göksjön
Kvarnriset
Bygdeträsk
Lillsele
Storsävarträsket
Hökmark
Stryksele
Sjöbrånet
Vebomark
Mångbyn
Bygdeträsket
Kålaboda
Kamsjö
Bygdsiljum
Lövånger
Avanäs
Hällnäs
Storsandsjö
Ytterträsk
Korssjön
Lövsele
Flarken
Långsele
Åkullsjön
Ånäset
Ledskär
Granö
Tegnäset
Botsmark
Skäran
Skarda
Skurträsk
Vindel-Ånäset
Hertsånger
Umeälven
Vindeln
Rickleån
Robe
Vännskär
Micklaträsk
Västra Sjulsmark
Gumark
Tvärålund
Stora Sandsjön
E12
E4
12
353
363
365
373
383
94
95

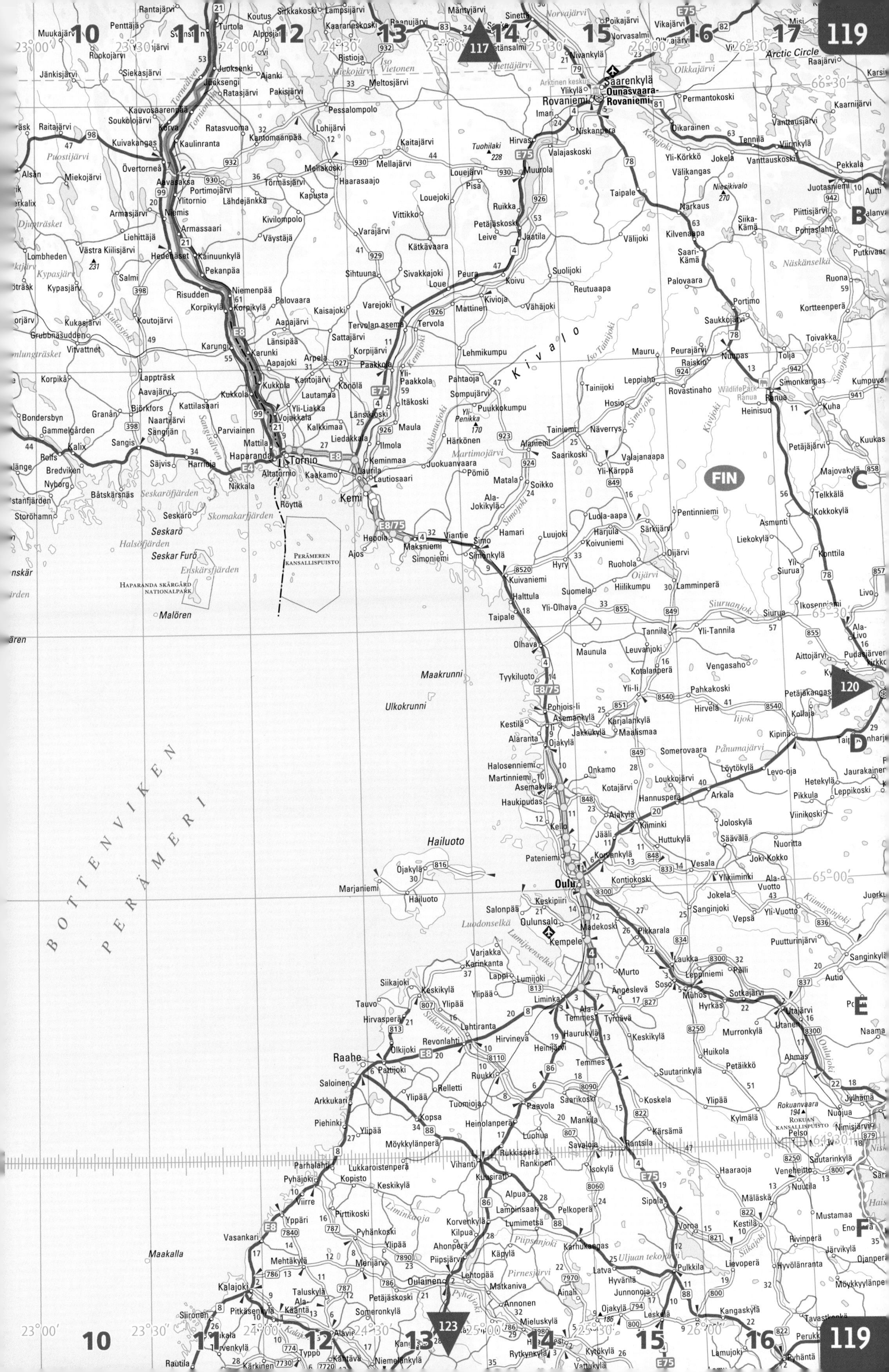

10
11
12
13
14
15
16
17
117
120
123
Arctic Circle
Rovaniemi
Saarenkylä
Ounasvaara-Rovaniemi
Arktinen keskus
Ylikylä
Tornio
Haparanda
Kemi
Keminmaa
Kalix
Simo
Kuivaniemi
Ii
Haukipudas
Kiiminki
Oulu
Oulunsalo
Kempele
Liminka
Muhos
Utajärvi
Raahe
Pattijoki
Vihanti
Oulainen
Kalajoki
Alavieska
Ranua
Tervola
Ylitornio
Övertorneå
Aavasaksa
Pello
Hailuoto
Marjaniemi
Maakrunni
Ulkokrunni
Seskarö
Seskar Furö
Malören
Haparanda skärgård nationalpark
Perämeren kansallispuisto
Rokuan kansallispuisto
Rokuanvaara 194
Tuohilaki 228
Niesikivalo 270
Yli-Penikka 170
Kivalo
Kemijoki
Simojoki
Iijoki
Oulujoki
Siikajoki
Pyhäjoki
Torneälven
Tornionjoki
Liminkaoja
Luodonselkä
Lumijoenselkä
Seskaröfjärden
Skomakarfjärden
Halsöfjärden
Enskärsfjärden
Puostijärvi
Oijärvi
Siuruanjoki
Pånumajärvi
Kiiminginjoki
Pirnesjärvi
Uljuan tekojärvi
Piipsanjoki
BOTTENVIKEN
PERÄMERI
FIN
Wildlife Park Ranua
E4
E8
E75
E8/75
23°00′
23°30′
24°00′
24°30′
25°00′
25°30′
26°00′
26°30′
66°30′
66°00′
65°30′
65°00′
64°30′
B
C
D
E
F

117
119
124
Rovaniemi
Saarenkylä
Ounasvaara-Rovaniemi
Arktinen keskus
Kivalo
Haparanda
Tornio
Kemi
Simo
Ranua
Pudasjärvi
Isö-Syöte-Pudasjärvi
Oulu
Kempele
Liminka
Raahe
Hailuoto
Muhos
Utajärvi
Vaala
Oulujärvi
Kalajoki
Oulainen
Vihanti
Ylitornio
Tervola
Keminmaa
Ii
Haukipudas
Kiiminki
Tyrnävä
Pulkkila
Rokuanvaara
Rokuan kansallispuisto
Perämeren kansallispuisto
Haparanda skärgård nationalpark
Bottenviken
Perämeri
Maakrunni
Ulkokrunni
Malören
Seskarö
Kalix
S
FIN
E8
E4
E75
E8/75
66°30′
66°00′
65°30′
65°00′
64°30′
23°30′
24°00′
24°30′
25°00′
25°30′
26°00′
26°30′
27°00′
B
C
D
E
F
2
3
4
5
6
7
8
9

10
11
12
13
14
15
16
17
28°00′
28°30′
29°00′
29°30′
30°00′
30°30′
31°00′
115
Arctic Circle
66°30′
66°00′
65°30′
65°00′
64°30′
B
C
D
E
F
RUS
viii
125
Joutsijärvi
Varpuvaara
Haaparanta
Räisälä
Suomutunturi
Suommu
Tonkopuro
Morottaja
Karhujärvi
Maaninkavaara
Kivelä
Palopera
Nolimo
Aittaniemi
Jumisko
Mourujärvi
Ristilä
Niirokumpu
Lehtiniemi
Karjalaisenniemi
Lamminvaara
Perä-Posio
Keski-Posio
Suolijärvet
Riisitunturin kansallispuisto
Ahola
Posio
Hietaniemi
Hyväniemi
Vasaraperä
Raistakka
Luonselkä
Kolkonjärvi
Mäntyjärvi
Livonniska
Kuloharju
Anetjärvi
Löytövaara
Sirniö
Kouva
Kumpujenselkä
Kynsijärvi
Kynsiperä
Pyhitys
Kostonjärvi
Syötteen kansallispuisto
Loukusa
Iso-Syöte
Syötekylä
Virkkunen
Koitila
Siekkinen
Taivalkoski
Isokumpu
Lehtovaara
Jurmu
Pintamo
Hautakylä
Poijula
Yli-Kurki
Hukijärvi
Pääaho
Puhos
Siivikko
Salmijärvi
Näljänkä
Kurkikylä
Jaurakkajärvi
Suolijärvi
Korpinen
Ränninvaara
Yrittäperä
Pyssyperä
Joukokylä
Neulikko
Aittokylä
Naulaperä
Puolanka
Leipivaara
Rasinkylä
Kurtto
Kytömäki
Väisälä
Väyrylä
Paljakka
Kangaskylä
Hyrynsalmi
Lietekylä
Oravivaara
Nalkki
Kotila
Uva
Törmänmäki
Raappananmäki
Uura
Ristijärvi
Kivesjärvi
Karjalanvaara
Saukkovaara
Pyhäntä
Vaarankylä
Melalahti
Paltamo
Mieslahti
Hämänmäki
Saviranta
Hannusranta
Paltaselkä
Kontiomäki
Paltaniemi
Kuluntalahti
Tuulimäki
Kajaani
Pohjavaara
Nakkurinvaara
Suovaara
Vuokatti
Sotkamo
Nuasjärvi
Hirvasvaara
Aholanvaara
Ritakorkia
Oulanka
Ruvanaho
Oulangan kansallispuisto
Hautajärvi
Niemelä
Palotunturi
Kolimiemi
Koramoniemi
Vallioniemi
Piiloperä
Patoniemi
Alakitka
Kitka
Kantojoki
Kallunki
Käylä
Säkkilä
Juuma
Oulankajoki
Liikasenvaara
Tolva
Yli-Kitka
Viitaranta
Suonnankylä
Kesämemenkylä
Virkkula
Rukatunturi
Ruka
Salminen
Rukajärvi
Oivanki
Soidinkumpu
Nissinvaara
Lohiranta
Livojärvi
Kurkijärvi
Kuusamo
Kuusamo-Ruka
Korhosenniemi
Majava
Jokilampi
Kynsivaara
Purnuvaara
Kuolio
Oijusluoma
Penttilänvaara
Pahkakumpu
Käsmä
Inkee
Vaarakylä
Särkelä
Polo
Arnijärvi
Jokijärvi
Tyrävaara
Tyrämäki
Tyräjärvi
Kurtti
Kuusijärvi
Latvajärvenperä
Keminperä
Korvuanjärvi
Pistö
Paranka
Lesovaara
Pyhäkylä
Korvua
Pyhäjärvi
Metsäkylä
Kivivaara
Piispajärvi
Leino
Mustavaara
Ahola
Saarikylä
Vaaranniva
Vääkiö
Leppälä
Ahjola
Naamankajärvi
Parkkila
Luokkala
Tervavaara
Ahelva
Losovaara
Alajärvi
Kannas
Pesiönranta
Pesiökylä
Kuurtola
Lonkka
Ämmänsaari
Suomussalmi
Palovaara
Lylykylä
Laaja
Korpikylä
Sakaravaara
Hoikka
Hyrynjärvi
Hakokylä
Nuottikylä
Laitala
Kyparävaara
Ollilanniemi
Jokikylä
Matkavaara
Koskenkylä
Mustavaara
Rampsankylä
Tapanikylä
Härmänkylä
Kusamonkylä
Hiisijärvi
Sipinen
Paakinmäki
Lemetinvaara
Heinämäki
Vuosanka
Koskenmäki
Huuhilonkylä
Kellojärvi
Ala-Vieksi
Juonto
Hietaperä
Ontojärvi
Soidinvaara
Kuhmo
Paljakka
Suorajärvi
Vuotunki
Jyrkänkoski
Lehto
Särkiluoma
Kiviperä
Määttälänvaara
Suininki
Säynäjä
Maivala
Heikkilä
Sossonniemi
Kärpänkylä
Muojärvi
Koskenkylä
Törmäsenvaara
Haukiniemi
Kemilä
Kortesalmi
Multiperä
Iivaara
Lusminki
Poussu
Soivio
Penikkajärvi
Tammela
Murtovaara
Irninniemi
Vaaraperä
Kurvinen
Teeriranta
Iijärvi
Hossa
Selkoskylä
Pajuvaara
Lavala
Juntusranta
Keträvaara
Pyykösskylä
Rasinvaara
Kiannanniemi
Lappi
Myllylahti
Aittovaara
Kiantajärvi
Näätävaara
Puras
Kotiranta
Raate
Mäkelänranta
Vuokkijärvi
Pyykkölänvaara
Ala-Vuokki
Jumaliskylä
Viitavaara
Keskinen
Moisiovaara
Pekankylä
Hirvivaara
Kuumu
Vartius
Lehtovaara
Änättijärvi
Iivantiira
Haukilahti
Lentiira
Korkana
Niva
Maaselkä
Sumsa
Kalliojoki
Timoniemi
Lentua
Vieksi
Juntinvaara
Viiksimo
Hirvola
Kämäränkylä
Marjokylä
Saarivaara
Veihtivaara
Kuivajärvi
Malahvianvaara
Lehtovaara
Pirttivaara
Tumcha
Oz. Ruvozero
Oz. Kundozero
Oz. Sokolozero
Kuma
Panajärvi Natsional'nyy Park
Olanga
Ozero Pyaozero
Ozero Tavayarvi
Sofporog
Pyaozerskiy
Tungozero
Poncha
Pista
Tukhkala
Oz. Okhtan''yarvi
Oz. Pistayarvi
Regozero
Kalevala
Voynitsa
Oz. Sredneye Kuyto
Oz. Verkhneye Kuyto
Voknavolok
Ozero Kento
Livo
Kostomuksha
Ozero Kamennoye
Oz. Kimasozero
Kimasozero
E63
5
20
843
863
941
945
947
950
8420
8400
800
858
862
8610
9190
9160
8980
8390
897
8950
9130
892
891
912
9110
904
888
8890
9070
89
9000
8800
899
870
78
6
9

2
3
4
5
6
7
8
9
118
19°30′
20°00′
20°30′
21°00′
21°30′
22°00′
22°30′
B
C
D
E
F
107
126
S
64°00′
63°30′
63°00′
62°30′
20′
10′
Södra Åbyn
Storbränan
Burträsk
Mjövattnet
Liusvattnet
Skötgrönnan
Vånören
Ekträsk
Rotsjön
Kvarnbyn
Kvarnriset
Vallen
Bjuröklubb
Storsävarträsk
Bygdeträsk
Hökmark
Lillsele
Mångbyn
Vebomark
Kålaboda
Sjöbränet
Kamsjö
Storsandsjö
Bygdeträsket
Bygdsiljum
Lövånger
Lövsele
Ytterträsk
Korssjön
Flarken
Ledskär
Långsele
Ånäset
Skäran
Hertsånger
Tegnäset
Botsmark
Åkullsjön
Skurträsk
Vindeln
Vindel-Ånäset
Robertsfors
Rickleån
Sikeå
Vännskär
Örträsk
Bjurfors
Mickelsträsk
Västra Sjulsmark
Gravmark
Skivsjön
Tvärålund
Stora Sandsjön
Öreström
Ramsele
Rödåsel
Selet
Kroksjö
Tavelsjö
Storarmsjö
Byggeå
Bygdefjärden
Bastuträsk
Bullmark
Stärkesmark
Bodbyn
Djäkneboda
Ratan
Ångermanbalen
Bjurholm
Balsjö
Flurkmark
Pengfors
Hissjön
Vitvattnet
Vännäsby
Vännäs
Brännland
Sävar
Ersmark
Sörfors
Angnäs
Brännland
Pengsjö
Hjäggsjö
Norrfjärden
Brattsbacka
Umeå
Täfteå
Hörnsjö
Röbäck
Innertavle
Östnäsfjärden
St Fjäderägg
Nyåker
Gräsmyr
Hössjö
Djäkneböle
Holmön
Hummelholm
Nyland
Stöcke
Täftefjärden
Västra Kvarken
Torrböle
Bjännberg
Holmsund
Ängesön
Klöse
Örsbäck
Sörmjöle
Ströмbäck
Obbola
Ledusjö
Brattfors
Bredskär
Lemelsjön
Ängersjö
Hörnefors
Grossgrunden
Byviken
Långed
Mjölefjärden
Salberg
Olofsfors
Nordmaling
Holmögadd
Flärke
Lögdeå
Rundvik
Bredvik
Norrbyn
Norrbyskär
Nyland
Ava
Rönnholm
Kråken
Öreffärden
Skademark
Järnäs
Snöan
Järnäsklubb
Västanå
Degerfjärden
Grundsuna
Fanbyn
Husum
Banafjäl
Ällön
Skeppsmalen
Norra Kvarken
Merenkurkku
Mickelsörarna
Valsörarna
Norra Gloppet
Östra Gloppet
Björkön
Björköby
Replot fjärden
Merenkurkku
Köklot
Brändövik
Replot
Norra Vallgrund
Södra Vallgrund
Södra Gloppet
Jungsund
Petsmo
Österhankmo
Maxmo (Maksamaa)
Kvevlax
Vassor
Korsholm (Mustasaari)
Vaasa (Vasa)
Sundom
Solf
Hälsingby
Rönnskären
Bergö
Bergön
Aminne
Malax (Maalahti)
Övermalax
Långåminne
Molpe
Petalax
Poola
Halsön
Korsnäs
Korsbäck
Sarvijoki
Nyby
Södra Björkön
Taklax
Harrström
Pörtom
Harjunkylä
Niemenkylä
Tjöby
Bodbacka
Närvijoki
Järvenpää
Rangsby
Övermark
Norrnäs
Östra Yttermark
Västra Yttermark
Grytskäret
Nämpnäs
Närpes
Karlä
Teuva
Riippi
Äystö
Gottböle
Perälä
Kaskinen (Kaskö)
Pjelax
Myrkky
Luovankylä
Karijoki
Tjöck
Kristinestad (Kristiinankaupunki)
Lappfjärd
Dagsmark
Träskvik
Härkmeri
Vanhakylä
Kärjenkoski
Skaftung
Vesijärvi
Ömossa
Suojoki
Kallträsk
Jakobstad (Pietarsaari)
Torsön
Sundby
Soklot
Nykarleby (Uusikaarlepyy)
Vexala
Monäs
Munsala
Ytterjeppo
Jeppo
Hirvlax
Monå
Pensala
Ekola
Östero
Oravais (Oravainen)
Särkimo
Oxkangar
Kimo
Komossa
Kuoppala
Tuckur
Vörå
Koskeby
Kaurajärvi
Kosola
Untamala
Lehmäjoki
Vähäkyrö
Tervajoki
Laihia
Isokyrö
Liipantönkkä
Orismala
Ylistaro
Kitinoja
Jakkula
Kylänpää
Jääskänjoki
Jokikylä
Jokiperä
Kivi-ja Levalamman tekojärvi
Munakka
Könni
Seinäjoki
Huissinkylä
Ilmajoki
Koskimäki
Nopankylä
Koskenkorva
Pojanluoma
Jurva
Panttila
Kampinkylä
Tuiskula
Kurikka
Luopa
Polvenkylä
Jyllintaival
Myllykylä
Norinkylä
Lohiluoma
Jalasjärvi
Kainasto
Kauhajoki
Aronkylä
Lamminmaa
Sahankylä
Keskikylä
Päntäne
Ikkeläjärvi
Ilvesjoki
Hyyppä
Panttikylä
Nummijärvi
Uuro
Nummikoski
Sara
Heikkilä
Kauhajärvi
Kauhanevan-Pohjankankaan kansallispuisto
Lauhanvuoren kansallispuisto
Lauhavuori 230
Villamo
Isojoki
Perä-Hyyppä
Karvia
Sarvela
Alkkia
Saarviluoma
Suomijärvi
Jyllinkoski
Honkajoki
E4
E8
E12
Ostrobotnia?
Hinjärv
Kyrönjoki
Isojoki
Kauhajoki

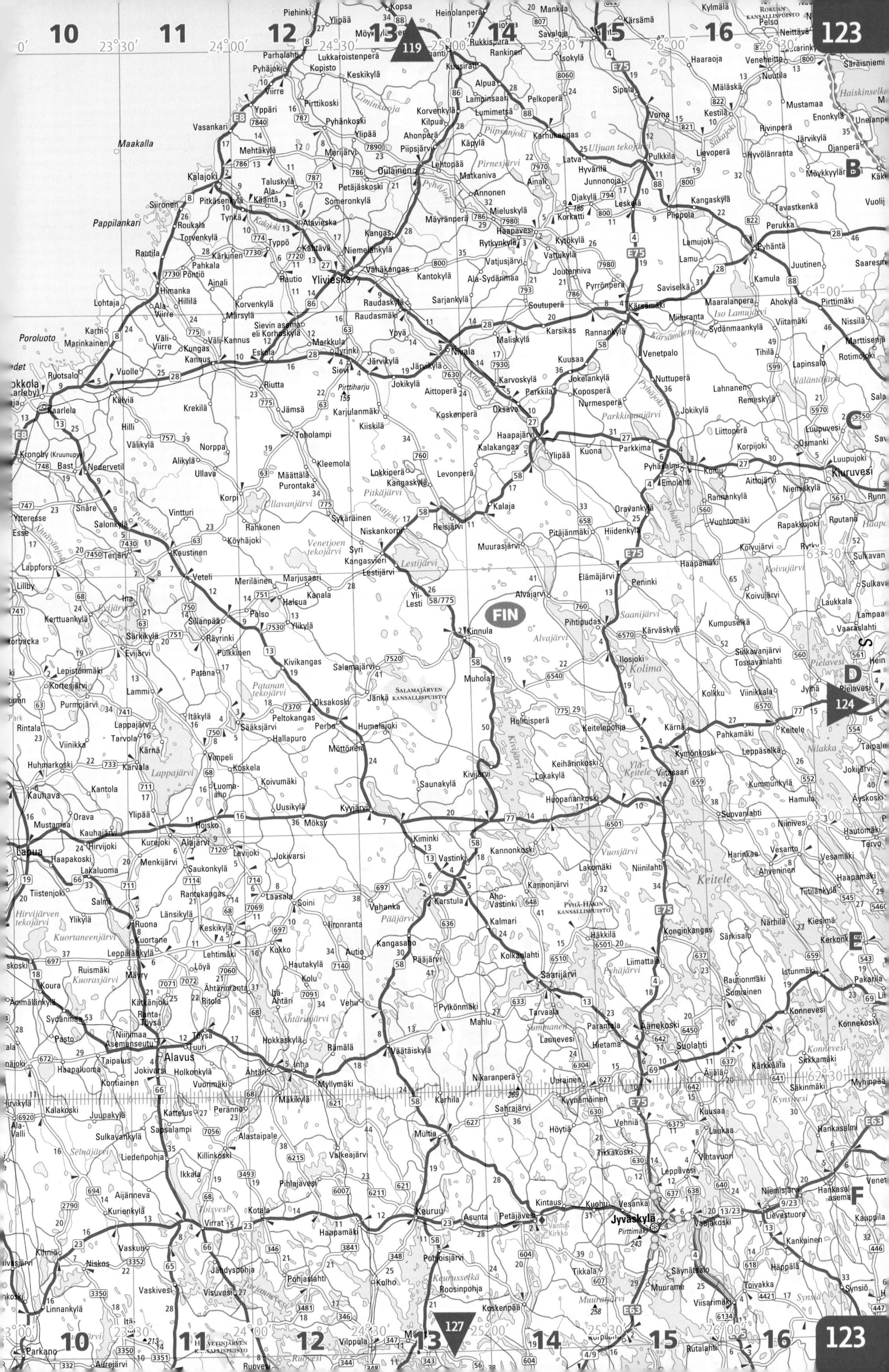
10
11
12
13
14
15
16
119
124
127
FIN
B
C
D
E
F
Piehinki
Kopsa
Heinolanperä
Mankila
Kylmälä
Rokuan kansallispuisto
Pelso
Neittävä
Kärsämä
Ylipää
Möykkylä
Rukkispera
Savaloja
Parhalahti
Lukkaroistenperä
Rankinen
Isokylä
Haaraoja
Veneheitto
Säräisniemi
Pyhäjoki
Kopisto
Keskikylä
Kuusirati
Nuutila
Viirre
Alpua
Sipola
Mäläskä
Yppäri
Pirttikoski
Liminkaoja
Lampinsaari
Pelkoperä
Kestilä
Mustamaa
Vasankari
Korvenkylä
Lumimetsä
Vorna
Enonkylä
Pyhänkoski
Kilpua
Siikajoki
Rivinperä
Maakalla
Ylipää
Ahonperä
Piipsanjoki
Korhukangas
Järvikylä
Mehtäkylä
Merijärvi
Piipsjärvi
Käpylä
Uljuan tekojärvi
Pulkkila
Lievoperä
Hyvölänranta
Ojanperä
Latva
Pirnesjärvi
Hyvärilä
Möykkyylä
Kalajoki
Taluskylä
Oulainen
Lehtopää
Matkaniva
Ainali
Junnonoja
Ala-Kääntä
Petäjäskoski
Pyhäjoki
Annonen
Ojakylä
Leskelä
Kangaskylä
Tavastkenkä
Siironen
Pitkäsenkylä
Someronkylä
Mieluskylä
Korkatti
Piippola
Perukka
Pappilankari
Roukala
Tynkä
Kalajoki
Alavieska
Mäyränperä
Haapavesi
Rytkynkylä
Kytökylä
Lamujoki
Pyhäntä
Torvenkylä
Typpö
Kangas
Vattukylä
Lamu
Rautila
Kärkinen
Kääntä
Niemelänkylä
Vatjusjärvi
Pahkala
Pöntiö
Vähäkangas
Kantokylä
Ala-Sydänmaa
Joutenniva
Juutinen
Saaresmäki
Ainali
Rautio
Ylivieska
Pyrrönperä
Saviselkä
Kamula
Himanka
Sarjankylä
Hillilä
Lohtaja
Ala-Viirre
Korvenkylä
Raudaskylä
Soutuperä
Kärsämäki
Maaralanpera
Ahokylä
Pirttimäki
Märsylä
Raudasmäki
Miiluranta
Iso Lamujärvi
Karhi
Sievin asema eli Korhoskylä
Ypyä
Karsikas
Rannankylä
Kärsämäenjoki
Sydänmaankylä
Viitamäki
Nissilä
Poroluoto
Marinkainen
Väli-Viirre
Väli-Kannus
Markkula
Maliskylä
Venetpalo
Tihilä
Marttisenjärvi
Kungas
Kannus
Eskola
Jyrinki
Järvikylä
Nivala
Järvikylä
Kuusaa
Lapinsalo
Rotimojoki
Vuolle
Sievi
Jokikylä
Karvoskylä
Jokelankylä
Nuttuperä
Nälänjärvi
Ruotsalo
Kokkola (Karleby)
Kälviä
Riutta
Pirttiharju
Aittoperä
Kalajoki
Parkkila
Koposperä
Lahnanen
Remeskylä
Kaarlela
Krekilä
Jämsä
Karjulanmäki
Nurmesperä
Parkkimanjärvi
Jokikylä
Hilli
Kiiskilä
Koskenperä
Oksava
Haapajärvi
Liittoperä
Luupuvesi
Välikylä
Norppa
Toholampi
Kalakangas
Parkkima
Korpijoki
Osmanki
Kronoby (Kruunupyy)
Bast
Nedervetil
Alikylä
Kleemola
Lokkiperä
Levonperä
Ylipää
Kuona
Pyhäsalmi
Komu
Luupujoki
Kiuruvesi
Ullava
Määttälä
Purontaka
Kangaskylä
Emolahti
Aittojärvi
Niemiskylä
Snåre
Korpi
Pitkäjärvi
Rannankylä
Ytteresse
Ullavanjärvi
Kalaja
Oravankylä
Esse
Salonkylä
Perhonjoki
Vintturi
Sykäräinen
Lestijoki
Reisjärvi
Vuohtomäki
Rapakkojoki
Ähtävänjoki
Rahkonen
Niskankorpi
Pitäjänmäki
Hiidenkylä
Routana
Köyhäjoki
Venetjoen tekojärvi
Syri
Muurasjärvi
Koivujärvi
Terjärv
Kaustinen
Kangasvieri
Lestijärvi
Haapamäki
Sulkavanjärvi
Lappfors
Lestijärvi
Elämäjärvi
Peninki
Koivujärvi
Sulkava
Lillby
Veteli
Meriläinen
Marjusaari
Yli-Lesti
Alvajärvi
Ina
Halsua
Kanala
Koivujärvi
Laukkala
Kerttuankylä
Evijärvi
Sillanpää
Polso
Ylikylä
Kinnula
Pihtipudas
Saanijärvi
Kärväskylä
Kumpuselkä
Vaaraslahti
Torbacka
Särkikylä
Räyrinki
Alvajärvi
Lepistönmäki
Evijärvi
Pulkkinen
Kivikangas
Salamajärvi
Muhola
Ilosjoki
Sulkavanjärvi
Tossavanlahti
Kortesjärvi
Patana
Kolima
Pielavesi
Lammi
Patanan tekojärvi
Salamajärven kansallispuisto
Jänkä
Kolkku
Viinikkala
Jylhä
Purmojärvi
Oksakoski
Holmisperä
Keitelepohja
Kärnä
Pahkamäki
Keitele
Lappajärvi
Itäkylä
Peltokangas
Rintala
Tarvola
Kärnä
Sääksjärvi
Perho
Humalajoki
Hallapuro
Kivijärvi
Viinikka
Vimpeli
Möttönen
Keihärinkoski
Kymönkoski
Leppäselkä
Ylä-Keitele
Viitasaari
Nilakka
Huhmarkoski
Karvala
Koskela
Lappajärvi
Lokakylä
Taipale
Kantola
Luoma-aho
Koivumäki
Saunakylä
Kivijärvi
Kummunkylä
Jokijärvi
Kauhava
Uusikylä
Huopanankoski
Hamula
Äyskoski
Orava
Ylipää
Kyyjärvi
Suovanlahti
Niinivesi
Mustamaa
Kauhajärvi
Hoisko
Möksy
Hautomäki
Hirvijoki
Kurejoki
Alajärvi
Levijoki
Kiminki
Kannonkoski
Tervo
Lapua
Haapakoski
Menkijärvi
Jokivarsi
Vastinki
Vuosjärvi
Harinkaa
Vesanto
Vesamäki
Lakaluoma
Saukonkylä
Lakomäki
Niinilahti
Ahveninen
Haapamäki
Tiistenjoki
Salmi
Rantakangas
Laasala
Soini
Vahanka
Karstula
Aho-Vastinki
Kannonjärvi
Keitele
Tiitilänkylä
Hirvijärven tekojärvi
Ylikylä
Ruona
Länsikylä
Ironranta
Pääjärvi
Kalmari
Pyhä-Häkin kansallispuisto
Närhilä
Kiesimä
Kuortane
Keskikylä
Kuortaneenjärvi
Häkkilä
Konginkangas
Särkisalo
Kerkonkoski
Leppälänkylä
Lehtimäki
Kukko
Autio
Kangasaho
Kolkanlahti
Liimattala
Ruismäki
Löyä
Hautakylä
Pääjärvi
Saarijärvi
Pyhäjärvi
Istunmäki
Pakarila
Koura
Kuorasjärvi
Mäyry
Kolu
Rautionmäki
Sumiainen
Ämmälänkylä
Kätkänjoki
Ähtärinranta
Itä-Ähtäri
Vehu
Pylkönmäki
Konnevesi
Sydänmaa
Ranta-Töysä
Ritola
Ähtärinjärvi
Mahlu
Tarvaala
Summanen
Parantala
Äänekoski
Konnekoski
Niinimaa
Asemanseutu
Töysä
Tuuri
Hokkaskylä
Rämälä
Väätäiskylä
Lannevesi
Hietama
Suolahti
Konnevesi
Pasto
Taipalus
Alavus
Inha
Ähtäri
Myllymäki
Nikaranperä
Urainen
Äijälä
Kärkkäälä
Sirkkamäki
Haapaluoma
Jokivarsi
Holkonkylä
Vuorimäki
Kontiainen
Mäkikylä
Karhila
Sahrajärvi
Kyynämöinen
Säkinmäki
Myhinpää
Hirvikylä
Kalakoski
Kattelus
Peränne
Kuusaa
Kynsivesi
Ala-Valli
Juupakylä
Sapsalampi
Vehniä
Höytiä
Laukaa
Hankasalmi
Sulkavankylä
Alastaipale
Multia
Tikkakoski
Vihtavuori
Seinäjärvi
Liedenpohja
Killinkoski
Valkeajärvi
Leppävesi
Ikkala
Pihlajavesi
Niemisjärvi
Hankasalmi asema
Aijänneva
Kotala
Kintaus
Kuohu
Vesanka
Kurienkylä
Töysvesi
Keuruu
Asunta
Petäjävesi
Vanha Kirkko
Jyväskylä
Vaajakoski
Lievestuore
Kauppila
Virrat
Haapamäki
Pirttimäki
Kankainen
Vaskuu
Jähdyspohja
Pohjoisjärvi
Kaurusselkä
Säynätsalo
Häppälä
Khmiö
Niskos
Pohjaslahti
Kolho
Roosinpohja
Tikkala
Muurame
Toivakka
Synsiö
Vaskivesi
Visuvesi
Muuratjärvi
Viisarimäki
Synsiä
Linnankylä
Itä-Aure
Koskenpää
Parkano
Helvetinjärven kansallispuisto
Aurejärvi
Ruovesi
Vilppula
Rutalahti
Korpilahti
E8
E75
E63
E12

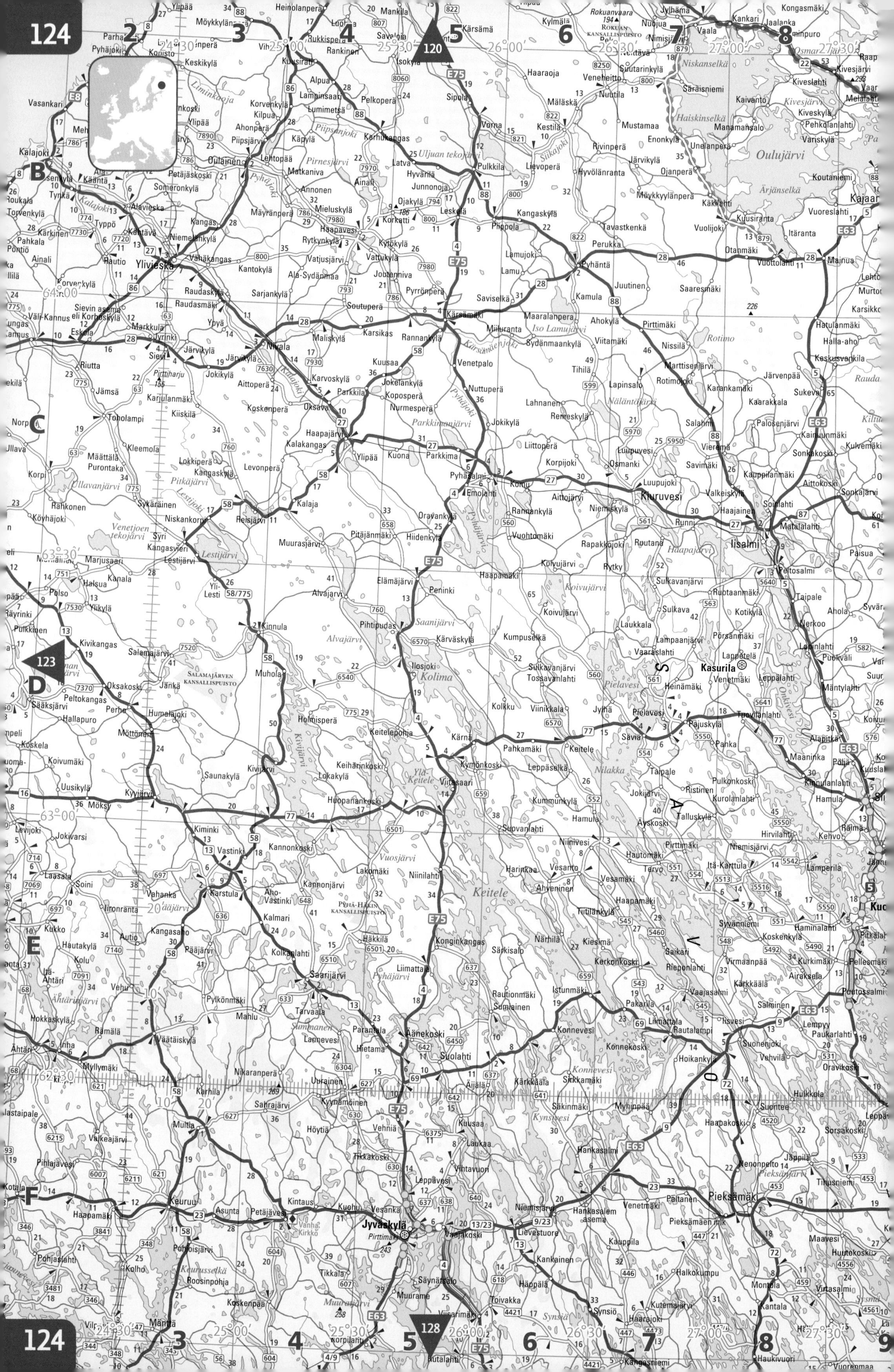
Kalajoki
Ylivieska
Oulainen
Nivala
Haapajärvi
Kärsämäki
Pyhäntä
Vaala
Oulujärvi
Kajaani
Vuolijoki
Pulkkila
Haapavesi
Reisjärvi
Pyhäsalmi
Kiuruvesi
Iisalmi
Sievi
Toholampi
Kannus
Lestijärvi
Kinnula
Pihtipudas
Kivijärvi
Viitasaari
Pielavesi
Kasurila
Nilsiä
Siilinjärvi
Keitele
Perho
Kyyjärvi
Karstula
Saarijärvi
Äänekoski
Suolahti
Konnevesi
Rautalampi
Vesanto
Tervo
Suonenjoki
Pieksämäki
Jyväskylä
Keuruu
Petäjävesi
Multia
Laukaa
Hankasalmi
Ähtäri
Soini
Alajärvi
Vimpeli
Mänttä
Muurame
Kangasniemi
Haukivuori
Halsua
Veteli
Lappajärvi
Jämsä
Vaajakoski
Toivakka
Kinnula
Pyhäjärvi
Pyhäjoki
Merijärvi
Rokua
Haapamäki
Uljuan tekojärvi
Keitele
Kolima
Alvajärvi
Vuosijärvi
Konnevesi
Salamajärven kansallispuisto
Pyhä-Häkin kansallispuisto
Rokuan kansallispuisto
E8
E63
E75
120
123
128
25°00′
25°30′
26°00′
26°30′
27°00′
27°30′
64°00′
63°30′
63°00′
62°30′
B
C
D
E
F
2
3
4
5
6
7
8
9

10
11
12
13
14
15
16
121
129
B
C
D
E
F
ix
FIN
RUS
Kostomuksha
Ozero Kamennoye
Oz. Kimasozero
Kimasozero
Kuhmo
Lentiira
Korkana
Maaselkä
Sumsa
Kalliojoki
Viiksimo
Juntinvaara
Hirvelä
Kämäränkylä
Kortevaara
Lammasjärvi
Kiekinkoski
Hukkajärvi
Haukela
Kesselinkylä
Oz. Roykul'skoye
Rastinkylä
Sivakka
Saunajärvi
Saarela
Riihivaara
Reboly
Oz. Leksozero
Lauvuskylä
Vepsänjärvi
Iso Tipasjärvi
Hiidenportin kansallispuisto
Mujejärvi
Jonkeri
Teljo
Petäiskylä
Kuohattijärvi
Savijärvi
Kivivaara
Tulos
Oz. Tulos
Kimovaara
Nurmes
Nurmijärvi
Oz. Sula
Vieki
Mätäsvaara
Pankajärvi
Lieksanjoki
Ruunaa
Lendery
Ozero Kuykasel'kya
Lieksa
Pankakoski
Hatunkylä
Kitsi
Inari
Shaverki
Pielinen
Paalasmaa
Juuka
Liukkunen
Pötsönvaara
Vuonislahti
Vuonisjärvi
Sokojärvi
Suomunjärvi
Patvinsuon kansallispuisto
Koli
Kolin kansallispuisto
Kelvä
Jaakonvaara
Naarva
Syväjärvi
Ukkola
Uimaharju
Kivilahti
Koitere
Hattuvaara
Käenkoski
Höytiäinen
Eno
Kontiolahti
Jakokoski
Ilomantsi
Möhkö
Ontronvaara
Petkeljärven kansallispuisto
Joensuu
Pyhäselkä
Outokumpu
Viinijärvi
Kontkala
Ylämylly
Liperi
Heinävaara
Keskijärvi
Koveró
Marjovaara
Maukkula
Hukkivaara
Tuupovaara
Mutalahti
Kiihtelysvaara
Sulkava
Rääkkylä
Orivesi
Onkamo
Tohmajärvi
Värtsilä
Vyartsilya
Korpisel'kya
Tolvayarvi
Saarivaara
Kitee
Puhos
Kesälahti
Savonranta
Rantasalmi
Linnansaaren kansallispuisto
Kolovesi
Koloveden kansallispuisto
Heinävesi
Vihtari
Kerma
Kermajärvi
Tahko
Nilsiä
Juankoski
Kaavi
Rautavaara
Valtimo
Sotkamo
Vuokatti
Kontiomäki
Paltamo
Ristijärvi
Hyrynsalmi
Pyhäntä
Mustavaara
Suomussalmi
Hiidenportti
Sapsojärvi
Ontojärvi
Lentua
Naulavaara
Maanselkä
Tiilikkajärven kansallispuisto
Ylä-Luosta
Sälevä
Rikkavesi
Suvasvesi
Haapavesi
Pyhäselkä
Heinoniemi
Paasselkä
Oz. Yanis'yarvi
Yanisyoki
28°00'
28°30'
29°00'
29°30'
30°00'
30°30'
31°00'
62°30'
63°00'
63°30'
64°00'

Kaskinen
Pjelax
Myrkky
Kauhajoki
Luovankylä
Sahankylä
Ikkelänjärvi
Ilvesjoki
Keskikylä
Tjöck
Karijoki
Kristinestad
(Kristiinankaupunki)
Lappfjärd
Dagsmark
Hyyppä
Panttikylä
Nummijärvi
Nummikoski
Sara
Uuro
Kauhajärvi
Heikkilä
Träskvik
Vanhakylä
Härkmeri
Kärjenkoski
Villamo
Lauhanvuoren kansallispuisto
Kauhanevan-Pohjankankaan kansallispuisto
Lauhavuori
Perä-Hyyppä
Sarvela
Karvia
Skaftung
Isojoki
Sarviluoma
Vesijärvi
Suomijärvi
Ömossa
Suojoki
Kodesjärvi
Jyllinkoski
Kantti
Sideby
Kallträsk
Honkajoki
Korvaluoma
Kuvaskangas
Lauttijärvi
Pyntäinen
Ala-Honkajoki
Kusijoki
Merikarvia
Tuorila
Siikainen
Pohjankangas
Ouran saaristo
Alakylä
Venesjärvi
Niinisalo
Jämijärvi
Leväsjoki
Kankaanpää
Köörtilä
Hämeenkangas
Honkakoski
Isojärvi
Vihteljärvi
Pomarkku
Ahlainen
Sävi
Lassila
Lavia
Reposaari
Noormarkku
Mäntyluoto
Pihlava
Söörmarkku
Harjakangas
Kyläsaari
Karhijärvi
Suodenniemi
Säppi
Preiviiki
Pori
Harjunpää
Viasvedenlahti
Kullaa
Putaja
Viasvesi
Kaasmarkku
Ulvila
Sääksjärvi
Kiikoinen
Niemenkylä
Friitala
Lattomeri
Nakkila
Luvia
Kauvatsa
Kiikka
Harjavalta
Äetsä
Kuivalahti
Riste
Keikyä
Olkiluoto
Panelia
Kokemäki
Puurijärven ja Isonsuon kansallispuisto
Irjanne
Peipohja
Lapijoki
Eurajoki
Kiukainen
Huittinen
Rauma
Vanha Rauma
Eura
Köyliönjärvi
Lappi
Sammallahdenmäki
Köyliö
Kankaanpää
Rihtniemi
Unaja
Iso-Vimma
Vuorenmaa
Kodiksami
Säkylä
Vampula
Vermuntila
Kodisjoki
Pyhäjärvi
Pyhäjoki
Ihode
Hinnerjoki
Otajärvi
Koskenkylä
Alastaro
Pyhäranta
Pyhämaa
Honkilahti
Kammela
Untamala
Heinijoki
Virttaa
Laitila
Yläne
Oripää
Lyökki
Laajoki
VARSINAIS-SUOMI
Vekara
Kalanti
Karjalankylä
Uusikaupunki
Uusikartano
Lahti
Karjalan kirkonkylä
Kurjenrahkan kansallispuisto
Isokari
Mynäjoki
Lokalahti
Pöytyä
Karinainen
Vehmaa
Mynämäki
Tortinmäki
Kaurissalo
Valpperi
Aura
Rautila
Pyhe
Mietoinen
Nousiainen
Vahto
Askainen
Paattinen
Kustavi
Taivassalo
Lemu
Masku
Tarvasjoki
Jurmo
Rusko
Maaria
Lieto
Etelä-Vartsala
Hakkenpää
Iniön aukko
Merimasku
Naantali
Raisio
Veritas Stadion (FC Inter Turku)
Åva
Fiskö
Brändö
Turun linna
Littoinen
Paimio
Geta
Turku (Åbo)
Piikkiö
Rymättylä
Kaarina
Bergö
Ödkarby
Saltvik
Enklinge
Torsholma
Björkö
Lappo
Kakskerta
Sauvo
Finström
Sund
Delet Teili
Kihti Skiftet
Godby
Vårdö
Kumlinge
Mossala
Pargas (Parainen)
Hammarland
Kastelholman linna
Finby
Karuna
Eckerö
Gölby
Seglinge
Houtsala
Torp
Houtskär
Jomala
Lumparn
Nagu
Tjuda
Eckerö
Önningby
Lumparland
Sottunga
Korpo
Attu
Mjösund
Kimito
Åland
Mariehamn
Jungfruskär
Storlandet
Överö
Korpoström
Kirjais
Östermark
Lemland
Björkboda
Dragsfjärd
Flaka
Degerby
Föglö
Dalsbruk (Taalintehdas)
Västanfjärd
Alskär
Stockholm
Hellsö
Aspö
Nötö
Ålands Hav
Kökar
Karlby
Gullkronafjärd
Högsåra
Hankoniemi
Kökarsfjärde
Björkö
Hitis
Helsinki
Jurmo
Skärgårdshavets nationalpark
Örö
Rosala
Hangö

123
128
131
9
10
11
12
13
14
15
A
B
C
D
E
F
23°30′
24°00′
24°30′
25°00′
25°30′
26°00′
62°00′
61°30′
61°00′
60°30′
60°00′
FIN
K U N T A
H Ä M E
U U S I M A A
P ä i j ä t - H ä m e
SUOMENLAHTI
Päijänne
Näsijärvi
Vanajavesi
Mallasvesi
Pyhäjärvi
Jyväskylä
Tampere
Nokia
Kangasala
Orivesi
Mänttä
Keuruu
Virrat
Ruovesi
Jämsä
Himos-Jämsä
Jämsänkoski
Kuhmoinen
Joutsa
Hartola
Sysmä
Heinola
Lahti
Hollola
Nastola
Orimattila
Valkeakoski
Toijala
Urjala
Forssa
Loimaa
Hämeenlinna
Riihimäki
Hyvinkää
Mäntsälä
Järvenpää
Kerava
Tuusula
Vantaa (Vanda)
Espoo (Esbo)
HELSINKI (HELSINGFORS)
Porvoo (Borgå)
Loviisa (Lovisa)
Kirkkonummi (Kyrkslätt)
Lohja
Salo
Karis
Ekenäs (Tammisaari)
Hanko
Somero
Parkano
Ylöjärvi
Pirkkala
Lempäälä
Suomen rautatiemuseo
Sankt-Peterburg
Mariehamn, Stockholm
Lübeck, Travemünde
Rostock, Tallinn
E12
E63
E75
E18

Jyväskylä
Keuruu
Petäjävesi
Kintaus
Vesanka
Vaajakoski
Lievestuore
Hankasalmi asema
Pieksämäen mlk
Kangasniemi
Haukivuori
Jämsä
Himos-Jämsä
Jämsänkoski
Korpilahti
Muurame
Säynätsalo
Toivakka
Joutsa
Hartola
Mikkeli
Mikkelin mlk
Otava
Ristiina
Pihlajasalo
Puula
Päijänne
Kuhmoinen
Orivesi
Heinola
Sysmä
Pertunmaa
Mäntyharju
Savitaipale
Lahti
Hollola
Nastola
Kuusankoski
Kouvola
Valkeala
Elimäki
Anjalankoski
Myllykoski
Hämeenlinna
Riihimäki
Hyvinkää
Mäntsälä
Järvenpää
Tuusula
Kerava
Orimattila
Porvoo (Borgå)
Loviisa (Lovisa)
Kotka
Hamina
Vaalimaa
Virolahti
Vantaa (Vanda)
Espoo (Esbo)
HELSINKI (HELSINGFORS)
Sibbo
Santahamina
Isosaari
Kirkonmaanselkä
Itäisen Suomenlahden kansallispuisto
SUOMENLAHTI
FINSKIY ZALIV
Ostrov Gogland
O. Moshchnyy
O. Bol'shoy Tyuters
O. Malyy Tyuters
Tallinn, Rostock
Tallinn, Rostock, Kaliningrad, Sassnitz, Lübeck
FIN
E63
E75
E12
E18
124
127
131
A
B
C
D
E
F
2
3
4
5
6
7
8
25°00′
25°30′
26°00′
26°30′
27°00′
27°30′
62°00′
61°30′
61°00′
60°30′
60°00′

9
10
11
12
13
14
15
A
B
C
D
E
F
125
132
ix
62°00′
61°30′
61°00′
60°30′
60°00′
28°30′
29°00′
29°30′
30°00′
30°30′
31°00′
Niinimäki
Syrjä
Kolvumäki
Kerma
Vihtari
Oravisalo
Kompakka
Tikkala
Öllölä
Korpiselkya
Tolvayarvi
Saarivaara
Pöllökkä
Varpasalo
Rasivaara
Suuri Onkamojärvi
Orivesi
Säimen
Tohmajärvi
Saario
Uusi-Värtsilä
Värtsilä
Vyartsilya
Viljolahti
Tiemassaari
Ahvensalmi
Torasalo
Linnansaaren kansallispuisto
Koloveden kansallispuisto
Savonranta
Heinoniemi
Paasselkä
Kokkolahti
Tolosenmäki
Ruppovaara
Puhos
Kitee
Vepsä
Korkeakangas
Oravi
Enonkoski
Rantasalmi
Juvola
Villala
Raikuu
Haukivesi
Rantasalmen asema
Varparanta
Makkola
Kumpuranta
Rauvanniemi
Rasti
Juurikka
Hyvönmäki
Yanisyoki
Oz. Yanis'yarvi
Suystamo
Ruskeala
Hiltula
Parkumäki
Ruokojärvi
Kerimäki
Kallislahti
Rinkilä
Olavinlinna
Savonlinna
Pihlajalahti
Hälvä
Kesälahti
Pyhäjärvi
Astikkala
Kuhakoski
Kyrsyä
Kulennoinen
Pitkälä
Puruvesi
Purujärvi
Uukuniemi
Kharlu
Lyaskelya
Sulkava
Hiukkajoki
Punkaharju
Niukkala
Khelyulya
Sortavala
Impilahti
Pihlajavesi
Ahvionsaari
Ruokoniemi
Putikko
Tarnala
Saari
Kiviapaja
Kirjavala
Saaren kk
Pitkyaranta
Ryhälä
Partalansaari
Lohilahti
Vuoriniemi
Särkisalmi
Viljakansaari
Särkilahti
Parikkala
Lakhdenpokh'ya
O. Putsari
Saarajärvi
Pohja-Lankila
Eräjärvi
Rautjärvi
Elisenvaara
Valaamskiy Monastyr'
O. Valaam
Luukkola
Syyspohja
Utula
Virmutjoki
Laikko
Kokkolanyoki
Ostrov Mantsinsari
Rautjärven kk
Miettilä
Ruokolahti
Savilahti
Saimaa
Khiytola
O. Kheynyasensari
O. Vossinansari
Rehula
Vehkataipale
Rauha
Imatra
Dymovka
Kuznechnoye
Joutseno
Svetogorsk
Lappeenranta
Konnunsuo
Lesogorskiy
Priozersk
Larionovo
Borodinskoye
Ladozhskoye Ozero
Hytti
Nuijamaa
Kamennogorsk
Mel'nikovo
Simola
Vainikkala
O. Konevits
Plodovoye
Vuoksa
Villala
Oz. Otradnoye
Seleznevo
Pal'tsevo
Vyborgskiy Zamok
Vyborg
Zhitkovo
Oz. Vuoksa
Oz. Sukhodol'skoye
Kondrat'yevo
Vysotsk
Krasnosel'skoye
Zaporozhskoye
Pyatirech'ye
Sosnovo
Sovetskiy
Oz. Glubokoye
Vyborgskiy Zaliv
O. Severnyy Berezovyy
Kirillovskoye
Kamenka
RUS
Primorsk
Pervomayskoye
Ryabovo
Polyany
Kuyvozi
O. Zapadnyy Berezovyy
O. Bol'shoy Berezovyy
Roshchino
Zelenogorsk
Komarovo
Repino
Vartemyagi
Toksovo
Mor'ye
Sertolovo
Pesochnyy
Kuz'molovskiy
Ladozhskoye Ozero
Rakh'ya
Sestroretsk
Pargolovo
Bukhta Petrokrepost'
O. Malyy
O. Lesnoy
Lisiy Nos
Vsevolozhsk
Kronshtadt
Sankt-Peterburg
Morozova
Shlissel'burg
Priladozhskiy
Lebyazh'ye
Lomonosov
Petrodvorets
Kirovsk
Dubrovka
Sosnovyy Bor
Metallostroy
Pontonnyy
Otradnoye
Kolpino
Mga
Ekaterininskiy Dvorets
E18
A118
A120
A121
A122
A124
A130
A131
A181
M11
P21
P23
3SD

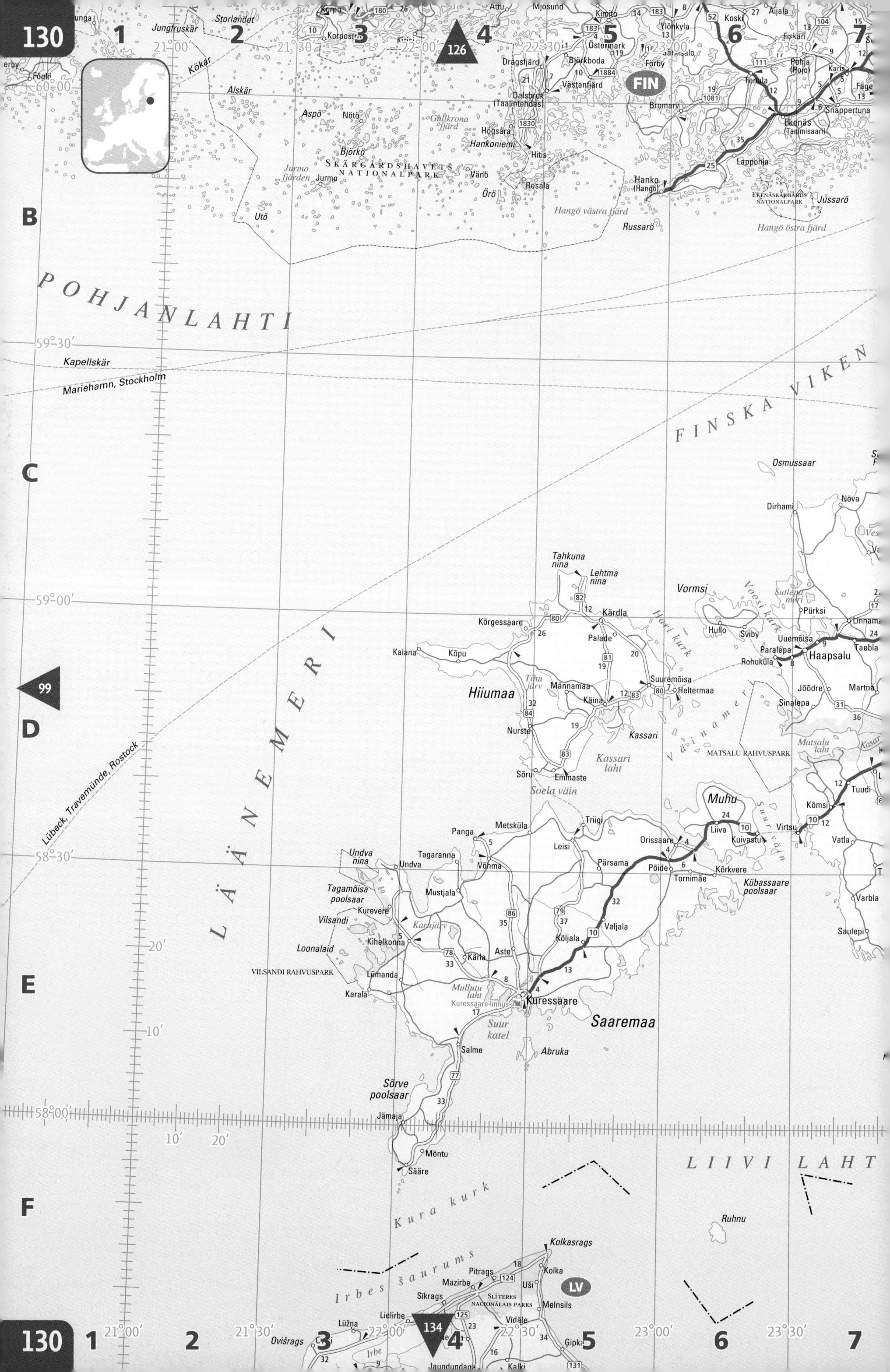

FIN
LV
POHJANLAHTI
FINSKA VIKEN
LÄÄNEMERI
LIIVI LAHT
SKÄRGÅRDSHAVETS NATIONALPARK
EKENÄSKÄRGÅRDS NATIONALPARK
MATSALU RAHVUSPARK
VILSANDI RAHVUSPARK
SLĪTERES NACIONĀLAIS PARKS
Kapellskär
Mariehamn, Stockholm
Lübeck, Travemünde, Rostock
Jungfruskär
Storlandet
Korpo
Korpoström
Kökar
Alskär
Aspö
Nötö
Gullkrona fjärd
Björkö
Jurmo fjärden
Jurmo
Utö
Högsåra
Hankoniemi
Hitis
Dragsfjärd
Dalsbruk (Taalintehdas)
Kimito
Östermark
Björkboda
Västanfjärd
Ylönkylä
Särkisalo
Förby
Bromarv
Koski
Aijala
Fiskari
Pohja (Pojo)
Karis
Tenhola
Ekenäs (Tammisaari)
Snappertuna
Lappohja
Hanko (Hangö)
Russarö
Jussarö
Hangö västra fjärd
Hangö östra fjärd
Vänö
Örö
Rosala
Osmussaar
Dirhami
Nõva
Tahkuna nina
Lehtma nina
Vormsi
Hullo
Sviby
Sutlepa meri
Pürksi
Vooši kurk
Hari kurk
Kärdla
Kõrgessaare
Palade
Kalana
Kõpu
Hiiumaa
Tihu järv
Männamaa
Käina
Suuremõisa
Heltermaa
Kassari
Kassari laht
Nurste
Sõru
Emmaste
Soela väin
Väinameri
Uuemõisa
Paralepa
Rohuküla
Haapsalu
Linnamäe
Taebla
Jõõdre
Martna
Sinalepa
Matsalu laht
Tuudi
Kõmsi
Virtsu
Vatla
Varbla
Saulepi
Muhu
Liiva
Kuivastu
Suur väin
Orissaare
Põide
Tornimäe
Kõrkvere
Kübassaare poolsaar
Triigi
Leisi
Pärsama
Metsküla
Panga
Tagaranna
Undva nina
Undva
Võhma
Tagamõisa poolsaar
Mustjala
Kurevere
Vilsandi
Karujärv
Kihelkonna
Loonalaid
Kärla
Aste
Kõljala
Valjala
Lümanda
Karala
Mullutu laht
Kuressaare
Kuressaare linnus
Saaremaa
Suur katel
Abruka
Salme
Sõrve poolsaar
Jämaja
Mõntu
Sääre
Kura kurk
Ruhnu
Irbes šaurums
Kolkasrags
Kolka
Pitrags
Mazirbe
Sīkrags
Uši
Melnsils
Lielirbe
Lūžņa
Vīdale
Ovišrags
Irbe
Gipka
60°00′
59°30′
59°00′
58°30′
58°00′
21°00′
21°30′
22°00′
22°30′
23°00′
23°30′
10′
20′
B
C
D
E
F
1
2
3
4
5
6
7
126
99
134

HELSINKI (HELSINGFORS)
Santahamina
Isosaari
Siuntio
Evitskog
Degerby
Inga (Inkoo)
Upinniemi
Porkkala
Porkkalafjärden
SUOMENLAHTI
SOOME LAHT
Sankt-Peterburg
Kotka
Ostrov Gogland
O. Bol'shoy Tyuters
O. Malyy Tyuters
RUS
Purekkari neem
Aegna
Prangli
Naissaar
Leppneeme
Viimsi
Haabneeme
Tallinna laht
TALLINN
Maardu
Muraste
Tabasalu
Harku
Keila-Joa
Laulasmaa
Klooga
Keila
Saue
Laagri
Jüri
Loo
Lagedi
Saku
Kiili
Vasalemma
Rummu
Padise
Kohila
Rapla
Kehra
Aegviidu
Kuusalu
Kolga
Loksa
Kunda
Viru-Nigula
Aseri
Kiviõli
Kohtla-Järve
Kukruse
Rakvere
Tapa
Tamsalu
Väike-Maarja
Pandivere kõrgustik
Kadrina
Haljala
Sõmeru
Vinni
Laekvere
Simuna
Avinurme
Mustvee
Peipsi järv
Paide
Türi
Järva-Jaani
Koeru
Anna
Põltsamaa
Jõgeva
Kuremaa
Palamuse
Vändra
Suure-Jaani
Viljandi
Võhma
Kolga-Jaani
Vitsjärv
Võrtsjärv
Tartu
Elva
Otepää
Otepää kõrgustik
Kambja
Nõo
Rõngu
Puka
Tõrva
Valga
Valka
Võru
Põlva
Räpina
Haanja kõrgustik
Suur Munamägi 318
Karula rahvuspark
Pärnu
Pärnu laht
Sindi
Audru
Uulu
Tori
Häädemeeste
Kabli
Treimani
Ikla
Ainaži
Manilaid
Soomaa rahvuspark
Abja-Paluoja
Mõisaküla
Karksi-Nuia
Kilingi-Nõmme
Sakala kõrgustik
Lahemaa rahvuspark
EST
LV
Mazsalaca
Rūjiena
Salacgrīva
Aloja
Staicele
Burtnieku ezers
Valmiera
Smiltene
Strenči
Ērgeme
E20
E67
E263
E264
127
132
135
B
C
D
E
F
8
9
10
11
12
13
14

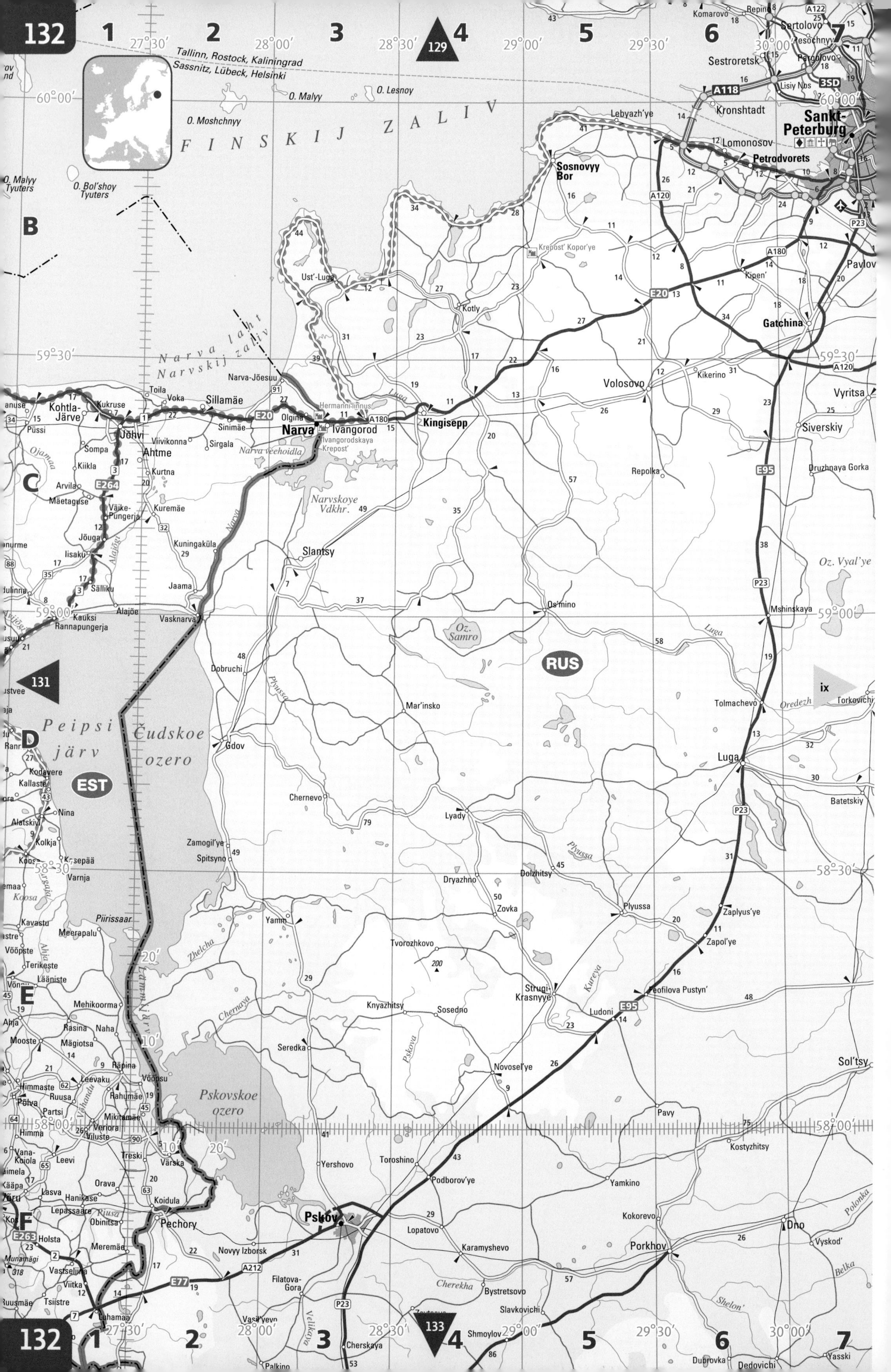
1
2
3
4
5
6
7
129
Tallinn, Rostock, Kaliningrad
Sassnitz, Lübeck, Helsinki
O. Malyy
O. Lesnoy
O. Moshchnyy
F I N S K I J Z A L I V
O. Malyy Tyuters
O. Bol'shoy Tyuters
Komarovo
Repino
Sertolovo
Pesochnyy
Sestroretsk
Pargolovo
Lisiy Nos
Kronshtadt
Lebyazh'ye
Sankt-Peterburg
Lomonosov
Petrodvorets
Sosnovyy Bor
Krepost' Kopor'ye
Pavlov
Ust'-Luga
Kotly
Kipen'
Gatchina
Narva laht
Narvskij zaliv
Narva-Jõesuu
Toila
Voka
Sillamäe
Kohtla-Järve
Kukruse
Jõhvi
Sinimäe
Olgina
Hermanni linnus
Narva
Ivangorod
Ivangorodskaya Krepost'
Kingisepp
Volosovo
Kikerino
Vyritsa
Siverskiy
Püssi
Ahtme
Viivikonna
Sirgala
Narva veehoidla
Sompa
Kiikla
Kurtna
Repolka
Druzhnaya Gorka
Arvila
Mäetaguse
Väike-Pungerja
Kuremäe
Narvskoye Vdkhr.
Narva
Jõuga
Iisaku
Alajõgi
Kuningaküla
Slantsy
Oz. Vyal'ye
Sälliku
Jaama
Kauksi
Rannapungerja
Alajõe
Vasknarva
Os'mino
Mshinskaya
Oz. Samro
Luga
RUS
131
Dobruchi
Plyussa
Mar'insko
Tolmachevo
Oredezh
Torkovichi
ix
Peipsi järv
Čudskoe ozero
Gdov
Luga
Kodavere
Kallaste
EST
Chernevo
Lyady
Batetskiy
Nina
Alatskivi
Kolkja
Kasepää
Varnja
Zamogil'ye
Spitsyno
Plyussa
Dolzhitsy
Dryazhno
Zovka
Plyussa
Zaplyus'ye
Zapol'ye
Koosa
Kavastu
Piirissaar
Meerapalu
Yamm
Tvorozhkovo
Võõpste
Terikeste
Lääniste
Zhelcha
Lämmijärv
Strugi-Krasnyye
Kureya
Teofilova Pustyn'
Mehikoorma
Knyazhitsy
Sosedno
Ludoni
Chernaya
Rasina
Naha
Mooste
Mägiotsa
Seredka
Pskova
Novosel'ye
Sol'tsy
Räpina
Himmaste
Leevaku
Ruusa
Võõpsu
Rahumäe
Põlva
Partsi
Mikitamäe
Pskovskoe ozero
Pavy
Veriora
Viluste
Himma
Kostyzhitsy
Vana-Koiola
Leevi
Treski
Värska
Yershovo
Toroshino
Podborov'ye
Yamkino
Orava
Lasva
Hanikase
Koidula
Võru
Lepassaare
Obinitsa
Piusa
Pechory
Pskov
Lopatovo
Kokorevo
Dno
Polonka
Holsta
Meremäe
Novyy Izborsk
Karamyshevo
Porkhov
Vyskod'
Munamägi
Vastseliina
Filatova-Gora
Cherekha
Bystretsovo
Belka
Viitka
Ruusmäe
Tsiistre
Luhamaa
Vasil'yevo
Velikaya
Zavelye
Slavkovichi
Shelon'
133
Shmoylov
Cherskaya
Palkino
Dubrovka
Dedovichi
Yasski
E20
E95
E264
E77
E263
A118
A120
A180
A212
P23
3SD
59°30'
59°00'
58°30'
58°00'
60°00'
27°30'
28°00'
28°30'
29°00'
29°30'
30°00'

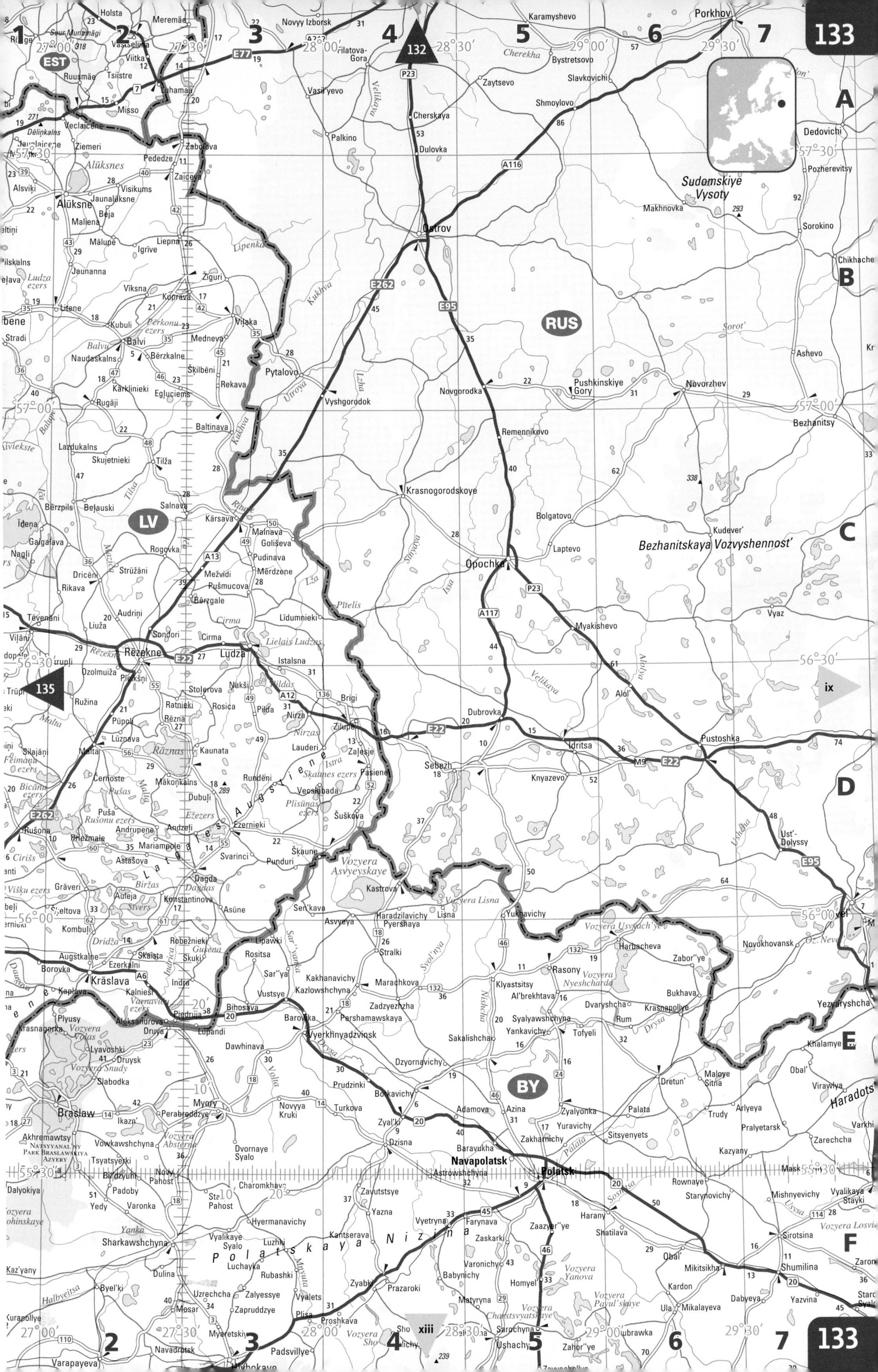
EST
LV
RUS
BY
Holsta
Meremäe
Novyy Izborsk
Karamyshevo
Porkhov
Vastseliina
Viitka
Filatova-Gora
Bystretsovo
Cherekha
Ruusmäe
Tsiistre
Luhamaa
Zaytsevo
Slavkovichi
Misso
Vasil'yevo
Shmoylovo
Cherskaya
Veclaicene
Dēliņkalns
Jaunlaicene
Ziemeri
Palkino
Dulovka
Dedovichi
Zaboļova
Pededze
Alūksnes
Zaiceva
Pozherevitsy
Sudomskiye Vysoty
Alsviķi
Visikums
Jaunalūksne
Alūksne
Maliena
Beja
Makhnovka
Ostrov
Sorokino
Mālupe
Igrīve
Liepna
Lipenka
Pilskalns
Jaunanna
Chikhachevo
Ludza ezers
Žiguri
Viksna
Kuprava
Litene
Kubuli
Perkonu ezers
Vilaka
Balvi
Medneva
Kukhva
Stradi
Balvu
Naudaskalns
Bērzkalne
Šķilbēni
Pytalovo
Utroya
Lzha
Sorot'
Ashevo
Kārklinieki
Rekava
Vyshgorodok
Novgorodka
Pushkinskiye Gory
Novorzhev
Rugāji
Egļuciems
Bezhanitsy
Baltinava
Remennikovo
Lazdukalns
Skujetnieki
Tilža
Tilsa
Krasnogorodskoye
Bērzpils
Bełauski
Salnava
Īdeņa
Kārsava
Malnava
Goliševa
Bolgatovo
Kudever'
Gaigalava
Rogovka
Pudinava
Laptevo
Bezhanitskaya Vozvyshennost'
Nagli
Dricēni
Strūžāni
Meždvidi
Mērdzene
Opochka
Rikava
Pušmucova
Bērzgale
Lza
Pītelis
Tēvenāni
Audriņi
Līdumnieki
Myakishevo
Vyaz
Viļāni
Liuža
Sondori
Cirma
Lielais Ludzas
Rēzekne
Ludza
Istalsna
Velikaya
Alol'
Dzolmuiža
Pleikšņi
Stolerova
Nukši
Rosica
Brigi
Ružina
Ratnieki
Rēzna
Pilda
Nirza
Zilupe
Dubrovka
Idritsa
Pustoshka
Pūpoli
Lūznava
Malta
Rāznas
Kaunata
Lauderi
Zaļesje
Pasiene
Sebezh
Knyazevo
Feimanu ezers
Silajāņi
Čerņoste
Makoņkalns
Dubuļi
Rundēni
Vecslabada
Plisūnas ezers
Šuškova
Puša
Rušonu ezers
Ežezers
Ezernieki
Rušona
Andrupene
Andzeli
Ust'-Dolyssy
Priežmale
Mariampole
Svarinci
Punduri
Škaune
Vozyera Asvyeyskaye
Astašova
Lubāna
Gorodets
Dagda
Kastrova
Vozyera Lisna
Gräveri
Auleja
Konstantinova
Asūne
Sen'kava
Haradzilavichy
Lisna
Yukhavichy
Vozyera Usvyach'ye
Šķeltova
Kombuļi
Asvyeya
Pyershaya
Novokhovansk
Dridža
Robežnieki
Lipawki
Stralki
Harbacheva
Zabor''ye
Augstkalne
Skaista
Skuķi
Rositsa
Rasony
Borovka
Ezerkalni
Krāslava
Indra
Sar''ya
Kakhanavichy
Marachkova
Klyastsitsy
Vozyera Nyeshcharda
Kaplava
Kalnieši
Varnaviči
Vustsye
Kazlowshchyna
Al'brekhtava
Bukhava
Plyusy
Piedruja
Bihosava
Zadzyezhzha
Dvaryshcha
Krasnapollye
Yezyaryshcha
Krasnagorka
Vozyera Volas
Aleksandrova
Druya
Lupandi
Barowka
Pershamawskaya
Syalyawshchyna
Yankavichy
Rum
Tofyeli
Lyavoshki
Druysk
Dawhinava
Vyerkhnyadzvinsk
Sakalishcha
Khalamyer
Vozyera Snudy
Slabodka
Dzyornavichy
Dretun'
Maloye Sitna
Obal'
Prudzinki
Borkavichy
Virawlya
Braslaw
Perabrodzye
Myory
Novyya Kruki
Turkova
Adamova
Azina
Zyalyonka
Palata
Trudy
Arlyeya
Haradotsk
Ikazn'
Zyal'ki
Yuravichy
Pralyetarsk
Akhremawtsy
Natsyyanal'ny Park Braslawskiya Azyery
Vowkawshchyna
Vozyera Absterna
Dzisna
Baravukha
Zakharnichy
Sitsyenyets
Zarechcha
Tsyatsyerki
Dvornaye Syalo
Navapolatsk
Kazyany
Bil'dzyuhi
Novy Pahost
Astrowshchyna
Polatsk
Mask
Dalyokiya
Padoby
Charomkhava
Zavutstsye
Rownaye
Starynovichy
Mishnyevichy
Vyalikaya Stayki
Yedy
Varonka
Stary Pahost
Yazna
Harany
Vozyera Losvida
Hyermanavichy
Vyetryna
Farynava
Zaazyer''ye
Sirotsina
Sharkawshchyna
Vyalikaye Syalo
Luzhki
Kantserava
Zaskarki
Shatilava
Polatskaya Nizina
Luchayka
Rubashki
Varonichy
Mikitsikha
Shumilina
Kaz'yany
Dulina
Zyabki
Prazaroki
Babynichy
Homyel'
Vozyera Yanova
Kardon
Byel'ki
Uzrechcha
Zalyessye
Zapruddzye
Vyalets
Vozyera Payul'skaye
Ula
Mikalayeva
Dabyeya
Yazvina
Mosar
Matyryna
Charstsvyatskaye
Plisa
Proshkava
Myaretski
Sarochyna
Zahor''ye
Navadrutsk
Ushachy
Padsvillye
Varapayeva
Hlybokaye
Lipenka
Bibaki
Malta
Rēzekne
Daugava
Yanka
Halbyeitsa
Volta
Dzisna
Drysa
Usvyacha
Ushcha
Alolya
Sorot'
Issa
Sinyaya
Velikaya
Kukhva
Nishcha
Obal'
Usysa
Sosnitsa
E77
E262
E95
E22
A116
A117
A13
A12
A6
P23
M9
27°00'
27°30'
28°00'
28°30'
29°00'
29°30'
57°30'
57°00'
56°30'
56°00'
55°30'
135
132
ix
xiii
1
2
3
4
5
6
7
A
B
C
D
E
F

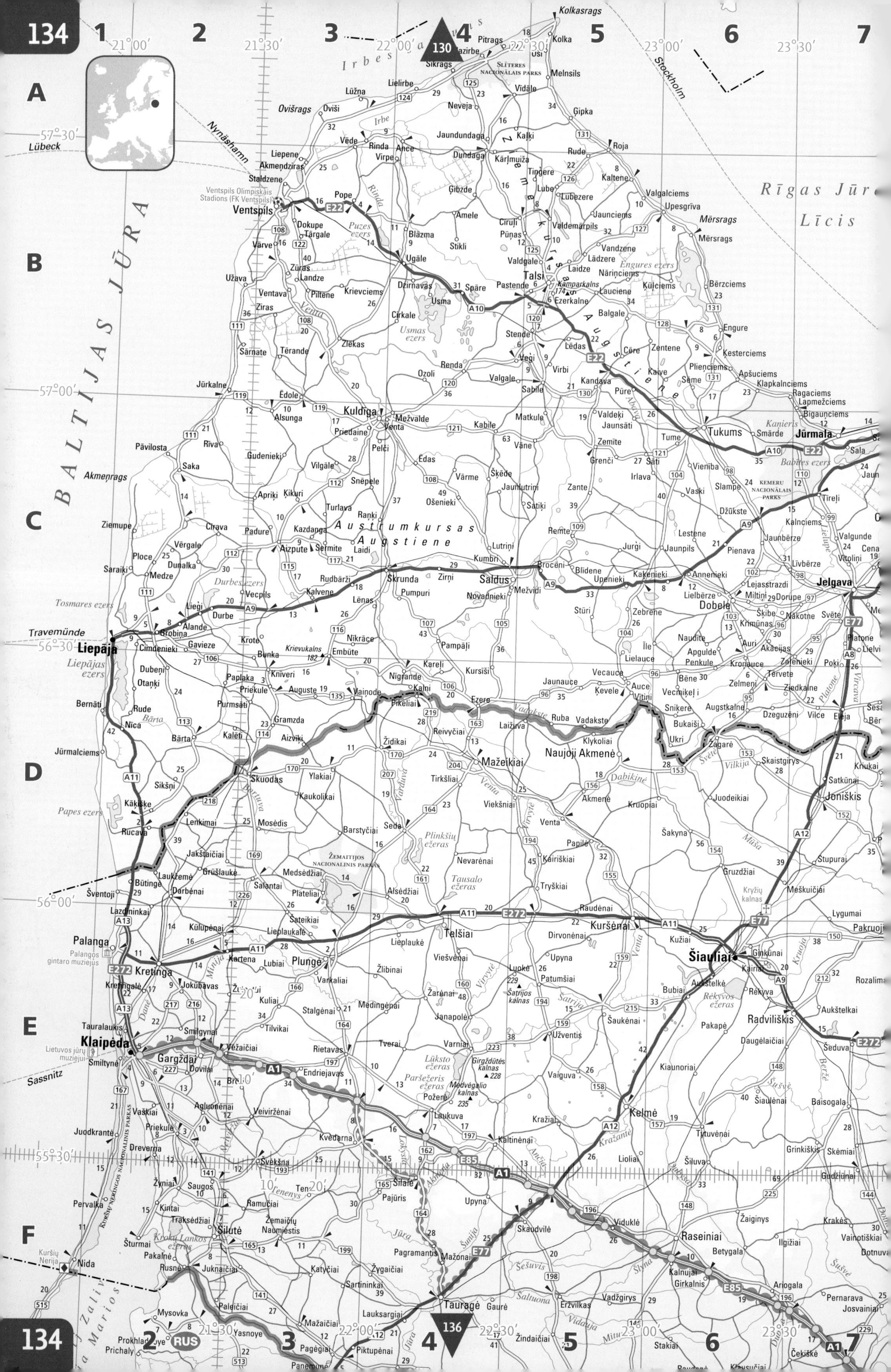

Kolkasrags
Kolka
Pitrags
Mazirbe
Sīkrags
Slīteres Nacionālais parks
Melnsils
Vīdāle
Ģipka
Roja
Stockholm
Nynäshamn
Lübeck
Irbes šaurums
Lielirbe
Lūžņa
Oviši
Ovišrags
Vēde
Rinda
Ance
Virpe
Jaundundaga
Dundaga
Kalķi
Kārļmuiža
Liepene
Akmeņdziras
Staldzene
Ventspils Olimpiskais Stadions (FK Ventspils)
Ventspils
Pope
Puzes ezers
Rude
Tingere
Kaltene
Valgalciems
Upesgrīva
Mērsrags
Rīgas Jūras Līcis
Ģibzde
Lube
Lubezere
Jaunciems
Amele
Ciruļi
Valdemārpils
Dokupe
Tārgale
Blāzma
Pūņas
Vandzene
Vārve
Stikli
Valdgale
Lādzere
Ugāle
Laidze
Nāriņciems
Engures ezers
Zūras
Landze
Talsi
Užava
Ventava
Piltene
Krievciems
Dzirnavas
Spāre
Pastende
Kamparkalns
Ķūļciems
Bērzciems
Lauciene
Ezerkalne
Usma
Ziras
Cirkale
Balgale
Usmas ezers
Stende
Engure
Ķesterciems
Sārnate
Tērande
Zlēkas
Lēdas
Cēre
Zentene
Apšuciems
Klapkalnciems
Ragaciems
Lapmežciems
Bigauņciems
Vegi
Virbi
Kalve
Plieņciems
Sēme
Renda
Ozoli
Valgale
Sabile
Kandava
Pūre
Jūrkalne
Ēdole
Alsunga
Kuldīga
Mežvalde
Venta
Priedaine
Kabile
Matkule
Valdeķi
Jaunsāti
Tukums
Smārde
Jūrmala
Kanieris
Sala
Pāvilosta
Rīva
Gudenieki
Pelči
Vāne
Zemīte
Grenči
Sāti
Tume
Vienība
Irlava
Slampe
Ķemeru Nacionālais parks
Babītes ezers
Akmeņrags
Saka
Vilgāle
Ēdas
Šķēde
Vārme
Jaunlutriņi
Zante
Vaski
Tīreļi
Apriķi
Ķikuri
Snēpele
Ošenieki
Satiķi
Turlava
Raņķi
Džūkste
Kalnciems
Ziemupe
Cīrava
Padure
Kazdanga
Austrumkursas Augstiene
Remte
Lestene
Jaunbērze
Valgunde
Vērgale
Aizpute
Sermīte
Laidi
Lutriņi
Jurģi
Jaunpils
Pienava
Cena
Ploce
Dunalka
Kumbri
Brocēni
Līvbērze
Vītoliņi
Saraiķi
Medze
Durbes ezers
Rudbārži
Skrunda
Zirņi
Saldus
Blīdene
Upenieki
Kakenieki
Annenieki
Lejasstrazdi
Jelgava
Vecpils
Kalvene
Pumpuri
Novadnieki
Mežvidi
Tosmares ezers
Liegi
Lēnas
Lielbērze
Miltiņi
Dorupe
Dobele
Durbe
Stūri
Zebrene
Šķibe
Nākotne
Svēte
Alande
Grobiņa
Travemünde
Liepāja
Cimdenieki
Gavieze
Krote
Nīkrāce
Pampāļi
Krimūnas
Platone
Lielvircava
Liepājas ezers
Bunka
Krievukalns
Embūte
Īle
Lielauce
Naudīte
Apgulde
Penkule
Auri
Akācijas
Zaļenieki
Dubeņi
Otaņķi
Kniveri
Nīgrande
Kareļi
Kursīši
Vecauce
Bēne
Kronauce
Tērvete
Pokaiņi
Paplaka
Priekule
Auguste
Vaiņode
Kalni
Jaunauce
Ķevele
Auce
Vecmikeļi
Zelmeņi
Ziedkalne
Bernāti
Rude
Purmsāti
Pikeliai
Ezere
Vadakste
Vītiņi
Sniķere
Augstkalne
Dzeguzēni
Vilce
Eleja
Nīca
Bārta
Gramzda
Reivyčiai
Laižuva
Ruba
Klykoliai
Bukaiši
Ukri
Žagarė
Kalēti
Aizviķi
Židikai
Mažeikiai
Naujoji Akmenė
Skaistgirys
Jūrmalciems
Skuodas
Ylakiai
Tirkšliai
Akmenė
Dabikinė
Kruopiai
Juodeikiai
Joniškis
Siksni
Kukoliai
Viekšniai
Papes ezers
Kāķišķe
Lenkimai
Mosėdis
Barstyčiai
Seda
Plinkšių ežeras
Venta
Papilė
Šakyna
Rucava
Žemaitijos Nacionalinis parkas
Jakštaičiai
Grūšlaukė
Medsėdžiai
Nevarėnai
Kairiškiai
Gruzdžiai
Stupurai
Laukžemė
Būtingė
Šventoji
Darbėnai
Salantai
Plateliai
Alsėdžiai
Tausalo ežeras
Tryškiai
Kryžių kalnas
Meškuičiai
Lazdininkai
Šateikiai
Telšiai
Raudėnai
Kuršėnai
Lygumai
Palanga
Palangos gintaro muziejus
Kūlupėnai
Lieplaukalė
Lieplaukė
Dirvonėnai
Kužiai
Pakruojis
Kretinga
Kartena
Lubiai
Plungė
Viešvėnai
Upyna
Šiauliai
Ginkūnai
Kairiai
Kretingalė
Jokūbavas
Varkaliai
Žlibinai
Luokė
Šatrijos kalnas
Patumšiai
Bubiai
Aukštelkė
Rėkyvos ežeras
Rėkyva
Radviliškis
Aukštelkai
Rozalimas
Tauralaukis
Kuliai
Stalgėnai
Medingėnai
Žarėnai
Janapolė
Šaukėnai
Pakapė
Klaipėda
Smilgynai
Tilvikai
Užventis
Daugėlaičiai
Šeduva
Lietuvos jūrų muziejus
Smiltynė
Gargždai
Vėžaičiai
Rietavas
Tverai
Varniai
Lūksto ežeras
Girgždūtės kalnas
Parševežeris ežeras
Medvėgalio kalnas
Kiaunoriai
Sassnitz
Dovilai
Endriejavas
Požerė
Vaiguva
Agluonėnai
Veiviržėnai
Laukuva
Kražiai
Kelmė
Šiaulėnai
Baisogala
Juodkrantė
Vaškiai
Priekulė
Kvėdarna
Kaltinėnai
Tytuvėnai
Dreverna
Švėkšna
Lioliai
Šiluva
Grinkiškis
Skėmiai
Kuršių Nerijos Nacionalinis parkas
Žyniai
Saugos
Ten
Silalė
Pajūris
Upyna
Gudžiūnai
Pervalka
Kintai
Ramučiai
Šilutė
Žemaičių Naumiestis
Skaudvilė
Viduklė
Raseiniai
Žaiginys
Krakės
Vainotiškiai
Dotnuva
Trakšėdžiai
Šturmai
Kuršių Nerija
Nida
Pakalnė
Rusnė
Juknaičiai
Katyčiai
Žygaičiai
Pagramantis
Mažonai
Betygala
Ilgižiai
Kalnujai
Girkalnis
Šešuvis
Šaltuona
Ariogala
Pernarava
Josvainiai
Kuršių Marios
Mysovka
Paleičiai
Sartininkai
Tauragė
Gaurė
Eržvilkas
Vadžgirys
Prokhladnoye
Prichaly
Yasnoye
Mažaičiai
Lauksargiai
Pagėgiai
Piktupėnai
Žindaičiai
Stakiai
Čekiškė
Vidauja
Mituva
Šušvė
Baltijas Jūra

8
9
10
11
12
13
131
A
B
C
D
E
F
LV
LT
EST
BY
133
137
Vecsalaca
Svētciems
Ungurpils
Korģene
Aloja
Urga
Vilzēni
Rencēni
Burtnieki
Turna
Lugaži
Seda
Strenči
KARULA RAHVUSPARK
Tsooru
Rõuge
Haanja kõrgustik
Ruusmäe
Pāle
Ārciems
Puikule
Matīši
Lizdēni
Ēvele
Hargla
Varstu
Mõniste
Krabi
Vecļaicene
Dēliņkalns
Viļķene
Ozoli
Dikļi
Bērzaine
Zilais kalns
Valmiermuiža
Jaunklidzis
Vijciems
Birzuļi
Ape
Jaunlaicene
Ziemeri
Mārīnkalns
Alūksne
Priedes
Pociems
Zilaiskalns
Dauguļi
Kocēni
Brenguļi
Valmiera
Trikāta
Plāņi
Lobērģi
Gaujiena
Trapene
Ozolaine
Umurga
Limbaži
Tūja
Lielezers
Cempi
Bilska
Dzeņi
Palsa
Vireši
Rubene
Kauguriēši
Līči
Mārsnēni
Smiltene
Alsviķi
Jaunalūksne
Liepupe
Ausmas
Vaidava
Blome
Vidaga
Ilzene
Maliena
Bēja
Dādes ezers
Sāruma ezers
Aijažu ezers
Rozula
Kūdums
Lode
Rozes
Silva
Palsmane
Zeltiņi
Mālupe
Vidriži
Straupe
Stalbe
Jānmuiža
Liepa
Plācis
Ungura ezers
Skulte
Vecskulte
Zvejniekciems
Lēdurga
Cēsis
Priekuļi
Rauna
Launkalne
Variņi
Sudala ezers
Pilskalns
Cēsu pils
Veselava
Sinole
Lejasciems
Beļava
Ludza ezers
Bīriņi
Līvi
Gaujas Nacionālais Parks
Līgatne
Rīdzene
Drusti
Gauja
Saulkrasti
Inciems
Ieriķi
Drabeši
Dzērbene
Jaunpiebalga
Ranka
Lizums
Blome
Gulbene
Litene
Lilaste
Ragana
Sigulda
Augšlīgatne
Ģikši
Taurene
Melnbārži
Abrupe
Slapjuma kalns
Druviena
Tirza
Šķieneri
Stradi
Dūņu ezers
Loja
Gauja
Carnikava
Murjāņi
Lorupe
Sērmūkši
Greiveri
Stāķi
Stari
Naudaskalns
Garciems
Sauļiņi
Ādaži
Vangaži
Inčukalns
Allaži
More
Nitaure
Skujene
Kaive
Vecpiebalga
Alauksts
Inesis
Sveķi
Jaungulbene
Ušuru ezers
Kīšezers
Baltezers
Garkalne
Allažmuiža
Mālpils
Vidzemes Centrālā Augstiene
Ineši
Liezēre
Kraukļi
Prūšiņi
Rīgas zoodārzs
Ropaži
Tumšupe
Liela Jugla
Sidgunda
Zaube
Jumurda
Ozolі
Cesvaine
Dzelzava
Aizpurve
Liede
Aiviekste
Lazdukalns
RĪGA
Ulbroka
Kastrāne
Ērgļi
Lauterе
Kusa
Biksēre
Lubāna
Mārupe
Salaspils
Saurieši
Suntaži
Ķieģelcepls
Līčupe
Gaiziņkalns
Madona
Lazdona
Ošupe
Ķeipene
Taurupe
Kāla ezers
Vestiena
Prauliena
Degumnieki
Bērzpils
Ismas
Ķekava
Saulkalne
Tinūži
Ikšķile
Ogre
Ogresgals
Laubere
Madliena
Sidrabiņi
Sausnēja
Bērzaune
Mārciena
Vecsaikava
Stalidzāni
Jaunolaine
Rīgas Ūdenskrātuve
Meņģele
Irši
Ideņa
Gaigalava
Baldone
Ķegums
Lielvārde
Veckrape
Lobe
Lobes ezers
Vecbebri
Odziena
Jaunkalsnava
Ļaudona
Barkava
Murmastiene
Lubānas ezers
Nagļi
Rikava
Dricēni
Baldones Muiža
Piebalgas
Lāčplēsis
Bormaņi
Odzes ezers
Aiviekste
Mētriena
Dimzukalns
Jumprava
Skrīveri
Koknese
Kriškalni
Aizkraukle
Rīteri
Pļaviņas
Antūži
Kokari
Varakļāni
Tēvenāni
Garoza
Zālīte
Vecumnieki
Birzgale
Jaunjelgava
Sērene
Sece
Staburags
Stukmaņi
Spuņģēni
Kūkas
Atašiene
Viļāni
Staļģene
Iecava
Stelpe
Radopole
Krupļi
Strēlnieki
Valle
Daudzeva
Daudzese
Jaunsēlpils
Sala
Ošāni
Jaunmuiža
Mežāre
Jēkabpils
Sīļukalns
Galēni
Code
Mežotne
Birzes
Vecsaule
Bārbele
Kurmene
Sunākste
Piksteres ezers
Birži
Vīpe
Turki
Atašā
Smelteri
Maltas Trūpi
Stabulnieki
Mēmele
Bauska
Mūsa
Bauskas pils
Skaistkalne
Nemunėlio Radviliškis
Ziemeļ Susēja
Jaunsilava
Rudzāti
Ritausmas
Svitene
Brunava
Ceraukste
Mēmele
Lielmēmele
Ērberģe
Ēkengrāve
Viesīte
Viesītes ezers
Leimaņi
Vidsala
Līvāni
Rožupe
Prikuļi
Anspoki
Riebiņi
Sīļajāņi
Adžūni
Kamarde
Īslīce
Mūsa
Apaščia
Medeikiai
Zalve
Sprogi
Lone
Sauka
Ormankalns
Saukas ezers
Zasa
Dignāja
Upenieki
Sutri
Fiemanka
Lielklapari
Līči
Preiļi
Feimaņu ezers
Gailmuiža
Bicānu ezers
Žeimelis
Lauksodis
Kiemėnai
Saločiai
Smilgiai
Širvėnos ežeras
Biržai
Nereta
Bērzieši
Mežgale
Liepas
Sudrabkalns
Slate
Dunava
Rimicāni
Vārkava
Kastīre
Jasmuiža
Rušona
Pabiržė
Silavēveri
Rite
Elkšņi
Aknīste
Liel Kalupes ezers
Pelēči
Ciriss
Vaškai
Kratiškiai
Papilys
Nemunėlis
Suvainiškis
Onuškis
Juodupė
Kraujas
Gārsene
Asare
Ancene
Rubeņi
Kaldabruņa
Nīcgale
Kalupe
Baltmuiža
Dubna
Vīganti
Viškī
Viškų ezers
Grāveri
Grūžai
Čedasai
Bebrene
Dviete
Dvietе
Ambeļi
Šķeltova
Joniškėlis
Pasvalys
Pandėlys
Lukštai
Subate
Ilze
Doļnaja
Aizgalis
Yabole
Malinovka
Bikernieki
Kon
Klovainiai
Vabalninkas
Daujėnai
Alizava
Lėvuo
Rokiškis
Obeliai
Eglaine
Ilūkste
Auzgulāni
Līksna
Lociki
Borovka
Augšzemes Augstiene
Pušalotas
Pumpėnai
Panemunėlis
Skapiškis
Rageliai
Šēdere
Pašulienе
Eglukalns
Svente
Stropi
Krauja
Daugavpils
Saliena
Pyvesa
Palėvenėlė
Anatazavė
Rauda
Svententes ezers
Kalkūni
Tanaji
Skrudaliena
Plys
Skaistgiriai
Kupiškis
Kamajai
Sartų ežeras
Čičirio ežeras
Medumi
Medumu ezers
Krasnagorka
Smilgiai
Karsakiškis
Subačius
Dvirgio ežeras
Jūžintai
Imbrados
Brigeņes ezers
Jānuciems
Sila ezers
Panevėžys
Dembava
Šimonys
Dusetos
Avilio ežeras
Zarasai
Demene
Kumbuli
Silene
Naujamiestis
Velžys
Upytė
Viešintų ežeras
Svėdasai
Samavo ežeras
Smalvas ežeras
Turmantas
Drisvjaty ozero
Vozyera Rychy
Myazhany
Kiršinas
Mažeikiai
Surdegis
Užpaliai
Indraju ežeras
Degučiai
Antalieptė
Smalvos
Visaginas
Drysvyaty
Juostininkai
Šventoji
Andrioniškis
Alauso ežeras
Vyžuonos
Antalieptės marios
Salakas
Vozyera Abolye
Natsyyanal'ny Park Braslawskiya Azyery
Akhremawtsy
Daktai
Raguva
Troškūnai
Daugailiai
Memiakalnis
Luodžio ežeras
Rimšė
Opsa
Krekenava
Traupis
Anykščiai
Rubikių ežeras
Utena
Dūkštas
Ramygala
Vadokliai
Leliūnai
Taurągnai
Tauragno ežeras
Dysnų ežeras
Prūto ežeras
Dalyokiya
Surviliškis
Truskava
Kavarskas
Nevėžos ežeras
Pakalniai
Piliakalnis
Aukštaitijos Nacionalinis Parkas
Dysnykščio ežeras
Vidzy
Šlapaberžė
Skiemonys
Kuktiškės
Rimšėnai
Naujasis Daugėliškis
Vozyera Bohinskaye
Taujėnai
Pagiriai
Alanta
Galuonų ežeras
Lūšių ežeras
Ignalina
Nevaišių kalnas
Didžiasalis
Kaz'yany
Sirutiškis
Balninkai
Stirnių ežeras
Linkmenys
Tverečius
Kėdainiai
Šėta
Vidiškiai
Toliejai
Labanoras
Kretuono ežeras
Ceikiniai
Kurapollye
Bartkuškiai
Ukmergė
Siesartis
Dūrių ežeras
Molėtai
Mindūnai
Kaltanėnai
Nociūnai
Bukonys
Želva
Videniškiai
Siesarties ežeras
Inturkė
Švenčionėliai
Svirkos
Rutiškis
Pabaisk
Šešuoliai
Švenčionys
Yareva
Pastavy
Vepriai
Išnaru ežeras
Žverno
Palyessye
Vandžiogala
Žirnajų ežeras
24°00′
24°30′
25°00′
25°30′
26°00′
26°30′
57°30′
57°00′
56°30′
56°00′
55°30′
E67
E264
E77
E22
E262
E272
A1
A2
A3
A4
A5
A6
A7
A8
A9
A10
A12
A13
A14
A17

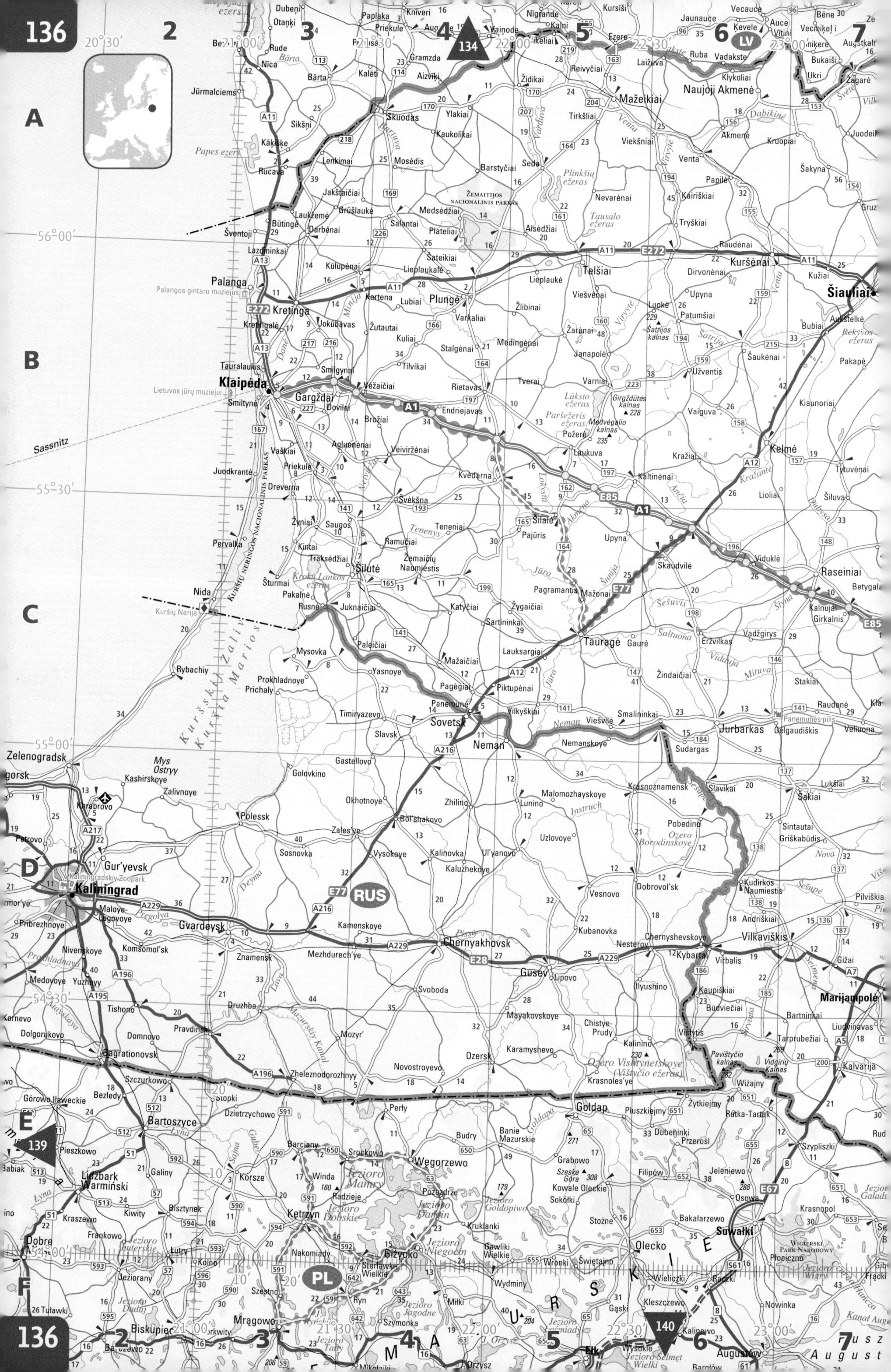
134
139
140
LV
RUS
PL
Klaipėda
Palanga
Kretinga
Skuodas
Mažeikiai
Naujoji Akmenė
Plungė
Telšiai
Kuršėnai
Šiauliai
Gargždai
Kelmė
Raseiniai
Šilalė
Šilutė
Tauragė
Jurbarkas
Šakiai
Nida
Kuršių Nerija
Sovetsk
Neman
Zelenogradsk
Kaliningrad
Gur'yevsk
Gvardeysk
Chernyakhovsk
Gusev
Vilkaviškis
Marijampolė
Kalvarija
Bagrationovsk
Pravdinsk
Ozersk
Gołdap
Węgorzewo
Kętrzyn
Giżycko
Bartoszyce
Lidzbark Warmiński
Mrągowo
Olecko
Suwałki
Ełk
Augustów
Sassnitz
Palangos gintaro muziejus
Lietuvos jūrų muziejus
Panemunės pilis
Kaliningradskiy Zoopark
Žemaitijos nacionalinis parkas
Kuršių neringos nacionalinis parkas
Wigierski Park Narodowy
Kurshskiy Zaliv
Kuršių Marios
Mys Ostryy
Ozero Vishtynetskoye (Vištyčio ežeras)
Jezioro Mamry
Jezioro Niegocin
Neman
Šešupė
Venta
Pregolya
E272
E85
E77
E28
E67
A1
A11
A12
A13
A229
A216
56°00′
55°30′
55°00′
54°30′
54°00′
20°30′
21°00′
21°30′
22°00′
22°30′
23°00′
A
B
C
D
E
F
2
3
4
5
6
7

LV
LT
BY
Daugavpils
Līvāni
Bauska
Biržai
Pasvalys
Joniškis
Rokiškis
Panevėžys
Kupiškis
Anykščiai
Utena
Visaginas
Ignalina
Kėdainiai
Ukmergė
Jonava
Kaunas
Molėtai
Švenčionėliai
Švenčionys
Širvintos
Elektrėnai
Trakai
VILNIUS
Prienai
Birštonas
Alytus
Varėna
Lazdijai
Druskininkai
Šalčininkai
Ashmyany
Lida
Pabradė
Nemenčinė
Zarasai
Aukštaitijos Nacionalinis Parkas
Dzūkija Nacionalinis Parkas
Natsyyanal'ny Park Narochanski
135
xiii
8
9
10
11
12
13
A
B
C
D
E
F

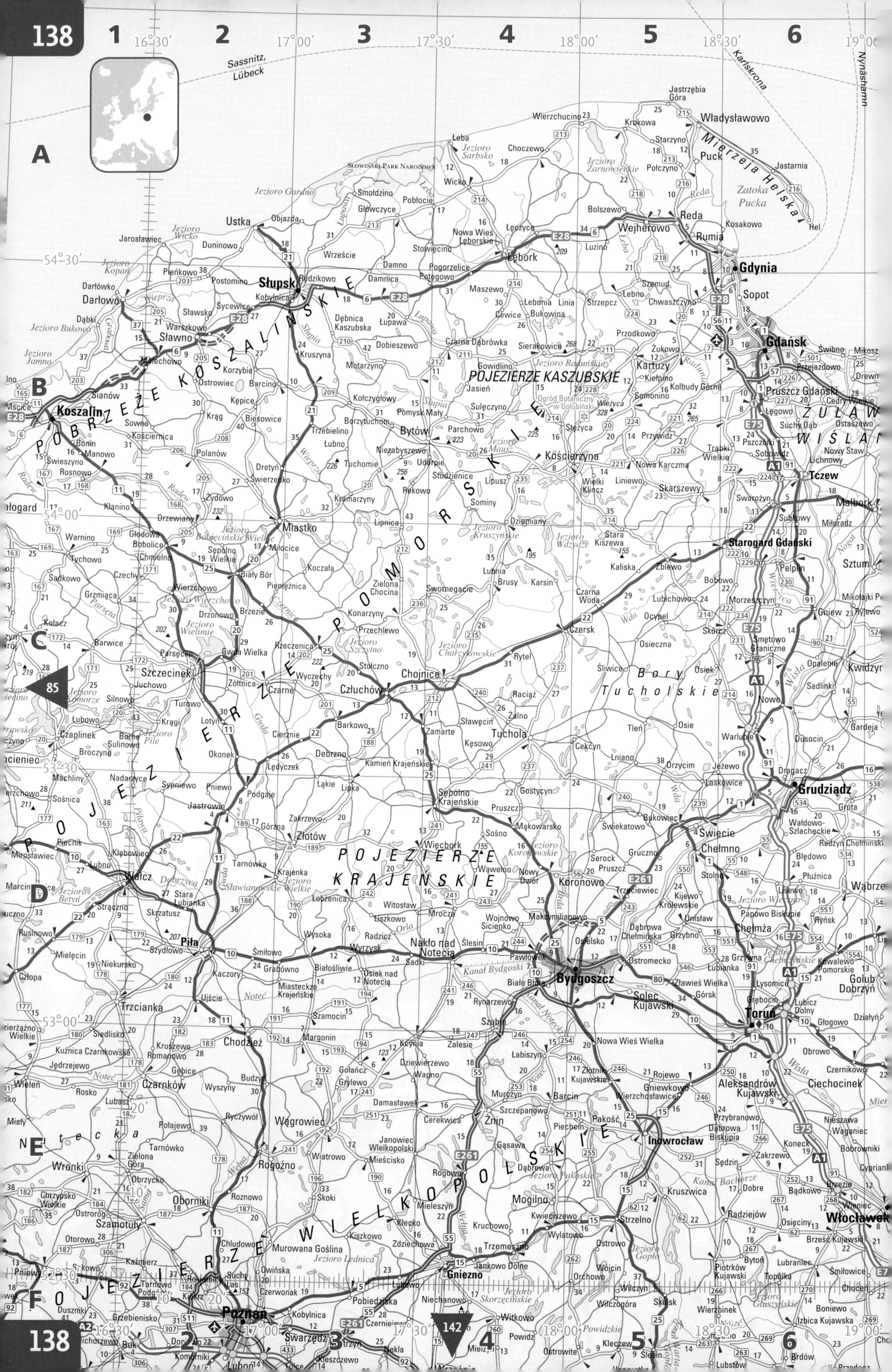
1
2
3
4
5
6
A
B
C
D
E
F
Sassnitz, Lübeck
Karlskrona
Nynäshamn
Słowiński Park Narodowy
Mierzeja Helska
Zatoka Pucka
Władysławowo
Puck
Hel
Jastarnia
Reda
Rumia
Wejherowo
Gdynia
Sopot
Gdańsk
Łeba
Lębork
Ustka
Słupsk
Darłowo
Sławno
Koszalin
Bytów
Kartuzy
Kościerzyna
Pruszcz Gdański
Tczew
Malbork
Starogard Gdański
Kwidzyn
Grudziądz
Chojnice
Człuchów
Czersk
Tuchola
Szczecinek
Miastko
Bobolice
Wałcz
Piła
Złotów
Nakło nad Notecią
Bydgoszcz
Toruń
Chełmno
Świecie
Chełmża
Inowrocław
Włocławek
Aleksandrów Kujawski
Ciechocinek
Gniezno
Poznań
Wągrowiec
Oborniki
Szamotuły
Czarnków
Chodzież
Trzcianka
Wronki
Rogoźno
Żnin
Mogilno
Strzelno
Kruszwica
Swarzędz
POBRZEŻE KOSZALIŃSKIE
POJEZIERZE KASZUBSKIE
POJEZIERZE POMORSKIE
POJEZIERZE KRAJEŃSKIE
POJEZIERZE WIELKOPOLSKIE
Bory Tucholskie
ŻUŁAWY WIŚLANE
Notecka
Kanał Bydgoski
85
142

Kurši Marios
Zatoka Dańska
Kaliningradskiy Zaliv
Zalew Wiślany
Mierzeja Wiślana
Baltiyskaya Kosa
RUS
PL
Kaliningrad
Svetlogorsk
Zelenogradsk
Pionerskiy
Baltiysk
Svetlyy
Gur'yevsk
Polessk
Gvardeysk
Chernyakhovsk
Znamensk
Pravdinsk
Bagrationovsk
Mamonovo
Zheleznodorozhnyy
Ozersk
Braniewo
Frombork
Elbląg
Pasłęk
Morąg
Orneta
Pieniężno
Górowo Iławeckie
Bartoszyce
Lidzbark Warmiński
Dobre Miasto
Biskupiec
Kętrzyn
Węgorzewo
Giżycko
Mrągowo
Mikołajki
Orzysz
Pisz
Ruciane-Nida
Olsztyn
Ostróda
Iława
Olsztynek
Szczytno
Pasym
Nidzica
Działdowo
Lidzbark
Lubawa
Nowe Miasto Lubawskie
Brodnica
Rypin
Żuromin
Mława
Przasnysz
Ciechanów
Maków Mazowiecki
Ostrołęka
Kolno
Nowogród
Ostrów Mazowiecka
Pułtusk
Wyszków
Płońsk
Sierpc
Płock
Raciąż
Nowy Dwór Mazowiecki
Legionowo
Radzymin
Wołomin
Łomianki
Węgrów
Łochów
Warmia
Pojezierze Iławskie
Pojezierze Mazurskie
Nizina
Jezioro Mamry
Jezioro Śniardwy
Jezioro Niegocin
Jezioro Zegrzyńskie
Jezioro Drużno
E28
E77
E67
A229
A196
A195
A217
A216
136
140
143

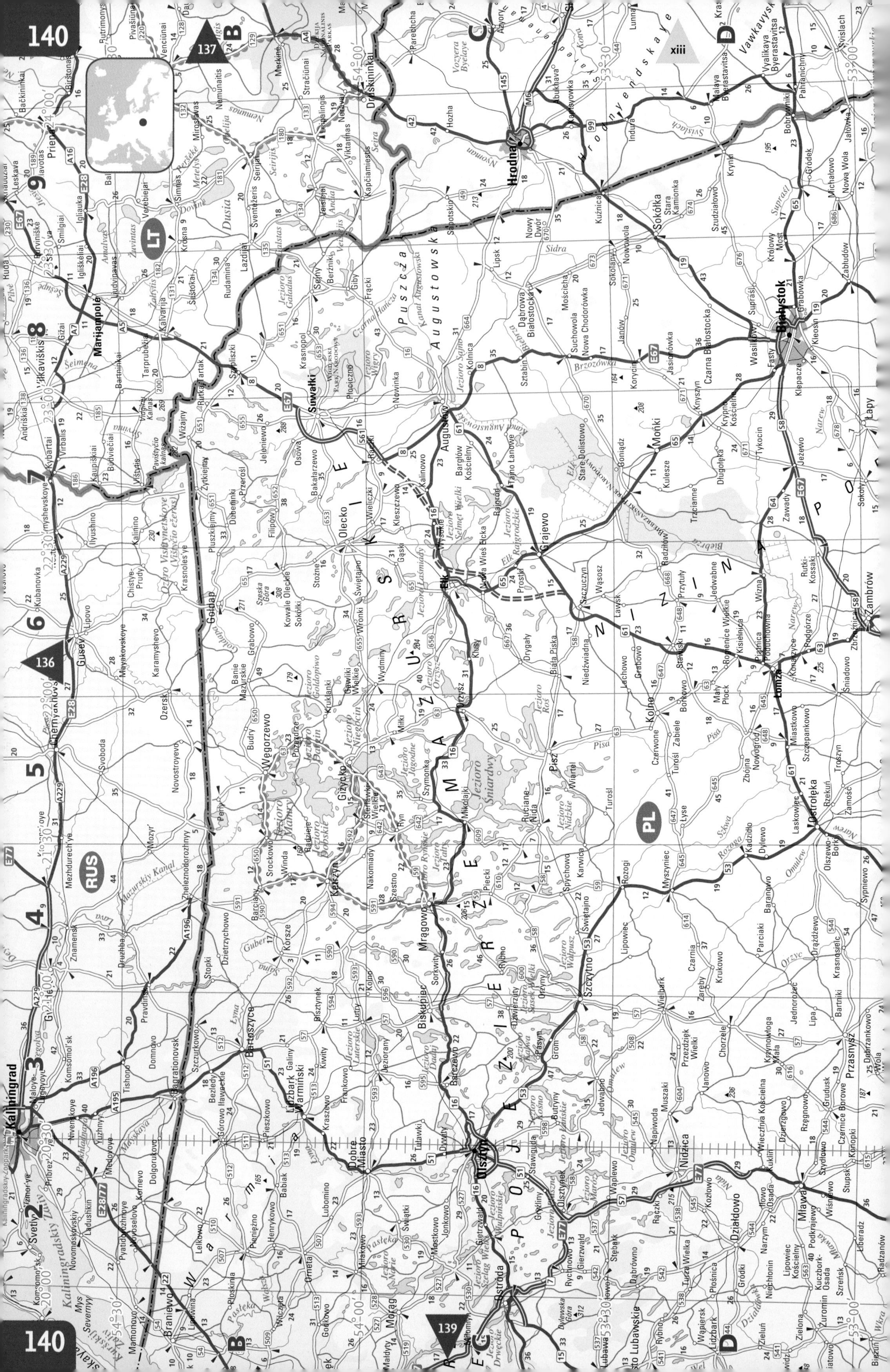
Kaliningrad
Svetlyy
Gvardeysk
Chernyakhovsk
Gusev
Nesterov
Sovetsk
Marijampolė
Vilkaviškis
Kalvarija
Lazdijai
Druskininkai
Hrodna
Sokółka
Białystok
Łapy
Suwałki
Augustów
Sejny
Olecko
Gołdap
Ełk
Grajewo
Mońki
Łomża
Zambrów
Kolno
Pisz
Giżycko
Węgorzewo
Kętrzyn
Mrągowo
Orzysz
Ruciane-Nida
Szczytno
Olsztyn
Bartoszyce
Lidzbark Warmiński
Dobre Miasto
Biskupiec
Ostróda
Morąg
Braniewo
Bagrationovsk
Nidzica
Działdowo
Mława
Przasnysz
Ostrołęka
Wizna
Kadzidło
RUS
LT
PL
W a r m i a
M a z u r y
P u s z c z a A u g u s t o w s k a
P o j e z i e r z e
Jezioro Śniardwy
Jezioro Mamry
Jezioro Niegocin
Jezioro Wigry
E28
E67
E77
A229
A196
B
C
D
137
136
139
xiii

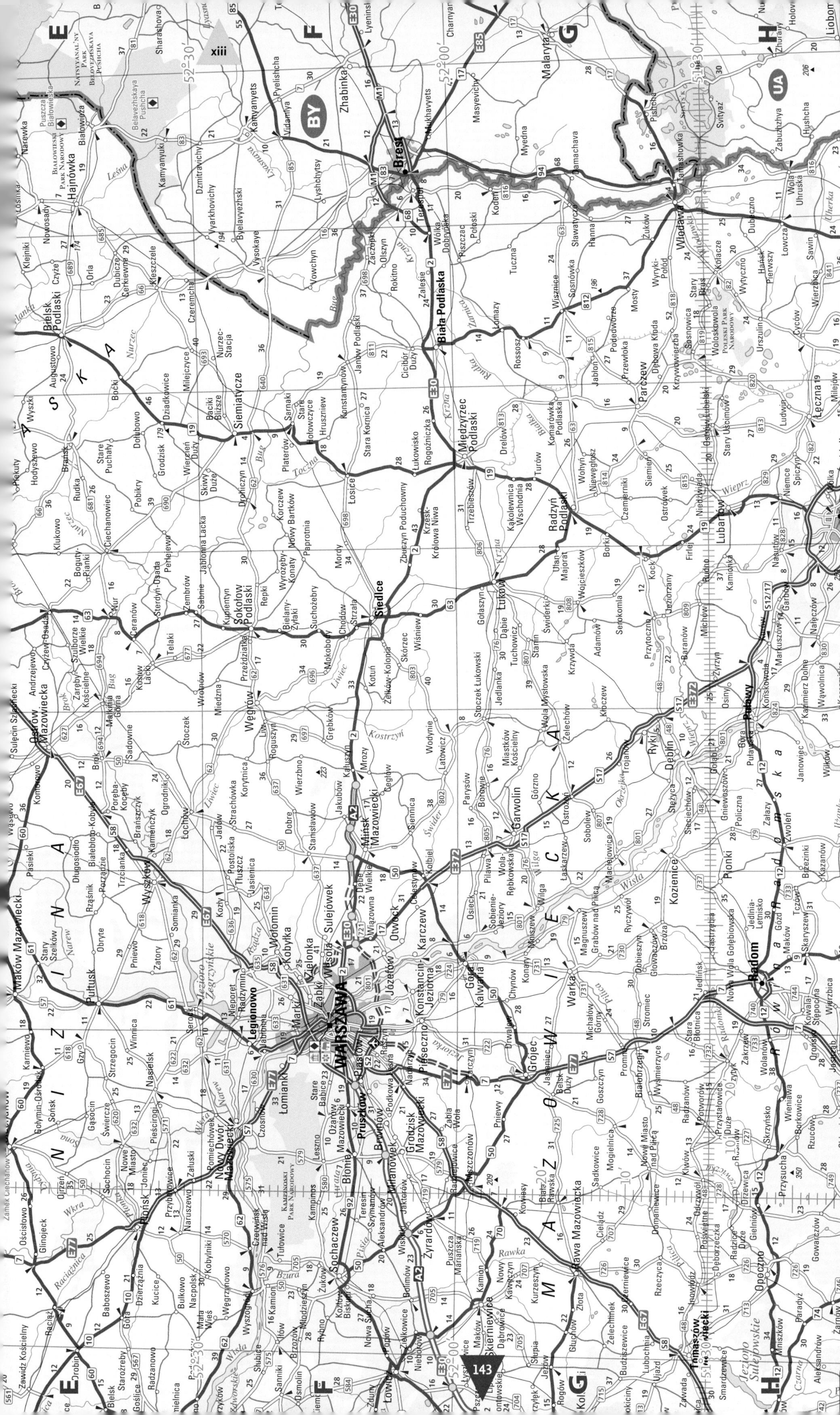
WARSZAWA
Brest
Siedlce
Biała Podlaska
Międzyrzec Podlaski
Lublin
Radom
Puławy
Chełm
Włodawa
Łuków
Garwolin
Mińsk Mazowiecki
Węgrów
Sokołów Podlaski
Siemiatycze
Bielsk Podlaski
Hajnówka
Ostrów Mazowiecka
Wyszków
Pułtusk
Legionowo
Płońsk
Sochaczew
Żyrardów
Skierniewice
Grójec
Rawa Mazowiecka
Opoczno
Kozienice
Dęblin
Ryki
Radzyń Podlaski
Parczew
Łęczna
Świdnik
Lubartów
Zwoleń
Szydłowiec
Skarżysko-Kamienna
Tomaszów Mazowiecki
Zabinka
Kamyanyets
Malaryta
Svityaz'
BY
UA
M A Z O W I E C K A
L U B E L S K A
P O D L A S K A
Z I E M I A
xiii
143
144

1
2
3
4
5
6
138
B
C
D
E
F
81
146
PL
CZ
Poznań
Oborniki
Szamotuły
Mogilno
Gniezno
Kłecko
Pobiedziska
Swarzędz
Luboń
Kórnik
Środa Wielkopolska
Września
Słupca
Konin
Koło
Pyzdry
Buk
Opalenica
Grodzisk Wielkopolski
Wolsztyn
Kościan
Śmigiel
Mosina
Śrem
Jarocin
Pleszew
Turek
Kalisz
Ostrów Wielkopolski
Sieradz
Leszno
Gostyń
Krotoszyn
Wschowa
Głogów
Rawicz
Góra
Milicz
Odolanów
Ostrzeszów
Kępno
Syców
Trzebnica
Oleśnica
Wieluń
Legnica
Lubin
Wołów
Wrocław
Jawor
Strzegom
Świdnica
Wałbrzych
Oława
Brzeg
Namysłów
Kluczbork
Olesno
Opole
Strzelin
Ząbkowice Śląskie
Kłodzko
Nysa
Prudnik
Głuchołazy
Krapkowice
Strzelce Opolskie
Kędzierzyn-Koźle
Głubczyce
Racibórz
Rybnik
Gliwice
Zabrze
Tarnowskie Góry
Lubliniec
Dzierżoniów
Bielawa
Jeseník
Krnov
Náchod
Kudowa-Zdrój
Nové Město nad Metují
Rychnov nad Kněžnou
Žamberk
Bruntál
Wodzisław Śląski
Żory
Jezioro Gopło
Jezioro Lednica
Jezioro Turawskie
Jezioro Otmuchowskie
Jezioro Nyskie
Wielkopolski Park Narodowy
Park Narodowy Gór Stołowych
Nizina Śląska
Wyżyna
Płaskowyż Głubczycki
Rychlebské Hory
Góry Bystrzyckie
Orlické Hory
Śnieżnik
Praděd
Sanktuarium Matki Bożej Licheńskiej
Zamek w Kórniku
Zamek w Uniejowie
52°30'
52°00'
51°30'
51°00'
50°30'
16°30'
17°00'
17°30'
18°00'
18°30'
E30
E261
E65
E67
E40
A2
A4
A8
A1

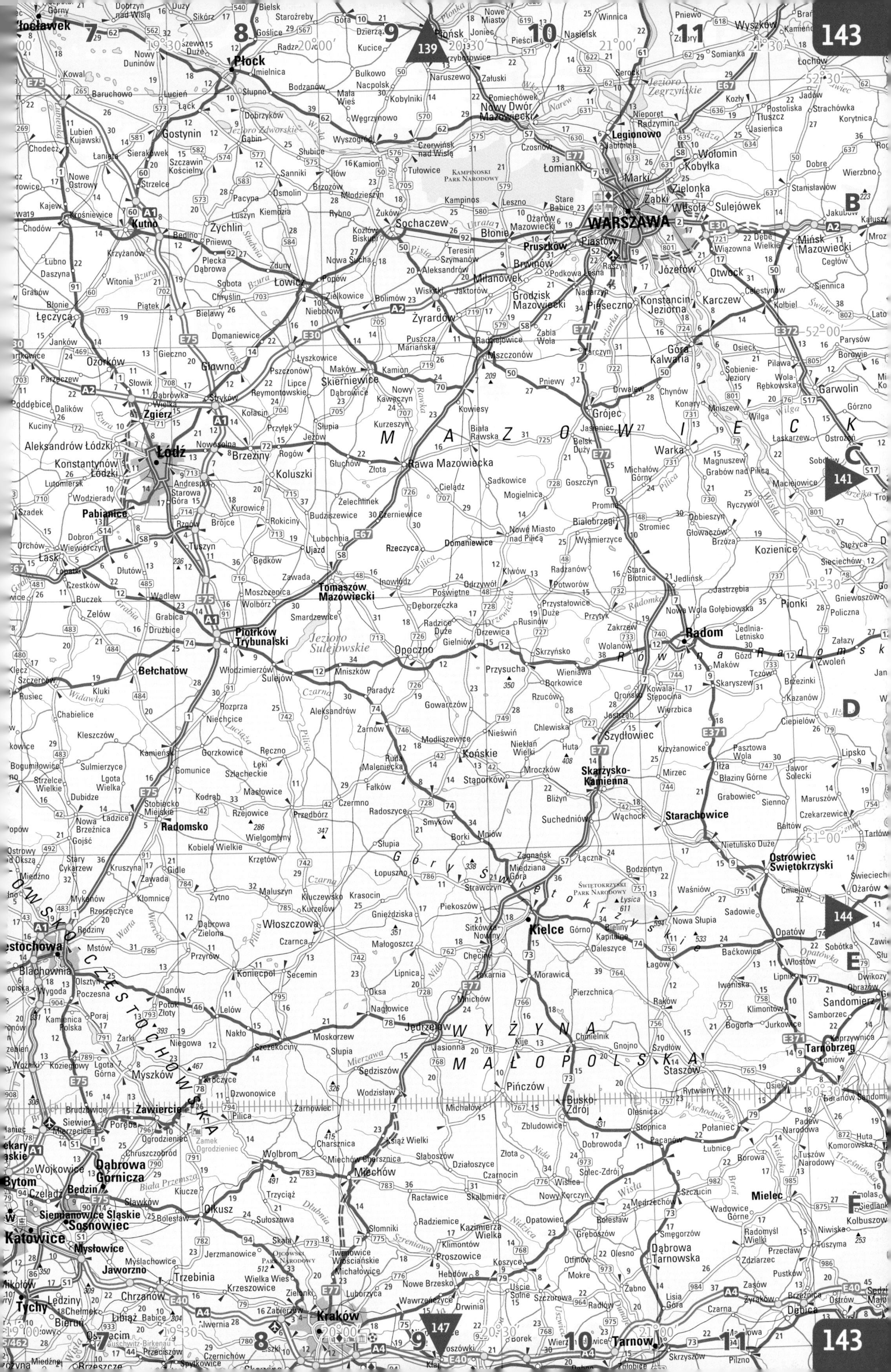
Włocławek
Płock
Płońsk
Nasielsk
Wyszków
Gostynin
Kutno
Łęczyca
Zgierz
Łódź
Pabianice
Konstantynów Łódzki
Aleksandrów Łódzki
Łask
Zelów
Bełchatów
Piotrków Trybunalski
Tomaszów Mazowiecki
Skierniewice
Łowicz
Głowno
Sochaczew
Żyrardów
Grodzisk Mazowiecki
Błonie
Pruszków
Piastów
WARSZAWA
Legionowo
Nowy Dwór Mazowiecki
Łomianki
Marki
Ząbki
Zielonka
Wołomin
Kobyłka
Sulejówek
Józefów
Otwock
Karczew
Piaseczno
Konstancin-Jeziorna
Góra Kalwaria
Grójec
Mińsk Mazowiecki
Garwolin
Warka
Rawa Mazowiecka
Brzeziny
Koluszki
Opoczno
Przysucha
Końskie
Radom
Pionki
Kozienice
Zwoleń
Szydłowiec
Skarżysko-Kamienna
Starachowice
Ostrowiec Świętokrzyski
Opatów
Sandomierz
Tarnobrzeg
Staszów
Kielce
Busko-Zdrój
Pińczów
Jędrzejów
Włoszczowa
Radomsko
Częstochowa
Myszków
Zawiercie
Dąbrowa Górnicza
Będzin
Sosnowiec
Katowice
Bytom
Mysłowice
Jaworzno
Tychy
Olkusz
Miechów
Kraków
Tarnów
Dąbrowa Tarnowska
Mielec
Dębica
Proszowice
Chrzanów
M A Z O W I E C K
R ó w n i n a R a d o m s k a
G ó r y Ś w i ę t o k r z y s k i e
W Y Ż Y N A M A Ł O P O L S K A
W Y Ż Y N A K R A K O W S K O - C Z Ę S T O C H O W S K A
Kampinoski Park Narodowy
Świętokrzyski Park Narodowy
Ojcowski Park Narodowy
Jezioro Sulejowskie
Jezioro Zegrzyńskie
Wisła
Pilica
Narew
Bzura
139
141
144
147
7
8
9
10
11
B
C
D
E
F

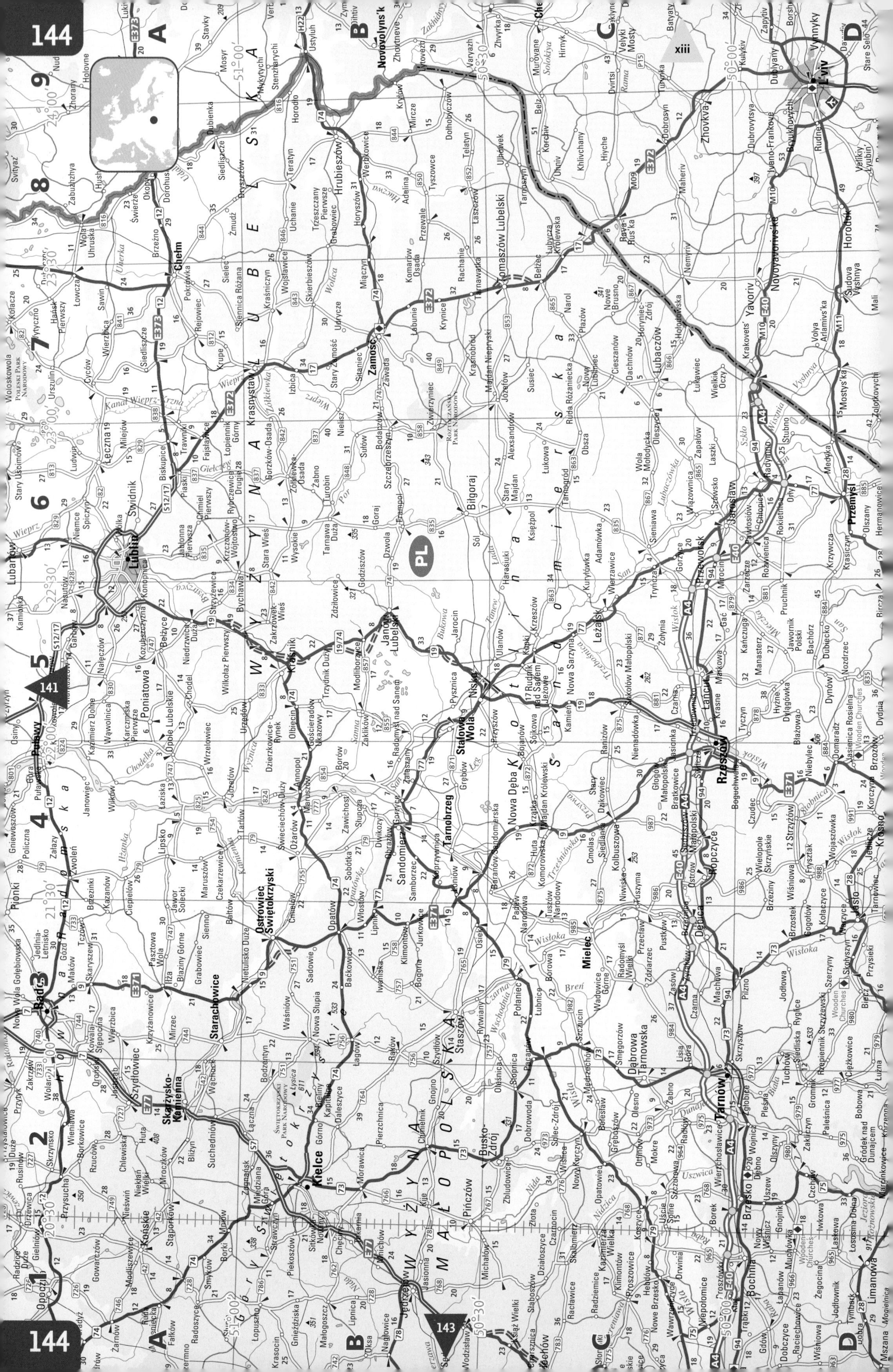
Lublin
Chełm
Zamość
Hrubieszów
Krasnystaw
Świdnik
Puławy
Radom
Kielce
Skarżysko-Kamienna
Starachowice
Ostrowiec Świętokrzyski
Sandomierz
Tarnobrzeg
Stalowa Wola
Nisko
Kraśnik
Janów Lubelski
Biłgoraj
Tomaszów Lubelski
Zwoleń
Szydłowiec
Końskie
Opoczno
Jędrzejów
Pińczów
Busko-Zdrój
Staszów
Połaniec
Mielec
Dębica
Ropczyce
Rzeszów
Łańcut
Leżajsk
Przeworsk
Jarosław
Przemyśl
Lubaczów
Tarnów
Dąbrowa Tarnowska
Brzesko
Bochnia
Limanowa
Jasło
Krosno
Strzyżów
Dynów
Rawa Rus'ka
Yavoriv
Novoyavorivs'ke
Horodok
Zhovkva
L'viv
Novovolyns'k
Ustyluh
Mostys'ka
PL
Roztoczański Park Narodowy
Świętokrzyski Park Narodowy
Poleski Park Narodowy
Wooden Churches
141
143
xiii
A
B
C
D
1
2
3
4
5
6
7
8
9

UA
SK
H
RO
Uzhhorod
Mukacheve
Stryy
Drohobych
Sambir
Sanok
Prešov
Košice
Miskolc
Nyíregyháza
Poprad
Michalovce
Humenné
Bardejov
Svidník
Berehove
Khust
Svalyava
Sátoraljaújhely
Sárospatak
Tokaj
Bieszczady
Beskidy
Slovenské Rudohorie
Zemplénihegység
BODROGKÖZ
RÉTKÖZ
SZAMOSKÖZ
152
151
147
xiii

1
2
3
4
5
6
A
B
C
D
E
F
142
149
77
CZ
A
Hradec Králové
Pardubice
Chrudim
Náchod
Kłodzko
Nysa
Opole
Kędzierzyn-Koźle
Racibórz
Opava
Ostrava
Havířov
Frýdek-Místek
Krnov
Bruntál
Šumperk
Jeseník
Głuchołazy
Prudnik
Głubczyce
Ústí nad Orlicí
Litomyšl
Svitavy
Moravská Třebová
Mohelnice
Zábřeh
Lanškroun
Uničov
Šternberk
Litovel
Olomouc
Prostějov
Přerov
Hranice
Nový Jičín
Valašské Meziříčí
Rožnov pod Radhoštěm
Vsetín
Zlín
Otrokovice
Kroměříž
Holešov
Vyškov
Boskovice
Blansko
Brno
Třebíč
Velké Meziříčí
Žďár nad Sázavou
Znojmo
Mikulov
Břeclav
Hodonín
Kyjov
Uherské Hradiště
Uherský Brod
Trenčín
Púchov
Myjava
Senica
Skalica
Malacky
Pezinok
Trnava
Piešťany
Hlohovec
Nitra
Sereď
Galanta
Šaľa
Senec
BRATISLAVA
Šamorín
Dunajská Streda
Mosonmagyaróvár
Mistelbach
Hollabrunn
Stockerau
Tulln
Klosterneuburg
WIEN
Schwechat
Mödling
Baden
Wiener Neustadt
Eisenstadt
Bruck an der Leitha
Neusiedl am See
Hrubý Jeseník
Oderské vrchy
MORAVA
Chřiby
Malé Karpaty
Považský Inovec
TRIBEČ
Ždánický Les
Žďárské Vrchy
Javorník
Moravskoslezské Beskydy
Marchfeld
Leithagebirge
KOWYŻ GŁUBCZYCKI
E442
E461
E462
E50/65
E65
E75
E50
E59
E49
E60
E58
E65/75
E575
E572
E67
D1
D2
D35
D46
D52
A1
A4
A5
A6
A21
M15
49°00'
48°30'
48°00'
50°00'
49°30'
16°00'
16°30'
17°00'
17°30'
18°00'

7
8
9
10
11
A
B
C
D
E
F
143
144
145
150
PL
SK
H
Kraków
Katowice
Tarnów
Nowy Sącz
Zakopane
TATRY
NÍZKE TATRY
SLOVENSKÉ RUDOHORIE
Žilina
Martin
Banská Bystrica
Poprad
Košice
Miskolc
Eger
Salgótarján
Lučenec
Zvolen
Bielsko-Biała
Tychy
Oświęcim
Wadowice
Nowy Targ
Ružomberok
Liptovský Mikuláš
Prievidza
Rožňava
Levoča
Kežmarok
Tatranská Lomnica
Dolný Kubín
Čadca
Cieszyn
Český Těšín
Třinec
Balassagyarmat
Bátonyterenye
Rimavská Sobota
Levice
Krynica
Gorlice
Bochnia
Wieliczka
Myślenice
Limanowa
Miechów
Olkusz
Zawiercie
Dąbrowa Górnicza
Sosnowiec
Jaworzno
Chrzanów
Rybnik
Żory
Jastrzębie-Zdrój
Beskid Sądecki
Levočské vrchy
Volovské vrchy
Slovenský kras
Cserehát
Bükk
Cserhát
Börzsöny
Veľká Fatra
Malá Fatra
Oravská Magura
Poľana
Javorie
Krupinská Planina
Štiavnické Vrchy
19°00′
19°30′
20°00′
20°30′
21°00′
50°00′
49°30′
49°00′
48°30′
48°00′

1
2
3
4
5
6
A
B
C
D
E
F
76
77
73
156
A
SLO
14°00′
14°30′
15°00′
15°30′
16°00′
47°30′
47°00′
46°30′
46°00′
45°30′
Gmunden
Schladming
Ramsau
Bad Aussee
Liezen
Admont
Rottenmann
Trieben
Eisenerz
Waidhofen an der Ybbs
Mariazell
St Sebastian
Mürzzuschlag
Krieglach
Kapfenberg
Bruck an der Mur
Leoben
Trofaiach
Knittelfeld
Judenburg
Zeltweg
Frohnleiten
Graz
Köflach
Voitsberg
Gleisdorf
Hartberg
Fürstenfeld
Wiener Neustadt
Neunkirchen
Ternitz
Gloggnitz
Bad Radkersburg
Leibnitz
Deutschlandsberg
Wolfsberg
St Andrä
Völkermarkt
Klagenfurt
Villach
St Veit an der Glan
Feldkirchen in Kärnten
Ferlach
Wörther See
Ossiacher See
Jesenice
Bled
Kranj
Škofja Loka
LJUBLJANA
Domžale
Kamnik
Trbovlje
Celje
Velenje
Slovenj Gradec
Dravograd
Maribor
Ptuj
Rogla
Krško
Brežice
Novo Mesto
Postojna
Trieste
Koper
Muggia
Sežana
Karlovac
Samobor
Zaprešić
ZAGREB
Velika Gorica
Zabok
Krapina
Platak
Delnice
Kočevje
Ribnica
Črnomelj
Metlika
Vogel
Kobla
Triglav
Tolmin
Idrija
Hochschwab
Ennstaler Alpen
Eisenerzer Alpen
Seckauer Alpen
Niedere Tauern
Sengsengebirge
Kräuterin
Fischbacher Alpen
Gleinalpe
Saualpe
Koralpe
Karawanken
Kamniške in Savinjske Alpe
Pohorje
Slovenske Gorice
Haloze
Zagorje
Medvednica
Žumberačka Gora
Samoborska Gora
Bela Krajina
Suha Krajina
Gorski Kotar
Javorniki
Brkini
Posavsko Hribovje
Julijske Alpe

146
150
157
SK
H
HR
Sopron
Eisenstadt
Győr
Mosonmagyaróvár
Komárno
Komárom
Tata
Tatabánya
Esztergom
Štúrovo
Szombathely
Sárvár
Celldömölk
Pápa
Zirc
Várpalota
Székesfehérvár
Veszprém
Ajka
Devecser
Körmend
Zalaegerszeg
Keszthely
Balatonfüred
Siófok
Tapolca
Sümeg
Nagykanizsa
Marcali
Kaposvár
Dombóvár
Szekszárd
Tolna
Paks
Dunaújváros
Dunaföldvár
Bonyhád
Pécs
Szigetvár
Komló
Mohács
Siklós
Barcs
Osijek
Virovitica
Slatina
Našice
Daruvar
Bjelovar
Koprivnica
Križevci
Kutina
Sisak
Varaždin
Čakovec
Lendava
Požega
Balaton
Bakony
Zselic
Ormánság
Drava
Dráva
Duna
Rába
Zala
Kőszeg
Sárbogárd
Oroszlány
Kisbér
Mór
Csorna
Kapuvár
Bicske
Neusiedler See
Fertő
Nagyatád
Belső-Somogy
Külső-Somogy
Völgység
Mecsek
Papuk
Moslavačka Gora
Bilogora
Hegyhát
Hetés
Göcsej
Őrség
Nagy-Berek
Kis-Alföld
Kemeneshát
Hanság
Velencei-tó
16°30′
17°00′
17°30′
18°00′
18°30′
47°30′
47°00′
46°30′
46°00′
45°30′
7
8
9
10
11
A
B
C
D
E
F

1
2
3
4
5
6
A
B
C
D
E
F
147
149
158
SK
H
SRB
HR
BUDAPEST
Miskolc
Eger
Salgótarján
Balassagyarmat
Lučenec
Rimavská Sobota
Vác
Esztergom
Štúrovo
Tatabánya
Székesfehérvár
Dunaújváros
Kecskemét
Szolnok
Cegléd
Nagykőrös
Jászberény
Gyöngyös
Hatvan
Gödöllő
Kiskunfélegyháza
Csongrád
Szentes
Hódmezővásárhely
Szeged
Makó
Kiskunhalas
Kalocsa
Kiskőrös
Paks
Szekszárd
Baja
Mohács
Pécs
Bonyhád
Subotica
Sombor
Senta
Kikinda
Orosháza
Szarvas
Mezőtúr
Tiszafüred
Mezőkövesd
Heves
Kazincbarcika
Ózd
Mátra
Bükk
Cserhát
Börzsöny
Krupinská planina
Ipeľská pahorkatina
Kiskunság
Nagykunság
Solti-síkság
Duna–Tisza köze
Bugac
Tolnai-hegyhát
Völgység
Mecsek
Geresdi-dombság
Zombor
Duna
Tisza
Maros
E60
E71
E73
E75
E77
E66
E662
E68
M0
M1
M3
M5
M6
M7
M31
M43
M44
19°00′
19°30′
20°00′
20°30′
48°00′
47°30′
47°00′
46°30′
46°00′

Sátoraljaújhely
Sárospatak
BODROGKÖZ
RÉTKÖZ
Tokaj
Szerencs
Kisvárda
Záhony
145
Berehove
Vynohradiv
Khust
UA
Vásárosnamény
Nyíregyháza
Mátészalka
SZAMOSKÖZ
NYÍRSÉG
Fehérgyarmat
Satu Mare
Câmpia Someşului
Carei
Câmpia Careiului
Nyírbátor
Hajdúnánás
Hajdúböszörmény
HAJDÚSÁG
HORTOBÁGY
Hortobágy
Tiszaújváros
Polgár
Debrecen
Hajdúszoboszló
Püspökladány
Berettyóújfalu
Marghita
Şimleu Silvaniei
Zalău
Jibou
152
Oradea
Munţii Plopişului
Munţii Meseşului
Aleşd
Huedin
Munţii Vlădeasa
Munţii Gilăului
Munţii Pădurea Craiului
NAGY-SÁRRÉT
KIS-SÁRRÉT
KÖRÖS-VIDÉK
Szeghalom
Békés
Békéscsaba
Gyula
Salonta
Beiuş
RO
Ştei
Munţii Codru-Moma
Munţii Bihor
Munţii Muntele Mare
Câmpeni
Abrud
Zlatna
Ineu
Chişineu-Criş
Sebiş
Munţii Zarandului
Brad
Munţii Metaliferi
Arad
Câmpia Aradului
Câmpia Vingăi
Pecica
Lipova
Dealurile Lipovei
Deva
Hunedoara
Orăştie
Timişoara
159
E60
E79
E671
E81
E68
E573
A1
M3
M35

UA
RO
H
145
151
160
Satu Mare
Baia Mare
Sighetu Marmației
Rakhiv
Yasinya
Borșa
Bistrița
Dej
Gherla
Cluj Napoca
Turda
Câmpia Turzii
Târgu Mureș
Reghin
Sighișoara
Mediaș
Alba Iulia
Aiud
Blaj
Sebeș
Sibiu
Făgăraș
Vatra Dornei
Toplița
Zalău
Huedin
Negrești-Oaș
Nǎsǎud
Beclean
Câmpeni
Zlatna
Odorheiu Secuiesc
Cristuru Secuiesc
Târnǎveni
Luduș
Sovata
Rupea
Agnita
Orǎștie
Munții Rodnei
Munții Călimani
Munții Gurghiului
Munții Maramureșului
Podișul Transilvaniei
Podișul Târnavelor
Munții Trascăului
Munții Apuseni
Munții Gilăului
Depresiunea Maramureșului
Wooden Churches
Biserica fortificatǎ
Stadionul Dan Păltinișanu (FC Timișoara)
E58
E60
E81
E576
E578
E68
A1
A3

7
8
9
10
11
xiii
Chernivtsi
Storozhynets
Siret
Rădăuţi
Suceava
Gura Humorului
Fălticeni
Botoşani
Dorohoi
Darabani
Săveni
Hârlău
Paşcani
Târgu Neamţ
Târgu Frumos
Iaşi
Ungheni
Piatra Neamţ
Roman
Bacău
Buhuşi
Moineşti
Comăneşti
Dărmăneşti
Târgu Ocna
Oneşti
Adjud
Vaslui
Bârlad
Huşi
Tecuci
Mărăşeşti
Panciu
Focşani
Miercurea-Ciuc
Gheorgheni
Sfântu Gheorghe
Târgu Secuiesc
Covasna
Baraolt
Bicaz
Bălţi
Edineţ
Briceni
Donduşeni
Drochia
Rîşcani
Glodeni
Făleşti
MD
Podişul Sucevei
Câmpia Moldovei
Coasta Iaşilor
Podişul Moldovei
Podişul Bârladului
Munţii Stânişoarei
Munţii Tarcăului
Munţii Goşmanului
Munţii Ciucului
Munţii Harghita
Munţii Berzunţi
Munţii Vrancei
Munţii Baraolt
Lacul Izvorul Muntelui
Lacul Stânca-Costeşti
Complexul Naţional Muzeal Moldova
E85
E58
E583
E574
E578
E581
E58/583
48°00'
47°30'
47°00'
46°30'
46°00'
26°00'
26°30'
27°00'
27°30'
A
B
C
D
E
F
154
161

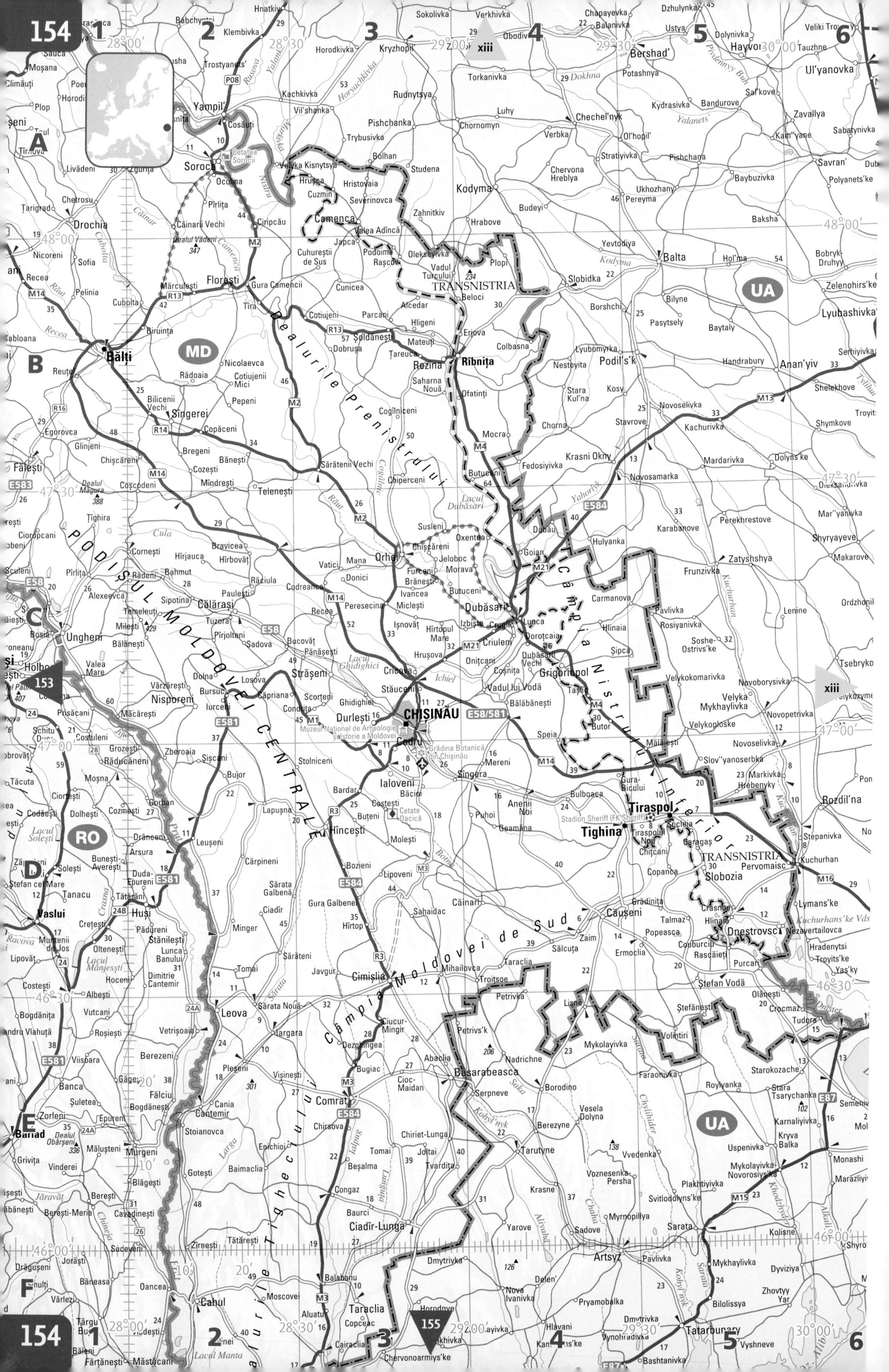
1
2
3
4
5
6
A
B
C
D
E
F
MD
RO
UA
TRANSNISTRIA
153
155
xiii
Yampil'
Soroca
Cetatea Sorocii
Cosăuți
Drochia
Florești
Bălți
Sîngerei
Fălești
Ungheni
Orhei
Călărași
Nisporeni
Strășeni
CHIȘINĂU
Muzeul Național de Arheologie și Istorie a Moldovei
Grădina Botanică din Chișinău
Codru
Durlești
Ialoveni
Cetate Dacică
Hîncești
Leova
Cimișlia
Basarabeasca
Comrat
Ciadîr-Lunga
Cantemir
Cahul
Taraclia
Vulcănești
Huși
Vaslui
Bîrlad
Rezina
Rîbnița
Dubăsari
Criuleni
Anenii Noi
Tiraspol
Tighina
Stadion Sheriff (FK Sheriff)
Slobozia
Căușeni
Ștefan Vodă
Grigoriopol
Dnestrovsc
Camenca
Kodyma
Balta
Bershad'
Ananʼyiv
Rozdil'na
Kuchurhan
Artsyz
Tatarbunary
Sarata
Tarutyne
Bilolissya
Dealurile Prenistrului
PODIȘUL MOLDOVEI CENTRALE
Cîmpia Nistrului Inferior
Cîmpia Moldovei de Sud
Dealurile Tigheciului
Lacul Dubăsari
Lacul Ghidighici
Lacul Manta
Nistru
Prut
Dnister
Răut
Cula
Ichel
Botna
Kuchurhan
Kodyma
Yahorlyk
M2
M3
M4
M14
M21
M13
M15
M16
R13
R14
R16
E58
E581
E583
E584
E58/581
E87
Dealul Vădeni 347
Dealul Măgura 388
Dealul Obârșeni 336
48°00'
47°30'
47°00'
46°30'
46°00'
28°00'
28°30'
29°00'
29°30'
30°00'

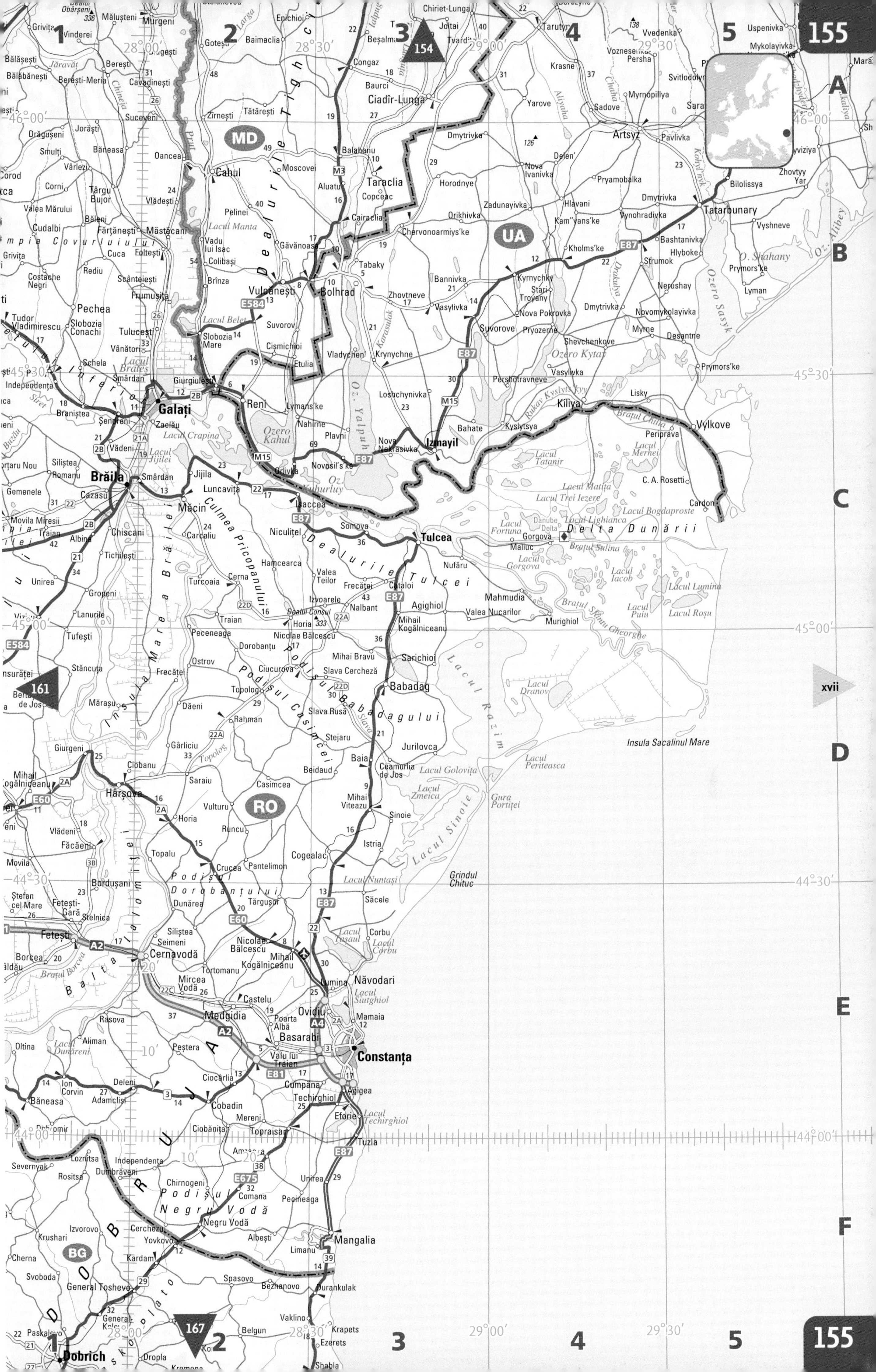
1
2
3
4
5
154
A
B
C
D
E
F
MD
UA
RO
BG
161
167
xvii
Galați
Brăila
Tulcea
Constanța
Izmayil
Kiliya
Vylkove
Reni
Bolhrad
Cahul
Vulcănești
Ciadîr-Lunga
Taraclia
Artsyz
Tatarbunary
Babadag
Măcin
Isaccea
Hârșova
Cernavodă
Medgidia
Mangalia
Năvodari
Mamaia
Ovidiu
Basarabi
Techirghiol
Eforie
Tuzla
Negru Vodă
Dobrich
General Toshevo
Fetești
Pechea
Tecuci
Delta Dunării
Lacul Razim
Lacul Sinoie
Ozero Kahul
Ozero Kytay
Ozero Sasyk
Oz. Yalpuh
Lacul Brateș
Dealurile Tulcei
Dealurile Tigheci
Podișul Babadagului
Podișul Casimcei
Podișul Dorobanțului
Podișul Negru Vodă
Culmea Pricopanului
Insula Mare a Brăilei
Balta Ialomiței
Insula Sacalinul Mare
Grindul Chituc
Gura Portiței
Brațul Chilia
Brațul Sulina
Brațul Sfântu Gheorghe
DOBRUJA
E87
E584
E60
E81
E675
M15
M3
A2
A4
45°30′
45°00′
44°30′
44°00′
46°00′
28°00′
28°30′
29°00′
29°30′

1
2
3
4
5
148
67
B
C
D
E
F
SLO
HR
14°30′
15°00′
15°30′
16°00′
16°30′
45°30′
45°00′
44°30′
44°00′
43°30′
20′
10′
MARE ADRIATICO
Venezia Trieste
Ancona
Rijeka
Opatija
Bakar
Kraljevica
Karlovac
Duga Resa
Ogulin
Delnice
Kočevje
Kočevje Reka
Črnomelj
Metlika
Bela Krajina
Gorski Kotar
Velika Kapela
Mala Kapela
Lička Jesenica
Plitvička Jezera
Korenica
Otočac
Gospić
Senj
Novi Vinodolski
Crikvenica
Krk
Cres
Lošinj
Mali Lošinj
Rab
Pag
Karlobag
Velebit
Lika
Ličko Polje
Zadar
Biograd na Moru
Benkovac
Bukovica
Ravni Kotari
Obrovac
Gračac
Knin
Drniš
Šibenik
Vodice
Primošten
Trogir
Split
Kaštel
Šolta
Brač
Hvar
Vis
Jabuka
Sveta Andrija
Ugljan
Pašman
Dugi Otok
Kornat
Murter
Silba
Olib
Molat
Ist
Sestrunj
Bihać
Cazin
Velika Kladuša
Bosanska Krupa
Bosanski Novi
Bosanski Petrovac
Bosansko Grahovo
Drvar
Glina
Petrinja
Sisak
Slunj
Topusko
Kordun
Banija
Zrinska Gora
Petrova Gora
Plješevica
Dinara
Promina
Svilaja
E65
E71
E61
E751
E761
A1
A6
A7
Kupa
Korana
Una
Krka
Zrmanja
Cetina
Kanal Velebitski
Zadarski Kanal
Splitski Kanal
Viški Kanal

6
7
8
9
10
149
B
C
158
D
E
163
F
162
BIH
MNE
SLAVONIJA
BOSANSKA POSAVINA
GORNJE
17°00′
17°30′
18°00′
18°30′
45°30′
45°00′
44°30′
44°00′
43°30′
Osijek
Vinkovci
Vukovar
Đakovo
Našice
Požega
Kutina
Novska
Nova Gradiška
Bosanska Gradiška
Slavonski Brod
Bosanski Brod
Županja
Brčko
Derventa
Prijedor
Banja Luka
Doboj
Gradačac
Tuzla
Lukavac
Zvornik
Gračanica
Prnjavor
Teslić
Jajce
Travnik
Zenica
Bugojno
Kupres
Livno
Visoko
SARAJEVO
Konjic
Mostar
Foča
Goražde
Čapljina
Metković
Makarska
Imotski
Tomislavgrad
Posušje
Gacko
Nevesinje
Kakanj
Zavidovići
Vareš
Olovo
Kladanj
Vlasenica
Sokolac
Pale
Trnovo
Jablanica
Ljubuški
Ploče
Omiš
Sava
Drina
Neretva
Bosna
Vrbas
Una
Kozara
Motajica
Psunj
Papuk
Krndija
Ozren
Majevica
Konjuh
Zvijezda
Vranica
Vlašić
Bjelašnica
Jahorina
Treskavica
Prenj
Čvrsnica
Čabulja
Zelengora
Durmitor
Romanija
Glasinac
Cincar
Vitorog
Kamešnica
Biokovo
Velebit
Trebević
Igman
E70
E73
E661
E761
E762
E65
E71
A1
A3
A5
A10
A2

1
2
3
4
5
6
A
B
C
D
E
F
150
149
157
163
H
HR
SRB
BIH
Szeged
Pécs
Baja
Mohács
Subotica
Sombor
Osijek
Vukovar
Vinkovci
Đakovo
Apatin
Kula
Vrbas
Bačka Topola
Senta
Kikinda
Novi Bečej
Bečej
Zrenjanin
Novi Sad
Petrovaradin
Sremski Karlovci
Ruma
Sremska Mitrovica
Šid
Ilok
Bačka Palanka
Županja
Brčko
Bijeljina
Zvornik
Loznica
Šabac
Valjevo
Tuzla
Lukavac
Gradačac
Gračanica
Obrenovac
Novo Beograd
Zemun
BEOGRAD
Pančevo
Lazarevac
Aranđelovac
Mladenovac
Gornji Milanovac
Čačak
Kraljevo
Užice
Požega
Arilje
Bajina Bašta
Višegrad
Rogatica
Goražde
Pale
SARAJEVO
Olovo
Vlasenica
Srebrenica
Ljubovija
Kladanj
Vareš
Živinice
Modriča
Slavonski Šamac
Bosanski Šamac
Beli Manastir
Siklós
Batina
Bezdan
Odžaci
Temerin
Titel
Inđija
Stara Pazova
Nova Pazova
Batajnica
Surčin
Ub
Kosjerić
Ivanjica
Zlatibor
Čajetina
Kamenica
Lučani
SEMBERIJA
MAČVA
POCERINA
JADAR
RAĐEVINA
TAMNAVA
TAKOVO
ŠUMADIJA
DRAGAČEVO
BANAT
SREM
POSAVINA
Fruška Gora
Dunav
Sava
Drina
Tisa
E70
E75
E73
E662
E761
E763
A1
A2
A3
M43
M6
44°00′
44°30′
45°00′
45°30′
46°00′
18°30′
19°00′
19°30′
20°00′
20°30′

Arad
Timișoara
Lipova
Lugoj
Reșița
Caransebeș
Oravița
Anina
Deva
Hunedoara
Simeria
Orăștie
Hațeg
Brad
Petroșani
Lupeni
Vulcan
Uricani
Orșova
Drobeta-Turnu Severin
Vidin
Calafat
Vršac
Kovin
Smederevo
Požarevac
Kragujevac
Jagodina
Ćuprija
Paraćin
Zaječar
Negotin
Bor
Majdanpek
Kladovo
Kula
Belgradchik
Câmpia Vingăi
Câmpia Timișului
Câmpia Gătaiei
Dealurile Lipovei
Dealurile Buziașului
Munții Poiana Ruscă
Munții Metaliferi
Munții Retezatului
Munții Godeanu
Munții Țarcului
Munții Cernei
Munții Mehedinți
Munții Almăjului
Munții Locvei
Munții Semenicului
Câmpia Blahniței
Platforma Jiului
Platforma Strehaiei
Iblatska Peščara
Braničevo
Pomoravlje
Homolje
Homoljske Planine
Kučajske Planine
Deli Jovan
Krajina
Resava
Ključ
Miroč
Lepenica
Dunav
Mureș
Timiș
Cerna
Jiu
RO
BG
E70
E68
E79
E673
E671
E75
E761
E771
A1
A6
151
160
164

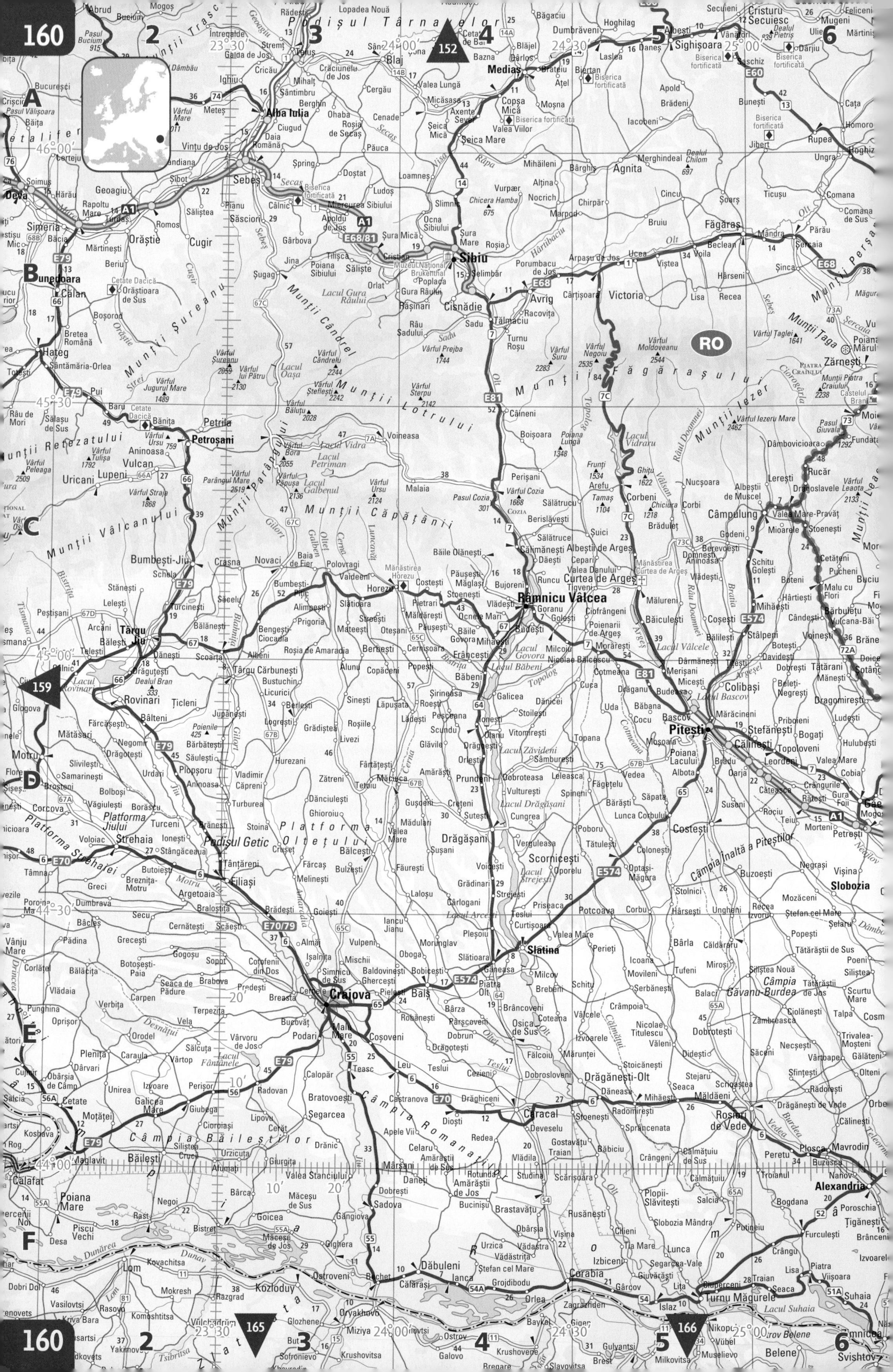

2
3
4
5
6
A
B
C
D
E
F
152
159
165
166
RO
Podișul Târnavelor
Alba Iulia
Mediaș
Sighișoara
Deva
Sebeș
Sibiu
Hunedoara
Hațeg
Făgăraș
Agnita
Victoria
Avrig
Cisnădie
Blaj
Petroșani
Vulcan
Lupeni
Uricani
Târgu Jiu
Motru
Rovinari
Râmnicu Vâlcea
Curtea de Argeș
Pitești
Câmpulung
Slatina
Craiova
Caracal
Filiași
Băilești
Calafat
Corabia
Turnu Măgurele
Alexandria
Roșiori de Vede
Drăgășani
Balș
Strehaia
Drăgănești-Olt
Costești
Slobozia
Munții Șureanu
Munții Cândrel
Munții Lotrului
Munții Căpățânii
Munții Parângului
Munții Vâlcanului
Munții Retezatului
Munții Făgărașului
Munții Iezer
Munții Țaga
Podișul Getic
Platforma Olteţului
Platforma Jiului
Câmpia Băileștilor
Câmpia Romanaţilor
Câmpia Înaltă a Piteștilor
Dunărea
Lom
Kozloduy
Oryakhovo
Nikopol
Svishtov
Belene
Vârful Negoiu 2535
Vârful Moldoveanu 2544
Parângul Mare 2519
Lacul Vidraru
Biserica fortificată
Cetate Dacică

Brașov
Sfântu Gheorghe
Târgu Secuiesc
Covasna
Onești
Adjud
Bârlad
Focșani
Mărășești
Panciu
Tecuci
Brăila
Râmnicu Sărat
Buzău
Nehoiu
Sinaia
Bușteni
Predeal
Câmpina
Vălenii de Munte
Ploiești
Mizil
Urziceni
Slobozia
Țăndărei
Fetești
Călărași
Silistra
Oltenița
Giurgiu
Ruse
Tutrakan
Dulovo
Isperikh
Kubrat
BUCUREȘTI
Voluntari
Otopeni
Buftea
Chitila
Popești-Leordeni
Jilava
Budești
Lehliu Gară
Moreni
Băicoi
Boldești-Scăeni
Comarnic
Breaza
Săcele
Munții Vrancei
Munții Siriului
Munții Ciucaș
Munții Baiului
Munții Bârsei
Câmpia Covurluiului
Câmpia Siretului
Câmpia Brăilei
Câmpia Bărăganului
Câmpia Buzăului
Câmpia Gheorghiței
Câmpia Ploieștilor
Câmpia Mostiștei
Câmpia Burnazului
Ludogorie
Dunărea
BG
153
155
167
7
8
9
10
11
A
B
C
D
E
F
26°00'
26°30'
27°00'
27°30'
46°00'
45°30'
45°00'
44°30'
44°00'
25°30'

1
2
3
4
5
A
B
C
D
E
F
157
63
HR
BIH
I
16°30′
17°00′
17°30′
18°00′
44°00′
43°30′
43°00′
42°30′
42°00′
20′
10′
Knin
Drniš
Sinj
Split
Trogir
Kaštel Stari
Kaštel Sućurac
Solin
Klis
Omiš
Dugi Rat
Podstrana
Stobreč
Šolta
Maslinica
Čiovo
Splitski Kanal
Brač
Supetar
Sutivan
Milna
Nerežišće
Pučišće
Povlja
Bol
Gornji Humac
Vidova Gora
Hvarski Kanal
Hvar
Stari Grad
Starogradsko Polje
Jelsa
Zavala
Zastražišće
Gdinj
Sućuraj
Šćedro
Pakleni Otoci
Rt Pelegrin
Viški Kanal
Vis
Rt Stončica
Korčulanski Kanal
Korčula
Vela Luka
Blato
Smokvica
Brna
Pupnat
Račišće
Lumbarda
Rt Velo Dance
Lastovski Kanal
Lastovo
Ubli
Prežba
Sušac
Palagruža
Ancona
Šibenik, Zadar
Makarska
Baška Voda
Tučepi
Podgora
Živogošće
Drvenik
Gradac
Ploče
Metković
Opuzen
Neum
Pelješac
Orebić
Trpanj
Ston
Ston
Mljet
Mljetski Kanal
Polače
Babino Polje
Sobra
Rt Goli
Neretvanski Kanal
Rt Lovišće
Lovište
Kučište
Rt Ražnjić
Trstenik
Žuljana
Janjina
Dubrovnik
Koločep
Lopud
Šipan
Jakljan
Slano
Cavtat
Čilipi
Molunat
Gruda
Herceg Novi
Oštri Rt
Boka Kotorska
Trebinje
Ljubinje
Stolac
Čapljina
Ljubuški
Međugorje
Čitluk
Mostar
Buna
Blagaj
Nevesinje
Konjic
Jablanica
Prozor
Posušje
Grude
Široki Brijeg
Imotski
Vrgorac
Tomislavgrad
Livno
Duvanjsko Polje
Buško Jezero
Kupres
Bugojno
Donji Vakuf
Jajce
Travnik
Novi Travnik
Zenica
Vitez
Busovača
Kakanj
Visoko
Kiseljak
Fojnica
Kreševo
Hadžići
Ilidža
Vogošća
SARAJEVO
Hrasnica
Trnovo
Kalinovik
Gacko
Bileća
Glamoč
Glamočko Polje
Kupreško Polje
Livanjsko Polje
Dinara
Vran
Čvrsnica
Prenj
Velež
Čabulja
Vranica
Bjelašnica
Treskavica
Visočica
Crvanj
Vučev
Zelengora
Biokovo
Mosor
Kozjak
Svilaja
Vlašić
Kruščica
Zvijezda
Raduša
Ljubuša
Bitovnja
Stolovac
Vrata
Vitorog
Cincar
Šator
Velika Golija
Hrbina
Cetina
Neretva
Rama
Vrbas
Bosna
Bijela
Blidinje Jezero
Ramsko Jezero
Jablaničko Jezero
Hutovo Blato
Deransko Jezero
Popovo
Dabarsko Polje
Vidoša
Snježnica
Zaba
Sveti Jure
1762
2228
2074
2088
1913
Vieste
Testa del Gargano
Bari
Igoumenitsa
E65
E71
E73
E761
E762
E661/761
E73/761
A1
A10

SRB
MNE
RKS
AL
NMK
PODGORICA
Shkodër
Kraljevo
Kragujevac
Čačak
Užice
Požega
Gornji Milanovac
Aranđelovac
Ivanjica
Novi Pazar
Raška
Sjenica
Nova Varoš
Prijepolje
Priboj
Višegrad
Goražde
Foča
Pljevlja
Žabljak
Bijelo Polje
Berane
Rožaje
Tutin
Mitrovicë
Pejë
Deçan
Gjakovë
Prizren
Rahovec
Suharekë
Nikšić
Cetinje
Kotor
Tivat
Budva
Bar
Ulcinj
Danilovgrad
Kolašin
Mojkovac
Plav
Gusinje
Kukës
Lezhë
Peshkopi
Tetovo
Gostivar
Bajina Bašta
Srebrenica
Vlasenica
Han-Pijesak
Rogatica
Sokolac
Kosjerić
Ljig
Topola
Vrnjačka Banja
Trstenik
Zubin Potok
Vushtrri
Klinë
Istog
Skenderaj
Drenica
Metohija
Prokletije
Pešter
Zlatibor
Zlatar
Javor
Golija
Kopaonik
Durmitor
Sinjajevina Planina
Prekornica
Komovi
Rumija
Lovćen
Skadarsko Jezero
Mokra Planina
Mokra Gora
Šar Planina
Dragačevo
Takovo
Šumadija
Podrinje
Tara
Drina
Lim
Ibar
E65/80
E761
E762
E763
E851
E761/763
158
164
168
A
B
C
D
E
F
6
7
8
9
10
19°00′
19°30′
20°00′
20°30′
44°00′
43°30′
43°00′
42°30′
42°00′

SRB
RKS
MNE
NMK
AL
159
163
168
169
Aranđelovac
Topola
Velika Plana
Svilajnac
Kragujevac
Jagodina
Ćuprija
Paraćin
Despotovac
Bor
Negotin
Zaječar
Knjaževac
Čačak
Kraljevo
Kruševac
Trstenik
Aleksinac
Niš
Prokuplje
Kuršumlija
Leskovac
Vlasotince
Pirot
Bela Palanka
Novi Pazar
Mitrovicë
Vushtrri
PRISHTINË
Fushë Kosovë
Pejë
Deçan
Gjakovë
Prizren
Suharekë
Ferizaj
Gjilan
Vranje
Bujanovac
Preševo
Kumanovo
Skopje
Tetovo
Gostivar
Sveti Nikole
Kočani
Štip
Kriva Palanka
Surdulica
Bosilegrad
Kukës
ŠUMADIJA
JASENICA
LEPENICA
RESAVA
GRUŽA
ŽUPA
TOPLICA
KOSOVO
METOHIJA
DRENICA
POLOG
TORBEŠIJA
ZAGLAVAK
KRAJIŠTE
SLAVIŠTE
Veliki Jastrebac
Homoljske Planine
Kučajske Planine
Suva Planina
Šar Planina
Osogovske Planine
Ovče Pole
Kukavica
Rtanj
Devica
Kopaonik

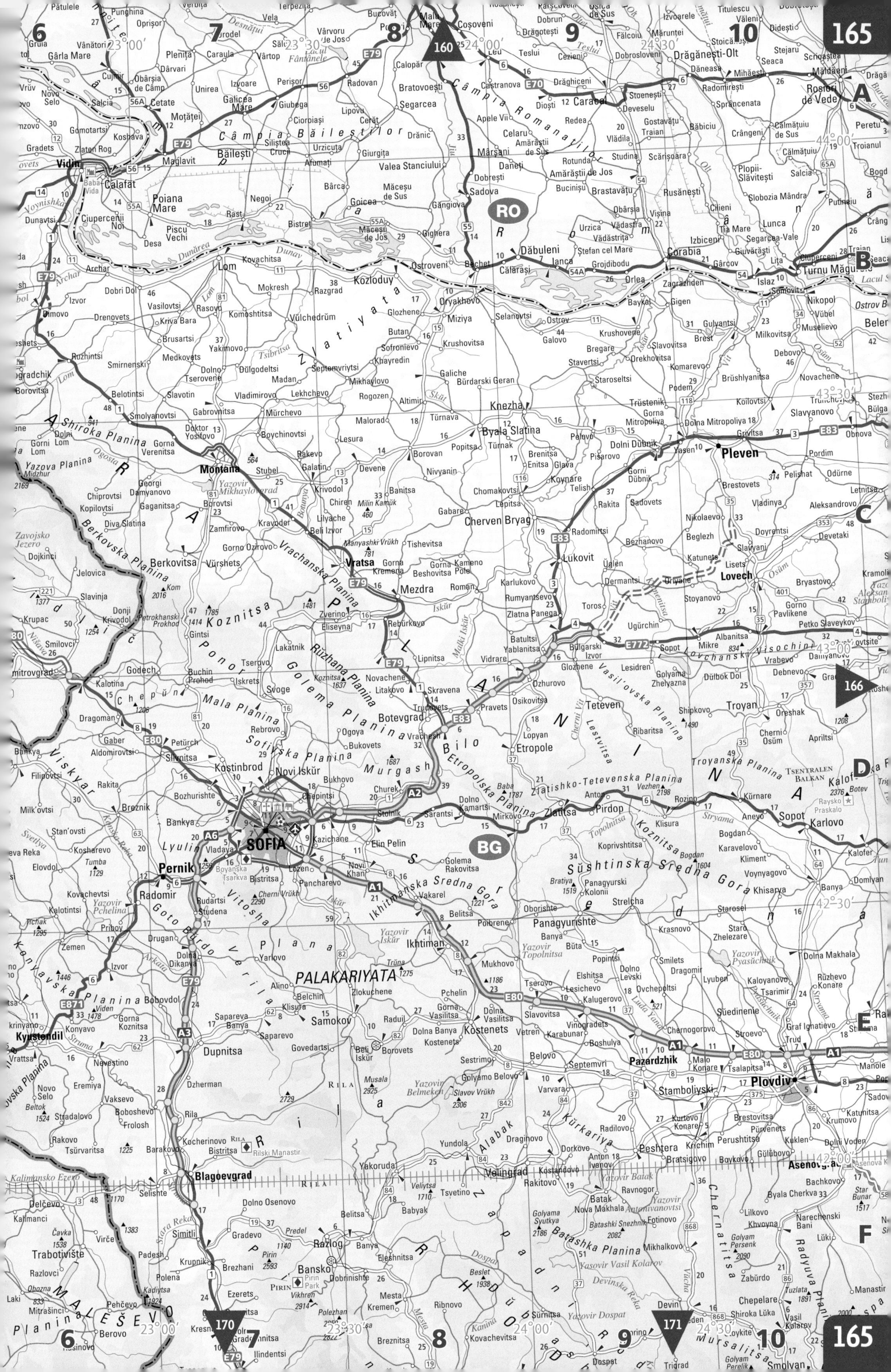

RO
BG
Vidin
Calafat
Băileşti
Câmpia Băileştilor
Câmpia Romanaţilor
Caracal
Drăgăneşti-Olt
Roşiori de Vede
Corabia
Turnu Măgurele
Dunărea
Dunav
Lom
Kozloduy
Oryakhovo
Nikopol
Zlatiya
Montana
Vratsa
Mezdra
Byala Slatina
Knezha
Cherven Bryag
Pleven
Lukovit
Lovech
Troyan
Teteven
Botevgrad
Etropole
Berkovitsa
Pirdop
Zlatitsa
Karlovo
Sopot
SOFIA
Pernik
Radomir
Kyustendil
Dupnitsa
Samokov
Ikhtiman
Kostenets
Pazardzhik
Plovdiv
Stamboliyski
Peshtera
Velingrad
Blagoevgrad
Razlog
Bansko
Dospat
Smolyan
Asenovgrad
PALAKARIYATA
Vitosha
Murgash
Sredna Gora
E79
E70
E80
E83
E772
E871
A1
A2
A3
A6
160
166
170
171

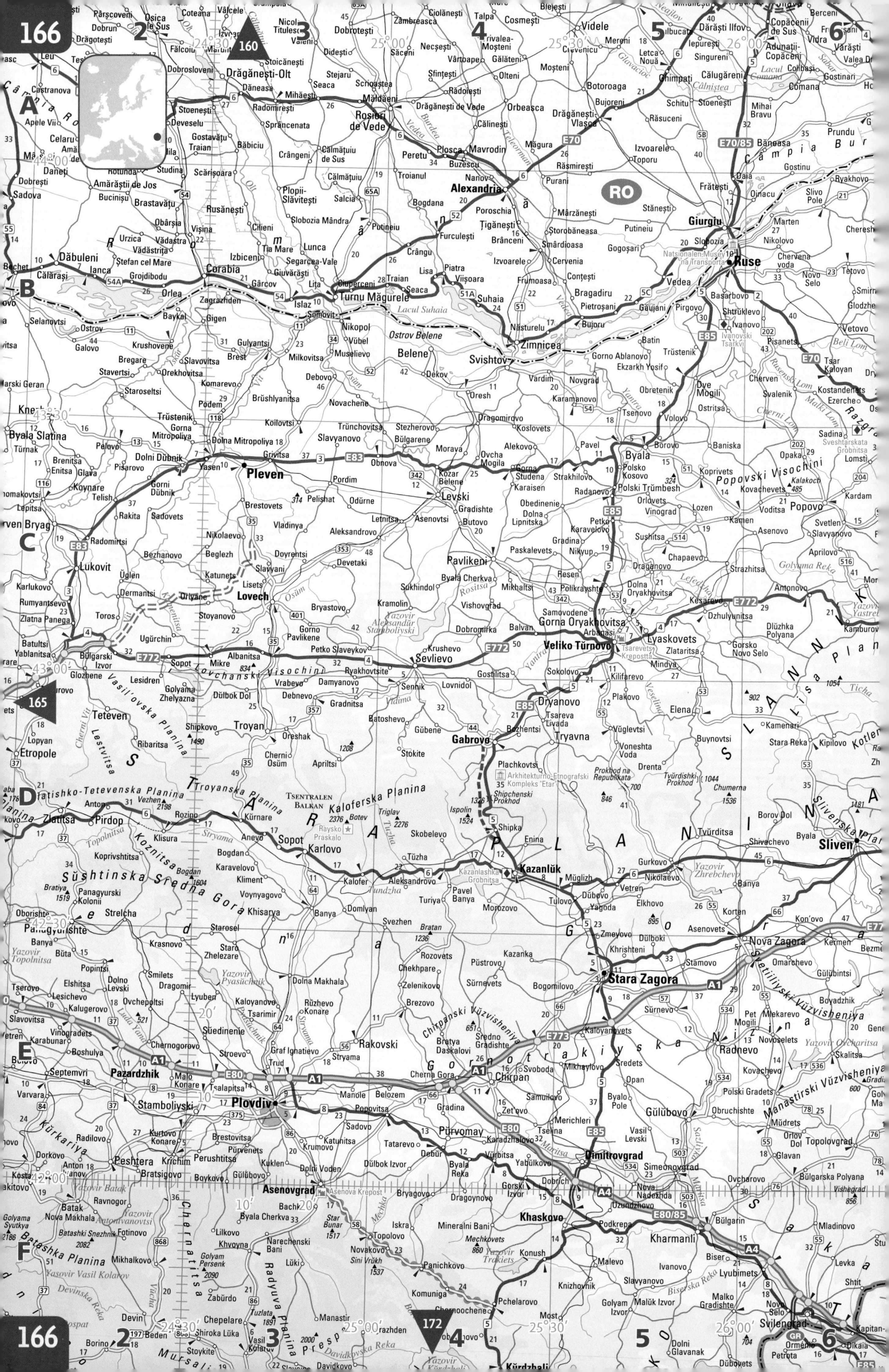
RO
Drăgănești-Olt
Roșiori de Vede
Alexandria
Giurgiu
Ruse
Corabia
Turnu Măgurele
Zimnicea
Svishtov
Nikopol
Belene
Pleven
Byala
Levski
Lukovit
Lovech
Sevlievo
Veliko Tŭrnovo
Gorna Oryakhovitsa
Lyaskovets
Pavlikeni
Popovo
Gabrovo
Dryanovo
Tryavna
Troyan
Teteven
Etropole
Elena
Kazanlŭk
Karlovo
Sopot
Pirdop
Zlatitsa
Sliven
Nova Zagora
Stara Zagora
Chirpan
Pazardzhik
Plovdiv
Asenovgrad
Dimitrovgrad
Khaskovo
Kharmanli
Svilengrad
Peshtera
Batak
Rakovski
Radnevo
Gŭlŭbovo
Pŭrvomay
Devin
Stamboliyski
Kaloferska Planina
Troyanska Planina
Sŭshtinska Sredna Gora
Lovchanski Visochini
Popovski Visochini
Arkhitekturno-Etnografski Kompleks "Etar"
Kazanlashka Grobnitsa
Natsionalen Muzey na Transporta
E70
E83
E85
E772
E773
E80
A1
A4
160
165
172

Constanța
Medgidia
Călărași
Silistra
Oltenița
Tutrakan
Mangalia
Negru Vodă
Dobrich
Balchik
Kavarna
Shabla
Nos Shabla
Nos Kaliakra
Razgrad
Shumen
Novi Pazar
Provadiya
Devnya
Varna
Varnenski Zaliv
Nos Galata
Veliki Preslav
Obzor
Nos Emine
Nesebŭr
Pomorie
Karnobat
Aytos
Burgas
Burgaski Zaliv
Sozopol
Sredets
Primorsko
Tsarevo
Akhtopol
Rezovo
Malko Tŭrnovo
Elkhovo
Kırklareli
İğneada
İğneada Burnu
Demirköy
Limanköy
DOBRUJA
DOBRUDZHANSKO PLATO
LUDOGORIE
Ludogorsko Plato
Provadiysko Plato
Kamchiyska Planina
Eminska Planina
Aytoska Planina
Karnobatska Planina
Bakadzhitsite
Medni Rid
STRANDZHA
Yıldız Dağları
Dervetski Vŭzvisheniya
ČERNO MORE
BG
TR
44°00′
43°30′
43°00′
42°30′
42°00′
27°00′
27°30′
28°00′
28°30′
A
B
C
D
E
F
7
8
9
10
11
161
173
xvii

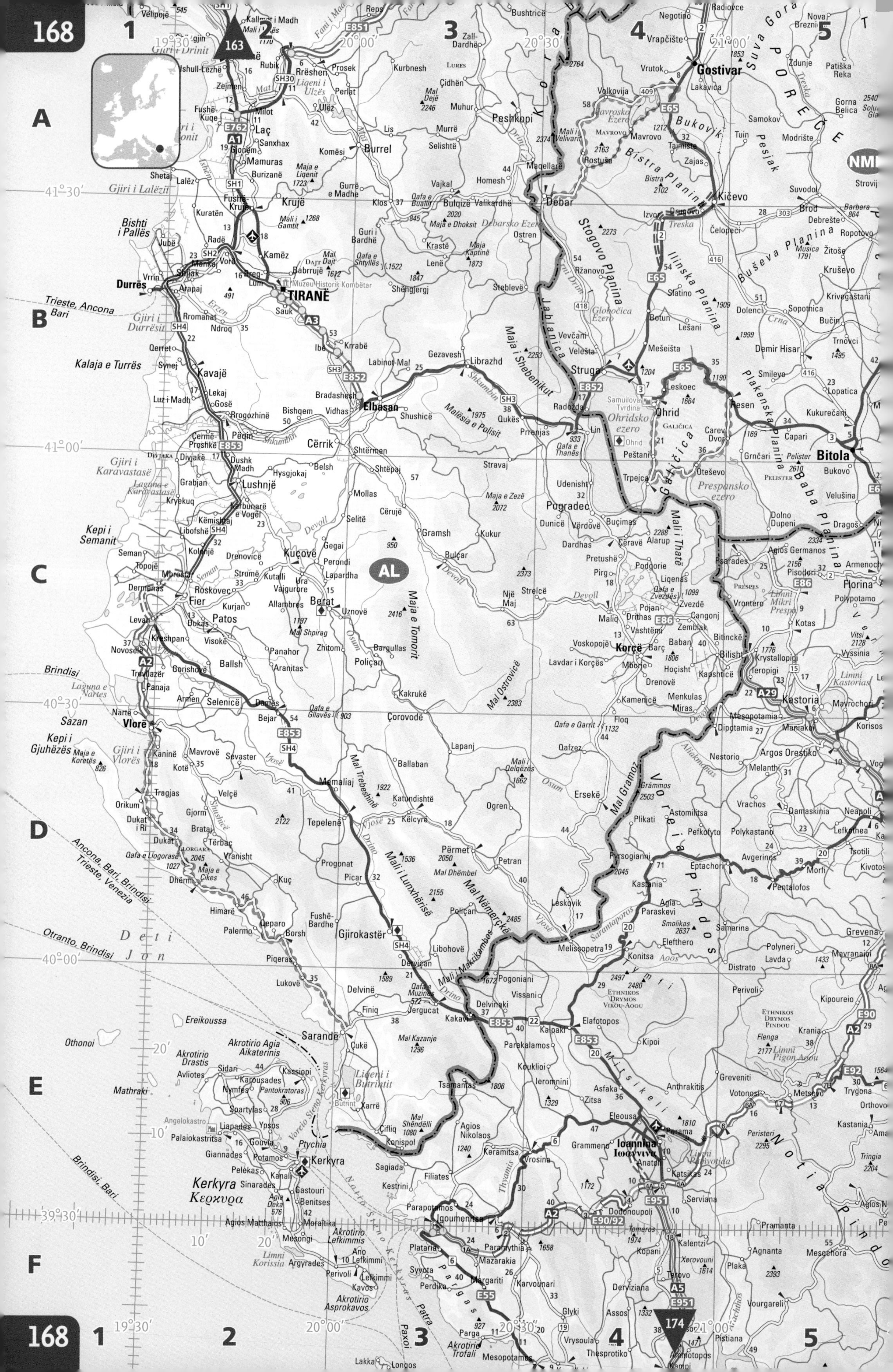
1
2
3
4
5
A
B
C
D
E
F
163
174
AL
NMK
19°30′
20°00′
20°30′
21°00′
41°30′
41°00′
40°30′
40°00′
39°30′
Velipojë
Kallmet i Madh
Gjiri i Drinit
Shëngjin
Lezhë
Rubik
Rrëshen
Prosek
Kurbnesh
Lures
Reps
Bushtricë
Negotino
Radiovce
Vrapčište
Gostivar
Suva Gora
Nova Breznica
Patiška Reka
Zdunje
Lakavica
Vrutok
Volkovija
Mavrovsko Ezero
Mavrovo
Bukovik
Tuin
Samokov
Modriište
Gorna Belica
Poreče
Pesjak
Peshkopi
Muhur
Çidhën
Mal Dejë
2246
Zall-Dardhë
Ulëz
Perlat
Lis
Burrel
Murrë
Selishtë
Komësi
Milot
Laç
Fushë-Kuqe
Zejmen
Mamuras
Sanxhax
Burizanë
Maja e Liqenit
1723
Gurrë e Madhe
Klos
Vajkal
Homesh
Maqellarë
Debar
Drugovo
Kičevo
Suvodol
Strovij
Brod
Debrešte
Barbara
864
Ropotovo
Sheta
Lalëz
Gjiri i Lalëzit
Fushë-Krujë
Krujë
Kuratën
Mali i Gamtit
1268
Qafa e Bualit
Bulqizë
Valikardhë
Maja e Dhoksit
2020
Debarsko Ezero
Ostren
Stogovo Planina
Bistra Planina
Bistra
2102
Izvor
Treska
Čelopeci
Buševa Planina
Musica
1791
Žitoše
Kruševo
Bishti i Pallës
Jubë
Radë
Kamëz
Dajt
Mal Dajt
1612
Qafa e Shtyllës
1522
Krastë
Lenë
Maja Kaptinë
1873
1847
Guri i Bardhë
2273
Ilinska Planina
Rzanovo
1909
Durrës
Vrrin
Shijak
Marikaj
Vora
Breg-Lum
Muzeu Historik Kombëtar
TIRANË
Sauk
Shëngjergj
Steblevë
Arapaj
491
Trieste, Ancona
Bari
Gjiri i Durrësit
Rromanat
Ndroq
Erzen
Jablanica
Crni Drim
Glonočica Ezero
Slatino
Botun
Lešani
Dolenci
Crna
Sopotnica
Krivogaštani
Bučin
Trnovci
1495
Demir Hisar
1999
Qerret
Kalaja e Turrës
Synej
Kavajë
Luz i Madh
Lekaj
Gosë
Ibë
Krrabë
Gezavesh
Librazhd
Labinot-Mal
Maja i Shebenikut
2253
Vevčani
Velešta
Struga
Mešeišta
1204
Smilevo
Lopatica
Bradashesh
Elbasan
Vidhas
Bishqem
Shkumbin
Shushicë
Qukës
Prrenjas
Radožda
Samuilova Tvrdina
Ohrid
Ohridsko ezero
Leskoec
1664
1190
Resen
Plakenska Planina
Kukurečani
Galičica
Carev Dvor
Capari
Bitola
1975
Malësia e Polisit
Qafa e Thanës
933
Lin
Rrogozhinë
Pëqin
Cërrik
Shtërmen
Çermë-Proshkë
Divjakë
Gjiri i Karavastasë
Laguna e Karavastasë
Dushk Madh
Belsh
Shtëpaj
Stravaj
Udenisht
Pogradec
Pestani
Trpejca
Otesevo
Prespansko ezero
Grnčari
Pelister
2610
Bukovo
Velušina
Grabjan
Lushnjë
Hysgjokaj
Mollas
Maja e Zezë
2072
Dunicë
Vërdovë
Buçimas
Mali i Thatë
Dolno Dupeni
Baba Planina
Dragoš
Kryekuq
Karbunarë e Vogël
Këmishtaj
Libofshë
Kepi i Semanit
Cërujë
Selitë
Devoll
Gramsh
Kukur
Dardhas
Çeravë
Alarup
2288
Psarades
Agios Germanos
2334
Seman
Topojë
Kolonjë
Drenovicë
Kuçovë
Gegai
Perondi
Lapardha
950
Bulçar
Pretushë
Pirg
Podgorie
Liqenas
1099
Pisoderi
Armenochori
Florina
Mbrostar
Dermenas
Roskovec
Strumë
Kutalli
Ura Vajgurore
2373
Strelcë
Një Maj
Qafa e Zvezdës
Zvezdë
Prespes
Limni Mikri Prespa
Polypotamo
Fier
Kurjan
Allambres
Berat
Uznovë
Maja e Tomorit
2416
Maliq
Pojan
Drithas
Cangonj
Vrontero
Kotas
Levan
Dukas
Patos
1197
Mal Shpirag
Zemblak
Vashtëm
E86
Voskopojë
Korçë
Baban
Bitinckë
Vitsi
2128
Vyssinia
Novosela
Kreshpan
Visokë
Panahor
Zhitom
Poliçan
Bargullas
Mal Ostrovicë
Lavdar i Korçës
Barç
Mborje
Hoçisht
1806
Bilisht
Kapshticë
Krystallopigi
Ieropigi
Brindisi
Trevllazër
Gorishovë
Ballsh
Aranitas
Drenovë
Limni Kastorias
Panaja
Laguna e Nartes
Armen
Selenicë
Damës
Kakrukë
2383
Kamenicë
Menkulas
Miras
Kastoria
Mavrochori
Narta
Sazan
Vlorë
Bejar
Qafa e Gllavës
903
Çorovodë
Qafa e Qarrit
1132
Floq
Mesopotamia
Dipotamia
Maniakoi
Korisos
Kepi i Gjuhëzës
Maja e Koretës
826
Gjiri i Vlorës
Kaninë
Mavrovë
Sevaster
Vjosë
Kotë
Lapanj
Qafzez
Mali i Qelqëzës
1662
Osum
Aliakmonas
Nestorio
Argos Orestiko
Melanthi
Orikum
Tragjas
Velçë
Memaliaj
Mal Trebeshinë
1922
Ballaban
Ersekë
Mal Gramoz
Grammos
2503
Vo reia Pindos
Vrachos
Damaskinia
Neapoli
Dukat i Ri
Gjorm
Brataj
2122
Tepelenë
Katundishtë
Këlcyrë
Ogren
Plikati
Astomiitsa
Pefkofyto
Polykastano
Lefkothea
Ancona, Bari, Brindisi
Trieste, Venezia
Dukat
Llogara
Qafa e Llogorasë
1027
2045
Tërbac
Vranisht
Maja e Çikës
Prognat
Mali i Lunxhërisë
1536
Përmet
2050
Mal Dhëmbel
Petran
Pyrsogianni
2045
Eptachori
Avgerinos
Tsotili
Morfi
Kivotos
Pentalofos
Dhërmi
Kuç
Picar
2155
Mal Nëmerçkë
Leskovik
Kastania
Agia Paraskevi
Smolikas
2637
Samarina
Grevena
Otranto, Brindisi
Himarë
Qeparo
Palermo
Borsh
Fushë-Bardhe
Gjirokastër
Poliçan
2485
Sarantaporos
Melissopetra
Elefthero
Polyneri
Deti Jon
Piqeras
Libohovë
Dervican
Mali i Makrikambos
1672
Pogoniani
Konitsa
Aoos
Tymfi
Distrato
Lavda
1433
Mavranaioi
Lukovë
Delvinë
1589
Qafa e Muzinës
572
Vissani
2497
2480
Ethnikos Drymos Vikou-Aoou
Perivoli
Kipoureio
Ereikoussa
Finiq
Jergucat
Delvinaki
Kakavi
E853
Kalpaki
Elafotopos
Ethnikos Drymos Pindou
E90
Krania
Othonoi
Akrotirio Agia Aikaterinis
Sarandë
Çukë
Mal Kazanje
1296
Parakalamos
Kipoi
Flenga
2177
Limni Pigon Aoou
Akrotirio Drastis
Sidari
Kassiopi
Avliotes
Karousades
Mathraki
Nymfes
Pantokratoras
906
Spartylas
Voreio Steno Kerkyras
Liqeni i Butrintit
Butrint
Xarrë
Tsamantas
1806
Kouklioi
Ieromnini
1329
Asfaka
Zitsa
Mitsikeli
Anthrakitis
Greveniti
Votonosi
Metsovo
Trygona
Orthovouni
Angelokastro
Liapades
Ypsos
Palaiokastritsa
Gouvia
Ptychia
Giannades
Potamos
Kerkyra
Pelekas
Kanali
Sinarades
Kerkyra
Κερκυρα
Agia Deka
576
Gastouri
Benitses
Çifliq
Mal Shëndëlli
1080
Konispol
Agios Nikolaos
1240
Keramitsa
Vrosina
Grammeno
Eleousa
1810
Perama
Ioannina
Ιωαννινα
Anatoli
Limni Pamvotida
Peristeri
2295
Notia Pindos
Kastania
Tringia
2204
Sagiada
Filiates
Thyamis
Katsikas
Serviana
1172
Kestrini
Notio Steno Kerkyras
Parapotamos
Igoumenitsa
Dodonoupoli
E951
E90/92
Agios Nikolaos
Agios Matthaios
Moraitika
Mesongi
Akrotirio Lefkimmis
Ano Lefkimmi
Lefkimmi
Limni Korissia
Argyrades
Perivoli
Kavos
Plataria
Paramythia
1658
Mazarakia
Tomaros
1974
Kopani
Kalentzi
Xerovouni
1614
Pramanta
Agnanta
Plaka
2393
Mesochora
Syvota
Perdika
Margariti
Karvounari
Dervisiani
Terovo
Vourgareli
Akrotirio Asprokavos
Pargas
E55
927
Parga
Glyki
Assos
1332
1471
Pistiana
Paxoi
Akrotirio Trofali
Mesopotamos
Vrysoula
Thesprotiko
Ammotopos
Kampi
Lakka
Longos
Patra

Veles
Sveti Nikole
Štip
Radoviš
Berovo
Pehčevo
Bansko
Sandanski
Melnik
Gotse Delchev
Petrich
Kulata
Negotino
Kavadarci
Strumica
Valandovo
Gevgelija
Bogdanci
Novi Dojran
Prilep
Edessa
Giannitsa
Kilkis
Serres
Nigrita
Lagkadas
Thessaloniki
Θεσσαλονικη
Kalamaria
Evosmos
Ampelokipoi
Naousa
Alexandreia
Veroia
Ptolemaida
Kozani
Siatista
Servia
Katerini
Litochoro
Leptokarya
Platamonas
Elassona
Tyrnavos
Larisa
Λαρισα
Trikala
Kalampaka
Meteora
Karditsa
Sofades
Farsala
Volos
Nea Ionia
Almyros
Nea Moudania
Polygyros
Kassandra
Thermaïkos Kolpos
Kolpos Kassandras
Olympos
Kissavos
Mavrovouni
Pieria
Vermio
Chasia
Kamvounia
Vertiskos
Kerdylio
Orvilos
Slavyanka
Belasica
Ogražden
Maleševo
Plačkovica Planina
Konečka Planina
Selečka Planina
Nidže
Kožuf
Mariovo
Tikveš
Limni Kerkini
Limni Koroneia
Limni Volvi
Limni Vegoritida
Limni Polyfytou
Lake Dojran
Kalymnos, Kos, Myrina, Rodos
Alonnisos
Skiathos
Agios Konstantinos
Pagasitikos
BG
GR
A1
A2
A25
E75
E79
E90
E65
E92
164
165
170
175
6
7
8
9
10
22°00′
22°30′
23°00′
23°30′
41°30′
41°00′
40°30′
40°00′
39°30′
A
B
C
D
E
F

164
165
169
175
NMK
GR
Kočani
Radoviš
Strumica
Negotino
Kavadarci
Demir Kapija
Valandovo
Gevgelija
Bogdanci
Gradsko
Berovo
Pehčevo
Plačkovica Planina
Maleševo
Maleshevska Planina
Belasica
Kožuf
Blagoevgrad
Simitli
Razlog
Bansko
Pirin
Gotse Delchev
Sandanski
Petrich
Kulata
Slavyanka
Orvilos
Kerkini
Limni Kerkini
Sidirokastro
Serres
Drama
Nigrita
Amfipoli
Kilkis
Polykastro
Edessa
Giannitsa
Naousa
Veroia
Alexandreia
Thessaloniki
Θεσσαλονικη
Kalamaria
Evosmos
Ampelokipoi
Lagkadas
Limni Koroneia
Limni Volvi
Kolpos Orfanou
Kolpos Thessalonikis
Thermaïkos Kolpos
Polygyros
Nea Moudania
Kassandra
Kolpos Kassandras
Sithonia
Kolpos Ierissou
Kolpos Agiou Orous
Akrotirio Pyrgos
Akrotirio Kassandras
Akrotirio Paliouri
Akra Drepano
Akrotirio Rigas
Akrotirio Arapis
Amouliani
Ouranoupoli
Katerini
Litochoro
Olympos
Kato Olympos
Elassona
Tyrnavos
Larisa
Λαρισα
Agia
Kissavos
Mavrovouni
Farsala
Sofades
Velestino
Nea Ionia
Volos
Pilio
Zagora
Voreies Sporades
Βορειοι Σποραδες
Skiathos
Alonnisos
E75
E79
E90
E65
E86
E92
A1
A2
A3
A25
40°00′
40°30′
41°00′
41°30′
39°30′
22°30′
23°00′
23°30′
24°00′
A
B
C
D
E
F
1
2
3
4
5

7
8
9
10
166
172
176
177
A
B
C
D
E
F
BG
GR
TR
24°30′
25°00′
25°30′
26°00′
41°30′
41°00′
40°30′
40°00′
39°30′
Rodopi
Gorna Arda
Zhŭlti Dyal
Iztochni Rodopi
Bolyarsko
Mŭglenik
Prespa
Radyuva planina
Mursalitsa
Thrakiko Pelagos
Saros Körfezi
Gelibolu Yarımadası
Gelibolu Yarımadası Tarihi Milli Parkı
Smolyan
Pamporovo
Chepelare
Devin
Madan
Rudozem
Zlatograd
Kŭrdzhali
Momchilgrad
Ardino
Dzhebel
Krumovgrad
Ivaylovgrad
Svilengrad
Harmanli
Lyubimets
Madzharovo
Edirne
Kastanies
Orestiada
Didymoteicho
Soufli
Feres
Alexandroupoli
Makri
Komotini
Xanthi
Iasmos
Sapes
Kavala
Καβαλα
Chrysoupoli
Keramoti
Thasos
Θασος
Limenaria
Potamia
Samothraki
Kamariotissa
Fengari 1600
Gökçeada
Kaleköy
İmroz
Uğurlu
Limnos
Λημνος
Myrina
Moudros
Agios Efstratios
Bozcaada
Çanakkale
Eceabat
Kilitbahir
Ezine
Ayvacık
Truva (Troy)
Keşan
İpsala
Enez
Paranesti
Drama
Stavroupoli
Kechrokampos
Akrotirio Pyrgos
Akrotirio Salonikios
Akrotirio Kipos
Akrotirio Plaka
Akrotirio Mourtzeflos
Akrotirio Trypiti
Oros Athos 2033
Mount Athos
Akrotirio Pines
Akrotirio Timiou Prodromou
Mytilini
Peiraias
Evvoia
Agios Konstantinos
Kalymnos, Kos, Rodos
Psathoura
Piperi
Kefalo Burnu
Baba Burnu
Seddülbahir
Kumkale
Kepez
Kolpos Kavalas
Diavlos Thasou
Limni Vistonida
Ormos Vistonias
Nestos
Evros
Meriç
Arda
Yazovir Kŭrdzhali
Yazovir Studen Kladenets
Yazovir Ivaylovgrad
E85
E90
E87
A2

2
3
4
5
166
A
B
C
D
E
F
25°00′
25°30′
26°00′
26°30′
41°30′
41°00′
40°30′
40°00′
39°30′
10′
20′
BG
GR
Khvoyna
Narechenski Bani
Golyam Persenk 2090
Devin
Shiroka Lùka
Beden
Manastir
Zagrazhden
Presp a
Slaveino
Davidkovo
Banite
Ardino
Kobilyane
Raykovo
Ustovo
Smilyan
Rudozem
Madan
Boriaeva
Arda
Dipotama
Nedelino
Zlatograd
Dzhebel
Momchilgrad
Kŭrdzhali
Yazovir Kŭrdzhali
Yazovir Studen Kladenets
Novakovo
Konush
Panichkovo
Komuniga
Pchelarovo
Chernoochene
Svobodinovo
Most
Malevo
Slavyanovo
Ivanovo
Malŭk Izvor
Golyam Izvor
Biser
Malko Gradishte
Dolni Glavanak
Dŭbovets
Madzharovo
Yazovir Ivaylovgrad
Popsko
Ivaylovgrad
Lyutitsa Zamŭka
Kamilski Dol
Krumovgrad
Tokachka
Avren
Gugutka
Mandritsa
Podkova
Benkovski
Dobromirtsi
Svilengrad
Kapitan-Andreevo
Novo Selo
Ormeni
Petrota
Dikaia
Pentalofos
Kastanies
Edirne
Plati
Komara
Kyprinos
Filakio
Rizia
Sterna
Nea Vyssa
Kavyli
Valtos
Neochori
Orestiada
Zoni
Ladi
Metaxades
Mani
Karoti
Sofiko
Pythio
Didymoteicho
Petrades
Mavrokklisi
Koufovouno
Protokklisi
Amori
Lavara
Mandra
Soufli
Kornofolia
Dadia
Lykofi
Lagyna
Küplü
Meriç
Subaşı
Büyükaltıağaç
Kurtbey
Hamidiye
Uzunköprü
Hasırcıarnavutköy
Lefkimmi
Tychero
Sultanköy
İbriktepe
Hacıköy
Peplos
Sarıcaali
İpsala
Paşayiğit
Beğendik
Feres
Paşaköy
Koyunyeri
Keşan
Karpuzlu
Kocahıdır
Çeltik Gölü
Orhaniye
Çamlıca
Enez
Yenice
Çavuşköy
Büyük Evren
Suluca
Mecidiye
Sultaniça
Karaincirli
Mikro Dereio
Mega Dereio
Kechros
Organi
Ano Drosini
Nea Santa
Fillyra
Aratos
Arriana
Arisvi
Sapes
Aisymi
Sykorrachi
Tsopan 628
Avantas
Loutros
Makri
Alexandroupoli
Maroneia
Agios Charalampos
Komotini
Kosmio
Venna
Mesti
Xylagani
Krovyli
Proskynites
Imeros
Fanari
Ormos Vistonias
Limni Vistonida
Amvrosia
Palladio
Porpi
Pagouria
Lagos
Mesi
Sostis
Polyantho
Iasmos
Amaxades
Ifaistos
Gratini
Dialampi
Selero
Kimmeria
Xanthi
Chrysa
Genisea
Vafaika
Melissa
Avdira
Evlalo
Avato
Neo Erasmio
Paralia Avdiron
Dasochori
Keramoti
Nea Karya
Agiasma
Chrysochori
Chrysoupoli
Nea Karvali
Kavala Καβαλα
Kolpos Kavalas
Perni
Paradeisos
Skopos
Platamonas
Lekani
Kechrokampos
Stavroupoli
Potamochori
Kentavros
Myki
Glavki
Echinos
Oraio
Pachni
Melivoia
Medousa
Thasopoula
Diavlos Thasou
Thasos
Thasos Θασος
Rachoni
Prinos
Kalyves
Panagia
Potamia
Akrotirio Pyrgos
Kallirachi
Theologos
Limenaria
Skala Marion
Koinyra
Akrotirio Babouras
Akrotirio Salonikios
171
RHODOPE MOUNTAINS
Iztochni Rodopi
Gorna Arda
Zhŭlti Dyal
Bolyarsko
Strumi Rd
Anatoliki Rodopi
Thrakiko Pelagos
Saros Körfezi
Kamariotissa
Samothraki
Therma
Fengari 1600
Rempoutsadika
Akrotirio Kipos
Lakkoma
Samothraki
Gökçeada
Kaleköy
İmroz
Kefalo Burnu
Uğurlu
Güneyli
Yeniköy
Fındıklı
Değirmendüzü
Tayfur
Gelibolu
Bayırköy
Karainebeyli
Büyükkemikli Burnu
Küçükanafarta
Büyükanafarta
Gelibolu Yarımadası
Yalova
Sulucа
Umurbey
Gelibolu Yarimadasi Tarihi Milli Parki
Eceabat
Kilitbahir
Çanakkale
Çanakkale Boğazı
Yapıldak
Hacıgelen
Alçıtepe
Kepez
Seddülbahir
Ilyas Burnu
İntepe
Kirazlı
Kayacı Dağı 877
Kumkale
Tevfikiye
Truva (Troy)
Pınarbaşı
Üvecik
Mahmudiye
Kuşçayır
Kumburun
Geyikli
Akköy
Bayramiç
Ezine
Gökçebayır
Türkmenli
Biga Yarımadası
Ahmetçeeli
Bahçeli
Sapanca
Tavaklı
Kösedere
Kavak Dağı 672
Ayvacık
Tuzla
Sazlı
Küçükkuyu
Tamış
Paşaköy
Gülpınar
Korubaşı
Baba Burnu
Bademli
Behramkale
Edremit Körfezi
Akrotirio Korakas
Alibey Adası
Ayvalık
Küçükköy
Sykaminia
Klelo
Vigla 968
Mantamados
Petra
Stypsi
Skoutaros
Agios
177
176
Bozcaada
İzmir
Mytilini
Peiraias
Evvoia
Agios Konstantinos
Kalamaria
Limnos Λημνος
Sideritis
Akrotirio Plaka
Akrotirio Mourtzeflos
Skopia 430
Plaka
Panagia
Atsiki
Kontopouli
Limni Alyki
Kornos
Kaspakas
Kalliopi
Myrina
Kontias
Moudros
Ormos Moudrou
Akrotirio Tigani
Akrotirio Agia Eirinis
Agios Efstratios
Akrotirio Trypiti
A2
A4
E90
E85
E87
E80/85
E85/90
550
110

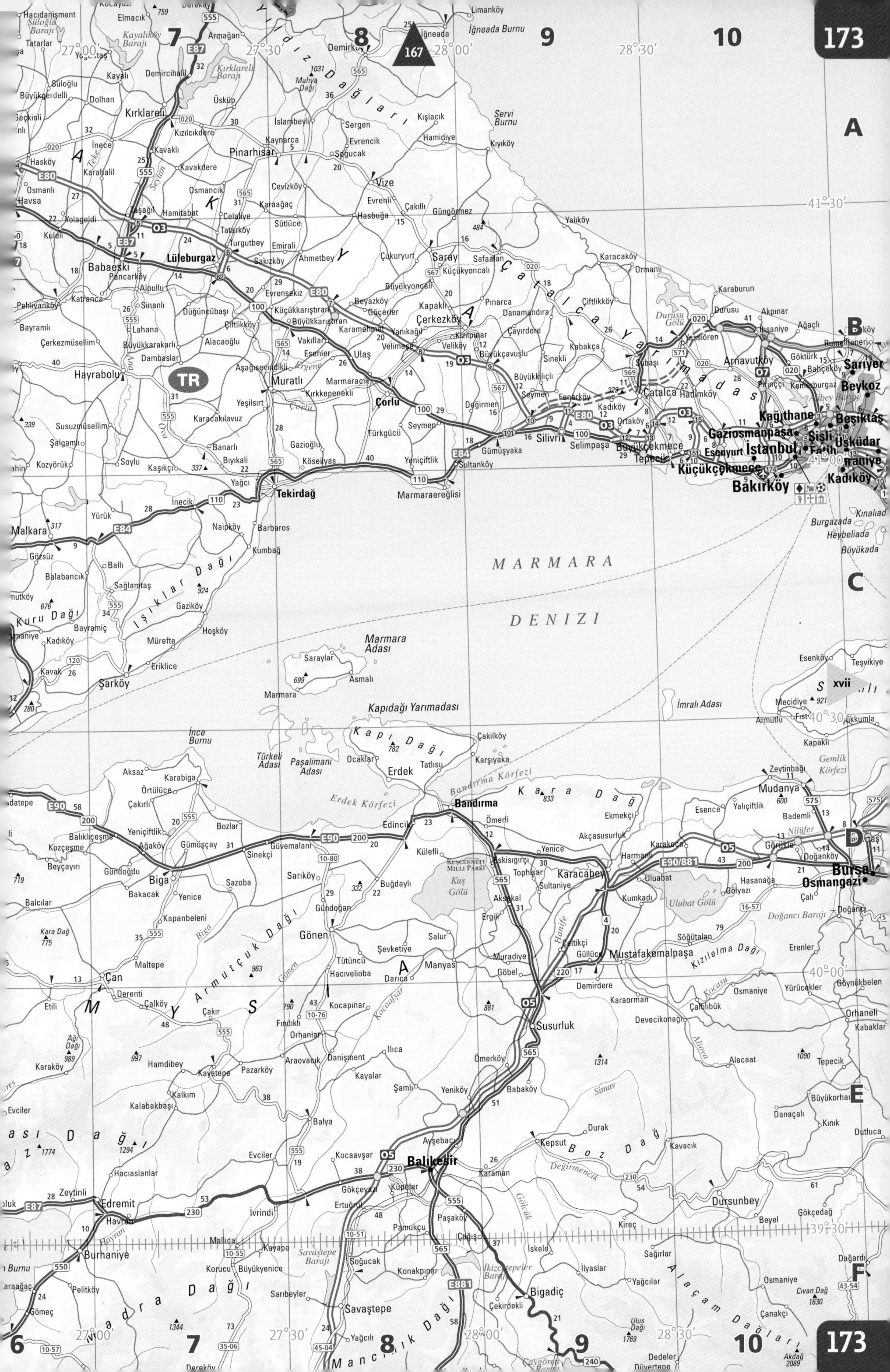

MARMARA
DENIZI
Marmara Adası
Kapıdağı Yarımadası
İmralı Adası
Türkeli Adası
Paşalimanı Adası
İnce Burnu
İğneada Burnu
Servi Burnu
Yıldız Dağları
Çatalca Yarımadası
Işıklar Dağı
Kuru Dağı
Kapı Dağı
Kara Dağ
Armutçuk Dağı
Boz Dağ
Madra Dağı
Alaçam Dağları
Kızılelma Dağı
Mancılık Dağı
Erdek Körfezi
Bandırma Körfezi
Gemlik Körfezi
Kuş Gölü
Kuşcenneti Milli Parkı
Ulubat Gölü
Durusu Gölü
Kayalıköy Barajı
Kırklareli Barajı
Süloğlu Barajı
Doğancı Barajı
Savaştepe Barajı
İkizcetepeler Barajı
Alibey Barajı
Kınalıada
Burgazada
Heybeliada
Büyükada
Kırklareli
Lüleburgaz
Babaeski
Pınarhisar
Vize
Saray
Çerkezköy
Çorlu
Muratlı
Tekirdağ
Marmaraereğlisi
Malkara
Hayrabolu
Şarköy
Silivri
Çatalca
Büyükçekmece
Küçükçekmece
Bakırköy
İstanbul
Gaziosmanpaşa
Kağıthane
Şişli
Beşiktaş
Fatih
Üsküdar
Sarıyer
Beykoz
Ümraniye
Kadıköy
Arnavutköy
Esenyurt
Tepecik
Selimpaşa
Gümüşyaka
Sultanköy
İğneada
Demirköy
Kıyıköy
Erdek
Bandırma
Biga
Çan
Gönen
Manyas
Susurluk
Karacabey
Mustafakemalpaşa
Mudanya
Bursa
Osmangazi
Balıkesir
Edremit
Havran
Burhaniye
Bigadiç
Savaştepe
Dursunbey
Kepsut
Balya
İvrindi
Armutlu
E80
E84
E87
E90
E90/881
E881
O3
O5
O7
27°00′
27°30′
28°00′
28°30′
41°30′
41°00′
40°30′
40°00′
39°30′
TR
167
xvii
A
B
C
D
E
F
6
7
8
9
10

LEFKADA
Λευκας
KEFALLONIA
Κεφαλληνια
ZAKYNTHOS
Ζακυνθος
Ithaki
Paxoi
Antipaxoi
Preveza
Arta
Lefkada
Argostoli
Zakynthos
Mesolongi
Agrinio
Nafpaktos
Patra
Πατρα
Aigio
Pyrgos
Amaliada
Tripoli
Kalamata
Karditsa
Lamia
Karpenisi
Amfissa
Kyparissia
Megalopoli
Amvrakikos Kolpos
Patraïkos Kolpos
Kyparissiakos Kolpos
Pelopònnisos
Πελοπόννησος
GR
168
169
178
Strofades
Voreies Echinades

6
7
8
9
170
A
B
C
D
E
176
179
23°00′
23°30′
24°00′
24°30′
39°00′
38°30′
38°00′
37°30′
37°00′
Voreies Sporades
Βορειοι Σποραδες
Skiathos
Skopelos
Alonnisos
Peristera
Skantzoura
Piperi
Kyra Panagia
Akrotirio Tamvouras
Gioura
Volos
Nea Ionia
Portaria
Zagora
Tsagkarada
Milies
Argalasti
Trikeri
Pagasitikos Kolpos
Almyros
Nea Anchialos
Velestino
Fylaki
Othrys
Lamia
Stylida
Molos
Kamena Vourla
Agios Konstantinos
Atalanti
Kallidromo
Amfikleia
Skyros
Linaria
Skyropoula
Akrotirio Kartsino
Agios Efstratios, Mytilini
Agios Efstratios
Istiaia
Oreoi
Aidipsos
Limni
Rovies
Mantoudi
Prokopi
Kandili
Dirfys
Kymi
Voreios Evvoïkos Kolpos
Notios Evvoïkos Kolpos
Chalkida
Eretria
Amarynthos
Aliveri
Karystos
Styra
Marmari
Ochi
EVVOIA
Ευβοια
Tinos
Petalioi
Kolpos Petalion
Makronisos
Livadeia
Orchomenos
Apoxirameni Limni Kopaïdas
Thiva
Elikonas
Kithaironas
Parnitha
Delfoi
Arachova
Distomo
Antikyra
Kolpos Antikyras
Kolpos Alkyonidon
Megara
Elefsina
Aspropyrgos
Mandra
Acharnes
Kifisia
Marousi
Chalandri
Nea Liosia
Peristeri
ATHINA
ΑΘΗΝΑ
Peiraias
ΠΕΙΡΑΙΑΣ
Kallithea
Glyfada
Voula
Vouliagmeni
Vari
Koropi
Markopoulo
Rafina
Spata
Porto Rafti
Keratea
Lavrio
Akra Sounio
Salamina
Aigina
Agistri
Saronikos Kolpos
Korinthos
Κορινθος
Kiato
Loutraki
Isthmia
Geraneia
Nemea
Argos
Nafplio
Tolo
Epidavros
Methana
Poros
Ydra
Spetses
Kranidi
Portocheli
Ermioni
Argolikos Kolpos
Astros
Leonidio
Parnonas
Arachnaio
Kea
Tzia
Κεα
Kythnos
Κυθνος
Serifos
Gyaro
Syros
Paros
Naxos
Myrtoo Pelagos
Kythira
Chania, Rethymno
Irakleio
Adamas
E75
E65
E94
E962
A1
A6
A7
A8
A11

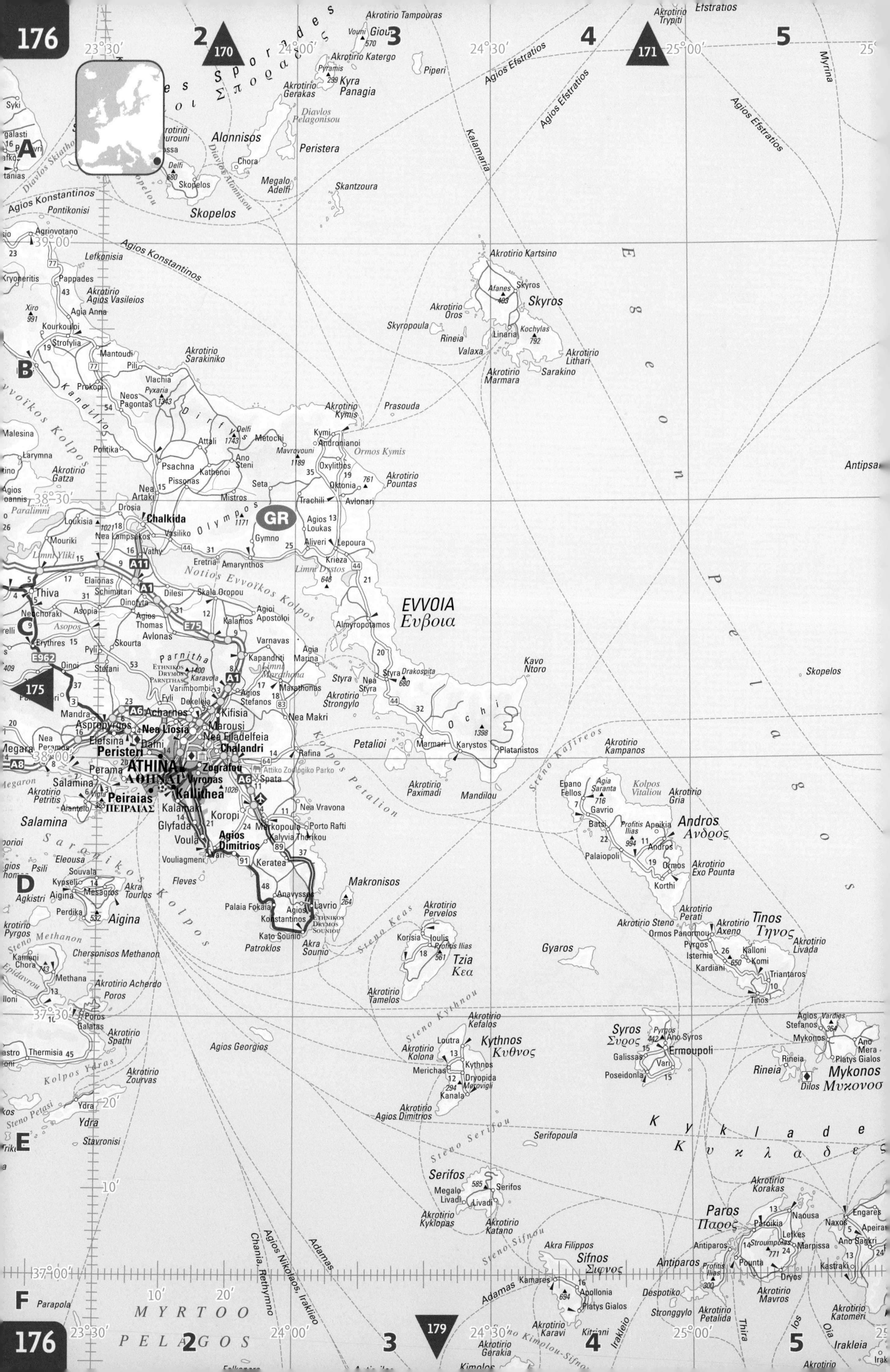
Sporades
Σποραδες
Akrotirio Tampouras
Giour
Akrotirio Katergo
Kyra Panagia
Akrotirio Gerakas
Piperi
Diavlos Pelagonisou
Alonnisos
Peristera
Chora
Megalo Adelfi
Skantzoura
Skopelos
Agios Efstratios
Akrotirio Trypiti
Efstratios
Myrina
Kalamaria
Agios Konstantinos
Pontikonisi
Agriovotano
Lefkonisia
Kryoneritis
Pappades
Akrotirio Agios Vasileios
Xiro
Agia Anna
Kourkouloi
Strofylia
Mantoudi
Pili
Akrotirio Sarakiniko
Prokopi
Vlachia
Pyxaria
Neos Pagontas
Dirfys
Delfi
Attali
Metochi
Mavrovouni
Kymi
Andronianoi
Ormos Kymis
Akrotirio Kymis
Prasouda
Politika
Psachna
Ano Steni
Kathenoi
Pissonas
Nea Artaki
Oxylithos
Oktonia
Avlonari
Akrotirio Pountas
Seta
Mistros
Trachili
Drosia
Chalkida
Olympos
GR
Agios Loukas
Gymno
Aliveri
Lepoura
Krieza
Limni Dystos
Loukisia
Mouriki
Nea Lampsakos
Vasiliko
Vathy
Eretria
Amarynthos
Limni Yliki
Notios Evvoikos Kolpos
Thiva
Elaionas
Schimatari
Dilesi
Skala Oropou
Neochoraki
Asopia
Oinofyta
Agios Thomas
Avlonas
Kalamos
Agioi Apostoloi
Almyropotamos
EVVOIA
Ευβοια
Erythres
Skourta
Pyli
Varnavas
Kapandriti
Agia Marina
Stefani
Parnitha
Karavola
Varimbombi
Marathonas
Limni Marathona
Agios Stefanos
Styra
Nea Styra
Drakospita
Akrotirio Strongylo
Kavo Ntoro
Ochi
Mandra
Aspropyrgos
Acharnes
Kifisia
Dekeleia
Fyli
Nea Makri
Marousi
Nea Liosia
Nea Filadelfeia
Elefsina
Dafni
Peristeri
Chalandri
Rafina
Petalioi
Marmari
Karystos
Platanistos
Nea Peramos
Megara
ATHINA
ΑΘΗΝΑΙ
Zografou
Attiko Zoologiko Parko
Perama
Salamina
Vyronas
Spata
Kallithea
Peiraias
ΠΕΙΡΑΙΑΣ
Akrotirio Petritis
Aianteio
Kalamaki
Koropi
Nea Vravona
Porto Rafti
Kalyvia Thorikou
Markopoulo
Glyfada
Voula
Agios Dimitrios
Vouliagmeni
Vari
Keratea
Kolpos Petalion
Akrotirio Paximadi
Mandilou
Saronikos Kolpos
Psili
Eleousa
Souvala
Kypseli
Aigina
Mesagros
Akra Tourlos
Fleves
Perdika
Agkistri
Anavyssos
Lavrio
Palaia Fokaia
Agios Konstantinos
Kato Sounio
Akra Sounio
Patroklos
Makronisos
Steno Keas
Korisia
Ioulis
Profitis Ilias
Tzia
Κεα
Akrotirio Pervelos
Akrotirio Tamelos
Chersonisos Methanon
Steno Methanon
Kameni Chora
Methana
Akrotirio Acherdo
Poros
Galatas
Akrotirio Spathi
Agios Georgios
Thermisia
Kolpos Ydras
Akrotirio Zourvas
Steno Petasi
Ydra
Stavronisi
Akrotirio Kartsino
Afanes
Skyros
Akrotirio Oros
Skyropoula
Rineia
Linaria
Kochylas
Valaxa
Akrotirio Lithari
Akrotirio Marmara
Sarakino
Egeon Pelagos
Antipsara
Skopelos
Steno Kafireos
Akrotirio Kampanos
Epano Fellos
Agia Saranta
Kolpos Vitaliou
Akrotirio Gria
Gavrio
Batsi
Profitis Ilias
Apoikia
Andros
Ανδρος
Palaiopoli
Ormos
Akrotirio Exo Pounta
Korthi
Akrotirio Perati
Akrotirio Steno
Ormos Panormou
Akrotirio Axeno
Tinos
Τηνος
Akrotirio Livada
Pyrgos
Isternia
Kalloni
Komi
Kardiani
Triantaros
Gyaros
Steno Kythnou
Akrotirio Kefalos
Loutra
Kythnos
Κυθνος
Akrotirio Kolona
Merichas
Dryopida
Merovigli
Kanala
Akrotirio Agios Dimitrios
Syros
Συρος
Pyrgos
Ano Syros
Ermoupoli
Galissas
Vari
Poseidonia
Agios Stefanos
Vardies
Mykonos
Ano Mera
Platys Gialos
Rineia
Dilos
Mykonos
Μυκονος
Kyklades
Κυκλαδες
Steno Serifou
Serifopoula
Serifos
Megalo Livadi
Livadi
Akrotirio Kyklopas
Akrotirio Katano
Steno Sifnou
Akra Filippos
Sifnos
Σιφνος
Kamares
Apollonia
Platys Gialos
Akrotirio Karavi
Kitriani
Akrotirio Gerakia
Kimolos
Adamas
Chania, Rethymno
Agios Nikolaos, Irakleio
Irakleio
Akrotirio Korakas
Paros
Παρος
Paroikia
Naousa
Lefkes
Marpissa
Antiparos
Stroumpias
Pounta
Dryos
Profitis Ilias
Akrotirio Mavros
Despotiko
Stronggylo
Akrotirio Petalida
Thira
Ios
Oia
Naxos
Engares
Apeiranthos
Ano Sagkri
Kastraki
Akrotirio Katomeri
Irakleia
MYRTOO PELAGOS
A
B
C
D
E
F
2
3
4
5
170
171
175
179

6
7
8
9
172
173
26°00′
26°30′
27°00′
27°30′
Akrotirio Korakas
Sykaminia
Petra
Akrotirio Fournia
Skoutaros
Stypsi
Mantamados
Agios Paraskevi
Antissa
Kalloni
Megalonisi
Sigri
Vatoussa
Profitis Ilias
799
Skala Kallonis
Mystegna
Pigi
Pamfylla
Eresos
Akrotirio Saratsina
Parakoila
Kolpos Kallonis
Skala Eresou
Agra
Mesotopos
Moria
LESVOS
Λεσβος
Vasilika
Polichnitos
Agiasos
Kolpos Geras
Palaiokipos
Mytilini
Profitis Ilias
968
Loutra
Kratigos
Akrotirio Kalloni
Vrisa
Pappados
Skopelos
Vatera
Akrotirio Agios Fokas
Akrotirio Agrilia
Plomari
Çanakkale
Mytilini Strait
Alibey Adası
Ayvalık
Küçükköy
Altınova
E87
Gömeç
Bağyüzü
Yukarıbey
Madra Dağı
1344
Dereköy
Göçbeyli
Kadıköy
Bergama
Bakır
Cinge
Turgutalp
Soma
Manca
Kırkağaç
Bakır
İyaslar
Poyrazcık
Kınık
Kabakum
Dikili
Bademli
Deliktaş
Yeniköy
Zeytindağ
Çandarlı
İsmailli
Yunt Dağı
1074
Zeytinliova
Süleymanlı
Erdelli
Kayalıoğlu
Mecidiye
Yenişakran
Aliağa
Karaköy
Güzelhisar Barajı
Osmancalı
Üçpınar
TR
Sarıçam
Pasaköy
Hacırahmanlı
İshakçelebi
Nuriye
Saruhanlı
Selimşahlar
Halitpaşa
Mütevelli
Koldere
Karaağaçlı
Yeniköy
Helvacı
Dumanlı Tepe
Yenifoça
Bağarası
Foça
Gediz
Muradiye
Kesik
Emiralem
Menemen
Manisa
Spil Dağı Milli Parkı
Seyrek
Koyundere
Yamanlar Dağı
1076
Sabuncubeli Geçidi
Aşağıçobanisa
Karaoğlanlı
Turgutlu
Tuzculu
Ulucak
Büyükçiğli
Uzun Ada
İzmir Körfezi
Kaklıç
Sasallı
Bornova
Karşıyaka
İzmir
Konak
Ulucak
Ansızca
Kemalpaşa
Armutlu
Ören
Bağyurdu
Narlıdere
Altındağ
Buca
Yukarıkızılca
1446
Kaynaklar
Boz Dağ
1337
Güzelbahçe
1017
Balçova
Gaziemir
Sarnıç
Dağkızılca
Görece
Menderes
Ayrancılar
Yazıbaşı
Bayındır
Kızılcaova
Yeniköy
Pancar
Seferihisar Barajı
Tekeli
Torbalı
Çırpı
Hasköy
Çaybaşı
Subaşı
Yeniçiftlik
Tahtalı Barajı
Değirmendere
Ahmetli
Ürkmez
Gümüşsuyu
Doğanbey
Ahmetbeyli
Özdere
Belevi
Selçuk
Kuşadası Körfezi
Kuşadası
Çamlık
Gökçealan
Ortaklar
Germencik
İncirliova
Acarlar
Turanlar
1016
Soğucak
Söke
Büyükmenderes
Yeniköy
Bıyıklı
Haydarlı
Bağarası
Davutlar
Güzelçamlı
Güllübahçe
Dilek Yarımadası Milli Parkı
1237
Tuzburgazı
Özbaşı
Doğanbey
Balat Ovası
Sarıkemer
Batı Menteşe
Camiçi Gölü
Balat
Akköy
Yeniköy
Çamiçi
İlbir Dağı
Kazıklı
1083
Selimiye
Yenihisar
Akbük Limanı
Güllük
Güllük Körfezi
181
Güvercinlik
Yalıkavak
Gölköy
Ortakent
Bodrum
Pınarlıbelen
Turgutreis
Kara Ada
37°00′
37°30′
38°00′
38°30′
39°00′
Psara
Profitis Ilias
531
Akrotirio Kampi
Kampia
Akrotirio Vamvakas
Marmaro
1297
Oinousses
Pasas
Akrotirio Melanios
Ano Kardamyla
Lagkada
Volissos
Vrontados
Anavatos
Nea Moni Chiou
773
Chios
Χιος
Lithi
Thymiana
Chios Strait
Vessa
Limenas
Kallimasia
Mesta
Armolia
Katarraktis
Nenita
Akrotirio Mesta
Pyrgi
Kalamoti
Komi
Emporeios
Akrotirio Oura
Tepeboz
Karaburun
Küçükbahçe
1218
Bozdağ
Kösedere
Mordoğan
Balıklıova
Kara Ada
Ildır
Özbek
Çeşme
Gülbahçe
Uzunkuyu
Urla
Bademler
Alaçatı
Zeytineli
Ulamış
Seferihisar
Kiran Dağları
662
Sığacık Körfezi
GR
Karlovasi
Avlakia
Leka
Kokkari
1153
Samos
Palaiokastro
Kallithea
Vigla
1433
Marathokampos
Mytilinioi
Vathy
Akrotirio Katavasi
Akrotirio Fanari
Pyrgos
Chora
Pythagoreio
Pagondas
Kolpos Marathokampou
Ikaria
Ικαρια
Perdiki
Armenistis
Evdilos
Efanos
1037
Agios Kirykos
Raches
Amalo
1033
Akrotirio Papas
Fournoi
Thymaina
Agios Minas
Samiopoula
Samos
Σαμοσ
Megalos Anthropofagos
Makronisi
Agathonisi
Dodekanisos
Δωδεκανησος
Petrokaravo
Anydros
Patmos
Arkoi
Leipsoi
Skala
Farmakonisi
Archangelos
Leros
Partheni
Agia Marina
Piganoussa
Lakki
Xirokampo
326
Akrotirio Tilos
Kalolimnos
Kalymnos
Arginonta
Telendos
Myrties
Chorio
678
Vathys
Plati
Pserimos
Kalymnos
Levitha
Rodos
Astypalaia
Akrotirio Stavri
Donousa
Agia Paraskevi
Koronos
Moutsouna
Danakos
Naxos
Ναξος
Kinaros
Mavria
Koufonisi
Liadi
Kato Agios Georgios
Keros
Schoinoussa
Chorafakia
821
Aigiali
Nikouria
Amorgos
Katapola
Kato Antikeri
180
Akrotirio Skandari
Kos
Antimacheia
Akrotirio Agios Fokas
846
Kardamaina
A
B
C
D
E
F
xvii

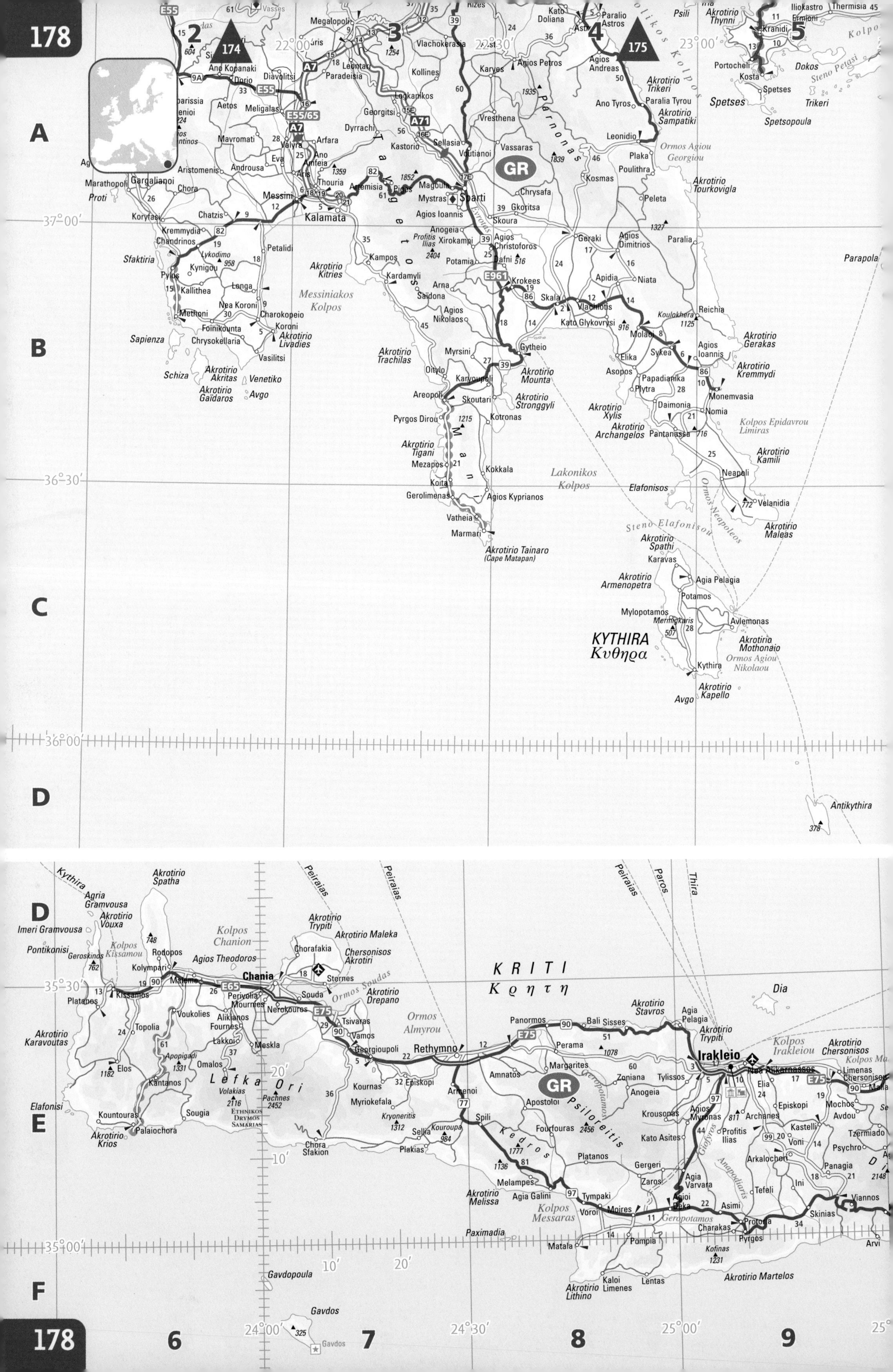

A
B
C
D
E
F
6
7
8
9
2
3
4
5
174
175
GR
37°00′
36°30′
36°00′
35°30′
35°00′
22°00′
22°30′
23°00′
24°00′
24°30′
25°00′
E55
Vasses
Megalopoli
Vlachokerasia
Kato Doliana
Paralio Astros
Psili
Akrotirio Thynni
Iliokastro
Thermisia
Kranidi
Ermioni
Ano Kopanaki
Dorio
Diavolitsi
Leontari
Paradeisia
Kollines
Karyes
Agios Petros
Agios Andreas
Portocheli
Kosta
Dokos
Spetses
Trikeri
Spetsopoula
Steno Petasi
Akrotirio Trikeri
Paralia Tyrou
Ano Tyros
Akrotirio Sampatiki
Leonidio
Ormos Agiou Georgiou
Plaka
Poulithra
Kyparissia
Aetos
Meligalas
Georgitsi
Logkanikos
Vresthena
Parnonas
Mavromati
Dyrrachi
Kastorio
Sellasia
Vassaras
Voutianoi
Arfara
Eva
Valyra
Ano Amfeia
Androusa
Aristomenis
Aris
Thouria
Artemisia
Piges
Magoula
Mystras
Sparti
Chrysafa
Kosmas
Akrotirio Tourkovigla
Marathopoli
Gargalianoi
Chora
Proti
Messini
Kalamata
Gkoritsa
Skoura
Peleta
Koryfasi
Chatzis
Agios Ioannis
Anogeia
Xirokampi
Profitis Ilias
Agios Christoforos
Geraki
Agios Dimitrios
Paralia
Parapola
Kremmydia
Chandrinos
Lykodimo
Kynigou
Petalidi
Kampos
Potamia
Dafni
Sfaktiria
Pylos
Akrotirio Kitries
Kardamyli
Krokees
Apidia
Niata
Kallithea
Longa
Arna
Saidona
Skala
Vlachiotis
Messiniakos Kolpos
Nea Koroni
Methoni
Charokopeio
Koroni
Agios Nikolaos
Kato Glykovrysi
Molaoi
Koulokhera
Reichia
Foinikounta
Akrotirio Livadies
Sapienza
Chrysokellaria
Vasilitsi
Akrotirio Trachilas
Myrsini
Gytheio
Elika
Sykea
Agios Ioannis
Akrotirio Gerakas
Oitylo
Asopos
Akrotirio Kremmydi
Schiza
Akrotirio Akritas
Venetiko
Akrotirio Gaidaros
Avgo
Karyoupoli
Akrotirio Mounta
Papadianika
Plytra
Monemvasia
Areopoli
Skoutari
Akrotirio Stronggyli
Daimonia
Nomia
Pyrgos Dirou
Kotronas
Akrotirio Xylis
Akrotirio Archangelos
Pantanassa
Kolpos Epidavrou Limiras
Mani
Akrotirio Tigani
Mezapos
Akrotirio Kamili
Kokkala
Lakonikos Kolpos
Neapoli
Koita
Gerolimenas
Agios Kyprianos
Elafonisos
Ormos Neapoleos
Velanidia
Vatheia
Marmari
Steno Elafonisou
Akrotirio Maleas
Akrotirio Tainaro (Cape Matapan)
Akrotirio Spathi
Karavas
Akrotirio Armenopetra
Agia Pelagia
Potamos
Mylopotamos
Mermigkaris
Avlemonas
KYTHIRA
Κυθηρα
Akrotirio Mothonaio
Ormos Agiou Nikolaou
Kythira
Akrotirio Kapello
Avgo
Antikythira
Kythira
Agria Gramvousa
Akrotirio Spatha
Akrotirio Vouxa
Imeri Gramvousa
Pontikonisi
Geroskinos
Kolpos Kissamou
Rodopos
Kolpos Chanion
Peiraias
Akrotirio Trypiti
Akrotirio Maleka
Chorafakia
Chersonisos Akrotiri
Kolympari
Agios Theodoros
Chania
Sternes
KRITI
Κρητη
Maleme
Kissamos
Platanos
Perivolia
Mournies
Souda
Ormos Soudas
Akrotirio Drepano
Nerokouros
Voukolies
Alikianos
Akrotirio Karavoutas
Topolia
Fournes
Tsivaras
Vamos
Ormos Almyrou
Panormos
Bali Sisses
Akrotirio Stavros
Agia Pelagia
Akrotirio Trypiti
Dia
Lakkoi
Meskla
Georgioupoli
Rethymno
Perama
Irakleio
Kolpos Irakleiou
Nea Alikarnassos
Akrotirio Chersonisos
Apopigadi
Omalos
Margarites
Tylissos
Elos
Lefka Ori
Amnatos
Zoniana
Anogeia
Elia
Chersonisos
Kantanos
Volakias
Ethnikos Drymos Samarias
Pachnes
Kournas
Episkopi
Armenoi
Psiloreitis
Mochos
Malia
Elafonisi
Myriokefala
Apostoloi
Episkopi
Avdou
Kountouras
Sougia
Kryoneritis
Kouroupa
Spili
Krousonas
Agios Myronas
Archanes
Kastelli
Tzermiado
Akrotirio Krios
Palaiochora
Chora Sfakion
Sellia
Plakias
Kedros
Fourfouras
Kato Asites
Profitis Ilias
Voni
Psychro
Platanos
Gergeri
Arkalochori
Panagia
Melampes
Zaros
Agia Varvara
Ini
Akrotirio Melissa
Agia Galini
Tympaki
Kolpos Messaras
Voroi
Moires
Agioi Deka
Asimi
Tefeli
Viannos
Geropotamos
Protoria
Skinias
Paximadia
Charakas
Pyrgos
Matala
Pompia
Kofinas
Arvi
Gavdopoula
Akrotirio Lithino
Kaloi Limenes
Lentas
Akrotirio Martelos
Gavdos
Gavdos

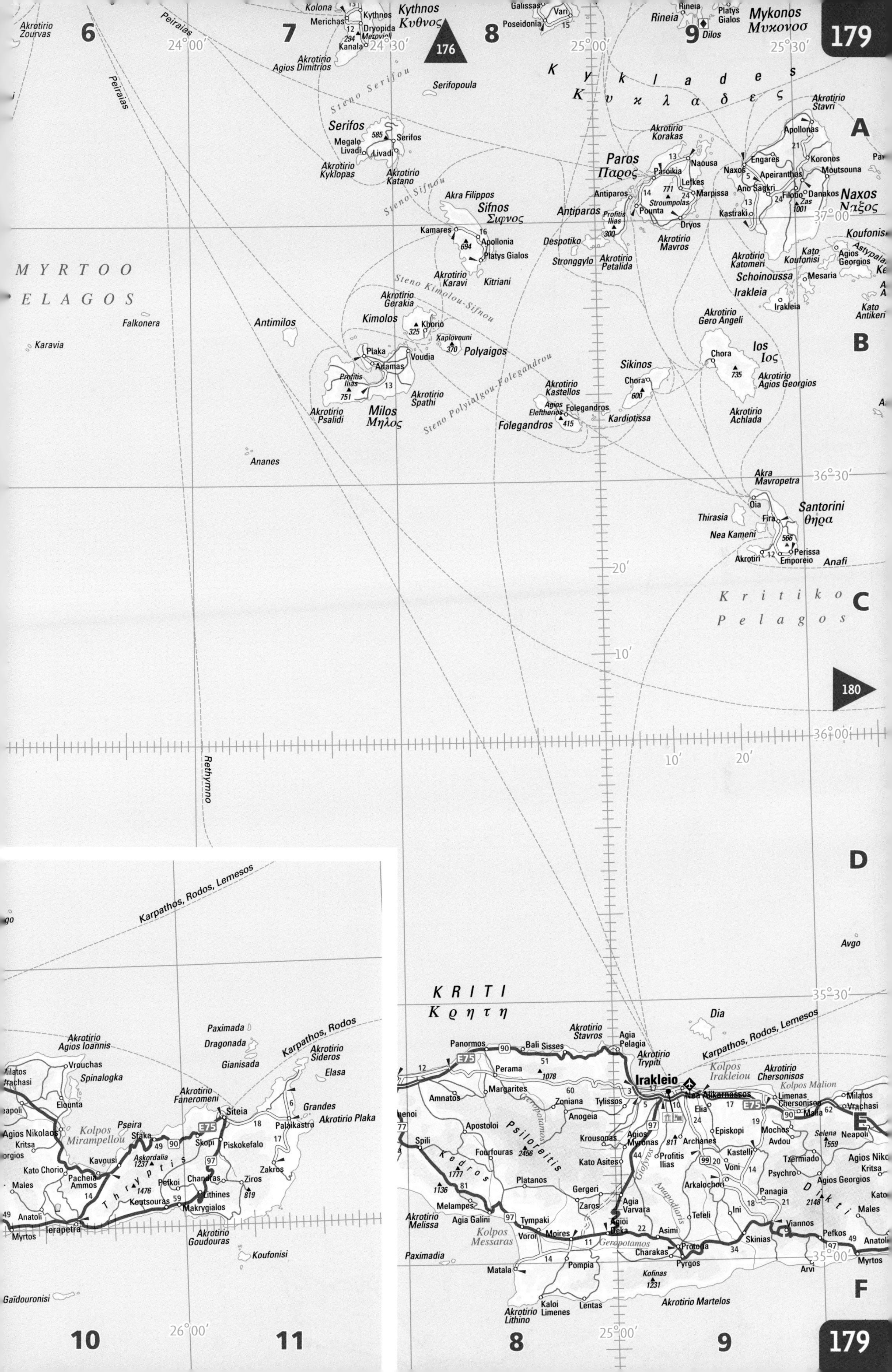
6
7
8
9
176
Kythnos
Κυθνος
Mykonos
Μυκονοσ
Akrotirio Zourvas
Peiraias
24°00′
24°30′
25°00′
25°30′
Kolona
Merichas
Kythnos
Dryopida
Merovigli
Kanala
Akrotirio Agios Dimitrios
Galissas
Vari
Poseidonia
Rineia
Platys Gialos
Dilos
Serifopoula
Steno Serifou
K y k l a d e s
Κ υ κ λ α δ ε ς
Serifos
Megalo Livadi
Livadi
Akrotirio Kyklopas
Akrotirio Katano
Steno Sifnou
Akra Filippos
Sifnos
Σιφνος
Kamares
Apollonia
Platys Gialos
Akrotirio Karavi
Kitriani
Paros
Παρος
Antiparos
Despotiko
Stronggylo
Akrotirio Petalida
Profitis Ilias
Akrotirio Korakas
Paroikia
Naousa
Lefkes
Marpissa
Stroumpolas
Pounta
Dryos
Akrotirio Mavros
Akrotirio Stavri
Apollonas
Engares
Koronos
Naxos
Apeiranthos
Moutsouna
Ano Sagkri
Filotio
Danakos
Zas
Kastraki
Naxos
Νaξος
37°00′
Koufonisi
Kato Koufonisi
Agios Georgios
Akrotirio Katomeri
Schoinoussa
Mesaria
Irakleia
Kato Antikeri
Astypalaia
A
B
C
D
E
F
MYRTOO
PELAGOS
Falkonera
Karavia
Antimilos
Akrotirio Gerakia
Kimolos
Steno Kimolou-Sifnou
Khorio
Xaplovouni
Polyaigos
Plaka
Adamas
Voudia
Profitis Ilias
Akrotirio Spathi
Akrotirio Psalidi
Milos
Μηλος
Steno Polyialgou-Folegandrou
Akrotirio Gero Angeli
Sikinos
Chora
Ios
Ιος
Chora
Akrotirio Agios Georgios
Akrotirio Kastellos
Agios Eleftherios
Folegandros
Kardiotissa
Akrotirio Achlada
Ananes
Akra Mavropetra
36°30′
Oia
Santorini
θηρα
Thirasia
Fira
Nea Kameni
Perissa
Akrotiri
Emporeio
Anafi
20′
Kritiko
Pelagos
10′
180
36°00′
Rethymno
Avgo
35°30′
KRITI
Κρητη
Dia
Karpathos, Rodos, Lemesos
Karpathos, Rodos
Akrotirio Agios Ioannis
Paximada
Dragonada
Gianisada
Akrotirio Sideros
Elasa
Milatos
Vrachasi
Vrouchas
Spinalogka
Elounta
Neapoli
Akrotirio Faneromeni
Siteia
Grandes
Akrotirio Plaka
Palaikastro
Agios Nikolaos
Kolpos Mirampellou
Pseira
Sfaka
Kritsa
Kavousi
Askordalia
Skopi
Piskokefalo
Kato Chorio
Pacheia Ammos
Thrypti
Chandras
Ziros
Zakros
Males
Petkoi
Lithines
Koutsouras
Makrygialos
Anatoli
Myrtos
Ierapetra
Akrotirio Goudouras
Koufonisi
Gaïdouronisi
26°00′
10
11
Akrotirio Stavros
Agia Pelagia
Akrotirio Trypiti
Panormos
Bali
Sisses
Perama
Margarites
Amnatos
Zoniana
Anogeia
Tylissos
Irakleio
Kolpos Irakleiou
Nea Alikarnassos
Akrotirio Chersonisos
Kolpos Malion
Limenas Chersonisou
Malia
Milatos
Vrachasi
Elia
Episkopi
Mochos
Avdou
Selena
Neapoli
Apostoloi
Psiloreitis
Krousonas
Agios Myronas
Archanes
Kastelli
Tzermiado
Agios Nikolaos
Kritsa
Spili
Fourfouras
Kedros
Kato Asites
Profitis Ilias
Voni
Psychro
Agios Georgios
Platanos
Gergeri
Arkalochori
Panagia
Dikti
Kato
Males
Melampes
Zaros
Agia Varvara
Anapodiaris
Ini
Agia Galini
Akrotirio Melissa
Tympaki
Kolpos Messaras
Voroi
Moires
Agioi Deka
Asimi
Tefeli
Viannos
Skinias
Pefkos
Anatoli
Geropotamos
Charakas
Protoria
Pyrgos
Myrtos
Arvi
35°00′
Paximadia
Matala
Pompia
Kofinas
Akrotirio Martelos
Kaloi Limenes
Lentas
Akrotirio Lithino
25°00′
8
9

Kyklades
Κυκλαδες
Dodekanisa
Δωδεκανα
Tinos
Syros
Mykonos
Μυκονοσ
Rineia
Dilos
Tragonisi
Ikaria
Ικαρια
Evdilos
Agios Kirykos
Fournoi
Thymaina
Patmos
Leipsoi
Paros
Παρος
Antiparos
Naxos
Ναξος
Sifnos
Σιφνος
Koufonisi
Schoinoussa
Irakleia
Keros
Donousa
Amorgos
Ios
Ιος
Sikinos
Folegandros
Polyaigos
Anydros
GR
Astypalaia
Kinaros
Levitha
Mavria
Santorini
θηρα
Thirasia
Nea Kameni
Oia
Fira
Anafi
Kritiko Pelagos
Pacheia
Makra
Adelfoi
Syrna
Tria Nisia
Peiraias
Sofrana
Karavonisia
Chamili
Divounia
Avgo
Dia
KRITI
Κρητη
Irakleio
Kolpos Irakleiou
Kolpos Malion
Kolpos Mirampellou
Agios Nikolaos
Psiloreitis
Dikti
Siteia
Palaikastro
Zakros
Ierapetra
Dragonada
Gianisada
Paximada
Elasa
Grandes
176
179

6
7
8
9
B
C
D
E
F
A
177
TR
xvii
27°00′
27°30′
28°00′
28°30′
37°00′
36°30′
36°00′
35°30′
Milas
Muğla
Yatağan
Bodrum
Marmaris
Datça
Köyceğiz
Ortaca
Dalaman
Çine
Eskiçine
Akçaova
Bağcılar
Turgut
Beçin
Güllük
Koruköy
Dörttepe
Güvercinlik
Karaova
Pınarlıbelen
Mazı
Ören
Pınarköy
Dağpınar
Yeniköy
Yerkesik
Yeşilyurt
Yenice
Ula
Yaraş
Portakallık
Gökova
Kıran
Karaböğürtlen
Kızılyaka
Toparlar
Yangı
Zeytinalanı
Beyobası
Demirli
Döğüşbelen
Hamit
Dalyan
Okçular
Bayır
Yalıkavak
Gölköy
Ortakent
Turgutreis
Kazıklı
Selimiye
Bahçeburun
Çamiçi
Yenihisar
Balat
Akköy
Yeniköy
Sarıkemer
Doğanbey
Tuzburgazı
Özbaşı
Ulukonak
Abak
Kahraman
Karpuzlu
Bölüntü
Soğukoluk
Tekeler
Hatipkışlası
Altıntaş
Haydere
Çayboyu
Kavaklıdere
Menteşe
Çamyayla
Göktepe
Gökçeören
Kayabaşı
Kapız
Muratlar
Yemişendere
Beyağaç
Karaköy
Kale
Hırka
Özlüce
Karaca
Beldibi
Armutalanı
Hisarönü
Orhaniye
Bozburun
Söğüt
Emecik
Yazıköy
İskandil Burnu
İnce Burun
Kara Ada
Akrotirio Skandari
Akrotirio Agios Fokas
Gökova Körfezi
Güllük Körfezi
Hisarönü Körfezi
Köyceğiz Gölü
Reşadiye Yarımadası
Bozburun Yarımadası
Yaran Dağı
İlbir Dağı
Menteşe Dağları
Gölgeli
Çetibeli Geçidi
Sakar Geçidi
Balan Dağı
Kızılbel Geçidi
Yılancık Adası
Kurtoğlu Burnu
Kapıkaya
Akbük Limanı
Kemer Barajı
Çamiçi Gölü
Karpuzlu Barajı
Atatürk Milli Parkı
Milli Parkı
Agathonisi
Farmakonisi
Leros
Partheni
Piganoussa
Xirokampo
Akrotirio Tilos
Kalolimnos
Kalymnos
Arginonta
Myrties
Chorio
Vathys
Plati
Pserimos
Kos
Κως
Asfendiou
Pyli
Mastichari
Antimacheia
Kardamaina
Kefalos
Kolpos Kefalou
Akrotirio Krykello
Gyali
Strongyli
Mandraki
Pergousa
Pacheia
Nisyros
Kandelioussa
Gaidouronisi
Akra Orfos
Megalo Chorio
Tilos
Akrotirio Trachilos
Antitilos
Nimos
Symi
Sesklio
Alimia
Chalki
Merovigli
Akrotirio Matsouka
Rodos
RODOS
Ροδος
Kremasti
Trianta
Paradeisi
Akrotirio Vodi
Koskinou
Akrotirio Nisi
Kalythies
Afantou
Kolympia
Maritsa
Psinthos
Soroni
Kalavarda
Kamiros
Salakos
Mandriko
Kritinia
Apollona
Archipoli
Emponas
Archangelos
Malona
Masari
Atavyros
Laerma
Kalathos
Lindos
Akrotirio Gkinas
Monolithos
Akrotirio Armenistis
Istrio
Profilia
Lardos
Asklipieio
Apolakkia
Vati
Gennadi
Skiadi
Lachania
Kattavia
Oros
Akrotirio Prasonisi
Antalya
Lemesos
Steno Karpathou
Astakida
Akrotirio Paraspori
Pachy Vouno
Saria
Akrotirio Agios Ioannis
Diafani
Olympos
Mesochori
Karpathos
Aperi
Pyles
Kali Limni
Arkasa
Karpathos
Menetes
Akrotirio Agios Theodoros
Armathia
Steno Kasou
Kasos
Fry
Akrotirio Kastelo

2
3
4
5
3°00′
3°30′
4°00′
4°30′
52°00′
51°30′
51°00′
50°30′
A
B
C
D
0 10 20 30 40 50 km
0 10 20 30 miles
Kingston upon Hull
Harwich
EUROPOORT
NL
B
F
18
184
Zaandam
Haarlem
AMS
Zandvoort
Heemstede
Hillegom
Noordwijkerhout
Noordwijk aan Zee
Noordwijk-Binnen
Katwijk aan Zee
Rijnsburg
Lisse
Aalsmeer
Uithoorn
Mijdrecht
Wassenaar
Leiden
Leiderdorp
Oegstgeest
Alphen aan den Rijn
Voorschoten
Leidschendam
'S-GRAVENHAGE
(DEN HAAG)
Rijswijk
Voorburg
Zoetermeer
Wateringen
Delft
Pijnacker
Monster
Naaldwijk
's-Gravenzande
Hoek van Holland
Waddinxveen
Gouda
Boskoop
Bodegraven
Woerden
Berkel
Bergschenhoek
Nieuwerkerk aan de IJssel
Capelle a an de IJssel
Schoonhoven
Maassluis
Schiedam
Vlaardingen
Rotterdam
Rozenburg
Krimpen aan de IJssel
Oostvoorne
Rockanje
Brielle
Hoogvliet
Spijkenisse
Ridderkerk
Alblasserdam
Hardinxveld-Giessendam
Hellevoetsluis
Goedereede
Ouddorp
Oud-Beijerland
Zwijndrecht
Papendrecht
Sliedrecht
Dordrecht
Middelharnis
Stellendam
Renesse
Brouwershaven
Burgh-Haamstede
Zierikzee
Nieuwerkerk
Oosterland
Bruinisse
Grevelingen
Oosterschelde
Noordbeveland
Domburg
Vrouwenpolder
Westkapelle
Middelburg
Veere
Goes
Vlissingen
Oost-Souburg
Tholen
St Maartensdijk
Steenbergen
Halsteren
Bergen op Zoom
Roosendaal
Oudenbosch
Zevenbergen
Breda
Etten-Leur
Willemstad
Klundert
Numansdorp
Raamsdonksveer
Made
Oosterhout
Teteringen
Rijen
Essen
Zundert
Wuustwezel
Kalmthout
Hoogstraten
Rijsbergen
Westerschelde
Borssele
Breskens
Terneuzen
Hulst
Knokke-Heist
Zeebrugge
Blankenberge
De Haan
Oostende
(Ostend)
Brugge
(Bruges)
Damme
Maldegem
Eeklo
Assenede
Zelzate
Stekene
St-Gillis-Waas
St-Niklaas
Beveren
Zwijndrecht
Antwerpen
(Anvers)
Brasschaat
Schoten
Schilde
Wommelgem
Mortsel
Edegem
Kapellen
Stabroek
Brecht
Westmalle
Zoersel
Herentals
Lille
Nijlen
Lier
Duffel
Boom
Rumst
Willebroek
Mechelen
(Malines)
Heist-op-den-Berg
Aarschot
Haacht
Leuven
(Louvain)
Lubbeek
Vilvoorde
Zaventem
Schaerbeek
BRUSSEL /
BRUXELLES
Molenbeek-St-Jean
Anderlecht
Ixelles
Uccle
Tervuren
Overijse
Forêt de Soignes
Waterloo
Braine-l'Alleud
Rixensart
Wavre
Grez-Doiceau
Jodoigne
Halle
Tubize
Nivelles
Genappe
Ottignies
Gembloux
Namur
Seneffe
La Louvière
Binche
Soignies
Braine-le-Comte
Enghien
Ath
Leuze-en-Hainaut
Beloeil
Lessines
Geraardsbergen
Ninove
Aalst
(Alost)
Dendermonde
Zele
Lokeren
Wetteren
Gent
(Gand)
Destelbergen
Melle
Merelbeke
Oosterzele
Zottegem
Oudenaarde
Ronse
Deinze
Nevele
Aalter
Tielt
Torhout
Diksmuide
Gistel
Zedelgem
Beernem
Roeselare
(Roulers)
Izegem
Ingelmunster
Waregem
Harelbeke
Kortrijk (Courtrai)
Menen
Wervik
Wevelgem
Moorslede
Zonnebeke
Ieper
Mouscron
Tourcoing
Roubaix
Armentières
Lille
Villeneuve-d'Ascq
Tournai
Péruwelz
Seclin
Orchies
Condé-sur-l'Escaut
St-Ghislain
Mons
Quaregnon
Fleurus
Charleroi

Almere
Harderwijk
Nunspeet
Heerde
Raalte
Nijverdal
Wierden
Oldenzaal
Bad Bentheim
Hilversum
Amersfoort
Apeldoorn
Deventer
Hengelo
Enschede
Gronau (Westfalen)
Utrecht
Zeist
Zutphen
Lochem
Haaksbergen
Ahaus
Ede
Arnhem
Doetinchem
Winterswijk
Stadtlohn
Gescher
Veenendaal
Culemborg
Tiel
Nijmegen
Emmerich
Bocholt
Borken
Kleve
Oss
's-Hertogenbosch
Goch
Wesel
Dorsten
Marl
Uden
Boxmeer
Xanten
Gladbeck
Herten
Gelsenkirchen
Veghel
Kevelaer
Dinslaken
Bottrop
Helmond
Venray
Geldern
Duisburg
Moers
Oberhausen
Essen
Eindhoven
Deurne
Mülheim an der Ruhr
Venlo
Krefeld
Weert
Roermond
Viersen
Mönchengladbach
Neuss
Düsseldorf
Ratingen
Mettmann
Hilden
Solingen
Langenfeld (Rheinland)
Dormagen
Grevenbroich
Leverkusen
Heinsberg
Erkelenz
Hückelhoven
Sittard
Geleen
Genk
Hasselt
Maastricht
Heerlen
Kerkrade
Aachen
Eschweiler
Düren
Jülich
Bergheim (Erft)
Köln
Kerpen
Hürth
Brühl
Wesseling
Erftstadt
Bonn
Tongeren
Liège (Luik)
Seraing
Verviers
Eupen
Euskirchen
Zülpich
Mechernich
Rheinbach
Monschau
Schleiden
Bad Münstereifel
Bad Neuenahr-Ahrweiler
Huy
Spa
Malmédy
Stolberg (Rheinland)
NATIONAAL PARK DE HOGE VELUWE
NATIONAAL PARK VELUWEZOOM
NATIONAAL PARK DE GROOTE PEEL
Hertogenwald
Hautes Fagnes

0 10 20 30 40 50 km
0 10 20 30 miles
A
B
C
D
E
1
2
3
4
5
182
19
20
Dordrecht
Breda
Tilburg
Roosendaal
Bergen op Zoom
Eindhoven
Helmond
Antwerpen (Anvers)
Mechelen (Malines)
St-Niklaas
Turnhout
Hasselt
Genk
Maastricht
Heerlen
Aachen
Sittard
Roermond
Venlo
BRUSSEL / BRUXELLES
Leuven (Louvain)
Liège (Luik)
Namur
Charleroi
Verviers
Malmédy
Huy
Dinant
Bastogne
Marche-en-Famenne
Rochefort
La Roche-en-Ardenne
St-Hubert
Neufchâteau
Bouillon
Chimay
Couvin
Philippeville
Tongeren
Sint-Truiden
Tienen
Waterloo
Nivelles
Wavre
Gembloux
Spa
Hautes Fagnes
Plateau de l'Ardenne (Ardennes)
Famenne
Fagne
Hertogenwald
Nationaal Park De Biesbosch
Nationaal Park De Groote Peel

Wesel
Dorsten
Marl
Recklinghausen
Gladbeck
Herten
Castrop-Rauxel
Gelsenkirchen
Lünen
Hamm
Ahlen
Ascheberg
Lüdinghausen
Werne
Bergkamen
Kamen
Unna
Soest
Werl
Lippstadt
Dinslaken
Bottrop
Herne
Dortmund
Essen
Bochum
Oberhausen
Duisburg
Moers
Mülheim an der Ruhr
Witten
Schwerte
Menden (Sauerland)
Arnsberg
Arnsberger Wald
Iserlohn
Hagen
Krefeld
Velbert
Ratingen
Wuppertal
Viersen
Düsseldorf
Neuss
Mönchengladbach
Remscheid
Solingen
Hilden
Langenfeld (Rheinland)
Dormagen
Grevenbroich
Leverkusen
Lüdenscheid
Plettenberg
Meschede
Schmallenberg
Lennestadt
Olpe
Attendorn
Gummersbach
Bergisch Gladbach
Köln
Bergheim (Erft)
Kerpen
Hürth
Brühl
Troisdorf
Siegburg
Siegen
Bonn
St Augustin
Königswinter
Euskirchen
Düren
Jülich
Zülpich
Bad Neuenahr-Ahrweiler
Remagen
Neuwied
Koblenz
Montabaur
Limburg an der Lahn
Weilburg
Herborn
Mayen
Boppard
Bad Ems
Lahnstein
Idstein
Wiesbaden
Mainz
Bingen am Rhein
Bad Kreuznach
Ingelheim am Rhein
Bad Schwalbach
Cochem
Wittlich
Bitburg
Daun
Gerolstein
Prüm
Simmern (Hunsrück)
Bernkastel-Kues
Traben-Trarbach
Eifel
Westerwald
Rothaargebirge
Taunus
Hunsrück
Haarstrang
Schneifel

185
184
26
27
1
2
3
4
A
B
C
D
E
0 10 20 30 40 50 km
0 10 20 30 miles
Trier
Saarbrücken
Kaiserslautern
Strasbourg
Metz
Nancy
Luxembourg
Thionville
Saarlouis
Neunkirchen
Homburg
Zweibrücken
Pirmasens
Sarreguemines
Forbach
Sarrebourg
Saverne
Haguenau
Lunéville
Bitburg
Wittlich
Idar-Oberstein
Bad Kreuznach
Bingen am Rhein
Boppard
Bad Schwalbach
Neustadt an der Weinstraße
Landau in der Pfalz
Offenburg
Molsheim
Obernai
Sélestat
Saint-Dié
GUTLAND
NORDPFÄLZER BERGLAND
Plateau Lorrain
HUNSRÜCK
Pfälzer Wald
Haardt
VOSGES
Petite Suisse Luxembourgeoise
Osburger Hochwald
Idarwald
Rheingaugebirge
L
F

Bad Homburg vor der Höhe
Friedrichsdorf
Wächtersbach
Bad Orb
Königstein im Taunus
Bad Vilbel
Langenselbold
Hanau
Offenbach am Main
Frankfurt am Main
Wiesbaden
Mainz
Rüsselsheim
Seligenstadt
Aschaffenburg
Hösbach
Gemünden am Main
Hammelburg
Karlstadt
Lohr am Main
Darmstadt
Dieburg
Marktheidenfeld
Würzburg
Kitzingen
Ochsenfurt
Miltenberg
Wertheim
Michelstadt
Erbach
Worms
Bensheim
Heppenheim (Bergstraße)
Weinheim
Mannheim
Ludwigshafen am Rhein
Heidelberg
Speyer
Walldürn
Buchen (Odenwald)
Tauberbischofsheim
Lauda-Königshofen
Bad Mergentheim
Eberbach
Mosbach
Sinsheim
Bruchsal
Bad Friedrichshall
Neckarsulm
Heilbronn
Öhringen
Künzelsau
Rothenburg ob der Tauber
Crailsheim
Schwäbisch Hall
Karlsruhe
Bretten
Pforzheim
Ludwigsburg
Backnang
Ellwangen (Jagst)
Aalen
Stuttgart
Esslingen am Neckar
Schwäbisch Gmünd
Göppingen
Heidenheim an der Brenz
Baden-Baden
Gernsbach
Sindelfingen
Böblingen
Calw
Nagold
Herrenberg
Tübingen
Reutlingen
Metzingen
Nürtingen
Kirchheim unter Teck
Geislingen an der Steige
Ulm
Neu-Ulm
Freudenstadt
Horb am Neckar
Rottenburg am Neckar
Hechingen
Balingen
Ehingen (Donau)
Blaubeuren
Münsingen
Spessart
Hohenloher Ebene
Schurwald
Welzheimer Wald
Albuch
Schwarzwald
D
A
B
C
D
E
5
6
7
8
9
78
75
74

A

Aachen D 183 D8
Aalen D 187 D9
Aalsmeer NL 182 A5
Aalst B 182 D4
Aalst NL 183 B6
Aalten NL 183 B9
Aalter B 182 C2
Aardenburg NL 182 C2
Aarle NL 183 C7
Aarschot B 182 D5
Aartrijke B 182 C2
Aartselaar B 182 C4
Abcoude NL 182 A5
Abreschviller F 186 D3
Abtsgmünd D 187 D8
Achel B 183 C6
Achern D 186 D5
Achstetten D 187 E8
Adegem B 182 C2
Adelmannsfelden D 187 D8
Adelsheim D 187 C7
Adenau D 185 D6
Aglasterhausen D 187 C6
Ahaus D 183 A10
Ahlen D 185 A8
Ahrbrück D 183 E9
Aichhalden D 187 E5
Aiglemont F 184 E2
Albergen NL 183 A9
Albertshofen D 187 B9
Albestroff F 186 D2
Albisheim (Pfrimm) D 186 B5
Alblasserdam NL 182 B5
Aldenhoven D 183 D8
Alf D 185 D7
Alfdorf D 187 D8
Alken B 183 D6
Allarmont F 186 E3
Allmendingen D 187 E8
Almelo NL 183 A9
Almere NL 183 A6
Almkerk NL 182 B5
Alost B 182 D4
Alpen D 183 B9
Alpenrod D 185 C8
Alphen NL 182 C5
Alphen aan den Rijn NL 182 A5
Alpirsbach D 187 E5
Alsbach D 187 B6
Alsdorf D 183 D8
Alsenborn D 186 C4
Alsenz D 186 B4
Alsheim D 185 E9
Alsting F 186 C2
Altena D 185 B8
Altenahr D 183 D9
Altenbuch D 187 B7
Altendiez D 185 D8
Altenglan D 186 B3
Altenheim D 186 E4
Altenkirchen (Westerwald) D 185 C8
Altenstadt D 187 A6
Altensteig D 187 D6
Altheim (Alb) D 187 D9
Althengstett D 187 D6
Altleiningen D 186 B5
Altrich D 185 E6
Alzenau in Unterfranken D 187 A7
Alzey D 186 B5
Amay B 183 D6
Amberloup B 184 D4
Ameide NL 182 B5
Amel B 184 D5
Amerongen NL 183 B6
Amersfoort NL 183 A6
Ammerbuch D 187 D6
Ammerzoden NL 183 B6
Amnéville F 186 C1
Amorbach D 187 B7
Amstelveen NL 182 A5
Amsterdam NL 182 A5
Amstetten D 187 D8
Andelst NL 183 B7
Andenne B 183 E6
Anderlecht B 182 D4
Anderlues B 182 E4
Andernach D 185 D7
Andlau F 186 E3
Anhée B 184 D2
Annœullin F 182 D1
Annweiler am Trifels D 186 C4
Anröchte D 185 A9
Ans B 183 D7
Anseremme B 184 D2
Antoing B 182 D2
Antwerpen B 182 C4
Anvers B 182 C4
Anzegem B 182 D2
Apeldoorn NL 183 A7
Appenweier D 186 D4
Arcen NL 183 C8
Ardooie B 182 D2
Arendonk B 183 C6
Argenthal D 185 E8
Armentières F 182 D1
Armsheim D 185 E9
Arnemuiden NL 182 C3
Arnhem NL 183 B7
Arnsberg D 185 B9
Arnstein D 187 B8
Arracourt F 186 D2
Arry F 186 C1
Arzbach D 185 D8
Arzfeld D 185 D5
As B 183 C7
Asbach D 185 C7
Aschaffenburg D 187 B7
Ascheberg D 185 A8
Asperen NL 183 B6
Assamstadt D 187 C8
Asse B 182 D4
Assenede B 182 C3
Assesse B 184 D3
Asten NL 183 C7
Ath B 182 D3
Attendorn D 185 B8
Aub D 187 B9
Aubel B 183 D7
Aubenton F 184 E1
Auby F 182 E2
Aulnois sur-Seille F 186 D1
Aura im Sinngrund D 187 A8
Auvelais B 182 E5
Auvillers-les-Forges F 184 E1
Avelgem B 182 D2
Avricourt F 186 D2
Awans B 183 D6
Axel NL 182 C3
Aywaille B 183 E7

B

Baarle-Hertog B 182 C5
Baarle-Nassau NL 182 C5
Baarn NL 183 A6
Babberich NL 183 B8
Babenhausen D 187 B6
Baccarat F 186 E2
Bacharach D 185 D8
Backnang D 187 D7
Bad Bentheim D 183 A10
Bad Bergzabern D 186 C4
Bad Berleburg D 185 B9
Bad Bertrich D 185 D7
Bad Boll D 187 D8
Bad Breisig D 185 D7
Bad Camberg D 185 D9
Bad Dürkheim D 187 C5
Bad Ems D 185 D8
Baden-Baden D 187 D5
Bad Friedrichshall D 187 C7
Bad Herrenalb D 187 D5
Badhoevedorp NL 182 A5
Bad Homburg vor der Höhe D 187 A6
Bad Honnef D 185 C7
Bad Hönningen D 185 C7
Bad Kissingen D 187 A9
Bad König D 187 B7
Bad Kreuznach D 185 E8
Bad Laasphe D 185 C9
Bad Liebenzell D 187 D6
Bad Marienberg (Westerwald) D 185 C8
Bad Mergentheim D 187 C8
Bad Münstereifel D 183 D9
Bad Neuenahr-Ahrweiler D 183 D10
Badonviller F 186 D2
Bad Orb D 187 A7
Bad Peterstal D 187 E5
Bad Rappenau D 187 C7
Bad Sassendorf D 185 A9
Bad Schönborn D 187 C6
Bad Schwalbach D 185 D9
Bad Sobernheim D 185 E8
Bad Überkingen D 187 D8
Bad Urach D 187 E7
Bad Vilbel D 187 A6
Bad Wildbad im Schwarzwald D 187 D6
Bad Wimpfen D 187 C7
Baelen B 183 D7
Baesweiler D 183 D8
Baiersbronn D 187 D5
Baillonville B 184 D3
Bakel NL 183 C7
Balen B 183 C6
Balingen D 187 E6
Balve D 185 B8
Bammental D 187 C6
Barneveld NL 183 A7
Baronville F 186 D2
Barr F 186 E3
Bartenstein D 187 C8
Bartholomä D 187 D8
Barvaux B 184 D3
Basècles B 182 D3
Bassenge B 183 D7
Bastogne B 184 D4
Bathmen NL 183 A8
Battice B 183 D7
Baumholder D 186 B3
Bausendorf D 185 D6
Bavel NL 182 B5
Bayon F 186 E1
Beaumont B 184 D1
Beauraing B 184 D2
Becherbach D 186 B4
Bechhofen D 186 C3
Bechtheim D 187 B5
Beckingen D 186 C2
Beckum D 185 A9
Bedburg D 183 D9
Bedburg-Hau D 183 B8
Beek NL 183 B7
Beek NL 183 B7
Beekbergen NL 183 A7
Beerfelden D 187 B6
Beernem B 182 C2
Beers NL 183 B7
Beerse B 182 C5
Beersel B 182 D4
Beerst B 182 C1
Beesd NL 183 B6
Begijnendijk B 182 C5
Behren-lès-Forbach F 186 C2
Beilstein D 187 C7
Beimerstetten D 187 E8
Belfeld NL 183 C8
Bell D 185 D7
Bell (Hunsrück) D 185 D7
Bellenberg D 187 E9
Belles-Forêts F 186 D2
Bellheim D 187 C5
Belœil B 182 D3
Beltheim D 185 D7
Beltrum NL 183 A9
Bemmel NL 183 B7
Bendorf D 185 D8
Beneden-Leeuwen NL 183 B6
Bénestroff F 186 D2
Benfeld F 186 E4
Bennebroek NL 182 A5
Bennekom NL 183 A7
Bensheim D 187 B6
Bentelo NL 183 A9
Berchem B 182 D3
Berg D 183 D9
Berg L 184 E5
Berg NL 183 D7
Berg NL 183 D7
Berg (Pfalz) D 187 D5
Bergen op Zoom NL 182 C4
Bergeyk NL 183 C6
Bergharen NL 183 B7
Berghaupten D 186 E4
Bergheim (Erft) D 183 D9
Berghem NL 183 B7
Berghülen D 187 E8
Bergisch Gladbach D 183 D10
Bergkamen D 185 A8
Bergneustadt D 185 B8
Bergschenhoek NL 182 B5
Bergtheim D 187 B9
Beringe NL 183 C7
Beringen B 183 C6
Berkel NL 182 B4
Berkel-Enschot NL 183 B6
Berlicum NL 183 B6
Bernissart B 182 E3
Bernkastel-Kues D 185 E7
Bernstadt D 187 D9
Bertogne B 184 D4
Bertrange L 186 B1
Bertrichamps F 186 E2
Bertrix B 184 E3
Beselich-Obertiefenbach D 185 D9
Besigheim D 187 D7
Bessenbach D 187 B7
Best NL 183 B6
Bestwig D 185 B9
Betschdorf F 186 D4
Bettelainville F 186 C1
Bettembourg L 186 B1
Bettendorf L 184 E5
Bettingen D 185 E5
Betzdorf D 185 C8
Betzdorf L 186 B1
Beuningen NL 183 B7
Beuvrages F 182 E2
Beveren B 182 C4
Beverlo B 183 C6
Bexbach D 186 C3
Biberach D 186 E5
Biblis D 187 B5
Bieber D 187 A7
Biebesheim am Rhein D 187 B5
Bietigheim D 187 D5
Bietigheim-Bissingen D 187 D7
Bièvre B 184 E3
Billigheim D 187 C7
Bilthoven NL 183 A6
Bilzen B 183 D7
Binche B 182 E4
Bingen am Rhein D 185 E8
Bingerden NL 183 B8
Birkenau D 187 B6
Birkenfeld D 186 B3
Birkenfeld D 187 B8
Birkenfeld D 187 D6
Birken-Honigsessen D 185 C8
Birresborn D 185 D6
Bischbrunn D 187 B7
Bischheim F 186 D4
Bischoffsheim F 186 E3
Bischofsheim D 185 E9
Bischwiller F 186 D4
Bisingen D 187 E6
Bissen L 184 E5
Bitburg D 185 E6
Bitche F 186 C3
Bladel NL 183 C6
Blainville-sur-l'Eau F 186 D1
Blâmont F 186 D2
Blankenberge B 182 C2
Blankenheim D 183 E9
Blankenrath D 185 D7
Blaricum NL 183 A6
Blaton B 182 D3
Blaubeuren D 187 E8
Blaufelden D 187 C8
Blaustein D 187 E8
Blegny B 183 D7
Bléharies B 182 D2
Bleialf D 185 D5
Bleidenstadt D 185 D9
Bleiswijk NL 182 A5
Blerick NL 183 C8
Bleskensgraaf NL 182 B5
Blieskastel D 186 C3
Bobenheim-Roxheim D 187 B5
Böblingen D 187 D7
Bocholt B 183 C7
Bocholt D 183 B9
Bochum D 185 B7
Bockenheim an der Weinstraße D 187 B5
Bodegraven NL 182 A5
Bodelshausen D 187 E6
Bodenheim D 185 E9
Boechout B 182 C4
Boekel NL 183 B7
Boekhoute B 182 C3
Bogny-sur-Meuse F 184 E2
Böhl D 187 C5
Bolanden D 186 B5
Bolnes NL 182 B5
Bomal B 184 D4
Bondorf D 187 D6
Bondues F 182 D2
Bönen D 185 A8
Bonheiden B 182 C5
Bonn D 183 D10
Bönnigheim D 187 C7
Boom B 182 C4
Boortmeerbeek B 182 D5
Boppard D 185 D8
Borculo NL 183 A9
Borg D 186 B1
Borgloon B 183 D6
Borken D 183 B9
Born NL 183 C7
Borne NL 183 A9
Bornem B 182 C4
Bornerbroek NL 183 A9
Bornheim D 183 D9
Bornhofen D 185 D8
Bornich D 185 D8
Borssele NL 182 C3
Boskoop NL 182 A5
Bottrop D 183 B9
Bouillon B 184 E3
Boulay-Moselle F 186 C1
Bourdonnay F 186 D2
Bourscheid L 184 E5
Bousse F 186 C1
Boussu B 182 E3
Boutersem B 182 D5
Bouxières-aux-Dames F 186 D1
Bouxwiller F 186 D3
Bouzonville F 186 C2
Bovigny B 184 D4
Boxberg D 187 C8
Boxmeer NL 183 B7
Boxtel NL 183 B6
Brachbach D 185 C8
Brackenheim D 187 C7
Braine-l'Alleud B 182 D4
Braine-le-Comte B 182 D4
Braives B 183 D6
Brakel B 182 D3
Brasschaat B 182 C4
Braubach D 185 D8
Brauneberg D 185 E6
Braunfels D 185 C9
Braunsbach D 187 C8
Brecht B 182 C5
Breckerfeld D 185 B7
Breda NL 182 B5
Bredene B 182 C1
Bredevoort NL 183 B9
Bree B 183 C7
Breidenbach F 186 C3
Breitenbach D 186 C3
Breitscheid D 183 C9
Breitscheid D 185 C7
Breitscheid D 185 C9
Bremm D 185 D7
Brensbach D 187 B6
Breskens NL 182 C3
Bretten D 187 C6
Bretzenheim D 185 E8
Bretzfeld D 187 C7
Breuberg-Neustadt D 187 B7
Breugel NL 183 B7
Breukelen NL 183 A6
Briedel D 185 D7
Brielle NL 182 B4
Brin-sur-Seille F 186 D1
Broekhuizenvorst NL 183 C8
Brohl D 185 D7
Brouvelieures F 186 E2
Brouwershaven NL 182 B3
Bruchköbel D 187 A6
Bruchmühlbach D 186 C3
Bruchsal D 187 C6
Bruchweiler-Bärenbach D 186 C4
Brücken D 186 B3
Brücken (Pfalz) D 186 C3
Brugelette B 182 D3
Bruges B 182 C2
Brugge B 182 C2
Brüggen D 183 C8
Brühl D 183 D9
Brühl D 187 C6
Bruinisse NL 182 B4
Brûly B 184 E2
Brumath F 186 D4
Brummen NL 183 A8
Brunehamel F 184 E1
Brunssum NL 183 D7
Brussel B 182 D4
Bruttig-Fankel D 185 D7
Bruxelles B 182 D4
Büchel D 185 D7
Buchen (Odenwald) D 187 B7
Büchenbeuren D 185 E7
Buchholz (Westerwald) D 185 C7
Budel NL 183 C7
Budenheim D 185 D9
Büdesheim D 187 A6
Buer D 183 B10
Buggenhout B 182 C4
Bühl D 186 D5
Bühlertal D 187 D5
Bühlertann D 187 C8
Bühlerzell D 187 C8
Bullay D 185 D7
Büllingen B 183 E8
Bundenbach D 185 E7
Bunschoten-Spakenburg NL 183 A6
Burbach D 185 C9
Burdinne B 183 D6
Buren NL 183 B6
Burgbrohl D 185 D7
Burgh-Haamstede NL 182 B3
Burgsinn D 187 A8
Bürgstadt D 187 B7
Burladingen D 187 E7
Bürstadt D 187 B5
Bussum NL 183 A6
Bütgenbach B 183 E8
Büttelborn D 187 B6
Bütthard D 187 B8
Buurse NL 183 A9

C

Calw D 187 D6
Capelle aan de IJssel NL 182 B5
Carling F 186 C2
Carlsberg D 186 C5
Carvin F 182 E1
Castrop-Rauxel D 185 A7
Cattenom F 186 C1
Ceintrey F 186 D1
Celles B 182 D2
Cerfontaine B 184 D1
Chaam NL 182 C5
Chaligny F 186 D1
Champigneulles F 186 D1
Chapelle-lez-Herlaimont B 182 E4
Charleroi B 182 E4
Charmes F 186 E1
Chastre B 182 D5
Château-Salins F 186 D2
Châtelet B 184 D2
Châtel-sur-Moselle F 186 E1
Châtenois F 186 E3
Chaudfontaine B 183 D7
Chavelot F 186 E1
Chièvres B 182 D3
Chimay B 184 D1
Chooz F 184 D2
Ciney B 184 D3
Cirey-sur-Vezouze F 186 D2
Clavier B 183 E6
Clervaux L 184 D5
Clinge NL 182 C4
Cochem D 185 D7
Coesfeld D 183 B10
Colijnsplaat NL 182 B3
Colroy-la-Grande F 186 E3
Comblain-au-Pont B 183 E7
Comines B 182 D1
Condé-sur-l'Escaut F 182 E3
Consdorf L 186 B1
Contwig D 186 C3
Cothen NL 183 A6
Courcelles B 182 E4
Courcelles-Chaussy F 186 C1
Courcelles-sur-Nied F 186 C1
Courrières F 182 E1
Courtrai B 182 D2
Court-St-Etienne B 182 D5
Couvin B 184 D2
Crailsheim D 187 C9
Creglingen D 187 C9
Créhange F 186 C2
Creutzwald F 186 C2
Crévéchamps F 186 D1
Cuijk NL 183 B7
Culemborg NL 183 B6
Custines F 186 D1
Cysoing F 182 D2

D

Daaden D 185 C8
Dabo F 186 D3
Dahlem D 185 D6
Dahlhausen D 183 C10
Dahn D 186 C4
Daknam B 182 C3
Daleiden D 184 D5
Dalhem B 183 D7
Dalstein F 186 C1
Damas-aux-Bois F 186 E1
Dambach-la-Ville F 186 E3
Damelevières F 186 D1
Damme B 182 C2
Darmstadt D 187 B6
Datteln D 185 A7
Daun D 185 D6
De Bilt NL 183 A6
Deerlijk B 182 D2
Deggingen D 187 D8
De Haan B 182 C2
Deidesheim D 187 C5
Deinze B 182 D3
Delden NL 183 A9
Delft NL 182 A4
Delme F 186 D1
De Meern NL 183 A6
Den Bommel NL 182 B4
Denderleeuw B 182 D4
Dendermonde B 182 C4
Den Dungen NL 183 B6
Denekamp NL 183 A10
Den Haag NL 182 A4
Denkendorf D 187 D7
Dentergem B 182 D2
Dernau D 183 D10
Dessel B 183 C6
De Steeg NL 183 A8
Destelbergen B 182 C3
Dettelbach D 187 B9
Dettenhausen D 187 D7
Dettingen an der Erms D 187 D7
Dettwiller F 186 D3
Deurne NL 183 C7
Deventer NL 183 A8
Deville F 184 E2
Dhron D 185 E6
Didam NL 183 B8
Dieblich D 185 D7
Dieburg D 187 B6
Diekirch L 184 E5
Dielheim D 187 C6
Diemen NL 182 A5
Dienheim D 185 E9
Diepenbeek B 183 D6
Diepenheim NL 183 A9
Diepenveen NL 183 A8
Dierdorf D 185 C8
Dieren NL 183 A8
Diessen NL 183 C6
Diest B 183 D6
Dietzenbach D 187 A6
Dietzhölztal-Ewersbach D 185 C9
Dieuze F 186 D2
Dikkebus B 182 D1
Diksmuide B 182 C1
Dilbeek B 182 D4
Dillenburg D 185 C9
Dillingen (Saar) D 186 C2
Dilsen B 183 C7
Dinant B 184 D2
Dinslaken D 183 B9
Dinteloord NL 182 B4
Dinther NL 183 B6
Dinxperlo NL 183 B8
Dirksland NL 182 B4
Dirmstein D 187 B5
Dison B 183 D7
Ditzingen D 187 D7
Dockweiler D 185 D6
Dodewaard NL 183 B7
Doesburg NL 183 A8
Doetinchem NL 183 B8
Doische B 184 D2
Dombasle-sur-Meurthe F 186 D1
Domburg NL 182 B3
Domèvre-sur-Vezouze F 186 D2
Dommershausen D 185 D7
Dongen NL 182 B5
Donk NL 183 B7
Donzdorf D 187 D8
Doorn NL 183 A6
Doornspijk NL 183 A7
Dordrecht NL 182 B5
Dorlisheim F 186 D3
Dormagen D 183 C9
Dornburg-Frickhofen D 185 C9
Dornhan D 187 E6
Dornstadt D 187 E8
Dornstetten D 187 E5
Dorsten D 183 B9
Dorstfeld D 185 A7
Dortmund D 185 A7
Dörzbach D 187 C8
Dossenheim D 187 C6
Dreieich D 187 A6
Dreis D 185 E6
Drensteinfurt D 185 A8
Dreumel NL 183 B6
Driebergen NL 183 A6
Driedorf D 185 C9
Drolshagen D 185 B8
Drongen B 182 C3
Drulingen F 186 D3
Drusenheim F 186 D4
Druten NL 183 B7
Dudelange L 186 C1
Dudeldorf D 185 E6
Duffel B 182 C5
Duisburg D 183 C9
Dümpelfeld D 183 E9
Düngenheim D 185 D7
Durbach D 186 D5
Durbuy B 184 D3
Düren D 183 D8
Durmersheim D 187 D5
Düsseldorf D 183 C9
Dussen NL 182 B5

E

Eberbach D 187 C6
Ebersbach an der Fils D 187 D8
Ebersmunster F 186 E4
Ebhausen D 187 D6
Écaussinnes-d'Enghien B 182 D4
Echt NL 183 C7
Echternach L 185 E5
Eckbolsheim F 186 D4
Ede NL 183 A7
Edegem B 182 C4
Edenkoben D 186 C5
Edesheim D 186 C5
Ediger-Eller D 185 D7
Eefde NL 183 A8
Eeklo B 182 C3
Eerbeek NL 183 A8
Eernegem B 182 C2
Eersel NL 183 C6
Eggenstein-Leopoldshafen D 187 C5
Eghezée B 182 D5
Ehingen (Donau) D 187 E8
Ehningen D 187 D6
Ehringshausen D 185 C9
Eibelstadt D 187 B9
Eibergen NL 183 A9
Eich D 187 B5
Eichenbühl D 187 B7
Eijsden NL 183 D7
Eindhoven NL 183 C6
Einville-au-Jard F 186 D1
Eisden B 183 D7
Eisenberg (Pfalz) D 186 B5
Eislingen (Fils) D 187 D8
Eitelborn D 185 D8
Eitorf D 185 C7
Ekeren B 182 C4
Eksaarde B 182 C3
Eksel B 183 C6
Elchingen D 187 E9
Elfershausen D 187 A8
Elkenroth D 185 C8
Ellenberg D 187 C9
Ellezelles B 182 D3
Ellwangen (Jagst) D 187 D9
Elsdorf D 183 D9
Elsenborn B 183 E8
Elsenfeld D 187 B7
Elsloo NL 183 D7
Elspeet NL 183 A7
Elst NL 183 B6
Elst NL 183 B7
Eltville am Rhein D 185 D9
Elz D 185 D9
Emmelshausen D 185 D8
Emmerich D 183 B8
Empel NL 183 B6
Empfingen D 187 E6
Emptinne B 184 D3
Emst NL 183 A7
Engden D 183 A10
Engelskirchen D 185 C7
Enghien B 182 D4
Engis B 183 D6
Engstingen D 187 E7
Eningen unter Achalm D 187 E7
Enkenbach D 186 C4
Enkirch D 185 E7
Ennepetal D 185 B7
Ennery F 186 C1
Enschede NL 183 A9
Ensdorf D 186 C2
Ense D 185 B9
Ensheim D 186 C3
Enter NL 183 A9
Enzklösterle D 187 D5
Epe NL 183 A7
Epfendorf D 187 E6
Eppelborn D 186 C2
Eppelheim D 187 C6
Eppenbrunn D 186 C4
Eppertshausen D 187 B6
Eppingen D 187 C6
Eppstein D 187 A5
Erbach D 187 B7
Erbach D 187 E8
Erftstadt D 183 D9
Erkelenz D 183 C8
Erlenbach am Main D 187 B7
Ermelo NL 183 A7
Erndtebrück D 185 C9
Erp NL 183 B7
Erpel D 185 C7
Erquelinnes B 184 D1
Erstein F 186 E4
Ertvelde B 182 C3
Erwitte D 185 A9
Erzhausen D 187 B6
Esch NL 183 B6
Eschau D 187 B7
Eschau F 186 E4
Eschborn D 187 A6
Eschenburg-Eibelshausen D 185 C9
Esch-sur-Sûre L 184 E4
Eschweiler D 183 D8
Eslohe (Sauerland) D 185 B9
Esneux B 183 D7
Essen B 182 C4
Essen D 183 C10
Essingen D 187 D9
Esslingen am Neckar D 187 D7
Estaimpuis B 182 D2
Estenfeld D 187 B9
Étival-Clairefontaine F 186 E2
Ettelbruck L 184 E5
Ettenheim D 186 E4
Etten-Leur NL 182 B5
Ettlingen D 187 D5
Ettringen D 185 D7
Eubigheim D 187 B8
Euerdorf D 187 A9
Eupen B 183 D8
Euskirchen D 183 D9
Eußenheim D 187 A8
Eutingen im Gäu D 187 E6
Everdingen NL 183 B6
Evergem B 182 C3

F

Faches-Thumesnil F 182 D2
Faid D 185 D7
Faimes B 183 D6
Falck F 186 C2
Fameck F 186 C1
Farciennes B 182 E5
Farébersviller F 186 C2
Faulbach D 187 B7
Faulquemont F 186 C2
Feilbingert D 185 E8
Fell D 186 B2
Fellbach D 187 D7
Fénétrange F 186 D3
Fépin F 184 D2
Ferrières B 183 E7
Ferschweiler D 185 E5
Fichtenberg D 187 D8
Fijnaart NL 182 B4
Finnentrop D 185 B8
Fischbach D 186 B3
Fischbach bei Dahn D 186 C4
Flavigny-sur-Moselle F 186 D1
Flein D 187 C7
Flémalle B 183 D6
Fléron B 183 D7
Flers-en-Escrebieux F 182 E2
Fleurus B 182 E5
Flines-lez-Raches F 182 E2
Florange F 186 C1
Floreffe B 182 E5
Florennes B 184 D2
Flörsbach D 187 A7
Flörsheim am Main D 187 A5
Flörsheim-Dalsheim D 187 B5
Focant B 184 D3
Föhren D 185 E6
Folschviller F 186 C2
Fontaine-l'Évêque B 182 E4
Forbach D 187 D5
Forbach F 186 C2
Forchtenberg D 187 C8
Forst D 187 C6
Fosses-la-Ville B 184 D2
Fraire B 184 D2
Frameries B 182 E3
Frammersbach D 187 A7
Francorchamps B 183 E7
Frankenthal (Pfalz) D 187 B5
Frankfurt am Main D 187 A6
Frasnes-lez-Buissenal B 182 D3
Frasnes-lez-Gosselies B 182 D4
Frechen D 183 D9
Freinsheim D 187 B5
Freisen D 186 B3
Freistroff F 186 C1
Fresnes-sur-Escaut F 182 E3
Freudenberg D 185 C8
Freudenberg D 187 B7
Freudenburg D 186 B2
Freudenstadt D 187 E5
Freyming-Merlebach F 186 C2
Friedewald D 185 C8
Friedrichsdorf D 187 A6
Friesenhagen D 185 C8
Friesenheim D 186 E4
Frisange L 186 B1
Frœschwiller F 186 D4
Fromelennes F 184 D2
Fröndenberg D 185 B8
Frouard F 186 D1
Fumay F 184 E2
Fürth D 187 B6

G

Gaanderen NL 183 B8
Gaggenau D 187 D5
Gaildorf D 187 D8
Gambsheim F 186 D4
Gammertingen D 187 E7
Gand B 182 C3
Ganshoren B 182 D4
Garderen NL 183 A7
Gärtringen D 187 D6
Gau-Algesheim D 185 E9
Gaukönigshofen D 187 B8
Gau-Odernheim D 185 E9
Gavere B 182 D3
Gebhardshain D 185 C8
Gechingen D 187 D6
Gedinne B 184 E2
Geel B 183 C6
Geertruidenberg NL 182 B5
Geesteren NL 183 A9
Geetbets B 183 D6
Geffen NL 183 B6
Geilenkirchen D 183 D8
Geiselbach D 187 A7
Geisenheim D 185 E8
Geislingen D 187 E6
Geislingen an der Steige D 187 D8
Geispolsheim F 186 D4
Gelchsheim D 187 B9
Geldermalsen NL 183 B6
Geldern D 183 B8
Geldersheim D 187 A9
Geldrop NL 183 C7
Geleen NL 183 D7
Gelnhausen D 187 A7
Gelsenkirchen D 183 B10
Gembloux B 182 D5
Gemert NL 183 B7
Gemmingen D 187 C6
Gemünden D 185 E7
Gemünden am Main D 187 A8
Genappe B 182 D4
Gendringen NL 183 B8
Gendt NL 183 B7
Gengenbach D 186 E5
Genk B 183 D7
Gennep NL 183 B7
Gensingen D 185 E8
Gent B 182 C3
Geraardsbergen B 182 D3
Gerabronn D 187 C8
Gerbéviller F 186 E2
Gerbrunn D 187 B8
Gerchsheim D 187 B8
Gerlingen D 187 D7
Germersheim D 187 C5
Gernsbach D 187 D5
Gernsheim D 187 B5
Gerolstein D 185 D6
Gerpinnes B 184 D2
Gersheim D 186 C3
Gerstetten D 187 D9
Gerstheim F 186 E4
Gescher D 183 B10
Gespunsart F 184 E2
Gesves B 184 D3
Gevelsberg D 185 B7
Ghislenghien B 182 D3
Giebelstadt D 187 B8
Gierle B 182 C5
Gillenfeld D 185 D6
Gilze NL 182 B5
Gingelom B 183 D6
Gingen an der Fils D 187 D8
Ginsheim D 185 E9
Gistel B 182 C1
Givet F 184 D2
Gladbeck D 183 B9
Glanerbrug NL 183 A9
Gläshütten D 187 A5
Goch D 183 B8

Goddelau D 187 B6
Goedereede NL 182 B3
Goes NL 182 B3
Göggingen D 187 D8
Goirle NL 183 B6
Göllheim D 186 B5
Gomadingen D 187 E7
Gomaringen D 187 E7
Gondelsheim D 187 C6
Gondershausen D 185 D7
Gondorf D 185 D7
Goor NL 183 A9
Göppingen D 187 D8
Gorinchem NL 182 B5
Gorssel NL 183 A8
Gorxheimertal D 187 B6
Gouda NL 182 A5
Goudswaard NL 182 B4
Gouvy B 184 D4
Graben-Neudorf D 187 C5
Grâce-Hollogne B 183 D6
Gräfendorf D 187 A8
Grafenrheinfeld D 187 B9
Grandvillers F 186 E2
Grave NL 183 B7
Greifenstein D 185 C9
Grevenbicht NL 183 C7
Grevenbroich D 183 C9
Grevenmacher L 186 B1
Grez-Doiceau B 182 D5
Gries F 186 D4
Griesbach D 187 E5
Griesheim D 187 B6
Grimbergen B 182 D4
Grobbendonk B 182 C5
Groenlo NL 183 A9
Groesbeek NL 183 B7
Gronau (Westfalen) D 183 A10
Groß-Bieberau D 187 B6
Großbottwar D 187 D7
Grosselfingen D 187 E6
Groß-Gerau D 187 B5
Großheubach D 187 B7
Großlangheim D 187 B9
Großlittgen D 185 D6
Großmaischeid D 185 C8
Großostheim D 187 B7
Großrinderfeld D 187 B8
Groß-Rohrheim D 187 B5
Großrosseln D 186 C2
Groß-Umstadt D 187 B6
Großwallstadt D 187 B7
Groß-Zimmern D 187 B6
Grostenquin F 186 D2
Grubbenvorst NL 183 C8
Grünsfeld D 187 B8
Grünstadt D 187 B5
Gschwend D 187 D8
Guénange F 186 C1
Güglingen D 187 C6
Gulpen NL 183 D7
Gummersbach D 185 B8
Gundelsheim D 187 C7
Gundershoffen F 186 D4
Guntersblum D 185 E9
Güntersleben D 187 B8
Gusterath D 186 B2
Gutach (Schwarzwaldbahn) D 187 E5

H

Haacht B 182 D5
Haaften NL 183 B6
Haaksbergen NL 183 A9
Haaltert B 182 D4
Haaren NL 183 B6
Haarlem NL 182 A5
Haastrecht NL 182 B5
Hachenburg D 185 C8
Hackenheim D 185 E8
Hadamar D 185 D9
Haelen NL 183 C7
Hagen D 185 B7
Hagenbach D 187 C5
Hagondange F 186 C1
Haguenau F 186 D4
Hahnstätten D 185 D9
Haibach D 187 B7
Haiger D 185 C9
Haigerloch D 187 E6
Haiterbach D 187 D6
Halen B 183 D6
Halfweg NL 182 A5
Halle B 182 D4
Halle NL 183 B8
Halluin B 182 D2
Halsenbach D 185 D8
Halsteren NL 182 B4
Halstroff F 186 C1
Haltern D 183 B10
Halver D 185 B7
Hambach F 186 C3
Hambrücken D 187 C6
Hamm D 185 A8
Hamm (Sieg) D 185 C8
Hamme B 182 C4
Hammelburg D 187 A8
Hamme-Mille B 182 D5
Hamminkeln D 183 B9
Hamoir B 183 E7
Hamois B 184 D3
Hamont B 183 C7
Hampont F 186 D2
Ham-sous-Varsberg F 186 C2
Ham-sur-Heure B 184 D1
Hanau D 187 A6
Handzame B 182 C2
Hannut B 183 D6
Han-sur-Nied F 186 D1
Hapert NL 183 C6
Haps NL 183 B7
Harderwijk NL 183 A7
Hardheim D 187 B7
Hardinxveld-Giessendam NL 182 B5
Harelbeke B 182 D2
Hargesheim D 185 E8
Hargimont B 184 D3
Hargnies F 184 D2
Harmelen NL 182 A5
Harnes F 182 E1
Haroué F 186 E1
Harthausen D 187 C5
Haslach im Kinzigtal D 186 E5
Hasselt B 183 D6
Haßloch D 187 C5
Haßmersheim D 187 C7
Hastière-Lavaux B 184 D2
Hattersheim am Main D 187 A5
Hattert D 185 C8
Hattingen D 183 C10
Hatzenbühl D 187 C5
Haubourdin F 182 D1
Hauenstein D 186 C4
Hausach D 187 E5
Hausen bei Würzburg D 187 B9
Haut-Fays B 184 D3
Havelange B 184 D3
Haversin B 184 D3
Hayange F 186 C1
Haybes F 184 D2
Hayingen D 187 E7
Hazerswoude-Rijndijk NL 182 A5
Hechingen D 187 E6
Hechtel B 183 C6
Heddesheim D 187 C6
Hedel NL 183 B6
Heek D 183 A10
Heel NL 183 C7
Heemstede NL 182 A5
Heenvliet NL 182 B4
Heer B 184 D2
Heerde NL 183 A8
Heerewaarden NL 183 B6
Heerlen NL 183 D7
Heers B 183 D6
Heesch NL 183 B7
Heeswijk NL 183 B6
Heeten NL 183 A8
Heeze NL 183 C7
Heidelberg D 187 C6
Heiden D 183 B9
Heidenheim an der Brenz D 187 D9
Heigenbrücken D 187 A7
Heilbronn D 187 C7
Heiligenhaus D 183 C9
Heimbach D 186 B3
Heimbuchenthal D 187 B7
Heimsheim D 187 D6
Heinkenszand NL 182 C3
Heino NL 183 A8
Heinsberg D 183 C8
Heisingen D 183 C10
Heist-op-den-Berg B 182 C5
Hekelgem B 182 D4
Helchteren B 183 C6
Heldenbergen D 187 A6
Hellendoorn NL 183 A8
Hellenthal D 183 E8
Hellevoetsluis NL 182 B4
Helmond NL 183 C7
Helmstadt D 187 B8
Heltersberg D 186 C4
Helvoirt NL 183 B6
Hem F 182 D2
Hemer D 185 B8
Hemsbach D 187 B6
Hengelo NL 183 A8
Hengelo NL 183 A9
Hengevelde NL 183 A9
Hénin-Beaumont F 182 E1
Hennef (Sieg) D 185 C7
Hennweiler D 185 E7
Heppen B 183 C6
Heppenheim (Bergstraße) D 187 B6
Herbeumont B 184 E3
Herborn D 185 C9
Herbrechtingen D 187 D9
Herdecke D 185 B7
Herdorf D 185 C8
Herent B 182 D5
Herentals B 182 C5
Herenthout B 182 C5
Herk-de-Stad B 183 D6
Herkenbosch NL 183 C8
Herkingen NL 182 B4
Hermersberg D 186 C4
Hermeskeil D 186 B2
Herne B 182 D4
Herne D 185 A7
Héron B 183 D6
Herrenberg D 187 D6
Herrlisheim F 186 D4
Herschbach D 185 C8
Herscheid D 185 B8
Herschweiler-Pettersheim D 186 C3
Herselt B 182 C5
Herstal B 183 D7
Herten D 183 B10
Herve B 183 D7
Herwijnen NL 183 B6
Herzele B 182 D3
Herzogenrath D 183 D8
Hespérange L 186 B1
Heßheim D 187 B5
Hettange-Grande F 186 C1
Hettenleidelheim D 186 B5
Hetzerath D 185 E6
Heubach D 187 D8
Heukelum NL 183 B6
Heusden B 183 C6
Heusden NL 183 B6
Heusenstamm D 187 A6
Heusweiler D 186 C2
Heythuysen NL 183 C7
Hilchenbach D 185 C9
Hilden D 183 C9
Hillegom NL 182 A5
Hillesheim D 185 D6
Hilsenheim F 186 E4
Hilvarenbeek NL 183 C6
Hilversum NL 183 A6
Hinterweidenthal D 186 C4
Hirrlingen D 187 E6
Hirschhorn (Neckar) D 187 C6
Hochfelden F 186 D4
Hochspeyer D 186 C4
Hochstadt (Pfalz) D 187 C5
Hochstetten-Dhaun D 185 E7
Höchst im Odenwald D 187 B6
Hockenheim D 187 C6
Hoek NL 182 C3
Hoek van Holland NL 182 B4
Hoenderloo NL 183 A7
Hœnheim F 186 D4
Hoensbroek NL 183 D7
Hœrdt F 186 D4
Hoeselt B 183 D6
Hoevelaken NL 183 A6
Hoeven NL 182 B5
Hof D 185 C9
Hofheim am Taunus D 187 A5
Hohberg D 186 E4
Höhn D 185 C8
Höhr-Grenzhausen D 185 D8
Hollange B 184 E4
Holten NL 183 A8
Holzappel D 185 D8
Holzgerlingen D 187 D7
Holzhausen an der Haide D 185 D8
Holzheim D 187 E9
Holzwickede D 185 A8
Hombourg-Budange F 186 C1
Hombourg-Haut F 186 C2
Homburg D 186 C3
Hoofddorp NL 182 A5
Hoogerheide NL 182 C4
Hoog-Keppel NL 183 B8
Hoogland NL 183 A6
Hoogstraten B 182 C5
Hoogvliet NL 182 B4
Hoornaar NL 182 B5
Hoppstädten D 186 B3
Horb am Neckar D 187 E6
Hörde D 185 B7
Hornbach D 186 C3
Horst NL 183 C8
Hösbach D 187 A7
Hosingen L 184 D5
Hotton B 184 D3
Houffalize B 184 D4
Houten NL 183 A6
Houthalen B 183 C6
Houthulst B 182 D1
Houyet B 184 D3
Hückelhoven D 183 C8
Hückeswagen D 185 B7
Huijbergen NL 182 C4
Huissen NL 183 B7
Huizen NL 183 A6
Hüls D 183 C8
Hulsberg NL 183 D7
Hulst NL 182 C4
Hummelo NL 183 A8
Hundsangen D 185 D8
Hünfelden-Kirberg D 185 D9
Hunsel NL 183 C7
Hunspach F 186 D4
Hünxe D 183 B9
Hürth D 183 D9
Hütschenhausen D 186 C3
Hüttisheim D 187 E8
Hüttlingen D 187 D9
Huy B 183 D6
Hymont F 186 E1

I

Ichenheim D 186 E4
Ichtegem B 182 C2
Idar-Oberstein D 186 B3
Idstein D 185 D9
Ieper B 182 D1
Iffezheim D 187 D5
Igel D 186 B2
Igersheim D 187 C8
Iggelheim D 187 C5
Igney F 186 E1
IJsselstein NL 183 A6
IJzendijke NL 182 C3
Illingen D 186 C3
Illingen D 187 D6
Illkirch-Graffenstaden F 186 D4
Ilsfeld D 187 C7
Incourt B 182 D5
Ingelfingen D 187 C8
Ingelheim am Rhein D 185 E9
Ingelmunster B 182 D2
Ingwiller F 186 D3
Insming F 186 D2
Iphofen D 187 B9
Ippesheim D 187 B9
Irrel D 185 E5
Irsch D 186 B2
Iserlohn D 185 B8
Ispringen D 187 D6
Isselburg D 183 B8
Issum D 183 B8
Ittre B 182 D4
Ixelles B 182 D4
Izegem B 182 D2

J

Jabbeke B 182 C2
Jagsthausen D 187 C7
Jagstzell D 187 C9
Jalhay B 183 D7
Jarville-la-Malgrange F 186 D1
Jemeppe B 182 E5
Jockgrim D 187 C5
Jodoigne B 182 D5
Jouy-aux-Arches F 186 C1
Jüchen D 183 C8
Jülich D 183 D8
Jungingen D 187 E7
Junglinster L 186 B1
Jünkerath D 185 D6
Juprelle B 183 D7
Jurbise B 182 D3

K

Kaarst D 183 C9
Kaatsheuvel NL 183 B6
Kahl am Main D 187 A7
Kaisersesch D 185 D7
Kaiserslautern D 186 C4
Kalkar D 183 B8
Kall D 183 D9
Kalmthout B 182 C4
Kamen D 185 A8
Kamerik NL 182 A5
Kamp D 185 D8
Kampenhout B 182 D5
Kämpfelbach D 187 D6
Kamp-Lintfort D 183 C9
Kandel D 187 C5
Kapelle NL 182 C3
Kapellen B 182 C4
Kapelle-op-den-Bos B 182 C4
Kappel D 185 E7
Kappel-Grafenhausen D 186 E4
Kappelrodeck D 186 D5
Kaprijke B 182 C3
Karben D 187 A6
Karden D 185 D7
Karlsbad D 187 D6
Karlsdorf-Neuthard D 187 C6
Karlsruhe D 187 C5
Karlstadt D 187 B8
Kastellaun D 185 D7
Kasterlee B 182 C5
Katwijk aan Zee NL 182 A4
Katzenelnbogen D 185 D8
Katzweiler D 186 B4
Kaub D 185 D8
Kaulille B 183 C7
Kautenbach L 184 E5
Kehl D 186 D4
Kehlen L 186 B1
Kehrig D 185 D7
Kelberg D 185 D6
Kelkheim (Taunus) D 187 A5
Kell D 186 B2
Kelmis B 183 D8
Kempen D 183 C8
Kempenich D 183 E10
Kenn D 185 E6
Kerkdriel NL 183 B6
Kerken D 183 C8
Kerkrade NL 183 D8
Kerkwijk NL 183 B6
Kerpen D 183 D9
Kessel B 182 C5
Kessel NL 183 C8
Kesteren NL 183 B7
Ketsch D 187 C6
Kettwig D 183 C9
Kevelaer D 183 B8
Kieldrecht B 182 C4
Kierspe D 185 B8
Kinderbeuern D 185 D7
Kindsbach D 186 C4
Kinrooi B 183 C7
Kippenheim D 186 E4
Kirchardt D 187 C6
Kirchberg (Hunsrück) D 185 E7
Kirchberg an der Jagst D 187 C8
Kirchellen D 183 B9
Kirchen (Sieg) D 185 C8
Kirchheim D 187 B8
Kirchheim am Neckar D 187 C7
Kirchheim-Bolanden D 186 B5
Kirchheim unter Teck D 187 D7
Kirchhundem D 185 B9
Kirchzell D 187 B7
Kirkel-Neuhäusel D 186 C3
Kirn D 185 E7
Kirschweiler D 186 B3
Kist D 187 B8
Kitzingen D 187 B9
Klaaswaal NL 182 B4
Klausen D 185 E6
Kleinblittersdorf D 186 C3
Kleinheubach D 187 B7
Kleinrinderfeld D 187 B8
Kleinwallstadt D 187 B7
Kleve D 183 B8
Klingenberg am Main D 187 B7
Kloetinge NL 182 C3
Kloosterzande NL 182 C4
Klotten D 185 D7
Klundert NL 182 B5
Knesselare B 182 C2
Knittlingen D 187 C6
Knokke-Heist B 182 C2
Kobern D 185 D7
Koblenz D 185 D8
Koekelare B 182 C1
Koersel B 183 C6
Koewacht NL 182 C3
Kolitzheim D 187 B9
Köln D 183 D9
Königheim D 187 B8
Königsbronn D 187 D9
Königstein im Taunus D 187 A5
Königswinter D 185 C7
Konz D 186 B2
Kootwijkerbroek NL 183 A7
Kopstal L 186 B1
Kordel D 185 E6
Kornwestheim D 187 D7
Körperich D 185 E5
Kortemark B 182 C2
Kortenhoef NL 183 A6
Kortessem B 183 D6
Kortgene NL 182 B3
Kortrijk B 182 D2
Kottenheim D 185 D7
Koudekerke NL 182 C3
Krabbendijke NL 182 C4
Kranenburg D 183 B8
Krautheim D 187 C8
Krefeld D 183 C9
Kreuzau D 183 D8
Kreuztal D 185 C8
Kreuzwertheim D 187 B8
Krimpen aan de IJssel NL 182 B5
Kronau D 187 C6
Kronberg im Taunus D 187 A5
Kröv D 185 E7
Kruft D 185 D7
Kruibeke B 182 C4
Kruiningen NL 182 C4
Kruishoutem B 182 D3
Kuchen D 187 D8
Külsheim D 187 B8
Kunrade NL 183 D7
Künzelsau D 187 C8
Kupferzell D 187 C8
Kuppenheim D 187 D5
Kürnach D 187 B9
Kürnbach D 187 C6
Kusel D 186 B3
Kusterdingen D 187 D7
Kuurne B 182 D2
Kwaadmechelen B 183 C6
Kyllburg D 185 D6

L

Laarne B 182 C3
La Broque F 186 E3
Lachen-Speyerdorf D 187 C5
Ladenburg D 187 C6
Lafrimbolle F 186 D3
Lage Mierde NL 183 C6
Lahnstein D 185 D8
Lahr (Schwarzwald) D 186 E4
Laichingen D 187 E8
Laifour F 184 E2
Lallaing F 182 E2
La Louvière B 182 E4
Lambersart F 182 D2
Lambrecht (Pfalz) D 186 C5
Lambsheim D 187 B5
Lampertheim D 187 B5
Lanaken B 183 D7
Landau in der Pfalz D 186 C5
Landen B 183 D6
Landersheim F 186 D3
Landgraaf NL 183 D8
Landscheid D 185 E6
Landsmeer NL 182 A5
Landstuhl D 186 C4
Langemark B 182 D1
Langen D 187 B6
Langenau D 187 E9
Langenaubach D 185 C9
Langenberg D 183 C10
Langenberg D 185 A9
Langenburg D 187 C8
Langenfeld (Rheinland) D 183 C9
Langenhahn D 185 C8
Langenlonsheim D 185 E8
Langenselbold D 187 A7
Langsur D 186 B2
Lannoy F 182 D2
La Petite-Pierre F 186 D3
Laren NL 183 A6
Laren NL 183 A8
La Roche-en-Ardenne B 184 D4
Larochette L 186 B1
Lasne B 182 D4
Lattrop NL 183 A9
Laubach D 185 D7
Lauda-Königshofen D 187 B8
Lauf D 186 D5
Laufach D 187 A7
Lauffen am Neckar D 187 C7
Lautenbach D 186 D5
Lauterbourg F 187 D5
Lauterecken D 186 B4
Lauterstein D 187 D8
La Wantzenau F 186 D4
Laxou F 186 D1
Lebach D 186 C2
Le Ban-St-Martin F 186 C1
Lebbeke B 182 C4
Lede B 182 D3
Ledegem B 182 D2
Leende NL 183 C7
Leerdam NL 183 B6
Leersum NL 183 A6
Leffinge B 182 C1
Leforest F 182 E2
Legden D 183 A10
Léglise B 184 E4
Lehmen D 185 D7
Le Hohwald F 186 E3
Leichlingen (Rheinland) D 183 C10
Leiden NL 182 A5
Leiderdorp NL 182 A5
Leidschendam NL 182 A4
Leimen D 187 C6
Leimuiden NL 182 A5
Leinfelden-Echterdingen D 187 D7
Leinzell D 187 D8
Leiwen D 185 E6
Lembeke B 182 C3
Lemberg D 186 C4
Lemberg F 186 C3
Lendelede B 182 D2
Léning F 186 D2
Lennestadt D 185 B9
Lenningen D 187 D7
Lens B 182 D3
Lent NL 183 B7
Leonberg D 187 D7
Leopoldsburg B 183 C6
Les Hautes-Rivières F 184 E2
Les Mazures F 184 E2
Lessines B 182 D3
Leun D 185 C9
Leusden NL 183 A6
Leutesdorf D 185 D7
Leuven B 182 D5
Leuze-en-Hainaut B 182 D3
Leverkusen D 183 C9
L'Hôpital F 186 C2
Libin B 184 E3
Libramont B 184 E3
Lichtaart B 182 C5
Lichtenau D 186 D5
Lichtenvoorde NL 183 B9
Lichtervelde B 182 C2
Liège B 183 D7
Liempde NL 183 B6
Lienden NL 183 B7
Lier B 182 C5
Lierneux B 184 D4
Lieser D 185 E7
Lieshout NL 183 B7
Liessel NL 183 C7
Ligneuville B 184 D5
Lille B 182 C5
Lille F 182 D2
Limbach D 186 C2
Limbach D 187 C7
Limbourg B 183 D7
Limburg an der Lahn D 185 D9
Limburgerhof D 187 C5
Lincent B 183 D6
Lindenfels D 187 B6
Lindlar D 185 B7
Lingenfeld D 187 C5
Lingolsheim F 186 D4
Linnich D 183 D8
Linz am Rhein D 185 C7
Lippstadt D 185 A9
Lisse NL 182 A5
Lissendorf D 185 D6
Lith NL 183 B6
Lixing-lès-St-Avold F 186 C2
Lobith NL 183 B8
Lochem NL 183 A8
Lochristi B 182 C3
Loenen NL 183 A8
Löf D 185 D7
Lohmar D 185 C7
Löhnberg D 185 C9
Lohr am Main D 187 B8
Lokeren B 182 C4
Lomme F 182 D1
Lommel B 183 C6
Londerzeel B 182 D4
Longeville-lès-St-Avold F 186 C2
Longlier B 184 E3
Lonneker NL 183 A9
Lonny F 184 E2
Lonsee D 187 D8
Lontzen B 183 D8
Loon op Zand NL 183 B6
Loos F 182 D2
Lopik NL 182 B5
Lorch D 185 D8
Lorch D 187 D8
Lorquin F 186 D2
Lorsch D 187 B6
Losheim D 186 B2
Loßburg D 187 E5
Losser NL 183 A9
Lotenhulle B 182 C2
Lottum NL 183 C8
Louvain B 182 D5
Louveigné B 183 D7
Lovendegem B 182 C3
Löwenstein D 187 C7
Lubbeek B 182 D5
Lüdenscheid D 185 B8
Lüdinghausen D 185 A7
Ludres F 186 D1
Ludwigsburg D 187 D7
Ludwigshafen am Rhein D 187 C5
Luik B 183 D7
Lummen B 183 D6
Lünebach D 185 D5
Lünen D 185 A8
Lunéville F 186 D1
Lunteren NL 183 A7
Luppy F 186 D1
Lustadt D 187 C5
Luttenberg NL 183 A8
Lützelbach D 187 B7
Lutzerath D 185 D7
Luxembourg L 186 B1
Luyksgestel NL 183 C6

M

Maarheeze NL 183 C7
Maarn NL 183 A6
Maarssen NL 183 A6
Maarssenbroek NL 183 A6
Maasbracht NL 183 C7
Maasbree NL 183 C8
Maasdam NL 182 B5
Maaseik B 183 C7
Maasland NL 182 B4
Maasmechelen B 183 D7
Maassluis NL 182 B4
Maastricht NL 183 D7
Machelen B 182 D4
Mackenbach D 186 C4
Made NL 182 B5
Magnières F 186 E2
Mahlberg D 186 E4
Maikammer D 186 C5
Mainaschaff D 187 B7
Mainbernheim D 187 B9
Mainhardt D 187 C8
Mainz D 185 D9
Maizières-lès-Metz F 186 C1
Malborn D 186 B2
Maldegem B 182 C2
Malden NL 183 B7
Malines B 182 C4
Malmédy B 183 E8
Malsch D 187 D5
Manage B 182 E4
Mandelbachtal-Ormesheim D 186 C3
Manderscheid D 185 D6
Manhay B 184 D4
Mannheim D 187 C5
Manternach L 186 B1
Marange-Silvange F 186 C1
Marbach am Neckar D 187 D7
Marche-en-Famenne B 184 D3
Marchiennes F 182 E2
Marchin B 183 E6
Marcq-en-Barœul F 182 D2
Margraten NL 183 D7
Mariembourg B 184 D2
Marienheide D 185 B8
Markelo NL 183 A9
Markgröningen D 187 D7
Marktbreit D 187 B9
Marktheidenfeld D 187 B8
Marktseft D 187 B9
Marl D 183 B10
Marlenheim F 186 D4
Marly F 186 C1
Marmoutier F 186 D3
Marnheim D 186 B5
Marpingen D 186 C3
Marsal F 186 D2
Martelange B 184 E4
Marxzell D 187 D5
Maßbach D 187 A9
Mastershausen D 185 D7
Mattaincourt F 186 E1
Maubert-Fontaine F 184 E1
Maulbronn D 187 D6
Maurik NL 183 B6
Maxéville F 186 D1
Maxsain D 185 C8
Mayen D 185 D7
Mayschoss D 183 D10
Mechelen B 182 C4
Mechelen NL 183 D7
Mechernich D 183 D9
Meckenheim D 183 D10
Meckesheim D 187 C6
Meddersheim D 186 B4
Meddo NL 183 A9
Meer B 182 C5
Meerbusch D 183 C9
Meerhout B 183 C6
Meerkerk NL 182 B5
Meerle B 182 C5
Meerlo NL 183 B8
Meerssen NL 183 D7
Meetkerke B 182 C2
Meeuwen B 183 C7
Megen NL 183 B7
Mehren D 185 D6
Mehring D 185 E6
Mehrstetten D 187 E8
Meijel NL 183 C7
Meinerzhagen D 185 B8
Meise B 182 D4
Meisenheim D 186 B4
Meißenheim D 186 E4
Melick NL 183 C8
Meliskerke NL 182 B3
Melle B 182 C3
Menden (Sauerland) D 185 B8
Mendig D 185 D7
Menen B 182 D2
Mengerskirchen D 185 C9
Ménil-sur-Belvitte F 186 E2
Menin B 182 D2
Merbes-le-Château B 184 D1
Merchtem B 182 D4
Mere B 182 D3
Merelbeke B 182 D3
Merenberg D 185 C9
Merklingen D 187 D8
Merksplas B 182 C5
Mersch L 186 B1
Mertert L 186 B1
Mertesdorf D 186 B2
Mertloch D 185 D7
Mertzwiller F 186 D4
Merzig D 186 C2
Meschede D 185 B9
Mespelbrunn D 187 B7
Metelen D 183 A10
Mettendorf D 185 E5
Mettet B 184 D2
Mettlach D 186 C2
Mettmann D 183 C9
Metz F 186 C1
Metzervisse F 186 C1
Metzingen D 187 D7
Meudt D 185 D8
Meulebeke B 182 D2
Michelbach an der Bilz D 187 C8
Michelfeld D 187 C8
Michelstadt D 187 B7
Middelbeers NL 183 C6
Middelburg NL 182 B3
Middelharnis NL 182 B4
Middelkerke B 182 C1
Miehlen D 185 D8
Mierlo NL 183 C7
Miesau D 186 C3
Miesenbach D 186 C4
Mijdrecht NL 182 A5
Mill NL 183 B7
Millingen aan de Rijn NL 183 B8
Milmort B 183 D7
Miltenberg D 187 B7
Minderhout B 182 C5
Minfeld D 186 C5
Mirecourt F 186 E1
Mittelsinn D 187 A8
Mittersheim F 186 D2
Möckmühl D 187 C7
Modave B 183 E6
Moerbeke B 182 C3
Moergestel NL 183 B6
Moerkerke B 182 C2
Moers D 183 C9
Mögglingen D 187 D8
Möglingen D 187 D7
Mol B 183 C6
Molenbeek-St-Jean B 182 D4
Molenstede B 183 C6
Molsheim F 186 D3
Mömbris D 187 A7
Momignies B 184 D1
Moncel-sur-Seille F 186 D1
Mönchengladbach D 183 C8
Mondorf-les-Bains L 186 B1
Mons B 182 E3
Monschau D 183 D8
Monsheim D 187 B5
Mönsheim D 187 D6
Monster NL 182 A4
Montabaur D 185 D8
Montcy-Notre-Dame F 184 E2
Montfoort NL 182 A5
Montfort NL 183 C7
Monthermé F 184 E2
Montignies-le-Tilleul B 184 D1
Montigny F 186 D2
Montigny-lès-Metz F 186 C1
Montzen B 183 D7
Monzelfeld D 185 E7
Monzingen D 185 E8
Mook NL 183 B7
Moorslede B 182 D2
Morbach D 185 E7
Mörfelden D 187 B6
Morhange F 186 D2
Morlanwelz B 182 E4
Mörlenbach D 187 B6
Morsbach D 185 C8
Mortsel B 182 C4
Mosbach D 187 C7
Mössingen D 187 E7
Mouscron B 182 D2
Moussey F 186 E3
Moyenmoutier F 186 E2
Much D 185 C7
Mudau D 187 B7
Müdelheim D 183 C9
Mudersbach D 185 C8
Muggensturm D 187 D5
Mühlacker D 187 D6
Mühlhausen D 187 C6
Mulfingen D 187 C8
Mülheim an der Ruhr D 183 C9
Mülheim-Kärlich D 185 D7
Münchweiler an der Rodalb D 186 C4
Munderkingen D 187 E8
Mundolsheim F 186 D4
Munkzwalm B 182 D3
Münnerstadt D 187 A9
Münsingen D 187 E7
Münster D 187 B6
Munstergeleen NL 183 D7
Münstermaifeld D 185 D7
Murrhardt D 187 D8
Müschenbach D 185 C8
Mutterstadt D 187 C5
Mutzig F 186 D3

N

Naaldwijk NL 182 B4
Naarden NL 183 A6
Nackenheim D 185 E9
Nagold D 187 D6
Nalbach D 186 C2
Namborn D 186 B3
Namur B 182 E5
Nancy F 186 D1
Nandrin B 183 D6
Nassau D 185 D8
Nassogne B 184 D3
Nastätten D 185 D8
Nauheim D 187 B5
Nauroth D 185 C8
Neckarbischofsheim D 187 C6
Neckargemünd D 187 C6
Neckarsteinach D 187 C6
Neckarsulm D 187 C7
Neckartenzlingen D 187 D7
Nederhorst den Berg NL 183 A6
Nederlangbroek NL 183 A6
Nederweert NL 183 C7
Neede NL 183 A9
Neer NL 183 C8
Neerijnen NL 183 B6
Neeroeteren B 183 C7
Neerpelt B 183 C6
Nellingen D 187 D8
Nentershausen D 185 D8
Neroth D 185 D6
Nersingen D 187 E9
Netphen D 185 C9
Nettersheim D 183 E9

Nettetal D 183 C8
Neubrunn D 187 B8
Neubulach D 187 D6
Neuenbürg D 187 D6
Neuenkirchen-Seelscheid D 185 C7
Neuenrade D 185 B8
Neuenstadt am Kocher D 187 C7
Neuenstein D 187 C8
Neuerburg D 185 D5
Neufchâteau B 184 E3
Neuffen D 187 D7
Neufmanil F 184 E2
Neufra D 187 E7
Neuhausen D 187 D6
Neuhofen D 187 C5
Neu-Isenburg D 187 A6
Neuler D 187 D9
Neumagen D 185 E6
Neunkirchen D 185 C9
Neunkirchen D 186 C3
Neuss D 183 C9
Neustadt (Wied) D 185 C7
Neustadt an der Weinstraße D 186 C5
Neu-Ulm D 187 E9
Neuves-Maisons F 186 D1
Neuweiler D 187 D6
Neuwied D 185 D7
Nevele B 182 C3
Newel D 185 E6
Niederanven L 186 B1
Niederbrechen D 185 D9
Niederbreitbach D 185 C7
Niederbronn-les-Bains F 186 D4
Niederfischbach D 185 C8
Niederkassel D 183 D10
Niederkirchen D 186 B4
Niederkrüchten D 183 C8
Niederneisen D 185 D9
Niedernhall D 187 C8
Niedernhausen D 185 D9
Nieder-Olm D 185 E9
Nieder-Rodenbach D 187 A7
Niederselters D 185 D9
Niederstetten D 187 C8
Niederwerrn D 187 A9
Niederwörresbach D 186 B3
Niederzissen D 185 D7
Niefern-Öschelbronn D 187 D6
Niel B 182 C4
Nierstein D 185 E9
Nieuw-Bergen NL 183 B8
Nieuwegein NL 183 A6
Nieuwerkerk NL 182 B4
Nieuwerkerk aan de IJssel NL 182 B5
Nieuwerkerken B 183 D6
Nieuwe-Tonge NL 182 B4
Nieuw-Heeten NL 183 A8
Nieuwkoop NL 182 A5
Nieuw-Loosdrecht NL 183 A6
Nieuw-Milligen NL 183 A7
Nieuw-Namen NL 182 C4
Nieuwveen NL 182 A5
Nieuw-Vennep NL 182 A5
Nieuw-Vossemeer NL 182 B4
Nievern D 185 D8
Nijkerk NL 183 A6
Nijlen B 182 C5
Nijmegen NL 183 B7
Nijverdal NL 183 A8
Nilvange F 186 C1
Ninove B 182 D4
Nismes B 184 D2
Nispen NL 182 C4
Nistelrode NL 183 B7
Nittel D 186 B1
Nivelles B 182 D4
Nohfelden D 186 B3
Noisseville F 186 C1
Nomeny F 186 D1
Nomexy F 186 E1
Nonnenweier D 186 E4
Nonnweiler D 186 B2
Noordwijk aan Zee NL 182 A4
Noordwijk-Binnen NL 182 A4
Noordwijkerhout NL 182 A5
Nootdorp NL 182 A4
Nordheim D 187 C7
Nordkirchen D 185 A8
Nouzonville F 184 E2
Noville B 182 D5
Nüdlingen D 187 A9
Nuenen NL 183 C7
Nuland NL 183 B6
Numansdorp NL 182 B4
Nunkirchen D 186 C2
Nunspeet NL 183 A7
Nürtingen D 187 D7
Nuth NL 183 D7

O

Oberderdingen D 187 C6
Oberfell D 185 D7
Oberharmersbach D 186 E5
Oberhausen D 183 C9
Oberhausen-Rheinhausen D 187 C5
Oberhoffen-sur-Moder F 186 D4
Oberkirch D 186 D5
Oberkochen D 187 D9
Obermoschel D 186 B4
Obernai F 186 E3
Obernburg am Main D 187 B7
Oberndorf am Neckar D 187 E6
Obernheim-Kirchenarnbach D 186 C4
Ober-Olm D 185 E9
Ober-Roden D 187 B6
Oberrot D 187 C8
Obersinn D 187 A8
Obersontheim D 187 C8
Oberstenfeld D 187 C7
Oberthal D 186 B3
Oberthulba D 187 A8
Obertshausen D 187 A6
Oberursel (Taunus) D 187 A6
Oberwesel D 185 D8
Oberwolfach D 187 E5
Obrigheim D 187 C7
Obrigheim (Pfalz) D 187 B5
Ochsenfurt D 187 B9
Ochtrup D 183 A10
Odernheim am Glan D 186 B4
Oedelem B 182 C2
Oeffelt NL 183 B7
Oegstgeest NL 182 A5
Oene NL 183 A8
Oerlenbach D 187 A9
Oestrich-Winkel D 185 D8
Offenbach am Main D 187 A6
Offenbach an der Queich D 187 C5
Offenburg D 186 E4
Ofterdingen D 187 E7
Oftersheim D 187 C6
Ogéviller F 186 D2
Ohey B 183 E6
Ohlsbach D 186 E4
Öhringen D 187 C7
Oignies F 182 E1
Oijen NL 183 B6
Oirschot NL 183 B6
Oisterwijk NL 183 B6
Oldenzaal NL 183 A9
Olen B 182 C5
Olfen D 185 A7
Olpe D 185 B8
Olst NL 183 A8
Onstmettingen D 187 E6
Ooltgensplaat NL 182 B4
Oostakker B 182 C3
Oostburg NL 182 C2
Oostende B 182 C1
Oosterbeek NL 183 B7
Oosterhout NL 182 B5
Oosterland NL 182 B4
Oosterzele B 182 D3
Oostham B 183 C6
Oostkamp B 182 C2
Oostkapelle NL 182 B3
Oostmalle B 182 C5
Oost-Souburg NL 182 C3
Oostvoorne NL 182 B4
Ootmarsum NL 183 A9
Opglabbeek B 183 C7
Opheusden NL 183 B7
Opitter B 183 C7
Oploo NL 183 B7
Opoeteren B 183 C7
Oppenau D 187 E5
Oppenheim D 185 E9
Oppenweiler D 187 D7
Opwijk B 182 D4
Orchies F 182 E2
Orenhofen D 185 E6
Oreye B 183 D6
Ortenberg D 186 E4
Osburg D 186 B2
Oss NL 183 B7
Ossendrecht NL 182 C4
Ostend B 182 C1
Osterburken D 187 C7
Ostfildern D 187 D7
Osthofen D 187 B5
Ostricourt F 182 E2
Östringen D 187 C6
Ostwald F 186 D4
Ötigheim D 187 D5
Ötisheim D 187 D6
Ottenheim D 186 E4
Ottenhöfen im Schwarzwald D 187 D5
Otterbach D 186 C4
Otterberg D 186 B4
Otterlo NL 183 A7
Ottersweier D 186 D5
Ottignies B 182 D5
Ottweiler D 186 C3
Oud-Beijerland NL 182 B4
Ouddorp NL 182 B3
Oudenaarde B 182 D3
Oudenbosch NL 182 B5
Oudenburg B 182 C2
Oude-Tonge NL 182 B4
Oudewater NL 182 A5
Oud-Gastel NL 182 B4
Oud-Turnhout B 182 C5
Oud-Vossemeer NL 182 B4
Oudzele B 182 C2
Ouffet B 183 E6
Oulder B 184 D5
Oupeye B 183 D7
Overath D 185 C7
Overdinkel NL 183 A10
Overijse B 182 D5
Overloon NL 183 B7
Overpelt B 183 C6
Ovezande NL 182 C3
Owen D 187 D7

P

Paal B 183 C6
Padoux F 186 E2
Paliseul B 184 E3
Palzem D 186 B1
Pange F 186 C1
Panningen NL 183 C7
Papendrecht NL 182 B5
Partenstein D 187 A8
Pâturages B 182 E3
Pecq B 182 D2
Peer B 183 C6
Pelm D 185 D6
Pepingen B 182 D4
Pepinster B 183 D7
Perl D 186 C1
Péruwelz B 182 D3
Perwez B 182 D5
Petite-Rosselle F 186 C2
Petitmont F 186 D2
Pexonne F 186 E2
Pfaffenhofen an der Roth D 187 E9
Pfaffenhoffen F 186 D4
Pfalzfeld D 185 D8
Pfalzgrafenweiler D 187 D6
Pfedelbach D 187 C7
Pforzheim D 187 D6
Pfronstetten D 187 E7
Pfullingen D 187 E7
Pfungstadt D 187 B6
Phalsbourg F 186 D3
Philippeville B 184 D2
Philippine NL 182 C3
Philippsburg D 187 C5
Piershil NL 182 B4
Piesport D 185 E6
Pijnacker NL 182 A4
Pirmasens D 186 C4
Pittem B 182 D2
Plaidt D 185 D7
Plettenberg D 185 B8
Pliezhausen D 187 D7
Plobsheim F 186 E4
Plochingen D 187 D7
Ploegsteert B 182 D1
Plüderhausen D 187 D8
Poederlee B 182 C5
Polch D 185 D7
Polsbroek NL 182 B5
Pompey F 186 D1
Pont-à-Celles B 182 D4
Pont-à-Marcq F 182 D2
Pont-de-Loup B 182 E5
Poppenhausen D 187 A9
Portieux F 186 E1
Posterholt NL 183 C8
Poussay F 186 E1
Pracht D 185 C8
Prinsenbeek NL 182 B5
Profondeville B 184 D2
Pronsfeld D 185 D5
Provenchères-sur-Fave F 186 E3
Prüm D 185 D5
Puderbach D 185 C8
Pulheim D 183 C9
Putte B 182 C5
Putte NL 182 C4
Puttelange-aux-Lacs F 186 C2
Putten NL 183 A7
Püttlingen D 186 C2
Puurs B 182 C4

Q

Quaregnon B 182 E3
Queidersbach D 186 C4
Quendorf D 183 A10
Quesnoy-sur-Deûle F 182 D2
Quierschied D 186 C3
Quiévrain B 182 E3
Quiévrechain F 182 E3

R

Raalte NL 183 A8
Raamsdonksveer NL 182 B5
Radevormwald D 185 B7
Raeren B 183 D8
Raesfeld D 183 B9
Ralingen D 185 E6
Rambervillers F 186 E2
Rambrouch L 184 E4
Ramillies B 182 D5
Rammelsbach D 186 B3
Rammingen D 187 D9
Ramstein D 186 C4
Rance B 184 D1
Randersacker D 187 B8
Rangendingen D 187 E6
Ransbach-Baumbach D 185 D8
Ranst B 182 C5
Raon-l'Étape F 186 E2
Rastatt D 187 D5
Ratingen D 183 C9
Raubach D 185 C8
Ravels B 182 C5
Ravenstein NL 183 B7
Rebecq B 182 D4
Réchicourt-le-Château F 186 D2
Recht B 184 D5
Rechtenbach D 187 B8
Recklinghausen D 183 B10
Réding F 186 D3
Rees D 183 B8
Rehlingen-Siersburg D 186 C2
Reichelsheim (Odenwald) D 187 B6
Reichenbach D 187 B6
Reichenberg D 187 B8
Reicholzheim D 187 B8
Reichshoffen F 186 D4
Reichstett F 186 D4
Reil D 185 D7
Reilingen D 187 C6
Reinheim D 187 B6
Reinsfeld D 186 B2
Reken D 183 B10
Rekken NL 183 A9
Remagen D 185 C7
Remich L 186 B1
Remicourt B 183 D6
Remouchamps B 183 E7
Remscheid D 183 C10
Renchen D 186 D5
Renesse NL 182 B3
Rengsdorf D 185 C7
Renkum NL 183 B7
Rennerod D 185 C9
Renningen D 187 D6
Renswoude NL 183 A7
Renwez F 184 E2
Retie B 183 C6
Reusel NL 183 C6
Reutlingen D 187 E7
Reuver NL 183 C8
Revin F 184 E2
Rhaunen D 185 E7
Rhede D 183 B9
Rheden NL 183 A8
Rheinau D 186 D4
Rheinbach D 183 D9
Rheinberg D 183 B9
Rheinböllen D 185 E8
Rheinbreitbach D 185 C7
Rheinbrohl D 185 D7
Rheinstetten D 187 D5
Rheinzabern D 187 C5
Rhenen NL 183 B7
Rhens D 185 D8
Rhinau F 186 E4
Rhisnes B 182 D5
Rhoon NL 182 B4
Richardménil F 186 D1
Ridderkerk NL 182 B5
Riegelsberg D 186 C2
Riemst B 183 D7
Rieneck D 187 A8
Riethoven NL 183 C6
Rijen NL 182 B5
Rijkevorsel B 182 C5
Rijnsburg NL 182 A4
Rijsbergen NL 182 B5
Rijsel F 182 D2
Rijssen NL 183 A9
Rijswijk NL 182 A4
Rilland NL 182 C4
Rimbach D 187 B6
Rimogne F 184 E2
Rips NL 183 B7
Rittersdorf D 185 D5
Rixensart B 182 D5
Rochefort B 184 D3
Rochehaut B 184 E3
Rochin F 182 D2
Rockanje NL 182 B4
Rockenhausen D 186 B4
Rocroi F 184 E2
Rodalben D 186 C4
Roermond NL 183 C7
Roeselare B 182 D2
Roetgen D 183 D8
Roggel NL 183 C7
Röhlingen D 187 D9
Rohrbach-lès-Bitche F 186 C3
Rombas F 186 C1
Rommerskirchen D 183 C9
Ronse B 182 D3
Roosendaal NL 182 B4
Rosée B 184 D2
Rosenfeld D 187 E6
Rosheim F 186 D3
Rosmalen NL 183 B6
Rösrath D 185 C7
Roßdorf D 187 B6
Rossum NL 183 B6
Rot am See D 187 C9
Rothenberg D 187 B6
Rothenbuch D 187 B7
Rothenburg ob der Tauber D 187 C9
Rothenfels D 187 B8
Rotheux-Rimière B 183 D6
Rotselaar B 182 D5
Rottenacker D 187 E8
Rottenburg am Neckar D 187 E6
Rottendorf D 187 B9
Rotterdam NL 182 B5
Röttingen D 187 B8
Roubaix F 182 D2
Roulers B 182 D2
Rouvroy F 182 E1
Rouvroy-sur-Audry F 184 E2
Rozenburg NL 182 B4
Rozendaal NL 183 A7
Ruddervoorde B 182 C2
Rudersberg D 187 D8
Rüdesheim D 185 E8
Ruiselede B 182 C2
Rülzheim D 187 C5
Rumes B 182 D2
Rumigny F 184 E1
Rumst B 182 C4
Runkel D 185 D9
Rüsselsheim D 187 A5
Rutesheim D 187 D6
Rüthen D 185 B9
Rütten-Scheid D 183 C9
Ruurlo NL 183 A8

S

Saales F 186 E3
Saarbrücken D 186 C2
Saarburg D 186 B2
Saarlouis D 186 C2
Saarwellingen D 186 C2
Sachsenheim D 187 D7
St-Amand-les-Eaux F 182 E2
St-Avold F 186 C2
St-Blaise-la-Roche F 186 E3
St-Clément F 186 D2
St-Dié F 186 E2
Ste-Marguerite F 186 E2
Ste-Marie-aux-Mines F 186 E3
St-Firmin F 186 E1
St-Ghislain B 182 E3
St-Hubert B 184 D3
St-Louis-lès-Bitche F 186 D3
St-Max F 186 D1
St-Michel F 184 E1
St-Michel-sur-Meurthe F 186 E2
St-Nicolas B 183 D7
St-Nicolas-de-Port F 186 D1
St-Oedenrode NL 183 B6
St-Quirin F 186 D3
St-Vith B 184 D5
Salmtal D 185 E6
Sandhausen D 187 C6
Sankt Augustin D 185 C7
Sankt Goar D 185 D8
Sankt Goarshausen D 185 D8
Sankt Ingbert D 186 C3
Sankt Julian D 186 B4
Sankt Katharinen D 185 C7
Sankt Wendel D 186 C3
Santpoort NL 182 A5
Sarralbe F 186 D3
Sarrebourg F 186 D3
Sarreguemines F 186 C3
Sarre-Union F 186 D3
Sart B 183 D7
Sasbach D 186 D5
Sasbachwalden D 186 D5
Sassenheim NL 182 A5
Sas Van Gent NL 182 C3
Satteldorf D 187 C9
Saulheim D 185 E9
Saverne F 186 D3
Schaafheim D 187 B7
Schaarsbergen NL 183 A7
Schaerbeek B 182 D4
Schaesberg NL 183 D8
Schaijk NL 183 B7
Schalkhaar NL 183 A8
Schalksmühle D 185 B8
Scharendijke NL 182 B3
Schebheim D 187 B9
Schefflenz D 187 C7
Schelklingen D 187 E8
Schenkenzell D 187 E5
Schermbeck D 183 B9
Scherpenheuvel B 182 D5
Scherpenzeel NL 183 A6
Scherwiller F 186 E3
Schiedam NL 182 B4
Schieren L 184 E5
Schifferstadt D 187 C5
Schiffweiler D 186 C3
Schijndel NL 183 B6
Schilde B 182 C5
Schillingen D 186 B2
Schiltach D 187 E5
Schiltigheim F 186 D4
Schinnen NL 183 D7
Schinveld NL 183 D7
Schipluiden NL 182 B4
Schirmeck F 186 E3
Schlangenbad D 185 D9
Schleiden D 183 D8
Schmallenberg D 185 B9
Schmelz D 186 C2
Schnelldorf D 187 C9
Schnürpflingen D 187 E8
Schoenberg B 185 D5
Schöllkrippen D 187 A7
Schömberg D 187 D6
Schönaich D 187 D7
Schondra D 187 A8
Schönecken D 185 D5
Schönenberg-Kübelberg D 186 C3
Schöntal D 187 C8
Schoondijke NL 182 C3
Schoonhoven NL 182 B5
Schorndorf D 187 D8
Schoten B 182 C4
Schriesheim D 187 C6
Schrozberg D 187 C8
Schuttertal D 186 E4
Schutterwald D 186 E4
Schüttorf D 183 A10
Schwäbisch Gmünd D 187 D8
Schwäbisch Hall D 187 C8
Schwaigern D 187 C7
Schwalbach D 186 C2
Schwegenheim D 187 C5
Schweich D 185 E6
Schweigen-Rechtenbach D 186 C4
Schweighouse-sur-Moder F 186 D4
Schweinfurt D 187 A9
Schwelm D 185 B7
Schwerte D 185 B8
Schwieberdingen D 187 D7
Seckach D 187 C7
Seclin F 182 D2
Seebach D 187 D5
Seeheim-Jugenheim D 187 B6
Seilles B 183 E6
Seinsheim D 187 B9
Sélestat F 186 E3
Seligenstadt D 187 A6
Selm D 185 A7
Selters (Westerwald) D 185 C8
Seltz F 186 D5
Senden D 187 E9
Seneffe B 182 D4
Senones F 186 E2
Seraing B 183 D7
Serooskerke NL 182 B3
Serrig D 186 B2
Sevenum NL 183 C8
's-Gravendeel NL 182 B5
's-Gravenhage NL 182 A4
's-Gravenmoer NL 182 B5
's-Gravenpolder NL 182 C3
's-Gravenvoeren B 183 D7
's-Gravenzande NL 182 B4
's-Heerenberg NL 183 B8
's-Heerenhoek NL 182 C3
's-Hertogenbosch NL 183 B6
Siebengewald NL 183 B8
Siegburg D 185 C7
Siegen D 185 C9
Sierck-les-Bains F 186 C1
Siershahn D 185 D8
Signy-le-Petit F 184 E1
Sijsele B 182 C2
Silenrieux B 184 D1
Simmerath D 183 D8
Simmern (Hunsrück) D 185 E8
Simpelveld NL 183 D7
Sindelfingen D 187 D6
Singhofen D 185 D8
Sinn D 185 C9
Sinsheim D 187 C6
Sint Annaland NL 182 B4
Sint Anthonis NL 183 B7
Sint-Genesius-Rode B 182 D4
Sint-Gillis-Waas B 182 C4
Sint-Huibrechts-Lille B 183 C6
Sint Jansteen NL 182 C4
Sint-Katelijne-Waver B 182 C5
Sint-Laureins B 182 C3
Sint-Lenaarts B 182 C5
Sint Maartensdijk NL 182 B4
Sint-Margriete B 182 C3
Sint-Maria-Lierde B 182 D3
Sint-Martens-Latem B 182 C3
Sint Michielsgestel NL 183 B6
Sint-Niklaas B 182 C4
Sint Odilienberg NL 183 C8
Sint-Pauwels B 182 C4
Sint Philipsland NL 182 B4
Sint-Pieters-Leeuw B 182 D4
Sint-Truiden B 183 D6
Sinzheim D 187 D5
Sinzig D 185 C7
Sittard NL 183 D7
Sivry B 184 D1
Sleidinge B 182 C3
Sliedrecht NL 182 B5
Sluis NL 182 C2
Sluiskil NL 182 C3
Soerendonk NL 183 C7
Soest D 185 A9
Soest NL 183 A6
Soesterberg NL 183 A6
Soheit-Tinlot B 183 E6
Sohren D 185 E7
Soignies B 182 D4
Solingen D 183 C10
Sombreffe B 182 D5
Someren NL 183 C7
Somme-Leuze B 184 D3
Somzée B 184 D1
Son NL 183 B6
Soufflenheim F 186 D4
Soultz-sous-Forêts F 186 D4
Soumagne B 183 D7
Spa B 183 E7
Spabrücken D 185 E8
Spay D 185 D8
Speicher D 185 E6
Speyer D 187 C5
Spiere B 182 D2
Spiesen-Elversberg D 186 C3
Spijkenisse NL 182 B4
Spontin B 184 D3
Spraitbach D 187 D8
Sprendlingen D 185 E8
Sprimont B 183 D7
Sprockhövel D 185 B7
Stabroek B 182 C4
Staden B 182 D2
Stadtkyll D 185 D6
Stadtlohn D 183 B9
Staig D 187 E8
Standdaarbuiten NL 182 B5
Stavelot B 184 D4
Stavenisse NL 182 B4
Steenbergen NL 182 B4
Steenderen NL 183 A8
Stein NL 183 D7
Steinach D 186 E5
Steinfeld D 186 C5
Steinfeld D 187 B8
Steinheim am Albuch D 187 D9
Steinheim an der Murr D 187 D7
Steinsfeld D 187 C9
Steinwenden D 186 C4
Stekene B 182 C4
Stellendam NL 182 B4
Stevensweert NL 183 C7
Stimpfach D 187 C9
Stiring-Wendel F 186 C2
Stockstadt am Rhein D 187 B5
Stolberg (Rheinland) D 183 D8
Stoumont B 183 E7
Straelen D 183 C8
Straimont B 184 E3
Stramproy NL 183 C7
Strasbourg F 186 D4
Strassen L 186 B1
Straßenhaus D 185 C8
Strijen NL 182 B5
Stromberg D 185 E8
Stuttgart D 187 D7
Sturzelbronn F 186 C4
Suddendorf D 183 A10
Südlohn D 183 B9
Sulz am Neckar D 187 E6
Sulzbach am Main D 187 B7
Sulzbach an der Murr D 187 C7
Sulzbach-Laufen D 187 D8
Sulzbach/Saar D 186 C3
Sulzfeld D 187 C6
Sulzthal D 187 A9
Sundern (Sauerland) D 185 B9
Susteren NL 183 C7
Swalmen NL 183 C8

T

Taintrux F 186 E2
Talange F 186 C1
Tamm D 187 D7
Tantonville F 186 E1
Tauberbischofsheim D 187 B8
Tawern D 186 B2
Tegelen NL 183 C8
Tellin B 184 D3
Templeuve F 182 D2
Temse B 182 C4
Tenneville B 184 D4
Ter Aar NL 182 A5
Terborg-Silvolde NL 183 B8
Terheijden NL 182 B5
Terneuzen NL 182 C3
Tervuren B 182 D5
Tessenderlo B 183 C6
Testelt B 182 C5
Teteringen NL 182 B5
Thaleischweiler-Fröschen D 186 C4
Thalfang D 186 B2
Thaon-les-Vosges F 186 E1
't Harde NL 183 A7
Theux B 183 D7
Thionville F 186 C1
Tholen NL 182 B4
Tholey D 186 C3
Thommen B 184 D5
Thorn NL 183 C7
Thuin B 184 D1
Thüngen D 187 B8
Thüngersheim D 187 B8
Tiefenbronn D 187 D6
Tiel NL 183 B6
Tielen B 182 C5
Tielt B 182 D2
Tienen B 182 D5
Tilburg NL 183 B6
Tongeren B 183 D6
Tönisvorst D 183 C8
Torhout B 182 C2
Tourcoing F 182 D2
Tournai B 182 D2
Traar D 183 C9
Traben D 185 E7
Trarbach D 185 E7
Trebur D 187 B5
Treis D 185 D7
Tremelo B 182 D5
Trier D 186 B2
Trierweiler D 186 B2
Trippstadt D 186 C4
Trittenheim D 185 E6
Trochtelfingen D 187 E7
Troisdorf D 183 D10
Troisfontaines F 186 D3
Trois-Ponts B 184 D4
Troisvierges L 184 D5
Trooz B 183 D7
Truchtersheim F 186 D4
Trulben D 186 C4
Tubbergen NL 183 A9
Tübingen D 187 D7
Tubize B 182 D4
Turnhout B 182 C5
Twello NL 183 A8

U

Übach-Palenberg D 183 D8
Überherrn D 186 C2
Ubstadt-Weiher D 187 C6
Uccle B 182 D4
Üchtelhausen D 187 A9
Uckange F 186 C1
Uddel NL 183 A7
Uden NL 183 B7
Udenhout NL 183 B6
Üdersdorf D 185 D6
Uettingen D 187 B8
Uffenheim D 187 B9
Uhingen D 187 D8
Uithoorn NL 182 A5
Ulft NL 183 B8
Ulicoten NL 182 C5
Ulm D 187 E8
Ulmen D 185 D6
Ulvenhout NL 182 B5
Undingen D 187 E7
Unkel D 185 C7
Unna D 185 A8
Unnau D 185 C8
Untermünkheim D 187 C8
Unterpleichfeld D 187 B9
Urbach D 185 C8
Urbar D 185 D8
Urberach D 187 B6
Utrecht NL 183 A6
Üxheim D 185 D6

V

Vaals NL 183 D8
Vaassen NL 183 A7
Valkenburg NL 183 D7
Valkenswaard NL 183 C6
Vallendar D 185 D8
Vandœvre-lès-Nancy F 186 D1
Varik NL 183 B6
Varsseveld NL 183 B8
Vaux-sur-Sûre B 184 E4
Veenendaal NL 183 A7
Veere NL 182 B3
Veerle B 182 C5
Veghel NL 183 B7
Velbert D 183 C10
Veldegem B 182 C2
Velden NL 183 C8
Veldhoven NL 183 C6
Velen D 183 B9
Vellberg D 187 C8
Velp NL 183 B7
Vendenheim F 186 D4
Venlo NL 183 C8
Venray NL 183 B7
Vergaville F 186 D2
Verlaine B 183 D6
Verny F 186 C1
Verviers B 183 D7
Vessem NL 183 C6
Vettelschoss D 185 C7
Vianden L 184 E5
Vianen NL 183 B6
Vic-sur-Seille F 186 D2
Vielsalm B 184 D4
Vierlingsbeek NL 183 B7
Viernheim D 187 B6
Viersen D 183 C8
Vieux-Condé F 182 E3
Vigy F 186 C1
Villé F 186 E3
Villeneuve-d'Ascq F 182 D2
Villers-le-Bouillet B 183 D6
Villers-lès-Nancy F 186 D1
Villmar D 185 D9
Vilvoorde B 182 D4
Vincey F 186 E1
Vinkt B 182 C2
Vinningen D 186 C4
Vireux-Molhain F 184 D2
Vireux-Wallerand F 184 D2
Visé B 183 D7
Vlaardingen NL 182 B4
Vleuten NL 183 A6
Vlijmen NL 183 B6
Vlissingen NL 182 C3
Voerde (Niederrhein) D 183 B9
Vogelenzang NL 182 A5
Vogelweh D 186 C4
Vöhringen D 187 E6
Vöhringen D 187 E9
Volkach D 187 B9
Volkel NL 183 B7
Völklingen D 186 C2
Volmunster F 186 C3
Voorburg NL 182 A4
Voorhout NL 182 A4
Voorschoten NL 182 A4
Voorst NL 183 A8
Voorthuizen NL 183 A7
Vorden NL 183 A8
Vorst B 183 C6
Vosselaar B 182 C5
Vrasene B 182 C4
Vreden D 183 A9
Vreeland NL 183 A6
Vresse B 184 E2
Vriezenveen NL 183 A9
Vrouwenpolder NL 182 B3
Vught NL 183 B6

W

Waalre NL 183 C6
Waalwijk NL 183 B6
Waarschoot B 182 C3
Wachenheim an der Weinstraße D 187 C5
Wachtebeke B 182 C3
Wächtersbach D 187 A7
Waddinxveen NL 182 A5
Wadern D 186 B2
Wadersloh D 185 A9
Wadgassen D 186 C2
Wageningen NL 183 B7
Waghäusel D 187 C6
Waiblingen D 187 D7
Waibstadt D 187 C6
Waigolshausen D 187 B9
Waimes B 183 E8
Walcourt B 184 D1
Waldachtal D 187 E6
Waldböckelheim D 185 E8
Waldbreitbach D 185 C7
Waldbröl D 185 C8
Waldbrunn-Lahr D 185 C9
Waldbüttelbrunn D 187 B8
Waldenbuch D 187 D7
Waldenburg D 187 C8
Waldesch D 185 D8
Waldfischbach-Burgalben D 186 C4
Wald-Michelbach D 187 B6
Waldmohr D 186 C3
Waldrach D 186 B2
Waldsee D 187 C5
Waldstetten D 187 D8
Walferdange L 186 B1
Walldorf D 187 A6
Walldorf D 187 C6
Walldürn D 187 B7
Wallhausen D 185 E8
Wallhausen D 187 C9
Wamel NL 183 B6
Wandre B 183 D7
Wanne-Eikel D 183 B10
Wanroij NL 183 B7
Wanssum NL 183 B8
Wanze B 183 D6
Wapenveld NL 183 A8
Waregem B 182 D2
Waremme B 183 D6
Warmond NL 182 A5
Warnsveld NL 183 A8
Warstein D 185 B9
Wartmannsroth D 187 A8
Wäschenbeuren D 187 D8
Waspik NL 182 B5
Wasseiges B 183 D6
Wasselonne F 186 D3

Wassenaar *NL* **182** A4
Wassenberg *D* **183** C8
Wasseralfingen *D* **187** D9
Wasserbillig *D* **186** B2
Wasserliesch *D* **186** B2
Wasserlosen *D* **187** A9
Wateringen *NL* **182** A4
Waterland-Oudeman *B* **182** C3
Waterloo *B* **182** D4
Watten-Scheid *D* **183** C10
Wavre *B* **182** D5
Wavrin *F* **182** D1
Waxweiler *D* **185** D5
Waziers *F* **182** E2
Weelde *B* **182** C5
Weerselo *NL* **183** A9
Weert *NL* **183** C7
Weesp *NL* **183** A6
Weeze *D* **183** B8
Wegberg *D* **183** C8
Wehl *NL* **183** B8
Weibern *D* **183** E10
Weibersbrunn *D* **187** B7
Weidenstetten *D* **187** D8
Weidenthal *D* **186** C4
Weiersbach *D* **186** B3
Weikersheim *D* **187** C8
Weilbach *D* **187** B7
Weilburg *D* **185** D9
Weil der Stadt *D* **187** D6
Weilerbach *D* **186** C4
Weilerswist *D* **183** D9
Weilheim an der Teck *D* **187** D8
Weilmünster *D* **185** D9
Weinbach *D* **185** D9
Weingarten (Baden) *D* **187** C6
Weinheim *D* **187** B6
Weinsberg *D* **187** C7
Weinsheim *D* **185** D5
Weinsheim *D* **185** E8
Weinstadt *D* **187** D7
Weiskirchen *D* **186** B2
Weissach *D* **187** D6
Weißenhorn *D* **187** E9
Weißenthurm *D* **185** D7
Weiswampach *L* **184** D5
Weitbruch *F* **186** D4
Weitefeld *D* **185** C8
Weiterstadt *D* **187** B6
Wekerom *NL* **183** A7
Welkenraedt *B* **183** D7
Well *NL* **183** B8
Wellen *B* **183** D6
Wellin *B* **184** D3
Welling *D* **185** D7
Welschbillig *D* **185** E6
Welver *D* **185** A8
Welzheim *D* **187** D8
Wemeldinge *NL* **182** B4
Wendelsheim *D* **186** B5
Wenden *D* **185** C8
Wendlingen am Neckar *D* **187** D7
Wenduine *B* **182** C2
Wengsel (Isterberg) *D* **183** A10
Wépion *B* **182** E5
Werbach *D* **187** B8
Werbomont *B* **184** D4
Werdohl *D* **185** B8
Werkendam *NL* **182** B5
Werl *D* **185** A8
Wermelskirchen *D* **185** B7
Wernau *D* **187** D7
Werne *D* **185** A8
Werneck *D* **187** B9
Wertheim *D* **187** B8
Wervik *B* **182** D2
Wesel *D* **183** B9
Wesepe *NL* **183** A8
Wesseling *D* **183** D9
Wessem *NL* **183** C7
Westerburg *D* **185** C8
Westerheim *D* **187** D8
Westerhoven *NL* **183** C6
Westerlo *B* **182** C5
Westerstetten *D* **187** D8
Westervoort *NL* **183** B7
Westhausen *D* **187** D9
Westhofen *D* **187** B5
Westhoffen *F* **186** D3
Westkapelle *NL* **182** B2
Westmalle *B* **182** C5
Wetter (Ruhr) *D* **185** B7
Wetteren *B* **182** C3
Wevelgem *B* **182** D2
Weyerbusch *D* **185** C8
Weyersheim *F* **186** D4
Wichelen *B* **182** C3
Wickede (Ruhr) *D* **185** B8
Wiehl *D* **185** C8
Wielsbeke *B* **182** D2
Wierden *NL* **183** A9
Wiernsheim *D* **187** D6
Wiesbaden *D* **185** D9
Wiesen *D* **187** A7
Wiesensteig *D* **187** D8
Wiesloch *D* **187** C6
Wijchen *NL* **183** B7
Wijhe *NL* **183** A8
Wijk bij Duurstede *NL* **183** B6
Wijk en Aalburg *NL* **183** B6
Wildberg *D* **187** D6
Wilhelminadorp *NL* **183** C6
Willebroek *B* **182** C4
Willemstad *NL* **182** B4
Willich *D* **183** C9
Willstätt *D* **186** D4
Wilnis *NL* **182** A5
Wilnsdorf *D* **185** C9
Wilp *NL* **183** A8
Wiltingen *D* **186** B2
Wiltz *L* **184** E4
Wincheringen *D* **186** B1
Wincrange *L* **184** D4
Windesheim *D* **185** E8
Windhagen *D* **185** C7
Wingene *B* **182** C2
Wingen-sur-Moder *F* **186** D3
Winnenden *D* **187** D7
Winningen *D* **185** D8
Winnweiler *D* **186** B4
Winssen *NL* **183** B7
Winterswijk *NL* **183** B9
Wintrich *D* **185** E6
Wipperfürth *D* **185** B7
Wirges *D* **185** D8
Wissembourg *F* **186** C4
Wissen *D* **185** C8
Wissenkerke *NL* **182** B3
Witten *D* **185** B7
Wittighausen *D* **187** B8
Wittlich *D* **185** E6
Woensdrecht *NL* **182** C4
Woerden *NL* **182** A5
Wœrth *F* **186** D4
Woippy *F* **186** C1
Wolfach *D* **187** E5
Wolfstein *D* **186** B4
Wolpertshausen *D* **187** C8
Wolphaartsdijk *NL* **182** B3
Wommelgem *B* **182** C5
Wormeldange *L* **186** B1
Worms *D* **187** B5
Wörrstadt *D* **185** E9
Wortel *B* **182** C5
Wörth am Main *D* **187** B7
Wörth am Rhein *D* **187** C5
Woudenberg *NL* **183** A6
Woudrichem *NL* **182** B5
Woustviller *F* **186** C3
Wouw *NL* **182** B4
Wuppertal *D* **183** C10
Würselen *D* **183** D8
Würzburg *D* **187** B8
Wüstenrot *D* **187** C7
Wuustwezel *B* **182** C5

X

Xanten *D* **183** B8

Y

Yerseke *NL* **182** C4
Ysselsteyn *NL* **183** C7
Yutz *F* **186** C1
Yvoir *B* **184** D2

Z

Zaamslag *NL* **182** C3
Zaandam *NL* **182** A5
Zaltbommel *NL* **183** B6
Zandhoven *B* **182** C5
Zandvliet *B* **182** C4
Zandvoort *NL* **182** A5
Zarren *B* **182** C1
Zaventem *B* **182** D4
Zeddam *NL* **183** B8
Zedelgem *B* **182** C2
Zeebrugge *B* **182** C2
Zeeland *NL* **183** B7
Zeewolde *NL* **183** A7
Zeiskam *D* **187** C5
Zeist *NL* **183** A6
Zeitlofs *D* **187** A8
Zele *B* **182** C4
Zelhem *NL* **183** A8
Zell (Mosel) *D* **185** D7
Zell am Harmersbach *D* **186** E5
Zell am Main *D* **187** B8
Zellingen *D* **187** B8
Zeltingen-Rachtig *D* **185** E7
Zelzate *B* **182** C3
Zemmer *D* **185** E6
Zemst *B* **182** D4
Zerf *D* **186** B2
Zevenaar *NL* **183** B8
Zevenbergen *NL* **182** B5
Zierikzee *NL* **182** B3
Zoelen *NL* **183** B6
Zoersel *B* **182** C5
Zoetermeer *NL* **182** A4
Zolder *B* **183** C6
Zomergem *B* **182** C3
Zonhoven *B* **183** D6
Zonnebeke *B* **182** D1
Zornheim *D* **185** E9
Zottegem *B* **182** D3
Zoutleeuw *B* **183** D6
Zuid-Beijerland *NL* **182** B4
Zuidland *NL* **182** B4
Zuienkerke *B* **182** C2
Zülpich *D* **183** D9
Zulte *B* **182** D2
Zundert *NL* **182** C5
Zutendaal *B* **183** D7
Zutphen *NL* **183** A8
Zweibrücken *D* **186** C3
Zwevegem *B* **182** D2
Zwevezele *B* **182** C2
Zwiefalten *D* **187** E7
Zwijndrecht *B* **182** C4
Zwijndrecht *NL* **182** B5
Zwingenberg *D* **187** B6

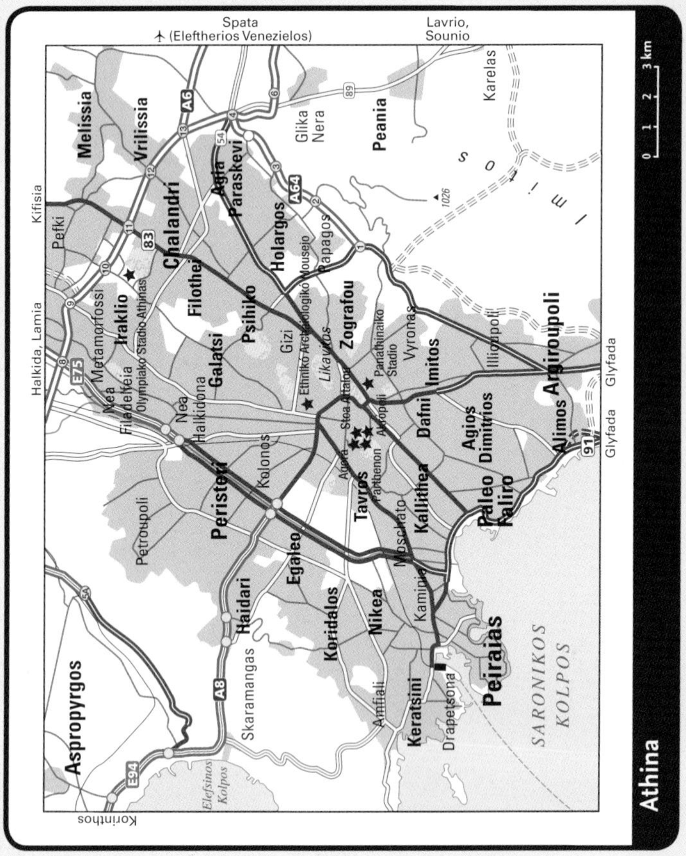
Athina
Spata
(Eleftherios Venezielos)
Lavrio, Sounio
Kifisia
Halkida, Lamia
Glyfada
Korinthos
0 1 2 3 km
Melissia
Vrilissia
Pefki
Iraklio
Chalandri
Agia Paraskevi
Holargos
Papagos
Glika Nera
Peania
Karelas
Metamorfossi
Nea Filadelfeia
Olympiako Stadio Athinas
Nea Halkidona
Galatsi
Filothei
Psihiko
Gizi
Ethniko Archeologiko Mousejo
Likavitos
Zografou
Panathinaiko Stadio
Vyronas
Imitos
Ilioupoli
Argiroupoli
Stoa Attalou
Parthenon
Akropoli
Agora
Dafni
Agios Dimitrios
Alimos
Kalonos
Peristeri
Petroupoli
Egaleo
Tavros
Kallithea
Moschato
Paleo Faliro
Haidari
Koridalos
Nikea
Kaminia
Pireiaias
Drapetsona
Keratsini
Amfiali
Skaramangas
Aspropyrgos
Elefsinos Kolpos
SARONIKOS KOLPOS

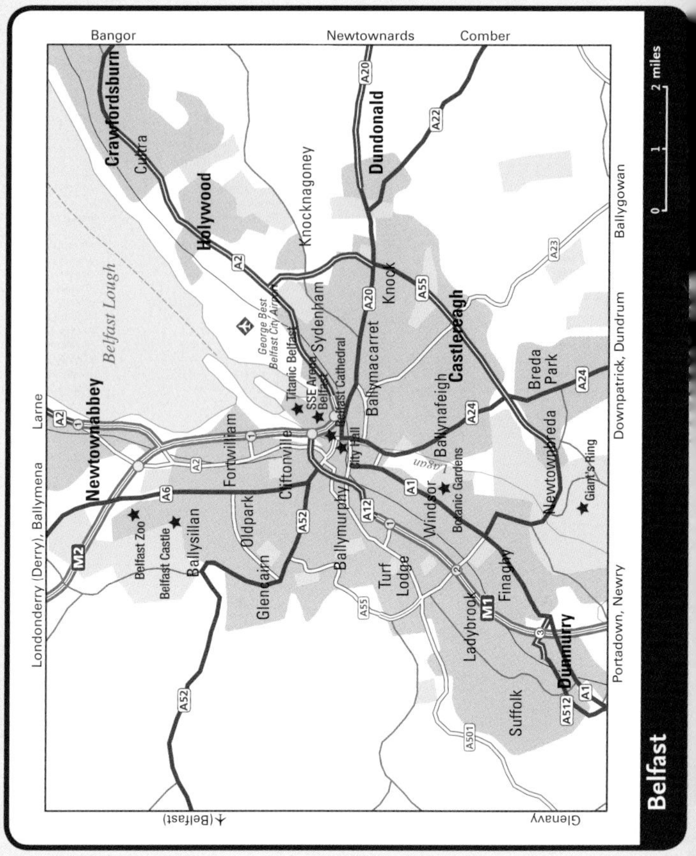
Belfast
Bangor
Newtownards
Comber
Larne
Londonderry (Derry), Ballymena
Ballygowan
Downpatrick, Dundrum
Portadown, Newry
Glenavy
(Belfast)
0 1 2 miles
Crawfordsburn
Cultra
Holywood
Dundonald
Knocknagoney
Belfast Lough
George Best Belfast City Airport
Titanic Belfast
SSE Arena Belfast
Sydenham
Knock
Castlereagh
Ballymacarret
Belfast Cathedral
City Hall
Newtownabbey
Fortwilliam
Cliftonville
Ballynafeigh
Breda Park
Belfast Zoo
Belfast Castle
Ballysillan
Oldpark
Ballymurphy
Windsor
Botanic Gardens
Newtownbreda
Giant's Ring
Glengormley
Turf Lodge
Finaghy
Ladybrook
Dunmurry
Suffolk

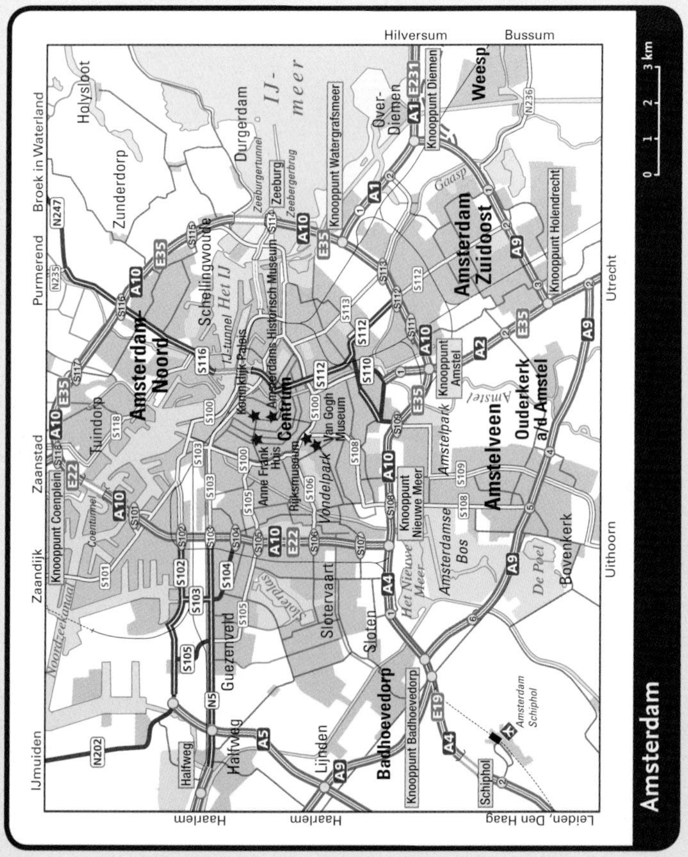
Amsterdam
IJmuiden
Zaandijk
Zaanstad
Purmerend
Broek in Waterland
Holysloot
Hilversum
Bussum
Utrecht
Uithoorn
Haarlem
Leiden, Den Haag
0 1 2 3 km
Zunderdorp
Durgerdam
IJ-meer
Knooppunt Watergraafsmeer
Over-Diemen
Knooppunt Diemen
Weesp
Schellingwoude
Zeeburg
Amsterdam Noord
Tuindorp
Knooppunt Coenplein
Het IJ
Koninklijk Paleis
Amsterdams Historisch Museum
Centrum
Anne Frank Huis
Van Gogh Museum
Rijksmuseum
Vondelpark
Amsterdam Zuidoost
Knooppunt Holendrecht
Knooppunt Amstel
Ouderkerk a/d Amstel
Amstelveen
Knooppunt Nieuwe Meer
Amsterdamse Bos
Bovenkerk
De Poel
Het Nieuwe Meer
Slotervaart
Sloten
Geuzenveld
Halfweg
Badhoevedorp
Knooppunt Badhoevedorp
Lijnden
Schiphol
Amsterdam Schiphol

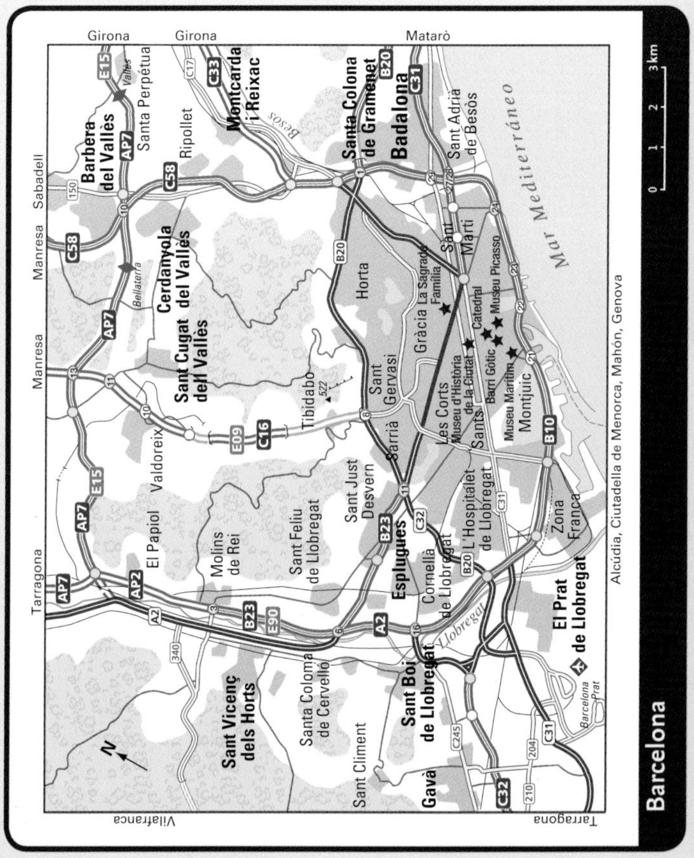
Barcelona
Girona
Mataró
Sabadell
Manresa
Tarragona
Vilafranca
Alcúdia, Ciutadella de Menorca, Mahón, Genova
0 1 2 3 km
Barberà del Vallès
Santa Perpètua
Ripollet
Montcada i Reixac
Santa Coloma de Gramenet
Badalona
Sant Adrià de Besòs
Cerdanyola del Vallès
Sant Cugat del Vallès
Horta
Sant Martí
La Sagrada Família
Gràcia
Catedral
Barri Gòtic
Museu Picasso
Museu Marítim
Montjuïc
Tibidabo
Sant Gervasi
Sarrià
Les Corts
Sants
Museu d'Història de la Ciutat
Valldoreix
El Papiol
Molins de Rei
Sant Feliu de Llobregat
Sant Just Desvern
Esplugues
Cornellà de Llobregat
L'Hospitalet de Llobregat
Zona Franca
El Prat de Llobregat
Sant Vicenç dels Horts
Santa Coloma de Cervelló
Sant Boi de Llobregat
Sant Climent
Gavà
Barcelona Prat
Mar Mediterráneo

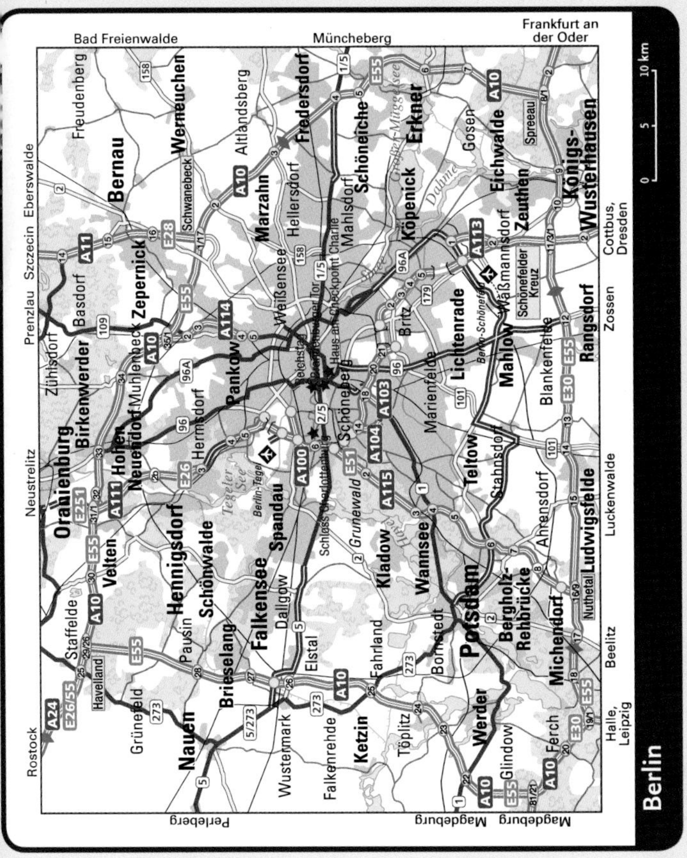
Berlin
Bad Freienwalde
Müncheberg
Frankfurt an der Oder
Rostock
Neustrelitz
Prenzlau Szczecin Eberswalde
Cottbus, Dresden
Zossen
Luckenwalde
Beelitz
Halle, Leipzig
Perleberg
Magdeburg
Oranienburg
Birkenwerder
Bernau
Zepernick
Werneuchen
Velten
Hennigsdorf
Falkensee
Spandau
Nauen
Brieselang
Ketzin
Potsdam
Werder
Michendorf
Ludwigsfelde
Teltow
Lichtenrade
Mahlow
Rangsdorf
Köpenick
Erkner
Fredersdorf
Marzahn
Pankow
Wannsee
Kladow
Schöneiche
Eichwalde
Zeuthen
Königs-Wusterhausen
Schönefelder Kreuz
Schloss Charlottenburg
Haus am Checkpoint Charlie
Berlin-Tegel
Berlin-Schönefeld
0 5 10 km

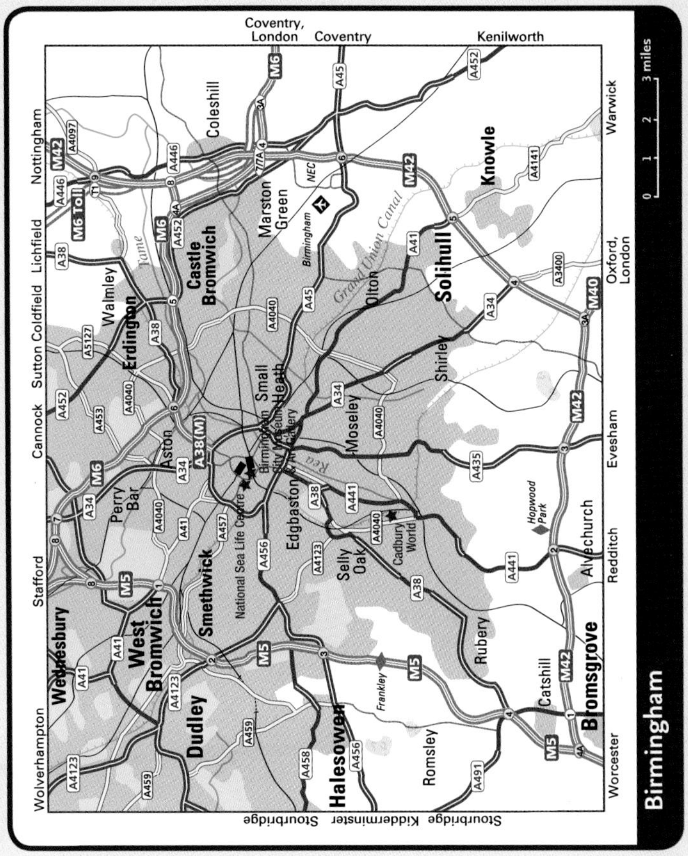
Birmingham
Coventry, London
Coventry
Kenilworth
Nottingham
Lichfield
Sutton Coldfield
Cannock
Stafford
Wolverhampton
Warwick
Oxford, London
Evesham
Redditch
Worcester
Stourbridge
Kidderminster
Coleshill
Castle Bromwich
Marston Green
Erdington
Walmley
Perry Barr
Aston
West Bromwich
Wednesbury
Dudley
Smethwick
Halesowen
Edgbaston
Selly Oak
Moseley
Small Heath
Solihull
Knowle
Olton
Shirley
Rubery
Romsley
Catshill
Bromsgrove
Alvechurch
Hopwood Park
Frankley
Cadbury World
National Sea Life Centre
Grand Union Canal
Birmingham
NEC
0 1 2 3 miles

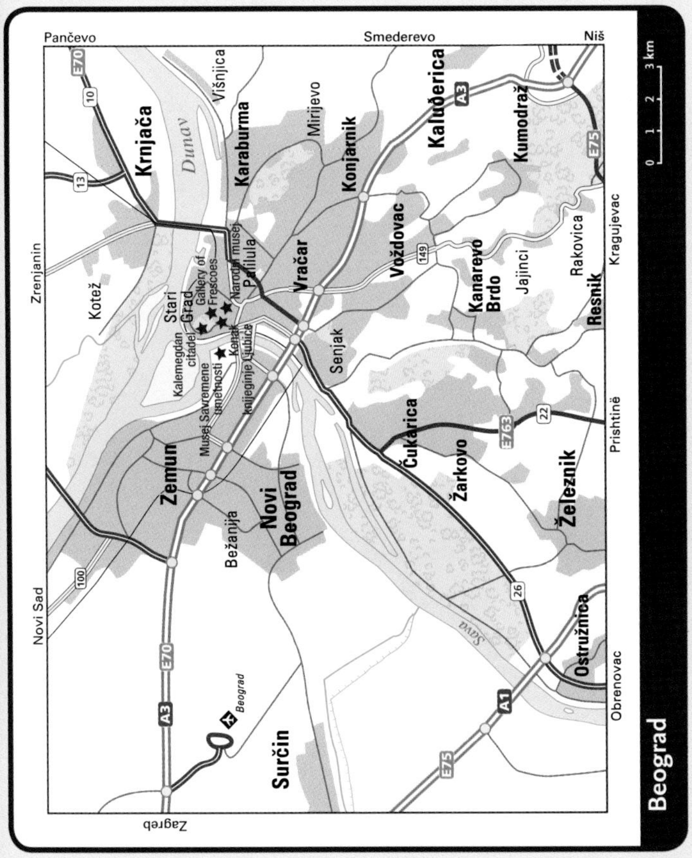
Beograd
Pančevo
Smederevo
Niš
Zrenjanin
Novi Sad
Zagreb
Obrenovac
Prishtinë
Kragujevac
Krnjača
Višnjica
Karaburma
Mirijevo
Konjarnik
Kaluđerica
Kumodraž
Voždovac
Vračar
Kanarevo Brdo
Jajinci
Rakovica
Resnik
Senjak
Čukarica
Žarkovo
Železnik
Zemun
Novi Beograd
Bežanija
Surčin
Ostružnica
Kotež
Stari Grad
Kalemegdan citadel
Dunav
Sava
Beograd
0 1 2 3 km

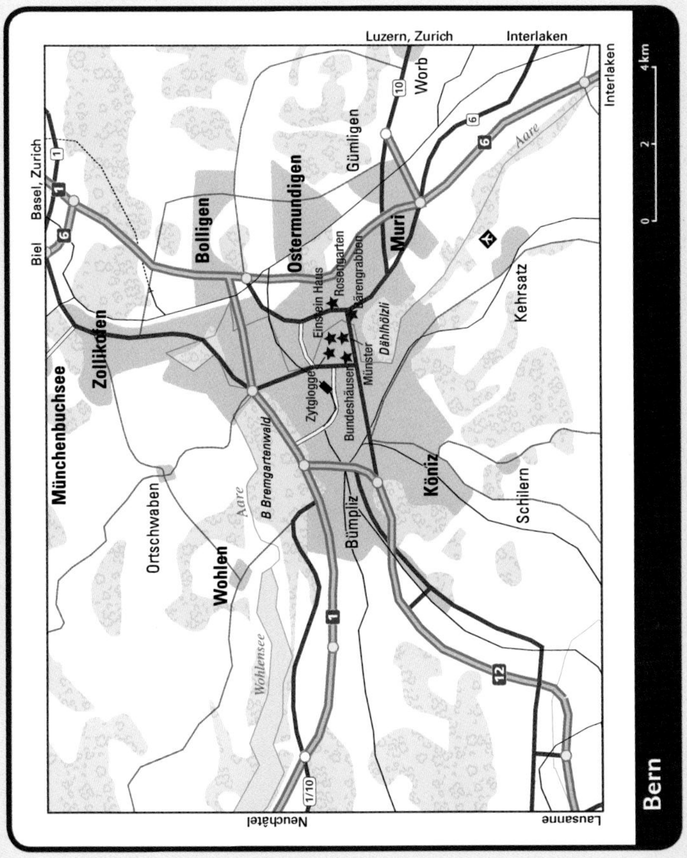
Bern
Biel
Basel, Zurich
Luzern, Zurich
Interlaken
Neuchâtel
Lausanne
Worb
Gümligen
Ostermundigen
Bolligen
Muri
Kehrsatz
Zollikofen
Münchenbuchsee
Köniz
Schliern
Bümpliz
Wohlen
Ortschwaben
Wohlensee
Aare
Bremgartenwald
Zytglogge
Bundeshäuser
Münster
Einstein Haus
Rosengarten
Bärengraben
Dählhölzli
0 2 4 km

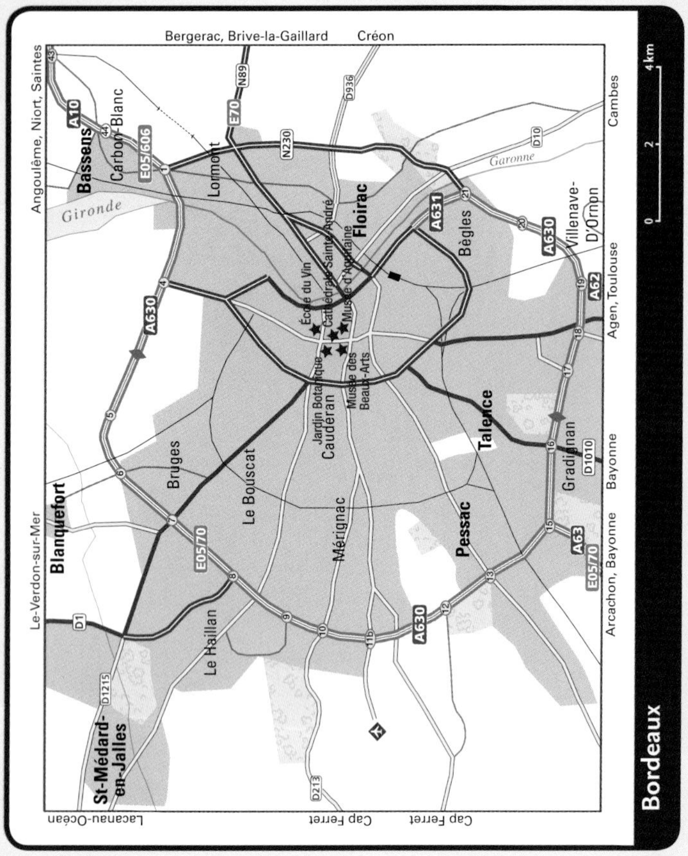
Bordeaux
Bergerac, Brive-la-Gaillard
Créon
Angoulême, Niort, Saintes
Le-Verdon-sur-Mer
Lacanau-Océan
Cap Ferret
Arcachon, Bayonne
Bayonne
Agen, Toulouse
Cambes
Bassens
Carbon-Blanc
Lormont
Floirac
Bègles
Villenave-D'Ornon
Blanquefort
Bruges
Le Bouscat
Caudéran
Mérignac
Pessac
Talence
Gradignan
Le Haillan
St-Médard-en-Jalles
Gironde
Garonne
Jardin Botanique
Musée des Beaux-Arts
École du Vin
Cathédrale Sainte-André
Musée d'Aquitaine

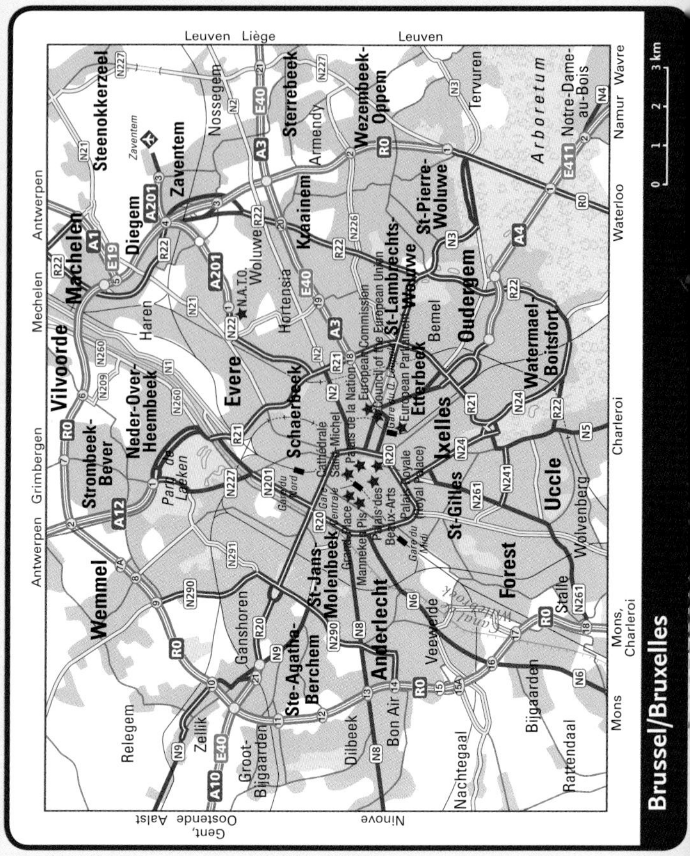
Brussel/Bruxelles
Leuven
Liège
Antwerpen
Mechelen
Grimbergen
Namur
Wavre
Waterloo
Charleroi
Mons, Charleroi
Mons
Ninove
Gent, Oostende
Aalst
Vilvoorde
Machelen
Diegem
Zaventem
Steenokkerzeel
Nossegem
Sterrebeek
Wezembeek-Oppem
Tervuren
Kraainem
Evere
Haren
Schaerbeek
Strombeek-Bever
Neder-Over-Heembeek
Wemmel
Ganshoren
St-Jans-Molenbeek
St-Agatha-Berchem
Anderlecht
Dilbeek
Zellik
Groot-Bijgaarden
Relegem
Bon Air
Veeweyde
St-Gilles
Ixelles
Etterbeek
Forest
Uccle
Watermael-Boitsfort
Oudergem
St-Pierre-Woluwe
St-Lambrechts-Woluwe
Woluwe
Hortensia
Bemel
Stalle
Wolvenberg
Nachtegaal
Bijgaarden
Rattendaal
Arboretum
Notre-Dame-au-Bois
Armendy
N.A.T.O.
European Commission
Council of the European Union
European Parliament
Palais de la Nation
Cathédrale
Manneken Pis
Grand-Place
Palais des Beaux-Arts
Palais Royale (Royal Palace)
Gare du Nord
Gare du Midi
Gare Centrale
Parc de Laeken

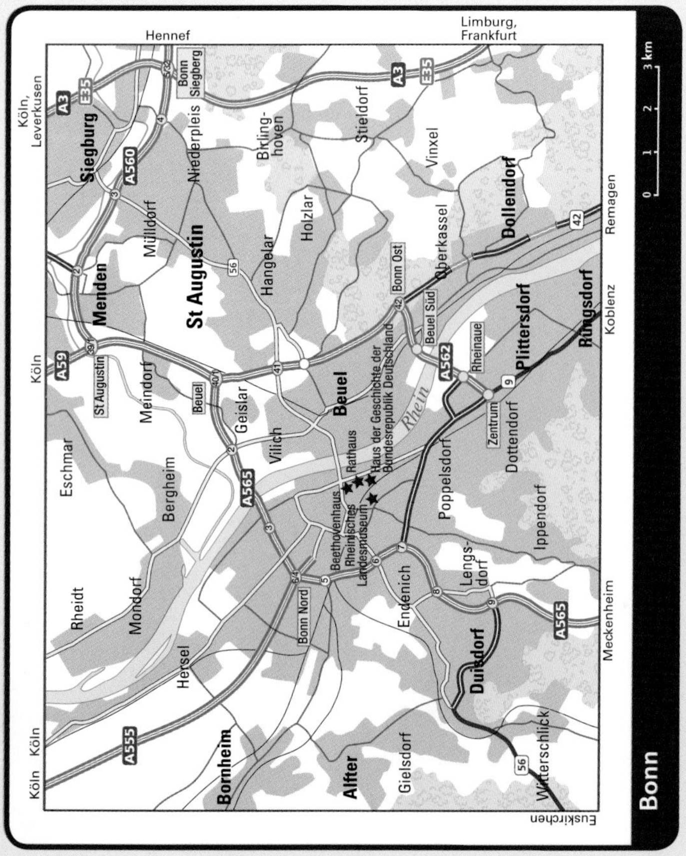
Bonn
Hennef
Limburg, Frankfurt
Köln, Leverkusen
Köln
Remagen
Koblenz
Meckenheim
Euskirchen
Siegburg
Menden
Mülldorf
Niederpleis
St Augustin
Meindorf
Geislar
Vilich
Beuel
Hangelar
Holzlar
Birlinghoven
Stieldorf
Vinxel
Oberkassel
Dollendorf
Plittersdorf
Rüngsdorf
Dottendorf
Poppelsdorf
Ippendorf
Lengsdorf
Endenich
Duisdorf
Witterschlick
Gielsdorf
Alfter
Bornheim
Hersel
Rheidt
Mondorf
Bergheim
Eschmar
Rhein
Beethovenhaus
Rathaus
Rheinisches Landesmuseum
Haus der Geschichte der Bundesrepublik Deutschland
Bonn Nord
Bonn Ost
Beuel Süd
Rheinaue
Zentrum

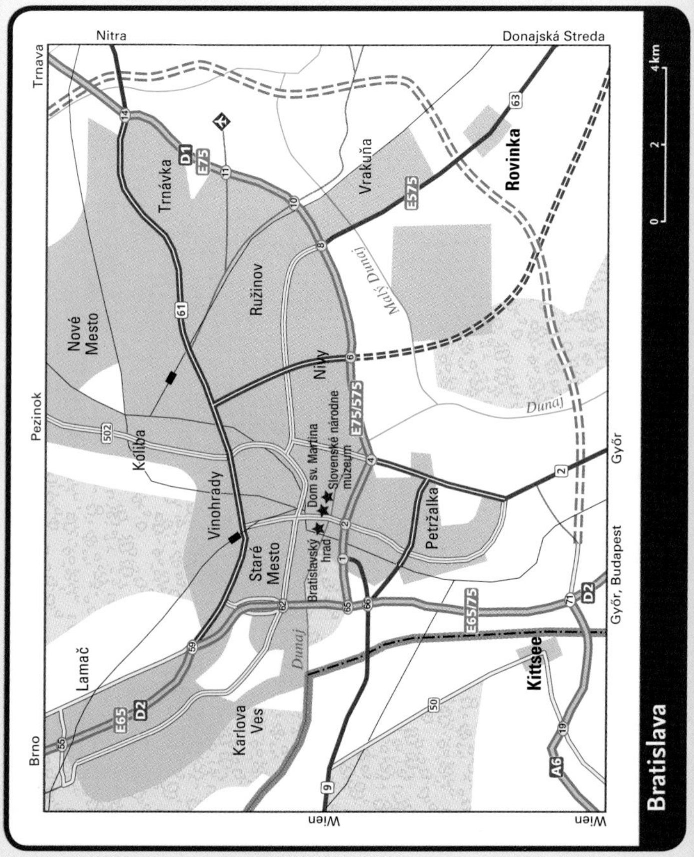
Bratislava
Nitra
Trnava
Donajská Streda
Pezinok
Brno
Wien
Győr
Győr, Budapest
Trnávka
Ružinov
Vrakuňa
Rovinka
Nové Mesto
Nivy
Koliba
Vinohrady
Staré Mesto
Petržalka
Lamač
Karlova Ves
Kittsee
Dunaj
Malý Dunaj
Bratislavský hrad
Dom sv. Martina
Slovenské národne múzeum

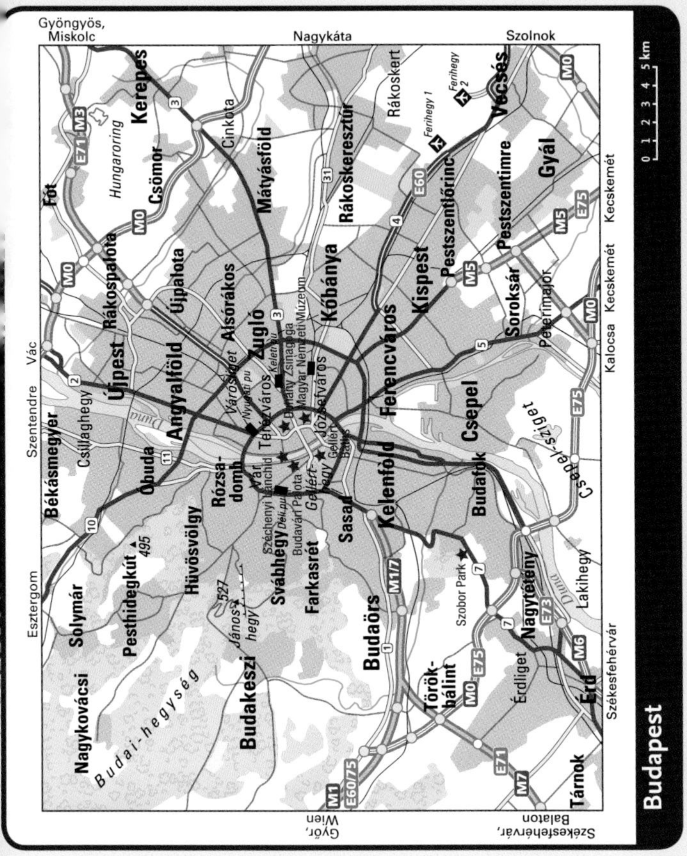
Budapest
Gyöngyös, Miskolc
Nagykáta
Szolnok
Esztergom
Szentendre
Vác
Kalocsa
Kecskemét
Székesfehérvár
Győr, Wien
Balaton Székesfehérvár,
0 1 2 3 4 5 km
Fót
Kerepes
Csömör
Hungaroring
Rákospalota
Újpalota
Mátyásföld
Cinkota
Rákoskeresztúr
Rákoskert
Ferihegy 1
Ferihegy 2
Vecsés
Gyál
Pestszentimre
Pestszentlőrinc
Kőbánya
Kispest
Soroksár
Pesterimajor
Újpest
Angyalföld
Alsórákos
Zugló
Ferencváros
Józsefváros
Csepel
Csepel-sziget
Békásmegyer
Csillaghegy
Óbuda
Rózsadomb
Terézváros
Kelenföld
Budafok
Budaörs
Sasad
Farkasrét
Svábhegy
Hűvösvölgy
Pesthidegkút
Solymár
Nagykovácsi
Budai-hegység
Budakeszi
Jánoshegy
Törökbálint
Érdliget
Nagytétény
Lakihegy
Szobor Park
Érd
Tárnok
Duna
495
527

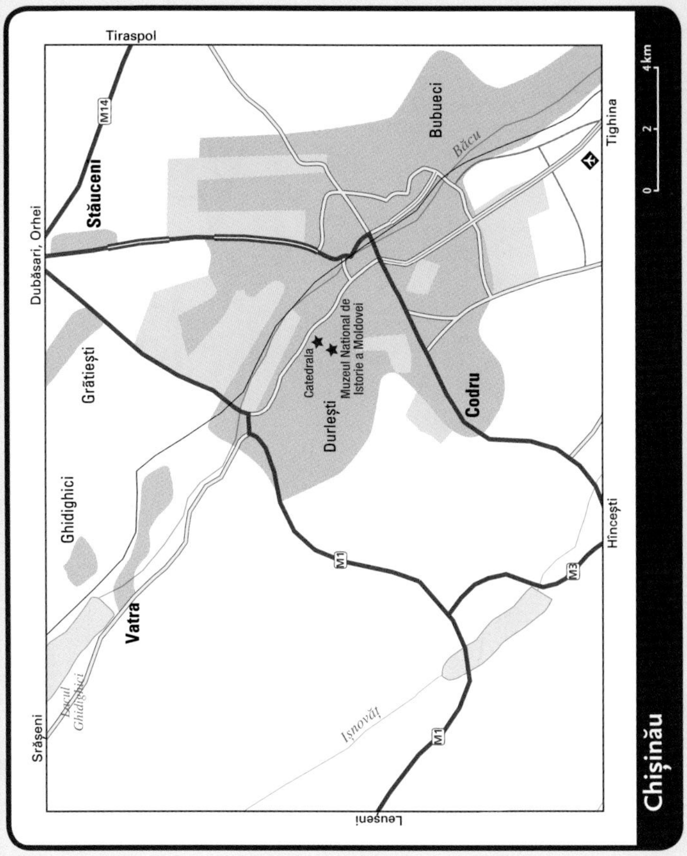
Chişinău
Tiraspol
Dubăsari, Orhei
Străşeni
Leuşeni
Hînceşti
Tighina
0 2 4 km
Stăuceni
Bubueci
Bîcu
Grătieşti
Ghidighici
Vatra
Codru
Durleşti
Catedrala
Muzeul Naţional de Istorie a Moldovei
Işnovăţ
M1
M3
M14

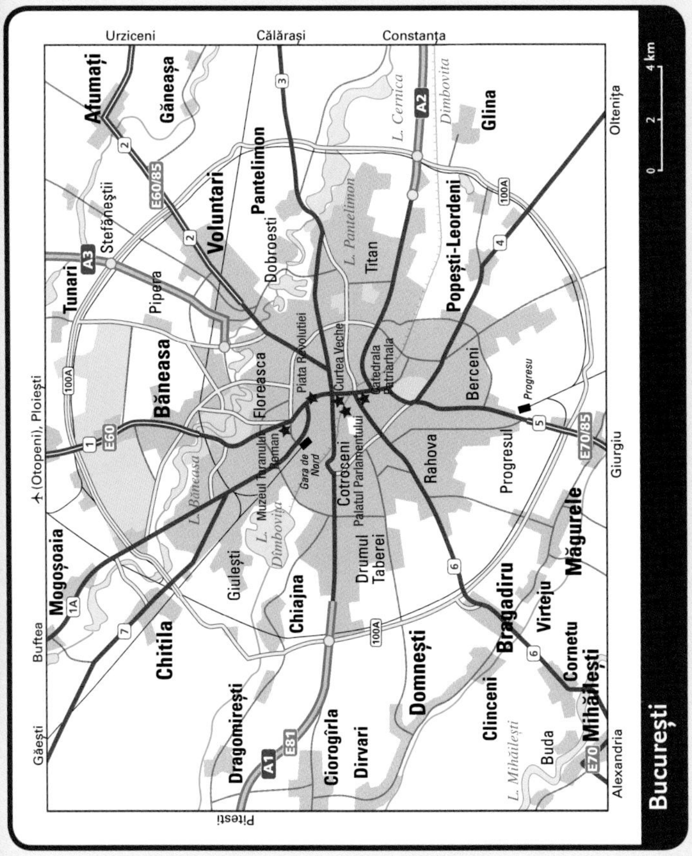
Bucureşti
Urziceni
Călăraşi
Constanţa
Olteniţa
Giurgiu
Alexandria
Piteşti
Găeşti
Buftea
(Otopeni), Ploieşti
0 2 4 km
Afumaţi
Găneasa
Ştefăneştii
Tunari
Voluntari
Pantelimon
Glina
Pipera
Dobroesti
Titan
Popeşti-Leordeni
Băneasa
Floreasca
Piata Revolutiei
Curtea Veche
Catedrala Patriarhala
Berceni
Progresu
Mogoşoaia
Chitila
Giuleşti
Chiajna
Cotroceni
Drumul Taberei
Rahova
Progresul
Măgurele
Bragadiru
Domneşti
Vîrteju
Cornetu
Mihăileşti
Clinceni
Buda
Dragomireşti
Ciorogîrla
Dirvari
Gara de Nord
Palatul Parlamentului
L. Cernica
L. Pantelimon
Dîmbovita
L. Mihăileşti

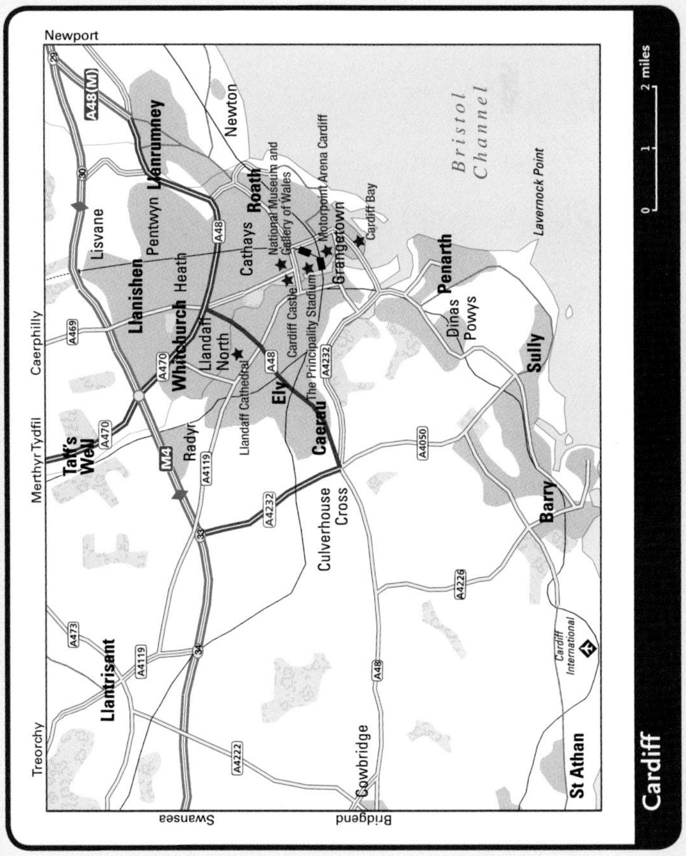
Cardiff
Newport
Caerphilly
Merthyr Tydfil
Treorchy
Swansea
Bridgend
0 1 2 miles
Newton
Llanrumney
Lisvane
Pentwyn
Llanishen
Heath
Whitchurch
Cathays
Roath
Llandaff North
Llandaff Cathedral
Ely
Caerau
Grangetown
National Museum and Gallery of Wales
Cardiff Castle
The Principality Stadium
Motorpoint Arena Cardiff
Cardiff Bay
Bristol Channel
Lavernock Point
Penarth
Dinas Powys
Sully
Barry
Taff's Well
Radyr
Culverhouse Cross
Llantrisant
Cowbridge
St Athan
Cardiff International

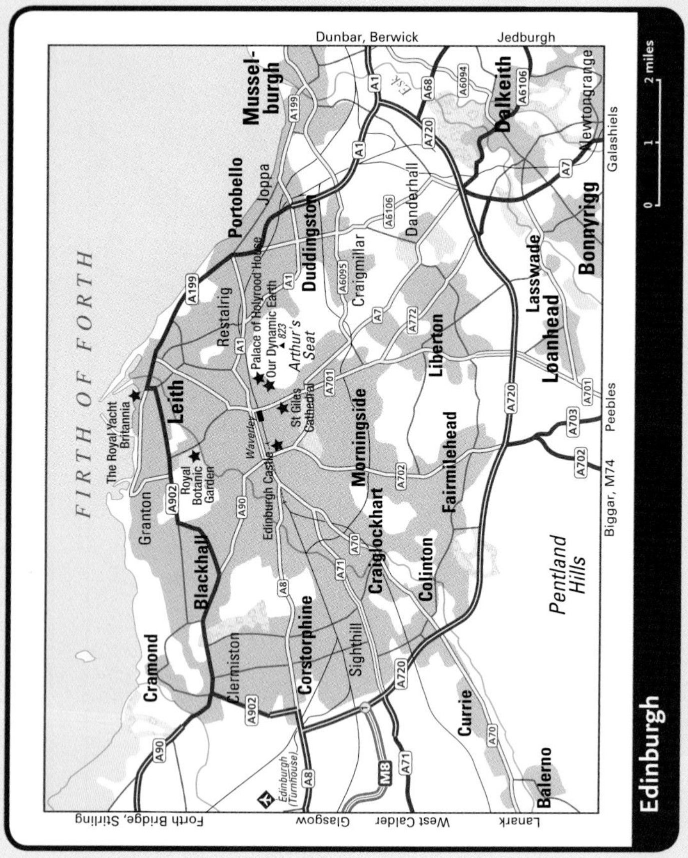
Edinburgh
FIRTH OF FORTH
Dunbar, Berwick
Jedburgh
Galashiels
Peebles
Biggar, M74
Lanark
West Calder
Glasgow
Forth Bridge, Stirling
Edinburgh (Turnhouse)
Musselburgh
Portobello
Joppa
Dalkeith
Newtongrange
Bonnyrigg
Lasswade
Loanhead
Danderhall
Duddingston
Craigmillar
Restalrig
Leith
The Royal Yacht Britannia
Granton
Royal Botanic Garden
Palace of Holyrood House
Our Dynamic Earth
Arthur's Seat
St Giles Cathedral
Waverley
Edinburgh Castle
Morningside
Liberton
Fairmilehead
Blackhall
Cramond
Clermiston
Corstorphine
Sighthill
Craiglockhart
Colinton
Currie
Balerno
Pentland Hills
0 1 2 miles

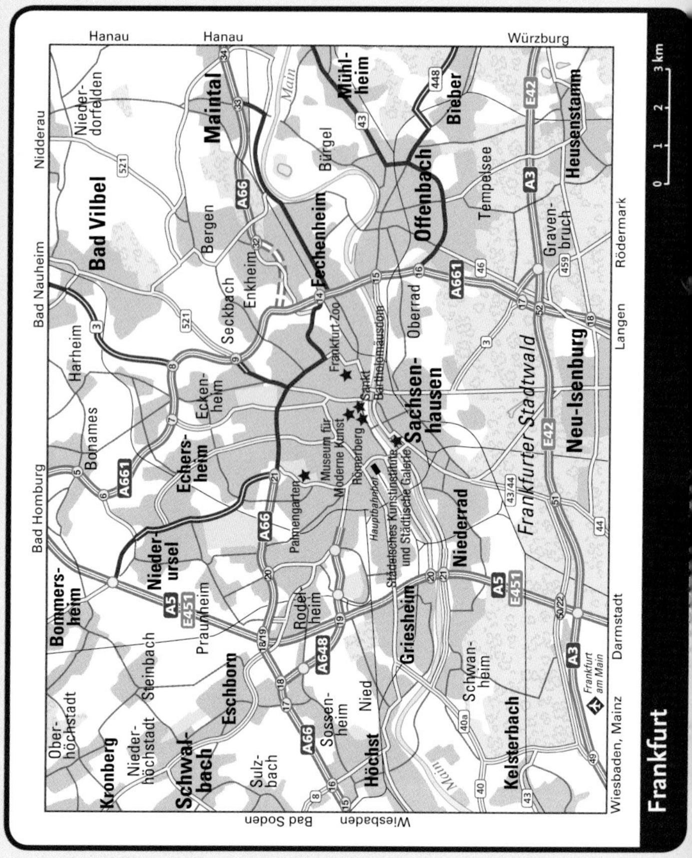
Frankfurt
Hanau
Würzburg
Nidderau
Bad Nauheim
Bad Homburg
Darmstadt
Rödermark
Langen
Wiesbaden, Mainz
Wiesbaden
Bad Soden
Nieder-dorfelden
Maintal
Mühlheim
Bürgel
Bieber
Offenbach
Heusenstamm
Tempelsee
Gravenbruch
Bad Vilbel
Bergen
Enkheim
Fechenheim
Seckbach
Oberrad
Harheim
Bonames
Eckenheim
Frankfurt Zoo
Sankt Bartholomäusdom
Römerberg
Museum für Moderne Kunst
Sachsenhausen
Städelsches Kunstinstitut und Städtische Galerie
Hauptbahnhof
Palmengarten
Eschersheim
Niederursel
Bommersheim
Frankfurter Stadtwald
Neu-Isenburg
Niederrad
Praunheim
Rödelheim
Griesheim
Schwanheim
Steinbach
Oberhöchstadt
Niederhöchstadt
Eschborn
Kronberg
Schwalbach
Sulzbach
Sossenheim
Nied
Höchst
Kelsterbach
Frankfurt am Main
Main
0 1 2 3 km

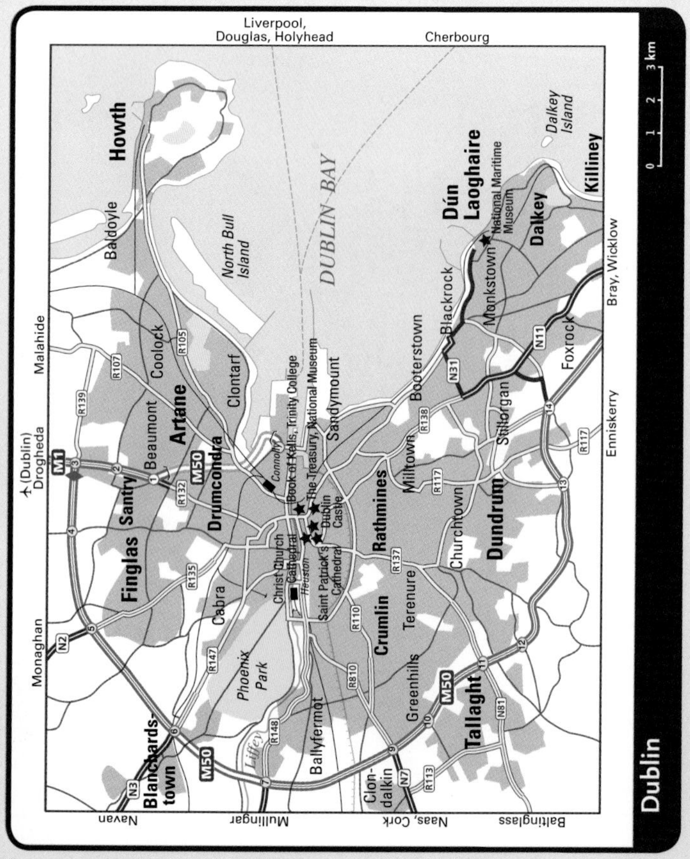
Dublin
DUBLIN BAY
Liverpool, Douglas, Holyhead
Cherbourg
(Dublin) Drogheda
Malahide
Monaghan
Navan
Mullingar
Naas, Cork
Baltinglass
Enniskerry
Bray, Wicklow
Howth
Baldoyle
North Bull Island
Dalkey Island
Killiney
Dalkey
Dún Laoghaire
National Maritime Museum
Monkstown
Blackrock
Foxrock
Stillorgan
Booterstown
Sandymount
Clontarf
Coolock
Artane
Beaumont
Santry
Finglas
Drumcondra
Connolly
Book of Kells, Trinity College
The Treasury, National Museum
Dublin Castle
Christ Church Cathedral
Heuston
Saint Patrick's Cathedral
Cabra
Phoenix Park
Liffey
Ballyfermot
Rathmines
Milltown
Churchtown
Dundrum
Terenure
Crumlin
Greenhills
Tallaght
Clondalkin
Blanchardstown
0 1 2 3 km

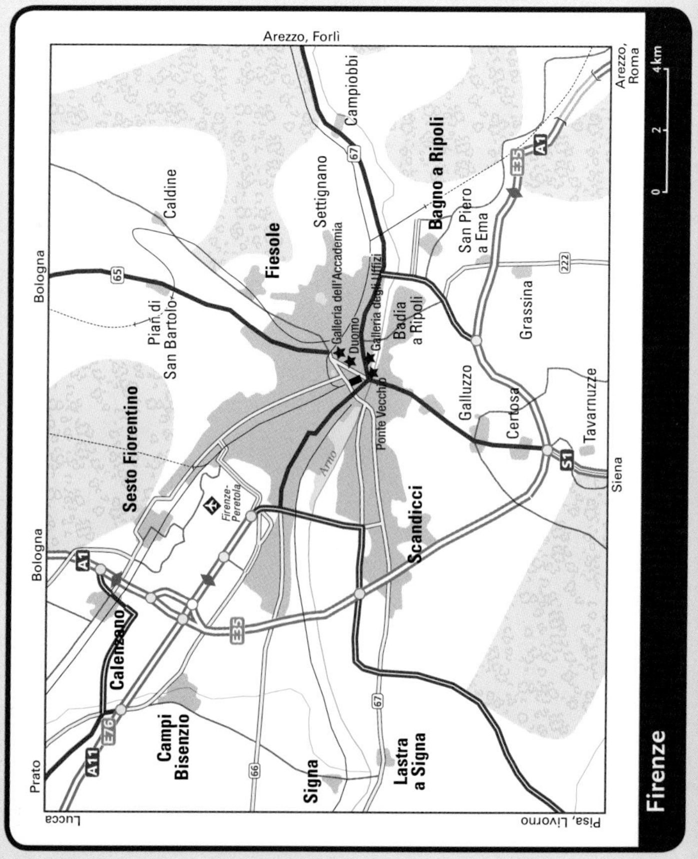
Firenze
Arezzo, Forlì
Arezzo, Roma
Bologna
Prato
Lucca
Pisa, Livorno
Siena
Campiobbi
Caldine
Settignano
Fiesole
Bagno a Ripoli
San Piero a Ema
Grassina
Badia a Ripoli
Galleria dell'Accademia
Duomo
Galleria degli Uffizi
Ponte Vecchio
Pian di San Bartolo
Sesto Fiorentino
Firenze-Peretola
Arno
Galluzzo
Certosa
Tavarnuzze
Scandicci
Calenzano
Campi Bisenzio
Signa
Lastra a Signa
0 2 4 km

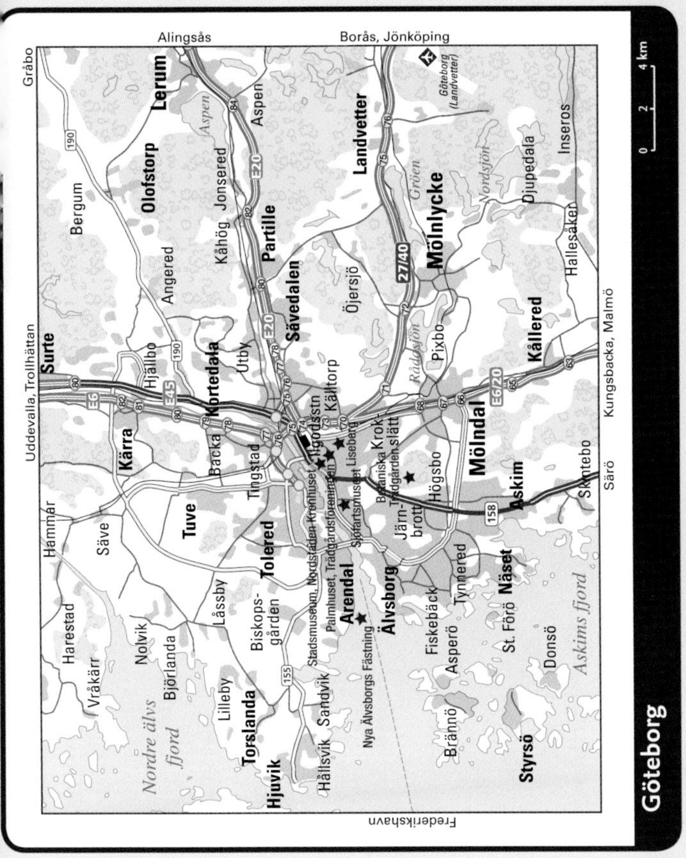
Göteborg
Alingsås
Borås, Jönköping
Uddevalla, Trollhättan
Kungsbacka, Malmö
Frederikshavn
Gråbo
Särö
Lerum
Olofstorp
Landvetter
Mölnlycke
Partille
Sävedalen
Kortedala
Surte
Kärra
Tuve
Torslanda
Hjuvik
Tolered
Arendal
Älvsborg
Mölndal
Askim
Näset
Kållered
Styrsö
Nordre älvs fjord
Askims fjord
Göteborg (Landvetter)

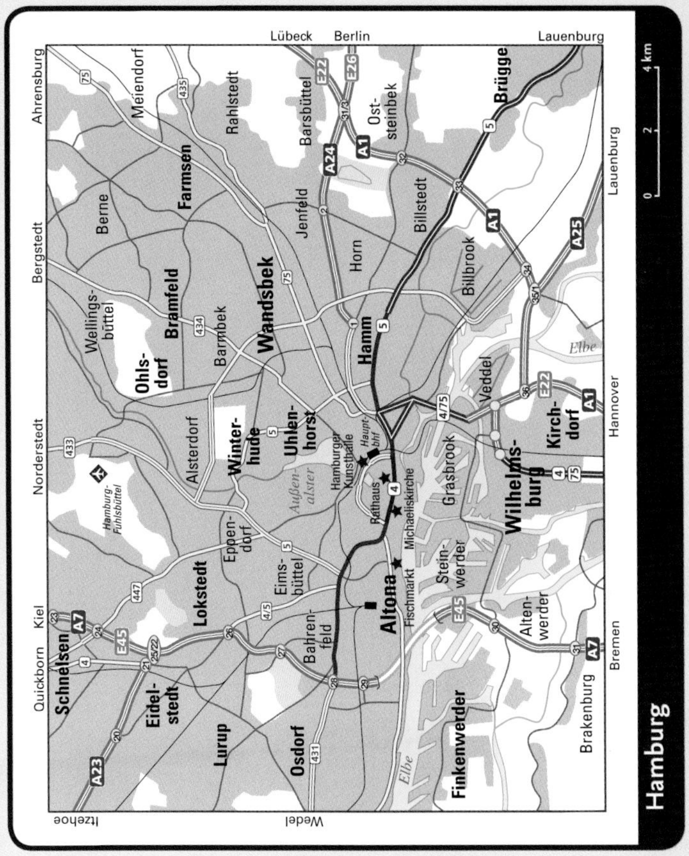
Hamburg
Lübeck
Berlin
Lauenburg
Ahrensburg
Bergstedt
Norderstedt
Quickborn
Kiel
Bremen
Hannover
Itzehoe
Wedel
Farmsen
Bramfeld
Wandsbek
Ohlsdorf
Winterhude
Uhlenhorst
Hamm
Brügge
Lokstedt
Schnelsen
Eidelstedt
Lurup
Osdorf
Altona
Wilhelmsburg
Kirchdorf
Finkenwerder
Elbe
Hamburg-Fuhlsbüttel

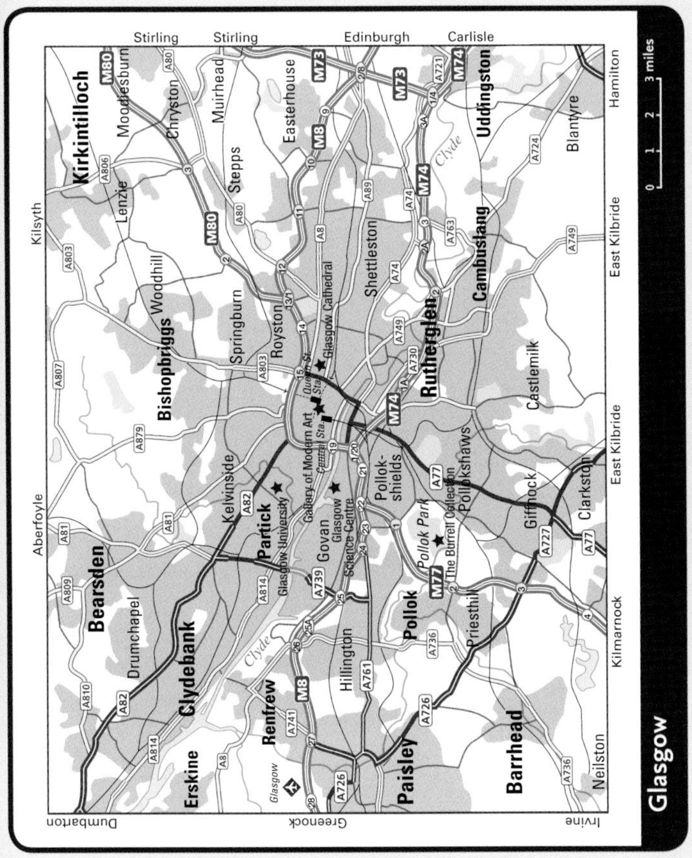
Glasgow
Stirling
Edinburgh
Carlisle
Kilsyth
Aberfoyle
Dumbarton
Greenock
Irvine
Kilmarnock
East Kilbride
Hamilton
Kirkintilloch
Bishopbriggs
Bearsden
Clydebank
Erskine
Renfrew
Paisley
Barrhead
Pollok
Partick
Rutherglen
Cambuslang
Uddingston
Clyde
Glasgow Cathedral
Gallery of Modern Art
Glasgow University
The Burrell Collection
Pollok Park

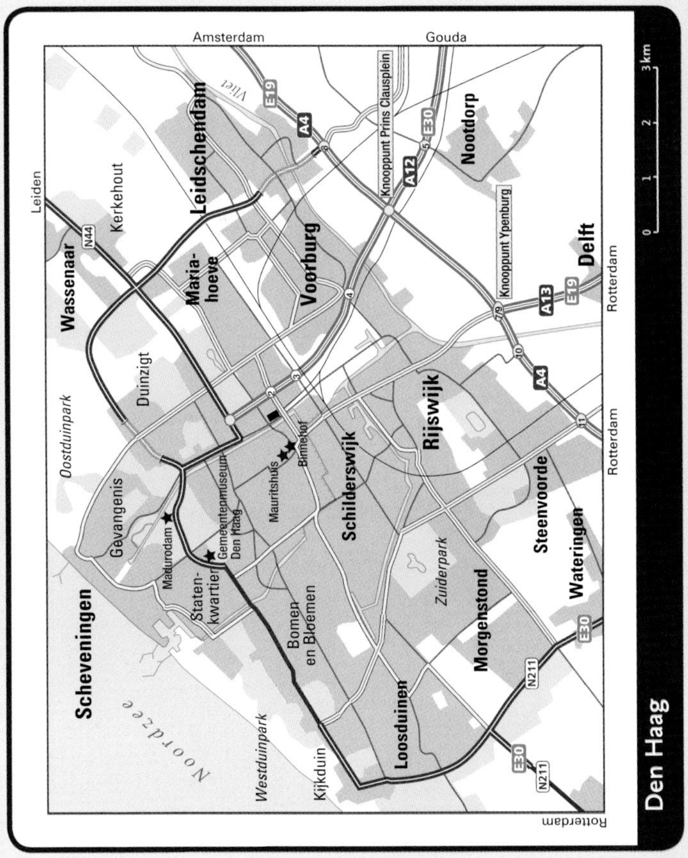
Den Haag
Amsterdam
Gouda
Leiden
Rotterdam
Scheveningen
Wassenaar
Leidschendam
Voorburg
Mariahoeve
Rijswijk
Schilderswijk
Loosduinen
Morgenstond
Wateringen
Steenvoorde
Delft
Nootdorp
Noordzee
Madurodam
Mauritshuis
Binnenhof
Knooppunt Prins Clausplein
Knooppunt Ypenburg

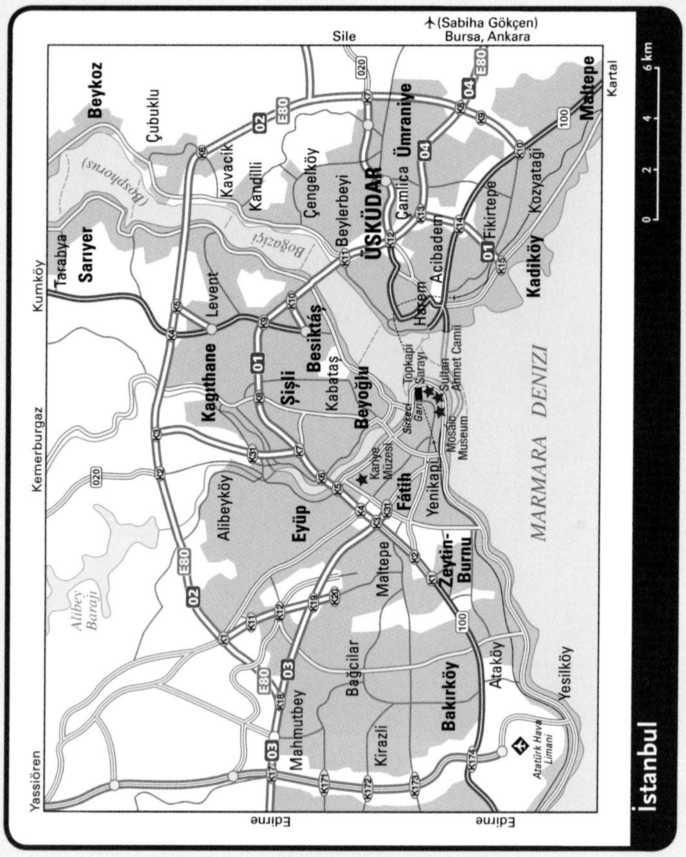
İstanbul
Sile
(Sabiha Gökçen) Bursa, Ankara
Beykoz
Çubuklu
Sarıyer
Tarabya
Kumköy
Kemerburgaz
Yassiören
Edirne
Kağıthane
Şişli
Beşiktaş
Beyoğlu
Üsküdar
Ümraniye
Kadıköy
Maltepe
Kartal
Eyüp
Fatih
Zeytinburnu
Bakırköy
Bağcılar
Kirazli
Mahmutbey
Ataköy
Yesilköy
Atatürk Hava Limanı
Alibeyköy
Alibey Barajı
Levent
Kavacık
Kandilli
Çengelköy
Beylerbeyi
Çamlıca
Acıbadem
Haseм
Fikirtepe
Kozyatağı
Kabataş
Topkapı Sarayı
Sirkeci Garı
Sultan Ahmet Camii
Mosaic Museum
Kariye Müzesi
Yenikapı
Maltepe
Boğaziçi
(Bosphorus)
MARMARA DENIZI
0 2 4 6 km

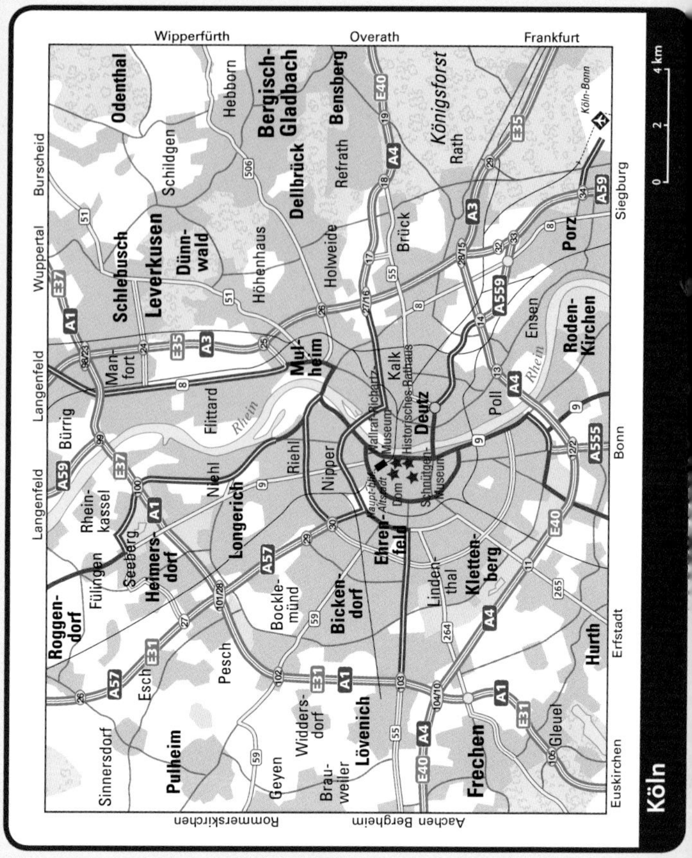
Köln
Wipperfürth
Overath
Frankfurt
Burscheid
Wuppertal
Langenfeld
Odenthal
Bergisch-Gladbach
Bensberg
Schildgen
Hebborn
Dellbrück
Refrath
Königsforst
Rath
Schlebusch
Leverkusen
Dünnwald
Höhenhaus
Holweide
Brück
Mülheim
Kalk
Deutz
Poll
Ensen
Porz
Roden-Kirchen
Siegburg
Köln-Bonn
Bonn
Bürrig
Manfort
Flittard
Rhein
Rheinkassel
Niehl
Riehl
Nippes
Dom
Hauptbf
Wallraf-Richartz Museum
Historisches Rathaus
Schnütgen Museum
Altstadt
Fühlingen
Seeberg
Heimersdorf
Longerich
Ehrenfeld
Roggendorf
Bocklemünd
Bickendorf
Lindenthal
Klettenberg
Pesch
Esch
Widdersdorf
Lövenich
Sinnersdorf
Pulheim
Geyen
Brauweiler
Frechen
Gleuel
Hürth
Erfstadt
Euskirchen
Aachen Bergheim
Rommerskirchen
0 2 4 km

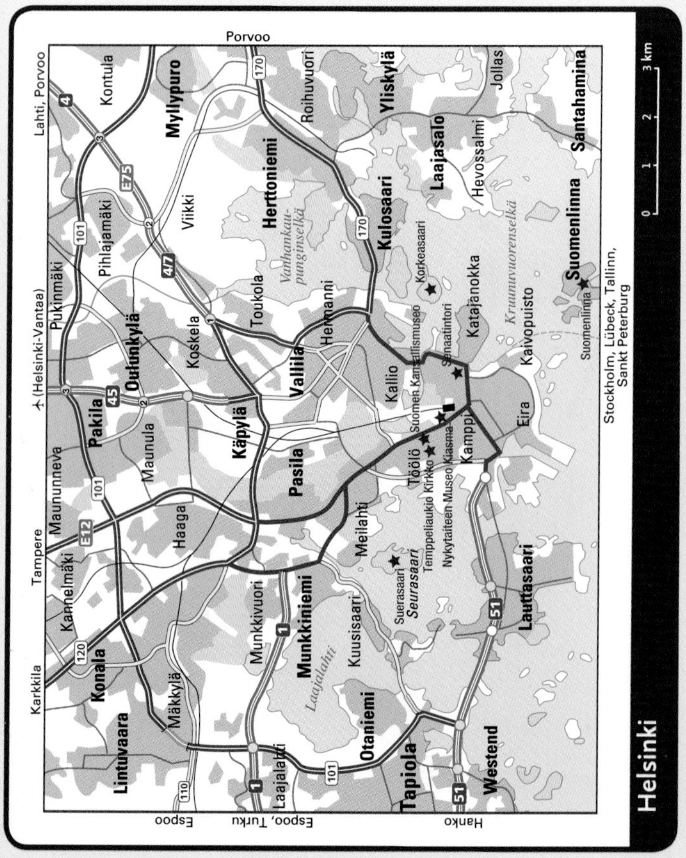
Helsinki
Porvoo
Lahti, Porvoo
(Helsinki-Vantaa)
Tampere
Karkkila
Espoo
Espoo, Turku
Hanko
Kontula
Myllypuro
Roihuvuori
Vuosaari
Jollas
Yliskylä
Laajasalo
Herttoniemi
Kulosaari
Viikki
Vanhankaupunginselkä
Pihlajamäki
Pukinmäki
Oulunkylä
Koskela
Toukola
Hermanni
Vallila
Käpylä
Pakila
Maunula
Pasila
Haaga
Maununeva
Kannelmäki
Konala
Mäkkylä
Lintuvaara
Munkkivuori
Munkkiniemi
Kuusisaari
Meilahti
Seurasaari
Laajalahti
Otaniemi
Tapiola
Westend
Lauttasaari
Laajalahti
Töölö
Kallio
Kamppi
Eira
Kaivopuisto
Katajanokka
Suomenlinna
Santahamina
Korkeasaari
Kruunuvuorenselkä
Hevossalmi
Temppeliaukio Kirkko
Kiasma
Nykytaiteen Museo
Suomen Kansallismuseo
Senaatintori
Stockholm, Lübeck, Tallinn, Sankt Peterburg
0 1 2 3 km

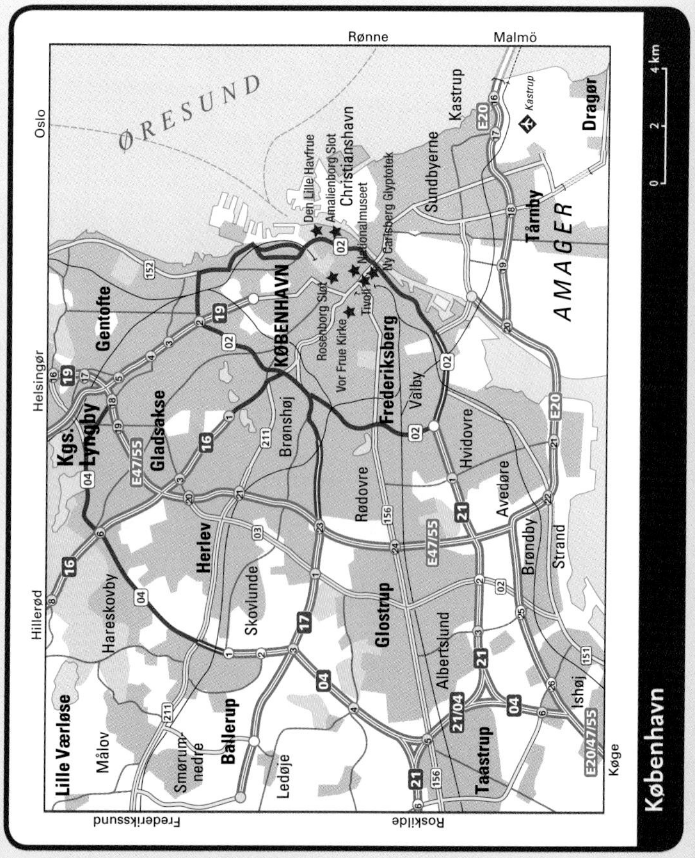
København
Rønne
Malmö
Oslo
Helsingør
Hillerød
Frederikssund
Roskilde
Køge
ØRESUND
Kastrup
Dragør
Tårnby
AMAGER
Sundbyerne
Christianshavn
Den Lille Havfrue
Amalienborg Slot
Nationalmuseet
Ny Carlsberg Glyptotek
Tivoli
Rosenborg Slot
Vor Frue Kirke
KØBENHAVN
Frederiksberg
Valby
Hvidovre
Avedøre
Brøndby Strand
Brøndby
Gentofte
Kgs. Lyngby
Gladsakse
Brønshøj
Rødovre
Herlev
Skovlunde
Glostrup
Albertslund
Hareskovby
Lille Værløse
Målov
Smørum-nedre
Ballerup
Ledøje
Taastrup
Ishøj
0 2 4 km

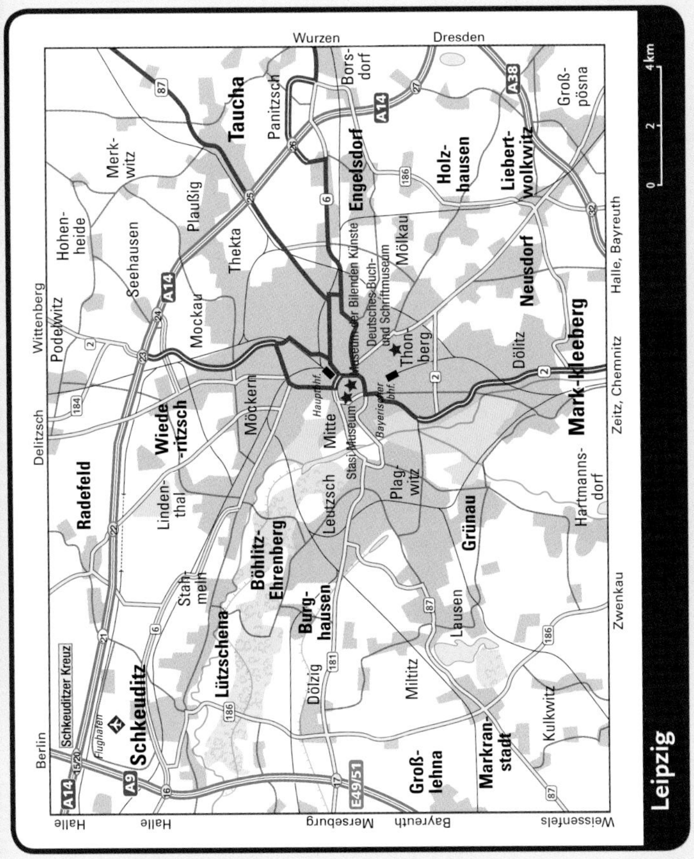
Berlin
Delitzsch
Wittenberg
Podelwitz
Hohen-heide
Schkeuditzer Kreuz
Radefeld
Flughafen
Schkeuditz
Seehausen
Merk-witz
Linden-thal
Wiede-ritzsch
Stah-meln
Mockau
Plaußig
Lützschena
Thekta
Taucha
Böhlitz-Ehrenberg
Möckern
Panitzsch
Dölzig
Burg-hausen
Leutzsch
Mitte
Hauptbhf.
Stasi Museum
Museum der Bildenden Künste
Engelsdorf
Bors-dorf
Bayerischer Bhf.
Deutsches Buch- und Schriftmuseum
Groß-lehna
Miltitz
Plag-witz
Thon-berg
Mölkau
Lausen
Grünau
Holz-hausen
Markran-stadt
Dölitz
Neusdorf
Liebert-wolkwitz
Kulkwitz
Hartmanns-dorf
Mark-kleeberg
Groß-pösna
Zwenkau
Zeitz, Chemnitz
Halle, Bayreuth
Halle
Merseburg
Bayreuth
Weissenfels
Wurzen
Dresden
Leipzig
0 2 4 km

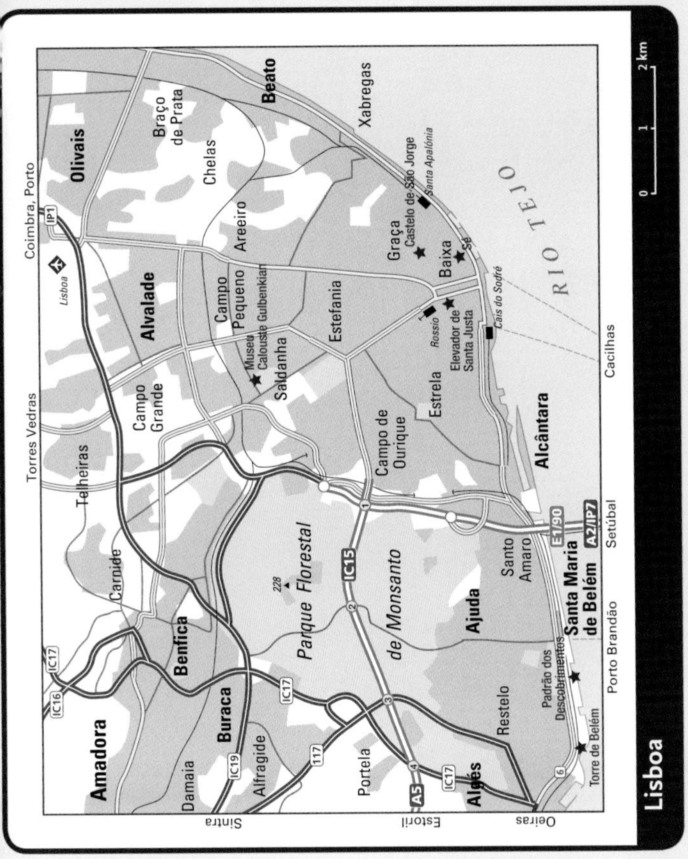
Torres Vedras
Coimbra, Porto
Lisboa
Amadora
Telheiras
Olivais
Carnide
Campo Grande
Alvalade
Braço de Prata
Damaia
Benfica
Chelas
Buraca
Campo Pequeno
Areeiro
Sintra
Alfragide
Museu Calouste Gulbenkian
Saldanha
Beato
Parque Florestal
Portela
Estefania
Xabregas
de Monsanto
Campo de Ourique
Graça
Castelo de São Jorge
Estoril
Estrela
Rossio
Santa Apolónia
Algés
Elevador de Santa Justa
Baixa
Sé
Ajuda
Restelo
Cais do Sodré
Santo Amaro
Oeiras
Alcântara
RIO TEJO
Padrão dos Descobrimentos
Santa Maria de Belém
Torre de Belém
Porto Brandão
Setúbal
Cacilhas
Lisboa
0 1 2 km

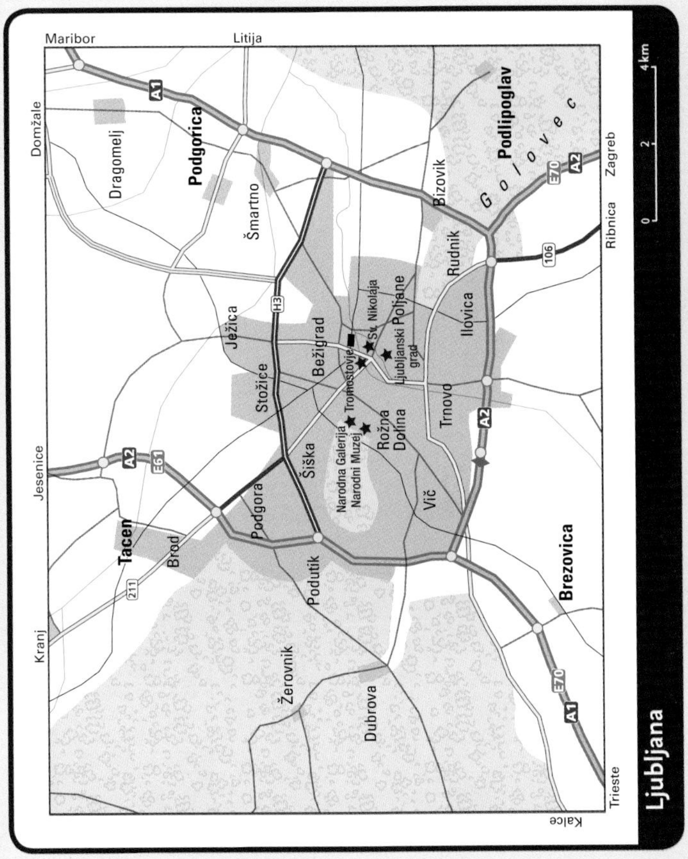
Kranj
Jesenice
Domžale
Maribor
Tacen
Dragomelj
Brod
Podgorica
Ježica
Podgora
Stožice
Šmartno
Litija
Žerovnik
Podutik
Šiška
Bežigrad
Narodna Galerija
Narodni Muzej
Tromostovje
Sv. Nikolaja
Dubrova
Rožna Dolina
Ljubljanski grad
Poljane
Vič
Bizovik
Trnovo
Rudnik
Ilovica
Golovec
Podlipoglav
Brezovica
Kalce
Trieste
Ribnica
Zagreb
Ljubljana
0 2 4 km

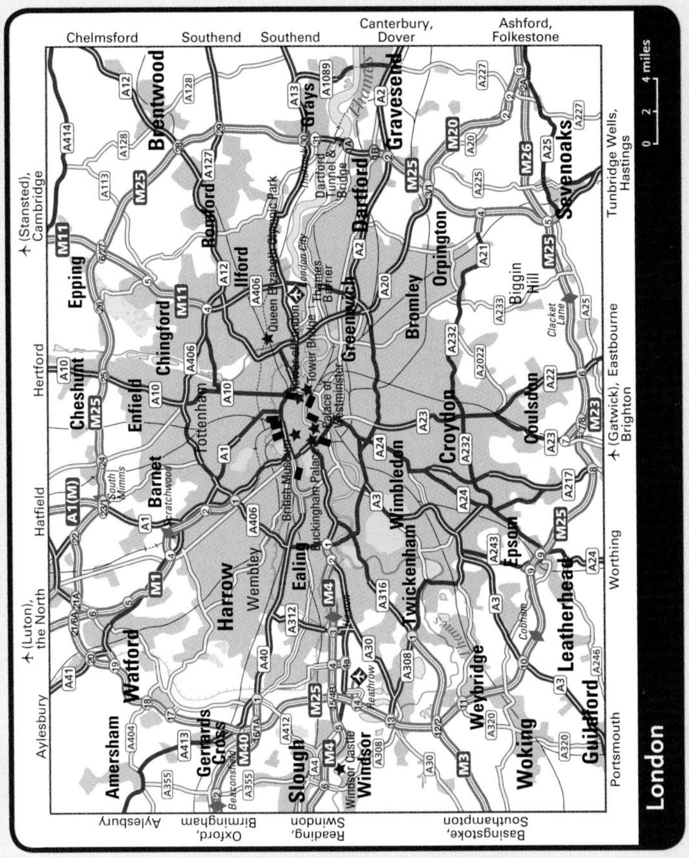
Aylesbury
(Luton), the North
Hatfield
Hertford
(Stansted), Cambridge
Cheshunt
Epping
Amersham
Watford
South Mimms
Chelmsford
Barnet
Enfield
Chingford
Brentwood
Gerrards Cross
Harrow
Tottenham
Romford
Southend
Beaconsfield
Wembley
Ilford
Queen Elizabeth Olympic Park
Slough
British Museum
Tower of London
London City
Grays
Ealing
Buckingham Palace
Tower Bridge
Thames Barrier
Windsor Castle
Palace of Westminster
Dartford Tunnel & Bridge
Windsor
Heathrow
Greenwich
Dartford
Twickenham
Wimbledon
Gravesend
Bromley
Croydon
Orpington
Weybridge
Epsom
Biggin Hill
Woking
Cobham
Coulsdon
Clacket Lane
Leatherhead
Sevenoaks
Guildford
Oxford, Birmingham
Reading, Swindon
Basingstoke, Southampton
Canterbury, Dover
Ashford, Folkestone
Portsmouth
Worthing
(Gatwick), Eastbourne Brighton
Tunbridge Wells, Hastings
London
0 2 4 miles

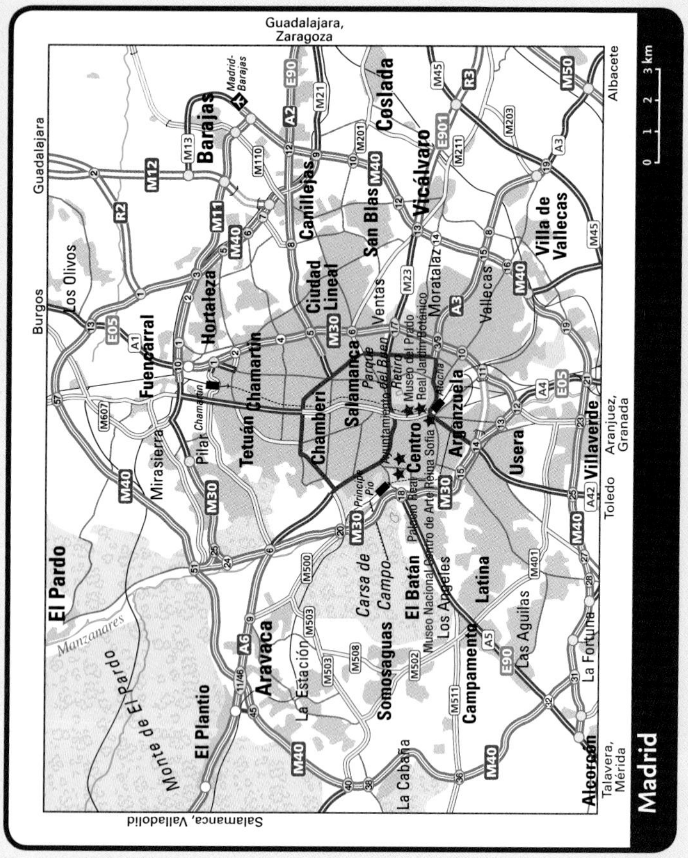
Madrid
Guadalajara, Zaragoza
Salamanca, Valladolid
Talavera, Mérida
Toledo
Aranjuez, Granada
Albacete
Burgos
Guadalajara
El Pardo
Aravaca
El Plantío
Fuencarral
Hortaleza
Barajas
Coslada
Vicálvaro
Canillejas
Chamartín
Tetuán
Chamberí
Salamanca
Centro
Arganzuela
Usera
Villaverde
Latina
Campamento
Somosaguas
Carabanchel
Villa de Vallecas
Ciudad Lineal
San Blas
Moratalaz
Mirasierra
Alcorcón
Casa de Campo
Manzanares
Monte de El Pardo
0 1 2 3 km

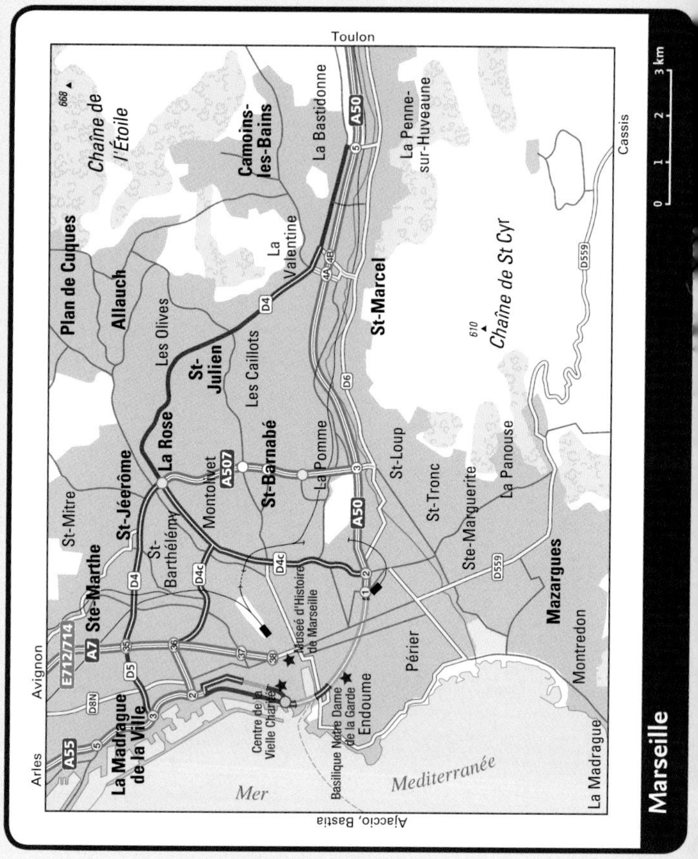
Marseille
Toulon
Ajaccio, Bastia
Arles
Avignon
Cassis
Mer Méditerranée
Chaîne de l'Etoile
Chaîne de St Cyr
Plan de Cuques
Allauch
Camoins-les-Bains
La Bastidonne
La Penne-sur-Huveaune
St-Marcel
St-Julien
La Rose
St-Jérôme
St-Barnabé
Les Olives
Les Caillots
La Pomme
St-Loup
St-Tronc
Ste-Marguerite
La Panouse
Mazargues
Montredon
La Madrague
Périer
Endoume
Ste-Marthe
St-Mitre
La Madrague de la Ville
Musée d'Histoire de Marseille
Basilique Notre Dame de la Garde
Centre de la Vieille Charité
0 1 2 3 km

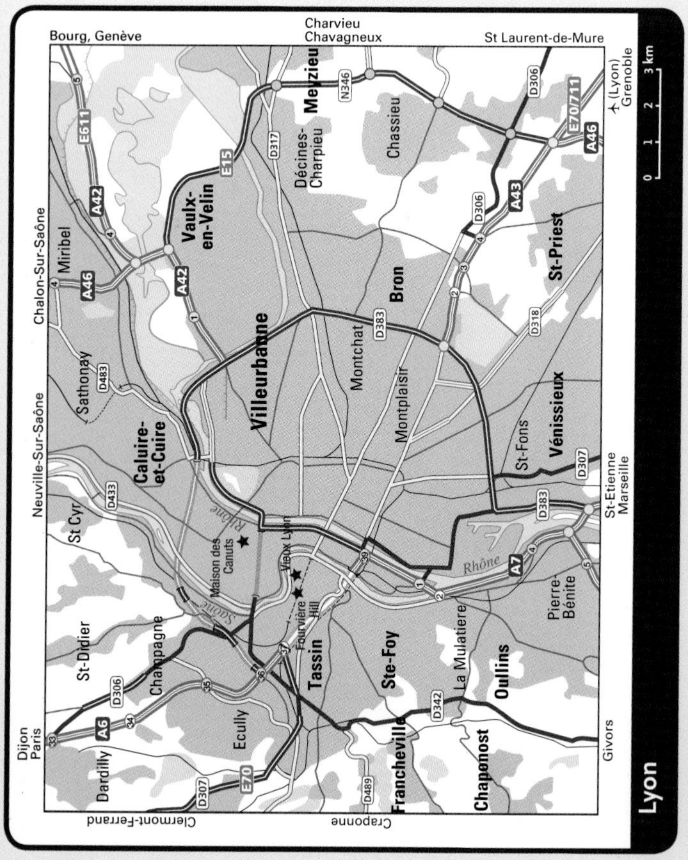
Lyon
Bourg, Genève
Charvieu Chavagneux
St Laurent-de-Mure
Clermont-Ferrand
Craponne
Dijon Paris
Neuville-Sur-Saône
Chalon-Sur-Saône
St-Etienne Marseille
Givors
(Lyon) Grenoble
Villeurbanne
Vaulx-en-Velin
Meyzieu
Décines-Charpieu
Chassieu
Bron
St-Priest
Vénissieux
St-Fons
Caluire-et-Cuire
Sathonay
Miribel
St Cyr
St-Didier
Champagne
Dardilly
Ecully
Tassin
Ste-Foy
Francheville
Chaponost
Oullins
La Mulatière
Pierre-Bénite
Montchat
Montplaisir
Fourvière Hill
Vieux Lyon
Maison des Canuts
Rhône
Saône
0 1 2 3 km

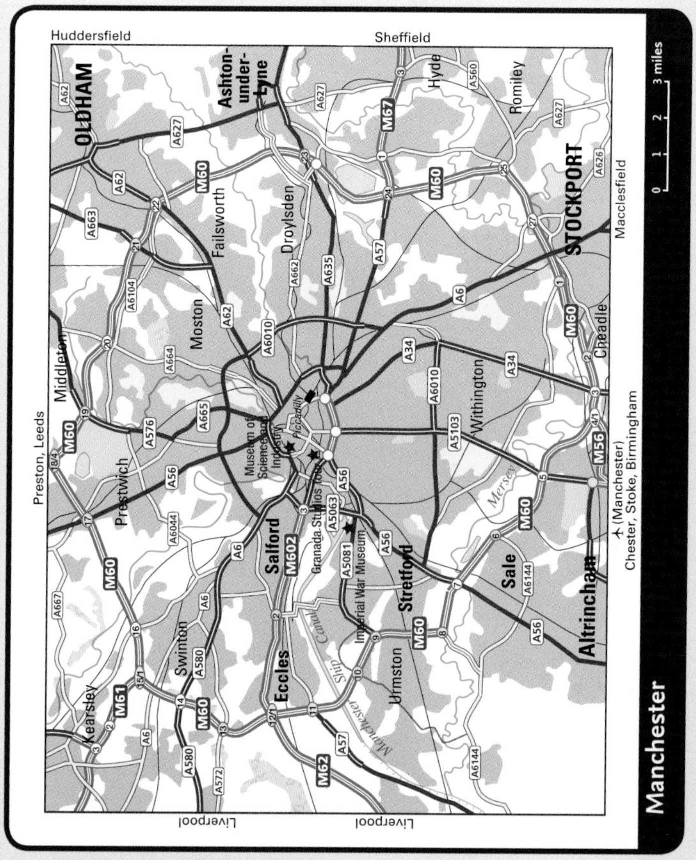
Manchester
Huddersfield
Sheffield
Liverpool
Preston, Leeds
Chester, Stoke, Birmingham
Macclesfield
Oldham
Ashton-under-Lyne
Hyde
Romiley
Stockport
Cheadle
Droylsden
Failsworth
Moston
Middleton
Prestwich
Salford
Eccles
Swinton
Kearsley
Stretford
Urmston
Sale
Altrincham
Withington
Museum of Science and Industry
Imperial War Museum
Granada Studios Tour
Manchester Ship Canal
Mersey
0 1 2 3 miles

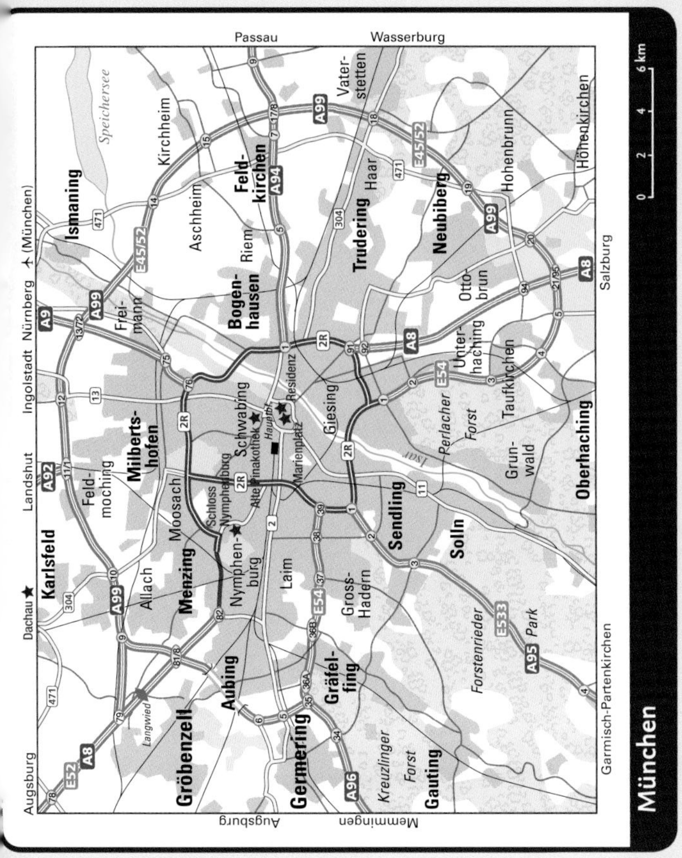
München
Augsburg
Landshut
Ingolstadt
Nürnberg
(München)
Passau
Wasserburg
Salzburg
Garmisch-Partenkirchen
Memmingen
0 2 4 6 km

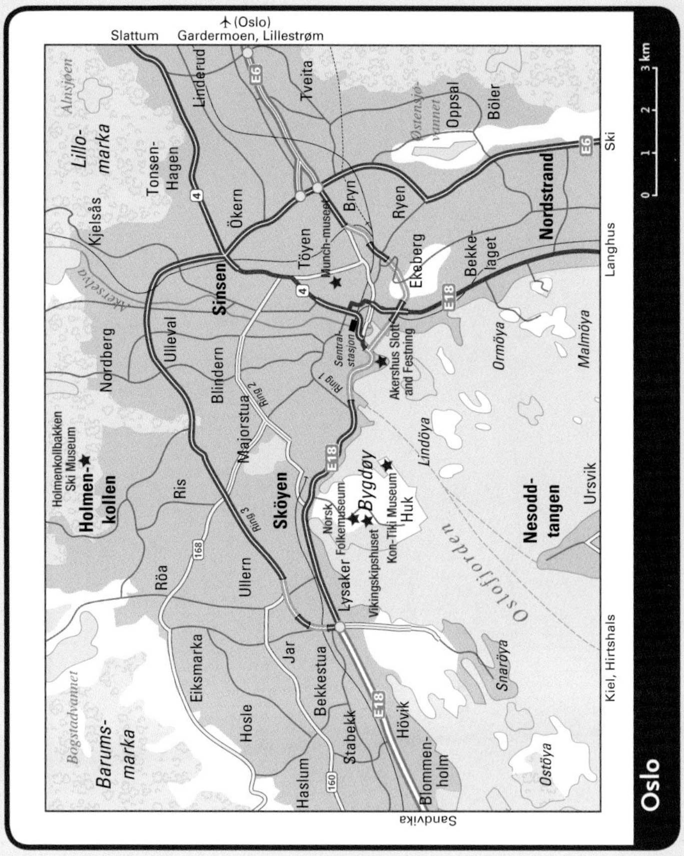
Oslo
Slattum
(Oslo) Gardermoen, Lillestrøm
Langhus
Ski
Kiel, Hirtshals
Sandvika
0 1 2 3 km

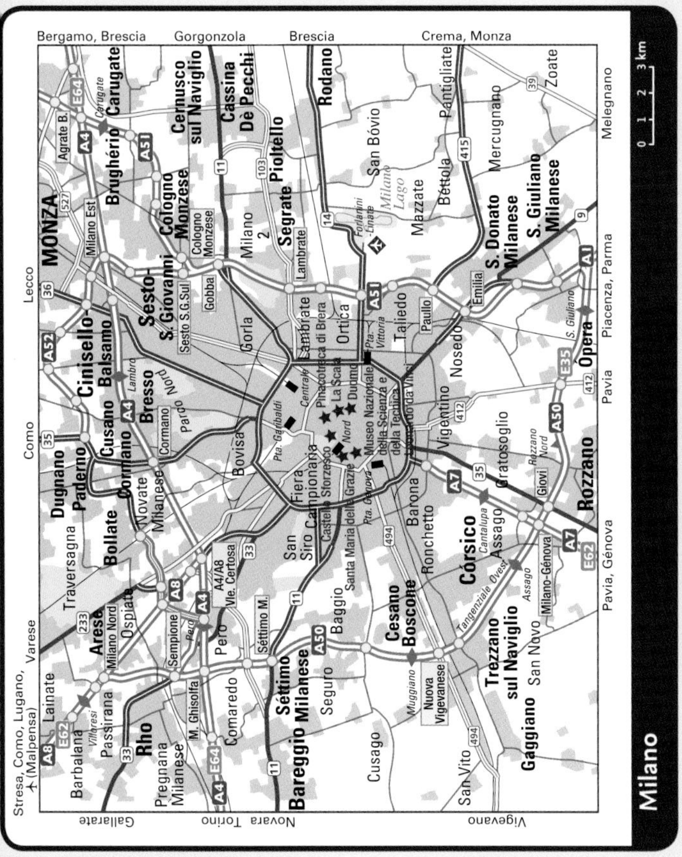
Milano
Stresa, Como, Lugano, Varese
(Malpensa)
Como
Lecco
Bergamo, Brescia
Gorgonzola
Brescia
Crema, Monza
Melegnano
Piacenza, Parma
Pavia
Pavia, Gênova
Gallarate
Novara
Torino
Vigevano
0 1 2 3 km

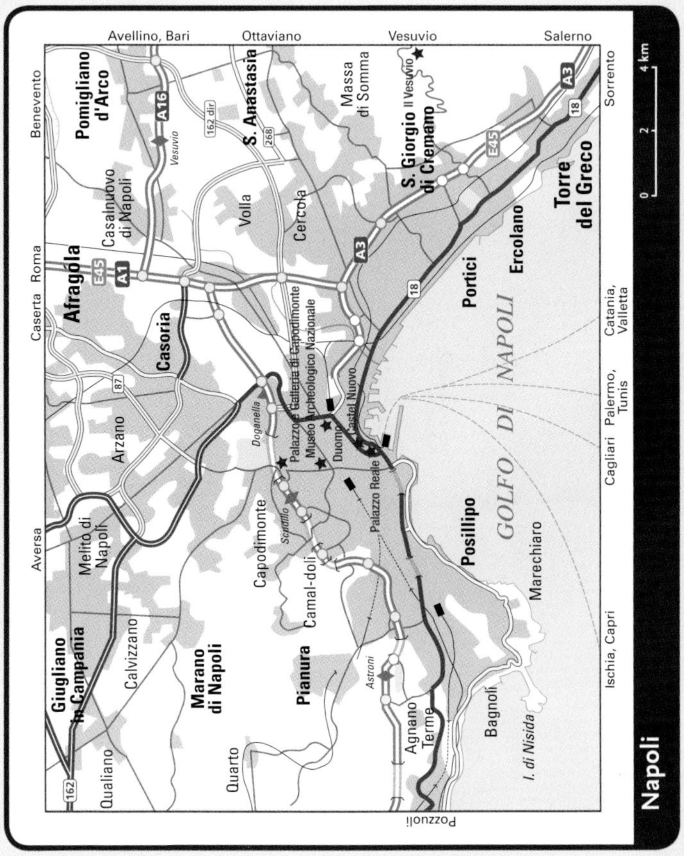
Napoli
Aversa
Caserta
Roma
Benevento
Avellino, Bari
Ottaviano
Vesuvio
Salerno
Sorrento
Catania, Valletta
Palermo, Tunis
Cagliari
Ischia, Capri
Pozzuoli
0 2 4 km

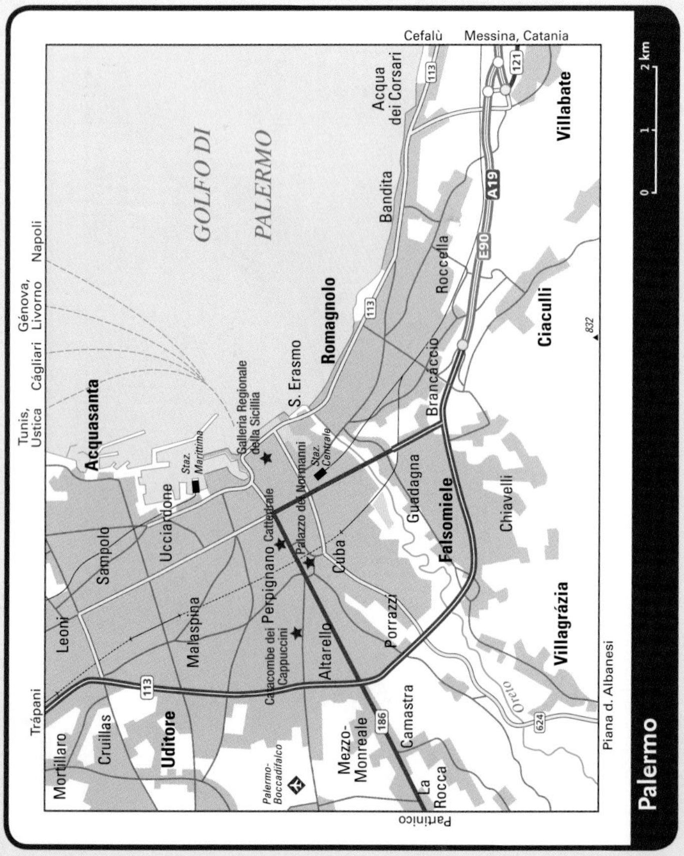
Palermo
GOLFO DI PALERMO
Trápani
Tunis, Ustica
Cágliari
Génova, Livorno
Napoli
Cefalù
Messina, Catania
Partinico
Piana d. Albanesi
Acquasanta
Romagnolo
Ciaculli
Villabate
Falsomiele
Villagrázia
Uditore
Cruillas
Mondello
Sampolo
Leoni
Malaspina
Altarello
Mezzo-Monreale
Camastra
La Rocca
Brancaccio
Roccella
Bandita
Acqua dei Corsari
Guadagna
Chiavelli
Porrazzi
Cuba
Ucciardone
S. Erasmo
Galleria Regionale della Sicilia
Cattedrale
Palazzo dei Normanni
Catacombe dei Cappuccini
Perpignano
Staz. Marittima
Staz. Centrale
Palermo-Boccadifalco
Oreto
832
0 1 2 km

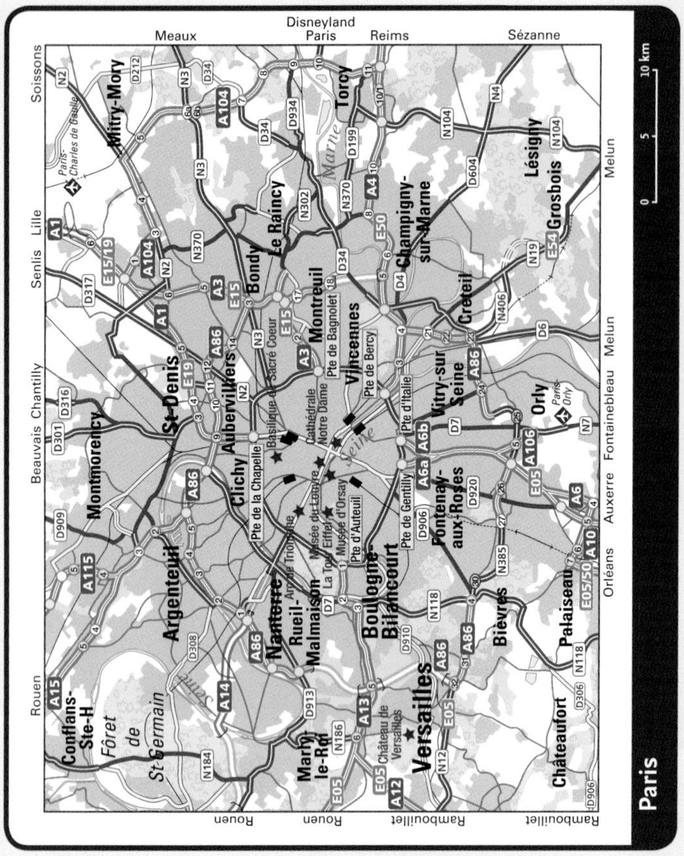
Paris
Meaux
Disneyland Paris
Reims
Sézanne
Soissons
Senlis
Lille
Beauvais
Chantilly
Rouen
Rambouillet
Orléans
Auxerre
Fontainebleau
Melun
Mitry-Mory
Paris-Charles de Gaulle
Le Raincy
Bondy
Torcy
Champigny-sur-Marne
Lésigny
Grosbois
Montreuil
Vincennes
Créteil
St-Denis
Aubervilliers
Montmorency
Clichy
Argenteuil
Conflans-Ste-H
Forêt de St-Germain
Nanterre
Rueil-Malmaison
Boulogne-Billancourt
Versailles
Marly-le-Roi
Château de Versailles
Vitry-sur-Seine
Orly
Paris-Orly
Fontenay-aux-Roses
Bièvres
Palaiseau
Châteaufort
Basilique du Sacré Coeur
Cathédrale Notre Dame
Musée du Louvre
Musée d'Orsay
Arc de Triomphe
La Tour Eiffel
Pte de la Chapelle
Pte de Bagnolet
Pte de Bercy
Pte d'Italie
Pte de Gentilly
Pte d'Auteuil
Seine
Marne
0 5 10 km

Podgorica
Bijelo Polje
Nikšić
Cetinje
Bar
Shkodër
Dinoša
Tuzi
Doljani
Rogami
Gorica
Botun
Gornji Kokoti
Millennium Bridge
Zeta
Morača
Cijevna
0 2 4 km

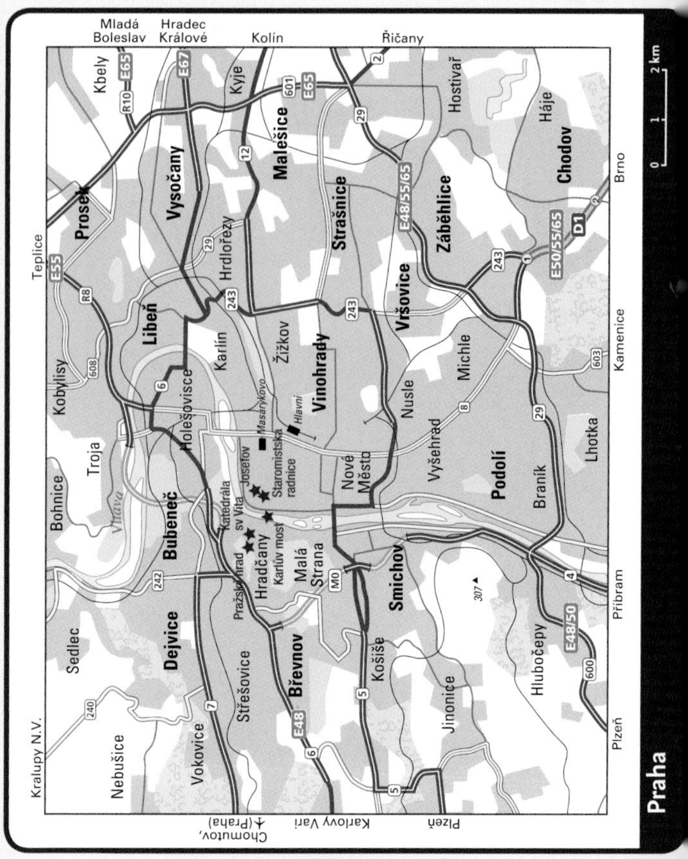
Praha
Mladá Boleslav
Hradec Králové
Kolín
Říčany
Teplice
Kralupy N.V.
Chomutov, (Praha)
Karlovy Vari
Plzeň
Příbram
Kamenice
Brno
Kbely
Kyje
Hostivař
Háje
Chodov
Prosek
Vysočany
Malešice
Strašnice
Záběhlice
Hrdlořezy
Libeň
Karlín
Žižkov
Vinohrady
Vršovice
Michle
Nusle
Vyšehrad
Podolí
Braník
Lhotka
Kobylisy
Troja
Bohnice
Holešovice
Bubeneč
Dejvice
Sedlec
Nebušice
Vokovice
Střešovice
Břevnov
Hradčany
Malá Strana
Nové Město
Smíchov
Košiře
Jinonice
Hlubočepy
Josefov
Staroměstská radnice
Katedrála sv Víta
Pražský hrad
Karlův most
Masarykovo
Hlavní
Vltava
0 1 2 km

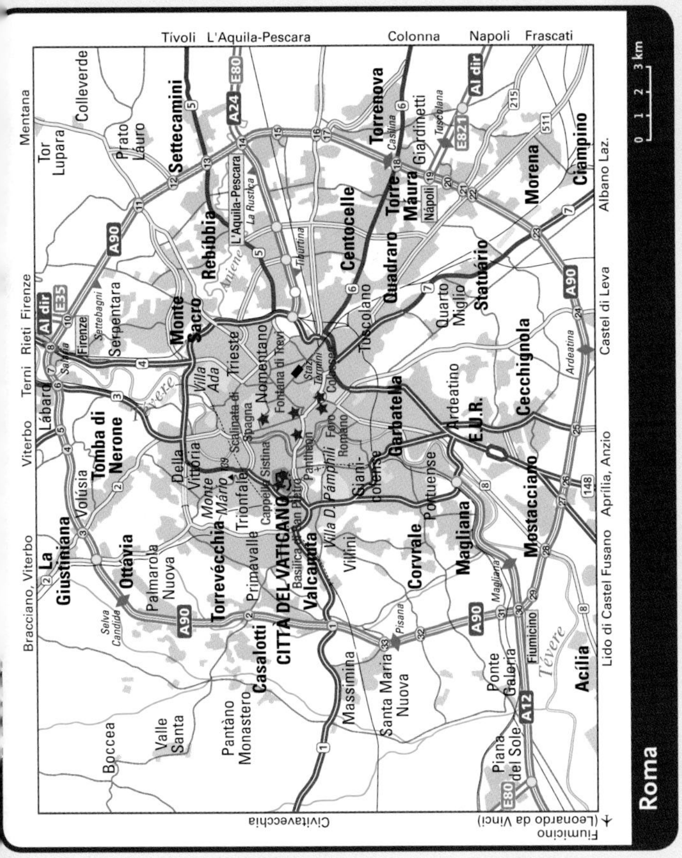
Roma

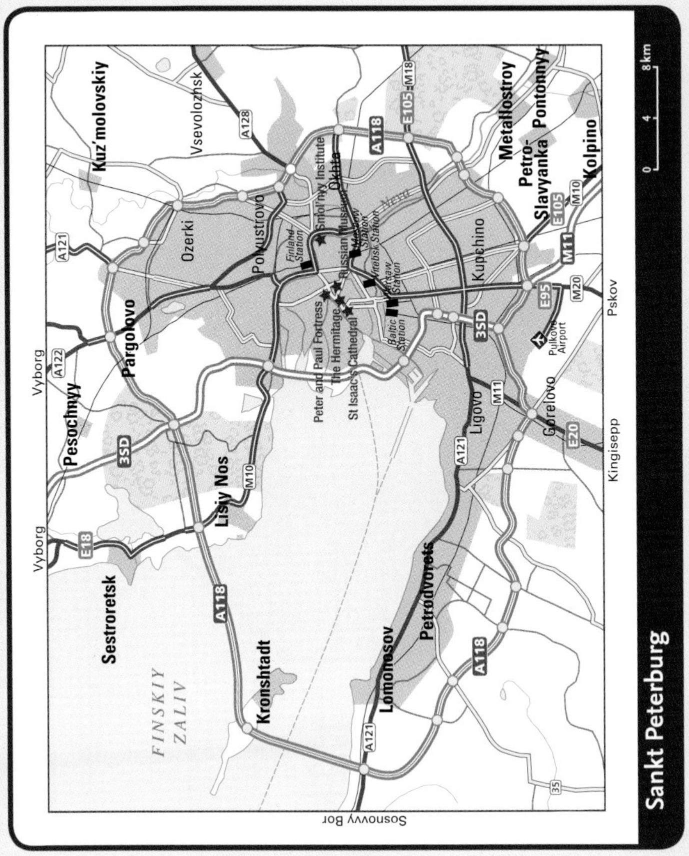
Sankt Peterburg

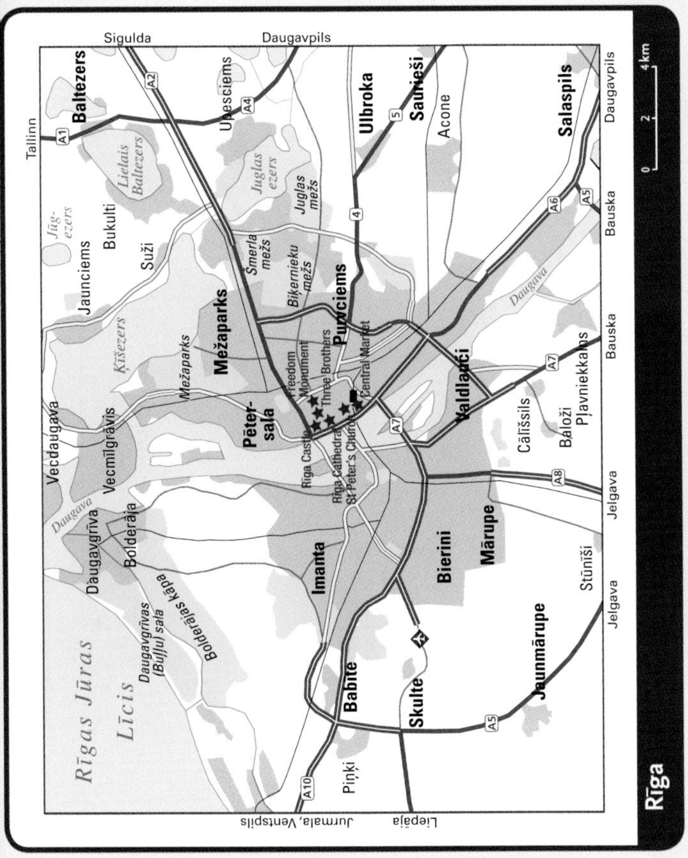
Rīga

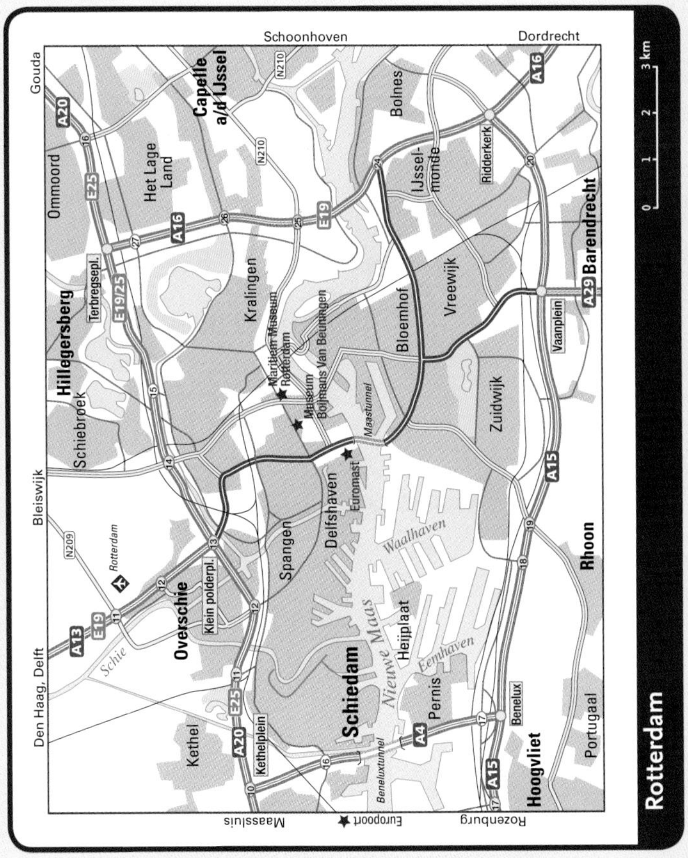
Rotterdam

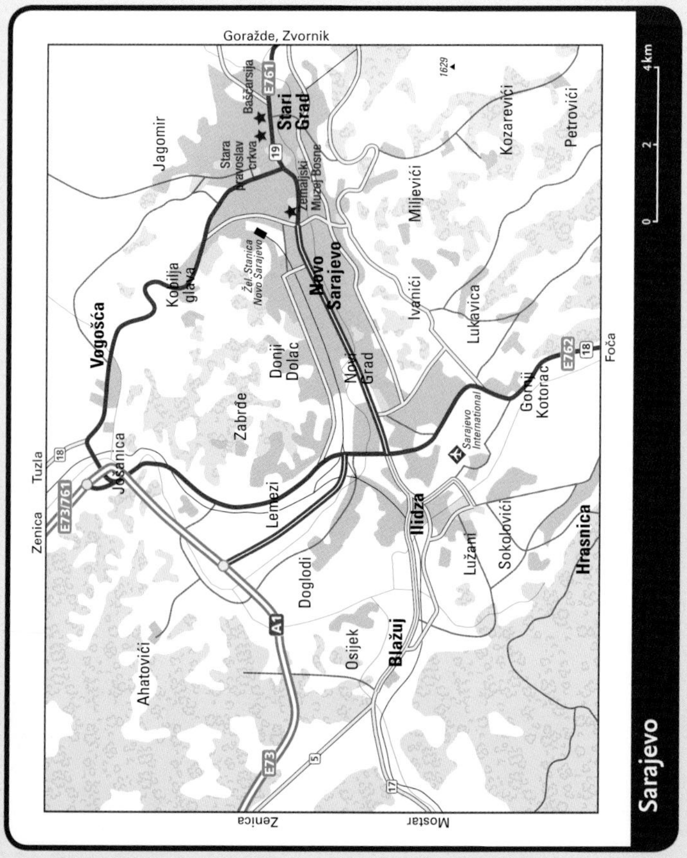
Sarajevo
Goražde, Zvornik
Zenica
Tuzla
Mostar
Foča
Vogošća
Jagomir
Stari Grad
Baščaršija
Stara Pravoslav crkva
Zemaljski Muzej Bosne
Žel Stanica Novo Sarajevo
Novo Sarajevo
Novi Grad
Kobilja glava
Donji Dolac
Zabrde
Jošanica
Lemezi
Doglodi
Osijek
Blažuj
Ahatovići
Ilidža
Lužani
Sokolovići
Hrasnica
Sarajevo International
Gornji Kotorac
Lukavica
Ivanići
Miljevići
Kozarevići
Petrovići
0 2 4 km

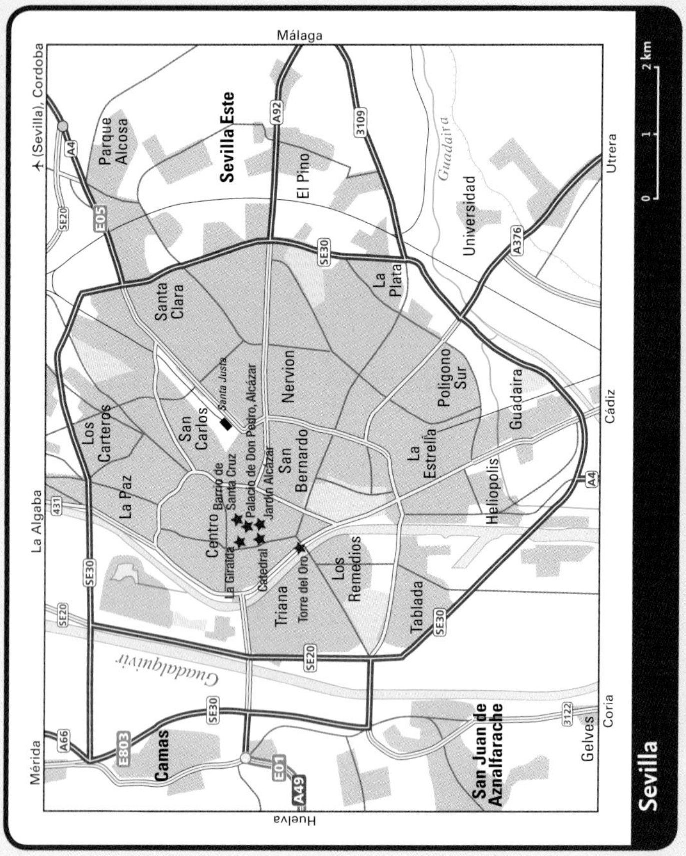
Sevilla
Málaga
Huelva
(Sevilla), Cordoba
Mérida
La Algaba
Utrera
Cádiz
Coria
Gelves
Camas
San Juan de Aznalfarache
Sevilla Este
Parque Alcosa
El Pino
Universidad
Santa Clara
La Plata
Nervion
Poligono Sur
Santa Justa
San Carlos
Los Carteros
La Paz
San Bernardo
La Estrella
Guadaira
Heliopolis
Centro
Barrio de Santa Cruz
Palacio de Don Pedro, Alcázar
Jardin Alcázar
La Giralda
Catedral
Torre del Oro
Triana
Los Remedios
Tablada
Guadalquivir
0 1 2 km

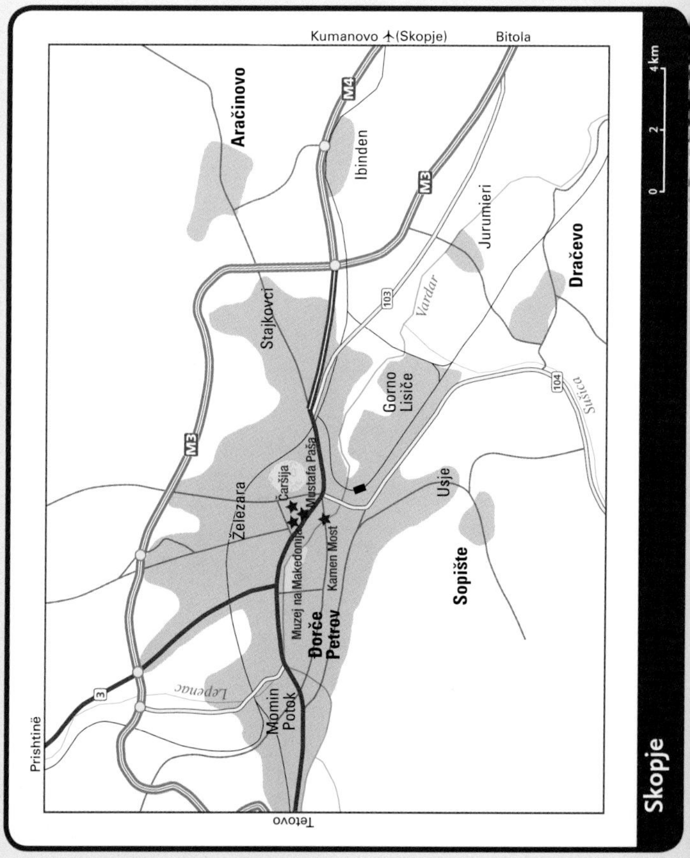
Skopje
Kumanovo (Skopje)
Bitola
Prishtinë
Tetovo
Aračinovo
Ibinden
Jurumieri
Dračevo
Stajkovci
Vardar
Gorno Lisiče
Železara
Čaršija
Mustafa Paša
Kamen Most
Muzej na Makedonija
Usje
Sopište
Đorče Petrov
Momin Potok
Lepenac
0 2 4 km

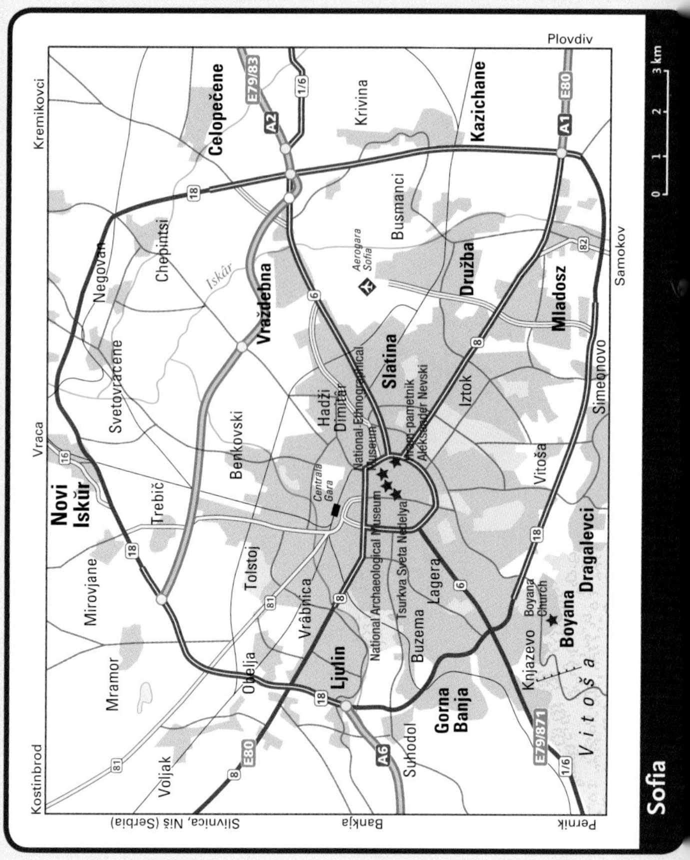
Sofia
Plovdiv
Kremikovci
Vraca
Kostinbrod
Slivnica, Niš (Serbia)
Bankja
Pernik
Samokov
Celopečene
Krivina
Kazichane
Chepintsi
Negovan
Busmanci
Aerogara Sofia
Vrazhdebna
Družba
Mladosz
Svetovračene
Slatina
Iztok
Simeonovo
Benkovski
Hadži Dimitar
National Ethnographical Museum
Hram-pametnik Aleksandar Nevski
Novi Iskăr
Trebič
Centralna Gara
National Archaeological Museum
Tsurkva Sveta Nedelya
Vitoša
Dragalevci
Mirovjane
Tolstoj
Vrabnica
Lagera
Boyana Church
Boyana
Mramor
Obelja
Ljulin
Buzema
Knjazevo
Gorna Banja
Suhodol
Voljak
0 1 2 3 km

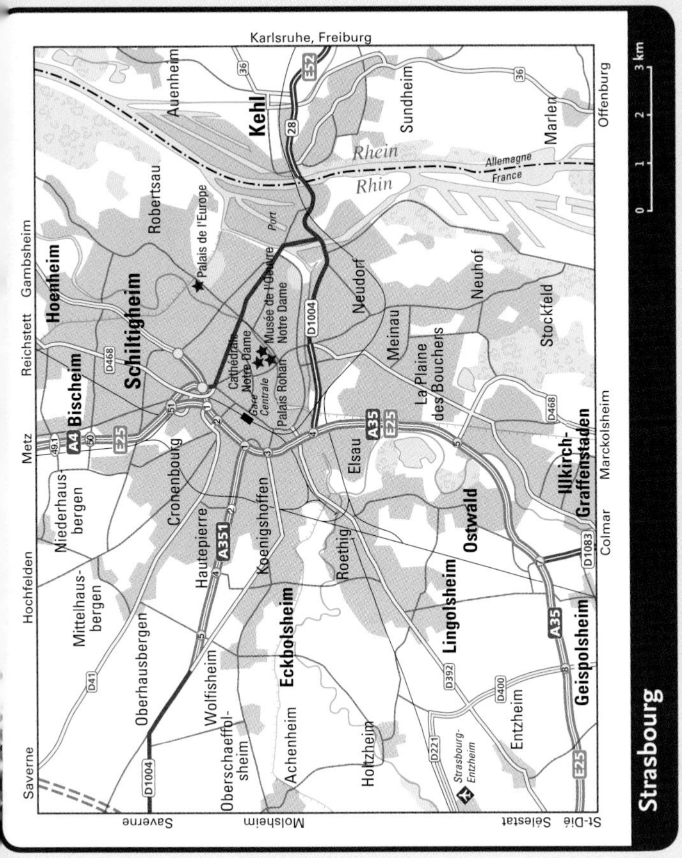
Strasbourg
Karlsruhe, Freiburg
Kehl
Rhein
Rhin
Allemagne
France
Offenburg
Schiltigheim
Bischheim
Hoenheim
Niederhausbergen
Mittelhausbergen
Oberhausbergen
Cronenbourg
Hautepierre
Koenigshoffen
Eckbolsheim
Wolfisheim
Oberschaeffolsheim
Achenheim
Holtzheim
Lingolsheim
Ostwald
Illkirch-Graffenstaden
Geispolsheim
Entzheim
Strasbourg-Entzheim
Neudorf
Meinau
Neuhof
Stockfeld
La Plaine des Bouchers
Robertsau
Palais de l'Europe
Cathédrale Notre Dame
Musée de l'Oeuvre Notre Dame
Palais Rohan
Gare Centrale
Port
Sundheim
Auenheim
Marlen
Elsau
Roethig
Saverne
Molsheim
St-Dié Sélestat
Colmar
Marckolsheim
Hochfelden
Metz
Reichstett
Gambsheim
0 1 2 3 km

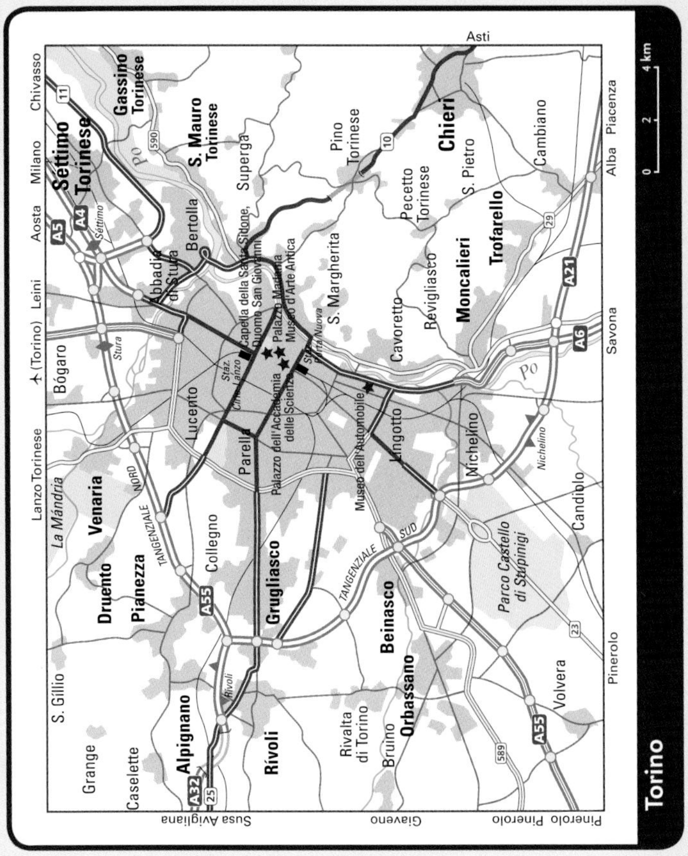
Torino
Asti
Chivasso
Milano
Aosta
Leini
(Torino)
Lanzo Torinese
Settimo Torinese
Gassino Torinese
S. Mauro Torinese
Superga
Pino Torinese
Chieri
Pecetto Torinese
Cambiano
S. Pietro
Trofarello
Moncalieri
Revigliasco
Cavoretto
Bertolla
Abbadia di Stura
Bógaro
Venaria
La Mandria
Druento
Pianezza
Collegno
Lucento
Parella
Grugliasco
Rivoli
Alpignano
Caselette
Grange
S. Gillio
Rivalta di Torino
Bruino
Orbassano
Beinasco
Volvera
Parco Castello di Stupinigi
Candiolo
Nichelino
Lingotto
Museo dell'Automobile
Palazzo dell'Accademia delle Scienze
Palazzo Madama
Museo d'Arte Antica
Cappella della Santa Sindone
Duomo San Giovanni
S. Margherita
Po
Stura
TANGENZIALE NORD
TANGENZIALE SUD
Susa Avigliana
Giaveno
Pinerolo
Savona
Alba
Piacenza
0 2 4 km

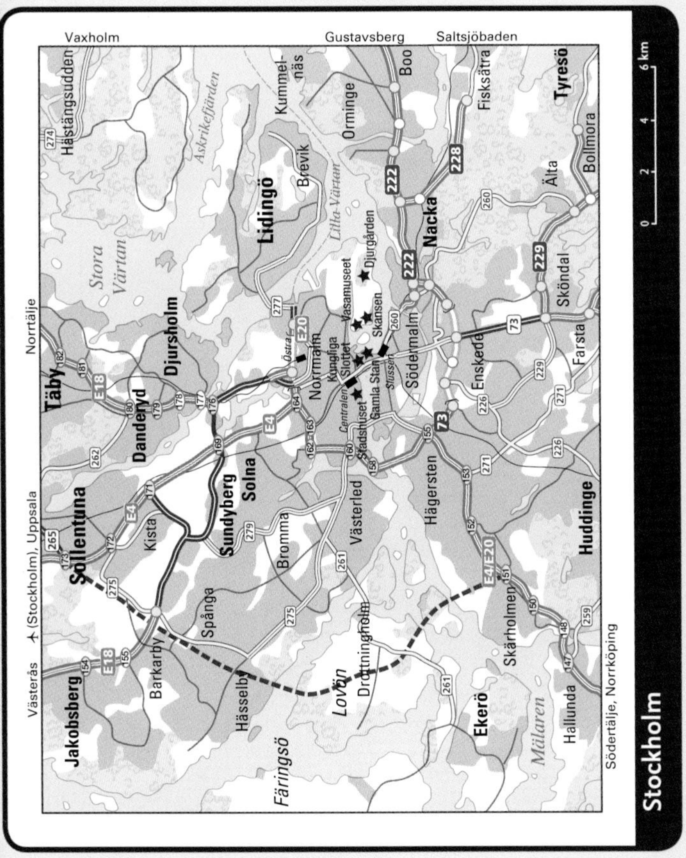
Stockholm
Vaxholm
Gustavsberg
Saltsjöbaden
Norrtälje
Västerås
(Stockholm), Uppsala
Södertälje, Norrköping
Jakobsberg
Sollentuna
Täby
Danderyd
Djursholm
Lidingö
Kista
Sundbyberg
Solna
Bromma
Spånga
Barkarby
Hässelby
Lovön
Drottningholm
Färingsö
Ekerö
Mälaren
Hallunda
Skärholmen
Huddinge
Hägersten
Västerled
Stadshuset
Centralen
Norrmalm
Kungliga Slottet
Gamla Stan
Slussen
Östra
Vasamuseet
Skansen
Djurgården
Södermalm
Enskede
Farsta
Sköndal
Nacka
Älta
Bollmora
Tyresö
Fisksätra
Boo
Orminge
Brevik
Kummelnäs
Hästängsudden
Stora Värtan
Lilla Värtan
Askrikefjärden
0 2 4 6 km

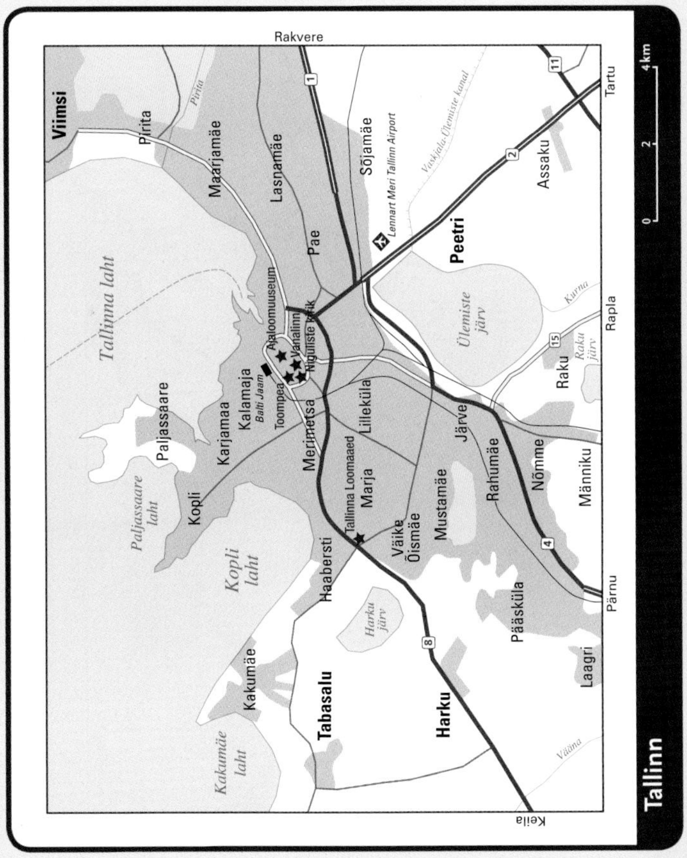
Tallinn
Rakvere
Tartu
Rapla
Pärnu
Keila
Viimsi
Pirita
Maarjamäe
Lasnamäe
Sõjamäe
Lennart Meri Tallinn Airport
Peetri
Assaku
Ülemiste järv
Raku
Pae
Ajaloomuuseum
Raekoda
Niguliste kirik
Balti Jaam
Kalamaja
Karjamaa
Paljassaare
Paljassaare laht
Kopli
Kopli laht
Toompea
Merimetsa
Lilleküla
Järve
Rahumäe
Nõmme
Männiku
Marja
Tallinna Loomaaed
Väike Õismäe
Mustamäe
Haabersti
Harku järv
Pääsküla
Laagri
Tabasalu
Kakumäe
Kakumäe laht
Harku
Tallinna laht
0 2 4 km

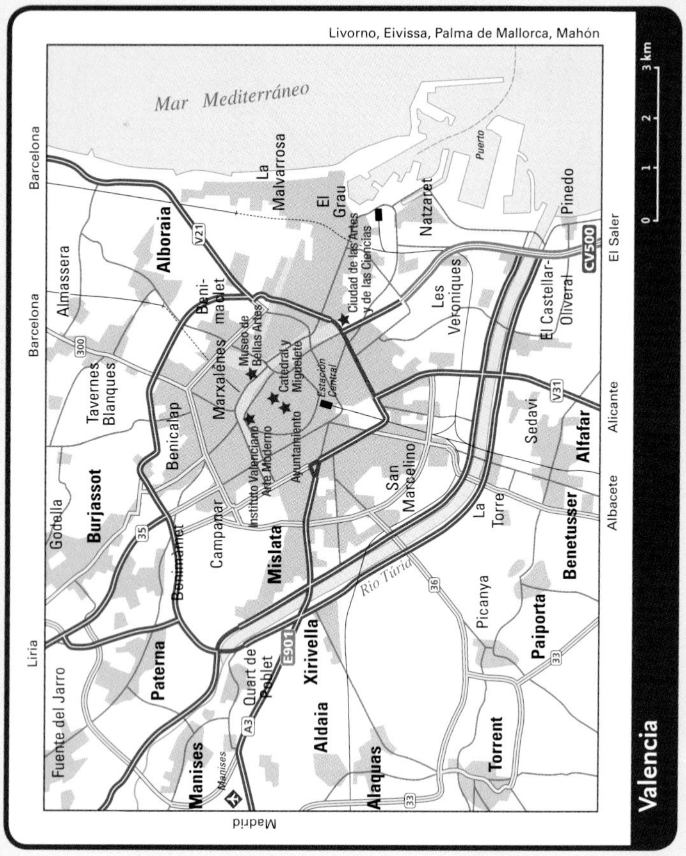
Valencia
Mar Mediterráneo
Livorno, Eivissa, Palma de Mallorca, Mahón
Barcelona
Madrid
Alicante
Albacete
El Saler
Liria
Burjassot
Alboraia
Mislata
Paterna
Manises
Xirivella
Aldaia
Torrent
Paiporta
Benetusser
Alfafar
Río Turia
0 1 2 3 km

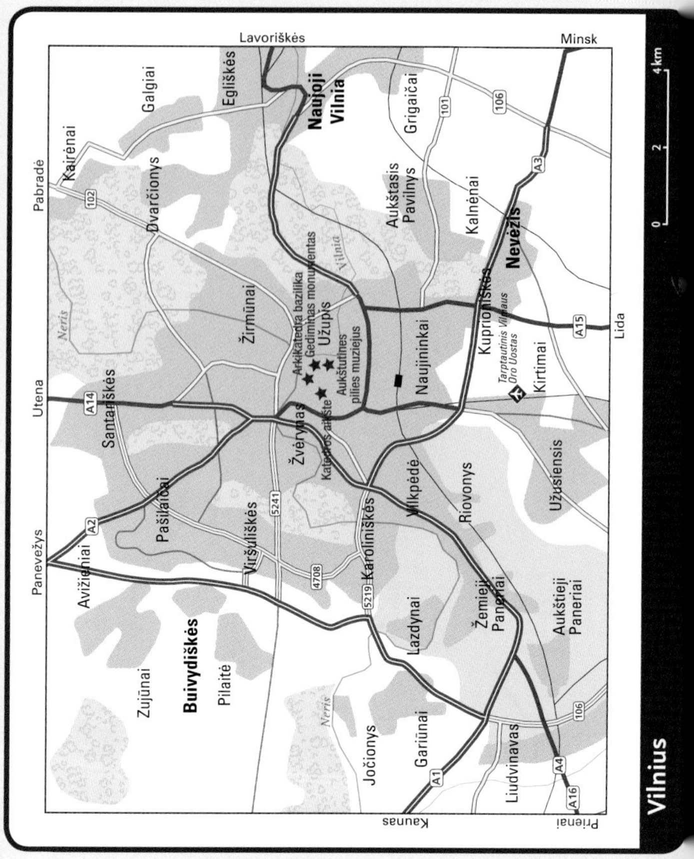
Vilnius
Lavoriškės
Minsk
Pabradė
Utena
Panevežys
Kaunas
Prienai
Lida
Naujoji Vilnia
Nevėžis
Buivydiškės
Karoliniškės
Žvėrynas
Užupis
Naujininkai
Vilkpėdė
Neris
0 2 4 km

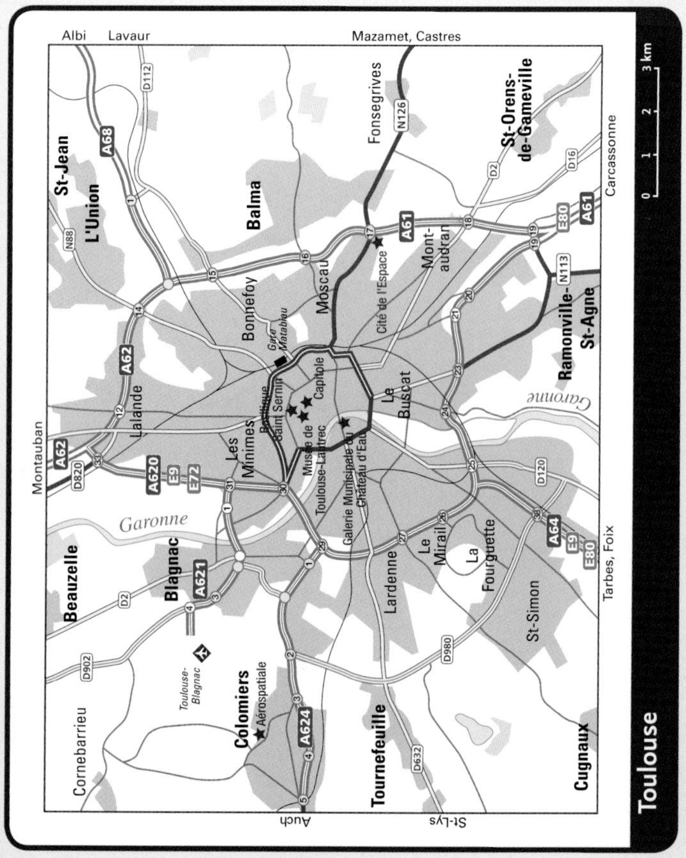
Toulouse
Albi
Lavaur
Mazamet, Castres
Montauban
Carcassonne
Tarbes, Foix
Auch
St-Lys
Garonne
St-Jean
L'Union
Balma
Blagnac
Beauzelle
Colomiers
Tournefeuille
Cugnaux
Ramonville-St-Agne
St-Orens-de-Gameville
Toulouse-Blagnac
0 1 2 3 km

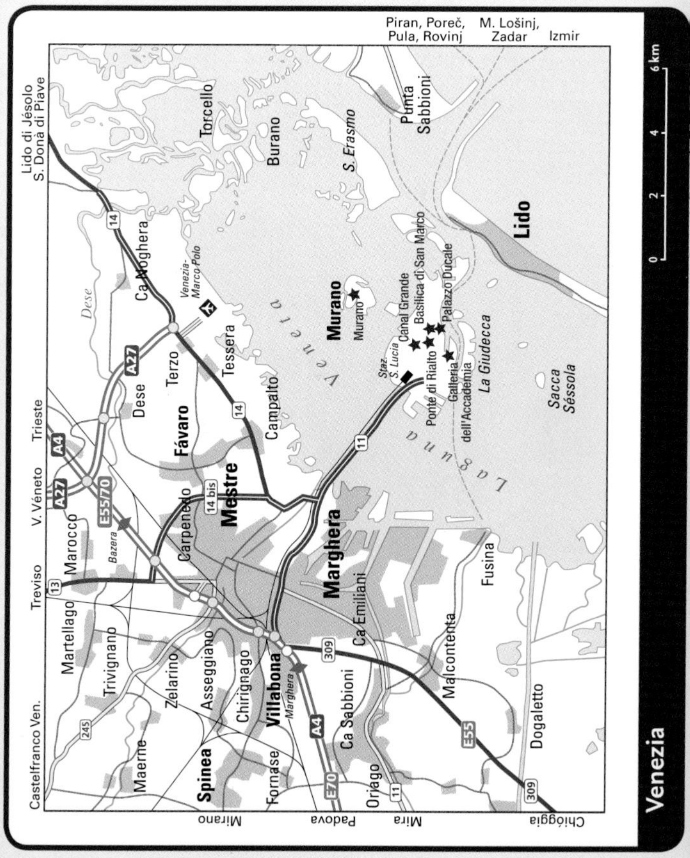
Venezia
Castelfranco Ven.
Treviso
V. Véneto
Trieste
Lido di Jésolo
S. Donà di Piave
Piran, Poreč, Pula, Rovinj
M. Lošinj, Zadar
Izmir
Mirano
Padova
Mira
Chióggia
Mestre
Marghera
Murano
Burano
Torcello
Lido
Laguna Veneta
La Giudecca
Venezia-Marco Polo
0 2 4 6 km

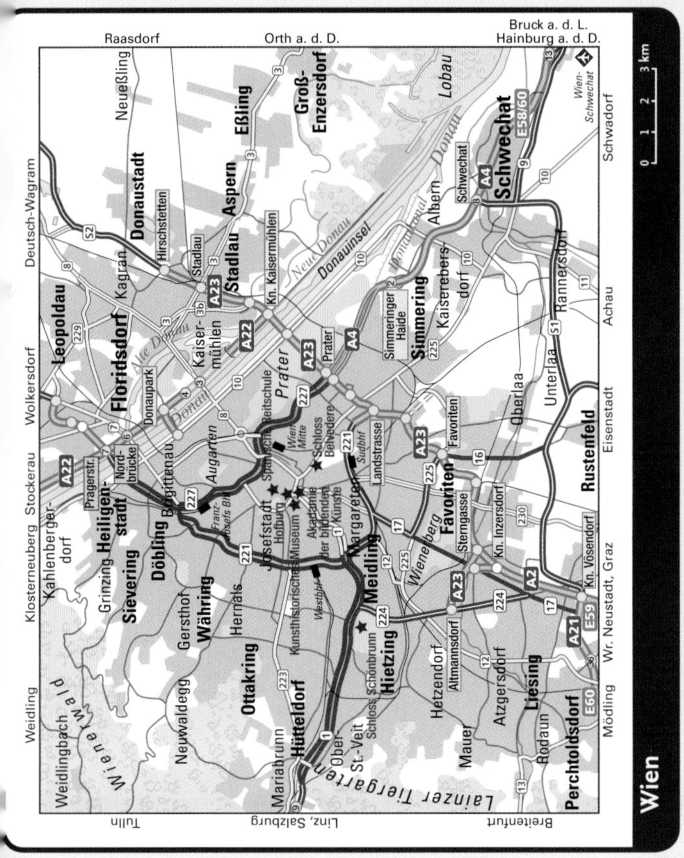
Wien
Raasdorf
Orth a. d. D.
Bruck a. d. L.
Hainburg a. d. D.
Tulln
Linz, Salzburg
Breitenfurt
Weidling
Klosterneuberg
Stockerau
Wolkersdorf
Deutsch-Wagram
Mödling
Wr. Neustadt, Graz
Eisenstadt
Achau
Schwadorf
Floridsdorf
Leopoldau
Donaustadt
Stadlau
Aspern
Eßling
Groß-Enzersdorf
Schwechat
Simmering
Favoriten
Meidling
Hietzing
Hütteldorf
Ottakring
Währing
Döbling
Sievering
Heiligenstadt
Liesing
Perchtoldsdorf
Rustenfeld
Prater
Lobau
Lainzer Tiergarten
Wienerwald
Josefstadt
Margareten
Landstrasse
Schloss Schönbrunn
Schloss Belvedere
0 1 2 3 km

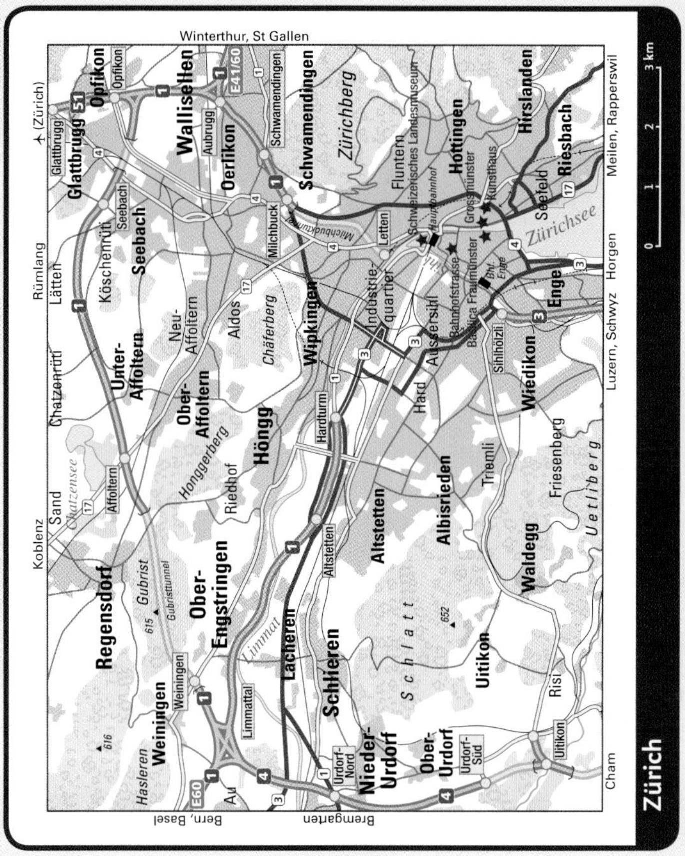
Zürich
Winterthur, St Gallen
Bern, Basel
Bremgarten
Koblenz
Rümlang
Cham
Luzern, Schwyz
Horgen
Meilen, Rapperswil
Opfikon
Glattbrugg
Wallisellen
Oerlikon
Schwamendingen
Seebach
Affoltern
Höngg
Wipkingen
Regensdorf
Ober-Engstringen
Weiningen
Schlieren
Altstetten
Albisrieden
Wiedikon
Enge
Riesbach
Hottingen
Hirslanden
Zürichsee
Zürichberg
Uetliberg
Limmat
Uitikon
Waldegg
Nieder-Urdorf
Ober-Urdorf
0 1 2 3 km

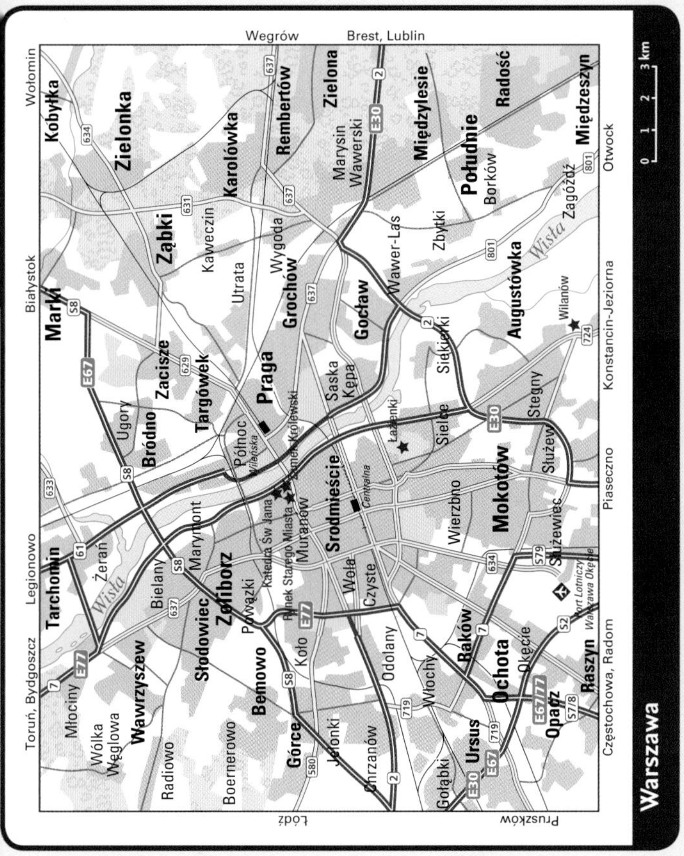
Warszawa
Toruń, Bydgoszcz
Legionowo
Białystok
Wołomin
Wegrów
Brest, Lublin
Łódź
Pruszków
Częstochowa, Radom
Piaseczno
Konstancin-Jeziorna
Otwock
Praga
Śródmieście
Mokotów
Ochota
Wola
Żoliborz
Bemowo
Targówek
Bródno
Zielonka
Ząbki
Marki
Kobyłka
Rembertów
Wawer
Ursus
Wilanów
Wisła
0 1 2 3 km

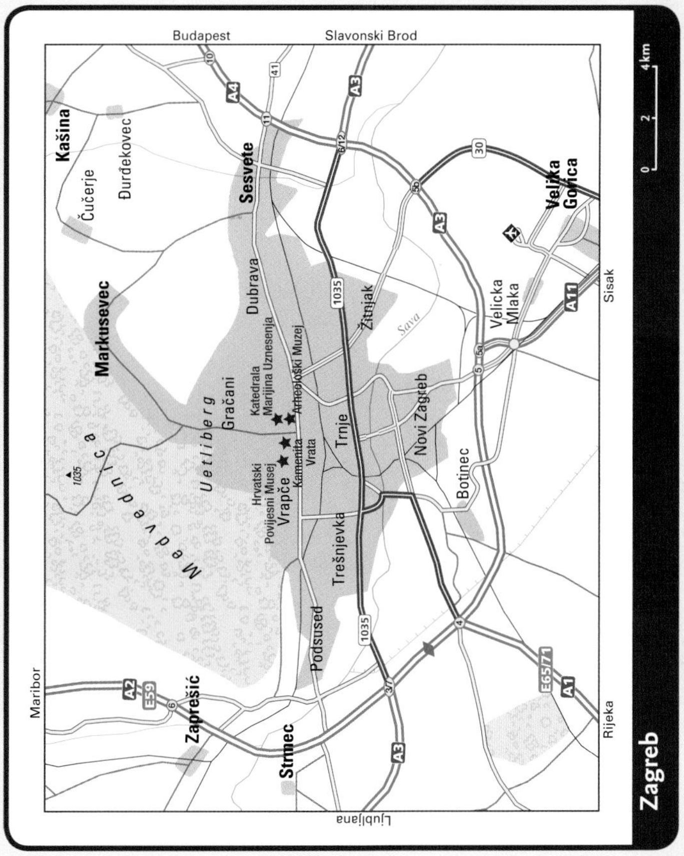
Zagreb
Maribor
Budapest
Slavonski Brod
Ljubljana
Rijeka
Sisak
Zaprešić
Strmec
Podsused
Trešnjevka
Vrapče
Trnje
Novi Zagreb
Botinec
Sesvete
Kašina
Markuševec
Dubrava
Žitnjak
Sava
Velika Gorica
Velicka Mlaka
Medvednica
0 2 4 km

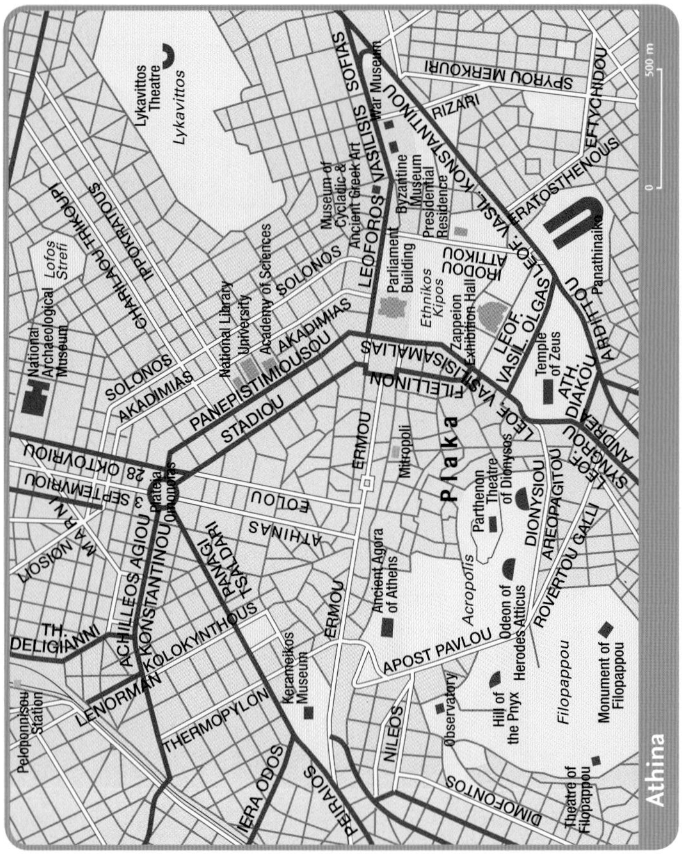
Athina
500 m
Lykavittos Theatre
Lykavittos
National Archaeological Museum
Lofos Strefi
Plaka
Acropolis
Parthenon
Theatre of Dionysos
Odeon of Herodes Atticus
Ancient Agora of Athens
Keramikos Museum
Hill of the Phyx
Observatory
Filopappou
Monument of Filopappou
Theatro of Filopappou
Temple of Zeus
Panathinaiko
Zappeion Exhibition Hall
Ethnikos Kipos
Parliament Building
Byzantine Museum
Presidential Residence
Museum of Cycladic & Ancient Greek Art
War Museum
National Library
University
Academy of Sciences
Mitropoli
Peloponnisou Station
Plateia Omonias
ERMOU
STADIOU
AKADIMIAS
PANEPISTIMIOU
SOLONOS
VASILISIS SOFIAS
LEOFOROS
28 OKTOVRIOU
3 SEPTEMVRIOU
EOLOU
ATHINAS
PIREOS
IERA ODOS
THERMOPYLON
LENORMAN
KOLOKYNTHOUS
ACHILLEOS
AGIOU KONSTANTINOU
TH. DELIGIANNI
APOST PAVLOU
DIONYSIOU AREOPAGITOU
ROVERTOU GALLI
DIMOFONTOS
NILEOS
FILELLINON
AMALIAS
VASIL. OLGAS
VASIL. KONSTANTINOU
ERATOSTHENOUS
EFTYCHIDOU
RIZARI
SPYROU MERKOURI
IPPOKRATOUS
CHARILAOU TRIKOUPI
ARDITTOU
SYNGROU ANDREA
ATH. DIAKOU
IRODOU ATTIKOU

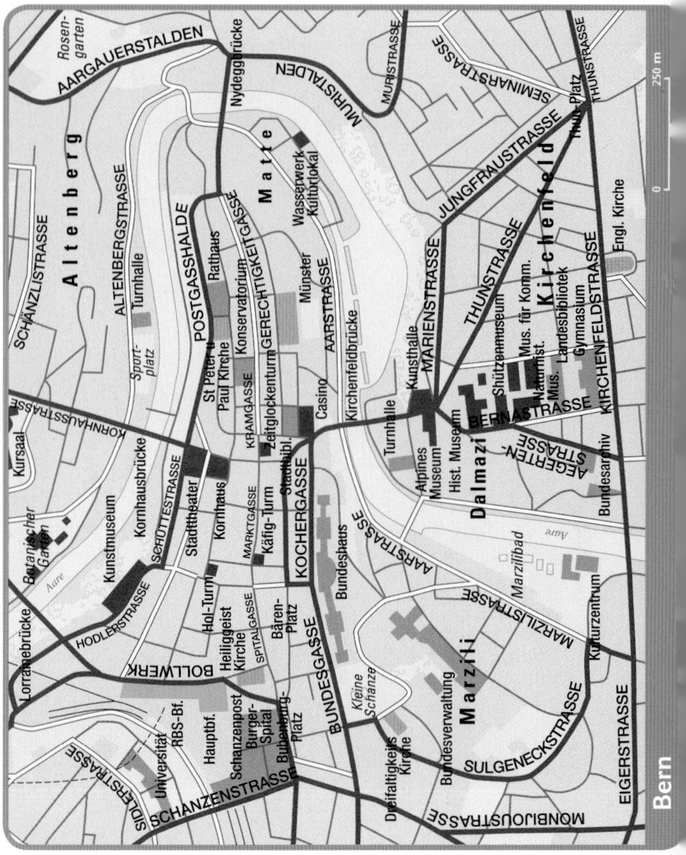
Bern
250 m
Rosengarten
AARGAUERSTALDEN
Altenberg
ALTENBERGSTRASSE
SCHÄNZLISTRASSE
Nydeggbrücke
MURISTALDEN
MURISTRASSE
Matte
Wasserwerk Kulturlokal
Rathaus
Münster
Konservatorium
Casino
Kirchenfeldbrücke
POSTGASSHALDE
GERECHTIGKEITGASSE
KRAMGASSE
Zeitglockenturm
Käfig-Turm
Stadttheater
Kornhaus
Kornhausbrücke
Kunstmuseum
Botanischer Garten
Kursaal
Lorrainebrücke
Heiliggeist Kirche
Bären-Platz
Bundeshaus
Burger-Spital
Hauptbf.
Universität
SCHANZENSTRASSE
BOLLWERK
KOCHERGASSE
BUNDESGASSE
AARSTRASSE
Marzili
Marzilibad
Kleine Schanze
Dreifaltigkeits Kirche
Bundesverwaltung
SULGENECKSTRASSE
MONBIJOUSTRASSE
EIGERSTRASSE
Dalmazi
Alpines Museum
Hist. Museum
Kunsthalle
MARIENSTRASSE
Kirchenfeld
Landesbibliotek
Gymnasium
KIRCHENFELDSTRASSE
Bundesarchiv
Engl. Kirche
THUNSTRASSE
JUNGFRAUSTRASSE
Thunplatz
Kurzentrum

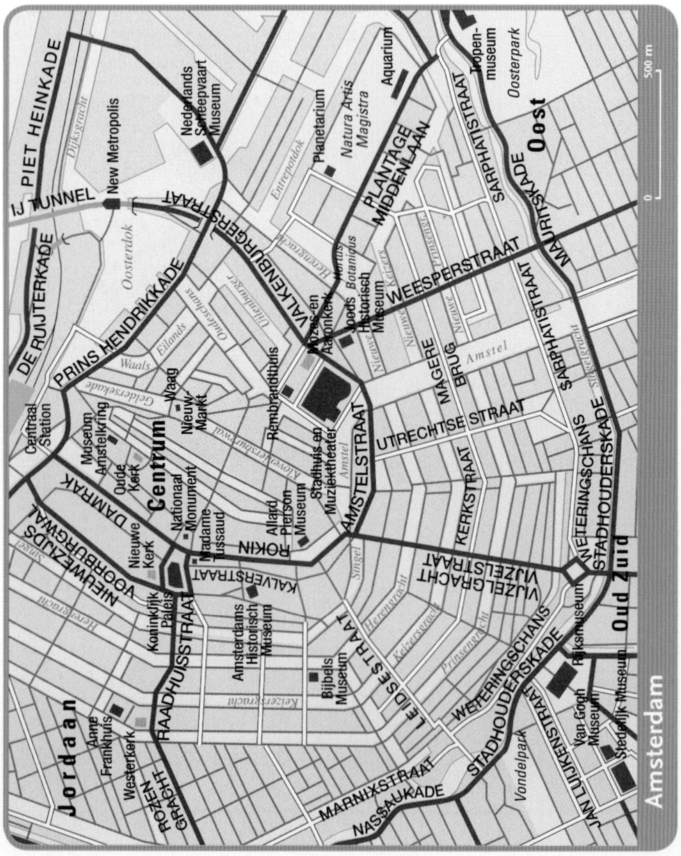
Amsterdam
500 m
Jordaan
Centrum
Oost
Oud Zuid
PIET HEINKADE
IJ TUNNEL
New Metropolis
Nederlands Scheepvaart Museum
Planetarium
Natura Artis Magistra
Aquarium
Tropenmuseum
Oosterpark
PLANTAGE MIDDENLAAN
SARPHATISTRAAT
MAURITSKADE
WEESPERSTRAAT
VALKENBURGERSTRAAT
PRINS HENDRIKKADE
DE RUIJTERKADE
Centraal Station
Museum Amstelkring
Oude Kerk
Waag
Nieuw Markt
Rembrandthuis
Stadhuis en Muziektheater
Joods Historisch Museum
Hortus Botanicus
Nationaal Monument
Madame Tussaud
Nieuwe Kerk
Koninklijk Paleis
DAMRAK
ROKIN
KALVERSTRAAT
Allard Pierson Museum
Amsterdams Historisch Museum
Bijbels Museum
Anne Frankhuis
Westerkerk
RAADHUISSTRAAT
ROZENGRACHT
LEIDSESTRAAT
AMSTELSTRAAT
UTRECHTSE STRAAT
MAGERE BRUG
KERKSTRAAT
VIJZELSTRAAT
VIJZELGRACHT
WETERINGSCHANS
STADHOUDERSKADE
Rijksmuseum
Van Gogh Museum
Stedelijk Museum
Vondelpark
JAN LUIJKENSTRAAT
MARNIXSTRAAT
NASSAUKADE
NIEUWEZIJDS VOORBURGWAL

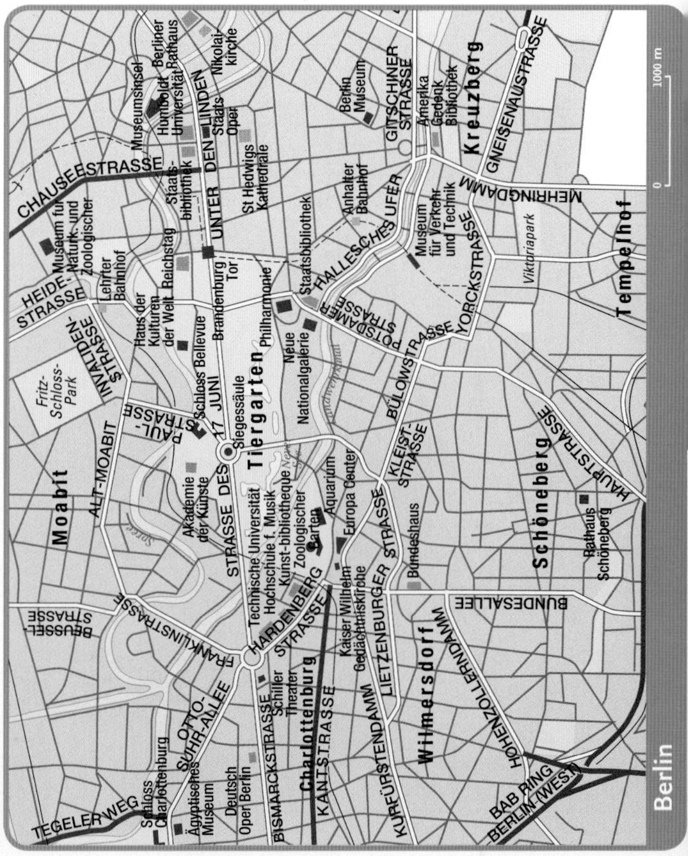
Berlin
1000 m
Moabit
Tiergarten
Charlottenburg
Wilmersdorf
Schöneberg
Kreuzberg
Tempelhof
CHAUSSEESTRASSE
Museum für Naturkunde
Zoologischer Garten
Lehrter Bahnhof
Haus der Kulturen der Welt
Reichstag
Brandenburg Tor
UNTER DEN LINDEN
Museumsinsel
Humboldt Universität
Berliner Rathaus
Nikolaikirche
Staatsbibliothek
Staats Oper
St Hedwigs Kathedrale
Anhalter Bahnhof
Berlin Museum
GITSCHINER STRASSE
Amerika Gedenk Bibliothek
GNEISENAUSTRASSE
MEHRINGDAMM
Museum für Verkehr und Technik
YORCKSTRASSE
Viktoriapark
HALLESCHES UFER
POTSDAMER STRASSE
Philharmonie
Neue Nationalgalerie
Siegessäule
STRASSE DES 17. JUNI
Schloss Bellevue
Fritz-Schloss-Park
INVALIDENSTRASSE
HEIDESTRASSE
ALT-MOABIT
Akademie der Künste
Technische Universität
Hochschule f. Musik
Kunstbibliothek
Aquarium
Europa Center
Kaiser Wilhelm Gedächtniskirche
BÜLOWSTRASSE
KLEISTSTRASSE
Bundeshaus
HAUPTSTRASSE
Rathaus Schöneberg
BUNDESALLEE
HOHENZOLLERNDAMM
KURFÜRSTENDAMM
LIETZENBURGER STRASSE
KANTSTRASSE
HARDENBERGSTRASSE
Schiller Theater
Deutsch Oper Berlin
BISMARCKSTRASSE
OTTO-SUHR-ALLEE
Schloss Charlottenburg
Ägyptisches Museum
TEGELER WEG
FRANKLINSTRASSE
BEUSSELSTRASSE
BAB RING BERLIN/WEST

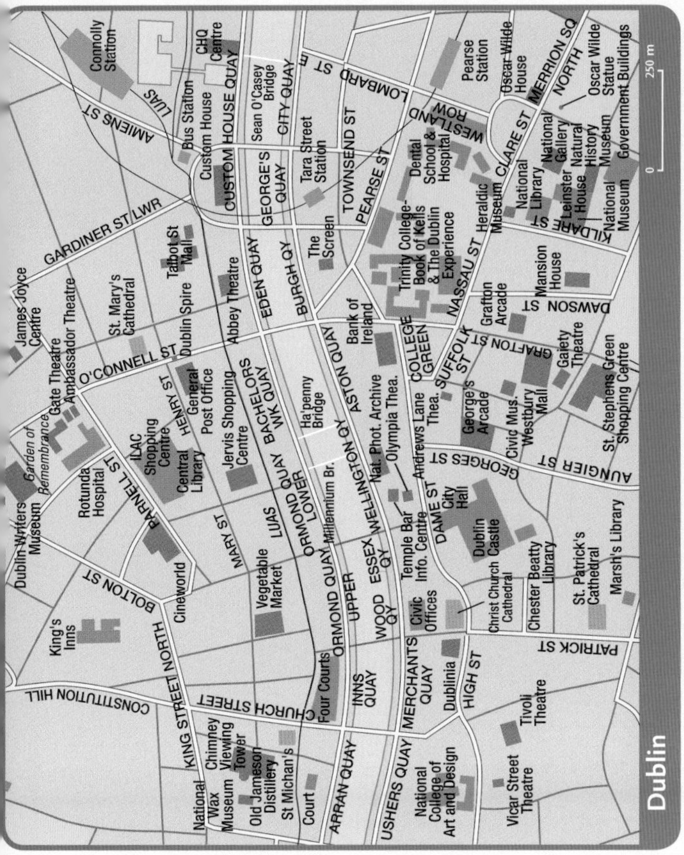
Dublin
0
250 m
O'CONNELL ST
GARDINER ST/LWR
CUSTOM HOUSE QUAY
GEORGE'S QUAY
CITY QUAY
TOWNSEND ST
PEARSE ST
NASSAU ST
DAWSON ST
GRAFTON ST
DAME ST
HIGH ST
PATRICK ST
CHURCH STREET
CONSTITUTION HILL
KING STREET NORTH
BOLTON ST
PARNELL ST
HENRY ST
MARY ST
ORMOND QUAY
WELLINGTON QY
ASTON QUAY
BACHELORS WK QUAY
EDEN QUAY
BURGH QY
USHERS QUAY
ARRAN QUAY
INNS QUAY
MERCHANTS QUAY
WOOD QY
ESSEX QY
AUNGIER ST
GEORGES ST
KILDARE ST
CLARE ST
MERRION SQ NORTH
WESTLAND ROW
LOMBARD ST E
AMIENS ST
LUAS
Connolly Station
CHQ Centre
Bus Station
Custom House
Sean O'Casey Bridge
Tara Street Station
Pearse Station
Oscar Wilde House
Oscar Wilde Statue
Government Buildings
National Gallery
National History Museum
National Museum
Leinster House
National Library
Heraldic Museum
Dental School & Hospital
Trinity College-Book of Kells & The Dublin Experience
Mansion House
Grafton Arcade
Gaiety Theatre
St. Stephens Green Shopping Centre
George's Arcade
Westbury Mall
Civic Mus.
Bank of Ireland
The Screen
Ha'penny Bridge
Nat. Phot. Archive
Olympia Thea.
Andrews Lane Thea.
Temple Bar Info. Centre
City Hall
Dublin Castle
Chester Beatty Library
St. Patrick's Cathedral
Marsh's Library
Christ Church Cathedral
Civic Offices
Dublinia
Tivoli Theatre
Vicar Street Theatre
National College of Art and Design
Four Courts
Court
St Michan's
Old Jameson Distillery
Chimney Viewing Tower
National Wax Museum
King's Inns
Cineworld
Vegetable Market
Millennium Br.
Jervis Shopping Centre
Abbey Theatre
Central Library
ILAC Shopping Centre
General Post Office
Dublin Spire
Talbot St Mall
St. Mary's Cathedral
Rotunda Hospital
Dublin Writers Museum
Garden of Remembrance
Gate Theatre
Ambassador Theatre
James Joyce Centre

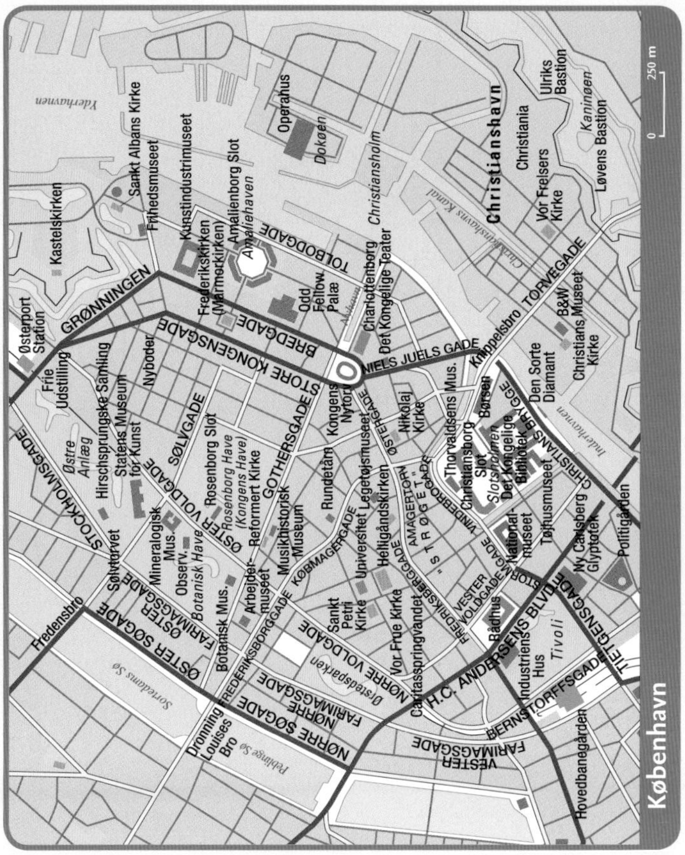
København
0
250 m
Christianshavn
Christiania
Vor Frelsers Kirke
Løvens Bastion
Uriks Bastion
Operahus
Dokøen
Amalienborg Slot
Amaliehaven
Frederikskirken (Marmorkirken)
Kunstindustrimuseet
Frihedsmuseet
Sankt Albans Kirke
Kastelskirken
Østerport Station
GRØNNINGEN
BREDGADE
TOLDBODGADE
STORE KONGENSGADE
NIELS JUELS GADE
Odd Fellow Palæ
Charlottenborg
Det Kongelige Teater
Kongens Nytorv
Nyboder
SØLVGADE
GOTHERSGADE
Frie Udstilling
Østre Anlæg
Hirschsprungske Samling
Statens Museum for Kunst
Rosenborg Slot
Rosenborg Have (Kongens Have)
Reformert Kirke
Mineralogisk Mus.
Observ.
Botanisk Have
Botanisk Mus.
Arbejder-museet
Musikhistorisk Museum
Rundetårn
Nikolaj Kirke
Børsen
Den Sorte Diamant
Christians Kirke
B&W Museet
TORVEGADE
Knippelsbro
Thorvaldsens Mus.
Christiansborg Slot
Det Kongelige Bibliotek
Nationalmuseet
Tøjhusmuseet
Ny Carlsberg Glyptotek
Politigården
Helligåndskirken
Universitet
Sankt Petri Kirke
Vor Frue Kirke
Caritasspringvandet
Rådhus
Industriens Hus
Tivoli
H.C. ANDERSENS BLVD
BERNSTORFFSGADE
Hovedbanegården
VESTER FARIMAGSGADE
NØRRE FARIMAGSGADE
NØRRE SØGADE
ØSTER SØGADE
Ørstedsparken
Dronning Louises Bro
Sortedams Sø
Peblinge Sø
Fredensbro
STOCKHOLMSGADE
ØSTER VOLDGADE
ØSTER FARIMAGSGADE
Sølvtorvet
FREDERIKSBORGGADE
NØRRE VOLDGADE
KØBMAGERGADE
AMAGERTORV
STRØGET
ØSTERGADE
VESTER VOLDGADE
STORMGADE
TIETGENSGADE
Christianshavns Kanal
Inderhavnen
Kaninøen

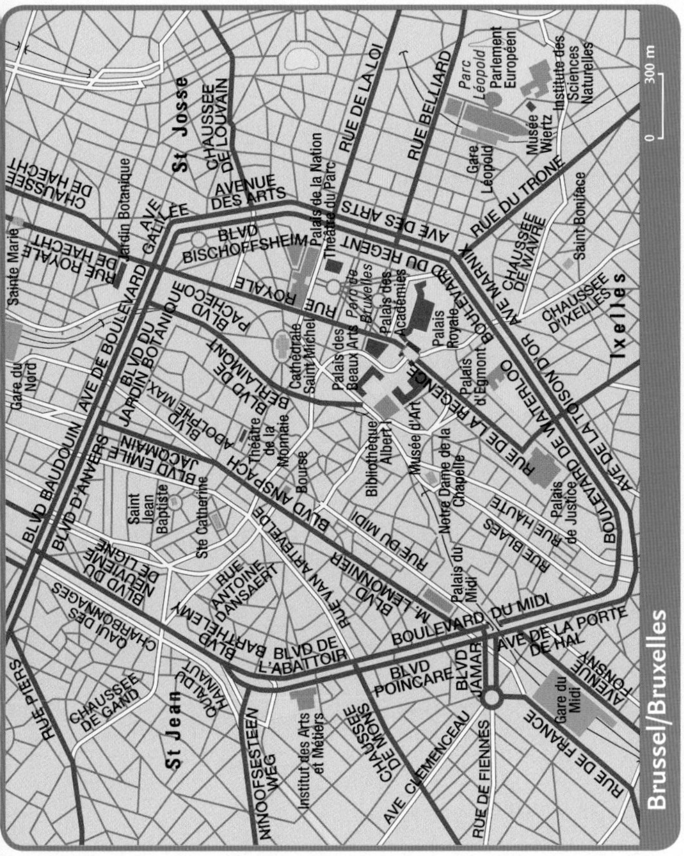
Brussel/Bruxelles
0
300 m
St Josse
St Jean
Ixelles
CHAUSSEE DE LOUVAIN
AVENUE DES ARTS
RUE DE LA LOI
RUE BELLIARD
AVE DES ARTS
RUE DU TRONE
CHAUSSEE DE WAVRE
CHAUSSEE D'IXELLES
AVE MARNIX
BOULEVARD DU REGENT
BLVD BISCHOFFSHEIM
RUE ROYALE
BLVD PACHECO
BLVD DU JARDIN BOTANIQUE
AVE GALILEE
CHAUSSEE DE HAECHT
AVE DE BOULEVARD
BLVD BAUDOUIN
BLVD D'ANVERS
BLVD EMILE JACQMAIN
BLVD ADOLPHE MAX
BLVD DE BERLAIMONT
BLVD ANSPACH
RUE DU MIDI
BLVD M. LEMONNIER
RUE VAN ARTEVELDE
RUE ANTOINE DANSAERT
BLVD DE NIEUWE LIGNE
QUAI DES CHARBONNAGES
BLVD BARTHELEMY
BLVD DE L'ABATTOIR
CHAUSSEE DE GAND
RUE PIERS
QUAI DU HAINAUT
NINOOFSESTEEN WEG
CHAUSSEE DE MONS
AVE CLEMENCEAU
RUE DE FIENNES
BLVD POINCARE
BLVD JAMAR
BOULEVARD DU MIDI
AVE DE LA PORTE DE HAL
AVENUE FONSNY
RUE DE FRANCE
BOULEVARD DE WATERLOO
AVE DE LA TOISON D'OR
RUE DE LA REGENCE
RUE HAUTE
RUE BLAES
Gare du Midi
Institut des Arts et Métiers
Palais du Midi
Palais de Justice
Notre Dame de la Chapelle
Musée d'Art
Bibliothèque Albert I
Bourse
Théâtre de la Monnaie
Ste Catherine
Saint Jean Baptiste
Gare du Nord
Sainte Marie
Jardin Botanique
Cathédrale Saint-Michel
Palais des Beaux Arts
Parc de Bruxelles
Palais des Académies
Palais Royal
Palais d'Egmont
Palais de la Nation
Théâtre du Parc
Saint-Boniface
Gare Léopold
Parc Léopold
Parlement Européen
Musée Wiertz
Institute des Sciences Naturelles

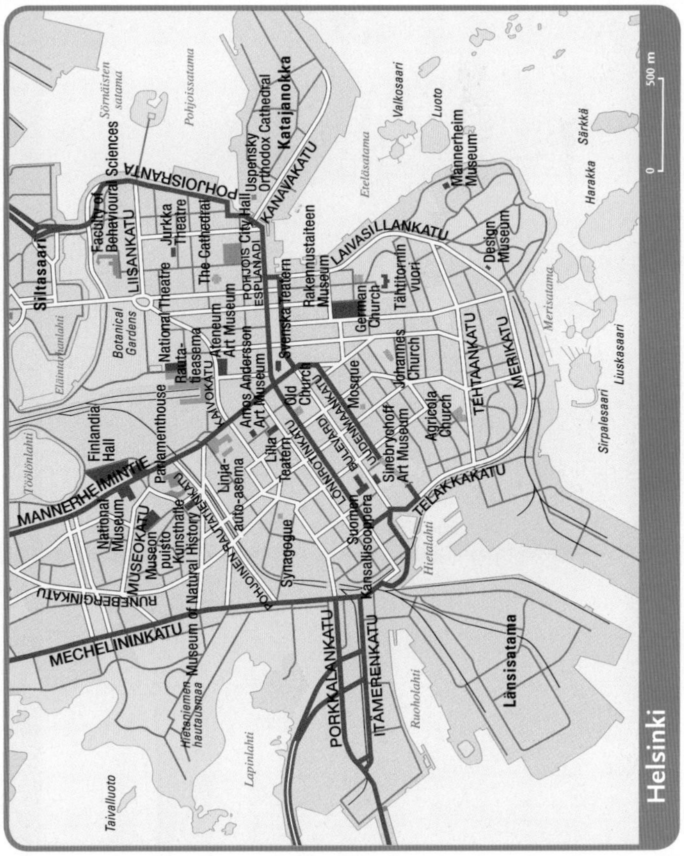
Helsinki
0
500 m
Siltasaari
Katajanokka
Länsisatama
Taivalluoto
Pohjoissatama
Eteläsatama
Valkosaari
Luoto
Särkkä
Harakka
Sirpalesaari
Liuskasaari
Merisatama
Hietalahti
Ruoholahti
Lapinlahti
Töölönlahti
Eläintarhanlahti
Sörnäisten satama
POHJOISRANTA
KANAVAKATU
LIISANKATU
LAIVASILLANKATU
MERIKATU
TEHTAANKATU
TELAKKAKATU
MANNERHEIMINTIE
MUSEOKATU
RUNEBERGINKATU
MECHELININKATU
PORKKALANKATU
ITÄMERENKATU
LÖNNROTINKATU
BULEVARDI
POHJOISESPLANADI
ESPLANADI
Uspensky Orthodox Cathedral
City Hall
The Cathedral
Jurkka Theatre
Faculty of Behavioural Sciences
Botanical Gardens
National Theatre
Ateneum Art Museum
Rautatieasema
Svenska Teatern
Rakennustaiteen Museum
German Church
Tähtitornin Vuori
Design Museum
Mannerheim Museum
Amos Anderson Art Museum
Old Church
Lilla Teatern
Mosque
Johannes Church
Agricola Church
Sinebrychoff Art Museum
Linja-auto-asema
Synagogue
Suomen Kansallisooppera
Finlandia Hall
Parliamenthouse
Kunsthalle
National Museum
Museum of Natural History
Hietaniemen hautausmaa

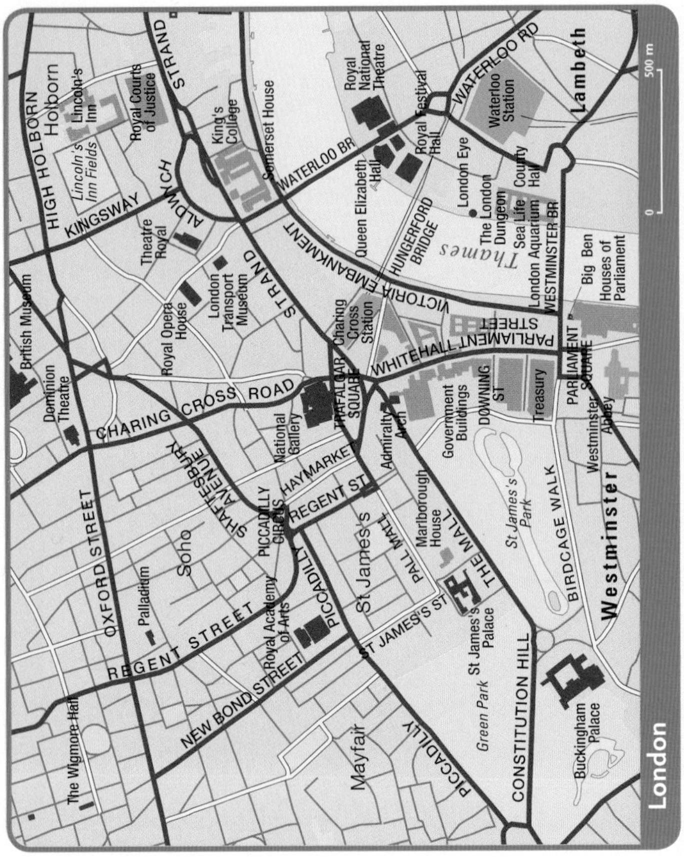
London
0
500 m
HIGH HOLBORN
Holborn
Lincoln's Inn
Lincoln's Inn Fields
Royal Courts of Justice
STRAND
KINGSWAY
ALDWYCH
King's College
Somerset House
Royal National Theatre
WATERLOO BR
WATERLOO RD
Royal Festival Hall
Queen Elizabeth Hall
London Eye
Waterloo Station
Lambeth
County Hall
The London Dungeon
Sea Life London Aquarium
WESTMINSTER BR
Big Ben
Houses of Parliament
HUNGERFORD BRIDGE
Thames
VICTORIA EMBANKMENT
Theatre Royal
London Transport Museum
Royal Opera House
British Museum
Dominion Theatre
CHARING CROSS ROAD
Charing Cross Station
TRAFALGAR SQUARE
WHITEHALL
PARLIAMENT STREET
PARLIAMENT SQUARE
National Gallery
Admiralty Arch
Government Buildings
DOWNING ST
Treasury
Westminster Abbey
SHAFTESBURY AVENUE
HAYMARKET
REGENT ST
PICCADILLY CIRCUS
OXFORD STREET
Soho
Palladium
REGENT STREET
Royal Academy of Arts
PICCADILLY
St. James's
PALL MALL
Marlborough House
St James's Park
BIRDCAGE WALK
Westminster
THE MALL
ST JAMES'S ST
St James's Palace
NEW BOND STREET
Mayfair
Green Park
CONSTITUTION HILL
Buckingham Palace
The Wigmore Hall

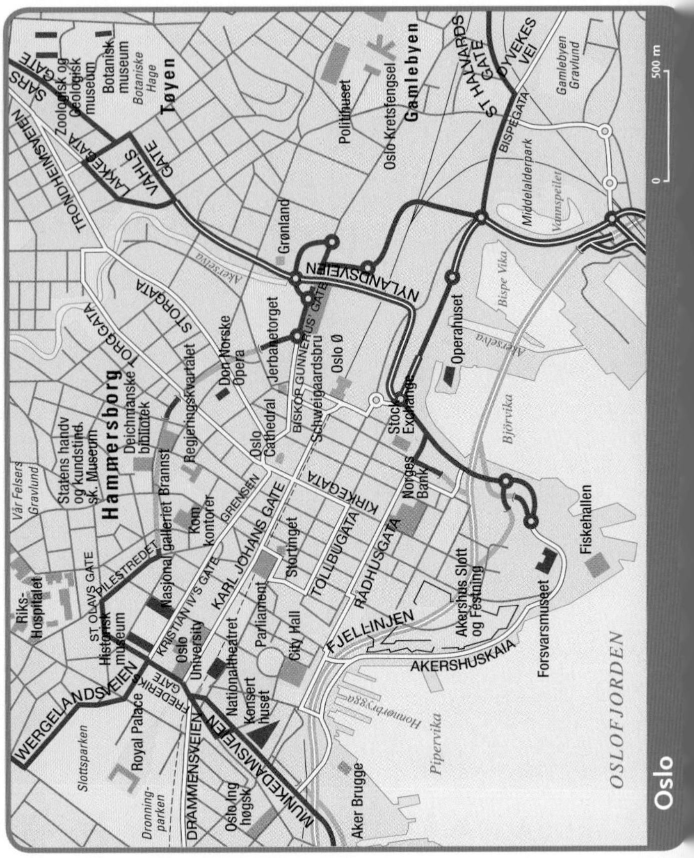
Oslo
0
500 m
SARS GATE
Zoologisk og Geologisk museum
Botanisk museum
Botaniske Hage
Tøyen
TRONDHEIMSVEIEN
LAKKEGATA
VAHLS GATE
Politihuset
Oslo Kretsfengsel
Gamlebyen
ST HALVARDS GATE
OSLOVEIEN
BISPEGATA
Middelalderpark
Gamlebyen Gravlund
Grønland
NYLANDSVEIEN
STORGATA
TORGGATA
Hammersborg
Deichmanske bibliotek
Regjeringskvartalet
Den Norske Opera
Jernbanetorget
Oslo Ø
Operahuset
BISKOP GUNNERUS' GATE
Schweigaardsbru
Oslo Cathedral
Stock Exchange
Norges Bank
Vår Frelsers Gravlund
Statens handv og kundstind. sk. Museum
Galleriet Branist
Kom kontorer
GRENSEN
KARL JOHANS GATE
KIRKEGATA
Stortinget
TOLLBUGATA
RÅDHUSGATA
Fiskehallen
Riks-Hospitalet
ST OLAVS GATE
PILESTREDET
Nasjonalgalleriet
KRISTIAN IV'S GATE
Historisk museum
Oslo University
Parliament
City Hall
FJELLINJEN
Akershus Slott og Festning
Forsvarsmuseet
AKERSHUSKAIA
WERGELANDSVEIEN
Nationaltheatret
Konserthuset
FREDERIKS GATE
Slottsparken
Royal Palace
Dronningparken
DRAMMENSVEIEN
MUNKEDAMSVEIEN
Oslo ing høgsk
Aker Brugge
Pipervika
OSLOFJORDEN

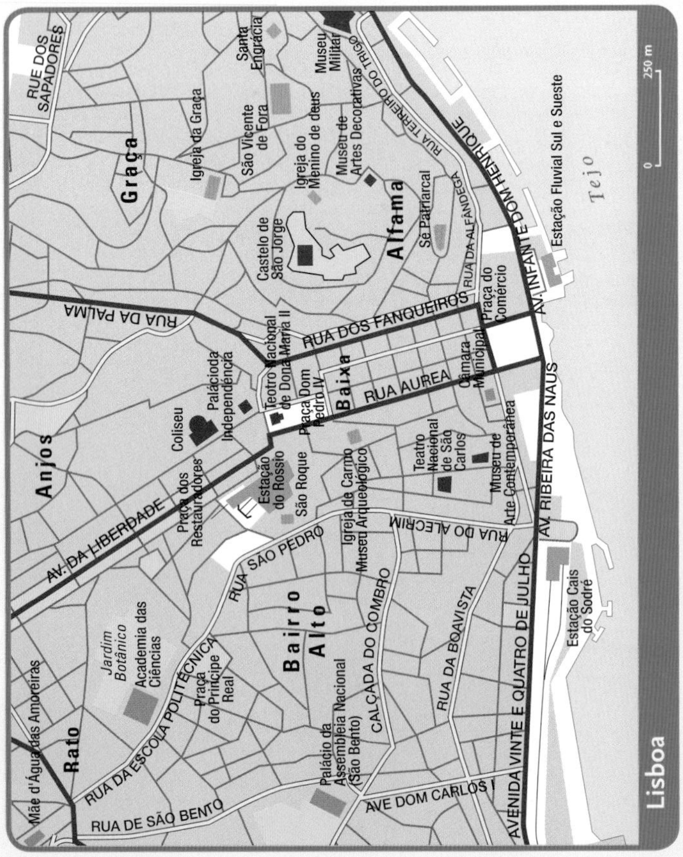
Lisboa
0
250 m
RUE DOS SAPADORES
Graça
Santa Engrácia
Museu Militar
Igreja da Graça
São Vicente de Fora
Igreja do Menino de deus
Museu de Artes Decorativas
Castelo de São Jorge
Alfama
Sé Patriarcal
RUA DA ALFÂNDEGA
Tejo
Estação Fluvial Sul e Sueste
RUA DA PALMA
RUA DOS FANQUEIROS
Praça do Comércio
AV. INFANTE DOM HENRIQUE
Palácio da Independência
Teatro Nacional de Dona Maria II
Baixa
RUA AUREA
Câmara Municipal
Coliseu
Praça Dom Pedro IV
Anjos
Praça dos Restauradores
Estação do Rossio
São Roque
Igreja do Carmo
Museu Arqueológico
Teatro Nacional de São Carlos
Museu de Arte Contemporânea
AV. RIBEIRA DAS NAUS
AV. DA LIBERDADE
RUA SÃO PEDRO
RUA DO ALECRIM
Bairro Alto
CALÇADA DO COMBRO
RUA DA BOAVISTA
AVENIDA VINTE E QUATRO DE JULHO
Estação Cais do Sodré
Jardim Botânico
Academia das Ciências
Praça do Príncipe Real
RUA DA ESCOLA POLITÉCNICA
Rato
Mãe d'Água das Amoreiras
Palácio da Assembleia Nacional (São Bento)
AVE DOM CARLOS I
RUA DE SÃO BENTO

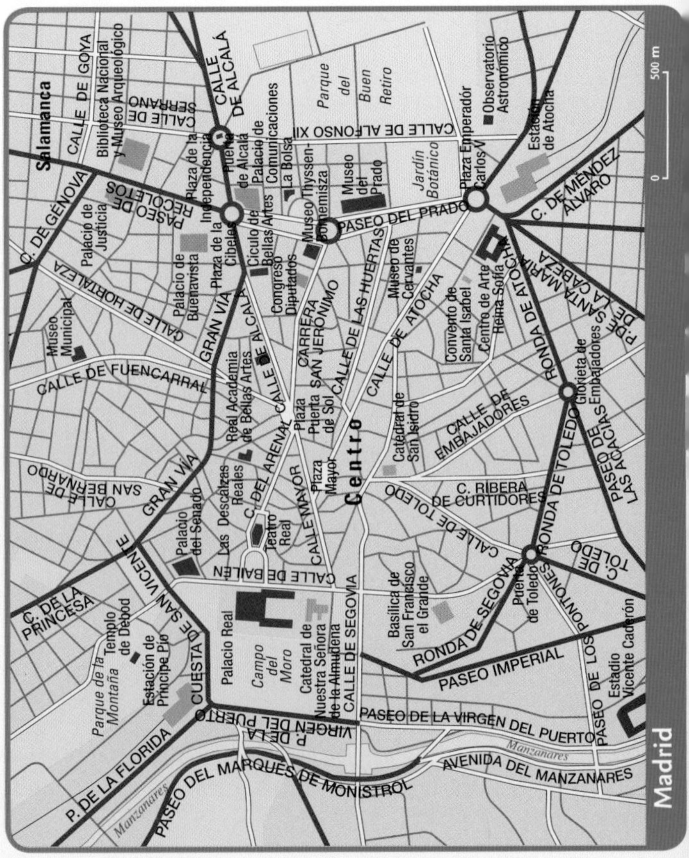
Madrid
0
500 m
Salamanca
CALLE DE GOYA
Biblioteca Nacional y Museo Arqueológico
CALLE DE SERRANO
CALLE DE ALCALÁ
Puerta de Alcalá
Plaza de la Independencia
Parque del Buen Retiro
CALLE DE ALFONSO XII
Observatorio Astronómico
Estación de Atocha
C. DE GÉNOVA
PASEO DE RECOLETOS
Palacio de Justicia
Plaza de Cibeles
Palacio de Comunicaciones
La Bolsa
Museo Thyssen-Bornemisza
Museo del Prado
PASEO DEL PRADO
Jardín Botánico
Plaza Emperador Carlos V
C. DE MÉNDEZ ALVARO
Palacio de Buenavista
Círculo de Bellas Artes
Congreso Diputados
CALLE DE HORTALEZA
Museo Municipal
GRAN VÍA
CARRERA SAN JERÓNIMO
CALLE DE LAS HUERTAS
Museo de Cervantes
CALLE DE ATOCHA
Convento de Santa Isabel
Centro de Arte Reina Sofía
RONDA DE ATOCHA
P. DE SANTA MARÍA DE LA CABEZA
CALLE DE FUENCARRAL
Real Academia de Bellas Artes
Plaza Puerta del Sol
Glorieta de Embajadores
CALLE DE EMBAJADORES
CALLE DE SAN BERNARDO
Las Descalzas Reales
Plaza Mayor
Centro
Catedral de San Isidro
C. RIBERA DE CURTIDORES
PASEO DE LAS ACACIAS
Palacio del Senado
Teatro Real
CALLE MAYOR
CALLE DE TOLEDO
RONDA DE TOLEDO
CALLE DE BAILÉN
C. DE LA PRINCESA
Templo de Debod
Palacio Real
Campo del Moro
Catedral de Nuestra Señora de la Almudena
CALLE DE SEGOVIA
Basílica de San Francisco el Grande
RONDA DE SEGOVIA
Puerta de Toledo
C. DE TOLEDO
Estación de Príncipe Pío
Parque de la Montaña
CUESTA DE SAN VICENTE
PASEO IMPERIAL
P. DE LA VIRGEN DEL PUERTO
PASEO DE LA VIRGEN DEL PUERTO
Estadio Vicente Calderón
P. DE LA FLORIDA
PASEO DEL MARQUÉS DE MONISTROL
Manzanares
AVENIDA DEL MANZANARES

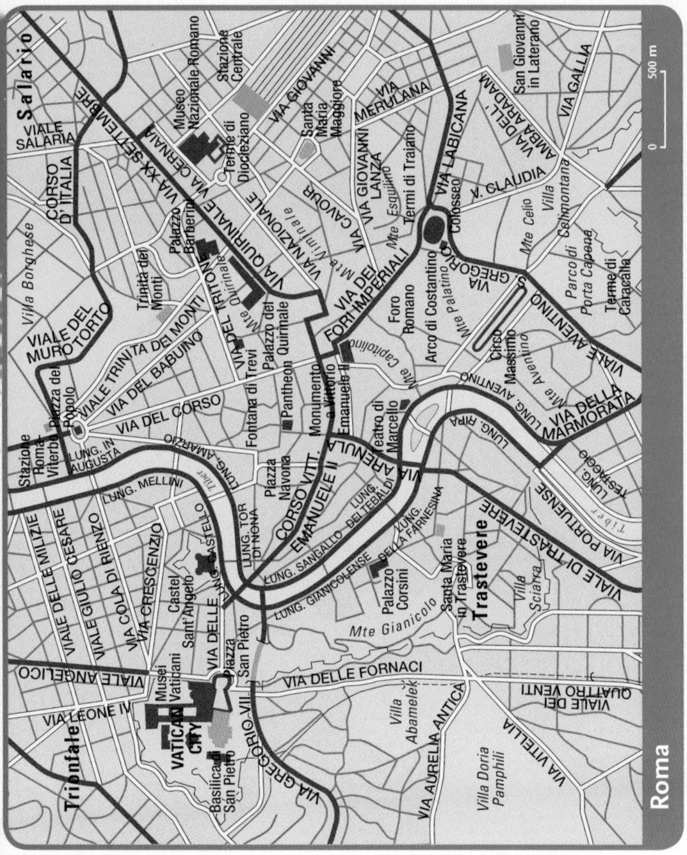
Roma
0 500 m
Salario
Trastevere
Trionfale
VATICANO
CITTÀ
Colosseo
Foro Romano
Pantheon
Fontana di Trevi
Piazza Navona
Castel Sant'Angelo
Stazione Centrale
Villa Borghese
Tiber

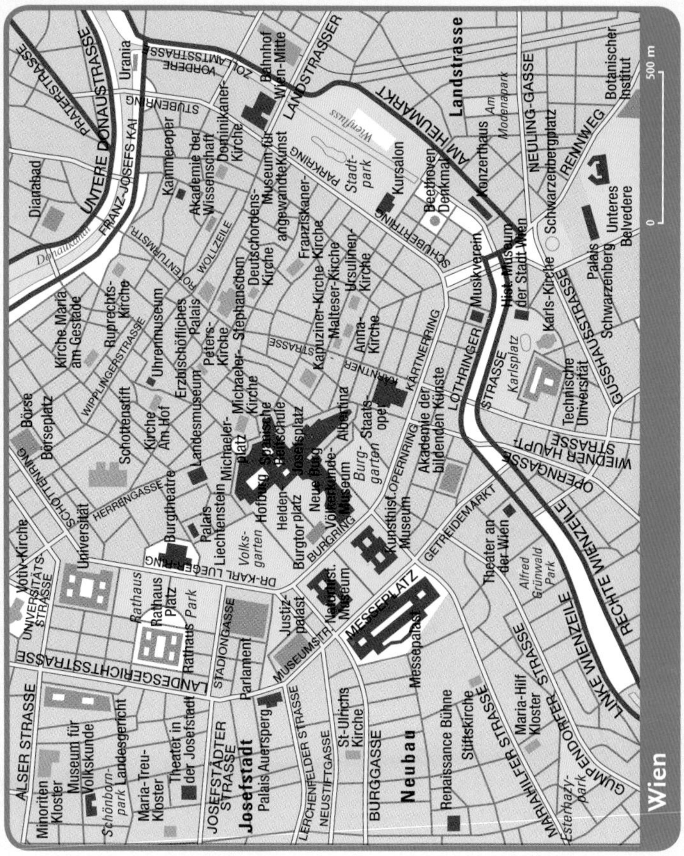
Wien
0 500 m
Landstrasse
Josefstadt
Neubau
Stephansdom
Hofburg
Rathaus
Parlament
Universität
Staatsoper
Karlsplatz
Karls-Kirche
Messeplatz
Donaukanal

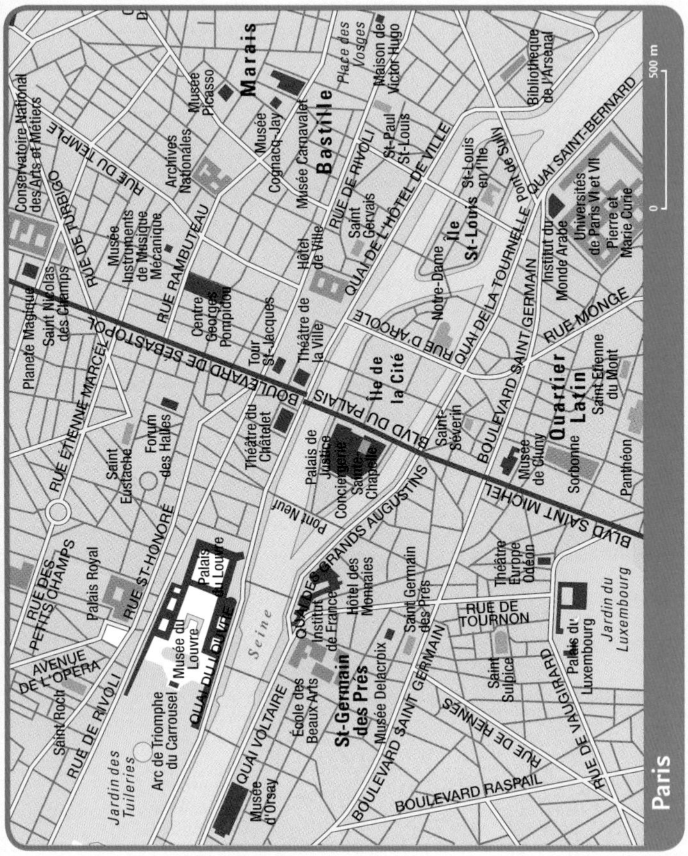
Paris
0 500 m
Marais
Bastille
Île de la Cité
Île St-Louis
Quartier Latin
St-Germain des Prés
Musée du Louvre
Musée d'Orsay
Centre Georges Pompidou
Notre-Dame
Panthéon
Seine
Jardin des Tuileries
Jardin du Luxembourg

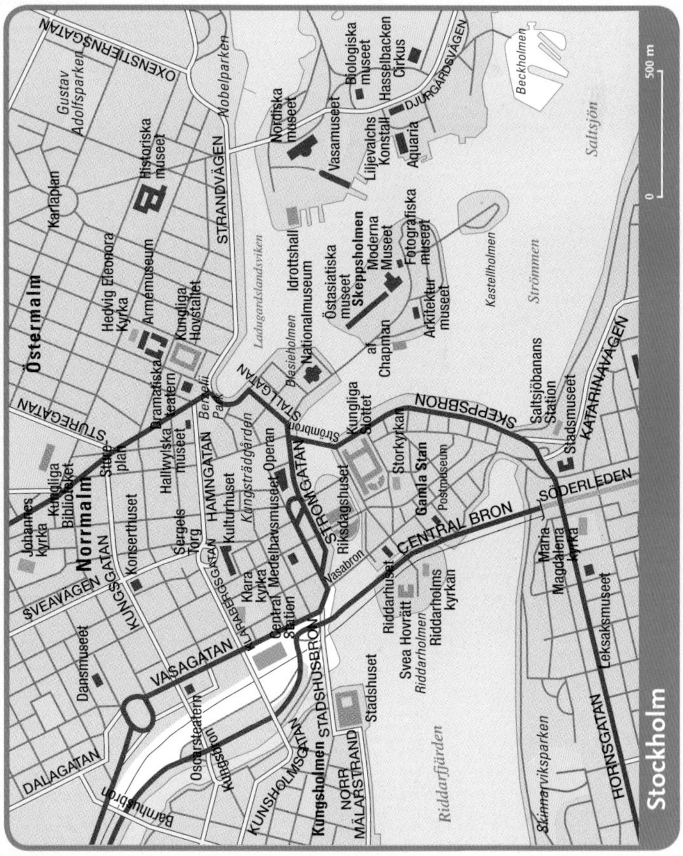
Stockholm
0 500 m
Östermalm
Norrmalm
Kungsholmen
Skeppsholmen
Gamla Stan
Stadshuset
Nationalmuseum
Vasamuseet
Nordiska museet
Historiska museet
Riddarfjärden
Saltsjön
Strömmen

A

Å N 104 F7
Å N 110 E4
Å N 111 B12
Å N 111 C13
Aabenraa DK 86 E4
Aabybro DK 86 A5
Aachen D 20 C6
Aadorf CH 27 F10
Aakirkeby DK 89 E7
Aalborg DK 86 A5
Aalen D 75 E7
Aalestrup DK 86 B4
Aalsmeer NL 16 D3
Aalst B 19 C9
Aalst NL 183 B6
Aalten NL 17 E7
Aalter B 19 B7
Äänekoski FIN 123 E15
Aapajärvi FIN 115 D2
Aapajärvi FIN 119 B12
Aapajoki FIN 119 B12
Aapua S 117 E11
Aarau CH 27 F9
Aarberg CH 31 A11
Aardenburg NL 19 B7
Aareavaara S 117 D10
Aarhus DK 86 C6
Aarle NL 16 F5
A Armada E 38 B3
Aars DK 86 B5
Aarschot B 19 C10
Aartrijke B 182 C2
Aartselaar B 19 B9
Aarup DK 86 E6
Aarwangen CH 27 F8
Aasleagh IRL 6 E3
Ääsmäe EST 131 C9
Aaspere EST 131 C12
Aatsinki FIN 115 E5
Aavajärvi S 119 C11
Aavasaksa FIN 119 B11
Aba H 149 B11
Abaclia MD 154 E3
Abades E 46 C4
Abadín E 38 B5
Abadiño-Zelaieta E 41 B6
Abádszalók H 150 C6
A Baiuca E 38 B3
Abak TR 181 A7
Abalar TR 172 A6
Abánades E 47 C8
Abanilla E 56 E2
Abano Terme I 66 B4
Abarán E 55 C10
A Barrela E 38 C4
Abasár H 150 B5
Abaújszántó H 145 G3
Abbadia San Salvatore I 62 B1
Abbasanta I 64 C2
Abbekås S 87 E13
Abbeville F 18 D4
Abbey IRL 6 F6
Abbeydorney IRL 8 D3
Abbeyfeale IRL 8 D4
Abbeyleix IRL 9 C8
Abbey Town GB 5 F10
Abbiategrasso I 69 C6
Abborrberg S 109 F12
Abborreberget S 98 D8
Abborrträsk S 109 F17
Abbotsbury GB 13 D9
Abbots Langley GB 15 D8
Abcoude NL 16 D3
Abejar E 40 E6
Abejuela E 48 E3
Abela P 50 C2
Abelvær N 105 B10
Abenberg D 75 D8
Abenójar E 54 B4
Abensberg D 75 E10
Aberaeron GB 12 A6
Aberaman GB 13 B8
Aberchirder GB 3 K11
Aberdare GB 13 B8
Aberdaron GB 10 F2
Aberdeen GB 3 L12
Aberdovey GB 10 F3
Aberfeldy GB 5 B9
Aberffraw GB 10 E3
Aberford GB 11 D9
Aberfoyle GB 5 C8
Abergavenny GB 13 B8
Abergele GB 10 E4
Åberget S 109 E18
Abergwaun GB 12 B5
Abergynolwyn GB 10 F4
Aberlady GB 5 C11
Aberlour GB 3 L10
Abernethy GB 5 C10
Aberporth GB 12 A5
Abersoch GB 10 F2
Abertamy CZ 75 B12
Abertawe GB 13 B7
Abertillery GB 13 B8
Abertura E 45 F9
Aberuthven GB 5 C9
Aberystwyth GB 12 A6
Abetone I 66 D2
Abfaltersbach A 72 C6
Abhainnsuidhe GB 2 K2
Abia de la Obispalía E 47 D8
Abiego E 42 C3
Abild DK 86 F3
Abilly F 29 B7
Abingdon GB 13 B12
Abington GB 5 E9
Abisko Östra S 111 D16
Abja-Paluoja EST 131 E10
Abla E 55 E7
Ablis F 24 C6
Ablitas E 41 E8
Abmelaseter N 112 E6
Abo FIN 126 E7
Åbo S 103 C10
Åbodarna S 107 E14
Åbogen N 96 B7
Abondance F 31 C10
Abony H 150 C5
Åbosjö S 107 D13
Aboyne GB 5 A11
Abragão P 44 B4
Abram RO 151 C9
Abrămuț RO 151 C9
Abrantes P 44 F4
Abraur S 109 D16
Abreiro P 38 F5
Abreschviller F 27 C7
Abrest F 30 C3
Abriès F 31 F10
Abrigada P 44 F2
Abriola I 60 B5
Abrucena E 55 E7
Abrud RO 151 E11
Abrupe LV 135 B11
Absam A 72 B4
Absberg D 75 D8
Absdorf A 77 F9
Abtenau A 73 A7
Abtsgmünd D 74 E6
Abukhava BY 140 C10
Åby S 89 A7
Åby S 93 B8
Åbyen DK 90 D7
Åbyggeby S 103 E13
Åbyn S 118 D6
Åbytorp S 92 A6
Acaill IRL 6 E3
A Cañiza E 38 D3
A Carballa E 38 B2
Acarlar TR 177 D10
A Carreira E 38 B3
Acâș RO 151 B10
Acate I 58 E5
Accadia I 60 A4
Acceglio I 36 C5
Accettura I 60 C6
Acciano I 62 C5
Acciaroli I 60 C4
Accous F 32 E4
Accrington GB 11 D7
Accumoli I 62 B4
Acebo E 45 D7
Acedera E 45 F9
Acedo E 32 E1
Acehuche E 45 E7
Aceituna E 45 D8
Acered E 47 B9
Acerenza I 60 B5
Acerno I 60 B4
Acerra I 60 B2
Aceuchal E 51 B7
Ach A 76 F3
Achadh Mòr GB 2 J3
A Chan E 38 D3
Acharacle GB 4 B5
Acharnes GR 175 C8
Achavanich GB 3 J10
Achel B 183 C6
Achenkirch A 72 A4
Achern D 27 C9
Acheux-en-Amiénois F 18 D6
Achicourt F 18 D6
Achill IRL 6 E3
Achilleio GR 175 A6
Achim D 17 B12
Achintee GB 2 L6
Achladochori GR 169 B10
Achladokampos GR 175 D6
Achnacroish GB 4 B6
Achnasheen GB 2 K6
Achosnich GB 4 B4
Achstetten D 71 A9
Achtrup D 82 A6
Aci Castello I 59 D7
Aci Catena I 59 D7
Acireale I 59 D7
Aci Sant'Antonio I 59 D7
Aci Trezza I 59 D7
Acktjära S 103 D11
Acle GB 15 B12
A Coruña E 38 B3
Acquacalda I 59 B6
Acqualagna I 67 E6
Acquanegra sul Chiese I 66 B1
Acquapendente I 62 B1
Acquappesa I 60 E5
Acquaro I 59 B9
Acquarossa CH 71 E7
Acquasanta Terme I 62 B4
Acquasparta I 62 B3
Acquaviva Picena I 62 B5
Acquedolci I 59 C6
Acquigny F 24 B5
Acqui Terme I 37 B8
Acri I 61 E6
A Cruz do Incio E 38 C5
Ács H 149 A10
Acsa H 150 B3
Acuto I 62 D4
Ada SRB 150 F5
Adács H 150 B4
Adahuesca E 42 C3
Adak S 109 F16
Ådalsliden S 107 E11
Adamas GR 179 B7
Adamclisi RO 155 E1
Adamov CZ 77 D11
Adamova BY 133 E4
Adamów PL 141 G6
Adamówka PL 144 C6
Adamstown IRL 9 D9
Adămuș RO 152 E4
Adamuz E 53 A7
Adâncata RO 153 B8
Adâncata RO 161 D8
Ádánd H 149 C10
Adanero E 46 C3
Adão P 45 D6
Adare IRL 8 C5
Adatepe TR 173 D6
Adaúfe P 38 E3
Adavere EST 131 D11
Ādaži LV 135 B8
Adderbury GB 13 A12
Addlestone GB 15 E8
Adegem B 182 C2
Adelboden CH 31 C12
Adelebsen D 78 C6
Adelfia I 61 A7
Adelina PL 144 B8
Adelmannsfelden D 187 D8
Adelschlag D 75 E9
Adelsheim D 27 B11
Adelsried D 75 F8
Ademuz E 47 D10
Adenau D 21 D7
Adendorf D 83 D8
Adendro GR 169 C8
Adenstedt D 78 C6
Adjud RO 153 E10
Adlešiči SLO 148 E4
Adliswil CH 27 F10
Adlkofen D 75 E11
Admont A 73 A9
Adolfsström S 109 D12
Adony H 149 B11
Adorf D 75 B11
Adorf (Diemelsee) D 17 F11
Adoufe P 38 F4
Adra E 55 F6
Adradas E 41 F7
Adrados E 40 F3
Adrano I 59 D6
Adria I 66 B5
Adriani GR 171 B6
Adriers F 29 C7
Aduard NL 17 B6
Adulsbruk N 101 E14
Ådum DK 86 D3
Adunați RO 161 C7
Adunații-Copăceni RO 161 E8
Adutiškis LT 135 F13
Adzaneta de Albaida E 56 D4
Adžūni LV 135 D8
Aegviidu EST 131 C11
Aerino GR 169 F8
Ærøskøbing DK 86 F6
Aerzen D 17 D12
A Escusa E 38 C2
A Esfarrapada E 38 D2
A Estrada E 38 C3
Aetos GR 169 C6
Aetos GR 174 B3
Aetos GR 174 E4
Äetsä FIN 126 C8
Afantou GR 181 D8
Åfarnes N 100 A7
A Feira do Monte E 38 B4
Affing D 75 F8
Afife P 38 E2
Afissos GR 169 F9
Åfjord N 104 D8
Aflenz Kurort A 73 A11
A Fonsagrada E 38 B5
A Forxa E 38 D4
A Forxa E 38 D4
Åfoss N 90 A6
Afragola I 60 B2
Afritz A 73 C8
Afumați RO 160 E2
Afumați RO 161 D8
Afytos GR 169 D9
Aga D 79 E11
Ağaçli TR 173 B10
Ağaköy TR 173 D7
Agalas GR 174 D2
Agallas E 45 D8
A Gándara E 38 B3
A Gándara de Altea E 38 A3
Agapia RO 153 C8
Agăș RO 153 D8
Ágasegyháza H 150 D3
Agde F 34 D5
Agen F 33 B7
Àger E 42 C5
Agerbæk DK 86 D3
Agerskov DK 86 E4
Agersted DK 86 A6
Ågerup DK 87 D10
Ágfalva H 149 A7
Aggersund DK 86 A4
Aggius I 64 B3
Aggsbach Markt A 77 F8
Aghaboe IRL 9 C7
Aghagallon GB 7 C10
Aghalee GB 7 C10
Aghanloo GB 4 E3
Aghaville IRL 8 E4
Aghern IRL 8 D6
Aghione F 37 G10
Aghireșu RO 151 D11
Aghleam IRL 6 D2
Aghnagar Bridge IRL 8 E2
Agia GR 169 E8
Agia Anna GR 175 B7
Agia Anna GR 175 C6
Agia Effimia GR 174 C2
Agia Efthymia GR 174 C5
Agia Galini GR 178 E8
Agia Kyriaki GR 174 E4
Agia Marina GR 175 B6
Agia Marina GR 175 C9
Agia Marina GR 177 E8
Agia Paraskevi GR 168 D4
Agia Paraskevi GR 174 A3
Agia Paraskevi GR 177 E6
Agia Pelagia GR 178 C4
Agia Pelagia GR 178 E9
Agiasma GR 171 C7
Agiasos GR 177 A7
Agia Triada GR 174 D4
Agia Triada GR 175 D6
Agia Varvara GR 169 D7
Agia Varvara GR 178 E9
Agigea RO 155 E3
Agighiol RO 155 C3
Agino Selo BIH 157 C7
Agiofyllo GR 169 E6
Agioi Anargyroi GR 169 E7
Agioi Apostoloi GR 175 C8
Agioi Deka GR 178 E8
Agioi Theodoroi GR 169 E5
Agioi Theodoroi GR 175 A6
Agioi Theodoroi GR 175 D7
Agiokampos GR 169 E8
Agiokampos GR 175 B7
Agionori GR 175 D6
Agios Andreas GR 175 E6
Agios Athanasios GR 169 C8
Agios Athanasios GR 171 B6
Agios Charalampos GR 171 C9
Agios Christoforos GR 175 F5
Agios Dimitrios GR 169 D7
Agios Dimitrios GR 175 D8
Agios Dimitrios GR 175 F6
Agios Efstratios GR 171 E7
Agios Georgios GR 169 C7
Agios Georgios GR 174 B4
Agios Georgios GR 175 C6
Agios Georgios GR 177 F6
Agios Georgios GR 178 E9
Agios Germanos GR 168 C5
Agios Ioannis GR 174 E5
Agios Ioannis GR 175 C7
Agios Ioannis GR 178 B4
Agios Kirykos GR 177 D7
Agios Konstantinos GR 174 B3
Agios Konstantinos GR 174 D5
Agios Konstantinos GR 175 B6
Agios Konstantinos GR 175 D9
Agios Kyprianos GR 178 C3
Agios Leon GR 174 D2
Agios Loukas GR 169 C7
Agios Loukas GR 175 C9
Agios Mamas GR 169 D9
Agios Matthaios GR 168 F2
Agios Myronas GR 178 E9
Agios Nikolaos GR 168 E3
Agios Nikolaos GR 168 E5
Agios Nikolaos GR 169 D10
Agios Nikolaos GR 174 B2
Agios Nikolaos GR 174 B4
Agios Nikolaos GR 174 B4
Agios Nikolaos GR 178 B3
Agios Nikolaos GR 179 E10
Agios Panteleïmonas GR 169 C6
Agios Paraskevi GR 171 F10
Agios Petros GR 169 C8
Agios Petros GR 174 B2
Agios Petros GR 175 E6
Agios Spyridonas GR 169 D7
Agios Spyridonas GR 174 A2
Agios Stefanos GR 175 C8
Agios Stefanos GR 176 E5
Agios Thomas GR 175 C8
Agios Vasileios GR 169 C9
Agios Vasileios GR 175 D6
Agira I 59 D6
Agivey GB 4 E3
Agkathia GR 169 C7
Agkistro GR 169 B9
Aglapsvik N 111 B15
Aglasterhausen D 187 C6
Agle N 105 C13
Aglen N 105 B10
Agliana I 66 E3
Aglientu I 64 A3
Aglish IRL 9 D7
Agluonėnai LT 134 E2
Agnadello I 69 C8
Agnagar Bridge IRL 8 E2
Agnanta GR 168 F5
Agnantero GR 169 F6
Agneaux F 23 B9
Agnita RO 152 F5
Agno CH 69 A6
Agnone I 63 D6
Agolada E 38 C3
Agoncillo E 32 F1
Agon-Coutainville F 23 B8
Agordo I 72 D5
Agost E 56 E3
Agos-Vidalos F 32 D5
Ågotnes N 94 B2
Agra GR 177 A7
Agramón E 55 C9
Agramunt E 42 D6
Agrate Brianza I 69 B7
Agreda E 41 E8
Agrés E 56 D4
Agria GR 169 F9
Agridi GR 174 D4
Agrigento I 58 E4
Agrij RO 151 C11
Agrili GR 174 E4
Agrinio GR 174 B3
Agriovotano GR 175 A7
Agrochão P 39 E5
Agropoli I 60 C3
Ågskaret N 108 C5
Aguadulce E 53 B7
Aguadulce E 55 F7
A Guarda E 38 E2
Aguarón E 41 F9
Aguas E 42 C3
Águas Belas P 44 E4
Aguas de Busot E 56 D4
Águas de Moura P 50 B2
Águas Frias P 38 E5
Aguaviva E 42 F3
A Gudiña E 38 D5
Agudo E 54 B3
Águeda P 44 C4
Aguessac F 34 B5
Agugliano I 67 E7
Aguiar P 50 C4
Aguiar da Beira P 44 C5
Aguilafuente E 46 B4
Aguilar de Alfambra E 42 F2
Aguilar de Campóo E 40 C3
Aguilar de la Frontera E 53 A7
Aguilar del Río Alhama E 41 E8
Águilas E 55 E9
Agullana E 34 F4
Agullent E 56 D3
Aha S 109 F14
Ahafona IRL 8 C3
Aham D 75 E11
Ahascragh IRL 6 F6
Ahaus D 17 D8
Åheim N 100 B3
Ahelva FIN 121 E11
Ahigal E 45 D8
Ahigal de Villarino E 45 B8
Ahillones E 51 C8
Ahja EST 131 E14
Ahjola FIN 121 D12
Ahlainen FIN 126 B6
Ahlatli TR 167 E8
Ahlbeck D 84 C6
Ahlbeck D 84 C6
Ahlden (Aller) D 82 E7
Ahlen D 17 E9
Ahlerstedt D 17 B12
Ahlhorn D 17 C10
Ahmas FIN 119 E17
Ahmavaara FIN 115 E4
Ahmetbey TR 173 B8
Ahmetbeyli TR 177 C9
Ahmetçeeli TR 172 E6
Ahmetli TR 177 C9
Ahmovaara FIN 125 D13
Ahnsbeck D 79 A7
Ahoghill GB 4 F4
Ahoinen FIN 127 D11
Ahokylä FIN 123 C17
Ahola FIN 121 B11
Ahola FIN 121 C13
Ahola FIN 121 D13
Ahola FIN 124 D9
Aholanvaara FIN 115 E5
Ahonperä FIN 119 F13
Ahorn D 75 B8
Aho-Vastinki FIN 123 E14
Ahrbrück D 21 D7
Ahrensbök D 83 B9
Ahrensburg D 83 C8
Ahrenshagen D 83 B13
Ahrenshoop D 83 B12
Ähtäri FIN 123 E12
Ähtärinranta FIN 123 E12
Ahtme EST 132 C1
Ahula EST 131 C11
Ahun F 29 C10
Åhus S 88 D6
Ahveninen FIN 123 E16
Ahvenisto FIN 127 C16
Ahvensalmi FIN 125 F10
Ahvenselkä FIN 115 E4
Ahvenvittikko FIN 115 D4
Ahvionsaari FIN 129 B10
Aiani GR 169 D6
Aianteio GR 175 D7
Aibar E 32 E3
Aibl A 73 C11
Aichach D 75 F9
Aichhalden D 27 D9
Aichstetten D 71 B10
Ai'dejav'ri N 117 A10
Aidenbach D 76 E4
Aidipsos GR 175 B7
Aidone I 58 E5
Aidonochori GR 169 C10
Aidt DK 86 C5
Aidu EST 131 D12
Aiello Calabro I 59 A9
Aielo de Malferit E 56 D3
Aieta I 60 D5
Aiffres F 28 C5
Aigeira GR 174 C5
Aigen im Ennstal A 73 A9
Aigen im Mühlkreis A 76 E5
Aigiali GR 177 F6
Aigina GR 175 D7
Aiginio GR 169 D8
Aigio GR 174 C5
Aigle CH 31 C10
Aiglemont F 184 E2
Aignan F 33 C6
Aignay-le-Duc F 25 E12
Aigre F 28 D6
Aigrefeuille-d'Aunis F 28 C4
Aigrefeuille-sur-Maine F 28 A3
A Igrexa E 38 D3
Aiguafreda E 43 D8
Aiguebelle F 31 D9
Aigueblanche F 31 D10
Aigueperse F 30 C3
Aigues-Mortes F 35 C7
Aigues-Vives F 33 E9
Aigues-Vives F 34 D4
Aigues-Vives F 35 C7
Aiguilhe F 30 E4
Aiguilles F 31 F10
Aiguillon F 33 B6
Aigurande F 29 C9
Äijäjoki FIN 116 B10
Äijälä FIN 123 E16
Aijala FIN 127 E9
Aijänneva FIN 123 F11
Aillant-sur-Tholon F 25 E9
Aillas F 32 B5
Aillevillers-et-Lyaumont F 26 E5
Ailly-le-Haut-Clocher F 18 D4
Ailly-sur-Noye F 18 E5
Ailly-sur-Somme F 18 E5
Ailt an Chorráin IRL 6 C6
Aimargues F 35 C7
Aime F 31 D10
Ainali FIN 119 F14
Ainali FIN 123 B11
Ainay-le-Château F 29 B11
Ainaži LV 131 F8
Aindling D 75 E8
Ainet A 73 C6
Ainsa E 33 F6
Ainzón E 41 E9
Airaines F 18 E4
Airaksela FIN 124 E8
Airasca I 31 F11
Aird Asaig GB 2 K3
Airdrie GB 5 D9
Aire-sur-l'Adour F 32 C5
Aire-sur-la-Lys F 18 C5
Airidh a'Bhruaich GB 2 J3
Airola I 60 A3
Airole I 37 D7
Airolo CH 71 D7
Airvault F 28 B5
Aisey-sur-Seine F 25 E12
Aïssey F 26 F5
Aisymi GR 171 B9
Aisy-sur-Armançon F 25 E11
Aitamännikkö FIN 117 D12
Aita Mare RO 153 F7
Aiterhofen D 75 E12
Aith GB 3 E14
Aith GB 3 G11
Aitolahti FIN 127 B10
Aitoliko GR 174 C3
Aiton RO 152 D3
Aitona E 42 E4
Aitoo FIN 127 C11
Aitrach D 71 B10
Aitrang D 71 B11
Aittaniemi FIN 121 B10
Aittijoki FIN 113 D17
Aittojärvi FIN 119 D17
Aittojärvi FIN 123 C16
Aittokoski FIN 124 C8
Aittokylä FIN 121 E10
Aittoperä FIN 123 C13
Aittovaara FIN 121 D13
Aiud RO 152 E3
Aiviekste LV 135 C11
Aix-en-Othe F 25 D10
Aix-en-Provence F 35 C9
Aixe-sur-Vienne F 29 D8
Aix-les-Bains F 31 D8
Aizenay F 28 B2
Aizkraukle LV 135 C10
Aizpún E 32 E2
Aizpurve LV 135 C12
Aizpute LV 134 C3
Aizvīķi LV 134 D3
Ajaccio F 37 H9
Ajanki FIN 117 E12
Ajankijärvi FIN 117 E12
Ajat F 29 E8
Ajaureforsen S 109 E10
Ajdovščina SLO 73 E8
Ajka H 149 B9
Ajo E 40 B4
Ajofrín E 46 E5
Ajos FIN 119 C13
Akācijas LV 134 C6
Åkarp S 87 D12
Äkäsjokisuu FIN 117 D11
Äkäslompolo FIN 117 C12
Akasztó H 150 D3
Akçaova TR 181 B7
Akçasusurluk TR 173 D9
Akeld GB 5 D12
Aken D 79 C11
Åkerbränna S 107 D11
Åkerby S 99 B9
Åkerholmen S 118 C6
Åkersberga S 99 D10
Akersjön S 105 D16
Åkers styckebruk S 98 D8
Åkerstrømmen N 101 C14
Akheloy BG 167 D9
Akhremawtsy BY 133 E2
Akhtopol BG 167 E9
Akkan S 109 F12
Akkarfjord N 113 B12
Akkarvik N 112 C5
Akkasæter N 111 B16
Akkavare S 109 E17
Akkerhaugen N 95 D10
Akköy TR 171 E10
Akköy TR 177 E9
Akkrum NL 16 B5
Akmeņdziras LV 134 B3
Akmenė LT 134 D5
Åknes N 110 C9
Aknīste LV 135 D11
Akonkoski FIN 121 F13
Akonpohja FIN 125 D10
Akpinar TR 173 B10
Akraifnio GR 175 C7
Åkran N 105 D12
Akrata GR 174 C5
Åkrehamn N 94 D2
Akrini GR 169 D6
Akrolimni GR 169 C7
Akropotamos GR 170 C6
Akrotiri GR 179 C9
Aksakal TR 173 D9
Aksaz TR 173 D7
Aksdal N 94 D2
Aksnes N 104 F4
Akujärvi FIN 114 F3
Åkullsjön S 118 F5
Åkvisslan S 107 E13
Ål N 101 E9
Ala I 69 B11
Ala S 93 E13
Alacaat TR 173 E10
Alacant E 56 E4
Alacaoğlu TR 173 B7
Alaçatı TR 177 C7
Alà dei Sardi I 64 B3
Ala di Stura I 31 E11
Alaejos E 39 F9
Alagna Valsesia I 68 B4
A Lagoa E 38 C2
Alagoa P 44 F5
Alagón E 41 E9
Alahärmä FIN 122 D9
Ala-Honkajoki FIN 126 B7
Alaigne F 33 D10
Alaior E 57 B13
Alájar E 51 D6
Alajärvi FIN 117 E15
Alajärvi FIN 121 E12
Alajärvi FIN 123 D11
Alajõe EST 132 C1
Ala-Jokikylä FIN 119 C14
Ala-Kääntä FIN 119 F12
Ala-Keyritty FIN 125 D10
Alakurtti RUS 115 E8
Alakylä FIN 117 D13
Alakylä FIN 119 D15
Alakylä FIN 126 B6
Ala-Livo FIN 119 D17
Alameda E 53 B7
Alameda de Cervera E 47 F6
Alameda de la Sagra E 46 D5
Alamedilla E 55 D6
Alamillo E 54 B3
Alan HR 67 B10
Ala-Nampa FIN 117 E16
Alanäs S 106 C9
Alande LV 134 C2
Alandroal P 50 B5
Ålandsbro S 103 A14
Alange E 51 B7
Alaniemi FIN 119 C14
Alanís E 51 C8
Alanta LT 135 F10
Alap H 149 C11
Alapitkä FIN 124 D9
Alaquàs E 48 F4
Alaranta FIN 119 D14
Alaraz E 45 C10
Alarcón E 47 E8
Alar del Rey E 40 C3
Alaró E 49 E10
Alarup AL 168 C4
Ålåsen S 106 D7
Alaskylä FIN 127 B8
Alassio I 37 C8
Alastaipale FIN 123 F11
Alastaro FIN 126 D8
Ala-Sydänmaa FIN 123 B14
Alata F 37 H9
Ala-Temmes FIN 119 E15
Alatoz E 47 F10
Alatri I 62 D4
Alatskivi EST 131 D14
Alattyán H 150 C5
Ala-Valli FIN 123 F9
Alavattnet S 106 C9
Alavere EST 131 C10
Ala-Vieksi FIN 121 F12
Alavieska FIN 119 F12
Ala-Viirre FIN 123 B11
Ala-Vuokki FIN 121 E13
Ala-Vuotto FIN 119 D16
Alavus FIN 123 E11
Alba I 37 B8
Alba Adriatica I 62 B5
Albac RO 151 E10
Albacete E 55 A9
Albacken S 103 A11
Alba de Tormes E 45 C9
Albæk DK 90 D7
Albagiara I 64 D2
Albaida E 56 D4
Alba Iulia RO 152 E3
Albaladejo E 55 B7
Alba-la-Romaine F 35 A8
Albalate de Arzobispo E 42 E3
Albalate de Cinca E 42 D4
Albalate de las Nogueras E 47 D8
Albalate de Zorita E 47 D7
Albalatillo E 42 D3
Alban F 33 C10
Albánchez E 55 E8
Albanella I 60 C4
Albanitsa BG 165 C10
Albano di Lucania I 60 B6
Albano Laziale I 62 D3
Albano Vercellese I 68 C5
Albanyà E 43 C9
Albaredo per San Marco I 69 A8
Albaret-le-Comtal F 30 F3
Albareto I 69 E8
Albaret-Ste-Marie F 30 F3
Albaron F 35 C7
Albarracín E 47 D10
Albatana E 55 B9
Albatàrrec E 42 D5
Albatera E 56 E3
Albbruck D 27 E9
Albelda E 42 D4
Albelda de Iregua E 41 D7
Albella E 32 F5
Albendea E 47 C8
Albendín E 53 A8
Albenga I 37 C8
Albeni RO 160 C3
Albens F 31 D8
Albentosa E 48 D3
Ålberga S 93 B9
Alberga S 98 D6
Albergaria-a-Velha P 44 C4
Albergaria dos Doze P 44 E3
Albergen NL 183 A9
Alberic E 48 F4
Alberndorf in der Riedmark A 77 F6
Albernoa P 50 D4
Albero Alto E 41 D11
Alberobello I 61 B8
Alberona I 60 A4
Alberoni I 66 B5
Alberschwende A 71 C9
Albersdorf D 82 B6
Albert F 18 E6
Albertacce F 37 G9
Alberta Ligure I 37 B10
Albertirsa H 150 C4
Albertshofen D 187 B9
Albertville F 31 D9
Alberuela de Tubo E 42 D3
Albesa E 42 D5
Albești RO 152 E5
Albești RO 153 B10
Albești RO 153 D11
Albești RO 155 F2
Albești RO 161 D10
Albeștii de Argeș RO 160 C5
Albeștii de Muscel RO 160 C6
Albești-Paleologu RO 161 D8
Albestroff F 27 C6
Albi F 33 C10
Albias F 33 B8
Albidona I 61 D6
Albignasego I 66 B4
Albina RO 155 C1
Albino I 69 B8
Albires E 39 D9
Albisheim (Pfrimm) D 21 E10
Albisola Marina I 37 C9
Albisola Superiore I 37 C9
Alblasserdam NL 16 E3
Ålbo S 98 B7
Albocàsser E 48 D5
Alboloduy E 55 E7
Albolote E 53 B9
Albon F 30 E6
Albondón E 55 F6
Alboraya E 48 E4
Alborea E 47 F10
Albota RO 160 D5
Albox E 55 E8
Albrechtice nad Orlicí CZ 77 B10
Al'brekhtava BY 133 E5
Albstadt D 27 D11
Albu EST 131 C11
Albudeite E 55 C10
Albufeira P 50 E3
Albujón E 56 F2
Albuñol E 55 F6
Albuñuelas E 53 C9
Alburquerque E 45 F7
Alby S 89 C11
Alby S 103 A9
Alby-sur-Chéran F 31 D9
Alcácer E 48 F4
Alcácer do Sal P 50 C2
Alcáçovas P 50 C3
Alcadozo E 55 B9
Alcafozes P 45 E6
Alcaine E 42 F2
Alcains P 44 E6
Alcalá de Guadaira E 51 E8
Alcalá de Gurrea E 41 D10
Alcalá de Henares E 46 D6
Alcalá del Júcar E 47 F10
Alcalá de los Gazules E 52 D5
Alcalá del Río E 51 D8
Alcalá del Valle E 51 F9
Alcalà de Xivert E 48 D5
Alcalá la Real E 53 B9
Alcalalí E 56 D4
Alcamo I 58 D2
Alcampell E 42 D4
Alcanadre E 32 F1
Alcanede P 44 F3
Alcanena P 44 F3
Alcanhões P 44 F3
Alcañices E 39 E7
Alcañiz E 42 E3
Alcántara E 45 E7
Alcantarilla E 56 F2
Alcantud E 47 C8
Alcaracejos E 54 C3
Alcara li Fusi I 59 C6
Alcaraz E 55 B8
Alcaria Ruiva P 50 D4
Alcarràs E 42 D5
Alcaucín E 53 C8
Alcaudete E 53 A8
Alcaudete de la Jara E 46 E3
Alçay-Alçabéhéty-Sunharette F 32 D4
Alcázar del Rey E 47 D7
Alcázar de San Juan E 47 F6
Alcedar MD 154 B3
Alcester GB 13 A11
Alcıtepe TR 171 D10
Alcoba E 46 F4
Alcobaça P 44 E3
Alcobendas E 46 C5
Alcocer E 47 D7
Alcocero de Mola E 40 D5
Alcochete P 50 B2
Alcoentre P 44 F3
Alcoi E 56 D4
Alcolea E 53 A7
Alcolea E 55 F7
Alcolea de Calatrava E 54 B4
Alcolea de Cinca E 42 D4
Alcolea del Pinar E 47 B8
Alcolea del Río E 51 D8
Alcollarín E 45 F9
Alconchel E 51 B5
Alcóntar E 55 E7
Alcorcón E 46 D5
Alcorisa E 42 F3
Alcoroches E 47 C9
Alcossebre E 48 D5
Alcoutim P 50 E5
Alcover E 42 E6
Alcoy E 56 D4
Alcsútdoboz H 149 B11
Alcubierre E 41 E11
Alcubilla de Avellaneda E 40 E5
Alcubillas E 55 B6
Alcublas E 48 E3
Alcúdia E 57 B11
Alcudia de Guadix E 55 E6
Alcudia de Monteagud E 55 E8
Alcuéscar E 45 F8
Aldbrough GB 11 D11
Aldeacentenera E 45 E9

Aldeadávila de la Ribera E 45 B7
Aldea del Cano E 45 F8
Aldea del Fresno E 46 D4
Aldea del Obispo E 45 C7
Aldea del Rey E 54 B5
Aldea de Trujillo E 45 E9
Aldealafuente E 41 E7
Aldealpozo E 41 E7
Aldeamayor de San Martín E 39 E10
Aldeanueva de Barbarroya E 45 E10
Aldeanueva de Ebro E 41 D8
Aldeanueva de Figueroa E 45 B9
Aldeanueva de la Vera E 45 D9
Aldeanueva del Camino E 45 D9
Aldeanueva de San Bartolomé E 45 E10
Aldeaquemada E 55 C6
Aldea Real E 46 B4
Aldearrodrigo E 45 B9
Aldeaseca E 46 B3
Aldeatejada E 45 C9
Aldeavieja E 46 C4
Aldeburgh GB 15 C12
Aldehuela de la Bóveda E 45 C8
Aldehuela de Yeltes E 45 C8
Aldeia da Mata P 44 F5
Aldeia da Ponte P 45 D7
Aldeia de João Pires P 45 D6
Aldeia do Bispo P 45 D6
Aldeia dos Elvas P 50 D3
Aldeia dos Fernandes P 50 D3
Aldeia dos Palheiros P 50 D3
Aldeia Velha P 44 F4
Aldenhoven D 20 C6
Aldeno I 69 B11
Alderbury GB 13 C11
Alderholt GB 13 D11
Alderley Edge GB 11 E7
Aldersbach D 76 E4
Aldershot GB 15 E7
Aldinac SRB 164 B5
Aldinci NMK 164 F3
Aldingham GB 10 C5
Aldomirovtsi BG 165 D6
Aldover E 42 F5
Aldridge GB 11 F8
Aldudes F 32 D3
Åle DK 86 D5
Åled S 87 B11
Aledo E 55 D9
Alekovo BG 161 F10
Alekovo BG 166 C4
Aleksandriškės LT 137 D10
Aleksandrova LV 133 E2
Aleksandrovac SRB 159 E7
Aleksandrovac SRB 163 C11
Aleksandrovo BG 165 C10
Aleksandrovo BG 166 D4
Aleksandrovo BG 167 E7
Aleksandrów PL 141 F2
Aleksandrów PL 141 H1
Aleksandrów Kujawski PL 138 E6
Aleksandrów Łódzki PL 143 C7
Aleksa Šantić SRB 150 F3
Aleksinac SRB 164 B4
Ålem S 89 B10
Ålen N 101 A14
Alençon F 23 D12
Alenquer P 44 F3
Alénya F 34 E4
Alerheim D 75 E8
Aléria F 37 G11
Alerre E 41 D11
Alès F 35 B7
Ales I 64 D2
Aleșd RO 151 C9
Alesón E 41 D6
Alessandria I 37 B9
Alessandria del Carretto I 61 D6
Alessandria della Rocca I 58 D3
Alessano I 61 D10
Ålesund N 100 B4
Alet-les-Bains F 33 D10
Alexandreia GR 169 C7
Alexandria GB 4 D7
Alexandria RO 160 F6
Alexandroupoli GR 171 C9
Alexandru Vlahuță RO 153 E11
Alexeevca MD 153 C11
Alexeni RO 161 D9
Alexandrów PL 144 C6
Alezio I 61 C10
Alf D 21 D8
Alfacar E 53 B9
Alfafar E 48 F4
Alfaiates P 45 D7
Alfajarín E 41 E10
Alfambra E 42 F1
Alfambras P 50 E2
Alfamén E 41 F9
Alfândega da Fé P 39 F6
Alfántega E 42 D4
Alfarim P 50 C1
Alfaro E 41 D8
Alfarràs E 42 D5
Alfatar BG 161 F10
Alfdorf D 74 E6
Alfedena I 62 D6
Alfeizerão P 44 E2
Alfeld (Leine) D 78 C6
Alfena P 44 B3
Alferce P 50 E3
Alfhausen D 17 C9
Alfonsine I 66 D5
Alford GB 3 L11
Alford GB 11 E12
Alforja E 42 E5
Alfredshem S 107 E15
Alfreton GB 11 E9
Alfta S 103 D11
Alfundão P 50 C3
Algaida E 57 B10
Algajola F 37 F9
Algámitas E 53 B6
Algar E 52 C5
Algarås S 92 B4
Ålgård N 94 E3
Algarinejo E 53 B8
Algarrobo E 53 C8
Algatocín E 53 C6
Algeciras E 53 D6
Algemesí E 48 F4
Ålgered S 103 B12
Algermissen D 79 B6
Algerri E 42 D5
Algestrup DK 87 E10
Algete E 46 C6
Alghero I 64 B1
Älghult S 89 A9
Alginet E 48 F4
Ålgnäs S 103 D12
Algodonales E 51 F9
Algodor P 50 D4
Algora E 47 C7
Algorta E 40 B6
Algoso P 39 F6
Algoz P 50 E3
Algrange F 20 F6
Alguaire E 42 D5
Alguazas E 56 E2
Algueirão-Mem Martins P 50 B1
Algueña E 56 E3
Algutsrum S 89 B11
Alhabia E 55 F7
Alhama de Almería E 55 F7
Alhama de Aragón E 41 F8
Alhama de Granada E 53 B9
Alhama de Murcia E 55 D10
Alhambra E 55 B6
Alhamn S 118 D7
Alhaurín de la Torre E 53 C7
Alhaurín el Grande E 53 C7
Alhendín E 53 B9
Alhojärvi FIN 127 B13
Alhóndiga E 47 C7
Ålhult S 92 D7
Alía E 45 F10
Alia I 58 D4
Aliaga E 42 F2
Aliağa TR 177 B8
Aliaguilla E 47 E10
Aliano I 60 C6
Aliartos GR 175 C7
Alibunar SRB 159 C6
Alicante E 56 E4
Alicún de Ortega E 55 D6
Alife I 60 A2
Alija del Infantado E 39 D8
Alijó P 38 F5
Alikianos GR 178 E6
Alikylä FIN 123 C11
Aliman RO 155 E1
Alimena I 58 D5
Aliminusa I 58 D4
Alimpești RO 160 C3
Alingsås S 91 D12
Alino BG 165 E7
Alionys 1 LT 137 C11
Aliseda E 45 F7
Alistrati GR 170 B5
Alì Terme I 59 C7
Aliveri GR 175 C9
Alizava LT 135 E10
Aljaraque E 51 E5
Aljezur P 50 E2
Aljinović SRB 163 C8
Aljubarrota P 44 E3
Aljucén E 51 A7
Aljustrel P 50 D3
Alken B 19 C11
Alkkia FIN 122 F9
Alkmaar NL 16 C3
Allai I 64 D2
Allaire F 23 E7
Allambres AL 168 C2
Allan F 35 A8
Allanche F 30 E2
Allariz E 38 D4
Allarmont F 27 D7
Allassac F 29 E8
Allaži LV 135 B9
Allažmuiža LV 135 B9
Alle CH 27 F7
Alleghe I 72 D5
Allègre F 30 E4
Alleins F 35 C9
Allemond F 31 E9
Allen IRL 7 F9
Allendale Town GB 5 F12
Allendorf (Eder) D 21 B11
Allenheads GB 5 F12
Allensbach D 27 E11
Allentsteig A 77 E8
Allenwood IRL 7 F9
Allepuz E 42 G2
Allerona I 62 B1
Allersberg D 75 D9
Allershausen D 75 F10
Allerslev DK 87 E10
Allevard F 31 E9
Allex F 30 F6
Allibaudières F 25 C11
Alligny-en-Morvan F 25 F11
Allihies IRL 8 E2
Allingåbro DK 86 C6
Allinges F 31 C9
Allinge-Sandvig DK 89 E7
Alliste I 61 D10
Allmendingen D 74 F6
Allo E 32 E1
Alloa GB 5 C9
Allogny F 25 F7
Ålloluokta S 109 B17
Allonby GB 5 F10
Allonnes F 23 E12
Allonnes F 23 F12
Allons F 32 B5
Allos F 36 C5
Allouе F 29 C7
Alloza E 42 F2
Allschwil CH 27 E8
Allsta S 103 A15
Allstad N 110 D6
Allstedt D 79 D9
Allumiere I 62 C1
Alluy F 30 A4
Almacelles E 42 D4
Almáchar E 53 C8
Almada P 50 B1
Almadén E 54 B3
Almadén de la Plata E 51 D7
Almadenejos E 54 B3
Almagro E 54 B5
Almăj RO 160 E3
Almajano E 41 E7
Almalaguês P 44 D4
Almaluez E 41 F7
Almansa E 56 D2
Almansil P 50 E3
Almanza E 39 C9
Almaraz E 45 E9
Almargen E 53 B6
Almarza E 41 E7
Almaș RO 151 E9
Almásfüzitő H 149 A10
Almașu RO 151 D11
Almașu Mare RO 151 E11
Almazán E 41 F6
Almazora E 48 E4
Almazul E 41 E7
Almedina E 55 B7
Almedinilla E 53 B8
Almeida de Sayago E 39 F7
Almeirim P 44 F3
Almelo NL 17 D7
Almenar E 42 D5
Almenara E 48 E4
Almenar de Soria E 41 E7
Almendra E 45 B8
Almendra P 45 B6
Almendral E 51 B6
Almendralejo E 51 B7
Almendricos E 55 E9
Almendros E 47 E7
Almere NL 16 D4
Almería E 55 F8
Almerimar E 55 F7
Älmestad S 91 D13
Älmhult S 88 B6
Almind DK 86 D4
Almkerk NL 16 E3
Ålmo N 104 E4
Almodôvar P 50 D3
Almodóvar del Campo E 54 B4
Almodóvar del Pinar E 47 E9
Almodóvar del Río E 53 A6
Almofala P 44 C5
Almogía E 53 C7
Almograve P 50 D2
Almoguera E 47 D7
Almoharín E 45 F8
Almonacid de la Sierra E 41 F9
Almonacid del Marquesado E 47 E7
Almonacid del Zorita E 47 D7
Almonacid de Toledo E 46 E5
Almonaster la Real E 51 D6
Almondsbury GB 13 B9
Almonte E 51 E6
Almoradí E 56 E3
Almorchón E 51 B9
Almorox E 46 D4
Álmosd H 151 C8
Almoster P 44 E4
Almsele S 107 C12
Almsjönäs S 107 E14
Älmsta S 99 C11
Almstedt D 79 B6
Almudema E 55 C9
Almudévar E 41 D10
Almuñécar E 53 C9
Almunge S 99 C10
Almuniente E 41 E11
Almünster A 73 A8
Almuradiel E 55 B6
Almussafes E 48 F4
Almvik S 93 D9
Almyropotamos GR 175 C9
Almyros GR 175 A6
Alnes N 100 B4
Alness GB 3 K8
Alnwick GB 5 E13
Alobras E 47 D10
Alocén E 47 C7
Aloja LV 131 F9
Alol' RUS 133 D6
Alonia GR 169 D8
Álora E 53 C7
Alós d'Ensil E 33 E8
Alosno E 51 D5
Alost B 19 C9
Alost B 182 D4
Alovera E 47 C6
Alozaina E 53 C7
Alp E 33 F9
Alpalhão P 44 F5
Alpanseque E 41 F6
Alpbach A 72 B4
Alpedrinha P 44 D6
Alpedriz P 44 E3
Alpen D 17 E7
Alpenrod D 21 C9
Alpens E 43 C8
Alpera E 56 D2
Alphen NL 16 F3
Alphen aan den Rijn NL 16 D3
Alpiarça P 44 F3
Alpirsbach D 27 D9
Alpnach CH 70 D6
Alposjärvi FIN 117 E12
Alpua FIN 119 F14
Alpuente E 47 E11
Alpullu TR 173 B7
Alquería de la Condesa E 56 D4
Alquerías E 56 E2
Alqueva P 50 C4
Alquife E 55 E6
Alrance F 34 B4
Alrewas GB 11 F8
Als DK 86 B6
Alsager GB 11 E7
Alsån S 119 B9
Alsbach D 187 B6
Alsdorf D 20 C6
Alsėdžiai LT 134 D4
Alsen S 105 E15
Alsenborn D 21 F9
Alseno I 69 D8
Alsenz D 21 E9
Alsfeld D 21 C12
Alsheim D 185 E9
Alsike S 99 C9
Alsjö S 103 B11
Alsleben (Saale) D 79 C10
Alslev DK 86 D2
Alsmo N 100 D6
Alsónémedi H 150 C3
Alsópáhok H 149 C8
Alsos N 108 A8
Alsóvadász H 145 G2
Alsózsolca H 145 G2
Ålsrode DK 87 C7
Ålstad N 110 E9
Alstad S 87 E12
Alstahaug N 108 E3
Alstakan S 97 C8
Alster S 97 D10
Alsterbro S 89 B9
Alstermo S 89 B9
Alsting F 186 C2
Alston GB 5 F12
Alsunga LV 134 C3
Alsvåg N 110 C9
Alsvik N 108 B7
Alsviķi LV 133 B1
Alta N 113 D11
Älta S 99 D10
Altafulla E 43 E6
Altamura I 61 B7
Altare I 37 C8
Altatornio FIN 119 C12
Altaussee A 73 A8
Altavilla Irpina I 60 B3
Altavilla Silentina I 60 B4
Altdöbern D 80 C6
Altdorf CH 71 D7
Altdorf D 75 E11
Altdorf bei Nürnberg D 75 D9
Alt Duvenstedt D 82 B7
Alte P 50 E3
Altea E 56 D4
Altefähr D 84 B4
Alteglofsheim D 75 E11
Alteidet N 112 C9
Altena D 17 F9
Altenahr D 21 C7
Altenau D 79 C7
Altenberg D 80 E5
Altenberge D 17 D8
Altenbruch-Westerende D 17 A11
Altenbuch D 74 C5
Altenburg D 79 E11
Altendiez D 21 D9
Altenfeld D 75 A8
Altenfelden A 76 F5
Altenglan D 21 E8
Altenhagen D 83 B11
Altenheim D 27 D8
Altenhof D 84 E5
Altenholz D 83 B8
Altenkirchen D 84 A4
Altenkirchen (Westerwald) D 21 C9
Altenkrempe D 83 B9
Altenkunstadt D 75 B9
Altenmarkt an der Triesting A 77 F9
Altenmarkt bei Sankt Gallen A 73 A10
Altenmarkt im Pongau A 73 B7
Altenmedingen D 83 D9
Altenmünster D 75 F8
Altenstadt D 21 D11
Altenstadt D 71 A10
Altenstadt D 71 B11
Altensteig D 27 C10
Altentreptow D 84 C4
Alter do Chão P 44 F5
Altes Lager D 80 B4
Altevik N 111 C12
Altfraunhofen D 75 F11
Altheim A 76 F4
Altheim D 27 D11
Altheim (Alb) D 187 D9
Althengstett D 187 D6
Althofen A 73 C9
Altier F 35 B6
Altimir BG 165 B8
Altîna RO 152 F4
Altindag TR 177 C9
Altinoluk TR 172 E6
Altinova TR 177 A8
Altintaş TR 181 A8
Altkirch F 27 E7
Alt Krenzlin D 83 D10
Altlandsberg D 80 A5
Altleiningen D 21 E10
Altmannstein D 75 E10
Altnaharra GB 2 J8
Altofonte I 58 C3
Altomonte I 60 D6
Altomünster D 75 F9
Alton GB 11 F8
Alton GB 14 E7
Altopascio I 66 E2
Altorricón E 42 D4
Altötting D 75 F12
Altrich D 185 E6
Altrincham GB 11 E7
Alt Ruppin D 84 E3
Altsasu E 32 E1
Alt Schwerin D 83 C12
Altshausen D 71 B9
Altstätten CH 71 C9
Alttajärvi S 116 C5
Altura E 48 E4
Altusried D 71 B10
Alu EST 131 C9
Aluatu MD 154 F3
Alūksne LV 133 B2
Ålund S 118 D6
Alunda S 99 B10
Aluniș RO 152 C3
Aluniș RO 152 D5
Aluniș RO 161 C7
Alunu RO 160 C3
Alustante E 47 C9
Alva S 93 E12
Alvaiázere P 44 E4
Alvajarvi FIN 123 D14
Alvalade P 50 D3
Alvaneu CH 71 D9
Alvängen S 91 D11
Alvarenga P 44 C4
Álvares P 44 D4
Álvaro P 44 E5
Alvdal N 101 B13
Älvdalen S 102 D7
Alvega P 44 F4
Alveley GB 13 A10
Alvelos P 38 E2
Alverca P 50 B1
Alverca da Beira P 45 C6
Alvesta S 88 B7
Alvestad N 111 C11
Alvestorp S 97 C12
Alvettula FIN 127 C11
Alvhem S 91 C11
Älvho S 102 D8
Alviano I 62 B2
Alvie GB 3 L9
Alvignac F 29 F9
Ålvik N 94 B4
Alvik S 102 E8
Alvik S 103 B13
Alvik S 118 C7
Alvito I 62 D5
Alvito P 50 C4
Älvkarleby S 103 E13
Älvkarleö S 99 A8
Alvnes N 108 B9
Alvnes N 110 E9
Alvoco da Serra P 44 D5
Älvros S 102 B8
Älvsbyn S 118 C6
Älvsered S 87 A11
Ålvund N 101 A9
Ålvundeid N 101 A9
Alwernia PL 143 F8
Alyki GR 174 A3
Alyth GB 5 B10
Alytus LT 137 E9
Alzenau in Unterfranken D 21 D12
Alzey D 21 E10
Alzira E 48 F4
Alzon F 34 C5
Alzonne F 33 D10
Åmådalen S 102 D8
Amadora P 50 B1
Amaiur-Maia E 32 D3
Åmål S 91 A12
Åmål S 91 B12
Amalfi I 60 B3
Amaliada GR 174 D3
Amaliapoli GR 175 A6
Amalo GR 177 D6
Amance F 26 E5
Amancey F 31 A9
Amandola I 62 B4
Amantea I 60 E6
Amara RO 161 D10
Amarante P 38 F3
Amarantos GR 168 E5
Amărăști RO 160 D4
Amărăștii de Jos RO 160 F4
Amărăștii de Sus RO 160 F4
Amareleja P 51 C5
Amares P 38 E3
Amaroni I 59 B9
Amaru RO 161 D9
Amarynthos GR 175 C8
Amaseno I 62 E4
Amatrice I 62 B4
Amaxades GR 171 B8
Amay B 19 C11
Ambasaguas E 39 C9
Ambazac F 29 D8
Ambel E 41 E8
Ambeļi LV 135 D13
Amberg D 75 D10
Ambergate GB 11 E9
Ambérieu-en-Bugey F 31 D7
Amberloup B 19 D12
Ambert F 30 D4
Ambès F 28 E4
Ambierle F 30 C4
Ambillou F 24 F3
Ambjörby S 97 B9
Ambjörnarp S 91 E13
Ambla EST 131 C11
Amblainville F 24 B7
Amble GB 5 E13
Ambleside GB 10 C6
Ambleteuse F 15 F12
Amboise F 24 F4
Ambon F 22 E6
Ambrault F 29 B9
Ambrières-les-Vallées F 23 D10
Ambronay F 31 C7
Ambrosden GB 13 B12
Åmdals Verk N 95 D8
Ameglia I 69 E8
Ameide NL 182 B5
Ameixial P 50 E4
Amel B 20 D6
Amele LV 134 B4
Amelia I 62 B2
Amélie-les-Bains-Palalda F 34 F4
Amelinghausen D 83 D8
Amêndoa P 44 E4
Amendoeira P 50 D4
Amendolara I 61 D7
Amer E 43 C9
Amerang D 75 G11
A Merca E 38 D4
Amerongen NL 183 B6
Amersfoort NL 16 D4
Amersham GB 15 D7
Amesbury GB 13 C11
Amfikleia GR 175 B6
Amfilochia GR 174 B3
Amfipoli GR 169 C10
Amfissa GR 174 B5
Amieira P 50 C4
Amiens F 18 E5
Amilly F 25 E8
Åminne FIN 122 E7
Åminne S 87 A14
Åmland N 94 F5
Åmli N 90 A3
Åmli N 90 B3
Amlwch GB 10 E3
Ämmäläнkylä FIN 123 E9
Ammanford GB 12 B7
Ämmänsaari FIN 121 E12
Ammarnäs S 109 E11
Åmmeberg S 92 B6
Ammenäs S 91 C10
Ammerbuch D 187 D6
Ammern D 79 D7
Ammersbek D 83 C8
Ammerzoden NL 183 B6
Ammochori GR 169 C5
Ammotopos GR 168 F4
Ammoudia GR 169 B9
Amnatos GR 178 E8
Amnéville F 186 C1
Amoeiro E 38 D4
Amonde P 38 E2
Amorbach D 21 E12
Amorebieta E 40 B6
Amorgos GR 177 F6
Amori GR 171 B10
Åmot N 94 C7
Åmot N 95 B11
Åmot N 95 C11
Åmot S 103 E11
Åmotfors S 96 C7
Amou F 32 C4
Åmøyhamn N 108 C5
Ampelakia GR 169 E8
Ampeleia GR 169 F7
Ampelokipoi GR 169 C8
Ampelonas GR 169 E7
Ampezzo I 73 D6
Ampfing D 75 F11
Ampflwang im Hausruckwald A 76 F5
Amplepuis F 30 D5
Amposta E 42 F5
Ampthill GB 15 C8
Ampudia E 39 E10
Ampuero E 40 B5
Ampus F 36 D4
Amriswil CH 27 E11
Åmsele S 107 B16
Åmsosen N 94 D3
Amstelveen NL 16 D3
Amsterdam NL 16 D3
Amstetten A 77 F7
Amstetten D 187 D8
Amulree GB 5 B9
Amurrio E 40 B6
Amusco E 40 D3
Amvrosia GR 171 B8
Amygdaleonas GR 171 C6
Amygdalia GR 174 C5
Åmynnet S 107 E15
Amyntaio GR 169 C6
Amzacea RO 155 F2
Anacapri I 60 B2
Anadia P 44 D4
Anafi GR 180 D3
Anafonitria GR 174 D2
Anagaire IRL 6 B6
Anagni I 62 D4
An Aird Mhóir IRL 6 F3
Añana-Gesaltza E 40 C6
Anan'yiv UA 154 B5
Anarcs H 145 G5
Anargyroi GR 169 C6
Anarrachi GR 169 D6
Ånäset S 118 F6
Åna-Sira N 94 F4
Anatazavė LT 135 E11
Anatoli GR 168 E4
Anatoli GR 169 E8
Anatoli GR 179 E10
Anatoliki Fragkista GR 174 B4
Anatoliko GR 169 C6
Anatoliko GR 169 C8
Anavatos GR 177 C7
Anavra GR 174 A5
Anavra GR 175 A6
Anavyssos GR 175 D8
Anaya de Alba E 45 C10
An Baile Breac IRL 8 E2
An Baile Nua IRL 8 D5
An Bhlarna IRL 8 E5
An Bun Beag IRL 6 B6
An Cabhán IRL 7 E8
An Caiseal IRL 6 F3
An Caisleánn Riabhach IRL 6 E6
An Caisléan Nua IRL 7 F10
An Caisléan Nua IRL 8 D4
An Cathair IRL 9 D7
Ance LV 134 A4
Ancelle F 36 B4
Ancene LV 135 D11
Ancenis F 23 F9
Ancerville F 26 C3
An Charraig IRL 6 C5
An Cheathru Rua IRL 6 F3
An Chill IRL 7 F9
Ancín E 32 E1
An Cionn Garbh IRL 6 C6
An Clochán IRL 7 C7
An Clochán Liath IRL 6 C6
An Cóbh IRL 8 E6
An Coimín IRL 7 C7
An Coireán IRL 8 E2
Ancona I 67 E8
Ancroft GB 5 D13
Ancrum GB 5 D11
Ancy-le-Franc F 25 E11
Anda N 100 C4
Andalo I 69 A11
Åndalsnes N 100 A7
Andau A 149 A8
Andavías E 39 E8
Anddalsvågen N 108 E3
Andebu N 95 D12
Andechs D 75 G9
Andeer CH 71 D8
Andelfingen CH 27 E10
Andelot-Blancheville F 26 D3
Andelst NL 16 E5
Andenes N 111 B11
Andenne B 19 D11
Anderlecht B 19 C9
Anderlues B 19 D9
Andermatt CH 71 D7
Andernach D 185 D7
Andernos-les-Bains F 28 F3
Andersbo S 99 B9
Anderslöv S 87 E12
Anderstorp S 88 A5
Andervenne D 17 C9
Andfiskå N 108 D7
Andijk NL 16 C4
Andilly-en-Bassigny F 26 E4
Andlau F 27 D7
Andoain E 32 D1
Andocs H 149 C9
Andolsheim F 27 D7
Andorf A 76 F5
Andørja N 111 C13
Andorno Micca I 68 B5
Andorra E 42 F3
Andorra la Vella AND 33 E9
Andosilla E 32 F2
Andouillé F 23 D10
Andover GB 13 C12
Andrano I 61 D10
Andrășești RO 161 D10
Andratx E 49 E9
Andravida GR 174 D3
Andreas GBM 10 C3
Andreiașu de Jos RO 153 F9
Andrespol PL 143 C8
Andrest F 33 D6
Andretta I 60 B4
Andria I 60 A6
Andrid RO 151 B9
Andrieșeni RO 153 B10
Andrijaševci HR 157 B10
Andrijevica MNE 163 D8
Andrioniškis LT 135 E10
Andriškiai LT 136 D6
Andritsaina GR 174 E4
Andronianoi GR 175 B9
Andros GR 176 D4
Androusa GR 174 E4
Andrup DK 86 D3
Andrupene LV 133 D2
Andrychów PL 147 B8
Andrzejewo PL 141 E6
Andselv N 111 B15
Andsnes N 112 C7
An Dúchoraidh IRL 6 C6
Andújar E 53 A8
Anduze F 35 B6
Andzeļi LV 133 D3
An Eachléim IRL 6 D2
Åneby N 95 B13
Aneby S 92 D5
Anela I 64 C3
Anenii Noi MD 154 D4
Ånes N 104 E4
Anet F 24 C5
Anetjärvi FIN 121 C10
Anevo BG 165 D10
Aneza GR 174 A2
An Fál Carrach IRL 6 B6
An Féar Bán IRL 7 F7
An Fhairche IRL 6 E4
Anfo I 69 B9
Ång S 92 D5
Anga S 93 E13
Ånge S 103 A10
Ånge S 105 E16
Ånge S 109 E14
An Geata Mór IRL 6 D2
Ängebo S 103 C11
Angeja P 44 C3
Ängelholm S 87 C11
Angeli FIN 113 F16
Angelniemi FIN 127 E8
Angelochori GR 169 C7
Angelokastro GR 174 B3
Angelokastro GR 175 D7
Ängelsberg S 97 C15
Angelstad S 87 B13
Angely F 25 E11
Anger D 73 A6
Angera I 68 B6
Angermünde D 84 D6
Angern D 79 B10
Angern an der March A 77 F11
Angers F 23 F10
Ångersjö S 102 C8
Ängersjö S 122 C3
Angersnes N 108 D4
Angervikko FIN 125 D10
Angerville F 24 D7
Ängesån S 116 E8
Ängeslevä FIN 119 E15
Ängesträsk S 118 B8
Anghiari I 66 E5
Anglade F 28 E4
Angle GB 9 E12
Anglès E 43 D9
Anglès F 34 C4
Anglesola E 42 D5
Anglesona E 42 D6
Angles-sur-l'Anglin F 29 B7
Anglet F 32 D2
Angliers F 29 B6
Anglure F 25 C10
Angnäs S 107 D16
Angoisse F 29 E8
Ångom S 103 B13
An Gort IRL 6 F5
Angoulême F 29 D6
Angoulins F 28 C3
Angri I 60 B3
Angrie F 23 E10
Angüés E 42 C3
Anguiano E 40 D6
Anguillara Sabazia I 62 C2
Anguillara Veneta I 66 B4
Anguita E 47 B8
Angvik N 100 A8
Anha P 38 E2
Anhée B 19 D10
Anholt DK 87 B9
Aniane F 35 C6
Aniche F 19 D7
Anif A 73 A7
Anina RO 159 C8
Aninoasa RO 160 C2
Aninoasa RO 160 C5
Aninoasa RO 160 D2
Aninoasa RO 161 D6
Anizy-le-Château F 19 E7
Anjalankoski FIN 128 D6
Anjan S 105 D13
Anjum NL 16 B6
Ankaran SLO 73 E8
Ankarede Kapell S 105 B16
Ankarsrum S 93 D8
Ankarsund S 109 F12
Ankarsvik S 103 B13
Ankenes N 111 D13
Ankerlia N 112 E6
Ankershagen D 84 D3
Anklam D 84 C5
Ankum D 17 C9
Anlaby GB 11 D11
An Leadhb Gharbh IRL 6 C5
Anlezy F 30 B4
An Longfort IRL 7 E7
An Mám IRL 6 E3
An Mhala Raithní IRL 6 E3
An Móta IRL 7 F7
An Muileann gCearr IRL 7 E8
Ånn S 105 E13
Anna E 56 C3
Anna EST 131 C11
Annaberg A 77 G8
Annaberg-Buchholtz D 80 E4
Annaburg D 80 C4
Annagassan IRL 7 E10
Annagry IRL 6 B6
Annahilt GB 7 D10
Annahütte D 80 C5
Annalong GB 7 D11
Annamoe IRL 7 F10
Annan GB 5 F10
Anna Paulowna NL 16 C3
Annarode D 79 C9
An Nás IRL 7 F9
Annayalla IRL 7 D9
Annbank GB 4 E7
Anneberg S 91 D11
Anneberg S 92 D5
Annecy F 31 D9
Annecy-le-Vieux F 31 D9
Annefors S 103 D11
Annelund S 91 D13
Annemasse F 31 C9
Annen NL 17 B7
Annenieki LV 134 C6
Annestown IRL 9 D8
Anneyron F 30 E6
Annikvere EST 131 C12
Annœullin F 182 D1
Annonay F 30 E6
Annonen FIN 119 F14
Annopol PL 144 B4
Annot F 36 D5
Annweiler am Trifels D 21 F9
Ano Agios Vlasios GR 174 B4
Ano Amfeia GR 174 E5
Ano Chora GR 174 B4
Ano Diakofto GR 174 C5
Ano Drosini GR 171 B9
Anoeta E 32 D1
Anogeia GR 174 F5
Anogeia GR 178 E8
Ano Kalliniki GR 168 C5
Ano Kardamyla GR 177 B7
Ano Kavallari GR 169 C9
Ano Komi GR 169 D6
Ano Kopanaki GR 174 E4
Ano Lechonia GR 169 F9
Ano Lefkimmi GR 168 F3
Ano Mera GR 176 E5
Añón E 41 E8
Ano Poroia GR 169 B9
Anor F 19 E9
Añora E 54 C3
Ano Sagkri GR 176 E5
Ano Steni GR 175 B8

Ano Syros GR 176 E4
Ano Trikala GR 174 D5
Ano Tyros GR 175 E6
Anould F 27 D6
Añover de Tajo E 46 E5
Ano Vrontou GR 169 B10
Anquela del Ducado E 47 C8
Anras A 72 C6
An Rinn IRL 9 D7
Anröchte D 185 A9
An Ros IRL 7 E10
Ans B 19 C12
Ans DK 86 C5
Ansac-sur-Vienne F 29 D7
Ansager DK 86 D3
Ansbach D 75 D8
An Sciobairin IRL 8 E4
Anse F 30 D6
Ansedonia I 65 C4
Anseremme B 19 D10
Ansfelden A 76 F6
Ansião P 44 E4
Ansizca TR 177 C9
Ansjö S 103 A11
Ansnes N 111 B15
Ansó E 32 E4
An Spidéal IRL 6 F4
Anspoki LV 135 D13
Ansprung D 80 E4
Ånstad N 110 C8
Anstruther GB 5 C11
Ånsvik N 109 B9
Antalieptė LT 135 E11
Antanhol P 44 D4
An tAonach IRL 8 C6
Antas E 55 E9
Antas P 38 E2
Antas P 44 C6
Antas de Ulla E 38 C4
An Teampall Mór IRL 9 C7
An Tearmann IRL 7 B7
Antequera E 53 B7
Anterselva di Sopra I 72 C5
Anthéor F 36 E5
Anthien F 25 F10
Anthili GR 175 B5
Anthotopos GR 175 A6
Anthrakitis GR 168 E4
Antibes F 36 D6
Antigonos GR 169 C6
Antikyra GR 175 C6
Antillo I 59 D7
Antimacheia GR 177 F9
An tInbhear Mór IRL 9 C10
Antiparos GR 176 E5
Antirrio GR 174 C4
Antisanti F 37 G10
Antissa GR 171 F9
Antjärn S 103 A14
Antnäs S 118 C7
Antoing B 19 C7
Antol SK 147 E7
Anton BG 165 D9
Anton Ivanov BG 165 E9
Antonivka UA 145 F6
Antonne-et-Trigonant F 29 E7
Antonovo BG 166 C6
Antony F 25 C7
Antraigues-sur-Volane F 30 F5
Antrain F 23 D9
Antrim GB 4 F4
Antrodoco I 62 C4
An tSeanga Mheáin IRL 6 C6
Antsla EST 131 F13
Anttis S 116 D9
Anttola FIN 128 B8
An Tulch IRL 9 C9
Antully F 30 B5
Antunovac Tenjski HR 149 F11
Antuži LV 135 C11
Antwerpen B 19 B9
Antzuola E 32 D1
An Uaimh IRL 7 E9
Anvers B 19 B9
Anvers B 182 C4
Anvin F 18 D5
Anykščiai LT 135 E10
Anzano di Puglia I 60 A4
Anzat-le-Luguet F 30 E3
Anzegem B 19 C7
Anzère CH 31 C11
Anzi I 60 B5
Anzin F 19 D7
Anzing D 75 F10
Anzio I 62 E3
Aoiz E 32 E3
Aoradh GB 4 D4
Aós E 32 E3
Aosta I 31 D11
Aouste-sur-Sye F 31 F7
Apa RO 151 B11
Apagy H 145 H4
Apahida RO 152 D3
Apaj H 150 C3
Apața RO 153 F7
Apateu RO 151 D8
Apátfalva H 150 E6
Apatin SRB 158 B2
Apatovac HR 149 D7
Apc H 150 B4
Ape LV 131 F13
Apecchio I 66 E5
A Pedreira E 38 D3
Apeiranthos GR 177 E6
Apeldoorn NL 16 D5
Apelern D 17 D12
Apele Vii RO 160 E4
Apen D 17 B9
Apenburg D 83 E10
Apensen D 82 D7
Aperi GR 181 E6
A Peroxa E 38 D4
Apgulde LV 134 C6
Apice I 60 A3
A Picota E 38 C2
Apidia GR 175 F6
Apiro I 67 F7
Aplared S 91 D13
A Pobla de Brollón E 38 C5
A Pobra de San Xiao E 38 C5
A Pobra de Trives E 38 D5
A Pobra do Caramiñal E 38 C2
Apoikia GR 176 D4
Apolakkia GR 181 D7
Apold RO 152 E5
Apolda D 79 D10
Apoldu de Jos RO 152 F3
Apollona GR 181 D7
Apollonas GR 177 E6
Apollonia GR 176 F4
A Pontenova E 38 B5
A Pontepedra E 38 B2
Áporka H 150 C3
Apostag H 149 C11
Apostoloi GR 178 E8
Äppelbo S 97 B11
Appenweier D 186 D4
Appenzell CH 27 F11
Appiano sulla Strada del Vino I 72 D3
Appietto F 37 G9
Appignano I 67 F7
Appingedam NL 17 B7
Appleby-in-Westmorland GB 10 B7
Appleby Magna GB 11 F8
Applecross GB 2 L5
Appledore GB 12 C6
Appledore GB 15 E10
Apprieu F 31 E7
Apremont-la-Forêt F 26 C4
Aprica I 69 A9
Apricena I 63 D8
Aprigliano I 61 E6
Apriķi LV 134 C3
Aprilia I 62 D3
Aprilovo BG 166 C6
Apriltsi BG 165 D10
A Proba E 39 C6
Apsalos GR 169 C7
Apšuciems LV 134 B6
Apt F 35 C9
Aquaviva delle Fonti I 61 B7
Aquilonia I 60 B4
Aquilué E 32 F5
Aquino I 62 E5
Aracena E 51 D6
Arachnaio GR 175 D6
Arachova GR 175 C6
Aračinovo NMK 164 E4
Arad RO 151 E7
Aradac SRB 158 C5
Arådalen S 102 A6
Aradeo I 61 C10
Aragnouet F 33 E6
Aragona I 58 E4
Aragoncillo E 47 C8
Araia E 32 E1
A Ramallosa E 38 C2
Aramits F 32 D4
Aramon F 35 C8
Aranda de Duero E 40 E4
Aranda de Moncayo E 41 E8
Aranđelovac SRB 158 E6
Aranhas P 45 D6
Aranitas AL 168 C2
Aranjuez E 46 D5
Arano E 32 D2
Aranzueque E 47 D6
Araovacik TR 173 E7
Arapaj AL 168 B2
Arapiles E 45 C9
Aras E 32 E1
Aras de Alpuente E 47 E10
Arasvika N 104 E4
Aratos GR 171 B9
Araules F 30 E5
Aravete EST 131 C11
Aravissos GR 169 C7
Arazede P 44 D3
Arbanasi BG 166 C5
Arbas F 33 E7
Arbatax I 64 D4
Arbeca E 42 D5
Arbecey F 26 E4
Arbedo CH 69 A7
Arbéost F 32 E5
Arberg D 75 D8
Arbesbach A 77 E7
Arbeteta E 47 C8
Arboga S 97 D14
Arbois F 31 B8
Arboleas E 55 E8
Arbon CH 27 E11
Arbore RO 153 B7
Arborea I 64 D2
Arborio I 68 C5
Årbostad N 111 C13
Arbrå S 103 D11
Arbroath GB 5 B11
Arbúcies E 43 D9
Arbus I 64 D2
Årby DK 87 D8
Årbyn S 118 C8
Arcachon F 32 A3
Arcangues F 32 D2
Arcani RO 159 C11
Arce I 62 D5
Arcen NL 16 F6
Arc-en-Barrois F 26 E3
Arces F 28 D4
Arces-Dilo F 25 D10
Arc-et-Senans F 31 A8
Arcevia I 67 E6
Archaia Epidavros GR 175 D7
Archaia Korinthos GR 175 D6
Archaia Olympia GR 174 D4
Archanes GR 178 E9
Archangelos GR 181 D8
Archar BG 159 F10
Archena E 55 C10
Archiac F 28 D5
Archidona E 53 B8
Archipoli GR 181 D8
Archiș RO 151 E9
Archivel E 55 C9
Arcidosso I 65 B5
Arciems LV 131 F9
Arcis-sur-Aube F 25 C11
Arc-lès-Gray F 26 F4
Arco I 69 B10
Arco de Baúlhe P 38 F4
Arcola I 69 E8
Arçon F 31 B9
Arçonnay F 23 D12
Arcos E 40 D4
Arcos P 50 B4
Arcos de Jalón E 47 B8
Arcos de la Frontera E 52 C5
Arcos de las Salinas E 47 E10
Arcos de Valdevez P 38 E3
Arcozelo P 38 E2
Arcozelo P 38 E2
Arc-sur-Tille F 26 F3
Arcusa E 33 F6
Arda BG 171 B7
Ardagger Markt A 77 F7
Ardagh IRL 8 D4
Årdal N 100 C4
Ardala S 91 C13
Ardales E 53 C7
Årdalstangen N 100 D7
Ardanairy IRL 9 C10
Ardanaz E 32 E3
Ard an Rátha IRL 6 C6
Ardara I 64 B2
Ardara IRL 6 C6
Ardauli I 64 C2
Ardea I 62 D3
Ardee IRL 7 E9
Ardeluța RO 153 D8
Arden DK 86 B5
Arden GB 4 C7
Ardentes F 29 B9
Ardeoani RO 153 D9
Ardersier GB 3 K8
Ardes F 30 E3
Ardez CH 71 D10
Ardfern GB 4 C5
Ardfert IRL 8 D3
Ardfinnan IRL 9 D7
Ardgay GB 3 K8
Ardglass GB 7 D11
Ardgroom IRL 8 E3
Ardino BG 171 A8
Ardkeen GB 7 D11
Ardlui GB 4 C7
Ardlussa GB 4 C5
Ardmair GB 2 K6
Ardminish GB 4 D5
Ardmore IRL 6 F3
Ardmore IRL 9 E7
Ardon CH 31 C11
Ardooie B 19 C7
Ardore I 59 C9
Ardpatrick IRL 8 D5
Ardrahan IRL 6 F5
Ardre S 93 E13
Ardres F 18 C4
Ardrishaig GB 4 C6
Ardrossan GB 4 D7
Ardscull IRL 7 F9
Ardtoe GB 4 B5
Ardu EST 131 C10
Ardud RO 151 B10
Ardusat RO 151 B11
Ardvasar GB 4 A5
Are EST 131 D9
Åre S 105 E14
Areatza E 40 B6
Arefu RO 160 C5
Areias P 44 E4
Aremark N 96 D6
Arén E 42 C5
Arenas de Iguña E 40 B3
Arenas del Rey E 53 C9
Arenas de San Juan E 46 F6
Arenas de San Pedro E 45 D10
Arendal N 90 C4
Arendonk B 16 F4
Arendsee (Altmark) D 83 E10
Arengosse F 32 B4
Arenillas E 40 F6
Arenshausen D 79 D6
Arentorp S 91 C12
Arentsminde DK 86 A5
Arenys de Mar E 43 D9
Arenzano I 37 C9
Areopoli GR 178 B3
Areosa P 38 E2
Ares E 38 B3
Arès F 28 F3
Ares del Maestre E 48 D4
Aresing D 75 E9
Arespalditza E 40 B5
Arethousa GR 169 C10
Arette F 32 D4
Arette-Pierre-St-Martin F 32 E4
Aretxabaleta E 41 B7
Arevalillo E 45 C10
Arévalo E 46 B3
Arezzo I 66 F4
Arfara GR 174 E5
Arfons F 33 D10
Årfor N 105 B11
Argalasti GR 169 F9
Argallón E 51 C9
Argamasilla de Alba E 47 F6
Argamasilla de Calatrava E 54 B4
Argamasón E 55 B8
Arganda del Rey E 46 D6
Arganil P 44 D4
Arganza E 39 C6
Årgård N 105 C10
Argegno I 69 B7
Argelès-Gazost F 32 D5
Argelès-sur-Mer F 34 E5
Argeliers F 34 D4
Argelita E 48 D4
Argenbühl D 71 B9
Argences F 23 B11
Argenta I 66 C4
Argentan F 23 C11
Argentat F 29 E9
Argente E 47 C10
Argentera I 36 C5
Argenteuil F 25 C7
Argenthal D 21 E9
Argentiera I 64 B1
Argentière F 31 D10
Argentine F 31 E9
Argenton-les-Vallées F 28 B5
Argenton-sur-Creuse F 29 B9
Argentre F 23 D10
Argentré-du-Plessis F 23 D9
Argent-sur-Sauldre F 25 E7
Argés E 46 E4
Argetoaia RO 160 D2
Arginonta GR 177 E8
Argonay F 31 D9
Argos GR 175 D6
Argos Orestiko GR 168 D5
Argostoli GR 174 C1
Argouges F 23 D9
Arguedas E 41 D8
Argueil F 18 E4
Arguellite E 55 C8
Arguís E 32 F5
Arguisuelas E 47 E9
Argujillo E 39 F8
Argyrades GR 168 F2
Argyroupoli GR 169 E7
Århult S 89 A10
Århus DK 86 C6
Ariano Irpino I 60 A4
Ariano nel Polesine I 66 C5
Ariany E 57 B11
Aribe E 32 E3
Ariccia I 62 D3
Aridaia GR 169 C7
Arieșeni RO 151 E10
Arignac F 33 E9
Arija E 40 C4
Arild S 87 C11
Arileod GB 4 B3
Arilje SRB 158 F5
Arinagour GB 4 B3
Ariniș RO 151 C11
Ariño E 42 E2
Arinsal AND 33 E8
Arinthod F 31 C8
Ariogala LT 134 F6
Aris GR 174 E5
Arisaig GB 4 B5
Aristomenis GR 174 E4
Arisvi GR 171 B9
Aritzo I 64 D3
Ariz P 44 C5
Ariza E 41 F7
Arizgoiti E 40 B6
Arizola E 32 E2
Årjäng S 96 D7
Arjeplog S 109 D14
Arjona E 53 A8
Arjonilla E 53 A8
Arkala FIN 119 D16
Arkalochori GR 178 E9
Arkasa GR 181 F6
Arkelstorp S 88 C6
Arkesini GR 180 C3
Arkitsa GR 175 B7
Arkkukari FIN 119 E12
Arklow IRL 9 C10
Arkna EST 131 C12
Arkösund S 93 C9
Ärla S 98 D7
Arlanc F 30 E4
Arlanzón E 40 D5
Arle (Großheide) D 17 A8
Arlena di Castro I 62 C1
Arles F 35 C8
Arleuf F 30 A5
Arleux F 19 D7
Arligbo S 98 B8
Arló H 145 G1
Arlon B 19 E12
Arluno I 69 B6
Arlyeya BY 133 E6
Armação de Pêra P 50 E3
Armadale GB 5 D9
Armağan TR 167 F8
Armagh GB 7 D9
Armallones E 47 C8
Armamar P 44 B5
Armășești RO 161 D9
Armasjärvi S 119 B11
Armassaari FIN 119 B11
Armen AL 168 C2
Armenioi GR 174 E4
Armeniș RO 159 C9
Armenistis GR 177 D7
Armeno I 68 B5
Armenochori GR 168 C5
Armenoi GR 178 E7
Armenteros E 45 C10
Armentières F 18 C6
Armento I 60 C6
Armilla E 53 B9
Armissan F 34 D5
Armolia GR 177 C7
Armoy GB 4 E4
Armsheim D 185 E9
Armuña E 46 B4
Armungia I 64 D3
Armunia E 39 C8
Armutalani TR 181 C8
Armutlu TR 173 C10
Armutlu TR 177 C10
Arna GR 174 F5
Arnac-Pompadour F 29 E8
Arnad I 68 B4
Arnage F 23 E12
Arnaia GR 169 D10
Årnäs S 91 B14
Årnäs S 102 D5
Årnäs S 102 E5
Arnäsvall S 107 E15
Arnavutköy TR 173 B10
Arnay-le-Duc F 25 F11
Arnberg S 107 B16
Arnborg DK 86 C3
Arnbruck D 76 D3
Arneburg D 83 E12
Arnedillo E 41 D7
Arnedo E 41 D7
Arnéguy F 32 D3
Arnemark S 118 D6
Arnemuiden NL 16 F1
Arnes E 42 F4
Årnes N 95 B14
Årnes N 104 F5
Årnes N 111 B15
Arnfels A 148 C4
Arnhem NL 16 E5
Arnionys 1 LT 137 C12
Arnissa GR 169 C6
Arnö S 93 B10
Arnol GB 2 J3
Arnold GB 11 E9
Arnoldstein A 73 C8
Arnót H 145 G2
Arnöviken S 103 C13
Arnoyhamn N 112 C6
Arnprior GB 5 C8
Arnsberg D 17 F10
Arnschwang D 76 D3
Arnstadt D 79 E8
Arnstein D 74 C6
Arnstorf D 76 E3
Arnum DK 86 E3
Aroania GR 174 D5
Aroktő H 151 B6
Arola FIN 113 D20
Arolla CH 31 C11
Arolsen D 17 F12
Aron F 23 D10
Arona I 68 B6
Aroneanu RO 153 C11
Aronkylä FIN 122 F8
Åros N 95 C12
Arosa CH 71 D9
Arosa P 38 E3
Årosjåkk S 111 E17
Arouca P 44 C4
Årøybukta N 111 A19
Årøysund N 90 A7
Arpajon F 25 C7
Arpajon-sur-Cère F 29 F10
Arpașu de Jos RO 152 F5
Arpela FIN 119 B12
Arpino I 62 D5
Arquata del Tronto I 62 B4
Arquata Scrivia I 37 B9
Arques F 18 C5
Arques F 33 E10
Arques-la-Bataille F 18 E3
Arquillos E 55 C6
Arrabalde E 39 D8
Arracourt F 26 C6
Arradon F 22 E6
Arraiolos P 50 B4
Arrakoski FIN 127 C13
Arranhó P 50 B1
Arras F 18 D6
Arrasate E 41 B7
Ärre DK 86 D3
Arreau F 33 E6
Arredondo E 40 B4
Arrën AL 163 F9
Årrenjarka S 109 C15
Arrentières F 25 D12
Arriach A 73 C8
Arriana GR 171 B9
Arriate E 53 C6
Arrifana P 45 C6
Arrigny F 25 C12
Arrigorriaga E 40 B6
Arrild DK 86 E3
Arriondas E 39 B9
Arroba de los Montes E 46 F3
Arrochar GB 4 C7
Arronches P 45 F6
Arrone I 62 B3
Arroniz E 32 E1
Arrou F 24 D5
Arroyal E 40 C3
Arroyo de la Luz E 45 E7
Arroyo del Ojanco E 55 C7
Arroyo de San Serván E 51 B7
Arroyomolinos de León E 51 C7
Arruda dos Vinhos P 50 B1
Arry F 186 C1
Årsandøy N 105 A12
Ärsdale DK 89 E8
Arseni GR 169 C7
Ars-en-Ré F 28 C2
Årset N 105 A11
Arsiè I 72 E4
Arsiero I 69 B11
Årslev DK 86 E6
Arsoli I 62 C4
Ars-sur-Formans F 30 D6
Ars-sur-Moselle F 26 B5
Årstein N 111 C14
Årsunda S 98 A7
Arsura RO 153 D12
Arsvågen N 94 D2
Artà E 57 B11
Arta GR 174 A2
Artajona E 32 E2
Artana E 48 E4
Artannes-sur-Indre F 24 F4
Artemisia GR 174 E5
Artemisio GR 174 D5
Artemisio GR 175 A7
Artèn I 72 D4
Artena I 62 D3
Artenay F 24 D6
Artern (Unstrut) D 79 D9
Artés E 43 D7
Artesa de Segre E 42 D6
Artesiano GR 169 F6
Arth CH 71 C7
Arthez-d'Asson F 32 D5
Arthez-de-Béarn F 32 D4
Arthon F 29 B9
Arthon-en-Retz F 23 F8
Artieda E 32 E4
Artigarvan GB 4 F2
Artigat F 33 D8
Artix F 32 D4
Artjärvi FIN 127 D15
Artled S 103 E9
Artlenburg D 83 D8
Artogne I 69 B9
Årtrik S 107 E11
Artsyz UA 154 F4
Artziniega E 40 B5
A Rúa E 38 D5
Arudy F 32 D5
Arukülä EST 131 C10
Arukülä EST 131 C12
Arundel GB 15 F7
Årvågen N 104 E5
Arvagh IRL 7 E7
Arvån S 107 B16
Arvesund S 105 E16
Arveyres F 28 F5
Arvi GR 178 F9
Arvidsjaur S 109 E17
Arvidsträsk S 118 C5
Arvieu F 34 B4
Arvieux F 31 F10
Årvik N 100 B3
Arvika S 97 C8
Årviksand N 112 C6
Arvila EST 131 C14
Åryd S 89 B7
Åryd S 89 C8
Arzachena I 64 A3
Arzacq-Arraziguet F 32 C5
Arzana I 64 D4
Aržano HR 157 E7
Arzbach D 21 D9
Arzberg D 75 B11
Arzberg D 80 C4
Arzfeld D 20 D6
Arzignano I 72 E3
Arzl im Pitztal A 71 C11
Arzúa E 38 C3
As B 19 B12
Aš CZ 75 B11
Ås N 95 C13
Ås N 105 E11
Ås S 96 C7
Ås S 97 C12
Ås S 106 E7
Ås S 107 E11
Åsa N 95 B12
Åsa S 91 E11
Asaa DK 86 A6
Aşağıçobanisa TR 177 B10
Aşağısevindikli TR 173 B8
Åsan N 105 B12
Ašanja SRB 158 D5
Asare LV 135 D11
Åsarna S 102 A7
Åsarp S 91 C14
Asasp-Arros F 32 D4
Asbach D 21 C8
Åsbacka S 103 D11
Åsby S 87 A10
Asby S 92 D6
Ascain F 32 D2
Ascea I 60 C4
Aschach an der Donau A 76 F6
Aschaffenburg D 21 E12
Aschbach Markt A 77 F7
Ascheberg D 17 E9
Ascheberg (Holstein) D 83 B8
Aschères-le-Marché F 24 D7
Aschersleben D 79 C9
Așchileu RO 151 D11
Asciano I 66 F4
Ascó E 42 E5
Asco F 37 G10
Ascoli Piceno I 62 B5
Ascoli Satriano I 60 A5
Ascona CH 68 A6
Ascou F 33 E9
As Covas E 38 D2
Åse N 111 B10
Åsebyn S 96 D7
Åseda S 89 A8
Åsegg N 105 C9
Åsele S 107 C12
Åselet S 118 D4
Asemakylä FIN 119 D14
Asemankylä FIN 119 D14
Asemanseutu FIN 123 E11
Åsen N 105 D10
Åsen S 102 C7
Åsen S 102 D6
Åsen S 106 E7
Åsen S 109 E16
Åsenbruk S 91 B11
Asendorf D 17 C12
Asenovets BG 166 D5
Asenovgrad BG 165 E10
Asenovo BG 166 C6
Asenovtsi BG 165 C11
Åseral N 90 B1
Aseri EST 131 C13
A Serra de Outes E 38 C2
Asfaka GR 168 E4
Asfeld F 19 F9
Asfendiou GR 177 F9
Asferg DK 86 B5
Asgårstrand N 95 D12
Ash GB 15 E7
Åshammar S 103 E12
Ashbourne GB 11 E8
Ashbourne IRL 7 E10
Ashburton GB 13 D7
Ashbury GB 13 B11
Ashby de la Zouch GB 11 F9
Ashcott GB 13 C9
Ashevo RUS 133 B7
Ashford GB 13 D11
Ashford GB 15 E10
Ashford IRL 7 F10
Ashford IRL 8 D4
Ashill GB 15 B10
Ashington GB 5 E13
Ashkirk GB 5 E11
Ashley GB 15 C9
Ashmyany BY 137 D13
Ashmyany BY 137 E12
Ashton-under-Lyne GB 11 E7
Ashurst GB 13 D11
Ashwick GB 13 C9
Asiago I 72 E4
Asikkala FIN 127 C14
Asilah MA 52 F4
Asimi GR 178 E9
Asín E 32 F3
Asiros GR 169 C9
Ask N 95 B14
Aska FIN 117 D17
Askainen FIN 126 D6
Askeaton IRL 8 C5
Asker N 95 C12
Askern GB 11 D9
Askersby S 92 A6
Askersund S 92 B5
Åskilje S 107 B13
Askim N 95 C14
Asklipieio GR 175 D7
Asklipieio GR 181 D7
Åskogen S 118 C7
Askola FIN 127 D14
Åsköping S 92 A8
Askos GR 169 C9
Askvoll N 100 D2
Aslakkala FIN 113 E16
Aslestad N 94 D7
Åsli N 101 E11
Åsljunga S 87 C12
Asmali TR 173 C8
Åsmansbo S 97 B13
Åsmarka N 101 D13
Asmunti FIN 119 C17
Asnæs DK 87 D8
As Neves E 38 B3
As Neves E 38 D3
As Nogais E 38 C5
Asola I 66 B1
Asolo I 72 E4
Asopia GR 175 C8
Asopos GR 178 B4
Asos GR 174 C2
Åsottbalom H 150 E4
Asp DK 86 C3
Aspa S 93 B10
Aspa bruk S 92 B5
Aspach A 76 F4
Aspan S 102 B8
Aspang-Markt A 148 A6
Asparn an der Zaya A 77 E10
Asparukhovo BG 167 D8
Aspås S 106 E6
Aspatria GB 5 F10
Aspe E 56 E3
Aspe S 97 B8
Aspeå S 107 E12
Aspele S 107 D14
Asperen NL 183 B6
Aspet F 33 D7
Asphyltan S 97 C11
Aspliden S 109 F17
Aspliden S 118 B7
Aspnäs S 99 B8
Aspnäs S 103 A14
As Pontes de García Rodríguez E 38 B4
Aspremont F 35 A10
Aspres-sur-Buëch F 35 A10
Aspropyrgos GR 175 C8
Asprovalta GR 169 C10
Aspudden S 116 E3
As Rodrigas E 38 B5
Assamstadt D 74 D6
Asse B 19 C9
Assebakti N 113 E15
Asseiceira P 44 E4
Assemini I 64 E3
Assen NL 17 B7
Assendelft NL 16 D3
Assenede B 16 F1
Assens DK 86 B6
Assens DK 86 E5
Assentoft DK 86 C6
Assérac F 23 F7
Assergi I 62 C5
Assesse B 19 D11
Assier F 33 A9
Assisi I 62 A3
Åssjö S 103 B12
Åsskard N 104 E5
Aßlar D 21 C10
Assling A 73 C6
Asso I 69 B7
Asson F 32 D5
Assoro I 58 D5
Assos GR 168 F4
Assumar P 44 F6
Åsta N 101 D14
Astaffort F 33 B7
Astakos GR 174 B3
Åstan N 104 E7
Astašova LV 133 D2
Aste EST 130 E4
Åsteby S 97 B9
Astee IRL 8 C3
Asten A 76 F6
Asten NL 16 F5
Asti I 37 B8
Astikkala FIN 129 B12
Aştileu RO 151 C9
Astomilitsa GR 168 D4
Aston Clinton GB 15 D7
Astorga E 39 D7
Åstorp S 87 C11
Åstrand S 97 B9
Astravyets BY 137 D12
Astrazup RKS 163 E10
Astros GR 175 E6
Astrowna BY 133 F7
Astrowshchyna BY 133 F4
Astrup DK 86 B5
Astrup DK 86 C3
Astrup DK 90 E7
Astudillo E 40 D3
Astypalaia GR 180 C4
Asuaju de Sus RO 151 B11
Asūne LV 133 D3
Asuni I 64 D2
Asunta FIN 123 F13
Ásványráró H 146 F5
Asvestopetra GR 169 D6
Asvyeya BY 133 D4
Aszaló H 145 G2
Aszód H 150 B3
Atalaia P 44 F4
Atalaia P 44 F5
Atalanti GR 175 B7
Atalaya del Cañavate E 47 E8
Ataquines E 46 B3
Atarfe E 53 B9
Atašiene LV 135 C12
Atea E 47 B9
Ateca E 41 F8
A Teixeira E 38 D5
Ațel RO 152 E4
Ateleta I 63 D6
Atella I 60 B5
Atena Lucana I 60 C5
Återvänningen S 103 A13
Atessa I 63 C6
Ath B 19 C8
Athani GR 174 B2
Áth an Sceire IRL 7 F10
Athboy IRL 7 E9
Athea IRL 8 D4
Athenry IRL 6 F5
Athenstedt D 79 C8
Atheras GR 174 C1
Atherington GB 12 D6
Atherstone GB 11 F8
Athies F 18 E6
Athies-sous-Laon F 19 E8
Athikia GR 175 D6
Athina GR 175 D8
Athis-de-l'Orne F 23 C11
Athleague IRL 6 E6
Athlone IRL 7 F7
Áth Trasna IRL 8 D4
Athy IRL 7 G9
Athyra GR 169 C8
Atid RO 152 E6
Atienza E 47 B7
Atina I 62 D5
Atintiș RO 152 E4
Atjiken S 107 A9
Atkár H 150 B4
Atna N 101 C13
Åtorp S 92 A4
Atouguia da Baleia P 44 F2
Åtran S 87 A11
Åträsk S 118 B7
Åträsk S 118 D5
Atri I 62 B5
Atripalda I 60 B3
Atsiki GR 171 E8
Attadale GB 2 L6
Attala H 149 D10
Attali GR 175 B8
Attanagh IRL 9 C8
Attavalley IRL 6 D3
Attendorn D 21 B9
Attenkirchen D 75 E10
Attersee A 73 A8
Attert B 19 E12
Attica GB 7 D10
Attigliano I 62 B2
Attignat F 31 C7
Attigny F 19 F10
Attleborough GB 15 B11
Attnang A 76 F5
Åttonträsk S 107 C14
Attu FIN 126 E7
Atur F 29 E7
Åtvidaberg S 92 C7
Atzara I 64 D3
Atzenbrugg A 77 F9
Atzendorf D 79 C10
Atzeneta del Maestrat E 48 D4
Au A 71 C9
Au CH 71 C9
Aub D 75 C7
Aubagne F 35 D10
Aubange B 19 E12
Aube F 24 C4
Aubel B 183 D7
Aubenas F 35 A7
Aubenton F 19 E9
Aubergenville F 24 C6
Auberive F 26 E3
Aubeterre-sur-Dronne F 29 E6
Aubiet F 33 C7
Aubignan F 35 B9
Aubigné-Racan F 23 E12
Aubignosc F 35 B10
Aubigny F 28 B3
Aubigny-en-Artois F 18 D6
Aubigny-sur-Nère F 25 F7
Aubin F 33 A10
Aubonne CH 31 B9
Aubord F 35 C7
Auboué F 20 F5
Aubusson F 29 D10

Auby F 19 D7
Aucamville F 33 C8
Auce LV 134 D5
Auch F 33 C7
Auchallater GB 5 B10
Auchenbreck GB 4 D6
Auchencairn GB 5 F9
Auchencrow GB 5 D12
Auchnagatt GB 3 L12
Auchterarder GB 5 C9
Auchtermuchty GB 5 C10
Auchy-au-Bois F 18 C5
Aucun F 32 E5
Audenge F 32 A3
Auderville F 23 A8
Audeux F 26 F4
Audevälja EST 131 C8
Audierne F 22 D2
Audincourt F 27 F6
Audlem GB 10 F6
Audley GB 11 E7
Audnedal N 90 C1
Audon F 32 C4
Audresselles F 15 F12
Audriņi LV 133 C2
Audru EST 131 E8
Audruicq F 18 C5
Audun-le-Roman F 20 F5
Aue D 79 E12
Auerbach D 75 A11
Auerbach in der Oberpfalz D 75 C10
Auersthal A 77 F11
Auffay F 18 E3
Aufhausen D 75 E11
Augbrim IRL 6 F5
Auggen D 27 E8
Augher GB 7 D8
Aughnacloy GB 7 D9
Aughrim IRL 6 F5
Aughrim IRL 9 C10
Aughton GB 11 E9
Augignac F 29 D7
Augsburg D 75 F8
Augšlīgatne LV 135 B10
Augstkalne LV 133 E2
Augstkalne LV 134 D6
Augusta I 59 E7
Auguste LV 134 D3
Augustenborg DK 86 F5
Augustów PL 136 F6
Augustowo PL 141 E8
Augustusburg D 80 E4
Auho FIN 121 E10
Aukan N 104 E4
Aukra N 100 A5
Aukrug D 82 B7
Aukštadvaris LT 137 D10
Aukštelkai LT 134 E7
Aukštelkė LT 134 E6
Auktsjaur S 109 E17
Auleja LV 133 D2
Aulendorf D 71 B9
Auletta I 60 B4
Aulla I 69 E8
Aullène F 37 H10
Aulnat F 30 D3
Aulnay F 28 C5
Aulnay-sous-Bois F 25 C8
Aulnois sur-Seille F 26 C5
Aulnoye-Aymeries F 19 D8
Aulon F 33 D7
Aulosen D 83 E11
Ault F 18 D3
Aultbea GB 2 K5
Aultguish Inn GB 2 K7
Aulus-les-Bains F 33 E8
Auma D 79 E10
Aumale F 18 E4
Aumetz F 20 F5
Aumont F 31 B8
Aumont-Aubrac F 30 F3
Aumühle D 83 C8
Aunay-en-Bazois F 25 F10
Aunay-sur-Odon F 23 B10
Auneau F 24 D6
Aunegrenda N 105 F10
Aunfoss N 105 B13
Auning DK 86 C6
Auñón E 47 C7
Aups F 36 D4
Aura FIN 126 D8
Aurach D 75 D7
Aurach bei Kitzbühel A 72 B5
Aura im Sinngrund D 74 B6
Auran N 105 E9
Auray F 22 E6
Aurdal N 101 E10
Aure N 104 E5
Aurec-sur-Loire F 30 E5
Aureilhan F 33 D6
Aureille F 35 C8
Aurejärvi FIN 123 G10
Aurel F 35 A9
Aurel F 35 B9
Aurensan F 32 C5
Aureosen N 100 A6
Auri LV 134 C6
Aurich D 17 B8
Aurignac F 33 D7
Aurillac F 29 F10
Auriol F 35 D10
Aurisina I 73 E8
Auritz E 32 E3
Aurland N 100 E6
Aurolzmünster A 76 F4
Auron F 36 C5
Auronzo di Cadore I 72 C5
Auros F 32 A5
Auroux F 30 F4
Aurskog N 95 C14
Ausa-Corno I 73 E7
Ausejo E 32 F1
Auşeu RO 151 C10
Ausleben D 79 B9
Ausmas LV 135 B9
Ausonia I 62 E5
Außervillgraten A 72 C5
Aussillon F 33 C10
Aussonne F 33 C8
Austafjord N 105 B9
Austbø N 95 C8
Austborg N 105 C15
Austertana N 114 C5
Austis I 64 C3
Austmannli N 94 C5
Austnes N 100 A4
Austnes N 105 B15
Austnes N 111 C12
Austråt N 104 D7
Austsmøla N 104 E4
Auterive F 33 D8
Authon F 24 E4
Authon F 36 C4
Authon-du-Perche F 24 D4
Autio FIN 119 E17
Autio FIN 123 E13
Autol E 41 D7
Autrans F 31 E8
Autreville F 26 D4
Autrey-lès-Gray F 26 F3
Autry F 19 F10
Autti FIN 119 B18
Auttoinen FIN 127 C13
Autun F 30 B5
Auve F 25 B12
Auvelais B 19 D10
Auvers-le-Hamon F 23 E11
Auvillar F 33 B7
Auvillers-les-Forges F 184 E1
Auxerre F 25 E10
Auxi-le-Château F 18 D5
Auxonne F 26 F3
Auxy F 30 B5
Auzances F 29 C10
Auzat F 33 E8
Auzat-la-Combelle F 30 E3
Aužguļāni LV 135 E12
Auzon F 30 E3
Åva FIN 126 E5
Ava S 107 D16
Avafors S 118 B8
Availles-Limouzine F 29 C7
Avaldsnes N 94 D2
Avallon F 25 E10
Avan S 118 C7
Avanäs S 107 C17
Avanca P 44 C3
Avançon F 36 B4
Avantas GR 171 C9
Avant-lès-Ramerupt F 25 D11
Avasjö S 107 C11
Avato GR 171 C7
Avaträsk S 107 C10
Avaviken S 109 E16
Avdira GR 171 C7
Avdou GR 178 E9
A Veiga E 39 D6
Aveiras de Cima P 44 F3
Aveiro P 44 C3
Avelar P 44 E4
Avelãs de Caminho P 44 D4
Aveleda P 38 E3
Aveleda P 39 E6
Avelgem B 19 C7
Avella I 60 B3
Avellino I 60 B3
Avenay-Val-d'Or F 25 B11
Avenches CH 31 B11
Avenhorn NL 16 C3
Avenida do Marqués de Figueroa E 38 A3
Avermes F 30 B3
Avers CH 71 E9
Aversa I 60 B2
Avesnes-le-Comte F 18 D6
Avesnes-sur-Helpe F 19 D8
Avesta S 98 B6
Åvestbo S 97 C14
Avetrano I 61 C9
Avezzano I 62 C4
Avgerinos GR 168 D5
Avià E 43 C7
Aviano I 73 D6
Aviemore GB 3 L9
Avigliana I 31 E11
Avigliano I 60 B5
Avigliano Umbro I 62 B2
Avignon F 35 C8
Ávila E 46 C3
A Vila da Igrexa E 38 A4
Avilés E 39 A8
Avilley F 26 F5
Avintes P 44 B3
Avinurme EST 131 D13
Avinyó E 43 D7
Avio I 69 B10
Avion F 18 D6
Avioth F 19 E11
Avis P 44 F5
Avispea EST 131 C12
Åvist FIN 122 D9
Avize F 25 C11
Avižieniai LT 137 D11
Avlakia GR 177 D8
Avlemonas GR 178 C5
Avliotes GR 168 E2
Avlonari GR 175 B9
Avlonas GR 175 C8
Avlum DK 86 C3
Avoca IRL 9 C10
Avoine F 23 F12
Avola I 59 F7
Avon F 25 D8
Avonmouth GB 13 B9
Avord F 29 A11
Avoriaz F 31 C10
Avoudrey F 26 F5
Avrămeni RO 153 A9
Avrămești RO 152 E6
Avram Iancu RO 151 D8
Avram Iancu RO 151 E10
Avranches F 23 C9
Avren BG 171 B9
Avricourt F 186 D2
Avrig RO 152 F4
Avril F 20 F5
Avrillé F 23 E10
Avrillé F 28 C3
Avtovac BIH 157 F10
Av'že N 112 E10
Awans B 183 D6
Axams A 72 B3
Axat F 33 E10
Axel NL 16 F1
Axente Sever RO 152 E4
Axintele RO 161 D9
Axioupoli GR 169 C8
Ax-les-Thermes F 33 E9
Axmar S 103 D13
Axmarsbruk S 103 D13
Axminster GB 13 D9
Axos GR 169 C7
Axvall S 91 C14
Ayamonte E 50 E5
Aycliffe GB 5 F13
Aydat F 30 D2
Aydemir BG 161 E10
Ayen F 29 E8
Ayerbe E 32 F4
Aying D 72 A4
Aylesbury GB 15 D7
Ayllón E 40 F5
Aylsham GB 15 B11
Aymavilles I 31 D11
Ayna E 55 B8
Aynac F 29 F9
Ayoo de Vidriales E 39 D7
Ayora E 47 F10
Ayr GB 4 E7
Ayrancilar TR 177 C9
Ayron F 28 B6
Ayşebaci TR 173 E8
Aysgarth GB 11 C8
Äyskoski FIN 123 D17
Äystö FIN 122 F7
Aytos BG 167 D8
Aytré F 28 C3
Ayvacık TR 171 E10
Ayvalık TR 172 F6
Aywaille B 19 D12
Azagra E 32 F2
Azaila E 41 F11
Azambuja P 44 F3
Azanja SRB 159 E6
Azanúy E 42 D4
Azaruja P 50 B4
Azatlı TR 172 B6
Azay-le-Ferron F 29 B8
Azay-le-Rideau F 24 F3
Azé F 23 E10
Azerables F 29 C8
Azina BY 133 E5
Azinhaga P 44 F3
Azinhal P 50 E5
Azinheira dos Barros P 50 C3
Azinhoso P 39 F6
Azkoitia E 32 D1
Aznalcázar E 51 E7
Aznalcóllar E 51 D7
Azóia P 50 C1
Azpeitia E 32 D1
Azuaga E 51 C8
Azuara E 41 F10
Azuel E 54 C4
Azuelo E 32 E1
Azuga RO 161 C7
Azuqueca de Henares E 47 C6
Azur F 32 C3
Azután E 45 E10
Azy-le-Vif F 30 B3
Azyory BY 140 C10
Azzano Decimo I 73 E6
Azzone I 69 B9

B

Baalberge D 79 C10
Baâlon F 19 F11
Baar CH 27 F10
Baarle-Hertog B 16 F3
Baarle-Nassau NL 16 F3
Baarn NL 16 D4
Baba Ana RO 161 D8
Babadag RO 155 D3
Babaeski TR 173 B7
Babaköy TR 173 E9
Baban AL 168 C4
Băbana RO 160 D5
Babberich NL 183 B8
Babchyntsi UA 154 A2
Babenhausen D 21 E11
Băbeni RO 151 C11
Băbeni RO 160 D4
Babiak PL 136 E1
Babiak PL 138 F6
Babice CZ 146 C4
Babice PL 143 F7
Babice nad Svitavou CZ 77 D11
Babići BIH 157 D7
Băbiciu RO 160 E5
Babilafuente E 45 C10
Babimost PL 81 B9
Babín SK 147 C8
Babina SRB 164 D5
Babina Greda HR 157 B10
Babino Polje HR 162 D4
Babīte LV 135 C7
Babno Polje SLO 73 E10
Babócsa H 149 D8
Bábolna H 149 A9
Baborów PL 142 F4
Baboszewo PL 139 E9
Babót H 149 A8
Babrrujë AL 168 B2
Babtai LT 137 C8
Babuk BG 161 E10
Babušnica SRB 164 C5
Babyak BG 165 F8
Babynichy BY 133 F4
Bać MNE 163 D9
Bač SRB 158 C3
Băcani RO 153 E11
Bacares E 55 E8
Bacău RO 153 D9
Baccarat F 27 D6
Baceno I 68 A5
Băcești RO 153 D10
Bach A 71 C10
Bacharach D 21 D9
Bachkovo BG 165 F10
Bachórz PL 144 D5
Băcia RO 151 F11
Baciki Bliższe PL 141 F7
Băcioi MD 154 D3
Baciu RO 152 D3
Bäck S 105 E16
Backa S 91 E10
Backa S 97 A9
Backa S 97 B9
Backaland GB 3 G11
Bačka Palanka SRB 158 C3
Backaryd S 89 C8
Bačka Topola SRB 150 F4
Backberg S 103 E12
Backe S 107 D10
Bäckebo S 89 B10
Bäckefors S 91 B11
Bäckhammar S 91 A15
Bački Breg SRB 150 F2
Bački Brestovac SRB 158 B3
Bački Jarak SRB 158 C4
Bački Monoštor SRB 150 F2
Bačkininkai LT 137 D8
Bački Petrovac SRB 158 C4
Bäcklund S 109 E17
Bäckmark S 107 A11
Backnang D 27 C11
Bäcknäs S 109 F17
Bačko Dobro Polje SRB 158 B4
Bačko Gradište SRB 158 B5
Bačko Novo Selo SRB 157 B11
Bačko Petrovo Selo SRB 158 B5
Baćkowice PL 143 E11
Backträsk S 118 C6
Bäckvallen S 102 B8
Băcleș RO 159 E11
Bacoli I 60 B2
Bacqueville-en-Caux F 18 E2
Bácsalmás H 150 E3
Bácsbokod H 150 E3
Bácsborsód H 150 E3
Bacúch SK 147 D9
Baczyna PL 85 E8
Bada S 97 B9
Bad Abbach D 75 E11
Bad Aibling D 72 A5
Badajoz E 51 B6
Badalona E 43 E8
Badalucco I 37 D7
Bádames E 40 B5
Badarán E 40 D6
Bad Aussee A 73 A8
Bad Bayersoien D 71 B12
Bad Bederkesa D 17 A11
Bad Belzig D 79 B12
Bad Bentheim D 17 D8
Bad Bergzabern D 27 B8
Bad Berka D 79 E9
Bad Berleburg D 21 B10
Bad Berneck im Fichtelgebirge D 75 B10
Bad Bertrich D 21 D8
Bad Bevensen D 83 D9
Bad Bibra D 79 D10
Bad Birnbach D 76 F4
Bad Blankenburg D 79 E9
Bad Blumau A 148 B6
Bad Bocklet D 75 B7
Bad Boll D 74 E6
Bad Brambach D 75 B11
Bad Bramstedt D 83 C7
Bad Breisig D 185 D7
Bad Brückenau D 74 B6
Bad Buchau D 71 A9
Bad Camberg D 21 D10
Badcaul GB 2 K6
Badderen N 112 D9
Bad Doberan D 83 B11
Bad Driburg D 17 E12
Bad Düben D 79 C12
Bad Dürkheim D 21 F10
Bad Dürrenberg D 79 D11
Bad Dürrheim D 27 D10
Badeborn D 79 C9
Badefols-d'Ans F 29 E8
Bad Elster D 75 B11
Bademler TR 177 C8
Bademli TR 171 F10
Bademli TR 173 D10
Bademli TR 177 B8
Bad Ems D 21 D9
Baden A 77 F10
Baden CH 27 F9
Baden F 22 E6
Bádenas E 47 B10
Baden-Baden D 27 C9
Bad Endorf D 72 A5
Badenscoth GB 3 L12
Badenweiler D 27 E8
Baderna HR 67 B8
Badersleben D 79 C8
Badesi I 64 B2
Bad Essen D 17 D10
Bădeuți RO 153 B7
Bad Fallingbostel D 82 E7
Bad Feilnbach D 72 A5
Bad Frankenhausen (Kyffhäuser) D 79 D9
Bad Freienwalde D 84 E6
Bad Friedrichshall D 21 F12
Bad Füssing D 76 F4
Bad Gams A 73 C11
Bad Gandersheim D 79 C7
Badgastein A 73 B7
Bad Gleichenberg A 148 C5
Bad Goisern A 73 A8
Bad Griesbach im Rottal D 76 F4
Bad Grönenbach D 71 B10
Bad Großpertholz A 77 E7
Bad Grund (Harz) D 79 C7
Bad Hall A 76 F6
Bad Harzburg D 79 C8
Bad Herrenalb D 27 C9
Bad Hersfeld D 78 E6
Bad Hindelang D 71 B10
Badhoevedorp NL 182 A5
Bad Hofgastein A 73 B7
Bad Homburg vor der Höhe D 21 D11
Bad Honnef D 21 C8
Bad Hönningen D 185 C7
Badia I 72 C4
Badia Calavena I 69 B11
Badia Gran E 49 F10
Badia Polesine I 66 B3
Badia Tedalda I 66 E5
Bad Iburg D 17 D10
Bădiceni MD 153 A12
Badín SK 147 D8
Bad Ischl A 73 A8
Bad Karlshafen D 78 C5
Bad Kissingen D 75 B7
Bad Kleinen D 83 C10
Bad Kleinkirchheim A 73 C8
Bad König D 21 E12
Bad Königshofen im Grabfeld D 75 B7
Bad Kösen D 79 D10
Bad Köstritz D 79 E11
Bad Kötzting D 76 D3
Bądkowo PL 138 E6
Bad Kreuzen A 77 F7
Bad Kreuznach D 21 E9
Bad Krozingen D 27 E8
Bad Laasphe D 21 C10
Bad Laer D 17 D10
Bad Langensalza D 79 D8
Bad Lauchstädt D 79 D10
Bad Lausick D 79 D12
Bad Lauterberg im Harz D 79 C7
Bad Leonfelden A 76 E6
Bad Liebenstein D 79 E7
Bad Liebenwerda D 80 C4
Bad Liebenzell D 27 C10
Bad Lippspringe D 17 E11
Badljevina HR 149 E8
Bad Lobenstein D 75 B10
Bad Marienberg (Westerwald) D 21 C9
Bad Mergentheim D 74 D6
Bad Mitterndorf A 73 A8
Bad Münder am Deister D 78 B5
Bad Münstereifel D 21 C7
Bad Muskau D 81 C7
Bad Nauheim D 21 D11
Bad Nenndorf D 17 D12
Bad Neuenahr-Ahrweiler D 21 C8
Bad Neustadt an der Saale D 75 B7
Badolato I 59 B10
Badolatosa E 53 B7
Bad Oldesloe D 83 C8
Badonviller F 27 C6
Bad Orb D 21 D12
Badovinci SRB 158 D3
Bad Peterstal D 27 D9
Bad Pirawarth A 77 F11
Bad Pyrmont D 17 E12
Bad Radkersburg A 148 C5
Bad Ragaz CH 71 C9
Bad Rappenau D 187 C7
Bad Reichenhall D 73 A6
Bad Rodach D 75 B8
Bad Saarow-Pieskow D 80 B6
Bad Sachsa D 79 C8
Bad Säckingen D 27 E8
Bad Salzdetfurth D 79 B7
Bad Salzuflen D 17 D11
Bad Salzungen D 79 E7
Bad Sankt Leonhard im Lavanttal A 73 C10
Bad Sassendorf D 17 E10
Bad Schandau D 80 E6
Bad Schmiedeberg D 79 C12
Bad Schönborn D 187 C6
Bad Schussenried D 71 A9
Bad Schwalbach D 21 D10
Bad Schwartau D 83 C9
Bad Segeberg D 83 C8
Bad Sobernheim D 185 E8
Bad Soden-Salmünster D 74 B5
Bad Sooden-Allendorf D 79 D6
Bad Staffelstein D 75 B8
Bad Steben D 75 B10
Bad Sulza D 79 D10
Bad Sülze D 83 B13
Bad Tennstedt D 79 D8
Bad Tölz D 72 A4
Bad Überkingen D 187 D8
Badules E 47 B10
Bad Urach D 27 D11
Bad Vilbel D 21 D11
Bad Vöslau A 77 G10
Bad Waldsee D 71 B9
Bad Waltersdorf A 148 B6
Bad Wildbad im Schwarzwald D 187 D6
Bad Wildungen D 21 B12
Bad Wilsnack D 83 E11
Bad Wimpfen D 21 F12
Bad Windsheim D 75 C7
Bad Wörishofen D 71 B11
Bad Wurzach D 71 B9
Bad Zell A 77 F7
Bad Zurzach CH 27 E9
Bad Zwesten D 21 B12
Bad Zwischenahn D 17 B10
Bække DK 86 D4
Bækmarksbro DK 86 C2
Baelen B 183 D7
Bælum DK 86 B6
Baena E 53 A8
Bærums Verk N 95 C12
Baesweiler D 20 C6
Baeza E 53 A10
Baflo NL 17 B7
Bagà E 43 C7
Băgaciu RO 152 E4
Bagaladi I 59 C8
Bagamér H 151 C8
Bağarasi TR 177 B8
Bağarasi TR 177 D10
Bagard F 35 B7
Bağcılar TR 181 B8
Bâgé-le-Châtel F 30 C6
Bagenalstown IRL 9 C9
Bagenkop DK 83 A9
Bages F 34 E4
Baggå S 97 C14
Bagheria I 58 C4
Bagn N 101 E11
Bagnacavallo I 66 D4
Bagnac-sur-Célé F 33 A10
Bagnara Calabra I 59 C8
Bagnaria I 37 B10
Bagnaria Arsa I 73 E7
Bagnasco I 37 C8
Bagneaux-sur-Loing F 25 D8
Bagnères-de-Bigorre F 33 D6
Bagnères-de-Luchon F 33 E7
Bagni di Lucca I 66 D2
Bagni di Masino I 69 A8
Bagni di Rabbi I 71 E11
Bagno a Ripoli I 66 E3
Bagno di Romagna I 66 E4
Bagnoli del Trigno I 63 D6
Bagnoli di Sopra I 66 B4
Bagnoli Irpino I 60 B4
Bagnolo in Piano I 66 C2
Bagnolo Mella I 66 B1
Bagnolo Piemonte I 31 F11
Bagnolo San Vito I 66 B2
Bagnols-les-Bains F 35 A6
Bagnols-sur-Cèze F 35 B8
Bagnoregio I 62 B2
Bagod H 149 C7
Bagolino I 69 B9
Bagrationovsk RUS 136 E2
Bagrdan SRB 159 E7
Bagshot GB 15 E7
Báguena E 47 B10
Bágyogszovát H 149 A8
Bağyurdu TR 177 C10
Bağyüzü TR 173 F6
Bahabón de Esgueva E 40 E4
Bahate UA 155 C3
Bahçeburun TR 181 B7
Bahçeköy TR 173 B10
Bahçeli TR 171 E10
Bahíllo E 39 D10
Bahmut MD 153 C12
Bahna RO 153 D9
Bahnea RO 152 E4
Báhoň SK 146 E4
Bahrenborstel D 17 C11
Bahrendorf D 79 C10
Baia RO 153 C8
Baia RO 155 D3
Baia de Aramă RO 159 D10
Baia de Arieș RO 151 E11
Baia de Criș RO 151 E10
Baia de Fier RO 160 C3
Baia della Zagare I 63 D10
Baia Mare RO 152 B3
Baiano I 60 B3
Baiardo I 37 D7
Baia Sprie RO 152 B3
Băicoi RO 161 C7
Băiculești RO 160 C5
Baiersbronn D 27 C9
Baiersdorf D 75 C9
Baignes-Ste-Radegonde F 28 E5
Baigneux-les-Juifs F 25 E12
Baile an Bhiataigh IRL 7 E10
Baile an Bhuinneánaigh IRL 8 C3
Baile an Chinnéidigh IRL 7 F10
Baile an Dúlaigh IRL 6 F4
Baile an Fheirtéaraigh IRL 8 D2
Baile an Mhóta IRL 6 D5
Baile an Mhuilinn IRL 8 D2
Baile an Róba IRL 6 E4
Baile an Sceilg IRL 8 E2
Baile Átha an Rí IRL 6 F5
Baile Átha Buí IRL 7 E9
Baile Átha Cliath IRL 7 F10
Baile Átha Fhirdhia IRL 7 E9
Baile Átha Í IRL 7 G9
Baile Átha Luain IRL 7 F7
Baile Átha Troim IRL 7 E9
Baile Brigin IRL 7 E10
Baile Coimin IRL 7 F9
Băile Govora RO 160 C4
Băile Herculane RO 159 D9
Baile Loch Riach IRL 6 F5
Baile Mhartainn GB 2 K2
Baile Mhic Andáin IRL 9 C8
Baile Mhic Íre IRL 8 E4
Baile Mhistéale IRL 8 D6
Bailén E 54 C5
Baile na Finne IRL 6 C6
Baile na Lorgan IRL 7 D9
Băile Olănești RO 160 C4
Baile Órthaí IRL 7 E9
Băilești RO 160 E2
Băile Tușnad RO 153 E7
Baile Uílcín IRL 7 E9
Bailieborough IRL 7 E9
Baillargues F 35 C7
Bailleau-le-Pin F 24 D5
Bailleul F 18 C6
Baillonville B 19 D11
Bailo E 32 E4
Baimaclia MD 154 E2
Bainbridge GB 11 C7
Bain-de-Bretagne F 23 E8
Baindt D 71 B9
Bains F 30 E4
Bains-les-Bains F 26 D5
Bainton GB 11 D10
Baio E 38 B2
Baiona E 38 D2
Bais F 23 D9
Bais F 23 D11
Baiso I 66 D2
Băișoara RO 151 D11
Baisogala LT 134 E7
Băița RO 151 E10
Băița de sub Codru RO 151 B11
Baix F 35 A8
Baixa da Banheira P 50 B1
Baixas F 34 E4
Baj H 149 A10
Baja H 150 E2
Bajč SK 146 F6
Bajgorë RKS 164 D3
Bajina Bašta SRB 158 F4
Bajmok SRB 150 F3
Bajna H 149 A11
Bajót H 149 A11
Bajovo Polje MNE 157 F10
Bajram Curri AL 163 E9
Bajša SRB 150 F4
Bak H 149 C7
Baka SK 146 F5
Bakacak TR 173 D7
Bakałarzewo PL 136 E6
Bakar HR 67 B10
Bakel NL 16 F5
Bakir TR 177 A10
Bakırköy TR 173 C10
Bakkasund N 94 B2
Bakke N 111 A16
Bakkeby N 112 D6
Bakkejord N 111 A15
Bakken N 101 E15
Bakko N 95 C9
Bakonszeg H 151 C7
Bakonybél H 149 B9
Bakonycsernye H 149 B10
Bakonysárkány H 149 B10
Bakonyszentkirály H 149 B9
Bakonyszentlászló H 149 B9
Bakonyszombathely H 149 B9
Bakov nad Jizerou CZ 77 B7
Baks H 150 D5
Baksa H 149 E10
Baksha UA 154 A5
Baktalórántháza H 145 H5
Baktsjaur S 109 F17
Bakum D 17 C10
Bakvattnet S 105 D16
Bäl S 93 D13
Bala GB 10 F4
Bala RO 159 D10
Balabancık TR 173 C6
Bălăbănești MD 154 C4
Bălăbănești RO 153 E11
Balabanu MD 154 F3
Bălăceanu RO 161 C10
Balaci RO 160 E5
Bălăcița RO 159 E11
Balaciu RO 161 D9
Balaguer E 42 D5
Balallan GB 2 J3
Balan F 19 E10
Balan F 31 D7
Bălan RO 151 C11
Bălan RO 153 D7
Bălănești MD 153 C12
Bălănești RO 160 C2
Balanivka UA 154 A4
Balaruc-les-Bains F 35 D6
Bălășești RO 153 E11
Bălăsinești MD 153 A9
Balassagyarmat H 147 E8
Balástya H 150 E5
Balat TR 177 D9
Balaton H 145 G1
Balatonalmádi H 149 B10
Balatonberény H 149 C8
Balatonboglár H 149 C9
Balatonfőkajár H 149 B10
Balatonföldvár H 149 C9
Balatonfüred H 149 C9
Balatonfőzfő H 149 B10
Balatonkenese H 149 B10
Balatonlelle H 149 C9
Balatonszabadi H 149 C10
Balatonszárszó H 149 C9
Balatonvilágos H 149 C10
Bălăușeri RO 152 E5
Balazote E 55 B8
Balbeggie GB 5 C10
Balbieriškis LT 137 D8
Balbigny F 30 D5
Balbriggan IRL 7 E10
Balcani RO 153 D9
Bălcești RO 160 D3
Balchik BG 167 C10
Balcilar TR 173 D6
Balçova TR 177 C9
Balderton GB 11 E10
Baldock GB 15 D8
Baldone LV 135 C8
Baldones Muiža LV 135 C8
Baldovinești RO 160 E4
Bale HR 67 B8
Baleizão P 50 C4
Balemartine GB 4 C3
Balen B 19 B11
Băleni RO 153 F11
Băleni RO 161 D7
Balephuil GB 4 C3
Balerma E 55 F7
Bălești RO 159 C11
Balestrand N 100 D5
Balestrate I 58 C3
Balfour GB 3 G11
Balfron GB 5 C8
Balgale LV 134 B5
Balgown GB 2 K4
Bälgviken S 98 D6
Bali GR 178 E8
Baligród PL 145 E5
Balikesir TR 173 E8
Balıklıçeşme TR 173 D7
Balıkliova TR 177 C8
Bălilești RO 160 C5
Bälinge S 99 C9
Bälinge S 118 C7
Balingen D 27 D10
Balinka H 149 B10
Balinț RO 151 F8
Balintore GB 3 K9
Balje D 17 A12
Baljevac BIH 156 C4
Baljevac SRB 163 C10
Baljvine BIH 157 D7
Balk NL 16 C5
Balkány H 151 B8
Balkbrug NL 16 C6
Balla IRL 6 E4
Ballaban AL 168 D3
Ballabio I 69 B7
Ballachulish GB 4 B6
Ballaghaderreen IRL 6 E5
Ballaghkeen IRL 9 D10
Ballangen N 111 D12
Ballantrae GB 4 E6
Ballao I 64 D3
Ballasalla GBM 10 C2
Ballater GB 5 A10
Ballaugh GBM 10 C2
Balle DK 87 C7
Ballée F 23 E11
Ballee GB 7 D11
Ballen DK 86 D7
Ballenstedt D 79 C9
Balleroy F 23 B10
Ballerup DK 87 D10
Ballesteros de Calatrava E 54 B5
Balli TR 173 C7
Ballina IRL 6 D4
Ballina IRL 8 C6
Ballinaboy IRL 6 F2
Ballinafad IRL 6 D6
Ballinagar IRL 7 F8
Ballinagh IRL 7 E8
Ballinakill IRL 9 C8
Ballinalack IRL 7 E8
Ballinalee IRL 7 E7
Ballinamallard GB 7 D7
Ballinamore IRL 7 D7
Ballinamult IRL 9 D7
Ballinasloe IRL 6 F6
Ballincollig IRL 8 E5
Ballindine IRL 6 E5
Ballindooly IRL 6 F4
Ballineen IRL 8 E5
Ballingarry IRL 8 D5
Ballingarry IRL 9 C7
Ballingeary IRL 8 E4
Ballingry GB 5 C10
Ballingslöv S 87 C13
Ballingurteen IRL 8 E4
Ballinhassig IRL 8 E5
Ballinlough IRL 6 E5
Ballinluig GB 5 B9
Ballinrobe IRL 6 E4
Ballinskelligs IRL 8 E2
Ballinspittle IRL 8 E5
Ballintober IRL 6 E4
Ballintoy GB 4 E4
Ballintra IRL 6 C6
Ballintubber IRL 6 E4
Ballinure IRL 9 C7
Ballivor IRL 7 E9
Ballobar E 42 D4
Ballon F 23 D12
Ballon IRL 9 C9
Ballószög H 150 D4
Ballots F 23 E9
Ballsh AL 168 C2
Ballsnes N 111 A16
Ballstad N 110 D6
Ballstädt D 79 D8
Ballum DK 86 E3
Ballum NL 16 B5
Ballure IRL 6 C6
Ballybay IRL 7 D9
Ballybofey IRL 7 C7
Ballybrack IRL 7 F10
Ballybrack IRL 8 E2
Ballybrittas IRL 7 F8
Ballybunion IRL 8 C3
Ballybunnion IRL 8 C3
Ballycahill IRL 9 C7
Ballycanew IRL 9 C10
Ballycarry GB 4 F5
Ballycastle GB 4 E4
Ballycastle IRL 6 D4
Ballyclare GB 4 F5
Ballycolla IRL 9 C8
Ballyconneely IRL 6 F2
Ballyconnell IRL 7 D7
Ballycotton IRL 8 E6
Ballycroy IRL 6 D3
Ballydavid IRL 6 F6
Ballydehob IRL 8 E4
Ballydesmond IRL 8 D4
Ballydonegan IRL 8 E2
Ballyduff IRL 8 D3
Ballyduff IRL 8 D6
Ballyfarnan IRL 6 D6
Ballyfarnon IRL 6 D6
Ballyfeard IRL 8 E6

Ballyferriter IRL 8 D2
Ballyforan IRL 6 F6
Ballygar IRL 6 E6
Ballygarrett IRL 9 C10
Ballygawley GB 7 D8
Ballygeary IRL 9 D10
Ballyglass IRL 6 E5
Ballygorman IRL 4 E2
Ballygowan GB 7 C11
Ballyhaise IRL 7 D8
Ballyhalbert GB 7 D12
Ballyhale IRL 9 D8
Ballyhaunis IRL 6 E5
Ballyhean IRL 6 E4
Ballyheigue IRL 8 D3
Ballyjamesduff IRL 7 E8
Ballykeeran IRL 7 F7
Ballykelly GB 4 E2
Ballykilleen IRL 7 F8
Ballylanders IRL 8 D6
Ballylaneen IRL 9 D8
Ballylickey IRL 8 E4
Ballyliffen IRL 4 E2
Ballyliffin IRL 4 E2
Ballylynan IRL 9 C8
Ballymacarberry IRL 9 D7
Ballymacmague IRL 9 D7
Ballymadog IRL 9 E7
Ballymagorry GB 4 F2
Ballymahon IRL 7 E7
Ballymakeery IRL 8 E4
Ballymartin GB 7 D11
Ballymena GB 4 F4
Ballymoney GB 4 E3
Ballymore IRL 7 F7
Ballymote IRL 6 D5
Ballymurphy IRL 9 C9
Ballymurry IRL 6 E6
Ballynacally IRL 8 C4
Ballynafid IRL 7 E8
Ballynahinch GB 7 D11
Ballynahowen IRL 7 F7
Ballynakill IRL 7 F7
Ballynamona IRL 8 D5
Ballyneaner GB 4 F2
Ballynunty IRL 9 C7
Ballynure GB 4 F5
Ballyporeen IRL 8 D6
Ballyragget IRL 9 C8
Ballyroan IRL 9 C8
Ballyronan GB 4 F3
Ballyshannon IRL 6 C6
Ballyvaldon IRL 9 D10
Ballyvaughan IRL 6 F4
Ballyvoy GB 4 E4
Ballyvoyle IRL 9 D7
Ballywalter GB 7 C12
Ballyward GB 7 D10
Balma F 33 C9
Balmaha GB 4 C7
Balmaseda E 40 B5
Balmazújváros H 151 B7
Balme I 31 E11
Balmedie GB 3 L12
Balmuccia I 68 B5
Balnacra GB 2 L6
Balnapaling GB 3 K8
Balneario de Panticosa Huesca E 32 E5
Balninkai LT 135 F10
Balocco I 68 C5
Balogunyom H 149 B7
Balot F 25 E11
Balotaszállás H 150 E4
Baloteşti RO 161 D8
Balow D 83 D11
Balrath IRL 7 E10
Balş RO 160 E4
Balşa RO 151 E11
Balsa de Ves E 47 F10
Balsa Pintada E 56 F2
Balsareny E 43 D7
Balsfjord N 111 B17
Balsicas E 56 F3
Balsjö S 107 D16
Balsorano I 62 D5
Bålsta S 99 C9
Balsthal CH 27 F8
Balta RO 159 D10
Balta UA 154 B5
Balta Albă RO 161 C10
Balta Berilovac SRB 164 C5
Balta Doamnei RO 161 D8
Baltanás E 40 E3
Baltar E 38 E4
Baltasound GB 3 D15
Bălţăteşti RO 153 C8
Bălţaţi RO 153 C10
Bălteni RO 153 D11
Bălteni RO 159 D11
Baltezers LV 135 B8
Bălţi MD 153 B11
Baltimore IRL 8 F4
Baltinava LV 133 C3
Baltinglass IRL 9 C9
Baltiysk RUS 139 A8
Baltmuiža LV 135 D13
Baltoji Vokė LT 137 E11
Baltora S 99 C11
Bałtów PL 143 D12
Baltray IRL 7 E10
Băluşeni RO 153 B9
Balvan BG 166 C4
Bălvăneşti RO 159 D10
Balvano I 60 B5
Balve D 17 F9
Balvi LV 133 B2
Balvicar GB 4 C5
Balya TR 173 E8
Balzers FL 71 C9
Bamberg D 75 C8
Bamburgh GB 5 D13
Bammental D 21 F11
Bampini GR 174 B3
Bampton GB 13 B11
Bampton GB 13 D8
Bana H 149 A9
Banafjäl S 107 E16
Banagher IRL 7 F7
Banarli TR 173 B7
Banassac F 34 B5
Banatski Brestovac SRB 159 D6
Banatski Dvor SRB 158 B6
Banatski Karlovac SRB 159 C7
Banatsko Aranđelovo SRB 150 E5
Banatsko Karađorđevo SRB 158 B6
Banatsko Novo Selo SRB 159 D6
Banatsko Veliko Selo SRB 150 F6
Banbridge GB 7 D10
Banbury GB 13 A12
Banca RO 153 E11
Banchory GB 3 A12
Band RO 152 D4
Bande E 38 D4
Bandenitz D 83 D10
Bandholm DK 83 A10
Bandirma TR 173 D8
Bandol F 35 D10
Bandon IRL 8 E5
Bandurove UA 154 A5
Băneasa RO 153 F11
Băneasa RO 155 E1
Băneasa RO 161 E8
Băneşti MD 154 B2
Băneşti RO 161 C7
Banevo BG 167 D8
Banff GB 3 K11
Bångnäs S 106 B9
Bangor GB 4 F5
Bangor GB 10 E3
Bangor IRL 6 D3
Bangor Erris IRL 6 D3
Bangsund N 105 C10
Banham GB 15 C11
Bánhorváti H 145 G2
Bănia RO 159 D9
Banie PL 85 D7
Banie Mazurskie PL 136 E5
Baniska BG 166 C5
Bănişor RO 151 C10
Băniţa RO 159 C11
Banite BG 171 A8
Banitsa BG 165 C8
Banja BIH 158 F3
Banja SRB 163 B8
Banja Lučica BIH 157 D10
Banja Luka BIH 157 C7
Banjani SRB 158 D4
Banja Vrućia BIH 157 C8
Bankekind S 92 C7
Bankeryd S 92 D4
Bankfoot GB 5 B9
Bankya BG 165 D6
Bankya BG 165 D7
Banloc RO 159 C7
Bannalec F 22 E4
Bannay F 25 F8
Bannesdorf auf Fehmarn D 83 B10
Bannewitz D 80 E5
Bannivka UA 155 B3
Bannockburn GB 5 C9
Bañobárez E 45 C7
Bañón E 47 C10
Banon F 35 B10
Baños de la Encina E 54 C5
Baños de Molgas E 38 D4
Baños de Montemayor E 45 D9
Baños de Río Tobía E 40 D6
Baños de Valdearados E 40 E4
Bánov CZ 146 D5
Bánov SK 146 E6
Banova Jaruga HR 149 F7
Bánovce nad Bebravou SK 146 D6
Banoviči BIH 157 D10
Bánréve H 145 G1
Bansin D 84 C6
Banská Belá SK 147 E7
Banská Bystrica SK 147 D8
Banská Štiavnica SK 147 E7
Banské SK 145 F4
Bansko BG 165 F7
Bant NL 16 C5
Banteer IRL 8 D5
Banteln D 78 B6
Bantheville F 19 F11
Bantry IRL 8 E4
Banya BG 165 D10
Banya BG 165 E9
Banya BG 165 F8
Banya BG 166 D5
Banya BG 167 D9
Banyalbufar E 49 E10
Banyeres de Mariola E 56 D3
Banyliv UA 152 A6
Banyliv-Pidhirnyy UA 152 A7
Banyoles E 43 C9
Banyuls-sur-Mer F 34 F5
Banzi I 60 B6
Banzkow D 83 C11
Bapaume F 18 D6
Bar MNE 163 E7
Bara RO 151 F8
Bara RO 153 C10
Bara S 87 D12
Barabás H 145 G5
Baracska H 149 B11
Bărăganul RO 161 D11
Baragiano I 60 B5
Barahona E 41 F6
Barajas de Melo E 47 D7
Barajevo SRB 158 D5
Barakaldo E 40 B6
Barakovo BG 165 E7
Baralla E 38 C5
Barañain E 32 E2
Baranbio E 40 B6
Báránd H 151 C7
Baranello I 63 D7
Baranjsko Petrovo Selo HR 149 E10
Barano d'Ischia I 62 F5
Baranów PL 141 G6
Baranów PL 142 D5
Baranowo PL 139 D11
Baranów Sandomierska PL 143 F12
Barão de São João P 50 E2
Baraolt RO 153 E7
Baraqueville F 33 B10
Barásoain E 32 E2
Barassie GB 4 D7
Bărăşti RO 160 D5
Baravukha BY 133 E5
Barbacena P 51 B5
Barbadás E 38 D4
Barbadillo de Herreros E 40 D5
Barbadillo del Mercado E 40 D5
Barbadillo del Pez E 40 D5
Barban HR 67 B9
Barbarano Vicentino I 66 B4
Barbaraville GB 3 K8
Barbaros TR 173 C7
Barbaste F 33 B6
Barbastro E 42 C4
Barbat HR 67 C10
Barbate de Franco E 52 D5
Bărbăteşcu RO 161 D9
Bărbăteşti RO 160 D3
Barbatovac SRB 164 C3
Barbâtre F 28 B1
Bārbele LV 135 D9
Barbentane F 35 C8
Barberá del Vallès E 43 D8
Barberaz F 31 D8
Barberino di Mugello I 66 D3
Barbezieux-St-Hilaire F 28 E5
Barbonne-Fayel F 25 C10
Bărbuleţu RO 160 C6
Barbullush AL 163 F8
Barby (Elbe) D 79 C10
Barç AL 168 C4
Barca E 41 F6
Bârca RO 160 F3
Barcabo E 42 C4
Barcada BIH 157 B8
Barca de Alva P 45 B7
Bărcăneşti RO 161 D8
Bărcăneşti RO 161 D9
Barcani RO 161 B8
Barcarrota E 51 B6
Barcea RO 153 F10
Barcelinhos P 38 E2
Barcellona Pozzo di Gotto I 59 C7
Barcelona E 43 E8
Barcelonne-du-Gers F 32 C5
Barcelonnette F 36 C5
Barcelos P 38 E2
Bárcena del Monasterio E 39 B6
Bárcena de Pie de Concha E 40 B3
Barcenillas de Cerezos E 40 B4
Barchfeld D 79 E7
Barciany PL 136 E3
Barcillonnette F 35 B10
Barcin PL 138 E4
Barcino PL 85 B11
Barcis I 72 D6
Barcones E 40 F6
Barcos P 44 B5
Barcs H 149 E8
Barcus F 32 D4
Barczewo PL 136 F2
Bardal N 108 D5
Bardar MD 154 D3
Barde DK 86 C3
Bardejov SK 145 E3
Bárdena E 41 D9
Bardenitz D 80 B3
Bårdesø DK 86 D6
Bardi I 69 D8
Bardineto I 37 C8
Bardney GB 11 E11
Bardo PL 77 B11
Bardolino I 66 A2
Bardonecchia I 31 E10
Bardos F 32 D3
Bardowick D 83 D8
Bardsea GB 10 C5
Bárdudvarnok H 149 D9
Bare BIH 157 E10
Bare SRB 158 E6
Bare SRB 163 C8
Barefield IRL 8 C5
Barèges F 33 E6
Barenburg D 17 C11
Barendorf D 83 D9
Bärenklau D 81 C7
Bärenstein D 76 B4
Bärenstein D 80 E5
Barentin F 18 E2
Barenton F 23 C10
Barevo BIH 157 D7
Barfleur F 23 A9
Barga I 66 D1
Bargagli I 37 C10
Bargas E 46 E4
Bărgăuani RO 153 D9
Barge I 31 F11
Bargemon F 36 D5
Bargen CH 27 E10
Bargenstedt D 82 B6
Barghe I 69 B9
Bârghiş RO 152 F5
Bargischow D 84 C5
Bargłów Kościelny PL 140 C7
Bargoed GB 13 B8
Bargrennan GB 4 E7
Bargstedt D 17 B12
Bargteheide D 83 C8
Bargullas AL 168 C3
Barham GB 15 E11
Bar Hill GB 15 C9
Bari I 61 A7
Barić Draga HR 156 D3
Barile I 60 B5
Barilović HR 148 F5
Barinas E 56 E2
Båring DK 86 E5
Bari Sardo I 64 D4
Barisciano I 62 C5
Barjac F 35 B7
Bårjasnjar'ga N 113 D15
Barjols F 35 C11
Barkåkar N 95 D12
Barkåkra S 87 C11
Barkald N 101 C13
Barkarö S 98 C7
Barkava LV 135 C13
Barkelsby D 83 A7
Barkhyttan S 103 E11
Barkowo PL 85 C12
Barkston GB 11 F10
Bârla RO 160 E5
Bârlad RO 153 E11
Barleben D 79 B10
Bar-le-Duc F 26 C3
Barles F 36 C4
Barletta I 60 A6
Barley GB 15 C9
Barlinek PL 85 E8
Barlingbo S 93 D12
Barmouth GB 10 F3
Barmstedt D 82 C7
Bárna H 147 E9
Barna IRL 6 F4
Bârna RO 159 B9
Barnaderg IRL 6 F5
Barnard Castle GB 11 B8
Barnarp S 92 D4
Barnatra IRL 6 D3
Bärnau D 75 C11
Barnbach A 73 B11
Barneberg D 79 B9
Barneveld NL 16 D5
Barneville-Carteret F 23 B8
Barnewitz D 79 A12
Barneycarroll IRL 6 E5
Barnoldswick GB 11 D7
Bârnova RO 153 C11
Barnowko PL 85 E7
Barnsley GB 11 D9
Barnstädt D 79 D10
Barnstaple GB 12 C6
Barnstorf D 17 C11
Barntrup D 17 E12
Baronissi I 60 B3
Baronville F 26 C6
Baroševac SRB 158 E5
Barovo NMK 169 B7
Barowka BY 133 E3
Barqueros E 55 D10
Barr F 27 D7
Barr GB 4 E7
Barracas E 48 D3
Barrachina E 47 C10
Barraduff IRL 8 D4
Barrafranca I 58 E5
Barral E 38 D3
Barrali I 64 E3
Barranco do Velho P 50 E4
Barrancos P 51 C6
Barranda E 55 C9
Barrapoll GB 4 C3
Barrax E 55 A8
Barre-des-Cévennes F 35 B6
Barreiro P 50 B1
Bärrek S 98 B7
Barrême F 36 D4
Barrhead GB 5 D8
Barrhill GB 4 E7
Barriada Nueva E 43 D8
Bàrrio P 38 E2
Barrio del Peral E 56 F3
Barrio Mar E 48 E4
Barrit DK 86 D5
Barr na Trá IRL 6 D3
Barroca P 44 D5
Barroselas P 38 E2
Barrowby GB 11 F10
Barrow-in-Furness GB 10 C5
Barruecopardo E 45 B7
Barruelo de Santullan E 40 C3
Barry GB 13 C8
Barry IRL 7 E7
Bârsa RO 151 E9
Barsac F 32 A5
Bârsana RO 145 H9
Bârsău RO 151 B11
Barsbüttel D 83 C8
Bårse DK 87 E9
Barsele S 107 A12
Bârseşti RO 153 F9
Barsinghausen D 78 B5
Barßel D 17 B9
Barsta S 103 A15
Barstyčiai LT 134 D3
Bar-sur-Aube F 25 D12
Bar-sur-Seine F 25 D11
Bārta LV 134 D2
Bartenheim F 27 E7
Bartenstein D 74 D6
Barth D 83 B13
Bartholomä D 74 E6
Bartholomäberg A 71 C9
Bartkuškiai LT 135 F9
Bartkuškis LT 137 D10
Bartnes N 105 C10
Bartniki PL 139 D10
Bartninkai LT 136 E7
Barton GB 10 D6
Barton-upon-Humber GB 11 D11
Bartoszyce PL 136 E2
Baru RO 159 C11
Baruchowo PL 139 F7
Barulho P 45 F6
Barumini I 64 D3
Baruth D 80 B5
Barvas GB 2 J3
Barvaux B 19 D11
Barver D 17 C11
Barwedel D 79 A8
Barwice PL 85 C10
Barxeta E 56 C4
Bârza RO 160 E4
Bárzana E 39 B8
Bârzava RO 151 E9
Barzio I 69 B7
Bašaid SRB 158 B5
Basarabeasca MD 154 E3
Basarabi RO 155 E2
Basarbovo BG 161 F7
Bàscara E 43 C9
Bascharage L 20 E5
Baschi I 62 B2
Baschurch GB 10 F6
Basciano I 62 B5
Basconcillos del Tozo E 40 C4
Bascons F 32 C5
Bascous F 33 C6
Bascov RO 160 D5
Basdahl D 17 B12
Basècles B 19 C8
Basel CH 27 E8
Baselga di Pinè I 69 A11
Baselice I 60 A3
Bas-en-Basset F 30 E5
Băseşti RO 151 C11
Båsheim N 95 B10
Bashtanivka UA 154 F4
Basigo E 40 B6
Basildon GB 15 D9
Basiliano I 73 D7
Basingstoke GB 13 C12
Baška CZ 146 B6
Baška HR 67 C10
Baška Voda HR 157 F6
Baskemölla S 88 D6
Bäsksele S 107 B11
Bäsksjö S 107 B12
Basksjön S 107 E12
Baslow GB 11 E8
Bäsna S 97 A13
Bassacutena I 64 A3
Bassano del Grappa I 72 E4
Bassano Romano I 62 C2
Bassecourt CH 27 F7
Basse-Goulaine F 23 F9
Bassenge B 19 C12
Bassens F 28 F4
Bassiano I 62 D4
Bassoues F 33 C6
Bassum D 17 C11
Bassy F 31 D8
Bast FIN 123 C10
Båstad S 87 C11
Bastardo I 62 B3
Bastasi BIH 156 D5
Bastasi BIH 157 F10
Bastelica F 37 G10
Bastelicaccia F 37 H9
Bastennes F 32 C4
Bastfallet S 98 B7
Bastia F 37 F10
Bastia I 62 A3
Bastogne B 19 D12
Bastorf D 83 B11
Basttjärn S 97 B12
Bastumarks by S 118 E3
Bastuträsk S 107 C16
Bastuträsk S 118 E4
Báta H 149 D11
Bata RO 151 E9
Batajnica SRB 158 D5
Batak BG 165 F9
Batalha P 44 E3
Băţani RO 153 E7
Batăr RO 151 D8
Bătarci RO 145 G7
Båtas S 106 B8
Bátaszék H 149 D11
Batea E 42 E4
Batelov CZ 77 D8
Båteng N 113 C20
Baterno E 54 B3
Batetskiy RUS 132 D7
Bath GB 13 C10
Bathford GB 13 C10
Bathgate GB 5 D9
Bathmen NL 16 D6
Batin BG 161 F7
Batina HR 149 E11
Batizovce SK 145 E1
Batković BIH 158 D3
Batley GB 11 D8
Batllavë RKS 164 D3
Bátmonostor H 150 E2
Båtnfjordsøra N 100 A7
Batočina SRB 159 E7
Bátonyterenye H 147 F9
Bátorove Kosihy SK 146 F6
Batoş RO 152 D5
Batoshevo BG 166 D4
Bátovce SK 147 E7
Batovo BG 167 C9
Batrina HR 157 B8
Båtsfjord N 114 B7
Batsi GR 176 D4
Båtsjaur S 109 D13
Båtskärsnäs S 119 C10
Battenberg (Eder) D 21 B11
Bätterkinden CH 27 F8
Battice B 183 D7
Battipaglia I 60 B3
Battle GB 15 F9
Battonya H 151 E7
Batultsi BG 165 C9
Bátya H 150 E2
Batyatychi UA 144 C9
Batz-sur-Mer F 22 F7
Baucina I 58 D4
Baud F 22 E5
Bauduen F 36 D4
Bauen CH 71 D7
Baugé F 23 E11
Baugy F 25 F8
Bauladu I 64 C2
Baulon F 23 E8
Baume-les-Dames F 26 F5
Baumholder D 186 B3
Baunach D 75 C8
Baunei I 64 C4
Baurci MD 154 E3
Bausendorf D 21 D7
Bauska LV 135 D8
Băuţar RO 159 B10
Bautzen D 80 D6
Bavanište SRB 159 D6
Bavay F 19 D8
Bavel NL 182 B5
Baveno I 68 B6
Bavilliers F 27 E6
Bavorov CZ 76 D6
Bawdeswell GB 15 B11
Bawdsey GB 15 C11
Bawinkel D 17 C8
Bawn Cross Roads IRL 8 D5
Bayárcal E 55 E7
Bayarque E 55 E8
Baybuzivka UA 154 A5
Baye F 25 C10
Bayel F 25 D12
Bayerbach D 76 F4
Bayerbach bei Ergoldsbach D 75 E11
Bayerisch Eisenstein D 76 D4
Bayeux F 23 B10
Bayindir TR 177 C10
Bayir TR 181 B8
Bayirköy TR 172 D6
Baykal BG 160 F4
Bayon F 26 D5
Bayonne F 32 D3
Bayramiç TR 172 E6
Bayramiç TR 173 C6
Bayramli TR 173 B6
Bayreuth D 75 C10
Bayrischzell D 72 A5
Bayston Hill GB 10 F6
Baytaly UA 154 B5
Bayubas de Abajo E 40 E6
Baza E 55 D7
Bázakerettye H 149 C7
Bazas F 32 B5
Bazet F 33 D6
Baziège F 33 D9
Bazillac F 33 D6
Bazna RO 152 E4
Bazoches F 25 F10
Bazoches-au-Houlme F 23 C11
Bazoches-les-Gallerandes F 24 D7
Bazoches-sur-Hoëne F 24 C3
Bazougers F 23 D10
Bazouges F 23 E10
Bazzano I 66 D3
Beaconsfield GB 15 D7
Beadnell GB 5 D13
Beagh IRL 6 E5
Bealach A Doirín IRL 6 E5
Bealach Conglais IRL 9 C9
Bealach Feich IRL 7 C7
Bealaclugga IRL 6 F4
Béal an Átha IRL 6 D4
Béal an Mhuirthead IRL 6 D3
Béal Átha an Ghaorthaidh IRL 8 E4
Béal Átha Beithe IRL 7 D9
Béal Átha hAmhnais IRL 6 E5
Béal Átha Liag IRL 7 E7
Béal Átha na Muice IRL 6 E5
Béal Átha na Sluaighe IRL 6 F6
Béal Átha Seanaidh IRL 6 C6
Béal Deirg IRL 6 D3
Béal Easa IRL 6 E4
Bealnablath IRL 8 E5
Beaminster GB 13 D9
Beamud E 47 D9
Beanchar IRL 7 F7
Beantraí IRL 8 E4
Beariz E 38 D3
Bearna IRL 6 F4
Bearsden GB 5 D8
Beas E 51 E6
Beasain E 32 D1
Beas de Granada E 53 B10
Beas de Segura E 55 C7
Beateberg S 92 B4
Beattock GB 5 E10
Beaucaire F 35 C8
Beaucamps-le-Vieux F 18 E4
Beauchastel F 30 F6
Beaucouzé F 23 F10
Beaufay F 24 D3
Beaufort F 31 B7
Beaufort F 31 D10
Beaufort IRL 8 D3
Beaufort-en-Vallée F 23 F11
Beaugency F 24 E6
Beaujeu F 30 C6
Beaujeu F 36 C4
Beaujeu-St-Vallier-Pierrejux-et-Quitteur F 26 E4
Beaulieu F 35 C7
Beaulieu-lès-Loches F 24 F5
Beaulieu-sur-Dordogne F 29 F9
Beaulieu-sur-Loire F 25 E8
Beaulon F 30 B4
Beauly GB 2 L8
Beaumarchés F 33 C6
Beaumaris GB 10 E3
Beaumesnil F 24 B4
Beaumetz-lès-Loges F 18 D6
Beaumont B 19 D9
Beaumont F 23 A8
Beaumont F 29 B6
Beaumont F 29 F7
Beaumont-de-Lomagne F 33 C7
Beaumont-de-Pertuis F 35 C10
Beaumont-en-Argonne F 19 E11
Beaumont-en-Véron F 23 F12
Beaumont-le-Roger F 24 B4
Beaumont-lès-Valence F 30 F6
Beaumont-sur-Oise F 25 B7
Beaumont-sur-Sarthe F 23 D12
Beaune F 30 A6
Beaune-La Rolande F 25 D7
Beaupréau F 23 F10
Beauquesne F 18 D5
Beauraing B 19 D10
Beaurepaire F 31 E7
Beaurepaire-en-Bresse F 31 B7
Beaurières F 35 A10
Beausite F 26 C3
Beausoleil F 37 D6
Beautor F 19 E7
Beauvais F 18 F5
Beauval F 18 D5
Beauvezer F 36 C5
Beauville F 33 B7
Beauvoir-sur-Mer F 28 B1
Beauvoir-sur-Niort F 28 C5
Beauzac F 30 E5
Beauzelle F 33 C8
Beba Veche RO 150 E5
Bebertal D 79 B9
Bebington GB 10 E5
Bebra D 78 E6
Bebrene LV 135 D12
Bebrina HR 157 B8
Beccles GB 15 C12
Becedas E 45 D9
Beceite E 42 F4
Bečej SRB 158 B5
Beceni RO 161 C9
Becerreá E 38 C5
Becerril de Campos E 39 D10
Becherbach D 186 B4
Bécherel F 23 D8
Bechet RO 160 F3
Bechhofen D 21 F8
Bechhofen D 75 D8
Bechlín CZ 76 B6
Bechtheim D 21 E10
Bechyně CZ 77 D6
Becicherecu Mic RO 151 F7
Bečići MNE 163 E6
Becilla de Valderaduey E 39 D9
Beçin TR 181 B7
Beckdorf D 82 D7
Beckedorf D 17 D12
Beckeln D 17 C11
Beckingen D 21 F7
Beckingham GB 11 E10
Beckov SK 146 D5
Beckum D 17 E10
Beclean RO 152 C5
Beclean RO 152 F5
Bécon-les-Granits F 23 F10
Bečov CZ 76 B5
Becsehely H 149 D7
Becsvölgye H 149 C7
Bečváry CZ 77 C8
Bedale GB 11 C8
Bédar E 55 E9
Bédarieux F 34 C5
Bédarrides F 35 B8
Bedburg D 21 C7
Bedburg-Hau D 183 B8
Beddgelert GB 10 E3
Beddingestrand S 87 E12
Bédée F 23 D8
Bedekovčina HR 148 D5
Beden BG 165 F9
Beder DK 86 C6
Bedford GB 15 C8
Bedihošť CZ 77 D12
Będków PL 143 C8
Bedlington GB 5 E13
Bedlno PL 143 B8
Bedmar E 53 A10
Bednja HR 148 D5
Bédoin F 35 B9
Bedollo I 69 A11
Bedonia I 37 B11
Bedous F 32 D4
Bedsted DK 86 E4
Bedsted Stationsby DK 86 B2
Béduer F 33 A9
Bedum NL 17 B7
Bedwas GB 13 B8
Bedworth GB 13 A12
Będzin PL 143 F7
Będzino PL 85 B9
Beedenbostel D 79 A7
Beeford GB 11 D11
Beek NL 16 E5
Beek NL 16 E5
Beek NL 183 D7
Beekbergen NL 183 A7
Beelitz D 80 B3
Beendorf D 79 B9
Beenz D 84 D4
Beerfelden D 21 E11
Beernem B 19 B7
Beers NL 16 E5
Beerse B 16 F3
Beersel B 19 C9
Beerst B 182 C1
Beerta NL 17 B8
Beesd NL 183 B6
Beesenstedt D 79 C10
Beeskow D 80 B6
Beesten D 17 D9
Beeston GB 11 F9
Beetsterzwaag NL 16 B6
Beetzendorf D 83 E10
Bégaar F 32 C4
Bégadan F 28 E4
Begaljica SRB 158 D6
Bégard F 22 C5
Begejci SRB 158 B6
Begendik TR 172 C6
Begíjar E 53 A9
Begijnendijk B 19 B10
Beglezh BG 165 C10
Begnište NMK 169 B6
Begonte E 38 B4
Begur E 43 D10
Behramkale TR 171 F10
Behren-lès-Forbach F 27 B6
Behren-Lübchin D 83 B13
Behringen D 79 D8
Beica de Jos RO 152 D5
Beidaud RO 155 D3
Beierfeld D 79 E12
Beierstedt D 79 B8
Beilen NL 17 C7
Beilngries D 75 D9
Beilstein D 27 B11
Beimerstetten D 187 E8
Beinasco I 37 A7
Beinette I 37 C7
Beinwil CH 27 F9
Beirã P 44 F6
Beisfjord N 111 D14
Beisland N 90 C3
Beith GB 4 D7
Beitostølen N 101 D9
Beitstad N 105 C10
Beiuş RO 151 D9
Beja LV 133 B2
Beja P 50 C4
Bejar AL 168 D2
Béjar E 45 D9
Bejís E 48 E3
Bekecs H 145 G3
Békés H 151 D7
Békéscsaba H 151 D7
Békéssámson H 150 E6
Békésszentandrás H 150 D5
Bekkarfjord N 113 B19
Bekken N 101 C15
Bekkevoll N 114 D8
Belá SK 147 C7
Bélâbre F 29 B8
Bela Crkva SRB 159 D7
Beladice SK 146 E6
Belá-Dulice SK 147 C7
Belalcázar E 51 B9
Belá nad Cirochou SK 145 F5
Bělá nad Radbuzou CZ 75 C12
Belanovce NMK 164 E4
Belanovica SRB 158 E5
Bela Palanka SRB 164 C5
Bélapátfalva H 145 G1
Bělá pod Bezdězem CZ 77 A7
Bělá pod Pradědem CZ 77 B12
Belascoáin E 32 E2
Belauski LV 133 C2
Belava LV 135 B13
Belazaima do Chão P 44 C4
Belcaire F 33 E9
Belcastel F 33 B10
Belceşti RO 153 C10
Bełchatów PL 143 D7
Belchin BG 165 E7
Belchite E 41 F10
Bělčice CZ 76 C5
Belciugatele RO 161 E8
Belclare IRL 6 F5
Belcoo GB 7 D7
Belderg IRL 6 D3
Beldibi TR 181 C8
Beled H 149 B8
Belegiš SRB 158 C5
Belej HR 67 C9
Belene BG 160 F6
Bélesta F 33 E9
Beleţi-Negreşti RO 160 D6
Belevi TR 177 C9
Belezna H 149 D7
Belfast GB 7 C11
Belfeld NL 16 F6
Belford GB 5 D13
Belfort F 27 E6
Belfort-du-Quercy F 33 B9
Belforte del Chienti I 67 F7
Belgern D 80 D4
Belgershain D 79 D12
Belgioioso I 69 C7
Belgodère F 37 F10
Belgooly IRL 8 E6
Belgun BG 155 F2
Belhomert-Guéhouville F 24 C5
Beli HR 67 B9
Belianes E 42 D6
Belica HR 149 D7
Beli Iskŭr BG 165 E8
Beli Izvor BG 165 C7
Beli Manastir HR 149 E11
Belin RO 153 F7
Belin-Béliet F 32 B4
Belinchón E 47 D6
Belinţ RO 151 F8
Beli Potok SRB 164 B5
Beliş RO 151 D11
Belišće HR 149 E10
Belitsa BG 161 F9
Belitsa BG 165 D8
Belitsa BG 165 F8
Beliu RO 151 E9
Bělkovice-Laštany CZ 146 B4
Bell D 21 D8
Bell (Hunsrück) D 185 D7
Bella I 60 B5
Bellac F 29 C8
Bellacorick IRL 6 D3
Bellaghy GB 4 F3
Bellaghy IRL 6 E5
Bellagio I 69 B7
Bellahy IRL 6 E5
Bellanicë RKS 163 E10
Bellano I 69 A7

Bellante I 62 B5
Bellaria I 66 D5
Bellavary IRL 6 E4
Bellavista E 51 E8
Bellclaire d'Urgell E 42 D5
Belleek GB 7 D10
Bellegarde F 25 E7
Bellegarde F 35 C8
Bellegarde-en-Marche F 29 D10
Bellegarde-sur-Valserine F 31 C8
Belle-Isle-en-Terre F 22 C5
Bellême F 24 D4
Bellenaves F 30 C3
Bellenberg D 71 A10
Bellencombre F 18 E3
Bellerive-sur-Allier F 30 C3
Belles-Forêts F 27 C6
Belleu F 19 F7
Bellevaux F 31 C10
Belleville F 30 C6
Belleville-sur-Meuse F 26 B3
Belleville-sur-Vie F 28 B3
Bellevue-la-Montagne F 30 E4
Belley F 31 D8
Bellheim D 21 F10
Bellherbe F 26 F6
Bellignat F 31 C8
Bellinge DK 86 E6
Bellingham GB 5 E12
Bellingwolde NL 17 B8
Bellinzago Novarese I 68 B6
Bellinzona CH 69 A7
Bellizzi I 60 B3
Bell-Lloc d'Urgell E 42 D5
Bello E 47 C10
Bellobradë RKS 163 C10
Bellopojë RKS 163 D10
Bellou-en-Houlme F 23 C11
Bellpuig E 42 D6
Bellreguard E 56 D4
Bellshill GB 5 D8
Belluno I 72 D5
Bellver de Cerdanya E 33 F9
Bellvik S 107 C10
Belm D 17 D10
Bélmegyer H 151 D7
Bélmez E 51 C9
Bélmez de la Moraleda E 53 A10
Belmont GB 3 D15
Belmont-de-la-Loire F 30 C5
Belmonte E 39 B7
Belmonte E 47 E7
Belmonte P 45 D6
Belmonte Calabro I 60 E6
Belmonte del Sannio I 63 D6
Belmonte in Sabina I 62 C3
Belmontejo E 47 E8
Belmont-sur-Rance F 34 C4
Belmullet IRL 6 D3
Belo Brdo RKS 163 C10
Beloci MD 154 B4
Belœil B 19 C8
Belogradchik BG 159 F10
Beloiannisz H 149 B11
Belojin SRB 164 C3
Belorado E 40 D5
Beloslav BG 167 C9
Bělotín CZ 146 B5
Belotintsi BG 165 B6
Belovo BG 165 E9
Belozem BG 166 E4
Belp CH 31 B11
Belpasso I 59 D6
Belpech F 33 D9
Belper GB 11 E9
Belsay GB 5 E13
Belsh AL 168 C2
Belsk Duży PL 141 G3
Beltheim D 21 D8
Beltinci SLO 148 C6
Beltiug RO 151 B10
Beltra IRL 6 D5
Beltra IRL 6 E4
Beltrum NL 183 A9
Belturbet IRL 7 D8
Beluša SK 146 C6
Belušić SRB 159 F7
Belvédère-Campomoro F 37 H9
Belvedere Marittimo I 60 D5
Belvedere Ostrense I 67 E7
Belver de Cinca E 42 D4
Belver de los Montes E 39 E9
Belvès F 29 F8
Belvèze-du-Razès F 33 D10
Belvì I 64 D3
Belville IRL 6 D4
Belvís de la Jara E 46 E3
Belz F 22 E5
Belz UA 144 C9
Bełżec PL 144 C7
Bełżyce PL 141 H6
Bembibre E 38 B2
Bembibre E 39 C7
Bemmel NL 16 E5
Bemposta P 39 F7
Bemposta P 44 F4
Bempton GB 11 C11
Benabarre E 42 C4
Benacazón E 51 E7
Benahadux E 55 F8
Benahavís E 53 C6
Benalmádena E 53 C7
Benalúa de Guadix E 55 E6
Benalúa de las Villas E 53 B9
Benalup de Sidonia E 52 D5
Benamargosa E 53 C8
Benamaurel E 55 D7
Benamejí E 53 B7
Benamocarra E 53 C8
Benaocaz E 53 C6
Benaoján E 53 C6
Benasal E 48 D4
Benasau E 56 D4
Benasque E 33 E7
Benassay F 28 B6
Benatae E 55 C7
Benátky nad Jizerou CZ 77 B7
Benavente E 39 D8
Benavente P 50 B2
Benavides de Orbigo E 39 D8
Benavila P 44 F5
Benburb GB 7 D9
Bencatel P 50 B5
Bendorf D 21 D9
Bēne LV 134 D6
Benecko CZ 81 E9
Beneden-Leeuwen NL 16 E4
Benediktbeuren D 72 A3
Benedita P 44 F3
Benegiles E 39 E8
Bénéjacq F 32 D5
Benejama E 56 D3
Benejúzar E 56 E3
Benesat RO 151 C11
Benešov CZ 77 C7
Benešov nad Černou CZ 77 E7
Benešov nad Ploučnicí CZ 80 E6
Bénesse-Maremne F 32 C3
Benestare I 59 C9
Bénestroff F 27 C6
Benet F 28 C4
Benetutti I 64 C3
Bene Vagienna I 37 B7
Bénévent-l'Abbaye F 29 C9
Benevento I 60 A3
Benfeld F 27 D8
Benfica do Ribatejo P 44 F3
Bengești-Ciocadia RO 160 C3
Bengtsfors S 91 A11
Bengtsheden S 103 E10
Benia de Onís E 39 B10
Beniarbeig E 56 D5
Beniarrés E 56 D4
Beničanci HR 149 E10
Benicarló E 48 D5
Benicasim E 48 D5
Benidorm E 56 D4
Beniel E 56 E3
Benifaió E 48 F4
Benifallet E 42 F5
Benifallim E 56 D4
Benigánim E 56 D4
Benilloba E 56 D4
Benissa E 56 D5
Benissanet E 42 E5
Benitachell E 56 D5
Benitses GR 168 E2
Benizalón E 55 E8
Benizar y la Tercia E 55 C9
Benken CH 27 F11
Benkovac HR 156 D4
Benkovski BG 161 F10
Benkovski BG 171 B8
Benllech GB 10 E3
Benlloch E 48 D5
Bennebroek NL 182 A5
Bennekom NL 183 A7
Bennewitz D 79 D12
Bennungen D 79 D9
Bénodet F 22 E3
Benquerença P 45 D6
Benquerenças P 44 E5
Benquerencia de la Serena E 51 B9
Benquet F 32 C4
Bensafrim P 50 E2
Bensbyn S 118 C8
Bensdorf D 79 B11
Benshausen D 79 E8
Bensheim D 21 E11
Bensjö S 103 A9
Benson GB 13 B12
Bentelo NL 17 D7
Bentivoglio I 66 C3
Bentley GB 11 D9
Bentwisch D 83 B12
Bentzin D 84 C4
Beňuš SK 147 D9
Benzingerode D 79 C8
Beočin SRB 158 C4
Beograd SRB 158 D5
Bera de Bidasoa E 32 D2
Beragh GB 7 C8
Berane MNE 163 D8
Beranga E 40 B4
Berango E 40 B6
Berantevilla E 40 C6
Berat AL 168 C2
Bérat F 33 D8
Beratzhausen D 75 D10
Berbegal E 42 D3
Berbești RO 160 C3
Berca RO 161 C9
Bercedo E 40 B5
Bercel H 147 F8
Berceni RO 161 D8
Berceni RO 161 E8
Bercero E 39 E9
Berceto I 69 D8
Berchem B 19 C8
Berchidda I 64 B3
Berching D 75 D9
Berchtesgaden D 73 A7
Bérchules E 55 F6
Bercianos del Páramo E 39 D8
Berck F 15 G12
Bercu RO 145 H6
Berdal N 104 E6
Berdalen N 94 D6
Berducedo E 39 B6
Berdún E 32 E4
Bere Alston GB 12 E6
Beregdaróc H 145 G6
Bereguardo I 69 C7
Berehomet UA 152 A6
Berehove UA 145 G6
Berek HR 149 E7
Berekböszörmény H 151 C8
Berekfürdő H 150 C6
Beremend H 149 E10
Berești RO 153 E11
Berești-Meria RO 153 E11
Berești-Tazlău RO 153 E9
Berettyóújfalu H 151 C8
Berevoești RO 160 C5
Berezeni RO 154 E2
Berezyne UA 154 E4
Berg D 71 B9
Berg D 75 B10
Berg D 183 D9
Berg L 20 E6
Berg N 96 B7
Berg N 108 F3
Berg N 111 B13
Berg NL 19 C12
Berg NL 183 D7
Berg S 92 C8
Berg S 102 A7
Berg S 107 E10
Berg (Pfalz) D 27 C9
Berga D 79 D9
Berga D 79 E11
Berga E 43 C7
Berga S 89 A10
Bergagård S 87 B11
Bergaland N 94 D4
Bergama TR 177 A9
Bergamo I 69 B8
Bergantino I 66 B3
Bergara E 32 D1
Bergasa E 32 F1
Bergatreute D 71 B9
Berg bei Neumarkt in der Oberpfalz D 75 D9
Bergby S 103 E13
Berge D 17 C9
Berge D 83 D11
Berge E 42 F3
Berge S 102 A8
Berge S 105 D14
Bergeforsen S 103 A13
Bergeggi I 37 C8
Bergen D 73 A6
Bergen D 83 E7
Bergen D 84 B4
Bergen N 94 B2
Bergen NL 16 C3
Bergen (Dumme) D 83 E9
Bergen op Zoom NL 16 F2
Berger N 95 C12
Bergerac F 29 F6
Bergères-lès-Vertus F 25 C11
Bergesserin F 30 C6
Berget N 108 D6
Bergeyk NL 16 F4
Bergfors S 111 D18
Berghamn S 103 A15
Bergharen NL 183 B7
Berghaupten D 186 E4
Bergheim A 73 A7
Bergheim D 75 E9
Bergheim (Edertal) D 21 B12
Bergheim (Erft) D 21 C7
Berghem NL 16 E5
Berghem S 91 E12
Berghin RO 152 E3
Berghülen D 74 F6
Berg im Drautal A 73 C7
Bergisch Gladbach D 21 C8
Bergkamen D 17 E9
Bergkarlås S 102 D8
Bergkvara S 89 C10
Bergland S 107 A10
Berglia N 105 C15
Bergmo N 112 D7
Bergnäs S 109 E13
Bergnäset S 118 C8
Bergnäsudden S 109 E15
Bergnäsviken S 109 D15
Bergneustadt D 185 B8
Bergö FIN 99 B13
Bergö FIN 122 E6
Bergom S 107 E15
Bergsåker S 103 B13
Bergsäng S 97 B10
Bergsäter S 107 B12
Bergsbyn S 118 E6
Bergschenhoek NL 182 B5
Bergsgården S 103 E10
Bergshamra S 99 C11
Bergsjö S 103 C13
Bergsnov N 105 B9
Bergs slussar S 92 C7
Bergstod N 95 D9
Bergstrøm N 96 D6
Bergsviken S 118 D6
Bergtheim D 75 C7
Bergues F 18 C5
Bergün CH 71 D9
Bergvik S 103 D12
Bergviken S 109 D16
Bergwitz D 79 C12
Berhida H 149 B10
Beringe NL 183 C7
Beringel P 50 C4
Beringen B 19 B11
Berislăvești RO 160 C4
Beriu RO 151 F11
Berja E 55 F7
Berka D 79 E7
Berkåk N 101 A12
Berkel NL 16 E2
Berkel-Enschot NL 16 E4
Berkeley GB 13 B10
Berkenthin D 83 C9
Berkheim D 71 A10
Berkhout NL 16 C4
Berkovići BIH 157 F9
Berkovitsa BG 165 C7
Berlanga E 51 C8
Berlanga de Duero E 40 F6
Berlești RO 160 D3
Berlevåg N 114 B6
Berlicum NL 183 B6
Berlin D 80 A4
Berlingerode D 79 D7
Berliște RO 159 D7
Berlstedt D 79 D9
Bermatingen D 27 E11
Bermeo E 40 B6
Bermillo de Sayago E 39 F7
Bern CH 31 B11
Bernac-Dessus F 33 D6
Bernalda I 61 C7
Bernardos E 46 B4
Bernartice CZ 76 D6
Bernartice CZ 81 E9
Bernāti LV 134 D1
Bernau D 27 E9
Bernau D 84 E5
Bernau am Chiemsee D 72 A5
Bernaville F 18 D5
Bernay F 24 B4
Bernbeuren D 71 B11
Bernburg (Saale) D 79 C10
Berndorf A 77 G10
Berne D 17 B10
Bernecebaráti H 147 E7
Bernedo E 41 C7
Bernhardsthal A 77 E11
Bernhardswald D 75 D11
Bernin F 31 E8
Bernis F 35 C7
Bernisdale GB 2 L4
Bernissart B 19 D8
Bernitt D 83 C11
Bernkastel-Kues D 21 E8
Bernolákovo SK 146 E4
Bernsdorf D 80 D6
Bernshammar S 97 C14
Bernstadt D 74 E7
Bernstadt D 81 D7
Bernsteinstein A 148 B6
Beromünster CH 27 F9
Beronovo BG 167 D7
Beroun CZ 76 C6
Berovo NMK 165 F6
Berra I 66 C4
Berre-l'Étang F 35 D9
Berriedale GB 3 J9
Berrien F 22 D4
Berriozar E 32 E2
Berru F 19 F9
Berry-au-Bac F 19 F8
Bersenbrück D 17 C9
Bershad' UA 154 A5
Beršići SRB 158 E5
Bersone I 69 B10
Bērstele LV 135 D7
Bertamirans E 38 C2
Bertea RO 161 C7
Bertești de Jos RO 155 D1
Bertinoro I 66 D5
Bertnes N 108 B8
Bertogne B 19 D12
Bertrange L 186 B1
Bertrichamps F 27 D6
Bertrix B 19 E11
Běrunice CZ 77 B8
Berveni RO 151 B9
Bērvircava LV 134 D7
Berwick-upon-Tweed GB 5 D12
Bērzaine LV 131 F10
Berzasca RO 159 D8
Bērzaune LV 135 C12
Bērzciems LV 134 B6
Berzence H 149 D8
Bērzgale LV 133 C3
Bērzieši LV 135 D11
Bērzkalne LV 133 B2
Berźniki PL 137 E7
Berzovia RO 159 C8
Bērzpils LV 133 C2
Berzunți RO 153 E9
Beșalma MD 154 E3
Besalú E 43 C9
Besançon F 26 F5
Besande E 39 C10
Bescanó E 43 D9
Beselich-Obertiefenbach D 21 D10
Beseňov SK 146 E6
Besenyőtelek H 150 B5
Besenyszög H 150 C5
Besigheim D 27 C11
Beşiktaş TR 173 B11
Beška SRB 158 C5
Besko PL 145 D4
Besni Fok SRB 158 D5
Besnyő H 149 B11
Besozzo I 68 B6
Bessacarr GB 11 D9
Bessais-le-Fromental F 29 B10
Bessan F 34 D5
Bessay-sur-Allier F 30 C3
Bessbrook GB 7 D10
Besse F 31 E9
Besse-et-St-Anastaise F 30 D2
Bessèges F 35 B7
Bessenbach D 187 B7
Bessé-sur-Braye F 24 E4
Besse-sur-Issole F 36 E4
Bessières F 33 C9
Bessines-sur-Gartempe F 29 C8
Bessude I 64 B2
Best NL 16 E4
Bestensee D 80 B5
Bestorp S 92 C7
Bestwig D 17 F10
Bestwina PL 147 B8
Beszterec H 145 G4
Betanzos E 38 B3
Betelu E 32 D2
Bétera E 48 E4
Beteta E 47 C8
Bethausen RO 151 F8
Betheln D 78 B6
Bethesda GB 10 E3
Bethmale F 33 E8
Bethon F 25 C10
Béthune F 18 C6
Betna N 104 E4
Beton-Bazoches F 25 C9
Betschdorf F 186 D4
Betsele S 107 B15
Bettelainville F 186 C1
Bettembourg L 20 E6
Bettendorf L 20 E6
Bettingen D 20 E6
Bettna S 93 B9
Bettola I 37 B11
Betton F 23 D8
Bettyhill GB 3 H8
Bettystown IRL 7 E10
Betws-y-coed GB 10 E4
Betz F 25 B8
Betygala LT 134 F6
Betz F 25 B8
Betzdorf D 21 C9
Betzdorf L 186 B1
Betzenstein D 75 C9
Betzigau D 71 B10
Beucha D 79 D12
Beuil F 36 C5
Beuningen NL 16 E5
Beuren D 79 D7
Beuron D 27 D10
Beurville F 25 D12
Beuvrages F 182 E2
Beuvry F 18 C6
Beuzeville F 18 F1
Bevagna I 62 B3
Bevaix CH 31 B10
Beveren B 19 B9
Beverley GB 11 D11
Beverlo B 183 C6
Bevern D 78 C5
Beverstedt D 17 B11
Beverungen D 21 A12
Beverwijk NL 16 D3
Béville-le-Comte F 24 D6
Bewdley GB 13 A10
Bex CH 31 C11
Bexbach D 21 F8
Bexhill GB 15 F9
Beyağaç TR 181 B9
Beyazköy TR 173 B8
Beyçayiri TR 173 D6
Beyel TR 173 E10
Beyendorf D 79 B10
Beykoz TR 173 B11
Beynac-et-Cazenac F 29 F8
Beynat F 29 E9
Beynost F 31 D7
Beyoba TR 177 B10
Beyobasi TR 181 C9
Bezas E 47 D10
Bezau A 71 C9
Bezdan SRB 150 F2
Bezdead RO 161 C6
Bezdonys LT 137 D12
Bèze F 26 F3
Bezenye H 146 F4
Bezhanitsy RUS 133 C7
Bezhanovo BG 155 F2
Bezhanovo BG 165 C9
Béziers F 34 D5
Bezledy PL 136 E2
Bezmer BG 161 F10
Bezmer BG 166 E6
Bezouce F 35 C8
Bežovce SK 145 F5
Biadki PL 142 C4
Biała PL 142 F4
Biała-Parcela Pierwsza PL 142 D5
Biała Piska PL 139 C13
Biała Podlaska PL 141 F8
Biała Rawska PL 141 G2
Białe Błota PL 138 D4
Białebłoto-Kobyla PL 139 E12
Białka PL 145 E1
Białobrzegi PL 141 G3
Białogard PL 85 C9
Białośliwie PL 85 D12
Białowieża PL 141 E9
Biały Bór PL 85 C11
Biały Dunajec PL 147 C10
Białystok PL 140 D8
Biancavilla I 59 D6
Bianco I 59 C9
Biandrate I 68 C5
Bians-les-Usiers F 31 B9
Bianzè I 68 C5
Biar E 56 D3
Biarritz F 32 D2
Biarrotte F 32 C3
Biars-sur-Cère F 29 F9
Bias F 32 B3
Bias F 33 B7
Biasca CH 71 E7
Biatorbágy H 149 B11
Bibbiena I 66 E4
Bibbona I 66 F2
Biberach D 27 D9
Biberach an der Riß D 71 A9
Biberbach D 75 E8
Biberist CH 27 F8
Bibinje HR 156 D3
Bibione I 73 E7
Biblis D 21 E10
Bibury GB 13 B11
Bicaz RO 151 C11
Bicaz RO 153 D8
Bicaz-Chei RO 153 D7
Bicazu Ardelean RO 153 D7
Biccari I 60 A4
Bicester GB 13 B12
Bichiș RO 152 E4
Bichl D 72 A3
Bichlbach A 71 C11
Bickleigh GB 13 D7
Bicorp E 48 F3
Bicos P 50 D3
Bicske H 149 A11
Bicton GB 10 F6
Bidache F 32 D3
Bidart F 32 D2
Biddenden GB 15 E10
Biddinghuizen NL 16 D5
Biddulph GB 11 E7
Bideford GB 12 C6
Bidjovagge N 112 E10
Bidos F 32 D4
Bidovce SK 145 F3
Bie S 93 A8
Bieber D 21 D12
Biebesheim am Rhein D 21 E10
Biecz PL 144 D3
Biedenkopf D 21 C11
Biel CH 27 F7
Biel E 32 F4
Bielany-Żyłaki PL 141 F6
Bielawa PL 81 E11
Bielawy PL 143 B8
Bielefeld D 17 D11
Bielice PL 85 D7
Bieliny Kapitulne PL 143 E10
Biella I 68 B5
Bielle F 32 D5
Bielsa E 33 E6
Bielsk PL 139 E8
Bielsko-Biała PL 147 B8
Bielsk Podlaski PL 141 E8
Bienenbüttel D 83 D8
Bieniów PL 81 C8
Bienno I 69 B9
Bienservida E 55 B7
Bienvenida E 51 C7
Bierawa PL 142 F5
Bierdzany PL 142 E5
Bière CH 31 B9
Bierge E 42 C3
Bierné F 23 E10
Biersted DK 86 A5
Biert F 33 E8
Biertan RO 152 E5
Bieruń PL 143 F7
Bierutów PL 142 D4
Bierzwienna-Długa PL 142 B6
Bierzwnik PL 85 D9
Biesaidgohppi N 113 C16
Biescas E 32 E5
Biesenthal D 84 E5
Biesiekierz PL 85 B10
Biesles F 26 D3
Biesowice PL 85 B11
Biessenhofen D 71 B11
Bietigheim D 27 C9
Bietigheim-Bissingen D 27 C11
Bietikow D 84 D5
Bièvre B 19 E11
Bieżuń PL 139 E8
Biga TR 173 D7
Bigadiç TR 173 F9
Biganos F 32 A4
Bigastro E 56 E3
Bigauņciems LV 134 C7
Bigbury-on-Sea GB 13 E7
Biggar GB 5 D9
Biggleswade GB 15 C8
Bignan F 22 E6
Bignasco CH 71 E7
Bigor MNE 163 E7
Bigüézal E 32 E3
Biguglia F 37 F10
Bihać BIH 156 C4
Biharia RO 151 C8
Biharkeresztes H 151 C8
Biharnagybajom H 151 C7
Bihartorda H 151 C7
Biharugra H 151 D8
Bihosava BY 133 E3
Bijela MNE 163 E6
Bijele Poljane MNE 163 D6
Bijeljani BIH 157 F9
Bijeljina BIH 158 D3
Bijelo Brdo HR 149 E11
Bijelo Bucđje BIH 157 D8
Bijelo Polje MNE 163 C8
Biķernieki LV 135 E13
Bikovo SRB 150 F4
Biksēre LV 135 C12
Bílá Lhota CZ 77 C11
Bilalovac BIH 157 D9
Bilbao E 40 B6
Bilbo E 40 B6
Bilbor RO 153 C7
Bilca RO 153 B7
Bilciurești RO 161 D7
Bil'dzyuhi BY 133 F2
Bileća BIH 162 D5
Biled RO 151 F6
Biłgoraj PL 144 B6
Bilicenii Vechi MD 153 B12
Bílina CZ 80 E5
Bilisht AL 168 C4
Biljača SRB 164 E4
Bilje HR 149 E11
Bilky UA 145 G7
Billdal S 91 D10
Billerbeck D 17 E8
Billère F 32 D5
Billericay GB 15 D9
Billesholm S 87 C11
Billiat F 31 C8
Billigheim D 21 F12
Billingham GB 11 B9
Billinghay GB 11 E11
Billingsfors S 91 B11
Billingshurst GB 15 E8
Billom F 30 D3
Billsåsen S 105 F16
Billsbro S 92 A7
Billsta S 107 E15
Billum DK 86 D2
Billund DK 86 D4
Billy F 30 C3
Bilolissya UA 154 F5
Bílovec CZ 146 B6
Bílovice CZ 146 C5
Bilska LV 135 B11
Bilston GB 5 D10
Bilthoven NL 16 D4
Bilto N 112 E7
Bilton GB 11 D11
Bilyayivka UA 154 E6
Bilychi UA 145 E6
Bilyn UA 152 A4
Bilyne UA 154 B5
Bilzen B 19 C12
Bimbister GB 3 G10
Bíňa SK 147 F7
Binaced E 42 D4
Binas F 24 E5
Binasco I 69 C7
Binbrook GB 11 E11
Binche B 19 D9
Bindalseit N 105 A12
Bindlach D 75 C10
Bindslev DK 90 D7
Binefar E 42 D4
Bingen D 27 D11
Bingen am Rhein D 21 E9
Bingerden NL 183 B8
Bingham GB 11 F10
Binghamstown IRL 6 D2
Bingley GB 11 D8
Bingsjö S 103 D10
Binic F 22 C6
Biniés E 32 E4
Binissalem E 49 E10
Binnen D 17 C12
Binz D 84 B5
Binzen D 27 E8
Biograd na Moru HR 156 E3
Biokovina BIH 157 D7
Biol F 31 E7
Bionaz I 31 D11
Biorra IRL 7 F7
Biosca E 43 D6
Biot F 36 D6
Biota E 41 D9
Birchington GB 15 E11
Birchiș RO 151 F9
Bircza PL 144 D5
Birdhill IRL 8 C6
Birgittelyst DK 86 C4
Biri H 151 B8
Biri N 101 E13
Bĭrini LV 135 B9
Biristrand N 101 D12
Birkeland N 90 C3
Birkelse DK 86 A5
Birkenau D 187 B6
Birkenfeld D 21 E8
Birkenfeld D 27 C10
Birkenfeld D 74 C6
Birkenhead GB 10 E5
Birken-Honigsessen D 185 C8
Birkenwerder Berlin D 84 E4
Birkerød DK 87 D10
Birket DK 87 F8
Birketveit N 90 C2
Birkfeld A 148 B5
Birkungen D 79 D7
Birmingham GB 13 A11
Birnbaum A 73 C6
Biron F 33 A7
Birori I 64 C2
Birr IRL 7 F7
Birresborn D 21 D7
Birsay GB 3 G10
Birstall GB 11 F9
Birstein D 21 D12
Birštonas LT 137 D9
Birtavarre N 112 E6
Birtley GB 5 F13
Biruința MD 153 B12
Biržai LT 135 D9
Birzes LV 135 D8
Birzgale LV 135 C9
Birži LV 135 D11
Birzuļi LV 131 F12
Biš SLO 148 C5
Bisaccia I 60 A4
Bisacquino I 58 D3
Biscarrosse F 32 B3
Biscarrosse-Plage F 32 B3
Bisceglie I 61 A7
Bischberg D 75 C8
Bischbrunn D 187 B7
Bischhausen (Waldkappel) D 78 D6
Bischheim F 27 C8
Bischoffen D 21 C10
Bischofferode D 79 D7
Bischoffsheim F 186 E3
Bischofsheim D 21 E10
Bischofsheim an der Rhön D 74 B7
Bischofshofen A 73 B7
Bischofsmais D 76 E4
Bischofswerda D 80 D6
Bischofswiesen D 73 A6
Bischofszell CH 27 E11
Bischwiller F 27 C8
Bisenti I 62 B5
Biser BG 166 F5
Bisertsi BG 161 F9
Bishop Auckland GB 5 F13
Bishop's Castle GB 10 G6
Bishop's Cleeve GB 13 B10
Bishop's Lydeard GB 13 C8
Bishop's Stortford GB 15 D9
Bishop's Waltham GB 13 D12
Bishqem AL 168 B2
Bishtazhin RKS 163 E10
Bisignano I 60 D6
Bisingen D 27 D10
Biskupice PL 141 H7
Biskupice PL 142 D5
Biskupice SK 147 E9
Biskupiec PL 136 F2
Biskupiec PL 139 C7
Bislev DK 86 B5
Bismark (Altmark) D 83 E11
Bismervik N 113 B11
Bismo N 101 C8
Bisoca RO 161 B9
Bispgården S 107 E11
Bispingen D 83 D8
Bissen L 20 E6
Bissendorf D 17 D10
Bissendorf (Wedemark) D 78 A6
Bissingen D 75 E8
Bistagno I 37 B8
Bistarac BIH 157 C10
Bistra RO 151 E11
Bistra RO 152 B4
Bistreț RO 160 F3
Bistrets BG 167 E8
Bistrica BIH 157 B7
Bistrica BIH 157 C7
Bistrica BIH 157 E8
Bistrica BIH 157 E10
Bistrica SLO 73 D9
Bistrica SLO 148 D5
Bistričak BIH 157 D8
Bistrița RO 152 C5
Bistrița Bârgăului RO 152 C5
Bistritsa BG 165 D7
Bistritsa BG 165 E7
Bisztynek PL 136 E2
Bitburg D 21 E7
Bitche F 27 B7
Bitetto I 61 A7
Bitinckë AL 168 C4
Bitola NMK 168 B5
Bitonto I 61 A7
Bitritto I 61 A7
Bitschwiller-lès-Thann F 27 E7
Bitterfeld D 79 C11
Bitterstad N 110 C9
Bitti I 64 C3
Bittkau D 79 B10
Bitton GB 13 C10
Bitz D 27 D11
Biurrun E 32 E2
Bivio CH 71 E9
Bivolari RO 153 B10
Bivona I 58 D3
Bixad RO 145 H7
Bixad RO 153 E7
Bixter GB 3 E14
Biyikali TR 173 B7
Biyikli TR 177 D10
Bizanet F 34 D4
Bizanos F 32 D5
Bizovac HR 149 E10
Bjåen N 94 C6
Bjærangen N 108 C6
Bjæverskov DK 87 E10
Bjännberg S 122 C3
Bjarkøy N 111 C12
Bjärnum S 87 C13
Bjärred S 87 D12
Bjärsjölagård S 87 D13
Bjärtrå S 107 F13
Bjästa S 107 E15
Bjela BIH 157 F10
Bjelajci BIH 157 B6
Bjelopolje HR 156 C4
Bjelovar HR 149 E7
Bjergby DK 90 D7
Bjerge DK 87 D8
Bjerka N 108 D6
Bjerkvik N 111 C14
Bjerreby DK 86 F7
Bjerregrav DK 86 B5
Bjerringbro DK 86 C5
Bjøllånes N 108 C8
Bjoneroa N 95 A12
Bjønnes N 108 D7
Björbo S 97 B12
Björboholm S 91 D11
Bjordal N 94 E4
Bjørgen N 105 F9
Bjørgo N 101 E10
Björkå S 107 E13
Bjørkåsen N 111 C17
Bjørkåsen N 111 D12
Björkberg S 103 C9
Björkberg S 107 B13
Björkberg S 118 C5
Björkboda FIN 126 E8
Björke S 93 D12
Björke S 103 E13
Bjørkeflåta N 95 B9
Bjørkelangen N 95 C15
Bjørkeset N 95 C10
Bjørkestrand N 114 C4
Björketorp S 91 E12
Björkfors S 119 C10
Björkheden S 109 E12
Björkhöjden S 107 E10
Björkholmen S 109 C17
Björkland S 109 F16
Bjørklia N 105 E9
Björkliden S 111 D16
Björklinge S 99 B9
Björknäset S 107 F12
Bjørknes N 96 B6
Bjørknes N 114 D6
Björkö FIN 126 E4
Björköby FIN 122 D6
Björköby S 92 D5
Björkön S 103 B14
Björksele S 107 B15
Björksele S 107 D12
Björksjön S 107 E13
Björkstugan S 111 D15
Björkvik S 93 B9
Bjorli N 100 B8
Bjørn N 108 D4
Björna S 107 D15
Björnänge S 105 E14
Björndalen S 91 C11
Björneborg S 97 D11
Bjørnengen N 113 D11

Bjørnera N 111 C12
Bjørnes N 113 B18
Bjørnevatn N 114 D7
Bjørnfjell N 111 D15
Björnhult S 89 A10
Björnliden S 102 B3
Björnlunda S 93 A10
Björnön S 103 A9
Bjørnrå N 111 C10
Björnrike S 102 B6
Björnsjö S 107 D14
Bjørnskinn N 111 B10
Bjørnstad N 105 B14
Bjørnstad N 114 D9
Björsarv S 103 B11
Björsäter S 92 C8
Björsbo S 103 C12
Björsjö S 97 B13
Bjugn N 104 D7
Bjurå S 118 B8
Bjuråker S 103 C12
Bjurberget S 97 A8
Bjurfors S 107 C17
Bjurfors S 118 E5
Bjurholm S 107 D16
Bjursås S 103 E9
Bjurselet S 118 E6
Bjurträsk S 107 B17
Bjuv S 87 C11
Blace NMK 164 E3
Blace SRB 164 C3
Blachownia PL 143 E6
Black Bourton GB 13 B11
Black Bull IRL 7 F10
Blackburn GB 3 L12
Blackburn GB 5 D9
Blackburn GB 10 D7
Blackmoor Gate GB 13 C7
Blackpool GB 10 D5
Blackrock IRL 7 E10
Blackstad S 93 D8
Blacktown GB 7 C7
Blackwater IRL 9 D10
Blackwaterfoot GB 4 D6
Blackwood GB 13 B8
Bladel NL 16 F4
Blaenau Ffestiniog GB 10 F4
Blaenavon GB 13 B8
Blagaj BIH 157 F8
Blagaj Japra BIH 156 B5
Blagdon GB 13 C9
Blăgești RO 153 D9
Blăgești RO 153 E12
Blagnac F 33 C8
Blagoevgrad BG 165 E7
Blagoevo BG 166 C6
Blåhøj DK 86 D4
Blaibach D 75 D12
Blain F 23 F8
Blainville-sur-l'Eau F 186 D1
Blainville-sur-Mer F 23 B8
Blair Atholl GB 5 B9
Blairgowrie GB 5 B10
Blaj RO 152 E3
Blajan F 33 D7
Blăjani RO 161 C9
Blăjel RO 152 E4
Blăjeni RO 151 E10
Blakeney GB 13 B10
Blakeney GB 15 B11
Blakstad N 90 C4
Blâmont F 27 C6
Blan F 33 C10
Blanca E 55 C10
Blancafort F 25 E8
Blancas E 47 C10
Blandford Forum GB 13 D10
Blandiana RO 151 F11
Blanes E 43 D9
Blaney GB 7 D7
Blangy-sur-Bresle F 18 E4
Blankaholm S 93 D9
Blankenberg D 83 C11
Blankenberge B 19 B7
Blankenburg (Harz) D 79 C8
Blankenfelde D 80 B4
Blankenhain D 79 E9
Blankenhain D 79 E11
Blankenheim D 21 D7
Blankenrath D 21 D8
Blankensee D 84 D4
Blankenstein D 75 B10
Blanquefort F 28 F4
Blans DK 86 F5
Blansko CZ 77 D11
Blanzac-Porcheresse F 28 E6
Blanzay F 29 C6
Blanzy F 30 B5
Blaricum NL 183 A6
Blarney IRL 8 E5
Blasimon F 28 F5
Blåsjöfallet S 105 B16
Blåsmark S 118 D6
Błaszki PL 142 C5
Blatec NMK 164 F6
Blatets BG 167 D7
Blatna BIH 156 C5
Blatná CZ 76 D5
Blatné SK 146 E4
Blatnica BIH 157 D8
Blato HR 162 D2
Blaton B 182 D3
Blattniksele S 109 F14
Blaubeuren D 74 F6
Blaufelden D 74 D6
Blausasc F 37 D6
Blaustein D 187 E8
Blåvik S 92 C6
Blåviksjön S 107 B14
Blavozy F 30 E4
Blaye F 28 E4
Blaževo SRB 163 C10
Błaziny Górne PL 141 H4
Blāzma LV 134 B4
Blažovice CZ 77 D11
Błażowa PL 144 D5
Blázquez E 51 C9
Blažuj BIH 157 E9
Bleckåsen S 105 E15
Bleckede D 83 D9
Blecua E 42 C3
Bled SLO 73 D9
Błędowo PL 138 D6
Bledzew PL 81 A8
Blegny B 19 C12
Bléharies B 19 C7
Bleialf D 20 D6
Bleiburg A 73 C10
Bleicherode D 79 D8
Bleidenstadt D 185 D9
Bleik N 111 B10
Bleikvassli N 108 E6
Bleiswijk NL 182 A5
Blejești RO 161 E6
Blejoi RO 161 D8
Blekendorf D 83 B9
Bleket S 91 D10
Blender D 17 C12
Bléneau F 25 E8
Blénod-lès-Toul F 26 C4
Blenstrup DK 86 B6
Blentarp S 87 D13
Blera I 62 C2
Blérancourt F 19 E7
Bléré F 24 F4
Blerick NL 16 F6
Blesa E 42 E2
Bleskensgraaf NL 182 B5
Blesle F 30 E3
Blessington IRL 7 F9
Blet F 29 B11
Bletchley GB 15 D7
Blīdene LV 134 C5
Blidsberg S 91 D14
Blieskastel D 21 F8
Bligny F 25 D12
Bligny-sur-Ouche F 25 F12
Blikstorp S 91 C15
Bliksund N 90 C3
Blimea E 39 B8
Blindow D 84 D5
Blinja HR 149 F6
Blistrup DK 87 C10
Blixterboda S 97 D13
Blizanów PL 142 C5
Blížejov CZ 76 D3
Blížkovice CZ 77 E9
Bliznatsi BG 167 C9
Bliżyn PL 141 H3
Bllacë RKS 163 E10
Blois F 24 E5
Blokhus DK 86 A5
Blokzijl NL 16 C5
Blombacka S 97 C10
Blomberg D 17 E12
Blome LV 135 B11
Blome LV 135 B13
Blomsøy N 108 E3
Blomstermåla S 89 B10
Błonie PL 141 F3
Błonie PL 143 B7
Blönsdorf D 79 C12
Blötberget S 97 B13
Blousson-Sérian F 33 D6
Blovice CZ 76 C5
Blowatz D 83 C11
Bloxham GB 13 A12
Bludenz A 71 C9
Bludov CZ 77 C11
Blue Ball IRL 7 F7
Blumberg D 27 E10
Blumberg D 80 A5
Blumenhagen D 84 C5
Blumenholz D 84 D4
Blŭskovo BG 167 C8
Blyberg S 102 D7
Blyth GB 5 E13
Blyth GB 11 E9
Blyth Bridge GB 5 D10
Blyton GB 11 E10
Bø N 95 D10
Bø N 110 C8
Bo N 111 B10
Bø N 111 D12
Boada E 45 C8
Boadilla del Monte E 46 D5
Boadilla de Rioseco E 39 D10
Boal E 39 B6
Boalhosa P 38 E3
Boan MNE 163 D7
Boara Pisani I 66 B4
Boat of Garten GB 3 L9
Boa Vista P 44 E3
Boavista P 44 F2
Bobadilla E 53 B7
Bobâlna RO 152 C3
Bobbio I 37 B10
Bobbio Pellice I 31 F11
Bobenheim-Roxheim D 187 B5
Boberg S 107 E9
Boberka UA 145 E6
Bobicești RO 160 E4
Böbing D 71 B12
Bobingen D 71 A11
Bobitz D 83 C10
Bobivtsi UA 153 A7
Böblingen D 27 C11
Bobolice PL 85 C11
Boborás E 38 D3
Boboshevo BG 165 E7
Bobota HR 149 F11
Bobota RO 151 C10
Bobovdol BG 165 E7
Bobove UA 145 G6
Bobowa PL 144 D2
Bobowo PL 138 C6
Bobrov SK 147 C9
Bobrovec SK 147 C9
Bobrowice PL 81 C8
Bobrówko PL 85 E8
Bobrowniki PL 138 E6
Bobrowniki PL 140 D9
Bobryk-Druhyy UA 154 B6
Bocacara E 45 C8
Bocairent E 56 D3
Bočar SRB 150 F5
Bocchigliero I 61 E7
Boceguillas E 40 F4
Bocfölde H 149 C7
Bochnia PL 144 D1
Bocholt B 19 B12
Bocholt D 17 E7
Bochov CZ 76 B4
Bochum D 17 F8
Bockara S 89 A10
Bockenem D 79 B7
Bockenheim an der Weinstraße D 187 B5
Bockhammar S 97 C14
Bockhorn D 17 B10
Bockhorn D 75 F10
Bockhorst D 17 B9
Boćki PL 141 E8
Bocksjö S 92 B5
Bockträsk S 109 F15
Bocognano F 37 G10
Boconád H 150 B5
Bőcs H 145 G2
Bócsa H 150 D3
Bocșa RO 151 C10
Bocșa RO 159 C8
Bocsig RO 151 E8
Boczów PL 81 B7
Bod RO 153 F7
Böda S 89 A12
Boda S 103 A12
Boda S 103 D9
Boda bruk S 103 C12
Bodaczów PL 144 B7
Bodafors S 92 D5
Boda glasbruk S 89 B9
Bodajk H 149 B10
Bodåsgruvan S 98 B6
Bodbacka FIN 122 E6
Bodbyn S 122 B4
Boddam GB 3 F14
Boddam GB 3 L13
Boddin D 83 C10
Bodegraven NL 182 A5
Bodelshausen D 187 E6
Boden S 118 C7
Bodenfelde D 78 C6
Bodenham GB 13 A9
Bodenheim D 21 E10
Bodenkirchen D 75 F11
Bodenmais D 76 D4
Bodenteich D 83 E9
Bodenwerder D 78 C6
Bodenwöhr D 75 D11
Bodești RO 153 C8
Bodman D 27 E11
Bodmin GB 12 E5
Bodnegg D 71 B9
Bodø N 108 B7
Bodom N 105 D11
Bodonal de la Sierra E 51 C6
Bodoney GB 7 C8
Bodony H 147 F10
Bodroghalom H 145 G4
Bodrogkisfalud H 145 G3
Bodrum TR 177 E9
Bodsjö S 102 A8
Bodsjöbyn S 102 A8
Bodträskfors S 118 B5
Bódvaszilas H 145 F2
Bodyke IRL 8 C5
Bodzanów PL 139 E9
Bodzanów PL 142 F3
Bodzentyn PL 143 E10
Boé F 33 B7
Boechout B 19 B9
Boecillo E 39 E10
Boekel NL 16 E5
Boekhoute B 182 C3
Boën-sur-Lignon F 30 D5
Boeslunde DK 87 E8
Boeza E 39 C7
Boffres F 30 F6
Boffzen D 21 A12
Boftsa N 113 C21
Bogács H 145 H2
Bogajo E 45 C7
Bogarra E 55 B8
Bogați RO 160 D6
Bogatić SRB 158 D4
Bogatići BIH 157 E9
Bogatynia PL 81 E7
Boğaziçi TR 177 C10
Bogda RO 151 F8
Bogdan BG 165 D10
Bogdana RO 153 D11
Bogdana RO 160 F6
Bogdanci NMK 169 B8
Bogdand RO 151 C10
Bogdănești RO 153 E9
Bogdănești RO 154 E2
Bogdaniec PL 85 E8
Bogdănița RO 153 E11
Bogdan Vodă RO 152 B4
Boge S 93 D13
Bogen D 75 E12
Bogen N 105 A11
Bogen N 111 C12
Bogense DK 86 D6
Boggsjö S 106 E8
Boghești RO 153 E10
Bogilice BIH 158 F3
Bogliasco I 37 C10
Bognanco I 68 A5
Bognelv N 112 C9
Bognes N 111 D11
Bogniebrae GB 3 L11
Bognor Regis GB 15 F7
Bogny-sur-Meuse F 184 E2
Bogø DK 87 F10
Bogodol BIH 157 F8
Bogojevo SRB 157 A11
Bogomilovo BG 166 E5
Bogoria PL 143 E11
Bogorojca NMK 169 B8
Bogovina SRB 159 F8
Bogovinje NMK 163 F10
Bogoy N 110 E9
Bograngen S 102 E4
Boguchwała PL 144 D4
Bogumiłowice PL 143 D7
Boguszów-Gorce PL 81 E10
Boguty-Pianki PL 141 E6
Bogyiszló H 149 D11
Bohain-en-Vermandois F 19 E7
Bohars F 22 D3
Bohdalov CZ 77 D9
Bohdan UA 152 A4
Bohdíkov CZ 77 B11
Boherboy IRL 8 D4
Boherbue IRL 8 D4
Bohinjska Bistrica SLO 73 D8
Böhl D 187 C5
Böhlen D 79 D11
Böhme D 82 E6
Bohmte D 17 D10
Böhne D 79 A11
Bohola IRL 6 E4
Bohonal de Ibor E 45 E10
Böhönye H 149 D8
Bohoyo E 45 D10
Bohumín CZ 146 B6
Bohuňovice CZ 146 B4
Bohuslavice CZ 146 B6
Bohutín CZ 76 C5
Boianu Mare RO 151 C10
Boiro de Arriba E 38 C2
Boiscommun F 25 D7
Bois-d'Amont F 31 B9
Boisgervilly F 23 D7
Bois-Guillaume F 18 F3
Boișoara RO 160 C4
Boisset-et-Gaujac F 35 B7
Boissezon F 33 C10
Boitzenburg D 84 D5
Boiu Mare RO 152 C3
Boizenburg D 83 D9
Bojadła PL 81 C9
Bojano I 63 E6
Bojanów PL 144 C4
Bojanowo PL 81 C11
Bøjden DK 86 E6
Bojkovice CZ 146 C5
Bojná SK 146 D6
Bojnice SK 147 D7
Bojničky SK 146 E5
Bojnik SRB 164 C4
Bojszów PL 142 F5
Bojszowy PL 143 F7
Boka SRB 159 C6
Bokel D 17 B11
Böklund D 82 A7
Bokod H 149 A10
Bököny H 151 B8
Bokšić HR 149 E10
Boksjön S 109 E10
Bol HR 156 F6
Bölan S 103 D12
Bolanden D 186 B5
Bolandoz F 31 A9
Bolaños de Calatrava E 54 B5
Bolătău RO 153 D8
Bolayir TR 173 C6
Bolbaite E 56 C3
Bolbec F 18 E1
Bolboși RO 159 D11
Bölcske H 150 D2
Boldekow D 84 C5
Bolderslev DK 86 F4
Boldești-Grădiștea RO 161 D9
Boldești-Scăeni RO 161 C8
Boldog H 150 B4
Boldogkőváralja H 145 G3
Boldre GB 13 D11
Boldu RO 161 C10
Boldur RO 159 B8
Boldva H 145 G2
Böle S 99 B9
Böle S 102 B7
Böle S 105 D14
Böle S 105 E15
Böle S 118 C8
Böle S 118 D6
Bolea E 41 D10
Bolekhiv UA 145 E8
Boleráz SK 146 E5
Bolesław PL 143 F7
Bolesław PL 143 F10
Bolesławiec PL 81 D9
Bolesławiec PL 142 D5
Boleszkowice PL 84 E7
Bolga N 108 C5
Bolgatovo RUS 133 C5
Bolhan UA 154 A3
Bolhrad UA 155 B3
Boliden S 118 E4
Bolimów PL 141 F2
Bolintin-Deal RO 161 E7
Bolintin-Vale RO 161 E7
Boliqueime P 50 E3
Boljanić BIH 157 C9
Boljanići MNE 163 C7
Boljevac SRB 159 F8
Boljevci SRB 158 D5
Bölkow D 83 B11
Bołków PL 81 E10
Bollebygd S 91 D12
Bollène F 35 B8
Bollengo I 68 C4
Bollermoen N 108 D6
Bolligen CH 31 B11
Bolling DK 86 D3
Bollingstedt D 82 A6
Bollnäs S 103 D11
Bollsbyn S 91 A12
Bollstabruk S 107 E13
Bollullos Par del Condado E 51 E6
Bolnes NL 182 B5
Bolnhurst GB 15 C8
Bologna I 66 D3
Bologne F 26 D3
Bolognetta I 58 D3
Bolognola I 62 B4
Bolotana I 64 C2
Bolotești RO 153 F10
Bolsena I 62 B1
Bol'shakovo RUS 136 D4
Bolsover GB 11 E9
Bolsward NL 16 B5
Bolszewo PL 138 A5
Boltaña E 33 F6
Boltåsen N 111 C12
Boltenhagen D 83 C10
Boltigen CH 31 B11
Bolton GB 5 D11
Bolton GB 11 D7
Bolüntü TR 181 A7
Bolvașnița RO 159 C9
Bolventor GB 12 D5
Bóly H 149 E11
Bolyarovo BG 167 E7
Bolzano I 72 D3
Bomal B 19 D12
Bomba I 63 C6
Bombarral P 44 F2
Bomlitz D 82 E7
Bompas F 34 E4
Bompensiere I 58 E4
Bompietro I 58 D5
Bomporto I 66 C3
Bomsund S 107 E9
Bona F 30 A3
Bonaduz CH 71 D8
Bonakas N 113 C21
Bonäs S 103 E13
Bonanza E 52 C4
Boñar E 39 C9
Bonar Bridge GB 3 K8
Bonarcado I 64 C2
Bonares E 51 E6
Bonäs S 102 D7
Bonäset S 106 D8
Bonäset S 107 E15
Bonassola I 37 C11
Bonawe GB 4 C6
Bonboillon F 26 F4
Bonchamp-lès-Laval F 23 D10
Bonchester Bridge GB 5 E11
Boncourt CH 27 F7
Bondeno I 66 C3
Bondersbyn S 119 C9
Bonderup DK 86 A4
Bondorf D 187 D6
Bondsjö S 103 A14
Bondues F 182 D2
Bönebüttel D 83 B8
Bonefro I 63 D7
Bönen D 17 E9
Bo'ness GB 5 C9
Bonete E 55 B10
Bönhamn S 103 A15
Bonheiden B 19 B10
Boniches E 47 E9
Boniewo PL 138 F6
Bonifacio F 37 J10
Bonifati I 60 D5
Bönigen CH 70 D5
Bonin PL 85 B10
Bonn D 21 C8
Bonnåsjøen N 109 A10
Bonnat F 29 C9
Bonndorf im Schwarzwald D 27 E9
Bønnerup Strand DK 87 B7
Bonnes N 111 C15
Bonnet DK 86 B2
Bonnétable F 24 D3
Bonneuil-Matours F 29 B7
Bonneval F 24 D5
Bonneval F 31 D10
Bonneval-sur-Arc F 31 E11
Bonnevaux F 31 B9
Bonneville F 31 C9
Bonnieux F 35 C9
Bönnigheim D 27 B11
Bonnyrigg GB 5 D10
Bonny-sur-Loire F 25 E8
Bono F 22 E6
Bono I 64 C3
Bonorva I 64 C2
Bons-en-Chablais F 31 C9
Bonson F 30 D5
Bonțida RO 152 D3
Bőny H 149 A9
Bonyhád H 149 D11
Boo S 99 D10
Boock D 84 D6
Boom B 19 B9
Boortmeerbeek B 19 C10
Boos F 18 F3
Boostedt D 83 B8
Bootle GB 10 E6
Bopfingen D 75 E7
Boppard D 21 D9
Bor CZ 75 C12
Bor S 88 A6
Bor SRB 159 E9
Borač SRB 158 F6
Borås S 91 D12
Borăscu RO 160 D2
Borba P 50 B5
Borbjerg DK 86 C3
Borca RO 153 C7
Borča SRB 158 D5
Borcea RO 155 E1
Borchen D 17 E11
Borci BIH 157 C7
Borci BIH 157 E9
Börcs H 149 A9
Borculo NL 17 D7
Bordalba E 41 F7
Bordány H 150 E4
Bordeaux F 28 F4
Bordeira P 50 E2
Bordei Verde RO 161 C11
Bordelum D 82 A5
Bordères-Louron F 33 E6
Bordères-sur-l'Échez F 33 D6
Bordes F 32 D5
Bordes F 33 D6
Bordesholm D 83 B8
Bordești RO 161 B10
Bordighera I 37 D7
Bordils E 43 C9
Bording DK 86 C4
Bordón E 42 F3
Bordușani RO 155 E1
Bore I 69 D8
Boreham GB 15 D10
Borehamwood GB 15 D8
Borek PL 143 F10
Borek Strzeliński PL 81 E12
Borek Wielkopolski PL 81 C12
Boreland GB 5 E10
Borelva N 108 B8
Borensberg S 92 B6
Borg D 20 E6
Borgå FIN 127 E14
Borgafjäll S 106 B8
Borgentreich D 17 E12
Börger D 17 C9
Borger NL 17 C7
Borggård S 92 B7
Borghamn S 92 C5
Borgheim N 90 A7
Borghetto d'Arroscia I 37 C7
Borghetto di Borbera I 37 B9
Borghetto di Vara I 69 E8
Borghetto Santo Spirito I 37 C8
Borgholm S 89 B11
Borgholzhausen D 17 D10
Borgia I 59 B10
Borgloon B 19 C11
Børglum DK 90 E6
Borgo F 37 F10
Borgo a Mozzano I 66 E2
Borgo d'Ale I 68 C5
Borgoforte I 66 B2
Borgofranco d'Ivrea I 68 B4
Borgo Grappa I 61 C10
Borgo-lavezzaro I 68 C6
Borgomanero I 68 B5
Borgomaro I 37 D7
Borgone Susa I 31 E11
Borgonovo Val Tidone I 69 C7
Borgo Pace I 66 E5
Borgorose I 62 C4
Borgo San Dalmazzo I 37 C6
Borgo San Lorenzo I 66 E3
Borgo San Martino I 68 C6
Borgosesia I 68 B5
Borgo Tossignano I 66 D4
Borgo Val di Taro I 69 E8
Borgo Valsugana I 72 D3
Borgo Velino I 62 C4
Borgo Vercelli I 68 C5
Borgsjö S 103 A10
Borgsjö S 107 C13
Borgstedt D 82 B7
Borgstena S 91 D13
Borgue GB 5 F8
Borgvattnet S 107 E9
Borhaug N 94 F5
Boriaeva BG 171 B7
Borike BIH 157 E11
Borino BG 165 F9
Bořitov CZ 77 D11
Borja E 41 E8
Borjabad E 41 E7
Borjana SLO 73 D7
Borjelslandet S 118 C8
Borkan S 106 A8
Borkavichy BY 133 E4
Borken D 17 E7
Borken (Hessen) D 21 B12
Borkenes N 111 C11
Borki PL 141 G7
Borki PL 143 D9
Børkop DK 86 D5
Borkowice PL 141 H3
Borkowo PL 139 D12
Borkum D 17 A7
Borlänge S 97 B13
Borlești RO 153 D9
Bormani LV 135 C10
Børmarka N 104 C8
Bormio I 71 E10
Born D 79 B9
Born NL 183 C7
Borna D 79 D12
Borna D 80 D4
Born am Darß D 83 B13
Borne NL 17 D7
Bornem B 19 B9
Bornerbroek NL 17 D7
Bornes P 39 F6
Bornes de Aguiar P 38 E4
Borne Sulinowo PL 85 C11
Bornheim D 21 C7
Bornhofen D 21 D9
Bornhöved D 83 B8
Bornich D 185 D8
Bornos E 51 F8
Bornova TR 177 C9
Börnsen D 83 D8
Boroaia RO 153 C8
Borobia E 41 E8
Borod RO 151 D10
Borodino UA 154 E4
Borodinskoye RUS 129 C11
Borohrádek CZ 77 B10
Borojevići BIH 157 F8
Boronów PL 143 E6
Borore I 64 C2
Boroșneu Mare RO 153 F8
Boroszów PL 142 E5
Borota H 150 E3
Boroughbridge GB 11 C9
Borovan BG 165 C8
Borovany CZ 77 E7
Borov Dol BG 166 D6
Borovets BG 165 E8
Borovik HR 149 F10
Borovitsa BG 165 B6
Borovka LV 133 E1
Borovnica BIH 157 D9
Borovnica SLO 73 E9
Borovo BG 166 C5
Borovo Selo HR 157 B10
Borovtsi BG 165 C7
Borów PL 81 E11
Borów PL 144 B4
Borowa PL 143 F11
Borowie PL 141 G5
Borox E 46 D5
Borrby S 88 E6
Borre DK 87 F10
Borre N 95 D12
Borrentin D 84 C3
Borrèze F 29 F8
Borriol E 48 D4
Borris DK 86 D3
Borris IRL 9 C9
Borris-in-Ossory IRL 9 C7
Borrisokane IRL 6 G6
Borrisoleigh IRL 9 C7
Borrowdale GB 10 B5
Børrud N 96 C7
Börrum S 93 C9
Borș RO 151 C8
Børsa N 104 E8
Borșa RO 152 B5
Borșa RO 152 D3
Borša SK 145 G4
Borsbeek B 19 B10
Borsec RO 153 D7
Børselv N 113 C16
Borsh AL 168 D2
Borshchi UA 154 B5
Borshchovychi UA 144 D9
Boršice u Buchlovic CZ 146 C4
Borsio GR 174 B3
Borský Svätý Jur SK 77 E12
Borsodbóta H 145 G1
Borsodnádasd H 145 G1
Borsodszentgyörgy H 145 G1
Borsodszirák H 145 G2
Borsosberény H 147 F8
Borssele NL 182 C3
Borstel D 17 C11
Borth GB 10 G3
Bortigali I 64 C2
Bortigiadas I 64 B3
Bort-les-Orgues F 29 E10
Börtnan S 102 A6
Bortnen N 100 C2
Borum DK 86 C6
Borup DK 87 E9
Borve GB 2 L4
Borynya UA 145 E6
Boryslav UA 145 E7
Borzęciczki PL 81 C12
Borzonasca I 37 C10
Borzytuchom PL 85 B12
Bosa I 64 C2
Bošáca SK 146 D5
Bosa Marina I 64 C1
Bosanci RO 153 B8
Bosanka Rača BIH 158 D3
Bosanska Dubica BIH 157 B6
Bosanska Gradiška BIH 157 B7
Bosanska Kostajnica BIH 156 B6
Bosanska Krupa BIH 156 C5
Bosanski Brod BIH 157 B9
Bosanski Kobas BIH 157 B8
Bosanski Novi BIH 156 B5
Bosanski Petrovac BIH 156 C5
Bosanski Šamac BIH 157 B9
Bosansko Grahovo BIH 156 D5
Bošany SK 146 D6
Bősárkány H 149 A8
Bosau D 83 B8
Boscastle GB 12 D5
Bosco I 66 F5
Bosco Chiesanuova I 69 B11
Bosco Marengo I 37 B9
Boscotrecase I 60 B2
Bösdorf D 83 B8
Bösebo S 89 A9
Bösel D 17 B9
Boshulya BG 165 E9
Bosia RO 153 C11
Bosilegrad SRB 164 E5
Bosiljevo HR 148 F4
Boskoop NL 16 D3
Boskovice CZ 77 D11
Bošnjace SRB 164 D4
Bošnjaci HR 157 B10
Bošnjane SRB 159 F7
Bošnjane SRB 159 F7
Boșorod RO 159 B11
Bössbod S 102 D7
Bosset F 29 F6
Bossolasco I 37 B8
Bòssost E 33 E7
Bostad N 110 D6
Bostan BIH 157 F7
Bøstølen N 100 B6
Boston GB 11 F11
Boston Spa GB 11 D9
Bostrak N 90 A4
Bosundet S 107 C10
Botão P 44 D4
Boteå S 107 E13
Boteni RO 160 C6
Botesdale GB 15 C11
Botești RO 153 C9
Botești RO 160 C6
Botevgrad BG 165 D8
Botevo BG 167 C9
Bothel GB 5 F10
Boticas P 38 E4
Botiz RO 151 B10
Botiza RO 152 B4
Botn N 110 E9
Botn N 111 A18
Botn N 112 D4
Botngård N 104 D7
Botnhamn N 111 A14
Botoroaga RO 161 E7
Botorrita E 41 E9
Botoš SRB 158 C6
Botoșana RO 153 B7
Botoșani RO 153 B9
Botoșești-Paia RO 159 E11
Botricello I 61 F7
Bötsle S 103 A14
Botsmark S 118 F4
Bottendorf (Burgwald) D 21 B11
Bottesford GB 11 D10
Bottidda I 64 C3
Bottnaryd S 91 D14
Bottrop D 17 E7
Botun NMK 168 B4
Bötzingen D 27 D8
Bouafles F 24 B5
Boucau F 32 C3
Bouc-Bel-Air F 35 D9
Boucé F 23 C11
Bouchain F 19 D7
Bouchemaine F 23 F10
Bouchoir F 18 E6
Boudry CH 31 B10
Boué F 19 D8
Bouglon F 33 B6
Bouguenais F 23 F8
Bouillargues F 35 C7
Bouillon B 19 E11
Bouilly F 25 D10
Bouin F 28 B1
Boujailles F 31 B9
Boujan-sur-Libron F 34 D5
Boulay-Moselle F 26 B5
Boulazac F 29 E7
Boulbon F 35 C8
Bouligny F 19 F12
Bouloc F 33 C8
Boulogne-Billancourt F 25 C7
Boulogne-sur-Gesse F 33 D7
Boulogne-sur-Mer F 15 F12
Bouloire F 24 E4
Boulouris F 36 E5
Boult-aux-Bois F 19 F10
Boulzicourt F 19 E10
Bouniagues F 29 F7
Bøur FO 2 A2
Bourbon-Lancy F 30 B4
Bourbon-l'Archambault F 30 B3
Bourbonne-les-Bains F 26 E4
Bourbourg F 18 C5
Bourbriac F 22 D5
Bourcefranc-le-Chapus F 28 D3
Bourdeaux F 35 A9
Bourdeilles F 29 E7
Bourdonnay F 27 C6
Bouresse F 29 C7
Bourg F 28 E4
Bourg-Achard F 18 F2
Bourganeuf F 29 D9
Bourg-Argental F 30 E6
Bourg-de-Péage F 31 E7
Bourg-de-Thizy F 30 C5
Bourg-de-Visa F 33 B7
Bourg-Dun F 18 E2
Bourg-en-Bresse F 31 C7
Bourges F 29 A10
Bourg-et-Comin F 19 F8
Bourg-Lastic F 29 D11
Bourg-lès-Valence F 30 F6
Bourgneuf-en-Mauges F 23 F10
Bourgneuf-en-Retz F 28 A2
Bourgogne F 19 F9
Bourgoin-Jallieu F 31 D7
Bourg-St-Andéol F 35 B8
Bourg-St-Bernard F 33 C9
Bourg-St-Maurice F 31 D10
Bourgtheroulde-Infreville F 18 F2
Bourguébus F 23 B11
Bourgueil F 23 F12
Bourmont F 26 D4
Bourne GB 11 F11
Bournemouth GB 13 D11
Bournezeau F 28 B3
Bourran F 33 B6
Bourriot-Bergonce F 32 B5
Bourron-Marlotte F 25 D8
Bourscheid L 184 E5
Bourtange NL 17 B8
Bourton GB 13 C10
Boussac F 29 C10
Bousse F 186 C1
Boussens F 33 D7
Boussières F 26 F4
Boussois F 19 D9
Boussu B 19 D8
Boutersem B 19 C10
Bouveret CH 31 C10
Bouvières F 35 A9
Bouvron F 23 F8
Bouxières-aux-Dames F 26 C5
Bouxwiller F 27 C7
Bouy F 25 B11
Bouzonville F 21 F7
Bouzov CZ 77 C11
Bova I 59 C8
Bøvær N 111 B13
Bovalino I 59 C9
Bovallstrand S 91 C9
Bova Marina I 59 D8
Bovan SRB 159 F8
Bovec SLO 73 D8
Bóveda E 38 C5

Boveda E 40 C5
Bovegno I 69 B9
Bovenden D 78 C6
Bøverfjord N 104 E5
Boves F 18 E5
Boves I 37 C7
Bovigny B 20 D5
Boviken S 118 E6
Boville Ernica I 62 D4
Bovino I 60 A4
Bøvlingbjerg DK 86 C2
Bovolone I 66 B3
Bovrup DK 86 F5
Bow GB 3 H10
Bowes GB 11 B7
Bowmore GB 4 D4
Box FIN 127 E13
Boxberg D 81 D7
Boxberg D 187 C8
Boxdorf D 80 D5
Boxholm S 92 C6
Boxmeer NL 16 E5
Boxtel NL 16 E4
Boyadzhik BG 166 E6
Boyanovo BG 167 E7
Boychinovtsi BG 165 C7
Boykovo BG 165 E10
Boyle IRL 6 E6
Bøylefoss N 90 B4
Boynes F 25 D7
Boynitsa BG 159 F10
Bøyum N 100 D5
Božava HR 67 D10
Bozburun TR 181 C8
Bozeat GB 15 C7
Bozel F 31 E10
Boževac SRB 159 D7
Bożewo PL 139 E8
Bozhentsi BG 166 D4
Bozhurishte BG 165 D7
Božica SRB 164 D5
Božice CZ 77 E10
Bozieni MD 154 D3
Bozieni RO 153 D10
Bozioru RO 161 C8
Božjakovina HR 148 E6
Bozlar TR 173 D7
Bozouls F 34 B4
Bozovici RO 159 D9
Bozveliysko BG 167 C8
Bozzolo I 66 B1
Bra I 37 B7
Braås S 89 A8
Bråbo S 89 A10
Brabova RO 160 E2
Bracadale GB 2 L4
Bracciano I 62 C2
Brach F 28 E4
Brachbach D 185 C8
Bracieux F 24 E6
Bräcke S 103 A9
Brackenheim D 27 B11
Brackley GB 13 A12
Bracknagh IRL 7 F8
Bracknell GB 15 E7
Braco GB 5 C9
Brad RO 151 E10
Bradashesh AL 168 B3
Brădeanu RO 161 D9
Brădeni RO 152 E5
Brădești RO 152 E6
Brădești RO 160 E3
Bradford GB 11 D8
Bradford-on-Avon GB 13 C10
Bradpole GB 13 D9
Bradu RO 160 D5
Brădulet RO 160 C5
Brăduț RO 153 E7
Bradwell GB 15 B12
Bradwell Waterside GB 15 D10
Brae GB 3 E14
Brædstrup DK 86 D5
Braehead of Lunan GB 5 B11
Braemar GB 5 A10
Brăești RO 153 B8
Brăești RO 153 C10
Brăești RO 161 C9
Bràfim E 43 E6
Braga P 38 E3
Bragadiru RO 161 E7
Bragadiru RO 161 F7
Bragança P 39 E6
Bragar GB 2 J3
Brăhășești RO 153 E10
Brahlstorf D 83 D9
Brăila RO 155 C1
Brailsford GB 11 F8
Braine F 19 F8
Braine-l'Alleud B 19 C9
Braine-le-Comte B 19 C9
Braintree GB 15 D10
Braives B 19 C11
Brajkoviči BIH 157 D8
Brake (Unterweser) D 17 B10
Brakel B 19 C8
Brakel D 17 E12
Bräkne-Hoby S 89 C8
Brålanda S 91 B11
Bralin PL 142 D4
Brallo di Pregola I 37 B10
Bralos GR 174 B5
Braloștița RO 160 D3
Bram F 33 D10
Bramans F 31 E10
Bramberg am Wildkogel A 72 B5
Bramdrupdam DK 86 D4
Bramming DK 86 E3
Brampton GB 5 F11
Brampton GB 15 C12
Bramsche D 17 D8
Bramsche D 17 D10
Bramstedt D 17 B11
Bran RO 160 B6
Brånaberg S 109 E11
Branäs S 102 E4
Brancaleone I 59 D9
Brancaster GB 15 B10
Brânceni RO 160 F6
Brâncovenești RO 152 D5
Brâncoveni RO 160 E4
Brand A 71 C9
Brand D 75 C10
Brandal N 100 B4
Brändåsen S 102 B4
Brändbo S 103 B11
Brandbu N 95 B13
Brande DK 86 D4
Brande-Hörnerkirchen D 82 C7
Brandenberg A 72 B4
Brandenburg D 79 B12
Brand-Erbisdorf D 80 E4
Branderup DK 86 E4
Brandesburton GB 11 D11
Brandis D 80 C4
Brand-Nagelberg A 77 E8
Brando F 37 F10
Brändö FIN 126 E5
Brandon GB 15 C10
Brändön S 118 C8
Brändövik FIN 122 D6
Brandshagen D 84 B4
Brandstorp S 92 C4
Brandsvoll N 90 C2
Brandval N 96 B7
Brandvoll N 111 C15
Brandýs nad Labem-Stará Boleslav CZ 77 B7
Brandýs nad Orlicí CZ 77 B10
Branes N 96 A6
Brănești MD 154 C3
Brănești RO 160 C6
Brănești RO 160 D2
Brănești RO 161 E8
Branice PL 142 F4
Braniewo PL 139 B8
Branik SLO 73 E8
Brănișca RO 151 F10
Braniștea RO 152 C4
Braniștea RO 155 C1
Braniștea RO 161 D7
Brankas LV 134 C7
Bränna S 91 B11
Brännåker S 107 B9
Brännäs S 103 B11
Brännberg S 118 C6
Branne F 28 F5
Brännland S 107 D16
Brännland S 122 C4
Brañosera E 40 C3
Brańsk PL 141 E7
Branston GB 11 E11
Brańszczyk PL 139 E12
Brantevik S 88 D6
Brantice CZ 142 F4
Brantôme F 29 E7
Branzi I 69 A8
Braojos E 46 B5
Braone I 69 B9
Braskereidfoss N 101 E15
Braslaw BY 133 E2
Brașov RO 161 B7
Brassac F 33 C10
Brasschaat B 16 F2
Brassy F 25 F10
Brasta S 105 E16
Brastad S 91 C10
Brastavățu RO 160 F4
Břasy CZ 76 C5
Brataj AL 168 D2
Bratca RO 151 D10
Bråte N 95 C14
Brateiu RO 152 E4
Brateljevici BIH 157 D10
Brateș RO 153 F8
Bratislava SK 77 F12
Bratkowice PL 144 C4
Bratovoești RO 160 E3
Bratsigovo BG 165 E9
Brattåker S 107 A11
Brattbäcken S 107 C9
Bratten S 107 B14
Brattfors S 103 E12
Brattfors S 107 D17
Brattli N 114 D7
Brattmon S 102 E4
Bratton GB 13 C10
Brattsbacka S 107 D16
Brattsele S 107 D12
Brattset N 104 E5
Brattvåg N 100 A4
Bratunac BIH 158 E3
Brătușeni MD 153 A10
Bratya Daskalovi BG 166 E4
Braubach D 21 D9
Braud-et-St-Louis F 28 E4
Braunau am Inn A 76 F4
Brauneberg D 185 E6
Braunfels D 21 C10
Braunlage D 79 C8
Bräunlingen D 27 E9
Braunsbach D 187 C8
Braunsbedra D 79 D10
Braunschweig D 79 B8
Braunton GB 12 C6
Bravicea MD 154 C2
Bravnica BIH 157 D7
Bray IRL 7 F10
Bray-sur-Seine F 25 D9
Bray-sur-Somme F 18 E6
Brazatortas E 54 B4
Brazey-en-Plaine F 26 F3
Brazi RO 161 D8
Brazii RO 151 E9
Brazii RO 161 D8
Brbinj HR 67 D11
Brčigovo BIH 157 E11
Brčko BIH 157 C10
Brdów PL 138 F6
Bré IRL 7 F10
Brea E 41 E8
Brea de Tajo E 47 D6
Breaghva IRL 8 C3
Breascleit GB 2 J3
Breasta RO 160 E3
Breaza RO 152 B6
Breaza RO 152 D5
Breaza RO 161 C7
Breaza RO 161 C9
Brebeni RO 160 E4
Brebu RO 159 C8
Brebu RO 161 C7
Brebu Nou RO 159 C9
Brécey F 23 C9
Brech F 22 E6
Brechfa GB 12 B6
Brechin GB 5 B11
Brecht B 16 F3
Breckerfeld D 185 B7
Břeclav CZ 77 E11
Brecon GB 13 B8
Breda E 43 D9
Breda NL 16 E3
Bredared S 91 D12
Bredaryd S 87 A13
Bredbyn S 107 E14
Breddenberg D 17 C9
Breddin D 83 E12
Bredebro DK 86 E3
Bredene B 18 B6
Bredereiche D 84 D4
Bredevoort NL 17 E7
Bredkälen S 106 D8
Bredsätra S 89 B11
Bredsel S 118 C4
Bredsjö S 97 C12
Bredsjön S 103 A13
Bredstedt D 82 A5
Bredsten DK 86 D4
Bredträsk S 107 D15
Bredvik S 107 D17
Bredviken S 108 D8
Bredviken S 119 C10
Bree B 19 B12
Breese D 83 D11
Bregana HR 148 E5
Breganze I 72 E4
Bregare BG 165 B9
Bregeni MD 153 B12
Bregenz A 71 B9
Breg-Lum AL 163 E9
Breg-Lum AL 168 B2
Bregninge DK 86 F6
Bregovo BG 159 E10
Breguzzo I 69 B10
Bréhal F 23 C8
Bréhan F 22 D6
Brehna D 79 C11
Breidenbach D 21 C10
Breidenbach F 27 B7
Breidstrand N 111 C12
Breidvik N 108 B9
Breidvik N 110 C8
Breidvik N 110 E9
Breidvik N 111 D11
Breiholz D 82 B7
Breil CH 71 D8
Breil-sur-Roya F 37 D7
Breisach am Rhein D 27 D8
Breistein N 94 B2
Breitenbach CH 27 F8
Breitenbach D 21 F8
Breitenbach (Schauenburg) D 17 F12
Breitenbach am Herzberg D 78 E6
Breitenbach am Inn A 72 B4
Breitenberg D 76 E5
Breitenbrunn D 75 D10
Breitenburg D 82 C7
Breitenfelde D 83 C9
Breitengüßbach D 75 C8
Breitenhagen D 79 C10
Breitnau D 27 E9
Breitscheid D 183 C9
Breitscheid D 185 C7
Breitscheid D 185 C9
Breitungen D 79 E7
Breivik N 111 C12
Breivik N 112 B9
Breivikbotn N 112 B9
Breivikeidet N 111 A18
Brejning DK 86 D5
Brekka N 108 B9
Brekken N 101 A15
Brekken N 108 E5
Brekkestø N 90 C3
Brekkhus N 100 E4
Brekkvasseiv N 105 B14
Breklum D 82 A5
Brekovo SRB 158 F5
Breksillan N 105 B10
Brekstad N 104 D7
Brélès F 22 D2
Brelingen (Wedemark) D 78 A6
Bremdal DK 86 B3
Bremen D 17 B11
Bremerhaven D 17 A11
Bremervörde D 17 A12
Bremgarten CH 27 F9
Bremm D 21 D8
Bremnes N 94 C2
Bremnes N 110 C9
Brem-sur-Mer F 28 B2
Brenderup DK 86 E5
Brenes E 51 D8
Brenguli LV 131 F11
Brenitsa BG 165 C9
Brenna N 108 F5
Brenna N 110 D7
Brenna PL 147 B7
Brennero I 72 C4
Brennes N 112 D5
Brennfjell N 112 E5
Brenngam N 113 B19
Brennhaug N 101 C10
Brennmo N 105 E11
Brennsvik N 113 B13
Breno I 69 B9
Brénod F 31 C8
Brens F 33 C9
Brensbach D 187 B6
Brent Knoll GB 13 C9
Brentwood GB 15 D9
Brenzone I 69 B10
Bresalc RKS 164 E3
Brescello I 66 C2
Brescia I 66 A1
Breskens NL 16 F1
Bresnica SRB 158 F6
Bressana Bottarone I 69 C7
Bressanone I 72 C4
Bressols F 33 C8
Bressuire F 28 B5
Brest BG 160 F5
Brest BY 141 F9
Brest F 22 D3
Brestak BG 167 C9
Brestanica SLO 148 E4
Bresternica SLO 148 C5
Brestova HR 67 B9
Brestovac SRB 159 E9
Brestovac SRB 164 C4
Brestovac Požeški HR 149 F9
Brestovăț RO 151 F8
Brestovene BG 161 F9
Brestovets BG 165 C10
Brestovitsa BG 165 E10
Bretagne-d'Armagnac F 33 C6
Brețcu RO 153 E8
Bretea Română RO 159 B11
Breteil F 23 D8
Bretenoux F 29 F9
Breteuil F 18 E5
Breteuil F 24 C4
Brétignolles-sur-Mer F 28 B2
Bretnig D 80 D6
Bretocino E 39 E8
Bretoncelles F 24 D4
Bretten D 27 B10
Bretton GB 10 E6
Bretteville-sur-Laize F 23 B11
Bretzenheim D 185 E8
Bretzfeld D 187 C7
Breuberg-Neustadt D 21 E12
Breuches F 26 E5
Breugel NL 183 B7
Breuil-Cervinia I 68 B4
Breuil-Magné F 28 D4
Breuilpont F 24 C5
Breukelen NL 16 D4
Breum DK 86 B4
Breuna D 17 F12
Breuvannes-en-Bassigny F 26 D4
Brevens bruk S 92 A7
Brevik N 90 A6
Brevik S 92 C4
Brevik S 93 A12
Brevik S 99 D10
Breviken S 96 D7
Brevörde D 78 C5
Breza BIH 157 D9
Breza SK 147 C8
Brežde SRB 158 E5
Breze SLO 148 D4
Brezhani BG 165 F7
Březí CZ 77 E11
Brezičani BIH 157 B6
Brežice SLO 148 E5
Brezna SRB 163 B10
Breznica HR 148 D6
Breznica SK 145 E4
Březnice CZ 76 C5
Breznik BG 165 D6
Breznița-Motru RO 159 D11
Breznița-Ocol RO 159 D10
Breznitsa BG 165 F8
Březno CZ 76 B4
Brezno SK 147 D9
Brezoaele RO 161 D7
Brézolles F 24 C5
Březolupy CZ 146 C5
Březová CZ 146 D5
Březová nad Svitavou CZ 77 C11
Brezová pod Bradlom SK 146 D5
Brezovica SK 145 E2
Brezovica SK 147 C9
Brezovica SLO 73 D9
Brezovo BG 166 E4
Brezovo Polje BIH 157 C10
Brezovo Polje HR 156 B5
Briançon F 31 F10
Briare F 25 E8
Briatexte F 33 C9
Briceni MD 153 A10
Bricherasio I 31 F11
Bricon F 26 D2
Bricquebec F 23 B8
Brides-les-Bains F 31 E10
Brideswell IRL 6 F6
Bridgeland IRL 9 C9
Bridgend GB 4 C6
Bridgend GB 4 D4
Bridgend GB 13 B7
Bridge of Cally GB 5 B10
Bridge of Don GB 3 L12
Bridge of Dye GB 5 B11
Bridge of Earn GB 5 C10
Bridge of Orchy GB 4 B7
Bridge of Weir GB 4 D7
Bridgetown IRL 9 D9
Bridgnorth GB 11 F7
Bridgwater GB 13 C8
Břidličná CZ 146 B4
Bridlington GB 11 C11
Bridport GB 13 D9
Brie F 29 D6
Briec F 22 D4
Brie-Comte-Robert F 25 C8
Briedel D 185 D7
Brielle NL 16 E2
Brienne-le-Château F 25 D12
Briennon F 30 C5
Brienon-sur-Armançon F 25 D10
Brienz CH 70 D6
Brienza I 60 C5
Briesen D 80 B6
Brieske D 80 D5
Brieskow-Finkenheerd D 81 B7
Briesnig D 81 C7
Brietlingen D 83 D8
Briey F 20 F5
Brig CH 68 A4
Brigg GB 11 D11
Brighstone GB 13 D12
Brightlingsea GB 15 D11
Brighton GB 15 F8
Brigi LV 133 D4
Brignais F 30 D6
Brignogan-Plage F 22 C3
Brignoles F 36 E4
Brigstock GB 15 C7
Brihuega E 47 C7
Brijesta HR 162 D4
Brillon-en-Barrois F 26 C3
Brilon D 17 F11
Brimington GB 11 E9
Brimnes N 94 B5
Brinches P 50 C4
Brincones E 45 B8
Brindisi I 61 B9
Brindisi Montagna I 60 B5
Bringsinghaug N 100 B2
Bringsli N 108 B9
Brinian GB 3 G11
Brinje HR 67 B11
Brinkum D 17 B9
Brinkum D 17 B11
Brinlack IRL 6 B6
Brinon-sur-Beuvron F 25 F9
Brinon-sur-Sauldre F 25 E7
Brin-sur-Seille F 26 C5
Brînza MD 155 B2
Brînzeni MD 153 A10
Brion F 30 F3
Briones E 40 C6
Brionne F 24 B4
Brioude F 30 E3
Brioux-sur-Boutonne F 28 C5
Briouze F 23 C11
Briscous F 32 D3
Brisighella I 66 D4
Brissac-Quincé F 23 F11
Bristol GB 13 C9
Briston GB 15 B11
Britelo P 38 E3
Britof SLO 73 D9
Briton Ferry GB 13 B7
Brittas IRL 7 F10
Brittas Bay IRL 9 C10
Britvica BIH 157 F8
Britz D 84 E5
Brive-la-Gaillarde F 29 E9
Briviesca E 40 C5
Brix F 23 A8
Brixen im Thale A 72 B5
Brixham GB 13 E7
Brixworth GB 15 C7
Brka BIH 157 C10
Brložnik BIH 157 D11
Brna HR 162 D2
Brnaze HR 157 E6
Brněnec CZ 77 C11
Brniště CZ 81 E7
Brnjica SRB 159 D8
Brnjica SRB 163 C9
Brno CZ 77 D11
Bro S 93 D12
Bro S 99 C9
Broadford GB 2 L5
Broadford IRL 8 C5
Broadford IRL 8 D5
Broad Haven GB 9 E12
Broadheath GB 13 A10
Broadstairs GB 15 E11
Broadway GB 13 A11
Broadwey GB 13 D10
Broadwindsor GB 13 D9
Broager DK 86 F5
Broaryd S 87 A12
Broby S 88 C6
Broby S 99 C11
Brobyværk DK 86 E6
Broc CH 31 B11
Broćanac BIH 157 F7
Brocas F 32 B4
Brocēni LV 134 C5
Bröckel D 79 A7
Brockum D 17 D10
Brockworth GB 13 B10
Broczyno PL 85 D10
Brod BIH 157 F10
Brod NMK 168 A5
Brod NMK 169 C6
Brod RKS 163 F10
Brod RKS 164 E3
Brodalen S 91 C10
Brodarevo SRB 163 C8
Broddbo S 98 C6
Brodek u Prostějova CZ 77 D12
Broderstorf D 83 B12
Brodica SRB 159 E8
Brodick GB 4 D6
Brodilovo BG 167 E9
Brodina RO 152 B6
Brodnica PL 81 B11
Brodnica PL 139 D7
Brodosanë RKS 163 E10
Brodské SK 77 E12
Brodski Stubnik HR 157 B8
Brody PL 81 B8
Brody PL 81 C7
Broekhuizenvorst NL 183 C8
Broglie F 24 B4
Brohl D 185 D7
Brohm D 84 C5
Broin F 26 F3
Brójce PL 81 B9
Brojce PL 85 C8
Brójce PL 143 C8
Brok PL 139 E12
Brokdorf D 17 A12
Brokind S 92 C7
Brokka N 90 C2
Brokstedt D 83 C7
Brolo I 59 C6
Bromarv FIN 127 F9
Brome D 79 A8
Bromma N 95 B10
Bromnes N 112 C2
Bromölla S 88 C6
Brömsebro S 89 C10
Bromsgrove GB 13 A10
Bromyard GB 13 A9
Bron F 30 D6
Bronchales E 47 C9
Brønderslev DK 86 A5
Broni I 69 C7
Bronice PL 81 C7
Brønnøysund N 108 F3
Bronnytsya UA 154 A1
Brøns DK 86 E3
Bronte I 59 D6
Bronzani Majdan BIH 157 C6
Brooke GB 15 B11
Brookeborough GB 7 D8
Broons F 23 D7
Broquiès F 34 B4
Brora GB 3 J9
Brørup DK 86 E4
Brösarp S 88 D6
Broscăuți RO 153 B8
Broseley GB 10 F7
Broshniv Osada UA 145 F9
Brossac F 28 E5
Brøstadbotn N 111 B14
Broșteni RO 153 C7
Broșteni RO 153 F10
Broșteni RO 159 D10
Brotas P 50 B3
Brötjemark S 92 D4
Broto E 32 E5
Brottby S 99 C10
Brottes F 26 D3
Brotton GB 11 B10
Brøttum N 101 D13
Brou F 24 D5
Brough GB 3 H10
Brough GB 11 B7
Broughshane GB 4 F4
Broughton GB 5 D10
Broughton GB 10 E6
Broughton in Furness GB 10 C5
Broughtown GB 3 G11
Broughty Ferry GB 5 C11
Broumov CZ 81 E10
Brousseval F 26 D2
Broutzaiika GR 175 D6
Brouvelieures F 26 D6
Brouwershaven NL 16 E1
Brovst DK 86 A5
Brownhills GB 11 F8
Broxburn GB 5 D10
Brozany CZ 76 B6
Brozas E 45 E7
Brožiai LT 134 E3
Brozzo I 69 B9
Brštanovo HR 156 E5
Brtnice CZ 77 D9
Bruay-la-Bussière F 18 D6
Bruchhausen-Vilsen D 17 C12
Bruchköbel D 187 A6
Bruchmühlbach D 21 F8
Bruchsal D 27 B10
Bruchweiler-Bärenbach D 186 C4
Brück D 79 B12
Bruck an der Großglocknerstraße A 73 B6
Bruck an der Leitha A 77 F11
Bruck an der Mur A 73 B11
Brücken D 21 E8
Brücken (Helme) D 79 D9
Brücken (Pfalz) D 21 F8
Brückl A 73 C10
Bruckmühl D 72 A4
Brudzeń Duży PL 139 E8
Brudzew PL 142 B6
Brudzowice PL 143 E7
Brue-Auriac F 35 C10
Brüel D 83 C11
Bruère-Allichamps F 29 B10
Bruff IRL 8 D5
Brugelette B 182 D3
Bruges B 19 B7
Bruges B 182 C2
Brugg CH 27 F9
Brugge B 19 B7
Brüggen D 16 F6
Brüggen D 78 B6
Brugnato I 69 E8
Brugnera I 72 E6
Bruguières F 33 C8
Bruhagen N 104 E3
Brühl D 21 C7
Brühl D 187 C6
Bruinisse NL 16 E2
Bruiu RO 152 F5
Bruksvallarna S 102 A3
Brûlon F 23 E11
Brûly B 19 E10
Brumath F 27 C8
Brummen NL 183 A8
Brumov-Bylnice CZ 146 C6
Brumunddal N 101 E13
Brumundsag N 101 E13
Brunau D 83 E10
Brunava LV 135 D8
Brundby DK 86 D7
Brundish GB 15 C11
Brunehamel F 19 E9
Brunete E 46 D5
Brunflo S 106 E7
Brunico I 72 C4
Bruniquel F 33 B9
Brunkeberg N 95 D8
Brunn D 84 C4
Brunna S 99 C8
Brunna S 99 C9
Brunn am Gebirge A 77 F10
Brunnberg S 97 B10
Brunne S 103 A14
Brunnen CH 71 C7
Brunnsberg S 102 D6
Brunsberg S 97 C8
Brunsbüttel D 17 A12
Brunssum NL 20 C5
Bruntál CZ 142 G3
Bruravik N 94 B5
Bruree IRL 8 D5
Brus SRB 163 C11
Brusago I 69 A11
Brusand N 94 E3
Brušane HR 156 C3
Brusartsi BG 159 F11
Brüsewitz D 83 C10
Brŭshlen BG 161 F8
Brŭshlyanitsa BG 165 B10
Brusio CH 69 A9
Brusnik SRB 159 E9
Brusnica Velika BIH 157 B9
Brusno SK 147 D8
Brusque F 34 C4
Brussel B 19 C9
Brusson I 68 B4
Brüssow D 84 D6
Brusturi RO 151 C9
Brusturi-Drăgănești RO 153 C8
Brusturiv UA 152 A5
Brusturoasa RO 153 D8
Brusy PL 138 C4
Bruton GB 13 C10
Bruttig-Fankel D 21 D8
Bruvno HR 156 D4
Bruxelles B 19 C9
Bruyères F 26 D6
Bruz F 23 D8
Bruzaholm S 92 D6
Brvnište SK 146 C6
Brwinów PL 141 F3
Bryagovo BG 166 F4
Bryastovo BG 165 C10
Bryggerhaug N 111 B14
Brymbo GB 10 E5
Brynamman GB 13 B7
Bryne N 94 E3
Brynford GB 10 E5
Brynge S 107 E14
Bryngelhögen S 102 B7
Brynje S 102 A8
Brynje S 106 E7
Brynmawr GB 13 B8
Bryrup DK 86 C5
Bryukhovychi UA 144 D8
Brzan SRB 159 F7
Brza Palanka SRB 159 E9
Brzeće SRB 163 C10
Brzeg PL 142 E3
Brzeg Dolny PL 81 D11
Brześć Kujawski PL 138 E6
Brzesko PL 143 G10
Brzeszcze PL 143 G7
Brzezie PL 85 C11
Brzezie PL 138 E6
Brzezinki PL 141 H5
Brzeziny PL 142 C5
Brzeziny PL 143 C8
Brzeziny PL 144 D4
Brzeźnica PL 81 C8
Brzeźnica PL 143 F11
Brzeźnica PL 147 B9
Brzeźno PL 85 C9
Brzeźno PL 141 H9
Brzeźno PL 142 B5
Brzostek PL 144 D3
Brzotín SK 145 F1
Brzóza PL 141 G4
Brzozów PL 141 F2
Brzozów PL 144 D5
Brzozowiec PL 81 A8
Brzuze PL 139 D7
Bû F 24 C6
Bua S 87 A10
Buais F 23 C10
Buarcos P 44 D3
Buavågen N 94 C2
Bubbio I 37 B8
Bubiai LT 134 E6
Bubry F 22 E5
Bubwith GB 11 D10
Búč SK 149 A10
Buca TR 177 C9
Bučany SK 146 E5
Buccheri I 59 E6
Bucchianico I 63 C6
Buccinasco I 69 C7
Buccino I 60 B4
Bucecea RO 153 B8
Bucelas P 50 B1
Buceș RO 151 E10
Bucey-lès-Gy F 26 F4
Buch D 71 A10
Buch am Erlbach D 75 F11
Buchbach D 75 F11
Buchboden A 71 C9
Büchel D 21 D8
Büchen D 83 D9
Buchen (Odenwald) D 27 A11
Büchenbeuren D 185 E7
Buchholz D 83 D12
Buchholz (Aller) D 82 E7
Buchholz (Westerwald) D 21 C8
Buchin RO 159 C9
Buchin Prohod BG 165 D7
Buch in Tirol A 72 B4
Buchkirchen A 76 F6
Büchlberg D 76 E5
Buchloe D 71 A11
Buchlovice CZ 146 C4
Bucholz in der Nordheide D 83 D7
Buchs CH 71 C8
Buchy F 18 E3
Bučim NMK 164 F5
Buçimas AL 168 C4
Bučin NMK 168 B5
Bucine I 66 F4
Bucinișu RO 160 F4
Bučište NMK 164 F5
Bucium RO 151 E11
Buciumeni RO 153 F10
Buciumeni RO 161 C6
Buciumi RO 151 C11
Bučje SRB 159 F9
Bučje SRB 163 C7
Buckden GB 11 C7
Bückeburg D 17 D12
Bücken D 17 C12
Buckfastleigh GB 13 E7
Buckhaven GB 5 C10
Buckie GB 3 K11
Buckingham GB 14 D7
Buckley GB 10 E5
Buckode IRL 6 D6
Buckow Märkische Schweiz D 80 A6
Bückwitz D 83 E12
Bucoșnița RO 159 C9
Bucov RO 161 D8
Bucovăț MD 154 C2
Bucovăț RO 160 E3
Bucovica BIH 157 E7
Bučovice CZ 77 D12
Bucsa H 151 C7
Bucșani RO 161 D7
Bucșani RO 161 E7
Bucu RO 161 D11
Bucureșci RO 151 E10
București RO 161 E8
Bucy-lès-Pierrepont F 19 E8
Bucz PL 81 B10
Buczek PL 143 D7
Bud N 100 A5
Buda RO 161 B9
Budacu de Jos RO 152 C5
Budakalász H 150 B3
Budakeszi H 149 A11
Budakovo NMK 168 B5
Budaörs H 149 B11
Budapest H 150 C3
Budča SK 147 D8
Buddusò I 64 B3
Bude GB 12 D5
Budeasa RO 160 D5
Budel NL 16 F5
Büdelsdorf D 82 B7
Budenets' UA 153 A7
Budenheim D 21 D10
Budens P 50 E2
Büdesheim D 21 D11
Budești RO 152 B3
Budești RO 152 D4
Budești RO 160 C4
Budești RO 161 E8
Budeyi UA 154 A4
Budia E 47 C7
Budila RO 161 B7
Budimci HR 149 F10
Budimlić Japra BIH 156 C5
Budiná SK 147 E8
Büdingen D 21 D12
Budinšćina HR 148 D6
Budišov CZ 77 D9
Budišov nad Budišovkou CZ 146 B5
Budkovce SK 145 F4
Budleigh Salterton GB 13 D8
Budmerice SK 146 E4
Budoia I 72 D6
Budoni I 64 B4
Budrio I 66 C4
Budry PL 136 E4
Budureasa RO 151 D10
Buduslău RO 151 C9
Budva MNE 163 E6
Būdviečiai LT 136 D6
Budyně nad Ohří CZ 76 B6
Budziszewice PL 141 G1
Budzów PL 147 B9
Budzyń PL 85 E11
Bue N 94 E3
Bueña E 47 C10
Buenache de Alarcón E 47 E8
Buenache de la Sierra E 47 D8
Buenaventura E 46 D3
Buenavista de Valdavia E 39 C10
Buendía E 47 D7
Buer D 183 B10
Buer N 96 D6
Bueu E 38 D2
Bufleben D 79 D8
Buftea RO 161 D7
Bugac H 150 D4
Bugarra E 48 E3
Buğdayli TR 173 D8
Bugeat F 29 D9
Buggenhout B 182 C4
Buggerru I 64 E1
Buggingen D 27 E8
Bugiac MD 154 E3
Bugnara I 62 C5
Bugnein F 32 D4
Bugojno BIH 157 D7
Bugøyfjord N 114 D6
Bugøynes N 114 D7
Bugyi H 150 C3
Bühl D 27 C9
Bühlertal D 27 C9
Bühlertann D 74 D6
Bühlerzell D 74 D6

Buhoci RO 153 D10
Buhølen N 90 C1
Buhuși RO 153 D9
Buia I 73 D7
Builth Wells GB 13 A8
Buis-les-Baronnies F 35 B9
Buitenpost NL 16 B6
Buitrago del Lozoya E 46 C5
Buivydiškės LT 137 D11
Buivydžiai LT 137 D12
Buják H 147 F9
Bujalance E 53 A8
Bujan AL 163 E9
Bujanovac SRB 164 E4
Bujaraloz E 42 E3
Buje HR 67 B8
Bujor MD 154 D2
Bujoreni RO 160 C4
Bujoreni RO 161 E7
Bujoru RO 161 F7
Bük H 149 B7
Buk PL 81 B11
Bukaiši LV 134 D6
Bukhava BY 133 E6
Bukhovo BG 165 D8
Bukhovtsi BG 167 C7
Bükkábrány H 145 H2
Bükkösd H 149 D9
Bukksnes N 111 C10
Bükkszék H 145 H1
Bükkszentkereszt H 145 G2
Bükkzsérc H 145 H2
Buko D 79 C11
Bukonys LT 135 F8
Bukova Gora BIH 157 E7
Bukovče SRB 159 E10
Bukovec CZ 147 B7
Bukovets BG 165 D8
Bukovje SLO 73 E9
Bukovo NMK 168 C5
Buków PL 81 B9
Bukowe PL 142 B4
Bukowice PL 81 D12
Bukowiec PL 81 B9
Bukowiec PL 81 B10
Bukowiec PL 138 D5
Bukowina PL 138 B4
Bukowina Tatrzańska PL 145 E1
Bukownica PL 142 D5
Bukowsko PL 145 E5
Bülach CH 27 E10
Bulboaca MD 154 D4
Bulbucata RO 161 E7
Bulçar AL 168 C3
Buldoo GB 3 H9
Bulford GB 13 C11
Bŭlgarene BG 165 C11
Bŭlgarevo BG 167 C10
Bŭlgari BG 167 E9
Bŭlgarin BG 166 F5
Bŭlgarovo BG 167 D8
Bŭlgarska Polyana BG 166 E6
Bŭlgarski Izvor BG 165 C9
Bulgnéville F 26 D4
Bülkau D 17 A11
Bulkington GB 13 A12
Bulkowo PL 139 E9
Bullas E 55 C9
Bullaun IRL 6 F5
Bullay D 21 D8
Bulle CH 31 B11
Bullerup DK 86 E6
Büllingen B 20 D6
Bullmark S 122 B4
Bully-les-Mines F 18 D6
Bulqizë AL 168 A3
Bultei I 64 C3
Bulz RO 151 D10
Bulzești RO 160 D3
Bulzeștii de Sus RO 151 E10
Bulzi I 64 B2
Bumbești-Jiu RO 160 C2
Bumbești-Pițic RO 160 C3
Buna BIH 157 F8
Bunacurry IRL 6 E3
Bunalty IRL 6 D3
Bun an Churraigh IRL 6 E3
Bun an Phobail IRL 4 E2
Bun an Tábhairne IRL 8 E6
Bunbeg IRL 6 B6
Bunclody IRL 9 C9
Bun Clóidí IRL 9 C9
Buncrana IRL 4 E2
Bun Cranncha IRL 4 E2
Bunde D 17 B8
Bünde D 17 D11
Bundenbach D 21 E8
Bunderhee D 17 B8
Bun Dobhrain IRL 6 D6
Bundoran IRL 6 D6
Bunessan GB 4 C4
Bunești RO 152 E6
Bunești RO 153 B8
Bunești-Averești RO 153 D11
Bungay GB 15 C11
Bunge S 93 D14
Bunić HR 156 C4
Buniel E 40 D4
Bunila RO 159 B10
Bunka LV 134 D3
Bunkeflostrand S 87 D11
Bunkris S 102 D5
Bunmahon IRL 9 D8
Bunnaglass IRL 6 F5
Bun na hAbhna IRL 6 D3
Bunnahowen IRL 6 D3
Bun na Leaca IRL 6 B6
Bunnanaddan IRL 6 D5
Bunnanadden IRL 6 D5
Buñol E 48 F3
Bunschoten-Spakenburg NL 16 D4
Buntești RO 151 D10
Buntingford GB 15 D8
Bunyola E 49 E10
Buoač BIH 157 C7
Buochs CH 71 D6
Buollannjárga N 113 E15
Buonabitacolo I 60 C5
Buonalbergo I 60 A3
Buonconvento I 66 F3
Buonvicino I 60 D5
Bur DK 86 C2
Buran N 105 D11
Burbach D 21 C10
Burbage GB 13 C11
Burbáguena E 47 B10
Burcei I 64 E3
Bŭrdarski Geran BG 165 B8
Burdinne B 19 C11
Bureå S 118 E6
Bureåborg S 107 E13
Büren D 17 E11
Buren NL 183 B6
Büren an der Aare CH 27 F7
Bures GB 15 D10
Buresjön S 109 E14
Burfjord N 112 D9
Burford GB 13 B11
Burg D 80 C6
Burg (Dithmarschen) D 82 C6
Burganes de Valverde E 39 E8
Burgas BG 167 E8
Burgau A 148 B6
Burgau D 75 F7
Burgau P 50 E2
Burg auf Fehmarn D 83 B10
Burg bei Magdeburg D 79 B10
Burgberg im Allgäu D 71 B10
Burgbernheim D 75 D7
Burgbrohl D 185 D7
Burgdorf CH 70 C5
Burgdorf D 79 B7
Burgdorf D 79 B7
Burgebrach D 75 C8
Bürgel D 79 E10
Burgess Hill GB 15 F8
Burghausen D 76 F3
Burghclere GB 13 C12
Burghead GB 3 K10
Burgh-Haamstede NL 16 E1
Burgh le Marsh GB 11 E12
Burgio I 58 D3
Burgkirchen an der Alz D 75 F12
Burgkunstadt D 75 B9
Bürglen CH 27 E11
Bürglen CH 71 D7
Burglengenfeld D 75 D11
Burgohondo E 46 D3
Burgos E 40 D4
Burgos I 64 C2
Burgsalach D 75 D9
Burgsinn D 74 B6
Bürgstadt D 21 E12
Burgstädt D 79 E12
Burg Stargand D 84 D4
Burgsvik S 93 E12
Burgthann D 75 D9
Burgtonna D 79 D8
Burgui E 32 E3
Burguillos E 51 D8
Burguillos del Cerro E 51 C6
Burguillos de Toledo E 46 E5
Burgum NL 16 B6
Burgwindheim D 75 C8
Burhaniye TR 173 F6
Burhave (Butjadingen) D 17 A10
Buriasco I 31 F11
Burie F 28 D5
Burila Mare RO 159 E10
Burizanë AL 168 A2
Burjassot E 48 E4
Burjuc RO 151 F10
Burkardroth D 74 B6
Burkhardtsdorf D 80 E3
Burlada E 32 E2
Burladingen D 27 D11
Burlats F 33 C10
Bürmoos A 76 G3
Burnchurch IRL 9 C8
Burness GB 3 G11
Burnfoot GB 4 F3
Burnfoot IRL 4 E2
Burnham GB 15 D7
Burnham Market GB 15 B10
Burnham-on-Crouch GB 15 D10
Burnham-on-Sea GB 13 C9
Burniston GB 11 C11
Burnley GB 11 D7
Burntisland GB 5 C10
Burntwood Green GB 11 F8
Burón E 39 B9
Buronzo I 68 C5
Buros F 32 D5
Burovac SRB 159 E7
Burow D 84 C4
Burøysund N 112 C4
Burravoe GB 3 E14
Burrel AL 168 A3
Burren GB 7 D10
Burren IRL 6 F4
Burriana E 48 E4
Burry Port GB 12 B6
Bürs A 71 C9
Burs S 93 D13
Bursa TR 173 D11
Burscough Bridge GB 10 D6
Burseryd S 87 A12
Bursfelde D 78 C6
Bürstadt D 21 E10
Burstow GB 15 E8
Bursuc MD 154 C2
Burtnieki LV 131 F10
Burton-in-Kendal GB 10 C6
Burton Latimer GB 15 C7
Burtonport IRL 6 C6
Burton upon Trent GB 11 F8
Burträsk S 118 E5
Buru RO 152 D3
Burujón E 46 E4
Burwarton GB 13 A9
Burwash GB 15 F9
Burwell GB 15 C9
Burwick GB 3 H11
Bury GB 11 D7
Bury St Edmunds GB 15 C10
Burzenin PL 142 D6
Busachi I 64 C2
Busalla I 37 B9
Busana I 66 D1
Busanski Dubočac BIH 157 B8
Busca I 37 B6
Buscemi I 59 E6
Busdorf D 82 B7
Buseto Palizzolo I 58 C2
Buševec HR 148 E6
Busha UA 153 A12
Bushmills GB 4 E3
Bushtricë AL 163 F9
Bushtyna UA 145 G7
Busigny F 19 D7
Busilovac SRB 159 F7
Bušince SK 147 E9
Buskhyttan S 93 B9
Busko-Zdrój PL 143 F10
Buślary PL 85 C10
Bušletić BIH 157 C9
Busnes N 108 D6
Busot E 56 E4
Busovača BIH 157 D8
Bussang F 27 E6
Busseto I 69 C9
Bussière-Badil F 29 D7
Bussière-Galant F 29 D8
Bussière-Poitevine F 29 C7
Bussigny CH 31 B10
Bussi sul Tirino I 62 C5
Büßleben D 79 E9
Bussolengo I 66 B2
Bussoleno I 31 E11
Bussum NL 16 D4
Bussy-en-Othe F 25 D10
Bussy-le-Grand F 25 E12
Bușteni RO 161 C7
Bustillo del Páramo E 39 D8
Busto Arsizio I 69 B6
Bustuchin RO 160 D3
Busturi-Axpe E 41 B6
Büsum D 82 B5
Bŭta BG 165 E9
Butan BG 160 F3
Bușeni MD 154 D3
Buteni RO 151 E9
Butera I 58 E5
Butești MD 153 B10
Bütgenbach B 20 D6
Butimanu RO 161 D7
Būtingė LT 134 D2
Butlers Bridge IRL 7 D8
Butoiești RO 160 D2
Butor MD 154 C4
Butovo BG 166 C4
Bütow D 83 D12
Butrimonys LT 137 D9
Butrimonys LT 137 E11
Butryny PL 139 C10
Bütschwil CH 27 F11
Büttelborn D 187 B6
Buttelstedt D 79 D9
Buttermere GB 10 B5
Buttevant IRL 8 D5
Bütthard D 187 B8
Buttigliera d'Asti I 37 A7
Buttle S 93 E13
Buttstädt D 79 D9
Büttstedt D 79 D7
Butuceni MD 154 B4
Butuceni MD 154 C3
Buturugeni RO 161 E7
Butzbach D 21 D11
Bützow D 83 C11
Buurse NL 17 D7
Buvåg N 110 D9
Buvik N 111 A15
Buvika N 104 E8
Buxerolles F 29 B6
Buxheim D 71 B10
Buxières-les-Mines F 30 C2
Buxted GB 15 F9
Buxtehude D 82 D7
Buxton GB 11 E8
Buxy F 30 B6
Buynovtsi BG 166 D5
Büyükada TR 173 C11
Büyükaltiağaç TR 171 B10
Büyükanafarta TR 171 D10
Büyükbelen TR 177 B10
Büyükçavuşlu TR 173 B9
Büyükçekmece TR 173 B10
Büyükçiğli TR 177 C9
Büyükdöllük TR 167 F7
Büyük Evren TR 171 C10
Büyükgerdelli TR 167 F7
Büyükkarakarli TR 173 B7
Büyükkariştiran TR 173 B8
Büyükkiliçli TR 173 B9
Büyükorhan TR 173 E10
Büyükyenice TR 173 F7
Büyükyoncali TR 173 B8
Buza RO 152 D4
Buzançais F 29 B8
Buzancy F 19 F10
Buzău RO 161 C9
Buzescu RO 160 E6
Buzet HR 67 B8
Buzet-sur-Baïse F 33 B6
Buzet-sur-Tarn F 33 C9
Buziaș RO 159 B8
Buzica SK 145 F3
Bužim BIH 156 B5
Buzoești RO 160 D5
Buzsák H 149 C9
By N 104 D8
Byala BG 166 C5
Byala BG 166 D6
Byala BG 167 D9
Byala Cherkva BG 165 F10
Byala Cherkva BG 166 C4
Byala Reka BG 166 E4
Byala Reka BG 167 D7
Byala Slatina BG 165 C8
Byal Izvor BG 171 A8
Byalo Pole BG 166 E5
Byberget S 103 A9
Bybjerg DK 87 D9
Bychawa PL 144 A6
Bycina PL 142 F6
Byczyna PL 142 D5
Bydalen S 105 E15
Bydgoszcz PL 138 D5
Bye S 106 E7
Byelavyezhski BY 141 F8
Byel'ki BY 133 F2
Byenyakoni BY 137 E11
Byershty BY 137 F9
Byfield GB 13 A12
Bygdeå S 122 B5
Bygdeträsk S 118 F5
Bygdsiljum S 118 F5
Bygland N 90 B2
Byglandsfjord N 90 B2
Bygstad N 100 D3
Byhleguhre D 80 C6
Bykle N 94 D6
Bylchau GB 10 E4
Bylderup-Bov DK 86 F4
Byn S 97 B10
Byneset N 104 E8
Byremo N 90 C1
Byrkjedal N 94 E4
Byrkjelo N 100 C5
Byrknes N 100 E1
Byrtegrend N 94 C7
Byrum DK 87 A7
Byšice CZ 77 B7
Byske S 118 E6
Byssträsk S 107 C15
Bystřany CZ 80 E5
Bystré CZ 77 C10
Bystré SK 145 E4
Bystřec CZ 77 B11
Bystretsovo RUS 132 F4
Bystričany SK 147 D7
Bystřice CZ 77 C7
Bystřice CZ 147 B7
Bystřice nad Pernštejnem CZ 77 C10
Bystřice pod Hostýnem CZ 146 C5
Bystrička SK 147 C7
Bystrzyca PL 142 E3
Bystrzyca Kłodzka PL 77 B11
Bytča SK 147 C7
Bytnica PL 81 B8
Bytom PL 143 F6
Bytom Odrzański PL 81 C9
Bytoń PL 138 E6
Bytów PL 85 B12
Byvallen S 102 B7
Byviken S 107 D16
Byxelkrok S 89 A12
Bzenec CZ 146 D4
Bzince pod Javorinou SK 146 D5

C

Cabacés E 42 E5
Cabaj-Čápor SK 146 E6
Cabanac-et-Villagrains F 32 A4
Cabañaquinta E 39 B8
Cabañas del Castillo E 45 E9
Cabanas de Viriato P 44 D5
Cabañas Raras E 39 C6
Cabanes E 48 D5
Cabanillas E 41 D8
Cabannes F 35 C8
Čabar HR 73 E10
Cabasse F 36 E4
Cabeça Gorda P 50 D4
Cabeção P 50 B3
Cabeceiras de Basto P 38 E4
Cabeço de Vide P 44 F5
Cabella Ligure I 37 B10
Căbești RO 151 D9
Cabeza de Framontanos E 45 B8
Cabeza del Buey E 51 B9
Cabeza del Caballo E 45 B7
Cabeza la Vaca E 51 C7
Cabezamesada E 47 E6
Cabezarados E 54 B4
Cabezarrubias del Puerto E 54 B4
Cabezas del Villar E 45 C10
Cabezas Rubias E 51 D5
Cabezón de Cameros E 41 D6
Cabezón de la Sal E 40 B3
Cabezón de Liébana E 39 B10
Cabezuela del Valle E 45 D9
Čabiny SK 145 E4
Cabo de Palos E 56 F3
Cabolafuente E 47 B8
Cabra E 53 B8
Cabração P 38 E2
Cabra del Camp E 42 E6
Cabra del Santo Cristo E 55 D6
Cabra de Mora E 48 D3
Cabras I 64 D2
Cabrejas del Pinar E 40 E6
Cabrela P 50 B3
Cabrerets F 33 A9
Cabrières-d'Aigues F 35 C10
Cabril P 44 D5
Cabrillanes E 39 C7
Cabrillas E 45 C8
Cabuna HR 149 E9
Cacabelos E 39 C6
Čačak SRB 158 F5
Caçarelhos P 39 E7
Caccamo I 58 D4
Caccuri I 61 E7
Cacém P 50 B1
Cáceres E 45 F8
Cachopo P 50 E4
Čachtice SK 146 D5
Cacica RO 153 B7
Cacín E 53 B9
Čačinci HR 149 E9
Cadalso de los Vidrios E 46 D4
Cadamstown IRL 7 F7
Cadaqués E 43 C10
Cadaval P 44 F2
Čađavica BIH 157 D6
Čađavica HR 149 E9
Čađavica Gornja BIH 157 C11
Čadca SK 147 C7
Cadelbosco di Sopra I 66 C2
Cadenazzo CH 69 A6
Cadenberge D 17 A12
Cadenet F 35 C9
Cadeo I 69 D8
Cádiar E 55 F6
Cadillac F 32 A5
Cádiz E 52 C4
Cadolzburg D 75 D8
Cadoneghe I 66 B4
Cadours F 33 C8
Cadreita E 41 D8
Cadrete E 41 E10
Caen F 23 B11
Caerau GB 13 C8
Caerdydd GB 13 C8
Caerfyrddin GB 12 B6
Caergybi GB 10 E2
Caerhun GB 10 E4
Caerleon GB 13 B9
Caernarfon GB 10 E3
Caerphilly GB 13 B8
Cafasse I 31 E12
Caggiano I 60 B5
Çağiş TR 173 E8
Cagli I 66 E6
Cagliari I 64 E3
Čaglin HR 149 F9
Cagnac-les-Mines F 33 C10
Cagnano Varano I 63 D9
Cagnes-sur-Mer F 36 D6
Caherconlish IRL 8 C6
Cahermore IRL 8 E2
Cahir IRL 9 D7
Cahirsiveen IRL 8 E2
Cahors F 33 B8
Cahul MD 154 F2
Cahuzac-sur-Vère F 33 C9
Căianu RO 152 D3
Căianu Mic RO 152 C4
Caiazzo I 60 A2
Căinari MD 154 D4
Căinarii Vechi MD 153 A12
Căineni RO 160 C4
Căineni-Băi RO 161 C10
Caión E 38 B2
Cairaclia MD 154 F3
Cairanne F 35 B8
Cairnbaan GB 4 C6
Cairnryan GB 4 F6
Cairo Montenotte I 37 C8
Caiseal IRL 9 C7
Caisleán an Bharraigh IRL 6 E4
Caisleán an Chomair IRL 9 C8
Caisleán Uí Chonail IRL 8 C5
Caissargues F 35 C7
Caister-on-Sea GB 15 B12
Caistor GB 11 E11
Căiuți RO 153 E9
Caivano I 60 B2
Cajarc F 33 B9
Čajetina SRB 158 F4
Čajić BIH 157 E6
Čajkov SK 147 E7
Čajniče BIH 157 E11
Cajvana RO 153 B7
Čaka SK 146 E6
Čakajovce SK 146 E6
Çakılköy TR 173 D9
Çakilli TR 173 A8
Çakir TR 173 E7
Çakirli TR 173 D7
Çakmakköy TR 172 B6
Čakovec HR 149 D6
Cala E 51 D7
Calabardina E 55 E9
Calabritto I 60 B4
Calaceite E 42 E4
Calacuccia F 37 G10
Cala d'Oliva I 64 A1
Cala d'Or E 57 C11
Calaf E 43 D7
Calafat RO 159 F10
Calafell E 43 E7
Cala Figuera E 57 C11
Calafindești RO 153 B8
Cala Galdana E 57 B12
Calahonda E 53 C10
Calahorra E 32 F2
Calais F 15 F12
Calalzo di Cadore I 72 D5
Calamandrana I 37 B8
Cala Millor E 57 B11
Calamocha E 47 C10
Calamonaci I 58 D3
Calamonte E 51 B7
Cala Murada E 57 C11
Călan RO 151 F11
Calañas E 51 D6
Calanda E 42 F3
Calangianus I 64 B3
Calanna I 59 C8
Cala'n Porter E 57 B13
Calarașăuca MD 154 A1
Călărași MD 154 C2
Călărași RO 152 E3
Călărași RO 153 B10
Călărași RO 160 F4
Călărași RO 161 E10
Cala Ratjada E 57 B11
Calascibetta I 58 D5
Calasetta I 64 E1
Calasparra E 55 C9
Calatafimi I 58 D2
Calatayud E 41 F8
Călățele RO 151 D11
Calatorao E 41 E9
Calau D 80 C5
Calbe (Saale) D 79 C10
Calcatoggio F 37 G9
Calcinato I 66 B1
Calcio I 69 B8
Căldăraru RO 160 E5
Caldarola I 67 F7
Caldaro sulla Strada del Vino I 72 D3
Caldas da Rainha P 44 F2
Caldas de Reis E 38 C2
Caldas de Vizela P 38 F3
Caldbeck GB 5 F10
Caldearenas E 32 F4
Caldecott GB 11 F10
Caldelas P 38 E3
Caldelas Taipas P 38 F3
Calden D 21 B12
Caldercruix GB 5 D9
Caldes de Malavella E 43 D9
Caldes de Montbui E 43 D8
Caldes d'Estrac E 43 D9
Caldicot GB 13 B9
Caldogno I 72 E4
Caldonazzo I 69 A11
Calella E 43 D9
Calendário P 38 F2
Calenzana F 37 F9
Calenzano I 66 E3
Calera de León E 51 C7
Calera y Chozas E 45 E10
Caleruega E 40 E5
Calfsound GB 3 G11
Calgary GB 4 B4
Çali TR 173 D10
Calig E 42 G4
Călimănești RO 160 C4
Calimera I 61 C10
Călinești MD 153 B10
Călinești RO 152 B3
Călinești RO 160 D6
Călinești RO 160 E6
Călinești-Oaș RO 145 H7
Calitri I 60 B4
Calizzano I 37 C8
Çalköy TR 173 E7
Callac F 22 D5
Callain IRL 9 C8
Callan IRL 9 C8
Callander GB 5 C8
Callanish GB 2 J3
Callantsoog NL 16 C3
Callas F 36 D5
Callen F 32 B5
Callian F 36 D5
Calliano I 37 A8
Callington GB 12 D6
Callosa d'En Sarrià E 56 D4
Callosa de Segura E 56 E3
Čalma SRB 158 C4
Călmățuiu RO 160 F5
Călmățuiu de Sus RO 160 E5
Calmont F 33 B11
Calmont F 33 D9
Calne GB 13 C10
Câlnic RO 152 F3
Câlnic RO 159 D11
Calolziocorte I 69 B7
Calomarde E 47 D9
Calonge E 43 D10
Calopăr RO 160 E3
Čalovec SK 146 F5
Calpe E 56 D5
Caltabellotta I 58 D3
Caltagirone I 59 E6
Caltanissetta I 58 E5
Caltavuturo I 58 D4
Caltignaga I 68 B6
Çaltilibük TR 173 E10
Caltojar E 40 F6
Caltra IRL 6 F6
Călugăreni RO 161 E7
Caluso I 68 C4
Calvão P 44 D3
Calvarrasa de Abajo E 45 C9
Calvarrasa de Arriba E 45 C9
Calvello I 60 C5
Calverstown IRL 7 F9
Calvi F 37 F9
Calvi dell'Umbria I 62 C3
Calvignac F 33 B9
Calvinet F 29 F10
Calvini RO 161 C8
Calvi Risorta I 60 A2
Calvisson F 35 C7
Calvörde D 79 B9
Calvos E 38 E4
Calw D 27 C10
Calzada de Calatrava E 54 B5
Calzada de Valdunciel E 45 B9
Calzadilla E 45 D7
Calzadilla de los Barros E 51 C7
Camaldoli I 66 E4
Camaleño E 39 B10
Camallera E 43 C9
Camañas E 47 C10
Camăr RO 151 C10
Camarasa E 42 D5
Cămărașu RO 152 D4
Camarena E 46 D4
Camarena de la Sierra E 47 D10
Camarès F 34 C4
Camaret-sur-Aigues F 35 B8
Camaret-sur-Mer F 22 D2
Camarillas E 42 F2
Camariñas E 38 B1
Cămârzana RO 145 H7
Camarzana de Tera E 39 D7
Camas E 51 E7
Camastra I 58 E4
Cambados E 38 C2
Camberley GB 15 E7
Cambes F 28 F5
Cambil E 53 A9
Cambo-les-Bains F 32 D3
Camborne GB 12 E4
Cambra de Baixo P 44 C4
Cambrai F 19 D7
Cambre E 38 B3
Cambridge GB 15 C9
Cambrils E 42 E6
Cambron F 18 D4
Cambs D 83 C11
Camburg D 79 D10
Camelford GB 12 D5
Camenca MD 154 A3
Camerano I 67 E8
Cameri I 68 B6
Camerino I 67 F7
Camerles E 42 F5
Camerota I 60 C4
Çamiçi TR 177 E10
Camigliatello Silano I 61 E6
Camin D 83 D9
Caminha P 38 E2
Caminomorisco E 45 D8
Caminreal E 47 C10
Çamlica TR 172 C6
Çamlik TR 177 D9
Cammarata I 58 D4
Cammer D 79 B12
Cammin D 83 C12
Camogli I 37 C10
Camolin IRL 9 C10
Camon F 18 E5
Camors F 22 E6
Camp IRL 8 D3
Campagna I 60 B4
Campagnano di Roma I 62 C2
Campagnatico I 65 B4
Campagne F 29 F7
Campagne-lès-Hesdin F 15 G12
Campan F 33 D6
Campana I 61 E7
Campanario E 51 B8
Campanet E 57 B10
Câmpani RO 151 D10
Campano E 52 D4
Campaspero E 40 F3
Campbeltown GB 4 E5
Campbon F 23 F8
Campdevànol E 43 C8
Campeã P 38 F4
Campello E 56 E4
Campello sul Clitunne I 62 B3
Campelo P 44 E4
Campelos P 44 F2
Campénéac F 23 E7
Câmpeni RO 151 E11
Campertogno I 68 B5
Câmpia Turzii RO 152 D3
Campi Bisenzio I 66 E3
Campiglia Marittima I 65 A3
Campiglia Soana I 31 D12
Campillo de Alto Buey E 47 E9
Campillo de Arenas E 53 A9
Campillo de Dueñas E 47 C9
Campillo de Llerena E 51 B8
Campillos E 53 B7
Campillos-Paravientos E 47 E9
Câmpina RO 161 C7
Câmpineanca RO 153 F10
Campinho P 50 C5
Campisábalos E 40 F5
Campi Salentina I 61 C10
Campli I 62 B5
Campo E 33 F6
Campo P 38 F3
Campobasso I 63 D7
Campobello di Licata I 58 E4
Campobello di Mazara I 58 D2
Campodarsego I 66 A4
Campo de Caso E 39 B9
Campo de Criptana E 47 F6
Campo de San Pedro E 40 F4
Campodimele I 62 E5
Campo di Trens I 72 C3
Campodolcino I 71 E8
Campofelice di Roccella I 58 D4
Campofiorito I 58 D3
Campoformido I 73 D7
Campofranco I 58 D4
Campofrío E 51 D6
Campoli Appennino I 62 D5
Campo Ligure I 37 B9
Campolongo Maggiore I 66 B5
Campo Lugar E 45 F9
Campo Maior P 51 A5
Campomarino I 61 C9
Campomarino I 63 D8
Campomorone I 37 B9
Camponaraya E 39 C6
Camponogara I 66 B5
Campora San Giovanni I 59 A9
Camporeale I 58 D3
Campo Redondo P 50 D2
Camporgiano I 66 D1
Camporosso I 37 D7
Camporrells E 42 D5
Camporrobles E 47 E10
Campos E 57 C11
Campos P 38 E4
Camposampiero I 66 A4
Camposanto I 66 C3
Campotéjar E 53 B9
Campotosto I 62 B4
Campo Tures I 72 C4
Camprodon E 33 F10
Camptown GB 5 E11
Câmpulung RO 160 C6
Câmpulung la Tisa RO 145 H8
Câmpulung Moldovenesc RO 153 B7
Câmpuri RO 153 E9
Camrose GB 12 B4
Camuñas E 46 F6
Çamyayla TR 181 B8
Çan TR 173 D7
Čaňa SK 145 F3
Cañada E 56 D3
Cañada de Benatanduz E 42 F2
Cañada del Hoyo E 47 E9
Cañada Vellida E 42 F2
Čanak HR 156 C3
Çanakçi TR 173 F10
Çanakkale TR 171 D10
Canale I 37 B7
Canale-di-Verde F 37 G10
Canalejas del Arroyo E 47 D8
Canalejas de Peñafiel E 40 E3
Canals E 56 D3
Canals F 33 C8
Canàl San Bovo I 72 D4
Cañamares E 47 D8
Cañamero E 45 F10
Canaples F 18 D5
Canari F 37 F10
Canaro I 66 C4
Cañaveral E 45 E8
Cañaveral de León E 51 C6
Cañaveras E 47 D8
Cañaveruelas E 47 D7
Canazei I 72 D4
Cancale F 23 C8
Cancarix E 55 C9
Cancellara I 60 B5
Cancello ed Arnone I 60 A2
Cancon F 33 A7
Candanchú E 32 E4
Çandarli TR 177 B8
Candás E 39 A8
Candasnos E 42 D4
Candé F 23 E9
Candela I 60 A5
Candelario E 45 D9
Candeleda E 45 D10
Candelo I 68 B5
Candemil P 38 E2
Cândești RO 153 D9
Cândești RO 160 C6
Candia Lomellina I 68 C6
Candilichera E 41 E7
Candín E 39 C6
Canedo P 44 B4
Canelli I 37 B8
Canena E 55 C6
Canepina I 62 C2
Canero E 39 A7
Cănești RO 161 C9
Canet F 34 C5
Canet F 34 D4
Canet de Mar E 43 D9
Cañete E 47 D9
Cañete de las Torres E 53 A8
Cañete la Real E 53 C6
Canet-en-Roussillon F 34 E5
Canet lo Roig E 42 F4
Canet-Plage F 34 E5
Cangas E 38 D2
Cangas del Narcea E 39 B6
Cangas de Onís E 39 B9
Cangonj AL 168 C4
Canha P 50 B2
Canhestros P 50 C3
Cania MD 154 E2
Canicattì I 58 E4
Canicattini Bagni I 59 E7
Canicosa de la Sierra E 40 E5
Caniles E 55 E7
Canillas de Aceituno E 53 C8
Canino I 62 C1
Cañizal E 45 B10
Cañizares E 47 C8
Cañizo E 39 E9
Canjáyar E 55 E7
Canlia RO 161 E11
Canna I 61 C7
Cannara I 62 B3
Cannero Riviera I 68 A6
Cannes F 36 D6
Canneto I 59 C6
Canneto I 66 F2
Canneto sull'Oglio I 66 B1
Cannich GB 2 L7
Canningstown IRL 7 E8
Cannington GB 13 C8
Cannobio I 68 A6
Cannock GB 11 F7
Cano P 50 B4
Canolo I 59 C9
Canonbie GB 5 E11
Canosa di Puglia I 60 A6
Cánovas E 56 F2
Can Pastilla E 49 E10
Can Picafort E 57 B11
Canredondo E 47 C8
Cansano I 62 D6
Cantagallo I 66 D3
Cantalapiedra E 45 B10
Cantalejo E 40 F4
Cantalice I 62 C3
Cantalpino E 45 B10
Cantanhede P 44 D3
Cantavieja E 42 F3
Čantavir SRB 150 F4
Cantemir MD 154 E2
Cantenac F 28 E4
Canteras E 56 F2
Canterbury GB 15 E11
Cantiano I 66 F6
Cantillana E 51 D8
Cantimpalos E 46 B4
Cantoira I 31 E11
Cantoria E 55 E8
Cantù I 69 B7
Canvey Island GB 15 D10
Cany-Barville F 18 E2
Canyelles E 43 E7
Caolas GB 4 B3

Caorle I 73 E6
Capaccio I 60 C4
Capaci I 58 C3
Capafonts E 42 E6
Capalbio I 65 C4
Căpâlna RO 151 D9
Căpâlnița RO 153 E6
Capannoli I 66 E2
Capannori I 66 E2
Caparde BIH 157 D10
Capari NMK 168 B5
Caparica P 50 B1
Caparrosa P 44 C4
Caparroso E 32 F2
Cap-Blanc E 48 F4
Capbreton F 32 C3
Cap d'Agde F 34 D6
Capdenac F 33 A10
Capdenac-Gare F 33 A10
Capdepera E 57 B11
Capel Curig GB 10 E4
Capelins P 51 B5
Capelle aan de IJssel NL 16 E3
Capellen L 20 E6
Capel St Mary GB 15 C11
Capendu F 34 D4
Capestang F 34 D5
Capestrano I 62 C5
Cap Ferret F 32 A3
Capileira E 55 F6
Capilla E 54 B2
Capinha P 44 D6
Capistrello I 62 D4
Capizzi I 58 D5
Căpleni RO 151 B10
Čaplje BIH 157 C6
Čapljina BIH 157 F8
Capodimonte I 62 B1
Capo di Ponte I 69 A9
Capo d'Orlando I 59 C6
Capoliveri I 65 B2
Capolona I 66 E4
Caposele I 60 B4
Capoterra I 64 E2
Cappadocia I 62 C4
Cappagh White IRL 8 C6
Cappamore IRL 8 C6
Cappawhite IRL 8 C6
Cappeen IRL 8 E5
Cappelle sul Tavo I 62 C6
Cappeln (Oldenburg) D 17 C10
Cappercleuch GB 5 E10
Cappoquin IRL 9 D7
Capracotta I 63 D6
Capraia Isola I 65 A1
Capranica I 62 C2
Caprarola I 62 C2
Căpreni RO 160 D3
Capri I 60 B2
Căpriana MD 154 C2
Capriati a Volturno I 63 E6
Capri Leone I 59 C6
Caprino Bergamasco I 69 B7
Caprino Veronese I 69 B10
Captieux F 32 B5
Capua I 60 A2
Capurso I 61 A7
Căpușu Mare RO 151 D11
Capvern-les-Bains F 33 D6
Carabaña E 47 D6
Caracal RO 160 E4
Caracuel de Calatrava E 54 B4
Caragaș MD 154 D5
Caragele RO 161 D10
Caraglio I 37 C6
Caraman F 33 C9
Caramanico Terme I 62 C6
Caramulo P 44 C4
Cărand RO 151 E9
Caranga E 39 B7
Caranguejeira P 44 E3
Caransebeș RO 159 C9
Carantec F 22 C4
Carapelle I 60 A5
Carapinheira P 44 D3
Carasco I 37 C10
Carașova RO 159 C8
Caraula RO 159 E11
Caravaca de la Cruz E 55 C9
Caravaggio I 69 C8
Carbajales de Alba E 39 E8
Carballeda de Avia E 38 D3
Carballo E 38 B2
Carballo E 38 D4
Carbellino E 45 B8
Carbonera de Frentes E 41 E6
Carboneras E 55 F9
Carboneras de Guadazaón E 47 E9
Carbonero El Mayor E 46 B4
Carboneros E 54 C5
Carbonia I 64 E2
Carbonìn I 72 C5
Carbonne F 33 D8
Carbost GB 2 L4
Carbost GB 2 L4
Cărbunari RO 159 D8
Cărbunești RO 161 C8
Carbury IRL 7 F9
Carcaboso E 45 D8
Carcabuey E 53 B8
Carcaixent E 48 F4
Carcaliu RO 155 C2
Carcans F 28 E3
Carcans-Plage F 28 E3
Carção P 39 E6
Cárcar E 32 F2
Carcare I 37 C8
Carcassonne F 33 D10
Carcastillo E 32 F3
Carcelén E 47 F10
Carcès F 36 E4
Carchelejo E 53 A9
Carcoforo I 68 B5
Cardaillac F 29 F9
Çardak TR 172 D6
Cardedeu E 43 D8
Cardedu I 64 D4
Cardeña E 54 C4
Cardeñadijo E 40 D4
Cardenden GB 5 C10
Cardenete E 47 E9
Cardeñosa E 46 C3
Cardeto I 59 C8
Cardiff GB 13 C8
Cardigan GB 12 A5
Cardigos P 44 E4
Cardinale I 59 B9
Cardito I 62 D5
Cardon RO 155 C5
Cardona E 43 D7
Cardosas P 50 E2
Carei RO 151 B9
Carenas E 41 F8
Carentan F 23 B9
Carentoir F 23 E7
Carevdar HR 149 D7
Carev Dvor NMK 168 B5
Cargenbridge GB 5 E9
Cargèse F 37 G9
Carhaix-Plouguer F 22 D4
Caria P 44 D6
Cariati I 61 E7
Caridade P 50 C4
Carife I 60 A4
Carignan F 19 E11
Carignano I 37 B7
Cariñena E 41 F9
Carini I 58 C3
Carinish GB 2 K2
Cariño E 38 A4
Carinola I 60 A1
Carisio I 68 C5
Carisolo I 69 A10
Cârjiți RO 151 F10
Carland GB 7 C9
Carlanstown IRL 7 E9
Carlantino I 63 D7
Carlat F 29 F11
Carlentini I 59 E7
Carlet E 48 F3
Cârlibaba RO 152 B6
Cârligele RO 153 F10
Carling F 186 C2
Carlingford IRL 7 D10
Carlisle GB 5 F11
Carloforte I 64 E1
Cârlogani RO 160 D4
Cârlomănești RO 161 C9
Carlopoli I 59 A9
Carlops GB 5 D10
Carlow D 83 C9
Carlow IRL 9 C9
Carloway GB 2 J3
Carlsberg D 186 C5
Carlton GB 11 F9
Carlton Colville GB 15 C12
Carluke GB 5 D9
Carlux F 29 F8
Carmagnola I 37 B7
Carmanova MD 154 C5
Carmarthen GB 12 B6
Carmaux F 33 B10
Carmena E 46 E4
Cármenes E 39 C8
Carmiano I 61 C10
Carmona E 51 E8
Carmonita E 45 F8
Carmyllie GB 5 B11
Carnac F 22 E5
Carnagh GB 7 D9
Carndonagh IRL 4 E2
Carnew IRL 9 C10
Carnforth GB 10 C6
Carnières F 19 D7
Carnikava LV 135 B8
Carnlough GB 4 F5
Carno GB 10 F4
Carnota E 38 C1
Carnoules F 36 E4
Carnoustie GB 5 B11
Carnoux-en-Provence F 35 D10
Carnteel GB 7 D9
Carnwath GB 5 D9
Carolei I 60 E6
Carolles F 23 C8
Carona I 69 A8
Caronia I 58 C5
C. A. Rosetti RO 155 C5
C. A. Rosetti RO 161 C10
Carosino I 61 C8
Carovigno I 61 B9
Carovilli I 63 D6
Carpaneto Piacentino I 69 D8
Carpegna I 66 E5
Carpen RO 159 E11
Carpenedolo I 66 B1
Carpentras F 35 B9
Carpi I 66 C2
Carpignano Salentino I 61 C10
Carpignano Sesia I 68 B5
Cărpineni MD 154 D2
Cărpinet RO 151 E10
Carpineti I 66 D1
Carpineto Romano I 62 D4
Cărpiniș RO 151 F6
Carpino I 63 D9
Carpinone I 63 D6
Carpio E 40 F1
Carpiquet F 23 B11
Carquefou F 23 F9
Carqueiranne F 36 E4
Carracastle IRL 6 E5
Carracedelo E 39 C6
Carradale East GB 4 D6
Carragh IRL 7 F9
Carraig Airt IRL 7 B7
Carraig na Siuire IRL 9 D8
Carraig Thuathail IRL 8 E6
Carral E 38 B3
Carralevë RKS 163 E10
Carranque E 46 D5
Carrapateira P 50 E2
Carrapichana P 44 C6
Carrara I 69 E9
Carraroe IRL 6 F3
Carrascal del Obispo E 45 C9
Carrascosa E 47 C8
Carrascosa del Campo E 47 D7
Carratraca E 53 C7
Carrazeda de Ansiães P 45 B6
Carrazedo de Montenegro P 38 E5
Carrbridge GB 3 L9
Carreço P 38 E2
Carregado P 50 A2
Carregal do Sal P 44 D5
Carregueiros P 44 E4
Carreira P 44 E3
Carreña E 39 B10
Carreteira E 38 C4
Carriazo E 40 B4
Carrick IRL 6 C5
Carrick IRL 9 D9
Carrickart IRL 7 B7
Carrickfergus GB 4 F5
Carrickmacross IRL 7 E9
Carrickmore GB 4 F2
Carrick-on-Shannon IRL 6 E6
Carrick-on-Suir IRL 9 D8
Carriço P 44 E3
Carrigaholt IRL 8 C3
Carrigallen IRL 7 E7
Carriganima IRL 8 E4
Carriganimmy IRL 8 E4
Carrigart IRL 7 B7
Carrigkerry IRL 8 D4
Carrig Mhachaire IRL 7 E9
Carrigtohill IRL 8 E6
Carrigtwohill IRL 8 E6
Carrio E 38 B3
Carrión de Calatrava E 54 A5
Carrión de los Céspedes E 51 E7
Carrión de los Condes E 39 D10
Carrizo de la Ribera E 39 C8
Carrizosa E 55 B7
Carronbridge GB 5 E9
Carros F 37 D6
Carrouges F 23 C11
Carrowkeel IRL 4 E2
Carrowkeel IRL 7 B7
Carrowkennedy IRL 6 E3
Carrù I 37 C7
Carryduff GB 7 C11
Carry-le-Rouet F 35 D9
Cars F 28 E4
Carsac-Aillac F 29 F8
Carsluith GB 5 F8
Carsoli I 62 C4
Carspach F 27 E7
Carsphairn GB 5 E8
Carstairs GB 5 D9
Cartagena E 56 F3
Cártama E 53 C7
Cartaxo P 44 F3
Cartaya E 51 E5
Cartelègue F 28 E4
Carteret F 23 B8
Carterton GB 13 B11
Cartes E 40 B3
Cârțișoara RO 152 F5
Cartoceto I 67 E6
Carucedo E 39 D6
Carunchio I 63 D7
Carvalhal P 44 E4
Carvalhal P 50 C2
Carvalho de Egas P 38 F5
Carvalhosa P 38 F3
Carviçais P 45 B7
Carvin F 18 D6
Carvoeira P 44 F2
Carvoeiro P 50 E3
Čáry SK 77 E12
Casabermeja E 53 C8
Casabona I 61 E7
Casa Branca P 50 B3
Casa Branca P 50 B4
Casacalenda I 63 D7
Casagiove I 60 A2
Casaglione F 37 G9
Casa l'Abate I 61 C10
Casalanguida I 63 C6
Casalarreina E 40 C6
Casalbordino I 63 C7
Casalbore I 60 A4
Casalborgone I 68 C4
Casalbuono I 60 C5
Casalbuttano ed Uniti I 69 C8
Casàl Cermelli I 37 B9
Casàl di Principe I 60 A2
Casalecchio di Reno I 66 D3
Casale Monferrato I 68 C5
Casaletto Spartano I 60 C5
Casalfiumanese I 66 D4
Casalgrande I 66 C2
Casalgrasso I 37 B7
Casalmaggiore I 66 C1
Casalnuovo Monterotaro I 63 D8
Casalpusterlengo I 69 C8
Casalvecchio di Puglia I 63 D8
Casàl Velino I 60 C4
Casamassima I 61 B7
Casamozza F 37 F10
Casarabonela E 53 C7
Casarano I 61 C10
Casar de Cáceres E 45 E8
Casar de Palomero E 45 D8
Casarejos E 40 E5
Casares E 39 B7
Casares E 53 D6
Casares de las Hurdes E 45 D8
Casariche E 53 B7
Casarrubios del Monte E 46 D4
Casarsa della Delizia I 73 E6
Casarza Ligure I 37 C10
Casas Altas E 47 D10
Casas Bajas E 47 D10
Casas de Benítez E 47 F8
Casas de Don Pedro E 45 F10
Casas de Fernando Alonso E 47 F8
Casas de Haro E 47 F8
Casas de Juan Gil E 47 F10
Casas de Juan Núñez E 47 F9
Casas de Lázaro E 55 B8
Casas del Monte E 45 D9
Casas de los Pinos E 47 F8
Casas del Puerto E 56 E2
Casas de Millán E 45 E8
Casas de Reina E 51 C8
Casas de Ves E 47 F10
Casas-Ibáñez E 47 F10
Casasimarro E 47 F8
Casas Novas de Mares P 50 B5
Casasola de Arión E 39 E9
Casatejada E 45 E9
Casatenovo I 69 B7
Casavieja E 46 D3
Cascais P 50 B1
Cascante E 41 D8
Cascante del Río E 47 D10
Cascia I 62 B4
Casciana Terme I 66 E2
Cascina I 66 E2
Căscioarele RO 161 E8
Casebres P 50 B2
Caseda E 32 E3
Case della Marina I 64 E4
Casei Gerola I 37 A9
Cășeiu RO 152 C3
Casekow D 84 D6
Casella I 37 B9
Caselle in Pittari I 60 C5
Caselle Torinese I 68 C4
Case Perrone I 61 B7
Caseras E 42 E4
Caserta I 60 A2
Casével P 50 D3
Cashel IRL 6 E5
Cashel IRL 6 F3
Cashel IRL 7 B7
Cashel IRL 7 G8
Cashel IRL 9 C7
Cashla IRL 6 F5
Casillas E 46 D3
Casillas de Flores E 45 D7
Casimcea RO 155 D2
Cașin RO 153 E9
Casina I 66 C1
Casinos E 48 E3
Casla IRL 6 F3
Čáslav CZ 77 C8
Casnewydd GB 13 B9
Casola in Lunigiana I 66 D1
Casola Valsenio I 66 D4
Casole d'Elsa I 66 F3
Casoli I 63 C6
Casoria I 60 B2
Caspe E 42 E3
Casperia I 62 C3
Cassà de la Selva E 43 D9
Cassagnes-Bégonhès F 33 B11
Cassaniouze F 29 F10
Cassano allo Ionio I 61 D6
Cassano delle Murge I 61 B7
Cassano Magnano I 69 B6
Cassano Spinola I 37 B9
Cassaro I 59 E6
Cassel F 18 C5
Casseneuil F 33 B7
Casserres E 43 C7
Cassibile I 59 F7
Cassine I 37 B9
Cassino I 62 E5
Cassis F 35 D10
Cassola I 72 E4
Cassuéjouls F 30 F2
Častá SK 146 E4
Castagliona Olona I 69 B6
Castagnaro I 66 B3
Castagneto Carducci I 66 F2
Castagnole delle Lanze I 37 B8
Castagnole Monferrato I 37 B8
Castalla E 56 D3
Castañar de Ibor E 45 E10
Castañares de Rioja E 40 C6
Castanet-Tolosan F 33 C9
Castanheira P 44 C6
Castanheira de Pêra P 44 D4
Castano Primo I 68 B6
Castasegna CH 69 A8
Casteggio I 37 A10
Castejón E 41 D8
Castejón del Puente E 42 D4
Castejón de Monegros E 42 D3
Castejón de Sos E 33 E6
Castejón de Valdejasa E 41 E10
Castelbellino I 67 F7
Castèl Bolognese I 66 D4
Castelbuono I 58 D5
Castelcivita I 60 C4
Castèl d'Ario I 66 B2
Castel de Cabra E 42 F2
Casteldelfino I 36 B6
Castèl del Monte I 62 C5
Castèl del Piano I 65 B5
Castèl del Rio I 66 D4
Castèl di Iudica I 59 E6
Castèl di Lama I 62 B5
Castèl di Lucio I 58 D5
Castèl di Sangro I 62 D6
Casteleiro P 45 D6
Castelfidardo I 67 F8
Castelfiorentino I 66 E2
Castelflorite E 42 D3
Castèl Focognano I 66 E4
Castelforte I 62 E5
Castelfranci I 60 B4
Castelfranco di Sopra I 66 E4
Castelfranco di Sotto I 66 E2
Castelfranco Emilia I 66 C3
Castelfranco in Miscano I 60 A4
Castelfranco Veneto I 72 E4
Castèl Frentano I 63 C6
Castèl Gandolfo I 62 D3
Castelginest F 33 C8
Castèl Giorgio I 62 B1
Castèl Goffredo I 66 B1
Castelgrande I 60 B4
Casteljaloux F 33 B6
Castell D 75 C7
Castellabate I 60 C3
Castell'Alfero I 37 B8
Castellalto I 62 B5
Castellammare del Golfo I 58 C2
Castellammare di Stabia I 60 B2
Castellamonte I 68 C4
Castellana Grotte I 61 B8
Castellane F 36 D5
Castellaneta I 61 B7
Castellanos de Castro E 40 D3
Castellarano I 66 C2
Castellar de la Frontera E 53 D6
Castellar de la Muela E 47 C9
Castellar de la Ribera E 43 C6
Castellar de Santiago E 55 B6
Castellar de Santisteban E 55 C6
Castell'Arquato I 69 D8
Castell'Azzara I 62 B1
Castellazzo Bormida I 37 B9
Castelldans E 42 E5
Castell de Cabres E 42 F4
Castell de Castells E 56 D4
Castelldefels E 43 E7
Castell de Ferro E 55 F6
Castelleone I 69 C8
Castelletto sopra Ticino I 68 B6
Castellfort E 42 F3
Castellina in Chianti I 66 F3
Castellina Marittima I 66 F2
Castelliri I 62 D5
Castellnou de Bassella E 43 C6
Castellnovo E 48 E4
Castelló d'Argile I 66 C3
Castelló de Farfanya E 42 D5
Castelló de la Plana E 48 E4
Castelló d'Empúries E 43 C10
Castelló de Rugat E 56 D4
Castello di Annone I 37 B8
Castellón de la Plana E 48 E4
Castellote E 42 F3
Castello Tesino I 72 D4
Castellserà E 42 D5
Castellterçol E 43 D8
Castellucchio I 66 B2
Castelluccio dei Sauri I 60 A4
Castelluccio Inferiore I 60 C5
Castellucio Valmaggiore I 60 A4
Castell'Umberto I 59 C6
Castelluzzo I 58 C2
Castell-y-Nedd GB 13 B7
Castèl Madama I 62 D3
Castèl Maggiore I 66 C3
Castelmagno I 37 C6
Castelmassa I 66 B3
Castelmauro I 63 D7
Castelmoron-sur-Lot F 33 B6
Castelnau-Barbarens F 33 C7
Castelnaudary F 33 D9
Castelnau-d'Auzan F 33 C6
Castelnau-de-Médoc F 28 E4
Castelnau-de-Montmiral F 33 C9
Castelnau d'Estréfonds F 33 C8
Castelnau-le-Lez F 35 C6
Castelnau-Magnoac F 33 D7
Castelnau-Montratier F 33 B8
Castelnau-Rivière-Basse F 32 C5
Castelnovo di Sotto I 66 C2
Castelnovo ne'Monti I 66 D1
Castelnuovo Berardenga I 66 F4
Castelnuovo della Daunia I 63 D8
Castelnuovo di Garfagnana I 66 D1
Castelnuovo di Porto I 62 C3
Castelnuovo di Val di Cecina I 66 F2
Castelnuovo Don Bosco I 68 C4
Castelnuovo Rangone I 66 C2
Castelnuovo Scrivia I 37 B9
Castelo Bom P 45 C7
Castelo Branco P 39 F6
Castelo Branco P 44 E6
Castelo de Paiva P 44 B4
Castelo de Vide P 44 F6
Castelo do Neiva P 38 E2
Castelões P 44 B4
Castelplanio I 67 F7
Castelraimondo I 67 F7
Castèl Ritaldi I 62 B3
Castelrotto I 72 C4
Castelsagrat F 33 B7
Castèl San Giovanni I 69 C7
Castèl San Lorenzo I 60 C4
Castèl San Niccolò I 66 E4
Castèl San Pietro Terme I 66 D4
Castèl Sant'Angelo I 62 C4
Castelsantangelo sul Nera I 62 B4
Castelsaraceno I 60 C5
Castelsardo I 64 B2
Castelsarrasin F 33 B8
Castelseras E 42 F3
Casteltermini I 58 D4
Castelu RO 155 E2
Castelverde I 69 C8
Castelvetere in Val Fortore I 60 A3
Castelvetrano I 58 D2
Castelvetro Placentino I 69 C8
Castèl Viscardo I 62 B2
Castèl Volturno I 60 A1
Castenaso I 66 C3
Castéra-Verduzan F 33 C6
Castetnau-Camblong F 32 D4
Castets F 32 C3
Castiadas I 64 E4
Castielfabib E 47 D10
Castiello de Jaca E 32 E4
Castiglioncello I 66 F1
Castiglione dei Pepoli I 66 D3
Castiglione del Lago I 66 F5
Castiglione della Pescaia I 65 B3
Castiglione della Stiviere I 66 B1
Castiglione di Sicilia I 59 D7
Castiglione d'Orcia I 65 A5
Castiglione in Teverina I 62 B2
Castiglione Messer Marino I 63 D6
Castiglion Fiorentino I 66 F4
Castignano I 62 B5
Castilblanco E 45 F10
Castilblanco de los Arroyos E 51 D8
Castiliscar E 32 F3
Castilleja de la Cuesta E 51 E7
Castillejar E 55 D7
Castillejo de Martin Viejo E 45 C7
Castillejo de Mesleón E 40 F4
Castillejo de Robledo E 40 E5
Castillo de Bayuela E 46 D3
Castillo de Garcimuñoz E 47 E8
Castillo de Locubín E 53 A9
Castillon-en-Couserans F 33 E8
Castillon-la-Bataille F 28 F5
Castillonnès F 33 A7
Castillo-Nuevo E 32 E3
Castilruiz E 41 E7
Castione della Presolana I 69 B9
Castiòns di Strada I 73 E7
Castlebar IRL 6 E4
Castlebay GB 4 B2
Castlebellingham IRL 7 E10
Castleblakeney IRL 6 F6
Castleblayney IRL 7 D9
Castlebridge IRL 9 D10
Castle Carrock GB 5 F11
Castle Cary GB 13 C9
Castlecomer IRL 9 C8
Castleconnell IRL 8 C5
Castlecor IRL 8 D5
Castledawson GB 4 F3
Castlederg GB 4 F1
Castledermot IRL 9 C9
Castle Douglas GB 5 F9
Castleellis IRL 9 D10
Castlefinn IRL 4 F1
Castleford GB 11 D9
Castlegal IRL 6 D6
Castlegregory IRL 8 D2
Castlehill IRL 6 D4
Castleisland IRL 8 D4
Castle Kennedy GB 4 F7
Castlellis IRL 9 D10
Castlemaine IRL 8 D3
Castlemartin GB 12 B4
Castlemartyr IRL 8 E6
Castleplunket IRL 6 E6
Castlepollard IRL 7 E8
Castlerea IRL 6 E6
Castlereagh GB 7 C11
Castlerock GB 4 E3
Castletown GB 3 H10
Castletown GB 11 F7
Castletown GBM 10 C2
Castletown IRL 7 G8
Castletown Bere IRL 8 E3
Castletownshend IRL 8 E4
Castlewellan GB 7 D11
Castranova RO 160 E4
Castrejón de la Peña E 39 C10
Castrelo do Val E 38 E5
Castres F 33 C10
Castricum NL 16 C3
Castries F 35 C6
Castrignano del Capo I 61 D10
Castril E 55 D7
Castrillo de Don Juan E 40 E3
Castrillo de Duero E 40 E3
Castrillo de la Reina E 40 E5
Castrillo de la Vega E 40 E4
Castrillo Tejeriego E 40 E3
Castro I 61 C10
Castrobarto E 40 B5
Castrocalbón E 39 D8
Castro Caldelas E 38 D5
Castrocaro Terme I 66 D4
Castrocontrigo E 39 D7
Castro Daire P 44 C5
Castro dei Volsci I 62 D5
Castro del Río E 53 A8
Castro de Ouro E 38 A5
Castro de Rei E 38 B5
Castrofilippo I 58 E4
Castrogonzalo E 39 E8
Castrojeriz E 40 D3
Castro Laboreiro P 38 D3
Castro Marim P 50 E5
Castromocho E 39 D10
Castromonte E 39 E9
Castronuevo E 39 E8
Castronuño E 39 F9
Castronuovo di Sant'Andrea I 60 C6
Castronuovo di Sicilia I 58 D4
Castropignano I 63 D7
Castropodame E 39 C7
Castropol E 39 A5
Castrop-Rauxel D 17 E8
Castroreale I 59 C7
Castro-Urdiales E 40 B5
Castroverde E 38 B5
Castro Verde P 50 D3
Castroverde de Campos E 39 E9
Castrovillari I 60 D6
Castuera E 51 B8
Cața RO 152 E6
Catadau E 48 F3
Çatalca TR 173 B9
Catalina RO 153 F8
Cataloi RO 155 C3
Catania I 59 E7
Catanzaro I 59 B10
Catanzaro Marina I 59 B10
Catarroja E 48 F4
Cățcău RO 152 C3
Căteasca RO 160 D6
Catenanuova I 59 D6
Caterham GB 15 E8
Cateri F 37 F9
Cathair Dónall IRL 8 E2
Cathair na Mart IRL 6 E3
Cathair Saidhbhín IRL 8 E2
Catherdaniel IRL 8 E2
Catí E 42 G4
Čatići BIH 157 D9
Catignano I 62 C5
Cătina RO 152 D4
Cătina RO 161 C8
Cativelos P 44 C5
Catoira E 38 C2
Caton GB 10 C6
Catral E 56 E3
Cattenom F 20 F6
Catterfeld D 79 E8
Catterick GB 11 C8
Catterline GB 5 B12
Cattolica I 67 E6
Cattolica Eraclea I 58 E3
Cătunele RO 159 D10
Catus F 33 A8
Căuaș RO 151 B10
Caudan F 22 E5
Caudebec-lès-Elbeuf F 18 F3
Caudecoste F 33 B7
Caudete E 56 D3
Caudete de las Fuentes E 47 E10
Caudiel E 48 E3
Caudiès-de-Fenouillèdes F 33 E10
Caudry F 19 D7
Caujac F 33 D8
Caulnes F 23 D7
Caulonia I 59 C9
Caumont F 33 B8
Caumont F 33 C9
Caumont-l'Éventé F 23 B10
Caumont-sur-Durance F 35 C8
Caunes-Minervois F 34 D4
Cauro F 37 H9
Căușeni MD 154 D4
Causeway IRL 8 D3
Causeway Head GB 4 E3
Caussade F 33 B9
Cautano I 60 A3
Cauterets F 32 E5
Cava de'Tirreni I 60 B3
Cavadinești RO 153 E12
Cavaglià I 68 C5
Cavaillon F 35 C9
Cavalaire-sur-Mer F 36 E5
Cavaleiro P 50 D2
Cavalese I 72 D3
Cavallermaggiore I 37 B7
Cavallino I 66 B6
Cava Manara I 69 C7
Cavan IRL 7 E8
Cavanagarven IRL 7 D9
Cavargna I 69 A7
Cavarzere I 66 B5
Cavazzo Carnico I 73 D7
Cave I 62 D3
Cave del Predil I 73 D8
Caveirac F 35 C7
Cavezzo I 66 C3
Cavignac F 28 E5
Čavle HR 67 B9
Cavnic RO 152 B3
Cavour I 68 D3
Cavriago I 66 C2
Cavriglia I 66 E3
Cavtat HR 162 D5
Çavuşköy TR 171 C10
Cawdor GB 3 K9
Cawood GB 11 D9
Cawston GB 15 B11
Caxarias P 44 E3
Çaybaşi TR 177 C9
Çayboyu TR 181 B8
Cayeux-sur-Mer F 18 D4
Çayirdere TR 173 B9
Caylus F 33 B9
Cazalegas E 46 D3
Cazalilla E 53 A9
Cazalla de la Sierra E 51 D8
Cazals F 33 A8
Cazals F 33 B9
Căzănești RO 159 D10
Căzănești RO 161 D10
Cazasu RO 155 C1
Cazaubon F 32 C5
Cazères F 33 D8
Cazes-Mondenard F 33 B8
Cazilhac F 33 D10
Cazin BIH 156 C4
Cazis CH 71 D8
Cazma HR 149 E7
Cazorla E 55 D7
Cazoulès F 29 F8
Cea E 38 D4
Cea E 39 D10
Ceahlău RO 153 C7
Ceamurlia de Jos RO 155 D3
Ceanannus Mór IRL 7 E9
Ceann Toirc IRL 8 D5
Ceann Trá IRL 8 D2
Ceanu Mare RO 152 D3
Cearsiadar GB 2 J3
Ceatharlach IRL 9 C9
Ceaucé F 23 D10
Ceaușu de Câmpie RO 152 D5
Céaux-d'Allègre F 30 E4
Cébazat F 30 D3
Čebín CZ 77 D10
Cebolla E 46 E3
Čebovce SK 147 E8
Cebreros E 46 D4
Ceccano I 62 D4
Cece H 149 C11
Čečejovce SK 145 F3
Čechtice CZ 77 C8
Čechynce SK 146 E6
Cecina I 66 F2
Ceclavín E 45 E7
Cecuni MNE 163 D8
Cedães P 38 F5
Cēdasai LT 135 D10
Cedegolo I 69 A9
Cedeira E 38 A3
Cedillo E 44 E6
Cedillo del Condado E 46 D5
Cedrillas E 48 D3
Cedry Wielkie PL 138 B6
Cedynia PL 84 E6
Cee E 38 C1
Cefa RO 151 D8
Cefalù I 58 C5
Cefn-mawr GB 10 F5
Ceggia I 73 E6
Cegléd H 150 C4
Ceglédbercel H 150 C4
Ceglie Messapica I 61 B9
Cegłów PL 141 F5
Čegrane NMK 163 F10
Cehal RO 151 C10
Cehegín E 55 C9
Cehu Silvaniei RO 151 C11
Ceica RO 151 D9
Ceikiniai LT 135 F12
Ceilhes-et-Rocozels F 34 C5
Ceinos de Campos E 39 D9
Ceintrey F 26 C5
Ceira P 44 D4
Čejč CZ 77 E11
Čejkov SK 145 G4
Cekcyn PL 138 C5
Çekirdekli TR 173 F9
Čekiškė LT 134 F7
Ceków-Kolonia PL 142 C5
Celadas E 47 D10
Čeladná CZ 146 B6
Čelákovice CZ 77 B7
Celaliye TR 173 A7
Celano I 62 C5
Celanova E 38 D4
Čelarevo SRB 158 C4
Celaru RO 160 E4
Celbridge IRL 7 F9
Čelebić BIH 157 E6
Čelebići BIH 157 F10
Celeiros P 38 E3
Celenza Valfortore I 63 D7
Celestynów PL 141 F4
Čelič BIH 157 C10
Celico I 61 E6
Čelinac Donji BIH 157 C7
Celje SLO 148 D4
Cella E 47 D10
Celldömölk H 149 B8
Celle D 79 A7
Celle Ligure I 37 C9
Cellere I 62 C1
Celles B 19 C7
Celles-sur-Belle F 28 C5
Celles-sur-Ource F 25 D11
Cellettes F 24 E5
Cellino Attanasio I 62 B5
Cellole I 62 E5
Čelopeci NMK 168 B5
Čelopek NMK 164 F3
Celorico da Beira P 44 C6
Celorico de Basto P 38 F4
Celrà E 43 C9
Çeltikçi TR 173 D9
Cembra I 69 A11
Čemerno BIH 157 F10
Cempi LV 135 A11
Cénac-et-St-Julien F 29 F8
Cenad RO 150 E6
Cenade RO 152 E4
Cenas LV 134 C7
Cencenighe Agordino I 72 D4
Cendras F 35 B7
Cendrieux F 29 F7
Cenei RO 159 B6
Ceneselli I 66 B3
Cengio I 37 C8
Cenicero E 41 D6
Cenicientos E 46 D4
Čenta SRB 158 C5
Centallo I 37 B7
Centelles E 43 D8
Cento I 66 C3
Centola I 60 C4
Centuri F 37 F10
Centuripe I 59 D6
Cepagatti I 62 C6
Cepari RO 160 C5
Čepin HR 149 E11
Cepleniţa RO 153 C9
Čepovan SLO 73 D8
Ceppaloni I 60 A3
Ceppo Morelli I 68 B5
Ceprano I 62 D5
Čeptura RO 161 C8
Čeralije HR 149 E9
Cerami I 59 D6
Cerani BIH 157 C8
Cerano I 68 C6
Ceranów PL 141 E6
Cérans-Foulletourte F 23 E12
Cerasi I 59 C8
Ceraso I 60 C4
Cerașu RO 161 C8
Cerăt RO 160 E3
Ceraukste LV 135 D8
Çeravë AL 168 C4
Cerbăl RO 151 F10

Cerbère F 34 F5
Cercal P 44 F3
Cercal P 50 D2
Čerčany CZ 77 C7
Cercedilla E 46 C4
Cercemaggiore I 63 E7
Cerchezu RO 155 F2
Cerchiara di Calabria I 61 D6
Cerchio I 62 C5
Cercy-la-Tour F 30 B4
Cerda I 58 D4
Cerdanyola del Vallès E 43 E8
Cerdedo E 38 C3
Cerdeira P 44 D5
Cerdon F 25 E7
Cēre LV 134 B5
Cerea I 66 B3
Cered H 147 E9
Ceregnano I 66 B4
Cerekwica PL 85 E13
Cérences F 23 C9
Ceres GB 5 C11
Ceres I 31 E11
Ceresole Reale I 31 E11
Céreste F 35 C10
Céret F 34 F4
Čerević SRB 158 C4
Cerezo de Abajo E 46 B5
Cerezo de Arriba E 40 F4
Cerezo de Riotirón E 40 C5
Cerfontaine B 184 D1
Cergău RO 152 E3
Cergy F 24 B7
Cerhenice CZ 77 B8
Ceriale I 37 C8
Ceriana I 37 D7
Cerignola I 60 A5
Cérilly F 30 B2
Čerin BIH 157 F8
Cerisano I 60 E6
Cerisiers F 25 D9
Cerisy-la-Forêt F 23 B10
Cerisy-la-Salle F 23 B9
Cerizay F 28 B4
Çerkezköy TR 173 B9
Çerkezmüsellim TR 173 B7
Cerklje SLO 73 D9
Cerklje SLO 148 E5
Cerknica SLO 73 E9
Cerkno SLO 73 D8
Cerkwica PL 85 B8
Cermei RO 151 D8
Çermë-Proshkë AL 168 B2
Cermignano I 62 B5
Cërmjan RKS 163 E9
Cerna HR 157 B10
Cerna RO 155 C2
Cernache do Bonjardim P 44 E4
Černá Hora CZ 77 D11
Cernat RO 153 F8
Cernătești RO 160 E2
Cernătești RO 161 C9
Cernavodă RO 155 E2
Cernay F 27 E7
Cernay-en-Dormois F 19 F10
Černčice CZ 76 B5
Cernégula E 40 C4
Cernele RO 160 E3
Cernești RO 152 C3
Cernica RO 161 E8
Cernier CH 31 A10
Černík HR 157 B7
Černík SK 146 E6
Černilov CZ 77 B9
Cernișoara RO 160 C4
Cernobbio I 69 B7
Černoleuca MD 153 A11
Černošice CZ 76 C6
Černošín CZ 76 C3
Černovice CZ 77 D7
Černožice CZ 77 B9
Cerová SK 146 D4
Cerovac SRB 159 E6
Cerovak Tušilovički HR 148 F5
Ceroviljani BIH 157 B7
Cerovlje HR 67 B9
Cerovo SK 147 E8
Cerralbo E 45 C7
Cerreto d'Esi I 67 F6
Cerreto di Spoleto I 62 B3
Cerreto Sannita I 60 A3
Cerrigydrudion GB 10 E4
Cërrik AL 168 B2
Cerro al Volturno I 62 D6
Cersay F 28 A5
Cersosimo I 61 C6
Certaldo I 66 E3
Certeju de Sus RO 151 F10
Certești RO 153 E11
Certeze RO 145 H7
Certosa di Pavia I 69 C7
Certosa di Pesio I 37 C7
Ceru-Băcăinți RO 151 F11
Cërujë AL 168 C3
Cerva P 38 F4
Cervaro I 62 E5
Cervatos de la Cueza E 39 D10
Červená Voda CZ 77 B11
Cervenia RO 161 F6
Červená Voda CZ 77 C12
Červený Kostelec CZ 77 B10
Cervera E 42 D6
Cervera de la Cañada E 41 F8
Cervera del Llano E 47 E8
Cervera del Maestre E 48 D5
Cervera de los Montes E 46 D3
Cervera del Río Alhama E 41 D8
Cervera de Pisuerga E 40 C3
Cerveteri I 62 D2
Cervia I 66 D5
Cervignano del Friuli I 73 E7
Cervinara I 60 A3
Červiná Řečice CZ 77 C8
Cervione F 37 G10
Cervo E 38 A5
Cervo I 37 D8
Cervon F 25 F10
Cerzeto I 60 E6
Cesano Boscone I 69 C7
Cesano Maderno I 69 B7
Cesarò I 59 D6
Cesena I 66 D5
Cesenatico I 66 D5
Cesio I 37 C7
Cēsis LV 135 B10
Česká Kamenice CZ 80 E6
Česká Lípa CZ 81 E7
Česká Skalice CZ 77 B10
Česká Ves CZ 77 B12
České Brezovo SK 147 E9
České Budějovice CZ 77 E6
České Meziříčí CZ 77 B10
Český Brod CZ 77 B7
Český Dub CZ 81 E7
Český Krumlov CZ 76 E6
Český Těšín CZ 147 B7
Česljeva Bara SRB 159 D7
Çeşme TR 177 C7
Cespedosa E 45 C9
Cessalto I 73 E6
Cessenon-sur-Orb F 34 D5
Cessole I 37 B8
Cesson F 25 C8
Cesson-Sévigné F 23 D8
Cestas F 28 F4
Čestobrodica SRB 158 F5
Cesuras E 38 B3
Cesvaine LV 135 C12
Cetariu RO 151 C9
Cetate RO 152 C5
Cetate RO 159 E11
Cetatea de Baltă RO 152 E4
Cetățeni RO 160 C6
Cetina E 41 F8
Cetingrad HR 156 B4
Cetinje MNE 163 E6
Ceto I 69 A9
Ceton F 24 D4
Cetona I 62 B1
Cetraro I 60 D5
Ceuta WHAT 53 E6
Ceutí E 56 E2
Ceva I 37 C8
Cevico de la Torre E 40 E3
Cevico Navero E 40 E3
Cevins F 31 D9
Cevio CH 68 A6
Çevizköy TR 173 A8
Čevo MNE 163 D6
Cewice PL 85 B13
Ceyreste F 35 D10
Ceyzériat F 31 C7
Cezieni RO 160 E4
Chã P 38 E4
Chaam NL 16 F3
Chabanais F 29 D7
Chabeuil F 31 F7
Chabielice PL 143 D7
Chablis F 25 E10
Chabówka PL 147 B9
Chabreloche F 30 D4
Chabris F 24 F6
Chacim P 39 F6
Chagford GB 13 D7
Chagny F 30 B6
Chaïkali GR 174 C4
Chaillac F 29 C8
Chailland F 23 D10
Chaillé-les-Marais F 28 C3
Chailley F 25 D10
Chaintrix-Bierges F 25 C11
Chaironeia GR 175 C6
Chalabre F 33 E10
Chalais CH 31 C12
Chalais F 28 E6
Chalamera E 42 D4
Chalamont F 31 C7
Chalampé F 27 E8
Chalandri GR 175 C8
Chalandritsa GR 174 C4
Chalastra GR 169 C8
Chale GB 13 D12
Chaleix F 29 D7
Châlette-sur-Loing F 25 D8
Chalford GB 13 B10
Chalgrove GB 13 B12
Chaligny F 26 C5
Chalin PL 139 E7
Chalindrey F 26 E3
Chalivoy-Milon F 29 B11
Chalki GR 169 E8
Chalki GR 181 D7
Chalkiades GR 169 F7
Chalkiades GR 174 A2
Chalkida GR 175 C8
Chalkidona GR 169 C8
Chalkio GR 175 D6
Challans F 28 B2
Challerange F 19 F10
Challes-les-Eaux F 31 D8
Chalmoux F 30 B4
Chalonnes-sur-Loire F 23 F10
Châlons-en-Champagne F 25 C11
Chalon-sur-Saône F 30 B6
Châlus F 29 D7
Cham CH 27 F9
Cham D 75 D12
Chamalières F 30 D3
Chamaloc F 31 F7
Chamberet F 29 D9
Chambéria F 31 C8
Chambéry F 31 D8
Chambley-Bussières F 26 B4
Chambois F 23 C12
Chambon-sur-Voueize F 29 C10
Chambord F 24 E6
Chamboulive F 29 E9
Chambray-lès-Tours F 24 F4
Chambry F 19 E8
Chamesson F 25 E12
Chamonix-Mont-Blanc F 31 D10
Chamoux-sur-Gelon F 31 D9
Champagnac F 29 E10
Champagnac-de-Belair F 29 E7
Champagnac-le-Vieux F 30 E4
Champagne-Mouton F 29 D6
Champagne-sur-Seine F 25 D8
Champagney F 26 E6
Champagnole F 31 B8
Champaubert F 25 C10
Champdeniers-St-Denis F 28 C5
Champ-d'Oiseau F 25 E11
Champeix F 30 D3
Champéry CH 31 C10
Champex CH 31 C11
Champforgeuil F 30 B6
Champgenéteux F 23 D11
Champier F 31 E7
Champigné F 23 E10
Champignelles F 25 E9
Champigneulles F 186 D1
Champigny F 25 D9
Champlemy F 25 F9
Champlitte F 26 E4
Champniers F 29 D6
Champoléon F 31 F9
Champoluc I 68 B4
Champsecret F 23 C10
Champs-sur-Tarentaine-Marchal F 29 E11
Champs-sur-Yonne F 25 E10
Champ-sur-Drac F 31 E8
Champtoceaux F 23 F9
Chamrousse F 31 E8
Chamusca P 44 F4
Chanac F 34 B5
Chanas F 30 E6
Chança P 44 F5
Chanceaux F 25 E12
Chanceaux-sur-Choisille F 24 F4
Chancelade F 29 E7
Chancelaria P 44 E3
Chandras GR 179 E11
Chandrinos GR 174 F4
Chañe E 40 F3
Changé F 23 D10
Changé F 23 E12
Changy F 30 C5
Chania GR 178 D7
Chaniotis GR 169 D10
Chantada E 38 C4
Chantelle F 30 C3
Chantilly F 25 B7
Chantonnay F 28 B3
Chanu F 23 C10
Chaource F 25 D11
Chapaevo BG 166 C5
Chapayevka UA 154 A5
Chapel-en-le-Frith GB 11 E8
Chapelle-lez-Herlaimont B 182 E4
Chapeltown GB 11 E9
Chapinería E 46 D4
Charakas GR 178 E9
Charavgi GR 169 D6
Charbonnat F 30 B5
Charcenne F 26 F4
Charchilla F 31 C8
Chard GB 13 D9
Chardstock GB 13 D9
Charenton-du-Cher F 29 B11
Charfield GB 13 B10
Chargey-lès-Gray F 26 F4
Charlbury GB 13 B12
Charlemont GB 7 D9
Charleroi B 19 D9
Charlestown IRL 6 E5
Charleville IRL 8 D5
Charleville-Mézières F 19 E10
Charlieu F 30 C5
Charlottenberg S 96 C7
Charlton GB 13 C12
Charlton Kings GB 13 B10
Charly F 25 C9
Charmé F 29 D6
Charmes F 26 D5
Charmes-sur-Rhône F 30 F6
Charmey CH 31 B11
Charmouth GB 13 D9
Charmoy F 25 E9
Charnay-lès-Mâcon F 30 C6
Charny F 25 E9
Charokopeio GR 178 B2
Charolles F 30 C5
Charomkhava BY 133 F3
Charopo GR 169 B9
Chârost F 29 B10
Charquemont F 27 F6
Charrat CH 31 C11
Charrey-sur-Seine F 25 E12
Charrin F 30 B4
Charroux F 29 C6
Charsznica PL 143 F8
Chartres F 24 D5
Charvensod I 31 D11
Charvieu-Chavagneux F 31 D7
Charzyno PL 85 B9
Chassagne-Montrachet F 30 B6
Chasseneuil-sur-Bonnieure F 29 D6
Chasseradès F 35 A6
Chasse-sur-Rhône F 30 D6
Chassigny-Aisey F 26 E3
Chassillé F 23 D11
Chastre B 19 C10
Château-Arnoux F 35 B10
Châteaubernard F 28 D5
Châteaubourg F 23 D9
Châteaubriant F 23 E9
Château-Chinon F 30 A4
Château-d'Oex CH 31 C11
Château-d'Olonne F 28 B2
Château-du-Loir F 24 E3
Châteaudun F 24 D5
Châteaugiron F 23 D8
Château-Gontier F 23 E10
Château-Landon F 25 D8
Château-la-Vallière F 24 E3
Châteaulin F 22 D3
Châteaumeillant F 29 B10
Châteauneuf-de-Galaure F 31 E6
Châteauneuf-de-Randon F 35 A6
Châteauneuf-d'Ille-et-Vilaine F 23 C8
Châteauneuf-du-Faou F 22 D4
Châteauneuf-en-Thymerais F 24 C5
Châteauneuf-la-Forêt F 29 D9
Châteauneuf-les-Martigues F 35 D9
Châteauneuf-sur-Charente F 28 D5
Châteauneuf-sur-Cher F 29 B10
Châteauneuf-sur-Loire F 25 E7
Châteauneuf-sur-Sarthe F 23 E11
Châteauneuf-Val-de-Bargis F 25 F9
Châteauponsac F 29 C8
Château-Porcien F 19 E9
Châteauredon F 36 C4
Châteaurenard F 25 E8
Châteaurenard F 35 C8
Châteaurenaud F 31 B7
Château-Renault F 24 E4
Châteauroux F 29 B9
Châteauroux F 36 B5
Château-Salins F 26 C6
Château-Thierry F 25 B9
Châteauvillain F 25 D12
Châtel F 31 C10
Châtelaillon-Plage F 28 C3
Châtelaudren F 22 C6
Châtel-Censoir F 25 E10
Châteldon F 30 D4
Châtelet B 19 D10
Châtel-Gérard F 25 E11
Châtelguyon F 30 D3
Châtellerault F 29 B7
Châtel-Montagne F 30 C4
Châtel-St-Denis CH 31 B10
Châtel-sur-Moselle F 26 D5
Châtelus-Malvaleix F 29 C10
Châtenois F 26 D4
Châtenois F 27 D7
Châtenois-les-Forges F 27 E6
Châtenoy-le-Royal F 30 B6
Chatham GB 15 E10
Châtillon B 19 E12
Châtillon I 68 B4
Châtillon-Coligny F 25 E8
Châtillon-en-Bazois F 30 A4
Châtillon-en-Diois F 35 A9
Châtillon-en-Michaille F 31 C8
Châtillon-la-Palud F 31 D7
Châtillon-sur-Chalaronne F 31 C6
Châtillon-sur-Colmont F 23 D10
Châtillon-sur-Indre F 29 B8
Châtillon-sur-Loire F 25 E8
Châtillon-sur-Marne F 25 B10
Châtillon-sur-Seine F 25 E12
Châtillon-sur-Thouet F 28 B5
Chatte F 31 E7
Chatteris GB 15 C9
Chatton GB 5 D13
Chatuzange-le-Goubet F 31 F7
Chatzis GR 174 E4
Chauchina E 53 B9
Chaudenay F 26 E4
Chaudes-Aigues F 30 F3
Chaudeyrac F 35 A6
Chaudfontaine B 19 C12
Chauffailles F 30 C5
Chauffayer F 31 F9
Chaulnes F 18 E6
Chaumergy F 31 B7
Chaumont F 26 D3
Chaumont-en-Vexin F 18 F4
Chaumont-Porcien F 19 E9
Chaumont-sur-Aire F 26 C3
Chaumont-sur-Loire F 24 F5
Chaunay F 29 C6
Chauny F 19 E7
Chaussin F 31 B7
Chauvigny F 29 B7
Chavanay F 30 E6
Chavanges F 25 C12
Chavanoz F 31 D7
Chavari GR 174 D3
Chavelot F 26 D5
Chaves P 38 E5
Chazelles-sur-Lyon F 30 D5
Cheadle GB 11 F8
Cheb CZ 75 B11
Checa E 47 C9
Chechel'nyk UA 154 A4
Chęciny PL 143 E9
Chécy F 24 E7
Chedburgh GB 15 C10
Cheddar GB 13 C9
Chef-Boutonne F 28 C5
Chekhpare BG 166 E4
Cheles E 51 B5
Chella E 56 C3
Chełm PL 141 H8
Chełmek PL 143 F7
Chełmiec PL 145 D2
Chełmno PL 138 D5
Chełmno PL 142 B6
Chelmsford GB 15 D9
Chełmża PL 138 D6
Cheltenham GB 13 B10
Chelva E 47 E11
Chemazé F 23 E10
Chémery F 24 F5
Chémery-sur-Bar F 19 E10
Chemillé F 23 F10
Chemin F 31 B7
Cheminon F 25 C12
Chemiré-le-Gaudin F 23 E11
Chemnitz D 80 E3
Chenecey-Buillon F 26 F4
Chénérailles F 29 C10
Cheniménil F 26 D6
Chenôve F 26 F3
Cheny F 25 E10
Chepelare BG 165 F10
Chepintsi BG 165 D7
Chepstow GB 13 B9
Chepy F 25 C11
Chera E 48 E3
Chérac F 28 D5
Cherasco I 37 B7
Chéraute F 32 D4
Cherbourg-Octeville F 23 A8
Cheremule I 64 B2
Cherepkivtsi UA 153 A7
Chereshovo BG 161 F8
Cherlenivka UA 153 A8
Cherna BG 155 F1
Cherna Gora BG 166 E4
Chernevo BG 167 C9
Chernevo RUS 132 D3
Cherni Osŭm BG 165 D10
Cherni Vrŭkh BG 167 E8
Chernivtsi UA 153 A7
Chernogorovo BG 165 E9
Cherno More BG 167 D8
Chernoochene BG 166 F4
Chernyakhovsk RUS 136 D4
Chernyshevskoye RUS 136 D6
Chéroy F 25 D9
Cherskaya RUS 132 F3
Cherso GR 169 B8
Chert E 42 F4
Cherveix-Cubas F 29 E8
Cherven BG 161 F8
Chervena voda BG 161 F8
Cherven Bryag BG 165 C9
Cherventsi BG 167 B8
Cherves-Richemont F 28 D5
Chervona Hreblya UA 154 A4
Chervonoarmiys'ke UA 154 F3
Chervonohrad UA 144 C9
Chesham GB 15 D7
Cheshunt GB 15 D8
Chesley F 25 E11
Chessy-les-Prés F 25 D10
Cheste E 48 F3
Chester GB 10 E6
Chesterfield GB 11 E9
Chester-le-Street GB 5 F13
Chețani RO 152 E4
Chetrosu MD 153 A11
Chevagnes F 30 B4
Chevanceaux F 28 E5
Chevereșu Mare RO 159 B7
Chevillon F 26 C3
Chevilly F 24 D6
Chevreuse F 24 C7
Chew Magna GB 13 C9
Cheylade F 30 E2
Chezal-Benoît F 29 B10
Chèze F 32 E5
Chiajna RO 161 E8
Chiampo I 66 A3
Chianciano Terme I 62 A1
Chianni I 66 E2
Chiaramonte Gulfi I 59 E6
Chiaramonti I 64 B2
Chiaravalle I 67 E7
Chiaravalle Centrale I 59 B9
Chiari I 69 B8
Chiaromonte I 60 C6
Chiasso CH 69 B7
Chiavari I 37 C10
Chiavenno I 69 A7
Chiché F 28 B5
Chichester GB 15 F7
Chichiș RO 153 F7
Chiclana de la Frontera E 52 D4
Chiclana de Segura E 55 C6
Chieming D 72 A6
Chienes I 72 C4
Chieri I 37 A7
Chiesa in Valmalenco I 69 A8
Chieșd RO 151 C10
Chiesina Uzzanese I 66 E2
Chieti I 63 C6
Chieuti I 63 D8
Chieveley GB 13 C12
Chièvres B 19 C8
Chigwell GB 15 D9
Chiheru de Jos RO 152 D5
Chikhachevo RUS 133 B7
Chilches E 48 E4
Chilcompton GB 13 C9
Chilham GB 15 E10
Chiliile RO 161 C9
Chiliomodi GR 175 D6
Chilleurs-aux-Bois F 24 D7
Chillón E 54 B3
Chilluévar E 55 C6
Chiloeches E 47 C6
Chimay B 19 D9
Chimeneas E 53 B9
Chinanale I 36 B6
Chinchilla de Monte Aragón E 55 B9
Chinchón E 46 D6
Chindrieux F 31 D8
Chinon F 23 F12
Chinteni RO 152 D3
Chiochiș RO 152 D4
Chioggia I 66 B5
Chiojdeni RO 161 B9
Chiojdu RO 161 C8
Chiomonte I 31 E10
Chiona GR 174 C4
Chionata GR 174 C2
Chios GR 177 C7
Chiperceni MD 154 B3
Chipiona E 52 C4
Chippenham GB 13 C10
Chipping Campden GB 13 A11
Chipping Norton GB 13 B11
Chipping Ongar GB 15 D9
Chipping Sodbury GB 13 B10
Chippis CH 31 C12
Chiprana E 42 E3
Chiprovtsi BG 165 C6
Chirbury GB 10 F5
Chiren BG 165 C8
Chiriet-Lunga MD 154 E3
Chirivel E 55 D8
Chirk GB 10 F5
Chirnogeni RO 155 F2
Chirnogi RO 161 E9
Chirnside GB 5 D12
Chiroubles F 30 C6
Chirpan BG 166 E4
Chirpăr RO 152 F5
Chirsova MD 154 E3
Chiscani RO 155 C1
Chișcăreni MD 153 B12
Chișcăreni MD 154 C3
Chiselet RO 161 E9
Chișinău MD 154 C3
Chisindia RO 151 E9
Chișineu-Criș RO 151 D8
Chistye-Prudy RUS 136 E5
Chițcani MD 154 D5
Chitignano I 66 E4
Chitila RO 161 D7
Chiuiești RO 152 C3
Chiuro I 69 A8
Chiusa I 72 C4
Chiusa di Pesio I 37 C7
Chiusaforte I 73 D7
Chiusa Sclafani I 58 D3
Chiusavecchia I 37 D7
Chiusdino I 66 F3
Chiusi I 62 A1
Chiusi della Verna I 66 E4
Chiuza RO 152 C4
Chiva E 48 F3
Chivasso I 68 C4
Chizé F 28 C5
Chlebičov CZ 146 B5
Chlebnice SK 147 C8
Chlebowo PL 81 B7
Chlewiska PL 141 H3
Chłopice PL 144 D6
Chludowo PL 81 A11
Chlumčany CZ 76 C4
Chlumec CZ 80 E5
Chlumec nad Cidlinou CZ 77 B8
Chlum u Třeboně CZ 77 E7
Chmielnik PL 143 E10
Chmielno PL 85 C10
Chmiel Pierwszy PL 144 A6
Chminianske Jakubovany SK 145 F3
Chobienia PL 81 C10
Chobienice PL 81 B9
Choceň CZ 77 B10
Choceń PL 138 F7
Chocholná-Velčice SK 146 D5
Chocianów PL 81 D9
Chocicza PL 81 B12
Chociwel PL 85 D8
Chocz PL 142 C4
Choczewo PL 138 A4
Chodecz PL 138 F7
Chodel PL 141 H6
Chodov CZ 75 B12
Chodová Planá CZ 75 C12
Chodów PL 141 F6
Chodów PL 143 B7
Chodzież PL 85 E11
Chojna PL 84 E6
Chojnice PL 85 C13
Chojno PL 81 C12
Chojnów PL 81 D9
Cholet F 28 A4
Chomakovtsi BG 165 C9
Chomelix F 30 E4
Chomérac F 35 A8
Chomutov CZ 76 B4
Chonikas GR 175 D6
Chooz F 19 D10
Chop UA 145 G5
Chora GR 174 E4
Chora GR 175 A8
Chora GR 177 D8
Chora GR 179 B9
Chora GR 179 B9
Chorafakia GR 178 D7
Chora Sfakion GR 178 E7
Chorefto GR 169 F9
Chorges F 36 B4
Chorio GR 177 F8
Choristi GR 171 B6
Chorkówka PL 145 D4
Chorley GB 10 D6
Chorna UA 154 B4
Chorna Tysa UA 152 A4
Chornoholova UA 145 F6
Chornomyn UA 154 A4
Chorzele PL 139 D10
Chorzów PL 143 F6
Chorzyna PL 142 D6
Choszczno PL 85 D8
Chotča SK 145 E4
Chotěboř CZ 77 C9
Chotěšov CZ 76 C4
Chotín SK 149 A10
Chouilly F 25 B11
Chouni GR 174 B4
Chouto P 44 F4
Chouzy-sur-Cisse F 24 E5
Chovar E 48 E4
Choye F 26 F4
Chozas de Abajo E 39 C8
Chrást CZ 76 C4
Chrast CZ 77 C9
Chrastava CZ 81 E7
Chřibská CZ 81 E6
Christchurch GB 13 D11
Christiansfeld DK 86 E4
Christon Bank GB 5 E13
Chropyně CZ 146 C4
Chróścina PL 142 E3
Chrostkowo PL 139 E7
Chroustovice CZ 77 C9
Chrudim CZ 77 C9
Chruślin PL 143 B8
Chruszczobród PL 143 F7
Chrysa GR 171 B7
Chrysafa GR 175 E6
Chryso GR 169 B10
Chrysochorafa GR 169 B9
Chrysochori GR 171 C7
Chrysokellaria GR 178 B2
Chrysoupoli GR 171 C7
Chrzanów PL 143 F7
Chrząstowa Wielka PL 81 D12
Chrząstowice PL 142 E5
Chrzypsko Wielkie PL 81 A10
Chtelnica SK 146 D5
Chuchelná CZ 142 G5
Chudleigh GB 13 D7
Chudoba PL 142 E5
Chulilla E 48 E3
Chulmleigh GB 13 D7
Chuprene BG 165 B6
Chur CH 71 D9
Churchdown GB 13 B10
Church Hill IRL 7 C7
Church Stretton GB 10 F6
Churek BG 165 D8
Churwalden CH 71 D9
Chuzelles F 30 D6
Chvalčov CZ 146 C5
Chvaletice CZ 77 B8
Chvalšiny CZ 76 E6
Chwaszczyno PL 138 B5
Chynadiyeve UA 145 F6
Chyňava CZ 76 B6
Chýnov CZ 77 D7
Chynów PL 141 G4
Chyšky CZ 77 C6
Ciacova RO 159 B7
Ciadîr MD 154 D2
Ciadîr-Lunga MD 154 E3
Ciadoux F 33 D7
Ciampino I 62 D3
Cianciana I 58 D3
Ciasna PL 142 E6
Ciążeń PL 142 B4
Cibakháza H 150 D5
Ciborro P 50 B3
Ciboure F 32 D2
Cicagna I 37 C10
Cicărlău RO 151 B11
Cicciano I 60 B3
Cicerale I 60 C4
Ćićevac SRB 159 F7
Cicibór Duży PL 141 F8
Ciclova Română RO 159 C8
Čičov SK 149 A9
Çidhën AL 163 F9
Cidones E 41 E6
Ciechanów PL 139 E10
Ciechanowiec PL 141 E7
Ciechocinek PL 138 E6
Cielądz PL 141 G2
Ciempozuelos E 46 D5
Ciepielów PL 141 H5
Ciepłowody PL 81 E11
Čierna nad Tisou SK 145 G5
Čierne Kľačany SK 146 E6
Čierny Balog SK 147 D9
Cierp-Gaud F 33 E7
Cierznie PL 85 C12
Cieszanów PL 144 C7
Cieszków PL 81 C12
Cieszyn PL 142 D4
Cieszyn PL 147 B7
Cieutat F 33 D6
Cieux F 29 D8
Cieza E 55 C10
Cijżkowice PL 144 D2
Çifer SK 146 E5
Çifliq AL 168 E3
Çiftlikköy TR 173 B7
Çiftlikköy TR 173 B9
Cifuentes E 47 C7
Cigales E 39 E10
Cigánd H 145 G4
Cigliano I 68 C5
Cikó H 149 D11
Cilibia RO 161 C10
Cilieni RO 160 F5
Čilipi HR 162 D5
Čiližská Radvaň SK 146 F5
Cill Airne IRL 8 D4
Cillas E 47 C9
Cill Chainnigh IRL 9 C8
Cill Chaoi IRL 8 C3
Cill Charthaigh IRL 6 C5
Cill Chiaráin IRL 6 F3
Cill Choca IRL 7 F9
Cill Chomhghaill IRL 7 F10
Cill Chormaic IRL 7 F7
Cill Chuillin IRL 7 F9
Cill Dalua IRL 8 C6
Cill Dara IRL 7 F9
Cill Dhéagláin IRL 7 E10
Cill Droichid IRL 7 F9
Cille Bhrighde GB 2 L2
Cilleros E 45 D7
Cill Mhantáin IRL 7 G10
Cill Mocheallóg IRL 8 D5
Cill na Mallach IRL 8 D5
Cill Orglan IRL 8 D3
Cill Rois IRL 8 C4
Cill Rónáin IRL 6 F3
Cilybebyll GB 13 B7
Cimanes del Tejar E 39 C8
Cimballa E 47 B9
Cimdenieki LV 134 C2
Čimelice CZ 76 D6
Ciminna I 58 D4
Cimișlia MD 154 D3
Cimolais I 72 D5
Çinarcik TR 173 C11
Cinco Casas E 47 F6
Cinctorres E 42 F3
Cincu RO 152 F5
Cinderford GB 13 B10
Çine TR 181 A8
Ciñera E 39 C8
Ciney B 19 D11
Cinfães P 44 B4
Cinge TR 177 A9
Cingoli I 67 F7
Cinigiano I 65 B4
Cinisello Balsamo I 69 B7
Cinn Mhara IRL 6 F3
Cinobaňa SK 147 E9
Cinq-Mars-la-Pile F 24 F3
Cinquefrondi I 59 C9
Cintegabelle F 33 D9
Cintrey F 26 E4
Cintruénigo E 41 D8
Ciobănița RO 155 E2
Ciobanu RO 155 D1
Čiobiškis LT 137 D10
Ciocănești RO 161 D7
Ciocănești RO 161 E10
Ciocârlia RO 155 E2
Ciocârlia RO 161 D9
Ciochina RO 161 D10
Ciocile RO 161 D10
Cioc-Maidan MD 154 E3
Ciofrângeni RO 160 C5
Cióirtheach IRL 7 F7
Ciolănești RO 160 E6
Ciolpani RO 161 D8
Cionn tSáile IRL 8 E5
Ciorani RO 161 D8
Ciorăști RO 161 C10
Ciorogârla RO 161 E7
Cioroiași RO 160 E2
Cioropcani MD 153 C11
Ciortești RO 153 D11
Ciprian Porumbescu RO 153 B8
Cirat E 48 D4
Ciraugui E 32 E2
Cīrava LV 134 C2
Circello I 60 A3
Cirencester GB 13 B11
Cireșu RO 159 D10
Cireșu RO 161 D10
Cirey-sur-Blaise F 26 D2
Cirey-sur-Vezouze F 27 C6
Ciria E 41 E8
Ciriè I 68 C4
Cirigliano I 60 C6
Ciripcău MD 154 A2
Cirkale LV 134 B4
Cirma LV 133 C3
Cirò I 61 E8
Cirò Marina I 61 E8
Çirpi TR 177 C10
Ciruelos E 46 E5
Ciruelos del Pinar E 47 B8
Cīruļi LV 134 B4
Ciry-le-Noble F 30 B5
Cisano sul Neva I 37 C8
Cisek PL 142 F5
Cislău RO 161 C8
Cișmichioi MD 155 B2
Cisna PL 145 E5
Cisnădie RO 160 B4
Cisneros E 39 D10
Cisòn di Valmarino I 72 E5
Cissé F 29 B6
Cista Provo HR 157 E6
Cisterna di Latina I 62 D3
Cisternino I 61 B8
Cistierna E 39 C9
Citerna I 66 F5
Čitluk BIH 157 B6
Čitluk BIH 157 F8
Cittadella I 72 E4
Città della Pieve I 62 B2
Città di Castello I 66 F5
Cittanova I 59 C9
Cittareale I 62 B4
Città Sant'Angelo I 62 B6
Cittiglio I 68 B6
Ciucea RO 151 D10
Ciuchici RO 159 D8
Ciuciulea MD 153 B10
Ciucsângeorgiu RO 153 E7
Ciucur-Mingir MD 154 E3
Ciucurova RO 155 D2
Ciudad Real E 54 B5
Ciudad Rodrigo E 45 C7
Ciudanovița RO 159 C8
Ciugud RO 152 E3
Ciuhoi RO 151 C9
Ciulnița RO 161 D10
Ciumani RO 153 D7
Ciumeghiu RO 151 D8
Ciuperceni RO 159 D11
Ciuperceni RO 160 F5
Ciupercenii Noi RO 159 F10
Ciurila RO 152 D3
Ciuruleasa RO 151 E11
Ciutadella E 57 A12
Civaux F 29 C7
Cividale del Friuli I 73 D7
Civita I 61 D6
Civita Castellana I 62 C2
Civita d'Antino I 62 D4
Civitanova del Sannio I 63 D6
Civitanova Marche I 67 F8
Civitaquana I 62 C5
Civitavecchia I 62 C1
Civitella Casanova I 62 C5
Civitella del Tronto I 62 B5
Civitella di Romagna I 66 D4
Civitella in Val di Chiana I 66 F4

Civitella Roveto *I* 62 D4
Civray *F* 29 B10
Civray *F* 29 C6
Cizer *RO* 151 C10
Čížkovice *CZ* 76 B6
Čkyně *CZ* 76 D5
Clabhach *GB* 4 B3
Clachan *GB* 2 L4
Clachan *GB* 4 C7
Clachan of Glendaruel *GB* 4 C6
Clachtoll *GB* 2 J6
Clackmannan *GB* 5 C9
Clacton-on-Sea *GB* 15 D11
Cladich *GB* 4 C6
Clady *GB* 4 F1
Clady *GB* 4 F3
Claggan *GB* 4 B5
Clairac *F* 33 B6
Clairoix *F* 18 F6
Clairvaux-les-Lacs *F* 31 B8
Claix *F* 31 E8
Clamecy *F* 25 F10
Clane *IRL* 7 F9
Clans *F* 36 C6
Claonadh *IRL* 7 F9
Claonaig *GB* 4 D6
Clapham *GB* 11 C7
Clapham *GB* 15 C8
Clara *IRL* 7 F7
Clár Chlainne Mhuiris *IRL* 6 E5
Clarecastle *IRL* 8 C5
Claremorris *IRL* 6 E5
Claret *F* 35 B10
Claro *CH* 69 A7
Clary *F* 19 D7
Clashmore *IRL* 9 D7
Clashnessie *GB* 2 J6
Claudy *GB* 4 F2
Clausnitz *D* 80 E4
Claußnitz *D* 80 E3
Clausthal-Zellerfeld *D* 79 C7
Claut *I* 72 D6
Clauzetto *I* 73 D6
Clavering *GB* 15 D9
Clavier *B* 19 D11
Clay Cross *GB* 11 E9
Claydon *GB* 15 C11
Clayton *GB* 15 F8
Cleady *IRL* 8 E3
Cleat *GB* 3 H11
Cleator Moor *GB* 10 B4
Clécy *F* 23 C11
Cléder *F* 22 C3
Cleethorpes *GB* 11 D11
Clefmont *F* 26 D4
Cléguérec *F* 22 D5
Cleja *RO* 153 E9
Clelles *F* 31 F8
Clémency *L* 20 E5
Clenze *D* 83 E9
Cleobury Mortimer *GB* 13 A10
Cléon *F* 18 F3
Cléon-d'Andran *F* 35 A8
Cléré-les-Pins *F* 24 F3
Clères *F* 18 E3
Clérey *F* 25 D11
Clermain *F* 30 C6
Clermont *F* 18 F5
Clermont *F* 33 D8
Clermont-en-Argonne *F* 26 B3
Clermont-Ferrand *F* 30 D3
Clermont-l'Hérault *F* 34 C5
Clerval *F* 26 F6
Clervaux *L* 20 D6
Cléry-St-André *F* 24 E6
Cles *I* 72 D3
Clevedon *GB* 13 C9
Cleveleys *GB* 10 D5
Clifden *IRL* 6 F2
Cliffe *GB* 15 E9
Cliffoney *IRL* 6 D6
Climăuți *MD* 153 A11
Clinge *NL* 16 F2
Clingen *D* 79 D8
Clion *F* 29 B8
Clisson *F* 28 A3
Clitheroe *GB* 11 D7
Cloch na Rón *IRL* 6 F3
Clogh *GB* 4 F4
Clogh *IRL* 9 C7
Clogh *IRL* 9 C8
Clogh *IRL* 9 C10
Cloghan *IRL* 7 C7
Cloghan *IRL* 7 F7
Clogheen *IRL* 8 D7
Clogher *GB* 7 D8
Clogherhead *IRL* 7 E10
Cloghy *GB* 7 D12
Clohars-Carnoët *F* 22 E4
Clohernagh *IRL* 9 D8
Cloich na Coillte *IRL* 8 E5
Clonakilty *IRL* 8 E5
Clonaslee *IRL* 7 F7
Clonbern *IRL* 6 E5
Clonbulloge *IRL* 7 F8
Clonbur *IRL* 6 E4
Clondrohid *IRL* 8 E4
Clondulane *IRL* 8 D6
Clonea *IRL* 9 D8
Clonee *IRL* 7 F10
Cloneen *IRL* 9 D7
Clones *IRL* 7 D8
Clonmel *IRL* 9 D7
Clonmellon *IRL* 7 E8
Clonoulty *IRL* 9 C7
Clonroche *IRL* 9 D9
Clontibret *IRL* 7 D9
Clonygowan *IRL* 7 F8
Cloonbannin *IRL* 8 D4
Cloonboo *IRL* 6 F4
Cloonfad *IRL* 6 E5
Cloonfad *IRL* 6 F6
Cloonkeen *IRL* 6 E4
Cloppenburg *D* 17 C10
Closeburn *GB* 5 E9
Clough *GB* 7 D11
Cloughjordan *IRL* 8 C6
Cloughmills *GB* 4 E4
Cloughton *GB* 11 C11
Clova *GB* 5 B10
Clovelly *GB* 12 D6
Clovullin *GB* 4 B6
Cloyes-sur-le-Loir *F* 24 E5
Cloyne *IRL* 8 E6
Cluain Bú *IRL* 6 F4
Cluain Eois *IRL* 7 D8
Cluainín *IRL* 6 D6
Cluain Meala *IRL* 9 D7
Cluis *F* 29 B9
Cluj-Napoca *RO* 152 D3
Clumanc *F* 36 C4
Clun *GB* 13 A8
Cluny *F* 30 C6
Cluses *F* 31 C10
Clusone *I* 69 B8
Clydach *GB* 13 B7
Clydebank *GB* 5 D8
Clynderwen *GB* 12 B5
Clyro *GB* 13 A8
Ćmielów *PL* 143 E12
Cmolas *PL* 143 F12
Coachford *IRL* 8 E5
Coagh *GB* 4 F3
Coalburn *GB* 5 D9
Coalisland *GB* 7 C9
Coalville *GB* 11 F9
Coaña *E* 39 A6
Coarnele Caprei *RO* 153 C10
Coarraze *F* 32 D5
Coast *GB* 2 K5
Coatbridge *GB* 5 D8
Cobadin *RO* 155 E2
Cobani *MD* 153 B10
Cobeja *E* 46 D5
Cobeta *E* 47 C8
Cobh *IRL* 8 E6
Cobia *RO* 160 D6
Coburg *D* 75 B8
Coca *E* 46 B3
Cocentaina *E* 56 D4
Cochem *D* 21 D8
Cochirleanca *RO* 161 C10
Cociuba Mare *RO* 151 D9
Cockburnspath *GB* 5 D12
Cockenzie and Port Seton *GB* 5 D11
Cockerham *GB* 10 D6
Cockermouth *GB* 5 F10
Cockett *GB* 12 B7
Cocora *RO* 161 D10
Cocu *RO* 160 D5
Cocumont *F* 32 B6
Codăești *RO* 153 D11
Coddington *GB* 11 E10
Code *LV* 135 D8
Codevigo *I* 66 B5
Codigoro *I* 66 C5
Codlea *RO* 161 B6
Codogno *I* 69 C8
Codos *E* 41 F9
Codreanca *MD* 154 C3
Codroipo *I* 73 E6
Codrongianos *I* 64 B2
Codru *MD* 154 D3
Coesfeld *D* 17 E8
Coevorden *NL* 17 C7
Coëx *F* 28 B2
Cofrentes *E* 47 F10
Cogealac *RO* 155 D3
Cogeces del Monte *E* 40 E3
Coggeshall *GB* 15 D10
Coggia *F* 37 G9
Coggiola *I* 68 B5
Cogîlniceni *MD* 154 B3
Çöğmen *TR* 181 C10
Cognac *F* 28 D5
Cognac-la-Forêt *F* 29 D8
Cogne *I* 31 D11
Cognin *F* 31 D8
Cogoleto *I* 37 C9
Cogolin *F* 36 E5
Cogollos *E* 40 D4
Cogollos Vega *E* 53 B9
Cogolludo *E* 47 C6
Cogula *P* 45 C6
Coillan Chollaigh *IRL* 7 E9
Coimbra *P* 44 D4
Coimbrão *P* 44 E3
Coín *E* 53 C7
Coincy *F* 25 B9
Coja *P* 44 D5
Cojasca *RO* 161 D7
Cojocna *RO* 152 D3
Čoka *SRB* 150 F5
Colares *P* 50 B1
Colayrac-St-Cirq *F* 33 B7
Colbasna *MD* 154 B4
Cölbe *D* 21 C11
Colbitz *D* 79 B10
Colbordola *I* 67 E6
Colceag *RO* 161 D8
Colchester *GB* 15 D10
Coldingham *GB* 5 D12
Colditz *D* 79 D12
Coldstream *GB* 5 D12
Coleford *GB* 13 B9
Coleraine *GB* 4 E3
Colibași *MD* 155 B2
Colibași *RO* 160 D5
Colibași *RO* 161 E8
Colibița *RO* 152 C5
Colico *I* 69 A7
Coligny *F* 31 C7
Colijnsplaat *NL* 182 B3
Colindres *E* 40 B5
Colintraive *GB* 4 D6
Collado Hermoso *E* 46 B5
Collado Villalba *E* 46 C5
Collagna *I* 66 D1
Collanzo *E* 39 B8
Collarmele *I* 62 C5
Collazzone *I* 62 B2
Collecchio *I* 66 C1
Collecorvino *I* 62 C5
Colledara *I* 62 B5
Colle di Val d'Elsa *I* 66 F3
Colleferro *I* 62 D4
Collegno *I* 68 C4
Colle Isarco *I* 72 C3
Collelongo *I* 62 D5
Collepardo *I* 62 D4
Collepasso *I* 61 C10
Collesalvetti *I* 66 E1
Colle Sannita *I* 60 A3
Collesano *I* 58 D4
Colletorto *I* 63 D7
Colliano *I* 60 B4
Colli a Volturno *I* 62 D6
Collieston *GB* 3 L13
Collinas *I* 64 D2
Collinée *F* 22 D6
Collinghorst (Rhauderfehn) *D* 17 B9
Collio *I* 69 B9
Collioure *F* 34 E5
Collobrières *F* 36 E4
Collombey *CH* 31 C10
Collon *IRL* 7 E10
Collonges *F* 31 C8
Collonges-la-Rouge *F* 29 E9
Collooney *IRL* 6 D6
Colmar *F* 27 D7
Colmars *F* 36 C5
Colmberg *D* 75 D7
Colmeal *P* 44 D5
Colmenar *E* 53 C8
Colmenar del Arroyo *E* 46 D4
Colmenar de Montemayor *E* 45 D9
Colmenar de Oreja *E* 46 D6
Colmenar Viejo *E* 46 C5
Colméry *F* 25 F9
Colmonell *GB* 4 E7
Colne *GB* 11 D7
Colobraro *I* 61 C6
Cologna Veneta *I* 66 B3
Cologne *F* 33 C7
Cologno al Serio *I* 69 B8
Colombelles *F* 23 B11
Colombey-les-Belles *F* 26 C4
Colombey-les-Deux-Églises *F* 25 D12
Colombier *CH* 31 B10
Colombiès *F* 33 B10
Colombres *E* 39 B10
Colomers *E* 43 C9
Colomiers *F* 33 C8
Colonești *RO* 153 D10
Colonești *RO* 160 D5
Colònia de Sant Jordi *E* 57 C11
Colònia de Sant Pere *E* 57 B11
Colonnella *I* 62 B5
Colorno *I* 66 C1
Colos *P* 50 D3
Cölpin *D* 84 C4
Colquhar *GB* 5 D10
Colroy-la-Grande *F* 27 D7
Colsterworth *GB* 11 F10
Colți *RO* 161 C8
Coltishall *GB* 15 B11
Colunga *E* 39 B9
Colwyn Bay *GB* 10 E4
Coly *F* 29 E8
Colyford *GB* 13 D8
Comacchio *I* 66 C5
Comana *RO* 152 F6
Comana *RO* 155 F2
Comana *RO* 161 E8
Comana de Sus *RO* 152 F6
Comandău *RO* 153 F8
Comănești *RO* 153 E8
Comares *E* 53 C8
Comarna *RO* 153 C11
Comarnic *RO* 161 C7
Combeaufontaine *F* 26 E4
Combe Martin *GB* 12 C6
Comber *GB* 7 C11
Comberton *GB* 15 C9
Comblain-au-Pont *B* 19 D12
Comblanchien *F* 26 F2
Combles *F* 18 D6
Combloux *F* 31 D10
Combourg *F* 23 D8
Combronde *F* 30 D3
Comeglians *I* 73 C6
Comelico Superiore *I* 72 C6
Comillas *E* 40 B3
Comines *B* 18 C6
Comișani *RO* 161 D7
Comiso *I* 59 F6
Comitini *I* 58 E4
Comloșu Mare *RO* 150 F6
Commeen *IRL* 7 C7
Commenailles *F* 31 B7
Commensacq *F* 32 B4
Commentry *F* 30 C2
Commequiers *F* 28 B2
Commer *F* 23 D10
Commercy *F* 26 C4
Como *I* 69 B7
Cómpeta *E* 53 C9
Compiano *I* 37 B11
Compiègne *F* 18 F6
Compolibat *F* 33 B10
Comporta *P* 50 C2
Compreignac *F* 29 D8
Comps-sur-Artuby *F* 36 D5
Comrat *MD* 154 E3
Comrie *GB* 5 C9
Comunanza *I* 62 B4
Cona *I* 66 B5
Conca *F* 37 H10
Concarneau *F* 22 E4
Concas *I* 64 B4
Conceição *P* 50 E4
Concesio *I* 69 B9
Concha *E* 40 B5
Conches-en-Ouche *F* 24 C4
Concordia Sagittaria *I* 73 E6
Concorès *F* 33 A8
Concots *F* 33 B9
Condat *F* 30 E2
Condé-en-Brie *F* 25 B10
Condeixa-a-Nova *P* 44 D4
Condé-sur-Huisne *F* 24 D4
Condé-sur-l'Escaut *F* 182 E3
Condé-sur-Noireau *F* 23 C10
Condé-sur-Vire *F* 23 B9
Condino *I* 69 B10
Condofuri *I* 59 C8
Condom *F* 33 C6
Condove *I* 31 E11
Condrieu *F* 30 E6
Condrița *MD* 154 C3
Conegliano *I* 72 E5
Conflans-en-Jarnisy *F* 26 B4
Conflans-sur-Lanterne *F* 26 E5
Conflenti *I* 59 A9
Confolens *F* 29 C7
Cong *IRL* 6 E4
Congaz *MD* 154 E3
Congdon's Shop *GB* 12 D6
Congleton *GB* 11 E7
Congosto *E* 39 C7
Congosto de Valdavia *E* 39 C10
Congrier *F* 23 E9
Conil de la Frontera *E* 52 D4
Coningsby *GB* 11 E11
Coniston *GB* 10 C5
Conlie *F* 23 D11
Conliège *F* 31 B8
Conlig *GB* 4 F5
Connah's Quay *GB* 10 E5
Connantre *F* 25 C10
Connaux *F* 35 B8
Connel *GB* 4 C6
Connerré *F* 24 D3
Connolly *IRL* 8 C4
Connor *GB* 4 F4
Conon Bridge *GB* 2 K8
Conop *RO* 151 E8
Čonoplja *SRB* 150 F3
Conow *D* 84 D4
Conques *F* 33 A10
Conques-sur-Orbiel *F* 33 D10
Conquista *E* 54 C3
Consandolo *I* 66 C4
Consdorf *L* 186 B1
Conselice *I* 66 C4
Consell *E* 49 E10
Conselve *I* 66 B4
Consett *GB* 5 F13
Constância *P* 44 F4
Constanța *RO* 155 E3
Constantí *E* 42 E6
Constantim *P* 38 F4
Constantim *P* 39 E7
Constantina *E* 51 D8
Constantin Daicoviciu *RO* 159 B9
Constanzana *E* 46 C3
Consuegra *E* 46 F5
Contarina *I* 66 B5
Contes *F* 37 D6
Contessa Entellina *I* 58 D3
Conțești *RO* 161 D7
Conțești *RO* 161 F6
Conthey *CH* 31 C11
Contigliano *I* 62 C3
Contis-Plage *F* 32 B3
Contres *F* 24 F5
Contrexéville *F* 26 D4
Controne *I* 60 B4
Contursi Terme *I* 60 B4
Contwig *D* 21 F8
Conty *F* 18 E5
Conversano *I* 61 B8
Convoy *IRL* 7 C7
Conwy *GB* 10 E4
Conza della Campania *I* 60 B4
Cookstown *GB* 4 F3
Coola *IRL* 6 D6
Coolbaun *IRL* 6 G6
Coole *F* 25 C11
Coole *IRL* 7 E8
Coolmore *IRL* 6 C6
Coombe Bissett *GB* 13 C11
Cootehill *IRL* 7 D8
Copăcel *RO* 151 D9
Copăcele *RO* 159 C9
Copăceni *MD* 154 B2
Copăceni *RO* 160 D3
Copăcenii de Sus *RO* 161 E8
Copalnic-Mănăștur *RO* 152 B3
Copanca *MD* 154 D5
Copanello *I* 59 B10
Copceac *MD* 154 F3
Copertino *I* 61 C10
Çöpköy *TR* 173 B6
Copley *GB* 5 F13
Copons *E* 43 D7
Copparo *I* 66 C4
Coppeen *IRL* 8 E5
Copplestone *GB* 13 D7
Coppull *GB* 10 D6
Copșa Mică *RO* 152 E4
Copythorne *GB* 13 D11
Corabia *RO* 160 F4
Cora Chaitlín *IRL* 8 C5
Cora Droma Rúisc *IRL* 6 E6
Čoralići *BIH* 156 C4
Corato *I* 61 A6
Coray *F* 22 D4
Corbalán *E* 47 D11
Corbally *IRL* 6 D4
Corbasca *RO* 153 E10
Corbeanca *RO* 161 D8
Corbeil-Essonnes *F* 25 C7
Corbeilles *F* 25 D8
Corbeni *RO* 160 C5
Corbeny *F* 19 F8
Corbera *E* 48 F4
Corbera d'Ebre *E* 42 E4
Corbi *RO* 160 C5
Corbie *F* 18 E6
Corbières *CH* 31 B11
Corbières *F* 35 C10
Corbigny *F* 25 F10
Corbii Mari *RO* 161 D6
Corbița *RO* 153 E10
Corbridge *GB* 5 F12
Corbu *RO* 153 D7
Corbu *RO* 155 E3
Corbu *RO* 160 D5
Corby *GB* 11 G10
Corçà *E* 43 D10
Corcaigh *IRL* 8 E6
Corcelles-lès-Cîteaux *F* 26 F3
Corchiano *I* 62 C2
Corciano *I* 66 F5
Corcieux *F* 27 D6
Corcova *RO* 159 D11
Corcubión *E* 38 C1
Cordăreni *RO* 153 B9
Cordemais *F* 23 F8
Cordenòns *I* 73 E6
Cordes-sur-Ciel *F* 33 B9
Córdoba *E* 53 A7
Cordobilla de Lácara *E* 45 F8
Corduente *E* 47 C9
Cordun *RO* 153 D9
Coreglia Antelminelli *I* 66 D2
Corella *E* 41 D8
Coreses *E* 39 E8
Corestăuți *MD* 153 A10
Corfe Castle *GB* 13 D10
Corfinio *I* 62 C5
Cori *I* 62 D3
Coria *E* 45 E7
Coria del Río *E* 51 E7
Coriano *I* 66 E6
Corigliano Calabro *I* 61 D7
Corinaldo *I* 67 E7
Coripe *E* 51 F9
Corjeuți *MD* 153 A10
Cork *IRL* 8 E6
Corlătel *RO* 159 E10
Corlățeni *RO* 153 B9
Corlay *F* 22 D5
Corlea *IRL* 7 E7
Corleone *I* 58 D3
Corleto Perticara *I* 60 C6
Çorlu *TR* 173 B8
Cormatin *F* 30 B6
Cormeilles *F* 18 F1
Corme Porto *E* 38 B2
Cormicy *F* 19 F8
Cormons *I* 73 E7
Cormontreuil *F* 20 F2
Cornafulla *IRL* 6 F7
Cornago *E* 41 D7
Cornamona *IRL* 6 E4
Cornaredo *I* 69 B7
Cornas *F* 30 F6
Cornățelu *RO* 161 D7
Cornau *D* 17 C10
Cornea *RO* 159 C9
Cornedo all'Isarco *I* 72 D3
Cornedo Vicentino *I* 69 B11
Corneilla-del-Vercol *F* 34 E4
Cornellà de Llobregat *E* 43 E8
Cornellà de Terri *E* 43 C9
Cornellana *E* 39 B7
Cornereva *RO* 159 C9
Cornești *MD* 153 C12
Cornești *RO* 152 C3
Cornești *RO* 161 D7
Cornetu *RO* 161 E7
Corni *RO* 153 B9
Corni *RO* 153 F11
Corniglio *I* 69 E9
Cornimont *F* 27 E6
Cornu *RO* 161 C7
Cornuda *I* 72 E5
Cornudella de Montsant *E* 42 E5
Cornudilla *E* 40 C5
Cornu Luncii *RO* 153 C8
Cornus *F* 34 C5
Corod *RO* 153 F11
Corofin *IRL* 8 C4
Coroieni *RO* 152 C3
Coroisânmărtin *RO* 152 E5
Coron *F* 23 F10
Çorovodë *AL* 168 C3
Corps *F* 31 F8
Corps-Nuds *F* 23 E8
Corral de Almaguer *E* 47 E6
Corral de Calatrava *E* 54 B4
Corrales *E* 39 F8
Corral-Rubio *E* 55 B10
Corre *F* 26 E5
Correggio *I* 66 C2
Corrèze *F* 29 E9
Corridonia *I* 67 F8
Corrie *GB* 4 D6
Corris *GB* 10 F4
Corr na Móna *IRL* 6 E4
Corrobert *F* 25 C10
Corry *IRL* 6 D6
Corsano *I* 61 D10
Corseul *F* 23 D7
Corsham *GB* 13 C10
Corsico *I* 69 C7
Corsock *GB* 5 E9
Cortale *I* 59 B9
Corte *F* 37 G10
Corteconcepción *E* 51 D7
Corte de Peleas *E* 51 B6
Cortegada *E* 38 D3
Cortegana *E* 51 D6
Cortemilia *I* 37 B8
Corteno Golgi *I* 69 A9
Corteolona *I* 69 C7
Cortes *E* 41 E9
Cortes de Aragón *E* 42 F2
Cortes de Arenoso *E* 48 D3
Cortes de Baza *E* 55 D7
Cortes de la Frontera *E* 53 C6
Cortes de Pallás *E* 48 F3
Cortiçadas do Lavre *P* 50 B3
Cortijo de Arriba *E* 46 F4
Cortijos Nuevos *E* 55 C7
Cortina d'Ampezzo *I* 72 C5
Corton *GB* 15 B12
Cortona *I* 66 F4
Coruche *P* 50 B2
Corullón *E* 39 C6
Corund *RO* 152 E6
Corvara in Badia *I* 72 C4
Corvera *E* 56 F2
Corwen *GB* 10 F5
Coryton *GB* 15 D10
Cosa *E* 47 C10
Cosâmbești *RO* 161 D10
Cosăuți *MD* 154 A2
Coșbuc *RO* 152 C4
Cosby *GB* 11 F9
Coșcodeni *MD* 153 B12
Coscurita *E* 41 F7
Coșeiu *RO* 151 C11
Cosenza *I* 60 E6
Coșereni *RO* 161 D9
Coșești *RO* 160 C5
Coshieville *GB* 5 B9
Ćosići *BIH* 157 D8
Cosio di Arroscia *I* 37 C7
Coslada *E* 46 D5
Cosmești *RO* 153 F10
Cosmești *RO* 160 E6
Cosminele *RO* 161 C7
Cosne-Cours-sur-Loire *F* 25 F8
Cosne-d'Allier *F* 30 C2
Cosnița *MD* 154 C4
Cosoleto *I* 59 C8
Coșoveni *RO* 160 E3
Cossato *I* 68 B5
Cossé-le-Vivien *F* 23 E10
Cossoine *I* 64 C2
Cossonay *CH* 31 B10
Costacciaro *I* 67 F6
Costache Negri *RO* 153 F11
Costa da Caparica *P* 50 B1
Costa di Rovigo *I* 66 B4
Costa Volpino *I* 69 B9
Costeiu *RO* 151 F8
Costelloe *IRL* 6 F3
Costești *MD* 153 B10
Costești *MD* 154 D3
Costești *RO* 153 D11
Costești *RO* 160 C4
Costești *RO* 160 D5
Costești *RO* 161 C9
Costeștii din Vale *RO* 161 D6
Costigliole Saluzzo *I* 37 B6
Costișa *RO* 153 D9
Costuleni *RO* 153 C11
Cosuenda *E* 41 F9
Coswig *D* 79 C11
Coswig *D* 80 D5
Coteana *RO* 160 E4
Cotești *RO* 161 B10
Cothen *NL* 16 D4
Coti-Chiavari *F* 37 H9
Cotignac *F* 36 D4
Cotignola *I* 66 D4
Cotiujeni *MD* 154 B3
Cotiujenii Mici *MD* 154 B2
Cotmeana *RO* 160 D5
Cotnari *RO* 153 C9
Coțofănești *RO* 153 E9
Coțofenii din Dos *RO* 160 E3
Cotronei *I* 61 E7
Cottanello *I* 62 C3
Cottbus *D* 80 C6
Cottenham *GB* 15 C9
Cottesmore *GB* 11 F10
Cottingham *GB* 11 F10
Coțușca *RO* 153 A9
Coubon *F* 30 E4
Couburciu *MD* 154 D5
Couches *F* 30 B6
Couço *P* 50 B3
Coucy-le-Château-Auffrique *F* 19 E7
Coudekerque-Branche *F* 18 B5
Couëron *F* 23 F8
Couflens *F* 33 E8
Coufouleux *F* 33 C9
Couhé *F* 29 C6
Couiza *F* 33 E10
Coulaines *F* 23 D12
Coulanges-la-Vineuse *F* 25 E10
Coulanges-sur-Yonne *F* 25 E10
Coulaures *F* 29 E7
Couleuvre *F* 30 B2
Coullons *F* 25 E7
Coulmier-le-Sec *F* 25 E11
Coulmiers *F* 24 E6
Coulogne *F* 15 F12
Coulombiers *F* 29 C6
Coulombs *F* 24 C6
Coulommiers *F* 25 C9
Coulonges-sur-l'Autize *F* 28 C4
Coulounieix-Chamiers *F* 29 E7
Coulport *GB* 4 C7
Coupar Angus *GB* 5 B10
Couptrain *F* 23 D11
Coura *P* 38 E2
Courcelles *B* 182 E4
Courcelles-Chaussy *F* 26 B5
Courcelles-sur-Nied *F* 186 C1
Courchaton *F* 26 E6
Courchevel *F* 31 E10
Cour-Cheverny *F* 24 E5
Courcité *F* 23 D11
Courçon *F* 28 C4
Courcy *F* 19 F9
Courgains *F* 23 D12
Courgenay *CH* 27 F7
Courgenay *F* 25 D10
Courlay *F* 28 B4
Courmayeur *I* 31 D10
Courmelles *F* 19 F7
Cournon-d'Auvergne *F* 30 D3
Courpière *F* 30 D4
Courrendlin *CH* 27 F7
Courrensan *F* 33 C6
Courrières *F* 182 E1
Coursac *F* 29 E7
Coursan *F* 34 D5
Coursegoules *F* 36 D6
Courseulles-sur-Mer *F* 23 B11
Cours-la-Ville *F* 30 C5
Courson-les-Carrières *F* 25 E9
Court *CH* 27 F7
Courtalain *F* 24 D5
Courtelary *CH* 27 F7
Courtenay *F* 25 D9
Courthézon *F* 35 B8
Courtmacsherry *IRL* 8 E5
Courtomer *F* 24 C3
Courtown *IRL* 9 C10
Courtrai *B* 19 C7
Courtrai *B* 182 D2
Court-St-Etienne *B* 19 C10
Courville-sur-Eure *F* 24 D5
Cousance *F* 31 B7
Cousances-les-Forges *F* 26 C3
Coussac-Bonneval *F* 29 D8
Coussay-les-Bois *F* 29 B7
Coussegrey *F* 25 E11
Coussey *F* 26 D4
Coustouges *F* 34 F4
Coutances *F* 23 B9
Couterne *F* 23 C11
Couto de Cima *P* 44 C5
Coutras *F* 28 E5
Couvet *CH* 31 B10
Couvin *B* 19 D10
Couze-et-St-Front *F* 29 F7
Couzeix *F* 29 D8
Covaleda *E* 40 E6
Covarrubias *E* 40 D5
Covăsînț *RO* 151 E8
Covasna *RO* 153 F8
Cove *GB* 2 K5
Cove Bay *GB* 3 L12
Coventry *GB* 13 A11
Covilhã *P* 44 D6
Cowbit *GB* 11 F11
Cowbridge *GB* 13 C8
Cowdenbeath *GB* 5 C10
Cowes *GB* 13 D12
Cox *E* 56 E3
Cox *F* 33 C8
Coxheath *GB* 15 E9
Coxhoe *GB* 5 F13
Coylumbridge *GB* 3 L9
Cózar *E* 55 B6
Cozes *F* 28 D4
Cozești *MD* 154 B2
Cozieni *RO* 161 C9
Cozmești *RO* 153 D11
Cozzano *F* 37 H10
Craanford *IRL* 9 C10
Crăcăoani *RO* 153 C8
Crach *F* 22 E5
Crăciunelu de Jos *RO* 152 E3
Crăciunești *RO* 152 E5
Craco *I* 61 C6
Craidorolț *RO* 151 B10
Craig *GB* 2 L6
Craigavad *GB* 4 F5
Craigavon *GB* 7 D10
Craigellachie *GB* 3 L10
Craignure *GB* 4 C5
Crail *GB* 5 C11
Crailsheim *D* 75 D7
Craiova *RO* 160 E3
Craiva *RO* 151 D8
Cramlington *GB* 5 E13
Crâmpoia *RO* 160 E5
Cranage *GB* 11 E7
Cranagh *GB* 4 F2
Cranford *IRL* 7 B7
Crângeni *RO* 160 E5
Cran-Gevrier *F* 31 D9
Crângu *RO* 160 F6
Crângurile *RO* 160 D6
Cranleigh *GB* 15 E8
Crans-sur-Sierre *CH* 31 C11
Craon *F* 23 E10
Craonne *F* 19 F8
Craponne-sur-Arzon *F* 30 E4
Crask Inn *GB* 2 J7
Crasna *RO* 151 C10
Crasna *RO* 160 C3
Crasnoe *MD* 154 D5
Crathie *GB* 5 A10
Crato *P* 44 F5
Cravagliana *I* 68 B5
Cravant *F* 25 E10
Craven Arms *GB* 13 A9
Crawfordjohn *GB* 5 E9
Crawfordsburn *GB* 4 F5
Crawley *GB* 15 E8
Creaca *RO* 151 C11
Creagh *IRL* 8 E4
Creagorry *GB* 2 L2
Creamhghort *IRL* 7 B7
Créances *F* 23 B8
Créancey *F* 25 F12
Crecente *E* 38 D3
Crêches-sur-Saône *F* 30 C6
Crécy-en-Ponthieu *F* 18 D4
Crécy-la-Chapelle *F* 25 C8
Crécy-sur-Serre *F* 19 E8
Credenhill *GB* 13 A9
Crediton *GB* 13 D7
Creeslough *IRL* 7 B7
Creevagh *IRL* 6 D4
Creggan *GB* 4 F2
Creggan *GB* 7 D9
Cregganbaun *IRL* 6 E3
Creggs *IRL* 6 E6
Creglingen *D* 75 D7
Cregneash *GBM* 10 C2
Créhange *F* 186 C2
Creil *F* 18 F5
Creil *NL* 16 C5
Creissels *F* 34 B5
Crema *I* 69 C8
Cremeaux *F* 30 D4
Crémenes *E* 39 C9
Crémieu *F* 31 D7
Cremlingen *D* 79 B8
Cremona *I* 69 C9
Črenšovci *SLO* 148 C6
Créon *F* 28 F5
Crepaja *SRB* 158 C6
Crépey *F* 26 C4
Crépy *F* 19 E8
Crépy-en-Valois *F* 18 F6
Cres *HR* 67 C9
Crescentino *I* 68 C5
Crespina *I* 66 E2
Crespino *I* 66 C4
Crespos *E* 46 C3
Cressensac *F* 29 E9
Crest *F* 31 F7
Creswell *GB* 11 E9
Cretas *E* 42 F4
Créteil *F* 25 C7
Crețeni *RO* 160 D4
Crețești *RO* 153 D11
Creußen *D* 75 C10
Creutzwald *F* 21 F7
Creuzburg *D* 79 D7
Crevalcore *I* 66 C3
Crevant *F* 29 C9
Crévéchamps *F* 26 C5
Crèvecœur-le-Grand *F* 18 E5
Crevedia *RO* 161 D7
Crevedia Mare *RO* 161 E7
Crevenicu *RO* 161 E7
Crevillente *E* 56 E3
Crevoladossola *I* 68 A5
Crewe *GB* 10 E7
Crewkerne *GB* 13 D9
Crianlarich *GB* 4 C7
Cricău *RO* 152 E3
Criccieth *GB* 10 F3
Criciova *RO* 159 B9
Crickhowell *GB* 13 B8
Cricklade *GB* 13 B11
Cricova *MD* 154 C3
Crieff *GB* 5 C9
Criel-sur-Mer *F* 18 D3
Crikvenica *HR* 67 B10
Crimmitschau *D* 79 E11
Crimond *GB* 3 K13
Crinan *GB* 4 C5
Cringleford *GB* 15 B11
Crinitz *D* 80 C5
Cripán *E* 41 C7
Cripp's Corner *GB* 15 F10
Criquetot-l'Esneval *F* 18 E1
Crișcior *RO* 151 E10
Crișeni *RO* 151 C11
Crispiano *I* 61 B8
Crissolo *I* 31 F11
Cristești *RO* 152 D4
Cristești *RO* 153 B9
Cristești *RO* 153 C9
Cristian *RO* 152 F4
Cristian *RO* 161 B6
Cristinești *RO* 153 A8
Criștioru de Jos *RO* 151 E10
Cristóbal *E* 45 D9
Cristolț *RO* 151 C11
Cristuru Secuiesc *RO* 152 E6
Criuleni *MD* 154 C4
Criva *MD* 153 A9
Crivitz *D* 83 C11
Crkvice *BIH* 157 D8
Crkvice *HR* 162 D3
Crkvice *MNE* 163 D6
Crkvina *BIH* 157 B9
Crkvine *SRB* 163 C9
Crljivica *BIH* 156 D5
Črmošnjice *SLO* 73 E11
Črna *SLO* 73 D10
Crna Bara *SRB* 150 F5
Crna Bara *SRB* 158 D3
Crnac *HR* 149 E9
Crnajka *SRB* 159 E9
Crna Trava *SRB* 164 D5
Crnča *SRB* 158 E3
Crni Lug *BIH* 156 D6
Crni Lug *HR* 67 B10
Crnjelovo *BIH* 157 C11
Črnkovci *HR* 149 E10
Crnoklište *SRB* 164 C5
Črnomelj *SLO* 148 E4
Crock *D* 75 B8
Crocketford *GB* 5 E9
Crockets Town *IRL* 6 D4
Crockmore *IRL* 7 C7
Crocmaz *MD* 154 E5
Crocq *F* 29 D10
Crodo *I* 68 A5
Crofty *GB* 12 B6
Croghan *IRL* 6 E6
Crognaleto *I* 62 B4
Croisilles *F* 18 D6
Croithlí *IRL* 6 B6
Crolles *F* 31 E8
Crolly *IRL* 6 B6
Cromadh *IRL* 8 C5
Cromarty *GB* 3 K8
Cromer *GB* 15 B11
Cromhall *GB* 13 B10
Cronat *F* 30 B4
Crook *GB* 5 F13
Crookham *GB* 5 D12
Crookhaven *IRL* 8 F3
Crookstown *IRL* 8 E5
Croom *IRL* 8 C5
Cropalati *I* 61 D7
Cropani *I* 59 B10
Crosbost *GB* 2 J4

Crosby GB 10 E5
Crosia I 61 D7
Cross IRL 6 E4
Crossaig GB 4 D6
Crossakeel IRL 7 E8
Cross Barry IRL 8 E5
Crosscanonby GB 5 F10
Crossdoney IRL 7 E8
Crossgar GB 7 D11
Crossgare GB 4 E3
Crossgates GB 13 A8
Crosshands GB 5 D8
Crosshaven IRL 8 E6
Crosshill GB 4 E7
Cross Inn GB 12 A6
Cross Keys IRL 7 E9
Crossmaglen GB 7 D9
Crotone I 61 E8
Crots F 36 B4
Crottendorf D 76 B3
Croughton GB 13 B12
Croutelle F 29 B6
Crouy F 19 F7
Crouy-sur-Ourcq F 25 B9
Crowborough GB 15 E9
Crowland GB 11 F11
Crowle GB 11 D10
Crowthorne GB 15 E7
Croy GB 3 K8
Croyde GB 12 C6
Crozant F 29 C9
Crozes-Hermitage F 30 E6
Crozon F 22 D3
Cruas F 35 A8
Crucea RO 153 C7
Crucea RO 155 D2
Crucișor RO 151 B11
Crucoli I 61 E7
Cruden Bay GB 3 L13
Cruglic MD 154 C4
Crumlin GB 4 F4
Cruseilles F 31 C9
Crușeț RO 160 D3
Crusheen IRL 8 C5
Crusnes F 20 F5
Cruzy F 34 D4
Cruzy-le-Châtel F 25 E11
Crvenka SRB 158 B3
Crymych GB 12 B5
Csabacsőd H 150 D6
Csabrendek H 149 B8
Csákánydoroszló H 149 C7
Csákberény H 149 B10
Csákvár H 149 B10
Csanádapáca H 151 D6
Csanádpalota H 150 E6
Csány H 150 B4
Csanytelek H 150 D5
Császár H 149 A10
Császártöltés H 150 E3
Csátalja H 150 E2
Csávoly H 150 E3
Csécse H 147 F9
Csemő H 150 C4
Csengele H 150 D4
Csenger H 151 B10
Csengőd H 150 D3
Csépa H 150 D5
Csepreg H 149 B7
Cserépfalu H 145 H2
Cserhátsurány H 147 F8
Cserkeszőlő H 150 D5
Csernely H 145 G1
Csesztreg H 149 C7
Csetény H 149 B9
Csévharaszt H 150 C3
Csikéria H 150 E3
Csókakő H 149 B10
Csökmő H 151 C7
Csököly H 149 D9
Csokonyavisonta H 149 D8
Csokvaomány H 145 G1
Csolnok H 149 A11
Csólyospálos H 150 E4
Csongrád H 150 D5
Csopak H 149 C9
Csór H 149 B10
Csorna H 149 A8
Csörnyeföld H 149 D7
Csorvás H 150 D6
Csősz H 149 B10
Csót H 149 B9
Csurgó H 149 D8
Cuacos de Yuste E 45 D9
Cuadros E 39 C8
Cualedro E 38 E4
Cuarte de Huerva E 41 E10
Cuba P 50 C4
Cubalhão P 38 D3
Cubells E 42 D5
Cubjac F 29 E7
Cubla E 47 D10
Cubo de Bureba E 40 C5
Cubo de la Solana E 41 E7
Cubolta MD 153 B12
Cubzac-les-Ponts F 28 F5
Cuca RO 153 F11
Cuca RO 160 D5
Cucalón E 47 B10
Cucerdea RO 152 E4
Cuci RO 152 E4
Cuckfield GB 15 E8
Cucuron F 35 C9
Cucuteni RO 153 C9
Cudalbi RO 153 F11
Cudillero E 39 A7
Čudnići BIH 157 D8
Cudos F 32 B5
Cuéllar E 40 F3
Cuenca E 47 D8
Cuenca de Campos E 39 D9
Cuers F 36 E4
Cuerva E 46 E4
Cueva de Agreda E 41 E8
Cuevas Bajas E 53 B8
Cuevas de Almanzora E 55 E9
Cuevas del Becerro E 53 C6
Cuevas del Campo E 55 D7
Cuevas de San Clemente
E 40 D4
Cuevas de San Marcos E 53 B8
Cuevas Labradas E 42 G1
Cuffley GB 15 D8
Cugand F 28 A3
Cuges-les-Pins F 35 D10
Cugir RO 151 F11
Cuglieri I 64 C2
Cugnaux F 33 C8
Cuguen F 23 D8
Cuhureștii de Sus MD 154 B3
Cuijk NL 16 E5
Cúil an tSúdaire IRL 7 F8
Cuiseaux F 31 C7
Cuise-la-Motte F 18 F7
Cuisery F 31 B6
Cujmir RO 159 E10
Çukë AL 168 E3
Çukuryurt TR 173 B8
Culan F 29 B10
Culciu RO 151 B11
Culdaff IRL 4 E2
Culdrain GB 3 L11
Culemborg NL 16 E4
Culjković SRB 158 D4
Culla E 48 D4
Cullahill IRL 9 C8
Cúllar-Baza E 55 D7
Cullen GB 3 K11
Cullera E 48 F4
Cullivoe GB 3 D14
Cullompton GB 13 D8
Cully CH 31 C10
Cullybackey GB 4 F4
Cullyhanna GB 7 D9
Culmstock GB 13 D8
Culnaknock GB 2 K4
Culoz F 31 D8
Culswick GB 3 E13
Cumbernauld GB 5 D9
Cumbres de San Bartolomé
E 51 C6
Cumbres Mayores E 51 C6
Cumeada P 50 E3
Cumiana I 31 F11
Cumieira P 38 F4
Cuminestown GB 3 K12
Cumlosen D 83 D11
Cumnock GB 5 E8
Cumpăna RO 155 E3
Cunault F 23 F11
Cunegès F 29 F6
Cuneo I 37 C7
Cunewalde D 81 D7
Cunfin F 25 D12
Cungrea RO 160 D4
Cunha P 44 C6
Cunicea MD 154 B3
Čuništa BIH 157 D10
Cunit E 43 E7
Cunningsburgh GB 3 E14
Cuntis E 38 C2
Cuorgnè I 68 C4
Cupar GB 5 C10
Cupcina MD 153 A10
Cupello I 63 C7
Cupra Marittima I 62 A5
Cupramontana I 67 F7
Ćuprija SRB 159 F7
Cupșeni RO 152 B3
Cuq-Toulza F 33 C9
Curățele RO 151 D9
Curcani RO 161 E9
Curcuris I 64 D2
Cureggio I 68 B5
Cureșnița MD 153 A12
Curgy F 30 B5
Curinga I 59 B9
Curon Venosta I 71 D11
Curracloe IRL 9 D10
Curraghroe IRL 6 E6
Curragh West IRL 6 E5
Currás E 38 C2
Curry IRL 6 E5
Curry Rivel GB 13 C9
Cursi I 61 C10
Curtea RO 151 F9
Curtea de Argeș RO 160 C5
Curtici RO 151 E7
Curtișoara RO 160 E4
Curtuișeni RO 151 B9
Čurug SRB 158 C5
Cusano Mutri I 60 A3
Cushendall GB 4 E4
Cushendun GB 4 E4
Cushina IRL 7 F8
Cussac F 29 D7
Cusset F 30 C3
Cussy-les-Forges F 25 F11
Custines F 26 C5
Custonaci I 58 C2
Cutigliano I 66 D2
Cutro I 61 E7
Cutrofiano I 61 C10
Cuxac-Cabardès F 33 D10
Cuxac-d'Aude F 34 D4
Cuxhaven D 17 A11
Cuzăplac RO 151 D11
Cuza Vodă RO 161 E10
Cuzmin MD 154 A3
Cuzorn F 33 A7
Cvikov CZ 81 E7
Cwmafan GB 13 B7
Cwmbrân GB 13 B8
Cybinka PL 81 B7
Cybowo PL 85 D9
Cychry PL 85 E7
Cyców PL 141 H8
Cydweli GB 12 B6
Cynghordy GB 13 A7
Cynwyl Elfed GB 12 B6
Cyprianka PL 138 E7
Cysoing F 182 D2
Czacz PL 81 B11
Czajków PL 142 D5
Czaplinek PL 85 C10
Czarna PL 143 F11
Czarna PL 144 C5
Czarna Białostocka PL 140 D8
Czarna Dąbrówka PL 85 B13
Czarna Górna PL 145 E6
Czarna Woda PL 138 C5
Czarnca PL 143 E8
Czarne PL 85 C11
Czarnia PL 139 D11
Czarnków PL 85 E11
Czarnocin PL 143 F10
Czarnów PL 81 A7
Czarnowąsy PL 142 E4
Czarnożyły PL 142 D6
Czarny Bór PL 81 E10
Czarny Dunajec PL 147 C9
Czastary PL 142 D5
Czaszyn PL 145 E5
Czchów PL 144 D2
Czechowice-Dziedzice PL 147 B8
Czechy PL 85 C11
Czechy PL 143 C6
Czekarzewice PL 143 D12
Czeladź PL 143 F7
Czemierniki PL 141 G7
Czempiń PL 81 B11
Czeremcha PL 141 E8
Czermin PL 142 C4
Czermno PL 141 H2
Czernica PL 81 D12
Czernice Borowe PL 139 D10
Czernichów PL 143 G8
Czernichów PL 147 B8
Czerniejewo PL 85 F12
Czerniewice PL 141 G2
Czernikowo PL 138 E6
Czernina PL 81 C11
Czersk PL 138 C4
Czerwieńsk PL 81 B8
Czerwin PL 139 E12
Czerwińsk nad Wisłą PL 139 F9
Czerwionka-Leszczyny PL 142 F6
Czerwonak PL 81 B11
Czerwone PL 139 D12
Czestków PL 143 C7
Częstochowa PL 143 E7
Czeszów PL 81 D12
Człopa PL 85 D10
Człuchów PL 85 C12
Czmoń PL 81 B12
Czorsztyn PL 145 E1
Czosnów PL 139 F10
Czudec PL 144 D4
Czyże PL 141 E8
Czyżew-Osada PL 141 E6

D

Daaden D 185 C8
Dăbâca RO 152 D3
Dabar HR 156 C3
Dabar HR 156 E6
Dabas H 150 C3
Dabel D 83 C11
Dąbie PL 81 B8
Dąbie PL 141 G6
Dąbie PL 142 B6
Dąbki PL 85 B10
Dabo F 27 C7
Daborgrad BIH 157 C9
Dabrac BIH 157 D7
Dabravolya BY 140 E10
Dabrica BIH 157 F9
Dąbroszyn PL 81 A7
Dąbroszyn PL 142 B5
Dąbrowa PL 138 E4
Dąbrowa PL 142 E4
Dąbrowa PL 142 E4
Dąbrowa Białostocka PL 140 C8
Dąbrowa Biskupia PL 138 E6
Dąbrowa Chełmińska PL 138 D5
Dąbrowa Górnicza PL 143 F7
Dąbrowa Tarnowska PL 143 F10
Dąbrowa Zielona PL 143 E8
Dąbrowice PL 141 G2
Dąbrowice PL 143 B7
Dąbrówka Wielka PL 143 C7
Dąbrówka Wielkopolska
PL 81 B9
Dąbrówno PL 139 D9
Dăbuleni RO 160 F4
Dabyeya BY 133 F7
Dachau D 75 F9
Dachnów PL 144 C7
Dachrieden D 79 D7
Dachwig D 79 D8
Dačice CZ 77 D8
Dacre GB 5 F11
Dad H 149 A10
Dadia GR 171 B10
Dådran S 103 E10
Dăeni RO 155 D2
Dăești RO 160 C4
Dåfjord N 112 D3
Dafnes GR 174 C4
Dafni GR 171 D6
Dafni GR 174 D5
Dafni GR 175 C8
Dafni GR 175 F6
Dág H 149 A11
Daganzo de Arriba E 46 C6
Dağardi TR 173 F11
Dagâța RO 153 D10
Dagda LV 133 D3
Dagebüll D 82 A5
Dağkızılca TR 177 C9
Daglan F 29 F8
Daglösen S 97 C11
Dagmersellen CH 27 F8
Dağpınar TR 181 B8
Dagsmark FIN 122 F7
Dahlem D 21 D7
Dahlen D 80 D4
Dahlenburg D 83 D9
Dahlhausen D 183 C10
Dahme D 80 C4
Dahme D 83 B10
Dahn D 27 B8
Dähre D 83 E9
Daia RO 161 F7
Daia Română RO 152 E3
Daikanberg S 107 A10
Daikanvik S 107 A10
Dailly GB 4 E7
Daimiel E 46 F5
Daimonia GR 178 B4
Daingean IRL 7 F8
Daingean Uí Chúis IRL 8 D2
Dainville F 18 D6
Dainville-Bertheléville F 26 D4
Dairsie GB 5 C11
Daknam B 182 C3
Đakovo HR 149 F10
Dal N 95 B14
Dal S 107 E13
Đala SRB 150 E5
Dalaas A 71 C10
Dalabrog GB 2 L2
Dalaman TR 181 C9
Dalarö S 93 A12
Dala Rostock S 91 B11
Dalåsen S 102 A7
Dalasjö S 107 B11
Dalbe LV 135 C7
Dalbeattie GB 5 F9
Dalberg-Wendelstorf D 83 C10
Dalboșeț RO 159 D8
Dalby DK 86 D7
Dalby DK 87 E10
Dalby GBM 10 C2
Dalby S 87 D12
Dalbyn S 103 D9
Dalbyover DK 86 B6
Däldenäs S 92 A4
Dale GB 9 E12
Dale N 90 B3
Dale N 100 D2
Dale N 100 E3
Dale N 111 C11
Daleiden D 20 D6
Dalen N 90 A5
Dalen N 94 D7
Dalen NL 17 C7
Daleszyce PL 143 E10
Dalfors S 103 D9
Dalfsen NL 16 C6
Dalgety Bay GB 5 C10
Dalham GB 15 C10
Dalhem B 19 C12
Dalhem S 93 D13
Dalholen N 101 B11
Dalías E 55 F7
Dalików PL 143 C7
Dalj HR 157 B10
Dalkarlsberg S 97 D12
Dalkeith GB 5 D10
Dalkey IRL 7 F10
Dallas GB 3 K10
Dallgow D 80 A4
Dall Villaby DK 86 B5
Dalmally GB 4 C7
Dalmand H 149 D10
Dalmellington GB 5 E8
Dalmine I 69 B8
Dalmose DK 87 E8
Dalovice CZ 76 B3
Dalry GB 4 D7
Dalrymple GB 4 E7
Dalsbruk FIN 126 E8
Dalsbygda N 101 A14
Dalselv N 108 D6
Dalsjöfors S 91 D13
Dals Långed S 91 B11
Dalstein F 20 F6
Dalston GB 5 F11
Dalstorp S 91 D14
Dalstuga S 103 D10
Dalton-in-Furness GB 10 C5
Daluis F 36 C5
Dalum S 91 D13
Dalur FO 2 B3
Dalvadas FIN 113 D17
Dalwhinnie GB 5 B8
Dalyan TR 181 C9
Dalyokiya BY 135 F13
Dalystown IRL 6 F6
Damachava BY 141 G9
Damas-aux-Bois F 26 D5
Damasi GR 169 E7
Damaskinia GR 168 D5
Damasławek PL 85 E13
Damazan F 33 B6
Dambach-la-Ville F 186 E3
Dambaslar TR 173 B7
Dambeck D 83 D11
Dâmbovicioara RO 160 C6
Damelevières F 26 C5
Damerstown IRL 9 C8
Damery F 25 B10
Damës AL 168 C2
Damgan F 22 E6
Damhead GB 4 E3
Damhliag IRL 7 E10
Dămienești RO 153 D9
Damigny F 23 D12
Damjan RKS 163 E10
Dammarie F 24 D6
Dammartin-en-Goële F 25 B8
Damme B 19 B7
Damme D 17 C10
Damnica PL 85 B12
Damno PL 85 A12
Damp D 83 A7
Dampierre F 26 F4
Dampierre-sur-Linotte F 26 E5
Dampierre-sur-Salon F 26 E4
Damprichard F 27 F6
Damshagen D 83 C10
Damsholte DK 87 F10
Dämsta S 107 E13
Dămuc RO 153 D7
Damüls A 71 C9
Damvant CH 27 F6
Damville F 24 C5
Damvillers F 19 F11
Damwoude NL 16 B6
Damyanovo BG 165 D10
Danaçali TR 173 E10
Danakos GR 177 E6
Danamandira TR 173 B9
Danasjö S 109 E12
Dănciulești RO 160 D3
Dăneasa RO 160 E5
Daneș RO 152 E5
Danesfort IRL 7 E7
Dănești RO 153 D7
Dănești RO 153 D11
Dănești RO 160 D2
Daneți RO 160 F4
Dångebo S 89 B8
Dângeni RO 153 B9
Dangé-St-Romain F 29 B7
Danholn S 103 E10
Dănicei RO 160 D4
Daniec PL 142 E5
Danilovgrad MNE 163 D7
Dänischenhagen D 83 B8
Danişment TR 173 E8
Danjoutin F 27 E6
Dankerode D 79 C9
Danndorf D 79 B8
Dannemare DK 83 A10
Dannemarie F 27 E7
Dannemora S 99 B9
Dannenberg (Elbe) D 83 D10
Dannenwalde D 84 D4
Dány H 150 B4
Daon F 23 E10
Daoulas F 22 D3
Darabani RO 153 A9
Dărăști Ilfov RO 161 E8
Darbėnai LT 134 D2
Dar Ben Karricha el Behri
MA 53 E6
Darby's Bridge IRL 8 D2
Dar Chaoui MA 52 E5
Darda HR 149 E11
Dardesheim D 79 C8
Dardhas AL 168 C4
Darè I 69 A10
Darfo Boario Terme I 69 B9
Dargun D 83 C13
Darica TR 173 D8
Darici TR 173 F10
Dârjiu RO 152 E6
Darkley GB 7 D9
Darlington GB 11 B8
Dârlos RO 152 E4
Darłówko PL 85 B10
Darłowo PL 85 B10
Dărmănești RO 153 B8
Dărmănești RO 153 E8
Dărmănești RO 160 C5
Dărmănești RO 161 D7
Darmstadt D 21 E11
Darney F 26 D5
Darnieulles F 26 D5
Darnózseli H 146 F4
Daroca E 47 B10
Darova RO 159 B8
Darque P 38 E2
Darra GB 3 K12
Darragh IRL 8 C4
Darro E 55 E6
Dartford GB 15 E9
Dartmeet GB 13 D7
Dartmouth GB 13 E7
Darton GB 11 D8
Dartsel S 118 C4
Daruvar HR 149 E8
Dârvari RO 159 E11
Darwen GB 10 D7
Dascălu RO 161 D8
Dashava UA 145 E9
Dašice CZ 77 B9
Dasing D 75 F9
Dasochori GR 169 B9
Dasochori GR 171 C7
Dassel D 78 C6
Dassendorf D 83 D8
Dassow D 83 C9
Daszyna PL 143 B7
Datça TR 181 C7
Datteln D 17 E8
Datterode (Ringgau) D 79 D7
Daudzese LV 135 D10
Daudzeva LV 135 C10
Daugai LT 137 E9
Daugailiai LT 135 E11
Daugård DK 86 D5
Daugavpils LV 135 E13
Daugėlaičiai LT 134 E7
Dauguļi LV 135 A10
Daujėnai LT 135 E9
Daumazan-sur-Arize F 33 D8
Daumeray F 23 E11
Daun D 21 D7
Dauphin F 35 C10
Dava GB 3 L9
Daventry GB 13 A12
Davézieux F 30 E6
Davidești RO 160 C6
Davidkovo BG 165 F10
Daviot GB 3 L8
Davle CZ 76 C6
Davleia GR 175 B6
Dávod H 150 E2
Davoli I 59 B9
Davor HR 157 B8
Davos CH 71 D9
Davutlar TR 177 D9
Davydiv UA 144 D9
Dawhinava BY 133 E3
Dawlish GB 13 D8
Dax F 32 C3
Deal GB 15 E11
Dealu RO 152 E6
Dealu Morii RO 153 E10
Dearham GB 5 F10
Deauville F 23 B12
Deba E 32 D1
Debar NMK 168 A4
Debeli Lug SRB 159 E8
Debeljača SRB 158 C6
Debenham GB 15 C11
Dębe Wielkie PL 141 F4
Dębica PL 143 F11
De Bilt NL 16 D4
Dęblin PL 141 G5
Debnevo BG 165 D10
Dębnica Kaszubska PL 85 B12
Dębno PL 85 E7
Dębno PL 143 G10
Dęborzeczka PL 141 H2
Debovo BG 165 B10
Dębowa Kłoda PL 141 G8
Dębowa Łąka PL 138 D7
Dębowiec PL 147 B7
Debrc SRB 158 D4
Debrecen H 151 B8
Debrešte NMK 168 B5
Debrzno PL 85 C12
Dębsko PL 85 D9
Debŭr BG 166 E4
Deçan RKS 163 D9
Decazeville F 33 A10
Dechtice SK 146 D5
Decimomannu I 64 E2
Decimoputzu I 64 E2
Děčín CZ 80 E6
Decize F 30 B3
De Cocksdorp NL 16 B3
Decollatura I 59 A9
Decs H 149 D11
Deda RO 152 D5
Deddington GB 13 B12
Dedeleben D 79 B8
Dedeler TR 173 F9
Dedelow D 84 D5
Dedelstorf D 83 E9
Dedemsvaart NL 17 C6
Dédestapolcsány H 145 G2
Dedham GB 15 D10
Dedovichi RUS 132 F6
Deensen D 78 C6
Deerlijk B 19 C7
Dég H 149 C10
Degaña E 39 C6
Degeberga S 88 D6
Degerbäcken S 118 C6
Degerby FIN 99 B14
Degerby FIN 127 E11
Degerfors S 92 A4
Degerhamn S 89 C10
Degersjö S 107 D12
Degerträsk S 118 D4
Deggendorf D 76 E3
Deggingen D 74 E6
Değirmen TR 173 B9
Değirmendere TR 177 C9
Değirmendüzü TR 171 D10
Değirmenyeni TR 167 F7
Dego I 37 C8
Degučiai LT 135 E12
Degumnieki LV 135 C13
De Haan B 19 B7
Dehesa de Campoamor E 56 F3
Dehesas de Guadix E 55 D6
Deià E 49 E10
Deidesheim D 21 F10
Deifontes E 53 B9
Deilão P 39 E6
Deining D 75 D10
Deiningen D 75 E8
Deinste D 17 A12
Deinze B 19 C8
Deiva Marina I 37 C11
Dej RO 152 C3
Deje S 97 C9
Dejtár H 147 E8
Dekani SLO 67 A8
Dekeleia GR 175 C8
De Koog NL 16 B3
De Kooy NL 16 C3
Dekov BG 165 B11
Delabole GB 12 D5
Delary S 87 B13
Delbrück D 17 E11
Delčevo NMK 165 F6
Delden NL 17 D7
Délegyháza H 150 C3
Deleitosa E 45 E9
Đelekovec HR 149 D7
Delémont CH 27 F7
Delen' UA 154 F4
Deleni RO 153 C9
Deleni RO 155 E2
Deleria GR 169 E7
Delești RO 153 D11
Delfoi GR 175 C6
Delft NL 16 D2
Delfzijl NL 17 B7
Delia I 58 E4
Delianuova I 59 C8
Deliblato SRB 159 D7
Deliceto I 60 A4
Deligrad SRB 159 F8
Deliktaş TR 177 B8
Delingsdorf D 83 C8
Delitzsch D 79 C11
Delle F 27 E7
Delligsen D 78 C6
Dello I 66 B1
Delme F 26 C5
Delmenhorst D 17 B11
Delnice HR 67 B10
Delsbo S 103 C12
Deltebre E 42 F5
Delvin IRL 7 E8
Delvinaki GR 168 E3
Delvinë AL 168 E3
Demandice SK 147 E7
Demange-aux-Eaux F 26 C3
Dembava LT 135 E8
Demecser H 145 G4
De Meern NL 183 A6
Demen D 83 C11
Demene LV 135 E13
Demigny F 30 B6
Demiraj AL 163 E7
Demircihalil TR 167 F8
Demirdere TR 173 D9
Demirhanli TR 167 F7
Demir Hisar NMK 168 B5
Demir Kapija NMK 169 B7
Demirköy TR 167 F9
Demirli TR 181 C9
Demirtaş TR 173 D11
Demmin D 84 C4
Demonte I 37 C6
Dému F 33 C6
Denain F 19 D7
Denbigh GB 10 E5
Den Bommel NL 182 B4
Den Burg NL 16 B3
Denderleeuw B 182 D4
Dendermonde B 19 B9
Den Dungen NL 16 E4
Denekamp NL 17 D8
Denguin F 32 D5
Den Haag NL 16 D2
Den Haag NL 182 A4
Denham GB 15 D8
Den Ham NL 17 D7
Den Helder NL 16 C3
Denholm GB 5 E11
Denia E 56 D5
Denkendorf D 27 C11
Denkendorf D 75 E9
Denkingen D 27 D10
Denkingen D 27 E11
Denklingen D 71 B11
Dennewitz D 80 C4
Dennhausen (Fuldabrück)
D 78 D5
Denny GB 5 C9
Den Oever NL 16 C4
Densow D 84 D4
Densuș RO 159 B10
Denta RO 159 C7
Dentergem B 19 C7
Dentlein am Forst D 75 D7
Denver GB 11 F12
Denzlingen D 27 D8
Déols F 29 B9
De Panne B 18 B6
Deppis S 109 E18
Deråsbrenna N 105 C10
Derby GB 11 F9
Derecske H 151 C8
Dereham GB 15 B10
Derekegyház H 150 D5
Dereköy TR 167 F8
Dereköy TR 173 F7
Derenburg D 79 C8
Derenti TR 173 E7
De Rijp NL 16 C3
Dermantsi BG 165 C9
Dermbach D 79 E7
Dermenas AL 168 C2
Derna RO 151 C9
Dernau D 21 C8
Derreen IRL 6 D4
Derreendaragh IRL 8 E3
Derreeny Bridge IRL 8 E4
Derry GB 4 F2
Derrygonnelly GB 7 D7
Derrylin GB 7 D7
Derrymore IRL 8 D3
Derrynawilt GB 7 D8
Derryrush IRL 6 F3
Derrywode IRL 6 E5
Dersca RO 153 B8
Dersingham GB 11 F13
Dersum D 17 C8
Deruta I 62 B2
Dervaig GB 4 B4
Derval F 23 E8
Dervenakia GR 175 D6
Derveni GR 174 C5
Derventa BIH 157 C8
Derviçan AL 168 D3
Dervio I 69 A7
Derviziana GR 168 F4
Dervock GB 4 E4
Desa RO 159 F11
Desana I 68 C5
Desantne UA 155 B5
Descargamaría E 45 D8
Descartes F 29 B7
Desenzano del Garda I 66 B2
Désertines F 29 C11
Desești RO 152 B3
Desfina GR 175 C6
Deskati GR 169 E6
Deskle SLO 73 D8
Despotovac SRB 159 E7
Despotovo SRB 158 C4
Dessau D 79 C11
Dessel B 16 F4
De Steeg NL 16 D6
Destelbergen B 19 B8
Deštná CZ 77 D7
Destriana E 39 D7
Desulo I 64 C3
Desvres F 15 F12
Deszczno PL 85 E8
Deszk H 150 E5
Deta RO 159 C7
Detern D 17 B9
Detk H 150 B5
Detkovac HR 149 E9
Dětmarovice CZ 146 B6
Detmold D 17 E11
Dettelbach D 75 C7
Dettenhausen D 187 D7
Dettingen an der Erms D
187 D7
Dettmannsdorf D 83 B13
Dettum D 79 B8
Dettwiller F 186 D3
Detva SK 147 D8
Deurne NL 16 F5
Deutsch Evern D 83 D8
Deutschfeistritz A 148 B4
Deutschhof D 84 E3
Deutschkreutz A 149 A7
Deutschlandsberg A 73 C11
Deutschneudorf D 80 E4
Deutsch-Wagram A 77 F11
Deutzen D 79 D11
Deva RO 151 F10
Dévaványa H 151 C6
Devecikonağı TR 173 E10
Devecser H 149 B8
Devene BG 165 C8
Deventer NL 16 D6
Devesel RO 159 E10
Deveselu RO 160 E4
Devetaki BG 165 C10
Deville F 184 E2
Devil's Bridge GB 13 A7
Devin BG 165 F9
Devizes GB 13 C11
Devletliağaç TR 167 F8
Devnya BG 167 C9
Đevrske HR 156 E4
De Wijk NL 16 C6
Dewsbury GB 11 D8
Deza E 41 F7
Dežanovac HR 149 E8
Dezghingea MD 154 E3
Dezna RO 151 E9
Dhërmi AL 168 D2
Dhron D 185 E6
Diafani GR 181 E6
Diakofto GR 174 C5
Dialampi GR 171 B8
Diamante I 60 D5
Dianalund DK 87 D8
Diano d'Alba I 37 B8
Diano Marina I 37 D8
Diavata GR 169 C8
Diavolitsi GR 174 E4
Dichiseni RO 161 E11
Dicomano I 66 E3
Didam NL 16 E6
Didcot GB 13 B12
Didderse D 79 B7
Didești RO 160 E5
Didyma GR 175 E7
Didymoteicho GR 171 B10
Didžiasalis LT 135 F13
Die F 31 F7
Dieblich D 21 D8
Dieburg D 21 E11
Dieci RO 151 E9
Diedorf D 75 F8
Diego Álvaro E 45 C10
Diekhof D 83 C12
Diekholzen D 78 B6
Diekirch L 20 E6
Dielheim D 21 F11
Dielmissen D 78 C6
Dielsdorf CH 27 F9
Diemen NL 16 D3
Diémoz F 31 D7
Dienheim D 185 E9
Dienne F 30 E2
Dienville F 25 D12
Diepenau D 17 D11
Diepenbeek B 19 C11
Diepenheim NL 183 A9
Diepenveen NL 183 A8
Diepholz D 17 C10
Dieppe F 18 E3
Dierdorf D 21 C9
Dieren NL 16 D6
Dierhagen D 83 B12
Diesdorf D 83 E9
Dieskau D 79 D11
Diespeck D 75 C8
Diessen NL 183 C6
Dießen am Ammersee D 72 A3
Diessenhofen CH 27 E10
Diest B 19 C11
Dietachdorf A 77 F6
Dietenheim D 71 A10
Dietersburg D 76 E3
Dietfurt an der Altmühl D
75 D10
Dietikon CH 27 F9
Dietingen D 27 D10
Dietmanns A 77 E7
Dietmanns A 77 E8
Dietmannsried D 71 B10
Dietzenbach D 21 D11
Dietzhölztal-Ewersbach D
185 C9
Dieue-sur-Meuse F 26 B3
Dieulefit F 35 A9
Dieulouard F 26 C5
Dieuze F 26 C6
Dievenišķės LT 137 E12
Diever NL 16 C6
Diex A 73 C10
Diezma E 55 E6
Differdange L 20 E5
Digerberget S 97 B9
Digerberget S 102 A8
Digermulen N 110 D8
Digernes N 100 B5
Dignac F 29 D6
Dignāja LV 135 D12
Dignano I 73 D6
Digne-les-Bains F 36 C4

Digny F 24 C5
Digoin F 30 C4
Dihtiv UA 144 B9
Dijon F 26 F3
Dikaia GR 166 F6
Dikanäs S 107 A10
Dikancë RKS 163 E10
Dikili TR 177 A8
Dikkebus B 18 C6
Dikļi LV 131 F10
Diksmuide B 18 B6
Dilar E 53 B9
Dilbeek B 182 D4
Dilesi GR 175 C8
Dilinata GR 174 C2
Dillenburg D 21 C10
Dilling N 95 D13
Dillingen (Saar) D 21 F7
Dillingen an der Donau D 75 E7
Dilove UA 145 H9
Dilsen B 19 B12
Dimaro I 71 E11
Diminio GR 169 F8
Dimitrie Cantemir RO 153 D12
Dimitritsi GR 169 C9
Dimitrovgrad BG 166 E5
Dimitrovgrad SRB 165 C6
Dimitsana GR 174 D5
Dimovo BG 159 F10
Dimzukalns LV 135 C8
Dinami I 59 B9
Dinan F 23 D7
Dinant B 19 D10
Dinard F 23 C7
Dingé F 23 D8
Dingelstädt D 79 D7
Dingelstedt am Huy D 79 C8
Dingle IRL 8 D2
Dingle S 91 B10
Dingolfing D 75 E12
Dingtuna S 98 C6
Dingwall GB 2 K8
Dinjiška HR 67 D11
Dinkelsbühl D 75 D7
Dinkelscherben D 75 F8
Dinklage D 17 C10
Dinnet GB 5 A11
Dinslaken D 17 E7
Dinteloord NL 16 E2
Dinther NL 183 B6
Dinxperlo NL 17 E6
Diö S 88 B6
Dion GR 169 D7
Diósd H 149 B11
Diosig RO 151 C9
Diósjenő H 147 F8
Dioști RO 160 E4
Diou F 30 B4
Dipignano I 60 E6
Dipotama GR 171 B7
Dipotamia GR 168 D4
Dippach L 20 E6
Dippoldiswalde D 80 E5
Dirdal N 94 E4
Dirhami EST 130 C7
Dirivaara S 116 E8
Dirkshorn NL 16 C3
Dirksland NL 16 E2
Dirlewang D 71 A11
Dirmstein D 187 B5
Dirvonėnai LT 134 E5
Dischingen D 75 E7
Disentis Muster CH 71 D7
Diseröd S 91 D11
Dison B 19 C12
Diss GB 15 C11
Dissay F 29 B6
Dissay-sous-Courcillon F 24 E3
Dissen am Teutoburger Wald D 17 D10
Distington GB 10 B4
Distomo GR 175 C6
Distrato GR 168 D5
Ditfurt D 79 C9
Diträu RO 153 D7
Ditton GB 15 E9
Ditzingen D 27 C11
Divača SLO 73 E8
Divarata GR 174 C2
Diva Slatina BG 165 C6
Divci SRB 158 E5
Divčibare SRB 158 E5
Dives-sur-Mer F 23 B11
Dividalen N 111 C18
Divieto I 59 C7
Divín SK 147 E9
Divina SK 147 C7
Divion F 18 D6
Divišov CZ 77 C7
Divjakë AL 168 C2
Divonne-les-Bains F 31 C9
Divuša HR 156 B5
Dixmont F 25 D9
Dizy F 25 B10
Dizy-le-Gros F 19 E9
Djäkneboda S 122 B5
Djäkneböle S 122 C4
Djupen N 111 B18
Djupfjord N 110 C9
Djupfors S 109 E11
Djupsjö S 107 E14
Djuptjärn S 107 D15
Djupvik N 109 B10
Djupvik N 112 D5
Djupvik S 89 A11
Djura S 103 E8
Djurås S 97 A13
Djurmo S 97 A13
Djurö S 99 D11
Dlhá nad Oravou SK 147 C8
Dlouhá Loučka CZ 77 C12
Dlouhá Třebová CZ 77 C10
Długołęka PL 81 D12
Długołęka PL 140 D7
Długosiodło PL 139 E12
Dłutów PL 143 C7
Dlŭzhka Polyana BG 166 C6
Dmytrivka UA 154 F3
Dmytrivka UA 154 F4
Dmytrivka UA 155 B4
Dnestrovsc MD 154 D5
Dno RUS 132 F6
Doagh GB 4 F4
Doba RO 151 B10
Dobanovci SRB 158 D5
Dobârceni RO 153 B10
Dobârlău RO 153 F7
Dobbertin D 83 C12
Dobbiaco I 72 C5
Dobczyce PL 144 D1
Dobele LV 134 C6
Döbeln D 80 D4
Dobërçan RKS 164 E4
Doberlug-Kirchhain D 80 C5
Döbern D 81 C7
Dobersberg A 77 E8
Doberschütz D 79 D12
Dobiegniew PL 85 E9
Dobieszewo PL 85 B12
Dobieszyn PL 141 G4
Doboj BIH 157 C9
Dobova SLO 148 E5
Doboz H 151 D7
Dobrá CZ 146 B6
Dobra PL 85 C8
Dobra PL 142 C6
Dobra PL 144 D1
Dobra RO 151 F10
Dobra RO 161 D7
Dobra SRB 159 D8
Dobrá Niva SK 147 E8
Dobřany CZ 76 C4
Dobre PL 138 E6
Dobre PL 139 F12
Dobre Miasto PL 136 F1
Dobreni RO 153 D8
Dobrešinci NMK 169 A8
Dobrești RO 151 D9
Dobrești RO 160 D6
Dobrești RO 160 F3
Dobrevo NMK 164 E5
Dobrica SRB 159 C6
Dobričevo SRB 159 D7
Dobrich BG 155 F1
Dobrich BG 166 E5
Dobri Do SRB 164 D3
Dobri Dol BG 159 F11
Dobrin RO 151 C11
Dobrinishte BG 165 F8
Dobříš CZ 76 C6
Dobritz D 79 B11
Dobřív CZ 76 C5
Dobrljin BIH 156 B5
Dobrna SLO 73 D11
Dobrnič SLO 73 E10
Dobrnja BIH 157 C7
Dobrnja BIH 157 C10
Dobrnje SRB 159 E7
Dobro E 40 C4
Dobrodzień PL 142 E5
Döbrököz H 149 D10
Dobromierz PL 81 E10
Dobromir RO 155 E1
Dobromirka BG 166 C4
Dobromirtsi BG 171 B8
Dobromyl' UA 145 D6
Dobroń PL 143 C7
Dobron' UA 145 G5
Dobronín CZ 77 D9
Dobro Polje BIH 157 E10
Dobro Polje SRB 159 F9
Dobrošane NMK 164 E4
Dobrosloveni RO 160 E4
Dobrosyn UA 144 C8
Dobroszyce PL 81 D12
Dobroteasa RO 160 D4
Dobrotești RO 160 E5
Dobrotić SRB 164 C4
Dobrotich BG 167 C8
Dobrotino NMK 169 B6
Dobrotitsa BG 161 F9
Dobrovăț RO 153 D11
Dobrovci BIH 157 C9
Dobrovice CZ 77 B7
Dobrovnik SLO 149 C6
Dobrovol'sk RUS 136 D5
Dobrowoda PL 143 F10
Dobruchi RUS 132 D2
Dobrun BIH 158 F3
Dobrun RO 160 E4
Dobrușa MD 154 B3
Dobruševo NMK 169 B5
Dobruška CZ 77 B10
Dobrzankowo PL 139 E10
Dobrzany PL 85 D8
Dobrzeń Wielki PL 142 E4
Dobrzyca PL 142 C4
Dobrzyków PL 139 F8
Dobrzyń nad Wisłą PL 139 E7
Dobšiná SK 145 F1
Dóc H 150 E5
Docking GB 15 B10
Dockmyr S 103 A10
Docksta S 107 E14
Dockweiler D 21 D7
Doclin RO 159 C8
Doddington GB 5 D12
Dodewaard NL 183 B7
Dodonoupoli GR 168 E4
Dödre S 102 A8
Doesburg NL 16 D6
Doetinchem NL 16 E6
Dofteana RO 153 E9
Doğanbey TR 177 C8
Doğanbey TR 177 D9
Doğanci TR 173 D10
Doğanköy TR 173 D10
Döge H 145 G5
Dogliani I 37 B7
Dognecea RO 159 C8
Döğüşbelen TR 181 C9
Dohna D 80 E5
Dohňany SK 146 C6
Dohren D 17 C9
Doicești RO 160 D6
Doïrani GR 169 B8
Doire lorrais IRL 6 F3
Doische B 19 D10
Dojč SK 146 D4
Dojkinci SRB 165 C6
Dokka N 101 E12
Dokkas S 116 D6
Dokkedal DK 86 B6
Dokkum NL 16 B5
Doksy CZ 76 B6
Doksy CZ 81 E7
Doktor Yosifovo BG 165 C7
Dokupe LV 134 B3
Dolanog GB 10 F5
Dolbenmaen GB 10 F3
Dolceacqua I 37 D7
Dol-de-Bretagne F 23 C8
Dole BIH 157 D10
Dole F 26 F3
Dølemo N 90 B3
Dolenci NMK 168 B5
Dolenja Vas SLO 73 E10
Dolenjske Toplice SLO 73 E11
Dolgarrog GB 10 E4
Dolgellau GB 10 F4
Dolgen D 84 D4
Dolgorukovo RUS 136 E2
Dolhan TR 167 F8
Dolhasca RO 153 C9
Dolhești RO 153 C9
Dolhești RO 153 D11
Dołhobyczów PL 144 B9
Dolianova I 64 E3
Dolice PL 85 D8
Dolichi GR 169 D7
Doljani BIH 157 E8
Doljani HR 156 D5
Doljevac SRB 164 C4
Dolla IRL 8 C6
Dolle D 79 B10
Dollern D 82 C7
Döllnitz D 79 D11
Dollnstein D 75 E9
Dollon F 24 D4
Dolna MD 154 C2
Dolna Banya BG 165 E8
Dolna Dikanya BG 165 E7
Dolna Gradeshnitsa BG 165 F7
Dolnaja LV 135 D12
Dolná Krupá SK 146 E5
Dolna Lipnitska BG 166 C4
Dolna Makhala BG 165 E10
Dolna Melna BG 164 D6
Dolna Mitropoliya BG 165 C10
Dolna Oryakhovitsa BG 166 C5
Dolná Strehová SK 147 E8
Dolná Súča SK 146 D6
Dolná Tižina SK 147 C7
Dolna Vasilitsa BG 165 E8
Dolné Orešany SK 146 E4
Dolné Vestenice SK 146 D6
Dolní Bousov CZ 77 B8
Dolní Bukovsko CZ 77 D7
Dolní Čermná CZ 77 C11
Dolni Chiflik BG 167 D9
Dolní Dobrouč CZ 77 C11
Dolni Dŭbnik BG 165 C9
Dolní Dvořiště CZ 77 E6
Dolni Glavanak BG 166 F5
Dolní Kounice CZ 77 D10
Dolni Lom BG 165 C6
Dolní Loučky CZ 77 D10
Dolní Němčí CZ 146 D5
Dolní Podluží CZ 81 E7
Dolní Újezd CZ 77 C10
Dolní Újezd CZ 146 B5
Dolni Voden BG 165 E10
Dolní Žandov CZ 75 B12
Dolno Dupeni NMK 168 C5
Dolno Ezerovo BG 167 D8
Dolno Kamartsi BG 165 D8
Dolno Konjare NMK 164 F4
Dolno Levski BG 165 E9
Dolno Osenovo BG 165 F7
Dolno Selo BG 164 E5
Dolno Tserovene BG 159 F11
Dolno Uyno BG 164 E6
Dolný Hričov SK 147 C7
Dolný Kubín SK 147 C8
Dolný Pial SK 146 E6
Dolný Štál SK 146 F5
Dolo I 66 B5
Dolomieu F 31 D8
Dolores E 56 E3
Dolovo SRB 159 D6
Dölsach A 73 C6
Dolsk PL 81 C12
Dołubowo PL 141 E7
Dolus-d'Oléron F 28 D3
Dolyna UA 145 F8
Dolynivka UA 154 A5
Dolyns'ke UA 154 B5
Dolzhitsy RUS 132 D5
Domaháza H 147 E10
Domaniewice PL 141 G2
Domaniewice PL 143 B8
Domanín CZ 146 C4
Domaradz PL 144 D4
Domart-en-Ponthieu F 18 D5
Domaševo BIH 162 D5
Domašinec HR 149 D7
Domașnea RO 159 C9
Domaszek H 150 E5
Domaszków PL 77 B11
Domaszowice PL 142 D4
Domat Ems CH 71 D8
Domats F 25 D9
Domažlice CZ 76 D3
Dombås N 101 B10
Dombasle-en-Xaintois F 26 D4
Dombasle-sur-Meurthe F 186 D1
Dombegyház H 151 E7
Dombóvár H 149 D10
Dombrád H 145 G4
Dombresson CH 31 A10
Domburg NL 16 E1
Domegge di Cadore I 72 D5
Domeikava LT 137 D8
Domène F 31 E8
Domeniko GR 169 E7
Domérat F 29 C11
Domèvre-en-Haye F 26 C4
Domèvre-sur-Vezouze F 27 C6
Domfront F 23 C10
Domgermain F 26 C4
Domince HR 162 D3
Domingo Pérez E 46 E4
Dömitz D 83 D10
Domlyan BG 165 D10
Dommartin-le-Franc F 26 D2
Dommartin-Varimont F 25 C12
Domme F 29 F8
Dommershausen D 21 D8
Dommitzsch D 80 C3
Domnești RO 160 C5
Domnești RO 161 E7
Domnitsa GR 174 B4
Domnovo RUS 136 E2
Domodossola I 68 A5
Domokos GR 174 A5
Domont F 25 B7
Domoroc RKS 164 D4
Dömös H 149 A11
Domoszló H 147 F10
Dompcevrin F 26 C3
Dompierre-les-Ormes F 30 C5
Dompierre-sur-Besbre F 30 B4
Dompierre-sur-Mer F 28 C3
Dompierre-sur-Yon F 28 B3
Domrémy-la-Pucelle F 26 D4
Dömsöd H 150 C3
Domsühl D 83 D11
Domus de Maria I 64 F2
Domusnovas I 64 E2
Domvaina GR 175 C6
Domžale SLO 73 D10
Donagh GB 7 D8
Donaghadee GB 4 F5
Donaghmore GB 7 C9
Donaghmore IRL 7 F10
Don Álvaro E 51 B7
Doña Mencía E 53 A8
Donard IRL 7 F9
Donaueschingen D 27 E9
Donauwörth D 75 E8
Don Benito E 51 B8
Doncaster GB 11 D9
Donchery F 19 E10
Donduşeni MD 153 A11
Donegal IRL 6 C6
Doneraile IRL 8 D5
Doneztebe E 32 D2
Dønfoss N 100 C8
Dongen NL 16 E3
Donges F 23 F7
Dongo I 69 A7
Donici MD 154 C3
Doñinos de Salamanca E 45 C9
Donja Bela Reka SRB 159 E9
Donja Brela HR 157 F6
Donja Bukovica MNE 163 C7
Donja Dubrava HR 149 D7
Donja Kupčina HR 148 E5
Donja Lepenica BIH 157 B8
Donja Mahala BIH 157 B10
Donja Motičina HR 149 F10
Donja Šatornja SRB 158 E6
Donja Stubica HR 148 E5
Donja Višnjica HR 148 D6
Donja Vrijeska HR 149 E8
Donja Zelina HR 148 E6
Donje Pazarište HR 67 C11
Donjeux F 26 D3
Donji Andrijevci HR 157 B9
Donji Čaglić HR 149 F8
Donji Dubovnik BIH 156 C5
Donji Dušnik SRB 164 C5
Donji Kosinj HR 156 C3
Donji Krčin SRB 159 F7
Donji Krivodol SRB 165 C6
Donji Lapac HR 156 C4
Donji Miholjac HR 149 E10
Donji Milanovac SRB 159 E9
Donji Proložac HR 157 F7
Donji Rujani BIH 157 E6
Donji Seget HR 156 E5
Donji Srb HR 156 D5
Donji Striževac SRB 164 C5
Donji Svilaj BIH 157 B9
Donji Vakuf BIH 157 D7
Donji Vijačani BIH 157 C8
Donji Zemunik HR 156 D3
Donji Širovac HR 156 B5
Donk NL 183 B7
Donkerbroek NL 16 B6
Donnalucata I 59 F6
Donnas I 68 B4
Donnemarie-Dontilly F 25 D9
Donnersbach A 73 B9
Donnersdorf D 75 C7
Donohill IRL 8 C6
Donori I 64 E3
Donostia E 32 D2
Donskoye RUS 139 A8
Donville-les-Bains F 23 C8
Donzdorf D 74 E6
Donzenac F 29 E9
Donzère F 35 B8
Donzy F 25 F9
Dooagh IRL 6 E2
Doochary IRL 6 C6
Dooish GB 4 F2
Doolin IRL 6 F4
Doon IRL 8 C6
Doonbeg IRL 8 C3
Doorn NL 16 D4
Doornspijk NL 183 A7
Dopiewo PL 81 B11
Đorče Petrov NMK 164 E3
Dorchester GB 13 D10
Dørdal N 90 B5
Dordives F 25 D8
Dordrecht NL 16 E3
Dore-l'Église F 30 E4
Dörentrup D 17 D12
Dores GB 3 L8
Dorfen D 75 F11
Dorfgastein A 73 B7
Dorfmark D 82 E7
Dorf Mecklenburg D 83 C10
Dorf Zechlin D 83 D13
Dorgali I 64 C4
Dorgoș RO 151 E8
Dorio GR 174 E4
Dorking GB 15 E8
Dorkovo BG 165 E9
Dorlisheim F 186 D3
Dormagen D 21 B7
Dormánd H 150 B5
Dormans F 25 B10
Dor Mărunt RO 161 E9
Dorna-Arini RO 152 C6
Dorna Candrenilor RO 152 C6
Dornava SLO 148 D5
Dörnberg (Habichtswald) D 17 F12
Dornbirn A 71 C9
Dornburg (Saale) D 79 D10
Dornburg-Frickhofen D 185 C9
Dornbusch D 17 A12
Dorndorf D 79 E7
Dorndorf-Steudnitz D 79 D10
Dornelas P 38 E4
Dornes F 30 B3
Dornești RO 153 B8
Dornhan D 187 E6
Dornie GB 2 L5
Dornișoara RO 152 C6
Dörnitz D 79 B11
Dorno I 69 C6
Dornoch GB 3 K8
Dornstadt D 74 F6
Dornstetten D 27 D9
Dornum D 17 A8
Dornumersiel D 17 A8
Dorobanțu RO 155 D2
Dorobanțu RO 161 E9
Dorog H 149 A11
Dorogháza H 147 F9
Dorohoi RO 153 B8
Dorohusk PL 141 H9
Dorolț RO 151 B10
Doroțcaia MD 154 C4
Dorotea S 107 C10
Dörpen D 17 C8
Dorras N 112 D8
Dorris S 107 B9
Dorstadt D 79 B8
Dorsten D 17 E7
Dorstfeld D 185 A7
Dortan F 31 C8
Dortmund D 17 E8
Dörttepe TR 177 E10
Doruchów PL 142 D5
Dorum D 17 A11
Dorupe LV 134 C7
Dörverden D 17 C12
Dörzbach D 74 D6
Dos Aguas E 48 F3
Dosbarrios E 46 E6
Dos Hermanas E 51 E8
Dospat BG 165 F9
Dossenheim D 21 F11
Doștat RO 152 F3
Dos Torres E 54 C3
Døstrup DK 86 E3
Dotnuva LT 134 F7
Dotternhausen D 27 D10
Döttingen CH 27 E9
Douai F 19 D7
Douarnenez F 22 D3
Doubrava CZ 147 B7
Doubravice nad Svitavou CZ 77 D11
Doubs F 31 B9
Douchy F 25 E9
Douchy-les-Mines F 19 D7
Doucier F 31 B8
Doudeville F 18 E2
Doudleby nad Orlicí CZ 77 B10
Doué-la-Fontaine F 23 F11
Douglas GB 5 D9
Douglas GBM 10 C3
Douglas IRL 8 E6
Douglas Bridge GB 4 F2
Doulaincourt-Saucourt F 26 D3
Doulevant-le-Château F 25 D12
Doullens F 18 D5
Dounaiika GR 174 D3
Doune GB 5 C8
Dounreay GB 3 H9
Dour B 19 D8
Dourdan F 24 C7
Dourgne F 33 D10
Douriez F 18 D4
Doussard F 31 D9
Douvaine F 31 C9
Douvres-la-Délivrande F 23 B11
Douzy F 19 E11
Dovadola I 66 D4
Dover GB 15 E11
Dovhe UA 145 G7
Döviken S 103 A9
Dovilai LT 134 E2
Dovre N 101 C10
Dowally GB 5 B9
Downham Market GB 11 F12
Downpatrick GB 7 D11
Downton GB 13 D11
Dowra IRL 6 D6
Dowsby GB 11 F11
Doxato GR 171 B6
Doyet F 30 C2
Doyrentsi BG 165 C10
Dozulé F 23 B11
Drabeši LV 135 B10
Dråby DK 86 C7
Dračevo BIH 162 D5
Dračevo NMK 164 F4
Drachhausen D 80 C6
Drachselsried D 76 D4
Drachten NL 16 B6
Drag N 105 B10
Drag N 111 D11
Dragacz PL 138 C6
Dragalijevac BIH 157 C11
Dragalina RO 161 E10
Dragalovci BIH 157 C8
Drăgănești RO 151 D9
Drăgănești RO 153 F10
Drăgănești RO 161 D8
Drăgănești de Vede RO 160 E6
Drăgănești-Olt RO 160 E5
Drăgănești-Vlașca RO 161 E7
Draganići HR 148 E5
Draganovo BG 166 C5
Drăganu RO 160 D5
Drăgășani RO 160 D4
Dragash RKS 163 E10
Dragatuš SLO 67 A11
Drage D 83 D8
Drage HR 156 E4
Dragești RO 151 D9
Draghiceni RO 160 E4
Draginac SRB 158 D3
Draginje SRB 158 D4
Draginovo BG 165 E8
Dragland N 111 C11
Dragnes N 111 C10
Dragnić BIH 157 D7
Dragobi AL 163 E8
Dragočaj BIH 157 C7
Dragocvet SRB 159 F7
Dragodana RO 160 D6
Dragoești RO 160 D4
Dragoești RO 161 D9
Dragoevo BG 167 C7
Dragoevo NMK 164 F5
Drăgoiești RO 153 B8
Dragoman BG 165 D6
Dragomance NMK 164 E4
Dragomir BG 165 E9
Dragomirești RO 152 B4
Dragomirești RO 153 C9
Dragomirești RO 153 D10
Dragomirești RO 160 D6
Dragomirovo BG 166 B4
Dragoni I 60 A2
Dragør DK 87 D11
Dragoš NMK 168 C5
Dragoslavele RO 160 C6
Dragoș Vodă RO 161 E10
Drăgotești RO 159 D11
Drăgotești RO 160 E4
Dragotina HR 156 B5
Dragović HR 149 F8
Dragovishtitsa BG 165 E6
Dragoychintsi BG 164 D5
Dragoynovo BG 166 F4
Dragsfjärd FIN 126 E7
Draguignan F 36 D4
Drăgușeni RO 153 A9
Drăgușeni RO 153 C8
Drăgușeni RO 153 F11
Drăgutești RO 159 D11
Drahnsdorf D 80 C5
Drahovce SK 146 D5
Drahove UA 145 G8
Drahovica Donja BIH 157 C9
Drajna RO 161 C8
Draka BG 167 E8
Drakenburg D 17 C12
Drakseniċ BIH 157 B6
Dralfa BG 167 C6
Drama GR 170 B6
Drammen N 95 C12
Drânceni RO 153 D12
Drange N 94 F5
Drangedal N 90 A5
Drangstedt D 17 A11
Drănic RO 160 E3
Dranse D 83 D13
Dransfeld D 78 D6
Dranske D 84 A4
Draperstown GB 4 F3
Drasenhofen A 77 E11
Draßmarkt A 149 A6
Drávafok H 149 E9
Dravagen S 102 B6
Draviskos GR 170 C5
Dravograd SLO 73 C11
Drawno PL 85 D9
Drawsko PL 85 E10
Drawsko Pomorskie PL 85 C9
Drayton GB 15 B11
Drążdżewo PL 139 D11
Dražen Vrh SLO 148 C5
Draževac SRB 158 D5
Dražgoše SLO 73 D9
Drebber D 17 C10
Drebkau D 80 C6
Drégelypalánk H 147 E8
Dreieich D 21 D11
Dreileben D 79 B9
Dreis D 21 E7
Drelów PL 141 G7
Drelsdorf D 82 A6
Drem GB 5 C11
Drenchia I 73 D8
Drenovac SRB 159 F7
Drenovci HR 157 C10
Drenovë AL 168 C4
Drenovets BG 159 F10
Drenovicë AL 168 C2
Drenovo NMK 164 F4
Drenovo NMK 169 B6
Drense D 84 D5
Drensteinfurt D 17 E9
Drenta BG 166 D5
Drentwede D 17 C11
Drepano GR 169 D6
Drepano GR 175 D6
Dresden D 80 D5
Dretun' BY 133 E6
Dretyń PL 85 B11
Dreumel NL 183 B6
Dreux F 24 C5
Dreverna LT 134 E2
Drevja N 108 E5
Drevjesætra N 102 D4
Dřevohostice CZ 146 C5
Drevsjø N 102 C3
Drevvatn N 108 D5
Drewitz D 79 B11
Drewnica PL 138 B6
Drezdenko PL 85 E9
Drežnica BIH 157 E8
Drežnik SRB 158 F4
Driceni LV 133 C2
Dridu RO 161 D8
Driebergen NL 16 D4
Driebes E 47 D6
Driedorf D 185 C9
Drienov SK 145 F3
Drietoma SK 146 D5
Driffield GB 11 C11
Drimmo IRL 7 F7
Drimnin GB 4 B5
Drimoleague IRL 8 E4
Drinić BIH 156 C5
Drinjača BIH 157 D11
Drinovci BIH 157 F7
Dripsey IRL 8 E5
Drisht AL 163 E8
Dříteň CZ 76 D6
Drithas AL 168 C4
Driva N 101 A11
Drivstua N 101 B11
Drmno SRB 159 D7
Drnholec CZ 77 E11
Drniš HR 156 E5
Drnje HR 149 D7
Drnovice CZ 77 D11
Drnovice CZ 77 D11
Dro I 69 B10
Drøbak N 95 C13
Drobeta-Turnu Severin RO 159 D10
Drobin PL 139 E8
Drochia MD 153 A11
Drochtersen D 17 A12
Drogheda IRL 7 E10
Drohiczyn PL 141 F7
Drohobych UA 145 E8
Droichead Abhann IRL 8 C5
Droichead Átha IRL 7 E10
Droichead na Bandan IRL 8 E5
Droichead Nua IRL 7 F9
Droitwich Spa GB 13 A10
Drolshagen D 185 B8
Drolsum N 95 B12
Dromara GB 7 D10
Dromina IRL 8 D5
Drommahane IRL 8 D5
Drömme S 107 E14
Dromod IRL 7 E7
Dromore GB 7 C8
Dromore GB 7 D10
Dromore West IRL 6 D5
Dronero I 37 C6
Dronfield GB 11 E9
Drongan GB 5 E8
Drongen B 182 C3
Dronninglund DK 86 A6
Dronrijp NL 16 B5
Dronten NL 16 C5
Dropla BG 155 F2
Drosato GR 169 B8
Drosbacken S 102 C3
Drosendorf A 77 E9
Drosia GR 175 C8
Drösing A 77 E11
Drosopigi GR 168 C5
Droué F 24 D5
Droyßig D 79 D11
Drugan BG 165 E7
Drugovo NMK 168 B4
Druid GB 10 F5
Druimdrishaig GB 4 D5
Drulingen F 27 C7
Drumandoora IRL 6 G5
Drumanespick IRL 7 E8
Drumatober IRL 6 F6
Drumbeg GB 2 J6
Drumbilla IRL 7 D10
Drumcard GB 7 D7
Drumcollogher IRL 8 D5
Drumcondra IRL 7 E9
Drumconrath IRL 7 E9
Drumcree IRL 7 E8
Drumettaz-Clarafond F 31 D8
Drumevo BG 167 C8
Drumfree IRL 4 E2
Drumkeeran IRL 6 D6
Drumlea IRL 7 D7
Drumlish IRL 7 E7
Drumlithie GB 5 B12
Drummin IRL 9 D9
Drummore GB 4 F7
Drumnadrochit GB 2 L8
Drumquin GB 4 F2
Drumshanbo IRL 6 D6
Drung IRL 7 D8
Drusenheim F 27 C8
Druskininkai LT 137 F9
Drusti LV 135 B11
Druten NL 183 B7
Druviena LV 135 B12
Druya BY 133 E2
Druyes-les-Belles-Fontaines F 25 E9
Druysk BY 133 E2
Drużbice PL 143 D7
Druzhba RUS 136 E3
Druzhnaya Gorka RUS 132 C7
Družstevná pri Hornáde SK 145 F3
Drvenik HR 157 F7
Drwalew PL 141 G4
Drwinia PL 143 F9
Dryanovets BG 161 F8
Dryanovo BG 166 D4
Dryazhno RUS 132 E4
Drygały PL 139 C13
Drymaia GR 175 B6
Drymen GB 5 C8
Drymos GR 169 C8
Dryna N 100 A5
Dryopida GR 175 E9
Dryos GR 176 E5
Drysvyaty BY 135 E13
Dryszczów PL 144 A8
Drzewce PL 142 B6
Drzewiany PL 85 C11
Drzewica PL 141 H2
Drzonowo PL 85 C11
Drzycim PL 138 C5
Duagh IRL 8 D4
Dualchi I 64 C2
Dually IRL 9 C7
Duas Igrejas P 39 F7
Dub SRB 158 F4
Dubá CZ 77 A7
Dubăsari MD 154 C4
Dubăsarii Vechi MD 154 C4
Duba Stonska HR 162 D4
Dubău MD 154 C4
Dubeczno PL 141 H8
Düben D 79 C11
Duben D 80 C5
Dübendorf CH 27 F10
Dubeņi LV 134 D2
Dubeninki PL 136 E6
Dubí CZ 80 E5
Dubičiai LT 137 E10
Dubicko CZ 77 C11
Dubicze Cerkiewne PL 141 E8
Dubidze PL 143 D7
Dubiecko PL 144 D5
Dubienka PL 144 A8
Dubingiai LT 137 C11
Dubino I 69 A7
Dubivka UA 153 A8
Dublin IRL 7 F10
Dublje SRB 158 D4
Dublovice CZ 76 C6
Dublyany UA 144 D9
Dublyany UA 145 E7
Dubna LV 135 D13
Dub nad Moravou CZ 146 C4
Dubňany CZ 77 E12
Dubnica nad Váhom SK 146 D6
Dubník SK 146 F6
Dubošbica BIH 157 D9
Dubova RO 159 D9
Dubovac SRB 159 D7
Dubove UA 145 G8
Dŭbovets BG 166 F5
Dubovica SK 145 E2
Dŭbovo BG 166 D5
Dubovo SRB 164 C4
Dubovsko BIH 156 C5
Dubrava BIH 157 C8
Dubrava HR 149 E7
Dubrave BIH 157 C10
Dubrave BIH 157 D6
Dubrave BIH 157 D10
Dubravica BIH 157 D8
Dubravica HR 148 E5
Dubravica SRB 159 D7
Dúbravy SK 147 D8
Dubrawka BY 133 F6
Dubrovka RUS 129 F14
Dubrovka RUS 132 F6
Dubrovka RUS 133 D5
Dubrovnik HR 162 D5
Dubrovytsya UA 144 D8
Dubuļi LV 133 D3
Dubynove UA 154 A6
Ducey F 23 C9
Ducherow D 84 C5
Duchov CZ 80 E5
Duck End GB 15 D9
Duclair F 18 F2
Duda-Epureni RO 153 D12
Dudar H 149 B9
Duddo GB 5 D12
Dudelange L 20 F6
Dudeldorf D 21 E7
Duderstadt D 79 C7
Dudești RO 161 D10
Dudestii Vechi RO 150 E5
Dudince SK 147 E7
Düdingen CH 31 B11
Dudley GB 11 F7
Dudovica SRB 158 E5
Dueñas E 40 E2
Duesund N 100 E2
Dueville I 72 E4
Duffel B 19 B10
Dufftown GB 3 L10
Duga Poljana SRB 163 C9
Duga Resa HR 148 F5
Dugi Rat HR 156 F6
Dugny-sur-Meuse F 26 B3
Dugopolje HR 156 E6
Dugo Selo HR 148 E6
Düğüncübaşi TR 173 B7
Duhort-Bachen F 32 C5
Duino I 73 E8
Duirinish GB 2 L5
Duisburg D 17 F7
Dukas AL 168 C2
Dukat AL 168 D2
Dukat i Ri AL 168 D1

Dukla PL 145 D4
Dūkštas LT 135 E12
Dŭlbok Dol BG 165 D10
Dŭlboki BG 166 E5
Dŭlbok Izvor BG 166 E4
Dulcești RO 153 D9
Duleek IRL 7 E10
Dŭlgodeltsi BG 160 F2
Dŭlgopol BG 167 C8
Dulina BY 133 F2
Duljci BIH 157 D7
Dullingham GB 15 C9
Dülmen D 17 E8
Dulnain Bridge GB 3 L9
Dulovce SK 146 F6
Dulovka RUS 133 A4
Dulovo BG 161 F10
Dulverton GB 13 C7
Dumbarton GB 4 D7
Dumbrava RO 151 F9
Dumbrava RO 159 D11
Dumbrava RO 161 D8
Dumbrava Roșie RO 153 D8
Dumbrăveni RO 152 E5
Dumbrăveni RO 153 B8
Dumbrăveni RO 155 F1
Dumbrăveni RO 161 B10
Dumbrăvești RO 161 C7
Dumbrăvița RO 151 F7
Dumbrăvița RO 152 B3
Dumbrăvița RO 153 F6
Dumbría E 38 B1
Dumești RO 153 C10
Dumești RO 153 D10
Dumfries GB 5 E9
Dumitra RO 152 C4
Dumitrești RO 161 B9
Dummerstorf D 83 C12
Dumnicë e Poshtme RKS 164 D3
Dümpelfeld D 21 D7
Dun F 33 D9
Duna N 105 B11
Dunaegyháza H 149 C11
Dunaföldvár H 149 C11
Dunaharaszti H 150 C3
Dunajská Lužná SK 146 E4
Dunajská Streda SK 146 F5
Dunakeszi H 150 B3
Dunalka LV 134 C2
Dún an Rí IRL 7 E9
Dunapataj H 150 D3
Dunărea RO 155 E2
Dunaszeg H 149 A9
Dunaszekcső H 149 D11
Dunaszentbenedek H 149 C11
Dunaszentgyörgy H 149 C11
Dunasziget H 146 F4
Dunatetétlen H 150 D3
Dunaújváros H 149 C11
Dunava LV 135 D12
Dunavarsány H 150 C3
Dunavecse H 150 D2
Dunavtsi BG 159 F10
Dunbar GB 5 C11
Dunbeath GB 3 J10
Dunblane GB 5 C9
Dunboyne IRL 7 F10
Dún Búinne IRL 7 F10
Duncannon IRL 9 D9
Dún Chaoin IRL 8 D2
Dunchurch GB 13 A12
Duncormick IRL 9 D9
Dundaga LV 134 A4
Dundalk IRL 7 D10
Dún Dealgan IRL 7 D10
Dun Dealgan IRL 7 D10
Dundee GB 5 C11
Dunderland N 108 D8
Dundonald GB 7 C11
Dundreggan GB 2 L7
Dundrennan GB 5 F9
Dundrum GB 7 D11
Dundrum IRL 8 C6
Dunecht GB 3 L12
Dunes F 33 B7
Dunfanaghy IRL 7 B7
Dunfermline GB 5 C10
Dungannon GB 7 C9
Dún Garbhán IRL 9 D7
Dungarvan IRL 9 C8
Dungarvan IRL 9 D7
Düngenheim D 185 D7
Dungiven GB 4 F3
Dungloe IRL 6 C6
Dungourney IRL 8 E6
Dunholme GB 11 E11
Dunicë AL 168 C4
Dunières F 30 E5
Duninowo PL 85 A11
Dunje NMK 169 B6
Dunkeld GB 5 B9
Dunkerque F 18 B5
Dunkerrin IRL 9 C7
Dunkitt IRL 9 D8
Dún Laoghaire IRL 7 F10
Dunlavin IRL 7 F9
Dunleer IRL 7 E10
Dún Léire IRL 7 E10
Dun-le-Palestel F 29 C9
Dun-les-Places F 25 F11
Dunlop GB 4 D7
Dunloy GB 4 E4
Dún Mánmhaí IRL 8 E4
Dunmanway IRL 8 E4
Dún Mór IRL 9 D9
Dunmore IRL 6 E5
Dunmore East IRL 9 D9
Dunmurry GB 7 C11
Dunnamanagh GB 4 F2
Dún na nGall IRL 6 C6
Dunning GB 5 C9
Dunoon GB 4 D7
Dunquin IRL 8 D2
Duns GB 5 D12
Dunscore GB 5 E9
Dünsen D 17 C11
Dunshaughlin IRL 7 E9
Dunstable GB 15 D7
Dunster GB 13 C8
Dun-sur-Auron F 29 B11
Dun-sur-Meuse F 19 F11
Dunure GB 4 E7
Dunvant GB 12 B6
Dunvegan GB 2 L3
Duplica SLO 73 D10
Dupnitsa BG 165 E7
Durach D 71 B10
Durak TR 173 E9
Durana E 41 C6
Durance F 33 B6
Durango E 41 B6
Durankulak BG 155 F3
Duras F 33 A6
Durbach D 27 C9
Durban-Corbières F 34 E4
Durbe LV 134 C2
Durbuy B 184 D3
Dúrcal E 53 C9
Durdat-Larequille F 29 C11
Đurđenovac HR 149 E10
Đurđevac HR 149 D8
Đurđevića Tara MNE 163 C7
Đurđevik BIH 157 D10
Đurđevo SRB 158 C5
Đurđevo SRB 159 E6
Düren D 20 C6
Durfort F 35 C6
Durham GB 5 F13
Ďurkov SK 145 F3
Durlas IRL 9 C7
Durlești MD 154 C3
Durmanec HR 148 D5
Dürmentingen D 71 A9
Durmersheim D 27 C9
Durness GB 2 H7
Durnești RO 153 B10
Dürnkrut A 77 F11
Durrës AL 168 B1
Durrington GB 13 C11
Dürrlauingen D 75 F7
Durrow IRL 9 C8
Durrus IRL 8 E3
Dürrwangen D 75 D7
Dursley GB 13 B10
Dursunbey TR 173 E10
Durtal F 23 E11
Duruelo de la Sierra E 40 E6
Duruitoarea MD 153 B10
Durup DK 86 B3
Durusu TR 173 B10
Dusetos LT 135 E11
Dushk i Madh AL 168 C2
Dusina BIH 157 E8
Dŭskotna BG 167 D8
Duškovci SRB 158 F5
Dusmenys LT 137 E9
Dusnok H 150 E2
Dusocin PL 138 C6
Düsseldorf D 21 B7
Dussen NL 16 E3
Dußlingen D 187 E7
Düßnitz D 79 C12
Duszniki PL 81 B10
Dutluca TR 173 E11
Dutovlje SLO 73 E8
Duvberg S 102 B7
Duved S 105 E13
Düvertepe TR 173 F9
Duži BIH 162 D5
Dvärsätt S 106 E6
Dvaryshcha BY 133 E6
Dve Mogili BG 161 F7
Dverberg N 111 B10
Dviete LV 135 D12
Dvirtsi UA 144 C9
Dvor HR 156 B5
Dvorce CZ 146 B5
Dvornaye Syalo BY 133 E3
Dvorníky SK 146 E5
Dvory nad Šitavou SK 146 F6
Dvůr Králové CZ 77 B9
Dwikozy PL 144 B4
Dwingeloo NL 16 C6
Dyan GB 7 D9
Dyankovo BG 161 F9
Dybvad DK 90 E7
Dyce GB 3 L12
Dychów PL 81 C8
Dydnia PL 144 D5
Dyfjord N 113 B19
Dygowo PL 85 B9
Dyke GB 3 K9
Dykehead GB 5 B11
Dykhtynets' UA 152 A6
Dylągówka PL 144 D5
Dylaki PL 142 E5
Dylewo PL 139 D11
Dymchurch GB 15 E10
Dymock GB 13 B10
Dynäs S 107 F13
Dynivtsi UA 153 A8
Dynów PL 144 D5
Dyo F 30 C5
Dyping N 110 E9
Dyrnes N 104 E3
Dyrøyhamn N 111 B13
Dyrrachi GR 174 E5
Dyulevo BG 167 E8
Dyulino BG 167 D9
Dyviziya UA 154 F5
Dywity PL 136 F1
Dzeguzēni LV 134 D6
Dzelzava LV 135 C12
Dzeņi LV 135 B12
Dzērbene LV 135 B11
Dzhebel BG 171 A8
Dzherman BG 165 E7
Dzhulynka UA 154 A5
Dzhulyunitsa BG 166 C5
Dzhuriv UA 152 A6
Dzhurovo BG 165 D9
Dziadkowice PL 141 E7
Dziadowa Kłoda PL 142 D4
Działdowo PL 139 D9
Działoszyce PL 143 F9
Działoszyn PL 142 D6
Działyń PL 138 D7
Dziemiany PL 138 B4
Dziergowice PL 142 F5
Dzierząźnia PL 139 E9
Dzierżążno Wielkie PL 85 E10
Dzierzgoń PL 139 C7
Dzierzgowo PL 139 D10
Dzierzkowice-Rynek PL 144 B5
Dzierżoniów PL 81 E11
Dzietrzniki PL 142 D6
Dzietrzychowo PL 136 E3
Dziewierzewo PL 85 E13
Džigolj SRB 164 C4
Dzirnavas LV 134 B4
Dzisna BY 133 E4
Dziwnów PL 85 B7
Dzmitravichy BY 141 F9
Džūkste LV 134 C6
Džumajlija NMK 164 F4
Dźwierzuty PL 139 C10
Dźwirzyno PL 85 B8
Dzwola PL 144 B6
Dzwonowice PL 143 E8
Dzyornavichy BY 133 E4

E

Éadan Doire IRL 7 F8
Eaglesfield GB 5 E10
Eardisley GB 13 A8
Earith GB 15 C9
Earl Shilton GB 11 F9
Earlston GB 5 D11
Earl Stonham GB 15 C11
Earsairidh GB 4 B2
Easdale GB 4 C5
Easington GB 5 F14
Easington GB 11 D12
Easingwold GB 11 C9
Easky IRL 6 D5
Eastbourne GB 15 F9
Eastburn GB 11 D11
Eastfield GB 11 C11
Eastgate GB 5 F12
East Grinstead GB 15 E8
East Harling GB 15 C10
East Kilbride GB 5 D8
Eastleigh GB 13 D12
East Linton GB 5 D11
East Looe GB 12 E6
Eastoft GB 11 D10
Easton GB 13 D10
East Retford GB 11 E10
Eastriggs GB 5 F10
Eastry GB 15 E11
East Wemyss GB 5 C10
East Wittering GB 15 F7
Eastwood GB 11 E9
Eaton Socon GB 15 C8
Eaunes F 33 D8
Eauze F 33 C6
Ebberup DK 86 E5
Ebbs A 72 A5
Ebbw Vale GB 13 B8
Ebecik TR 181 A9
Ebeleben D 79 D8
Ebelsbach D 75 C8
Ebeltoft DK 86 C7
Ebene Reichenau A 73 C8
Ebenfurth A 77 G10
Eben im Pongau A 73 B7
Ebensee A 73 A8
Ebensfeld D 75 B8
Ebenthal A 73 C9
Ebenweiler D 71 B9
Eberau A 149 B6
Eberbach D 21 F11
Ebergötzen D 79 C7
Ebermannsdorf D 75 D10
Ebermannstadt D 75 C9
Ebern D 75 B8
Eberndorf A 73 C10
Ebersbach D 80 D5
Ebersbach D 81 D7
Ebersbach an der Fils D 74 E6
Ebersberg D 75 F10
Eberschwang A 76 F5
Ebersdorf A 148 B5
Ebersdorf D 17 A12
Ebersdorf D 75 B10
Ebersmunster F 186 E4
Eberstein A 73 C10
Eberswalde-Finow D 84 E5
Ebes H 151 C8
Ebhausen D 27 C10
Ebikon CH 27 F9
Ebnat-Kappel CH 27 F11
Eboli I 60 B4
Ebrach D 75 C7
Ebreichsdorf A 77 G10
Ébreuil F 30 C3
Ebsdorfergrund-Dreihausen D 21 C11
Ebstorf D 83 D8
Écaussinnes-d'Enghien B 182 D4
Ecclefechan GB 5 E10
Eccles GB 5 D12
Eccleshall GB 11 F7
Eceabat TR 171 D10
Echallens CH 31 B10
Echarri E 32 E2
Échauffour F 24 C3
Échenoz-la-Méline F 26 E5
Eching D 75 E11
Eching D 75 F10
Echinos GR 171 B7
Échiré F 28 C5
Échirolles F 31 E8
Échourgnac F 29 E6
Echsenbach A 77 E8
Echt GB 3 L12
Echt NL 19 B12
Echte D 79 C7
Echternach L 20 E6
Écija E 53 A6
Ečka SRB 158 C5
Eckartsberga D 79 D10
Eckbolsheim F 186 D4
Eckental D 75 C9
Eckernförde D 83 B7
Eckerö FIN 99 B13
Eckington GB 11 E9
Eckington GB 13 A10
Éclaron-Braucourt-Ste-Livière F 25 C12
Écommoy F 23 E12
Écos F 24 B6
Écouché F 23 C11
Écouflant F 23 E10
Écouis F 18 F3
Écrouves F 26 C4
Écs H 149 A9
Ecséd H 150 B4
Ecseg H 147 F9
Ecsegfalva H 151 C6
Ecser H 150 C3
Écueillé F 29 A8
Écuisses F 30 B6
Écury-sur-Coole F 25 C11
Ed S 91 B10
Ed S 107 E12
Eda glasbruk S 96 C7
Edam NL 16 C4
Edane S 97 C8
Ēdas LV 134 C4
Eddelak D 82 C6
Edderton GB 3 K8
Eddleston GB 5 D10
Ede NL 16 D5
Ede S 103 B12
Edebäck S 97 B10
Edefors S 118 B5
Edegem B 19 B9
Edelény H 145 G2
Edelschrott A 73 B11
Edemissen D 79 B7
Eden GB 4 F5
Eden S 107 D12
Edenderry IRL 7 F8
Edenkoben D 21 F10
Edermünde D 78 D5
Ederny GB 7 C7
Edesheim D 21 F10
Edessa GR 169 C7
Edewecht D 17 B9
Edewechterdamm D 17 B9
Edgeworthstown IRL 7 E7
Edgmond GB 11 F7
Ediger-Eller D 21 D8
Edinburgh GB 5 D10
Edincik TR 173 D8
Edineț MD 153 A10
Edirne TR 171 A11
Edland N 94 C7
Edling D 75 F11
Edlingham GB 5 E13
Edlitz A 148 A6
Edmondstown IRL 6 E5
Edmundbyers GB 5 F13
Ēdole LV 134 B3
Edolo I 69 A9
Edremit TR 173 E7
Edrosa P 39 E6
Edroso P 39 E6
Edsbro S 99 C10
Edsbruk S 93 C8
Edsbyn S 103 D10
Edsele S 107 E11
Edsken S 98 A6
Edsvalla S 97 D9
Edzell GB 5 B11
Eefde NL 183 A8
Eeklo B 19 B8
Eelde-Paterswolde NL 17 B7
Eerbeek NL 16 D6
Eernegem B 182 C2
Eersel NL 16 F4
Eferding A 76 F6
Effelder D 75 B9
Effeltrich D 75 C9
Effretikon CH 27 F10
Efkarpia GR 169 B8
Efkarpia GR 169 C10
Eforie RO 155 E3
Efpalio GR 174 C4
Efringen-Kirchen D 27 E8
Eftimie Murgu RO 159 D9
Efxeinoupoli GR 175 A6
Egby S 89 B11
Egebæk DK 86 E3
Egebjerg DK 86 D5
Egebjerg DK 87 D9
Egeln D 79 C9
Egense DK 86 B6
Eger H 145 H1
Egerbakta H 145 H1
Egernsund DK 86 F5
Egersund N 94 F4
Egerszalók H 145 H1
Egervár H 149 C7
Egeskov DK 86 D5
Egestorf D 83 D8
Egga N 111 B19
Eggby S 91 C14
Eggebek D 82 A6
Eggenburg A 77 E9
Eggenfelden D 75 F12
Eggenstein-Leopoldshafen D 27 B9
Eggersdorf D 79 C10
Eggersdorf bei Graz A 148 B5
Eggesbønes N 100 B3
Eggesin D 84 C6
Eggingen D 27 E9
Eggiwil CH 70 D5
Egglham D 76 E4
Eggolsheim D 75 C9
Eggstätt D 72 A5
Eggum N 110 D6
Eghezée B 19 C10
Eging am See D 76 E4
Eglaine LV 135 E12
Égletons F 29 E10
Egling D 72 A4
Eglingham GB 5 E13
Eglinton GB 4 E2
Eglisau CH 27 E10
Eglish GB 7 D9
Egluciems LV 133 B2
Eglwys Fach GB 10 F4
Eglwyswrw GB 12 A5
Egmond aan Zee NL 16 C3
Egna I 69 A11
Egorovca MD 153 B11
Egremont GB 10 C4
Egsmark DK 86 C7
Egtved DK 86 D4
Éguilles F 35 C9
Eguisheim F 27 D7
Éguzon-Chantôme F 29 C9
Egyek H 151 B6
Egyházaskozár H 149 D10
Ehekirchen D 75 E9
Ehingen D 75 D8
Ehingen (Donau) D 71 A9
Ehlen (Habichtswald) D 17 F12
Ehningen D 187 D6
Ehra-Lessien D 79 A8
Ehrenberg-Wüstensachsen D 74 B7
Ehrenburg D 17 C11
Ehrenfriedersdorf D 80 E3
Ehrenhausen A 148 C5
Ehringshausen D 21 C10
Eibar E 41 B7
Eibelstadt D 74 C7
Eibenstock D 75 B12
Eibergen NL 17 D7
Eibiswald A 148 C4
Eich D 21 E10
Eichenbarleben D 79 B9
Eichenbühl D 27 A11
Eichendorf D 76 E3
Eichenzell D 74 B6
Eichgraben A 77 F9
Eichigt D 75 B11
Eichstätt D 75 E9
Eichwalde D 80 B5
Eickendorf D 79 C10
Eicklingen D 79 A7
Eidapere EST 131 D9
Eide N 100 A6
Eide N 104 D8
Eide N 111 C11
Eidem N 108 E2
Eidet N 105 C15
Eidet N 105 C16
Eidet N 108 A9
Eidet N 110 D8
Eidfjord N 94 B6
EiŠi FO 2 A2
Eidkjosen N 111 A16
Eidsbugarden N 101 D8
Eidsdal N 100 B6
Eidsfjord N 110 C8
Eidsfoss N 95 C12
Eidshaug N 105 B10
Eidsnes N 112 C10
Eidsøra N 100 A8
Eidstranda N 111 A19
Eidsund N 94 D3
Eidsvåg N 100 A8
Eidsvoll N 95 B14
Eidsvoll Verk N 95 B14
Eidvågeid N 113 B12
Eigeltingen D 27 E10
Eigenrieden D 79 D7
Eijsden NL 183 D7
Eik N 94 D3
Eikelandsosen N 94 B3
Eiken N 94 F6
Eikesdal N 100 B8
Eikjaberg N 100 D6
Eikjeskog N 94 E4
Eikjil N 90 B1
Eiksund N 100 B3
Eilenburg D 79 D12
Eilenstedt D 79 C9
Eilsleben D 79 B9
Eime D 78 B6
Eimen D 78 C6
Eimke D 83 E8
Eina N 101 E13
Einacleit GB 2 J3
Einbeck D 78 C6
Eindhoven NL 16 F4
Einsiedeln CH 27 F10
Einville-au-Jard F 26 C5
Einvollen N 108 F3
Eisden B 183 D7
Eiselfing D 75 F11
Eisenach D 79 E7
Eisenberg D 79 E10
Eisenberg (Pfalz) D 21 E10
Eisenerz A 73 A10
Eisenhüttenstadt D 81 B7
Eisenkappel A 73 D10
Eisenstadt A 77 G11
Eisfeld D 75 B8
Eišiškės LT 137 E10
Eislandet N 100 E3
Eisleben, Lutherstadt D 79 C10
Eislingen (Fils) D 74 E6
Eisma EST 131 B12
Eitelborn D 21 D9
Eiterfeld D 78 E6
Eiternes N 105 B11
Eiterstraum N 108 E5
Eitorf D 21 C8
Eivinvik N 100 E2
Eivissa E 57 D7
Eja P 44 B4
Ejby DK 86 E5
Ejby DK 87 D9
Ejby DK 87 E10
Ejea de los Caballeros E 41 D9
Ejsing DK 86 B3
Ejstrupholm DK 86 D4
Ejulve E 42 F2
Ekeby S 87 C11
Ekeby S 92 A6
Ekeby S 99 D9
Ekeby-Almby S 97 D13
Ekedalen S 91 C14
Ekenäs FIN 127 F9
Ekenäs S 91 B13
Ekenäs S 93 B9
Ekenässjön S 92 E6
Ēkengrāve LV 135 D11
Ekeren B 182 C4
Ekerö S 99 D9
Eket S 87 C12
Ekkerøy N 114 C8
Ekmekçi TR 173 D9
Ekola FIN 122 D9
Ekorrträsk S 107 B16
Eksaarde B 182 C3
Eksel B 183 C6
Ekshärad S 97 B9
Eksjö S 92 D5
Eksta S 93 E12
Ekträsk S 118 F3
Ekzarkh-Antimovo BG 167 D7
Ekzarkh Yosif BG 161 F7
Elafos GR 169 D7
Elafotopos GR 168 E4
Elaiochori GR 171 C6
Elaionas GR 169 B10
Elaionas GR 174 B5
Elaionas GR 175 C7
El Álamo E 46 D5
El Algar E 56 F3
El Almendro E 51 D5
El Alquián E 55 F8
Elämäjärvi FIN 123 D15
El Arahal E 51 E8
El Arenal E 45 D10
Elassona GR 169 E7
El Astillero E 40 B4
Elateia GR 175 B6
Elati GR 169 E6
Elati GR 169 E6
Elatochori GR 169 D7
Elatou GR 174 B4
El Ballestero E 55 B8
El Barco de Ávila E 45 D9
El Barraco E 46 D3
Elbasan AL 168 B3
Elbergen D 17 D8
Elbeuf F 18 F3
Elbigenalp A 71 C10
Elbingerode (Harz) D 79 C8
Elbląg PL 139 B7
El Bodón E 45 D7
El Bonillo E 55 B7
El Bosque E 53 C6
El Bullaque E 46 F4
El Burgo E 53 C7
El Burgo de Ebro E 41 E10
El Burgo de Osma E 40 E5
El Burgo Ranero E 39 D9
El Buste E 41 E8
El Cabaco E 45 C8
El Cabildo y la Campana E 55 E9
El Cabo de Gata E 55 F8
El Campillo E 51 D6
El Campillo de la Jara E 45 E10
El Campo de Peñaranda E 45 C10
El Cañavate E 47 E8
El Carpio E 53 A8
El Carpio de Tajo E 46 E4
El Casar E 46 C6
El Casar de Escalona E 46 D3
El Castellar E 48 D3
El Castillo de las Guardas E 51 D7
El Catllar de Gaià E 43 E6
El Centenillo E 54 C5
El Cerro de Andévalo E 51 D6
Elche E 56 E3
Elche de la Sierra E 55 C8
Elchingen D 187 E9
Elciego E 41 C6
Elçili TR 172 B6
El Coronil E 51 E8
El Cubo de Don Sancho E 45 C8
El Cubo de Tierra del Vino E 39 F8
El Cuervo E 47 D10
El Cuervo E 51 F7
Elda E 56 E3
Eldalsosen N 100 D4
Eldena D 83 D10
Eldforsen S 97 B11
Eldingen D 83 E8
Eldsberga S 87 B12
Elduvík FO 2 A3
Elefsina GR 175 C8
Eleftheres GR 171 C6
Elefthero GR 168 D4
Eleftheroupoli GR 171 C6
Eleja LV 134 D7
El Ejido E 55 F7
Elek H 151 D7
Elektrėnai LT 137 D10
Elemir SRB 158 C5
Elena BG 166 D5
Elend D 79 C8
Eleousa GR 168 E4
El Escorial E 46 C4
Eleshnitsa BG 165 F8
El Espinar E 46 C4
El Estrecho E 56 F3
Elexalde E 40 B6
El Fendek MA 53 E5
Elfershausen D 187 A8
El Fresno E 46 C3
Elgå N 101 B15
El Garrobo E 51 D7
Elgershausen (Schauenburg) D 21 B12
Elgeta E 41 B7
Elgin GB 3 K10
Elgoibar E 32 D1
Elgol GB 2 L4
El Grado E 42 C4
El Granado E 50 D5
El Grau de Borriana E 48 E4
Elgsnes N 111 C11
El Herrumblar E 47 F9
El Hito E 47 E7
El Hoyo de Pinares E 46 C4
Elia GR 178 E9
Elice I 62 B5
Elie GB 5 C11
Elika GR 178 B4
Elimäki FIN 127 D15
Eling GB 13 D12
Elini I 64 D4
Elin Pelin BG 165 D8
Elisenvaara RUS 129 C12
Eliseyna BG 165 C8
Elizondo E 32 D2
Eljas E 45 D7
Ełk PL 136 F5
Elkenroth D 185 C8
Elkhovo BG 166 D5
Elkhovo BG 167 E7
Elkšņi LV 135 D11
Ellan S 99 B11
Elland GB 11 D8
Ellefeld D 75 B11
Ellenberg D 187 C9
Ellerau D 83 C7
Ellerbek D 83 C7
Ellesmere GB 10 F6
Ellesmere Port GB 10 E6
Ellezelles B 19 C8
Ellidshøj DK 86 B5
Elling DK 90 E7
Ellingen D 75 D8
Ellington GB 5 E13
El Llano E 38 B5
Ellmau A 72 A5
Ellon GB 3 L12
Ellös S 91 C9
El Losar del Barco E 45 D9
Elloughton GB 11 D10
Ellrich D 79 C8
Ellwangen (Jagst) D 75 E7
Ellwürden D 17 B10
Elm CH 71 D8
Elm D 17 A12
Elmacik TR 167 F8
El Masroig E 42 E5
Elmen A 71 C11
Elmenhorst D 83 B12
Elmenhorst D 83 C8
Elmenhorst D 83 C9
Elmenhorst D 83 C10
El Molar E 46 C5
El Molinillo E 46 F4
El Moral E 55 D8
El Morell E 42 E6
Elmshorn D 82 C7
Elne F 34 E4
Elnesvågen N 100 A6
Elorrio E 41 B6
Elorz E 32 E2
Elos GR 178 E6
El Oso E 46 C3
Előszállás H 149 C11
Elounta GR 179 E10
Elovdol BG 165 D6
Éloyes F 26 D6
El Palmar E 56 F2
El Palo E 53 C8
El Payo E 45 D7
El Pedernoso E 47 F7
El Pedroso E 51 D8
El Pedroso de la Armuña E 45 B10
El Peral E 47 E9
El Perdigón E 39 F8
El Perelló E 42 F5
El Perelló E 48 F4
Elpersbüttel D 82 B6
Elphin GB 2 J6
Elphin IRL 6 E6
El Picazo E 47 F8
El Pinell de Bray E 42 E5
El Piñero E 39 F8
El Pla de Santa María E 43 E6
El Pobo E 42 F2
El Pobo de Dueñas E 47 C9
El Pont d'Armentera E 43 E6
El Port E 48 E4
El Port de la Selva E 34 F5
El Prat de Llobregat E 43 E8
El Provencio E 47 F7
El Puente E 40 B5
El Puente de Arzobispo E 45 E10
El Puerto de Santa María E 52 C4
El Real de la Jara E 51 D7
El Real de San Vicente E 46 D3
El Recuenco E 47 C8
El Robledo E 46 F4
El Rocío E 51 E7
El Romeral E 46 E6
El Rompido E 51 E5
El Ronquillo E 51 D7
El Royo E 41 E6
El Rubio E 53 B7
El Sabinar E 41 D9
El Sabinar E 55 C8
El Saler E 48 F4
El Salobral E 55 B9
Els Arcs E 42 D5
El Saucejo E 53 B6
El Saugo E 45 D7
Elsdon GB 5 E12
Elsdorf D 21 C7
Elsenborn B 20 D6
Elsendorf D 75 E10
Elsenfeld D 21 E12
El Serrat AND 33 E9
Elsfjord N 108 D6
Elsfleth D 17 B10
Elshitsa BG 165 E9
Elsloo NL 183 D7
Elsnes N 111 B19
Elsnig D 80 C3
Elsnigk D 79 C11
El Soleràs E 42 E5
Elspeet NL 16 D5
Els Prats de Rei E 43 D7
Elst NL 16 E5
Elst NL 183 B6
Elster D 79 C12
Elsterberg D 79 E11
Elsterwerda D 80 D5
Elstra D 80 D6
El Tiemblo E 46 D4
Eltmann D 75 C8
El Toboso E 47 E7
Elton GB 11 F11
Elton IRL 8 D6
El Torno E 45 D9
El Trincheto E 46 F4
El Tumbalejo E 51 E6
Eltville am Rhein D 21 D10
Elva EST 131 E12
Elvål N 101 C14
Elvanfoot GB 5 E9
Elvas P 51 B5
Elvebakken N 113 D11
Elvegard N 111 D13
Elvekrok N 113 B17
Elvelund N 112 E6
Elvemund N 113 E16
Elven F 22 E6
El Vendrell E 43 E7
El Verger E 56 D5
Elverum N 101 E15
Elvesletta N 111 D12
Elvevoll N 111 B14
Elvevollen N 111 B18
El Villar de Arnedo E 32 F1
Elvington GB 11 D10
El Viso E 54 C3
El Viso del Alcor E 51 E8
Elvnes N 114 D8
Elx E 56 E3
Elxleben D 79 D8
Ely GB 13 C8
Ely GB 15 C9
Elz D 185 D9
Elzach D 27 D9
Elze D 78 B6
Elze (Wedemark) D 78 A6
Embid E 47 C9
Embid de Ariza E 41 F8
Embleton GB 5 E13
Embrun F 36 B4
Emburga LV 135 C7
Embūte LV 134 C3
Emden D 17 B8
Emecik TR 181 C7
Emiralem TR 177 B9
Emirali TR 173 B8
Emlichheim D 17 C7
Emly IRL 8 D6
Emmaboda S 89 B9
Emmaljunga S 87 C13
Emmanouil Pappas GR 169 B10
Emmaste EST 130 D5
Emmeloord NL 16 C5
Emmelsbüll-Horsbüll D 82 A5
Emmelshausen D 21 D9
Emmen CH 27 F9
Emmen NL 17 C7
Emmendingen D 27 D8
Emmer-Compascuum NL 17 C8
Emmerich D 16 E6
Emmoo IRL 6 E6
Emőd H 145 H2
Emolahti FIN 123 C15
Empel NL 16 E4
Empesos GR 174 A3
Empfingen D 187 E6
Empoli I 66 E2
Emponas GR 181 D7
Emporeio GR 179 C9
Emporeios GR 177 C7
Emptinne B 19 D11
Emsbüren D 17 D8
Emsdetten D 17 D9
Emsfors S 89 A10
Emskirchen D 75 C8
Emst NL 16 D5
Emstek D 17 C10
Emsworth GB 15 F7
Emtinghausen D 17 C11
Emtunga S 91 C12
Emyvale IRL 7 D9
Enafors S 105 E12
Enäjärvi FIN 128 D7
Enånger S 103 C13
Enarsvedjan S 105 D16
Encamp AND 33 E9
Encinas de Abajo E 45 C10
Encinasola E 51 C6
Encinas Reales E 53 B8
Encinedo E 39 D6
Enciso E 41 D7
Encs H 145 G3
Encsencs H 151 B9
Endingen D 27 D8
Endre S 93 D12
Endrefalva H 147 E9
Endriejavas LT 134 E3
Endrinal E 45 C9

Endzele LV 131 F10
Enebakk N 95 C14
Enego I 72 E4
Eneryda S 88 B6
Enese H 149 A8
Enez TR 171 C10
Enfesta E 38 C2
Enfield IRL 7 F9
Engan N 101 B11
Engan N 104 E4
Engan N 108 D3
Engares GR 176 E5
Engavågen N 108 C6
Engden D 183 A10
Engelberg CH 71 D6
Engelhartstetten A 77 F11
Engelhartszell A 76 E5
Engeln D 17 C11
Engelsberg D 75 F12
Engelskirchen D 21 C8
Engen D 27 E10
Enger D 17 D11
Engerdal N 101 C15
Engerdalssetra N 101 C15
Engerneset N 102 C3
Engersen D 79 A9
Engesland N 90 B3
Engesvang DK 86 C4
Enghien B 19 C9
Engis B 19 C11
Englefontaine F 19 D8
Engomer F 33 E8
Engstingen D 27 D11
Enguera E 56 D3
Enguidanos E 47 E9
Engure LV 134 B6
Engvik N 112 C2
Enhagen-Ekbacken S 98 C7
Enichioi MD 154 E2
Enina BG 166 D4
Eningen unter Achalm D 187 E7
Enitsa BG 165 C9
Enix E 55 F7
Enkenbach D 186 C4
Enkhuizen NL 16 C4
Enkirch D 21 E8
Enklinge FIN 99 B15
Enköping S 98 C8
Enmo N 101 A12
Enna I 58 D5
Ennepetal D 185 B7
Ennery F 186 C1
Ennezat F 30 D3
Ennigerloh D 17 E10
Ennis IRL 8 C5
Enniscorthy IRL 9 C9
Enniscrone IRL 6 D4
Enniskean IRL 8 E5
Enniskerry IRL 7 F10
Enniskillen GB 7 D7
Ennistymon IRL 8 C4
Enns A 77 F6
Eno FIN 125 E14
Enonkoski FIN 125 F11
Enonkylä FIN 119 F17
Enontekiö FIN 117 B11
Ens NL 16 C5
Enschede NL 17 D7
Ensdorf D 75 D10
Ensdorf D 186 C2
Ense D 17 F10
Ensheim D 21 F8
Ensisheim F 27 E7
Enskogen S 103 C9
Ensuès-la-Redonne F 35 D9
Enter NL 183 A9
Enterkinfoot GB 5 E9
Entlebuch CH 70 D6
Entracque I 37 C6
Entradas P 50 D3
Entraigues-sur-la-Sorgue F 35 B8
Entrains-sur-Nohain F 25 F9
Entrammes F 23 E10
Entraunes F 36 C5
Entraygues-sur-Truyère F 33 A11
Entrena E 41 D6
Entrevaux F 36 D5
Entroncamento P 44 F4
Envendos P 44 E5
Envermeu F 18 E3
Enviken S 103 E10
Enying H 149 C10
Enzklösterle D 27 C9
Eochaill IRL 9 E7
Eoropaidh GB 2 H4
Épaignes F 18 F1
Épalignes CH 31 B10
Epano Fellos GR 176 D4
Epanomi GR 169 D8
Epe NL 16 D5
Eperjes H 150 D6
Eperjeske H 145 G5
Épernay F 25 B10
Épernon F 24 C6
Epfendorf D 27 D10
Épieds-en-Beauce F 24 E6
Épierre F 31 E9
Épila E 41 E9
Épinac F 30 B6
Épinal F 26 D5
Epiry F 25 F10
Episcopia I 60 C6
Episkopi GR 169 C7
Episkopi GR 178 E7
Episkopi GR 178 E9
Epitalio GR 174 D3
Époisses F 25 E11
Epoo FIN 127 E14
Eppelborn D 21 F7
Eppelheim D 21 F11
Eppenbrunn D 186 C4
Eppertshausen D 21 E11
Eppeville F 19 E7
Epping GB 15 D9
Eppingen D 27 B10
Eppishausen D 71 A11
Eppstein D 21 D10
Epsom GB 15 E8
Eptachori GR 168 D5
Épuisay F 24 E4
Epureni RO 153 E11
Epworth GB 11 D10
Équeurdreville-Hainneville F 23 A8
Eraclea I 73 E6
Eraclea Mare I 67 A6
Eräjärvi FIN 127 B12
Eräjärvi FIN 129 C10
Erastvere EST 131 F13
Erateini GR 174 C5
Eratyra GR 169 D6
Erba I 69 B7
Erbach D 21 E12
Erbach D 74 F6
Erbendorf D 75 C11
Ērberģe LV 135 D10
Erbiceni RO 153 C10
Erbray F 23 E9
Erchie I 61 C9
Ercsi H 149 B11
Érd H 149 B11
Erdeborn D 79 D10
Erdek TR 173 D8
Erdelli TR 177 B10
Erdeven F 22 E5
Erdevik SRB 158 C3
Erding D 75 F10
Erdőkertes H 150 B3
Erdut HR 157 A11
Erdweg D 75 F9
Erdželija NMK 164 F5
Éréac F 23 D7
Eremitu RO 152 D5
Eremiya BG 165 E6
Erenler TR 173 D10
Eresos GR 177 A6
Eretreia GR 169 F8
Eretria GR 175 C8
Erfde D 82 B6
Erftstadt D 21 C7
Erfurt D 79 E9
Ērģeme LV 131 F11
Ergersheim D 75 C7
Ergili TR 173 D9
Ērgļi LV 135 C11
Ergoldsbach D 75 E11
Ergué-Gabéric F 22 D3
Erharting D 75 F12
Eriboll GB 2 J7
Erice E 32 E2
Erice I 58 C2
Ericeira P 50 B1
Eriklice TR 173 C7
Eriksberg S 107 A9
Erikslund S 103 A10
Eriksmåla S 89 B8
Erikssund S 99 C9
Ering D 76 F4
Eringsboda S 89 C8
Eriswil CH 70 C5
Erjova MD 154 B4
Erkelenz D 20 B6
Erkheim D 71 A10
Erkner D 80 B5
Erla E 41 D10
Erlach CH 31 A11
Erlangen D 75 C9
Erlauf A 77 F8
Erlbach D 75 B11
Erlenbach am Main D 187 B7
Erli I 37 C8
Ermelo NL 16 D5
Ermelo P 38 F4
Ermenonville F 25 B8
Ermesinde P 44 B3
Ermidas do Sado P 50 C3
Ermioni GR 175 E7
Ermoclia MD 154 D5
Ermoupoli GR 176 E4
Ermsleben D 79 C9
Ermua E 41 B6
Erndtebrück D 21 C10
Ernée F 23 D10
Ernei RO 152 D5
Ernestinovo HR 149 F11
Ernstbrunn A 77 E10
Erp NL 16 E5
Érpatak H 151 B8
Erpel D 21 C8
Erquelinnes B 184 D1
Erquy F 22 C7
Erra P 50 A3
Errenteria E 32 D2
Errezil E 32 D1
Erribera E 41 B7
Errill IRL 9 C7
Errindlev DK 83 A11
Erritsø DK 86 D5
Errogie GB 3 L8
Érsekcsanád H 150 E2
Ersekë AL 168 D4
Érsekvadkert H 147 E8
Ersfjord N 111 B13
Ersfjordbotn N 111 A16
Ersmark S 107 A11
Ersmark S 118 E5
Ersmark S 122 C4
Ersnäs S 118 C7
Erstein F 27 D8
Erstfeld CH 71 D7
Ersvik N 108 B7
Ertenvåg N 108 B7
Ertingen D 71 A8
Erto I 72 D5
Ertsjärv S 116 E8
Ertuğrul TR 173 E8
Ertvelde B 182 C3
Erula I 64 B2
Ervalla S 97 D13
Ervasti FIN 121 D9
Ervedosa do Douro P 44 B6
Ervenik HR 156 D4
Ervidel P 50 D3
Ervik N 104 E5
Ervillers F 18 D6
Ervy-le-Châtel F 25 D10
Erwitte D 17 E10
Erxleben D 79 B9
Erxleben D 83 E11
Erythres GR 175 C7
Erzhausen D 21 E11
Eržvilkas LT 134 F5
Esanatoglia I 67 F6
Esbjerg DK 86 E2
Esbo FIN 127 E12
Esbønderup DK 87 C10
Escairón E 38 C4
Escalante E 40 B5
Escalaplano I 64 D3
Escalhão P 45 C7
Escaló E 33 E8
Es Caló E 57 D8
Escalona E 46 D4
Escalona del Prado E 46 B4
Escalonilla E 46 E4
Escalos de Baixo P 44 E6
Escalos de Cima P 44 E6
Escamilla E 47 C7
Es Canar E 57 C8
Escañuela E 53 A8
Escariche E 47 D6
Escarigo P 45 D6
Escároz E 32 E3
Es Castell E 57 B13
Escatrón E 42 E3
Esch NL 183 B6
Eschau D 187 B7
Eschau F 186 E4
Eschborn D 187 A6
Esche D 17 C7
Escheburg D 83 D8
Eschede D 83 E8
Eschenbach CH 27 F9
Eschenburg-Eibelshausen D 21 C10
Eschenstruth (Helsa) D 78 D6
Eschershausen D 78 C6
Eschlkam D 76 D3
Escholzmatt CH 70 D5
Esch-sur-Alzette L 20 F5
Esch-sur-Sûre L 20 E5
Eschwege D 79 D7
Eschweiler D 20 C6
Escombreras E 56 F3
Escorca E 49 E10
Escorihuela E 42 F2
Escos F 32 D3
Escouloubre F 33 E10
Escource F 32 B3
Escout F 32 D4
Escragnolles F 36 D5
Escucha E 42 F2
Escurial E 45 F9
Escúzar E 53 B9
Esechioi RO 161 E10
Esence TR 173 D10
Esenköy TR 173 C10
Esenler TR 173 B8
Esens D 17 A9
Esenyurt TR 173 B10
Esgos E 38 D4
Esgueira P 44 C3
Esguevillas de Esgueva E 40 E3
Eskdalemuir GB 5 E10
Eskelhem S 93 E12
Eskiçine TR 181 A8
Eskilstrup DK 84 A1
Eskilstuna S 98 D7
Eskioba TR 177 C10
Eskisigirçi TR 173 D9
Eskogen S 99 C10
Eskola FIN 123 C12
Eskoriatza E 41 B6
Esku EST 131 D11
Eslarn D 75 C12
Eslava E 32 E3
Eslohe (Sauerland) D 17 F10
Eslöv S 87 D12
Es Mercadal E 57 B13
Es Migjorn Gran E 57 B13
Esnes F 19 D7
Esneux B 19 C12
Espa N 101 E14
Espadañedo E 39 D7
Espalion F 34 A4
Espaly-St-Marcel F 30 E4
Esparragalejo E 51 B7
Esparragosa E 51 B9
Esparragosa de la Serena E 51 B8
Esparreguera E 43 D7
Esparron F 35 C10
Esparza de Salazar E 32 E3
Espe DK 86 E6
Espedal N 94 E4
Espeja E 45 C7
Espeja de San Marcelino E 40 E5
Espejo E 53 A7
Espejón E 40 E5
Espel NL 16 C5
Espeland N 94 B2
Espelette F 32 D3
Espelkamp D 17 D11
Espenau D 78 D5
Espenes N 111 B14
Espera E 51 F8
Esperança P 45 F6
Espéraza F 33 E10
Espergærde DK 87 D11
Esperia I 62 E5
Espevik N 94 C3
Espezel F 33 E10
Espiel E 54 C3
Espinama E 39 B10
Espinasses F 36 C4
Espinhal P 44 D4
Espinho P 44 B3
Espinilla E 40 B3
Espinosa de Cerrato E 40 E4
Espinosa de Henares E 47 C6
Espinosa de los Monteros E 40 B4
Espinoso del Rey E 46 E3
Espira-de-l'Agly F 34 E4
Espírito Santo P 50 D4
Espite P 44 E3
Esplegares E 47 C8
Esplugues de Llobregat E 43 E8
Esplús E 42 D4
Espolla E 34 F5
Espondeilham F 34 D5
Esponellà E 43 C9
Espoo FIN 127 E12
Espoonlahti FIN 127 E12
Esporlatu I 64 C2
Esporles E 49 E10
Esposende P 38 E2
Espot E 33 E8
Esprels F 26 E5
Esquivias E 46 D5
Esrange S 116 C6
Essay F 23 C12
Esse FIN 123 C10
Essel D 82 E7
Essen B 16 F2
Essen D 17 F8
Essen (Oldenburg) D 17 C9
Essenbach D 75 E11
Essert F 27 E6
Essingen D 74 E7
Esslingen am Neckar D 27 C11
Essoyes F 25 D12
Essu EST 131 C12
Essvik S 103 B13
Estación de Baeza E 54 C5
Estadilla E 42 C4
Estagel F 34 E4
Estaimpuis B 19 C7
Estaing F 34 A4
Estaires F 18 C6
Estang F 32 C5
Estarreja P 44 C3
Estavayer-le-Lac CH 31 B10
Este I 66 B4
Este P 38 E3
Estela P 38 F2
Estella E 32 E1
Estellencs E 49 E10
Estenfeld D 187 B9
Estepa E 53 B7
Estepar E 40 D4
Estepona E 53 D6
Esteras de Medinaceli E 47 B8
Estercuel E 42 F2
Esternay F 25 C10
Esterri d'Àneu E 33 E8
Esterwegen D 17 C9
Esterzili I 64 D3
Estiavreilles F 30 E5
Estissac F 25 D10
Estivareilles F 29 C11
Estói P 50 E4
Estômbar P 50 E3
Estorf D 17 A12
Estorf D 17 C12
Estoril P 50 B1
Estoublon F 36 D4
Estrablin F 31 D6
Estrées-St-Denis F 18 F6
Estreito P 44 E5
Estrela P 51 C5
Estremera E 47 D6
Estremoz P 50 B4
Estriégala E 47 B7
Esvres F 24 F4
Esztár H 151 C8
Esztergom H 149 A11
Étables-sur-Mer F 22 C6
Étagnac F 29 D7
Étain F 19 F12
Étais-la-Sauvin F 25 E9
Étalante F 25 E12
Étalle B 19 E12
Étampes F 24 D7
Étang-sur-Arroux F 30 B5
Étaples F 15 F12
Étaules F 28 D3
Étauliers F 28 E4
Eteläinen FIN 127 C12
Etelä-Vartsala FIN 126 D5
Etelhem S 93 E13
Éternoz F 31 A9
Etes H 147 E9
Ethe B 19 E12
Etholmen N 91 A9
Etili TR 173 E6
Étival F 31 B8
Étival-Clairefontaine F 27 D6
Étivey F 25 E11
Etna N 101 E11
Etne N 94 C3
Étréchy F 24 D7
Étrépagny F 18 F4
Étretat F 23 A12
Étreux F 19 E8
Etrín Bajo E 51 B6
Etropole BG 165 D9
Etroubles I 31 D11
Ettelbruck L 20 E6
Ettenheim D 27 D8
Etten-Leur NL 16 E3
Ettington GB 13 A11
Ettlingen D 27 C9
Ettrick GB 5 E10
Ettringen D 21 D8
Etulia MD 155 B2
Étupes F 27 E6
Étuz F 26 F4
Etwall GB 11 F8
Etxalar E 32 D2
Etxarri-Aranatz E 32 E1
Etyek H 149 B11
Eu F 18 D3
Eubigheim D 74 C6
Euerdorf D 74 B7
Eugénie-les-Bains F 32 C5
Eugmo FIN 122 C9
Eulate E 32 E1
Eupen B 20 C6
Euper D 79 C12
Eura FIN 126 C7
Eurajoki FIN 126 C6
Eurasburg D 72 A3
Eurville-Bienville F 26 C3
Euskirchen D 21 C7
Eußenheim D 74 B6
Eutin D 83 B9
Eutingen im Gäu D 187 E6
Eutzsch D 79 C12
Euville F 26 C4
Eva GR 174 E4
Evanger N 100 E4
Evanton GB 3 K8
Évaux-les-Bains F 29 C10
Evciler TR 173 E6
Evciler TR 173 E7
Evdilos GR 177 D7
Ēvele LV 131 F11
Evenes N 111 D12
Evenesdal N 109 C10
Evenset N 108 B8
Evenskjær N 111 C12
Evenstad N 101 D14
Everdingen NL 183 B6
Everdrup DK 87 E9
Evergem B 19 B8
Everöd S 88 D6
Evertsberg S 102 D6
Evesham GB 13 A11
Évian-les-Bains F 31 C10
Evijärvi FIN 123 D10
Evisa F 37 G9
Evitskog FIN 127 E11
Evje N 90 B2
Evlalo GR 171 C7
Evolène CH 31 C12
Évora P 50 B4
Évora-Monte P 50 B4
Evosmos GR 169 C8
Évran F 23 D8
Évrecy F 23 B10
Evrencik TR 173 A8
Evrenli TR 173 A8
Evrensekiz TR 173 B7
Évreux F 24 B5
Évron F 23 D11
Evropos GR 169 C8
Evrostina GR 174 C5
Évry F 25 C7
Evzonoi GR 169 B8
Ewhurst GB 15 E8
Examilia GR 175 D6
Exaplatanos GR 169 C7
Exarchos GR 175 B6
Excideuil F 29 E8
Exebridge GB 13 C7
Exeter GB 13 D7
Exilles I 31 E10
Exloo NL 17 C7
Exmes F 23 C12
Exminster GB 13 D8
Exmouth GB 13 D8
Exochi GR 169 B10
Exochi GR 169 D7
Exo Chora GR 174 D2
Exo Vathy GR 180 C4
Extremo P 38 E3
Eydehavn N 90 B4
Eydelstedt D 17 C11
Eye GB 11 F11
Eye GB 15 C11
Eyemouth GB 5 D12
Eyeries IRL 8 E3
Eyguians F 35 B10
Eyguières F 35 C9
Eygurande-et-Gardedeuil F 29 E6
Eymet F 33 A6
Eymoutiers F 29 D9
Eynsham GB 13 B12
Eyragues F 35 C8
Eyrans F 28 E4
Eyrecourt IRL 6 F6
Eyrein F 29 E9
Eyzin-Pinet F 31 E6
Ezcaray E 40 D6
Ezerche BG 166 B6
Ezere LV 134 D4
Ežerėlis LT 137 D8
Ezerets BG 155 F3
Ezerets BG 165 F7
Ezeriș RO 159 C8
Ezerkalne LV 134 B5
Ezerkalni LV 133 E2
Ezernieki LV 133 D3
Ezine TR 171 E10
Ezkurra E 32 D2
Ézy-sur-Eure F 24 C5

F

Faaborg DK 86 E6
Fabara E 42 E4
Fabas F 33 D8
Fåberg N 100 C6
Fåberg N 101 D12
Fabero E 39 C6
Fábiánháza H 145 H5
Fabianki PL 138 E7
Fábiánsebestyén H 150 D5
Fåbodliden S 107 B13
Fåborg DK 86 D3
Fabrègues F 35 C6
Fabrezan F 34 D4
Fabriano I 67 F6
Fabrica di Roma I 62 C2
Fábricas de San Juan de Alcaraz E 55 B8
Fabrizia I 59 C9
Fabro I 62 B2
Făcăeni RO 155 D1
Faches-Thumesnil F 182 D2
Facinas E 52 D5
Fadd H 149 D11
Faedis I 73 D7
Fæfjord N 113 C13
Faenza I 66 D4
Faeto I 60 A4
Fafe P 38 F3
Fagagna I 73 D7
Făgăraș RO 152 F5
Fågelfors S 89 A9
Fågelmara S 89 C9
Fågelsjö S 102 C8
Fågelsta S 92 C6
Fågelsundet S 103 E14
Fageräs S 97 C9
Fagerdal S 106 D8
Fagerhaug N 101 A11
Fagerhult S 89 A9
Fagerhult S 91 C11
Fagerhult S 92 C4
Fagerli N 109 B11
Fagernes N 101 E10
Fagernes N 111 A17
Fagersanna S 92 C4
Fagersta S 97 C14
Fagervik FIN 127 E10
Fagervika N 108 D4
Fagerviken S 99 A9
Făget RO 151 F9
Făgețelu RO 160 D5
Fäggeby S 97 B14
Fåglavik S 91 C13
Fagnano Castello I 60 D6
Fagnières F 25 C11
Fahan IRL 4 E2
Fahrdorf D 82 A7
Fahrenkrug D 83 C8
Fahrenzhausen D 75 F10
Fahrland D 80 B4
Faicchio I 60 A2
Faid D 21 D8
Faido CH 71 E7
Failde P 39 E6
Faimes B 19 C11
Fain-lès-Montbard F 25 E11
Fains-Véel F 26 C3
Fairlie GB 4 D7
Fair Oak GB 13 D12
Faissault F 19 E10
Fajão P 44 D5
Fajarda P 50 B2
Fajsławice PL 144 A6
Fajsz H 149 D11
Fakenham GB 15 B10
Fåker S 106 F7
Fakiya BG 167 E8
Fakovići BIH 158 E4
Faksdal N 105 B10
Fakse DK 87 E10
Fakse Ladeplads DK 87 E10
Falaise F 23 C11
Falani GR 169 E7
Fålasjö S 107 E13
Falcade I 72 D4
Falcarragh IRL 6 B6
Falces E 32 F2
Fălciu RO 154 E2
Falck F 186 C2
Fălcoiu RO 160 E4
Falconara I 58 E5
Falconara Albanese I 60 E6
Falconara Marittima I 67 E7
Falcone I 59 C7
Faldsled DK 86 E6
Fale N 101 A9
Faleria I 62 C2
Falerna I 59 A9
Falerone I 62 A4
Falerum S 93 C8
Fălești MD 153 B11
Falkekeila N 114 C8
Falkenberg D 75 C11
Falkenberg D 75 F12
Falkenberg D 80 C4
Falkenberg S 87 B11
Falkenhagen D 83 D12
Falkenhain D 79 D12
Falkensee D 80 A4
Falkenstein D 75 B11
Falkenstein D 75 D11
Falkirk GB 5 D9
Falkland GB 5 C10
Falköping S 91 C14
Fałków PL 141 H2
Fall N 97 A8
Falla S 92 B7
Falleron F 28 B2
Fällfors S 118 D5
Fälloheden S 109 E15
Fällsvikhamnen S 103 A15
Falltorp S 97 A8
Falmenta I 68 A6
Falmouth GB 12 E4
Falset E 42 E5
Falstad N 105 D10
Fălticeni RO 153 C8
Falträsk S 107 B15
Falun S 103 E10
Famalicão P 44 D6
Fambach D 79 E7
Fameck F 20 F6
Fámjin FO 2 B3
Fana N 94 B2
Fanano I 66 D2
Fanari GR 171 C8
Fanbyn S 107 E16
Fångsjöbacken S 107 E11
Fängsjön S 107 E12
Fanjeaux F 33 D10
Fanlo E 32 E5
Fannrem N 104 E7
Fano I 67 E7
Fanore IRL 6 F4
Fanos GR 169 B7
Fântânele RO 151 E7
Fântânele RO 152 E5
Fântânele RO 153 B9
Fanthyttan S 97 C13
Fão P 38 E2
Fara Filiorum Petri I 63 C6
Fărăgău RO 152 D5
Fara in Sabina I 62 C3
Faraoani RO 153 E9
Faraonivka UA 154 E5
Fara San Martino I 63 C6
Farasdues E 41 D9
Fărău RO 152 E4
Fårberget S 107 C15
Fårbo S 93 E8
Fărcaș RO 160 D3
Fărcașa RO 151 B11
Fărcașa RO 153 C7
Fărcășești RO 159 D11
Farchant D 72 A3
Farciennes B 19 D10
Fardal N 90 A3
Fărdea RO 151 F9
Fardella I 60 C6
Fardhem S 93 E12
Fardrum IRL 7 F7
Farébersviller F 186 C2
Fareham GB 13 D12
Faremoutiers F 25 C9
Fårevejle DK 87 D8
Fårevejle Stationsby DK 87 D8
Fărgelanda S 91 B11
Fargues-St-Hilaire F 32 A5
Fårholmen S 118 C8
Fårhus DK 86 F4
Fårila S 103 C10
Faringdon GB 13 B11
Farini I 37 B11
Fariza de Sayago E 39 F7
Färjestaden S 89 B10
Farkadona GR 169 E7
Farlete E 41 E10
Färliug RO 159 B8
Färlöv S 88 C6
Färna S 97 C14
Färnäs S 102 D8
Farnborough GB 15 E7
Farndon GB 10 E6
Farnese I 62 B1
Farnham GB 15 E7
Farnstädt D 79 D10
Faro P 50 E4
Fårö S 93 D14
Faro do Alentejo P 50 C4
Fårösund S 93 D14
Farr GB 3 L8
Farra d'Alpago I 72 D5
Farranfore IRL 8 D3
Farre DK 86 C5
Farre DK 86 D4
Farsala GR 169 F7
Färsån S 107 E10
Farsø DK 86 B4
Farstrup DK 86 B4
Farsund N 94 F5
Fărtănești RO 153 F11
Fărtățești RO 160 D3
Fårup DK 86 B5
Fårvang DK 86 C5
Farynava BY 133 F5
Fasano I 61 B8
Fåset N 101 B13
Fåssjodal S 103 B13
Fasterholt DK 86 C4
Fasty PL 140 D8
Fatela P 44 D6
Fatih TR 173 B10
Fátima P 44 E3
Fatjas S 116 E4
Fatmomakke S 106 A8
Fatnica BIH 157 F9
Fättjaur S 106 A8
Faucogney-et-la-Mer F 26 E6
Faugères F 34 C5
Fauglia I 66 E2
Faugueroltes F 33 B6
Faulbach D 187 B7
Fauldhouse GB 5 D9
Faulenrost D 83 C13
Faulquemont F 26 B6
Fauquembergues F 18 C5
Faura E 48 E4
Făurei RO 153 D9
Făurei RO 161 C10
Făurești RO 160 D3
Fauske N 108 B9
Fauskevåg N 111 C12
Fauville-en-Caux F 18 E2
Faux F 29 F7
Faux-la-Montagne F 29 D9
Favaios P 38 F5
Favale di Malvaro I 37 C10
Fåvang N 101 D12
Favara E 48 F4
Favara I 58 E4
Faverges F 31 D9
Faverney F 26 E5
Faverolles F 30 F3
Faversham GB 15 E10
Favignana I 58 D1
Fawley GB 13 D12
Fay-de-Bretagne F 23 F8
Fayence F 36 D5
Fayl-Billot F 26 E4
Fayón E 42 E4
Fay-sur-Lignon F 30 F5
Fažana HR 67 C8
Fazeley GB 11 F8
Feakle IRL 8 C5
Fécamp F 18 E1
Feda N 94 F5
Fedamore IRL 8 C5
Fedje N 100 E1
Fedosiyivka UA 154 B4
Feeard IRL 8 C3
Feeny GB 4 F2
Fegen S 87 A12
Fégréac F 23 E7
Fegyvernek H 150 C6
Fehérgyarmat H 145 H6
Fehrbellin D 83 E13
Fehring A 148 C6
Feijó P 50 B1
Feilbingert D 21 E9
Feilitzsch D 75 B10
Feillens F 30 C6
Feissons-sur-Isère F 31 D9
Feistritz im Rosental A 73 C9
Feistritz ob Bleiburg A 73 C10
Feiteira P 50 E4
Feketić SRB 158 B4
Felanitx E 57 C11
Felchow D 84 D6
Felcsút H 149 B11
Feld am See A 73 C8
Feldbach A 148 C5
Feldballe DK 86 C7
Feldberg D 84 D4
Felde D 83 B7
Feldebrő H 147 F10
Feldioara RO 153 F7
Feldkirch A 71 C9
Feldkirchen in Kärnten A 73 C9
Feldkirchen-Westerham D 72 A4
Feldru RO 152 C5
Feleacu RO 152 D3
Felgar P 45 B7
Felgueiras P 38 F3
Felgyő H 150 D5
Feliceni RO 152 E6
Felindre GB 13 A8
Félines F 30 E4
Felino I 66 C1
Felitto I 60 C4
Félix E 55 F7
Felixdorf A 77 G10
Felixstowe GB 15 D11
Felizzano I 37 B8
Fell D 21 E7
Fellbach D 27 C11
Felletin F 29 D10
Fellingsbro S 97 D14
Felnac RO 151 E7
Felsberg D 21 B12
Felsődobsza H 145 G3
Felsőlajos H 150 C4
Felsőnyék H 149 C10
Felsőpakony H 150 C3
Felsőszentiván H 150 E3
Felsőszentmárton H 149 E9
Felsőtárkány H 145 H1
Felsőzsolca H 145 G2
Felsted DK 86 F4
Felton GB 5 E13
Feltre I 72 D4
Feltwell GB 11 G13
Femundsenden N 101 C15
Femundsundet N 101 C15
Fénay F 26 F3
Fendeille F 33 D9
Fene E 38 B3
Fenerköy TR 173 B9
Fenes N 111 C12
Fenestrelle I 31 E11
Fénétrange F 27 C7
Feneu F 23 E10
Fengersfors S 91 B11
Fenioux F 28 B5
Fenis I 31 D11
Fenit IRL 8 D3
Feniton GB 13 D8
Fensmark DK 87 E9
Fenstanton GB 15 C8
Fenwick GB 5 D13
Fényeslitke H 145 G5
Feofilova Pustyn' RUS 132 E5
Feolin Ferry GB 4 D4
Feonanagh IRL 8 D5
Fépin F 19 D10
Ferbane IRL 7 F7
Ferdinandea I 59 B9
Ferdinandovac HR 149 D8
Ferdinandshof D 84 C5
Fère-Champenoise F 25 C10
Fère-en-Tardenois F 25 B10
Férel F 23 F7
Ferentillo I 62 B3
Ferentino I 62 D4
Feres GR 171 C10
Férez E 55 C9
Feria E 51 B6
Feričanci HR 149 E9
Ferizaj RKS 164 E3
Ferlach A 73 C9
Fermignano I 66 E6
Fermo I 67 F8
Fermoselle E 39 F7
Fermoy IRL 8 D6
Fernáncaballero E 46 F5
Fernán Núñez E 53 A7
Ferndown GB 13 D11
Ferness GB 3 L9
Ferney-Voltaire F 31 C9
Fernitz A 148 C5
Ferns IRL 9 C9
Feroleto Antico I 59 B9
Ferrals-les-Corbières F 34 D4
Ferrandina I 61 C6
Ferrara I 66 C4
Ferrazzano I 63 D7
Ferreira E 38 A5
Ferreira do Alentejo P 50 C3

Ferreira do Zêzere *P* 44 E4
Ferrel *P* 44 F2
Ferreras de Abajo *E* 39 E7
Ferreras de Arriba *E* 39 E7
Ferrere *I* 37 B7
Ferreries *E* 57 B13
Ferreruela de Huerva *E* 47 B10
Ferreruela de Tábara *E* 39 E7
Ferrette *F* 27 E7
Ferriere *I* 37 B11
Ferrières *B* 19 D12
Ferrières *F* 25 D8
Ferritslet *DK* 86 E7
Ferrol *E* 38 B3
Ferrybank *IRL* 9 C10
Ferryhill *GB* 5 F13
Ferschweiler *D* 185 E5
Fertilia *I* 64 B1
Fertőd *H* 149 A7
Fertőrákos *H* 149 A7
Fertőszentmiklós *H* 149 A7
Ferwert *NL* 16 B5
Feshiebridge *GB* 3 L9
Fessenheim *F* 27 E8
Festieux *F* 19 E8
Festvåg *N* 108 B8
Fetești *MD* 153 A10
Fetești *RO* 155 E1
Fetești-Gară *RO* 155 E1
Fethard *IRL* 9 D7
Fethard *IRL* 9 D9
Fetsund *N* 95 C14
Fettercairn *GB* 5 B11
Feucht *D* 75 D9
Feuchtwangen *D* 75 D7
Feugarolles *F* 33 B6
Feuquières *F* 18 E4
Feuquières-en-Vimeu *F* 18 D4
Feurs *F* 30 D5
Fevåg *N* 104 D7
Fevik *N* 90 C4
Feytiat *F* 29 D8
Ffestiniog *GB* 10 F4
Ffostrasol *GB* 12 A6
Fiac *F* 33 C9
Fiamignano *I* 62 C4
Fiano *I* 31 E12
Fiano Romano *I* 62 C3
Fiavè *I* 69 B10
Ficarazzi *I* 58 C3
Ficarolo *I* 66 C3
Fichtelberg *D* 75 C10
Fichtenberg *D* 74 E6
Fichti *GR* 175 D6
Ficulle *I* 62 B2
Fiddown *IRL* 9 D8
Fide *S* 93 E12
Fidenza *I* 69 D9
Fidjeland *N* 94 E5
Fiè allo Sciliar *I* 72 C4
Fieberbrunn *A* 72 B6
Fieni *RO* 160 C6
Fier *AL* 168 C2
Fiera di Primiero *I* 72 D4
Fierbinți-Târg *RO* 161 D8
Fierzë *AL* 163 E9
Fiesch *CH* 70 E6
Fiesole *I* 66 E3
Fiesso Umbertiano *I* 66 C4
Figanières *F* 36 D4
Figari *F* 37 J10
Figeac *F* 33 A10
Figeholm *S* 93 E9
Figgio *N* 94 E3
Figline Valdarno *I* 66 E3
Figueira da Foz *P* 44 D3
Figueira de Castelo Rodrigo *P* 45 C7
Figueira e Barros *P* 44 F5
Figueiredo de Alva *P* 44 C5
Figueiró da Granja *P* 44 C6
Figueiró dos Vinhos *P* 44 E4
Figueres *E* 43 C9
Figueroles *E* 48 D4
Figueruela de Arriba *E* 39 E7
Fijnaart *NL* 182 B4
Filadelfia *I* 59 B9
Filakio *GR* 171 A10
Fil'akovo *SK* 147 E9
Filatova-Gora *RUS* 132 F3
Filattiera *I* 69 E8
Fildu de Jos *RO* 151 D11
Filettino *I* 62 D4
Filey *GB* 11 C11
Filiano *I* 60 B5
Filiași *RO* 160 D3
Filiates *GR* 168 E3
Filiatra *GR* 174 E4
Filicudi Porto *I* 59 B6
Filipeni *RO* 153 D10
Filipești *RO* 153 D9
Filipeștii de Pădure *RO* 161 D7
Filipeștii de Târg *RO* 161 D7
Filipjakov *HR* 156 E3
Filipovtsi *BG* 165 D6
Filipów *PL* 136 E6
Filippiada *GR* 174 A2
Filipstad *S* 97 C11
Filisur *CH* 71 D9
Fillan *N* 104 D5
Fillinges *F* 31 C9
Fillyra *GR* 171 B9
Filotas *GR* 169 C6
Filotio *GR* 177 E6
Filottrano *I* 67 F7
Filsbäck *S* 91 C13
Filskov *DK* 86 D4
Filsum *D* 17 B9
Filton *GB* 13 B9
Filzmoos *A* 73 B8
Fimber *GB* 11 C10
Finale *I* 58 C5
Finale Emilia *I* 66 C3
Finale Ligure *I* 37 C8
Fiñana *E* 55 E7
Finavon *GB* 5 B11
Finby *FIN* 99 B14
Finby *FIN* 127 E8
Findern *GB* 11 F8
Findhorn *GB* 3 K9
Findikli *TR* 172 D6
Findikli *TR* 173 E8
Findochty *GB* 3 K11
Findon *GB* 15 F8
Finestrat *E* 56 D4
Finhan *F* 33 C8
Finiq *AL* 168 E3
Finiș *RO* 151 D9
Finja *S* 87 C13
Finkenstein *A* 73 C8
Finnbacka *S* 103 D10
Finnbodarna *S* 102 E7
Finnböle *S* 98 B8
Finnbyen *N* 110 D5
Finnea *IRL* 7 E8
Finneby *S* 103 B9
Finnentrop *D* 21 B9
Finnerödja *S* 92 B4
Finnes *N* 108 C6
Finnes *N* 111 B13
Finnfjordeidet *N* 111 B15
Finnfors *S* 118 E4
Finngruvan *S* 102 E7
Finnholt *N* 96 B6
Finningham *GB* 15 C11
Finnkroken *N* 111 A17
Finnøy *N* 111 D9
Finnsådal *N* 90 C2
Finnsäter *S* 105 D15
Finnset *N* 101 B8
Finnset *N* 108 B7
Finnset *N* 110 D9
Finnseter *N* 111 C10
Finnshögst *S* 103 D9
Finnskog *N* 102 E3
Finnsnes *N* 111 B14
Finntorp *S* 96 D7
Finnträsk *S* 118 D6
Finnvik *N* 111 A16
Finnvika *N* 108 D4
Finnygaud *GB* 3 K11
Fino Mornasco *I* 69 B7
Finowfurt *D* 84 E5
Finse *N* 100 E7
Finsjö *S* 89 A10
Finspång *S* 92 B7
Finsterwalde *D* 80 C5
Finsterwolde *NL* 17 B8
Finström *FIN* 99 B13
Finta *RO* 161 D7
Fintel *D* 82 D7
Fintice *SK* 145 E3
Fintona *GB* 7 D8
Fintown *IRL* 6 C6
Finuge *IRL* 8 D3
Finvoy *GB* 4 E4
Fiodh Ard *IRL* 9 D7
Fionnphort *GB* 4 C4
Fiorano Modense *I* 66 C2
Fiorenzuola d'Arda *I* 69 D8
Fiplingkroken *N* 108 F6
Fira *GR* 179 C9
Firenze *I* 66 E3
Firenzuola *I* 66 D3
Firlej *PL* 141 G7
Firmi *F* 33 A10
Firminy *F* 30 E5
Firmo *I* 60 D6
Fiscal *E* 32 E5
Fischach *D* 75 F8
Fischbach *A* 148 B5
Fischbach *D* 21 E8
Fischbachau *D* 72 A4
Fischbach bei Dahn *D* 27 B8
Fischbeck *D* 79 A11
Fischen im Allgäu *D* 71 C10
Fishguard *GB* 12 B5
Fiskå *N* 100 B3
Fiskardo *GR* 174 C2
Fiskarheden *S* 102 D5
Fiskari *FIN* 127 E10
Fiskebäckskil *S* 91 C9
Fiskebøl *N* 110 D8
Fiskefjord *N* 110 C9
Fiskö *FIN* 126 E4
Fiskøy *N* 111 C11
Fisksätra *S* 99 D10
Fismes *F* 19 F8
Fisterra *E* 38 C1
Fistikli *TR* 173 D10
Fitero *E* 41 D8
Fitionești *RO* 153 F10
Fitjar *N* 94 C2
Fitou *F* 34 E4
Fitz-James *F* 18 F5
Fiuggi *I* 62 D4
Fiumalbo *I* 66 D2
Fiumefreddo Bruzio *I* 60 E6
Fiumefreddo di Sicilia *I* 59 D7
Fiumicino *I* 62 D2
Fiunary *GB* 4 B5
Fivemiletown *GB* 7 D8
Fivizzano *I* 66 D1
Fix-St-Geneys *F* 30 E4
Fizeșu Gherlii *RO* 152 C3
Fjær *N* 108 B8
Fjäl *S* 106 E7
Fjälkinge *S* 88 C6
Fjäll *S* 96 C7
Fjällåkern *S* 107 E14
Fjällåsen *S* 116 C4
Fjällbacka *S* 91 B9
Fjällnäs *S* 102 A3
Fjällsjö *S* 107 D10
Fjällsjönäs *S* 109 E12
Fjärås Kyrkby *S* 91 E11
Fjärdhundra *S* 98 C7
Fjätervålen *S* 102 C5
Fjell *N* 94 B2
Fjellbu *N* 111 D14
Fjelldal *N* 111 C12
Fjelle *N* 105 C10
Fjellerup *DK* 86 B7
Fjellnes *N* 108 B9
Fjellstad *N* 111 C15
Fjelsø *DK* 86 B4
Fjelsted *DK* 86 E6
Fjelstervang *DK* 86 C3
Fjelstrup *DK* 86 E5
Fjenneslev *DK* 87 E9
Fjerritslev *DK* 86 A4
Fjone *N* 90 A3
Fjordgard *N* 111 A14
Fjørvikan *N* 104 E4
Fjugesta *S* 92 A5
Flå *N* 95 B10
Flachau *A* 73 B7
Flachsmeer *D* 17 B8
Fladungen *D* 75 A7
Flagnac *F* 33 A10
Flaine *F* 31 C10
Flaka *FIN* 99 B14
Flakaberg *S* 116 E7
Flakaträsk *S* 107 C15
Flakaträsk *S* 109 F12
Flakk *N* 104 E8
Flakkebjerg *DK* 87 E8
Flakstad *N* 111 B13
Flåm *N* 100 E6
Flamanville *F* 23 A8
Flămânzi *RO* 153 B9
Flamborough *GB* 11 C11
Flamouria *GR* 169 C7
Flampouro *GR* 169 C10
Flärke *S* 107 D16
Flarken *S* 118 F5
Flästa *S* 103 D11
Flatabø *N* 94 B4
Flåten *N* 112 D6
Flatøydegard *N* 101 E11
Flått *N* 105 B12
Flattach *A* 73 C7
Flattnitz *A* 73 C9
Flatval *N* 104 D5
Flauenskjold *DK* 86 A6
Flavigny-sur-Moselle *F* 26 C5
Flavigny-sur-Ozerain *F* 25 E12
Flavin *F* 34 B4
Flawil *CH* 27 F11
Flayosc *F* 36 D4
Flechtingen *D* 79 B9
Flecken Zechlin *D* 83 D13
Fleet *GB* 15 E7
Fleetmark *D* 83 E10
Fleetwood *GB* 10 D5
Flein *D* 27 B11
Flekkefjord *N* 94 F5
Flémalle *B* 19 C11
Flen *S* 93 A9
Flensburg *D* 82 A6
Flenstad *N* 104 D8
Fleringe *S* 93 D13
Flermoen *N* 102 D4
Flerohopp *S* 89 B9
Fléron *B* 19 C12
Flers *F* 23 C10
Flers-en-Escrebieux *F* 182 E2
Flesberg *N* 95 C10
Flesnes *N* 111 C10
Flessau *D* 83 E11
Flesvik *N* 104 E6
Fleurance *F* 33 C7
Fleuré *F* 29 C7
Fleurie *F* 30 C6
Fleurier *CH* 31 B10
Fleurus *B* 19 D10
Fleury *F* 34 D5
Fleury-les-Aubrais *F* 24 E6
Fleury-sur-Andelle *F* 18 F3
Fléville-Lixières *F* 19 F12
Flieden *D* 74 B6
Fließ *A* 71 C11
Flimby *GB* 5 F9
Flims *CH* 71 D8
Flines-lez-Raches *F* 182 E2
Flint *GB* 10 E5
Flintbek *D* 83 B8
Flirey *F* 26 C4
Flisa *N* 102 E3
Flisby *S* 92 D5
Fliseryd *S* 89 A10
Flix *E* 42 E5
Flixecourt *F* 18 D5
Flize *F* 19 E10
Floby *S* 91 C13
Floda *S* 91 D11
Floda *S* 97 A12
Flodden *GB* 5 D12
Flogned *S* 96 C7
Flogny-la-Chapelle *F* 25 E10
Floh *D* 79 E7
Flöha *D* 80 E4
Floing *F* 19 E10
Floirac *F* 28 F4
Flokenes *N* 100 D2
Floq *AL* 168 C4
Flor *S* 103 B9
Florac *F* 35 B6
Florange *F* 20 F6
Floreffe *B* 19 D10
Florennes *B* 19 D10
Florenville *B* 19 E11
Flores de Ávila *E* 45 C10
Floresta *I* 59 D6
Florești *MD* 154 B2
Florești *RO* 152 D3
Florești *RO* 159 D10
Florești *RO* 161 C7
Florești-Stoenești *RO* 161 E7
Floriada *GR* 174 A3
Florida de Liébana *E* 45 B9
Floridia *I* 59 E7
Florina *GR* 168 C5
Florinas *I* 64 B2
Florø *N* 100 C2
Flörsbach *D* 74 B5
Flörsheim am Main *D* 187 A5
Flörsheim-Dalsheim *D* 187 B5
Flosjöhyttan *S* 97 C12
Flossenbürg *D* 75 C11
Flöthe *D* 79 B7
Flötningen *S* 102 C3
Flötuträsk *S* 118 D5
Floure *F* 33 D10
Flovika *N* 110 D9
Fluberg *N* 101 E12
Flüelen *CH* 71 D7
Flühli *CH* 70 D6
Flumeri *I* 60 A4
Flumet *F* 31 D10
Fluminimaggiore *I* 64 E2
Flums *CH* 27 F11
Fluren *S* 103 C11
Flurkmark *S* 122 C4
Flussio *I* 64 C2
Fly *DK* 86 C4
Flyggsjö *S* 107 D15
Flyinge *S* 87 D12
Flykälen *S* 106 D8
Flyn *S* 107 D10
Fobello *I* 68 B5
Foča *BIH* 157 F10
Foça *TR* 177 B8
Focant *B* 19 D11
Fochabers *GB* 3 K10
Focșani *RO* 153 F10
Focuri *RO* 153 C10
Foëcy *F* 24 F7
Foeni *RO* 159 B6
Foggia *I* 63 E9
Foglianise *I* 60 A3
Föglö *FIN* 99 B14
Fohnsdorf *A* 73 B10
Fohrde *D* 79 B11
Föhren *D* 21 E7
Foiano della Chiana *I* 66 F4
Foieni *RO* 151 B9
Foinikounta *GR* 178 B2
Foix *F* 33 E9
Fojnica *BIH* 157 E8
Foktő *H* 149 C11
Földeák *H* 150 E6
Foldereid *N* 105 B12
Földes *H* 151 C7
Fole *DK* 86 E3
Fole *S* 93 D13
Folegandros *GR* 179 B8
Folgaria *I* 69 B11
Folgoso de Courel *E* 38 C5
Folgoso de la Ribera *E* 39 C7
Folia *GR* 170 C6
Folignano *I* 62 B5
Foligno *I* 62 B3
Folkestad *N* 100 B4
Folkestone *GB* 15 E11
Folkingham *GB* 11 F11
Follafoss *N* 105 D10
Folldal *N* 101 B12
Follebu *N* 101 D12
Føllenslev *DK* 87 D8
Follina *I* 72 E5
Follingbo *S* 93 D12
Föllinge *S* 106 D7
Follonica *I* 65 B3
Folly Gate *GB* 12 D6
Fölsbyn *S* 96 D7
Folschviller *F* 26 B6
Folteşti *RO* 155 B2
Fonaïtika *GR* 174 D3
Fondevila *E* 38 E3
Fondi *I* 62 E4
Fondón *E* 55 F7
Föne *S* 103 C10
Fönebo *S* 103 C12
Fonelas *E* 55 E6
Fonfría *E* 39 E7
Fonfría *E* 42 E1
Fønhus *N* 101 E11
Fonn *N* 100 C5
Fonni *I* 64 C3
Fonroque *F* 29 F6
Fonsorbes *F* 33 C8
Fontaine *F* 27 E6
Fontaine *F* 31 E8
Fontainebleau *F* 25 D8
Fontaine-Française *F* 26 E3
Fontaine-le-Bourg *F* 18 E3
Fontaine-le-Dun *F* 18 E2
Fontaine-lès-Dijon *F* 26 F3
Fontaine-lès-Luxeuil *F* 26 E5
Fontaine-l'Évêque *B* 19 D9
Fontainemore *I* 68 B4
Fontaines *F* 25 E9
Fontaines *F* 30 B6
Fontan *F* 37 C7
Fontanar *E* 47 C6
Fontanarejo *E* 46 F3
Fontane *I* 37 C7
Fontanelice *I* 66 D4
Fontanellato *I* 66 C1
Fontanès *F* 35 C7
Fontanigorda *I* 37 B10
Fontanosas *E* 54 B3
Fontecchio *I* 62 C5
Fonte Díaz *E* 38 C3
Fontellas *E* 41 D8
Fontenay-le-Comte *F* 28 C4
Fontenilles *F* 33 C8
Fontenoy *F* 25 E9
Fontenoy-le-Château *F* 26 E5
Fontes *P* 44 E4
Fontevraud-l'Abbaye *F* 23 F12
Fontiveros *E* 46 C3
Font-Romeu-Odeillo-Via *F* 33 E10
Fontstown *IRL* 7 F9
Fontvieille *F* 35 C8
Fonyód *H* 149 C9
Fonz *E* 42 C4
Fonzaso *I* 72 D4
Foppolo *I* 69 A8
Forano *I* 62 C3
Forăști *RO* 153 C8
Forbach *D* 27 C9
Forbach *F* 27 B6
Förby *FIN* 126 E8
Forcall *E* 42 F3
Forcalquier *F* 35 C10
Forcarei *E* 38 C3
Force *I* 62 B4
Forchheim *D* 75 C9
Forchtenberg *D* 187 C8
Forchtenstein *A* 149 A6
Ford *GB* 4 C6
Ford *GB* 5 D12
Ford *IRL* 9 C10
Førde *N* 94 C2
Førde *N* 100 D3
Förderstedt *D* 79 C10
Fordham *GB* 15 C9
Fordingbridge *GB* 13 D11
Fordongianus *I* 64 D2
Fordoun *GB* 5 B12
Fore *N* 110 C7
Foreneset *N* 94 D4
Forenza *I* 60 B5
Føresvik *N* 94 D2
Forfar *GB* 5 B11
Forges-les-Eaux *F* 18 E4
Forgie *GB* 3 K10
Forino *I* 60 B3
Forio *I* 62 F5
Föritz *D* 75 B9
Forjães *P* 38 E2
Forkhill *GB* 7 D10
Førland *N* 94 F6
Forlev *DK* 87 E8
Forlì *I* 66 D5
Forlimpopoli *I* 66 D5
Formazza *I* 71 E6
Formby *GB* 10 D5
Formello *I* 62 C2
Formerie *F* 18 E4
Formia *I* 62 E5
Formiche Alto *E* 48 D3
Formicola *I* 60 A2
Formigine *I* 66 C2
Formigliana *I* 68 C5
Formignana *I* 66 C4
Formiguères *F* 33 E10
Formofoss *N* 105 C12
Fornåsa *S* 92 C6
Fornelli *I* 64 A1
Fornells *E* 57 A13
Fornells de la Selva *E* 43 D9
Fornes *N* 111 C10
Fornes *N* 111 C13
Forni Avoltri *I* 73 C6
Forni di Sopra *I* 72 D6
Forni di Sotto *I* 73 D6
Forno Alpi Graie *I* 31 E11
Forno di Zoldo *I* 72 D5
Fornos *P* 45 B7
Fornos de Algodres *P* 44 C5
Fornovo di Taro *I* 66 C1
Foros de Vale Figueira *P* 50 B3
Foros do Arrão *P* 44 F4
Forotic *RO* 159 C8
Forøy *N* 108 C6
Forra *N* 111 D13
Forráskút *H* 150 E4
Forres *GB* 3 K9
Forró *H* 145 G3
Fors *S* 98 B6
Fors *S* 107 E11
Fors *S* 107 E15
Forså *N* 111 C12
Forså *N* 111 D11
Forsand *N* 94 E4
Forsåsen *S* 106 D7
Forsbäck *S* 109 E9
Forsbacka *S* 103 E12
Forsbacken *S* 109 F11
Forsbakken *N* 111 C14
Forsby *FIN* 122 C9
Forsby *FIN* 127 E14
Forserum *S* 92 D4
Forset *N* 111 C15
Forshaga *S* 97 C9
Forshed *S* 118 B8
Forsheda *S* 87 A13
Forsholm *S* 107 B16
Forsinard *GB* 3 J9
Forsland *N* 108 D4
Førslev *DK* 87 E9
Förslöv *S* 87 C11
Forsmark *S* 99 B10
Forsmark *S* 109 F10
Forsmo *S* 107 E12
Forsnäs *S* 109 D16
Forsnäs *S* 109 E13
Forsnäs *S* 118 B5
Forsnes *N* 104 E4
Forsøl *N* 113 B12
Forssa *FIN* 127 D10
Forsse *S* 107 E11
Forssjö *S* 93 B8
Forst *D* 27 B10
Forst *D* 81 C7
Forstinning *D* 75 F10
Forsträskhed *S* 118 B8
Forsvik *S* 92 B4
Fortanete *E* 42 F2
Fort Augustus *GB* 2 L7
Forter *GB* 5 B10
Fortezza *I* 72 C4
Forth *GB* 5 D9
Fortios *P* 44 F6
Fort-Mahon-Plage *F* 18 D4
Fortrose *GB* 3 K8
Fortuna *E* 56 E2
Fortuneswell *GB* 13 D10
Fort William *GB* 4 B6
Forvik *N* 108 E3
Fos *F* 33 E7
Fosdinovo *I* 69 E9
Foskros *S* 102 B4
Foskvallen *S* 102 C4
Fosnavåg *N* 100 B3
Fosnesvågen *N* 105 B10
Fossacesia *I* 63 C6
Fossalta di Portogruaro *I* 73 E6
Fossano *I* 37 B7
Fossato di Vico *I* 67 F6
Fossby *N* 91 A10
Fosse *N* 94 B4
Fosser *N* 95 C14
Fosses-la-Ville *B* 19 D10
Fossheim *N* 112 D5
Fossiat *F* 31 C7
Fossing *N* 90 B5
Fossmork *N* 94 E4
Fossombrone *I* 67 E6
Fos-sur-Mer *F* 35 D8
Fót *H* 150 B3
Foteina *GR* 169 D7
Fotherby *GB* 11 E11
Fotinovo *BG* 165 F9
Fotolivos *GR* 170 B6
Foucarmont *F* 18 E4
Fouesnant *F* 22 E3
Foug *F* 26 C4
Fougères *F* 23 D9
Fougerolles *F* 26 E5
Fougerolles-du-Plessis *F* 23 D10
Fouilloy *F* 18 E6
Foulain *F* 26 D3
Foulayronnes *F* 33 B7
Fountain Cross *IRL* 8 C4
Fouras *F* 28 D3
Fourcès *F* 33 C6
Fourchambault *F* 30 A3
Four Elms *GB* 15 E9
Fourfouras *GR* 178 E8
Fourmies *F* 19 D9
Fourna *GR* 174 A4
Fournels *F* 30 F3
Fournes *GR* 178 E6
Fournoi *GR* 177 D7
Fourques *F* 34 E4
Fourques *F* 35 C8
Fours *F* 30 B4
Foustani *GR* 169 B7
Fownhope *GB* 13 A9
Foxdale *GBM* 10 C2
Foxford *IRL* 6 E4
Foyers *GB* 2 L8
Foygh *IRL* 7 E7
Foynes *IRL* 8 C4
Foz *E* 38 A5
Foz *P* 44 F4
Foz do Arelho *P* 44 F2
Foz Giraldo *P* 44 E5
Frabosa Soprana *I* 37 C7
Frącki *PL* 136 F7
Frades de la Sierra *E* 45 C9
Fraga *E* 42 D4
Fragagnano *I* 61 C8
Fraham *A* 76 F6
Frailes *E* 53 B9
Fraire *B* 19 D10
Fraize *F* 27 D7
Frameries *B* 19 D8
Framfjord *N* 100 D4
Framlev *DK* 86 C6
Framlingham *GB* 15 C11
Främlingshem *S* 98 A7
Frammersbach *D* 187 A7
Främmestad *S* 91 C12
Frampol *PL* 144 B6
Frampton *GB* 11 F11
Francavilla al Mare *I* 63 C6
Francavilla di Sicilia *I* 59 D7
Francavilla Fontana *I* 61 B9
Francavilla in Sinni *I* 60 C6
Francescas *F* 33 B6
Francești *RO* 160 C4
Franco *P* 38 F5
Francofonte *I* 59 E6
Francorchamps *B* 20 D5
Francoulès *F* 33 A8
Francova Lhota *CZ* 146 C6
Frändefors *S* 91 C11
Franeker *NL* 16 B5
Frangy *F* 31 C8
Frankenau *D* 21 B11
Frankenberg *D* 80 E4
Frankenberg (Eder) *D* 21 B11
Frankenburg am Hausruck *A* 76 F4
Frankenfels *A* 77 G8
Frankenheim *D* 75 A7
Frankenmarkt *A* 76 G4
Frankenthal (Pfalz) *D* 21 E10
Frankfurt am Main *D* 21 D11
Frankfurt an der Oder *D* 81 B7
Frankowo *PL* 136 E2
Frankrike *S* 105 D15
Frånö *S* 103 A14
Franois *F* 26 F4
Fränsta *S* 103 A11
Františkovy Lázně *CZ* 75 B11
Franzburg *D* 83 B13
Frascati *I* 62 D3
Frascineto *I* 60 D6
Fraserburgh *GB* 3 K12
Frasin *MD* 153 A11
Frasin *RO* 153 B7
Fråsinet *RO* 161 E9
Frasne *F* 31 B9
Frasnes-lez-Buissenal *B* 19 C8
Frasnes-lez-Gosselies *B* 19 C9
Frassinoro *I* 66 D2
Frasso Telesino *I* 60 A3
Frastanz *A* 71 C9
Frata *RO* 152 D4
Frătăuții Noi *RO* 153 B7
Frătăuții Vechi *RO* 153 B7
Fratel *P* 44 E5
Frătești *RO* 161 F7
Fratta Polesine *I* 66 B4
Fratta Todina *I* 62 B2
Fraubrunnen *CH* 31 A12
Frauenau *D* 76 E4
Frauenfeld *CH* 27 E10
Frauenkirchen *A* 77 G11
Frauental an der Laßnitz *A* 148 C4
Frauenwald *D* 79 E8
Fraunberg *D* 75 F10
Frayssinet-le-Gélat *F* 33 A8
Frecăței *RO* 155 C3
Frecăței *RO* 155 D2
Frechas *P* 38 F5
Frechen *D* 21 C7
Frechilla *E* 39 D10
Freckleton *GB* 10 D6
Fredensborg *DK* 87 D10
Fredericia *DK* 86 D5
Frederiks *DK* 86 C4
Frederiksberg *DK* 87 D11
Frederiksberg *DK* 87 E9
Frederikshavn *DK* 90 E8
Frederikssund *DK* 87 D10
Frederiksværk *DK* 87 D10
Fredersdorf *D* 80 A5
Fredrika *S* 107 C14
Fredriksberg *S* 97 B11
Fredriksdal *S* 92 D5
Fredrikstad *N* 91 A8
Freemount *IRL* 8 D5
Fregenal de la Sierra *E* 51 C6
Fregene *I* 62 D2
Freginals *E* 42 F5
Fréhel *F* 23 C7
Freiberg *D* 80 E4
Freiburg (Elbe) *D* 17 A12
Freiburg im Breisgau *D* 27 D8
Freienseinwald *D* 74 B5
Freienwill *D* 82 A6
Freihung *D* 75 C10
Freila *E* 55 D7
Freilassing *D* 73 A6
Freinsheim *D* 187 B5
Freisen *D* 21 E8
Freising *D* 75 F10
Freissinières *F* 31 F10
Freistadt *A* 77 E7
Freistatt *D* 17 C11
Freistroff *F* 20 F6
Freital *D* 80 E5
Freixedas *P* 45 C6
Freixianda *P* 44 E4
Freixiosa *P* 44 C5
Freixo *P* 38 E2
Freixo de Espada à Cinta *P* 45 B7
Fréjairolles *F* 33 C10
Frejlev *DK* 86 A5
Fréjus *F* 36 E5
Frekhaug *N* 94 A2
Frellstedt *D* 79 B8
Freluga *S* 103 D11
Fremdingen *D* 75 E7
Fremington *GB* 12 C6
Frenchpark *IRL* 6 E6
Frencq *F* 15 F12
Frensdorf *D* 75 C8
Frenštát pod Radhoštěm *CZ* 146 B6
Freren *D* 17 D9
Fresach *A* 73 C8
Fresagrandinaria *I* 63 D7
Freshford *IRL* 9 C8
Freshwater *GB* 13 D11
Fresnay-sur-Sarthe *F* 23 D12
Fresneda de la Sierra *E* 47 D8
Fresnedoso de Ibor *E* 45 E9
Fresnes-en-Woëvre *F* 26 B4
Fresnes-sur-Apance *F* 26 E4
Fresnes-sur-Escaut *F* 182 E3
Fresne-St-Mamès *F* 26 E4
Fresno Alhándiga *E* 45 C9
Fresno de la Ribera *E* 39 E8
Fresno de Sayago *E* 39 F8
Fresno el Viejo *E* 45 B10
Fresnoy-Folny *F* 18 E3
Fresnoy-le-Grand *F* 19 E7
Fresse-sur-Moselle *F* 27 E6
Fressingfield *GB* 15 C11
Fresvik *N* 100 D5
Freswick *GB* 3 H10
Fretigney-et-Velloreille *F* 26 F4
Freudenberg *D* 21 C9
Freudenberg *D* 187 B7
Freudenburg *D* 186 B2
Freudenstadt *D* 27 D9
Frévent *F* 18 D5
Freyburg (Unstrut) *D* 79 D10
Freyenstein *D* 83 D12
Freyming-Merlebach *F* 27 B6
Freyung *D* 76 E5
Friarfjorden *N* 113 C18
Frías *E* 40 C5
Fribourg *CH* 31 B11
Frick *CH* 27 E9
Fričovce *SK* 145 E2
Fridafors *S* 88 C7
Fridalen *N* 109 B9
Fridaythorpe *GB* 11 C10
Fridingen an der Donau *D* 27 D10
Fridlevstad *S* 89 C9
Fridolfing *D* 76 G3
Frieda (Meinhard) *D* 79 D7
Friedberg *A* 148 B6
Friedberg *D* 75 F8
Friedberg (Hessen) *D* 21 D11
Friedeburg *D* 17 B9
Friedeburg (Saale) *D* 79 C10
Friedenfels *D* 75 C11
Friedersdorf *D* 79 C11
Friedersdorf *D* 80 B5
Friedewald *D* 78 E6
Friedewald *D* 185 C8
Friedland *D* 78 D6
Friedland *D* 80 B6
Friedland *D* 84 C5
Friedrichroda *D* 79 E8
Friedrichsbrunn *D* 79 C9
Friedrichsdorf *D* 187 A6
Friedrichshafen *D* 71 B9
Friedrichskoog *D* 82 B5
Friedrichsruhe *D* 83 C11
Friedrichstadt *D* 82 B6
Friedrichswalde *D* 84 D5
Frielendorf *D* 21 C12
Friemar *D* 79 E8
Friesach *A* 73 C9
Friesack *D* 83 E13
Friesenhagen *D* 185 C8
Friesenheim *D* 27 D8
Friesenried *D* 71 B11
Friesoythe *D* 17 B9
Frifelt *DK* 86 E3
Frigento *I* 60 A4
Friggesund *S* 103 C12
Frigiliana *E* 53 C9
Frihetsli *N* 111 C18
Friitala *FIN* 126 C6
Frikes *GR* 174 C2
Frikstad *N* 90 B2
Frillesås *S* 91 E11
Frinnaryd *S* 92 D5
Frinton-on-Sea *GB* 15 D11
Friockheim *GB* 5 B11
Friol *E* 38 B4
Frisange *L* 20 E6
Fristad *S* 91 D13
Fritsla *S* 91 D12
Fritzens *A* 72 B4
Fritzlar *D* 21 B12
Friville-Escarbotin *F* 18 D4
Frizington *GB* 10 B5
FroŠba *FO* 2 B3
Frödinge *S* 92 D8
Frodsham *GB* 10 E6
Frœschwiller *F* 186 D4
Froges *F* 31 E8
Frogmore *GB* 15 E7
Frohburg *D* 79 D12
Frohnleiten *A* 148 B4
Froideconche *F* 26 E5
Froissy *F* 18 E5
Fröjel *S* 93 E12
Froland *N* 90 B4
Frolosh *BG* 165 E6
Frombork *PL* 139 B8
Frome *GB* 13 C10
Fromelennes *F* 184 D2
Fromentine *F* 28 B1
Frómista *E* 40 D3
Fröndenberg *D* 17 F9
Fronhausen *D* 21 C11
Fronsac *F* 28 F5
Fronsac *F* 33 E7
Fronteira *P* 44 F5
Frontenard *F* 31 B7
Frontenay-Rohan-Rohan *F* 28 C4
Frontenhausen *D* 75 E12
Frontignan *F* 35 D6
Fronton *F* 33 C8
Frösakull *S* 87 B11
Frose *D* 79 C9
Fröseke *S* 89 B9
Frosinone *I* 62 D4
Frøskeland *N* 110 C9
Frøslev *DK* 86 B3
Frösö *S* 106 E7
Frosolone *I* 63 D6
Frosta *N* 105 D9
Frostadheia *N* 104 E4
Frøstrup *DK* 86 A3
Frouard *F* 26 C5
Frövi *S* 97 D13
Frufällan *S* 91 D12
Fruges *F* 18 C5
Frumoasa *RO* 153 E7
Frumoasa *RO* 161 F6
Frumosu *RO* 153 B7
Frumușani *RO* 161 E8
Frumușica *RO* 153 B9
Frumușița *RO* 155 B2
Frunzivka *UA* 154 C5
Frutigen *CH* 70 D5
Fry *GR* 181 F5
Frýdek-Místek *CZ* 146 B6
Frýdlant *CZ* 81 E8
Frýdlant nad Ostravicí *CZ* 146 B6
Frygnowo *PL* 139 C9
Fryksås *S* 102 D8
Frymburk *CZ* 76 E6
Fryšták *CZ* 146 C5
Frysztak *PL* 144 D4
Fubine *I* 37 B8
Fucecchio *I* 66 E2
Fuchstal *D* 71 B11
Fuencaliente *E* 54 C4
Fuendejalón *E* 41 E9
Fuengirola *E* 53 C7
Fuenlabrada *E* 46 D5
Fuenmayor *E* 41 D6
Fuensalida *E* 46 D4
Fuensanta *E* 47 F8
Fuensanta *E* 55 D9
Fuensanta de Martos *E* 53 A9
Fuente-Álamo *E* 55 B10
Fuente Álamo *E* 56 F2
Fuentealbilla *E* 47 F9
Fuentecambrón *E* 40 E5
Fuentecén *E* 40 E4
Fuente de Cantos *E* 51 C7
Fuente del Arco *E* 51 C8
Fuente del Maestre *E* 51 B7
Fuente de Pedro Naharro *E* 47 E6
Fuente de Piedra *E* 53 B7
Fuente el Fresno *E* 46 F5
Fuente el Saz de Jarama *E* 46 C6

Fuente el Sol E 46 B3
Fuenteguinaldo E 45 D7
Fuentelapeña E 39 F9
Fuentelcésped E 40 E4
Fuentelespino de Haro E 47 E7
Fuentelespino de Moya E 47 E10
Fuentelmonge E 41 F7
Fuentenovilla E 47 D6
Fuente Obejuna E 51 C9
Fuente Palmera E 53 A6
Fuentepelayo E 46 B4
Fuentepinilla E 40 E6
Fuenterodos E 41 F10
Fuenterrebollo E 40 F4
Fuenterroble de Salvatierra E 45 C9
Fuentesaúco E 45 B10
Fuentesaúco de Fuentidueña E 40 F3
Fuentes-Claras E 47 C10
Fuentes de Andalucía E 51 E9
Fuentes de Ebro E 41 E10
Fuentes de Jiloca E 41 F8
Fuentes de León E 51 C6
Fuentes de Nava E 39 D10
Fuentes de Oñoro E 45 C7
Fuentes de Ropel E 39 E8
Fuentespalda E 42 F4
Fuente-Tójar E 53 A8
Fuente Vaqueros E 53 B9
Fuentidueña E 40 F4
Fuerte del Rey E 53 A9
Fuertescusa E 47 D8
Fügen A 72 B4
FuglafjørÞur FO 2 A3
Fugleberg N 111 C12
Fuglebjerg DK 87 E9
Fuglstad N 105 A13
Fuhrberg (Burgwedel) D 78 A6
Fulda D 74 A6
Fulford GB 11 D9
Fulga RO 161 D8
Fulham GB 15 E8
Fullbro S 93 A11
Fulnek CZ 146 B5
Fülöp H 151 B9
Fülöpháza H 150 D3
Fülöpszállás H 150 D3
Fulunäs S 102 D5
Fumay F 19 E10
Fumel F 33 B7
Fumone I 62 D4
Funäsdalen S 102 A4
Fundada P 44 E4
Fundão P 44 D6
Fundata RO 160 C6
Fundeni RO 161 B11
Fundeni RO 161 E8
Funder Kirkeby DK 86 C4
Fundulea RO 161 E9
Fundu Moldovei RO 152 B6
Funes E 32 F2
Funes I 72 C4
Funzie GB 3 D15
Furadouro P 44 C3
Furceni MD 154 C3
Furci I 63 C7
Furci Siculo I 59 D7
Furculești RO 160 F6
Furiani F 37 F10
Furnace GB 4 C6
Furnari I 59 C7
Furraleigh IRL 9 D8
Fürstenau D 17 C9
Fürstenberg D 21 A12
Fürstenberg D 84 D4
Fürstenberg (Lichtenfels) D 21 B11
Fürstenfeld A 148 B6
Fürstenfeldbruck D 75 F9
Fürstenwalde D 80 B6
Fürstenwerder D 84 D5
Fürstenzell D 76 E4
Furta H 151 C7
Furtan S 97 C8
Furtei I 64 D2
Fürth D 21 E11
Fürth D 75 D8
Furth D 75 E11
Furth bei Göttweig A 77 F9
Furth im Wald D 76 D3
Furtwangen im Schwarzwald D 27 D9
Furuberg S 103 B12
Furuby S 89 B8
Furudal N 111 B16
Furudal S 103 D9
Furudals bruk S 103 D9
Furuflaten N 111 B19
Furuögrund S 118 E6
Furusjö S 91 D14
Furusund S 99 C11
Furutangvikja N 105 B14
Furuvik S 103 E13
Fusa N 94 B3
Fuscaldo I 60 E6
Fushë-Arrëz AL 163 E9
Fushë-Bardhe AL 168 D3
Fushë Kosovë RKS 164 D3
Fushë-Krujë AL 168 B2
Fushë-Kuqe AL 168 A2
Fusignano I 66 D4
Fußach A 71 C9
Füssen D 71 B11
Fussy F 25 F7
Fustiñana E 41 D9
Futeau F 26 B3
Futog SRB 158 C4
Futrikelva N 111 A17
Füzesabony H 150 B5
Füzesgyarmat H 151 C7
Fužine HR 67 B10
Fyfield GB 15 D9
Fylaki GR 169 F8
Fyli GR 175 C8
Fyllinge S 87 B11
Fyllo GR 169 F7
Fynshav DK 86 F5
Fyrås S 106 D8
Fyrde N 100 B4
Fyresdal N 90 A3
Fyteies GR 174 B3
Fyvie GB 3 L12

G

Gaal A 73 B10
Gaanderen NL 183 B8
Gabaldón E 47 E9
Gabare BG 165 C8
Gabarret F 32 C6
Gabčíkovo SK 146 F5
Gabela BIH 157 F8
Gaber BG 165 D6
Gabia la Grande E 53 B9
Gabicce Mare I 67 E6
Gąbin PL 139 F8
Gablingen D 75 F8
Gablitz A 77 F10
Gáborján H 151 C8
Gabriac F 34 B4
Gabrnik SLO 148 D5
Gabrovnitsa BG 165 B7
Gabrovo BG 166 D4
Gaby I 68 B4
Gać PL 144 C5
Gacé F 23 C12
Gacko BIH 157 F10
Gåda S 103 B10
Gadbjerg DK 86 D4
Gäddede S 105 B16
Gäddträsk S 107 C15
Gadebusch D 83 C10
Gadmen CH 70 D6
Gadoni I 64 D3
Gádor E 55 F8
Gádoros H 150 D6
Gadstrup DK 87 D10
Gadžin Han SRB 164 C5
Gaeiras P 44 F2
Gærum DK 90 E7
Găești RO 160 D6
Gaeta I 62 E5
Gafanha da Boa Hora P 44 C3
Gafanha da Nazaré P 44 C3
Gafanha do Carmo P 44 C3
Gafanhoeira P 50 B3
Gåfete P 44 F5
Gaflenz A 73 A10
Gafsele S 107 C12
Gaganitsa BG 165 C7
Găgești RO 153 E11
Gaggenau D 27 C9
Gaggi I 59 D7
Gaggio Montano I 66 D2
Gaglianico I 68 B5
Gagliano Castelferrato I 59 D6
Gagliano del Capo I 61 D10
Gagnef S 103 E9
Gagnières F 35 B7
Gagsmark S 118 D6
Găiceana RO 153 E10
Gaigalava LV 133 C2
Gaildorf D 74 E6
Gaillac F 33 C9
Gaillac-d'Aveyron F 34 B4
Gaillard F 31 C9
Gaillimh IRL 6 F4
Gaillon F 24 B5
Gaiļmui LV 135 D13
Gaimersheim D 75 E9
Gainsborough GB 11 E10
Gaiole in Chianti I 66 F3
Gaios GR 174 A1
Gairloch GB 2 K5
Gairo I 64 D4
Gais CH 71 C8
Gais I 72 C4
Găiseni RO 161 D7
Gaishorn A 73 A10
Gaismas LV 135 C8
Gaj SRB 159 D7
Gajanejos E 47 C7
Gajary SK 77 F11
Gakovo SRB 150 F3
Galăbodarna S 102 A6
Galambok H 149 C8
Galan F 33 D6
Gălănești RO 153 B7
Gálaniitu N 112 F10
Galanta SK 146 E5
Galapagar E 46 C5
Galaroza E 51 D6
Galåsen N 102 D4
Galashiels GB 5 D11
Galasjö S 107 E14
Galata BG 167 C9
Galatades GR 169 C7
Galatas GR 175 D6
Galatas GR 175 E7
Gălăteni RO 160 E6
Galați RO 155 C2
Galații Bistriței RO 152 D4
Galati Mamertino I 59 C6
Galatin BG 165 C8
Galatina I 61 C10
Galatini GR 169 D6
Galatista GR 169 D9
Galatone I 61 C10
Gălăuțaș RO 152 D6
Galaxidi GR 174 C5
Galbally IRL 8 D6
Galbarra E 32 E1
Galbenu RO 161 C10
Gålberget S 107 D14
Gălbinași RO 161 C9
Galda de Jos RO 152 E3
Găldău RO 161 E11
Gål'din N 113 E12
Galeata I 66 E4
Galende E 39 D6
Galēni LV 135 D13
Galera E 55 D7
Galéria F 37 G9
Gălești RO 152 E5
Galewice PL 142 D5
Galgagyörk H 150 B3
Galgahévíz H 150 B4
Gălgău RO 152 C3
Galgon F 28 F5
Gal'gunjar'ga N 113 F16
Galicea RO 160 D4
Galicea Mare RO 160 E2
Galiche BG 165 B8
Galinduste E 45 C9
Galiny PL 136 E2
Galissas GR 176 E4
Galisteo E 45 E8
Gallarate I 68 B6
Gallardon F 24 C6
Gallargues-le-Montueux F 35 C7
Galleberg N 95 C12
Gallegos de Argañan E 45 C7
Gallegos de Solmirón E 45 C10
Galleno I 66 E2
Gälleråsen S 97 D11
Gallese I 62 C2
Gallian-en-Médoc F 28 E4
Galliate I 68 C6
Gallicano I 66 D1
Gallicano nel Lazio I 62 D3
Gallin D 83 C9
Gallin D 83 C12
Gallio I 72 E4
Gallipoli I 61 C10
Gällivare S 116 D5
Gallizien A 73 C10
Gallneukirchen A 76 F6
Gällö S 103 A9
Gällstad S 91 D13
Galluccio I 60 A1
Gallur E 41 E9
Galovo BG 160 F4
Galros IRL 7 F7
Gålsjö bruk S 107 E13
Galston GB 5 D8
Galtelli I 64 C4
Galten DK 86 C5
Galterud N 96 B6
Gåltjärn S 103 A13
Gåltjärn S 103 A14
Galtström S 103 B13
Galtür A 71 D10
Galve E 42 F2
Galve de Sorbe E 47 B6
Galveias P 44 F5
Galven S 103 D11
Gálvez E 46 E4
Galway IRL 6 F4
Gama E 40 B5
Gamaches F 18 E4
Gamarde-les-Bains F 32 C4
Gamás H 149 C9
Gambara I 66 B1
Gambarie I 59 C8
Gambassi Terme I 66 E2
Gambatesa I 63 D7
Gambettola I 66 D5
Gambolò I 69 C6
Gambsheim F 27 C8
Gaming A 77 G8
Gamleby S 93 D8
Gamlingay GB 15 C8
Gamlitz A 148 C5
Gammalkroppa S 97 C11
Gammelboning S 103 E11
Gammelgården S 119 C10
Gammelgarn S 93 E13
Gammel Rye DK 86 C5
Gammelsdorf D 75 E10
Gammelstaden S 118 C8
Gammelstilla S 98 B7
Gammertingen D 27 D11
Gams CH 71 C8
Gamvik N 112 C9
Gamvik N 113 A21
Gamvik N 113 B11
Gan F 32 D5
Ganagobie F 35 B10
Gand B 19 B8
Gand B 182 C3
Gandarela P 38 F3
Gandellino I 69 B8
Ganderkesee D 17 B11
Gandesa E 42 E4
Gandesbergen D 17 C12
Gandía E 56 D4
Gandino I 69 B8
Gandra P 38 D2
Gandrup DK 86 A6
Gandvik N 114 C6
Găneasa RO 160 E4
Găneasa RO 161 D8
Gănești RO 152 E4
Ganfei P 38 D2
Ganges F 35 C6
Gånghester S 91 D13
Gangi I 58 D5
Găngiova RO 160 F3
Gangkofen D 75 F12
Ganløse DK 87 D10
Gannat F 30 C3
Gänserndorf A 77 F11
Ganshoren B 19 C9
Gånsvik S 103 A15
Ganzlin D 83 D12
Gaoth Dobhair IRL 6 B6
Gap F 36 B4
Gaperhult S 91 B13
Gara H 150 E3
Garaballa E 47 E10
Garagarza E 32 D1
Garaguso I 60 B6
Gara Khitrino BG 167 C7
Gara Oreshets BG 159 F10
Gărbău RO 151 D11
Garbayuela E 46 F3
Garberg N 105 E10
Gârbou RO 151 C11
Gârbova RO 152 F3
Gârbovi RO 161 D9
Garbów PL 141 H6
Garbsen D 78 B6
Garching an der Alz D 75 F12
Garching bei München D 75 F10
Gârcina RO 153 D8
Garchizy F 30 A3
Garcia E 42 E5
Garciaz E 45 F9
Garciems LV 135 B8
Garcihernández E 45 C10
Garcillán E 46 C4
Garčin HR 157 B9
Garcinarro E 47 D7
Gârcov RO 160 F5
Garda I 69 B10
Gârda de Sus RO 151 E10
Gardanne F 35 D9
Gärdås S 102 E6
Gardby S 89 B11
Garde S 93 E13
Gärde S 105 D15
Gardeja PL 138 C6
Gardelegen D 79 A9
Gardenstown GB 3 K12
Garderen NL 183 A7
Garderhouse GB 3 E14
Gardermoen N 95 B14
Gardiki GR 174 B4
Garding D 82 B5
Gärdnäs S 106 C8
Gardone Riviera I 69 B10
Gardone Val Trompia I 69 B9
Gardonne F 29 F6
Gárdony H 149 B11
Gardouch F 33 D9
Gärdsjö S 92 B4
Gärdsjöbäcken S 109 F12
Gardsjönås S 109 F11
Gårdskär S 103 E14
Gårds Köpinge S 88 D6
Gärdslösa S 89 B11
Gårdstånga S 87 D12
Gåre N 102 A1
Garein F 32 B4
Gårelehöjden S 107 D11
Garelochhead GB 4 C7
Garéoult F 36 E4
Garešnica HR 149 E7
Garessio I 37 C8
Garforth GB 11 D9
Gargalianoi GR 174 E4
Gargáligas E 45 F9
Gargallo E 42 F2
Garganta la Olla E 45 D9
Gargazzone I 72 C3
Gargilesse-Dampierre F 29 B9
Gargnano I 69 B10
Gargnäs S 107 A13
Gargogečče N 113 C20
Gargždai LT 134 E2
Garijp NL 16 B5
Garkalne LV 135 B8
Gârla Mare RO 159 E10
Garlasco I 69 C6
Gârleni RO 153 D9
Garliava LT 137 D8
Gârliciu RO 155 D2
Garlieston GB 5 F8
Garlin F 32 C5
Garlitos E 54 B2
Garlstorf D 83 D8
Garmisch-Partenkirchen D 72 B3
Garnes N 100 B3
Gârnic RO 159 D8
Garoafa RO 153 F10
Garons F 35 C7
Garoza LV 135 C7
Garpenberg S 98 B6
Garphyttan S 97 D12
Garrafe de Torio E 39 C8
Garralda E 32 E3
Garrane IRL 8 E4
Garray E 41 E7
Garrel D 17 C10
Garrison GB 6 D6
Garristown IRL 7 E10
Garrovillas E 45 E7
Garrucha E 55 E9
Garrynahine GB 2 J3
Garryvoe IRL 8 E6
Gars am Inn D 75 F11
Gars am Kamp A 77 E9
Garsås S 102 E8
Garsdale Head GB 11 C7
Gârsene LV 135 D11
Gårslev DK 86 D5
Gärsnäs S 88 D6
Garstang GB 10 D6
Garstedt D 83 D8
Garten N 104 D7
Garth GB 13 A7
Garthmyl GB 10 F5
Gartland N 105 B12
Gartow D 83 D10
Gärtringen D 27 C10
Gartz D 84 D6
Garvagh GB 4 F3
Garvagh IRL 7 E7
Garvaghy GB 7 D8
Garvald GB 5 D11
Garvamore GB 5 A8
Garvão P 50 D3
Garvard GB 4 C4
Garvary GB 7 D7
Garve GB 2 K7
Garwolin PL 141 G5
Garz D 84 B4
Gąsawa PL 138 E4
Gåsbakken N 104 E7
Gaschurn A 71 D10
Gascueña E 47 D7
Gåsholma S 103 D13
Gasjö S 97 B14
Gaskeluokt S 107 A11
Gąski PL 136 F5
Gåsnes N 112 D8
Gåsnes N 113 A13
Gasny F 24 B6
Gąsocin PL 139 E10
Gasperina I 59 B10
Gaspoltshofen A 76 F5
Gasselte NL 17 C7
Gasselternijveen NL 17 C7
Gassino Torinese I 68 C4
Gassjö S 103 B9
Gassum DK 86 B6
Gastellovo RUS 136 C4
Gastes F 32 B3
Gastouni GR 174 D3
Gastouri GR 168 E2
Gata E 45 D7
Gata de Gorgos E 56 D5
Gătaia RO 159 C7
Gatchina RUS 132 B7
Gatehouse of Fleet GB 5 F8
Gátér H 150 D4
Gateshead GB 5 F13
Gátova E 48 E3
Gattendorf A 77 F11
Gatteo a Mare I 66 D5
Gattières F 37 D6
Gattinara I 68 B5
Gau-Algesheim D 185 E9
Gauchy F 19 E7
Gaucín E 53 C6
Gauja LV 135 B9
Găujani RO 161 F7
Gaujiena LV 131 F12
Gaukönigshofen D 74 C6
Gaulstad N 105 D12
Gau-Odernheim D 185 E9
Gaupne N 100 D6
Gaurė LT 134 F4
Gausvik N 111 C11
Gautestad N 90 B2
Gauting D 75 F9
Gauto S 109 D12
Gavà E 43 E8
Gavalou GR 174 B4
Găvănoasa MD 155 B2
Gavardo I 69 B9
Gavarnie F 32 E5
Gávavencsellő H 145 G4
Gavere B 19 C8
Gavi I 37 B9
Gavião P 44 F5
Gavieze LV 134 C2
Gavik S 103 A15
Gavirate I 68 B6
Gävle S 103 E13
Gavoi I 64 C3
Gavojdia RO 159 B9
Gavorrano I 65 B3
Gavray F 23 C9
Gavrio GR 176 D4
Gavrolimni GR 174 C4
Gåvsta S 99 C9
Gaweinstal A 77 F11
Gawliki Wielkie PL 136 E5
Gaworzyce PL 81 C9
Gåxsjö S 106 D8
Gaytaninovo BG 169 B10
Gayton GB 11 F13
Gaziemir TR 177 C9
Gaziköy TR 173 C7
Gazioğlu TR 173 B8
Gaziosmanpaşa TR 173 B10
Gazolaz E 32 E2
Gazoldo degli Ippoliti I 66 B2
Gazoros GR 169 B10
Gazzo Veronese I 66 B3
Gazzuolo I 66 B2
Gbelce SK 147 F7
Gbely SK 77 E12
Gdańsk PL 138 B6
Gdinj HR 157 F6
Gdov RUS 132 D2
Gdów PL 144 D1
Gdynia PL 138 A6
Geaca RO 152 D4
Gea de Albarracín E 47 D10
Geaidnovuohppi N 113 E12
Geamăna MD 154 D4
Geashill IRL 7 F8
Geaune F 32 C5
Gebesee D 79 D8
Gebhardshain D 21 C9
Gjbice PL 85 E11
Gechingen D 187 D6
Geçkinli TR 167 F7
Geddington GB 15 C7
Gédérlak H 149 C11
Gedern D 21 D12
Gedinne B 19 E10
Gedney Drove End GB 11 F12
Gèdre F 32 E6
Gedser DK 83 A11
Gedsted DK 86 B4
Gedved DK 86 D5
Geel B 19 B11
Geertruidenberg NL 16 E3
Geeste D 17 C8
Geesteren NL 183 A9
Geestgottberg D 83 E11
Geesthacht D 83 D8
Geetbets B 19 C11
Geffen NL 183 B6
Gefrees D 75 B10
Gefyra GR 169 C8
Gefyria GR 169 F7
Gegai AL 168 C2
Gegužinė LT 137 D9
Gehrde D 17 C10
Gehrden D 78 B6
Gehren D 79 E9
Geijersholm S 97 B10
Geilenkirchen D 20 C6
Geilo N 95 A8
Geiranger N 100 B6
Geisa D 78 E6
Geiselbach D 187 A7
Geiselhöring D 75 E11
Geiselwind D 75 C7
Geisenfeld D 75 E10
Geisenhausen D 75 F11
Geisenheim D 21 E9
Geising D 80 E5
Geisingen D 27 E10
Geislingen D 187 E6
Geislingen an der Steige D 74 E6
Geismar D 79 D7
Geisnes N 105 B11
Geispolsheim F 27 C8
Geistthal A 73 B11
Geithain D 79 D12
Geithus N 95 C11
Geitvågen N 108 B8
Gela I 58 E5
Gelbensande D 83 B12
Gelchsheim D 74 C7
Geldermalsen NL 16 E4
Geldern D 16 E6
Geldersheim D 75 B7
Geldrop NL 16 F5
Geleen NL 19 C12
Gelgaudiškis LT 136 C6
Gelibolu TR 172 D6
Gellénháza H 149 C7
Gelligaer GB 13 B8
Gelnhausen D 21 D12
Gelnica SK 145 F2
Gelos F 32 D5
Gelsa E 41 F11
Gelse H 149 C7
Gelsenkirchen D 17 E8
Gelsted DK 86 E5
Gelsted DK 87 E9
Geltendorf D 71 A12
Gelting D 83 A7
Geltow D 80 B3
Gelvonai LT 137 C10
Gembloux B 19 C10
Gemeaux F 26 F3
Gemenele RO 155 C1
Gémenos F 35 D10
Gemerská Hôrka SK 145 F1
Gemerská Poloma SK 145 F1
Gemert NL 16 E5
Gemla S 88 B7
Gemmingen D 187 C6
Gemona del Friuli I 73 D7
Gémozac F 28 D4
Gemünden D 21 E8
Gemünden am Main D 74 B6
Genappe B 19 C9
Genarp S 87 D12
Génave E 55 C7
Genazzano I 62 D3
Gençay F 29 C6
Gencsapáti H 149 B7
Gendrey F 26 F4
Gendringen NL 16 E6
Gendt NL 16 E5
Génelard F 30 B5
Genemuiden NL 16 C6
General-Inzovo BG 167 E6
General-Kolevo BG 155 F1
Generalski Stol HR 148 F4
General Toshevo BG 155 F2
Genestoso E 39 B7
Genêts F 23 C9
Genevad S 87 B12
Genève CH 31 C9
Genevilla E 32 E1
Genga I 67 F6
Gengenbach D 27 D9
Geniai LT 137 E8
Genisea GR 171 B7
Génissac F 28 F5
Genk B 19 C12
Genlis F 26 F3
Gennadi GR 181 D7
Gennep NL 16 E5
Genner DK 86 E4
Gennes F 23 F11
Gennes-sur-Seiche F 23 E9
Genola I 37 B7
Génolhac F 35 B6
Genoni I 64 D3
Genouillac F 29 C9
Genouillé F 29 C6
Genouilly F 24 F6
Genouilly F 30 B6
Genova I 37 C9
Genovés E 56 D4
Gensac F 28 F6
Gensingen D 185 E8
Gent B 19 B8
Genthin D 79 B11
Gentioux-Pigerolles F 29 D9
Genzano di Lucania I 60 B6
Genzano di Roma I 62 D3
Geoagiu RO 151 F11
George Enescu RO 153 A9
Georgensgmünd D 75 D9
Georgianoi GR 169 D7
Georgianoi GR 170 C6
Georgi Damyanovo BG 165 C7
Georgioupoli GR 178 E7
Georgitsi GR 174 E5
Georgsheil D 17 B8
Georgsmarienhütte D 17 D10
Ger E 33 F9
Ger F 23 C10
Ger F 32 D5
Gera D 79 E11
Geraardsbergen B 19 C8
Gerabronn D 74 D6
Gerace I 59 C9
Geraci Siculo I 58 D5
Gerakarou GR 169 C9
Geraki GR 175 F6
Gerakini GR 169 D9
Gérardmer F 27 D6
Geras A 77 E9
Gerasdorf bei Wien A 77 F10
Géraudot F 25 D11
Gerbéviller F 186 E2
Gerbrunn D 187 B8
Gerbstedt D 79 C10
Gérce H 149 B8
Gerchsheim D 74 C6
Gerdau D 83 E8
Gerena E 51 D7
Gerendás H 151 D6
Geresdlak H 149 D11
Geretsberg A 76 F3
Geretsried D 72 A3
Gérgal E 55 E7
Gergei I 64 D3
Gergeri GR 178 E8
Gerhardshofen D 75 C8
Gerindote E 46 E4
Geringswalde D 80 D3
Gerjen H 149 D11
Gerlev DK 87 D10
Gerlingen D 27 C11
Gerlos A 72 B5
Germas GR 168 D5
Germay F 26 D3
Germencik TR 177 D10
Germering D 75 F9
Germersheim D 21 F10
Gernika-Lumo E 41 B6
Gernrode D 79 C9
Gernsbach D 27 C9
Gernsheim D 187 B5
Gerola Alta I 69 A8
Gerolimenas GR 178 C3
Gerolsbach D 75 F9
Gerolstein D 21 D7
Gerolzhofen D 75 C7
Gerovo HR 67 A10
Gerpinnes B 19 D10
Gersau CH 71 D7
Gersfeld (Rhön) D 74 B6
Gersheim D 27 B7
Gersten D 17 C9
Gerstetten D 74 E7
Gerstheim F 186 E4
Gersthofen D 75 F8
Gerstungen D 79 E7
Gerswalde D 84 D5
Gerwisch D 79 B10
Gerzat F 30 D3
Gerzen D 75 E11
Gesäter S 91 B10
Gescher D 17 E8
Gesico I 64 D3
Gespunsart F 19 E10
Gessertshausen D 75 F8
Gestalgar E 48 E3
Gesté F 23 F9
Gesten DK 86 D4
Gesturi I 64 D3
Gesualdo I 60 A4
Gesunda S 102 E8
Gesves B 19 D11
Geszt H 151 D8
Gesztely H 145 G2
Geszteréd H 151 B8
Geta FIN 99 B13
Getafe E 46 D5
Getaria E 32 D1
Gétigné F 28 A3
Getinge S 87 B11
Getryggen S 103 D10
Getterum S 93 D8
Gettjärn S 97 C8
Gettorf D 83 B7
Gevelsberg D 17 F8
Gévezé F 23 D8
Gevgelija NMK 169 B7
Gevrey-Chambertin F 26 F2
Gex F 31 C9
Geyer D 80 E3
Geyikli TR 171 E10
Gezavesh AL 168 B3
Gföhl A 77 E8
Ghedi I 66 B1
Ghelari RO 159 B10
Ghelința RO 153 F8
Ghemme I 68 B5
Gheorghe Doja RO 161 D10
Gheorghe Lazăr RO 161 D10
Gheorgheni RO 153 D7
Gherăești RO 153 C9
Gherăseni RO 161 C9
Ghercești RO 160 E3
Ghergheasa RO 161 C10
Gherghița RO 161 D8
Gherla RO 152 C3
Gherța Mică RO 145 H7
Ghidfalău RO 153 F7
Ghidigeni RO 153 E10
Ghidighiei MD 154 C3
Ghiffa I 68 B6
Ghilarza I 64 C2
Ghimbav RO 161 B7
Ghimeș-Făget RO 153 D8
Ghimpați RO 161 E7
Ghindari RO 152 E5
Ghioroc RO 151 E8
Ghioroiu RO 160 D3
Ghiroda RO 151 F7
Ghislenghien B 19 C8
Ghisonaccia F 37 G10
Ghisoni F 37 G10
Ghizela RO 151 F8
Ghyvelde F 18 B6
Gialtra GR 175 B6
Giannades GR 168 E2
Giannitsa GR 169 C7
Giannouli GR 169 E7
Giano dell'Umbria I 62 B3
Giardini-Naxos I 59 D7
Giarmata RO 151 F7
Giarratana I 59 E6
Giarre I 59 D7
Giat F 29 D10
Giave I 64 C2
Giaveno I 31 E11
Giba I 64 E2
Gibellina Nuova I 58 D2
Gibostad N 111 B15
Gibraleón E 51 E6
Gibraltar GBZ 53 D6
Giby PL 136 E7
Ģibzde LV 134 B4
Gideå S 107 E15
Gideå bruk S 107 E16
Gideåkroken S 107 C12
Gidle PL 143 E7
Giebelstadt D 74 C6
Gieboldehausen D 79 C7
Gieczno PL 143 C7
Giedraičiai LT 137 C11
Gielniów PL 141 H2
Gielow D 83 C13
Gien F 25 E8
Giengen an der Brenz D 75 E7
Giera RO 159 C6
Gierle B 182 C5
Giersleben D 79 C10
Gierstädt D 79 D8
Gierzwałd PL 139 C9
Gießen D 21 C11
Gieten NL 17 B7
Gietrzwałd PL 139 C9
Gièvres F 24 F6
Giffnock GB 5 D8
Gifford GB 5 D11
Gifhorn D 79 B8
Gigean F 35 C6
Gigen BG 160 F4
Gighera RO 160 F3
Giglio Castello I 65 C3
Gignac F 35 C6
Gignac F 35 C10
Gignod I 31 D11
Gijón E 39 A8
Ģikši LV 135 B10
Gilău RO 151 D11
Gilching D 75 F9
Gilena E 53 B7
Gilette F 37 D6
Gilford GB 7 D10
Gilleleje DK 87 C10
Gillenfeld D 21 D7
Gillhov S 102 A8
Gillingham GB 13 C10
Gillingham GB 15 E10
Gilling West GB 11 C8
Gilly-sur-Isère F 31 D9
Gilly-sur-Loire F 30 B4
Gilmerton GB 5 C9
Gilså N 105 E11
Gilserberg D 21 C12
Gilsland GB 5 F11
Gilten D 82 E7
Gilwern GB 13 B8
Gilze NL 16 E3
Gimåt S 107 E15
Gimdalen S 103 A10
Gimigliano I 59 B10
Gimo S 99 B10
Gimont F 33 C7
Gimouille F 30 B3
Gimsøy N 110 D7
Ginasservis F 35 C10
Ginestas F 34 D4
Gingelom B 19 C11
Gingen an der Fils D 187 D8
Gingst D 84 B4
Ginkūnai LT 134 E6
Ginoles F 33 E10
Ginosa I 61 B7
Ginostra I 59 B7
Ginsheim D 185 E9
Gintsi BG 165 C7
Giões P 50 E4
Gioi I 60 C4
Gioia dei Marsi I 62 D5
Gioia del Colle I 61 B7
Gioia Sannitica I 60 A2
Gioia Tauro I 59 C8
Gioiosa Ionica I 59 C9
Gioiosa Marea I 59 C6
Giornico CH 71 E7
Giovinazzo I 61 A7
Ģipka LV 130 F5
Giraltovce SK 145 E4
Girancourt F 26 D5
Girasole I 64 D4
Girifalco I 59 B9
Girișu de Criș RO 151 C8
Girkalnis LT 134 F6
Giroc RO 159 B7
Giromagny F 27 E6
Girona E 43 D9
Gironde-sur-Dropt F 32 A5
Gironella E 43 C7
Giroussens F 33 C9
Girov RO 153 D9
Girvan GB 4 E7
Gislaved S 88 A5
Gislev DK 86 E7
Gislinge DK 87 D9
Gislövs strandmark S 87 E12
Gisloy N 110 C9
Gisors F 18 F4
Gissi I 63 C7
Gisslarbo S 97 C14
Gistad S 92 C7
Gistel B 18 B6
Gistrup DK 86 B5
Giswil CH 70 D6

Gittelde D 79 C7
Gittun S 109 D16
Giubega RO 160 E2
Giubiasco CH 69 A7
Giugliano in Campania I 60 B2
Giulești RO 152 B3
Giuliano di Roma I 62 D4
Giulianova I 62 B5
Giulvăz RO 159 B6
Giuncugnano I 66 D1
Giurgeni RO 155 D1
Giurgița RO 160 E3
Giurgiu RO 161 F7
Giurgiulești MD 155 C2
Giuvărăști RO 160 F5
Give DK 86 D4
Givet F 19 D10
Givors F 30 D6
Givry B 19 D9
Givry F 30 B6
Givry-en-Argonne F 25 C12
Givskud DK 86 D4
Gižai LT 136 D7
Giżałki PL 142 B4
Gizeux F 23 F12
Giżycko PL 136 E4
Gizzeria I 59 B9
Gjakovë RKS 163 E9
Gjærnes N 90 B5
Gjegjan AL 163 E9
Gjegjan AL 163 F9
Gjengstø N 104 E6
Gjerde N 100 C6
Gjerdebakken N 113 C11
Gjerdrum N 95 B14
Gjerlev DK 86 B6
Gjermungshamn N 94 B3
Gjern DK 86 C5
Gjerrild DK 87 C7
Gjerstad N 90 B5
Gjersvik N 105 B14
Gjesing DK 86 C6
Gjesvær N 113 A15
Gjevaldshaugen N 101 D15
Gjilan RKS 164 E3
Gjirokastër AL 168 D3
Gjógv FO 2 A3
Gjøl DK 86 A5
Gjøljelia N 104 D7
Gjølme N 104 E7
Gjonaj RKS 163 E10
Gjonëm AL 168 A2
Gjøra N 101 A10
Gjorm AL 168 D2
Gjøvåg N 94 B2
Gjøvik N 101 E13
Gjurakoc RKS 163 D9
Gjuvberget N 102 E3
Gkoritsa GR 175 E6
Gladbeck D 17 E7
Gladenbach D 21 C11
Gladsaxe DK 87 D10
Gladstad N 108 E2
Glainans F 26 F6
Glamis GB 5 B11
Glamoč BIH 157 D6
Glämos N 101 A14
Glamsbjerg DK 86 E6
Glandage F 35 A10
Glandon F 29 E8
Glandore IRL 8 E4
Glandorf D 17 D10
Glanegg A 73 C9
Glanerbrug NL 17 D7
Glanshammar S 97 D13
Glanworth IRL 8 D6
Glarryford GB 4 F4
Glarus CH 71 C8
Glasbury GB 13 A8
Glasgow GB 5 D8
Glashütten D 21 D10
Glashütten D 75 C9
Glaslough IRL 7 D9
Glassan IRL 7 F7
Glastonbury GB 13 C9
Glaubitz D 80 D4
Glauchau D 79 E12
Glava BG 165 C9
Glava S 97 C8
Glava glasbruk S 96 C7
Glavan BG 166 E6
Glăvănești RO 153 E10
Glavanovtsi BG 164 D6
Glavatićevo BIH 157 F9
Glavice HR 157 E6
Glavičice BIH 157 C11
Glăvile RO 160 D4
Glavinitsa BG 161 F9
Glavki GR 171 B7
Gleann Cholm Cille IRL 6 C5
Gleann Doimhin IRL 7 C7
Gleann na Muaidhe IRL 6 D3
Gleđica SRB 163 C9
Glein N 108 D4
Gleina D 79 D10
Gleisdorf A 148 B5
Gleizé F 30 D6
Glejbjerg DK 86 D3
Glemsford GB 15 C10
Glen S 102 A6
Glenade IRL 6 D6
Glenamaddy IRL 6 E5
Glenamoy IRL 6 D3
Glenariff GB 4 E4
Glenarm GB 4 F5
Glenavy GB 7 C10
Glenbarr GB 4 D5
Glenbeg GB 4 B5
Glenbeigh IRL 8 D3
Glencaple GB 5 E9
Glencar IRL 6 D6
Glencoe GB 4 B6
Glencolumbkille IRL 6 C5
Glendowan IRL 7 C7
Gleneagles GB 5 C9
Glenealy IRL 7 G10
Gleneely IRL 4 E2
Glenegedale GB 4 D4
Glenelg GB 2 L5
Glenfield GB 11 F9
Glenfinnan GB 4 B6
Glengarriff IRL 8 E3
Glengavlen IRL 7 D7
Glenhead GB 4 E2
Glenluce GB 4 F7
Glenmore IRL 9 D8
Glenoe GB 4 F5
Glenrothes GB 5 C10
Glenties IRL 6 C6
Glère F 27 F6
Glesborg DK 87 C7
Gletsch CH 71 D6
Glewitz D 84 B3
Glibaći MNE 163 C7
Glimåkra S 88 C6
Glimboca RO 159 C9
Glin IRL 8 C4
Glina HR 148 F6
Glina RO 161 E8
Glinde D 83 C8
Glindow D 79 B12
Glinjeni MD 153 B11
Glinojeck PL 139 E9
Glinsce IRL 6 F3
Glinsk IRL 6 F3
Glinton GB 11 F11
Glissjöberg S 102 B7
Gliwice PL 142 F6
Gllamnik RKS 164 D3
Glloboçicë RKS 164 E3
Gllogoc RKS 163 D10
Glodeanu-Sărat RO 161 D9
Glodeanu-Siliștea RO 161 D9
Glodeni MD 153 B11
Glodeni RO 152 D5
Glodeni RO 161 C6
Glödnitz A 73 C9
Głodowa PL 85 C11
Glodzhevo BG 161 F8
Gloggnitz A 148 A5
Glogova RO 159 D10
Glogovac SRB 159 E7
Głogów PL 81 C10
Głogówek PL 142 F4
Głogów Małopolski PL 144 C4
Glogowo PL 138 D6
Glomfjord N 108 C6
Glommen S 87 B10
Glommersträsk S 107 A17
Glonn D 75 G10
Glória P 50 B4
Glória do Ribatejo P 44 F3
Glos-la-Ferrière F 24 C4
Glossa GR 175 A8
Glössbo S 103 D12
Glossop GB 11 E8
Glöte S 102 B5
Glöthe D 79 C10
Glottra S 92 B6
Gloucester GB 13 B10
Glounthaune IRL 8 E6
Głowaczów PL 141 G4
Główczyce PL 85 A12
Glowe D 84 A4
Glöwen D 83 E12
Głowno PL 143 C8
Gložan SRB 158 C4
Glozhene BG 160 F3
Glozhene BG 165 C9
Głubczyce PL 142 F4
Głuchołazy PL 142 F3
Głuchów PL 141 G2
Glücksburg (Ostsee) D 82 A7
Glückstadt D 17 A12
Glud DK 86 D5
Gludsted DK 86 C4
Gluggvasshaugen N 108 E5
Glumslöv S 87 D11
Glumsø DK 87 E9
Glusburn GB 11 D8
Glušci SRB 158 D4
Głuszyca PL 81 E10
Glyfa GR 175 B6
Glyfada GR 175 D8
Glyki GR 168 F4
Glyn Ceiriog GB 10 F5
Glyngøre DK 86 B3
Glynn GB 4 F5
Glynn IRL 9 D9
Glynneath GB 13 B7
Gmünd A 73 C8
Gmünd A 77 E7
Gmund am Tegernsee D 72 A4
Gmunden A 73 A8
Gnarp S 103 B13
Gnarrenburg D 17 B12
Gneisenaustadt Schildau D 80 D3
Gnesta S 93 A10
Gniebing A 148 C5
Gniew PL 138 C6
Gniewkowo PL 138 E5
Gniewoszów PL 141 H5
Gnieżdziska PL 143 E9
Gniezno PL 85 E13
Gnisvärd S 93 D12
Gnocchetta I 66 C5
Gnoien D 83 C13
Gnojna PL 81 E12
Gnojnice BIH 157 F8
Gnojnik PL 144 D2
Gnojno PL 143 E10
Gnosall GB 11 F7
Gnosjö S 91 E14
Gnotzheim D 75 D8
Gnutz D 83 B7
Göbel TR 173 D9
Gobowen GB 10 F5
Göçbeyli TR 177 A9
Göcek TR 181 C9
Göçerler TR 173 B8
Goch D 16 E6
Gochsheim D 75 B7
Goczałkowice-Zdrój PL 147 B7
Göd H 150 B3
Godačica SRB 159 F6
Godal N 95 D11
Godalming GB 15 E7
Godby FIN 99 B13
Goddelau D 187 B6
Goddelsheim (Lichtenfels) D 21 B11
Godeanu RO 159 D10
Godech BG 165 C7
Godega di Sant'Urbano I 72 E5
Godegård S 92 B6
Godelleta E 48 F3
Godeni RO 160 C5
Goderville F 18 E1
Godiasco I 37 B10
Godimilje BIH 157 E11
Godinești RO 159 C10
Godinje MNE 163 E7
Godkowo PL 139 B8
Godmanchester GB 15 C8
Gödöllő H 150 B3
Godovič SLO 73 E9
Gödre H 149 D9
Godstone GB 15 E8
Goduš BIH 157 C10
Godziesze Wielkie PL 142 C5
Godziszów PL 144 B5
Goedereede NL 16 E1
Goes NL 16 E1
Göfritz an der Wild A 77 E8
Göggingen D 187 D8
Gogolin PL 142 F5
Gogołów PL 144 D4
Gogoșari RO 161 F7
Gogoșu RO 159 E10
Gogoșu RO 160 E2
Göhl D 83 B9
Gohor RO 153 E10
Gohrau D 79 C11
Göhrde D 83 D9
Göhren D 84 B5
Göhren-Lebbin D 83 D13
Goian MD 154 C4
Goicea RO 160 F3
Goiești RO 160 E3
Goirle NL 16 E4
Góis P 44 D4
Goito I 66 B2
Goizueta E 32 D2
Gojść PL 143 D7
Gökçealan TR 177 D9
Gökçebayır TR 171 E10
Gökçedağ TR 173 E10
Gökçeören TR 181 B9
Gökçeyazı TR 173 E8
Gokels D 82 B6
Gökova TR 181 B8
Göktepe TR 181 B9
Göktürk TR 173 B10
Gol N 101 E9
Gola HR 149 D8
Gołąb PL 141 H5
Golac SLO 67 A9
Golăiești RO 153 C11
Golaj AL 163 E9
Gołańcz PL 85 E12
Gołaszyn PL 141 G6
Golbey F 26 D5
Gölby FIN 99 B13
Gölcük TR 173 F8
Golčův Jeníkov CZ 77 C8
Golczewo PL 85 C7
Goldach CH 71 C8
Gołdap PL 136 E5
Goldbeck D 83 E11
Goldberg D 83 C12
Goldegg A 73 B7
Goldelund D 82 A6
Golden IRL 9 D7
Golden Pot GB 14 E7
Goldenstedt D 17 C10
Goleen IRL 8 F3
Golegã P 44 F4
Golemanovo BG 159 F9
Golema Rakovitsa BG 165 D8
Golema Rečica NMK 163 F10
Golenice PL 85 E7
Goleniów PL 85 C7
Golesh BG 161 F11
Golești RO 153 F10
Golești RO 160 C4
Golfo Aranci I 64 B4
Golina PL 142 B5
Golinhac F 33 A11
Gološeva LV 133 C3
Gölköy TR 177 E9
Gölle H 149 D10
Göllersdorf A 77 F10
Göllheim D 186 B5
Gollin D 83 C11
Göllin D 84 D5
Golling an der Salzach A 73 A7
Göllingen D 79 D9
Gollmitz D 84 D5
Golmes E 42 D5
Golnik SLO 73 D9
Gøløse DK 87 D10
Golovkino RUS 136 D3
Golpejas E 45 B9
Gols A 77 G11
Golspie GB 3 K9
Golßen D 80 C5
Golubac SRB 159 D8
Golub-Dobrzyń PL 138 D7
Golubić HR 156 D5
Golubinje SRB 159 D9
Golyama Zhelyazna BG 165 D9
Golyam Izvor BG 166 F5
Golyam Manastir BG 166 E6
Golyamo Belovo BG 165 E8
Gölyazı TR 173 D10
Gołymin-Ośrodek PL 139 E10
Golzow D 79 B12
Gomadingen D 27 D11
Gómara E 41 E7
Gomaringen D 187 E7
Gomati GR 169 D10
Gomba H 150 C4
Gömeç TR 173 F6
Gomecello E 45 B9
Gomes Aires P 50 D3
Gomirje HR 67 B11
Gommern D 79 B10
Gomotartsi BG 159 E10
Gomunice PL 143 D7
Gönc H 145 G3
Gonçalo P 44 D6
Goncelin F 31 E8
Gondelsheim D 187 C6
Gondershausen D 185 D7
Gondomar E 38 D2
Gondomar P 44 B3
Gondorf D 21 D8
Gondrecourt-le-Château F 26 C4
Gondreville F 26 C4
Gondrin F 33 C6
Gönen TR 173 D8
Gonfaron F 36 E4
Gonfreville-l'Orcher F 18 E1
Goni I 64 D3
Goniądz PL 140 D7
Gonnesa I 64 E1
Gonnoi GR 169 E7
Gonnosfanadiga I 64 E2
Gonnosnò I 64 D2
Gonsans F 26 F5
Gönyű H 149 A9
Gonzaga I 66 C2
Goodwick GB 12 A5
Goole GB 11 D10
Goonhavern GB 12 E4
Goor NL 17 D7
Gopegi E 40 C6
Göppingen D 74 E6
Gor E 55 E7
Góra PL 81 C11
Góra PL 139 E9
Gorafe E 55 E6
Goraj PL 144 B6
Góra Kalwaria PL 141 G4
Goranu RO 160 C4
Góra Puławska PL 141 H5
Gorawino PL 85 C8
Goražde BIH 157 E10
Gorban RO 153 D12
Görbeháza H 151 B7
Görcsöny H 149 E10
Gördalen S 102 C3
Gordaliza del Pino E 39 D9
Gordes F 35 C9
Gordinești MD 153 A10
Gørding DK 86 E3
Gordola CH 69 A6
Gordon GB 5 D11
Gordona I 69 A7
Gorebridge GB 5 D10
Görece TR 177 C9
Gorenja Straža SLO 73 E11
Gorenja vas SLO 73 D9
Gorey IRL 9 C10
Gőrgeteg H 149 D8
Gorgoglione I 60 C6
Gorgonzola I 69 B7
Gorgota RO 161 D8
Gorgova RO 155 C4
Gorica BIH 157 D7
Gorica BIH 157 F7
Gorica BIH 162 D5
Gorica MNE 163 E7
Goričan HR 149 D7
Gorinchem NL 16 E3
Gorino I 66 C5
Gorishovë AL 168 C2
Görisried D 71 B11
Goritsa BG 167 D9
Goritsa BG 167 D9
Göritz D 84 D5
Gorizia I 73 E8
Gorleben D 83 D10
Gørlev DK 87 D8
Gorlice PL 144 D3
Görlitz D 81 D7
Gorlosen D 83 D10
Gormanston IRL 7 E10
Gormanstown IRL 7 E10
Gormaz E 40 E6
Görmin D 84 C4
Gorna Belica NMK 164 F3
Gorna Beshovitsa BG 165 C8
Gorna Breznitsa BG 165 F7
Gorna Koznitsa BG 165 E6
Gorna Kremena BG 165 C8
Gorna Mitropoliya BG 165 C9
Gorna Oryakhovitsa BG 166 C5
Gorna Studena BG 166 C4
Gornau D 80 E4
Gorna Vasilitsa BG 165 E8
Gorna Verenitsa BG 165 C7
Gornești RO 152 D5
Gornet RO 161 C8
Gornet-Cricov RO 161 C8
Gorni Dŭbnik BG 165 C9
Gorni Lom BG 165 C6
Gornja Golubinja BIH 157 D8
Gornja Grabovica BIH 157 E8
Gornja Gračenica HR 149 E7
Gornja Ljubata SRB 164 D5
Gornja Ljuta BIH 157 E9
Gornjane SRB 159 E9
Gornja Ploča HR 156 D4
Gornja Radgona SLO 148 C5
Gornja Sanica BIH 157 C6
Gornja Slatina BIH 157 C9
Gornja Toponica SRB 164 C4
Gornja Trnava SRB 159 E6
Gornja Tuzla BIH 157 C10
Gornje Jelenje HR 67 B10
Gornje Peulje BIH 156 D5
Gornje Ratkovo BIH 157 C6
Gornje Vratno HR 148 D6
Gornji Agići BIH 156 C5
Gornji Babin Potok HR 156 C4
Gornji Breg SRB 150 F5
Gornji Dolac HR 157 E6
Gornji Grad SLO 73 D10
Gornji Humac HR 157 F6
Gornji Kosinj HR 156 C3
Gornji Lapac HR 156 C5
Gornji Lukavac BIH 157 F9
Gornji Majkovi HR 162 D4
Gornji Malovan BIH 157 E7
Gornji Matejevac SRB 164 C4
Gornji Milanovac SRB 158 E5
Gornji Očauš BIH 157 C8
Gornji Podgradći BIH 157 B7
Gornji Rajić HR 157 B7
Gornji Ribnik BIH 157 D6
Gornji Tkalec HR 149 E6
Gornji Vakuf BIH 157 E8
Górno PL 143 E10
Gorno Ablanovo BG 161 F7
Gorno Aleksandrovo BG 167 D7
Gorno Orizari NMK 164 F4
Gorno Ozirovo BG 165 C7
Gorno Pavlikene BG 165 C10
Goro I 66 C5
Gorobinci NMK 164 F4
Górowo Iławeckie PL 136 E2
Gorredijk NL 16 B6
Gorreto I 37 B10
Gorron F 23 D10
Görsbach D 79 D8
Gorseinon GB 12 B6
Górsk PL 138 D5
Gorska Polyana BG 167 E7
Gorski Izvor BG 166 E4
Gorsko Novo Selo BG 166 C5
Gorssel NL 16 D6
Gort IRL 6 F5
Gortahork IRL 6 B6
Gort an Choirce IRL 6 B6
Gortavoy Bridge GB 7 C9
Gorteen IRL 6 E5
Gorteen IRL 6 E6
Gorteeny IRL 6 F6
Gortin GB 4 F2
Goruia RO 159 C8
Görükle TR 173 D10
Gorun BG 167 B10
Görvik S 106 D9
Görwihl D 27 E9
Gorxheimertal D 21 E11
Gorzanów PL 77 B11
Gorze F 26 B5
Görzig D 79 C10
Görzke D 79 B11
Gorzkowice PL 143 D8
Gorzków-Osada PL 144 B7
Górzna PL 85 D11
Górzno PL 139 D8
Górzno PL 141 G5
Gorzów Śląski PL 142 D5
Gorzów Wielkopolski PL 85 E8
Górzyca PL 81 B7
Górzyca PL 85 C8
Gorzyce PL 144 B4
Gorzyce PL 144 C6
Gorzyce PL 146 B6
Gorzyń PL 81 A9
Górzyn PL 81 C7
Gosaldo I 72 D4
Gosau A 73 A8
Gosberton GB 11 F11
Gościeradów Ukazowy PL 144 B4
Gościm PL 85 E9
Gościno PL 85 B9
Gósciszów PL 81 D8
Gosdorf A 148 C5
Gosë AL 168 B2
Gosfield GB 15 D10
Gosforth GB 5 E13
Gosforth GB 10 C5
Goslar D 79 C7
Goślice PL 139 E8
Gosné F 23 D9
Gospić HR 156 C3
Gospođinci SRB 158 C4
Gosport GB 13 D12
Gössäter S 91 B13
Gossau CH 27 F11
Gössendorf A 148 C5
Gößl A 73 A8
Gostavățu RO 160 E5
Gostil AL 163 E9
Gostilitsa BG 166 C4
Gostinari RO 161 E8
Gostinu RO 161 E8
Gostivar NMK 163 F10
Göstling an der Ybbs A 73 A10
Gostovići BIH 157 D9
Gostycyn PL 138 D4
Gostyń PL 81 C12
Gostyń PL 85 B7
Gostynin PL 139 F7
Goszcz PL 142 D3
Goszczanów PL 142 C6
Goszczyn PL 141 G3
Göta S 91 C11
Göteborg S 91 D10
Götene S 91 B13
Gotești MD 154 E2
Gotha D 79 E8
Gothem S 93 D13
Götlunda S 97 D14
Gotse Delchev BG 169 A10
Gottböle FIN 122 F6
Götteszell D 76 E3
Gottfrieding D 75 E12
Göttingen D 78 C6
Gottmadingen D 27 E10
Gottne S 107 E14
Gøttrup DK 86 A4
Götzis A 71 C9
Gouarec F 22 D5
Gouda NL 16 D3
Goudswaard NL 182 B4
Gouesnou F 22 D3
Gouhenans F 26 E5
Goult F 35 C9
Goumenissa GR 169 C7
Goumois F 27 F6
Gourdan-Polignan F 33 D7
Gourdon F 29 F8
Gourdon GB 5 B12
Gourette F 32 E5
Gourgançon F 25 C11
Gouria GR 174 C3
Gourin F 22 D4
Gournay-en-Bray F 18 F4
Goussainville F 25 B7
Gout-Rossignol F 29 E6
Gouveia P 44 D5
Gouvia GR 168 E2
Gouvy B 20 D5
Gouzon F 29 C10
Gove P 44 B4
Goveđari HR 162 D3
Govedartsi BG 165 E7
Goven F 23 D8
Gowarczów PL 141 H2
Gowidlino PL 138 B4
Goworowo PL 139 E12
Gowran IRL 9 C8
Goxhill GB 11 D11
Göynükbelen TR 173 E11
Gözd PL 141 H4
Gozdnica PL 81 D8
Gozdowice PL 84 E6
Gözsüz TR 173 C6
Gozzano I 68 B5
Graal-Müritz D 83 B12
Grab BIH 157 F10
Grab BIH 162 D5
Graben-Neudorf D 187 C5
Grabica PL 143 D8
Grabjan AL 168 C2
Gråbo S 91 D11
Grabovac HR 157 F7
Grabovci SRB 158 D4
Grabovica SRB 159 E10
Grabow D 83 D11
Grabów PL 143 B7
Grabowiec PL 143 D11
Grabowiec PL 144 B8
Grabówka PL 140 D8
Grabów nad Pilicą PL 141 G4
Grabów nad Prosną PL 142 C5
Grabownica Starzeńska PL 144 D5
Grabowno PL 85 D12
Grabowno Wielkie PL 142 D3
Grabowo PL 136 E5
Grabowo PL 139 D13
Grabs CH 71 C8
Gračac HR 156 D4
Gračanica BIH 157 C9
Gračanica BIH 157 D10
Gračanica BIH 157 E8
Graçay F 24 F6
Grâce-Hollogne B 19 C11
Grâces F 22 C5
Graçianica BIH 157 E8
Gracze PL 142 E4
Grad SLO 148 C6
Gradac BIH 162 D5
Gradac HR 157 F7
Gradac SLO 148 E4
Gradačac BIH 157 C9
Gradara I 67 E6
Gräddö S 99 C12
Gradec HR 149 E6
Gradec NMK 169 B7
Gradefes E 39 C9
Gradets BG 159 E10
Gradets BG 167 D7
Gradevo BG 165 F7
Gradina BG 166 C5
Gradina BG 166 E4
Gradina BIH 157 F9
Gradina SRB 163 C9
Grădinari RO 159 C8
Grădinari RO 160 D4
Grădinița MD 154 D5
Gradishte BG 166 C4
Gradište HR 157 B10
Gradište SRB 164 B5
Gradište SRB 164 C5
Grădiștea RO 160 D3
Grădiștea RO 161 C10
Grădiștea RO 161 D8
Grădiștea RO 161 E10
Gradište Bekteško HR 149 F9
Gradnitsa BG 165 D10
Grado E 39 B7
Grado I 73 E7
Gradö S 97 B15
Gradojević SRB 158 D4
Gradoli I 62 B1
Gradsko NMK 169 A6
Gradskovo SRB 159 E9
Graena E 55 E6
Græsted DK 87 C10
Gräfelfing D 75 F9
Grafenau D 76 E4
Gräfenberg D 75 C9
Gräfendorf D 74 B6
Grafendorf bei Hartberg A 148 B5
Gräfenhainichen D 79 C11
Grafenhausen D 27 E9
Grafenrheinfeld D 187 B9
Gräfenroda D 79 E8
Grafenstein A 73 C9
Grafenwöhr D 75 C10
Grafenworth A 77 F9
Graffignano I 62 B2
Grafhorst D 79 B8
Graf Ignatievo BG 165 E10
Gräfinau-Angstedt D 79 E9
Grafing bei München D 75 F10
Grafrath D 75 F9
Gräfsnäs S 91 C11
Gräftåvallen S 105 E15
Gragnano I 60 B3
Grahovac MNE 163 D6
Grahovo MNE 163 D6
Grahovo SLO 73 D8
Gráig na Manach IRL 9 C9
Graigue IRL 9 C9
Graiguenamanagh IRL 9 C9
Grain GB 15 E10
Grainau D 71 C12
Grainet D 76 E5
Graissac F 30 F2
Graissessac F 34 C5
Graja de Iniesta E 47 E9
Grajal de Campos E 39 D9
Grajduri RO 153 D11
Grajewo PL 140 C6
Grällsta S 98 C7
Grålum N 95 D14
Gram DK 86 E4
Gramada BG 159 F10
Gramastettan A 76 F6
Gramat F 29 F9
Gramatikovo BG 167 E9
Grambow D 84 D6
Grămești RO 153 B8
Gramkow D 83 C10
Grammatiko GR 169 F7
Grammendorf D 83 B13
Grammenitsa GR 174 A2
Grammeno GR 168 E4
Grammichele I 59 E6
Gramsbergen NL 17 C7
Gramsh AL 168 C3
Gramzda LV 134 D3
Gramzow D 84 D6
Gran N 95 B13
Granabeg IRL 7 F10
Granada E 53 B9
Granån S 119 C10
Granard IRL 7 E8
Granarolo dell'Emilia I 66 C3
Granåsen S 107 C11
Granátula de Calatrava E 54 B5
Granberg S 118 D3
Granberget N 102 D3
Granbergsdal S 97 D12
Granbergsträsk S 107 A17
Grančarevo BIH 162 D5
Grancey-le-Château-Nouvelle F 26 E3
Grandas E 39 B6
Grandcamp-Maisy F 23 B9
Grand-Champ F 22 E6
Grand-Couronne F 18 F3
Grande-Synthe F 18 B5
Grande-Vabre F 33 A10
Grand-Fort-Philippe F 18 B5
Grand-Fougeray F 23 E8
Grándola P 50 C2
Grandpré F 19 F10
Grandpuits-Bailly-Carrois F 25 C8
Grandrieu F 30 F4
Grandris F 30 C5
Grandson CH 31 B10
Grandtully GB 5 B9
Grandvelle-et-le-Perrenot F 26 E5
Grandvillars F 27 E6
Grandvillers F 26 D6
Grandvilliers F 18 E4
Grañén E 41 E11
Grangärde S 97 B12
Grange IRL 7 E10
Grange IRL 9 E7
Grangemouth GB 5 C9
Grange-over-Sands GB 10 C6
Grängesberg S 97 B13
Granges-sur-Vologne F 27 D6
Grängshyttan S 97 C12
Grängsjö S 103 B13
Granhult S 116 D7
Granica BIH 162 D5
Grăniceri RO 151 D7
Grănicești RO 153 B8
Graninge S 107 E11
Granitola-Torretta I 58 D2
Granitsa GR 174 A4
Granja P 51 C5
Granja de Moreruela E 39 E8
Granja de Torrehermosa E 51 C8
Granja do Ulmeiro P 44 D3
Gränna S 92 C4
Grannäs S 107 A10
Grannäs S 109 E13
Granneset N 108 E6
Granö S 107 C16
Granollers E 43 D8
Granön S 103 D13
Granowiec PL 142 D4
Granowo PL 81 B11
Granschütz D 79 D11
Gransee D 84 D4
Granselet S 109 E14
Gränsgård S 109 F15
Gransjö S 107 A15
Gransjön S 103 B11
Gränssjö S 108 F8
Grantham GB 11 F10
Grantown-on-Spey GB 3 L9
Granträsk S 107 C14
Granträskmark S 118 D6
Grantshouse GB 5 D12
Granum S 88 C7
Granvik S 92 B5
Granville F 23 C8
Granvin N 94 A5
Grapska BIH 157 C9
Gräs S 97 C10
Grasbakken N 114 C5
Gräsgård S 89 C11
Grasleben D 79 B9
Gräsmarken S 97 B8
Grasmere GB 10 C5
Gräsmyr S 107 D17
Grassåmoen N 105 C14
Grassano I 60 B6
Grassau D 72 A5
Grasse F 36 D5
Grassington GB 11 C8
Gråssjö S 103 A10
Gråsten DK 86 F5
Grästorp S 91 C11
Gratallops E 42 E5
Gratangsbotn N 111 C14
Gratens F 33 D8
Gratia RO 161 E6
Gratini GR 171 B9
Gratkorn A 148 B4
Grätnäs S 107 E14
Gråträsk S 118 D3
Gratteri I 58 D4
Gratwein A 148 B4
Graulhet F 33 C9
Graupa D 80 D5
Graus E 42 C4
Grávalos E 41 D8
Gravberget N 102 E3
Gravbränna S 106 D7
Gravdal N 110 D6
Grave NL 16 E5
Gravedona I 69 A7
Gravelines F 18 C5
Gravellona Toce I 68 B5
Gravelotte F 26 B5
Gravens DK 86 D4
Grävenwiesbach D 21 D10
Grăveri LV 133 D2
Gravesend GB 15 E9
Gravia GR 174 B5
Gravigny F 24 B5
Gråvika N 100 E1
Gravina di Catania I 59 D7
Gravina in Puglia I 61 B6
Gravmark S 118 F4
Gray F 26 F4
Grayan-et-l'Hôpital F 28 E3
Grays GB 15 E9
Graz A 148 B4
Grazalema E 53 C6
Grążawy PL 139 D8
Grazzanise I 60 A2
Grčak SRB 163 C10
Grdelica SRB 164 D5
Greaca RO 161 E8
Greåker N 95 D14
Gréalou F 33 A9
Great Baddow GB 15 D10
Great Bircham GB 15 B10
Great Clifton GB 5 F10
Great Cornard GB 15 C10
Great Dunmow GB 15 D9
Great Glen GB 11 F9
Great Gonerby GB 11 F10
Greatham GB 11 B9
Great Harwood GB 11 D7
Great Haywood GB 11 F8
Great Linford GB 15 C7
Great Malvern GB 13 A10
Great Ponton GB 11 F10
Great Salkeld GB 5 F11
Great Shelford GB 15 C9
Great Torrington GB 12 D6
Great Wakering GB 15 D10
Great Yarmouth GB 15 B12
Grebănu RO 161 C9
Grebaštica HR 156 E4
Grebbestad S 91 B9
Grebci BIH 162 D5
Grebenac SRB 159 D7
Grebendorf (Meinhard) D 79 D7
Grebenhain D 21 D12
Grebenișu de Câmpie RO 152 D4
Grebenstein D 21 B12
Grebin D 83 B8
Grębków PL 141 F5
Grebo S 92 C7
Grjbocin PL 138 D6
Grjboszów PL 143 F10
Grjbów PL 144 B4
Greccio I 62 C3
Grecești RO 160 E2
Greci I 60 A4
Greci RO 159 D11
Gredelj BIH 157 F10
Greding D 75 D9
Gredstedbro DK 86 E3
Greencastle GB 4 F2
Greencastle GB 7 D10
Greencastle IRL 4 E3
Greene D 78 C6
Greengairs GB 5 D9
Greenhead GB 5 F11
Greenigo GB 3 H10
Greenisland GB 4 F5
Greenlaw GB 5 D12
Greenloaning GB 5 C9
Greenock GB 4 D7
Greenodd GB 10 C5
Greenore IRL 7 D10
Greenway GB 12 B5
Greggio I 68 C5
Greifenburg A 73 C7
Greifendorf D 80 D4
Greifenstein D 21 C10
Greiffenberg D 84 D5
Greifswald D 84 B4
Grein A 77 F7

Greiveri LV 135 B11
Greiz D 79 E11
Grejs DK 86 D5
Gremersdorf D 83 B9
Grenaa DK 87 C7
Grenade F 33 C8
Grenade-sur-l'Adour F 32 C5
Grenant F 26 E4
Grenås S 106 D8
Grenchen CH 27 F7
Grenči LV 134 C5
Grenoble F 31 E8
Grense-Jakobselv N 114 D9
Gréoux-les-Bains F 35 C10
Gresenhorst D 83 B12
Gress GB 2 J4
Gressan I 31 D11
Gresse D 83 D9
Gressoney-la-Trinite I 68 B4
Gressvik N 91 A8
Gresten A 77 G8
Grésy-sur-Aix F 31 D8
Grésy-sur-Isère F 31 D9
Gretna GB 5 F10
Greußen D 79 D8
Greux F 26 D4
Grevbäck S 92 C4
Greve in Chianti I 66 E3
Greven D 17 D9
Greven D 83 D9
Grevena GR 168 D5
Grevenbicht NL 183 C7
Grevenbroich D 21 B7
Greveniti GR 168 E5
Grevenmacher L 20 E6
Grevesmühlen D 83 C10
Greve Strand DK 87 D10
Grevie S 87 C11
Grevinge DK 87 D9
Greyabbey GB 7 C11
Greystoke GB 5 F11
Greystones IRL 7 F10
Grez-Doiceau B 19 C10
Grez-en-Bouère F 23 E10
Grgar SLO 73 D8
Grgurevci SRB 158 C4
Griegos E 47 D9
Gries F 27 C8
Gries am Brenner A 72 B3
Griesbach D 27 D9
Griesheim D 21 E11
Grieskirchen A 76 F5
Grießen D 81 C7
Griesstätt D 75 G11
Griffen A 73 C10
Grigiškės LT 137 D11
Grignan F 35 B8
Grigno I 72 D4
Grignols F 32 B5
Grigny F 30 D6
Grigoriopol MD 154 C4
Grijota E 40 D2
Grijpskerk NL 16 B6
Grillby S 98 C8
Grillon F 35 B8
Grimaldi I 60 E6
Grimaud F 36 E5
Grimbergen B 19 C9
Grimma D 79 D12
Grimmen D 84 B4
Grimoldby GB 11 E12
Grimsås S 91 E14
Grimsbu N 101 B12
Grimsby GB 11 D11
Grimslöv S 88 B7
Grimstad N 90 C4
Grimston GB 11 F13
Grimstorp S 92 D5
Grimstrup DK 86 D3
Grindafjord N 94 D2
Grindaheim N 101 D9
Grindal N 101 A11
Grindelwald CH 70 D6
Grinder N 96 B7
Grindjord N 111 D13
Grindsted DK 86 A6
Grindsted DK 86 D3
Grindu RO 161 D9
Grinkiškis LT 134 E7
Griñón E 46 D5
Grins A 71 C11
Grinsbol S 97 D8
Grinţieş RO 153 C7
Gripenberg S 92 D5
Grisén E 41 E9
Griškabūdis LT 136 D7
Grisolia I 60 D5
Grisolles F 33 C8
Grisslehamn S 99 B11
Gritley GB 3 H11
Griviţa RO 153 E11
Griviţa RO 153 F11
Griviţa RO 161 D10
Grivitsa BG 165 C10
Grkinja SRB 164 C4
Grljan SRB 159 F9
Grnčari NMK 168 B5
Grobbendonk B 19 B10
Gröbenzell D 75 F9
Grobiņa LV 134 C2
Gröbming A 73 B8
Gröbzig D 79 C10
Grocka SRB 158 D6
Grödby S 93 A11
Gródek PL 140 D9
Gródek nad Dunajcem PL 144 D2
Gröden D 80 D5
Grödig A 73 A7
Gröditz D 80 D4
Gródki PL 139 D9
Grodków PL 142 E3
Grodziczno PL 139 D8
Grodziec PL 142 B5
Grodzisk PL 141 E7
Grodzisk Mazowiecki PL 141 F3
Grodzisk Wielkopolski PL 81 B10
Groenlo NL 17 D7
Groesbeek NL 183 B7
Grohnde (Emmerthal) D 78 B5
Groitzsch D 79 D11
Groix F 22 E5
Grojdibodu RO 160 F4
Grójec PL 141 G3
Grom PL 139 C10
Gromadka PL 81 D9
Grömitz D 83 B9
Gromnik PL 144 D2
Gromo I 69 B8
Gronau (Westfalen) D 17 D8
Grønbjerg DK 86 C3
Grönbo S 118 D5
Gröndal S 108 E8
Grong N 105 C12
Grönhögen S 89 C10
Grønhøj DK 86 C4
Gröningen D 79 C9
Groningen NL 17 B7
Grønnemose DK 86 E6
Grønnes N 100 A6
Grønning N 110 E9
Grønningen N 104 D7
Gronowo PL 139 B7
Grönsinka S 98 B7
Grönskåra S 89 A9
Grönsta S 103 A11
Grønvik N 94 D4
Grönviken S 103 A9
Grönviken S 103 D12
Groomsport GB 4 F5
Grootegast NL 16 B6
Gropello Cairoli I 69 C6
Gropeni RO 155 C1
Gropniţa RO 153 C10
Grorud N 95 D11
Groscavallo I 31 E11
Groşi RO 152 B3
Grosio I 69 A9
Grošnica SRB 159 F6
Grosotto I 69 A9
Großaitingen D 71 A11
Groß Ammensleben D 79 B10
Großarl A 73 B7
Groß-Bieberau D 21 E11
Groß Börnecke D 79 C9
Großbothen D 79 D12
Großbottwar D 27 C11
Großbreitenbach D 79 E9
Großburgwedel (Burgwedel) D 78 B6
Groß Dölln D 84 E5
Grosselfingen D 27 D10
Großenaspe D 83 C7
Großenbrode D 83 B10
Großenehrich D 79 D8
Groß Engersdorf A 77 F11
Großengottern D 79 D8
Großenhain D 80 D5
Großenkneten D 17 C10
Großenlüder D 78 E6
Großensee D 83 C8
Großenstein D 79 E11
Großenwiehe D 82 A6
Groß-Enzersdorf A 77 F11
Grosseto I 65 B4
Grosseto-Prugna F 37 H9
Groß Fredenwalde D 84 D5
Großfurra D 79 D8
Groß-Gerau D 21 E10
Groß-Gerungs A 77 E7
Groß Glienicke D 80 B4
Großgmain D 73 A6
Groß Grönau D 83 C9
Großhabersdorf D 75 D8
Großhansdorf D 83 C8
Großharras A 77 E10
Großhartmannsdorf D 80 E4
Groß Heere (Heere) D 79 B7
Großhennersdorf D 81 E7
Groß-Hesepe D 17 C8
Großheubach D 187 B7
Grössjö S 107 F14
Großkarolinenfeld D 72 A5
Groß Kiesow D 84 B4
Großklein A 148 C4
Groß Köris D 80 B5
Groß Kreutz D 79 B12
Großkrut A 77 E11
Groß Lafferde (Lahstedt) D 79 B7
Großlangheim D 187 B9
Groß Leine D 80 B6
Groß Leuthen D 80 B6
Großlittgen D 21 D7
Großlohra D 79 D8
Großmaischeid D 185 C8
Großmehlen D 80 D5
Groß Miltzow D 84 C5
Groß Mohrdorf D 84 B3
Großmonra D 79 D9
Groß Naundorf D 80 C3
Großnaundorf D 80 D5
Groß Nemerow D 84 D4
Groß Oesingen D 79 A7
Großolbersdorf D 80 E4
Groß Oßnig D 80 C6
Großostheim D 21 E12
Großpetersdorf A 149 B6
Groß Plasten D 83 C13
Großraming A 73 A10
Großräschen D 80 C6
Großrinderfeld D 74 C6
Groß Roge D 83 C13
Groß-Rohrheim D 21 E10
Großröhrsdorf D 80 D6
Großrosseln D 186 C2
Großrudestedt D 79 D9
Großrußbach A 77 F10
Groß Sankt Florian A 148 C4
Groß Särchen D 80 D6
Großschirma D 80 E4
Großschönau A 77 E7
Groß Schönebeck D 84 E5
Groß Schwechten D 83 E11
Groß Schwülper (Schwülper) D 79 B7
Groß-Siegharts A 77 E8
Groß Stieten D 83 C10
Großthiemig D 80 D5
Großtreben D 80 C3
Groß Twülpstedt D 79 B8
Groß-Umstadt D 187 B6
Großwallstadt D 187 B7
Groß Warnow D 83 D11
Großweikersdorf A 77 F9
Groß Welle D 83 D12
Groß Wittensee D 82 B7
Groß Wokern D 83 C12
Großwudicke D 79 A11
Groß Wüstenfelde D 83 C13
Groß Ziethen D 84 E5
Groß-Zimmern D 187 B6
Grostenquin F 27 C6
Grosuplje SLO 73 E10
Grøtavær N 111 C11
Grotfjord N 111 A16
Grötholen S 102 C4
Grötingen S 103 A9
Grotli N 100 B7
Grötlingbo S 93 E12
Grøtnesdalen N 111 A18
Grottaferrata I 62 D3
Grottaglie I 61 B8
Grottaminarda I 60 A4
Grottammare I 62 B5
Grottazzolina I 62 A5
Grotte I 58 E4
Grotte di Castro I 62 B1
Grotteria I 59 C9
Grottole I 61 B6
Grou NL 16 B5
Grova N 90 A4
Grove GB 13 B12
Grövelsjön S 102 B3
Grovfjord N 111 C13
Grozd'ovo BG 167 C9
Grozeşti RO 153 D12
Grub am Forst D 75 B9
Grubbenvorst NL 183 C8
Grubbnäsudden S 119 B10
Grube D 83 B10
Grubišno Polje HR 149 E8
Gruczno PL 138 D5
Gruda HR 162 D5
Grude BIH 157 F7
Grudusk PL 139 D10
Grudziądz PL 138 D6
Gruey-lès-Surance F 26 D5
Grugliasco I 68 C4
Gruia RO 159 E10
Gruissan F 34 D5
Gruiu RO 161 D8
Grullos E 39 B7
Grumăzeşti RO 153 C8
Grumbach D 80 D5
Grumo Appula I 61 A7
Grums S 97 D9
Grünau A 73 A8
Grünau A 77 F9
Grünberg D 21 C11
Grünburg A 76 G6
Grundagssätern S 102 B4
Grundfors S 106 A8
Grundfors S 107 B13
Grundforsen S 102 D4
Grundsanden S 118 B5
Grundsel S 118 C4
Grundsjö S 107 C11
Grundsuna S 107 E16
Grundsund S 91 C9
Grundtjärn S 107 D12
Grundträsk S 107 A16
Grundträsk S 109 F17
Grundträsk S 118 B7
Grundvattnet S 118 C4
Grünendeich D 82 C7
Grünewald D 80 D5
Grünewalde D 80 C5
Grungebru N 94 C7
Grünheide D 80 B5
Grünkraut D 71 B9
Grunnfarnes N 111 B12
Grunnfjord N 112 C4
Grunnførfjord N 110 D8
Grunow D 80 B6
Grünsfeld D 74 C6
Grünstadt D 21 E10
Grünwald D 75 F10
Grupčin NMK 164 F3
Grury F 30 B4
Grūšlaukė LT 134 D2
Grußendorf (Sassenburg) D 79 A8
Gruta PL 138 D6
Gruvberget S 103 D11
Gruyères CH 31 B11
Gruža SRB 159 F6
Grūžai LT 135 D8
Gruzdžiai LT 134 D6
Grybów PL 145 D2
Grycksbo S 103 E9
Gryfice PL 85 C8
Gryfino PL 84 D6
Gryfów Śląski PL 81 D8
Grygov CZ 146 B4
Grylewo PL 85 E12
Gryllefjord N 111 B13
Grynberget S 107 C11
Gryt S 93 C9
Grytan S 106 E7
Grytgöl S 92 B7
Grythyttan S 97 C12
Gryts bruk S 92 B6
Grytsjö S 106 A9
Gryttjom S 99 B8
Gryżliny PL 139 C9
Grzebienisko PL 81 B11
Grzmiąca PL 85 C10
Grzybno PL 84 D7
Grzybno PL 138 D5
Grzymiszew PL 142 B5
Grzywna PL 138 D6
Gschnitz A 72 B3
Gschwandt A 73 A8
Gschwend D 74 E6
Gstaad CH 31 C11
Gsteig CH 31 C11
Guadahortuna E 53 A10
Guadajoz E 51 D8
Guadalajara E 47 C6
Guadalaviar E 47 D9
Guadalcanal E 51 C8
Guadalcázar E 53 A7
Guadalest E 56 D4
Guadalmez E 54 B3
Guadarrama E 46 C4
Guadassuar E 48 F4
Guadix E 55 E6
Guaire IRL 9 C10
Guájar-Faraguit E 53 C9
Gualäv S 88 C6
Gualdo Cattaneo I 62 B3
Gualdo Tadino I 67 F6
Gualtieri I 66 C2
Guarcino I 62 D4
Guarda P 45 C6
Guardamar del Segura E 56 E3
Guardavalle I 59 B9
Guardea I 62 B2
Guardiagrele I 63 C6
Guardia Lombardi I 60 B4
Guardia Perticara I 60 C6
Guardia Piemontese I 60 E6
Guardia Sanframondi I 60 A3
Guardias Viejas E 55 F7
Guardiola de Berguedà E 43 C7
Guardo E 39 C10
Guardramiro E 45 B8
Guareña E 51 B7
Guaro E 53 C7
Guarromán E 54 C5
Guasila I 64 D3
Guastalla I 66 C2
Gubaveeny IRL 7 D7
Gubbhögen S 106 C9
Gubbio I 66 F6
Gubbträsk S 107 A13
Guben D 81 C7
Gübene BG 166 D4
Gubin PL 81 C7
Guča SRB 158 F5
Guča Gora BIH 157 D8
Gudar E 48 D3
Gudavac BIH 156 C5
Gudbjerg DK 86 E7
Gudenieki LV 134 C3
Guderup DK 86 F5
Gudhem S 91 C14
Gudhjem DK 89 E7
Gudiena LT 137 D9
Gudinge S 99 A9
Gudme DK 87 E7
Gudmont-Villiers F 26 D3
Gudow D 83 C9
Gudum DK 86 B2
Gudumholm DK 86 B6
Gudvangen N 100 E5
Gudžiūnai LT 134 E7
Guebwiller F 27 E7
Guégon F 22 E6
Güéjar-Sierra E 53 B10
Guémar F 27 D7
Guémené-Penfao F 23 E8
Guémené-sur-Scorff F 22 D5
Guénange F 20 F6
Güeñes E 40 B5
Guenrouet F 23 E8
Guer F 23 E7
Guérande F 22 F7
Guéret F 29 C9
Guérigny F 25 F9
Guerri de la Sal E 33 F8
Güesa E 32 E3
Gueugnon F 30 B5
Gugeşti RO 161 B10
Güglingen D 27 B10
Guglionesi I 63 D7
Gugutka BG 171 B9
Gühlen-Glienicke D 83 D13
Guia P 44 E3
Guia P 50 E3
Guichen F 23 E8
Guidel F 22 E5
Guide Post GB 5 E13
Guidizzolo I 66 B2
Guidonia-Montecelio I 62 D3
Guiglia I 66 D2
Guignen F 23 E8
Guignes F 25 C8
Guignicourt F 19 F8
Guijo de Coria E 45 D8
Guijo de Galisteo E 45 D8
Guijo de Granadilla E 45 D8
Guijuelo E 45 C9
Guildford GB 15 E7
Guilers F 22 D2
Guilherand F 30 F6
Guilhofrei P 38 E3
Guilhovai P 44 C3
Guillaumes F 36 C5
Guillena E 51 D7
Guillestre F 36 B5
Guilliers F 22 D7
Guillon F 25 E11
Guillos F 32 A4
Guilvinec F 22 E3
Guimarães P 38 F3
Guînes F 15 F12
Guingamp F 22 C5
Guipavas F 22 D3
Guipry F 23 E8
Guisando E 45 D10
Guisborough GB 11 B9
Guiscard F 19 E7
Guise F 19 E8
Guisseny F 22 C3
Guissona E 42 D6
Guist GB 15 B10
Guitiriz E 38 B4
Guîtres F 28 E5
Gujan-Mestras F 32 A3
Gulács H 145 G5
Gülbahçe TR 177 C8
Gulbene LV 135 B13
Guldager DK 86 D2
Guldborg DK 84 A1
Gulgamme N 113 B16
Gulianca RO 161 C11
Gülitz D 83 D11
Gullabo S 89 C9
Gullane GB 5 C11
Gullberg S 103 D10
Gullbrå N 100 E4
Gullbrandstorp S 87 B11
Gullbranna S 87 B11
Gulleråsen S 103 D9
Gullholmen N 111 C10
Gullön S 109 E15
Gullringen S 92 D7
Gullspång S 91 B15
Gullträsk S 118 B6
Güllübahçe TR 177 D9
Güllüce TR 173 D9
Güllük TR 177 E10
Gullverket N 95 B14
Gulpen NL 183 D7
Gülpinar TR 171 E10
Gulsele S 107 D12
Gulsvik N 95 B11
Gültz D 84 C4
Gülübintsi BG 166 E6
Gülübovo BG 165 E10
Gülübovo BG 166 E5
Gulyantsi BG 160 F5
Gülzow D 83 C12
Gumhöjden S 97 B10
Gumiel de Hizán E 40 E4
Gumiel de Mercado E 40 E4
Gummark S 118 E5
Gummersbach D 21 B9
Gumpelstadt D 79 E7
Gumtow D 83 E12
Gümüşçay TR 173 D7
Gümüşsuyu TR 177 C9
Gümüşyaka TR 173 B9
Gümzovo BG 159 E10
Gunaroš SRB 150 F4
Gundelfingen D 27 D8
Gundelfingen an der Donau D 75 E7
Gundelsheim D 21 F12
Gundershoffen F 27 C8
Gundinci HR 157 B9
Gündoğan TR 173 D8
Gündoğdu TR 173 D7
Gundsømagle DK 87 D10
Güneyli TR 172 D6
Güngörmez TR 173 B8
Gunja HR 157 C10
Gunnarn S 107 A13
Gunnarnes N 113 A13
Gunnarsbo S 103 C11
Gunnarsbyn S 118 B7
Gunnarskog S 97 C8
Gunnarvattnet S 105 C16
Gunnebo S 93 D9
Günstedt D 79 D9
Güntersberge D 79 C8
Guntersblum D 185 E9
Guntersdorf A 77 E10
Güntersleben D 187 B8
Guntramsdorf A 77 F10
Günzburg D 75 F7
Gunzenhausen D 75 D8
Gura-Bicului MD 154 D4
Gura Caliţei RO 161 B9
Gura Camencii MD 154 B2
Gura Foii RO 160 D6
Gura Galbenei MD 154 D3
Gurahonţ RO 151 E9
Gura Humorului RO 153 B7
Gura Ocniţei RO 161 D7
Gura Râului RO 152 F3
Gurasada RO 151 F10
Gura Şuţii RO 161 D7
Gura Teghii RO 161 C8
Gura Vadului RO 161 C8
Gura Văii RO 153 E9
Gura Vitioarei RO 161 C8
Gurbăneşti RO 161 E9
Gurghiu RO 152 D5
Guri i Bardhë AL 168 B3
Guri i Zi AL 163 E8
Gurk A 73 C9
Gurkovo BG 166 D5
Gurkovo BG 167 C10
Gŭrlyano BG 164 E6
Gurrea de Gállego E 41 D10
Gurrë e Madhe AL 168 A3
Gurteen IRL 6 E6
Gur'yevsk RUS 136 D2
Gusborn D 83 D10
Gušće HR 149 F7
Güsen D 79 B10
Gusev RUS 136 D5
Gusinje MNE 163 D8
Guşoeni RO 160 D4
Gusow D 80 A6
Guspini I 64 D2
Gussago I 69 B9
Gusselby S 97 C13
Güssing A 149 B6
Gussola I 66 B1
Gussvattnet S 105 C16
Gußwerk A 148 A4
Gustavsberg S 99 D10
Gustavsfors S 97 B10
Güsten D 79 C10
Gusterath D 21 E7
Güstrow D 83 C12
Gusum S 93 C8
Gutach (Schwarzwaldbahn) D 187 E5
Gutau A 77 F7
Gutcher GB 3 D14
Güterfelde D 80 B4
Güterglück D 79 C10
Gütersloh D 17 E10
Guthrie GB 5 B11
Gutorfölde H 149 C7
Gutow D 83 C12
Guttannen CH 70 D6
Guttaring A 73 C10
Gützkow D 84 C4
Guvåg N 110 C8
Güvemalani TR 173 D7
Güvercinlik TR 177 E10
Guxhagen D 78 D5
Güzelbahçe TR 177 C8
Güzelçamlı TR 177 D9
Gvardeysk RUS 136 D3
Gvarv N 95 D10
Gvozd HR 148 F5
Gvozd MNE 163 D7
Gvozdansko HR 156 B5
Gwda Wielka PL 85 C11
Gweedore IRL 6 B6
Gwithian GB 12 E4
Gy F 26 F4
Gyál H 150 C3
Gyarmat H 149 B8
Gyékényes H 149 D8
Gyenesdiás H 149 C8
Gyermely H 149 A11
Gyé-sur-Seine F 25 D11
Gyhum D 17 B12
Gyljen S 118 B9
Gylling DK 86 D6
Gymno GR 175 C8
Gyomaendrőd H 150 D6
Gyömöre H 149 A9
Gyömrő H 150 C3
Gyöngyös H 150 B4
Gyöngyöspata H 150 B4
Gyönk H 149 C10
Győr H 149 A9
Györköny H 149 C11
Győrság H 149 A9
Győrszemere H 149 A9
Győrtelek H 145 H5
Győrújbarát H 149 A9
Győrújfalu H 149 A9
Győrzámoly H 149 A9
Gyrstinge DK 87 E9
Gysinge S 98 B7
Gytheio GR 178 B4
Gyttorp S 97 C12
Gyueshevo BG 164 E5
Gyula H 151 D7
Gyulaháza H 145 G5
Gyulaj H 149 D10
Gyúró H 149 B11
Gzy PL 139 E10

H

Haabneeme EST 131 B9
Haacht B 19 C10
Häädemeeste EST 131 E8
Haaften NL 183 B6
Haag A 77 F7
Haag am Hausruck A 76 F5
Haag in Oberbayern D 75 F11
Haajainen FIN 124 C7
Haaksbergen NL 17 D7
Haaltert B 19 C9
Haanja EST 131 F14
Haapajärvi FIN 123 C14
Haapa-Kimola FIN 127 D15
Haapakoski FIN 123 E10
Haapakoski FIN 124 F8
Haapakumpu FIN 115 D3
Haapalahti FIN 113 E19
Haapaluoma FIN 123 E10
Haapamäki FIN 123 C16
Haapamäki FIN 123 E17
Haapamäki FIN 123 F12
Haapamäki FIN 125 E10
Haaparanta FIN 115 E3
Haapavesi FIN 119 F14
Haapsalu EST 130 D7
Haar D 75 F10
Haarajoki FIN 123 F17
Haarajoki FIN 127 E13
Haaraoja FIN 119 F16
Haarasaajo FIN 119 B12
Haarbach D 76 E4
Haarby DK 86 E6
Haaren NL 183 B6
Haarlem NL 16 D3
Haastrecht NL 16 E3
Haavisto FIN 127 D11
Habaja EST 131 C10
Habartov CZ 75 B12
Habas F 32 C4
Habay-la-Neuve B 19 E12
Häbbersliden S 118 E4
Habiller TR 167 F7
Hablingbo S 93 E12
Habo S 91 D15
Håbol S 91 B11
Habovka SK 147 C9
Habry CZ 77 C8
Habsheim F 27 E7
Hachenburg D 21 C9
Haciaslanlar TR 173 E7
Hacidanişment TR 167 F7
Hacigelen TR 172 D6
Haciköy TR 172 C6
Hacinas E 40 E5
Hacirahmanli TR 177 B10
Haciumur TR 167 F7
Hacivelioba TR 173 D8
Hackås S 102 A8
Hackenheim D 21 E9
Hacketstown IRL 9 C9
Hackleton GB 15 C7
Hacksjö S 107 B12
Hadamar D 21 D10
Hadanberg S 107 D14
Haddebo S 92 B6
Haddington GB 5 D11
Haddiscoe GB 15 B12
Haderslev DK 86 E4
Haderup DK 86 C3
Hadimköy TR 173 B10
Hadleigh GB 15 C10
Hadley GB 10 F7
Hadol F 26 D5
Hadres A 77 E10
Hadsel N 110 C8
Hadsten DK 86 C6
Hadsund DK 86 B6
Hadžići BIH 157 E9
Haelen NL 183 C7
Hafnerbach A 77 F8
Haftersbol S 97 C10
Haga S 98 B8
Haganj HR 149 E7
Hagaström S 103 E13
Hagby S 89 B10
Hagebyhöga S 92 C5
Hagen D 17 F8
Hagenbach D 187 C5
Hagenburg D 17 D12
Hagenow D 83 D10
Hagenwerder D 81 D7
Hageri EST 131 C9
Hägerstad S 92 C7
Hagetaubin F 32 C4
Hagetmau F 32 C4
Hagfors S 97 B10
Häggås S 107 C11
Häggdånger S 103 A14
Häggebäcken S 98 B6
Häggenås S 106 E7
Häggnäset S 105 C16
Häggsåsen S 105 E16
Häggsjön S 105 D13
Häggsjövik S 105 D16
Häghig RO 153 F7
Hagley GB 13 A9
Hagondange F 20 F6
Hagsta S 103 E13
Haguenau F 27 C8
Hahausen D 79 C7
Hahnbach D 75 C10
Hahnstätten D 185 D9
Hahót H 149 C7
Haibach D 21 E12
Haibach D 75 D12
Haidmühle D 76 E5
Haiger D 21 C10
Haigerloch D 27 D10
Häijää FIN 127 B9
Hailsham GB 15 F9
Hailuoto FIN 119 D13
Haiming D 76 F3
Haimoo FIN 127 E11
Haina D 75 B8
Haina (Kloster) D 21 B11
Hainburg an der Donau A 77 F11
Hainfeld A 77 F9
Hainichen D 80 E4
Haiterbach D 187 D6
Haitzendorf A 77 F9
Hajala FIN 127 E8
Hajdúböszörmény H 151 B8
Hajdúdorog H 151 B8
Hajdúhadház H 151 B8
Hajdúnánás H 145 H3
Hajdúsámson H 151 B8
Hajdúszoboszló H 151 C7
Hajdúszovát H 151 C7
Hajmáskér H 149 B10
Hajmel AL 163 F8
Hajnáčka SK 147 E9
Hajnoc RKS 164 D4
Hajnówka PL 141 E9
Hajós H 150 E3
Hakadal N 95 B13
Håkafot S 105 C16
Håkansvallen S 102 B7
Håkavik N 111 C14
Hakkas S 116 E7
Hakkenpää FIN 126 D6
Häkkilä FIN 123 E14
Hakokylä FIN 121 E12
Håkøybotn N 111 A16
Håksberg S 97 B13
Hakstabben N 112 C11
Håkvik N 111 D13
Halahora de Sus MD 153 A10
Håland N 94 C4
Halapić BIH 157 D6
Halászi H 146 F4
Halásztelek H 150 C2
Hălăuceşti RO 153 C9
Halbe D 80 B5
Halbenrain A 148 C5
Hålberg S 109 F18
Halberstadt D 79 C9
Halbjerg DK 90 E7
Halblech D 71 B11
Halbturn A 77 G11
Hălchiu RO 153 F7
Hald DK 86 B4
Hald DK 86 B6
Haldarsvik FO 2 A2
Hald Ege DK 86 C4
Halden N 91 A9
Haldensleben D 79 B9
Hale GB 11 E7
Halen B 183 D6
Halenkov CZ 146 C6
Halenkovice CZ 146 C4
Halesowen GB 13 A10
Halesworth GB 15 C12
Halfing D 72 A5
Halfway IRL 8 E5
Halfweg NL 16 D3
Halhjem N 94 B2
Halič SK 147 E9
Halifax GB 11 D8
Halikko FIN 127 E9
Halimba H 149 B9
Halitpaşa TR 177 B10
Haljala EST 131 C12
Häljarp S 87 D11
Halkia FIN 127 D13
Halkirk GB 3 H10
Halkivaha FIN 127 C9
Halkokumpu FIN 124 F7
Hall S 93 D13
Hälla S 107 D12
Halla-aho FIN 124 C9
Hallabro S 89 C8
Hällabrottet S 92 A6
Halla Heberg S 91 E10
Halland GB 15 F9
Hålland S 105 E14
Hallapuro FIN 123 D12
Hällaryd S 89 C7
Hällbacken S 105 E16
Hällbacken S 109 D12
Hällberga S 98 D7
Hällbo S 103 D11
Hallbodarna S 105 E15
Hällbybrunn S 98 D6
Halle B 19 C9
Halle D 78 C6
Halle NL 183 B8
Halle (Saale) D 79 D10
Halle (Westfalen) D 17 D10
Hällefors S 97 C12
Hälleforsnäs S 93 A9
Hallein A 73 A7
Hällekis S 91 B13
Hällen S 103 E14
Hallen S 105 E16
Hallenberg D 21 B11
Hallencourt F 18 E4
Halle-Neustadt D 79 D10
Hallerndorf D 75 C8
Hällesjö S 103 A11
Hällestad S 92 B7
Hällevadsholm S 91 B10
Hällevik S 88 C7
Hälleviksstrand S 91 C9
Hall-Häxåsen S 106 D8
Hallingby N 95 B12
Hallingeberg S 93 D8
Hällinmäki FIN 124 F9
Hall in Tirol A 72 B4
Hällnäs S 107 C17
Hällnäs S 109 D15
Hällnäs S 109 E13
Hallom S 102 A7
Hallow GB 13 A10
Hällsbäck S 97 D8
Hallsberg S 92 A6
Hällsjö S 107 E13
Hållsta S 98 D6
Hallstahammar S 98 C6
Hallstatt A 73 A8
Hallstavik S 99 B11
Halltorp S 89 C10
Halluin B 19 C7
Hallund DK 86 A6
Hällvik S 109 D14
Hallviken S 106 D8
Hallworthy GB 12 D5
Hălmăgel RO 151 E10
Hălmagiu RO 151 E10
Halmeu RO 145 H7
Halmstad S 87 B11
Halna S 92 B4
Halosenniemi FIN 119 D14
Halosenranta FIN 115 E2
Halovo SRB 159 F9
Hals DK 86 B6
Halsa N 104 E4
Halsenbach D 21 D9
Hal'shany BY 137 E13
Hälsingby FIN 122 D7
Hålsjö S 103 C12
Halsøy N 108 E5
Halsskov DK 87 E8
Halstead GB 15 D10
Halstenbek D 83 C7
Halsteren NL 16 E2
Halstroff F 20 F6
Halsua FIN 123 D12
Haltern D 17 E8
Halttula FIN 119 C14
Haltwhistle GB 5 F12
Haluna FIN 125 D10
Hälvä FIN 129 B11
Halvarsgårdarna S 97 B13
Halver D 21 B8
Halvrimmen DK 86 A5
Halwell GB 13 E7
Halže CZ 75 C12
Ham F 19 E7
Ham GB 3 E12
Hamar N 101 E14
Hamari FIN 119 C14
Hamarøy N 108 D5
Hamarøy N 111 D10
Hambach F 27 B7
Hambergen D 17 B11
Hamble-le-Rice GB 13 D12
Hambrücken D 21 F11
Hambühren D 79 A6
Hamburg D 83 C7
Hamburgsund S 91 B9
Hambye F 23 C9
Hamcearca RO 155 C2
Hamdibey TR 173 E7
Hämeenkoski FIN 127 C13

Hämeenkyrö FIN 127 B9
Hämeenlinna FIN 127 D11
Hämelhausen D 17 C12
Hameln D 17 D12
Hämerten D 79 A10
Hamica HR 148 E5
Hamidiye TR 167 F9
Hamidiye TR 172 B6
Hamilton GB 5 D8
Hamilton's Bawn GB 7 D9
Hamina FIN 128 D7
Haminalahti FIN 124 E9
Hamit TR 181 C9
Hamitabat TR 173 A7
Hamlagrø N 94 A4
Hamlot N 111 D10
Hamm D 17 E9
Hamm (Sieg) D 185 C8
Hammar S 92 B5
Hammarland FIN 99 B13
Hammarn S 97 C12
Hammarnäs S 105 E16
Hammarsbyn S 102 E5
Hammarstrand S 107 E10
Hammarvika N 104 D5
Hamme B 19 B9
Hammel DK 86 C5
Hammelburg D 74 B6
Hammelev DK 86 E4
Hammelspring D 84 D4
Hamme-Mille B 19 C10
Hammenhög S 88 D6
Hammer N 105 C12
Hammerbrücke D 75 B11
Hammerdal S 106 D8
Hammerfest N 113 B12
Hammershøj DK 86 C5
Hammerum DK 86 C4
Hamminkeln D 17 E7
Hamn N 108 E3
Hamn N 111 B13
Hamna N 114 B8
Hamnavoe GB 3 D14
Hamnavoe GB 3 E14
Hamnbukt N 112 C8
Hamnbukta N 111 B18
Hamneidet N 112 D6
Hamnes N 105 B10
Hamnes N 108 E4
Hamnes N 112 D6
Hamningberg N 114 B9
Hamnøy N 110 E5
Hamnvågnes N 111 B16
Hamoir B 19 D12
Hamois B 19 D11
Hamont B 16 F5
Hampen DK 86 C4
Hampetorp S 92 A7
Hämpjäkk S 116 D4
Hampont F 26 C6
Hampreston GB 13 D11
Hamra S 93 F12
Hamra S 103 C9
Hamrångefjärden S 103 E13
Hamre N 112 C4
Hamry nad Sázavou CZ 77 C9
Ham-sous-Varsberg F 186 C2
Hamstreet GB 15 E10
Hamsund N 111 D10
Ham-sur-Heure B 19 D9
Hamula FIN 123 D16
Hamula FIN 124 D9
Hamzabeyli TR 167 F7
Hanaskog S 88 C6
Hanau D 187 A6
Handbjerg DK 86 C3
Handeloh D 83 D7
Handen S 93 A12
Handest DK 86 B5
Handewitt D 82 A6
Handlová SK 147 D7
Handog S 106 E7
Handöl S 105 E12
Handrabury UA 154 B5
Handrup D 17 C9
Handsjö S 102 B8
Handstein N 108 D4
Handzame B 182 C2
Hanebo S 103 D12
Hanerau-Hademarschen D 82 B6
Hanestad N 101 C13
Hănești RO 153 B9
Hangastenmaa FIN 128 B7
Hangelsberg D 80 B5
Hånger S 87 A13
Hangö FIN 127 F8
Hangony H 145 G1
Hangu RO 153 C8
Hangvar S 93 D13
Hanhikoski FIN 115 E2
Hanhimaa FIN 117 C14
Han i Elezit RKS 164 E3
Hanikase EST 132 F1
Haniska SK 145 F3
Hankamäki FIN 125 D10
Hankasalem asema FIN 123 F16
Hankasalmi FIN 123 F16
Hankensbüttel D 83 E9
Han Knežica BIH 157 B6
Hanko FIN 127 F8
Hanna PL 141 G9
Hannäs S 93 C8
Hannover D 78 B6
Hannoversch Münden D 78 D6
Hannukainen FIN 117 C11
Hannusperä FIN 119 D15
Hannusranta FIN 121 F10
Hannut B 19 C11
Hanøy N 110 D9
Han-Pijesak BIH 157 D10
Hanshagen D 83 C10
Hańsk Pierwszy PL 141 H8
Hansnes N 112 D4
Hanstedt D 83 D8
Hanstholm DK 86 A3
Han-sur-Nied F 26 C5
Hanušovce nad Topľou SK 145 E4
Hanušovice CZ 77 B11
Hanvec F 22 D3
Haparanda S 119 C12
Hapert NL 183 C6
Häppälä FIN 123 F16
Happburg D 75 D9
Happisburgh GB 15 B12
Haps NL 183 B7
Hapträsk S 118 B4
Hara S 106 E6
Härad S 98 D7
Haradok BY 133 F7
Harads S 118 B5
Häradsbäck S 88 B6
Häradsbygden S 103 E9
Haradshammar S 93 B9
Haradzilavichy Pyershaya BY 133 D4
Haraldseng N 112 B9
Haram N 100 A4
Harang N 104 E6
Harany BY 133 F6
Harasiuki PL 144 C5
Hărău RO 151 F10
Haraudden S 116 E3
Harbacheva BY 133 E6
Harbak N 104 C8
Harbke D 79 B9
Harbo S 98 B8
Harboør DK 86 B2
Harbost GB 2 J4
Harburg (Schwaben) D 75 E8
Harbury GB 13 A12
Hard A 71 C9
Hardbakke N 100 D1
Hardegg A 77 E9
Hardegsen D 78 C6
Hardelot-Plage F 15 F12
Hardenberg NL 17 C7
Harderwijk NL 16 D5
Hardheim D 27 A11
Hardinxveld-Giessendam NL 182 B5
Hardt D 27 D9
Hareid N 100 B4
Harelbeke B 19 C7
Haren NL 17 B7
Haren (Ems) D 17 C8
Hare Street GB 15 D9
Harestua N 95 B13
Harfleur F 23 A12
Harg S 99 B10
Hargesheim D 21 E9
Hargimont B 19 D11
Hargla EST 131 F12
Hargnies F 19 D10
Hargshamn S 99 B10
Harichovce SK 145 F2
Harinkaa FIN 123 E16
Harjakangas FIN 126 B6
Härjäro S 99 D8
Härjåsjön S 102 C7
Harjavalta FIN 126 C7
Harjula FIN 119 C15
Harjumaa FIN 128 B7
Harjunkylä FIN 122 E7
Harjunpää FIN 126 C6
Harju-Risti EST 131 C7
Harka H 149 A7
Härkäjoki FIN 115 D2
Harkakötöny H 150 E4
Harkány H 149 E10
Härkmeri FIN 122 F6
Härkönen FIN 119 C13
Harku EST 131 C9
Hârlău RO 153 C9
Harlech GB 10 F3
Harleston GB 15 C11
Hårlev DK 87 E10
Harlingen NL 16 B4
Harlow GB 15 D9
Harly F 19 E7
Hărman RO 153 F7
Harmånger S 103 C13
Härmänkylä FIN 121 F13
Harmanli TR 173 D9
Härmänmäki FIN 121 F11
Harmannsdorf A 77 F10
Harmelen NL 182 A5
Harmoinen FIN 127 C13
Harmsdorf D 83 C9
Harmston GB 11 E10
Harnes F 18 D6
Härnösand S 103 A14
Haro E 40 C6
Harodz'ki BY 137 E13
Haroldswick GB 3 D15
Haroué F 26 D5
Härpe FIN 127 E14
Harpefoss N 101 C11
Harpenden GB 15 D8
Harplinge S 87 B11
Harpstedt D 17 C11
Harra D 75 B10
Harrachov CZ 81 E8
Harran N 105 B13
Harre DK 86 B3
Harridslev DK 86 C6
Harrietfield GB 5 C9
Harrioja S 119 C11
Harrislee D 82 A6
Harrogate GB 11 D8
Harrsjö S 106 B9
Harrström FIN 122 E6
Harrvik S 107 A10
Harsa S 103 C10
Hårsbäck S 98 C7
Harsefeld D 82 D7
Hârseni RO 152 F6
Harsești RO 160 D5
Harsleben D 79 C9
Hårslev DK 86 D6
Hârșova RO 155 D1
Harsprånget S 116 E3
Harstad N 111 C12
Harsum D 78 B6
Harsvik N 104 C8
Harta H 150 D3
Hartberg A 148 B5
Hårte S 103 C13
Hartenholm D 83 C8
Hartha D 80 D3
Harthausen D 21 F10
Hartheim D 27 E8
Hârtiești RO 160 C6
Hart im Zillertal A 72 B4
Hartkirchen A 76 F5
Hartland GB 12 D6
Hartlepool GB 11 B9
Hartmanice CZ 76 D4
Hartola FIN 127 B15
Harwich GB 15 D11
Harzgerode D 79 C9
Hasanağa TR 173 D10
Hasbuğa TR 173 A8
Haselünne D 17 C8
Hasirciarnavutköy TR 171 B10
Håsjö S 107 F10
Hasköy TR 173 A6
Hasköy TR 177 C9
Haslach an der Mühl A 76 E6
Haslach im Kinzigtal D 27 D9
Hasle CH 70 C5
Hasle DK 88 E7
Haslemere GB 15 E7
Haslev DK 87 E9
Hasloh D 83 C7
Hasløya N 104 E2
Haslund DK 86 C6
Hășmaș RO 151 D9
Hasparren F 32 D3
Haßbergen D 17 C12
Hassel (Weser) D 17 C12
Hassela S 103 B12
Hassela kyrkby S 103 B12
Hasselfelde D 79 C8
Hasselfors S 92 A5
Hasselt B 19 C11
Hasselt NL 16 C6
Haßfurt D 75 B8
Hassi FIN 127 B13
Hässjö S 103 A14
Haßleben D 79 D9
Haßleben D 84 D5
Hässleholm S 87 C13
Hasslö S 89 C8
Haßloch D 21 F10
Hasslöv S 87 C12
Haßmersheim D 187 C7
Hästbo S 103 E13
Hästholmen S 92 C5
Hastière-Lavaux B 19 D10
Hastings GB 15 F10
Hästnäs S 97 D14
Hästrup DK 86 E6
Hästveda S 87 C13
Hasvåg N 105 C9
Hasvik N 112 C9
Hať CZ 146 B6
Hat' UA 145 G6
Hațeg RO 159 B10
Hatfield GB 11 D10
Hatherleigh GB 12 D6
Hätilä FIN 127 C11
Hatipkışlası TR 181 B7
Hatsola FIN 128 B8
Hattarvík FO 2 A4
Hattem NL 16 D6
Hattersheim am Main D 21 D10
Hattert D 21 C9
Hattfjelldal N 108 E6
Hatting DK 86 D5
Hattingen D 17 F8
Hatton GB 3 L13
Hattstedt D 82 A6
Hattula FIN 127 C11
Hattuvaara FIN 125 E16
Hatulanmäki FIN 124 C8
Hatunkylä FIN 125 D15
Hatvan H 150 B4
Hatzenbühl D 27 B9
Hatzendorf A 148 C6
Hatzfeld (Eder) D 21 C11
Haubourdin F 18 C6
Hauenstein D 186 C4
Haugan N 105 D9
Haugastøl N 94 A7
Hauge N 94 F4
Hauge N 114 E6
Haugen N 110 D7
Haugesund N 94 D2
Haugh of Urr GB 5 F9
Haugland N 108 D5
Haugli N 111 C15
Haugnes N 111 B11
Haugnes N 112 C6
Haugset N 112 D7
Hauho FIN 127 C12
Haukå N 100 C2
Haukela FIN 125 B14
Haukeligrend N 94 C7
Haukijärvi FIN 127 B9
Haukilahti FIN 121 F13
Haukiniemi FIN 121 C13
Haukipudas FIN 119 D14
Haukivaara FIN 125 E15
Haukivuori FIN 124 F8
Haukøy N 111 D11
Haulerwijk NL 16 B6
Haurukylä FIN 119 E15
Haus A 73 B8
Haus N 94 B2
Hausach D 187 E5
Hausen D 75 E11
Hausen bei Würzburg D 187 B9
Häusern D 27 E9
Hausham D 72 A4
Hausjärvi FIN 127 D12
Hauske N 94 D3
Hausleiten A 77 F10
Hausmannstätten A 148 C5
Hautajärvi FIN 115 E6
Hautakylä FIN 121 D10
Hautakylä FIN 123 E12
Haute-Amance F 26 E4
Hautefort F 29 E8
Hauterives F 31 E7
Hauteville-Lompnes F 31 D8
Haut-Fays B 184 D3
Hautmont F 19 D8
Hautomäki FIN 123 E17
Haux F 32 D4
Hauzenberg D 76 E5
Havant GB 14 F7
Havârna RO 153 A9
Havbro DK 86 B4
Havdhem S 93 E12
Håvdna N 113 C15
Havelange B 19 D11
Havelberg D 83 E12
Havelte NL 16 C6
Håven S 103 C9
Haverdal S 87 B11
Haverfordwest GB 12 B5
Haverhill GB 15 C9
Haverlah D 79 B7
Haverö S 103 B9
Haversin B 19 D11
Haverslev DK 86 B5
Håverud S 91 B11
Havířov CZ 146 B6
Havixbeck D 17 E8
Hävla S 92 B7
Havlíčkův Brod CZ 77 C9
Havndal DK 86 B6
Havneby DK 86 E3
Havnebyen DK 87 D8
Havnsø DK 87 D8
Havøysund N 113 A14
Håvra S 103 C10
Havran TR 173 E7
Havrebjerg DK 87 E8
Havsa TR 173 A6
Havsskogen S 99 B11
Havtun N 94 B2
Hawarden GB 10 E5
Hawes GB 11 C7
Hawick GB 5 E11
Hawkhurst GB 15 E10
Hawkinge GB 15 E11
Haxby GB 11 C9
Hayange F 20 F6
Haybes F 184 D2
Haydarli TR 177 D10
Haydere TR 181 A8
Haydon Bridge GB 5 F12
Haydon Wick GB 13 B11
Hayingen D 71 A8
Hayle GB 12 E4
Hay-on-Wye GB 13 A8
Hayrabolu TR 173 B7
Hayton GB 11 D10
Hayvoron UA 154 A5
Haywards Heath GB 15 F8
Hazebrouck F 18 C6
Hazerswoude-Rijndijk NL 182 A5
Haźlach PL 147 B7
Hažlín SK 145 E3
Hazlov CZ 75 B11
Heacham GB 11 F12
Headcorn GB 15 E10
Headford IRL 6 F4
Healeyfield GB 5 F13
Heanor GB 11 E9
Heathfield GB 15 F9
Hebdów PL 143 F9
Hebenhausen (Neu-Eichenberg) D 78 D6
Heberg S 87 B11
Hebertsfelden D 76 F3
Hebnes N 94 D3
Heby S 98 C7
Hèches F 33 D6
Hechingen D 27 D10
Hecho E 32 E4
Hechtel B 19 B11
Hechthausen D 17 A12
Heckelberg D 84 E5
Heckington GB 11 F11
Hedared S 91 D12
Hedberg S 109 F16
Heddesheim D 21 F11
Hédé F 23 D8
Hede S 98 B6
Hede S 102 B6
Hedekas S 91 B10
Hedel NL 16 E4
Hedemora S 97 B14
Heden DK 86 E6
Heden S 102 C4
Heden S 118 C7
Hedenäset S 119 B11
Hedensbyn S 118 B9
Hedensted DK 86 D5
Hedersleben D 79 C9
Hédervár H 146 F4
Hedesunda S 98 B8
Hedeviken S 102 B6
Hedge End GB 13 D12
Hedlunda S 107 B15
Hedmark S 107 B13
Hedsjön S 103 E12
Hee DK 86 C2
Heeg NL 16 C5
Heek D 17 D8
Heel NL 183 C7
Heemsen D 17 C12
Heemskerk NL 16 C3
Heemstede NL 16 D3
Heenvliet NL 182 B4
Heer B 19 D10
Heerde NL 16 D6
Heerenveen NL 16 C5
Heerewaarden NL 183 B6
Heerhugowaard NL 16 C3
Heerlen NL 20 C5
Heers B 19 C11
Heesch NL 16 E5
Heeslingen D 17 B12
Heeßen D 17 D12
Heeswijk NL 16 E4
Heeten NL 183 A8
Heeze NL 16 F5
Heggeli N 111 B13
Heggem N 104 E4
Heggenes N 101 D10
Heggjabygda N 100 C4
Heggland N 90 A5
Heggmoen N 108 B8
Hegra N 105 E10
Hegyeshalom H 146 F4
Hehlen D 78 C5
Heia N 105 C12
Heia N 111 B17
Heide D 82 B6
Heideck D 75 D9
Heidelberg D 21 F11
Heiden D 17 E7
Heidenau D 80 E5
Heidenheim D 75 D8
Heidenheim an der Brenz D 75 E7
Heidenreichstein A 77 E8
Heigenbrücken D 187 A7
Heikendorf D 83 B8
Heikkilä FIN 121 C14
Heikkilä FIN 122 F7
Heiland N 90 B4
Heilbronn D 27 B11
Heilbrunn A 148 B5
Heiligenberg D 27 E11
Heiligenfelde D 83 E10
Heiligenhafen D 83 B9
Heiligenhaus D 17 F7
Heiligenkreuz am Waasen A 148 C5
Heiligenkreuz im Lafnitztal A 148 C6
Heiligenstadt Heilbad D 79 D7
Heiligenstedten D 82 C6
Heiloo NL 16 C3
Heilsbronn D 75 D8
Heiltz-le-Maurupt F 25 C12
Heim N 104 E6
Heimbach D 21 E8
Heimbuchenthal D 187 B7
Heimdal N 100 E3
Heimdal N 104 E8
Heimertingen D 71 A10
Heimseta N 100 C3
Heimsheim D 187 D6
Heinade D 78 C6
Heinämaa FIN 127 D14
Heinämäki FIN 121 F12
Heinämäki FIN 123 D17
Heinävaara FIN 125 E14
Heinävesi FIN 125 F11
Heinebach (Alheim) D 78 D6
Heinersbrück D 81 C7
Heinersdorf D 80 B6
Heinersreuth D 75 C10
Heinijärvi FIN 119 E14
Heinijoki FIN 126 D7
Heiningen D 79 B8
Heinisuo FIN 119 C16
Heinkenszand NL 16 F1
Heinlahti FIN 128 E6
Heino NL 183 A8
Heinola FIN 127 C15
Heinolan kirkonkylä FIN 127 C15
Heinolanperä FIN 119 E14
Heinoniemi FIN 125 F13
Heinsberg D 20 B6
Heinsen D 78 C5
Heinsnes N 105 B12
Heisingen D 183 C10
Heistadmoen N 95 C11
Heist-op-den-Berg B 19 B10
Heitersheim D 27 E8
Heituinlahti FIN 128 C8
Hejls DK 86 E5
Hejnice CZ 81 E8
Hejnsvig DK 86 D4
Hejőpapi H 145 H2
Hejsager DK 86 E5
Hekelgem B 19 C9
Hel PL 138 A6
Helbra D 79 C9
Helchteren B 183 C6
Heldburg D 75 B8
Heldenbergen D 21 D11
Heldrungen D 79 D9
Helechal E 51 B9
Helegiu RO 153 E9
Helensburgh GB 4 C7
Helfenberg A 76 E6
Helgenes N 110 C9
Helgeroa N 90 B6
Helgum S 107 E11
Hell N 105 E9
Hella N 100 D5
Helland N 104 E5
Helland N 111 D11
Hellanmaa FIN 122 D9
Hellarmo N 109 B10
Helle N 90 B5
Hellebæk DK 87 C11
Hellefjord N 113 B11
Hellendoorn NL 183 A8
Hellenthal D 20 D6
Hellenurme EST 131 E12
Hellesøy N 100 E1
Hellested DK 87 E10
Hellesvik N 104 D5
Hellesylt N 100 B5
Hellevad DK 86 E4
Hellevoetsluis NL 16 E2
Helligskogen N 112 E6
Hellín E 55 B9
Hellingly GB 15 F9
Hellnes N 112 C6
Hellsö FIN 126 F4
Hellvi S 93 D13
Hellvik N 94 F3
Helmbrechts D 75 B10
Helme EST 131 E11
Helmond NL 16 F5
Helmsdale GB 3 J9
Helmsley GB 11 C9
Helmstadt D 74 C6
Helmstedt D 79 B9
Heľpa SK 147 D9
Helppi FIN 117 D13
Helpringham GB 11 F11
Helse D 82 C6
Helsingborg S 87 C11
Helsinge DK 87 C10
Helsingfors FIN 127 E12
Helsingør DK 87 C11
Helsinki FIN 127 E12
Helstad N 105 A12
Helston GB 12 E4
Heltermaa EST 130 D6
Heltersberg D 21 F9
Helvaci TR 177 B9
Helvécia H 150 D4
Helvoirt NL 183 B6
Hem DK 86 B3
Hem F 182 D2
Hemau D 75 D10
Hemavan S 108 E9
Hemeiuș RO 153 D9
Hemel Hempstead GB 15 D8
Hemer D 185 B8
Hemfjäll S 109 E12
Hemfjällstangen S 102 D5
Hemhofen D 75 C8
Hemling S 107 D15
Hemme D 82 B6
Hemmet DK 86 D2
Hemmingen D 78 B6
Hemmingen S 107 B17
Hemmingsmark S 118 D6
Hemmoor D 17 A12
Hemnesberget N 108 D6
Hemnestad N 111 C11
Hempnall GB 15 C11
Hempstead GB 15 C9
Hemsbach D 21 E11
Hemsbünde D 82 D6
Hemsby GB 15 B12
Hemse S 93 E12
Hemsedal N 101 E9
Hemsjö S 107 D14
Hemslingen D 82 D7
Hemsloh D 17 C11
Hemsö S 103 A15
Hemyock GB 13 D8
Henån S 91 C10
Hénanbihen F 23 C7
Henarejos E 47 E10
Hencida H 151 C8
Hendaye F 32 D2
Hendon GB 15 D8
Hengelo NL 16 D6
Hengelo NL 17 D7
Hengersberg D 76 E4
Hengevelde NL 183 A9
Henggart CH 27 E10
Hengoed GB 13 B8
Hénin-Beaumont F 18 D6
Henley-on-Thames GB 15 D7
Hennan S 103 B10
Henndorf am Wallersee A 73 A7
Hennebont F 22 E5
Hennef (Sieg) D 21 C8
Hennes N 110 C9
Henne Stationsby DK 86 D2
Hennezel F 26 D5
Hennickendorf D 80 B4
Hennigsdorf Berlin D 80 A4
Henningskälen S 106 D8
Henningsvær N 110 D7
Hennseid N 90 A5
Hennset N 104 E4
Hennstedt D 82 B6
Hennweiler D 21 E8
Henrichemont F 25 F8
Henryków PL 81 E12
Henrykowo PL 139 B9
Henstridge GB 13 D10
Hepola FIN 119 C13
Heppen B 183 C6
Heppenheim (Bergstraße) D 21 E11
Herálec CZ 77 C8
Herálec CZ 77 C9
Herbault F 24 E5
Herbertingen D 27 D11
Herbertstown IRL 8 C6
Herbés E 42 F3
Herbeumont B 184 E3
Herbignac F 23 F7
Herbolzheim D 27 D8
Herborn D 21 C10
Herbrechtingen D 75 E7
Herbstein D 21 C12
Herby PL 142 E6
Herceghalom H 149 A11
Herceg-Novi MNE 162 E6
Hercegovac HR 149 E8
Hercegszántó H 150 F2
Herdecke D 17 F8
Herdorf D 21 C9
Hereclean RO 151 C11
Heréd H 150 B4
Hereford GB 13 A9
Héreg H 149 A11
Herencia E 46 F6
Herend H 149 B9
Herent B 19 C10
Herentals B 19 B10
Herenthout B 182 C5
Hérépian F 34 C5
Herford D 17 D11
Hergatz D 71 B9
Hergiswil CH 70 D6
Herguijuela E 45 F9
Héric F 23 F8
Héricourt F 27 E6
Hérimoncourt F 27 F6
Heringen (Helme) D 79 D8
Heringen (Werra) D 79 E7
Heringsdorf D 83 B10
Heringsdorf D 84 C6
Heriot GB 5 D11
Herisau CH 27 F11
Hérisson F 29 B11
Herk-de-Stad B 19 C11
Herkenbosch NL 183 C8
Herkingen NL 182 B4
Herleshausen D 79 D7
Herlev DK 87 D10
Herlufmagle DK 87 E9
Herm F 32 C3
Hermagor A 73 C7
Hermannsburg D 83 E8
Hermanovce SK 145 E3
Hermanowice PL 144 D6
Hermansverk N 100 D5
Heřmanův Městec CZ 77 C9
Herment F 29 D11
Hermersberg D 186 C4
Hermeskeil D 21 E7
Hermisende E 39 E6
Hermsdorf D 79 E10
Hernád H 150 C3
Hernádnémeti H 145 G2
Hernani E 32 D2
Hernansancho E 46 C3
Herne B 19 C9
Herne D 17 E8
Herne Bay GB 15 E11
Herning DK 86 C3
Heroldsbach D 75 C8
Héron B 19 C11
Hérouville-St-Clair F 23 B11
Herøy N 100 B3
Herpf D 79 E7
Herrala FIN 127 D13
Herramélluri E 40 C5
Herräng S 99 B11
Herré F 32 C5
Herre N 90 A6
Herrenberg D 27 C10
Herrera E 53 B7
Herrera del Duque E 45 F10
Herrera de los Navarros E 42 E1
Herrera de Pisuerga E 40 C3
Herrería E 47 C9
Herreruela E 45 F7
Herrestad S 91 C10
Herrieden D 75 D8
Herringbotn N 108 E6
Herrlisheim F 186 D4
Herrljunga S 91 C13
Herrnhut D 81 D7
Herrö S 102 B7
Herrsching am Ammersee D 75 G9
Herrskog S 103 A15
Herrvik S 93 E13
Herry F 25 F8
Hersbruck D 75 C9
Herschbach D 21 C9
Herscheid D 21 B9
Herschweiler-Pettersheim D 186 C3
Herselt B 19 B10
Herslev DK 86 D5
Herstal B 19 C12
Herstmonceux GB 15 F9
Herston GB 3 H11
Herten D 17 E8
Hertford GB 15 D8
Hertník SK 145 E3
Hertsa UA 153 A8
Hertsånger S 118 F6
Hertsjö S 103 D11
Herve B 19 C12
Hervik N 94 D3
Herwijnen NL 183 B6
Herzberg D 80 C4
Herzberg D 83 C11
Herzberg D 84 E3
Herzberg am Harz D 79 C7
Herzebrock-Clarholz D 17 E10
Herzele B 19 C8
Herzfelde D 80 B5
Herzhorn D 17 A12
Herzlake D 17 C9
Herzogenaurach D 75 C8
Herzogenbuchsee CH 27 F8
Herzogenburg A 77 F9
Herzogenrath D 183 D8
Herzsprung D 83 D12
Hesdin F 18 D5
Hesel D 17 B9
Hesjeberg N 111 C13
Hesjestranda N 100 A6
Heskestad N 94 F4
Hespérange L 20 E6
Heßdorf D 75 C8
Hesselager DK 87 E7
Hessen D 79 B8
Hessfjorden N 112 D3
Heßheim D 21 E10
Hessisch Lichtenau D 78 D6
Hessisch Oldendorf D 17 D12
Hest N 100 D3
Hestenesøyri N 100 C4
Hestnes N 104 D5
Hestøy N 108 E3
Hestra S 91 E14
Hestra S 92 D6
Hestvik N 105 B10
Hestvika N 104 D6
Heswall GB 10 E5
Hetekylä FIN 119 D17
Hetés H 149 D9
Hethersett GB 15 B11
Hetlingen D 82 C7
Hettange-Grande F 186 C1
Hettenleidelheim D 186 B5
Hettenshausen D 75 E10
Hettingen D 27 D11
Hetton GB 11 C7
Hettstedt D 79 C10
Hetzerath D 21 E7
Heubach D 187 D8
Heuchelheim D 21 C11
Heuchin F 18 D5
Heudicourt-sous-les-Côtes F 26 C4
Heukelum NL 16 E4
Heusden B 19 B11
Heusden NL 183 B6
Heusenstamm D 21 D11
Heustreu D 75 B7
Heusweiler D 186 C2
Heves H 150 B5
Hévíz H 149 C8
Hevlín CZ 77 E10
Hexham GB 5 F12
Heyrieux F 31 D7
Heysham GB 10 C6
Heythuysen NL 19 B12
Heywood GB 11 D7
Hida RO 151 C11
Hidas H 149 D10
Hidasnémeti H 145 G3
Hiddenhausen D 17 D11
Hiddensee D 84 A4
Hidirköylü TR 177 D10
Hidișelu de Sus RO 151 D9
Hieflau A 73 A10
Hiendelaencina E 47 B7
Hiersac F 28 D5
Hietakangas FIN 115 D3
Hietama FIN 123 E15
Hietanen FIN 117 D11
Hietanen FIN 128 B7
Hietaniemi FIN 115 D6
Hietaniemi FIN 121 B11
Hietaperä FIN 121 F13
Higham Ferrers GB 15 C7
Highampton GB 12 D6
High Bentham GB 10 C6
Highbridge GB 13 C9
Highclere GB 13 C12
High Halden GB 15 E10
High Hawsker GB 11 C10
High Hesket GB 5 F11
High Lorton GB 5 F10
Highnam GB 13 B10
Highworth GB 13 B11
High Wycombe GB 15 D7
Higuera de Arjona E 53 A9
Higuera de la Serena E 51 B8
Higuera de la Sierra E 51 D7
Higuera de Llerena E 51 C8
Higuera de Vargas E 51 C6
Higuera la Real E 51 C6
Higueruela E 55 B10
Higueruelas E 48 E3
Hihnavaara FIN 115 D4
Hiidenkylä FIN 123 C15
Hiidenlahti FIN 125 E10
Hiilikumpu FIN 119 C15
Hiirikylä FIN 125 C10
Hiirola FIN 128 B7
Hiisijärvi FIN 121 F12
Híjar E 42 E3
Hikiä FIN 127 D12
Hilbersdorf D 80 E4
Hilchenbach D 21 C10
Hildburghausen D 75 B8
Hilden D 21 B7
Hilders D 79 E7
Hilderthorpe GB 11 C11
Hildesheim D 78 B6
Hilgertshausen D 75 F9
Hilișeu-Horia RO 153 A8
Hiliuți MD 153 B10
Hillared S 91 D13
Hille D 17 D11
Hille S 103 E13
Hillebola S 99 B9
Hillegom NL 16 D3
Hillerød DK 87 D10
Hillerse D 79 B7
Hillerslev DK 86 A3
Hillerslev DK 86 E6
Hillerstorp S 88 A5
Hilleshamn N 111 C13
Hillesheim D 21 D7
Hillesøy N 111 A15
Hillevik S 103 E13
Hilli FIN 123 C11
Hillilä FIN 123 B11
Hill of Fearn GB 3 K9
Hillosensalmi FIN 128 C6
Hillsand S 106 C8
Hillsborough GB 7 D10
Hillside GB 5 B12
Hillswick GB 3 E14
Hilltown GB 7 D10
Hilpoltstein D 75 D9
Hilsenheim F 186 E4
Hilton GB 11 F8
Hiltpoltstein D 75 C9
Hiltula FIN 129 B9
Hilvarenbeek NL 183 C6
Hilversum NL 16 D4
Himalansaari FIN 128 C8
Himanka FIN 123 B11
Himarë AL 168 D2
Himberg A 77 F10
Himbergen D 83 D9
Himesháza H 149 D11
Himma EST 131 F14

Himmaste EST 131 E14
Himmelberg A 73 C9
Himmelpforten D 17 A12
Hîncești MD 154 D3
Hinckley GB 11 F9
Hindås S 91 D11
Hindenburg D 83 E11
Hinderwell GB 11 B10
Hindhead GB 15 E7
Hindley GB 10 D6
Hindon GB 13 C10
Hindrem N 104 D8
Hinganmaa FIN 117 D15
Hingham GB 15 B10
Hinnerjöki FIN 126 C6
Hinnerup DK 86 C6
Hinneryd S 87 B13
Hinojal E 45 E8
Hinojales E 51 C6
Hinojares E 55 D7
Hinojasas de Calatrava E 54 B4
Hinojos E 51 E7
Hinojosa E 47 B9
Hinojosa de Duero E 45 C7
Hinojosa de Jarque E 42 F2
Hinojosa del Duque E 51 B9
Hinojosa del Valle E 51 C7
Hinojosa de San Vicente
E 46 D3
Hinova RO 159 D10
Hinte D 17 B8
Hinterhermsdorf D 80 E6
Hinternah D 75 A8
Hinterrhein CH 71 D8
Hintersee A 73 A7
Hintersee D 84 C6
Hinterweidenthal D 186 C4
Hinterzarten D 27 E9
Hinthaara FIN 127 E13
Hinwil CH 27 F10
Hinx F 32 C4
Hippolytushoef NL 16 C3
Hîrbovăț MD 154 C2
Hîrjauca MD 154 C2
Hirka TR 181 B9
Hirnyk UA 144 C9
Hirrlingen D 27 D10
Hirschaid D 75 C9
Hirschau D 75 C10
Hirschberg D 75 B10
Hirschfeld D 80 D5
Hirschhorn (Neckar) D 187 C6
Hirsilä FIN 127 B11
Hirsingue F 27 E7
Hirson F 19 E9
Hîrtop MD 154 D3
Hîrtopul Mare MD 154 C3
Hirtshals DK 90 D6
Hirvas FIN 119 B14
Hirvaskoski FIN 120 D9
Hirvasperä FIN 119 E13
Hirvasvaara FIN 115 E5
Hirvelä FIN 119 D16
Hirvelä FIN 121 F14
Hirvensalmi FIN 128 B6
Hirviäkuru FIN 115 D1
Hirvihaara FIN 127 D13
Hirvijoki FIN 123 E10
Hirvikylä FIN 123 F9
Hirvilahti FIN 124 D8
Hirvineva FIN 119 E14
Hirvivaara FIN 121 E13
Hirvlax FIN 122 D8
Hirwaun GB 13 B7
Hirzenhain D 21 D12
Hisarönü TR 181 C8
Hishult S 87 C12
Hissjön S 122 C4
Histon GB 15 C9
Hita E 47 C6
Hitchin GB 15 D8
Hitis FIN 126 F8
Hittarp S 87 C11
Hittisau A 71 C9
Hitzacker D 83 D10
Hitzendorf A 148 B4
Hitzhusen D 83 C7
Hiukkajoki FIN 129 B12
Hiyche UA 144 C8
Hjåggsjö S 122 C3
Hjallerup DK 86 A6
Hjältevad S 92 D6
Hjärnarp S 87 C11
Hjärsås S 88 C6
Hjärtum S 91 C11
Hjarup DK 86 E4
Hjelle N 100 C6
Hjellestad N 94 B2
Hjellsand N 110 C8
Hjelmeland N 94 D4
Hjelset N 100 A7
Hjerkinn N 101 B11
Hjerm DK 86 C3
Hjo S 92 C4
Hjordkær DK 86 E4
Hjørring DK 90 E7
Hjorted S 93 D8
Hjortkvarn S 92 B6
Hjortsberga S 88 B6
Hjørungavåg N 100 B4
Hjuvik S 91 D10
Hlavani UA 154 F4
Hlebine HR 149 D7
Hligeni MD 154 B3
Hlinaia MD 153 A10
Hlinaia MD 154 C4
Hlinaia MD 154 D5
Hliník nad Hronom SK 147 D7
Hlinné SK 145 F4
Hlinsko CZ 77 C9
Hlohovec SK 146 E5
Hlubočky CZ 146 B4
Hluboká nad Vltavou CZ 77 D6
Hlučín CZ 146 B6
Hlyboka UA 153 A7
Hlybokaye BY 133 F3
Hlyboke UA 155 B5
Hnatkiv UA 154 A2
Hněvotín CZ 77 C12
Hniezdné SK 145 E2
Hnizdychiv UA 145 E9
Hnojník CZ 147 B7
Hnúšťa SK 147 D9
Hobol H 149 D9
Hobøl N 95 C13
Hobro DK 86 B5
Hoburg S 93 F12
Hoçë e Qytetit RKS 163 E10
Hoceni RO 153 D12
Hochdonn D 82 B6
Hochdorf CH 27 F9
Hochdorf D 71 A9
Hochfelden F 27 C8
Höchheim D 75 B7
Hochspeyer D 186 C4
Hochstadt (Pfalz) D 187 C5
Höchstadt an der Aisch D 75 C8
Höchstädt an der Donau
D 75 E8
Hochstetten-Dhaun D 21 E8
Höchst im Odenwald D 187 B6
Hoçisht AL 168 C4
Hockenheim D 187 C6
Hoczew PL 145 E5
Hodac RO 152 D5
Hodalen N 101 B14
Hoddesdon GB 15 D8
Hodejov SK 147 E10
Hodenhagen D 82 E7
Hodkovice nad Mohelkou
CZ 81 E8
Hódmezővásárhely H 150 E5
Hodnet GB 10 F6
Hodod RO 151 C11
Hodonice CZ 77 E10
Hodonín CZ 77 E12
Hodoșa RO 152 D5
Hodruša-Hámre SK 147 E7
Hodsager DK 86 C3
Hodyszewo PL 141 E7
Hoek NL 16 F1
Hoek van Holland NL 16 E2
Hoem N 104 F4
Hoenderloo NL 183 A7
Hœnheim F 186 D4
Hoensbroek NL 19 C12
Hœrdt F 186 D4
Hoeselt B 19 C11
Hoevelaken NL 16 D4
Hoeven NL 16 E3
Hof D 21 C10
Hof D 75 B10
Hof N 95 C12
Hofbieber D 78 E6
Hoffstad N 104 C8
Hofgeismar D 21 B12
Hofheim am Taunus D 21 D10
Hofheim in Unterfranken
D 75 B8
Hofles N 105 B11
Hofors S 98 A6
Hofsøy N 111 B13
Hofterup S 87 D11
Höganäs S 87 C11
Högås S 108 E9
Högbacka S 103 D12
Högbo S 103 E12
Högboda S 97 C9
Högbränna S 109 F15
Högen S 103 C13
Högfors S 97 B15
Högfors S 97 C13
Hoghilag RO 152 E5
Hoghiz RO 152 F6
Høgild DK 86 C3
Högland S 107 B9
Höglekardallen S 105 E15
Høgli N 111 B14
Höglunda S 107 E9
Hogosht RKS 164 D4
Hogrun S 105 D16
Högsåra FIN 126 F7
Högsäter S 91 B11
Högsäter S 96 C6
Högsäter S 97 D8
Hogsby S 89 A10
Högset N 104 F3
Högsjö S 92 A7
Högsjö S 103 A14
Hogstad S 92 C6
Hogstorp S 91 C10
Högträsk S 116 E5
Högvålen S 102 B4
Hőgyész H 149 C10
Hohberg D 186 E4
Hohen-Altheim D 75 E8
Hohenaspe D 82 C7
Hohenau D 76 E5
Hohenau an der March A 77 E11
Hohenberg A 77 G9
Hohenbocka D 80 D6
Hohenbucko D 80 C4
Hohenburg D 75 D10
Hohendorf D 84 B5
Hoheneich A 77 E8
Hohenems A 71 C9
Hohenfels D 75 D10
Hohenfurch D 71 B11
Hohengöhren D 79 A11
Hohenhameln D 79 B7
Hohenkammer D 75 F10
Hohenkirchen D 17 A9
Höhenkirchen-Siegertsbrunn
D 75 F10
Hohenleuben D 79 E11
Hohenlockstedt D 82 C7
Hohenmocker D 84 C4
Hohenmölsen D 79 D11
Hohennauen D 83 E12
Hohenpeißenberg D 71 B12
Hohenroth D 75 B7
Hohensaaten D 84 E6
Hohenseeden D 79 B11
Hohenstein-Ernstthal D 79 E12
Hohenthann D 75 E11
Hohenthurm D 79 C11
Hohen Wangelin D 83 C12
Hohenwart D 75 E9
Hohenwarth D 76 D3
Hohenwestedt D 82 B7
Höhn D 21 C9
Hohn D 82 B7
Hohne D 79 A7
Hohnhorst D 17 D12
Hohnstorf (Elbe) D 83 D9
Höhr-Grenzhausen D 21 D9
Hohwacht (Ostsee) D 83 B9
Hoikankylä FIN 124 E7
Hoikka FIN 121 E12
Hoisdorf D 83 C8
Hoisko FIN 123 D11
Højby DK 86 E6
Højby DK 87 D9
Højer DK 86 F3
Højmark DK 86 C2
Højslev DK 86 B4
Højslev Stationsby DK 86 B4
Hok S 92 D4
Hökåsen S 98 C7
Hökerum S 91 D13
Hökhult S 91 A13
Hökhuvud S 99 B10
Hokka FIN 128 B6
Hokkaskylä FIN 123 E12
Hokksund N 95 C11
Hokland N 111 C11
Hökmark S 118 F6
Hökön S 88 C6
Hol N 101 E8
Hol N 111 C11
Holand N 110 D9
Holandsvika N 108 E5
Holasovice CZ 142 G4
Holbæk DK 86 B6
Holbæk DK 87 D9
Holbeach GB 11 F12
Holboca RO 153 C11
Holbøl DK 86 F4
Holbrook GB 15 D11
Holdorf D 17 C10
Holeby DK 83 A10
Hølen N 95 C13
Holešov CZ 146 C5
Holevik N 100 D1
Holguera E 45 E8
Holič SK 77 E12
Holice CZ 77 B9
Höljes S 102 E4
Holkestad N 110 E8
Holkonkylä FIN 123 E11
Hollabrunn A 77 E10
Hollandscheveld NL 17 C7
Hollange B 19 E12
Hollås N 105 C11
Holle D 79 B7
Høllen N 90 C2
Hollenbach D 75 F9
Hollenbek D 83 C9
Hollenegg A 73 C11
Hollenstedt D 82 D7
Hollenstein an der Ybbs
A 73 A10
Hollern-Twielenfleth D 82 C7
Hollfeld D 75 C9
Hollingstedt D 82 B6
Hollington GB 15 F10
Hollingworth GB 11 E8
Hollóháza H 145 F3
Hollola FIN 127 D14
Hollum NL 16 B5
Hollybush GB 4 E7
Hollyford IRL 8 C6
Hollywood IRL 7 F9
Holm D 82 C7
Holm DK 86 E5
Holm N 105 A12
Holm N 110 C9
Holm S 103 A12
Holm S 107 E13
Hol'ma UA 154 B5
Holmajärvi S 111 E18
Holme-Olstrup DK 87 E9
Holme-on-Spalding-Moor
GB 11 D10
Holmestrand N 95 D12
Holmfirth GB 11 D8
Holmfors S 118 D4
Holmisperä FIN 123 D14
Holmsjö S 89 C9
Holmsjö S 107 A14
Holmsjö S 107 D12
Holmsund S 122 C4
Holmsvattnet S 118 B4
Holmsveden S 103 D12
Holmträsk S 107 B16
Hölö S 93 A11
Holod RO 151 D9
Hołodowska PL 144 C7
Holoșnița MD 153 A12
Holoubkov CZ 76 C5
Holovets'ko UA 145 E6
Holovne UA 141 H10
Holsbybrunn S 92 E6
Holsljunga S 91 E12
Holsta EST 131 F14
Holstebro DK 86 C3
Holsted DK 86 D3
Hölstein CH 27 F8
Holsworthy GB 12 D6
Holt GB 10 E6
Holt GB 15 B11
Holt N 111 B16
Holt N 111 B17
Holte DK 87 D10
Holten NL 17 D6
Holtet N 102 E3
Holtgast D 17 A9
Holthusen D 83 C10
Holtsee D 83 B7
Holungen D 79 D7
Holwerd NL 16 B5
Holycross IRL 9 C7
Holyhead GB 10 E2
Holywell GB 7 D7
Holywell GB 10 E5
Holywood GB 4 F5
Holzappel D 185 D8
Holzen D 78 C6
Holzgerlingen D 187 D7
Holzhausen an der Haide
D 21 D9
Holzheim D 21 D11
Holzheim D 75 E8
Holzheim D 75 E8
Holzheim D 75 F7
Holzkirchen D 72 A4
Holzminden D 21 A12
Holzthaleben D 79 D8
Holzweißig D 79 C11
Holzwickede D 17 E9
Hom DK 87 E9
Homberg (Efze) D 21 B12
Homberg (Ohm) D 21 C11
Hombourg-Budange F 186 C1
Hombourg-Haut F 186 C2
Homburg D 21 F8
Homécourt F 20 F5
Homersfield GB 15 C11
Homesh AL 168 A3
Hommelstø N 108 F4
Hommelvik N 105 E9
Hommersåk N 94 E3
Homna S 103 D10
Homocea RO 153 E10
Homokmégy H 150 E3
Homokszentgyörgy H 149 D9
Homoroade RO 151 B11
Homorod RO 152 E6
Homrogd H 145 G2
Homyel' BY 133 F5
Hondarribia E 32 D2
Hondón de las Nieves E 56 E3
Hondón de los Frailes E 56 E3
Hondschoote F 18 C6
Hône I 68 B4
Hønefoss N 95 B12
Honfleur F 23 B12
Høng DK 87 D8
Honiton GB 13 D8
Honkajoki FIN 122 G8
Honkakoski FIN 126 B7
Honkakylä FIN 122 E9
Honkilahti FIN 126 D7
Honley GB 11 D8
Honningsvåg N 100 B2
Honningsvåg N 113 B16
Hönö S 91 D10
Honoratka PL 142 B5
Honrubia E 47 E8
Honrubia de la Cuesta E 40 F4
Hønseby N 113 B11
Hontacillas E 47 E8
Hontalbilla E 40 F3
Hontanaya E 47 E7
Hontianske Nemce SK 147 E7
Hontoria de la Cantera E 40 D4
Hontoria del Pinar E 40 E5
Hontoria de Valdearados
E 40 E4
Hoofddorp NL 16 D3
Hoogerheide NL 16 F2
Hoogersmilde NL 16 C6
Hoogeveen NL 17 C6
Hoogezand-Sappemeer
NL 17 B7
Hoogkarspel NL 16 C4
Hoog-Keppel NL 183 B8
Hoogkerk NL 17 B6
Hoogland NL 183 A6
Hoogstede D 17 C7
Hoogstraten B 16 F3
Hoogvliet NL 16 E2
Hook GB 11 D10
Hook GB 14 E7
Hooksiel D 17 A10
Höör S 87 D13
Hoorn NL 16 C4
Hoornaar NL 182 B5
Hopârta RO 152 E3
Hope GB 10 E5
Hope N 100 E3
Hopeman GB 3 K10
Hopen N 111 E10
Hopfgarten im Brixental
A 72 B5
Hopfgarten in Defereggen
A 72 C6
Hopland N 100 C4
Hoppstädten D 21 E8
Hoppula FIN 115 F2
Hopseidet N 113 B20
Hopsten D 17 D9
Hopton GB 15 B12
Hoptonheath GB 13 A9
Hoptrup DK 86 E4
Horam GB 15 F9
Horažďovice CZ 76 D5
Horb am Neckar D 27 D10
Horbova UA 153 A8
Hörbranz A 71 B9
Hørby DK 90 E7
Hörby S 87 D13
Horcajo de las Torres E 45 B10
Horcajo de los Montes E 46 F3
Horcajo de Santiago E 47 E7
Horcajo Medianero E 45 C10
Horda N 94 C5
Horda S 88 A6
Hörde D 185 B7
Horden GB 11 B9
Hordum DK 86 B3
Horea RO 151 E10
Horeb GB 12 A6
Horești MD 153 C11
Horezu RO 160 C3
Horgen CH 27 F10
Horgenzell D 71 B9
Horgești RO 153 E10
Horgoš SRB 150 E4
Horia RO 153 D9
Horia RO 155 C2
Horia RO 155 D2
Hořice CZ 77 B9
Horinchove UA 145 G7
Horitschon A 149 A7
Horjul SLO 73 D9
Horka D 81 D7
Hôrka SK 145 E1
Hörken S 97 B12
Horley GB 15 E8
Hörlitz D 80 C5
Hormakumpu FIN 117 C14
Hormilla E 40 D6
Horn A 77 E9
Horn N 95 A12
Horn N 108 F3
Horn S 92 D7
Hornachos E 51 B7
Hornachuelos E 51 D9
Horná Kraľová SK 146 E5
Horná Potôň SK 146 E4
Horná Streda SK 146 D5
Horná Štubňa SK 147 D7
Horná Súča SK 146 D5
Horná Ves SK 146 D6
Hornbach D 21 F8
Horn-Bad Meinberg D 17 E11
Hornbæk DK 87 C10
Hornburg D 79 B8
Hornby GB 10 C6
Horncastle GB 11 E11
Horndal N 109 A10
Horndal S 98 B6
Horndean GB 14 F6
Horne DK 86 D3
Horne DK 86 E6
Horne DK 90 D6
Horneburg D 82 C7
Hörnefors S 122 C3
Horné Obdokovce SK 146 E6
Horné Orešany SK 146 E4
Horné Saliby SK 146 E5
Horné Srnie SK 146 C6
Horní Bečva CZ 146 C6
Horní Benešov CZ 146 B5
Horní Beřkovice CZ 76 B6
Horní Cerekev CZ 77 D8
Horní Jelení CZ 77 B10
Horní Jiřetín CZ 80 E5
Horní Lideč CZ 146 C6
Horní Maršov CZ 81 E9
Horní Moštěnice CZ 146 C4
Hornindal N 100 C5
Hørning DK 86 C6
Horní Planá CZ 76 E6
Horní Slavkov CZ 75 B12
Horní Štěpánov CZ 77 C11
Horní Stropnice CZ 77 E7
Horní Suchá CZ 146 B6
Hornmyr S 107 C14
Hornnäs S 97 B9
Hornnes N 90 B2
Hornön S 103 A14
Hornos E 55 C7
Hornow D 81 C7
Hornoy-le-Bourg F 18 E4
Hornsea GB 11 D11
Hörnsjö S 107 D17
Hornslet DK 86 C6
Hornstorf D 83 C11
Hornsyld DK 86 D5
Hörnum D 82 A4
Hornum DK 86 B4
Horný Bar SK 146 F4
Horný Tisovník SK 147 E8
Horný Vadičov SK 147 C7
Horoatu Crasnei RO 151 C10
Horodiște MD 153 A11
Horodiște MD 153 B10
Horodkivka UA 154 A3
Horodło PL 144 B9
Horodniceni RO 153 B8
Horodnye UA 154 F3
Horodok UA 144 D8
Horoměřice CZ 76 B6
Horonda UA 145 G6
Horonkylä FIN 122 E7
Hořovice CZ 76 C5
Horrabridge GB 12 D6
Horreby DK 83 A11
Horred S 91 E11
Hörsching A 76 F6
Horsdal N 108 B7
Horseleap IRL 6 F5
Horsens DK 86 D5
Horsforth GB 11 D8
Horsham GB 15 E8
Hørsholm DK 87 D10
Hörsingen D 79 B9
Horslunde DK 87 F8
Horsmanaho FIN 125 E12
Horsnes N 111 B18
Horšovský Týn CZ 76 C3
Horsskog S 98 B8
Horst NL 16 F6
Horst (Holstein) D 82 C7
Horstedt D 17 B12
Hörstel D 17 D9
Horstmar D 17 D8
Hort H 150 B4
Horten N 95 D12
Hortezuela E 40 F6
Hortigüela E 40 D5
Hortlax S 118 D6
Hortobágy H 151 B7
Horton in Ribblesdale GB 11 C7
Høruphav DK 86 F5
Hørve DK 87 D8
Hörvik S 89 C7
Horw CH 70 C6
Horwich GB 10 D6
Horyniec-Zdrój PL 144 C7
Horyszów PL 144 B8
Hösbach D 21 D12
Hosena D 80 D6
Hosenfeld D 74 A5
Hoset N 108 B8
Hosingen L 20 D6
Hosio FIN 119 C15
Hosjö S 106 E8
Hosjöbottnarna S 105 E15
Hosköy TR 173 C7
Hospital IRL 8 D6
Hossa FIN 121 D14
Hössjö S 122 C3
Hossjön S 107 D9
Hoßkirch D 27 E11
Hosszúhetény H 149 D10
Hosszúpályi H 151 C8
Hosszúpereszteg H 149 B8
Hošťálková CZ 146 C5
Hostalric E 43 D9
Hostens F 32 B4
Hostěradice CZ 77 E10
Hostie SK 146 E6
Hostinné CZ 81 E9
Hošťka CZ 76 B6
Hostomice CZ 76 C6
Hostomice CZ 80 E5
Hoston N 104 E7
Höstoppen S 106 C8
Hostouň CZ 75 C12
Hostrupskov DK 86 E4
Höstsätern S 102 C4
Hot AL 163 E8
Hotarele RO 161 E8
Hoting S 107 C10
Hotinja vas SLO 148 D5
Hotonj BIH 162 D4
Hotton B 19 D11
Hou DK 86 A6
Houbie GB 3 D15
Houdain F 18 D6
Houdan F 24 C6
Houdelaincourt F 26 C3
Houécourt F 26 D4
Houeillès F 32 B6
Houeydets F 33 D6
Houffalize B 19 D12
Houghton le Spring GB 5 F14
Houghton Regis GB 15 D7
Houlbjerg DK 86 C5
Houlgate F 23 B11
Hourtin F 28 E3
Hourtin-Plage F 28 E3
Houten NL 16 D4
Houthalen B 19 B11
Houthulst B 18 C6
Houton GB 3 H10
Houtsala FIN 126 E6
Houtskär FIN 126 E5
Houyet B 184 D3
Hov DK 86 D6
Hov N 101 E12
Hov N 108 D4
Hov N 111 A18
Hova S 92 B4
Hovborg DK 86 D3
Hovda N 94 D4
Hovde N 90 B4
Hovden N 110 C8
Hovdevik N 100 B2
Hove GB 15 F8
Hovedgård DK 86 D5
Hövelhof D 17 E11
Hoven DK 86 D3
Hoveton GB 15 B11
Hovězí CZ 146 C6
Hovid S 103 B13
Hovin N 104 E8
Hovingham GB 11 C10
Hovmantorp S 89 B8
Hovringen N 101 C10
Hovslund Stationsby DK 86 E4
Hovsta S 97 D13
Howden GB 11 D10
Howth IRL 7 F10
Höxter D 17 E12
Hoya D 17 C12
Hoya Gonzalo E 55 B9
Høyanger N 100 D4
Høydal N 90 A5
Hoyerswerda D 80 D6
Hoylake GB 10 E5
Høylandet N 105 B12
Hoym D 79 C9
Hoyocasero E 46 D3
Hoyo de Manzanares E 46 C5
Hoyos E 45 D7
Hoyos del Espino E 45 D10
Höytiä FIN 123 F14
Hoyvik FO 2 A3
Hozha BY 137 F8
Hrabove UA 154 A4
Hrabyně CZ 146 B6
Hradec Králové CZ 77 B9
Hradec nad Moravicí CZ 146 B5
Hradec nad Svitavou CZ 77 C10
Hrádek CZ 147 B7
Hrádek nad Nisou CZ 81 E7
Hradenytsi UA 154 D6
Hradešice CZ 76 D5
Hradište SK 146 D6
Hradište pod Vrátnom SK
146 D5
Hradištko CZ 76 C6
Hraň SK 145 F4
Hranice CZ 75 B11
Hranice CZ 146 B5
Hranovnica SK 145 F1
Hrasnica BIH 157 E9
Hrastnik SLO 73 D11
Hrawzhyshki BY 137 E12
Hrebenyky UA 154 D5
Hreljin HR 67 B10
Hrhov SK 145 F2
Hrimne UA 145 D8
Hriňová SK 147 D9
Hristovaia MD 154 A3
Hrnjadi BIH 156 D5
Hrob CZ 80 E5
Hrochot SK 147 D8
Hrochův Týnec CZ 77 C9
Hrodna BY 140 C9
Hromnice CZ 76 C4
Hronec SK 147 D9
Hronov CZ 77 B10
Hronovce SK 147 E7
Hronský Beň Beňx SK 147 E7
Hrotovice CZ 77 D10
Hroznová Lhota CZ 146 D4
Hrtkovci SRB 158 D4
Hrubieszów PL 144 B8
Hrușca MD 154 A3
Hrušky CZ 77 E11
Hrușova MD 154 C3
Hrušovany SK 146 E6
Hrušovany nad Jevišovkou
CZ 77 E10
Hruštín SK 147 C8
Hruszniew PL 141 F7
Hrvaćani BIH 157 C7
Hrvace HR 156 E6
Hrvatska Dubica HR 157 B6
Hrvatska Kostajnica HR 156 B6
Hrynyava UA 152 B5
Huaröd S 88 D5
Huarte E 32 E2
Hubová SK 147 C8
Hückelhoven D 20 B6
Hückeswagen D 21 B8
Hucknall GB 11 E9
Hucksjöåsen S 103 A10
Hucqueliers F 15 F12
Huddersfield GB 11 D8
Hüde D 17 C10
Hude (Oldenburg) D 17 B10
Hudești RO 153 A9
Hudiksvall S 103 C13
Huécija E 55 F7
Huedin RO 151 D11
Huélago E 55 E6
Huelgoat F 22 D4
Huelma E 53 A10
Huelva E 51 E6
Huelves E 47 D7
Huércal de Almería E 55 F8
Huércal-Overa E 55 E9
Huérguina E 47 D9
Huérmeces E 40 C4
Huerta del Marquesada E 47 D9
Huerta del Rey E 40 E5
Huerta de Valdecarábanos
E 46 E5
Huertahernando E 47 C8
Huerto E 42 D3
Huesa E 55 D6
Huesa del Común E 42 E2
Huesca E 41 D11
Huéscar E 55 D7
Huete E 47 D7
Huétor-Tájar E 53 B8
Huétor-Vega E 53 B9
Huévar E 51 E7
Hüfingen D 27 E9
Hufthamar N 94 B2
Hugh Town GB 12 F2
Hugulia N 101 D11
Hugyag H 147 E8
Huhdasjärvi FIN 127 C16
Huhmarkoski FIN 123 D10
Huhtamo FIN 127 C8
Huhti FIN 127 C10
Huhtilampi FIN 125 F14
Huhus FIN 125 E15
Huijbergen NL 182 C4
Huikola FIN 119 E16
Huisheim D 75 E8
Huisinis GB 2 K2
Huissen NL 16 E5
Huissinkylä FIN 122 E8
Huittinen FIN 126 C8
Huizen NL 16 D4
Hujakkala FIN 128 D8
Hukijärvi FIN 121 D10
Hukkajärvi FIN 125 B14
Hulín CZ 146 C4
Hulja EST 131 C12
Huljen S 103 B12
Hulkkola FIN 124 E8
Hull GB 11 D11
Hüllhorst D 17 D11
Hullo EST 130 D6
Hullsjön S 103 A12
Hüls D 183 C8
Hulsberg NL 183 D7
Hulst NL 16 F2
Hult S 91 A15
Hult S 92 D6
Hulterstad S 89 C11
Hultsfred S 92 D7
Hulu S 91 D13
Hulubești RO 160 D6
Hulyanka UA 154 C4
Hum BIH 157 F10
Hum BIH 162 D5
Humalajoki FIN 123 D13
Humanes de Madrid E 46 D5
Humanes de Mohernando
E 47 C6
Humberston GB 11 D11
Humbie GB 5 D11
Humble DK 83 A9
Humenné SK 145 F4
Humilladero E 53 B7
Humlebæk DK 87 D11
Humlegårdsstrand S 103 D13
Humlum DK 86 B3
Hummelholm S 107 D17
Hummelo NL 183 A8
Hummelsta S 98 C7
Hummuli EST 131 F12
Hum na Sutli HR 148 D5
Humpolec CZ 77 C8
Humppila FIN 127 D9
Humshaugh GB 5 E12
Huncovce SK 145 E1
Hundåla N 108 E4
Hundberg N 111 B18
Hundberg S 109 F16
Hundborg DK 86 B3
Hundeluft D 79 C11
Hunderdorf D 75 E12
Hundested DK 87 D9
Hundholmen N 111 D11
Hundorp N 101 C11
Hundsangen D 21 D9
Hundshübel D 79 E12
Hundsjön S 118 C7
Hundslund DK 86 D6
Hundvin N 100 E2
Hune DK 86 A5
Hunedoara RO 151 F10
Hünfeld D 78 E6
Hünfelden-Kirberg D 21 D10
Hunge S 103 A9
Hungen D 21 D11
Hungerford GB 13 C11
Hunnebostrand S 91 C9
Hunsel NL 19 B12
Hunspach F 27 C8
Hunstanton GB 11 F12
Huntingdon GB 15 C8
Huntlosen D 17 C10
Huntly GB 3 L11
Hünxe D 183 B9
Hunya H 151 D6
Huopanankoski FIN 123 D15
Hüpstedt D 79 D7
Hurbanovo SK 146 F6
Hurdal N 95 B14
Hurdalsverk N 95 B14
Hurezani RO 160 D3
Huriel F 29 C10
Hurissalo FIN 128 C8
Hurler's Cross IRL 8 C5
Hursley GB 13 C12
Hurst Green GB 15 E9
Hurstpierpoint GB 15 F8
Hurteles E 41 D7
Hürth D 21 C7
Huruiești RO 153 E10
Huruksela FIN 128 D6
Hurup DK 86 B2
Hurva S 87 D12
Husā S 105 E14
Husås S 106 E7
Husasău de Tinca RO 151 D8
Husbands Bosworth GB 13 A12
Husberget S 102 B6
Husbondliden S 107 B15
Husby D 82 A7
Husby S 97 B15
Husby S 99 B9
Hushcha UA 141 H9
Huși RO 153 D12
Husinec CZ 76 D5
Husjorda N 111 D9
Huskvarna S 92 D4
Husnes N 94 C3
Husnicioara RO 159 D10
Husøy N 108 D3
Hussjö S 103 A14
Hustopeče CZ 77 E11
Hustopeče nad Bečvou CZ
146 B5
Husum D 17 C12
Husum D 82 B6
Husum S 107 E16
Husvik N 108 E4
Huta PL 141 H3
Huta Komorowska PL 143 F12
Hutisko-Solanec CZ 146 C6
Hutovo BIH 162 D4
Hütschenhausen D 186 C3
Hüttau A 73 B7
Hüttenberg A 73 C10
Hüttisheim D 74 F6
Hüttlingen D 75 E7
Huttoft GB 11 E12
Hüttschlag A 73 B7
Huttukylä FIN 119 D15
Huttwil CH 27 F8
Huuhilonkylä FIN 121 F13
Huuki S 117 D11
Huutijärvi FIN 127 C11
Huutokoski FIN 124 F9
Huutokoski FIN 125 E12
Huutoniemi FIN 113 E18
Huvåsen S 118 D4
Hüven D 17 C9
Huwniki PL 145 D6
Huy B 19 C11
Hvalpsund DK 86 B4
Hvalsø DK 87 D9
Hvalvik FO 2 A2
Hvam DK 86 B5
Hvannasund FO 2 A3
Hvar HR 156 F5
Hvidbjerg DK 86 B3
Hvide Sande DK 86 C2
Hvidovre DK 87 D10
Hvilsom DK 86 B5
Hvittingfoss N 95 D11
Hvorslev DK 86 C5
Hwlffordd GB 12 B5
Hybe SK 147 C9
Hybo S 103 C11
Hycklinge S 92 D7
Hyères F 36 E4
Hyermanavichy BY 133 F3

Hyervyaty BY 137 D13
Hylen N 94 C5
Hylleråsen N 102 C3
Hyllestad N 100 D2
Hyllinge DK 87 E9
Hyllinge S 87 C11
Hyltebruk S 87 A12
Hymont F 26 D5
Hyönölä FIN 127 E10
Hyrkäs FIN 119 E16
Hyry FIN 119 C14
Hyrynsalmi FIN 121 E11
Hysgjokaj AL 168 C2
Hyssna S 91 D12
Hythe GB 13 D12
Hythe GB 15 E11
Hytti FIN 129 D9
Hyttön S 99 B8
Hyväneula FIN 127 D13
Hyvääniemi FIN 121 B11
Hyvärilä FIN 119 F15
Hyvikkälä FIN 127 D12
Hyvinkää FIN 127 D12
Hyvölänranta FIN 119 F16
Hyvönmäki FIN 129 B12
Hyypiö FIN 115 E1
Hyyppä FIN 122 F8
Hyżne PL 144 D5

I

Iablanița RO 159 D9
Iabloana MD 153 B11
Iacobeni RO 152 C6
Iacobeni RO 152 E5
Ialoveni MD 154 D3
Iam RO 159 C7
Ianca RO 160 F4
Ianca RO 161 C10
Iancu Jianu RO 160 E4
Iara RO 152 D3
Iargara MD 154 E2
Iarova MD 153 A12
Iași RO 153 C11
Iasmos GR 171 B8
Ibahernando E 45 F9
Iballë AL 163 E9
Ibănești RO 152 D5
Ibănești RO 153 A8
Ibarra E 32 D1
Ibbenbüren D 17 D9
Ibdes E 47 B9
Ibë AL 168 B2
Ibeas de Juarros E 40 D4
Ibestad N 111 C13
Ibi E 56 D3
Ibos F 32 D5
Ibrány H 145 G4
İbriktepe TR 171 B10
Ibros E 53 A10
Ibstock GB 11 F9
Ichenhausen D 75 F7
Ichenheim D 186 E4
Ichtegem B 18 B7
Icking D 72 A3
Icklesham GB 15 F10
Icklingham GB 15 C10
Iclănzel RO 152 D4
Iclod RO 152 D3
Icoana RO 160 E5
Icușești RO 153 D9
Idanha-a-Nova P 45 E6
Idanha-a-Velha P 45 E6
Idar-Oberstein D 21 E8
Ideciu de Jos RO 152 D5
Iden D 83 E11
Īdeņa LV 133 C1
Idenor S 103 C13
Idestrup DK 83 A11
Idiazabal E 32 D1
Idivuoma S 116 B8
Idkerberget S 97 B13
Idmiston GB 13 C11
Idocin E 32 E3
Idom DK 86 C2
Idoš SRB 150 F5
Idre S 102 C4
Idrigil GB 2 K4
Idrija SLO 73 D9
Idritsa RUS 133 D5
Idro I 69 B9
Idstedt D 82 A7
Idstein D 21 D10
Idvattnet S 107 C12
Iecava LV 135 C8
Iedera RO 161 C7
Ieper B 18 C6
Iepurești RO 161 E7
Ierapetra GR 179 E10
Ieriķi LV 135 B10
Ierissos GR 170 D5
Iernut RO 152 E4
Ieromnini GR 168 E4
Ieropigi GR 168 C5
Ieșelnița RO 159 D9
Ifaistos GR 171 E8
Iffendic F 23 D7
Iffezheim D 187 D5
Ifjord N 113 C19
Ifs F 23 B11
Ifta D 79 D7
Ig SLO 73 E10
Igal H 149 C9
Igalo MNE 162 E6
Igar H 149 C11
Igé F 24 D4
Igea E 41 D7
Igel D 186 B2
Igelfors S 92 B7
Igelstorp S 91 C14
Igensdorf D 75 C9
Igerøy N 108 E3
Igersheim D 74 D6
Iggelheim D 187 C5
Iggensbach D 76 E4
Iggesund S 103 C13
Ighiu RO 152 E3
Igis CH 71 D9
Iglesias I 64 E2
Igliauka LT 137 D8
Igling D 71 A11
Igliškėliai LT 137 D8
Ignalina LT 135 F12
Ignatievo BG 167 C9
İğneada TR 167 F9
Ignești RO 151 E9
Igney F 26 D5
Igornay F 30 A5
Igoumenitsa GR 168 E3
Igralishte BG 169 A9
Igrejinha P 50 B4
Igrici H 145 H2
Igrīve LV 133 B2
Igualada E 43 D7
Igualeja E 53 C6
Igueña E 39 C7
Iguerande F 30 C5
Iharosberény H 149 D8
Ihľany SK 145 E2
Ihlienworth D 17 A11
Ihlowerhörn (Ihlow) D 17 B9
Ihode FIN 126 D6
Iholdy F 32 D3
Ihrhove D 17 B8
Ihrlerstein D 75 E10
İhsaniye TR 173 B10
Ii FIN 119 D14
Iijärvi FIN 113 E20
Iinattijärvi FIN 121 D9
Iironranta FIN 123 E12
Iisalmi FIN 124 C8
Iisvesi FIN 124 E8
Iitti FIN 127 D15
Iitto FIN 116 A6
Iivantiira FIN 121 F13
IJlst NL 16 B5
IJmuiden NL 16 D3
IJsselmuiden NL 16 C5
IJsselstein NL 16 D4
IJzendijke NL 16 F1
Ikaalinen FIN 127 B9
Ikast DK 86 C4
Ikazn' BY 133 E2
Ikervár H 149 B7
İkhtiman BG 165 E8
İkizdere TR 177 D10
Ikkala FIN 123 F11
Ikkala FIN 127 E11
Ikkeläjärvi FIN 122 F9
Ikla EST 131 F8
Ikornes N 100 B5
Ikosenniemi FIN 119 C17
Ikrény H 149 A9
Ikšķile LV 135 C8
Ilandža SRB 159 C6
Ilanz CH 71 D8
Ilava SK 146 D6
Iława PL 139 C8
Ilbono I 64 D4
Ilchester GB 13 C9
Ildir TR 177 C7
Īle LV 134 C6
Ileana RO 161 D9
Ileanda RO 152 C3
Ilfeld D 79 C8
Ilford GB 15 D9
Ilfracombe GB 12 C6
Ilgižiai LT 134 F6
Ílhavo P 44 C3
Ilia RO 151 F10
Ilica TR 173 E8
Ilidža BIH 157 E9
Ilieni RO 153 F7
Ilijaš BIH 157 E9
Ilindentsi BG 165 F7
Iliokastro GR 175 E7
Ilirska Bistrica SLO 73 E9
Ilk H 145 G5
Ilkeston GB 11 F9
Ilkley GB 11 D8
Illana E 47 D7
Illar E 55 F7
Illats F 32 A5
Illerrieden D 71 A10
Illertissen D 71 A10
Illescas E 46 D5
Ille-sur-Têt F 34 E4
Illiers-Combray F 24 D5
Illingen D 21 F8
Illingen D 187 D6
Illkirch-Graffenstaden F 27 C8
Illmensee D 27 E11
Illmitz A 149 A7
Íllora E 53 B9
Illschwang D 75 D10
Illueca E 41 E8
Illzach F 27 E7
Ilmajoki FIN 122 E9
Ilmatsalu EST 131 E13
Ilmenau D 79 E8
Ilminster GB 13 D9
Ilmmünster D 75 F10
Ilmola FIN 119 C13
Il'nytsya UA 145 G7
Ilok HR 158 C3
Ilola FIN 127 E14
Ilomantsi FIN 125 E15
Ilosjoki FIN 123 D15
Ilovăț RO 159 D10
Ilovica NMK 169 B8
Ilovice BIH 157 E9
Ilovița RO 159 D9
Iłów PL 139 F9
Iłowa PL 81 C8
Iłowo Osada PL 139 D9
Ilsbo S 103 C13
Ilsede D 79 B7
Ilsenburg (Harz) D 79 C8
Ilseng N 101 E14
Ilsfeld D 27 B11
Ilskov DK 86 C4
Ilūkste LV 135 E12
Ilva Mare RO 152 C5
Ilva Mică RO 152 C5
Ilvesjoki FIN 122 F9
İlyaslar TR 173 F9
Ilyushino RUS 136 D6
Ilz A 148 B5
Iłża PL 141 H4
Ilze LV 135 D12
Ilzene LV 135 B13
Imari FIN 119 B15
Imatra FIN 129 C10
Imavere EST 131 D11
Imbradas LT 135 E12
Imeľ SK 146 F6
Imèr I 72 D4
Imeros GR 171 C8
Imielnica PL 139 E8
Immeln S 88 C6
Immendingen D 27 E10
Immenhausen D 78 D5
Immenreuth D 75 C10
Immenstaad am Bodensee D 27 E11
Immenstadt im Allgäu D 71 B10
Immingham GB 11 D11
Imnäs S 107 D11
Imola I 66 D4
Imotski HR 157 F7
Imperia I 37 D8
Imphy F 30 B3
Impilakhti RUS 129 B15
Impiö FIN 120 C9
Impruneta I 66 E3
Imrehegy H 150 E3
İmroz TR 171 D9
Imst A 71 C11
Ina FIN 123 D11
Inagh IRL 8 C4
Ináncs H 145 G3
Inárcs H 150 C3
Inari FIN 113 F19
Inari FIN 125 D15
Inca E 57 B10
Inch IRL 8 D3
Inch IRL 9 C10
Inchbare GB 5 B11
Incheville F 18 D3
Inchigeelagh IRL 8 E4
Inchnadamph GB 2 J7
Inciems LV 135 B9
Incinillas E 40 C4
İncirliova TR 177 D10
Incisa in Val d'Arno I 66 E3
Incourt B 19 C10
Inčukalns LV 135 B9
Indal S 103 A13
Indalsto N 100 E2
Independența RO 155 C1
Independența RO 155 F2
Inđija SRB 158 C5
Indra LV 133 E3
Indreabhán IRL 6 F4
Indre Arna N 94 B2
Indre Billefjord N 113 C15
Indre Brenna N 113 B16
Indre Kårvik N 111 A16
Indre Kiberg N 114 C9
Indre Kjæs N 113 B16
Indre Sortvik N 113 B15
Indura BY 140 D9
Indzhe Voyvoda BG 167 E8
İnece TR 167 F8
İnecik TR 173 C7
Ineši LV 135 B11
Ineu RO 151 C9
Ineu RO 151 E8
Infiesto E 39 B9
Ingå FIN 127 E11
Ingared S 91 D11
Ingatestone GB 15 D9
Ingatorp S 92 D6
Ingelfingen D 187 C8
Ingelheim am Rhein D 21 E10
Ingelmunster B 19 C7
Ingelstad S 89 B7
Ingenes N 94 B3
Ingersheim F 27 D7
Ingleton GB 5 F13
Ingleton GB 10 C7
Ingoldmells GB 11 E12
Ingolsbenning S 97 B14
Ingolstadt D 75 E9
Ingrandes F 23 F10
Ingrandes F 29 B7
Ingstrup DK 90 E6
Inguiniel F 22 E5
Ingulsvatn N 105 B14
Ingwiller F 27 C7
Inha FIN 123 E12
Ini GR 178 E9
Iniesta E 47 F9
Inis IRL 8 C5
Inis Córthaidh IRL 9 C9
Inis Díomáin IRL 8 C4
Inistioge IRL 9 D8
Injevo NMK 169 A7
Inkberrow GB 13 A11
Inke H 149 D8
Inkee FIN 121 C12
Inkere FIN 127 E9
Inkoo FIN 127 E11
Inndyr N 108 B7
Innerbraz A 71 C9
Innerleithen GB 5 D10
Innernzell D 76 E4
Innertällmo S 107 D13
Innertavle S 122 C4
Innertkirchen CH 70 D6
Innervik S 109 E14
Innervillgraten A 72 C5
Innhavet N 111 E10
Inniscrone IRL 6 D4
Innishannon IRL 8 E5
Innsbruck A 72 B3
Innset N 111 C16
Inntorget N 108 F3
Inowłódz PL 141 G2
Inowrocław PL 138 E5
Ins CH 31 A11
Insch GB 3 L11
Insjön S 103 E9
Ińsko PL 85 D9
Insming F 27 C6
Instefjord N 100 E2
Instinción E 55 F7
Însurăței RO 161 D11
İntepe TR 171 D10
Interlaken CH 70 D5
Întorsura Buzăului RO 161 B8
Întregalde RO 151 E11
Introbio I 69 B7
Inturkė LT 135 F11
Inver IRL 6 C6
Inverallochy GB 3 K13
Inveran IRL 6 F4
Inveraray GB 4 C6
Inverarity GB 5 B11
Inverarnan GB 4 C7
Inverbervie GB 5 B12
Invercassley GB 2 K7
Invercharnan GB 4 B6
Invergarry GB 4 A7
Invergordon GB 3 K8
Inverkeilor GB 5 B11
Inverkeithing GB 5 C10
Invermoriston GB 2 L7
Inverness GB 3 L8
Inverurie GB 3 L12
Inviken S 106 B8
Inzell D 73 A6
Inzigkofen D 27 D11
Inzing A 72 B3
Inzinzac-Lochrist F 22 E5
Ioannina GR 168 E4
Ion Corvin RO 155 E1
Ionești RO 153 D9
Ionești RO 160 D2
Ionești RO 160 D4
Ion Luca Caragiale RO 161 D7
Ion Roată RO 161 D9
Iordăcheanu RO 161 C8
Ioulis GR 175 D9
Ip RO 151 C10
Ipatele RO 153 D10
Iphofen D 187 B9
Ipiķi LV 131 E10
Ipotești RO 153 B8
Ipotești RO 153 B9
Ippesheim D 75 C7
Ipplepen GB 13 E7
Ipsala TR 171 C10
Ipsheim D 75 C7
Ipstones GB 11 E8
Ipswich GB 15 C11
Irakleia GR 169 B9
Irakleia GR 174 B5
Irakleia GR 176 F5
Irakleio GR 178 E9
Irancy F 25 E10
Iratoșu RO 151 E7
Irdning A 73 A9
Irechekovo BG 167 E7
Iregszemcse H 149 C10
Irgoli I 64 C4
Iria GR 175 E7
Irig SRB 158 C4
Irishtown IRL 6 E5
Irissarry F 32 D3
Irjanne FIN 126 C6
Irlava LV 134 C5
Irlbach D 75 E12
Irninniemi FIN 121 C13
Irodouër F 23 D8
Ironbridge GB 10 F7
Irrel D 20 E6
Irsch D 21 E7
Irsee D 71 B11
Irshava UA 145 G7
Irši LV 135 C11
Irsina I 60 B6
Irsta S 98 C7
Irueste E 47 C7
Irun E 32 D2
Iruña E 32 E2
Irurozqui E 32 E3
Irurtzun E 32 E2
Irvine GB 4 D7
Irvinestown GB 7 D7
Irxleben D 79 B9
Isaba E 32 E4
Isaccea RO 155 C2
Isačić BIH 156 C4
Işalnița RO 160 E3
Isane N 100 C3
Isaris GR 174 E4
Isaszeg H 150 B3
Isätra S 98 C7
Isbergues F 18 C5
Isbister GB 3 D14
Iscar E 40 F2
Isches F 26 D4
Ischgl A 71 C10
Ischia I 60 B1
Ischia di Castro I 62 B1
Ischitella I 63 D9
Isdes F 25 E7
Iselvmoen N 111 C16
Isen D 75 F11
Is-en-Bassigny F 26 D3
Isenbüttel D 79 B8
Isenvad DK 86 C4
Iseo I 69 B9
Iserlohn D 17 F9
Isernhagen D 78 B6
Isernia I 63 D6
Isfjorden N 100 A7
İshakçelebi TR 177 B10
Ishull-Lezhë AL 163 F8
Isigny-sur-Mer F 23 B9
Ișili I 64 D3
İskele TR 173 F9
İskender TR 172 A6
Iškoras N 113 E16
Iskra BG 166 F4
Iskrets BG 165 D7
Isla Cristina E 51 E5
İslambeyli TR 167 F9
Isla Plana E 56 F2
Išlaužas LT 137 D8
Islaz RO 160 F5
Isle F 29 D8
Isle of Whithorn GB 5 F8
Isleryd S 92 C4
Isles-sur-Suippe F 19 F9
Īslīce LV 135 D8
İsmailli TR 177 B9
Ismaning D 75 F10
Ismundsundet S 106 E8
Isna P 44 E5
Isnäs FIN 127 E15
Isnello I 58 D5
Ișnovăț MD 154 C3
Isny im Allgäu D 71 B10
Iso-Äiniö FIN 127 C13
Iso-Evo FIN 127 C13
Isohalme FIN 115 E3
Isojoki FIN 122 F7
Isokumpu FIN 121 C11
Isokylä FIN 115 E3
Isokylä FIN 119 F14
Isokyrö FIN 122 E8
Isola F 36 C6
Isola 2000 F 37 C6
Isola d'Asti I 37 B8
Isola del Gran Sasso d'Italia I 62 B5
Isola della Scala I 66 B3
Isola delle Femmine I 58 C3
Isola del Liri I 62 D5
Isola di Capo Rizzuto I 61 F8
Isola del Cantone I 37 B9
Isona E 42 C6
Isopalo FIN 115 D2
Isorella I 66 B1
Iso-Vimma FIN 126 C7
Ispagnac F 35 B6
Isperikh BG 161 F9
Ispica I 59 F6
Ispoure F 32 D3
Ispra I 68 B6
Ispringen D 27 C10
Issakka FIN 125 C10
Isselburg D 17 E6
Issigeac F 29 F7
Issime I 68 B4
Isso E 55 C9
Issogne I 68 B4
Issoire F 30 D3
Issoudun F 29 B9
Issum D 17 E6
Is-sur-Tille F 26 E3
Issy-l'Évêque F 30 B4
Istalsna LV 133 D3
İstán E 53 C7
İstanbul TR 173 B10
Istead Rise GB 15 E9
Istebna PL 147 B7
Istebné SK 147 C8
Istenmezeje H 147 E10
Isternia GR 176 D5
Isthmia GR 175 D7
Istiaia GR 175 B7
Istibanja NMK 164 F5
Istog RKS 163 D9
Istres F 35 C8
Istria RO 155 D3
Istrio GR 181 D7
Istunmäki FIN 123 E16
Isuerre E 32 F3
Iszkaszentgyörgy H 149 B10
Itä-Ähtäri FIN 123 E12
Itä-Aure FIN 123 F10
Itä-Karttula FIN 124 E8
Itäkoski FIN 119 C13
Itäkoski FIN 125 C9
Itäkylä FIN 123 D11
Itäranta FIN 115 F2
Itäranta FIN 120 F9
Itea GR 169 C6
Itea GR 169 D6
Itea GR 169 F7
Itea GR 174 C5
Itero de la Vega E 40 D3
Iteuil F 29 C6
Ithaki GR 174 C2
Itrabo E 53 C9
Itri I 62 E5
Itterbeck D 17 C7
Ittireddu I 64 B2
Ittiri I 64 B2
Ittre B 19 C9
Ituero de Azaba E 45 D7
Itzehoe D 82 C7
Itzstedt D 83 C8
Iurceni MD 154 C2
Ivalo FIN 115 A3
Ivalon Matti FIN 117 B15
Iván H 149 B7
Ivana Franka UA 145 E7
Ivancea MD 154 C3
Ivančice CZ 77 D10
Ivančići BIH 157 D9
Iváncsa H 149 B11
Ivanec HR 148 D6
Ivănești RO 153 D10
Ivangorod RUS 132 C3
Ivanić-Grad HR 149 E6
Ivanivka UA 145 G6
Ivanjica SRB 163 B9
Ivanjska BIH 157 C7
Ivankovo HR 149 F11
Ivano-Frankove UA 144 D8
Ivanovice na Hané CZ 77 D12
Ivanovo BG 161 F7
Ivanovo BG 166 F5
Ivanovo BG 167 C7
Ivanovo SRB 158 D6
Ivanska HR 149 E7
Ivanski BG 167 C8
Ivarrud N 108 F6
Ivarsbjörke S 97 C9
Ivars d'Urgell E 42 D5
Ivaylovgrad BG 171 A10
Iveland N 90 C2
Iver GB 15 D7
Ivești RO 153 E11
Ivești RO 153 F11
Ivrea I 68 C4
İvrindi TR 173 E7
Ivry-la-Bataille F 24 C5
Ivry-sur-Seine F 25 C7
Ivybridge GB 13 E7
Iwaniska PL 143 E11
Iwanowice Włościańskie PL 143 F8
Iwkowa PL 144 D2
Iwye BY 137 F12
Ixelles B 19 C9
Ixworth GB 15 C10
İyaslar TR 177 A10
Iža SK 149 A10
Iza UA 145 G7
Izarra E 40 C6
Izbica PL 144 B7
Izbica Kujawska PL 138 F6
Izbiceni RO 160 F5
Izbicko PL 142 E5
Izbiște MD 154 C4
Izbište SRB 159 C7
Izbižno BIH 157 E10
Izeaux F 31 E7
Izeda P 39 E6
Izegem B 19 C7
Izernore F 31 C8
Izeron F 31 E7
Izgrev BG 161 F9
Izgrev BG 167 E9
Iž Mali HR 67 D11
Izmayil UA 155 C3
İzmir TR 177 C9
Iznájar E 53 B8
Iznalloz E 53 B9
Izola SLO 67 A8
Izsák H 150 D3
Izsófalva H 145 G2
Izvoare RO 160 E2
Izvoarele RO 155 C3
Izvoarele RO 160 E5
Izvoarele RO 160 F6
Izvoarele RO 161 C8
Izvoarele RO 161 E7
Izvoarele Sucevei RO 152 B6
Izvor BG 159 F10
Izvor BG 165 E6
Izvor NMK 168 B4
Izvor NMK 169 A6
Izvor SRB 159 F8
Izvorovo BG 155 F1
Izvoru RO 160 E6
Izvoru Bârzii RO 159 D10
Izvoru Berheciului RO 153 D10
Izvoru Crișului RO 151 D11

J

Jääjärvi FIN 114 D6
Jaakonvaara FIN 125 D14
Jaala FIN 127 C15
Jaalanka FIN 120 D9
Jaalanka FIN 120 E9
Jääli FIN 119 D15
Jaama EST 132 C2
Jääskänjoki FIN 122 E9
Jääskö FIN 117 D14
Jaatila FIN 119 B14
Jabaga E 47 D8
Jabalanac HR 67 C10
Jabaloyas E 47 D10
Jabalquinto E 53 A9
Jabbeke B 19 B7
Jabel D 83 C13
Jablan Do BIH 162 D5
Jablanica BIH 157 E8
Jabłoń PL 141 G8
Jablonec nad Jizerou CZ 81 E8
Jablonec nad Nisou CZ 81 E8
Jablonica SK 146 D4
Jabłonka PL 147 C9
Jabłonka Kościelna PL 140 E6
Jabłonna PL 139 F10
Jabłonna Lacka PL 141 F6
Jabłonna Pierwsza PL 141 H7
Jablonné nad Orlicí CZ 77 B11
Jablonné v Podještědí CZ 81 E7
Jablonové SK 77 F12
Jabłonowo Pomorskie PL 139 D7
Jablūnka CZ 146 C5
Jablunkov CZ 147 B7
Jabugo E 51 D6
Jabuka BIH 157 E10
Jabuka SRB 158 D6
Jabuka SRB 163 C7
Jabukovac HR 149 F6
Jabukovac SRB 159 E9
Jabukovik SRB 164 D5
Jaca E 32 E4
Jachenau D 72 A3
Jáchymov CZ 76 B3
Jacovce SK 146 D6
Jäderfors S 103 E12
Jadów PL 139 F12
Jädraås S 103 E11
Jadranska Lešnica SRB 158 D3
Jadraque E 47 C7
Jægerspris DK 87 D9
Jægervatnet N 111 A18
Jaén E 53 A9
Jägala EST 131 C10
Jagare BIH 157 C7
Jagerberg A 148 C5
Jagodina SRB 159 F7
Jagodnjak HR 149 E11
Jagodzin PL 81 D8
Jagsthausen D 27 B11
Jagstzell D 75 D7
Jähdyspohja FIN 123 F11
Jahnsfelde D 80 A6
Jahodná SK 146 E5
Jah-Salih AL 163 E9
Jajce BIH 157 D7
Ják H 149 B7
Jakabszállás H 150 D4
Jäkälävaara FIN 121 C10
Jakkukylä FIN 119 D15
Jakkula FIN 122 E8
Jäkkvik S 109 D12
Jaklovce SK 145 F3
Jakobsbakken N 109 B10
Jakobsnes N 114 D8
Jakobstad FIN 122 C9
Jakokoski FIN 125 E13
Jakovlje HR 148 E5
Jakšić HR 149 F9
Jakštaičiai LT 134 D2
Jaktorów PL 141 F3
Jakubany SK 145 E2
Jakubov SK 77 F11
Jakubów PL 141 F5
Jalance E 47 F10
Jalasjärvi FIN 122 F9
Jalhay B 20 C5
Jaligny-sur-Besbre F 30 C4
Jallais F 23 F10
Jalovik SRB 158 D4
Jałówka PL 140 D9
Jalubí CZ 146 C4
Jämaja EST 130 E4
Jämäs FIN 125 B12
Jämejala EST 131 E11
Jameln D 83 D10
Jamena SRB 157 C11
Jamestown IRL 7 F8
Jametz F 19 F11
Jamielnik PL 139 C7
Jämijärvi FIN 126 B8
Jamilena E 53 A9
Jäminkipohja FIN 127 B11
Jämjö S 89 C9
Jammerdal N 96 B7
Jamník SK 145 F2
Jämsä FIN 123 C12
Jämsä FIN 127 B13
Jämsänkoski FIN 127 B13
Jämshög S 88 C7
Jämtön S 118 C8
Jamu Mare RO 159 C7
Janakkala FIN 127 D12
Janapolē LT 134 E4
Jånd H 145 G5
Jandelsbrunn D 76 E5
Janderup DK 86 D2
Jäneda EST 131 C11
Jänickendorf D 80 B4
Janja BIH 158 D3
Janjevë RKS 164 D3
Janjići BIH 157 D8
Janjina HR 162 D3
Jänkä FIN 123 D13
Jänkälä FIN 115 D3
Jänkisjärvi S 116 E10
Jánkmajtis H 145 H6
Janków PL 143 B7
Jankowo Dolne PL 138 E4
Jāņmuiža LV 135 B10
Jännevirta FIN 125 E9
Jánoshalma H 150 E3
Jánosháza H 149 B8
Jánoshida H 150 C5
Jánossomorja H 149 A8
Janovice nad Úhlavou CZ 76 D4
Janów PL 140 D8
Janów PL 143 E7
Janowice Wielkie PL 81 E9
Janowiec PL 141 H5
Janowiec Wielkopolski PL 85 E12
Janów Lubelski PL 144 B5
Janowo PL 139 D10
Janów Podlaski PL 141 F8
Jansjö S 107 D10
Jänsmässholmen S 105 D15
Jāņuciems LV 135 E13
Janville F 24 D6
Janzé F 23 E9
Japca MD 154 B3
Jäppilä FIN 124 F8
Jaraba E 47 B9
Jaraczewo PL 81 C12
Jarafuel E 47 F10
Jaraicejo E 45 E9
Jaraiz de la Vera E 45 D9
Järämä S 116 B6
Jarandilla de la Vera E 45 D9
Järbo S 103 E12
Járdánháza H 145 G1
Jard-sur-Mer F 28 C2
Jaren N 95 B13
Jarfjordbotn N 114 D8
Jårgastat N 113 E16
Jargeau F 24 E7
Jarhoinen FIN 117 E11
Jarhois S 117 E11
Jariștea RO 153 F10
Jarkovac SRB 159 C6
Järkvissle S 103 A12
Järlåsa S 98 C8
Järlepa EST 131 C9
Jarmen D 84 C4
Jarménil F 26 D6
Jarmina HR 149 F11
Järna S 93 A11
Järna S 97 A11
Jarnac F 28 D5
Jarnages F 29 C10
Järnäs S 107 E17
Järnäsklubb S 107 E17
Järnforsen S 92 E7
Jarny F 26 B4
Jarocin PL 142 C4
Jarocin PL 144 B5
Jarok SK 146 E5
Jaroměř CZ 77 B9
Jaroměřice CZ 77 C11
Jaroměřice nad Rokytnou CZ 77 D9
Jaroslavice CZ 77 E10
Jarosław PL 144 C6
Jarosławiec PL 85 A11
Jarošov nad Nežárkou CZ 77 D8
Jarovnice SK 145 E3
Järpås S 91 C12
Järpbyn S 105 E14
Järpen S 105 E14
Järpliden S 102 E3
Jarplund-Weding D 82 A6
Jarque E 41 E8
Jarrow GB 5 F14
Järva-Jaani EST 131 C11
Järvakandi EST 131 D9
Järvberget S 107 D13
Järvenpää FIN 117 C12
Järvenpää FIN 122 E7
Järvenpää FIN 124 C8
Järvenpää FIN 125 D10
Järvenpää FIN 127 E13
Järvikylä FIN 119 F17
Järvikylä FIN 123 C13
Järvikylä FIN 123 C13
Jarville-la-Malgrange F 26 C5
Järvirova FIN 117 D12
Järvsand S 107 C9
Järvsjö S 107 B12
Järvsö S 103 C11
Järvsta S 103 E13
Järvtjärn S 118 E5
Järvträsk S 107 A16
Jarzé F 23 E11
Jaša Tomić SRB 159 C6
Jasen BIH 162 D5
Jasenak HR 67 B11
Jasenica BIH 156 C5
Jasenovac HR 157 B6
Jasenovo SRB 159 D7
Jasenovo SRB 163 B8
Jasień PL 81 C8
Jasień PL 85 B13
Jasienica PL 139 F11
Jasienica PL 147 B7
Jasienica Rosielna PL 144 D4
Jasieniec PL 141 G3
Jasika SRB 159 F7
Jasionka PL 144 C5
Jasionna PL 143 E9
Jasionówka PL 140 D8
Jašliska PL 145 E4
Jasło PL 144 D3
Jašlūnai LT 137 E11
Jasmuiža LV 135 D13
Jasov SK 145 F2
Jasová SK 146 F6
Jassans-Riottier F 30 D6
Jasseron F 31 C7
Jastarnia PL 138 A6
Jastrebarsko HR 148 E5
Jastrowie PL 85 D11
Jastrząb PL 141 H3
Jastrzębia PL 141 H4
Jastrzębia Góra PL 138 A5
Jastrzębie-Zdrój PL 147 B7
Jászapáti H 150 B5
Jászárokszállás H 150 B4
Jászberény H 150 C4
Jászboldogháza H 150 C4
Jászfényszaru H 150 B4
Jászjákóhalma H 150 B5
Jászkarajenő H 150 C5
Jászkisér H 150 C5
Jászladány H 150 C5
Jászszentandrás H 150 B5
Jászszentlászló H 150 D4
Jásztelek H 150 C5
Jatar E 53 C9
Jättendal S 103 C13
Jättensjö S 103 B10
Jatuni FIN 116 B9
Jatzke D 84 C5
Jatznick D 84 C5
Jaulín E 41 F10
Jaun CH 31 B11
Jaunalūksne LV 133 B2
Jaunanna LV 133 B2
Jaunauce LV 134 D5
Jaunay-Clan F 29 B6
Jaunbērze LV 134 C6
Jaunciems LV 134 B5
Jaundundaga LV 134 B4
Jaungulbene LV 135 B13
Jaunjelgava LV 135 C10
Jaunkalsnava LV 135 C11
Jaunklidzis LV 131 F11
Jaunlaicene LV 131 F13
Jaunlutriņi LV 134 C4
Jaunmārupe LV 135 C7
Jaunmuiža LV 135 C11
Jaunolaine LV 135 C7
Jaunpiebalga LV 135 B12
Jaunpils LV 134 C6
Jaunsāti LV 134 C5
Jaunsēlpils LV 135 C11
Jaunsilava LV 135 D12
Jauntsarats E 32 E2
Jaurakainen FIN 119 D17
Jaurakkajärvi FIN 121 D10
Jaurrieta E 32 E3
Jausiers F 36 C5
Javalí Viejo E 56 F2
Javarus FIN 115 E1
Jávea-Xàbia E 56 D5

Jävenitz D 79 A10
Javerlhac-et-la-Chapelle-St-Robert F 29 D7
Javgur MD 154 D3
Javier E 32 E3
Javorani BIH 157 C7
Javorník CZ 77 B12
Jävre S 118 D6
Javron-les-Chapelles F 23 D11
Jawor PL 81 D10
Jawornik Polski PL 144 D5
Jawor Solecki PL 141 H4
Jaworzno PL 142 D6
Jaworzno PL 143 F7
Jaworzyna Śląska PL 81 E10
Jayena E 53 C9
Jazeneuil F 28 C6
Jebel RO 159 B7
Jebjerg DK 86 B4
Jedburgh GB 5 E11
Jedlanka PL 141 G6
Jedlicze PL 144 D4
Jedlina-Zdrój PL 81 E10
Jedlińsk PL 141 G4
Jedlnia-Letnisko PL 141 H4
Jedlová CZ 77 C10
Jedľové Kostolany SK 146 E6
Jednorożec PL 139 D11
Jedovnice CZ 77 D11
Jędrzejewo PL 85 E10
Jędrzejów PL 143 E9
Jédula E 52 C5
Jedwabne PL 140 D6
Jedwabno PL 139 C10
Jeesiö FIN 117 D16
Jeesiöjärvi FIN 117 C14
Jegălia RO 161 E11
Jegun F 33 C6
Jegunovce NMK 164 E3
Jejsing DK 86 F3
Jēkabpils LV 135 C11
Jektvik N 108 C5
Jelah BIH 157 C8
Jelašca BIH 157 F9
Jelcz-Laskowice PL 81 D12
Jelenia Góra PL 81 E9
Jeleniewo PL 136 E6
Jelenin PL 81 C8
Jelenje HR 67 B9
Jeleśnia PL 147 B8
Jelgava LV 134 C7
Jelka SK 146 E5
Jelling DK 86 D4
Jeloboc MD 154 C3
Jelovica SRB 165 C6
Jełowa PL 142 E5
Jels DK 86 E4
Jelsa HR 157 F6
Jelšane SLO 67 A9
Jelšava SK 145 F1
Jelsi I 63 D7
Jemeppe B 19 D10
Jemgum D 17 B8
Jemielnica PL 142 E5
Jemielno PL 81 C11
Jemnice CZ 77 D9
Jena D 79 E10
Jenbach A 72 B4
Jeneč CZ 76 B6
Jengen D 71 B11
Jenikowo PL 85 C8
Jennersdorf A 148 C6
Jenny S 93 D9
Jenő H 149 B10
Jensvoll N 101 A15
Jeppo FIN 122 D9
Jērcēni LV 131 F11
Jerchel D 79 B9
Jerez de la Frontera E 52 C4
Jerez del Marquesado E 55 E6
Jerez de los Caballeros E 51 C6
Jerfojaur S 109 E16
Jergol N 113 E14
Jergucat AL 168 E3
Jeri LV 131 F10
Jérica E 48 E3
Jerichow D 79 A11
Jerka PL 81 C11
Jernved DK 86 E3
Jerslev DK 87 D8
Jerslev DK 90 E7
Jerstad N 110 C9
Jerte E 45 D9
Jerup DK 90 D7
Jerzens A 71 C11
Jerzmanowa PL 81 C10
Jerzmanowice PL 143 F8
Jerzu I 64 D4
Jesenice CZ 76 B4
Jesenice CZ 77 C7
Jesenice HR 156 D4
Jesenice HR 156 F6
Jesenice SLO 73 D9
Jeseník CZ 77 B12
Jeseník nad Odrou CZ 146 B5
Jesenské SK 147 E10
Jeserig D 79 B11
Jeserig D 79 B12
Jesi I 67 E7
Jesionowo PL 85 D8
Jesolo I 66 A6
Jessen D 80 C3
Jessheim N 95 B14
Jeßnitz D 79 C11
Jesteburg D 83 D7
Jettingen-Scheppach D 75 F7
Jeumont F 19 D9
Jevenstedt D 82 B7
Jever D 17 A9
Jevíčko CZ 77 C11
Jevišovice CZ 77 E10
Jevnaker N 95 B12
Jezera BIH 157 D8
Jezerane HR 67 B11
Jezerc RKS 164 E3
Jezero BIH 157 D7
Jezero HR 156 B3
Jeżewo PL 138 C5
Jeżewo PL 140 D7
Jeziorany PL 136 F2
Jeziorzany PL 141 G6
Jeżów PL 141 G1
Jeżowe PL 144 C5
Jeżów Sudecki PL 81 E9
Jiana RO 159 E10
Jibert RO 152 E6
Jibou RO 151 C11
Jichişu de Jos RO 152 C3
Jičín CZ 77 B8
Jidvei RO 152 E4
Jieznas LT 137 D9
Jihlava CZ 77 D9
Jijila RO 155 C2
Jijona-Xixona E 56 D4
Jilava RO 161 E8
Jilavele RO 161 D9
Jilemnice CZ 81 E9
Jílové CZ 80 E6
Jílové u Prahy CZ 77 C7
Jiltjaur S 109 E12
Jimbolia RO 150 F6
Jimena E 53 A10
Jimena de la Frontera E 53 D6
Jimramov CZ 77 C10
Jina RO 152 F3
Jince CZ 76 C5
Jindřichov CZ 77 B12
Jindřichov CZ 142 F4
Jindřichův Hradec CZ 77 D8
Jiřkov CZ 81 E7
Jirkov CZ 76 A4
Jirlău RO 161 C10
Jirnsum NL 16 B5
Jirny CZ 77 B7
Jistebnice CZ 77 D7
Jistebník CZ 146 B6
Jitia RO 161 B9
Jlajkovci SRB 163 C10
Joachimsthal D 84 E5
Joane P 38 F3
Job F 30 D4
Jobbágyi H 147 F9
Jobsbo S 97 B13
Jochberg A 72 B5
Jocketa D 79 E11
Jockfall S 116 E9
Jockgrim D 27 B9
Jódar E 55 D6
Jodłowa PL 144 D3
Jodłownik PL 144 D1
Jodoigne B 19 C10
Joensuu FIN 125 E13
Jõepere EST 131 C12
Joesjö S 108 E8
Joeström S 108 E8
Jõesuu EST 131 E9
Jœuf F 20 F6
Jõgeva EST 131 D12
Jõgua EST 131 C14
Johanngeorgenstadt D 75 B12
Johannisfors S 99 B10
Johannishus S 89 C8
Johanniskirchen D 76 E3
Johansfors S 89 B9
John o'Groats GB 3 H10
Johnston GB 12 B5
Johnstone GB 4 D7
Johnstown IRL 9 C7
Johnstown IRL 9 C10
Johovac BIH 158 D3
Jöhstadt D 76 A4
Jõhvi EST 131 C14
Joigny F 25 E9
Joinville F 26 D3
Joița RO 161 E7
Jokela FIN 119 B16
Jokela FIN 119 E16
Jokela FIN 127 D12
Jokelankylä FIN 123 C14
Jøkelfjordeidet N 112 C9
Jokijärvi FIN 121 C12
Jokijärvi FIN 123 D17
Joki-Kokko FIN 119 D16
Jokikunta FIN 127 E11
Jokikylä FIN 121 E11
Jokikylä FIN 122 E8
Jokikylä FIN 123 C13
Jokikylä FIN 123 C15
Jokilampi FIN 121 C12
Jokimaa FIN 127 D12
Jokioinen FIN 127 D9
Jokiperä FIN 122 E8
Jokipii FIN 122 E9
Jokivarsi FIN 123 E11
Jokivarsi FIN 123 E12
Jokkmokk S 116 E3
Jokūbavas LT 134 E2
Jolanda di Savoia I 66 C4
Jolanki FIN 117 E13
Jolda P 38 E3
Joloskylä FIN 119 D16
Joltai MD 154 E3
Jomala FIN 99 B13
Jømna N 101 E15
Jona CH 27 F10
Jönåker S 93 B9
Jonava LT 137 C9
Joncy F 30 B6
Jondal N 94 B4
Jonesborough GB 7 D10
Joniec PL 139 E10
Joniškėlis LT 135 D8
Joniškis LT 134 D7
Joniškis LT 137 C12
Jonkeri FIN 125 C13
Jönköping S 92 D4
Jonkowo PL 139 C9
Jonku FIN 120 D9
Jonquières F 35 B8
Jonsberg S 93 B9
Jonsered S 91 D11
Jonslund S 91 C12
Jonstorp S 87 C11
Jonzac F 28 E5
Jõõdre EST 130 D7
Joppolo I 59 B8
Jorăşti RO 153 F11
Jorba E 43 D7
Jorcas E 42 F2
Jordanów PL 147 B9
Jordanów Śląski PL 81 E11
Jordbro S 99 D10
Jordbru N 108 B9
Jordbruna N 108 D8
Jördenstorf D 83 C13
Jordet N 102 D3
Jork D 82 C7
Jörlanda S 91 D10
Jormvattnet S 105 B16
Jörn S 118 D4
Joroinen FIN 125 F9
Jørpeland N 94 D4
Jorquera E 47 F9
Jørstadmoen N 101 D12
Jošanica BIH 157 E9
Jošanička Banja SRB 163 C10
Jošavka BIH 157 C7
Joseni RO 153 D6
Josenii Bârgăului RO 152 C5
Josifovo NMK 169 B7
Josipdol HR 156 B3
Josipovac HR 149 E11
Josnes F 24 E6
Jössefors S 96 C8
Josselin F 22 E6
Jossund N 105 C9
Josvainiai LT 134 F7
Jota N 101 D15
Jou P 38 F5
Jouarre F 25 C9
Joué-lès-Tours F 24 F4
Joué-sur-Erdre F 23 E9
Jougne F 31 B9
Joukokylä FIN 121 D10
Jouques F 35 C10
Joure NL 16 C5
Journiac F 29 F7
Joutenniva FIN 123 B15
Joutsa FIN 127 B15
Joutseno FIN 129 C10
Joutsijärvi FIN 115 E3
Joux-la-Ville F 25 E10
Jouy F 24 C6
Jouy-aux-Arches F 26 B5
Jouy-le-Potier F 24 E6
Jøvik N 111 A18
Jøvik N 111 B13
Joyeuse F 35 B7
Joze F 30 D3
Józefów PL 141 F4
Józefów PL 144 A4
Józefów PL 144 C7
Juankoski FIN 125 D10
Juan-les-Pins F 36 D6
Juban AL 163 E8
Jubë AL 168 B1
Jübek D 82 A6
Jublains F 23 D11
Jubrique E 53 C6
Jüchen D 20 B6
Juchowo PL 85 C10
Jüchsen D 75 B8
Jucu RO 152 D3
Judaberg N 94 D3
Judenbach D 75 B9
Judenburg A 73 B10
Judinsalo FIN 127 B14
Juelsminde DK 86 D6
Jugon-les-Lacs F 23 D7
Jugorje SLO 148 E4
Jugureni RO 161 C8
Juhonpieti S 116 D10
Juhtimäki FIN 127 B9
Juillac F 29 E8
Juillan F 32 D6
Jujurieux F 31 C7
Jukkasjärvi S 116 C5
Juknaičiai LT 134 F3
Juksjaur S 109 E10
Jukua FIN 121 C9
Julåsen S 103 B10
Julbach A 76 E5
Jule N 105 C15
Jülich D 20 C6
Juliénas F 30 C6
Jullouville F 23 C8
Jumaliskylä FIN 121 E13
Jumeaux F 30 E3
Jumilhac-le-Grand F 29 E8
Jumilla E 55 C10
Juminen FIN 125 D9
Jumisko FIN 121 B11
Jumprava LV 135 C9
Jumurda LV 135 C11
Juncal P 44 E3
Juncosa E 42 E5
Juneda E 42 D5
Jung S 91 C13
Jungingen D 27 D11
Junglinster L 20 E6
Jungsund FIN 122 D7
Junik RKS 163 E9
Juniskär S 103 B13
Juniville F 19 F9
Jünkerath D 21 D7
Junkerdal N 109 C10
Junnonoja FIN 119 F15
Junosuando S 116 D9
Junqueira P 50 E5
Junsele S 107 D11
Juntinvaara FIN 121 F15
Juntusranta FIN 121 D13
Juodeikiai LT 134 D6
Juodkrantė LT 134 E2
Juodšiliai LT 137 D11
Juodupė LT 135 D11
Juoksengi S 117 E11
Juoksenki FIN 117 E11
Juokslahti FIN 127 B13
Juokuanvaara FIN 119 C13
Juonto FIN 121 F13
Juorkuna FIN 120 E8
Juornaankylä FIN 127 D14
Juostininkai LT 135 E9
Juotasniemi FIN 119 B17
Jupânești RO 160 D3
Jupilles F 24 E3
Juprelle B 19 C12
Jurançon F 32 D5
Jurbarkas LT 136 C6
Jurbise B 19 C8
Jürgenshagen D 83 C11
Jürgenstorf D 84 C3
Jurģi LV 134 C5
Jüri EST 131 C9
Jurignac F 28 D5
Jurilovca RO 155 D3
Jurjevo HR 67 C10
Jūrkalne LV 134 B2
Jurklošter SLO 148 D4
Jurkowice PL 143 E11
Jūrmala LV 134 C7
Jūrmalciems LV 134 D2
Jurmo FIN 126 D5
Jurmo FIN 126 F6
Jurmu FIN 121 D10
Jurovski Brod HR 148 E4
Jursla S 93 B8
Jurva FIN 122 E7
Jussac F 29 F10
Jussey F 26 E4
Juta H 149 D9
Jüterbog D 80 C4
Jutis S 109 D13
Jutrosin PL 81 C12
Jutsajaure S 116 D3
Juujärvi FIN 120 B9
Juuka FIN 125 D12
Juuma FIN 121 B13
Juupajoki FIN 127 B11
Juupakylä FIN 123 F10
Juurikka FIN 125 G14
Juurikkalahti FIN 125 B10
Juurikkamäki FIN 125 E10
Juurikorpi FIN 128 D6
Juuru EST 131 C9
Juustovaara FIN 117 D13
Juutinen FIN 123 B17
Juva FIN 128 B8
Juvanådammet S 107 D12
Juvigné F 23 D9
Juvigny-le-Tertre F 23 C9
Juvigny-sous-Andaine F 23 C10
Juvola FIN 125 F11
Juzennecourt F 26 D2
Juzet-d'Izaut F 33 E7
Jūžintai LT 135 E11
Jyderup DK 87 D8
Jylhä FIN 123 D17
Jylhämä FIN 119 E17
Jyllinge DK 87 D10
Jyllinkoski FIN 122 F8
Jyllintaival FIN 122 E8
Jyrinki FIN 123 C12
Jyrkänkoski FIN 121 B14
Jyrkänkylä FIN 125 B13
Jyrkkä FIN 125 C9
Jystrup DK 87 D9
Jyväskylä FIN 123 F15

K

Kaagjärve EST 131 F12
Kaakamo FIN 119 C12
Kaalepi EST 131 C11
Kaamanen FIN 113 E19
Kaamasjoki FIN 113 E19
Kaamasmukka FIN 113 E18
Kaanaa FIN 127 B11
Kääntöjärvi S 116 D7
Kääpa EST 131 F14
Kääpälä FIN 128 C6
Kaarakkala FIN 124 C8
Kaaraneskoski FIN 117 E12
Käärdi EST 131 E12
Kaarepere EST 131 D13
Kaaresuvanto FIN 116 B9
Kaarina FIN 126 E7
Kaarlela FIN 123 C10
Käärmelehto FIN 117 D15
Kaarnevaara S 117 C10
Kaarnijärvi FIN 115 F1
Kaarßen D 83 D10
Kaarst D 21 B7
Kaasmarkku FIN 126 C7
Kaatsheuvel NL 16 E4
Kaava FIN 113 D18
Kaavi FIN 125 E10
Kaba H 151 C7
Kabakça TR 173 B9
Kabaklar TR 173 E11
Kabakum TR 177 A8
Kabala EST 131 D11
Kåbdalis S 118 B4
Kabelvåg N 110 D7
Kaberneeme EST 131 B10
Kabile LV 134 C4
Kableshkovo BG 167 D9
Kabli EST 131 E8
Kać SRB 158 C4
Kaçanik RKS 164 E3
Kačarevo SRB 158 D6
Kachkivka UA 154 A2
Kachurivka UA 154 B5
Kačice CZ 76 B5
Käckelbäcksmon S 103 A13
Kaczory PL 85 D11
Kadaň CZ 76 B4
Kadarkút H 149 D9
Kadıköy TR 173 B9
Kadıköy TR 173 C6
Kadıköy TR 173 C11
Kadıköy TR 177 A9
Kadila EST 131 C12
Kadrifakovo NMK 164 F5
Kadrina EST 131 C12
Kadzidło PL 139 D11
Käenkoski FIN 125 E15
Kaerepere EST 131 D9
Kåfjord N 112 D11
Kåfjord N 113 B16
Kåfjorddalen N 112 E6
Kåge S 118 E5
Kågeröd S 87 D12
Kaggebo S 93 D9
Kağıthane TR 173 B10
Kagkadi GR 174 C3
Kahla D 79 E9
Kahl am Main D 187 A7
Kähög S 91 D11
Kahraman TR 181 A8
Kähtävä FIN 119 F12
Kaïafa GR 174 D4
Käina EST 130 D5
Kainasto FIN 122 F8
Kainourgio GR 174 B3
Kainulasjärvi S 116 D9
Kainuunkylä FIN 119 B11
Kainuunmäki FIN 124 C8
Kaipiainen FIN 128 D7
Kaipola FIN 127 B13
Kairala FIN 115 D2
Kairiai LT 134 E6
Kairiškiai LT 134 D5
Kaisajoki FIN 119 B12
Kaisepakte S 111 D17
Kaisersesch D 21 D8
Kaiserslautern D 21 F9
Kaisheim D 75 E8
Kaišiadorys LT 137 D9
Kaisma EST 131 D9
Kaitainen FIN 124 F9
Kaitainsalmi FIN 121 F11
Kaitajärvi FIN 119 B13
Kaitum S 116 C4
Kaivanto FIN 120 F9
Kaive LV 134 B6
Kaive LV 135 B11
Kajaani FIN 121 F10
Kajal SK 146 E5
Kajanki FIN 117 B11
Kajdacs H 149 C11
Kajew PL 143 B7
Kajoo FIN 125 D12
Kájov CZ 76 E6
Kakanj BIH 157 D9
Kakasd H 149 D11
Kakavi AL 168 E3
Kakenieki LV 134 C6
Kakenstorf D 82 D7
Kakerbeck D 83 E10
Kakhanavichy BY 133 E4
Kakilahti FIN 120 F8
Kākišķe LV 134 D2
Kaklıç TR 177 C8
Kąkolewnica Wschodnia PL 141 G7
Kąkolewo PL 81 C11
Kakovatos GR 174 E4
Kakrukë AL 168 C3
Kakskerta FIN 126 E7
Kakslauttanen FIN 115 B2
Kakucs H 150 C3
Kál H 150 B5
Käl S 107 D12
Kälä FIN 127 B15
Kalabakbaşi TR 173 E7
Kålaboda S 118 F5
Kalače MNE 163 D9
Kala Dendra GR 169 B9
Kalaja FIN 123 C14
Kalajärvi FIN 127 E12
Kalajoki FIN 119 F11
Kalak N 113 B19
Kalakangas FIN 123 C14
Kalakoski FIN 123 F10
Kalamaki GR 169 E8
Kalamaki GR 174 D2
Kalamaki GR 175 D8
Kalamaria GR 169 C8
Kalamata GR 174 E5
Kalamos GR 175 C8
Kalamoti GR 177 C7
Kalamoto GR 169 C9
Kalampaka GR 169 E6
Kalampaki GR 171 B6
Kalana EST 130 D4
Kalandra GR 169 E9
Kala Nera GR 169 F9
Kalanistra GR 174 C4
Kalanti FIN 126 D6
Kälarne S 107 F10
Kalathos GR 181 D8
Kalavarda GR 181 D7
Kalavryta GR 174 C5
Kaława PL 81 B9
Kalbe (Milde) D 83 E10
Kalce SLO 73 E9
Kalchevo BG 167 E7
Káld H 149 B8
Kaldabruņa LV 135 D12
Kaldbak FO 2 A3
Kaldfarnes N 111 B12
Kaldfarnes N 111 B13
Kaldfjord N 111 A16
Kaldslett N 111 A16
Kaldvåg N 111 D10
Kaldvik N 111 D11
Kale TR 181 B9
Kalefeld D 79 C7
Kaleköy TR 171 D9
Kälen S 103 A8
Kälen S 103 B11
Kälen S 118 D6
Kalentzi GR 168 F4
Kalesija BIH 157 D10
Kalesmeno GR 174 B4
Kalēti LV 134 D2
Kalety PL 143 E6
Kalevala RUS 121 D17
Kali GR 169 C7
Kali HR 156 D3
Kalianoi GR 175 D5
Kalimanci NMK 165 F6
Kalimash AL 163 E9
Kaliningrad RUS 136 D2
Kalinino RUS 134 F3
Kalinovik BIH 157 F9
Kalinovka RUS 136 D4
Kalinowa PL 142 C5
Kalinowo PL 136 F6
Kaliska PL 138 C5
Kalisz PL 142 C5
Kalisz Pomorski PL 85 D9
Kalita EST 131 E8
Kali Vrysi GR 170 B5
Kalix S 119 C10
Kalixforsen S 116 C4
Kalkar D 16 E6
Kalkhorst D 83 C10
Kalki LV 130 F4
Kalkiainen FIN 115 E3
Kalkim TR 173 E7
Kalkkimaa FIN 119 C12
Kalkkinen FIN 127 C14
Kałków PL 77 B12
Kalkūni LV 135 E12
Kall D 21 C7
Kall S 105 E14
Källa S 89 A11
Kallaste EST 131 D14
Kallax S 118 C8
Källberget S 102 A6
Källbomark S 118 D6
Källby FIN 122 C9
Källby S 91 B13
Kalle N 110 D7
Källeboda S 96 D7
Kållekärr S 91 C10
Källered S 91 D11
Källerud S 91 A12
Kallham A 76 F5
Kallifoni GR 169 F6
Kallifytos GR 171 B6
Kallimasia GR 177 C7
Kallinge S 89 C8
Kalliojoki FIN 121 F15
Kalliopi GR 171 E8
Kalliosalmi FIN 117 E17
Kallirachi GR 171 C7
Kallislahti FIN 129 B10
Kallithea GR 169 D8
Kallithea GR 169 D9
Kallithea GR 169 E7
Kallithea GR 174 D4
Kallithea GR 174 F4
Kallithea GR 175 D8
Kallithea GR 177 D8
Kallithiro GR 169 F6
Kalljord N 110 C9
Kallmet i Madh AL 163 F8
Kallmünz D 75 D10
Kallo FIN 117 D12
Kálló H 150 B3
Kallön S 109 E15
Kalloni GR 171 F10
Kalloni GR 175 D7
Kalloni GR 176 D5
Kállósemjén H 145 H4
Kallsedet S 105 D13
Källsjön S 103 E11
Kallträsk FIN 122 F7
Kallunki FIN 115 E5
Kallunki FIN 121 B13
Kálmánháza H 145 H4
Kalmar S 89 B10
Kalmari FIN 123 E14
Kalmthout B 16 F2
Kalna SRB 164 C5
Kalna SRB 164 D5
Kalná nad Hronom SK 147 E7
Kalnciems LV 134 C7
Kalni LV 134 D4
Kalnieši LV 133 E2
Kalnujai LT 134 F6
Kalocsa H 150 D2
Kalofer BG 165 D10
Kaloi Limenes GR 178 F8
Kaloneri GR 169 D5
Kalo Nero GR 174 E4
Kalos Agros GR 170 B6
Kalotina BG 165 C6
Kalotintsi BG 165 D6
Kaloyanovets BG 166 E5
Kaloyanovo BG 165 E10
Káloz H 149 C10
Kalpaki GR 168 E4
Kalpio FIN 121 E10
Kals am Großglockner A 73 B6
Kaltanėnai LT 135 F11
Kaltbrunn CH 27 F11
Kaltene LV 134 B5
Kaltenkirchen D 83 C7
Kaltennordheim D 79 E7
Kaltensundheim D 79 E7
Kaltinėnai LT 134 E4
Kaluđerica SRB 158 D6
Kalugerovo BG 165 E9
Kalundborg DK 87 D8
Kalupe LV 135 D13
Kałuszyn PL 141 F5
Kaluzhskoye RUS 136 D4
Kalvåg N 100 C1
Kalvarija LT 136 E7
Kalvatn N 100 B4
Kalveliai LT 137 D12
Kalvene LV 134 C3
Kalvi EST 131 C13
Kälviä FIN 123 C10
Kalvik N 109 A10
Kalvitsa FIN 128 B7
Kalvola FIN 127 C11
Kalvträsk S 107 B17
Kalwang A 73 B10
Kalwaria Zebrzydowska PL 147 B9
Kalymnos GR 177 F8
Kalyny UA 145 G8
Kalythies GR 181 D8
Kalyves GR 171 C7
Kalyvia GR 174 B3
Kalyvia GR 174 B3
Kalyvia GR 174 D5
Kalyvia Thorikou GR 175 D8
Kamajai LT 135 E11
Kämäränkylä FIN 121 F14
Kamarde LV 135 D8
Kamares GR 174 C4
Kamares GR 175 F10
Kamariotissa GR 171 D8
Kambja EST 131 E13
Kamburovo BG 166 C6
Kamen BG 166 C5
Kamen D 17 E9
Kamenari BG 166 D6
Kamena Vourla GR 175 B6
Kamen Bryag BG 167 C11
Kamencia SRB 158 F6
Kamenec pod Vtáčnikom SK 147 D7
Kamengrad BIH 156 C6
Kamenica BIH 156 D5
Kamenica BIH 157 D9
Kamenica BIH 158 F3
Kamenica NMK 164 E6
Kamenica SK 145 E2
Kamenica SRB 158 E4
Kamenica SRB 164 C5
Kamenica nad Cirochou SK 145 F4
Kamenica nad Hronom SK 147 F7
Kamenicë AL 168 C4
Kamenice CZ 77 C7
Kamenice CZ 77 D9
Kamenicë RKS 164 D4
Kamenice nad Lipou CZ 77 D8
Kamenična SK 146 F6
Kamenín SK 147 F7
Kamenka RUS 129 E11
Kamenná Poruba SK 147 C7
Kamennogorsk RUS 129 D11
Kamenný Most SK 147 F7
Kamenný Přívoz CZ 77 C7
Kamenný Újezd CZ 77 E6
Kameno BG 167 D8
Kameno Pole BG 165 C8
Kamenovo BG 161 F8
Kamensko BIH 157 D9
Kamensko HR 149 F8
Kamensko HR 157 E6
Kamenskoye RUS 136 D4
Kamenz D 80 D6
Kamerik NL 182 A5
Kamern D 83 E12
Kames GB 4 D6
Kamëz AL 168 B2
Kamičak BIH 157 C6
Kamicë-Flakë AL 163 E7
Kamień PL 144 C5
Kamieńczyk PL 139 E12
Kamienica PL 145 D1
Kamienica Polska PL 143 E7
Kamieniec PL 81 B10
Kamieniec Ząbkowicki PL 77 A11
Kamienka SK 145 E2
Kamień Krajeński PL 85 C13
Kamienna Góra PL 81 E10
Kamiennik PL 81 E12
Kamień Pomorski PL 85 C7
Kamieńsk PL 143 D8
Kamień Wielkie PL 81 A7
Kamilski Dol BG 171 A10
Kamion PL 139 F9
Kamion PL 141 G2
Kamionka PL 141 H6
Kamiros GR 181 D7
Kamlunge S 119 B9
Kammela FIN 126 D5
Kammen N 112 C4
Kamnik SLO 73 D10
Kamno SLO 73 D8
Kamøyvær N 113 A16
Kamp D 185 D8
Kampanis GR 169 C8
Kampen D 86 F2
Kampen NL 16 C5
Kampenhout B 182 D5
Kämpfelbach D 187 D6
Kampi GR 174 A2
Kampia GR 177 B6
Kampinkylä FIN 122 E8
Kampinos PL 141 F2
Kamp-Lintfort D 17 F7
Kampos GR 174 C5
Kampos GR 174 F5
Kampvoll N 111 B14
Kamsjö S 118 F3
Kamula FIN 123 B16
Kamut H 151 D6
Kam''yane UA 154 A5
Kam''yans'ke UA 154 F4
Kamyanyets BY 141 F9
Kamyanyuki BY 141 E9
Kanaküla EST 131 E10
Kanal SLO 73 D8
Kanala FIN 123 D12
Kanala GR 175 E9
Kanali GR 168 E2
Kanali GR 174 A2
Kanalia GR 169 F8
Kanallaki GR 168 F4
Kanan S 109 F10
Kanatlarci NMK 169 B6
Kańczuga PL 144 D5
Kandava LV 134 B5
Kandel D 27 B9
Kandelin D 84 B4
Kandern D 27 E8
Kandersteg CH 70 E5
Kandila GR 174 B2
Kandila GR 174 D5
Kandle EST 131 B12
Kanepi EST 131 F13
Kanestraum N 104 E4
Kanfanar HR 67 B8
Kangas FIN 119 F13
Kangas FIN 122 D9
Kangasaho FIN 123 E13
Kangasala FIN 127 C11
Kangaskylä FIN 119 F16
Kangaskylä FIN 121 E11
Kangaskylä FIN 123 C13
Kangaslahti FIN 125 D10
Kangaslampi FIN 125 F10
Kangasniemi FIN 123 G17
Kangasvieri FIN 123 C13
Kangos S 116 D9
Kangosjärvi FIN 117 C11
Kanianka SK 147 D7
Kaninë AL 168 D2
Kanjiža SRB 150 E5
Kankaanpää FIN 126 B7
Kankaanpää FIN 126 C7
Kankainen FIN 123 F16
Kankari FIN 120 E8
Kånna S 87 B13
Kannas FIN 121 E12
Känne S 103 B9
Kannonjärvi FIN 123 E14
Kannonkoski FIN 123 E14
Kannus FIN 123 C11
Kannusjärvi FIN 128 D7
Kannuskoski FIN 128 D7
Kanpantxua E 41 B6
Kanstad N 111 D10
Kanstadbotn N 111 C10
Kantala FIN 124 F8
Kantanos GR 178 E6
Kantele FIN 127 D14
Kantens NL 17 B7
Kantia GR 175 D6
Kantojärvi FIN 119 C12
Kantojoki FIN 121 B13
Kantokylä FIN 123 B13
Kantola FIN 123 D10
Kantomaanpää FIN 119 B12
Kantorneset N 111 B17
Kantserava BY 133 F4
Kantti FIN 122 F9
Kanturk IRL 8 D5
Kaolinovo BG 161 F10
Kaona SRB 158 F5
Kaonik BIH 157 D8
Kaonik SRB 164 B3
Kapakli TR 173 B8
Kapakli TR 173 D10
Kapanbeleni TR 173 D7
Kapandriti GR 175 C8
Kaparelli GR 175 C7
Kapčiamiestis LT 137 F8
Kapelle NL 16 F1
Kapellen B 16 F2
Kapelle-op-den-Bos B 182 C4
Kapellskär S 99 C12
Kapfenberg A 148 B4
Kapikargin TR 181 C9
Kapitan-Andreevo BG 166 F6
Kapiz TR 181 B9
Kaplava LV 133 E2
Kaplice CZ 77 E7
Kapljuh BIH 156 C5
Kápolna H 150 B5
Kápolnásnyék H 149 B11
Kaposfő H 149 D9
Kaposmérő H 149 D9
Kaposszekcső H 149 D10
Kaposvár H 149 D9
Kapp N 101 E13
Kappel D 21 E8
Kappel-Grafenhausen D 186 E4
Kappeln D 83 A7
Kappelrodeck D 186 D5
Kappl A 71 C10
Kåpponis S 118 B4
Kaprijke B 16 F1
Kaprun A 73 B6
Kapshticë AL 168 C5
Kapsia GR 174 D5
Kaptol HR 149 F9
Kaptsyowka BY 140 C9
Kapušany SK 145 E3
Kapusta FIN 119 B12
Kapuvár H 149 A8
Käpylä FIN 119 F14
Karaağaç TR 173 A7
Karaağaç TR 173 F6
Karaağaçli TR 177 B9
Karabanove UA 154 C5
Karabiga TR 173 D7
Karaböğürtlen TR 181 B9
Karabunar BG 165 E9
Karaburun TR 173 B10
Karaburun TR 177 B7
Karaca TR 181 C8
Karacabey TR 173 D9
Karacadağ TR 167 F9
Karacakilavuz TR 173 B7
Karacaköy TR 173 B9
Karád H 149 C9
Karadzhalovo BG 166 E4
Karahalil TR 173 A7
Karaincirli TR 171 C10
Karainebeyli TR 171 D10
Karaisen BG 166 C4
Karakaja BIH 157 D11
Karakasim TR 172 A6
Karakaya TR 173 F9
Karakoca TR 173 D10
Karaköy TR 173 E6
Karaköy TR 177 B9

Karaköy TR 181 B9
Karakurt TR 177 A10
Karala EST 130 E3
Karaman TR 173 E9
Karamanovo BG 166 B5
Karamehmet TR 173 B8
Karamyshevo RUS 132 F4
Karamyshevo RUS 136 E5
Karancsberény H 147 E9
Karancskeszi H 147 E9
Karancslapujtő H 147 E9
Karancsság H 147 E9
Karankamäki FIN 124 C8
Karaoğlanli TR 177 B10
Karaorman TR 173 E9
Karaova TR 177 E10
Karapchiv UA 152 A6
Karapelit BG 161 F11
Karasjok N 113 E15
Karatoulas GR 174 D4
Karats S 109 C16
Karavas GR 178 C4
Karavelovo BG 165 D10
Karavelovo BG 167 E7
Käravete EST 131 C11
Karavomylos GR 175 B6
Karavukovo SRB 157 B11
Karben D 21 D11
Kårberg S 92 B5
Karbinci NMK 164 F5
Kårböle S 103 C9
Kårböleskog S 103 C9
Karbow-Vietlübbe D 83 D12
Karbunarë e Vogël AL 168 C2
Karby D 83 A7
Karby DK 86 B3
Karby S 99 C10
Karcag H 151 C6
Karcsa H 145 G4
Karczew PL 141 F4
Karczmiska Pierwsze PL 141 H6
Kärda S 87 A13
Kardakata GR 174 C1
Kardam BG 155 F2
Kardam BG 166 C6
Kardamaina GR 177 F9
Kardamyli GR 174 F5
Kardašova Řečice CZ 77 D7
Karden D 21 D8
Kardiani GR 176 D5
Kardis S 117 E11
Karditsa GR 169 F6
Karditsomagoula GR 169 F6
Kärdla EST 130 D5
Kardon BY 133 F6
Kardos H 150 D6
Kardoskút H 150 E6
Karegasnjarga FIN 113 E16
Kareli LV 134 D4
Karesuando S 116 B8
Kargowa PL 81 B9
Karhi FIN 123 C10
Karhila FIN 123 F13
Karhujärvi FIN 115 F4
Karhukangas FIN 119 F14
Karhula FIN 128 D6
Kariani GR 170 C5
Karigasniemi FIN 113 E16
Karihaugen N 111 D12
Karijoki FIN 122 F7
Karinainen FIN 126 D8
Käringberg S 107 A12
Kåringen N 111 D10
Käringsjön S 102 B3
Käringsjövallen S 102 B4
Karinkanta FIN 119 E13
Karis FIN 127 E10
Karise DK 87 E10
Karisjärvi FIN 127 D11
Karitaina GR 174 E5
Karitsa GR 169 D7
Karjalaisenniemi FIN 121 B11
Karjalan kirkonkylä FIN 126 D7
Karjalankylä FIN 119 D15
Karjalankylä FIN 126 D7
Karjalanvaara FIN 120 B9
Karjalanvaara FIN 121 F10
Karjalohja FIN 127 E10
Kärjenkoski FIN 122 F7
Karjulanmäki FIN 123 C13
Karkalou GR 174 D5
Kärki LV 131 F11
Karkinen FIN 119 F12
Kärkkäala FIN 123 E16
Kärkkäälä FIN 124 E8
Karkkila FIN 127 D11
Karkku FIN 127 C9
Kärklinieki LV 133 B2
Kärkölä FIN 127 D10
Kärkölä FIN 127 D13
Karksi EST 131 E11
Karksi-Nuia EST 131 E11
Kårkul S 118 B5
Kärla EST 130 E4
Karlå FIN 122 F7
Karlby FIN 126 F4
Karlebotn N 114 C5
Karleby FIN 123 C10
Karlholmsbruk S 99 A9
Karlino PL 85 B9
Kārļmuiža LV 134 B4
Karlobag HR 67 C11
Karlovac HR 148 F5
Karlovasi GR 177 D8
Karlovice CZ 142 F3
Karlovo BG 165 D10
Karlovy Vary CZ 76 B3
Karłowice PL 142 E4
Karlsbäck S 107 D15
Karlsbad D 27 C10
Karlsberg S 103 C9
Karlsborg S 92 B5
Karlsburg D 84 C5
Karlsdal S 97 D12
Karlsdorf-Neuthard D 27 B10
Karlsfeld D 75 F9
Karlsfors S 103 C9
Karlshagen D 84 B5
Karlshamn S 89 C7
Karlshöfen D 17 B12
Karlskoga S 97 D12
Karlskrona S 89 C9
Karlsøy N 112 C4
Karlsruhe D 27 B9
Karlstad S 97 D10
Karlstadt D 74 C6
Karlstein an der Thaya A 77 E8
Karlstetten A 77 F9
Karlukovo BG 165 C9
Karmansbo S 97 C14
Karmas S 109 B17
Karmėlava LT 137 D9
Kärnä FIN 123 D11
Kärnä FIN 123 D15
Kärna S 91 D10
Karnaliyivka UA 154 E6
Karnice PL 85 B8
Karniewo PL 139 E10
Karnjarga FIN 113 D19
Karnobat BG 167 D7
Karojba HR 67 B8
Karolinka CZ 146 C6
Karonsbo S 107 B15
Karoti GR 171 B10
Karousades GR 168 E2
Karow D 79 B11
Karow D 83 C12
Karpacz PL 81 E9
Kärpänkylä FIN 121 C14
Karpathos GR 181 E6
Karpenisi GR 174 B4
Karperi GR 169 B9
Karpero GR 169 E6
Kärppälä FIN 127 C9
Karpuzlu TR 171 C10
Karpuzlu TR 181 A7
Kärrbackstrand S 102 E4
Karrebæksminde DK 87 E9
Karrenzin D 83 D11
Kärrsjö S 107 D15
Karsakiškis LT 135 E9
Kärsämä FIN 119 E15
Kärsämäki FIN 123 C15
Kärsava LV 133 C3
Karsikas FIN 123 C14
Karsikkoniemi FIN 117 C11
Karsikkovaara FIN 124 B9
Karsimus FIN 115 E2
Karsin PL 138 C4
Karşiyaka TR 173 D9
Karşiyaka TR 177 C9
Karsko PL 85 E8
Kårsta S 99 C10
Karstädt D 83 D10
Karstädt D 83 D11
Kärstna EST 131 E11
Karstula FIN 123 E13
Karszew PL 142 B6
Kartal H 150 B4
Kartavoll N 94 E3
Kartena LT 134 E2
Kartitsch A 72 C6
Kartuzy PL 138 B5
Käru EST 131 D10
Käru EST 131 D12
Karuna FIN 126 E8
Karungi S 119 B11
Karunki FIN 119 B12
Karup DK 86 C4
Kårvåg N 104 E3
Karvala FIN 123 D11
Kärväskylä FIN 123 D15
Karvia FIN 122 F9
Kårvikhamn N 111 B15
Karviná CZ 147 B7
Karvoskylä FIN 123 C14
Karvounari GR 168 F3
Karwica PL 139 C11
Karya GR 169 E7
Karya GR 174 B2
Karya GR 175 D6
Karyes GR 171 D6
Karyes GR 175 E5
Karyotissa GR 169 C7
Karyoupoli GR 178 B3
Karystos GR 175 C9
Kås DK 86 A5
Kašalj SRB 163 C10
Kasejovice CZ 76 D5
Kasendorf D 75 B9
Kasepää EST 131 D14
Kasfjord N 111 C11
Kashirskoye RUS 136 D2
Kaşikçi TR 173 B7
Kašina HR 148 E6
Kaskantyú H 150 D3
Kaskats S 116 F4
Kaskii FIN 129 B9
Kaskinen FIN 122 F6
Kaskö FIN 122 F6
Käsmä FIN 121 C12
Käsmo N 108 B9
Kåsmolia N 108 B9
Käsmu EST 131 B11
Kaspakas GR 171 E8
Kašperské Hory CZ 76 D5
Kaspichan BG 167 C8
Kassa S 117 D11
Kassandreia GR 169 D9
Kasseedorf D 83 B9
Kassel D 78 D6
Kassiopi GR 168 E2
Kastania GR 168 D4
Kastania GR 168 E5
Kastania GR 169 D7
Kastania GR 169 F6
Kastanies GR 171 A10
Kastanochori GR 169 C10
Kastari FIN 127 C13
Kastellaun D 21 D8
Kastelli GR 178 E9
Kastellia GR 174 B5
Kaštel Stari HR 156 E5
Kaštel Sućurac HR 156 E5
Kaštel Šegarski HR 156 D4
Kasterlee B 16 F3
Kastīre LV 135 D13
Kastl D 75 D10
Kastlösa S 89 C10
Kastneshamn N 111 C13
Kastorf D 83 C9
Kastoria GR 168 C5
Kastorio GR 174 E5
Kastraki GR 174 B3
Kastraki GR 176 E5
Kastrāne LV 135 C10
Kastre EST 131 E14
Kastri GR 169 E8
Kastri GR 175 E6
Kastro GR 175 C7
Kastrosykia GR 174 A2
Kastrova BY 133 D4
Kaszaper H 150 E6
Kaszczor PL 81 C10
Katafyto GR 169 B10
Katajamäki FIN 125 D10
Katakolo GR 174 D3
Kåtaliden S 109 F15
Kataloinen FIN 127 C12
Katapola GR 177 F6
Katarraktis GR 177 C7
Kåtaselet S 118 D3
Katastari GR 174 D2
Katerini GR 169 D8
Katerma FIN 125 B12
Kathenoi GR 175 B8
Kathlow D 81 C6
Kätkänjoki FIN 123 E11
Kätkäsuvanto FIN 117 B10
Kätkävaara FIN 119 B13
Kätkesuando S 117 B10
Katlenburg-Lindau D 79 C7
Kátlovce SK 146 D5
Kato Achaïa GR 174 C4
Kato Alepochori GR 175 C7
Kato Asites GR 178 E9
Katochi GR 174 C3
Kato Chorio GR 179 E10
Kato Doliana GR 175 E6
Kato Glykovrysi GR 178 B4
Kato Kamila GR 169 B9
Kato Makrinou GR 174 C4
Kato Nevrokopi GR 169 B10
Kato Sounio GR 175 D9
Kato Tithorea GR 175 B6
Katouna GR 174 B3
Kato Vermio GR 169 C7
Katovice CZ 76 D5
Kato Vlasia GR 174 C4
Kato Vrontou GR 169 B10
Katowice PL 143 F7
Katranca TR 173 B7
Katrineberg S 103 D11
Katrineholm S 93 B8
Katrineholm S 103 E13
Katsdorf A 77 F6
Katsikas GR 168 E4
Kattavia GR 181 E7
Kattbo S 102 E7
Kattelus FIN 123 F11
Kattilasaari S 119 C11
Kättilstad S 92 C7
Kättilstorp S 91 C14
Kattisavan S 107 B14
Kattisträsk S 118 E3
Katundishtë AL 168 D3
Katunets BG 165 C10
Katunitsa BG 165 E10
Katuntsi BG 169 B9
Katwijk aan Zee NL 16 D2
Katyčiai LT 134 F3
Katymár H 150 E3
Kąty Wrocławskie PL 81 D11
Katzenelnbogen D 21 D9
Katzweiler D 21 E9
Kaub D 21 D9
Kaufbeuren D 71 B11
Kaufungen D 78 D6
Kaugurieši LV 135 B11
Kauhajärvi FIN 122 E8
Kauhajärvi FIN 123 D10
Kauhajoki FIN 122 F8
Kauhava FIN 123 D10
Kaukalampi FIN 127 D13
Kaukolikai LT 134 D3
Kaukonen FIN 117 D13
Kauksi EST 131 C14
Kaulille B 183 C7
Kaulinranta FIN 119 B11
Kaulsdorf D 79 E9
Kaunas LT 137 D8
Kaunata LV 133 D3
Kauniainen FIN 127 E12
Kaunisjoensuu S 117 D11
Kaunisvaara S 117 D10
Kaupanger N 100 D6
Kaupiškiai LT 136 D6
Kauppila FIN 123 F17
Kauppilanmäki FIN 124 C8
Kaurajärvi FIN 122 D9
Kaurissalo FIN 126 D5
Kaustinen FIN 123 C11
Kautenbach L 184 E5
Kautokeino N 112 E11
Kautzen A 77 E8
Kauvatsa FIN 126 C8
Kauvosaarenpää FIN 119 B11
Kavacik TR 172 B6
Kavacik TR 173 E9
Kavadarci NMK 169 B7
Kavajë AL 168 B2
Kavak TR 173 C6
Kavakdere TR 173 A7
Kavakli TR 173 A7
Kavaklidere TR 181 B8
Kavala GR 171 C6
Kavarna BG 167 C10
Kavarskas LT 135 F9
Kavasilas GR 174 D3
Kavastu EST 131 E14
Kavelstorf D 83 C12
Kävlinge S 87 D12
Kavos GR 168 F3
Kavousi GR 179 E10
Kavs'ke UA 145 E8
Kavyli GR 171 A11
Kaxås S 105 D15
Käxed S 107 E14
Kaxholmen S 92 D4
Kayabaşi TR 181 B9
Kayalar TR 173 E8
Kayali TR 167 F8
Kayalioğlu TR 177 B10
Kayapa TR 173 F7
Kayatepe TR 173 E7
Käylä FIN 121 B13
Käymäjärvi S 116 D9
Kayna D 79 E11
Kaynaklar TR 177 C9
Kaynarca TR 173 A7
Kaynardzha BG 161 F10
Käyrämö FIN 117 E16
Kaysersberg F 27 D7
Kazanka BG 166 E4
Kazanlŭk BG 166 D4
Kazanów PL 141 H4
Kazár H 147 E9
Kazdanga LV 134 C3
Kazichane BG 165 D7
Kazikli TR 177 E9
Kazimierza Wielka PL 143 F9
Kazimierz Biskupi PL 142 B5
Kazimierz Dolne PL 141 H5
Kazincbarcika H 145 G2
Kazlowshchyna BY 133 E4
Kazlų Rūda LT 137 D7
Kaźmierz PL 81 A11
Kaznějov CZ 76 C4
Kazyany BY 133 E7
Kaz'yany BY 135 F13
Kçirë AL 163 E8
Kcynia PL 85 E12
Kdyně CZ 76 D4
Keadue IRL 6 D6
Keady GB 7 D9
Kealkill IRL 8 E4
Kebal S 91 B9
Kecel H 150 D3
Kecerovce SK 145 F3
Kechrokampos GR 171 B7
Kechros GR 171 B9
Kecskéd H 149 A10
Kecskemét H 150 D4
Kėdainiai LT 135 F7
Kedros GR 174 A5
Kędzierzyn-Koźle PL 142 F5
Keele GB 11 E7
Keenagh IRL 7 E7
Keeni EST 131 F12
Kefalos GR 181 C5
Kefalovryso GR 169 E7
Kefenrod D 21 D12
Kefermarkt A 77 F7
Ķegums LV 135 C9
Kegworth GB 11 F9
Kehidakustány H 149 C8
Kehl D 27 C8
Kehlen L 20 E6
Kehra EST 131 C10
Kehrig D 21 D8
Kehtna EST 131 D9
Kehvo FIN 124 D9
Keighley GB 11 D8
Keihärinkoski FIN 123 D15
Keikyä FIN 126 C8
Keila EST 131 C8
Keila-Joa EST 131 C8
Keillmore GB 4 D5
Keinäsperä FIN 119 D17
Ķeipene LV 135 C10
Ķeiprod N 111 C14
Keiss GB 3 H10
Keitele FIN 123 D16
Keitelepohja FIN 123 D15
Keith GB 3 K11
Kék H 145 G4
Ķekava LV 135 C8
Kékcse H 145 G5
Kelankylä FIN 119 C18
Kelberg D 21 D7
Kelbra (Kyffhäuser) D 79 D9
Kelč CZ 146 C5
Këlcyrë AL 168 D3
Kelebia H 150 E4
Kelechyn UA 145 F7
Kelheim D 75 E10
Kelkheim (Taunus) D 187 A5
Kell D 21 E7
Kellas GB 3 K10
Kellas GB 5 B11
Kellenhusen D 83 B10
Kelli GB 169 C6
Kellinghusen D 82 C7
Kellmünz an der Iller D 71 A10
Kello FIN 119 D14
Kellokoski FIN 127 D13
Kelloniemi FIN 115 E3
Kelloniemi FIN 117 D11
Kelloselkä FIN 115 E5
Kells GB 4 F4
Kells IRL 7 E9
Kells IRL 8 E2
Kells IRL 9 C8
Kelmė LT 134 E5
Kelmis B 20 C6
Kelontekemä FIN 117 C15
Kelottijärvi FIN 116 A8
Kelso GB 5 D12
Kelujärvi FIN 115 D2
Kelvä FIN 125 D14
Kelvedon GB 15 D10
Kemalpaşa TR 177 C9
Kemberg D 79 C12
Kemecse H 145 G4
Kemence H 147 E7
Kemenesmagasi H 149 B8
Kemenessömjén H 149 B8
Kemerburgaz TR 173 B10
Kémes H 149 E10
Kemeten A 148 B6
Kemi FIN 119 C13
Kemihaara FIN 115 C5
Kemijärvi FIN 115 E2
Kemilä FIN 121 C14
Keminmaa FIN 119 C13
Keminperä FIN 121 D12
Këmishtaj AL 168 C2
Kemmel B 18 C6
Kemnath D 75 C10
Kemnay GB 3 L12
Kemnitz D 81 D7
Kemnitz D 84 B5
Kempele FIN 119 E15
Kempen D 16 F6
Kempenich D 21 D8
Kempsey GB 13 A10
Kempston GB 15 C8
Kempten (Allgäu) D 71 B10
Kendal GB 10 C6
Kenderes H 150 C6
Kendice SK 145 F3
Kenézlő H 145 G4
Kenfig GB 13 B7
Kengis S 117 D10
Kengyet H 150 C5
Kenilworth GB 13 A11
Kenmare IRL 8 E3
Kenmore GB 5 B9
Kenn D 21 E7
Kennacraig GB 4 D6
Kensaleyre GB 2 L4
Kensworth GB 15 D7
Kentavros GR 171 B7
Kentriko GR 169 B8
Kentro GR 174 D3
Kenyeri H 149 B8
Kenzingen D 27 D8
Kepez TR 171 D10
Kępice PL 85 B11
Kępno PL 142 D4
Kepsut TR 173 E9
Keqekollë RKS 164 D3
Keramitsa GR 168 E3
Keramoti GR 171 C7
Keräntöjärvi S 116 C9
Kerasia GR 169 D6
Kerasona GR 168 F4
Keräs-Sieppi FIN 117 B11
Keratea GR 175 D8
Kerava FIN 127 E13
Kerecsend H 147 F10
Kerekegyháza H 150 D3
Kerepestarcsa H 150 B3
Kerets'ky UA 145 G7
Kergu EST 131 D9
Keri GR 174 D2
Kerimäki FIN 129 B11
Kerisalo FIN 125 F9
Kerkdriel NL 16 E4
Kerkejaure S 118 B3
Kerken D 16 F6
Kerkini GR 169 B9
Kerkkoo FIN 127 E14
Kerkonkoski FIN 123 E17
Kerkrade NL 20 C6
Kerkwijk NL 183 B6
Kerkyra GR 168 E2
Kerlouan F 22 C3
Kerma FIN 125 F11
Kermen BG 166 D6
Kernascléden F 22 D5
Kernavė LT 137 D10
Kernhof A 148 A5
Kerns CH 70 D6
Kerpen D 21 C7
Kerrykeel IRL 7 B7
Kershopefoot GB 5 E11
Kersilö FIN 117 C17
Kerspleben D 79 D9
Kerstinbo S 98 B7
Kerteminde DK 86 E7
Kertészsziget H 151 C7
Kertezi GR 174 D4
Kerttuankylä FIN 123 D10
Kerzers CH 31 B11
Kesälahti FIN 129 B12
Keşan TR 172 C6
Kesäniemenkylä FIN 121 B12
Kesarevo BG 166 C5
Kesasjärv S 118 B8
Kesh GB 7 C7
Kesh IRL 6 D6
Kesik TR 177 B8
Keskijärvi FIN 125 E14
Keskikylä FIN 119 E13
Keskikylä FIN 119 E15
Keskikylä FIN 119 F13
Keskikylä FIN 122 F9
Keskikylä FIN 123 E11
Keskinen FIN 121 E13
Keskipiiri FIN 119 E14
Keski-Posio FIN 121 B11
Keskusvankila FIN 124 C8
Kjsowo PL 138 C4
Kessel B 182 C5
Kessel NL 183 C8
Kesselinkylä FIN 125 C14
Kessingland GB 15 C12
Ķesterciems LV 134 B6
Kesteren NL 183 B7
Kestilä FIN 119 D14
Kestilä FIN 119 F16
Kestrini GR 168 E3
Keswick GB 10 B5
Keszthely H 149 C8
Kesztölc H 149 A11
Kétegyháza H 151 D7
Kéthely H 149 C8
Ketola FIN 115 E2
Ketomella FIN 117 B12
Keträvaara FIN 121 D13
Kętrzyn PL 136 E3
Ketsch D 21 F11
Kétsoprony H 151 D6
Kettering GB 15 C7
Kettershausen D 71 A10
Kettinge DK 83 A11
Kettletoft GB 3 G11
Kettlewell GB 11 C7
Kettwig D 183 C9
Kęty PL 147 B8
Ketzin D 79 B12
Keula D 79 D8
Keuruu FIN 123 F13
Keutschach am See A 73 C9
Keväjärvi FIN 114 F3
Kevelaer D 16 E6
Ķevele LV 134 D5
Kevermes H 151 E7
Kevo FIN 113 D19
Keynsham GB 13 C9
Keyritty FIN 125 D10
Kežmarok SK 145 E1
Khadzhidimovo BG 169 A10
Khalamyer"ye BY 133 E7
Kharlu RUS 129 B14
Kharmanli BG 166 F5
Khaskovo BG 166 F5
Khayredin BG 160 F3
Khelyulya RUS 129 B14
Khisarya BG 165 D10
Khiytola RUS 129 C12
Khlivchany UA 144 C8
Kholmets' UA 145 F5
Kholms'ke UA 155 B4
Khorio GR 179 B8
Khrabrovo RUS 136 D2
Khrishteni BG 166 E5
Khust UA 145 G7
Khvoyna BG 165 F10
Khyriv UA 145 D6
Kiannanniemi FIN 121 D13
Kiato GR 175 C6
Kiaunoriai LT 134 E6
Kibæk DK 86 C3
Kibworth Harcourt GB 11 F10
Kiby N 114 C7
Kičevo NMK 168 A4
Kichenitsa BG 161 F8
Kichevo BG 167 C9
Kidderminster GB 13 A10
Kidlington GB 13 B12
Kidričevo SLO 148 D5
Kidsgrove GB 11 E7
Kidwelly GB 12 B6
Kiefersfelden D 72 A5
Ķieģeļceplis LV 135 C10
Kiekinkoski FIN 125 B14
Kiekrz PL 81 B11
Kiel D 83 B8
Kielajoki FIN 113 E18
Kielce PL 143 E10
Kiełczygłów PL 143 D6
Kielder GB 5 E11
Kieldrecht B 182 C4
Kiełpino PL 138 B5
Kiemėnai LT 135 D8
Kiemozia PL 141 F1
Kienberg D 75 F11
Kierinki FIN 117 D15
Kierspe D 21 B9
Kieselbach D 79 E7
Kiesilä FIN 128 C7
Kiesimä FIN 123 E17
Kietrz PL 142 F5
Kietz D 81 A7
Kifisia GR 175 C8
Kifjord N 113 B19
Kihelkonna EST 130 E4
Kihlanki FIN 117 C11
Kihlanki S 117 C10
Kihlepa EST 131 E8
Kihlevere EST 131 C12
Kihniö FIN 123 F10
Kiihtelysvaara FIN 125 F14
Kiikala FIN 127 E10
Kiikka FIN 126 C8
Kiikla EST 131 C14
Kiikoinen FIN 126 C8
Kiili EST 131 C9
Kiiminki FIN 119 D15
Kiisa EST 131 C9
Kiiskilä FIN 123 C13
Kiistala FIN 117 C14
Kiiu EST 131 C10
Kiiu-Aabla EST 131 B11
Kije PL 143 E10
Kijevë RKS 163 D10
Kijevo HR 156 E5
Kijewo Królewskie PL 138 D5
Kikerino RUS 132 C6
Kikinda SRB 150 F5
Kików PL 138 E7
Kikorze PL 85 C8
Ķikuri LV 134 C3
Kil N 90 B5
Kil S 97 C9
Kilafors S 103 D12
Kilargue IRL 6 D6
Kilb A 77 F8
Kilbaha IRL 8 C3
Kilbeggan IRL 7 F8
Kilbeheny IRL 8 D6
Kilberry GB 4 D5
Kilberry IRL 7 F8
Kilbirnie GB 4 D7
Kilboghamn N 108 D5
Kilbotn N 111 C12
Kilbrittain IRL 8 E5
Kilby S 99 B10
Kilcar IRL 6 C5
Kilchoan GB 4 B4
Kilchrenan GB 4 C6
Kilcock IRL 7 F9
Kilcolgan IRL 6 F5
Kilcommon IRL 9 D7
Kilconnell IRL 6 F6
Kilconney IRL 7 D8
Kilcoole IRL 7 F10
Kilcormac IRL 7 F7
Kilcreggan GB 4 D7
Kilcullen IRL 7 F9
Kildare IRL 7 F9
Kildavin IRL 9 C9
Kilden DK 90 E7
Kildimo New IRL 8 C5
Kildonan Lodge GB 3 J9
Kile N 90 A2
Kilen N 95 D9
Kilfenora IRL 6 G4
Kilfinan GB 4 D6
Kilfinnane IRL 8 D6
Kilforsen S 107 D11
Kilgarvan IRL 8 E4
Kilgetty GB 12 B5
Kilglass IRL 6 E6
Kilglass IRL 6 F6
Kilham GB 5 D12
Kilidülbahir TR 171 D10
Kilifarevo BG 166 C5
Kilingi-Nõmme EST 131 E9
Kiliya UA 155 C4
Kilkea IRL 9 C9
Kilkee IRL 8 C3
Kilkeel GB 7 D11
Kilkelly IRL 6 E5
Kilkenny IRL 9 C8
Kilkerrin IRL 6 E5
Kilkhampton GB 12 D6
Kilkieran IRL 6 F3
Kilkinlea IRL 8 D4
Kilkis GR 169 C8
Kilkishen IRL 8 C5
Kill IRL 7 F9
Kill IRL 9 D8
Killabunane IRL 8 E3
Killadysert IRL 8 C4
Killagan Bridge GB 4 E4
Killala IRL 6 D4
Killaloe IRL 8 C6
Killamerry IRL 9 D8
Killann IRL 9 C9
Killarga IRL 6 D6
Killarney IRL 8 D4
Killavullen IRL 8 D5
Killeagh IRL 8 E7
Killean GB 4 D5
Killearn GB 5 C8
Killeberg S 88 C6
Killeenleagh IRL 8 E4
Killeigh IRL 7 F8
Killen GB 7 C7
Killenaule IRL 9 C7
Killerrig IRL 9 C9
Killeshandra IRL 7 D7
Killichonan GB 5 B8
Killiecrankie GB 5 B9
Killimor IRL 6 F6
Killin GB 5 C8
Killinaboy IRL 6 G4
Killinchy GB 7 D11
Killinge S 116 C4
Killingworth GB 5 E13
Killinick IRL 9 D10
Killinkoski FIN 123 F11
Killorglin IRL 8 D3
Killough GB 7 D11
Killough IRL 7 F10
Killucan IRL 7 E8
Killukin IRL 6 E6
Killundine GB 4 B5
Killurin IRL 9 D9
Killybegs IRL 6 C6
Killyclogher GB 4 F2
Killylea GB 7 D9
Kilmacanogue IRL 7 F10
Kilmacrenan IRL 7 B7
Kilmacthomas IRL 9 D8
Kilmaganny IRL 9 D8
Kilmaine IRL 6 E4
Kilmaley IRL 8 C4
Kilmallock IRL 8 D5
Kilmaluag GB 2 K4
Kilmarnock GB 4 D8
Kilmartin GB 4 C6
Kilmeague IRL 7 F9
Kilmeedy IRL 8 D5
Kilmelford GB 4 C6
Kilmichael IRL 8 E4
Kilmihill IRL 8 C4
Kilmona IRL 8 E5
Kilmoon IRL 7 E10
Kilmore IRL 8 C5
Kilmore IRL 9 D9
Kilmore Quay IRL 9 D9
Kilmuckridge IRL 9 C10
Kilmurry IRL 8 C5
Kilmurry McMahon IRL 8 C4
Kilnaboy IRL 6 G4
Kilnaleck IRL 7 E8
Kilnamanagh IRL 9 C10
Kilninian GB 4 B4
Kilninver GB 4 C5
Kilnock IRL 6 E5
Kiloran GB 4 C4
Kilpelä FIN 115 D4
Kilpilahti FIN 127 E14
Kilpisjärvi FIN 112 E6
Kilpua FIN 119 F13
Kilquiggin IRL 9 C9
Kilrane IRL 9 D10
Kilrea GB 4 F3
Kilrean IRL 6 C6
Kilreekill IRL 6 F6
Kilrenny GB 5 C11
Kilronan IRL 6 F3
Kilrush IRL 8 C4
Kilsallagh IRL 6 E5
Kilsaran IRL 7 E10
Kilshanchoe IRL 7 F9
Kilshanny IRL 6 G4
Kilskeer IRL 7 E9
Kilsmo S 92 A7
Kilsund N 90 B4
Kilsyth GB 5 D8
Kiltartan IRL 6 F5
Kiltealy IRL 9 C9
Kiltegan IRL 9 C9
Kiltimagh IRL 6 E5
Kiltogan IRL 9 C9
Kiltoom IRL 6 F6
Kiltsi EST 131 C12
Kiltullagh IRL 6 F5
Kilvakkala FIN 127 B9
Kilvenaapa FIN 119 B16
Kilvo S 116 E6
Kilwaughter GB 4 F5
Kilwinning GB 4 D7
Kilworth IRL 8 D6
Kimasozero RUS 121 F17
Kimberley GB 15 B11
Kimbolton GB 15 C8
Kiminki FIN 123 E13
Kimito FIN 126 E8
Kimle H 146 F4
Kimmeria GR 171 B7
Kimo FIN 122 D8
Kimola FIN 127 C15
Kimonkylä FIN 127 D15
Kimovaara RUS 125 C16
Kimpton GB 15 D8
Kimstad S 92 B7
Kinahmo FIN 125 E13
Kinbrace GB 3 J9
Kincardine GB 5 C9
Kincraig GB 3 L9
Kincses H 149 B10
Kindberg A 148 A4
Kindelbrück D 79 D9
Kinderbeuern D 21 D8
Kinding D 75 E9
Kindsbach D 186 C4
Kindsjön S 102 E4
Kineta GR 175 D7
Kingarrow IRL 6 C6
Kingarth GB 4 D6
Kingisepp RUS 132 C4
Kingsbridge GB 13 E7
Kingsclere GB 13 C12
Kingscourt IRL 7 E9
Kingskerswell GB 13 E7
Kingsland IRL 6 E6
King's Lynn GB 11 F12
Kingsnorth GB 15 E10
Kingsteignton GB 13 D7
Kingsthorne GB 13 B9
Kingston GB 3 K10
Kingston Bagpuize GB 13 B12
Kingston Seymour GB 13 C9
Kingston upon Hull GB 11 D11
Kingswear GB 13 E7
Kingswood GB 13 C9
Kings Worthy GB 13 C12
Kington GB 13 A8
Kingussie GB 5 A8
Kingwilliamstown IRL 8 D4
Kinik TR 173 E10
Kinik TR 177 A9
Kinisjärvi FIN 117 D14
Kinloch GB 4 A4
Kinlochard GB 4 C8
Kinlochewe GB 2 K6
Kinlochleven GB 4 B7
Kinloch Rannoch GB 5 B8
Kinloss GB 3 K9
Kinlough IRL 6 D6
Kinn N 111 C10
Kinna S 91 D12
Kinnared S 87 A12
Kinnarp S 91 C14
Kinnarumma S 91 D12
Kinnegad IRL 7 F8
Kinnitty IRL 7 F7
Kinnula FIN 123 D13
Kinnulanlahti FIN 124 D8
Kinrooi B 19 B12
Kinross GB 5 C10
Kinsale IRL 8 E5
Kinsalebeg IRL 9 E7
Kinsarvik N 94 B5
Kintai LT 134 F2
Kintaus FIN 123 F14
Kintbury GB 13 C12
Kintore GB 3 L12
Kinvara IRL 6 F5
Kinvarra IRL 6 F3
Kioni GR 174 C2
Kipen' RUS 132 B6
Kipfenberg D 75 E9
Kipilovo BG 166 D6
Kipinä FIN 119 D17
Kipoi GR 168 E4
Kipoureio GR 168 E5
Kippel CH 70 E5
Kippen GB 5 C8
Kippenheim D 27 D8
Kir AL 163 E8
Kirakkajärvi FIN 114 D5
Kirakkakongäs FIN 113 F19
Királd H 145 G1
Királyegyháza H 149 D9
Királyhegyes H 150 E6
Kiran N 104 C8
Kiran TR 181 B8
Kirazli TR 172 D6
Kirbla EST 131 D7
Kirby Muxloe GB 11 F9
Kircasalih TR 173 B6
Kirchanschöring D 73 A6
Kirchardt D 21 F11

Kirchbach A 73 C7
Kirchbach in Steiermark A 148 C5
Kirchberg CH 27 F11
Kirchberg CH 31 A12
Kirchberg D 76 E4
Kirchberg D 79 E12
Kirchberg (Hunsrück) D 185 E7
Kirchberg am Wagram A 77 F9
Kirchberg am Walde A 77 E8
Kirchberg am Wechsel A 148 A5
Kirchberg an der Jagst D 74 D6
Kirchberg an der Pielach A 77 F8
Kirchberg an der Raab A 148 C5
Kirchbichl A 72 A5
Kirchdorf D 17 C11
Kirchdorf D 83 C10
Kirchdorf an der Iller D 71 A10
Kirchdorf an der Krems A 73 A9
Kirchdorf im Wald D 76 E4
Kirchdorf in Tirol A 72 A5
Kirchehrenbach D 75 C9
Kirchellen D 183 B9
Kirchen (Sieg) D 21 C9
Kirchenlamitz D 75 B10
Kirchenthumbach D 75 C10
Kirchgellersen D 83 D8
Kirchhain D 21 C11
Kirchheim D 74 C6
Kirchheim D 78 E6
Kirchheim am Neckar D 187 C7
Kirchheim bei München D 75 F10
Kirchheim-Bolanden D 21 E10
Kirchheim unter Teck D 27 C11
Kirchhundem D 21 B10
Kirchlauter D 75 B8
Kirchlinteln D 17 C12
Kirch Mulsow D 83 C11
Kirchohsen (Emmerthal) D 78 B5
Kirchroth D 75 E12
Kirchschlag in der Buckligen Welt A 148 A6
Kirchseelte D 17 C11
Kirchtimke D 17 B12
Kirchwalsede D 17 B12
Kirchweidach D 75 F12
Kirchwistedt D 17 B11
Kirchzarten D 27 E8
Kirchzell D 21 E12
Kircubbin GB 7 D11
Kireç TR 173 E9
Kiremitçisalih TR 172 B6
Kirillovskoye RUS 129 E11
Kirjais FIN 126 E6
Kirjavala FIN 129 B12
Kirkağaç TR 177 A10
Kirkbean GB 5 F9
Kirkbride GB 5 F10
Kirkby GB 10 E6
Kirkby in Ashfield GB 11 E9
Kirkby Lonsdale GB 10 C6
Kirkbymoorside GB 11 C10
Kirkby Stephen GB 11 C7
Kirkby Thore GB 5 F11
Kirkcaldy GB 5 C10
Kirkcolm GB 4 F6
Kirkconnel GB 5 E8
Kirkcudbright GB 5 F8
Kirkeby DK 86 E7
Kirkehamn N 94 F5
Kirke Helsinge DK 87 D8
Kirke Hyllinge DK 87 D9
Kirkel-Neuhäusel D 186 C3
Kirkenær N 96 B7
Kirkenes N 114 D8
Kirke Såby DK 87 D9
Kirke Stillinge DK 87 E8
Kirkham GB 10 D6
Kirkinner GB 5 F8
Kirkintilloch GB 5 D8
Kirkjubøur FO 2 B3
Kirkkavak TR 173 B6
Kirkkepenekli TR 173 B8
Kirkkonummi FIN 127 E11
Kirklareli TR 167 F8
Kirkmichael GB 4 E7
Kirkmichael GB 5 B9
Kirk Michael GBM 10 C2
Kirknewton GB 5 D12
Kirkoswald GB 5 F11
Kirkpatrick-Fleming GB 5 E10
Kirkton GB 4 C5
Kirkton of Durris GB 5 A12
Kirkton of Glenisla GB 5 B10
Kirkton of Skene GB 3 L12
Kirktown of Auchterless GB 3 L12
Kirktown of Deskford GB 3 K11
Kirkwall GB 3 H11
Kirn D 21 E8
Kirnujärvi S 116 D10
Kirovsk RUS 129 F14
Kirriemuir GB 5 B10
Kirschweiler D 21 E8
Kirtik S 118 B5
Kirtlington GB 13 B12
Kirton GB 15 C11
Kirton in Lindsey GB 11 E10
Kirtorf D 21 C12
Kiruna S 116 C4
Kisa S 92 D7
Kisač SRB 158 C4
Kisar H 145 G6
Kisbér H 149 A10
Kiseljak BIH 157 C10
Kiseljak BIH 157 C11
Kiseljak BIH 157 E9
Kisgyőr H 145 G2
Kishkeam IRL 8 D4
Kisielice PL 139 C7
Kisielnica PL 139 D13
Kisko FIN 127 E9
Kisköre H 150 B5
Kiskőrös H 150 D3
Kiskunfélegyháza H 150 D4
Kiskunhalas H 150 E3
Kiskunlacháza H 150 C3
Kiskunmajsa H 150 E4
Kişlacik TR 167 F9
Kisláng H 149 C10
Kisléta H 151 B8
Kislőd H 149 B9
Kismarja H 151 C8
Kisnána H 147 F10
Kisovec SLO 73 D10
Kissakoski FIN 128 B6
Kissamos GR 178 E6
Kissenbrück D 79 B8
Kißlegg D 71 B9
Kisszállás H 150 E3
Kist D 187 B8
Kistanje HR 156 E4
Kistelek H 150 E4
Kistokaj H 145 G2
Kistrand N 113 C15
Kisújszállás H 150 C6
Kisvárda H 145 G5
Kisvarsány H 145 G5
Kiszkowo PL 81 A12
Kiszombor H 150 E5
Kitee FIN 125 F14
Kiten BG 167 E9
Kitinoja FIN 122 E9
Kitka FIN 121 B12
Kitkiöjärvi S 116 C10
Kitros GR 169 D8
Kitsi FIN 125 D15
Kittajaur S 118 B3
Kittelfjäll S 106 A8
Kittilä FIN 117 C13
Kittsee A 77 F12
Kitula FIN 127 E10
Kitzbühel A 72 B5
Kitzen D 79 D11
Kitzingen D 75 C7
Kitzscher D 79 D12
Kiucze PL 143 F8
Kiukainen FIN 126 C7
Kiurujärvi FIN 115 D2
Kiuruvesi FIN 123 C17
Kivarinjärvi FIN 121 E10
Kivelä FIN 115 F4
Kiveri GR 175 D6
Kivesjärvi FIN 121 F9
Kiveskylä FIN 121 F9
Kiveslahti FIN 120 F9
Kiviapaja FIN 129 B10
Kivijärvi FIN 123 D14
Kivijärvi S 116 E10
Kivik S 88 D6
Kivikangas FIN 123 D12
Kivilahti FIN 125 E14
Kivilompolo FIN 117 A10
Kivilompolo FIN 119 B12
Kivilompolo N 117 A10
Kivioja FIN 119 B14
Kiviõli EST 131 C13
Kiviperä FIN 121 B14
Kivivaara FIN 121 D11
Kivivaara FIN 125 C14
Kivi-Vigala EST 131 D8
Kivotos GR 168 D5
Kiwity PL 136 E2
Kiyiköy TR 173 A9
Kizilcaova TR 177 C10
Kizilcikdere TR 167 F8
Kizilpinar TR 173 B8
Kizilyaka TR 181 B8
Kjækan N 112 D9
Kjåmes N 111 D11
Kjeldebotn N 111 D12
Kjelkenes N 100 C2
Kjelkvik N 111 D11
Kjellerup DK 86 C4
Kjelling N 108 B7
Kjemmoen N 102 D2
Kjengsnes N 111 C11
Kjerknesvågen N 105 D10
Kjerret N 96 B7
Kjerringdal N 112 C9
Kjerringholmen N 113 B12
Kjerringøy N 108 A8
Kjerringvåg N 104 D5
Kjerringvik N 110 C9
Kjerringvik N 111 D12
Kjerstad N 111 D11
Kjølebrønn N 90 B5
Kjølen N 91 A9
Kjøllefjord N 113 B19
Kjølstad N 101 D10
Kjøpsvik N 111 D11
Kjøra N 104 E7
Kjøsvika N 105 A12
Kjulaås S 98 D7
Klaaswaal NL 16 E2
Kľačno SK 147 D7
Kladanj BIH 157 D10
Kläden D 79 A10
Kladnica SRB 163 C9
Kladnice HR 156 E5
Kladno CZ 76 B6
Kladovo SRB 159 D10
Kladruby CZ 76 C3
Klæbu N 104 E8
Klagenfurt A 73 C9
Klågerup S 87 D12
Klaipėda LT 134 E2
Kłaj PL 143 G9
Klakksjorda N 110 C8
Klaksvík FO 2 A3
Klamila FIN 128 D7
Klana HR 67 B9
Klanac HR 156 C3
Klanino PL 85 B10
Klanjec HR 148 D5
Klanxbüll D 86 F3
Klapkalnciems LV 134 B6
Kläppsjö S 107 D12
Klärke S 103 A12
Klarup DK 86 A6
Klašnice BIH 157 C7
Klasov SK 146 E6
Klässbol S 97 C8
Klášterec nad Ohří CZ 76 B4
Kláštor pod Znievom SK 147 D7
Klátova Nová Ves SK 146 D6
Klatovy CZ 76 D4
Klaukkala FIN 127 E12
Klaus an der Pyhrnbahn A 73 A9
Klausdorf D 80 B4
Klausdorf D 84 B4
Klausen D 21 E7
Klausen Leopoldsdorf A 77 F10
Klausučiai LT 136 C7
Klauvnes N 112 D6
Klazienaveen NL 17 C7
Kłębowiec PL 85 D10
Klecko PL 81 A12
Kljcz PL 143 D7
Kleczew PL 138 F5
Kleemola FIN 123 C12
Kleidi GR 169 C8
Kleinarl A 73 B7
Klein Berßen D 17 C8
Kleinblittersdorf D 27 B7
Klein Bünzow D 84 C5
Kleinfurra D 79 D8
Kleinheubach D 21 E12
Kleinjena D 79 D10
Klein Kreutz D 79 B12
Kleinlobming A 73 B10
Kleinmachnow D 80 B4
Kleinpaschleben D 79 C10
Kleinreifling A 73 A10
Kleinrinderfeld D 187 B8
Klein Rönnau D 83 C8
Klein Sankt Paul A 73 C10
Kleinwallstadt D 21 E12
Kleinwelka D 80 D6
Kleinzell A 77 G9
Kleio GR 171 F10
Kleisoura GR 168 C5
Kleitoria GR 174 D5
Kleiva N 110 C9
Kleive N 100 A7
Klejniki PL 141 E8
Klejtrup DK 86 B5
Klek SRB 158 C5
Klembivka UA 154 A2
Klemensker DK 89 E7
Klenči pod Čerchovem CZ 75 D12
Klenica PL 81 C9
Klenike SRB 164 E4
Klenje SRB 158 D3
Klenovec SK 147 D9
Klenovice na Hané CZ 77 D12
Kleosin PL 140 D8
Klepacze PL 140 D8
Kleppe N 94 E3
Kleppestø N 94 B2
Kleppstad N 110 D7
Klępsk PL 81 B9
Kleszczele PL 141 E8
Kleszczewo PL 81 B12
Kleszczewo PL 136 F6
Kleszczów PL 143 D7
Klettwitz D 80 C5
Kleve D 16 E6
Klevshult S 92 E4
Kličevac SRB 159 D7
Kličevo MNE 163 D6
Klieken D 79 C11
Klietz D 83 E12
Klikuszowa PL 147 B9
Klim DK 86 A4
Kliment BG 161 F10
Kliment BG 165 D10
Klimentovo BG 167 C9
Klimkovice CZ 146 B6
Klimontów PL 143 E11
Klimontów PL 143 F9
Klimpfjäll S 106 A7
Klin SK 147 C8
Klinča Sela HR 148 E5
Klinë RKS 163 D10
Klinë e Epërme RKS 163 D10
Klingenberg D 80 E5
Klingenberg am Main D 21 E12
Klingenthal D 75 B11
Klingersel S 118 B7
Klingre S 107 E15
Klink D 83 D13
Klinkby DK 86 B2
Klinte S 93 E12
Klintebjerg DK 86 E6
Klintehamn S 93 E12
Kliplev DK 86 F4
Klippan S 87 C12
Klippen S 107 C13
Klippen S 108 E9
Klippinge DK 87 E10
Klis HR 156 E6
Klisura BG 165 D9
Klisura BG 165 E7
Klisura SRB 164 D5
Klitmøller DK 86 A3
Klitten D 81 D7
Klitten S 102 D7
Klixbüll D 82 A5
Kljajićevo SRB 150 F3
Ključ BIH 157 C6
Klokot RKS 164 E3
Klobouky CZ 77 E11
Kłobuck PL 143 E6
Klobuk BIH 157 F7
Klöch A 148 C5
Klockestrand S 103 A14
Klockrike S 92 C6
Kłoczew PL 141 G5
Kłodawa PL 85 E8
Kłodawa PL 143 B6
Kłodzko PL 77 B11
Kloetinge NL 16 F1
Kløfta N 95 B14
Klokkarstua N 95 C12
Klokkerholm DK 86 A6
Klokočevac SRB 159 E9
Klokočevci HR 149 E10
Klokočov SK 147 C7
Kłomnice PL 143 E7
Klonowa PL 142 D5
Klooga EST 131 C8
Kloosterhaar NL 17 D7
Kloosterzande NL 16 F2
Klos AL 163 F9
Klos AL 168 B3
Klöse S 107 D16
Kloštar Ivanić HR 149 E6
Kloštar Podravski HR 149 E8
Kloster DK 86 C2
Klosterfelde D 84 E4
Klosterhäseler D 79 D10
Klösterle A 71 C10
Klosterlechfeld D 71 A11
Klostermansfeld D 79 C9
Klosterneuburg A 77 F10
Klosters CH 71 D9
Kloster Zinna D 80 B4
Kloten CH 27 F10
Kloten S 97 C13
Klotten D 21 D8
Klötze (Altmark) D 79 A9
Klovainiai LT 135 E7
Klovborg DK 86 D4
Klövverträsk S 118 C6
Klømvoen N 108 E6
Klövsjö S 102 A7
Klubbfors S 118 D5
Klubbvik N 114 C6
Kluczbork PL 142 E5
Kluczewsko PL 143 E8
Kluki PL 143 D7
Kluknava SK 145 F2
Klukowo PL 141 E7
Klumpen S 106 D7
Klundert NL 16 E3
Klungsten S 99 A10
Klupe BIH 157 C8
Kluse D 17 C8
Klušov SK 145 E3
Klusy PL 139 C13
Klutsjön S 102 B4
Klütz D 83 C10
Klwów PL 141 G3
Klyastsitsy BY 133 E5
Klykoliai LT 134 D5
Klynivka UA 153 A7
Knaben N 94 E6
Knåda S 103 D10
Knaften S 107 C15
Knäred S 87 B12
Knaresborough GB 11 C9
Knarrevik N 94 B2
Knarrlagsund N 104 D6
Knätten S 102 B7
Knebel DK 86 C6
Knesebeck D 83 E9
Knesselare B 19 B7
Knetzgau D 75 C8
Knežak SLO 73 E9
Kneževi Vinogradi HR 149 E11
Kneževo HR 149 E11
Knezha BG 165 C9
Kněžice CZ 77 D9
Knežina BIH 157 D10
Kněžmost CZ 77 B8
Knić SRB 158 F6
Knidi GR 169 D6
Knighton GB 13 A8
Knin HR 156 D5
Knislinge S 88 C6
Knittelfeld A 73 B10
Knittlingen D 27 B10
Knīveri LV 134 D3
Knivsta S 99 C9
Knizhovnik BG 166 F5
Knjaževac SRB 164 B5
Knock GB 4 C5
Knock IRL 6 E5
Knock IRL 8 C4
Knockalough IRL 8 C4
Knockanevin IRL 8 D6
Knockban GB 2 K7
Knockbrack IRL 7 C7
Knockbridge IRL 7 E10
Knockcroghery IRL 6 E6
Knocklong IRL 8 D6
Knockmoyle IRL 6 F6
Knocknaboul IRL 8 D4
Knocknacarry GB 4 E4
Knocknacree IRL 9 C9
Knocknagree IRL 8 D4
Knocks IRL 8 E5
Knocktopher IRL 9 D8
Knokke-Heist B 19 B7
Knoppe S 103 B12
Knorrendorf D 84 C4
Knottingley GB 11 D9
Knowle GB 13 A11
Knucklas GB 13 A8
Knud DK 86 B4
Knurów PL 142 F6
Knutbränna S 106 D7
Knutby S 99 C10
Knutsbol S 97 D12
Knutsford GB 11 E7
Knyazevo RUS 133 D5
Knyazhe UA 152 A6
Knyazhevo BG 167 E6
Knyazhitsy RUS 132 E4
Knyszyn PL 140 D7
Kobaky UA 152 A6
Kobarid SLO 73 D8
Kobatovci BIH 157 C7
Kobbelveid N 109 A10
Kobbevågnes N 111 B16
Kobbfoss N 114 E7
Kobela EST 131 F12
København DK 87 D11
Kobenz A 73 B10
Kobeřice CZ 142 G5
Kobern D 185 D7
Kobersdorf A 149 A6
Kobiele Wielkie PL 143 D8
Kobierzyce PL 81 E11
Kobilyane BG 171 A8
Kobiór PL 143 F6
Koblenz D 21 D9
Kobrow D 83 C11
Kobyla Góra PL 142 D4
Kobylanka PL 85 D7
Kobylany PL 145 D4
Kobylets'ka Polyana UA 145 G9
Kobylin PL 81 C12
Kobyłka PL 139 F11
Kobylnica PL 81 B12
Kobylnica PL 85 B12
Kobylniki PL 139 F9
Kocaavşar TR 173 E8
Kocahidir TR 171 C10
Kočani NMK 164 F5
Kocapinar TR 173 E8
Koçarli TR 177 D10
Kocayazi TR 167 E8
Kocayazi TR 167 F8
Koceljevo SRB 158 E4
Kocēni LV 135 A10
Kočerin BIH 157 F8
Kočevje SLO 73 E10
Kočevska Reka SLO 73 E10
Kochanowice PL 142 E6
Kochel am See D 72 A3
Kocherinovo BG 165 E7
Kochmar BG 161 F10
Kochovo BG 167 C7
Kock PL 141 G6
Kočovce SK 146 D5
Kocs H 149 A10
Kocsér H 150 C4
Kocsola H 149 C10
Kocsord H 145 H5
Koczała PL 85 C12
Kodavere EST 131 D14
Kode S 91 D10
Kodeń PL 141 G9
Kodersdorf D 81 D7
Kodesjärvi FIN 122 F8
Kodiksami FIN 126 C6
Kodisjoki FIN 126 C6
Köditz D 75 B10
Kodrąb PL 143 D8
Kodyma UA 154 A4
Koekelare B 18 B6
Koersel B 183 C6
Koeru EST 131 D12
Koewacht NL 182 C3
Kofçaz TR 167 F8
Köflach A 73 B11
Kog SLO 148 D6
Køge DK 87 E10
Koglhof A 148 B5
Kohila EST 131 C9
Kohlberg D 75 C11
Köhlen D 17 A11
Kohren-Sahlis D 79 D12
Kohtla-Järve EST 131 C14
Koidula EST 132 F2
Koigi EST 131 D11
Koijärvi FIN 127 D10
Koikkala FIN 128 B8
Koiliomeno GR 174 D2
Koilovtsi BG 165 C10
Koimisi GR 169 B9
Koirakoski FIN 124 C9
Koita GR 178 B3
Koitila FIN 121 C11
Koivu FIN 119 B14
Koivujärvi FIN 123 C16
Koivujärvi FIN 123 D16
Koivumäki FIN 123 D12
Koivumäki FIN 124 D9
Koivumäki FIN 125 F11
Koivuniemi FIN 119 C15
Köja S 107 F13
Kojanlanti FIN 125 E11
Kojetín CZ 146 C4
Kóka H 150 C4
Kökar FIN 126 F4
Kokari LV 135 C13
Kokava nad Rimavicou SK 147 D9
Kokelv N 113 B14
Kokemäki FIN 126 C7
Kokkala GR 178 B3
Kokkari GR 177 D8
Kokkinochoma GR 171 C6
Kokkino Nero GR 169 E8
Kokkokylä FIN 119 C17
Kokkola FIN 123 C10
Kokkolahti FIN 125 F12
Kokkosniva FIN 115 D2
Kokkotoi GR 175 A6
Kokkovaara FIN 117 D13
Köklot FIN 122 D7
Koknese LV 135 C10
Kokonvaara FIN 125 E12
Kokora EST 131 D14
Kokorevo RUS 132 F6
Kokory CZ 146 C4
Kokrica SLO 73 D9
Koksijde B 18 B6
Kokträsk S 109 F16
Kola BIH 157 C7
Kołacin PL 141 G1
Kołacz PL 85 C10
Kołacze PL 141 H8
Kołaczkowo PL 142 B4
Kołaczyce PL 144 D3
Kolaka GR 175 B7
Koláre SK 147 E8
Kolari FIN 117 D11
Kolari S 117 D11
Kolari SRB 159 D6
Kolárovice SK 147 C7
Kolarovo BG 169 B9
Kolárovo SK 146 F5
Kolåsen S 105 D13
Kolašin MNE 163 D8
Kolbäck S 98 C6
Kołbacz PL 85 D7
Kołbaskowo PL 84 D6
Kolbermoor D 72 A5
Kołbiel PL 141 F4
Kolbotn N 95 C13
Kolbu N 101 E13
Kolbudy Górne PL 138 B5
Kolbuszowa PL 144 C4
Kølby DK 86 B4
Kol'chyne UA 145 G6
Kölcse H 145 G6
Kołczygłowy PL 85 B12
Kołczyn PL 81 A8
Koldby DK 86 B3
Koldere TR 177 B10
Kolding DK 86 E4
Koler S 118 D5
Kölesd H 149 C11
Kolesjan AL 163 F9
Koleska BIH 157 F9
Kolforsen S 103 E12
Kolga EST 131 C11
Kolga-Aabla EST 131 B11
Kolga-Jaani EST 131 D11
Kolho FIN 123 F13
Koli FIN 125 D13
Kolín CZ 77 B8
Kolíňany SK 146 E6
Kolind DK 86 C7
Kolindros GR 169 D7
Kolinec CZ 76 D4
Kolinkivtsi UA 153 A8
Koliri GR 174 D3
Kolisne UA 154 E5
Kolitzheim D 75 C7
Köljala EST 130 E5
Koljane HR 156 E5
Kolka LV 130 F5
Kølkær DK 86 C4
Kolkanlahti FIN 123 E14
Kölked H 149 E11
Kolkja EST 131 D14
Kolkku FIN 123 D16
Kolkonjärvi FIN 121 B10
Kolkwitz D 80 C6
Kollaja FIN 119 D17
Kölleda D 79 D9
Kollines GR 174 E5
Kölln-Reisiek D 82 C7
Kolltveit N 94 B2
Kollund DK 82 A6
Kolmisoppi FIN 124 D9
Köln D 21 C7
Kolnica PL 140 C8
Kolno PL 136 F2
Kolno PL 139 D12
Kolo BIH 157 E7
Koło PL 142 B6
Kołobrzeg PL 85 B9
Kolochau D 80 C4
Kolochava UA 145 G8
Kolonjë AL 168 C2
Kolonowskie PL 142 E5
Kölösen S 102 B4
Kolpino RUS 129 F14
Kolsätter S 102 B8
Kolsh AL 163 E9
Kölsillre S 103 B9
Kölsjön S 103 B11
Kolsko PL 81 C9
Kölsta S 97 C15
Kolsva S 97 C14
Kölsvallen S 102 C6
Kölsvallen S 102 C7
Kolt DK 86 C6
Kolta SK 146 E6
Kolu FIN 123 E12
Kolunič BIH 156 C5
Koluszki PL 141 G1
Koluvere EST 131 D8
Kölvallen S 102 B5
Kolvereid N 105 B11
Kolvik N 113 C15
Kølvrå DK 86 C4
Kolympari GR 178 D6
Kolympia GR 181 D8
Komádi H 151 C7
Komagfjord N 113 C11
Komagvær N 114 C9
Komańcza PL 145 E5
Komanos GR 169 D6
Komar BIH 157 D7
Komara GR 171 A10
Komarani SRB 163 C8
Komarevo BG 165 B10
Komarica BIH 157 C8
Komárno SK 149 A10
Komarno UA 145 D8
Komárom H 149 A10
Komárov CZ 76 C5
Komarovo RUS 129 E12
Komarówka Podlaska PL 141 G7
Komarów Osada PL 144 B7
Kombulj LV 133 E2
Komen SLO 73 E8
Komësi AL 168 A2
Komi GR 176 D5
Komi GR 177 C7
Komin HR 148 D6
Komin HR 157 F8
Komiža HR 63 A10
Komjatice SK 146 E6
Komletinci HR 157 B10
Komló H 149 D10
Kömlő H 150 B5
Kömlőd H 149 A10
Kommeno GR 174 A3
Komnina GR 169 C6
Komoran RKS 163 D10
Komorniki PL 81 B11
Komorowo PL 139 E12
Komorzno PL 142 D5
Komoshtitsa BG 160 F2
Komossa FIN 122 D9
Komotini GR 171 B8
Kompakka FIN 125 F13
Kompelusvaara S 116 D8
Kömpöc H 150 E4
Kompoti GR 174 A3
Komprachcice PL 142 E4
Kõmsi EST 130 D7
Komsomol'sk RUS 136 D2
Komsomol'sk RUS 139 A9
Komsomol's'k UA 145 G8
Komu FIN 123 C16
Komula FIN 125 C10
Komunari BG 167 C8
Komuniga BG 166 F4
Komylio GR 174 B2
Konak TR 177 C9
Konakpinar TR 173 F8
Konare BG 155 F2
Konary PL 141 G4
Konarzyce PL 139 D13
Konarzyny PL 85 C12
Koncanica HR 149 E8
Konče NMK 169 A7
Kondolovo BG 167 E9
Kondoros H 150 D6
Kondratowice PL 81 E11
Kondrat'yevo RUS 129 D9
Kondrić HR 157 B9
Koneck PL 138 E6
Køng DK 87 E9
Konga S 89 B8
Köngäs FIN 115 E1
Köngäs FIN 117 C13
Kongasmäki FIN 121 E9
Kongens Lyngby DK 87 D11
Kongerslev DK 86 B6
Konginkangas FIN 123 E15
Kongsberg N 95 C11
Kongselva N 110 D9
Kongsfjord N 114 B6
Kongslia N 101 D9
Kongsmoen N 105 B12
Kongsvik N 111 C11
Kongsvinger N 96 B7
Kongsvoll N 104 D6
Konice CZ 77 C11
Koniecpol PL 143 E8
Königheim D 187 B8
Königsberg in Bayern D 75 B8
Königsborn D 79 B10
Königsbronn D 75 E7
Königsbrück D 80 D5
Königsbrunn D 75 F8
Königsdorf D 72 A3
Königsee D 79 E9
Königsfeld im Schwarzwald D 27 D9
Königshofen D 79 D10
Königshütte D 79 C8
Königslutter am Elm D 79 B8
Königsmoos D 75 E9
Königssee D 73 A6
Königstein D 75 C10
Königstein D 80 E6
Königstein im Taunus D 187 A5
Königswartha D 80 D6
Königswiesen A 77 F7
Königswinter D 21 C8
Königs Wusterhausen D 80 B5
Konin PL 142 B5
Konispol AL 168 E3
Konitsa GR 168 D4
Könitz D 79 E10
Köniz CH 31 B11
Konjevrate HR 156 E5
Konjic BIH 157 E8
Konjsko BIH 157 E7
Konjsko BIH 162 D5
Konnekoski FIN 123 E17
Könnern D 79 C10
Konnevesi FIN 123 E16
Könni FIN 122 E9
Konnunsuo FIN 129 C10
Konnuslahti FIN 125 E9
Könölä FIN 119 C12
Konolfingen CH 70 D5
Konopiska PL 143 E7
Konopište NMK 169 B7
Konopki PL 139 D9
Konopnica PL 141 H6
Konopnica PL 142 D6
Konotop PL 81 C9
Konotop PL 85 D9
Kon'ovo BG 166 D6
Końskie PL 141 H2
Konsko NMK 169 B7
Końskowola PL 141 H6
Konsmo N 90 C1
Konstancin-Jeziorna PL 141 F4
Konstantinova LV 133 D2
Konstantinovy Lázně CZ 76 C3
Konstantynów PL 141 F8
Konstantynów Łódzki PL 143 C7
Konstanz D 27 E11
Kontariotissa GR 169 D7
Kontiainen FIN 123 E10
Kontias GR 171 E8
Kontinjoki FIN 121 F10
Kontiokoski FIN 119 D15
Kontiolahti FIN 125 E13
Kontiomäki FIN 121 F11
Kontkala FIN 125 E12
Kontopouli GR 171 E8
Kontovazaina GR 174 D4
Konttajärvi FIN 117 E12
Konttila FIN 119 C17
Konttimäki FIN 125 D9
Konush BG 166 F4
Kóny H 149 A8
Konyár H 151 C8
Konyavo BG 165 E6
Konz D 21 E7
Konzell D 75 D12
Koog aan de Zaan NL 16 D3
Koonga EST 131 D8
Köörtilä FIN 126 B6
Koosa EST 131 D14
Kootstertille NL 16 B6
Kootwijkerbroek NL 183 A7
Kopani GR 168 F4
Kopanica PL 81 B9
Kopanos GR 169 C7
Kopardal N 108 D4
Koparnes N 100 B3
Kopčany SK 77 E12
Koper SLO 67 A8
Kopervik N 94 D2
Kópháza H 149 A7
Kopice PL 142 E3
Kopidlno CZ 77 B8
Kopilovtsi BG 165 C6
Köping S 97 C15
Köpingebro S 88 E5
Köpingsvik S 89 B11
Kopisto FIN 119 F12
Kopki PL 144 C5
Koplik AL 163 E7
Koplik i Sipërm AL 163 E7
Köpmanholm S 99 C11
Köpmanholmen S 107 E15
Koporiće RKS 163 C10
Koporiqë RKS 163 C10
Koposperä FIN 123 C14
Koppang N 101 C14
Koppangen N 111 A19
Kopparberg S 97 C13
Kopparmora S 99 D11
Kopparnäs S 118 D6
Koppelo FIN 114 F3
Koppera N 105 E11
Koppl A 73 A7
Koppom S 96 C7
Koprivets BG 166 C5
Koprivlen BG 169 A10
Koprivnica HR 149 D7
Kopřivnice CZ 146 B6
Koprivshtitsa BG 165 D9
Koprzywnica PL 143 E12
Kopsa FIN 119 E13
Kopstal L 186 B1
Kõpu EST 130 D7
Kõpu EST 131 E10
Koraj BIH 157 C10
Koramoniemi FIN 121 B12
Korbach D 17 F11
Korbevac SRB 164 D5
Korbovo SRB 159 D10
Korčanica BIH 156 C5
Korçë AL 168 C4
Korchiv UA 144 C8
Körchow D 83 D10
Korčula HR 162 D3
Korczew PL 141 F7
Korczyna PL 144 D4
Kordel D 185 E6
Korenita SRB 158 E3
Kořenov CZ 81 E8
Korentokylä FIN 120 D9
Korentovaara FIN 125 E16
Koretin RKS 164 D4
Korfantów PL 142 F4
Korfos GR 175 D7
Korgen N 108 D6
Korğene LV 131 F9
Kõrgessaare EST 130 D4
Korholanmäki FIN 121 F10
Korhosenniemi FIN 121 C12
Koria FIN 128 D6
Korinos GR 169 D8
Korinth DK 86 E6
Korinthos GR 175 D6
Korisia GR 175 D9
Korisos GR 168 D5
Korita BIH 156 D5
Korita BIH 157 F9
Korita HR 162 D4
Korita MNE 163 E8
Korithi GR 174 D2
Korkana FIN 121 F15
Korkatti FIN 119 F15
Korkeakangas FIN 125 F14
Korkeakoski FIN 127 B11
Korkee FIN 127 D13
Körkvere EST 130 E6
Körle D 78 D6
Körmend H 149 B7
Kormista GR 170 C6
Kormu FIN 127 D12
Korňa SK 147 C7
Kornalovychi UA 145 D7
Körner D 79 D8
Korneuburg A 77 F10
Kornevo RUS 136 E1
Kórnik PL 81 B12
Kornitsa BG 165 F8
Kornofolia GR 171 B10
Kornos GR 171 E8
Kornsjø N 91 B10
Kornwestheim D 27 C11
Környe H 149 A10
Koroleve UA 145 G7
Koromačno HR 67 C9
Koroncó H 149 A9
Koroneia GR 175 C6
Koroni GR 178 B2
Koronisia GR 174 A2
Koronos GR 177 E6
Koronouda GR 169 C9
Koronowo PL 138 D4
Koropi GR 175 D8
Körösladány H 151 D7
Körösszakál H 151 C8
Körösszegapáti H 151 C8
Köröstarcsa H 151 D7
Koroviya UA 153 A7

Korpela FIN 117 B14
Körperich D 20 E6
Korpi FIN 123 C12
Korpijärvi FIN 119 B13
Korpijoki FIN 123 C16
Korpikå S 119 C10
Korpikylä FIN 119 B11
Korpikylä FIN 121 E12
Korpikylä S 119 B11
Korpilahti FIN 123 F15
Korpilombolo S 116 E10
Korpilompolo FIN 117 E13
Korpinen FIN 121 D10
Korpinen FIN 125 D10
Korpisel'kya RUS 125 F16
Korpivaara FIN 125 E12
Korpo FIN 126 E6
Korpoström FIN 126 E6
Korsåmon S 103 A12
Korsbäck FIN 122 E6
Korsberga S 89 A8
Korsberga S 91 C15
Korsgården S 103 E10
Korsholm FIN 122 D7
Korskrogen S 103 C10
Korsmyrbränna S 106 E8
Korsnäs FIN 122 E6
Korsnes N 111 D11
Korso FIN 127 E13
Korsør DK 87 E8
Korssjön S 118 F5
Korssund N 100 D1
Korsträsk S 118 C5
Korsveggen N 104 E8
Korsvoll N 104 E4
Korsze PL 136 E3
Kortemark B 19 B7
Korten BG 166 D5
Kortenhoef NL 16 D4
Kortesalmi FIN 121 C14
Kortesjärvi FIN 123 D10
Kortessem B 19 C11
Kortevaara FIN 125 B13
Kortgene NL 16 E1
Korthi GR 176 D4
Kortrijk B 19 C7
Kortteenperä FIN 119 B17
Kortteinen FIN 125 D11
Korubaşi TR 171 E10
Korucu TR 173 F7
Koruköy TR 173 C6
Koruköy TR 177 E10
Korva S 119 B11
Korvakumpu FIN 115 D2
Korvala FIN 117 E16
Korvaluoma FIN 126 B8
Kõrveküla EST 131 E13
Korvenkylä FIN 119 D15
Korvenkylä FIN 119 F14
Korvenkylä FIN 123 B12
Korvua FIN 121 D12
Koryčany CZ 77 D12
Korycin PL 140 D8
Koryfasi GR 174 E4
Koryfi GR 169 C8
Korytnica PL 139 F12
Korzenna PL 144 D2
Korzeńsko PL 81 C11
Korzunovo RUS 114 E9
Korzybie PL 85 B11
Kos GR 177 F9
Kosakowo PL 138 A6
Kosanica MNE 163 C7
Košarovce SK 145 E4
Kösching D 75 E10
Kościan PL 81 B11
Kościelec PL 142 B6
Kościelna Wieś PL 142 C5
Kościernica PL 85 B10
Kościerzyna PL 138 B4
Kosd H 150 B3
Kose EST 131 C10
Kose EST 131 F14
Košeca SK 146 C6
Košecké Podhradie SK 146 D6
Kösedere TR 171 E10
Kösedere TR 177 B8
Köseilyas TR 173 B8
Kosel D 82 A7
Koselji BIH 157 E9
Koserow D 84 B6
Košetice CZ 77 C8
Kosharevo BG 165 D6
Koshava BG 159 E11
Košice SK 145 F3
Kosiv UA 152 A6
Kosivs'ka Polyana UA 145 G9
Kosjerić SRB 158 F4
Koška HR 149 E10
Koskama FIN 117 C14
Koskeby FIN 122 D8
Koskela FIN 119 E15
Koskela FIN 123 D11
Koskenkorva FIN 122 E8
Koskenkylä FIN 117 C16
Koskenkylä FIN 121 C14
Koskenkylä FIN 121 F11
Koskenkylä FIN 124 E8
Koskenkylä FIN 126 D7
Koskenmäki FIN 121 F13
Koskenniska FIN 113 F17
Koskenpää FIN 123 F14
Koskenperä FIN 123 C14
Koski FIN 127 D9
Koski FIN 127 E9
Koskimäki FIN 122 E7
Koskinou GR 181 D8
Koskioinen FIN 127 C9
Koškovce SK 145 E4
Koskue FIN 122 F9
Koskullskulle S 116 D5
Koslovets BG 166 C4
Kosmach UA 152 A5
Kosman BIH 157 F10
Kosmas GR 175 E6
Kosmio GR 171 B8
Kosmonosy CZ 77 B7
Kosola FIN 122 D9
Kosova Hora CZ 77 C6
Kosovo HR 156 E5
Kosovska Kamenicë RKS 164 D4
Kosów Lacki PL 141 E6
Koßdorf D 80 D4
Kössen A 72 A5
Kosta GR 175 E7
Kosta S 89 B8
Kostakioi GR 174 A2
Koštálov CZ 81 E8
Kostamo FIN 115 E2
Kostandenets BG 166 B6
Kostandovo BG 165 E9
Kostanjevac HR 148 E4
Kostanjevica SLO 148 E4
Kostel SLO 67 A10
Kostelec nad Černými Lesy CZ 77 C7
Kostelec nad Orlicí CZ 77 B10
Kostelec na Hané CZ 77 C12
Kostenets BG 165 E8
Kostenets BG 165 E8
Kostice CZ 77 E11
Kostinbrod BG 165 D7
Kostolac SRB 159 D7
Kostolné Kračany SK 146 F5
Kostomłoty PL 81 D11
Kostomuksha RUS 121 E16
Kostrzyn PL 81 A7
Kostrzyn PL 81 B12
Kostyzhitsy RUS 132 F6
Kosula FIN 125 E11
Košute HR 157 E6
Kosy UA 154 B5
Kosyny UA 145 G5
Koszalin PL 85 B10
Koszjcin PL 142 E6
Kőszeg H 149 B7
Koszyce PL 143 F10
Kotajärvi FIN 119 D15
Kotala FIN 115 D5
Kotala FIN 123 F12
Kotalanperä FIN 119 D15
Kotas GR 168 C5
Kotë AL 168 D2
Kötegyán H 151 D7
Kotel BG 167 D6
Kőtelek H 150 C5
Kotelow D 84 C5
Kotešová SK 147 C7
Köthen (Anhalt) D 79 C10
Kotikylä FIN 124 D8
Kotila FIN 121 E10
Kotiranta FIN 121 E13
Kotka FIN 128 E6
Kotlin PL 142 C4
Kotly RUS 132 B4
Kotor MNE 163 E6
Kotoriba HR 149 D7
Kotorsko BIH 157 C9
Kotor Varoš BIH 157 C7
Kotraža SRB 158 F5
Kotronas GR 178 B3
Kötschach A 73 C7
Kotsøy N 105 F9
Kottenheim D 185 D7
Kottes A 77 F8
Köttmannsdorf A 73 C9
Köttsjön S 107 E10
Kotuń PL 141 F6
Koudekerke NL 16 F1
Koudum NL 16 C4
Koufalia GR 169 C8
Koufovouno GR 171 B10
Kougsta S 105 E15
Kouklioi GR 168 E4
Koumanis GR 174 D4
Koura FIN 123 E10
Kouřim CZ 77 C7
Kourkouloi GR 175 B7
Kournas GR 178 E7
Koutaniemi FIN 121 F10
Koutojärvi S 119 B10
Koutsochero GR 169 E7
Koutsopodi GR 175 D6
Koutsouras GR 179 E10
Koutus FIN 117 E12
Kouva FIN 121 C10
Kouvola FIN 128 D6
Kovachevets BG 166 C6
Kovachevitsa BG 165 F8
Kovachevo BG 166 E6
Kovachevtsi BG 165 D6
Kovachitsa BG 160 F2
Kovači BIH 157 E7
Kovačica SRB 158 C6
Kővágószőlős H 149 D10
Kovallberget S 107 B13
Kovanj BIH 157 E10
Kovarce SK 146 E6
Kovářov CZ 76 C6
Kovdor RUS 115 C8
Kovelahti FIN 126 B8
Kovero FIN 125 E15
Kovilj SRB 158 C5
Kovin SRB 159 D6
Kovjoki FIN 122 C9
Kovland S 103 B13
Kövra S 102 A7
Kovren MNE 163 C8
Kowal PL 139 E7
Kowala-Stępocina PL 141 H4
Kowale PL 142 D5
Kowale Oleckie PL 136 E5
Kowale-Pańskie PL 142 C6
Kowalewo Pomorskie PL 138 D6
Kowalów PL 81 B7
Kowary PL 81 E9
Kowiesy PL 141 G2
Köyceğiz TR 181 C9
Köyhäjoki FIN 123 C11
Köyliö FIN 126 C7
Koynare BG 165 C9
Koyundere TR 177 B9
Koyunyeri TR 171 C10
Kozani GR 169 D6
Kozarac BIH 157 C6
Kozarac HR 149 E11
Kozar Belene BG 166 C4
Kozármisleny H 149 D10
Kozárovce SK 147 E7
Kozçeşme TR 173 D6
Kozica HR 157 F7
Koziegłowy PL 143 E7
Kozielice PL 85 D7
Kozienice PL 141 G5
Kozina SLO 73 E8
Kožlany CZ 76 C5
Kozloduy BG 160 F3
Kozłów Biskupi PL 141 F2
Kozłowo PL 139 D9
Kozluk BIH 157 C11
Kozły PL 139 F11
Koźminek PL 142 C5
Koźmin Wielkopowski PL 142 C3
Koz'ove UA 145 F7
Kozubszczyzna PL 141 H6
Kożuchów PL 81 C9
Kožuhe BIH 157 C9
Kozy PL 147 B8
Kozyörük TR 173 B6
Krabbendijke NL 16 F2
Krabi EST 131 F13
Kräckelbäcken S 102 C7
Krackow D 84 D6
Kraddsele S 109 E12
Kraftsdorf D 79 E10
Krąg PL 85 B11
Kragelund DK 86 C4
Kragerø N 90 B5
Krągi PL 85 C11
Kragujevac SRB 159 E6
Kraj HR 156 E6
Kraj HR 157 F7
Krajenka PL 85 D12
Krajišnik SRB 159 C6
Krajnik Dolny PL 84 D6
Krakača BIH 156 B4
Kråkberget N 110 C8
Kråken S 122 C3
Kråkenes N 100 B2
Kråkerøy N 91 A8
Krakės LT 134 F7
Krakhella N 100 D2
Kråklingbo S 93 E13
Kråklivollen N 105 E9
Kråkmoen N 111 E10
Krakovets' UA 144 D7
Kraków PL 143 F8
Krakow am See D 83 C12
Kråksmåla S 89 A9
Kråkstad N 95 C13
Kralevo BG 167 C7
Králíky CZ 77 B11
Kraljeva BIH 157 D9
Kraljevica HR 67 B10
Kraljevo SRB 158 F6
Kralovice CZ 76 C4
Kráľovský Chlmec SK 145 G4
Kralupy nad Vltavou CZ 76 B6
Králův Dvůr CZ 76 C6
Kramarzyny PL 85 B12
Kramfors S 103 A14
Kramolin BG 166 C4
Krampenes N 114 C8
Kramsach A 72 B4
Kramsk PL 142 B5
Kramvik N 114 C9
Kranenburg D 16 E6
Kranevo BG 167 C10
Krångfors S 118 E4
Krania GR 168 E5
Krania Elassonas GR 169 E6
Kranichfeld D 79 E9
Kranidi GR 175 E7
Kranj SLO 73 D9
Kranjska Gora SLO 73 D8
Krapanj HR 156 E4
Krapets BG 155 F3
Krąpiel PL 85 D8
Krapina HR 148 D5
Krapinske Toplice HR 148 D5
Krapkowice PL 142 F4
Krašić HR 148 E5
Krasiczyn PL 144 D6
Krasiv UA 145 D8
Krāslava LV 133 E2
Kraslice CZ 75 B12
Krasnagorka BY 133 E2
Krásná Hora nad Vltavou CZ 76 C6
Krasnapollye BY 133 E6
Krasne PL 139 E10
Krasne PL 144 C5
Krasne UA 154 E4
Kraśniczyn PL 144 B7
Kraśnik PL 144 B5
Krasni Okny UA 154 B4
Krasnobród PL 144 B7
Krasnogorodskoye RUS 133 C4
Krásnohorské Podhradie SK 145 F2
Krasnoles'ye RUS 136 E5
Krásno nad Kysucou SK 147 C7
Krasnopol PL 136 E7
Krasno Polje HR 67 C11
Krasnosel'skoye RUS 129 D11
Krasnosielc PL 139 D11
Krasnovo BG 165 E9
Krasnoyil's'k UA 153 A7
Krasnoznamensk RUS 136 D5
Krasnystaw PL 144 B7
Krasocin PL 143 E9
Krastë AL 168 B3
Kraszewice PL 142 C5
Kraszewo PL 136 E2
Kratigos GR 177 A8
Kratiškiai LT 135 D9
Kratovo NMK 164 E5
Kratte masugn S 98 B6
Krauchenwies D 27 D11
Krauja LV 135 E13
Kraujas LV 135 D11
Kraukļi LV 135 B12
Krauschwitz D 81 C7
Krautheim D 74 D6
Kravaře CZ 146 B6
Kravarsko HR 148 E6
Kravoder BG 165 C7
Kraymorie BG 167 E8
Kražiai LT 134 E5
Krčina BIH 157 C11
Krefeld D 17 F7
Kreiensen D 78 C6
Krekenava LT 135 E8
Krekhovychi UA 145 E9
Krekilä FIN 123 C11
Kremasti GR 181 D8
Kremen BG 165 F8
Kremena BG 155 F2
Kremintsi UA 152 A5
Kremmydia GR 174 F4
Kremna SRB 158 F4
Kremnica SK 147 D7
Krempe D 82 C7
Kremperheide D 17 A12
Krempna PL 145 D4
Krems an der Donau A 77 F9
Kremsbrücke A 73 C8
Kremsmünster A 76 F6
Křepice CZ 77 E11
Krepoljin SRB 159 E8
Kreševo BIH 157 E9
Kreshpan AL 168 C2
Křešice CZ 76 A6
Kresna BG 165 F7
Kresnice SLO 73 D10
Kressbronn am Bodensee D 71 B9
Krestena GR 174 D4
Kretinga LT 134 E2
Kretingalė LT 134 E2
Kreuth D 72 A4
Kreuzau D 20 C6
Kreuzlingen CH 27 E11
Kreuztal D 21 C9
Kreuzwertheim D 74 C6
Kreva BY 137 E13
Krezluk BIH 157 D7
Krichim BG 165 E9
Krieglach A 148 A5
Kriegstetten CH 27 F8
Krien D 84 C4
Kriens CH 70 C6
Krievciems LV 134 B3
Krieza GR 175 C9
Krikello GR 174 B4
Krikellos GR 174 B3
Krimpen aan de IJssel NL 16 E3
Krimūnas LV 134 C6
Křinec CZ 77 B8
Krinida GR 170 C5
Krinides GR 171 B6
Kriškalni LV 135 C11
Kriškovci BIH 157 C7
Kristberg S 92 B6
Kristdala S 93 E8
Kristiansand N 90 C2
Kristianstad S 88 C6
Kristiansund N 104 E3
Kristiinankaupunki FIN 122 F6
Kristineberg S 107 A15
Kristinefors S 97 B8
Kristinehamn S 97 D11
Kristinestad FIN 122 F6
Kristoni GR 169 C8
Kristvallabrunn S 89 B10
Kritinia GR 181 D7
Kritsa GR 179 E10
Kritzmow D 83 B12
Kriukai LT 134 D7
Kriūkai LT 137 C7
Kriva Bara BG 159 F11
Krivača BIH 157 G9
Kriva Feja SRB 164 D5
Krivaja BIH 157 D9
Kriváň SK 147 D8
Krivany SK 145 E2
Kriva Palanka NMK 164 E5
Krivelj SRB 159 E9
Krivi Put HR 67 B10
Krivi Vir SRB 159 F8
Krivodol BG 165 C7
Krivogaštani NMK 168 B5
Krivolak NMK 169 A7
Križ HR 149 E7
Křižanov CZ 77 D10
Križevci HR 149 D7
Křížová CZ 77 C9
Križpolje HR 67 B11
Krk HR 67 B10
Krka SLO 73 E10
Krmčina HR 156 D3
Krnča SK 146 D6
Krnica HR 67 C9
Krnjača SRB 158 D6
Krnja Jela MNE 163 D7
Krnjak HR 148 F5
Krnjeuša BIH 156 C5
Krnjevo SRB 159 E7
Krnov CZ 142 F4
Krobia PL 81 C11
Kroczyce PL 143 E8
Krøderen N 95 B11
Krofdorf Gleiberg D 21 C11
Krog S 103 B9
Krögis D 80 D4
Krok S 105 E14
Krokees GR 175 F6
Krokeide N 94 B2
Krokek S 93 B8
Kroken N 100 D6
Kroken N 108 F7
Krokfors S 108 E9
Krokfors S 118 B5
Krokio GR 175 A6
Kroknäs S 102 A8
Kroknes N 114 C9
Krokom S 106 E6
Krokos GR 169 D6
Krokowa PL 138 A5
Kroksjö S 107 B13
Kroksjö S 107 D15
Kroksjö S 118 F4
Krokstadelva N 95 C12
Krokstadøra N 104 E7
Krokstranda N 108 D9
Krokströmmen S 102 B8
Kroktjärn S 118 B4
Kroktråsk S 118 C6
Królowy Most PL 140 D8
Krölpa D 79 E10
Kroměříž CZ 146 C4
Krommenie NL 16 C3
Krompachy SK 145 F2
Kromsdorf D 79 E9
Kronach D 75 B9
Kronau D 187 C6
Kronauce LV 134 C6
Kronberg im Taunus D 187 A5
Kronlund S 109 E14
Kronoby FIN 123 C10
Kronprinzenkoog D 82 C5
Kronshagen D 83 B8
Kronshtadt RUS 129 F12
Kronstorf A 77 F6
Kropa SLO 73 D9
Kröpelin D 83 B11
Kropp D 82 B7
Kroppenstedt D 79 C9
Kropstädt D 79 C12
Krościenko nad Dunajcem PL 145 E1
Kröslin D 84 B5
Krosna LT 137 E8
Krośnice PL 81 D12
Krośniewice PL 143 B7
Krosno PL 144 D4
Krosno Odrzańskie PL 81 B8
Krossen D 79 E10
Krossen N 90 C2
Krossen N 95 C8
Krossmoen N 94 E4
Krostitz D 79 D11
Krote LV 134 C3
Krotoszyce PL 81 D10
Krotoszyn PL 142 C3
Krottendorf A 148 B5
Krouna CZ 77 C10
Krousonas GR 178 E8
Kröv D 21 E8
Krovik S 111 E19
Krovyli GR 171 C9
Krrabë AL 168 B2
Krš HR 156 C3
Kršan HR 67 B9
Krško SLO 148 E4
Krstac MNE 157 F10
Krstinja HR 156 B4
Krtova BIH 157 C9
Kruchowo PL 138 E4
Krüden D 83 E11
Kruft D 185 D7
Kruibeke B 19 B9
Kruiningen NL 16 F2
Kruishoutem B 19 C8
Krujë AL 168 A2
Krukenychi UA 144 D7
Kruklanki PL 136 E4
Krukowo PL 139 D11
Krumbach A 71 C9
Krumbach A 148 A6
Krumbach (Schwaben) D 71 A10
Krumë AL 163 E9
Krummesse D 83 C9
Krumovgrad BG 171 B9
Krumovo BG 165 E10
Krumovo BG 166 E6
Krumpa (Geiseltal) D 79 D10
Krumvíř CZ 77 E11
Krün D 72 A3
Krunderup DK 86 C3
Kruonis LT 137 D9
Kruopiai LT 134 D6
Krupac BIH 157 E9
Krupac SRB 165 C6
Krupa na Vrbasu BIH 157 C7
Krupanj SRB 158 E3
Krupava BY 137 F11
Krupe PL 144 A7
Krupina SK 147 E8
Krupište NMK 164 F5
Krupka CZ 80 E5
Krupnik BG 165 F7
Kruså DK 82 A6
Kruševac SRB 164 B3
Kruševica SRB 158 E5
Kruševo NMK 168 B5
Kruševo Grdo BIH 157 D8
Krushari BG 155 F1
Krushë e Madhe RKS 164 E2
Krushel'nytsya UA 145 E8
Krushevets BG 167 E8
Krushevo BG 166 C4
Krushovene BG 160 F4
Krushovitsa BG 160 F3
Krušovce SK 146 D6
Kruszewo PL 85 E11
Kruszwica PL 138 E5
Kruszyna PL 85 B12
Kruszyna PL 143 E7
Krutådal N 108 E7
Krute MNE 163 E7
Kruunupyy FIN 123 C10
Kružlov SK 145 E3
Krya Vrysi GR 169 C7
Kryekuq AL 168 C2
Kryezi AL 163 E9
Kryłów PL 144 B9
Krynica PL 145 E2
Krynica Morska PL 139 B7
Krynice PL 144 B7
Krynki PL 140 D9
Krynychne UA 155 B3
Kryoneri GR 175 D6
Kryoneritis GR 175 B7
Kryopigi GR 169 D9
Krypno Kościelne PL 140 D7
Kryry CZ 76 B4
Krystad N 110 D5
Krystallopigi GR 168 C5
Kryva Balka UA 154 E5
Kryve Ozero UA 154 B6
Kryvorivnya UA 152 A5
Kryzhopil' UA 154 A3
Kržanja MNE 163 D7
Krzanowice PL 142 F5
Krzątka PL 144 C4
Krzczonów-Wójtostwo PL 144 A6
Krzęcin PL 85 D9
Krzelów PL 81 D11
Krzemieniewo PL 81 C11
Krzepice PL 142 E6
Krzepielów PL 81 C10
Krzesk-Królowa Niwa PL 141 F7
Krzeszów PL 81 E10
Krzeszów PL 144 C5
Krzeszowice PL 143 F8
Krzeszyce PL 81 A8
Krzętów PL 143 E8
Krzykosy PL 81 B12
Krzynowłoga Mała PL 139 D10
Krzystkowice PL 81 C8
Krzywcza PL 144 D6
Krzywda PL 141 G6
Krzywiń PL 81 C11
Krzywin PL 84 D6
Krzywowierzba PL 141 G8
Krzyżanów PL 143 B7
Krzyżanowice PL 141 H4
Krzyżanowice PL 146 B6
KrzyżKrzyż PL 85 E10
Ksar Sghir MA 53 E5
Książ Wielki PL 143 F9
Książ Wielkopolski PL 81 B12
Ksiżpol PL 144 C6
Kubanovka RUS 136 D5
Kubbe S 107 D14
Kübekháza H 150 E5
Kublichy BY 133 F4
Küblis CH 71 D9
Kubrat BG 161 F8
Kubuli LV 133 B2
Kuç AL 168 D2
Kučevo SRB 159 E8
Kuchen D 74 E6
Kuchl A 73 A7
Kuchurhan UA 154 D5
Kuchyňa SK 77 F12
Kucice PL 139 E9
Kuciny PL 143 C7
Kučište HR 162 D3
Kuçovë AL 168 C2
Küçükanafarta TR 171 D10
Küçükbahçe TR 177 B7
Küçükçekmece TR 173 B10
Küçükkariştiran TR 173 B7
Küçükkemerdere TR 177 C10
Küçükköy TR 172 F6
Küçükkumla TR 173 D11
Küçükkuyu TR 172 E6
Küçükyoncali TR 173 B8
Kucura SRB 158 B4
Kuczbork-Osada PL 139 D9
Kudever' RUS 133 C6
Kudirkos Naumiestis LT 136 D6
Kudowa-Zdrój PL 77 B10
Kūdums LV 135 B10
Kufstein A 72 A5
Kuggerud N 96 B6
Kuggören S 103 C14
Kuha FIN 119 C17
Kuhakoski FIN 129 B9
Kühbach D 75 F9
Kuhbier D 83 D12
Kuhfelde D 83 E10
Kühlungsborn D 83 B11
Kuhmalahti FIN 127 B12
Kuhmo FIN 121 F14
Kuhmoinen FIN 127 B13
Kühndorf D 79 E7
Kühren D 79 D12
Kuhs D 83 C12
Kuhstedt D 17 B11
Kuijõe EST 131 C7
Kuimetsa EST 131 C10
Kuinre NL 16 C5
Kuivajärvi FIN 121 E15
Kuivajõe EST 131 C10
Kuivakangas S 119 B11
Kuivalahti FIN 126 C6
Kuivaniemi FIN 119 C14
Kuivanto FIN 127 D15
Kuivasjärvi FIN 123 F9
Kuivastu EST 130 D6
Kujakowice Dolne PL 142 D5
Kūkas LV 135 C12
Kukasjärvi FIN 117 D15
Kukasjärvi S 119 B10
Kukës AL 163 E9
Kukko FIN 123 E12
Kukkola FIN 119 C12
Kukkola S 119 C12
Kuklen BG 165 E10
Kuklin PL 139 D9
Kuklinów PL 81 C12
Kukliš NMK 169 B8
Kukljić HR 156 D4
Kukljica HR 156 D3
Kukljin SRB 164 B3
Kukmirn A 148 B6
Kukruse EST 131 C14
Kuktiškės LT 135 F11
Kukulje BIH 157 C7
Kukur AL 168 C3
Kukurečani NMK 168 B5
Kula BG 159 F9
Kula HR 149 F9
Kula SRB 158 B4
Kulaši BIH 157 C8
Kulata BG 169 B9
Kulautuva LT 137 D8
Kūļciems LV 134 B6
Kuldīga LV 134 C3
Külefli TR 173 D8
Kuleli TR 173 B6
Kulennoinen FIN 129 B11
Kulen Vakuf BIH 156 C5
Kulesze PL 140 D7
Kulho FIN 125 E13
Kulia N 105 D9
Kuliai LT 134 E3
Kulju FIN 127 C10
Kullaa FIN 126 C7
Kullamaa EST 131 D8
Kulleseid N 94 C2
Kulltorp S 88 A5
Kulmain D 75 C10
Kulmbach D 75 B9
Kuloharju FIN 121 C11
Külsheim D 27 A12
Kultima FIN 116 B9
Kuluntalahti FIN 121 F10
Kūlupėnai LT 134 E2
Kulva LT 137 C9
Kulvemäki FIN 124 C9
Kulykiv UA 144 D9
Kumachevo RUS 139 A9
Kumane SRB 158 B5
Kumanica SRB 163 C9
Kumanovo NMK 164 E4
Kumbağ TR 173 C7
Kumberg A 148 B5
Kumbri LV 134 C4
Kumbuļi LV 135 E13
Kumburun TR 171 E10
Kumhausen D 75 E11
Kumkadi TR 173 D9
Kumkale TR 171 E10
Kumköy TR 173 B11
Kumla S 92 A6
Kumla kyrkby S 98 C7
Kumlinge FIN 99 B15
Kummer D 83 D10
Kummerow D 83 C13
Kummersdorf-Alexanderdorf D 80 B4
Kummersdorf Gut D 80 B4
Kummunkylä FIN 123 D16
Kumpuranta FIN 125 G12
Kumpuselkä FIN 123 D16
Kumpuvaara FIN 119 C18
Kumrovec HR 148 D5
Kunadacs H 150 D3
Kunágota H 151 E7
Kunbaja H 150 E3
Kunbaracs H 150 D3
Kunčina CZ 77 C11
Kunda EST 131 B13
Kunes N 113 C18
Kunfehértó H 150 E3
Kungälv S 91 D10
Kungas FIN 123 C11
Kungsängen S 99 D9
Kungsäter S 88 A3
Kungsbacka S 91 E11
Kungsberg S 103 E11
Kungsfors S 103 E12
Kungsgården S 103 D12
Kungsgården S 103 E12
Kungshamn S 91 C9
Kungshult S 87 D12
Kungsör S 98 D6
Kunhegyes H 150 C6
Kunice PL 81 D10
Kunín CZ 146 B5
Kuningaküla EST 132 C2
Kuniów PL 142 E5
Kunmadaras H 150 C6
Kunovice CZ 146 C4
Kunowice PL 81 B7
Kunowo PL 81 C12
Kunpeszér H 150 C3
Kunrade NL 183 D7
Kunrau D 79 A9
Kunštát CZ 77 C11
Kunszállás H 150 D4
Kunszentmárton H 150 D5
Kunszentmiklós H 150 C3
Kunsziget H 149 A9
Kunvald CZ 77 B11
Kunžak CZ 77 D8
Künzell D 74 A6
Künzelsau D 74 D6
Künzing D 76 E4
Kuohatti FIN 125 C12
Kuohu FIN 123 F14
Kuoksajärvi FIN 117 E15
Kuoksu S 116 C7
Kuolayarvi RUS 115 E6
Kuolio FIN 121 C12
Kuomiokoski FIN 128 C7
Kuona FIN 123 C15
Kuopio FIN 124 E9
Kuoppala FIN 122 D9
Kuorevesi FIN 127 B12
Kuortane FIN 123 E11
Kuortti FIN 127 C15
Kuosku FIN 115 D4
Kuossakåbba S 116 D4
Kuouka S 116 E5
Kup PL 142 E4
Kupari HR 162 D5
Küpeler TR 173 E8
Kupferberg D 75 B10
Kupferzell D 74 D6
Kupientyn PL 141 F6
Kupinec HR 148 E5
Kupinovo SRB 158 D5
Kupiškis LT 135 E9
Kupjak HR 67 B10
Küplü TR 171 B10
Kuppenheim D 27 C9
Kuprava LV 133 B3
Kupres BIH 157 D7
Kuprešani BIH 157 D7
Küps D 75 B9
Kurapollye BY 135 F13
Kuratën AL 168 B2
Kurbnesh AL 163 F9
Kurd H 149 D10
Kürdzhali BG 171 A8
Kurejoki FIN 123 D11
Kuremaa EST 131 D13
Kuremäe EST 132 C2
Kuressaare EST 130 E4
Kurevere EST 130 E3
Kurienkylä FIN 123 F10
Kurikka FIN 122 E8
Kuřim CZ 77 D11
Kurima SK 145 E3
Kurjala FIN 125 E10
Kurjan AL 168 C2
Kurki FIN 121 D10
Kurkiharju FIN 125 E9
Kurkikylä FIN 121 D11
Kurkimäki FIN 124 E9
Kurmene LV 135 D9
Kürnach D 187 B9
Kürnare BG 165 D10
Kürnbach D 27 B10
Kurolanlahti FIN 124 D8
Kuropta RUS 115 D9
Kurort Bad Gottleuba D 80 E5
Kurort Kipsdorf D 80 E5
Kurort Oberwiesenthal D 76 B3
Kurort Schmalkalden D 79 E7
Kurort Steinbach-Hallenberg D 79 E8
Kurów PL 141 H6
Kurowice PL 143 C8
Kurravaara S 116 C4
Kurrokvejk S 109 E14
Kuršėnai LT 134 D5
Kursīši LV 134 D4
Kursu FIN 115 E4
Kuršumlija SRB 164 C3
Kuršumlijska Banja SRB 164 C3
Kurtakko FIN 117 D12
Kurtbey TR 172 B6
Kurtna EST 132 C2
Kurtovo Konare BG 165 E9
Kurtti FIN 121 D11
Kurtto FIN 121 E11
Kurtzea E 40 B6
Kuru FIN 127 B10
Kurvinen FIN 121 C14
Kuryłówka PL 144 C5
Kurzelów PL 143 E8
Kurzeszyn PL 141 G2
Kurzętnik PL 139 D8
Kusa LV 135 C12
Kusadak SRB 159 E6
Kuşadasi TR 177 D9
Kuşçayir TR 172 E6
Kusel D 21 E8
Kusey D 79 A9
Kusfors S 118 E4
Kushnytsya UA 145 G7
Kušići SRB 163 C9
Kuside MNE 163 D6
Kuślin PL 81 B10
Kusmark S 118 E5
Küsnacht CH 27 F10
Küssnacht CH 27 F9
Kustavi FIN 126 D5
Küsten D 83 E10
Kusterdingen D 27 C11
Kuštilj SRB 159 C7
Kuta BIH 157 E10
Kutalli AL 168 C2
Kutas H 149 D8
Kutemajärvi FIN 124 F7
Kutenholz D 17 B12
Kuti MNE 163 D8
Kutina HR 149 F7
Kutjevo HR 149 F9
Kutlovo SRB 159 E6
Kutná Hora CZ 77 C8
Kutno PL 143 B7
Kutrikko FIN 115 E5
Kuttainen S 116 B9
Kuttanen FIN 116 B9
Kuttura FIN 117 B16
Kúty SK 77 E12
Kuty UA 152 A6
Kuukasjärvi FIN 119 C17
Kuumu FIN 121 E14
Kuurne B 19 C7
Kuurtola FIN 121 D12
Kuusaa FIN 123 C15
Kuusaa FIN 123 F15
Kuusajärvi FIN 117 C14
Kuusajoki FIN 117 C14
Kuusalu EST 131 C10
Kuusamo FIN 121 C13
Kuusamonkylä FIN 121 F13
Kuusankoski FIN 128 D6
Kuusijärvi FIN 121 D11
Kuusijoki FIN 126 B8
Kuusiku EST 131 D9
Kuusiranta FIN 120 F9
Kuusirati FIN 119 F14
Kuusivaara FIN 115 E2
Kuusjärvi FIN 125 E11
Kuusjoki FIN 127 D9
Kuuslahti FIN 124 D9
Kuvansi FIN 125 F9
Kuvaskangas FIN 126 B6
Kuyka UA 153 A7
Kuyvozi RUS 129 E13
Kužiai LT 134 E6
Kuzmice SK 145 F4

Kuzmin *SRB* 158 C3
Kuźmina *PL* 145 D5
Kuz'molovskiy *RUS* 129 E13
Kuznechnoye *RUS* 129 C12
Kuźnia Raciborska *PL* 142 F5
Kuźnica *PL* 140 C9
Kuźnica Czarnkowska *PL* 85 E11
Kväcklingen *S* 103 A12
Kværkeby *DK* 87 E9
Kværndrup *DK* 86 E7
Kvalfors *N* 108 E5
Kvalnes *N* 110 D6
Kvalnes *N* 110 E8
Kvalnes *N* 111 B11
Kvalnes *N* 114 C8
Kvaløyhamn *N* 108 E3
Kvaloysletta *N* 111 A16
Kvaløyvågen *N* 111 A16
Kvalsaukan *N* 111 C10
Kvalsund *N* 113 B12
Kvalsvik *N* 100 B3
Kvalvåg *N* 104 E3
Kvalvik *N* 111 A19
Kvam *N* 101 C11
Kvannås *N* 111 B14
Kvanndal *N* 94 B5
Kvanne *N* 101 A9
Kvannli *N* 105 A14
Kvänum *S* 91 C13
Kvarnberg *S* 102 D8
Kvarnbyn *S* 118 F4
Kvarnriset *S* 118 F5
Kvarnsand *S* 99 B11
Kvarnsjö *S* 102 A7
Kvarntäkt *S* 103 E10
Kvarntorp *S* 92 A6
Kvarv *N* 108 B8
Kvarv *N* 109 B10
Kvasice *CZ* 146 C4
Kvasy *UA* 152 A4
Kveaune *N* 105 C15
Kvėdarna *LT* 134 E3
Kveinsjøen *N* 105 A12
Kvelde *N* 90 A6
Kveli *N* 105 B15
Kvenvær *N* 104 D4
Kvevlax *FIN* 122 D7
Kvibille *S* 87 B11
Kvicksund *S* 98 D6
Kvidinge *S* 87 C12
Kvikkjokk *S* 109 C14
Kvillsfors *S* 92 E7
Kvinesdal *N* 94 F5
Kvinlog *N* 94 E5
Kvissleby *S* 103 B13
Kvisvik *N* 104 E3
Kvitblik *N* 109 B10
Kviteberg *N* 112 D8
Kviteseid *N* 95 D8
Kvitnes *N* 110 C9
Kvitnes *N* 112 C5
Kvitsøy *N* 94 D2
Kvívík *FO* 2 A2
Kvorning *DK* 86 C5
Kwaadmechelen *B* 19 B11
Kwidzyn *PL* 138 C6
Kwieciszewo *PL* 138 E5
Kwilcz *PL* 81 A10
Kyan *S* 103 D10
Kybartai *LT* 136 D6
Kycklingvattnet *S* 105 B16
Kydrasivka *UA* 154 A5
Kyjov *CZ* 77 D12
Kyläinpää *FIN* 122 E8
Kylänlahti *FIN* 125 D13
Kyläsaari *FIN* 126 B6
Kyleakin *GB* 2 L5
Kyle of Lochalsh *GB* 2 L5
Kylerhea *GB* 2 L5
Kylestrome *GB* 2 J6
Kylland *N* 90 B1
Kyllburg *D* 21 D7
Kyllini *GR* 174 D3
Kylmäkoski *FIN* 127 C10
Kylmälä *FIN* 119 E16
Kymi *GR* 175 B9
Kymina *GR* 169 C8
Kyminlinna *FIN* 128 D6
Kymönkoski *FIN* 123 D15
Kyndby Huse *DK* 87 D9
Kyngäs *FIN* 119 D17
Kynsiperä *FIN* 121 C11
Kynsivaara *FIN* 121 C11
Kynšperk nad Ohří *CZ* 75 B12
Kypärävaara *FIN* 121 E12
Kyparissia *GR* 174 E4
Kypasjärv *S* 119 B10
Kyprinos *GR* 171 A10
Kypseli *GR* 175 D7
Kyrgia *GR* 171 B6
Kyriaki *GR* 175 C6
Kyritz *D* 83 E12
Kyrkås *S* 106 E7
Kyrkhult *S* 88 C7
Kyrksæterøra *N* 104 E6
Kyrkslätt *FIN* 127 E11
Kyrksten *S* 97 D11
Kyrnychky *UA* 155 B4
Kyröskoski *FIN* 127 B9
Kyrsyä *FIN* 129 B9
Kyslytsya *UA* 155 C4
Kysucké Nové Mesto *SK* 147 C7
Kysucký Lieskovec *SK* 147 C7
Kytäjä *FIN* 127 D12
Kythira *GR* 178 C4
Kythnos *GR* 175 E9
Kytökylä *FIN* 119 F15
Kytömäki *FIN* 121 E11
Kyustendil *BG* 165 E6
Kyyjärvi *FIN* 123 D13
Kyynämöinen *FIN* 123 F14
Kyynärö *FIN* 127 C12

L

Laa an der Thaya *A* 77 E10
Laaber *D* 75 D10
La Adrada *E* 46 D3
Laage *D* 83 C12
Laagri *EST* 131 C9
Laaja *FIN* 121 E12
Laajoki *FIN* 126 D7
Laakajärvi *FIN* 125 C10
La Alberca *E* 45 C8
La Alberca *E* 56 F2
La Alberca de Záncara *E* 47 E8
La Alberguería de Argañán *E* 45 D7
La Albuera *E* 51 B6
La Aldehuela *E* 45 D10
La Algaba *E* 51 E7
La Aliseda de Tormes *E* 45 D10
La Aljorra *E* 56 F2
La Almarcha *E* 47 E8
La Almolda *E* 42 D3
La Almunia de Doña Godina *E* 41 F9
Laanila *FIN* 115 B2
Lääniste *EST* 131 E14
La Antilla *E* 51 E5
Laapas *FIN* 128 D8
Laarkirchen *A* 76 G5
Laarne *B* 19 B8
Laasala *FIN* 123 E12
Laaslich *D* 83 D11
Laatre *EST* 131 E10
Laatre *EST* 131 F12
Laatzen *D* 78 B6
Laax *CH* 71 D8
La Azohía *E* 56 F2
La Baconnière *F* 23 D10
Labajos *E* 46 C3
La Balme-de-Sillingy *F* 31 D9
La Bañeza *E* 39 D8
Labanoras *LT* 135 F11
La Barre-de-Monts *F* 28 B1
La Barre-en-Ouche *F* 24 C4
La Barthe-de-Neste *F* 33 D6
Labarthe-Rivière *F* 33 D7
La Bassée *F* 18 C6
La Bastide-Clairence *F* 32 D3
Labastide-d'Anjou *F* 33 D9
Labastide-d'Armagnac *F* 32 C5
La Bastide-de Bousignac *F* 33 D9
La Bastide-de-Sérou *F* 33 D8
La Bastide-l'Évêque *F* 33 B10
Labastide-Murat *F* 33 A9
La Bastide-Puylaurent *F* 35 A6
Labastide-Rouairoux *F* 34 D4
Labastide-St-Pierre *F* 33 C8
La Bastide-sur-l'Hers *F* 33 E9
La Bâthie *F* 31 D9
La Bâtie-Neuve *F* 36 B4
Lábatlan *H* 149 A10
Labatut-Rivière *F* 32 C6
La Baule-Escoublac *F* 23 F7
La Bazoche-Gouet *F* 24 D4
La Bazoge *F* 23 D12
L'Abbaye *CH* 31 B9
Labégude *F* 35 A7
La Bégude-de-Mazenc *F* 35 A8
Labenne *F* 32 C3
La Bérarde *F* 31 F9
Labergement-lès-Seurre *F* 31 A7
Laberget *N* 111 C13
La Bernerie-en-Retz *F* 28 A1
Laberweinting *D* 75 E11
Labin *HR* 67 B9
Labinot-Mal *AL* 168 B3
La Bisbal de Falset *E* 42 E5
La Bisbal del Penedès *E* 43 E6
La Bisbal d'Empordà *E* 43 D10
Łabiszyn *PL* 138 E4
Lablachère *F* 35 B7
Laboe *D* 83 B8
La Bonneville-sur-Iton *F* 24 C5
La Bouëxière *F* 23 D9
Labouheyre *F* 32 B4
La Bouilladisse *F* 35 D10
La Bourboule *F* 30 D2
Laboutarie *F* 33 C10
La Bóveda de Toro *E* 39 F9
Łabowa *PL* 145 D2
La Brède *F* 32 A4
La Bréole *F* 36 C4
La Bresse *F* 27 D6
La Brillanne *F* 35 C10
Labrit *F* 32 B4
La Broque *F* 27 D7
La Bruffière *F* 28 A3
Labruguière *F* 33 C10
L'Absie *F* 28 B4
La Buisse *F* 31 E8
Łabunie *PL* 144 B7
La Bussière *F* 25 E8
Läby *S* 99 B9
Laç *AL* 163 E8
Laç *AL* 168 A2
La Cabrera *E* 46 C5
La Caillère-St-Hilaire *F* 28 B4
Lacalahorra *E* 55 E6
La Caletta *I* 64 B4
Lacalm *F* 30 F2
La Calmette *F* 35 C7
La Calzada de Oropesa *E* 45 E10
La Campana *E* 51 D9
La Cañada de San Urbano *E* 55 F8
La Cañada de Verich *E* 42 F3
Lacanau *F* 28 F3
Lacanau-Océan *F* 28 E3
Lacanche *F* 25 F12
La Canourgue *F* 34 B5
La Capelle *F* 19 E8
Lacapelle-Barrès *F* 30 F2
Lacapelle-Marival *F* 29 F9
Laćarak *SRB* 158 C4
La Caridad *E* 39 A6
La Carlota *E* 53 A7
La Carolina *E* 54 C5
Lacaune *F* 34 C4
La Cavada *E* 40 B4
La Cavalerie *F* 34 B5
Lacave *F* 29 F9
Lacco Ameno *I* 62 F5
Laceby *GB* 11 D11
Lacedonia *I* 60 A4
La Cellera de Ter *E* 43 D9
La Celle-St-Avant *F* 29 A7
La Cerca *E* 40 C5
La Cerollera *E* 42 F3
Laces *I* 71 D11
La Chaise-Dieu *F* 30 E4
La Chaize-le-Vicomte *F* 28 B3
La Chambre *F* 31 E9
Lachania *GR* 181 E7
La Chapelaude *F* 29 C11
La Chapelle *F* 19 E11
La Chapelle-aux-Bois *F* 26 D5
La Chapelle-aux-Saints *F* 29 F9
La Chapelle-d'Abondance *F* 31 C10
La Chapelle-d'Aligné *F* 23 E11
La Chapelle-d'Angillon *F* 25 F7
La Chapelle-de-Guinchay *F* 30 C6
La Chapelle-des-Fougeretz *F* 23 D8
La Chapelle-en-Valgaudémar *F* 31 F9
La Chapelle-en-Vercors *F* 31 F7
La Chapelle-la-Reine *F* 25 D8
La Chapelle-Laurent *F* 30 E3
Lachapelle-sous-Aubenas *F* 35 A7
La Chapelle-St-André *F* 25 F9
La Chapelle-St-Laurent *F* 28 B5
La Chapelle-St-Luc *F* 25 D11
La Chapelle-St-Quillain *F* 26 F4
La Chapelle-St-Ursin *F* 29 A10
La Chapelle-sur-Erdre *F* 23 F8
Lachar *E* 53 B9
La Charité-sur-Loire *F* 25 F9
La Chartre-sur-le-Loir *F* 24 E4
La Châtaigneraie *F* 28 B4
La Châtre *F* 29 B9
La Châtre-Langlin *F* 29 C8
La Chaume *F* 25 E12
La Chaussée-St-Victor *F* 24 E5
La Chaussée-sur-Marne *F* 25 C12
La Chaux-de-Fonds *CH* 27 F6
La Chaux-du-Dombief *F* 31 B8
Lachendorf *D* 79 A7
Lachen-Speyerdorf *D* 21 F10
La Cheppe *F* 25 B12
La Chèze *F* 22 D6
Lachowo *PL* 139 D13
Lacići *HR* 149 E10
La Cierva *E* 47 D9
La Ciotat *F* 35 D10
La Cisterniga *E* 39 E10
Lack *GB* 7 C7
Łąck *PL* 139 F8
Lackamore *IRL* 8 C6
Läckeby *S* 89 B10
Łącko *PL* 145 D1
La Clayette *F* 30 C5
La Clusaz *F* 31 D9
La Cluse *F* 35 A10
La Cluse-et-Mijoux *F* 31 B9
La Codosera *E* 45 F6
La Concha *E* 40 B4
La Condamine-Châtelard *F* 36 C5
Laconi *I* 64 D3
La Coquille *F* 29 D7
La Coronada *E* 51 B8
La Coronada *E* 51 C9
La Côte-St-André *F* 31 E7
La-Couarde-sur-Mer *F* 28 C3
La Couronne *F* 28 D6
Lacourt *F* 33 E8
La Courtine *F* 29 D10
La Couture-Boussey *F* 24 C5
Lāčplēsis *LV* 135 C9
Lacq *F* 32 D4
La Crau *F* 36 E4
La Crèche *F* 28 C5
Lacroix-Barrez *F* 29 F11
La Croixille *F* 23 D9
La Croix-Valmer *F* 36 E5
Lacrouzette *F* 33 C10
La Cumbre *E* 45 F9
Łączna *PL* 143 E10
Łącznik *PL* 142 F4
Ladánybene *H* 150 C3
Ladbergen *D* 17 D9
Ladce *SK* 146 C6
Lądek *PL* 142 B4
Lądek-Zdrój *PL* 77 B11
Ladelund *D* 82 A6
Ladenburg *D* 21 F11
Lădeşti *RO* 160 D4
Ladi *GR* 171 B10
Ladignac-le-Long *F* 29 D8
Ladinhac *F* 29 F11
Ladispoli *I* 62 D2
Ladoeiro *P* 45 E6
Ladomirová *SK* 145 E4
Ladon *F* 25 D8
Ladozhskoye Ozero *RUS* 129 E15
Ladushkin *RUS* 139 A9
Ladybank *GB* 5 C10
Ladykirk *GB* 5 D12
Ladysford *GB* 3 K12
Lādzere *LV* 134 B5
Ładzice *PL* 143 D7
Ładzin *PL* 84 C7
Laekvere *EST* 131 C13
La Encina *E* 56 D3
Laer *D* 17 D8
La Ercina *E* 39 C9
Lærdalsøyri *N* 100 D6
Laerma *GR* 181 D7
Laerru *I* 64 B2
La Espina *E* 39 B7
La Estación *E* 43 D8
La Estrella *E* 45 E10
Laeva *EST* 131 E12
La Fare-les-Oliviers *F* 35 C9
La Farlède *F* 36 E4
La Fatarrella *E* 42 E4
La Faurie *F* 35 A10
La Faute-sur-Mer *F* 28 C3
La Felipa *E* 47 F9
La Fère *F* 19 E7
La Ferrière *F* 28 B3
La Ferrière-aux-Etangs *F* 23 C10
La Ferté-Alais *F* 25 D7
La Ferté-Bernard *F* 24 D4
La Ferté-Frênel *F* 24 C4
La Ferté-Gaucher *F* 25 C9
La Ferté-Imbault *F* 24 F6
La Ferté-Loupière *F* 25 E9
La Ferté-Macé *F* 23 C11
La-Ferté-Milon *F* 25 B9
La Ferté-sous-Jouarre *F* 25 C9
La Ferté-St-Aubin *F* 24 E6
La Ferté-St-Cyr *F* 24 E6
Laferté-sur-Amance *F* 26 E4
Laferté-sur-Aube *F* 25 D12
La Férte-Vidame *F* 24 C4
La Ferté-Villeneuil *F* 24 E5
Lafitole *F* 33 D6
Lafkos *GR* 175 A7
La Flèche *F* 23 E11
Lafnitz *A* 148 B6
La Fontaine-St-Martin *F* 23 E12
La Font de la Figuera *E* 56 D3
La Force *F* 29 F6
La Forêt-sur-Sèvre *F* 28 B4
La Forge *F* 26 D6
Laforsen *S* 103 C10
Lafortunada *E* 33 E6
La Fouillade *F* 33 B10
La Foux-d'Allos *F* 36 C5
Lafrançaise *F* 33 B8
La Fregeneda *E* 45 C7
La Fresneda *E* 42 F4
Lafrimbolle *F* 27 C7
La Frontera *E* 47 D8
La Fuente de San Esteban *E* 45 C8
La Fuliola *E* 42 D6
La Gacilly *F* 23 E7
La Galera *E* 42 F4
Lagan *S* 87 B13
La Garde *F* 36 E4
La Garde-Adhémar *F* 35 B8
La Garde-Freinet *F* 36 E4
Lagardelle-sur-Lèze *F* 33 D8
Lagarelhos *P* 38 E5
Lagares da Beira *P* 44 D5
La Garnache *F* 28 B2
La Garriga *E* 43 D8
Lagarrigue *F* 33 C10
La Gaubretière *F* 28 B3
Lagavara *GB* 4 E4
Lage *D* 17 D7
Lage *D* 17 E11
Lagedi *EST* 131 C9
Lage Mierde *NL* 16 F4
Lagerfors *S* 91 B15
Lagfors *S* 103 A13
Lagg *GB* 4 E6
Laggan *GB* 4 A7
Laggan *GB* 5 A8
Lagganulva *GB* 4 C4
Laggarberg *S* 103 B13
Laghey *IRL* 6 C6
Laghtgeorge *IRL* 6 F5
Łagiewniki *PL* 81 E11
La Gineta *E* 47 F9
Lagkada *GR* 177 C7
Lagkadas *GR* 169 C9
Lagkadia *GR* 174 D5
La Glacerie *F* 23 A8
Lagnieu *F* 31 D7
Lagny-sur-Marne *F* 25 C8
Lago *I* 60 E6
Lagoa *P* 39 F6
Lagoa *P* 50 E3
Lagoaça *P* 45 B7
Lago Menor *E* 57 B11
Lagonegro *I* 60 C5
Lagor *F* 32 D4
Lagorce *F* 35 B7
Lagord *F* 28 C3
La Gornal *E* 43 E7
Lagos *GR* 171 B8
Lagos *P* 50 E2
Lagosanto *I* 66 C5
Łagów *PL* 81 B8
Łagów *PL* 143 E11
Lagrán *E* 41 C6
La Granada de Riotinto *E* 51 D7
La Granadella *E* 42 E5
La Grand-Croix *F* 30 D6
La Grande-Combe *F* 35 B7
La Grande-Motte *F* 35 C7
La Granja d'Escarp *E* 42 E4
La Granjuela *E* 51 C9
Lagrasse *F* 34 D4
La Grave *F* 31 E9
Lägsta *S* 107 D14
La Guarda *E* 51 B8
Laguardia *E* 41 C6
La Guardia *E* 46 E6
La Guardia de Jaén *E* 53 A9
Laguarta *E* 32 F5
Laguenne *F* 29 E9
Laguépie *F* 33 B9
La Guerche-de-Bretagne *F* 23 E9
La Guerche-sur-l'Aubois *F* 30 B2
Laguiole *F* 30 F2
Laguna Dalga *E* 39 D8
Laguna de Duero *E* 39 E10
Laguna de Negrillos *E* 39 D8
Lagundo *I* 72 C3
Lagunilla *E* 45 D9
Lagyna *GR* 169 C9
Lagyna *GR* 171 B10
La Haba *E* 51 B8
Lahana *TR* 173 B7
La Haye-du-Puits *F* 23 B8
La Haye-Pesnel *F* 23 C9
Lähdejänkkä *FIN* 119 B12
Lähden *D* 17 C9
Lahenpää *S* 116 E10
Laheycourt *F* 26 C3
La Higuera *E* 55 B10
Lahinch *IRL* 8 C4
La Hiniesta *E* 39 E8
La Hinojosa *E* 47 E8
Lahnajärvi *S* 116 E8
Lahnalahti *FIN* 124 F9
Lahnanen *FIN* 123 C16
Lahnasjärvi *FIN* 125 C9
Lahnasuando *S* 116 E9
Lahnstein *D* 21 D9
Lahntal-Goßfelden *D* 21 C11
Laholm *S* 87 C12
Lahonci *SLO* 148 D6
La Horcajada *E* 45 D10
La Horra *E* 40 E4
Lahr (Schwarzwald) *D* 27 D8
Lähte *EST* 131 E13
Lahti *FIN* 126 D6
Lahti *FIN* 127 D14
Lahtiranta *FIN* 119 E13
Laichingen *D* 74 F6
Laide *GB* 2 K5
Laidi *LV* 134 C3
Laidze *LV* 134 B5
Laifour *F* 184 E2
L'Aigle *F* 24 C4
La Iglesuela *E* 46 D3
La Iglesuela del Cid *E* 42 G3
Laignes *F* 25 E11
Laigueglia *I* 37 D8
L'Aiguillon-sur-Mer *F* 28 C3
Laihia *FIN* 122 E8
Laikko *FIN* 129 C11
Laiksjö *S* 107 C11
Lailly-en-Val *F* 24 E6
Laimont *F* 26 C3
Lainate *I* 69 B7
Lainio *S* 116 C8
Laino Borgo *I* 60 D5
Lairg *GB* 3 J8
La Iruela *E* 55 D7
Laisbäck *S* 107 A12
Laisheden *S* 109 E14
Laissac *F* 34 B4
Laisvall *S* 109 D13
Laisvalls by *S* 109 D13
Laitala *FIN* 121 E12
Laitikkala *FIN* 127 C11
Laitila *FIN* 126 D6
Laiuse *EST* 131 D13
Laives *I* 72 D3
Laižuva *LT* 134 D5
La Jana *E* 42 F4
La Jarrie *F* 28 C3
Lajatico *I* 66 F2
La Javie *F* 36 C4
Lajeosa *P* 45 D7
Lajeosa do Mondego *P* 45 C6
Lajkovac *SRB* 158 E5
La Jonchère-St-Maurice *F* 29 C8
La Jonquera *E* 34 F4
Lajoskomárom *H* 149 C10
Lajosmizse *H* 150 C4
La Jumellière *F* 23 F10
Lakaluoma *FIN* 123 E10
Lakatnik *BG* 165 C7
Lakaträsk *S* 118 B6
Lakavica *NMK* 163 F10
Lakavica *NMK* 169 A7
Lakenheath *GB* 15 C10
Lakhdenpokh'ya *RUS* 129 B13
Laki *NMK* 165 F6
Łąkie *PL* 85 D12
Lakitelek *H* 150 D4
Lakka *GR* 168 F3
Lakki *GR* 177 E8
Lakkoi *GR* 178 E6
Lakkoma *GR* 169 D9
Lakkoma *GR* 171 D9
Lakkopetra *GR* 174 C3
Łąkociny *PL* 142 C4
Lakomäki *FIN* 123 E15
Łąkorz *PL* 139 D7
Lakšárska Nová Ves *SK* 146 D4
Lakselv *N* 113 C14
Lakselvsletta *N* 111 B18
Laksfors *N* 108 E5
Laktaši *BIH* 157 C7
Lakuntza *E* 32 E1
La Lantejuela *E* 51 E9
La Lapa *E* 51 C6
Lalapaşa *TR* 167 F7
Lalas *GR* 174 D4
L'Albagés *E* 42 E5
Lalbenque *F* 33 B9
L'Alcora *E* 48 D4
L'Alcudia *E* 48 F3
L'Alcudia de Crespins *E* 56 D3
Lalevade-d'Ardèche *F* 35 A7
Lalëz *AL* 168 A2
L'Alfàs del Pi *E* 56 D4
Lalín *E* 38 C3
Lalinac *SRB* 164 C5
Lalinde *F* 29 F7
La Línea de la Concepción *E* 53 D6
Lalioti *GR* 175 C6
Lallaing *F* 19 D7
Lalley *F* 31 F8
Lalm *N* 101 C10
La Londe-les-Maures *F* 36 E4
Laloşu *RO* 160 D4
Laloubère *F* 33 D6
La Loupe *F* 24 D5
Lalouvesc *F* 30 E6
La Louvière *B* 19 D9
Lalove *UA* 145 G6
La Loye *F* 31 A8
L'Alpe-d'Huez *F* 31 E9
Lalueza *E* 42 D3
La Luisiana *E* 51 D9
Laluque *F* 32 C4
Lam *D* 76 D4
La Machine *F* 30 B3
La Maddalena *I* 64 A3
Lama dei Peligni *I* 63 C6
La Magdalena *E* 39 C8
Lamagistère *F* 33 B7
La Malène *F* 34 B5
Lamalou-les-Bains *F* 34 C5
Lama Mocogno *I* 66 D2
La Manga del Mar Menor *E* 56 F3
Lamanon *F* 35 C9
La Marche *F* 25 F9
Lamarche *F* 26 D4
Lamarche-sur-Saône *F* 26 F3
Lamargelle *F* 25 E12
Lamarque *F* 28 E4
Lamas *P* 44 C3
La Massana *AND* 33 E9
Lamastre *F* 30 F6
La Mata *E* 46 E4
La Mata de los Olmos *E* 42 F3
La Matilla *E* 46 B5
Lambach *A* 76 F5
Lamballe *F* 22 D6
Lambersart *F* 18 C7
Lambesc *F* 35 C9
Lambia *GR* 174 D4
Łambinowice *PL* 142 E4
Lamborn *S* 103 E10
Lambourn *GB* 13 B11
Lambrecht (Pfalz) *D* 186 C5
Lambsheim *D* 21 E10
Lamego *P* 44 B5
La Meilleraye-de-Bretagne *F* 23 E9
Lameiras *P* 45 C6
Lamerdingen *D* 71 A11
L'Ametlla de Mar *E* 42 F5
Lamezia *I* 59 B9
Lamia *GR* 174 B5
Lamiako *E* 40 B6
La Milesse *F* 23 D12
Lamlash *GB* 4 D6
Lammhult *S* 88 A7
Lammi *FIN* 123 D11
Lammi *FIN* 127 C13
Lamminkoski *FIN* 123 F10
Lamminmaa *FIN* 122 F8
Lamminperä *FIN* 119 C16
Lamminvaara *FIN* 121 B10
La Mojonera *E* 55 F7
La Môle *F* 36 E4
Lamon *I* 72 D4
La Mongie *F* 33 E6
La Monnerie-le-Montel *F* 30 D4
La Morera *E* 51 B6
Lamothe *F* 30 E3
La Mothe-Achard *F* 28 B2
Lamothe-Cassel *F* 33 A8
La Mothe-St-Héray *F* 28 C5
Lamotte-Beuvron *F* 24 E7
La Motte-Chalancon *F* 35 B9
La Motte-du-Caire *F* 35 B11
Lamovita *BIH* 157 C6
Lampaanjärvi *FIN* 124 D7
Lampaul *F* 22 D1
Lampaul-Guimiliau *F* 22 D3
Lampaul-Plouarzel *F* 22 D2
Lampeland *N* 95 C11
Lamperila *FIN* 124 E8
Lampertheim *D* 21 E10
Lampertswalde *D* 80 D5
Lampeter *GB* 12 A6
Lampinou *GR* 169 F9
Lampinsaari *FIN* 119 F14
Lampiselkä *FIN* 115 D1
Lamprechtshausen *A* 76 G3
Lampsijärvi *FIN* 117 E13
Lamsfeld-Groß Liebitz *D* 80 C6
Lamspringe *D* 79 C7
Lamstedt *D* 17 A12
Lamu *FIN* 119 F16
La Mudarra *E* 39 E10
La Muela *E* 41 E9
Lamujoki *FIN* 119 F16
La Mure *F* 31 F8
Lamure-sur-Azergues *F* 30 C5
Lana *I* 72 C3
Lanabukt *N* 114 D8
Lanaja *E* 41 E11
Lanaken *B* 19 C12
Lanarce *F* 30 F5
Lanark *GB* 5 D9
La Nava *E* 51 D6
La Nava de Ricomalillo *E* 46 E3
La Nava de Santiago *E* 45 F8
Lancaster *GB* 10 C6
Lanchester *GB* 5 F13
Lanciano *I* 63 C6
Lanckorona *PL* 147 B9
Łańcut *PL* 144 C5
Lancy *CH* 31 C9
Landau an der Isar *D* 75 E12
Landau in der Pfalz *D* 21 F10
Landbobyn *S* 102 E7
Lande *N* 105 A13
Landeck *A* 71 C11
Landeleau *F* 22 D4
Landen *B* 183 D6
Landerneau *F* 22 D3
Landersheim *F* 27 C7
Landeryd *S* 87 A12
Landesbergen *D* 17 C12
Landete *E* 47 E10
Landévant *F* 22 E5
Landgraaf *NL* 20 C6
Landiras *F* 32 A5
Landivisiau *F* 22 C3
Landivy *F* 23 D9
Landkirchen auf Fehmarn *D* 83 B10
Landön *S* 105 D16
Landos *F* 30 F4
Landquart *CH* 71 D9
Landrecies *F* 19 D8
Landres *F* 19 F12
Landsberg am Lech *D* 71 A11
Landsbro *S* 92 E5
Landscheid *D* 185 E6
Landshut *D* 75 E11
Landskrona *S* 87 D11
Landsmeer *NL* 182 A5
Landstuhl *D* 21 F9
Landudec *F* 22 D3
Landvetter *S* 91 D11
Landze *LV* 134 B3
Lanesborough *IRL* 7 E7
Lanesøyra *N* 112 C4
Lanester *F* 22 E5
La Neuve-Lyre *F* 24 C4
La Neuveville *CH* 31 A11
La Neuville-au-Pont *F* 25 B12
Laneuville-sur-Meuse *F* 19 F11
Lång *S* 97 D9
Langå *DK* 86 C5
Langa *E* 46 B3
Långå *S* 102 B5
Langa de Duero *E* 40 E5
Långalma *S* 99 B10
Långaminne *FIN* 122 E7
Långan *S* 105 D16
Langangen *N* 90 A6
Långås *S* 87 B10
Langasjö *S* 89 B8
Langau *A* 77 E9
Långbäck *S* 107 A11
Långbäcken *S* 107 C14
Langballig *D* 82 A7
Långban *S* 97 C11
Långbo *S* 103 C10
Långbo *S* 103 D12
Langbunes *N* 114 C9
Langburkersdorf *D* 80 D6
Langdorf *D* 76 D4
Langeac *F* 30 E3
Langeais *F* 24 F3
Langebæk *DK* 87 F10
Långed *S* 107 D17
Langedijk *NL* 16 C3
Langeid *N* 90 B2
Längelmäki *FIN* 127 B12
Langeln *D* 79 C8
Langelsheim *D* 79 C7
Langemark *B* 18 C6
Langemyr *N* 90 B3
Langen *D* 17 A11
Langen *D* 21 E11
Langenaltheim *D* 75 E8
Langenau *D* 75 F7
Langenaubach *D* 185 C9
Langenberg *D* 17 E10
Langenberg *D* 183 C10
Langenburg *D* 74 D6
Langenenslingen *D* 27 D11
Langenes *N* 110 B9
Längenfeld *A* 71 C11
Langenfeld (Rheinland) *D* 21 B7
Langenhagen *D* 78 B6
Langenhahn *D* 185 C8
Langenhorn *D* 82 A5
Langenleuba-Oberhain *D* 79 E12
Langenlois *A* 77 F9
Langenlonsheim *D* 185 E8
Langennaundorf *D* 80 C4
Langenneufnach *D* 71 A11
Langenorla *D* 79 E10
Langenpreising *D* 75 F10
Langenselbold *D* 21 D12
Langenthal *CH* 27 F8
Langenwang *A* 148 A5
Langenweddingen *D* 79 B10
Langenzenn *D* 75 D8
Langenzersdorf *A* 77 F10
Langeoog *D* 17 A8
Langeskov *DK* 86 E7
Langesund *N* 90 A6
Langevåg *N* 94 C2
Langevåg *N* 100 B4
Langewiesen *D* 79 E8
Langfjordbotn *N* 112 C9
Langgöns *D* 21 D11
Langhagen *D* 83 C12
Langham *GB* 11 F10
Langhamn *N* 111 B14
Långhed *S* 103 D11
Långhem *S* 91 D13
Langhirano *I* 66 C1
Langholm *GB* 5 E11
Langhus *N* 95 C13
Långlöt *S* 89 B11
Långnäs *S* 98 A6
Langnau *CH* 70 D5
Langnes *N* 111 B15
Langnes *N* 114 C4
Langnes *N* 114 D7
Langø *DK* 83 A10
Langogne *F* 30 F4
Langoiran *F* 28 F5
Langon *F* 32 A5
Langport *GB* 13 C9
Langreo *E* 39 B8
Langres *F* 26 E3
Langschlag *A* 77 E7
Långsel *S* 118 B8
Långsele *S* 107 C15
Långsele *S* 107 E12
Langset *N* 95 B14
Langset *N* 108 D5
Langset *N* 109 B9
Långshyttan *S* 97 B15
Långsjöby *S* 107 A11
Långskog *S* 103 B12
Langslett *N* 112 D6
Langstrand *N* 112 B11
Långsund *S* 118 D7
Langsur *D* 186 B2
Langtoft *GB* 11 C11
Långträsk *S* 107 A16
Långträsk *S* 118 C7
Långträsk *S* 118 D4
Langueux *F* 22 D6
Languidic *F* 22 E5
Languilla *E* 40 F5
Langula *D* 79 D7
Långvattnet *S* 107 D11
Långvattnet *S* 107 D13
Långvattnet *S* 118 E4
Långviken *S* 109 E15
Långviksmon *S* 107 D15
Långvinds bruk *S* 103 D13
Langwarden (Butjadingen) *D* 17 A10
Langwathby *GB* 5 F11
Langwedel *D* 17 C12
Langwedel *D* 83 B7
Langweid am Lech *D* 75 F8
Łanijta *PL* 139 F7
Lanivet *GB* 12 E5
Lanjarón *E* 53 C10
Lankojärvi *FIN* 117 E12
Lanloup *F* 22 C6
Lanmeur *F* 22 C4
Lanna *S* 87 A13
Lanna *S* 92 A5
Länna *S* 99 C9
Lannach *A* 148 C4
Lannavaara *S* 116 B7
Lannemezan *F* 33 D6
Lannepax *F* 33 C6
Lannevesi *FIN* 123 E14
Lannilis *F* 22 C2
Lannion *F* 22 C5
Lannoy *F* 19 C7
Lanobre *F* 29 E11
La Nocle-Maulaix *F* 30 B4
Lanouaille *F* 29 E8
Lánov *CZ* 81 E9
Lansån *S* 116 F8
Lansargues *F* 35 C7
Lansen *D* 83 D13
Länsikioski *FIN* 119 C13
Länsikylä *FIN* 123 E11
Länsipää *FIN* 119 B12
Länsiranta *FIN* 117 D16
Länsi-Teisko *FIN* 127 B10
Lansjärv *S* 116 E8
Lanškroun *CZ* 77 C11
Lanslebourg-Mont-Cenis *F* 31 E10
Lanta *F* 33 C9
Lantadilla *E* 40 D3
Lanton *F* 28 F3
Lantosque *F* 37 D6
Lantriac *F* 30 E5
Lanty *F* 30 B4
La Nucía *E* 56 D4
Lanuéjouls *F* 33 B10
Lanurile *RO* 155 C1
Lanusei *I* 64 D4
Lanuvio *I* 62 D3
Lanvollon *F* 22 C6
Łany *PL* 142 F5
Lánycsók *H* 149 D11
Lanz *D* 83 D11
Lanzahita *E* 46 D3
Lanžhot *CZ* 77 E11
Lanzo Torinese *I* 31 E11
Laon *F* 19 E8
Laons *F* 24 C5
La Paca *E* 55 D9
La Pacaudière *F* 30 C4
Lapajärvi *FIN* 115 E4
Lapalisse *F* 30 C4
La Pallice *F* 28 C3
La Palma *E* 56 F3
La Palma del Condado *E* 51 E6
La Palme *F* 34 E4
Lapalud *F* 35 B8
La Palud-sur-Verdon *F* 36 D4
Lapanj *AL* 168 D3
Łapanów *PL* 144 D1
Lapardha *AL* 168 C2
La Parra *E* 51 B6
La Parra de Las Vegas *E* 47 E8
Lapas *GR* 174 C3
La Pellerine *F* 23 D9
La Penne *F* 36 D5
La Peraleja *E* 47 D7
La Pesga *E* 45 D8
La Petite-Pierre *F* 27 C7
La Peza *E* 55 E6
Lapford *GB* 13 D7
Lapijoki *FIN* 126 C6
La Pinilla *E* 56 F2
Lapinjärvi *FIN* 127 D15
Lapinkylä *FIN* 127 E11
Lapinlahti *FIN* 124 D8
Lapinneva *FIN* 123 G9
Lapinsalo *FIN* 123 C17
La Plagne *F* 31 D10
La Plaza *E* 39 B7
Laplume *F* 33 B7
Lapmežciems *LV* 134 B7
La Pobla de Claramunt *E* 43 D7
La Pobla del Duc *E* 56 D4
La Pobla de Lillet *E* 43 C7
La Pobla de Montornès *E* 43 E6
La Pobla de Segur *E* 42 C5
La Pobla de Vallbona *E* 48 E3
La Pola de Gordón *E* 39 C8
La Pommeraye *F* 23 F10
La Porta *F* 37 G10
La Portellada *E* 42 F4
La Portera *E* 47 F10

Lapoş RO 161 C8
La Pouëze F 23 E10
Lapoutroie F 27 D7
Lapovo SRB 159 E7
Lappajärvi FIN 123 D11
Lappe S 92 A7
Lappea FIN 117 D11
Lappeenranta FIN 129 C9
Lappersdorf D 75 D11
Lappetelä FIN 124 D8
Lappfjärd FIN 122 F7
Lappfors FIN 123 C10
Lappi FIN 119 E14
Lappi FIN 121 D13
Lappi FIN 126 C6
Lappila FIN 127 D13
Lappo FIN 126 E5
Lappohja FIN 127 F9
Lappträsk S 119 B11
Lappuluobbal N 113 E13
La Preste F 33 F10
La Proveda de Soria E 41 D7
Lâpseki TR 172 D6
Laptevo RUS 133 C5
Lapua FIN 123 E10
La Puebla de Almoradiel E 47 E6
La Puebla de Arganzón E 40 C6
La Puebla de Cazalla E 51 E9
La Puebla de los Infantes E 51 D9
La Puebla del Río E 51 E7
La Puebla de Montalbán E 46 E4
La Puebla de Valdavia E 39 C10
La Puebla de Valverde E 48 D3
La Puerta de Segura E 55 C7
Lăpugiu de Jos RO 151 F10
La Punt CH 71 D9
Lăpuş RO 152 C4
Lăpuşata RO 160 D4
Lapuşna MD 154 D2
Lăpuşnicel RO 159 D9
Lăpuşnicu Mare RO 159 D8
Łapy PL 140 E7
L'Aquila I 62 C4
Laracha E 38 B2
Laracor IRL 7 E9
Laragh IRL 7 F10
Laragne-Montéglin F 35 B10
La Rambla E 53 A7
Laranueva E 47 C7
La Rasa E 40 E5
La Ravoire F 31 D8
Larbert GB 5 C9
L'Arboç E 43 E7
L'Arbresle F 30 D6
Lärbro S 93 D13
Larceveau-Arros-Cibits F 32 D3
Larchamp F 23 D9
Larchant F 25 D8
Larche F 29 E8
Larche F 36 C5
Lardaro I 69 B10
Larderello I 66 F2
Lardero E 41 D7
Lardos GR 181 D8
Laredo E 40 B5
La Redorte F 34 D4
Laren NL 16 D4
Laren NL 183 A8
La Réole F 32 A5
Larga MD 153 A9
Largan IRL 6 D5
L'Argentière-la-Bessée F 31 F10
Largoward GB 5 C11
Largs GB 4 D7
Largu RO 161 D10
Lari I 66 E2
Lariano I 62 D3
La Riba E 42 E6
La Riba de Escalote E 40 F6
La Ricamarie F 30 E5
La Riche F 24 F4
La Rinconada E 51 E8
Larino I 63 D7
Larionovo RUS 129 D13
Larisa GR 169 E7
Larkhall GB 5 D9
Larkollen N 95 D13
Larling GB 15 C10
L'Armentera E 43 C10
Larmor-Plage F 22 E5
Larne GB 4 F5
La Robla E 39 C8
La Roca de la Sierra E 45 F7
La Roche CH 31 B11
La Roche-Bernard F 23 E7
La Roche-Canillac F 29 E9
La Roche-Chalais F 28 E6
La Roche-de-Rame F 31 F10
La Roche-Derrien F 22 C5
La Roche-des-Arnauds F 35 A10
La Roche-en-Ardenne B 19 D12
La Rochefoucauld F 29 D6
La Rochelle F 28 C3
Larochemillay F 30 B5
La Roche-Posay F 29 B7
La Rochepot F 30 B6
La Roche-sur-Foron F 31 C9
La Roche-sur-Yon F 28 B3
La Rochette F 31 E9
Larochette L 20 E6
La Roda E 47 F8
La Roda de Andalucía E 53 B7
La Roë F 23 E9
Laroles E 55 E7
La Romana E 56 E3
La Romieu F 33 C6
Laroquebrou F 29 F10
Laroque-d'Olmes F 33 E9
La Roque-Ste-Marguerite F 34 B5
Laroque-Timbaut F 33 B7
La Rouquette F 33 B9
Larraga E 32 E2
Larrasoaina E 32 E2
Larrau F 32 D4
Larrazet F 33 C8
Larressore F 32 D3
Larrión E 32 E1
Larsbo S 97 B14
Larseng N 111 A16
Larsmo FIN 122 C9
Larsnes N 100 B3
Laruns F 32 E5
Laruscade F 28 E5
Larv S 91 C13
Larva E 55 D6
Larvik N 90 A7
Larymna GR 175 B7
Lasà I 71 D11
Lasalle F 35 B6
La Salle I 31 D11
La Salle les Alpes F 31 F10
La Salvetat-Peyralès F 33 B10
La Salvetat-sur-Agout F 34 C4
La Salzadella E 48 D5
Läsänkoski FIN 128 B6
Las Arenas E 39 B10
La Sauvetat-du-Dropt F 33 A6
La Savina E 57 D7
Lasberg A 77 F7
Las Berlanas E 46 C3
Låsby DK 86 C5
Las Cabezas de San Juan E 51 F8
Lascari I 58 D4
Las Casas E 48 E4
Lascuarre E 42 C5
La Seca E 39 F10
La Secuita E 43 E6
La Séguinière F 28 A4
La Selva del Camp E 42 E6
La Selve F 33 B11
La Sènia E 42 F4
La Seyne-sur-Mer F 35 D10
Las Herencias E 46 E3
Łasin PL 138 C7
Lasinja HR 148 E5
Łask PL 143 C7
Łaskarzew PL 141 G5
Laško SLO 148 D4
Laskowa PL 144 D1
Laskowice PL 138 D5
Laskowiec PL 139 D12
Las Labores E 46 F5
Laslea RO 152 E5
Las Majadas E 47 D8
Las Menas E 55 E8
Las Mesas E 47 F7
Las Navas de la Concepción E 51 D9
Las Navas del Marqués E 46 C4
Lasne B 182 D4
Las Negras E 55 F9
La Solana E 55 B6
La Souterraine F 29 C8
Lasovo SRB 159 F9
Lasowice Małe PL 142 E5
Las Palas E 56 F2
Las Pedroñeras E 47 F7
Las Pedrosas E 41 D10
La Spezia I 69 E8
Las Plassas I 64 D2
Las Rotas E 56 D5
Las Rozas de Madrid E 46 C5
Lassahn D 83 C9
Lassan D 84 C5
Lassay-les-Châteaux F 23 D11
Lassemoen N 105 B13
Lässerud S 96 C7
Lasseube F 32 D5
Lassigny F 18 E6
Lassila FIN 126 B7
Lassing A 73 A9
Lassing A 73 A10
Laßnitzhöhe A 148 B5
Lastebasse I 69 B11
Las Terreras E 55 D9
Las Torres de Cotillas E 56 E2
Lastours F 33 D10
Lastovo HR 162 D2
Lastra a Signa I 66 E3
Lastras de Cuéllar E 40 F3
Lastrup D 17 C9
Lastukoski FIN 125 D10
Lastva BIH 162 D5
La Suze-sur-Sarthe F 23 E12
Lašva BIH 157 D8
Lasva EST 131 F14
Las Veguillas E 45 C9
Las Ventas con Peña Aguilera E 46 E4
Las Ventas de San Julián E 45 D10
Łaszczów PL 144 B8
Laszki PL 144 C6
Laterza I 61 B7
La Teste-de-Buch F 32 A3
Lathen D 17 C8
Latheron GB 3 J10
Latheronwheel GB 3 J10
La Thuile I 31 D10
Lathus F 29 C7
Latiano I 61 B9
Latikberg S 107 B12
Latillé F 28 B6
Latina I 62 E3
Latisana I 73 E7
Latorpsbruk S 97 D12
La Torre de Cabdella E 33 F7
La Torre de Esteban Hambrán E 46 D4
La Torre de l'Espanyol E 42 E5
La Tour-Blanche F 29 E6
La Tour-d'Auvergne F 29 D11
Latour-de-France F 34 E4
La Tour-du-Crieu F 33 D9
La Tour-du-Pin F 31 D7
La Tour-sur-Orb F 34 C5
Latowicz PL 141 F5
La Tranche-sur-Mer F 28 C3
La Tremblade F 28 D3
La Trimouille F 29 C8
La Trinité F 37 D6
La Trinité-Porhoët F 22 D6
La Trinité-sur-Mer F 22 E5
Latronico I 60 C6
Latronquière F 29 F10
Lattarico I 60 E6
Lattes F 35 C6
Lattomeri FIN 126 C6
Lattrop NL 183 A9
La Turballe F 22 F7
Latva FIN 119 F15
Latva FIN 120 C9
Latvajärvenperä FIN 121 D11
Laubach D 21 C11
Laubach D 21 D8
Lauben D 71 A10
Laubere LV 135 C10
Laubusch D 80 D6
Lauchhammer D 80 D5
Lauchringen D 27 E9
Lauciene LV 134 B5
Lauda-Königshofen D 74 C6
Lauder GB 5 D11
Lauderi LV 133 D4
Laudio E 40 B6
Laudona LV 135 C12
Laudun F 35 B8
Lauenau D 17 D12
Lauenbrück D 82 D7
Lauenburg (Elbe) D 83 D9
Lauenförde D 21 A12
Lauf D 186 D5
Laufach D 187 A7
Lauf an der Pegnitz D 75 C9
Laufen CH 27 F8
Laufenburg CH 27 E9
Lauffen am Neckar D 187 C7
Laugnac F 33 B7
Lauingen (Donau) D 75 E7
Laujar de Andarax E 55 F7
Laukaa FIN 123 F15
Laukeng N 112 D9
Lauker S 118 C3
Laukka FIN 119 E15
Laukkala FIN 123 D17
Laukkoski FIN 127 E13
Laukkuluspa S 111 E18
Laukna EST 131 D8
Lauksargiai LT 134 F4
Laukslett N 111 A17
Lauksletta N 112 C6
Lauksodis LT 135 D8
Laukuva LT 134 E4
Laukvik N 105 C9
Laukvik N 110 D7
Laukvik N 110 E8
Laukvik N 111 A14
Laukvik N 113 C11
Laukvik N 114 B6
Laukžemė LT 134 D2
Laulasmaa EST 131 C8
Launac F 33 C8
Launceston GB 12 D6
La Unión E 56 F3
Launkalne LV 135 B11
Launonen FIN 127 D12
Laupen CH 31 B11
Laupheim D 71 A9
Laupstad N 110 D8
Lauragh IRL 8 E3
Lauraguel F 33 D10
Laurbjerg DK 86 C5
Laureana di Borrello I 59 C9
Laurencekirk GB 5 B12
Laurencetown IRL 6 F6
Laurens F 34 C5
Laurenzana I 60 C5
Lauria I 60 C5
Laurière F 29 C8
Laurieston GB 5 F8
Laurila FIN 119 C13
Laurino I 60 C4
Lauris F 35 C9
Laurito I 60 C4
Lausanne CH 31 B10
Lauscha D 75 B9
Laußig D 79 C12
Laußnitz D 80 D5
Laussonne F 30 F5
Laussou F 33 A7
Lauta D 80 D6
Lautamaa FIN 119 C12
Lautenbach D 27 C9
Lauter D 79 E12
Lauterbourg F 27 C9
Lauterbrunnen CH 70 D5
Lautere LV 135 C12
Lauterecken D 186 B4
Lauterhofen D 75 D10
Lautersbach (Hessen) D 78 E5
Lauterstein D 187 D8
Lautertal D 75 B8
Lautiosaari FIN 119 C13
Lautrec F 33 C10
Lauttavaara FIN 121 E9
Lauttijärvi FIN 126 B6
Lauve N 90 A7
Lauvsnes N 105 C9
Lauvstad N 100 B3
Lauvuskylä FIN 125 C13
Lauvvik N 94 E4
Lauzerte F 33 B8
Lauzès F 33 A9
Lauzun F 33 A6
Lavagna I 37 C10
Laval F 23 D10
Lavala FIN 121 D14
Lavalette F 33 D10
La Valette-du-Var F 35 D10
La Vall d'Uixó E 48 E4
La Valle I 72 C4
Lavamünd A 73 C10
Lavangen N 111 C14
Lavangsnes N 111 C13
Lavara GR 171 B10
Lavardac F 33 B6
Lavassaare EST 131 D8
Lavaur F 33 C9
Lavaveix-les-Mines F 29 C10
Lavda GR 168 D5
Lavdar i Korçës AL 168 C4
La Vecilla E 39 C9
La Vega E 39 B8
La Vega E 39 B8
La Vega E 39 B10
Lavelanet F 33 E9
La Vellés E 45 B9
Lavello I 60 A5
Laven DK 86 C5
Lavena Ponte Tresa I 69 B6
Lavenham GB 15 C10
Laveno I 68 B6
La Ventosa E 47 D8
La Verdière F 35 C10
La Vernarède F 35 B6
La Verpillière F 31 D7
La Verrie F 28 B4
La Veuve F 25 B11
Lavia FIN 126 B8
Laviano I 60 B4
La Victoria E 53 A7
La Vid E 40 E5
Lavik N 111 B14
La Vila Joiosa E 56 D4
La Villa de Don Fadrique E 47 E6
La Ville-aux-Clercs F 24 E5
La Villedieu F 30 F4
La Villedieu-du-Clain F 29 C6
La Villedieu-en-Fontenette F 26 E5
Lavinio-Lido di Enea I 62 E3
Laviron F 26 F6
Lavis I 69 A11
Lavit F 33 C7
Lavoriškės LT 137 D12
La Voulte-sur-Rhône F 30 F6
Lavoûte-Chilhac F 30 E3
Lavoûte-sur-Loire F 30 E4
Lavradio P 50 B1
Lavre P 50 B3
Lavrio GR 175 D9
Lavsjö S 107 C11
La Wantzenau F 186 D4
Lawers GB 5 B8
Lawford GB 15 D11
Lawrencetown GB 7 D10
Ławsk PL 140 D6
Ławszowa PL 81 D8
Ławy PL 85 E7
Laxå S 92 B5
Laxbäcken S 107 B10
Laxe E 38 B2
Laxey GBM 10 C3
Laxford Bridge GB 2 J6
Laxnäs S 108 E9
Laxne S 93 A10
Laxo GB 3 E14
Laxou F 26 C5
Laxsjö S 106 D7
Laxvik S 87 B11
Laxviken S 106 D7
Layana E 32 F3
La Yesa E 48 E3
Läyliäinen FIN 127 D11
Layos E 46 E4
Layrac F 33 B7
Laz HR 148 E6
Laza E 38 D5
Laza RO 153 D11
Lazagurría E 32 F1
Lazarata GR 174 B2
Lăzarea RO 153 D7
Lăzăreni RO 151 D9
Lazarevac SRB 158 E5
Lazarev Krst MNE 163 D7
Lazarevo SRB 158 C6
Lazdijai LT 137 E8
Lazdininkai LT 134 E2
Lazdona LV 135 C12
Lazdukalns LV 133 C2
Lazeshchyna UA 152 A4
Lazise I 66 B2
Łaziska PL 141 H5
Łaziska Górne PL 142 F6
Lazkao E 32 D1
Lázně Bělohrad CZ 77 B9
Lázně Bohdaneč CZ 77 B9
Lázně Kynžvart CZ 75 B12
Laznica SRB 159 E8
Lazonby GB 5 F11
Lazuri RO 151 B10
Lazuri de Beiuş RO 151 D9
Leabgarrow IRL 6 C5
Leacht Seoirse IRL 6 F5
Leadburn GB 5 D10
Leadenham GB 11 E10
Leadhills GB 5 E9
Leamhcán IRL 7 F10
Leamington Spa, Royal GB 13 A11
Leányfalu H 150 B3
Leap IRL 8 E4
Leasingham GB 11 E11
Leatherhead GB 15 E8
Leavvajohka N 113 D17
Łeba PL 85 A13
Lebach D 21 F7
Lebane SRB 164 D4
Le Ban-St-Martin F 186 C1
Le Barp F 32 A4
Le Bar-sur-Loup F 36 D5
Lebbeke B 19 B9
Le Béage F 30 F5
Le Beausset F 35 D10
Lebedivka UA 154 F6
Lébényimiklós H 149 A8
Lebesby N 113 B18
Le Bez F 33 C10
Lebiez F 18 D4
Le Biot F 31 C10
Le Blanc F 29 B8
Le Bleymard F 35 B6
Łebno PL 138 B5
Le Bois-d'Oingt F 30 D6
Le Bois-Plage-en-Ré F 28 C3
Le Boréon F 37 C6
Lębork PL 85 A13
Le Boulou F 34 E4
Le Boupère F 28 B4
Le Bourg F 29 F9
Le Bourg-d'Oisans F 31 E9
Le Bourget-du-Lac F 31 D8
Le Bousquet-d'Orb F 34 C5
Le Breuil F 25 C10
Le Breuil F 30 B5
Lebrija E 51 F7
Lebring-Sankt Margarethen A 148 C5
Le Brouilh-Monbert F 33 C6
Le Brusquet F 36 C4
Lebução P 38 E5
Le Bugue F 29 F7
Le Buisson F 34 A5
Le Buisson-de-Cadouin F 29 F7
Łebunia PL 138 B4
Lebus D 81 B7
Lebusa D 80 C4
Lebyazh'ye RUS 129 F11
Leça da Palmeira P 44 B3
Leça do Bailio P 44 B3
Le Cannet F 36 D6
Le Cannet-des-Maures F 36 E4
Le Castellet F 35 D10
Le Cateau-Cambrésis F 19 D8
Le Catelet F 19 D7
Le Caylar F 34 C5
Le Cayrol F 34 A4
Lecce I 61 C10
Lecco I 69 B7
Lece SRB 164 D4
Lécera E 42 E2
Lech A 71 C10
Lechaina GR 174 D3
Lechaio GR 175 D6
Le Chambon-Feugerolles F 30 E5
Le Chambon-sur-Lignon F 30 E5
Lechaschau A 71 C11
Le Château-d'Oléron F 28 D3
Le Châtelard F 31 D9
Le Châtelet F 29 B10
Lechbruck D 71 B11
Le Chêne F 25 C11
Le Chesne F 19 E10
Le Cheylard F 30 F5
Le Cheylas F 31 E8
Lechința RO 152 C4
Lechlade GB 13 B11
Lechovo GR 169 C5
Lechtingen (Wallenhorst) D 17 D10
Leciñena E 41 E10
Leck D 82 A5
Leckaun IRL 6 D6
Leckmelm GB 2 K6
Le Clapier F 34 C5
Le Collet-de-Dèze F 35 B6
Le Conquet F 22 D2
Le Coteau F 30 C5
Le Coudray-St-Germer F 18 F4
Lécousse F 23 D9
Le Crès F 35 C6
Le Creusot F 30 B5
Lecrín E 53 C9
Le Croisic F 22 F6
Le Crotoy F 18 D4
Lectoure F 33 C7
Łęczna PL 141 H7
Łęczyca PL 143 B7
Łęczyce PL 138 A4
Ledaig GB 4 C6
Ledaña E 47 F9
Ledanca E 47 C7
Lēdas LV 134 B5
Ledbury GB 13 A10
Lede B 19 C8
Ledeč nad Sázavou CZ 77 C8
Ledegem B 182 D2
Ledenice BIH 157 C9
Ledenice CZ 77 E7
Lédergues F 33 B10
Ledesma E 45 B9
Lédignan F 35 C7
Ledigos E 39 D10
Ledmore GB 2 J7
Lednica SK 146 C6
Lednice CZ 77 E11
Lednické Rovne SK 146 C6
Le Donjon F 30 C4
Le Dorat F 29 C8
Ledrada E 45 D9
Lēdurga LV 135 B9
Ledusjö S 107 D16
Ledvattsfors S 109 F16
Lędyczek PL 85 C11
Lędzin PL 85 B8
Lędziny PL 143 F7
Leeds GB 11 D8
Leedstown GB 12 E4
Leek GB 11 E7
Leek NL 16 B6
Leeming GB 11 C8
Lee Moor GB 12 E6
Leende NL 16 F5
Leer (Ostfriesland) D 17 B8
Leerdam NL 16 E4
Leersum NL 183 A6
Leese D 17 C12
Leeuwarden NL 16 B5
Leevaku EST 131 E14
Leevi EST 131 F14
Leezen D 83 C8
Leezen D 83 C10
Le Faou F 22 D3
Le Faouët F 22 D5
Le Fenouiller F 28 B2
Leffinge B 182 C1
Lefkada GR 174 B2
Lefkes GR 176 E5
Lefkimmi GR 168 F3
Lefkimmi GR 171 B10
Lefkonas GR 169 B10
Lefkopigi GR 169 D6
Lefkothea GR 168 D5
Lefktra GR 175 C7
Le Fleix F 29 F6
Le Folgoët F 22 C3
Leforest F 182 E2
Le Fossat F 33 D8
Le Fousseret F 33 D8
Le Fugeret F 36 C5
Le Fuilet F 23 F9
Leganés E 46 D5
Leganiel E 47 D7
Legau D 71 B10
Le Gault-Soigny F 25 C10
Le Gault-St-Denis F 24 D5
Legazpi E 32 D1
Legde D 83 E11
Legden D 17 D8
Legé F 28 B2
Lège-Cap-Ferret F 28 F3
Le Genest-St-Isle F 23 D10
Leggs GB 7 C7
Legionowo PL 139 F10
Léglise B 19 E12
Legnago I 66 B3
Legnano I 69 B6
Legnica PL 81 D10
Legnickie Pole PL 81 D10
Le Gond-Pontouvre F 29 D6
Łęgowo PL 138 B6
Legrad HR 149 D7
Le Grand-Bornand F 31 D9
Le Grand-Bourg F 29 C9
Le Grand-Lemps F 31 E7
Le Grand-Lucé F 24 E3
Le Grand-Pressigny F 29 B7
Le Grand-Quevilly F 18 F3
Le Grand-Serre F 31 E7
Le Grau-du-Roi F 35 C7
Le Gros Theil F 18 F2
Le Gua F 31 E8
Legutiano E 41 C6
Legyesbénye H 145 G3
Le Havre F 23 A12
Lehe D 82 B6
Lehliu RO 161 E9
Lehliu-Gară RO 161 E9
Lehmäjoki FIN 122 D8
Lehmen D 21 D8
Lehmikumpu FIN 119 B14
Lehmivaara FIN 117 E11
Lehmo FIN 125 E13
Lehndorf D 79 E11
Lehnice SK 146 E4
Lehnin D 79 B12
Le Hohwald F 27 D7
Léhon F 23 D7
Le Horps F 23 D11
Lehota SK 146 E5
Le Houga F 32 C5
Lehrberg D 75 D8
Lehre D 79 B8
Lehrte D 78 B6
Lehsen D 83 D10
Lehtimäki FIN 123 E11
Lehtiniemi FIN 121 B10
Lehto FIN 121 B14
Lehtopää FIN 119 F13
Lehtovaara FIN 117 D17
Lehtovaara FIN 121 C10
Lehtovaara FIN 121 D11
Lehtovaara FIN 121 F14
Lehtovaara FIN 124 B9
Lehtovaara FIN 125 D11
Lehtse EST 131 C11
Leianokladi GR 174 B5
Leibertingen D 27 D11
Leiblfing D 75 E11
Leibnitz A 148 C5
Leicester GB 11 F9
Leichlingen (Rheinland) D 183 C10
Leiden NL 16 D3
Leiderdorp NL 16 D3
Leidschendam NL 16 D2
Leie EST 131 E12
Leifear IRL 4 F2
Leiferde D 79 B7
Leigh GB 10 E6
Leighlinbridge IRL 9 C9
Leighton Buzzard GB 15 D7
Leikanger N 100 B2
Leikanger N 100 D5
Léim an Bhradáin IRL 7 F10
Leimaņi LV 135 D11
Leimen D 21 F11
Leimuiden NL 182 A5
Leinburg D 75 D9
Leine N 101 D9
Leinefelde D 79 D7
Leinfelden-Echterdingen D 187 D7
Leinì I 68 C4
Leino FIN 121 D12
Leinzell D 74 E6
Leioa E 40 B6
Leipalingis LT 137 E8
Leipheim D 75 F7
Leipivaara FIN 121 E10
Leipojärvi S 116 D6
Leipzig D 79 D11
Leira N 101 E10
Leira N 104 E4
Leira N 108 D5
Leirado E 38 D3
Leiråmoen N 108 C8
Leiranger N 110 E8
Leirbotn N 113 C11
Leiria P 44 E3
Leirlia N 105 B15
Leiro E 38 D3
Leirvåg N 100 E2
Leirvík FO 2 A3
Leirvik N 94 C2
Leirvik N 100 D2
Leirvik N 105 B11
Leirvika N 108 D6
Leisach A 73 C6
Leisi EST 130 D5
Leisnig D 80 D3
Leißling D 79 D10
Leiston GB 15 C12
Leitir Ceanainn IRL 7 C7
Leitir Mhic an Bhaird IRL 6 C6
Leitrim IRL 6 D6
Leitza E 32 D2
Leitzkau D 79 B10
Leive FIN 119 B14
Leivonmäki FIN 127 B15
Leivset N 108 B9
Leiwen D 21 E7
Leixlip IRL 7 F10
Lejasciems LV 135 B13
Lejasstrazdi LV 134 C6
Leka GR 177 D8
Lekaj AL 168 B2
Lekangen N 111 B13
Lekani GR 171 B7
Łęka Opatowska PL 142 D5
Lekárovce SK 145 F5
Łękawica PL 147 B8
Lekbibaj AL 163 E8
Lekėčiai LT 137 D7
Lekenik HR 148 E6
Lekeryd S 92 D4
Lekhchevo BG 165 B8
Łęki Szlacheckie PL 143 D8
Leknes N 100 B5
Łęknica PL 81 C7
Lekoes N 110 D6
Lekowo PL 85 C9
Leksand S 103 E9
Leksvik N 105 D9
Lekunberri E 32 D2
Leland N 108 D4
Le Langon F 28 C4
Le Lardin-St-Lazare F 29 E8
Le Lauzet-Ubaye F 36 C4
Le Lavandou F 36 E4
Leleasca RO 160 D4
Leles SK 145 G5
Lelești RO 159 C11
Le Leuy F 32 C4
Lelice PL 139 E8
Le Lion-d'Angers F 23 E10
Leliūnai LT 135 F10
Lelkowo PL 139 B9
Lelle EST 131 D9
Le Locle CH 31 A10
Le Louroux-Béconnais F 23 E10
Lelów PL 143 E8
Le Luc F 36 E4
Le Lude F 23 E12
Lelystad NL 16 C4
Lem DK 86 C2
Le Malzieu-Ville F 30 F3
Le Mans F 23 D12
Le Markstein F 27 E7
Le Martinet F 35 B7
Le Mas-d'Agenais F 33 B6
Le Mas-d'Azil F 33 D8
Le Masnau-Massuguiès F 34 C4
Le Massegros F 34 B5
Le Mayet-de-Montagne F 30 C4
Le May-sur-Èvre F 23 F10
Lembach im Mühlkreis A 76 E5
Lembeke B 182 C3
Lemberg D 27 B8
Lemberg F 27 B7
Lembeye F 32 D5
Lembras F 29 F7
Lembruch D 17 C10
Lemele NL 16 D6
Lemelerveld NL 16 D6
Le Mêle-sur-Sarthe F 24 C3
Le Merlerault F 23 C12
Le Mesnil-sur-Oger F 25 C11
Lemetinvaara FIN 121 F12
Lemgo D 17 D11
Lemi FIN 128 C8
Lemierzyce PL 81 A7
Lemland FIN 99 B14
Lemmenjoki FIN 117 A16
Lemmer NL 16 C5
Lemnia RO 153 E8
Le Molay-Littry F 23 B10
Le Monastier F 34 A5
Le Monastier-sur-Gazeille F 30 F4
Le Monêtier-les-Bains F 31 F10
Le Montet F 30 C3
Lempäälä FIN 127 C10
Lempdes F 30 D3
Lempdes F 30 E3
Lempyy FIN 124 E8
Lemu FIN 126 D6
Le Muy F 36 E5
Lemvig DK 86 B2
Lemwerder D 17 B11
Lemybrien IRL 9 D7
Lena N 101 E13
Lenart SLO 148 C5
Lēnas LV 134 C3
Lenauheim RO 150 F6
Lencloître F 29 B6
Lencouacq F 32 B5
Lend A 73 B7
Lendak SK 145 E1
Lendava SLO 149 C6
Lendelede B 182 D2
Lendery RUS 125 D16
Lendinara I 66 B4
Lendum DK 90 E7
Lenë AL 168 B3
Lenešice CZ 76 B5
Le Neubourg F 24 B4
Lengau A 72 B6
Lengau A 76 F4
Lengdorf D 75 F11
Lengefeld D 80 E4
Lengenes N 111 D13
Lengenfeld D 79 E11
Lengenwang D 71 B11
Lengerich D 17 C9
Lengerich D 17 D9
Lenggries D 72 A4
Lengnau CH 27 F7
Lengyeltóti H 149 C9
Lenham GB 15 E10
Lenhovda S 89 B8
Lenine UA 154 C5
Léning F 27 C6
Le Nizan F 32 B5
Lenk CH 31 C11
Lenkimai LT 134 D2
Lenna I 69 B8
Lennartsfors S 96 D6
Lennartsnäs S 99 D9
Lenne D 78 C6
Lennestadt D 21 B10
Lenningen D 27 C11
Lennsjö S 103 B12
Leno I 66 B1
Le Noirmont CH 27 F6
Lenola I 62 E4
Le Nouvion-en-Thiérache F 19 D8
Lens B 19 C8
Lens F 18 D6
Lensahn D 83 B9
Lensvik N 104 D7
Lent F 31 C7
Lent NL 183 B7
Lentas GR 178 F8
Lenti H 149 C7
Lentiai I 72 D5
Lentiira FIN 121 F14
Lenting D 75 E9
Lentini I 59 E7
Lentvaris LT 137 D11
Lenvik N 111 C13
Lenzburg CH 27 F9
Lenzen D 83 D10
Lenzing A 76 G5
Lenzkirch D 27 E9
Leoben A 73 B11
Leoben A 73 C8
Leobendorf A 77 F10
Leobersdorf A 77 G10
Leogang A 73 B6
Léognan F 28 F4
Leominster GB 13 A9
León E 39 C8
Léon F 32 C3
Leonberg D 27 C11
Léoncel F 31 F7
Leonding A 76 F6
Leonessa I 62 B3
Leonforte I 58 D5
Leonidio GR 175 E6
Leontari GR 174 A5
Leontari GR 174 E5
Leopoldov SK 146 E5
Leopoldsburg B 19 B11
Leopoldsdorf im Marchfelde A 77 F11
Leopoldshagen D 84 C5
Leopoldshöhe D 17 D11
Leorda RO 153 B8
Leordeni RO 160 D6
Leordina RO 152 B4
Leova MD 154 E2
Leovo Brdo MNE 157 F11
Lepaa FIN 127 C11
Le Palais F 22 F5
Le Palais-sur-Vienne F 29 D8
Le Pallet F 23 F9
Le Parcq F 18 D5
Lepassaare EST 132 F1
Le Passage F 33 B7
Le Pavillon-Ste-Julie F 25 D10
Lepe E 51 E5
Le Péage-de-Roussillon F 30 E6
Le Pellerin F 23 F8
Le Périer F 31 F8
Le Perthus F 34 F4
Le Pertre F 23 D9
Le Petit-Quevilly F 18 F3
Le Pian-Médoc F 28 F4
Le Pin-au-Haras F 23 C12
L'Épine F 35 B10
Le Pin-la-Garenne F 24 D4
Lepistönmäki FIN 123 D10
Lepitsa BG 165 C9
Le Pizou F 28 E6
Le Plan F 33 D8
Le Plessis-Belleville F 25 B8
Le Poët F 35 B10
Lepoglava HR 148 D6
Le Poinçonnet F 29 B9
Le Poiré-sur-Vie F 28 B2
Le Pont-de-Beauvoisin F 31 D8
Le Pont-de-Claix F 31 E8
Le Pont-de-Monvert F 35 B6
Le Pontet F 35 C8
Leporano I 61 C8
Le Porge F 28 F3
Le Porge-Océan F 28 F3
Le Portel F 15 F12
Leposavić RKS 163 C10
Leposaviq RKS 163 C10
Le Pouldu F 22 E4
Le Pouliguen F 22 F7
Lepoura GR 175 C9

Le Pouzin F 30 F6
Leppäjärvi FIN 117 B10
Leppäkoski FIN 127 D12
Leppälä FIN 113 D19
Leppälä FIN 121 D11
Leppälähkylä FIN 123 E11
Leppälahti FIN 124 D8
Leppälahti FIN 125 F12
Leppäselkä FIN 123 D16
Leppävesi FIN 123 F15
Leppävirta FIN 124 F9
Leppiaho FIN 119 C15
Leppikoski FIN 119 D17
Leppiniemi FIN 119 E16
Leppneeme EST 131 B9
Lepsala FIN 127 C15
Lepsämä FIN 127 E12
Lepsény H 149 B10
Leptokarya GR 169 D8
Le Puy-en-Velay F 30 E4
Le Puy-Notre-Dame F 23 F11
Le Quesnoy F 19 D8
Lequile I 61 C10
Ler N 104 E8
Le Raincy F 25 C8
Léran F 33 E9
Lerberget S 87 C11
Lercara Friddi I 58 D4
Lerdala S 91 C14
Léré F 25 F8
Le Relecq-Kerhuon F 22 D3
Lereşti RO 160 C6
Lerici I 69 E8
Lérida E 42 D5
Lerín E 32 F2
Lerkaka S 89 B11
Lerma E 40 D4
Lerm-et Musset F 32 B5
Lermoos A 71 C11
Lerot S 96 C7
Le Rouget F 29 F10
Lérouville F 26 C4
Le Rozier F 34 B5
Lerum S 91 D11
Le Russey F 26 F6
Lervik N 95 D13
Lerwick GB 3 E14
Lesa I 68 B6
Les Abrets F 31 D8
Les Aix-d'Angillon F 25 F8
Lešak RKS 163 C10
Lesaka E 32 D2
Les Andelys F 18 F3
Les Angles F 33 E10
Les Angles F 35 C8
Lešani NMK 168 B4
Les Arcs F 31 D10
Les Arcs F 36 E4
Les Aubiers F 28 B4
Les Avellanes E 42 D5
Les Avenières F 31 D8
Les Bondons F 35 B6
Les Bordes F 25 E7
Les Borges Blanques E 42 D5
Les Borges del Camp E 42 E6
Les Bouchoux F 31 C8
Les Brenets CH 31 A10
Lesbury GB 5 E13
Les Cabannes F 33 E9
L'Escala E 43 C10
L'Escale F 35 B11
Les Cammazes F 33 D10
Lescar F 32 D5
L'Escarène F 37 D6
Les Cases d'Alcanar E 42 F5
Lesce SLO 73 D9
Lesconil F 22 E3
Les Contamines-Montjoie F 31 D10
Les Coves de Vinromà E 48 D5
Lescun F 32 E4
Lescure-d'Albigeois F 33 C10
Les Deux-Alpes F 31 E9
Les Diablerets CH 31 C11
Les Échelles F 31 E8
Les Églisottes-et-Chalaures F 28 E5
Le Sel-de-Bretagne F 23 E8
Le Sen F 32 B4
Le Sentier CH 31 B9
Les Éparges F 26 B4
Les Epesses F 28 B4
Les Escaldes AND 33 E9
Les Essards-Taignevaux F 31 B7
Les Essarts F 28 B3
Le Seu d'Urgell E 33 F8
Les Eyzies-de-Tayac-Sireuil F 29 F8
Les Fins F 31 A10
Les Forges F 26 D5
Les Fourgs F 31 B9
Les Gets F 31 C10
Leshak RKS 163 C10
Leshan RKS 163 D9
Les Hautes-Rivières F 184 E2
Les Herbiers F 28 B3
Les Houches F 31 D10
Lesichevo BG 165 E9
Lesično SLO 148 D5
Lesidren BG 165 D9
Lesina I 63 D8
Les Issambres F 36 E5
Lesja N 101 B9
Lesjöfors S 97 C11
Leskava LT 137 D8
Leskelä FIN 119 F15
Lesko PL 145 E5
Leskoec NMK 168 B4
Leskova SRB 163 C9
Leskovac SRB 164 D4
Leskovik AL 168 D4
Leskovo BG 161 F11
Les Landes-Genusson F 28 B3
Leslie GB 5 C10
Les Lucs-sur-Boulogne F 28 B3
Lesmahagow GB 5 D9
Les Maillys F 26 F3
Les Marches F 31 E9
Les Martres-de-Veyre F 30 D3
Les Matelles F 35 C6
Les Mazures F 184 E2
Les Mées F 35 B10
Les Menuires F 31 E10
Lesmont F 25 D11
Les Mureaux F 24 C6
Lešná CZ 146 B5
Leśna PL 81 D8
Lesneven F 22 C3
Leśnica PL 142 F5
Lešnica SRB 158 D3
Leśniów Wielki PL 81 C8
Lesogorskiy RUS 129 C10
Les Ollières-sur-Eyrieux F 30 F6
Lesovaara FIN 121 D13
Lesovo BG 167 F7
Lesparre-Médoc F 28 E4
Les Peintures F 28 E5
Les Pennes-Mirabeau F 35 D9
Lesperon F 32 C3
Lespezi RO 153 C9
Les Pieux F 23 A8
Lespignan F 34 D5
Lespinassière F 34 D4
Les Planches-en-Montagne F 31 B9
Les Planes d'Hostoles E 43 C9
L'Espluga Calba E 42 E6
L'Espluga de Francolí E 42 E6
Les Ponts-de-Cé F 23 F10
Les Ponts-de-Martel CH 31 A10
Les Preses E 43 C8
Lespugue F 33 D7
Les Rosiers-sur-Loire F 23 F11
Les Rousses F 31 C9
Les Sables-d'Olonne F 28 C2
Lessach A 73 B8
Les Salles-du-Gardon F 35 B7
Lessay F 23 B8
Lessebo S 89 B8
Les Sièges F 25 D10
Lessines B 19 C8
Les Sorinières F 23 F8
Lestene LV 134 C6
Les Ternes F 30 E3
Les Thuiles F 36 C5
Lestijärvi FIN 123 C13
Leština CZ 77 C11
Lestrade F 34 B4
Les Trois-Moutiers F 24 F3
Leşu RO 152 C5
Lesura BG 165 C8
Les Vans F 35 B7
Les Vignes F 34 B5
Leszczyn PL 85 C9
Leszno PL 81 C11
Leszno PL 141 F3
Leszno Górne PL 81 D9
Létavértes H 151 C8
Letca RO 151 C11
Leţcani RO 153 C10
Letca Nouă RO 161 E7
Letchworth Garden City GB 15 D8
Letea Veche RO 153 D9
Le Teich F 32 A3
Le Teil F 35 A8
Le Teilleul F 23 C10
Le Temple F 28 F4
Letenye H 149 D7
Le Theil F 24 D4
Le-Theil-de-Bretagne F 23 E9
Le Thillot F 27 E6
Le Tholy F 27 D6
Le Thor F 35 C8
Letino I 63 E6
Letkés H 147 F7
Letnitsa BG 165 C11
Letoianni I 59 D7
Letonice CZ 77 D11
Le Touquet-Paris-Plage F 15 F12
Le Touvet F 31 E8
Letovice CZ 77 C11
L'Étrat F 30 E5
Le Trayas F 36 E5
Le Tréport F 18 D3
Letsbo S 103 C10
Letschin D 80 A6
Letterfinish IRL 8 E3
Letterkenny IRL 7 C7
Lettermacaward IRL 6 C6
Letterston GB 12 B5
Letur E 55 C8
Le Tuzan F 32 B4
Letzlingen D 79 B9
Leu RO 160 E4
Leuc F 33 D10
Leucate F 34 E5
Leuchars GB 5 C11
Leuchtenberg D 75 C11
Leud RO 152 B4
Leuenberg D 84 E5
Leuglay F 25 E12
Leuk CH 68 A4
Leukerbad CH 70 E5
Leumrabhagh GB 2 J4
Leun D 185 C9
Leuna D 79 D11
Leusden NL 16 D4
Leuşeni MD 154 D2
Leutasch A 72 B3
Leutenberg D 79 E9
Leutershausen D 75 D7
Leutesdorf D 185 D7
Leutkirch im Allgäu D 71 B10
Leuvanjoki FIN 119 D15
Leuven B 19 C10
Leuze-en-Hainaut B 19 C8
Le Val F 36 E4
Levan AL 168 C1
Levänen FIN 128 C8
Levang N 108 D5
Levanger N 105 D10
Levanjska Varoš HR 149 F10
Levanto FIN 127 D13
Levanto I 37 C11
Leva Reka BG 165 D6
Leväsjoki FIN 126 B6
Levél H 146 F4
Levelek H 145 H4
Leven GB 5 C11
Leven GB 11 D11
Levens F 37 D6
Levens GB 10 C6
Levenwick GB 3 F14
Leverano I 61 C10
Leverburgh GB 2 K2
Le-Verdon-sur-Mer F 28 D3
Leverkusen D 21 B7
Le Vernet F 33 D9
Lèves F 24 D5
Levet F 29 B10
Levice SK 147 E7
Levico Terme I 69 A11
Levidi GR 174 D5
Levie F 37 H10
Levier F 31 B9
Le Vigan F 35 C6
Lévignac F 33 C8
Lévignacq F 32 B3
Levijoki FIN 123 E11
Le Ville I 66 F5
Levinovac HR 149 E8
Le-Vivier-sur-Mer F 23 C8
Levka BG 166 F6
Levkogeia GR 170 B5
Levoča SK 145 E2
Levonperä FIN 123 C14
Levo-oja FIN 119 D16
Levroux F 29 B9
Levski BG 166 C4
Levunovo BG 169 B9
Lewes GB 15 F9
Lewin Brzeski PL 142 E4
Lewin Kłodzki PL 77 B10
Leyburn GB 11 C8
Leyland GB 10 D6
Leyme F 29 F9
Leysin CH 31 C11
Leytron CH 31 C11
Ležajsk PL 144 C5
Lézan F 35 B7
Lézat-sur-Lèze F 33 D8
Lezay F 28 C5
Lezhë AL 163 F8
Lézignan-Corbières F 34 D4
Lezoux F 30 D3
Lezuza E 55 B8
Lgota Górna PL 143 E7
Lgota Wielka PL 143 D7
Lhenice CZ 76 D6
Lherm F 33 D8
L'Hermenault F 28 B4
L'Honor-de-Cos F 33 B8
L'Hôpital F 186 C2
L'Horme F 30 E6
Lhospitalet F 33 B8
L'Hospitalet de l'Infant E 42 F5
L'Hospitalet de Llobregat E 43 E8
L'Hospitalet-du-Larzac F 34 C5
L'Hospitalet-près-l'Andorre F 33 E9
L'Hostal del Alls E 42 F5
L'Huisserie F 23 D10
Lhuître F 25 C11
Lia N 111 C14
Liabøen N 104 E4
Liancourt F 18 F5
Liapades GR 168 E2
Liart F 19 E9
Liarvåg N 94 D3
Liatorp S 88 B6
Liatroim IRL 6 D6
Libáň CZ 77 B8
Libatse EST 131 D8
Libberton GB 5 D9
Libčany CZ 77 B9
Libčeves CZ 76 B5
Liberadz PL 139 D9
Liberec CZ 81 E8
Liběšice CZ 80 E6
Libiąż PL 143 F7
Libice nad Cidlinou CZ 77 B8
Libin B 19 E11
Libina CZ 77 C12
Libochovice CZ 76 B6
Libofshë AL 168 C2
Libohovë AL 168 D3
Libouchec CZ 80 E6
Libourne F 28 F5
Libramont B 19 E11
Librazhd AL 168 B3
Librilla E 55 D10
Libros E 47 D10
Licata I 58 E4
Licciana Nardi I 69 E9
Licenza I 62 C3
Liceras E 40 F5
Lich D 21 C11
Lichfield GB 11 F8
Lichnov CZ 142 F4
Lichnowy PL 138 B6
Lichtaart B 182 C5
Lichte D 75 A9
Lichtenau D 17 E11
Lichtenau D 27 C9
Lichtenau im Waldviertel A 77 E8
Lichtenfels D 75 B9
Lichtenstein D 79 E12
Lichtentanne D 79 E11
Lichtenvoorde NL 17 E7
Lichtenwörth A 77 G10
Lichterfelde D 84 E5
Lichtervelde B 19 B7
Līči LV 135 B10
Līči LV 135 D13
Lička Jesenica HR 156 C3
Lički Osik HR 156 C3
Licko Lešće HR 156 C3
Licodia Eubea I 59 E6
Licques F 15 F12
Līčupe LV 135 C10
Licurici RO 160 D3
Lida BY 137 F11
Lidečko CZ 146 C6
Liden S 103 A12
Lidhult S 87 B12
Lidingö S 99 D10
Lidköping S 91 B13
Lido I 66 B5
Lido Adriano I 66 D5
Lido di Classe I 66 D5
Lido di Foce Verde I 62 E3
Lido di Jesolo I 66 A6
Lido di Metaponto I 61 C7
Lido di Ostia I 62 D2
Lido di Siponto I 63 D9
Lido di Spina I 66 C5
Lidoriki GR 174 B5
Lidsälen S 102 E5
Lidsjöberg S 106 C8
Līdumnieki LV 133 C3
Lidzbark PL 139 D8
Lidzbark Warmiński PL 136 E2
Liebenau D 17 C12
Liebenau D 17 F12
Liebenburg D 79 B7
Liebenfels A 73 C9
Liebenwalde D 84 E4
Lieberose D 80 C6
Liebertwolkwitz D 79 D11
Liebling RO 159 B7
Lieboch A 148 C4
Liebstadt D 80 E5
Liedakkala FIN 119 C13
Liédena E 32 E3
Liedenpohja FIN 123 F11
Liège B 19 C12
Lieģi LV 134 C2
Liehittäjä S 119 B10
Liekokylä FIN 119 C16
Lieksa FIN 125 D14
Lielauce LV 134 C5
Lielbērze LV 134 C6
Lielirbe LV 130 F4
Lielklapari LV 135 D13
Lielmēmele LV 135 D10
Lielvārde LV 135 C9
Lielvircava LV 134 C7
Liempde NL 183 B6
Lien S 105 D15
Lien S 107 E10
Lienden NL 183 B7
Lienen D 17 D9
Lienz A 73 C6
Liepa LV 135 B10
Liepāja LV 134 C2
Liepāre LV 134 C7
Liepas LV 135 D12
Liepe D 84 E5
Liepen D 84 C4
Liepene LV 134 B3
Liepgarten D 84 C6
Liepimäjärvi FIN 117 B11
Lieplaukalė LT 134 E3
Lieplaukė LT 134 E4
Liepna LV 133 B2
Lieponys LT 137 E10
Liepupe LV 135 B8
Lier B 19 B10
Lier N 96 B7
Lierbyen N 95 C12
Liernais F 25 F11
Lierneux B 19 D12
Liesek SK 147 C9
Lieser D 21 E8
Lieshout NL 183 B7
Lieso FIN 127 C12
Liessel NL 16 F5
Liestal CH 27 F8
Lieštany SK 146 D6
Liești RO 161 B11
Lietavská Lúčka SK 147 C7
Lietekylä FIN 121 E11
Lieto FIN 126 D7
Liétor E 55 B9
Lievestuore FIN 123 F16
Lievoperä FIN 119 F16
Liezen A 73 A9
Liezēre LV 135 B12
Liffol-le-Grand F 26 D4
Lifford IRL 4 F2
Liffré F 23 D8
Lifton GB 12 D6
Ligardes F 33 B6
Līgatne LV 135 B10
Ligist A 73 C11
Lignano Pineta I 73 E7
Lignano Sabbiadoro I 73 E7
Lignan-sur-Orb F 34 D5
Ligné F 23 F9
Ligneuville B 20 D6
Lignières F 29 B10
Ligny-en-Barrois F 26 C3
Ligny-le-Châtel F 25 E10
Ligonchio I 66 D1
Ligota PL 142 C4
Ligowo PL 139 E7
Ligueil F 29 A7
Ligugé F 29 B6
Lihme DK 86 B3
Lihula EST 130 D7
Liigvalla EST 131 C12
Liikasenvaara FIN 121 B14
Liikavaara S 116 D6
Liimattala FIN 123 E15
Liimattala FIN 123 E17
Liipantönkkä FIN 122 E9
Liittoperä FIN 123 C16
Liiva EST 130 D6
Lijar E 55 E8
Liješće BIH 157 B9
Lijeska BIH 158 F3
Lijeva Rijeka MNE 163 D7
Lijevi Dubravčak HR 149 E6
Likavka SK 147 C8
Likenäs S 102 E5
Līksna LV 135 E12
Lilaia GR 175 B5
Liland N 110 D6
Liland N 111 D12
Lilaste LV 135 B8
L'Île-Bouchard F 24 F3
L'Île-Rousse F 37 F9
Lilienfeld A 77 F9
Lilienthal D 17 B11
Liljendal FIN 127 D15
Liljendal S 97 B11
Lilkovo BG 165 F10
Lillå S 118 B5
Lilla Edet S 91 C11
Lillåfors S 118 B6
Lilla Tjärby S 87 B12
Lillby FIN 123 D10
Lille B 16 F3
Lille F 19 C7
Lillebo N 102 C3
Lillebonne F 18 E2
Lillehammer N 101 D12
Lillers F 18 C5
Lillesand N 90 C3
Lilleshall GB 11 F7
Lille Skensved DK 87 D10
Lillestrøm N 95 C14
Lille Værløse DK 87 D10
Lillfjäten S 102 C4
Lillhamra S 102 C8
Lillhärdal S 102 C7
Lillholmsjö S 105 D16
Lillholmträsk S 107 B16
Lilliesleaf GB 5 D11
Lillkågeträsk S 118 E5
Lillkyrka S 98 C8
Lillmörtsjö S 103 B11
Lillo E 47 E6
Lillögda S 107 C13
Lillpite S 118 D6
Lillroten S 103 A14
Lillsaivis S 118 B7
Lillsele S 107 C16
Lillselet S 116 E9
Lillsjöhögen S 106 E8
Lillskog S 103 C9
Lillström S 103 B12
Lillsved S 102 A7
Lillviken S 109 C11
Lilyache BG 165 C8
Lilyak BG 167 C6
Lilyanovo BG 169 A9
Lima S 102 E5
Limana I 72 D5
Limanköy TR 167 F10
Limanowa PL 144 D1
Limanu RO 155 F3
Limatola I 60 A2
Limavady GB 4 E3
Limay F 24 B6
Limbach D 21 F12
Limbach D 186 C2
Limbach-Oberfrohna D 79 E12
Limbadi I 59 B8
Limbaži LV 135 A9
Limbourg B 20 C5
Limburg an der Lahn D 21 D10
Limburgerhof D 187 C5
Lime DK 86 C6
Limedsforsen S 102 E5
Limenaria GR 171 C7
Limenas GR 177 C6
Limenas Chersonisou GR 178 E9
Limerick IRL 8 C5
Limingen N 105 B15
Limingoån S 116 E9
Liminka FIN 119 E14
Liminpuro FIN 120 E9
Limmared S 91 D13
Limmen NL 16 C3
Limnes GR 175 D6
Limni GR 175 B7
Limnochori GR 169 C6
Limoges F 29 D8
Limogne-en-Quercy F 33 B9
Limone Piemonte I 37 C7
Limonest F 30 D6
Limone sul Garda I 69 B10
Limosano I 63 D7
Limoux F 33 D10
Limpias E 40 B5
Lin AL 168 B4
Linå DK 86 C5
Lina älv S 116 D4
Linakhamari RUS 114 D10
Linards F 29 D9
Linares E 54 C5
Linares de Mora E 48 D3
Linares de Riofrío E 45 C9
Linaria GR 175 B10
Lincent B 19 C11
Lincoln GB 11 E10
Lind DK 86 C3
Lindas N 100 E2
Lindau D 79 B11
Lindau D 82 A7
Lindau (Bodensee) D 71 B9
Lindberg D 76 D4
Linde DK 86 C2
Lindelse DK 87 F7
Linden D 21 C11
Linden D 82 B6
Lindenberg D 80 B6
Lindenberg D 83 D12
Lindenberg im Allgäu D 71 B9
Lindenfels D 21 E11
Lindern (Oldenburg) D 17 C9
Lindesberg S 97 C13
Lindesnäs S 97 B12
Lindewitt D 82 A6
Lindfield GB 15 E8
Lindholmen S 99 C10
Lindi EST 131 E8
Lindknud DK 86 D4
Lindkoski FIN 127 D15
Lindlar D 21 B8
Lindome S 91 D11
Lindores GB 5 C10
Lindos GR 181 D8
Lindoso P 38 E3
Lindow D 84 E3
Lindsdal S 89 B10
Lindsjö S 103 B12
Lindstedt D 79 A10
Lindved DK 86 D5
Lindwedel D 78 A6
Linge N 100 B6
Lingen (Ems) D 17 C8
Lingenfeld D 21 F10
Lingfield GB 15 E8
Linghed S 103 E10
Linghem S 92 C7
Lingolsheim F 27 C8
Lingrasmo N 111 B18
Linguaglossa I 59 D7
Linguizzetta F 37 G10
Linhares P 44 C6
Linia PL 138 B4
Liniewo PL 138 B5
Linkmenys LT 135 F11
Linköping S 92 C7
Linksness GB 3 H10
Linkuva LT 135 D7
Linlithgow GB 5 D9
Linna EST 131 E11
Linnamäe EST 130 D7
Linnamäe EST 131 F13
Linnankylä FIN 123 F10
Linneryd S 89 B8
Linnich D 20 C6
Linow D 83 D13
Linsell S 102 B6
Linsidemore GB 2 K8
Linthal CH 71 D8
Linthe D 79 B12
Lintig D 17 A11
Lintrup DK 86 E3
Lintula FIN 117 C14
Lintzoain E 32 E3
Linum D 84 E3
Linxe F 32 C3
Linyola E 42 D5
Linz A 76 F6
Linz am Rhein D 21 C8
Lioboml' UA 141 H10
Lioliai LT 134 E5
Lioni I 60 B4
Lion-sur-Mer F 23 B11
Liorac-sur-Louyre F 29 F7
Lios Mór IRL 9 D7
Lios Póil IRL 8 D2
Lios Tuathail IRL 8 D4
Lipa BIH 157 E7
Lipa PL 139 D10
Lipănești RO 161 C8
Lipany SK 145 E2
Lipar SRB 158 B4
Lipari I 59 C6
Lipawki BY 133 E3
Lipcani MD 153 A9
Lipce Reymontowskie PL 141 G1
Liperi FIN 125 E12
Liphook GB 15 E7
Lipiany PL 85 D7
Lipik HR 149 F8
Lipinki PL 144 D3
Lipinki Łużyckie PL 81 C8
Lipiny PL 81 C9
Lipjan RKS 164 D3
Lipka PL 85 D12
Lipki Wielkie PL 85 E9
Lipkovo NMK 164 E4
Lipnica BIH 157 D9
Lipnica PL 85 C12
Lipnica PL 138 D7
Lipnica PL 143 E9
Lipnik PL 143 E11
Lipník nad Bečvou CZ 146 B5
Lipniţa RO 161 E11
Lipnitsa BG 165 C8
Lipno PL 81 C11
Lipno PL 139 E7
Lipolist SRB 158 D4
Liposthey F 32 B4
Lipova RO 151 E8
Lipova RO 153 D10
Lipová SK 146 E6
Lipovac HR 157 B11
Lipovac SRB 164 B4
Lipová-Lázně CZ 77 B12
Lipovăţ RO 153 D11
Lipovec CZ 77 D11
Lipoveni MD 154 D3
Lipovljani HR 149 F7
Lipovo RUS 136 D5
Lipovu RO 160 E3
Lipowiec PL 139 D11
Lipowiec Kościelny PL 139 D9
Lipowina PL 139 B8
Lippoldsberg (Wahlsburg) D 78 C6
Lippstadt D 17 E10
Lipsk PL 140 C8
Lipsko PL 141 H5
Liptál CZ 146 C5
Liptovská Kokava SK 147 C9
Liptovská Lúžna SK 147 D8
Liptovská Osada SK 147 D8
Liptovská Teplička SK 147 D10
Liptovské Revúce SK 147 D8
Liptovský Hrádok SK 147 C9
Liptovský Mikuláš SK 147 C9
Lipusz PL 138 B4
Lipůvka CZ 77 D11
Liqenas AL 168 C4
Liré F 23 F9
Lis AL 168 A3
Lisa RO 152 F5
Lisa RO 160 F6
Lisac BIH 157 D8
Lisac HR 162 D4
Lisaku EST 131 C14
Lisacul IRL 6 E5
Lisbane GB 7 C11
Lisbellaw GB 7 D7
Lisboa P 50 B1
Lisburn GB 7 C10
Liscannor IRL 8 C4
Liscarney IRL 6 E3
Liscarroll IRL 8 D5
Lisciano Niccone I 66 F5
Lişcoteanca RO 161 C11
Lisdoonvarna IRL 6 F4
Liseleje DK 87 C9
Lisets BG 165 C10
Lisewo PL 138 D6
Lisgarode IRL 8 C6
Lisgoold IRL 8 E6
Lisia Góra PL 143 F11
Lisiįcice PL 142 F4
Lisieux F 23 B12
Lisiy Nos RUS 129 E13
Lisjö S 97 C15
Liskeard GB 12 E6
Lisková SK 147 C8
Lisków PL 142 C5
Lisky UA 155 C4
Lisle F 29 E7
Lislea GB 4 F3
L'Isle-Adam F 25 B7
L'Isle-de-Noé F 33 C6
L'Isle-d'Espagnac F 29 D6
L'Isle-en-Dodon F 33 D7
L'Isle-Jourdain F 29 C7
L'Isle-Jourdain F 33 C8
L'Isle-sur-la-Sorgue F 35 C9
L'Isle-sur-le-Doubs F 26 F6
L'Isle-sur-Serein F 25 E11
Lisle-sur-Tarn F 33 C9
Lisma FIN 117 B14
Lismakin IRL 9 C7
Lismanaapa FIN 117 D17
Lismarka N 101 D13
Lismore IRL 9 D7
Lisna BY 133 D4
Lisnagry IRL 8 C5
Lisnakill IRL 9 D8
Lisnarrick GB 7 D7
Lisnaskea GB 7 D8
Lisne UA 154 E4
Lišov CZ 77 D7
Lisów PL 142 E5
Lispole IRL 8 D2
Lisronagh IRL 9 D7
Lisryan IRL 7 E8
Liss GB 15 E7
Lissan GB 4 F3
Lisse NL 16 D3
Lissendorf D 185 D6
Lisskogsbrändan S 97 A10
Lissone I 69 B7
Lissycasey IRL 8 C4
List D 86 E2
Listed DK 89 E8
Listerby S 89 C8
Listerlin IRL 9 D8
Listowel IRL 8 D4
Listrac-Médoc F 28 E4
Listry IRL 8 D3
Liszki PL 143 F8
Liszkowo PL 85 D12
Lit S 106 E7
Liţa RO 160 F5
Litakovo BG 165 D8
Litava SK 147 E8
Litene LV 133 B2
Liteni RO 153 B9
Litér H 149 B9
Lit-et-Mixe F 32 B3
Lith NL 183 B6
Lithakia GR 174 D2
Lithi GR 177 C7
Lithines GR 179 E11
Litija SLO 73 D10
Litke H 147 E9
Litlefjord N 113 B14
Litmalahti FIN 125 E9
Litmaniemi FIN 125 E10
Litochoro GR 169 D8
Litoměřice CZ 76 A6
Litomyšl CZ 77 C10
Litovel CZ 77 C12
Litschau A 77 E8
Littau CH 70 C6
Littleborough GB 11 D7
Littlehampton GB 15 F7
Littlemill GB 3 K9
Littlemore GB 13 B12
Little Oakley GB 15 D11
Littleport GB 15 C9
Littlestone-on-Sea GB 15 F10
Littleton IRL 9 C7
Littoinen FIN 126 E7
Litva BIH 157 D10
Litvínov CZ 80 E5
Litzendorf D 75 C9
Liudvinavas LT 136 E7
Liukkunen FIN 125 D14
Liuža LV 133 C2
Livada RO 145 H7
Livada RO 151 E7
Livadaki GR 174 D4
Livadeia GR 175 C6
Livădeni MD 153 A11
Livadero GR 169 D6
Livadero GR 171 B6
Livadi GR 169 D7
Livadi GR 175 E10
Livadia GR 169 B9
Livanates GR 175 B7
Līvāni LV 135 D12
Livari MNE 163 E7
Livarot F 23 B12
Līvbērze LV 134 C6
Livernon F 33 A9
Liverpool GB 10 E6
Livezeni RO 152 D5
Livezi RO 153 E9
Livezi RO 160 D3
Livezile RO 152 C5
Livezile RO 152 E3
Livezile RO 159 D10
Līvi LV 135 B10
Livigno I 71 D10
Livingston GB 5 D9
Livno BIH 157 E7
Livo FIN 119 C17
Livold SLO 73 E10
Livonniska FIN 121 C10
Livorno I 66 E1
Livorno Ferraris I 68 C5
Livron-sur-Drôme F 30 F6
Liw PL 139 F12
Lixing-lès-St-Avold F 186 C2
Lixnaw IRL 8 D3
Lixouri GR 174 C1
Lizard GB 12 F4
Lizarraga E 32 E1
Lizdēni LV 131 F10
Lizums LV 135 B12
Lizy-sur-Ourcq F 25 B9
Lizzanello I 61 C10
Lizzano I 61 C8
Ljaljenča BIH 157 C11
Ljeskode Vode BIH 157 C8
Ljig SRB 158 E5
Ljønes N 108 B8
Ljørdal N 102 D4
Ljosland N 90 B1
Ljøsne N 100 D7
Ljuberađa SRB 164 C5
Ljubija BIH 156 C6
Ljubinje BIH 162 D5
Ljubiš SRB 158 F4
Ljubljana SLO 73 D10
Ljubogošta BIH 157 E10
Ljubovija SRB 158 E3
Ljubuški BIH 157 F8
Ljugarn S 93 E13
Ljung S 91 D13
Ljungå S 103 A11
Ljungaverk S 103 B11
Ljungby S 87 B13
Ljungby S 109 F15
Ljungbyhed S 87 C12
Ljungbyholm S 89 B10
Ljungdalen S 102 A4
Ljungsarp S 91 D14
Ljungsbro S 92 B7
Ljungskile S 91 C10
Ljupina HR 157 B7
Ljuša BIH 157 D7
Ljusâ S 118 C7
Ljušči Palanka BIH 156 C5
Ljusdal S 103 C11
Ljusfallshammar S 92 B7
Ljusne S 103 D13
Ljusnedal S 102 A4
Ljustorp S 103 A13
Ljusträsk S 118 C3
Ljusvattnet S 118 E6
Ljuti Dolac BIH 157 F8
Ljutomer SLO 148 C6
Llabjan RKS 164 D3
Llagostera E 43 D9
Llamas de la Ribera E 39 C8
Llanaelhaearn GB 10 F3
Llanarth GB 12 A6
Llanarthney GB 12 B6
Llanbadarn Fawr GB 12 A6
Llanbadrig GB 10 E3
Llanbedr GB 10 F3
Llanbedrog GB 10 F3
Llanberis GB 10 E3
Llanbister GB 13 A8
Llanblethian GB 13 C8
Llançà E 34 F5
Llandanwg GB 10 F3
Llandderfel GB 10 F4
Llandeilo GB 12 B7
Llandissilio GB 12 B5
Llandovery GB 13 B7
Llandrillo GB 10 F5
Llandrindod Wells GB 13 A8
Llandudno GB 10 E4
Llandwrog GB 10 E3
Llandysul GB 12 A6
Llanegwad GB 12 B6
Llaneilian GB 10 E3
Llanelli GB 12 B6
Llanelltyd GB 10 F4
Llanelwy GB 10 E5
Llanes E 39 B10
Llanfaelog GB 10 E3
Llanfair Caereinion GB 10 F5
Llanfairfechan GB 10 E4
Llanfairpwllgwyngyll GB 10 E3
Llanfair Talhaiarn GB 10 E4
Llanfihangel-ar-arth GB 12 A6
Llanfyllin GB 10 F5
Llangadfan GB 10 F5
Llangadog GB 13 B7
Llangefni GB 10 E3
Llangeler GB 12 A6
Llangelynin GB 10 F3
Llangoed GB 10 E3
Llangollen GB 10 F5
Llangurig GB 13 A7
Llangynidr GB 13 B8
Llanidloes GB 13 A7
Llanilar GB 12 A6
Llanishen GB 13 B8

Llanllwchaiarn GB 10 F5
Llanllyfni GB 10 E3
Llannerch-y-medd GB 10 E3
Llan-non GB 12 A6
Llannon GB 12 B6
Llanrhaeadr-ym-Mochnant GB 10 F5
Llanrhidian GB 12 B6
Llanrhystud GB 12 A6
Llanrug GB 10 E3
Llanrumney GB 13 B8
Llanrwst GB 10 E4
Llansanffraid Glan Conwy GB 10 E4
Llansannan GB 10 E4
Llansawel GB 12 A6
Llantilio Pertholey GB 13 B8
Llantrisant GB 13 B8
Llantwit Major GB 13 C8
Llanuwchllyn GB 10 F4
Llanwddyn GB 10 F5
Llanwenog GB 12 A6
Llanwnda GB 10 E3
Llanwnog GB 10 F5
Llanwrtyd Wells GB 13 A7
Llanybydder GB 12 A6
Llapushnik RKS 163 D10
Llardecans E 42 E5
Llaurí E 48 F4
Llavorsí E 33 E8
Llay GB 10 E5
Lledrod GB 12 A7
Lleida E 42 D5
Llera E 51 C7
Llerena E 51 C7
Llíria E 48 E3
Llívia E 33 F9
Llodio E 40 B6
Llombai E 48 F3
Lloret de Mar E 43 D9
Lloseta E 49 E10
Llubí E 57 B11
Llucmajor E 57 C10
Lniano PL 138 C5
Lo B 18 C6
Loamneș RO 152 F4
Loano I 37 C8
Loarre E 32 F4
Löbau D 81 D7
Lobbæk DK 89 E7
Lobe LV 135 C10
Löbejün D 79 C10
Lobera de Onsella E 32 F3
Lobērģi LV 131 F12
Łobez PL 85 C9
Lobith NL 183 B8
Löbnitz D 83 B13
Łobodno PL 143 E6
Lobón E 51 B6
Lobonäs S 103 C9
Loburg D 79 B11
Łobżenica PL 85 D12
Locana I 31 E11
Locarno CH 68 A6
Locate di Triulzi I 69 C7
Loccum (Rehburg-Loccum) D 17 D12
Loceri I 64 D4
Lochaline GB 4 B5
Lochau A 71 B9
Lochawe GB 4 C6
Lochboisdale GB 2 L2
Lochcarron GB 2 L5
Lochdon GB 4 C5
Lochearnhead GB 5 C8
Lochem NL 16 D6
Lochen A 76 F4
Lochend GB 3 L8
Loches F 24 F4
Loch Garman IRL 9 D10
Lochgelly GB 5 C10
Lochgilphead GB 4 C6
Lochgoilhead GB 4 C7
Lochinver GB 2 J6
Lochmaben GB 5 E10
Lochmaddy GB 2 K2
Lochovice CZ 76 C5
Łochów PL 139 E12
Lochranza GB 4 D6
Lochristi B 19 B8
Loch Sgioport GB 2 L2
Lociki LV 135 E13
Lockenhaus A 149 B6
Lockerbie GB 5 E10
Lockne S 106 E7
Löcknitz D 84 D6
Locks Heath GB 13 D12
Lockton GB 11 C10
Locmaria-Plouzané F 22 D2
Locmariaquer F 22 E6
Locminé F 22 E6
Locorotondo I 61 B8
Locquirec F 22 C4
Locri I 59 C9
Locronan F 22 D3
Loctudy F 22 E3
Loculi I 64 C4
Löddeköpinge S 87 D12
Lödderitz D 79 C10
Loddin D 84 B6
Lødding N 105 B10
Loddiswell GB 13 E7
Loddon GB 15 B11
Lodè I 64 B4
Lode LV 135 B10
Loděnice CZ 76 B6
Löderup S 88 E6
Lodève F 34 C5
Lodi I 69 C8
Løding N 108 B8
Lødingen N 111 D10
Lodi Vecchio I 69 C7
Lodosa E 32 F1
Lödöse S 91 C11
Łodygowice PL 147 B8
Łódź PL 143 C7
Loeches E 46 D6
Loenen NL 183 A8
Löf D 21 D8
Løfallstrand N 94 B4
Lofer A 73 A6
Löffingen D 27 E9
Lofos GR 169 D7
Lofsdalen S 102 B5
Loftahammar S 93 D9
Lofthus N 94 B5
Lofthus N 111 E10
Loftus GB 11 B10
Log SLO 73 D8
Loga N 94 F5
Logan GB 5 E8
Logatec SLO 73 E9
Lögda S 107 C14
Lögdeå S 107 D16
Loggerheads GB 11 F7
Loghill IRL 8 C4
Logkanikos GR 174 E5
Logofteni MD 153 B11
Logrești RO 160 D3
Logron F 24 D5
Logroño E 41 D7
Logrosán E 45 F10
Løgstør DK 86 B4
Løgstrup DK 86 B4
Løgten DK 86 C6
Løgumkloster DK 86 E3
Lohals DK 87 E7
Lohberg D 76 D4
Lohéac F 23 E8
Lohe-Rickelshof D 82 B6
Lohfelden D 78 D6
Lohijärvi FIN 119 B12
Lohilahti FIN 129 B10
Lohiluoma FIN 122 E8
Lohiniva FIN 117 D13
Lohiranta FIN 121 B12
Lohja FIN 127 E11
Lohjan kunta FIN 127 E11
Lohmar D 21 C8
Lohme D 84 A5
Lohmen D 80 E6
Lohmen D 83 C12
Löhnberg D 21 C10
Löhne D 17 D11
Lohne (Oldenburg) D 17 C10
Lohra D 21 C11
Lohr am Main D 74 C6
Lohsa D 80 D6
Lohtaja FIN 123 B11
Lohusuu EST 131 D14
Loiano I 66 D3
Loigny-la-Bataille F 24 D6
Loimaa FIN 127 D9
Loimaan kunta FIN 127 D8
Loiré F 23 E10
Loiri-Porto San Paolo I 64 B3
Loiron F 23 D10
Loisy-sur-Marne F 25 C12
Loitz D 84 C4
Loivos P 38 E5
Loivos do Monte P 44 B5
Loja E 53 B8
Loja LV 135 B9
Løjt Kirkeby DK 86 E4
Loka brunn S 97 C11
Lokakylä FIN 123 D14
Lokalahti FIN 126 D5
Lokavec SLO 73 E8
Lokca SK 147 C8
Loke S 106 F7
Løken N 95 C14
Lokeren B 19 B9
Loket CZ 75 B12
Lokev SLO 73 E8
Lokka FIN 115 C3
Løkken DK 90 E6
Løkken N 104 E7
Lokkiperä FIN 123 C13
Lőkösháza H 151 E7
Lokrume S 93 D13
Loksa EST 131 B11
Løksa N 111 C14
Løksebotn N 111 C14
Lokuta EST 131 D9
Lokuti EST 131 C9
Lokve HR 67 B10
Lokve SLO 73 D8
Lokve SRB 159 C7
Løkvoll N 112 D6
Lolishniy Shepit UA 152 A6
Lollar D 21 C11
L'Olleria E 56 D3
Lom BG 159 F11
Lom N 101 C9
Łomazy PL 141 G8
Lombez F 33 D7
Lombheden S 119 B9
Lomborg DK 86 B2
Lomello I 68 C6
Lomen N 101 D9
Łomianki PL 139 F10
Lomma S 87 D12
Lommatzsch D 80 D4
Lomme F 18 C6
Lommel B 19 B11
Łomnica PL 81 B9
Lomnice CZ 77 D10
Lomnice nad Lužnicí CZ 77 D7
Lomnice nad Popelkou CZ 77 A8
Lomonosov RUS 129 F12
Lompolo FIN 117 B13
Lomsdalen N 101 E12
Lomsjö S 107 C11
Lomsti BG 166 C6
Lomträsk S 109 E18
Lomträsk S 119 B9
Łomża PL 139 D13
Lonato I 66 B1
Lønborg DK 86 D2
Lončari BIH 157 C10
Lončarica HR 149 E8
Londa I 66 E4
Londerzeel B 19 C9
Londinières F 18 E3
London GB 15 D8
Londonderry GB 4 F2
Lone LV 135 D10
Long F 18 D4
Longa GR 174 F4
Longages F 33 D8
Longare I 66 B4
Longares E 41 F9
Longarone I 72 D5
Long Ashton GB 13 C9
Long Bennington GB 11 F10
Longbridge Deverill GB 13 C10
Longchaumois F 31 C8
Long Compton GB 13 B11
Long Crendon GB 14 D6
Long Eaton GB 11 F9
Longeau-Percey F 26 E3
Longecourt-en-Plaine F 26 F3
Longerak N 90 B2
Longeville-en-Barrois F 26 C3
Longeville-lès-St-Avold F 186 C2
Longeville-sur-Mer F 28 C3
Longford IRL 7 E7
Longframlington GB 5 E13
Longhope GB 3 H10
Longhope GB 13 B10
Longhorsley GB 5 E13
Longhoughton GB 5 E13
Long Itchington GB 13 A12
Longlier B 19 E11
Long Melford GB 15 C10
Longmorn GB 3 K10
Longny-au-Perche F 24 C4
Longobardi I 60 E6
Longobucco I 61 E7
Longomel P 44 F5
Longos GR 168 F3
Longos Vales P 38 D3
Long Preston GB 11 C7
Longré F 28 C5
Longridge GB 10 D6
Longroiva P 45 C6
Long Stratton GB 15 C11
Long Sutton GB 11 F12
Longton GB 10 D6
Longtown GB 5 E11
Longueau F 18 E5
Longué-Jumelles F 23 F11
Longuenesse F 18 C5
Longueville F 25 C9
Longueville-sur-Scie F 18 E3
Longuyon F 19 F12
Longwood IRL 7 F9
Longwy F 19 E12
Lonigo I 66 B3
Lonin N 95 C10
Löningen D 17 C9
Łoniów PL 143 E12
Lonja HR 149 F7
Lonjica HR 149 E6
Lonkan N 110 C9
Lonkka FIN 121 D13
Lonlay-l'Abbaye F 23 C10
Lönneberga S 92 D7
Lonneker NL 183 A9
Lonny F 184 E2
Lons F 32 D5
Lönsboda S 88 C6
Lonsee D 74 E6
Lons-le-Saunier F 31 B8
Lønstrup DK 90 E6
Lontzen B 183 D8
Lónya H 145 G5
Loo EST 131 C9
Loon op Zand NL 16 E4
Loos F 182 D2
Loosdorf A 77 F8
Loose GB 15 E10
Lopadea Nouă RO 152 E3
Lopar HR 67 C10
Lopare BIH 157 C10
Lopătari RO 161 C9
Lopate NMK 164 E4
Lopatica NMK 168 B5
Łopatki PL 143 C7
Lopatnic MD 153 A10
Lopatovo RUS 132 F4
Lopcombe Corner GB 13 C11
Lõpe EST 131 D7
Lopera E 53 A8
Łopiennik Górny PL 144 A7
Lopigna F 37 G9
Lopik NL 182 B5
Loppa N 112 C7
Loppersum NL 17 B7
Loppi FIN 127 D11
Lopra FO 2 C3
Lopushna UA 152 A6
Łopuszno PL 143 E9
Lopyan BG 165 D9
Lora N 101 B9
Lora del Río E 51 D8
Loranca de Tajuña E 47 D6
Lorås S 106 E8
Lörby S 88 C7
Lorca E 55 D9
Lorch D 21 D9
Lorch D 74 E6
Lorcha E 56 D4
Lordelo P 38 F4
Lordosa P 44 C5
Lørenskog N 95 C13
Loreo I 66 B5
Loreto I 67 F8
Loreto Aprutino I 62 C5
Lorgues F 36 D4
Lorient F 22 E5
Lorignac F 28 E4
Loriguilla E 48 E3
Lőrinci H 150 B4
Loriol-sur-Drôme F 30 F6
Lormes F 25 F10
Loro Ciuffenna I 66 E4
Loro Piceno I 67 F7
Lorquin F 186 D2
Lörrach D 27 E8
Lorrez-le-Bocage-Préaux F 25 D8
Lorris F 25 E8
Lorsch D 21 E11
Lørslev DK 90 E7
Lörstrand S 103 C11
Lörudden S 103 B14
Lorup D 17 C9
Lorupe LV 135 B9
Los S 103 C9
Losacino E 39 E7
Losa del Obispo E 48 E3
Los Alcázares E 56 F3
Los Algezares E 56 F2
Los Arcos E 32 E1
Losar de la Vera E 45 D9
Los Arenales del Sol E 56 E4
Los Barrios E 53 D6
Los Barrios de Luna E 39 C8
Los Belones E 56 F3
Los Cantareros E 55 D10
Los Corrales E 53 B7
Los Corrales de Buelna E 40 B3
Loscos E 42 E1
Los Dolores E 56 F2
Løset N 101 D14
Los Gallardos E 55 E9
Loshchynivka UA 155 C3
Losheim D 21 E7
Los Hinojosos E 47 E7
Łosice PL 141 F7
Łosinka PL 141 E9
Łosiów PL 142 E4
Los Maldonados E 56 F2
Los Molinos E 46 C4
Losna N 101 D12
Los Navalmorales E 46 E3
Los Navalucillos E 46 E3
Løsning DK 86 D5
Losomäki FIN 125 D11
Losone CH 68 A6
Łososina Dolna PL 144 D2
Losova MD 154 C2
Losovaara FIN 121 E11
Los Palacios y Villafranca E 51 E8
Los Pandos E 40 B4
Los Pedrones E 47 F10
Los Pozuelos de Calatrava E 54 B5
Los Rábanos E 41 E7
Los Royos E 55 D8
Los Santos E 45 C9
Los Santos de Maimona E 51 C7
Loßburg D 27 D9
Losse F 32 B5
Losser NL 17 D7
Lossiemouth GB 3 K10
Lößnitz D 79 E12
Lostallo CH 69 A7
Loštice CZ 77 C11
Los Tojos E 40 B3
Lostwithiel GB 12 E5
Los Villares E 53 A9
Los Yébenes E 46 E5
Löt S 89 B11
Lote N 100 C4
Loten N 94 D2
Løten N 101 E14
Lotenhulle B 182 C2
Loth GB 3 G11
Lothmore GB 3 J9
Lotorp S 92 B7
Lotte D 17 D9
Lottefors S 103 D11
Löttorp S 89 A11
Lottstetten D 27 E10
Lottum NL 183 C8
Lotyń PL 85 C11
Lotzorai I 64 D4
Louannec F 22 C5
Loučeň CZ 77 B8
Loučná nad Desnou CZ 77 B12
Loučovice CZ 76 E6
Loudéac F 22 D6
Loudes F 30 E4
Loudun F 28 A6
Loué F 23 E11
Loue FIN 119 B13
Louejärvi FIN 119 B14
Louejoki FIN 119 B14
Loughborough GB 11 F9
Loughbrickland GB 7 D10
Lougher IRL 8 D3
Loughgall GB 7 D9
Loughglinn IRL 6 E5
Loughrea IRL 6 F5
Loughton GB 15 D9
Lougratte F 33 A7
Louhans F 31 B7
Louka CZ 146 D4
Loukas GR 174 D5
Loukisia GR 175 C7
Loukkojärvi FIN 119 D15
Loukusa FIN 121 C10
Loulans F 26 F5
Loulay F 28 C4
Loulé P 50 E3
Louny CZ 76 B5
Loupiac F 32 A5
Lourdes F 32 D5
Lourdoueix-St-Pierre F 29 C9
Louriçal P 44 D3
Lourinhã P 44 F2
Lourmarin F 35 C9
Louros GR 174 A2
Loury F 24 E7
Lousã P 44 D4
Lousa P 50 B1
Lousada P 38 F3
Louth GB 11 E11
Louth IRL 7 E9
Loutra GR 175 E9
Loutra GR 177 A8
Loutra Aidipsou GR 175 B7
Loutra Eleftheron GR 170 C6
Loutraki GR 169 C6
Loutraki GR 174 B3
Loutraki GR 175 D6
Loutra Kyllinis GR 174 D3
Loutra Smokovou GR 174 A5
Loutra Ypatis GR 174 B5
Loutro GR 169 C7
Loutro GR 169 E6
Loutro GR 174 B3
Loutros GR 171 C10
Louvain B 19 C10
Louvain B 182 D5
Louveigné B 183 D7
Louverné F 23 D10
Louvie-Juzon F 32 D5
Louviers F 18 F3
Louvigné-du-Désert F 23 D9
Louvroil F 19 D8
Louze F 25 D12
Lov DK 87 E9
Lövånger S 118 F6
Lovas HR 157 B11
Lovasberény H 149 B11
Lovászi H 149 C7
Lovászpatona H 149 B9
Lovberg S 106 A7
Lövberga S 107 D9
Lovćenac SRB 158 B4
Lovčica-Trubín SK 147 D7
Løve DK 87 E8
Lovech BG 165 C10
Løvel DK 86 B4
Lovendegem B 19 B8
Lovere I 69 B9
Lovero I 69 A9
Lövestad S 88 D5
Loviisa FIN 127 E15
Lovik N 111 C10
Lovikka S 116 D9
Lovinac HR 156 D4
Lovinobaňa SK 147 E9
Lovisa FIN 127 E15
Lovište HR 157 F7
Lovliden S 107 B11
Løvlund N 101 D11
Lövnäs S 102 D5
Lövnäs S 107 B9
Lövnäs S 109 D14
Lövnäsvallen S 102 C6
Lovnidol BG 166 D4
Lövő H 149 A7
Lovosice CZ 76 A6
Lovraeid N 94 D4
Lovran HR 67 B9
Lovreč HR 67 B8
Lovreć HR 157 F7
Lovrenc SLO 148 C4
Lovrin RO 150 F6
Lövsele S 118 F6
Lövsjö S 106 B8
Lövsjön S 97 B12
Lövstabruk S 99 B9
Lövstalöt S 99 C9
Lövstrand S 107 C10
Lövtjärn S 103 D11
Lovund N 108 D3
Lövvik S 103 A15
Lövvik S 107 C9
Łowcza PL 141 H8
Löwenberg D 84 E4
Löwenstein D 27 B11
Lower Ballinderry GB 7 C10
Lower Cam GB 13 B10
Lower Kilchattan GB 4 C4
Lowestoft GB 15 C12
Lowick GB 5 D13
Łowicz PL 141 F1
Low Street GB 15 B11
Łowyń PL 81 B9
Loxstedt D 17 B11
Löyä FIN 123 E11
Loyettes F 31 D7
Loymola RUS 129 B16
Löytö FIN 128 B7
Löytökylä FIN 119 D16
Löytövaara FIN 121 C11
Lozarevo BG 167 D7
Lozen BG 165 D7
Lozen BG 166 C5
Lozenets BG 167 E9
Lozna RO 151 C11
Lozna SRB 159 F6
Loznica SRB 158 D3
Loznitsa BG 155 F1
Loznitsa BG 167 C7
Lozorno SK 77 F12
Lozovac HR 156 E4
Lozovik SRB 159 E7
Lozoya E 46 C5
Lozoyuela E 46 C5
Lozuvata UA 154 A6
Lozzo di Cadore I 72 D5
Lú IRL 7 E9
Luanco E 39 A8
Luarca E 39 A6
Lubaczów PL 144 C7
Lubań PL 81 D8
Lubāna LV 135 C13
Lubanowo PL 84 D7
Lübars D 79 B11
Lubartów PL 141 H7
Lubasz PL 85 E11
Lubawa PL 139 C8
Lubawka PL 81 E10
Lübbecke D 17 D11
Lubbeek B 19 C10
Lübben D 80 C5
Lübbenau D 80 C5
Lübbow D 83 E10
Lubczyna PL 85 C7
Lube LV 134 B5
Lübeck D 83 C9
Ľubeľa SK 147 C8
Lubenec CZ 76 B4
Lubeník SK 145 F1
Lubersac F 29 E8
Lübesse D 83 D10
Lubezere LV 134 B5
Lubiai LT 134 E3
Lubián E 39 D6
Łubianka PL 138 D6
Lubichowo PL 138 C5
Lubicz Dolny PL 138 D6
Lubijcin PL 81 C9
Lubień PL 147 B9
Lubień Kujawski PL 139 F7
Lubieszewo PL 85 D9
Lubiń PL 81 C11
Lubin PL 81 D10
Lubina SK 146 D5
Lubiszyn PL 85 E7
Lublin PL 141 H7
Lubliniec PL 142 E6
Lubmin D 84 B5
Lubnia PL 138 C4
Łubniany PL 142 E5
Lubnica NMK 169 A7
Lubnica SRB 159 F9
Łubnice PL 143 F11
Lubniewice PL 81 A8
Łubno PL 85 B12
Łubno PL 85 D10
Łubno PL 143 B7
Lubochnia PL 141 G2
Lubomierz PL 81 D9
Lubomino PL 139 B9
Luboń PL 81 B11
Luborzyca PL 143 F9
Ľubotice SK 145 E3
Ľubotín SK 145 E2
Lubowidz PL 139 D8
Łubowo PL 85 C10
Łubowo PL 85 E12
Lubraniec PL 138 E6
Lubrín E 55 E8
Lubrza PL 81 B8
Lubrza PL 142 F4
Lubsko PL 81 C7
Lübstorf D 83 C10
Lubstów PL 138 F5
Lubsza PL 142 E4
Lübtheen D 83 D10
Luby CZ 75 B11
Lubycza Królewska PL 144 C8
Lübz D 83 D12
Luc F 33 B11
Luc F 35 A6
Lucainena de las Torres E 55 E8
Lucan IRL 7 F10
Lučani SRB 158 F5
Lúcar E 55 E8
Luçay-le-Mâle F 24 F5
Lucca I 66 E2
Lucca Sicula I 58 D3
Lucé F 24 D5
Luče SLO 73 D10
Lucena E 53 B8
Lucena de Jalón E 41 E9
Lucena del Cid E 48 D4
Lucena del Puerto E 51 E6
Lucenay-lès-Aix F 30 B3
Lucenay-l'Évêque F 25 F11
Luc-en-Diois F 35 A9
Lučenec SK 147 E9
Luceni E 41 E9
Lucera I 63 D8
Lucéram F 37 D6
Lucey F 26 C4
Lucfalva H 147 E9
Luchayka BY 133 F3
Luché-Pringé F 23 E12
Lucheux F 18 D5
Lüchow D 83 E10
Luchy F 18 E5
Luciana E 54 B4
Lucień PL 139 F7
Lucieni RO 161 D6
Lucignano I 66 F4
Lucija SLO 67 A8
Lucillo de Somoza E 39 D7
Lučine SLO 73 D9
Lucito I 63 D7
Luciu RO 161 D10
Lucka D 79 D11
Luckau D 80 C5
Luckenwalde D 80 B4
Lucksta S 103 B13
Lückstedt D 83 E11
Lúčky SK 147 C8
Luco dei Marsi I 62 D4
Luçon F 28 C3
Lucq-de-Béarn F 32 D4
Luc-sur-Mer F 23 B11
Lucy-le-Bois F 25 E10
Ludag GB 2 L2
Ludanice SK 146 E6
Ludányhalászi H 147 E9
Ludbreg HR 149 D7
Lüdenscheid D 21 B9
Lüderitz D 79 A10
Lüdersdorf D 83 C9
Ludești RO 160 D6
Ludgershall GB 13 C11
Lüdinghausen D 17 E8
Ludlow GB 13 A9
Ludogortsi BG 161 F9
Ludoni RUS 132 E5
Ludoș RO 152 F3
Ludres F 186 D1
Luduș RO 152 E4
Ludvigsborg S 87 D13
Ludvika S 97 B13
Ludwigsau-Friedlos D 78 E6
Ludwigsburg D 27 C11
Ludwigsfelde D 80 B4
Ludwigshafen D 27 E11
Ludwigshafen am Rhein D 21 F10
Ludwigslust D 83 D10
Ludwigsstadt D 75 B9
Ludwin PL 141 H7
Ludza LV 133 C3
Lüe F 32 B4
Luelmo E 39 F7
Lüerdissen D 78 C6
Luesia E 32 F3
Lueta RO 153 E6
Lug BIH 162 D5
Lug HR 149 E11
Luga RUS 132 D6
Lugagnano Val d'Arda I 69 D8
Lugano CH 69 A6
Lüganuse EST 131 C14
Lugau D 79 E12
Lugaži LV 131 F11
Lügde D 17 E12
Luglon F 32 B4
Lugnano in Teverina I 62 B2
Lugnås S 91 B14
Lugnvik S 103 A14
Lugnvik S 106 E7
Lugny-lès-Charolles F 30 C5
Lugo E 38 B4
Lugo I 66 D4
Lugo-di-Nazza F 37 G10
Lugoj RO 159 B8
Lugones E 39 B8
Lugos F 32 B4
Lugrin F 31 C10
Lugros E 55 E6
Luhačovice CZ 146 C5
Luhalahti FIN 127 B9
Luhamaa EST 132 F1
Luhanka FIN 127 B14
Luhden D 17 D12
Luhe-Wildenau D 75 C11
Lühmannsdorf D 84 B5
Luhtapohja FIN 125 E15
Luhtikylä FIN 127 D13
Luhy UA 152 A4
Luhy UA 154 A4
Luica RO 161 E9
Luica RO 161 E9
Luik B 19 C12
Luik B 183 D7
Luikonlahti FIN 125 E11
Luimneach IRL 8 C5
Luino I 68 B6
Luintra E 38 D4
Luiro FIN 115 C4
Luiro FIN 115 D3
Luisant F 24 D5
Luizi Călugăra RO 153 D9
Luka BIH 157 F9
Luka SRB 159 E9
Lukácsháza H 149 B7
Luka nad Jihlavou CZ 77 D9
Lukavac BIH 157 C10
Lukavec CZ 77 C8
Lukavica BIH 157 C9
Łukawiec PL 144 C7
Luke NMK 164 E5
Lukeswell IRL 9 D8
Lŭki BG 165 F10
Lukivtsi UA 152 A6
Lukkaroistenperä FIN 119 F13
Lukov CZ 146 C5
Lukovë AL 168 E2
Lukovit BG 165 C9
Lukovo HR 67 C10
Lukovo SRB 159 F8
Lukovo SRB 163 C11
Lukovo Šugare HR 67 D11
Lukovytsya UA 153 A8
Łuków PL 141 G6
Łukowa PL 144 C6
Łukowisko PL 141 F7
Lukšiai LT 136 D7
Lukštai LT 135 D11
Luky UA 145 D7
Lula I 64 C3
Luleå S 118 C8
Lüleburgaz TR 173 B7
Lüllemäe EST 131 F12
Lullymore IRL 7 F9
Lümanda EST 130 E4
Lumbarda HR 162 D3
Lumbier E 32 E3
Lumbrales E 45 C7
Lumbreras E 41 D6
Lumbres F 18 C5
Lumby DK 86 E6
Lumezzane I 69 B9
Lumijoki FIN 119 E14
Lumimetsä FIN 119 F14
Lumina RO 155 E3
Lumio F 37 F9
Lummelunda S 93 D12
Lummen B 19 C11
Lumparland FIN 99 B14
Lumphanan GB 3 L11
Lumpiaque E 41 E9
Lumpzig D 79 E11
Lumsheden S 103 E11
Luna E 41 D10
Luna RO 152 D3
Lunamatrona I 64 D2
Lunano I 66 E5
Lunas F 34 C5
Lunca MD 154 C4
Lunca RO 151 D9
Lunca RO 152 D5
Lunca RO 153 B9
Lunca RO 160 F5
Lunca Banului RO 154 D2
Lunca Bradului RO 152 D6
Lunca Cernii de Jos RO 159 B10
Lunca Corbului RO 160 D5
Lunca de Jos RO 153 D7
Lunca de Sus RO 153 D7
Lunca Ilvei RO 152 C5
Lunca Mureșului RO 152 E3
Luncavița RO 155 C2
Luncavița RO 159 C9
Luncoiu de Jos RO 151 E10
Lund DK 86 D5
Lund N 105 B11
Lund N 110 E8
Lund N 111 C15
Lund S 87 D12
Lundamo N 104 E8
Lundbjörken S 102 E8
Lundby DK 86 F7
Lundby DK 87 E9
Lunde DK 86 D2
Lunde DK 86 E6
Lunde N 95 D10
Lunde N 111 C16
Lunde S 103 A14
Lundeborg DK 87 E7
Lundebyvollen N 102 E3
Lundegård N 94 F6
Lunden D 82 B6
Lunderskov DK 86 E4
Lundin Links GB 5 C11
Lundsbrunn S 91 C13
Lundsjön S 106 D7
Lünebach D 20 D6
Lüneburg D 83 D8
Lunel F 35 C7
Lünen D 17 E9
Lunery F 29 B10
Lunéville F 26 C5
Lungani RO 153 C10
Lunger S 97 D14
Lungern CH 70 D6
Lungro I 60 D6
Lungsjön S 107 E10
Lungulețu RO 161 D7
Lunino RUS 136 D5
L'Union F 33 C8
Lunkkaus FIN 115 D3
Lunna BY 140 D10
Lunnäset S 102 A5
Lünne D 17 D8
Lunneborg N 111 B16
Lunow D 84 E6
Lunteren NL 183 A7
Luogosanto I 64 A3
Luohua FIN 119 E14
Luokė LT 134 E5
Luokkala FIN 121 D11
Luola-aapa FIN 119 C15
Luoma-aho FIN 123 D11
Luopa FIN 122 E9
Luopajärvi FIN 122 E9
Luopioinen FIN 127 C12
Luostari RUS 114 E10
Luosto FIN 115 D1
Luosu FIN 117 C12
Luotolahti FIN 128 C8
Luovankylä FIN 122 F7
Luovttejohka N 113 C21
Lupac RO 159 C8
Lupandi LV 133 E3
Łupawa PL 85 B12
Lupeni RO 152 E6
Lupeni RO 159 C11
Lupiac F 33 C6
Lupiñén E 41 D10
Lupión E 53 A9
Łupków PL 145 E5
Lupoglav HR 67 B9
Łupowo PL 85 E8
Luppa D 80 D3
Lupporperä FIN 121 D9
Luppy F 26 C5
Lupșa RO 151 E11
Lupșanu RO 161 E9
Luque E 53 A8
Luras I 64 B3
Lurbe-St-Christau F 32 D4
Lurcy-Lévis F 30 B2
Lure F 26 E5
Lurgan GB 7 D10
Lurgan IRL 6 E6
Luri F 37 F10
Lurøy N 108 D4
Lurs F 35 C10
Lurudal N 105 C13
Lury-sur-Arnon F 24 F7
Lusca IRL 7 E10
Lusciano I 60 B2
Luserna San Giovanni I 31 F11
Lushnjë AL 168 C2
Lusi FIN 127 C15
Lusignan F 29 C6
Lusigny-sur-Barse F 25 D11
Lusk IRL 7 E10
Lus-la-Croix-Haute F 35 A10
Lusminki FIN 121 C14
Lusnić BIH 157 E6
Luso P 44 D4
Luspa FIN 116 B8
Luspebryggan S 109 B18
Lussac F 28 F5
Lussac-les-Châteaux F 29 C7
Lussac-les-Églises F 29 C8
Lussan F 35 B7
Lüssow D 83 C12
Lusta GB 2 K3
Lustad N 105 C12
Lustadt D 187 C5
Lustenau A 71 C9
Luster N 100 D6
Lustivere EST 131 D12
Łuszkowo PL 81 B11
Luszyn PL 143 B8
Lutago I 72 C4
Lütau D 83 D9
Lütetsburg D 17 A8
Lutherstadt Wittenberg D 79 C12

Lütjenburg D 83 B9
Lutnes N 102 D4
Lutocin PL 139 E8
Lutomiersk PL 143 C7
Luton GB 15 D8
Lutowiska PL 145 E6
Lutriņi LV 134 C4
Lutry PL 136 E2
Luttenberg NL 183 A8
Lutter am Barenberge D 79 C7
Lutterbach F 27 E7
Lutterworth GB 13 A12
Lututów PL 142 D5
Lützelbach D 21 E12
Lützen D 79 D11
Lutzerath D 21 D8
Lutzingen D 75 E8
Lutzmannsburg A 149 B7
Lützow D 83 C10
Luua EST 131 D13
Luujoki FIN 119 C14
Luukkola FIN 129 C9
Luukkonen FIN 129 B9
Luumäen kk FIN 128 D8
Luumäki FIN 128 D8
Luunja EST 131 E13
Luupujoki FIN 123 C17
Luupuvesi FIN 123 C17
Luusniemi FIN 124 G7
Luusua FIN 115 F2
Luvia FIN 126 C6
Luvos S 109 C16
Lux F 26 F3
Luxembourg L 20 E6
Luxe-Sumberraute F 32 D3
Luxeuil-les-Bains F 26 E5
Luxey F 32 B4
Luyego de Somoza E 39 D7
Luyksgestel NL 183 C6
Luz P 50 E2
Luz P 50 E4
Luz P 51 C5
Luzaga E 47 C8
Lužani HR 157 B8
Luzarches F 25 B7
Luz-Ardiden F 32 E5
Luže CZ 77 C10
Luzech F 33 B8
Lužec nad Vltavou CZ 76 B6
Luzenac F 33 E9
Luzern CH 70 C6
Luzhany UA 153 A7
Luzhki BY 133 F3
Luzianes P 50 D3
Luz i Madh AL 168 B2
Luzino PL 138 A5
Luzmela E 40 B3
Łużna PL 144 D3
Lūžņa LV 130 F3
Lūznava LV 133 D2
Luzón E 47 B8
Luz-St-Sauveur F 32 E6
Luzy F 30 B4
Luzzara I 66 C2
Luzzi I 60 E6
L'viv UA 144 D9
Lwówek PL 81 B10
Lwówek Śląski PL 81 D9
Lyady RUS 132 D4
Lyaskelya RUS 129 B15
Lyaskovets BG 166 C5
Lyavoshki BY 133 E2
Lybokhora UA 145 F6
Lybster GB 3 J10
Lychen D 84 D4
Lycksaberg S 107 A14
Lycksele S 107 B15
Lydd GB 15 F10
Lydersley DK 87 E10
Lydford GB 12 D6
Lydney GB 13 B9
Lyeninski BY 141 F10
Lyfjord N 111 A16
Lygna N 95 B13
Lygumai LT 134 D7
Lykofi GR 171 B10
Lykoporia GR 175 C6
Lyly FIN 127 B11
Lylykylä FIN 121 E11
Lyman UA 155 B5
Lymans'ke UA 154 D5
Lymans'ke UA 155 C2
Lyme Regis GB 13 D9
Lymington GB 13 D11
Lymm GB 10 E7
Lynäs S 103 D12
Lyndhurst GB 13 D11
Lyne DK 86 D3
Lyneham GB 13 B11
Lynemore GB 3 L9
Lyness GB 3 H10
Lyngby DK 87 C7
Lyngdal N 94 F6
Lyngmoen N 112 D5
Lyngså DK 86 A7
Lyngseidet N 111 A19
Lyngsnes N 105 B10
Lynmouth GB 13 C7
Lynton GB 13 C7
Lyntupy BY 137 C13
Lyökki FIN 126 D5
Lyon F 30 D6
Lyons-la-Forêt F 18 F3
Lyrestad S 91 B15
Lyrkeia GR 175 D6
Lysabild DK 86 F6
Lysá pod Makytou SK 146 C6
Lyse PL 139 D12
Lysebotn N 94 D5
Lysekil S 91 C9
Lyshchytsy BY 141 F9
Lysice CZ 77 D11
Lysnes N 111 B14
Łysomice PL 138 D6
Lysøysund N 104 D7
Lysroll N 111 D11
Lyss CH 31 A11
Lysvik S 97 B9
Łyszkowice PL 141 G1
Lytchett Minster GB 13 D10
Lytham St Anne's GB 10 D5
Lytovezh UA 144 B9
Lyubashivka UA 154 B6
Lyuben BG 165 E10
Lyubimets BG 166 F6
Lyublino RUS 136 D1
Lyubomyrka UA 154 B4
Lyubyntsi UA 145 E8
Lyulyakovo BG 167 D8

M

Maakeski FIN 127 C13
Maalahti FIN 122 E7
Maalismaa FIN 119 D15
Maam IRL 6 E3
Maaninka FIN 124 D8
Maaninkavaara FIN 115 F4
Maanselkä FIN 125 C10
Maaralanpera FIN 123 C16
Maardu EST 131 B10
Maarheeze NL 183 C7
Maaria FIN 126 D7
Maarianvaara FIN 125 E11
Maarn NL 183 A6
Maarssen NL 16 D4
Maarssenbroek NL 183 A6
Maas IRL 6 C6
Maasbracht NL 19 B12
Maasbree NL 16 F6
Maasdam NL 182 B5
Maaseik B 19 B12
Maaselkä FIN 121 F14
Maasen D 17 C11
Maasland NL 16 E2
Maasmechelen B 19 C12
Maassluis NL 16 E2
Maastricht NL 19 C12
Määttälä FIN 123 C12
Määttälänvaara FIN 121 B14
Maavesi FIN 124 F9
Mablethorpe GB 11 E12
Macael E 55 E8
Maçanet de Cabrenys E 34 F4
Maçanet de la Selva E 43 D9
Mação P 44 E5
Măcărești MD 153 C11
Macastre E 48 F3
Maccagno I 68 A6
Macchiagodena I 63 D6
Macclesfield GB 11 E7
Macduff GB 3 K12
Macea RO 151 E7
Maceda E 38 D4
Maceda P 44 C3
Macedo de Cavaleiros P 39 E6
Maceira P 44 C6
Maceira P 44 E3
Macelj HR 148 D5
Macerata I 67 F7
Macerata Feltria I 66 E5
Măceșu de Jos RO 160 F3
Măceșu de Sus RO 160 F3
Machados P 50 C5
Machairas GR 174 B3
Machault F 19 F10
Machecoul F 28 B2
Machelen B 182 D4
Machen GB 13 B8
Machern D 79 D12
Machliny PL 85 D10
Machov CZ 77 A10
Machowa PL 143 F11
Machrihanish GB 4 E5
Machynlleth GB 10 F4
Maciejowice PL 141 G5
Măcin RO 155 C2
Macinaggio F 37 F10
Măciuca RO 160 D4
Mačkatica SRB 164 D5
Mackenbach D 21 F9
Mackenrode D 79 C8
Mačkovci SLO 148 C6
Macomer I 64 C2
Mâcon F 30 C6
Macosquin GB 4 E3
Macotera E 45 C10
Macroom IRL 8 E5
Macugnaga I 68 B4
Mačvanska Mitrovica SRB 158 D4
Mačvanski Pričinović SRB 158 D4
Mád H 145 G3
Madan BG 165 B7
Madan BG 171 A7
Mădan S 103 A15
Madängsholm S 91 C14
Madara BG 167 C8
Madaras H 150 E3
Mădăraș RO 151 D8
Mădărjac RO 153 C10
Maddalena Spiaggia I 64 E3
Maddaloni I 60 A2
Made NL 16 E3
Madekoski FIN 119 E15
Madeley GB 10 F7
Mäder A 71 C9
Madetkoski FIN 115 C1
Madiran F 32 C5
Madley GB 13 A9
Madliena LV 135 C10
Madocsa H 150 D2
Madona LV 135 C12
Madonna di Campiglio I 69 A10
Madrid E 46 D5
Madridejos E 46 F5
Madrigal de las Altas Torres E 45 B11
Madrigal de la Vera E 45 D10
Madrigal del Monte E 40 D4
Madrigalejo E 45 F9
Madrigueras E 47 F9
Madroñera E 45 F9
Mădulari RO 160 D4
Madzharovo BG 171 A9
Mæl N 95 C9
Maël-Carhaix F 22 D5
Maella E 42 E4
Maello E 46 C3
Maenclochog GB 12 B5
Maenza I 62 D4
Mære N 105 D10
Măeriște RO 151 C10
Mäetaguse EST 131 C14
Maeztu E 41 C7
Mafra P 50 B1
Magacela E 51 B8
Magallón E 41 E9
Magaluf E 49 E10
Magaña E 41 E7
Magašici BIH 158 E3
Magaz E 40 E3
Magdala D 79 E9
Magdeburg D 79 B10
Magdeburgerforth D 79 B11
Magenta I 69 C6
Magescq F 32 C3
Măgești RO 151 C9
Maggia CH 68 A6
Maghera GB 4 F3
Magherafelt GB 4 F3
Magheralin GB 7 D10
Măgherani RO 152 D5
Maghery GB 7 C9
Maghull GB 10 D6
Magione I 66 F5
Măgiotsa EST 132 E1
Măgirești RO 153 D9
Magisano I 59 A10
Maglaj BIH 157 C9
Magland F 31 C10
Maglavit RO 159 E11
Magliano de'Marsi I 62 C4
Magliano in Toscana I 65 B4
Magliano Sabina I 62 C2
Magliĉ SRB 158 F6
Maglie I 61 C10
Maglód H 150 C3
Magnac-Laval F 29 C8
Magné F 28 C4
Magnières F 26 D6
Magnor N 96 C7
Magnuszew PL 141 G4
Magny-Cours F 30 B3
Magny-en-Vexin F 24 B6
Mágocs H 149 D10
Magoula GR 174 E5
Magstrup DK 86 E4
Magueija P 44 B5
Maguilla E 51 C8
Maguiresbridge GB 7 D8
Măgura RO 153 D9
Măgura RO 160 E6
Măgura Ilvei RO 152 C5
Măgurele RO 164 D3
Măgurele RO 161 C8
Măgurele RO 161 E8
Măgureni RO 161 C7
Măguri-Răcătău RO 151 D11
Magy H 145 H4
Magyaralmás H 149 B10
Magyaratád H 149 D9
Magyarbánhegyes H 151 E6
Magyarbóly H 149 E10
Magyaregregy H 149 D10
Magyarhomorog H 151 C8
Magyarkeszi H 149 C10
Magyarnándor H 147 F8
Magyarpolány H 149 B9
Magyarszék H 149 D10
Mahala UA 153 A8
Maheriv UA 144 C8
Mahíde E 39 E7
Mahlberg D 186 E4
Mahlsdorf D 83 E10
Mahlu FIN 123 E14
Mahlwinkel D 79 B10
Mahmudia RO 155 C4
Mahmudiye TR 171 E10
Mahmutköy TR 173 C6
Mahón E 57 B13
Mahora E 47 F9
Mahovo HR 149 E6
Mähring D 75 C12
Mahtra EST 131 C10
Maia P 44 B3
Maials E 42 E5
Măicănești RO 161 C10
Maîche F 27 F6
Maida I 59 B9
Maiden Bradley GB 13 C10
Maidenhead GB 15 D7
Maiden Newton GB 13 D9
Maidens GB 4 E7
Maidstone GB 15 E10
Maienfeld CH 71 C9
Maierato I 59 B9
Maierhöfen D 71 B10
Maieru RO 152 C5
Măieruș RO 153 F7
Maigh Chromtha IRL 8 E5
Maigh Cuilinn IRL 6 F4
Maiglean Rátha IRL 7 F8
Maignelay-Montigny F 18 E6
Maijanen FIN 117 D14
Maikammer D 186 C5
Maillas F 32 B5
Maillebois F 24 C5
Maillezais F 28 C4
Mailly-le-Camp F 25 C11
Mailly-le-Château F 25 E10
Mailly-Maillet F 18 D6
Mailovac SRB 159 D7
Mainaschaff D 187 B7
Mainbernheim D 75 C7
Mainburg D 75 E10
Mainham IRL 7 F9
Mainhardt D 74 D6
Mainiemi FIN 127 B16
Mainistir Eimhín IRL 7 F8
Mainistir Fhear Maí IRL 8 D6
Mainistir Laoise IRL 9 C8
Mainistir na Búille IRL 6 E6
Mainistir na Corann IRL 8 E6
Mainistir na Feile IRL 8 D4
Männikkö S 116 D8
Mainsat F 29 C10
Maintenon F 24 C6
Mainua FIN 121 F9
Mainvilliers F 24 D5
Mainz D 21 D10
Maiolati Spontini I 67 F7
Maiorca P 44 D3
Maiorga P 44 E3
Mairena del Alcor E 51 E8
Maisach D 75 F9
Maishofen A 73 B6
Maišiagala LT 137 D11
Maissau A 77 E9
Maisse F 25 D7
Maissin B 184 E3
Maivala FIN 121 B14
Maizières-lès-Metz F 186 C1
Majadahonda E 46 D5
Majadas de Tiétar E 45 E9
Majava FIN 121 C12
Majavatn N 105 A14
Majdan BIH 157 D7
Majdan Królewski PL 144 C4
Majdan Niepryski PL 144 C7
Majdanpek SRB 159 E8
Majovakylä FIN 119 C17
Majs H 149 E11
Majšperk SLO 148 D5
Majtum S 109 D18
Makád H 149 B11
Makarove UA 145 G6
Makarove UA 154 C6
Makarska HR 157 F7
Mäkelänranta FIN 121 E13
Makhnovka RUS 133 B6
Mäkikylä FIN 123 E12
Makkola FIN 125 G11
Makkoshotyka H 145 G4
Makkum NL 16 B4
Maklár H 147 F10
Makljenovac BIH 157 C9
Makó H 150 E5
Makoc RKS 164 D3
Mākoņkalns LV 133 D2
Mąkoszyce PL 142 E4
Makov SK 147 C7
Maków PL 141 G2
Maków PL 141 H4
Mąkowarsko PL 138 D4
Maków Mazowiecki PL 139 E11
Maków Podhalański PL 147 B9
Makrakomi GR 174 B5
Makresh BG 159 F10
Makri GR 171 C9
Makrisia GR 174 D4
Makrochori GR 169 C7
Makrychori GR 169 E7
Makrygialos GR 169 D8
Makrygialos GR 179 E10
Makrynitsa GR 169 F8
Makryrrachi GR 174 A5
Maksamaa FIN 122 D8
Maksniemi FIN 119 C13
Maksymilianowo PL 138 D5
Malá E 53 B9
Mala IRL 8 D5
Mala S 87 C13
Malå S 107 A15
Mala Bosna SRB 150 E4
Mala Čista HR 156 E4
Malacky SK 77 F12
Málaga E 53 C8
Malagón E 46 F5
Malahide IRL 7 F10
Malahviānvaara FIN 121 E14
Malaia RO 160 C4
Mălăiești MD 154 D5
Málainn Bhig IRL 6 C5
Málainn Mhóir IRL 6 C5
Mala Kladuša BIH 156 B4
Malalbergo I 66 C4
Malá Lehota SK 147 D7
Malamocco I 66 B5
Malancourt F 19 F11
Malandrino GR 174 C5
Malangen N 111 B16
Malangseidet N 111 B16
Malanów PL 142 C5
Malansac F 23 E7
Malaryta BY 141 G10
Mäläskä FIN 119 F16
Mala Subotica HR 149 D7
Malaucène F 35 B9
Malaunay F 18 E3
Malaussanne F 32 C5
Malåvaara FIN 115 E4
Malåvännäs S 107 A14
Mała Wieś PL 139 F9
Malax FIN 122 E7
Malaya Byerastavitsa BY 140 D9
Malbekkvatn N 114 E7
Malbork PL 138 B7
Malborn D 21 E7
Malbouzon F 30 F3
Malbuisson F 31 B9
Malcesine I 69 B10
Malchin D 83 C13
Malchow D 83 D12
Malcocinado E 51 C8
Malcov SK 145 E3
Malczyce PL 81 D10
Măldăeni RO 160 E5
Măldărești RO 160 C4
Maldegem B 19 B7
Malden NL 16 E5
Maldon GB 15 D10
Małdyty PL 139 C8
Malè I 71 E11
Malechowo PL 85 B11
Malejàn E 41 E8
Maleme GR 178 D6
Malemort-du-Comtat F 35 B9
Malemort-sur-Corrèze F 29 E9
Malente D 83 B9
Målerås S 89 B9
Males GR 179 E10
Malesco I 68 A6
Malesherbes F 25 D7
Malesina GR 175 B7
Malestroit F 23 E7
Maletto I 59 D6
Malevo BG 166 F5
Malexander S 92 C6
Malfa I 59 B6
Malgersdorf D 75 E12
Malgovik S 107 B10
Malgrat de Mar E 43 D9
Malhadas P 39 E7
Malia GR 178 E9
Malicorne-sur-Sarthe F 23 E11
Maliena LV 133 B2
Mali Iđoš SRB 158 B4
Malijai F 36 C4
Målilla S 92 E7
Mali Lošinj HR 67 C9
Mali Mokryany UA 144 D7
Malin IRL 4 E2
Malin Beg IRL 6 C5
Mălinec SK 147 D9
Malines B 19 B9
Malines B 182 C4
Mălini RO 153 C8
Malin More IRL 6 C5
Malinovka LV 135 E13
Malinska HR 67 B10
Maliq AL 168 C4
Malishevë RKS 163 E10
Maliskylä FIN 123 C14
Malissard F 30 F6
Maliuc RO 155 C4
Mali Zvornik SRB 157 D11
Maljasalmi FIN 125 E11
Malkara TR 173 C6
Małkinia Górna PL 139 E13
Malko Gradishte BG 166 F5
Malko Tŭrnovo BG 167 F9
Mallaig GB 4 A5
Mållångsbo S 103 D10
Mallén E 41 E9
Mallentin D 83 C10
Mallersdorf D 75 E11
Malles Venosta I 71 D11
Mallica TR 173 F7
Malling DK 86 C6
Malliß D 83 D10
Mallnitz A 73 C7
Mallow IRL 8 D5
Mallusjoki FIN 127 D14
Mallwyd GB 10 F4
Malm N 105 C10
Malmån S 107 E12
Malmbäck S 92 D4
Malmberget S 116 D5
Malmby S 98 D8
Malmédy B 20 D6
Malmein N 94 E4
Malmesbury GB 13 B10
Malmköping S 93 A9
Malmö S 87 D12
Malmslätt S 92 C7
Malnaș RO 153 E7
Malnate I 69 B6
Malnava LV 133 C3
Malnes N 110 C8
Malo I 69 B11
Malo Crniće SRB 159 D7
Małogoszcz PL 143 E9
Malo Konare BG 165 E9
Małomice PL 81 C8
Malomir BG 167 E7
Malomozhayskoye RUS 136 D5
Malón E 41 E8
Malona GR 181 D8
Malonno I 69 A9
Malonty CZ 77 E7
Malorad BG 165 C8
Malošište SRB 164 C4
Malo Titavo BIH 156 D5
Malovăț RO 159 D10
Måløy N 100 C2
Maloye-Lugovoye RUS 136 D2
Maloye Sitna BY 133 E6
Malpartida P 45 C7
Malpartida de Cáceres E 45 F8
Malpartida de la Serena E 51 B8
Malpartida de Plasencia E 45 E8
Malpas GB 10 E6
Malpica E 38 B2
Malpica de Tajo E 46 E3
Malpica do Tejo P 44 E6
Målpils LV 135 B9
Malsch D 27 C9
Målselv N 111 B16
Malsfeld D 78 D6
Malšice CZ 77 D7
Målsnes N 111 B16
Målsryd S 91 D13
Målsta S 106 E7
Malta A 73 C8
Malta LV 133 D2
Malta P 45 C6
Maltas Trūpi LV 135 D13
Maltby GB 11 E9
Maltby le Marsh GB 11 E12
Maltepe TR 173 D7
Malterdingen D 27 D8
Malters CH 70 C6
Malton GB 11 C10
Malu cu Flori RO 160 C6
Maluenda E 41 F8
Malŭk Izvor BG 166 F5
Malu Mare RO 160 E3
Malung S 102 E6
Malungsfors S 102 E6
Mălupe LV 133 B2
Mălureni RO 160 C5
Mălușteni RO 153 E11
Małuszów PL 81 B8
Maluszyn PL 143 E8
Malva E 39 E9
Malvaglia CH 71 E7
Malveira P 50 B1
Malvik N 105 E9
Malý Horeš SK 145 G4
Mályi H 145 G2
Mały Płock PL 139 D13
Malý Šariš SK 145 E3
Malyy Bereznyy UA 145 F5
Mamaia RO 155 E3
Mamarchevo BG 167 E7
Mamarrosa P 44 D3
Mambrilla de Castejón E 40 E4
Mamer L 20 E6
Mamers F 24 D3
Mamići BIH 157 F8
Mamirolle F 26 F5
Mammaste EST 131 E14
Mammendorf D 75 F9
Mammola I 59 C9
Mamoiada I 64 C3
Mamone I 64 B3
Mamonovo RUS 139 B8
Mamuras AL 168 A2
Mamushë RKS 163 E10
Mana MD 154 C3
Maňa SK 146 E6
Manacor E 57 B11
Manage B 19 D9
Manamansalo FIN 120 F9
Mañaria E 41 B6
Mänäs S 97 A9
Manasia RO 161 D9
Manasterz PL 144 D5
Manastir BG 165 F10
Mănăstirea RO 161 E9
Mănăstirea Cașin RO 153 E9
Mănăstirea Humorului RO 153 B7
Manastirica SRB 159 D7
Manastirsko BG 167 C7
Mănăștiur RO 151 F9
Mancera de Abajo E 45 C10
Mancha Real E 53 A9
Manchester GB 11 E7
Manching D 75 E9
Manchita E 51 B7
Manciano I 65 B5
Manciet F 33 C6
Mandal N 90 C1
Mandalen N 100 A6
Mandalo GR 169 C7
Mandas I 64 D3
Mandatoriccio I 61 E7
Mandayona E 47 C7
Mandelbachtal-Ormesheim D 186 C3
Mandelieu-la-Napoule F 36 D5
Mandello del Lario I 69 B7
Manderscheid D 21 D7
Mandeure F 27 F6
Mandino Selo BIH 157 E7
Mándok H 145 G5
Mandra GR 175 C7
Mândra RO 152 F6
Mandraki GR 181 C6
Mandres-en-Barrois F 26 D3
Mandriko GR 181 D7
Mandritsa BG 171 B10
Manduria I 61 C9
Mane F 33 D7
Mane F 35 C10
Manea GB 11 G12
Măneciu RO 161 C7
Manerbio I 66 B1
Mañeru E 32 E2
Mănești RO 160 D6
Mănești RO 161 D7
Manětín CZ 76 C4
Manfredonia I 63 D9
Mangalia RO 155 F3
Manganeses de la Lampreana E 39 E8
Manganeses de la Polvorosa E 39 D8
Mångberg S 102 E8
Mångbyn S 118 F6
Manger N 100 E2
Mangiennes F 19 F12
Mangotsfield GB 13 C9
Mångsbodarna S 102 D6
Mangualde P 44 C5
Manhay B 19 D12
Manhuelles F 26 B4
Mani GR 171 B10
Maniace I 59 D6
Maniago I 73 D6
Maniakoi GR 168 D5
Manieczki PL 81 B11
Manilva E 53 D6
Manisa TR 177 B9
Manises E 48 E4
Manjärvträsk S 118 C4
Manjaur S 107 B16
Mank A 77 F8
Mānkarbo S 99 B8
Mankila FIN 119 E15
Manlay F 25 F11
Manlleu E 43 D8
Manna GR 175 D6
Männamaa EST 130 D5
Mannersdorf an der Rabnitz A 149 B7
Mannheim D 21 F10
Männikuste EST 131 E8
Manningtree GB 15 D11
Manolada GR 174 C3
Manole BG 165 E10
Manoleasa RO 153 B10
Manoppello I 62 C6
Manorbier GB 12 B5
Manorhamilton IRL 6 D6
Manosque F 35 C10
Manowo PL 85 B10
Manresa E 43 D7
Månsåsen S 105 E16
Manschnow D 81 A7
Mansfeld D 79 C9
Mansfield GB 11 E9
Mansfield Woodhouse GB 11 E9
Mansilla E 40 D6
Mansilla de las Mulas E 39 D9
Mansle F 29 D6
Manso F 37 G9
Mansonville F 33 B7
Mansores P 44 C4
Manston GB 13 D10
Månsträsk S 109 E16
Mantamados GR 171 F10
Mantasia GR 174 A5
Manteigas P 44 D5
Mantel D 75 C11
Manternach L 186 B1
Mantes-la-Jolie F 24 C6
Mantes-la-Ville F 24 C6
Manthelan F 24 F4
Mantila FIN 122 F9
Mantoche F 26 F4
Mantorp S 92 C6
Mantoudi GR 175 B7
Mantova I 66 B2
Mäntsälä FIN 127 D13
Mänttä FIN 123 F13
Mäntyharju FIN 128 C6
Mäntyjärvi FIN 117 E14
Mäntyjärvi FIN 121 B10
Mäntylahti FIN 124 D8
Mäntyluoto FIN 126 B5
Mäntyvaara S 116 E7
Manuel E 56 C4
Manulla IRL 6 E4
Mány H 149 A11
Manyas TR 173 D8
Manzac-sur-Vern F 29 E7
Mânzălești RO 161 C9
Manzanal de Arriba E 39 E7
Manzanal del Puerto E 39 C7
Manzanares E 55 A6
Manzanares el Real E 46 C5
Manzaneda E 38 D5
Manzanedo E 40 C4
Manzaneque E 46 E5
Manzanera E 48 D3
Manzanilla E 51 E7
Manzano I 73 E7
Manzat F 30 D2
Manziana I 62 C2
Manziat F 30 C6
Maó E 57 B13
Mäo EST 131 D11
Maoča BIH 157 C10
Maqellarë AL 168 A3
Maqueda E 46 D4
Mar P 38 E2
Mara I 64 C2
Marac F 26 E3
Maracalagonis I 64 E3
Marachkova BY 133 E4
Mărăcineni RO 160 D5
Mărăcineni RO 161 C9
Maradik SRB 158 C5
Maråker S 103 D13
Maranchón E 47 B8
Maranello I 66 C2
Marange-Silvange F 186 C1
Maranhão P 50 A4
Marano I 66 D3
Marano di Napoli I 60 B2
Marano sul Panaro I 66 D2
Marans F 28 C4
Maranville F 25 D12
Mărășești RO 153 F10
Mărașu RO 155 D1
Maratea I 60 D5
Marateca P 50 B2
Marathea GR 169 E6
Marathias GR 174 C5
Marathokampos GR 177 D8
Marathonas GR 175 C8
Marathopoli GR 174 E4
Maraussan F 34 D5
Maraye-en-Othe F 25 D10
Marazion GB 12 E4
Marazliyivka UA 154 E6
Marbach CH 70 D5
Marbach am Neckar D 27 C11
Marbäck S 91 D13
Marbella E 53 C7
Marboz F 31 C7
Marburg an der Lahn D 21 C11
Marby S 105 E16
Marça E 42 E5
Marcali H 149 C8
Marcaltő H 149 B8
Marčana HR 67 C8
Marcaria I 66 B2
Marcăuți MD 153 A10
Marcellina I 62 C3
Marcelová SK 149 A10
Marcenais F 28 E5
Marcenat F 30 E2
March GB 11 F12
Marchamalo E 47 C6
Marchaux F 26 F5
Marche-en-Famenne B 19 D11
Marchegg A 77 F11
Marchena E 51 E9
Marchenoir F 24 E5
Marcheprime F 28 F4
Marchiennes F 19 D7
Marchin B 19 D11
Marchtrenk A 76 F6
Marciac F 33 C6
Marciana I 65 B2
Marciana Marina I 65 B2
Marcianise I 60 A2
Marciano della Chiana I 66 F4
Mărciena LV 135 C12
Marcigny F 30 C5
Marcilhac-sur-Célé F 33 A9
Marcilla E 32 F2
Marcillac F 28 E4
Marcillac-la-Croisille F 29 E10
Marcillac-Vallon F 33 B10
Marcillat-en-Combraille F 29 C11
Marcilly-en-Gault F 24 F6
Marcilly-en-Villette F 24 E7
Marcilly-le-Hayer F 25 D10
Marcilly-sur-Eure F 24 C5
Marcinkonys LT 137 E9
Marcinkowice PL 85 D10
Marcinkowice PL 144 D2
Marcinowice PL 81 E11
Marciszów PL 81 E10
Marck F 18 C4
Marckolsheim F 27 D8
Marco de Canaveses P 44 B4
Marcoing F 19 D7
Marcòn I 66 A5
Marcoux F 36 C4
Marcq-en-Barœul F 19 C7
Mărculești MD 153 B12
Mårdaklev S 87 A11
Mardarivka UA 154 B5
Mardeuil F 25 B10
Mårdsele S 107 B16
Mårdsjö S 106 E9
Mårdsjö S 107 C11
Mårdudden S 118 B6
Marebbe I 72 C4
Marennes F 28 D3
Maresfield GB 15 F9
Mareuil F 29 E6
Mareuil-sur-Arnon F 29 B10
Mareuil-sur-Ay F 25 B11
Mareuil-sur-Lay-Dissais F 28 B3
Marey-sur-Tille F 26 E3
Marga RO 159 B9
Margarites GR 178 E8
Mărgăritești RO 161 C9
Margariti GR 168 F3
Margate GB 15 E11
Mărgău RO 151 D10
Margecany SK 145 F3
Margerie-Hancourt F 25 C12
Margherita di Savoia I 60 A6
Marghita RO 151 C9
Margina RO 151 F9
Marginea RO 153 B7
Mărgineni RO 153 D9
Mărgineni RO 153 D9
Margionys LT 137 F9
Margone I 31 E11
Margonin PL 85 E12
Margraten NL 19 C12
Marguerittes F 35 C7
Margut F 19 E11
Marhaň SK 145 E3
María E 55 D8
Mariac F 30 F5
Mariager DK 86 B5
Maria Lankowitz A 73 B11
Maria Luggau A 73 C6
Marialva P 45 C6
Mariampole LV 133 D2
Mariana E 47 D8
Mariannelund S 92 D7
Mariano Comense I 69 B7
Marianopoli I 58 D4
Marianowo PL 85 D8
Mariánské Lázně CZ 75 C12
Mariapfarr A 73 B8
Maria Saal A 73 C9
Mariazell A 148 A4
Maribo DK 83 A10
Maribor SLO 148 C5
Marieberg S 92 A6
Marieby S 106 E7
Mariefred S 98 D8
Mariehamn FIN 99 B13
Marieholm S 87 D12
Marieholm S 91 E14
Mariemburg B 19 D10
Marienberg D 80 E4
Marienhafe D 17 A8
Marienhagen D 78 B6
Marienheide D 21 B9
Mariental D 79 B8
Mariestad S 91 B14
Marifjøra N 100 D6
Marigliano I 60 B2
Marignana F 37 G9
Marignane F 35 D9
Marigné-Laillé F 24 E3
Marigny F 23 B9
Marigny-le-Châtel F 25 D10
Marijampolė LT 136 D7
Marikaj AL 168 B2
Marikostinovo BG 169 B9
Marín E 38 D2
Marina di Alberese I 65 B4
Marina di Amendolara I 61 D7
Marina di Arbus I 64 D1
Marina di Camerota I 60 C4
Marina di Campo I 65 B2
Marina di Carrara I 69 E9
Marina di Castagneto Donoratico I 66 F2
Marina di Cecina I 66 F1
Marina di Chieuti I 63 D8
Marina di Gioiosa Ionica I 59 C9
Marina di Grosseto I 65 B3
Marina di Leuca I 61 D10
Marina di Massa I 69 E9
Marina di Novaglie I 61 D10

Marina di Palma I 58 E4
Marina di Pulsano I 61 C8
Marina di Ragusa I 59 F6
Marina di Ravenna I 66 C5
Marinaleda E 53 B7
Marina Palmense I 67 F8
Marina Romea I 66 C5
Marina Schiavonea I 61 D7
Marinella I 58 D2
Marineo I 58 D3
Marines E 48 E3
Marines F 24 B6
Maringues F 30 D3
Marinha das Ondas P 44 D3
Marinha Grande P 44 E3
Marinhas P 38 E2
Marinići HR 67 B9
Marinka BG 167 E8
Marinkainen FIN 123 C10
Māriņkalns LV 133 B1
Marino I 62 D3
Mar'insko RUS 132 D4
Mariotto I 61 A7
Mărişelu RO 152 C5
Maritsa GR 181 D8
Marizy F 30 B5
Märja EST 131 E13
Marjaliza E 46 E5
Märjamaa EST 131 D8
Marjaniemi FIN 119 D13
Marjokylä FIN 121 E14
Marjonieemi FIN 127 C14
Marjovaara FIN 125 E15
Marjusaari FIN 123 D12
Mark GB 13 C9
Mark S 107 B10
Markaryd S 87 C13
Markaz H 147 F10
Markby FIN 122 D9
Markdorf D 27 E11
Markebäck S 92 B5
Markelo NL 17 D7
Market Deeping GB 11 F11
Market Drayton GB 10 F7
Market Harborough GB 15 C7
Markethill GB 7 D9
Market Rasen GB 11 E11
Market Warsop GB 11 E9
Market Weighton GB 11 D10
Markgröningen D 27 C11
Markhus N 94 C4
Marki PL 139 F11
Markina-Xemein E 41 B7
Markinch GB 5 C10
Märkisch Buchholz D 80 B5
Markitta S 116 D7
Markivka UA 154 D5
Markkina FIN 116 B8
Markkleeberg D 79 D11
Markkula FIN 123 C12
Marklohe D 17 C12
Marknesse NL 16 C5
Markneukirchen D 75 B11
Markopoulo GR 175 D8
Markovac SRB 159 C7
Markovac SRB 159 E7
Markovac Našički HR 149 E10
Markovac Trojstveni HR 149 E7
Markowa PL 144 C5
Markranstädt D 79 D11
Marksuhl D 79 E7
Markt Allhau A 148 B6
Marktbergel D 75 D7
Markt Berolzheim D 75 D8
Markt Bibart D 75 C7
Marktbreit D 187 B9
Markt Erlbach D 75 D8
Markt Hartmannsdorf A 148 B5
Marktheidenfeld D 74 C6
Markt Indersdorf D 75 F9
Marktjärn S 103 A11
Marktl D 76 F3
Marktleugast D 75 B10
Marktoberdorf D 71 B11
Marktoffingen D 75 E7
Marktredwitz D 75 B11
Markt Rettenbach D 71 B10
Markt Sankt Martin A 149 A6
Markt Schwaben D 75 F10
Marktseft D 75 C7
Markt Wald D 71 A11
Markusevec HR 148 E6
Markušica HR 149 F11
Markušovce SK 145 F2
Markuszów PL 141 H6
Marl D 17 D10
Marl D 17 E8
Marlborough GB 13 C11
Marldon GB 13 E7
Marle F 19 E8
Marlengo I 72 C3
Marlenheim F 27 C8
Marlhes F 30 E5
Marlishausen D 79 E9
Marlow D 83 B13
Marlow GB 15 D7
Marly CH 31 B11
Marly F 19 D8
Marly F 26 B5
Marma S 99 B8
Marmagne F 25 F7
Marmagne F 30 B5
Marmande F 33 A6
Marmara GR 174 B5
Marmara TR 173 C8
Marmaracik TR 173 B8
Marmaraereğlisi TR 173 C8
Marmari GR 175 C9
Marmaris TR 181 C8
Marmaro GR 177 B7
Marmelar P 50 C4
Marmeleira P 44 F3
Marmelete P 50 E2
Marmirolo I 66 B2
Marmolejo E 53 A8
Marmoutier F 27 C7
Marnardal N 90 C2
Marnäs S 103 E10
Marnay F 26 F4
Marne D 82 C6
Marne-la-Vallée F 25 C8
Marnes N 108 B7
Marnheim D 21 E10
Marnitz D 83 D11
Maroldsweisach D 75 B8
Marolles-les-Braults F 23 D12
Maromme F 18 F3
Maroneia GR 171 C9
Maroslele H 150 E5
Marostica I 72 E4
Maroué F 22 D6
Marousi GR 175 C8
Marpingen D 21 F8
Marpissa GR 176 E5
Marple GB 11 E7
Marpod RO 152 F5
Marquartstein D 72 A5
Marquion F 19 D7
Marquise F 15 F12
Marquixanes F 33 E10
Marradi I 66 D4
Marrasjärvi FIN 117 E14
Marraskoski FIN 117 E14
Marrubiu I 64 D2
Marrum NL 16 B5
Mârşa RO 161 E7
Marsac-en-Livradois F 30 E4
Marsac-sur-Don F 23 E8
Marsaglia I 37 B10
Marsal F 26 C6
Marsala I 58 D1
Mârşani RO 160 E4
Marsannay-la-Côte F 26 F2
Marsanne F 35 A8
Marsberg D 17 F11
Marsciano I 62 B2
Marseillan F 35 D6
Marseille F 35 D9
Marseille-en-Beauvaisis F 18 E4
Marsico Nuovo I 60 C5
Marsico Vetere I 60 C5
Marsillargues F 35 C7
Marsjärv S 118 B8
Mårslet DK 86 C6
Mārsnēni LV 135 B11
Marssac-sur-Tarn F 33 C10
Märsta S 99 C9
Marstal DK 83 A9
Märstetten CH 27 E11
Marston GB 13 B12
Marstrand S 91 D10
Marstrup DK 86 E4
Märsylä FIN 123 C11
Marta I 62 B1
Mårtanberg S 103 E9
Martano I 61 C10
Martel F 29 F9
Martelange B 19 E12
Martellago I 66 A5
Martello I 71 D11
Mártély H 150 E5
Marten BG 161 F8
Martfeld D 17 C12
Martfű H 150 C5
Marthon F 29 D6
Martiago E 45 D8
Martignacco I 73 D7
Martigné-Briand F 23 F11
Martigné-Ferchaud F 23 E9
Martigné-sur-Mayenne F 23 D10
Martigny CH 31 C11
Martigny-le-Comte F 30 B5
Martigny-les-Bains F 26 D4
Martigny-les-Gerbonvaux F 26 D4
Martigues F 35 D9
Martiherrero E 46 C3
Martil MA 53 E6
Martim Longo P 50 E4
Martin SK 147 C7
Martina Franca I 61 B8
Martin Brod BIH 156 C5
Martinchel P 44 E4
Martinci SRB 158 C3
Martinci Čepinski HR 149 E10
Martín de la Jara E 53 B7
Martín del Río E 42 F2
Martín de Yeltes E 45 C8
Martinengo I 69 B8
Martineşti RO 151 F11
Martinet E 33 F9
Martinfeld D 79 D7
Martingança P 44 E3
Martiniş RO 152 E6
Martín Muñoz de las Posadas E 46 B3
Martinniemi FIN 119 D14
Martino GR 175 B7
Martinporra E 39 B8
Martinsberg A 77 F8
Martinšćica HR 67 C9
Martinsicuro I 62 B5
Martis I 64 B2
Martizay F 29 B8
Martley GB 13 A10
Martna EST 130 D7
Martock GB 13 D9
Martonvaara FIN 125 D12
Martorell E 43 E7
Martos E 53 A9
Martres-Tolosane F 33 D8
Mårtsbo S 103 E13
Martti FIN 115 D4
Marttila FIN 127 D8
Marttila FIN 127 D13
Marttisenjärvi FIN 124 C7
Marugán E 46 C4
Maruggio I 61 C9
Marum NL 16 B6
Marum S 99 C12
Mărunţei RO 160 E4
Mārupe LV 135 C8
Maruszów PL 143 D12
Maruszów PL 144 B4
Marvão P 44 F6
Marvejols F 34 A5
Marville F 19 F11
Marxheim D 75 E8
Marxzell D 27 C9
Märy FIN 127 E9
Mar''yanivka UA 154 C6
Marykirk GB 5 B11
Marynychi UA 152 A6
Marypark GB 3 L10
Maryport GB 5 F10
Marywell GB 5 A11
Marzabotto I 66 D3
Marzahna D 79 B12
Marzahne D 79 A12
Marzamemi I 59 F7
Marzan F 23 E7
Mărzăneşti RO 161 F6
Marzling D 75 F10
Masa E 40 C4
Masainas I 64 E2
Masalavés E 48 F3
Masari GR 181 D8
Mas-Cabardès F 33 D10
Mascali I 59 D7
Mascalucia I 59 D7
Mascaraque E 46 E5
Mascarenhas P 38 E5
Maschito I 60 B5
Masclat F 29 F8
Mas de Barberans E 42 F4
Mas de las Matas E 42 F3
Masegosa E 47 C8
Masegoso E 55 B8
Masegoso de Tajuña E 47 C7
Maselheim D 71 A9
Masera I 68 A5
Maserada sul Piave I 72 E5
Masevaux F 27 E6
Masfjorden N 100 E2
Masham GB 11 C8
Masi N 113 E12
Maside E 38 D3
Masi Torello I 66 C4
Maskalyanyaty BY 133 E7
Maskaur S 109 E14
Masku FIN 126 D7
Maslenika HR 156 D4
Maslinica HR 156 F5
Masłoc RO 151 F7
Maslovare BIH 157 C8
Masłowice PL 143 D8
Masone I 37 B9
Masquefa E 43 E7
Massa I 69 E9
Massa Fiscaglia I 66 C5
Massafra I 61 B8
Massa Lombarda I 66 D4
Massa Lubrense I 60 B2
Massamagrell E 48 E4
Massa Marittimo I 65 A3
Massa Martana I 62 B3
Massarosa I 66 E1
Massat F 33 E8
Massay F 24 F6
Maßbach D 75 B7
Masseret F 29 D9
Masseube F 33 D7
Massford GB 7 D10
Massiac F 30 E3
Massiaru EST 131 F9
Massimino I 37 C8
Massing D 75 F12
Mas-St-Chély F 34 B5
Măstăcani RO 155 B2
Mastershausen D 185 D7
Masterud N 96 B7
Mastichari GR 177 F9
Mastrevik N 100 E1
Masua I 64 E1
Masugnsbyn S 116 D8
Masullas I 64 D2
Måsvik N 112 D2
Masyevichy BY 141 G9
Maszewo PL 81 B7
Maszewo PL 85 B13
Maszewo PL 85 D8
Maszewo Duże PL 139 E8
Matabuena E 46 B5
Matadepera E 43 D8
Mataguži MNE 163 E7
Matala FIN 119 C14
Matala GR 178 F8
Matalalahti FIN 124 C8
Matalascañas E 51 E6
Matalebreras E 41 E7
Matallana de Valmadrigal E 39 D9
Matamala de Almazán E 41 E6
Matamorosa E 40 C3
Mataporquera E 40 C3
Matapozuelos E 39 F10
Matara FIN 125 D12
Mataragka GR 169 F7
Mataragka GR 174 B3
Mataraselkä FIN 117 C17
Mataró E 43 D8
Mataruge MNE 163 C7
Mataruška Banja SRB 158 F6
Mătăsari RO 159 D11
Mătăsaru RO 161 D6
Mätäsvaara FIN 125 D13
Matca RO 153 F11
Mateeşti RO 160 C3
Matei RO 152 D4
Matelica I 67 F7
Matera I 61 B7
Materija SLO 73 E9
Mateševo MNE 163 D8
Mátészalka H 145 H5
Mateuţi MD 154 B3
Matfors S 103 B13
Matha F 28 D5
Mathay F 27 F6
Mathi I 68 C4
Matignon F 23 C7
Matigny F 18 E7
Matilda FIN 127 E8
Matinlompolo FIN 117 E12
Matino I 61 C10
Matīši LV 131 F10
Matkaniva FIN 119 F14
Matkavaara FIN 121 E12
Matku FIN 127 D10
Matkule LV 134 C5
Matlock GB 11 E8
Matosinhos P 44 B3
Matour F 30 C5
Mátraballa H 147 F10
Mátraderecske H 147 F10
Mátramindszent H 147 F9
Matrand N 96 B7
Mátraszele H 147 E9
Mátraszőlős H 147 F9
Mátraterenye H 147 E9
Mátraverebély H 147 F9
Matre N 94 C3
Matre N 100 E3
Matrei am Brenner A 72 B3
Matrei in Osttirol A 72 B6
Matsdal S 109 F10
Matsouki GR 174 B3
Matt CH 71 D8
Mattaincourt F 26 D5
Mattersburg A 149 A6
Mattighofen A 76 F4
Mattila S 119 C12
Mattilanmäki FIN 115 E4
Mattinata I 63 D10
Mattinen FIN 119 B13
Mattisudden S 116 E3
Mattmar S 105 E15
Mattsmyra S 103 D9
Måttsund S 118 C7
Matuizos LT 137 E10
Matulji HR 67 B9
Matúškovo SK 146 E5
Matyryna BY 133 F5
Maubert-Fontaine F 19 E9
Maubeuge F 19 D8
Maubourguet F 32 D6
Maubuisson F 28 E3
Mauchline GB 5 D8
Maud GB 3 K12
Mauerbach A 77 F10
Mauerkirchen A 76 F4
Mauerstetten D 71 B11
Maughold GBM 10 C3
Mauguio F 35 C7
Maukkula FIN 125 E15
Maula FIN 119 C13
Maulbronn D 27 C10
Mauléon F 28 B4
Mauléon-Barousse F 33 E7
Mauléon-d'Armagnac F 32 C5
Mauléon-Licharre F 32 D4
Maulévrier F 28 A4
Maum IRL 6 E3
Mauna FIN 116 B8
Maunu S 116 B8
Maunujärvi FIN 117 D14
Maunula FIN 119 D15
Maura N 95 B13
Maure-de-Bretagne F 23 E8
Maureillas-las-Illas F 34 F4
Măureni RO 159 C8
Maurens F 29 F6
Mauriac F 28 F5
Mauriac F 29 E10
Mauricemills IRL 8 C4
Maurik NL 183 B6
Maurnes N 110 C9
Mauron F 23 D7
Mauroux F 33 B8
Maurs F 29 F10
Maurset N 94 B6
Maurstad N 100 C2
Mauru FIN 119 B15
Maury F 34 E4
Mautern an der Donau A 77 F9
Mauterndorf A 73 B8
Mautern in Steiermark A 73 B10
Mauth D 76 E5
Mauthausen A 77 F7
Mauthen A 73 C7
Mauves F 30 E6
Mauvezin F 33 C7
Mauvoisin CH 31 C11
Mauzé-sur-le-Mignon F 28 C4
Mavranaioi GR 168 D5
Mavrochori GR 168 C5
Mavrodendri GR 169 D6
Mavrodin RO 160 E6
Mavrokklisi GR 171 B10
Mavromati GR 174 E4
Mavrommati GR 169 F6
Mavrommati GR 175 C7
Mavrothalassa GR 169 C10
Mavrovë AL 168 D2
Mavrovo NMK 163 F10
Mavrovouni GR 169 C7
Mavrovouni GR 169 E7
Maxent F 23 E7
Maxéville F 186 D1
Maxial P 44 F2
Maxieira P 44 E5
Măxineni RO 161 C11
Maxmo FIN 122 D8
Maxsain D 185 C8
Mayakovskoye RUS 136 D5
Maybole GB 4 E7
Maydan UA 145 F7
Mayen D 21 D8
Mayenne F 23 D10
Mayet F 23 E12
Mayfield GB 15 E9
Mayobridge GB 7 D10
Mayorga E 39 D9
Mäyränperä FIN 119 F14
Mayres F 35 A7
Mayrhofen A 72 B4
Mäyry FIN 123 E10
Mayschoss D 21 C8
May's Corner GB 7 D10
Máza H 149 D10
Mazagón E 51 E6
Mazagran F 19 F10
Mažaičiai LT 134 F3
Mazaleón E 42 E4
Mazamet F 33 D10
Mazan F 35 B9
Mazara del Vallo I 58 D2
Mazarakia GR 168 F3
Mazarambroz E 46 E4
Mazarete E 47 C8
Mazarrón E 56 F2
Mazé F 23 F11
Mažeikiai LT 134 D4
Mažeiniai LT 135 E8
Mazères F 33 D9
Mazerolles F 32 D5
Mazeyrolles F 33 A8
Mazi TR 181 B7
Mazières-en-Gâtine F 28 B5
Mazirbe LV 130 F4
Mažonai LT 134 F4
Mazsalaca LV 131 F10
Mažučište NMK 169 B5
Mazzano I 66 A1
Mazzano Romano I 62 C2
Mazzarino I 58 E5
Mazzarrone I 59 E6
Mazzo di Valtellina I 69 A9
Mborje AL 168 C4
Mbrostar AL 168 C2
Mdiq MA 53 E6
Meadela P 38 E2
Mealhada P 44 D4
Mealsgate GB 5 F10
Meana Sardo I 64 D3
Meare GB 13 C9
Measham GB 11 F8
Meåstrand S 107 E11
Meaulne F 29 B11
Méaulte F 18 E6
Meaux F 25 C8
Meauzac F 33 B8
Mechelen B 19 B9
Mechelen NL 183 D7
Mechernich D 21 C7
Mechowo PL 85 C8
Mechterstädt D 79 E8
Mecidiye TR 172 C6
Mecidiye TR 173 C10
Mecidiye TR 177 B10
Měčín CZ 76 D4
Mecina-Bombarón E 55 F6
Mjcinka PL 81 D10
Meckenbeuren D 71 B9
Meckenheim D 21 C8
Meckesheim D 187 C6
Meco E 46 C6
Mecseknádasd H 149 D10
Meda P 45 C6
Međa SRB 159 B6
Medåker S 97 D14
Međas BIH 157 D10
Meddersheim D 21 E9
Meddo NL 183 A9
Mede I 68 C6
Medebach D 21 B11
Međeđa BIH 158 F3
Medeikiai LT 135 D9
Medelås S 107 B14
Medelim P 45 D6
Medellín E 51 B8
Medemblik NL 16 C4
Medena-Selišta BIH 157 D6
Medeno Polje BIH 156 C5
Medenychi UA 145 E8
Međeš BIH 158 D3
Medesano I 66 C1
Medgidia RO 155 E2
Medgyesbodzás H 151 D6
Medgyesegyháza H 151 E7
Medhamn S 91 A14
Mediana E 41 F10
Mediaş RO 152 E4
Medicina I 66 D4
Medieşu Aurit RO 151 B11
Medinaceli E 47 B8
Medina de las Torres E 51 C7
Medina del Campo E 39 F10
Medina de Pomar E 40 C5
Medina de Rioseco E 39 E9
Medina-Sidonia E 52 D5
Medingėnai LT 134 E4
Medinilla E 45 D9
Medininkai LT 137 D12
Mediona E 43 E7
Médis F 28 D4
Medkovets BG 159 F11
Medle S 118 E5
Medlov CZ 77 C12
Medneva LV 133 B3
Medolla I 66 C3
Medousa GR 171 B8
Medovoye RUS 136 D1
Mjdrzechów PL 143 F10
Medsēdžiai LT 134 D3
Medskog S 103 E12
Medstugan S 105 D12
Međugorje BIH 157 F8
Međuhana SRB 164 C3
Medulin HR 67 C8
Međumajdan HR 156 B5
Medumi LV 135 E12
Meduno I 73 D6
Međureče SRB 163 B9
Međuvođe BIH 157 B6
Medveđa SRB 159 E7
Medveđa SRB 159 F7
Medveđa SRB 164 D4
Medviđa HR 156 D4
Medvode SLO 73 D9
Medyka PL 144 D6
Medze LV 134 C2
Medzev SK 145 F2
Medzibrod SK 147 D8
Medzilaborce SK 145 E4
Meenaclady IRL 6 B6
Meenavean IRL 6 C5
Meer B 182 C5
Meerane D 79 E11
Meerapalu EST 132 E1
Meerbeck D 17 D12
Meerbusch D 17 F7
Meerhout B 183 C6
Meerkerk NL 182 B5
Meerle B 182 C5
Meerlo NL 183 B8
Meersburg D 27 E11
Meerssen NL 19 C12
Meetkerke B 182 C2
Meeuwen B 19 B12
Mefjordvær N 111 A13
Mega Dereio GR 171 B10
Megala Kalyvia GR 169 F6
Megali Panagia GR 169 D10
Megali Volvi GR 169 C9
Megalochori GR 169 E6
Megalo Chorio GR 174 B4
Megalo Chorio GR 181 D6
Megalo Livadi GR 175 E9
Megalopoli GR 174 E5
Megara GR 175 C7
Megardsaætra N 105 C13
Megen NL 183 B7
Megève F 31 D10
Megyaszó H 145 G3
Mehadia RO 159 D9
Mehadica RO 159 C9
Mehamn N 113 A20
Mehedeby S 99 B8
Mehikoorma EST 132 E1
Méhkerék H 151 D7
Mehren D 21 D7
Mehring D 21 E7
Mehrstetten D 74 F6
Mehtäkylä FIN 119 F12
Mehun-sur-Yèvre F 25 F7
Meidrim GB 12 B6
Meigh GB 7 D10
Meigle GB 5 B10
Meijel NL 16 F5
Meikleour GB 5 B10
Meilen CH 27 F10
Meilhan F 32 C4
Meillac F 23 D8
Meillant F 29 B10
Meillerie F 31 C10
Meimoa P 45 D6
Meina I 68 B6
Meine D 79 B8
Meinersen D 79 B7
Meinerzhagen D 185 B8
Meiningen D 79 E7
Meira E 38 B5
Meiringen CH 70 D6
Meisdorf D 79 C9
Meise B 182 D4
Meisenheim D 21 E9
Meißen D 80 D4
Meißenheim D 186 E4
Meitingen D 75 E8
Meix-devant-Virton B 19 E11
Mejlby DK 86 C6
Mejorada E 46 D3
Mejorada del Campo E 46 D6
Mejrup DK 86 C3
Meka Gruda BIH 157 F9
Mekinje SLO 73 D10
Mel I 72 D5
Melalahti FIN 121 F10
Melampes GR 178 E8
Melanthi GR 168 D5
Melay F 23 F10
Melay F 26 E4
Melazzo I 37 B8
Melbå N 111 C11
Melbourn GB 15 C9
Melbu N 110 C8
Melby GB 3 E13
Melchow D 84 E5
Meldal N 104 E7
Meldola I 66 D5
Meldorf D 82 B6
Mele I 37 C9
Melegnano I 69 C7
Melenci SRB 158 B5
Melendugno I 61 C10
Melfi I 60 B5
Melfjordbotn N 108 C6
Melgaço P 38 D3
Melgar de Arriba E 39 D9
Melgar de Fernamental E 40 D3
Melgar de Tera E 39 E7
Melgven F 22 E4
Melhus N 104 E8
Melia GR 169 E8
Meliana E 48 E4
Melick NL 20 B6
Melicucco I 59 C9
Mélida E 32 F2
Melide E 38 C4
Melides P 50 C2
Meligalas GR 174 E4
Meliki GR 169 C7
Melilli I 59 E7
Melineşti RO 160 D3
Mélisey F 26 E6
Meliskerke NL 182 B3
Melissa GR 171 B7
Melissa I 61 E8
Melissano I 61 D10
Melissochori GR 175 C7
Melissopetra GR 168 D4
Melitaia GR 174 A5
Meliti GR 169 C6
Melito di Porto Salvo I 59 D8
Melivoia GR 169 E8
Melivoia GR 171 B7
Melk A 77 F8
Melkadalen N 111 D12
Melkefoss N 114 E7
Melksham GB 13 C10
Mellac F 22 E4
Mellajärvi FIN 119 B13
Mellakoski FIN 119 B12
Mellanfjärden S 103 C13
Mellansel S 107 E14
Mellansjö S 103 B10
Mellanström S 109 E15
Mellau A 71 C9
Mellbystrand S 87 B11
Melle B 19 B8
Melle D 17 D10
Melle F 28 C5
Mellen D 83 D11
Mellenbach-Glasbach D 79 E9
Mellendorf (Wedemark) D 78 A6
Mellensee D 80 B4
Mellerud S 91 B11
Mellerup DK 86 B6
Mellgård S 103 A9
Mellilä FIN 127 D8
Mellin D 79 A8
Mellingen D 79 E9
Mellösa S 93 A9
Mellrichstadt D 75 B7
Melmerby GB 5 F11
Melnbārži LV 135 B11
Melnica SRB 159 E7
Melnik BG 169 A9
Mělník CZ 77 B6
Mel'nikovo RUS 129 D12
Melnitsa BG 167 E7
Melnsils LV 130 F5
Melón E 38 D3
Meloy N 110 C9
Meløysund N 108 C6
Melrand F 22 E5
Melres P 44 B4
Melrose GB 5 D11
Mels CH 71 C8
Melsdorf D 83 B8
Melsungen D 78 D6
Melsvik N 112 C11
Meltaus FIN 117 E14
Meltham GB 11 D8
Melton GB 15 C11
Melton Mowbray GB 11 F10
Meltosjärvi FIN 117 E13
Melun F 25 C8
Melvaig GB 2 K5
Melvich GB 3 H9
Mélykút H 150 E3
Melzo I 69 C7
Memaliaj AL 168 D2
Membrey F 26 E4
Membrilla E 55 B6
Membrío E 45 E6
Mēmele LV 135 D8
Memleben D 79 D9
Memmelsdorf D 75 C8
Memmingen D 71 B10
Memmingerberg D 71 B10
Memsie GB 3 K12
Menaggio I 69 A7
Menai Bridge GB 10 E3
Menaldum NL 16 B5
Menars F 24 E5
Menasalbas E 46 E4
Menat F 30 C2
Menata I 66 C5
Mendavia E 32 F1
Mende F 34 A6
Menden (Sauerland) D 17 F9
Mendenitsa GR 175 B6
Menderes TR 177 C9
Mendig D 21 D8
Mendiga P 44 E3
Mendigorría E 32 E2
Menditte F 32 D4
Mendrisio CH 69 B6
Ménéac F 22 D7
Menemen TR 177 B9
Menen B 19 C7
Menesjärvi FIN 117 A16
Ménesplet F 29 E6
Ménessaire F 25 F11
Menet F 29 E11
Menetes GR 181 F6
Menetou-Salon F 25 F7
Menfi I 58 D2
Mengabril E 51 B8
Mengele LV 135 C10
Mengen D 27 D11
Mengerskirchen D 21 C10
Mengeš SLO 73 D10
Mengíbar E 53 A9
Menidi GR 174 A3
Ménigoute F 28 C5
Ménil-la-Tour F 26 C4
Ménil-sur-Belvitte F 26 D6
Menin B 19 C7
Menin B 182 D2
Menkijärvi FIN 123 E11
Menkulas AL 168 C4
Mennecy F 25 C7
Mennetou-sur-Cher F 24 F6
Menou F 25 F9
Mens F 31 F8
Mensignac F 29 E7
Menslage D 17 C9
Mentana I 62 C3
Menteroda D 79 D8
Menteşe TR 181 B8
Menton F 37 D7
Méntrida E 46 D4
Menznau CH 70 C6
Méobecq F 29 B8
Meolo I 72 E5
Méounes-les-Montrieux F 35 D10
Meppel NL 16 C6
Meppen D 17 C8
Mequinenza E 42 E4
Mer F 24 E6
Mera RO 153 F9
Merag HR 67 C9
Meråker N 105 E11
Meråkervollen N 105 E11
Merano I 72 C3
Méraq F 32 C5
Merasjärvi S 116 C7
Merasjärvi S 117 C10
Merate I 69 B7
Merbes-le-Château B 19 D9
Mercadillo E 40 B5
Mercatale I 66 F5
Mercatello sul Metauro I 66 E5
Mercatino Conca I 66 E6
Mercato San Severino I 60 B3
Mercato Saraceno I 66 E5
Merćez SRB 163 C11
Merching D 71 A11
Merchtem B 19 C9
Mercœur F 29 E9
Mercogliano I 60 B3
Mercuès F 33 B8
Merdrignac F 22 D7
Mērdzene LV 133 C3
Mere B 19 C8
Mere GB 13 C10
Méreau F 24 F7
Merei RO 161 C9
Merelbeke B 19 C8
Meremäe EST 132 F2
Merenberg D 185 C9
Mereni MD 154 D4
Mereni RO 155 E2
Mereni RO 161 E7
Mérens-les-Vals F 33 E9
Mereşti RO 153 E6
Méréville F 24 D7
Merghindeal RO 152 F5
Mergozzo I 68 B5
Meria F 37 F10
Méribel-les-Allues F 31 E10
Meriç TR 171 B10
Merichas GR 175 E9
Merichleri BG 166 E4
Mérida E 51 B7
Meriden GB 13 A11
Merijärvi FIN 119 F12
Merikarvia FIN 126 B6
Meriläinen FIN 123 D12
Merimasku FIN 126 E6
Měřín CZ 77 D9
Mering D 71 A11
Merişani RO 160 D5
Mérk H 151 B9
Merkendorf A 148 C5
Merkendorf D 75 D8
Merkenes S 109 C11
Merkinė LT 137 E9
Merklín CZ 76 C4
Merklingen D 74 E6
Merksplas B 182 C5
Merlara I 66 B3
Merlevenez F 22 E5
Merlines F 29 D10
Mern DK 87 E10
Mērnieki LV 131 F8
Mernye H 149 C9
Merošina SRB 164 C4
Merrey F 26 D4
Mersch L 20 E6
Merseburg (Saale) D 79 D10
Mersinbeleni TR 177 D10
Mers-les-Bains F 18 D3
Mērsrags LV 134 B6
Mertajärvi S 116 B8
Mertert L 20 E6
Mertesdorf D 186 B2
Merthyr Tydfil GB 13 B8
Mertingen D 75 E8
Mertloch D 185 D7
Mértola P 50 D4
Mertzwiller F 186 D4
Méru F 18 F5
Mervans F 31 B7
Mervent F 28 B4
Merville F 18 C6
Merville F 33 C8
Méry-sur-Seine F 25 C10
Merzen D 17 D9
Merzig D 21 F7
Mesagne I 61 B9
Mesagros GR 175 D8
Mésanger F 23 F9
Mesão Frio P 44 B5
Mesaria GR 177 F6
Meschede D 17 F10
Meschers-sur-Gironde F 28 D4
Mešeišta NMK 168 B4
Meselefors S 107 C11
Mesenikolas GR 169 F6
Meseşenii de Jos RO 151 C10
Mesgrigny F 25 D10
Mesi GR 171 C8
Mesići BIH 157 E11
Mesihovina BIH 157 E7
Mesimeri GR 169 D9
Mesinge DK 86 E7
Meskla GR 178 E6
Meškuičiai LT 134 D6
Meslay-du-Maine F 23 E10
Mesocco CH 71 E8
Mesochora GR 168 F5
Mesochori GR 169 E7
Mesochori GR 181 E6
Mesola I 66 C5
Mesolongi GR 174 C3

Mesongi GR 168 F2
Mesopotamia GR 168 C5
Mesopotamos GR 168 F4
Mesoraca I 59 A10
Mesotopos GR 177 A7
Mespelbrunn D 187 B7
Mesquer F 22 F7
Messac F 23 E8
Messanges F 32 C3
Meßdorf D 83 E11
Messei F 23 C10
Messeix F 29 D11
Messejana P 50 D3
Messina I 59 C8
Messincourt F 19 E11
Messingen D 17 D8
Messini GR 174 E5
Meßkirch D 27 E11
Messlingen S 102 A4
Meßstetten D 27 D10
Mesta BG 165 F8
Mesta GR 177 C6
Mestanza E 54 B4
Městec Králové CZ 77 B8
Mestervik N 111 B16
Mesti GR 171 C9
Mestlin D 83 C11
Město Albrechtice CZ 142 F4
Město Touškov CZ 76 C4
Mestre I 66 B5
Mesves-sur-Loire F 25 F8
Mesztegnyő H 149 C8
Meta I 60 B2
Métabief F 31 B9
Metagkitsi GR 169 D10
Metajna HR 67 C11
Metalliko GR 169 B8
Metallostroy RUS 129 F14
Metaxades GR 171 B10
Metelen D 17 D8
Meteș RO 151 E11
Metfield GB 15 C11
Methana GR 175 D7
Metheringham GB 11 E11
Methlick GB 3 L12
Methoni GR 178 B2
Methven GB 5 C9
Methwold GB 11 F13
Metković HR 157 F8
Metlika SLO 148 E4
Metnitz A 73 C9
Metochi GR 174 C3
Metochi GR 175 B8
Metovnica SRB 159 F9
Mētriena LV 135 C12
Metsäkansa FIN 127 C10
Metsäkylä FIN 121 D11
Metsäkylä FIN 128 D7
Metsälä FIN 120 C9
Metsämaa FIN 127 D9
Metschow D 84 C3
Metsküla EST 130 D5
Metslawier NL 16 B6
Metsovo GR 168 E5
Mettäjärvi S 117 E11
Mettendorf D 20 E6
Mettenheim D 75 F11
Mettet B 19 D10
Mettevoll N 112 D7
Mettingen D 17 D9
Mettlach D 21 F7
Mettmann D 17 F7
Mettray F 24 F4
Metz F 26 B5
Metzervisse F 20 F6
Metzingen D 27 C11
Meudt D 185 D8
Meulan F 24 B6
Meulebeke B 19 C7
Meung-sur-Loire F 24 E6
Meursault F 30 B6
Meuselwitz D 79 D11
Meuzac F 29 D8
Mevagissey GB 12 E5
Mexborough GB 11 E9
Meximieux F 31 D7
Mey GB 3 H10
Meyenburg D 83 D12
Meylan F 31 E8
Meymac F 29 D10
Meyrargues F 35 C10
Meyreuil F 35 D10
Meyronnes F 36 C5
Meyrueis F 34 B5
Meyssac F 29 E9
Meysse F 35 A8
Meythet F 31 D9
Mezapos GR 178 B3
Mežāre LV 135 C12
Mežciems LV 134 C7
Mezdra BG 165 C8
Mèze F 35 D6
Mézel F 36 D4
Mežgale LV 135 D11
Mezhdurech'ye RUS 136 D4
Meziboří CZ 80 E5
Mežica SLO 73 C10
Mézidon-Canon F 23 B11
Mézières-en-Brenne F 29 B8
Mézières-sur-Issoire F 29 C7
Mézilhac F 30 F5
Mézilles F 25 E9
Meziměstí CZ 81 E10
Mézin F 33 B6
Mezio P 44 C5
Mezőberény H 151 D7
Mezőcsát H 147 F11
Mezőcsokonya H 149 D9
Mezőfalva H 149 C11
Mezőgyán H 151 D8
Mezőhegyes H 150 E6
Mezőkeresztes H 145 H2
Mezőkovácsháza H 151 E6
Mezőkövesd H 147 F11
Mezőlak H 149 B8
Mezőnyárád H 145 H2
Mezőörs H 149 A9
Mézos F 32 B3
Mezőszemere H 150 B6
Mezőszentgyörgy H 149 B10
Mezőszilas H 149 C10
Mezőtárkány H 150 B5
Mežotne LV 135 D8
Mezőtúr H 150 D6
Mezőzombor H 145 G3
Mezquita de Jarque E 42 F2
Mežvalde LV 134 C4
Mežvidi LV 133 C3
Mežvidi LV 134 C4
Mezzana I 69 A10
Mezzanego I 37 C10
Mezzano I 72 D4
Mezzocorona I 69 A11
Mezzojuso I 58 D3
Mezzoldo I 69 A8
Mezzolombardo I 69 A11
Mga RUS 129 F15
Miączyn PL 144 B8
Miajadas E 45 F9
Mialet F 29 D7
Miały PL 85 E10
Miasteczko Krajeńskie PL 85 D12
Miastko PL 85 B11
Miastków Kościelny PL 141 G5
Miastkowo PL 139 D12
Miavaig GB 2 J3
Mica RO 152 C3
Mica RO 152 E4
Micăsasa RO 152 E4
Micești RO 160 D5
Micestii de Câmpie RO 152 D4
Michaľany SK 145 F4
Michalová SK 147 D9
Michalovce SK 145 F4
Michałów PL 143 F9
Michałów Górny PL 141 G4
Michałowice PL 142 E3
Michałowice PL 143 F8
Michałowo PL 140 D9
Michelau in Oberfranken D 75 B9
Michelbach an der Bilz D 74 D6
Micheldorf A 73 C9
Micheldorf in Oberösterreich A 73 A9
Michelfeld D 74 D6
Michelstadt D 21 E12
Michendorf D 80 B4
Michorzewo PL 81 B10
Michów PL 141 G6
Mickelspiltom FIN 127 D15
Mickelsträsk S 118 F4
Mickleton GB 5 F12
Mickleton GB 13 A11
Miclești MD 154 C3
Midbea GB 3 G11
Middagsbukt N 111 B17
Middelbeers NL 183 C6
Middelburg NL 16 E1
Middelfart DK 86 D5
Middelharnis NL 16 E2
Middelkerke B 18 B6
Middelstum NL 17 B7
Middenbeemster NL 16 C3
Middenmeer NL 16 C4
Middleham GB 11 C8
Middlemarsh GB 13 D10
Middlesbrough GB 11 B9
Middleton GB 11 D7
Middleton Cheney GB 13 A12
Middleton in Teesdale GB 5 F12
Middletown GB 7 D9
Middlewich GB 10 E7
Midhurst GB 15 F7
Midleton IRL 8 E6
Midlum D 17 A11
Midsund N 100 A5
Midtgård N 114 D8
Midtskogberget N 102 D3
Mišvágur FO 2 A2
Midwolda NL 17 B8
Mid Yell GB 3 D14
Miechów PL 143 F9
Miechów Charsznica PL 143 F8
Miedes E 41 F9
Miedziana Góra PL 143 E10
Miedzichowo PL 81 B9
Miedzna PL 139 F13
Miedźna PL 143 G7
Miedźno PL 143 E6
Mijdzybórz PL 142 D4
Mijdzychód PL 81 A9
Mijdzylesie PL 77 B11
Mijdzyrzec Podlaski PL 141 G7
Mijdzyrzecz PL 81 B9
Mijdzyzdroje PL 84 C6
Miehikkälä FIN 128 D8
Miehlen D 185 D8
Miejsce Piastowe PL 145 D4
Miejska Górka PL 81 C11
Mijkinia PL 81 D11
Miekojärvi S 119 B10
Miélan F 33 D6
Mielec PL 143 F11
Mieljcin PL 85 D10
Mieleszyn PL 85 E12
Mielno PL 85 B10
Mieluskylä FIN 119 F14
Mielżyn PL 138 F4
Mieming A 71 C12
Mierasjärvi FIN 113 D19
Mieraslompolo FIN 113 D19
Miercurea-Ciuc RO 153 E7
Miercurea Nirajului RO 152 D5
Miercurea Sibiului RO 152 F3
Mieres E 39 B8
Mieres E 43 C9
Mierlo NL 16 F5
Mierojärvi N 113 E11
Mieroszów PL 81 E10
Miers F 29 F9
Mierzjcice PL 143 F7
Mierzyn PL 84 D6
Miesau D 186 C3
Miesbach D 72 A4
Mieścisko PL 85 E12
Miesenbach D 186 C4
Mieslahti FIN 121 F10
Miessaure S 116 E4
Mieste D 79 B9
Mieszków PL 142 B3
Mieszkowice PL 84 E6
Mietingen D 71 A9
Mietków PL 81 E11
Mietoinen FIN 126 D6
Miettilä FIN 129 C11
Mieussy F 31 C10
Mieza E 45 B7
Migennes F 25 E10
Miglianico I 63 C6
Migliarino I 66 C4
Migliaro I 66 C4
Miglionica I 61 B6
Mignaloux-Beauvoir F 29 B6
Mignano Monte Lungo I 60 A1
Migné-Auxances F 29 B6
Mignovillard F 31 B9
Miguel Esteban E 47 E6
Miguelturra E 54 B5
Migushino RUS 133 E7
Mihăești RO 160 C4
Mihăești RO 160 C6
Mihăești RO 160 E5
Mihai Bravu RO 155 D3
Mihai Bravu RO 161 E8
Mihăileni RO 152 F4
Mihăileni RO 153 B8
Mihăileni RO 153 E7
Mihăilești RO 161 D9
Mihăilești RO 161 E7
Mihail Kogălniceanu RO 155 C3
Mihail Kogălniceanu RO 155 D1
Mihail Kogălniceanu RO 155 E2
Mihailovca MD 154 D3
Mihai Viteazu RO 152 D3
Mihai Viteazu RO 155 D3
Mihajlovac SRB 159 D6
Mihajlovac SRB 159 E9
Mihajlovo SRB 158 C5
Mihălășeni RO 153 B10
Mihálď H 149 D8
Mihalț RO 152 E3
Mihályi H 149 A8
Mihesu de Câmpie RO 152 D4
Mihla D 79 D7
Miiluranta FIN 123 C16
Mijares E 46 D3
Mijas E 53 C7
Mijdrecht NL 16 D3
Mijoska MNE 163 D7
Mikalayeva BY 133 F6
Mikepércs H 151 C8
Mikhalishki BY 137 D13
Mikhalkovo BG 165 F9
Mikhaltsi BG 166 C4
Mikhaylovo BG 165 B8
Mikhaylovo BG 166 E5
Mikitamäe EST 132 E2
Mikitsikha BY 133 F6
Mikkeli FIN 128 B7
Mikkelin mlk FIN 128 B7
Mikkelvik N 112 C3
Mikkola FIN 117 D16
Mikladalur FO 2 A3
Miklavž SLO 148 C5
Miklebostad N 111 C13
Mikleuš HR 149 E9
Mikołajki PL 136 F4
Mikołajki Pomorskie PL 139 C7
Mikołów PL 143 F6
Mikoszewo PL 138 B6
Mikre BG 165 C10
Mikri Volvi GR 169 C10
Mikro Dereio GR 171 B10
Mikrokambos GR 169 C8
Mikromilia GR 170 B6
Mikropoli GR 169 B10
Mikrothives GR 169 F8
Mikrovalto GR 169 D6
Mikstat PL 142 C4
Mikuláš CZ 77 C8
Mikulasovice CZ 80 E6
Mikulčice CZ 77 E12
Mikulov CZ 77 E11
Mikulovice CZ 142 F3
Mikušovce SK 146 C6
Miladinovci NMK 164 F4
Milagro E 41 D8
Milagros E 40 E4
Miłakowo PL 139 B9
Milano I 69 C7
Milano Marittima I 66 D5
Milanówek PL 141 F3
Milaș RO 152 D4
Milas TR 181 B7
Milatkoviće SRB 163 C10
Milatos GR 179 E10
Milazzo I 59 C7
Milborne Port GB 13 D10
Milcoiu RO 160 C4
Milcov RO 160 E4
Milcovul RO 161 B10
Mildenhall GB 15 C10
Mildstedt D 82 B6
Mileanca RO 153 A9
Milejczyce PL 141 E8
Milejewo PL 139 B8
Milejów PL 141 H7
Milena I 58 E4
Milești MD 153 C12
Milestone IRL 8 C6
Mileto I 59 B9
Milevsko CZ 76 D6
Milfield GB 5 D12
Milfontes P 50 D2
Milford IRL 7 B7
Milford IRL 8 D5
Milford Haven GB 12 B4
Milhão P 39 E6
Milhaud F 35 C7
Milići BIH 157 D11
Milicz PL 81 C12
Milies GR 169 F9
Milíkov CZ 147 B7
Milín CZ 76 C6
Milina GR 175 A7
Milis I 64 C2
Militello in Val di Catania I 59 E6
Miliyeve UA 152 A6
Milizac F 22 D2
Miljana HR 148 D5
Miljeno BIH 157 E11
Miljevina BIH 157 E10
Milkel D 81 D6
Miłki PL 136 F4
Milkovitsa BG 160 F5
Milk'ovtsi BG 165 D6
Mill NL 16 E5
Millares E 48 F3
Millas F 34 E4
Millau F 34 B5
Millay F 30 B5
Millbrook GB 12 E6
Millbrook IRL 7 E8
Millesimo I 37 C8
Millevaches F 29 D10
Millford GB 7 D9
Millhouse GB 4 D6
Millières F 26 D3
Millingen aan de Rijn NL 183 B8
Millisle GB 7 C11
Millom GB 10 C5
Milloshevë RKS 164 D3
Millport GB 4 D7
Millstatt A 73 C8
Millstreet IRL 8 D4
Millstreet IRL 9 D7
Milltown IRL 6 E5
Milltown IRL 7 F9
Milltown IRL 8 D2
Milltown IRL 8 D3
Milltown Malbay IRL 8 C4
Milly-la-Forêt F 25 D7
Milmarcos E 47 B9
Milmersdorf D 84 D5
Milmort B 183 D7
Milna HR 156 F5
Milnathort GB 5 C10
Milngavie GB 5 D8
Milnthorpe GB 10 C6
Milo I 59 D7
Miłocice PL 85 C11
Milohnić HR 67 B9
Miłomłyn PL 139 C8
Miłoradz PL 138 B6
Miloșești RO 161 D10
Miłosław PL 142 B3
Milot AL 163 F8
Milotice CZ 77 E12
Milovaig GB 2 L3
Milovice CZ 77 B7
Milow D 79 A11
Milow D 83 D11
Milówka PL 147 B8
Miltach D 75 D12
Miltenberg D 21 E12
Miltiņi LV 134 C6
Milton GB 2 L8
Milton GB 5 B9
Milton Keynes GB 15 C7
Miltzow D 84 B4
Milutinovac SRB 159 F7
Milverton GB 13 C8
Milz D 75 B8
Mimetiz E 40 B5
Mimizan F 32 B3
Mimizan-Plage F 32 B3
Mimoň CZ 81 E7
Mina de São Domingos P 50 D5
Mín an Chladaigh IRL 6 B6
Minas de Riotinto E 51 D6
Minateda E 55 C9
Minaya E 47 F8
Minde P 44 E3
Mindelheim D 71 A10
Mindelstetten D 75 E10
Minden D 17 D11
Minderhout B 182 C5
Mindnes N 108 E3
Mindrești MD 154 B2
Mindszent H 150 D5
Mindszentgodisa H 149 D10
Mindtangen N 108 E3
Mindūnai LT 135 F11
Mindya BG 166 C5
Minehead GB 13 C8
Mineo I 59 E6
Mineralni Bani BG 166 F4
Minerbio I 66 C3
Minervino Murge I 60 A6
Minfeld D 27 B9
Minger MD 154 D2
Minglanilla E 47 E9
Mingorría E 46 C3
Miniac-Morvan F 23 C8
Minićevo SRB 159 F9
Mín na bhFiann IRL 6 C5
Minne S 103 B9
Minnertsga NL 16 B5
Minnesund N 95 B14
Minnigaff GB 4 F8
Minot F 25 E12
Mińsk Mazowiecki PL 141 F5
Minsterley GB 10 F6
Mintiloglio GR 174 C4
Mintiu Gherlii RO 152 C3
Mintlaw GB 3 K13
Mintraching D 75 E11
Minturno I 62 E5
Minucciano I 66 D1
Minusio CH 68 A6
Mioarele RO 160 C6
Mionica SRB 158 E5
Mionnay F 30 D6
Mios F 32 A4
Mira E 47 E10
Mira I 66 B5
Mira P 44 D3
Mirabeau F 35 C10
Mirabel E 45 E8
Mirabel F 33 B8
Mirabel-aux-Baronnies F 35 B9
Mirabella Eclano I 60 A4
Mirabella Imbaccari I 58 E5
Miradoux F 33 C7
Miraflores de la Sierra E 46 C5
Miralcamp E 42 D5
Miramare I 66 D6
Miramas F 35 C9
Mirambeau F 28 E4
Mirambel E 42 F3
Miramont-de-Guyenne F 33 A6
Miranda de Arga E 32 F2
Miranda de Ebro E 40 C6
Miranda do Corvo P 44 D4
Miranda do Douro P 39 E7
Mirande F 33 C6
Mirandela P 38 F5
Mirandilla E 51 A7
Mirandola I 66 C3
Mirandol-Bourgnounac F 33 B10
Miranje HR 156 E4
Mirano I 66 B5
Miras AL 168 C4
Mirash RKS 164 E3
Mirăslău RO 152 E3
Miratovac SRB 164 E4
Miravci NMK 169 B7
Miravet E 42 E5
Miravete de la Sierra E 42 F2
Mircea Vodă RO 155 E2
Mircea Vodă RO 161 C10
Mircești RO 153 C9
Mircze PL 144 B8
Mirebeau F 26 F3
Mirebeau F 29 B6
Mirecourt F 26 D5
Mirepoix F 33 D9
Mireșu Mare RO 151 C11
Mířetice CZ 77 C9
Mireval F 35 C6
Miričina BIH 157 C9
Mirkovci HR 157 B10
Mirkovo BG 165 D9
Mirlović Zagora HR 156 E5
Mirna SLO 73 E11
Mirna Peč SLO 73 E11
Mirocin PL 144 C6
Mirocin Górny PL 81 C9
Mironeasa RO 153 D10
Miroševce SRB 164 D4
Miroși RO 160 E5
Miroslava RO 153 C10
Miroslavas LT 137 E8
Mirosławiec PL 85 D10
Miroslovești RO 153 C9
Mirošov CZ 76 C5
Mirotice CZ 76 D6
Mirovice CZ 76 C6
Mirovtsi BG 167 C8
Mirow D 83 D13
Mirșid RO 151 C11
Mirsk PL 81 E8
Mirto Crosia I 61 D7
Mirueña de los Infanzones E 45 C10
Mirzec PL 141 H4
Misano Adriatico I 67 E6
Mișca RO 151 D8
Mischii RO 160 E3
Miserey-Salines F 26 F4
Mishnyevichy BY 133 F7
Misi FIN 117 E17
Misilmeri I 58 C3
Mišinci BIH 157 C8
Miske H 150 E3
Miskolc H 145 G2
Mislina HR 162 D4
Mislinja SLO 73 D11
Mišnjak HR 67 C10
Mison F 35 B10
Missanello I 60 C6
Missenträsk S 107 A17
Missillac F 23 F7
Misso EST 131 F14
Mistelbach A 77 E11
Mistelgau D 75 C9
Misten N 108 B8
Misterbianco I 59 D7
Misterhult S 93 E9
Misterton GB 11 E10
Mistretta I 58 D5
Mistros GR 175 B8
Misurina I 72 C5
Misvær N 108 B9
Mitandersfors S 96 B7
Mitchelstown IRL 8 D6
Mithymna GR 171 F10
Mitoc RO 153 A10
Mitrašinci NMK 165 F6
Mitreni RO 161 E9
Mitropoli GR 169 F6
Mitrousi GR 169 B9
Mitrova Reka SRB 163 C9
Mitrovicë RKS 163 D10
Mitry-Mory F 25 C8
Mittådalen S 102 A4
Mittelberg A 71 C10
Mittelberg A 71 D11
Mittelbiberach D 71 A9
Mittelkalbach D 74 B6
Mittelsinn D 187 A8
Mittelwald D 72 B3
Mittenwalde D 80 B5
Mittenwalde D 84 D5
Mitterbach am Erlaufsee A 148 A4
Mitterding A 76 F4
Mitterdorf im Mürztal A 148 A5
Mittersheim F 27 C6
Mittersill A 72 B5
Mitterskirchen D 75 F12
Mitterteich D 75 C11
Mittet N 100 A7
Mittiliden S 105 B16
Mittweida D 80 E3
Mitwitz D 75 B9
Mizhhir"ya UA 145 F8
Mizil RO 161 C8
Miziya BG 160 F3
Mjällby S 88 C7
Mjällom S 107 F14
Mjedë AL 163 F8
Mjelde N 110 E9
Mjelde N 111 A15
Mjöbäck S 88 A3
Mjölby S 92 C6
Mjølfell N 100 E5
Mjølnarodden N 110 D5
Mjönäs S 97 C10
Mjøndalen N 95 C12
Mjønes N 108 B8
Mjösjöby S 107 D15
Mjösund FIN 126 E7
Mjötråsk S 119 B9
Mjövattnet S 103 A14
Mjövattnet S 118 E5
Mladá Boleslav CZ 77 B7
Mladá Vožice CZ 77 C7
Mladé Buky CZ 81 E9
Mladenovac SRB 158 E6
Mladenovo SRB 158 C3
Mladikovine BIH 157 D8
Mladinovo BG 166 F6
Mlado Nagoričane NMK 164 E4
Mława PL 139 D9
Mlekarevo BG 166 E6
Mlinice BIH 157 D7
Mliniště BIH 157 D6
Młodzieszyn PL 141 F2
Młynary PL 139 B8
Młynarze PL 139 E11
Mlynys'ka UA 145 E6
Mnichovice CZ 77 C7
Mnichovo Hradiště CZ 77 A7
Mnichów PL 143 E9
Mniów PL 143 D9
Mníšek nad Hnilcom SK 145 F2
Mníšek pod Brdy CZ 76 C6
Mniszew PL 141 G4
Mniszków PL 141 H2
Mo N 100 E3
Mo S 103 D12
Mo S 103 E12
Mo S 107 D11
Mo S 107 E11
Moacșa RO 153 F7
Moaña E 38 D2
Moara RO 153 B8
Moara Domnească MD 153 B10
Moara Vlăsiei RO 161 D8
Moate IRL 7 F7
Mobberley GB 11 E7
Moča SK 149 A10
Moçarria P 44 F3
Mocejón E 46 E5
Močenok SK 146 E5
Mochales E 47 B9
Mochos GR 178 E9
Mochowo PL 139 E8
Mochy PL 81 B10
Mociu RO 152 D4
Möckern D 79 B10
Mockfjärd S 97 A12
Möckmühl D 27 B11
Mockrehna D 79 C12
Mockträsk S 118 C7
Moclín E 53 B9
Moclinejo E 53 C8
Mocra MD 154 B4
Mocsa H 149 A10
Modane F 31 E10
Modave B 19 D11
Modbury GB 13 E7
Modelu RO 161 E10
Modena I 66 C2
Modi GR 175 B6
Modica I 59 F6
Modigliana I 66 D4
Modliborzyce PL 144 B5
Mödling A 77 F10
Modliszewice PL 141 H2
Modra SK 146 E4
Modran BIH 157 C8
Modrany SK 146 F6
Modreeny IRL 8 C6
Modriach A 73 C11
Modriča BIH 157 C9
Modrište NMK 168 A5
Modruš HR 156 B3
Modrý Kameň SK 147 E8
Modugno I 61 A7
Moëlan-sur-Mer F 22 E4
Moelfre GB 10 E3
Moelv N 101 E13
Moen N 105 D12
Moen N 111 B16
Moena I 72 D4
Moerbeke B 182 C3
Moergestel NL 16 E4
Moerkerke B 182 C2
Moers D 17 F7
Moffat GB 5 E10
Mofreita P 39 E6
Moftin RO 151 B10
Mogadouro P 39 F6
Mogata S 93 C8
Mögelin D 79 A11
Møgeltønder DK 86 F3
Mogenstrup DK 87 E9
Moggio Udinese I 73 D7
Mögglingen D 187 D8
Mogielnica PL 141 G3
Mogila NMK 168 B5
Mogilany PL 147 B9
Mogilishte BG 167 C10
Mogilno PL 138 E4
Mogila I 66 C2
Mogliano I 67 F7
Mogliano Veneto I 66 A5
Möglingen D 187 D7
Mogón E 55 C6
Mogorella I 64 D2
Mogoș RO 151 E11
Mogoșani RO 160 D6
Mogoșești RO 153 C10
Mogoșești-Siret RO 153 C9
Mogoșoaia RO 161 D7
Moguer E 51 E6
Mogyoród H 150 B3
Mohács H 149 E11
Moharque E 55 C9
Mohed S 103 D12
Moheda S 88 A7
Mohedas de Granadilla E 45 D8
Mohedas de la Jara E 45 E10
Mohelnice CZ 77 C11
Mohelno CZ 77 D10
Mohernando E 47 C6
Mohil IRL 9 C8
Mohill IRL 7 E7
Möhkö FIN 125 E16
Möhlau D 79 C11
Möhlin CH 27 E8
Moholm S 91 B15
Mohora H 147 F8
Mohorn D 80 E4
Mohyliv Podil's'kyy UA 154 A1
Moi N 94 F5
Moi N 94 F6
Moià E 43 D8
Moiano I 60 A3
Moieciu RO 160 C6
Moimenta da Beira P 44 C5
Moinești RO 153 E8
Moingt F 30 D5
Móinteach Mílic IRL 7 F8
Moira GB 7 D10
Mo i Rana N 108 D7
Moirans F 31 E8
Moirans-en-Montagne F 31 C8
Moirax F 33 B7
Moires GR 178 E8
Mõisaküla EST 131 E10
Moisburg D 82 D7
Moisdon-la-Rivière F 23 E9
Moisei RO 152 B5
Moisiovaara FIN 121 E13
Moislains F 18 E6
Moissac F 33 B8
Moissac-Bellevue F 36 D4
Moissey F 26 F4
Moïta F 37 G10
Moita P 44 D4
Moita P 44 E3
Moita P 50 B2
Moixent-Mogente E 56 D3
Mojácar E 55 E9
Mojados E 39 F10
Mojkovac MNE 163 D8
Mojmírovce SK 146 E6
Mojstrana SLO 73 D8
Mojzesovo SK 146 E6
Møkkevik N 110 D6
Möklinta S 98 B7
Mokobody PL 141 F6
Mokrá Hora CZ 77 D11
Mokrance SK 145 F3
Mokre PL 143 F10
Mokren BG 167 D7
Mokresh BG 160 F2
Mokrievo NMK 169 B8
Mokrin SRB 150 F5
Mokro BIH 157 E10
Mokronog SLO 73 E11
Mokronoge BIH 156 D5
Mokronoge BIH 157 E7
Möksy FIN 123 D12
Mol B 19 B11
Mol SRB 150 F5
Mola di Bari I 61 A8
Molaoi GR 178 B4
Molare I 37 B9
Molares P 38 F4
Molbergen D 17 C9
Mölbling A 73 C9
Mølby DK 86 E4
Mold GB 10 E5
Moldava nad Bodvou SK 145 F2
Molde N 100 A6
Moldjord N 108 B8
Moldova Nouă RO 159 D8
Moldova-Sulița RO 152 B6
Moldoveni RO 153 D9
Moldovița RO 153 B7
Møldrup DK 86 B5
Moldvik N 111 C11
Moledo P 38 E2
Moledo P 44 C5
Molelos P 44 C4
Molenbeek-St-Jean B 182 D4
Molenstede B 183 C6
Molescroft GB 11 D11
Molești MD 154 D3
Molėtai LT 135 F10
Molfetta I 61 A7
Molfsee D 83 B8
Moliden S 107 E14
Molières F 29 F9
Molières F 33 B8
Molières-sur-Cèze F 35 B7
Moliets-et-Maa F 32 C3
Molina Aterno I 62 C5
Molina de Aragón E 47 C9
Molina de Segura E 56 E2
Molina di Ledro I 69 B10
Molinara I 60 A3
Molinaseca E 39 C7
Molinella I 66 C4
Molines-en-Queyras F 31 F10
Molinet F 30 C4
Molinges F 31 C8
Molinicos E 55 C8
Molini di Tures I 72 C4
Molino de Villobas E 32 F5
Molinos E 42 F3
Molinos de Rei E 43 E8
Moliterno I 60 C5
Molitg-les-Bains F 33 E10
Molkojärvi FIN 117 D14
Molkom S 97 C10
Mollas AL 168 C3
Mölle S 87 C11
Molledo E 40 B3
Möllenbeck D 84 D4
Möllenhagen D 84 C3
Mollerussa E 42 D5
Molles F 30 C4
Mollet del Vallès E 43 D8
Molliens-Dreuil F 18 E5
Mollis CH 27 F11
Molln A 73 A9
Mölln D 83 C9
Mölln D 84 C4
Molló E 33 F10
Möllösund S 91 C9
Mölltorp S 92 C4
Mölnbo S 93 A10
Mölnlycke S 91 D11
Molnytsya UA 153 A8
Moloha UA 154 E6
Molompize F 30 E3
Molos GR 175 B6
Moloy F 26 E2
Molpe FIN 122 E6
Molschleben D 79 D8
Molsheim F 186 D3
Molunat HR 162 E5
Molve HR 149 D8
Molveno I 69 A10
Molvízar E 53 C9
Mombaldone I 37 B8
Mombeltrán E 45 D10
Mombercelli I 37 B8
Mömbris D 21 D12
Mombuey E 39 D7
Momchilgrad BG 171 A8
Momignies B 19 D9
Momo I 68 B6
Monå FIN 122 D8
Monachil E 53 B9
Monacia-d'Aullène F 37 H10
Monaghan IRL 7 D9
Monamolin IRL 9 C10
Monäs FIN 122 D8
Monashi UA 154 E6
Monasterace I 59 C10
Monasterevin IRL 7 F8
Monastir I 64 E3
Monastiraki GR 174 B2
Monbahus F 33 A7
Monbazillac F 29 F6
Moncada E 48 E4
Moncalieri I 37 A7
Moncalvo I 68 C5
Monção P 38 D3
Moncarapacho P 50 E4
Moncaut F 33 B6
Moncel-sur-Seille F 26 C5
Mönchengladbach D 20 B6
Mönchhof A 77 G11
Monchio delle Corti I 66 D1
Monchique P 50 E2
Mönchsdeggingen D 75 E8
Monclar F 33 B7
Moncofa E 48 E4
Moncontour F 22 D6
Moncontour F 28 B5
Moncoutant F 28 B4
Moncrabeau F 33 B6
Monda E 53 C7
Mondariz E 38 D3
Mondariz-Balneario E 38 D3
Mondavezan F 33 D8
Mondavio I 67 E6
Mondéjar E 47 D6
Mondello I 58 C3
Mondeville F 23 B11
Mondolfo I 67 E7
Mondoñedo E 38 B5
Mondorf-les-Bains L 20 E6
Mondoubleau F 24 E4
Mondovì I 37 C7
Mondragon F 35 B8
Mondragone I 62 E5
Mondsee A 73 A7
Monea GB 7 D7
Moneasa RO 151 E9
Moneen IRL 6 F5
Moneglia I 37 C10
Monegrillo E 41 E11
Monein F 32 D4
Monemvasia GR 178 B5
Monesiglio I 37 C8
Monesterio E 51 C7
Monestier-de-Clermont F 31 F8
Monestiés F 33 B10
Monéteau F 25 E10
Moneygall IRL 9 C7
Moneymore GB 4 F3
Moneyneany GB 4 F3
Moneyreagh GB 7 C11
Monfalcone I 73 E8
Monfecorvino Rovella I 60 B3
Monflanquin F 33 A7
Monfort F 33 C7
Monforte P 44 F6

Monforte da Beira *P* 45 E6
Monforte d'Alba *I* 37 B7
Monforte del Cid *E* 56 E3
Monforte de Lemos *E* 38 C4
Monforte de Moyuela *E* 42 E2
Monfortinho *P* 45 D7
Monghidoro *I* 66 D3
Mongrando *I* 68 B5
Mongstad *N* 100 E2
Monguelfo *I* 72 C5
Monheim *D* 75 E8
Moniaive *GB* 5 E9
Monieux *F* 35 B9
Monifieth *GB* 5 C11
Monilea *IRL* 7 E8
Mõniste *EST* 131 F13
Monistrol-d'Allier *F* 30 F4
Monistrol de Calders *E* 43 D8
Monistrol de Montserrat *E* 43 D7
Monistrol-sur-Loire *F* 30 E5
Monivea *IRL* 6 F5
Mönkeberg *D* 83 B8
Mońki *PL* 140 D7
Monkokehampton *GB* 12 D6
Monléon-Magnoac *F* 33 D7
Monmouth *GB* 13 B9
Monnaie *F* 24 E4
Mönni *FIN* 125 E14
Monninkylä *FIN* 127 E14
Monok *H* 145 G3
Monolithos *GR* 181 D7
Monopoli *I* 61 B8
Monor *H* 150 C3
Monor *RO* 152 D5
Monostorapáti *H* 149 C9
Monostorpályi *H* 151 C8
Monóvar *E* 56 E3
Monpazier *F* 33 A7
Monreal *E* 32 E3
Monreal del Campo *E* 47 C10
Monreale *I* 58 C3
Monreith *GB* 4 F7
Monroy *E* 45 E8
Monroyo *E* 42 F3
Mons *B* 19 D8
Mons *F* 34 C4
Mons *F* 36 D5
Monsampolo del Tronto *I* 62 B5
Monsaraz *P* 51 C5
Monschau *D* 20 C6
Monsec *F* 29 E7
Monségur *F* 33 A6
Monselice *I* 66 B4
Monsempron-Libos *F* 33 B7
Monserrat *E* 48 F3
Monsheim *D* 187 B5
Mönsheim *D* 187 D6
Mønsted *DK* 86 C4
Monster *NL* 16 D2
Mönsterås *S* 89 A10
Monsummano Terme *I* 66 E2
Monta *I* 37 B7
Montabaur *D* 21 D9
Montaberner *E* 56 D4
Montady *F* 34 D5
Montagnac *F* 34 D5
Montagnana *I* 66 B3
Montagne *F* 28 F5
Montagney *F* 26 F4
Montagnol *F* 34 C5
Montagrier *F* 29 E6
Montaigu *F* 28 B3
Montaigu-de-Quercy *F* 33 B8
Montaigut *F* 30 C2
Montaigut-sur-Save *F* 33 C8
Montaione *I* 66 E2
Montalbán *E* 42 F2
Montalbán de Córdoba *E* 53 A7
Montalbano Elicona *I* 59 C7
Montalbano Jonico *I* 61 C7
Montalbo *E* 47 E7
Montalcino *I* 65 A4
Montale *I* 66 E3
Montalegre *P* 38 E4
Montalieu-Vercieu *F* 31 D7
Montalivet-les-Bains *F* 28 E3
Montallegro *I* 58 E3
Montalto delle Marche *I* 62 B5
Montalto di Castro *I* 65 C5
Montalto Marina *I* 65 C5
Montalto Uffugo *I* 60 E6
Montalvão *P* 44 E5
Montamarta *E* 39 E8
Montana *BG* 165 C7
Montana *CH* 31 C11
Montanejos *E* 48 D3
Montaner *F* 32 D5
Montano Antilia *I* 60 C4
Montans *F* 33 C9
Montaquila *I* 62 D6
Montargil *P* 44 F4
Montargis *F* 25 E8
Montastruc-la-Conseillère *F* 33 C9
Montataire *F* 18 F5
Montauban *F* 33 B8
Montauban-de-Bretagne *F* 23 D7
Montaudin *F* 23 D10
Montauriol *F* 33 A7
Montauroux *F* 36 D5
Montaut *F* 32 C4
Montaut *F* 32 D5
Montaut *F* 33 D9
Montayral *F* 33 B7
Montazzoli *I* 63 D6
Montbard *F* 25 E11
Montbarrey *F* 31 A8
Montbazens *F* 33 B10
Montbazin *F* 35 C6
Montbazon *F* 24 F4
Montbéliard *F* 27 E6
Montbenoît *F* 31 B9
Montbeton *F* 33 B8
Montblanc *E* 42 E6
Montboucher-sur-Jabron *F* 35 A8
Montbozon *F* 26 F5
Montbrió del Camp *E* 42 E6
Montbrison *F* 30 D5
Montbron *F* 29 D7
Montbrun *F* 33 A9
Montbrun-les-Bains *F* 35 B9
Montcada i Reixac *E* 43 E8
Montcavrel *F* 15 F12
Montceau-les-Mines *F* 30 B5
Montcenis *F* 30 B5
Montchanin *F* 30 B5
Montcornet *F* 19 E9
Montcresson *F* 25 E8
Montcuq *F* 33 B8
Montcy-Notre-Dame *F* 19 E10
Montdardier *F* 35 C6
Mont-Dauphin *F* 36 B5
Mont-de-Marsan *F* 32 C5
Montdidier *F* 18 E6
Mont-Dore *F* 30 D2
Monteagudo *E* 41 E8
Monteagudo de las Salinas *E* 47 E9
Monteagudo de las Vicarías *E* 41 F7
Montealegre del Castillo *E* 55 B10
Montebello Ionico *I* 59 D8
Montebello Vicentino *I* 66 B3
Montebelluna *I* 72 E5
Montebourg *F* 23 B9
Montebruno *I* 37 B10
Montecalvo in Foglia *I* 66 E6
Montecalvo Irpino *I* 60 A4
Monte-Carlo *MC* 37 D6
Montecarotto *I* 67 E7
Montecassiano *I* 67 F7
Monte Castello di Vibio *I* 62 B2
Montecastrilli *I* 62 B2
Montecatini Terme *I* 66 E2
Montecatini Val di Cecina *I* 66 F2
Montecchio *I* 67 E6
Montecchio Emilia *I* 66 C1
Montecchio Maggiore *I* 66 A3
Montech *F* 33 C8
Montechiaro d'Asti *I* 37 A8
Montechiarugolo *I* 66 C1
Montecilfone *I* 63 D7
Montecorice *I* 60 C3
Montecosaro *I* 67 F8
Montecreale Valcellina *I* 73 D6
Montecreto *I* 66 D2
Monte da Pedra *P* 44 F5
Monte das Flores *P* 50 B4
Montederramo *E* 38 D5
Monte di Procida *I* 60 B2
Monte do Trigo *P* 50 C4
Montefalco *I* 62 B3
Montefalcone di Val Fortore *I* 60 A4
Montefalcone nel Sannio *I* 63 D7
Montefano *I* 67 F7
Montefelcino *I* 67 E6
Montefiascone *I* 62 B2
Montefiore dell'Aso *I* 62 A5
Montefiorino *I* 66 D2
Montefortino *I* 62 B4
Montefranco *I* 62 B3
Montefrío *E* 53 B8
Montegiordano *I* 61 C7
Montegiorgio *I* 67 F8
Monte Gordo *P* 50 E5
Montegranaro *I* 67 F8
Montegrotto Terme *I* 66 B4
Montehermoso *E* 45 D8
Monteiasi *I* 61 C8
Monteils *F* 33 B9
Monteiros *P* 44 A5
Montejaque *E* 53 C6
Montejícar *E* 53 A10
Montejo de la Sierra *E* 46 B5
Montelabbate *I* 67 E6
Montelanico *I* 62 D4
Montelavar *P* 50 B1
Montel-de-Gelat *F* 29 D11
Monteleone di Puglia *I* 60 A4
Monteleone di Spoleto *I* 62 B3
Monteleone d'Orvieto *I* 62 B2
Monteleone Rocca Doria *I* 64 C2
Montelepre *I* 58 C3
Montelibretti *I* 62 C3
Montélier *F* 31 F7
Montélimar *F* 35 A8
Montella *I* 60 B4
Montellano *E* 51 E8
Montels *F* 33 D8
Montelupo Fiorentino *I* 66 E3
Montelupone *I* 67 F8
Montemaggiore Belsito *I* 58 D4
Montemagno *I* 37 B8
Montemarciano *I* 67 E7
Montemayor *E* 53 A7
Montemayor de Pililla *E* 40 E3
Montemboeuf *F* 29 D7
Montemesola *I* 61 B8
Montemiletto *I* 60 A3
Montemilone *I* 60 A5
Montemolín *E* 51 C7
Montemonaco *I* 62 B4
Montemor-o-Novo *P* 50 B3
Montemurlo *I* 66 E3
Montemurro *I* 60 C5
Montenay *F* 23 D10
Montendre *F* 28 E5
Montenegro de Cameros *E* 40 D6
Montenero di Bisaccia *I* 63 D7
Montenerodomo *I* 63 C6
Monte Porzio *I* 67 E7
Monteprandone *I* 62 B5
Montepulciano *I* 62 A1
Monterblanc *F* 22 E6
Monterchi *I* 66 F5
Monte Real *P* 44 E3
Montereale *I* 62 B4
Montereau-fault-Yonne *F* 25 D8
Monte Redondo *P* 44 E3
Monterenzio *I* 66 D3
Monteriggioni *I* 66 F3
Monteroduni *I* 63 D6
Monte Romano *I* 62 C1
Monteroni d'Arbia *I* 66 F3
Monteroni di Lecce *I* 61 C10
Monterosso Almo *I* 59 E6
Monterosso Calabro *I* 59 B9
Monterotondo *I* 62 C3
Monterotondo Marittimo *I* 66 F2
Monterrei *E* 38 E5
Monterroso *E* 38 C4
Monterrubio de la Serena *E* 51 B9
Monterubbiano *I* 62 A5
Montesa *E* 56 D3
Monte San Biagio *I* 62 E4
Monte San Giovanni Campano *I* 62 D5
Montesano Salentino *I* 61 D10
Montesano sulla Marcellana *I* 60 C5
Monte San Savino *I* 66 F4
Monte Santa Maria Tiberina *I* 66 F5
Monte Sant'Angelo *I* 63 D9
Monte San Vito *I* 67 E7
Montesarchio *I* 60 A3
Montescaglioso *I* 61 B7
Montesclaros *E* 46 D3
Montescudaio *I* 66 F2
Montese *I* 66 D2
Montesilvano *I* 63 B6
Montespertoli *I* 66 E3
Montesquieu *F* 33 B8
Montesquieu-Volvestre *F* 33 D8
Montesquiou *F* 33 C6
Montes Velhos *P* 50 D3
Monteux *F* 35 B8
Montevago *I* 58 D2
Montevarchi *I* 66 E4
Montevecchia *I* 64 D2
Monteverde *I* 60 A5
Montevil *P* 50 C2
Montfaucon *F* 23 F9
Montfaucon *F* 29 F9
Montfaucon-d'Argonne *F* 19 F11
Montfaucon-en-Velay *F* 30 E5
Montferran-Savès *F* 33 C7
Montferrat *F* 36 D4
Montferrier *F* 33 E9
Montfoort *NL* 182 A5
Montfort *F* 23 D8
Montfort *F* 32 D4
Montfort *NL* 183 C7
Montfort-en-Chalosse *F* 32 C4
Montfort-l'Amaury *F* 24 C6
Montfort-le-Gesnois *F* 24 D3
Montfort-sur-Risle *F* 18 F2
Montgai *E* 42 D5
Montgaillard *F* 33 D6
Montgaillard *F* 33 E9
Montgenèvre *F* 31 F10
Montgeron *F* 25 C7
Montgiscard *F* 33 D9
Montgivray *F* 29 B9
Montgomery *GB* 10 F5
Montguyon *F* 28 E5
Monthermé *F* 19 E10
Monthey *CH* 31 C10
Monthois *F* 19 F10
Monthureux-sur-Saône *F* 26 D4
Monti *I* 64 B3
Monticelli d'Ongina *I* 69 C8
Monticello *F* 37 F9
Montichiari *I* 66 B1
Monticiano *I* 65 A4
Montiel *E* 55 B7
Montier-en-Der *F* 25 D12
Montieri *I* 65 A4
Montiers-sur-Saulx *F* 26 C3
Montiglio *I* 68 C5
Montignac *F* 29 E8
Montignies-le-Tilleul *B* 19 D9
Montignoso *I* 66 D1
Montigny *F* 27 C6
Montigny-la-Resie *F* 25 E10
Montigny-le-Roi *F* 26 D3
Montigny-lès-Metz *F* 26 B5
Montigny-Mornay-Villeneuve-sur-Vingeanne *F* 26 E3
Montigny-sur-Aube *F* 25 E12
Montijo *E* 51 B6
Montijo *P* 50 B2
Montilla *E* 53 A7
Montillana *E* 53 A9
Montivilliers *F* 23 A12
Montizón *E* 55 C6
Montjaux *F* 34 B4
Montjean *F* 23 D10
Montjovet *I* 68 B4
Montlaur *F* 34 D4
Montlieu-la-Garde *F* 28 E5
Mont-Louis *F* 33 E10
Montluçon *F* 29 C11
Montluel *F* 31 D7
Montmarault *F* 30 C2
Montmartin-sur-Mer *F* 23 C8
Montmédy *F* 19 E11
Montmélian *F* 31 D9
Montmelo *E* 43 D8
Montmeryran *F* 31 F6
Montmeyan *F* 36 D4
Montmirail *F* 24 D4
Montmirail *F* 25 C10
Montmirey-le-Château *F* 26 F4
Montmoreau-St-Cybard *F* 29 E6
Montmorillon *F* 29 C7
Montmorin *F* 35 B10
Montmorot *F* 31 B8
Montmort-Lucy *F* 25 C10
Montoir-de-Bretagne *F* 23 F7
Montoire-sur-le-Loir *F* 24 E4
Montoison *F* 30 F6
Montoito *P* 50 B4
Montola *FIN* 124 F8
Montón *E* 47 B10
Montone *I* 66 F5
Montopoli di Sabina *I* 62 C3
Montorio al Vomano *I* 62 B5
Montoro *E* 53 A8
Montory *F* 32 D4
Montournais *F* 28 B4
Montpelier *IRL* 8 C6
Montpellier *F* 35 C6
Montpeyroux *F* 34 A4
Montpezat *F* 33 B7
Montpézat *F* 33 D7
Montpezat-de-Quercy *F* 33 B8
Montpezat-sous-Bauzon *F* 30 F5
Montpon-Ménestérol *F* 29 E6
Montpont-en-Bresse *F* 31 B7
Mont-ras *E* 43 D10
Montréal *F* 25 E11
Montréal *F* 33 C6
Montréal *F* 33 D10
Montredon-Labessonnié *F* 33 C10
Montregard *F* 30 E5
Montréjeau *F* 33 D7
Montrésor *F* 24 F5
Montresta *I* 64 C2
Montret *F* 31 B7
Montreuil *F* 15 G12
Montreuil-Bellay *F* 23 F11
Montreuil-Juigné *F* 23 E10
Montreux *CH* 31 C10
Montrevault *F* 23 F9
Montrevel-en-Bresse *F* 31 C7
Montrichard *F* 24 F5
Montricoux *F* 33 B9
Montriond *F* 31 C10
Mont-roig del Camp *E* 42 E5
Montrond *F* 31 B8
Montrond-les-Bains *F* 30 D5
Montrose *GB* 5 B12
Montroy *E* 48 F3
Monts *F* 24 F4
Montsalvy *F* 29 F10
Montsauche-les-Settons *F* 25 F11
Montségur *F* 33 E9
Montseny *E* 43 D8
Montsoué *F* 32 C4
Mont-sous-Vaudrey *F* 31 B8
Monts-sur-Guesnes *F* 29 B6
Mont-St-Aignan *F* 18 F3
Mont-St-Jean *F* 25 F11
Mont-St-Martin *F* 19 E12
Mont-St-Vincent *F* 30 B5
Montsûrs *F* 23 D10
Montsuzain *F* 25 D11
Mõntu *EST* 130 F4
Montuïri *E* 57 B10
Montvalent *F* 29 F9
Montville *F* 18 E3
Montzen *B* 183 D7
Montzéville *F* 20 F4
Monza *I* 69 B7
Monzelfeld *D* 21 E8
Monzingen *D* 21 E9
Monzón *E* 42 D4
Monzón de Campos *E* 40 D3
Mook *NL* 183 B7
Moone *IRL* 7 G9
Moordorf (Südbrookmerland) *D* 17 B8
Moorends *GB* 11 D10
Moorenweis *D* 75 F9
Moorfields *GB* 4 F4
Moorrege *D* 82 C7
Moorslede *B* 19 C7
Moorweg *D* 17 A9
Moos *D* 76 E3
Moosbach *D* 75 C11
Moosburg *A* 73 C9
Moosburg an der Isar *D* 75 F10
Moosinning *D* 75 F10
Mooste *EST* 131 E14
Mór *H* 149 B10
Mora *E* 46 E5
Mora *P* 50 B3
Mora *S* 97 B14
Mora *S* 102 D8
Móra d'Ebre *E* 42 E5
Mora de Rubielos *E* 48 D3
Moradillo de Roa *E* 40 E4
Morąg *PL* 139 C8
Mórahalom *H* 150 E4
Moraice *MNE* 163 C7
Moraira *E* 56 D5
Morais *P* 39 E6
Moraïtika *GR* 168 E2
Morakovo *MNE* 163 D7
Moral de Calatrava *E* 54 B5
Moraleda de Zafayona *E* 53 B9
Moraleja *E* 45 D7
Moraleja del Vino *E* 39 F8
Moraleja de Sayago *E* 45 B9
Morales de Campos *E* 39 E9
Morales del Vino *E* 39 F8
Morales de Toro *E* 39 E9
Morales de Valverde *E* 39 E8
Moralina *E* 39 F7
Moräng *S* 118 D3
Morano Calabro *I* 60 D6
Morano sul Po *I* 68 C5
Morar *GB* 4 B5
Morărești *RO* 160 C5
Morasverdes *E* 45 C8
Morata de Jalón *E* 41 F9
Morata de Tajuña *E* 46 D6
Moratalla *E* 55 C9
Morava *BG* 166 C4
Morava *MD* 154 C4
Morava *SLO* 73 E10
Moravany *CZ* 77 B9
Moravany *CZ* 77 D11
Moravany *SK* 145 F4
Moravče *SLO* 73 E10
Moravice *HR* 67 B11
Moravița *RO* 159 C7
Moravka *BG* 166 C6
Morávka *CZ* 147 B7
Moravská Třebová *CZ* 77 C11
Moravské Budějovice *CZ* 77 D9
Moravské Lieskové *SK* 146 D5
MoravskýMoravskýx *CZ* 146 B4
Moravský Svätý Ján *SK* 77 E12
Morawica *PL* 143 E10
Morbach *D* 21 E8
Morbegno *I* 69 A8
Morbier *F* 31 B9
Mörbisch am See *A* 149 A7
Mörby *S* 99 C10
Mörbylånga *S* 89 B10
Morcenx *F* 32 B4
Morciano di Leuca *I* 61 D10
Morciano di Romagna *I* 66 E6
Morcone *I* 60 A3
Mordelles *F* 23 D8
Mordoğan *TR* 177 B8
Mordy *PL* 141 F7
More *LV* 135 B10
Moréac *F* 22 E6
Moreanes *P* 50 D4
Morebattle *GB* 5 D12
Morecambe *GB* 10 C6
Moreda *E* 39 B8
Moreda *E* 55 E6
Morée *F* 24 E5
Mörel *CH* 70 E6
Morella *E* 42 F3
Moreni *RO* 161 D7
Morenish *GB* 5 C8
Morentín *E* 32 E1
Moreruela de Tábara *E* 39 E8
Mores *I* 64 B2
Morestel *F* 31 D7
Moretonhampstead *GB* 13 D7
Moreton-in-Marsh *GB* 13 B11
Moret-sur-Loing *F* 25 D8
Moretta *I* 37 B7
Moreuil *F* 18 E5
Morez *F* 31 B9
Morfa Nefyn *GB* 10 F2
Morfasso *I* 69 D8
Mörfelden *D* 187 B6
Morfi *GR* 168 D5
Morfi *GR* 168 F3
Morfovouni *GR* 169 F6
Morgat *F* 22 D2
Morgedal *N* 95 D8
Morges *CH* 31 B10
Morgex *I* 31 D11
Morgongåva *S* 98 C7
Morhange *F* 26 C6
Mori *I* 69 B10
Moria *GR* 177 A8
Moricone *I* 62 C3
Morienval *F* 18 F6
Moriles *E* 53 B7
Morinë *AL* 163 E10
Morinë *RKS* 163 E9
Moringen *D* 78 C6
Morino *I* 62 D4
Moritzburg *D* 80 D5
Morjärv *S* 118 B9
Mork *N* 104 F3
Mørke *DK* 86 C6
Morkkaperä *FIN* 115 E1
Mørkøv *DK* 87 D9
Morkovice *CZ* 77 D12
Mörkret *S* 102 C4
Morlaàs *F* 32 D5
Morlaix *F* 22 C4
Morlanne *F* 32 C4
Morlanwelz *B* 19 D9
Mörlenbach *D* 21 E11
Morley *F* 26 C3
Morley *GB* 11 D8
Morley's Bridge *IRL* 8 E4
Mörlunda *S* 89 A9
Mormanno *I* 60 D6
Mormant *F* 25 C8
Mormoiron *F* 35 B9
Mornant *F* 30 D6
Mornas *F* 35 B8
Mornese *I* 37 B9
Moroeni *RO* 161 C6
Morolo *I* 62 D4
Morón de Almazán *E* 41 F7
Morón de la Frontera *E* 51 E9
Moros *E* 41 F8
Morosaglia *F* 37 G10
Morottaja *FIN* 115 E4
Morović *SRB* 158 C3
Morozova *RUS* 129 F14
Morozovo *BG* 166 D4
Morozzo *I* 37 C7
Morpeth *GB* 5 E13
Mørrevatnet *N* 104 D8
Morrfjord *N* 110 D8
Morriston *GB* 13 B7
Morrovalle *I* 67 F8
Mörrum *S* 89 C7
Morsbach *D* 21 C9
Morschen *D* 78 D6
Morshyn *UA* 145 E8
Mörsil *S* 105 E15
Morskoga *S* 97 C13
Morskogen *N* 95 B14
Morsum *D* 17 C12
Mørsvikbotn *N* 111 E10
Mortagne-au-Perche *F* 24 C4
Mortagne-sur-Gironde *F* 28 E4
Mortagne-sur-Sèvre *F* 28 A4
Mortágua *P* 44 D4
Mortain *F* 23 C10
Mortara *I* 68 C6
Morteau *F* 31 A10
Morteaux-Coulibœuf *F* 23 C11
Mörtebo *S* 103 E12
Mortegliano *I* 73 E7
Mortelle *I* 59 C8
Morteni *RO* 160 D6
Mortensnes *N* 112 C11
Mortensnes *N* 114 C6
Mortimer's Cross *GB* 13 A9
Morton *GB* 11 F11
Mortrée *F* 23 C12
Mörtschach *A* 73 C6
Mortsel *B* 19 B9
Mörtsjön *S* 106 D7
Mortsund *N* 110 D6
Morud *DK* 86 E6
Morunglav *RO* 160 E4
Morville *GB* 10 F7
Mor'ye *RUS* 129 E15
Moryń *PL* 84 E6
Morzeszczyn *PL* 138 C6
Morzine *F* 31 C10
Moșana *MD* 153 A11
Mosar *BY* 133 F2
Mosås *S* 92 A6
Mosätt *S* 102 B7
Mosbach *D* 21 F12
Mosbjerg *DK* 90 D7
Mosborough *GB* 11 E9
Mosby *N* 90 C2
Moscavide *P* 50 B1
Moščenica *HR* 149 F6
Mošćenička Draga *HR* 67 B9
Moschopotamos *GR* 169 D7
Mosciano Sant'Angelo *I* 62 B5
Mościcha *PL* 140 C8
Moscovei *MD* 154 F2
Moscow *GB* 5 D8
Moseby *DK* 86 A5
Mosėdis *LT* 134 D3
Mosel *D* 79 E11
Möser *D* 79 B10
Mosina *PL* 81 B11
Mosjö *S* 107 E13
Mosjøen *N* 108 E5
Moskaret *N* 101 B12
Mosko *BIH* 162 D5
Moskorzew *PL* 143 E8
Moskosel *S* 109 E17
Moskuvaara *FIN* 115 C1
Moslavna Podravska *HR* 149 E9
Moșna *RO* 152 E4
Moșna *RO* 153 D11
Moșnița Nouă *RO* 159 B7
Moșoaia *RO* 160 D5
Moso in Passiria *I* 72 C3
Mosonmagyaróvár *H* 146 F4
Mosonszolnok *H* 146 F4
Mošovce *SK* 147 D7
Mosqueruela *E* 48 D4
Moss *N* 95 D13
Mossala *FIN* 126 E5
Mossat *GB* 3 L11
Mossbo *S* 103 D11
Mössingen *D* 27 D11
Mossley *GB* 4 F5
Mossley *GB* 11 D7
Moss-side *GB* 4 E4
Mosstakan *S* 96 C7
Most *BG* 166 F5
Most *CZ* 76 A5
Mostar *BIH* 157 F8
Mosteiro *E* 38 B5
Mosteiro *P* 44 E5
Mosteiro *P* 50 D4
Mostek *CZ* 77 B9
Moșteni *RO* 161 E7
Mosterhamn *N* 94 C2
Mostkowo *PL* 85 E8
Mostkowo *PL* 139 C9
Most na Soči *SLO* 73 D8
Móstoles *E* 46 D5
Mosty *PL* 141 G8
Mostys'ka *UA* 144 D7
Mosty u Jablunkova *CZ* 147 B7
Mosvik *N* 105 D10
Mosyr *UA* 144 A9
Moszczenica *PL* 143 C8
Mota del Cuervo *E* 47 F7
Mota del Marqués *E* 39 E9
Moțăieni *RO* 160 C6
Motala *S* 92 B6
Motarzyno *PL* 85 B12
Moțătei *RO* 159 E11
Moțca *RO* 153 C9
Motherwell *GB* 5 D9
Môtiers *CH* 31 B10
Motike *BIH* 156 D6
Motike *BIH* 157 C7
Motilla del Palancar *E* 47 E9
Motilleja *E* 47 F9
Motjärnshyttan *S* 97 C10
Motoșeni *RO* 153 E10
Motovun *HR* 67 B8
Motril *E* 53 C9
Motru *RO* 159 D10
Motta Montecorvino *I* 63 D8
Motta San Giovanni *I* 59 C8
Motta Visconti *I* 69 C6
Motten *D* 74 B6
Möttingen *D* 75 E8
Mottola *I* 61 B8
Möttönen *FIN* 123 D13
Mötz *A* 71 C11
Mou *DK* 86 B6
Moucha *GR* 174 A4
Mouchamps *F* 28 B3
Mouchan *F* 33 C6
Moudon *CH* 31 B10
Moudros *GR* 171 E8
Mougins *F* 36 D6
Mouhijärvi *FIN* 127 B9
Moularès *F* 33 B10
Moulay *F* 23 D10
Mouleydier *F* 29 F7
Mouliherne *F* 23 F12
Moulin-Neuf *F* 33 D9
Moulins *F* 30 B3
Moulins-Engilbert *F* 30 B4
Moulins-la-Marche *F* 24 C3
Moulis-en-Médoc *F* 28 E4
Moulismes *F* 29 C7
Moult *F* 23 B11
Moulton *GB* 15 C7
Moulton *GB* 15 C9
Mountbellew *IRL* 6 F6
Mount Bellew *IRL* 6 F6
Mountbenger *GB* 5 D10
Mountcharles *IRL* 6 C6
Mountcollins *IRL* 8 D4
Mount Hamilton *GB* 4 F2
Mountjoy *GB* 4 F2
Mountjoy *GB* 7 C9
Mountmellick *IRL* 7 F8
Mount Norris *GB* 7 D10
Mount Nugent *IRL* 7 E8
Mountrath *IRL* 7 F8
Mountshannon *IRL* 8 C6
Mountsorrel *GB* 11 F9
Moura *P* 50 C5
Mourão *P* 51 C5
Mourenx *F* 32 D4
Mouriès *F* 35 C8
Mouries *GR* 169 B8
Mouriki *GR* 175 C7
Mourisca do Vouga *P* 44 C4
Mouriscas *P* 44 E4
Mournies *GR* 178 E7
Mourujärvi *FIN* 121 B11
Mouscron *B* 19 C7
Moussac *F* 35 C7
Moussey *F* 27 D7
Moussoulens *F* 33 D10
Moussy *F* 25 F9
Moustéru *F* 22 C5
Moustey *F* 32 B4
Moustheni *GR* 170 C6
Moustiers-Ste-Marie *F* 36 D4
Mouthe *F* 31 B9
Mouthier-Haute-Pierre *F* 31 A9
Mouthiers-sur-Boëme *F* 29 D6
Mouthoumet *F* 34 E4
Moutier *CH* 27 F7
Moutier-d'Ahun *F* 29 C10
Moûtiers *F* 31 E10
Moutiers-les-Mauxfaits *F* 28 C3
Moutnice *CZ* 77 D11
Moutsouna *GR* 177 E6
Moux *F* 34 D4
Moux-en-Morvan *F* 25 F11
Mouy *F* 18 F5
Mouzaki *GR* 169 F6
Mouzaki *GR* 174 D4
Mouzay *F* 19 F11
Mouzon *F* 19 E11
Moviken *S* 103 C12
Movila *RO* 155 D1
Movila Miresii *RO* 155 C1
Movileni *RO* 153 C10
Movileni *RO* 153 F10
Movileni *RO* 160 E5
Movilița *RO* 153 F10
Movilița *RO* 161 D8
Moville *IRL* 4 E2
Movollen *N* 105 F11
Mowtie *GB* 5 B12
Moy *GB* 3 L8
Moy *GB* 7 D9
Moya *E* 47 E10
Moyard *IRL* 6 E2
Moyasta *IRL* 8 C3
Moycullen *IRL* 6 F4
Moy-de-l'Aisne *F* 19 E7
Moyenmoutier *F* 27 D6
Moyenneville *F* 18 D4
Moygashel *GB* 7 D9
Moyivka *UA* 154 A2
Möykkylänperä *FIN* 119 E13
Möykkyylänperä *FIN* 119 F17
Moylaw *IRL* 6 D4
Moylett *IRL* 7 E8
Moylough *IRL* 6 F5
Moymore *IRL* 8 C5
Moyne *IRL* 7 E7
Moyvalley *IRL* 7 F9
Moyvore *IRL* 7 E7
Mozac *F* 30 D3
Mozăceni *RO* 160 D6
Mozárbez *E* 45 C9
Mozelj *SLO* 73 E10
Mozelos *P* 44 C5
Mozgovo *SRB* 159 F8
Mozirje *SLO* 73 D10
Mozoncillo *E* 46 B4
Mozsgó *H* 149 D9
Mozyr' *RUS* 136 E3
Mračaj *BIH* 157 E7
Mrągowo *PL* 136 F3
Mrákov *CZ* 76 D3
Mrakovica *BIH* 157 B6
Mramor *BIH* 157 F8
Mramorak *SRB* 159 D6
Mratinje *MNE* 157 F10
Mrčajevci *SRB* 158 F6
Mrežičko *NMK* 169 B6
Mrkalji *BIH* 157 D10
Mrkonjić=-Grad *BIH* 157 D7
Mrkopalj *HR* 67 B10
Mrmoš *SRB* 164 B3
Mrocza *PL* 85 D13
Mroczeń *PL* 142 D4
Mroczków *PL* 141 H3
Mroczno *PL* 139 D8
Mrozy *PL* 141 F5
Mścice *PL* 85 B10
Mściwojów *PL* 81 D10
Mšené Lázně *CZ* 76 B6
Mšeno *CZ* 77 B7
Mshinskaya *RUS* 132 C6
Mstów *PL* 143 E7
Mszana *PL* 147 B7
Mszana Dolna *PL* 144 D1
Mszczonów *PL* 141 G3
Muccia *I* 62 A4
Much *D* 21 C8
Muchalls *GB* 5 A12
Mucharz *PL* 147 B9
Mücheln (Geiseltal) *D* 79 D10
Muchow *D* 83 D11
Muchówka *PL* 144 D1
Much Wenlock *GB* 10 F6
Mucientes *E* 39 E10
Mücka *D* 81 D7
Mücke Große-Eichen *D* 21 C12
Mücke-Nieder-Ohmen *D* 21 C12
Muckross *IRL* 8 D4
Múcsony *H* 145 G2
Mudanya *TR* 173 D10
Mudau *D* 187 B7
Müdelheim *D* 183 C9
Müden (Aller) *D* 79 A7
Müden (Örtze) *D* 83 E8
Mudersbach *D* 185 C8
Mŭdrets *BG* 166 E6
Muel *E* 41 F9
Muelas del Pan *E* 39 E8
Muff *IRL* 4 E2
Muga de Sayago *E* 39 F7
Mugardos *E* 38 B3
Muge *P* 44 F3
Mügeln *D* 80 C4
Mügeln *D* 80 D4
Mugeni *RO* 152 E6
Muggensturm *D* 187 D5
Muggia *I* 73 E8
Muğla *TR* 181 B8
Mŭglen *BG* 167 D8
Mŭglizh *BG* 166 D5
Mugron *F* 32 C4
Mühlacker *D* 27 C10
Mühlanger *D* 79 C12
Mühlbachl *A* 72 B3
Mühlberg *D* 79 E8
Mühlberg *D* 80 D4
Mühldorf *A* 73 C7
Mühldorf am Inn *D* 75 F12
Mühldorf bei Feldbach *A* 148 C5
Mühlen *A* 73 B10
Mühlenbeck *D* 84 E4
Mühlhausen *D* 21 F11
Mühlhausen *D* 75 D9
Mühlhausen (Thüringen) *D* 79 D7
Mühltroff *D* 75 A10
Muhola *FIN* 123 D14
Muhos *FIN* 119 E15
Muhr am See *D* 75 D8
Muhur *AL* 163 F9
Muineachán *IRL* 7 D9
Muine Bheag *IRL* 9 C9
Muiños *E* 38 E4
Muirdrum *GB* 5 B11
Muirhead *GB* 5 C10
Muirkirk *GB* 5 D8
Muir of Ord *GB* 2 K8
Muizon *F* 19 F8
Mujdić *BIH* 157 D7
Mujejärvi *FIN* 125 C12
Mukacheve *UA* 145 G6
Mukařov *CZ* 77 C7
Mukhavyets *BY* 141 F9
Mukhovo *BG* 165 E8
Mukkala *FIN* 115 D5
Mukkavaara *FIN* 115 D4
Mula *E* 55 C10
Mulbarton *GB* 15 B11
Muleby *DK* 88 E7
Mulešići *BIH* 157 C9
Mulfingen *D* 74 D6
Mülheim an der Ruhr *D* 17 F7
Mülheim-Kärlich *D* 185 D7
Mulhouse *F* 27 E7
Muljava *SLO* 73 E10
Mullach Íde *IRL* 7 F10
Mullagh *IRL* 7 E9
Mullagh *IRL* 7 F9
Mullaghroe *IRL* 6 E6
Mullany's Cross *IRL* 6 D5
Mullartown *GB* 7 D11
Müllheim *D* 27 E8
Mullhyttan *S* 92 A5
Mullingar *IRL* 7 E8
Mullion *GB* 12 E4
Müllrose *D* 80 B6
Mullsjö *S* 91 D14
Mulrany *IRL* 6 E3
Mulsanne *F* 23 E12
Mulseryd *S* 91 D14
Multia *FIN* 123 F13
Multiperä *FIN* 121 C15
Mümliswil *CH* 27 F8
Munakka *FIN* 122 E9
Muñana *E* 45 C10
Munapirtti *FIN* 128 E6
Münchberg *D* 75 B10
Müncheberg *D* 80 A6
München *D* 75 F10
Münchenbernsdorf *D* 79 E10
Münchenbuchsee *CH* 31 A11
Münchhausen *D* 21 C11
Münchsteinach *D* 75 C8
Münchweiler an der Rodalb *D* 186 C4
Münchwilen *CH* 27 F11
Mundaka *E* 41 B6
Munderkingen *D* 187 E8
Mundesley *GB* 15 B11
Mundford *GB* 15 B10
Mundheim *N* 94 B3
Mundolsheim *F* 27 C8
Munebrega *E* 41 F8
Munera *E* 55 A8

Mungia E 40 B6
Mungret IRL 8 C5
Muñico E 45 C10
Muniesa E 42 E2
Munilla E 41 D7
Munka-Ljungby S 87 C11
Munkbyn S 103 B11
Munkebakken N 114 D6
Munkebo DK 86 E7
Munkedal S 91 C10
Munken N 104 D6
Munkflohögen S 106 D7
Munkfors S 97 C10
Munklia N 111 D14
Munksund S 118 D7
Munktorp S 98 C6
Munkzwalm B 19 C8
Munne FIN 128 C7
Münnerstadt D 75 B7
Munningen D 75 E8
Muñogalindo E 46 C3
Munsala FIN 122 D8
Münsingen CH 31 B12
Münsingen D 74 F5
Münster A 72 B4
Münster CH 70 E6
Münster D 17 E9
Münster D 21 E11
Münster D 83 E8
Munster F 27 D7
Münsterdorf D 82 C7
Munstergeleen NL 183 D7
Münsterhausen D 75 F7
Münstermaifeld D 185 D7
Muntendam NL 17 B7
Munteni RO 153 F10
Munteni-Buzău RO 161 D9
Muntenii de Jos RO 153 D11
Münzenberg D 21 D11
Münzkirchen A 76 F5
Muodoslompolo S 117 C10
Muonio FIN 117 C11
Muonionalusta S 117 C11
Muotathal CH 71 D7
Muotkajärvi FIN 117 B10
Muotkavaara FIN 117 C12
Mur SRB 163 C9
Muradiye TR 173 D9
Muradiye TR 177 B9
Murakeresztúr H 149 D7
Muráň SK 147 D10
Muras E 38 B4
Murasson F 34 C4
Muraste EST 131 C8
Muraszemenye H 149 D7
Murat F 30 E2
Muratlar TR 181 B9
Muratli TR 173 B7
Murato F 37 F10
Murat-sur-Vèbre F 34 C4
Murau A 73 B9
Muravera I 64 E4
Murazzano I 37 C8
Murça P 38 F5
Murchante E 41 D8
Mŭrchevo BG 165 B7
Murchin D 84 C5
Murcia E 56 F2
Murczyn PL 138 E4
Mur-de-Barrez F 29 F11
Mûr-de-Bretagne F 22 D6
Mur-de-Sologne F 24 F6
Mureck A 148 C5
Mürefte TR 173 C7
Muret F 33 D8
Murgeni RO 153 E12
Murgenthal CH 27 F8
Murgești RO 161 C9
Murgia E 40 C6
Muri CH 27 F9
Muri CH 31 B11
Murias de Paredes E 39 C7
Muriedas E 40 B4
Murighiol RO 155 C4
Murillo de Río Leza E 32 F1
Murillo el Fruto E 32 F3
Murino MNE 163 D8
Murisengo I 68 C5
Murjāņi LV 135 B9
Murjek S 116 F5
Murley GB 7 D8
Murlo I 66 F3
Murmastiene LV 135 C13
Murnau am Staffelsee D 72 A3
Muro E 57 B11
Muro F 37 F9
Muro P 38 F2
Muro de Alcoy E 56 D4
Murol F 30 D2
Murole FIN 127 B10
Muro Lucano I 60 B4
Muron F 28 C4
Murony H 151 D7
Muros E 38 C1
Muros E 39 A7
Muros I 64 B2
Murovane UA 144 C9
Murów PL 142 E4
Murowana Goślina PL 81 A12
Murrë AL 168 A3
Murrhardt D 74 E6
Murronkylä FIN 119 E16
Murrough IRL 6 F4
Mursalli TR 177 D10
Mûrs-Erigné F 23 F10
Murska Sobota SLO 148 C6
Mursko Središće HR 149 C6
Murtas E 55 F6
Murtede P 44 D4
Murten CH 31 B11
Murter HR 156 E4
Murtino NMK 169 B8
Murto FIN 119 E15
Murtolahti FIN 125 D9
Murtomäki FIN 124 B9
Murtovaara FIN 121 C13
Murumoen N 105 C16
Murvica HR 156 D3
Murviel-lès-Béziers F 34 D5
Mürzsteg A 148 A5
Murzynowo PL 81 A8
Mürzzuschlag A 148 A5
Mūsa LV 135 D8
Musbury GB 13 D8
Müschenbach D 185 C8
Musei I 64 E2
Muselievo BG 160 F5
Mushtisht RKS 163 E10
Musile di Piave I 72 E6
Muskö S 93 B12
Mussalo FIN 128 E6
Musselburgh GB 5 D10
Musselkanaal NL 17 C8
Mussidan F 29 E6
Mussomeli I 58 D4
Musson B 19 E12
Mussy-sur-Seine F 25 E12
Mustafakemalpaşa TR 173 D9
Müstair CH 71 D10
Mustamaa FIN 119 F17
Mustamaa FIN 123 D10
Mustasaari FIN 122 D7
Mustavaara FIN 121 D12
Mustavaara FIN 121 F12
Mustinlahti FIN 125 E10
Mustjala EST 130 E4
Mustla EST 131 E11
Mustola FIN 114 F4
Mustolanmäki FIN 125 C10
Mustolanmutka FIN 125 B10
Mustvee EST 131 D13
Muszaki PL 139 D10
Muszyna PL 145 E2
Muta SLO 73 C11
Mutala FIN 127 B10
Mutalahti FIN 125 F16
Mütevelli TR 177 B10
Muthill GB 5 C9
Mutilva Baja E 32 E2
Mutné SK 147 C8
Mutriku E 32 D1
Mutterstadt D 21 F10
Mutxamel E 56 E4
Mutzig F 27 C7
Mutzschen D 80 D3
Muuga EST 131 C13
Muukajärvi S 116 E10
Muuksi EST 131 B11
Muurame FIN 123 F15
Muurasjärvi FIN 123 C14
Muurikkala FIN 128 D8
Muurla FIN 127 E9
Muurola FIN 119 B14
Muurola FIN 128 D8
Muuruvesi FIN 125 D10
Muxía E 38 B1
Muzillac F 22 E7
Mužla SK 149 A11
Myahuny BY 137 C14
Myakishevo RUS 133 C5
Myaretskiya BY 133 F3
Myazhany BY 135 E13
Mybster GB 3 J10
Myckelgensjö S 107 D13
Myckle S 118 E5
Myedna BY 141 G9
Myggenäs S 91 C10
Myggsjö S 102 C8
Myhinpää FIN 124 F7
Myjava SK 146 D5
Mykanów PL 143 E7
Mykhal'cha UA 153 A7
Mykhaylivka UA 154 F5
Myki GR 171 B7
Myklebostad N 110 E9
Mykolayiv UA 145 D8
Mykolayivka UA 154 E4
Mykolayivka-Novorosiys'ka UA 154 E5
Mykonos GR 176 E5
Mykulychyn UA 152 A5
Mykytychi UA 144 B9
Myllykoski FIN 128 D6
Myllykylä FIN 122 E8
Myllykylä FIN 127 E10
Myllykylä FIN 128 D7
Myllylahti FIN 121 D13
Myllymäki FIN 123 E12
Myloi GR 175 D6
Mylopotamos GR 178 C4
Mynämäki FIN 126 D7
Mynttilä FIN 128 C6
Myon F 31 A8
Myory BY 133 E3
Myra GR 169 F8
Myrås S 109 E14
Myre N 110 C9
Myre N 111 B10
Myresjö S 92 E5
Myrhaug N 101 A14
Myrheden S 118 D4
Myrhult S 92 B4
Myrina GR 171 E8
Myriokefala GR 178 E7
Myrkky FIN 122 F7
Myrland N 110 D5
Myrland N 110 D9
Myrland N 111 C10
Myrlandshaugen N 111 C13
Myrmoen N 101 A15
Myrne UA 155 B4
Myrnes N 112 C9
Myrnopillya UA 154 E4
Myrsini GR 174 D3
Myrsini GR 178 B3
Myrskylä FIN 127 D14
Myrties GR 177 F8
Myrtos GR 179 E10
Myrviken S 105 E16
Mysen N 95 C14
Myshall IRL 9 C9
Myślachowice PL 143 F7
Mysłakowice PL 81 E9
Myślenice PL 147 B9
Myślibórz PL 85 E7
Myślice PL 139 C8
Mysłowice PL 143 F7
Mysovka RUS 134 F2
Myssjö S 102 A7
Mystegna GR 177 A7
Mystras GR 174 E5
Myszków PL 143 E7
Myszyniec PL 139 D11
Mytikas GR 174 B2
Mytilini GR 177 A8
Mytilinioi GR 177 D8
Mýtna SK 147 E9
Mýto CZ 76 C5

N

Nå N 94 B5
Naaldwijk NL 16 E2
Naamankylä FIN 119 E17
Naamijoki FIN 117 E11
Naantali FIN 126 E7
Naapurinvaara FIN 121 F11
Naarden NL 183 A6
Näärinki FIN 128 B8
Naarn im Machlande A 77 F7
Naartijärvi S 119 C11
Naarva FIN 125 D16
Naas IRL 7 F9
Näätämö FIN 114 D6
Näätänmaa FIN 125 F10
Näätävaara FIN 121 E13
Nabburg D 75 D11
Nábrád H 145 G5
Na Cealla Beaga IRL 6 C6
Načeradec CZ 77 C7
Nacha BY 137 E10
Náchod CZ 77 B10
Nacina Ves SK 145 F4
Näckådalen S 102 D7
Nackel D 83 E13
Nackenheim D 185 E9
Näcksjö S 103 C12
Na Clocha Liathe IRL 7 F10
Nacpolsk PL 139 E9
Nad IRL 8 D5
Nadalj SRB 158 C4
Nadarzyce PL 85 D11
Nadarzyn PL 141 F3
Naddvik N 100 D7
Nadeș RO 152 E5
Nădlac RO 150 E6
Nădrag RO 159 B9
Nadrichne UA 154 E4
Nádudvar H 151 C7
Năeni RO 161 C8
Nærbø N 94 E3
Næroset N 101 E13
Nærsnes N 95 C13
Næsbjerg DK 86 D3
Næstved DK 87 E9
Näfels CH 27 F11
Nafferton GB 11 C11
Nafpaktos GR 174 C4
Nafplio GR 175 D6
Nagele NL 16 C5
Naggen S 103 B11
Naglarby S 97 B14
Na Gleannta IRL 6 C6
Nagli LV 133 C1
Nagłowice PL 143 E9
Nagold D 27 C10
Nagore E 32 E3
Nago-Torbole I 69 B10
Nagu FIN 126 E6
Nagyatád H 149 D8
Nagybajom H 149 D9
Nagybánhegyes H 151 E6
Nagybaracska H 149 D11
Nagybarca H 145 G2
Nagyberény H 149 C10
Nagyberki H 149 D10
Nagycenk H 149 A7
Nagycsécs H 145 H2
Nagycserkesz H 145 H4
Nagydobos H 145 G5
Nagydorog H 149 C11
Nagyecsed H 145 H5
Nagyfüged H 150 B5
Nagyhalász H 145 G4
Nagyharsány H 149 E10
Nagyhegyes H 151 B7
Nagyigmánd H 149 A10
Nagyiván H 151 C6
Nagykálló H 145 H4
Nagykanizsa H 149 D7
Nagykapornak H 149 C7
Nagykáta H 150 C4
Nagykereki H 151 C8
Nagykónyi H 149 C10
Nagykőrös H 150 C4
Nagykörű H 150 C5
Nagykovácsi H 149 A11
Nagylak H 150 E6
Nagylóc H 147 E9
Nagylók H 149 C11
Nagylózs H 149 A7
Nagymágocs H 150 D5
Nagymaros H 149 A11
Nagynyárád H 149 E11
Nagyoroszi H 147 F8
Nagyrécse H 149 C8
Nagyréde H 150 B4
Nagyszénás H 150 D6
Nagyszokoly H 149 C10
Nagytarcsa H 150 B3
Nagytőke H 150 D5
Nagyvarsány H 145 G5
Nagyvázsony H 149 C9
Nagyvisnyó H 145 G1
Naha EST 132 E1
Naharros E 47 D8
Nahe D 83 C8
Nahirne UA 155 C2
Nahrendorf D 83 D9
Naidaș RO 159 D8
Naila D 75 B10
Nailloux F 33 D9
Nailsworth GB 13 B10
Naimakka S 116 A7
Naintré F 29 B6
Naipköy TR 173 C7
Nairn GB 3 K9
Naives-Rosières F 26 C3
Naizin F 22 E6
Najac F 33 B9
Nájera E 40 D6
Näkkälä FIN 117 A11
Nakkerud N 95 B12
Nakkila FIN 126 C7
Náklo CZ 77 C12
Nakło PL 143 E8
Naklo SLO 73 D9
Nakło nad Notecią PL 85 D13
Nakomiady PL 136 E3
Näkotne LV 134 C6
Nakovo SRB 150 F6
Nakskov DK 83 A10
Nalbach D 186 C2
Nalbant RO 155 C3
Nalda E 41 D7
Nälden S 105 E16
Nałęczów PL 141 H6
Nálepkovo SK 145 F2
Näljänkä FIN 121 D11
Nalkki FIN 121 E10
Nalliers F 28 C3
Nalžovské Hory CZ 76 D5
Namborn D 21 E8
Nambroca E 46 E5
Namdalseid N 105 C10
Náměšť nad Oslavou CZ 77 D10
Náměšť na Hané CZ 77 C12
Námestovo SK 147 C8
Nämpnäs FIN 122 E6
Namsos N 105 C11
Namsskogan N 105 B14
Namsvatn N 105 B15
Namur B 19 D10
Namysłów PL 142 D4
Nana RO 161 E9
Nána SK 147 F7
Nançay F 24 F7
Nanclares de la Oca E 40 C6
Nancy F 26 C5
Nandrin B 183 D6
Nănești RO 161 B10
Nangis F 25 C9
Nannestad N 95 B13
Nanov RO 160 F6
Nans-les-Pins F 35 D10
Nant F 34 B5
Nanterre F 25 C7
Nantes F 23 F8
Nanteuil-le-Haudouin F 25 B8
Nantiat F 29 C8
Nantua F 31 C8
Nantwich GB 10 E6
Naousa GR 169 C7
Naousa GR 176 E5
Napajedla CZ 146 C5
Napiwoda PL 139 D9
Napkor H 145 H4
Napola I 58 D2
Napoli I 60 B2
Napp N 110 D5
Năpradea RO 151 C11
Náquera E 48 E4
När S 93 E13
Nåra N 100 D1
Nárai H 149 B7
Narberth GB 12 B5
Narbolia I 64 C2
Narbonne F 34 D5
Narbonne-Plage F 34 D5
Narborough GB 15 B10
Narbuvoll N 101 B14
Narcao I 64 E2
Narcy F 25 F9
Nardò I 61 C10
Narechenski Bani BG 165 F10
Narew PL 140 E9
Narewka PL 141 E9
Närhilä FIN 123 E16
Narin IRL 6 C6
Nāriņciems LV 134 B5
Narkaus FIN 119 B16
Narken S 116 E9
Narlıdere TR 177 C9
Narni I 62 B3
Naro I 58 E4
Narol PL 144 C7
Närpes FIN 122 F6
Narrosse F 32 C3
Narta HR 149 E7
Nartë AL 168 D1
Năruja RO 153 F9
Naruska FIN 115 D6
Naruszewo PL 139 E9
Narva EST 132 C3
Narva FIN 127 C10
Narva-Jõesuu EST 132 C3
Närvijoki FIN 122 E7
Narvik N 111 D13
Narzole I 37 B7
Narzym PL 139 D9
Näs FIN 99 B14
Nås N 90 A5
Nås S 93 E12
Nås S 97 B12
Näs S 102 A8
Näsåker S 107 E11
Năsăud RO 152 C4
Nasavrky CZ 77 C9
Näsberg S 103 C10
Nasbinals F 34 A5
Näs bruk S 98 B6
Näsby S 89 C10
Na Sceirí IRL 7 E10
Näset S 103 D9
Nashec RKS 163 E10
Našice HR 149 F10
Nasielsk PL 139 E10
Näske S 107 E15
Näsliden S 107 A16
Naso I 59 C6
Nassau D 21 D9
Nassereith A 71 C11
Nässja S 92 C5
Nässjö S 92 D5
Nässjö S 107 D10
Nassogne B 19 D11
Nästansjö S 107 B11
Nastätten D 185 D8
Nästeln S 102 A7
Nastola FIN 127 D14
Năsturelu RO 161 F6
Näsum S 88 C7
Nasutów PL 141 H6
Näsviken S 103 C12
Näsviken S 106 D9
Naszály H 149 A10
Natalinci SRB 159 E6
Nateby GB 11 C7
Naters CH 68 A4
Nattavaara S 116 E5
Nattavaara by S 116 E6
Nattheim D 75 E7
Nättraby S 89 C9
Naturno I 71 D11
Naucelle F 33 B10
Naucelles F 29 F10
Naudaskalns LV 133 B2
Nauders A 71 D11
Naudīte LV 134 C6
Nauen D 79 A12
Nauendorf D 79 C10
Nauheim D 21 E10
Naujac-sur-Mer F 28 E3
Naujamiestis LT 135 E8
Naujasis Daugėliškis LT 135 F12
Naujoji Akmenė LT 134 D5
Naujoji Vilnia LT 137 D11
Naukšēni LV 131 F10
Naul IRL 7 E10
Naulaperä FIN 121 E10
Naulavaara FIN 125 C10
Naumburg (Hessen) D 17 F12
Naumburg (Saale) D 79 D10
Naundorf D 80 D4
Naundorf D 80 E4
Naunhof D 79 D12
Nauroth D 21 C9
Naurstad N 108 B8
Naustbukta N 105 B11
Naustdal N 100 C3
Nauste N 101 A8
Nautijaur S 109 C17
Nautsi RUS 114 E6
Nautsund N 100 D2
Nava E 39 B9
Navacepeda de Tormes E 45 D10
Navaconcejo E 45 D9
Nava de Arévalo E 46 C3
Nava de la Asunción E 46 B4
Nava del Rey E 39 F9
Nava de Sotrobal E 45 C10
Navadrutsk BY 133 F2
Navafría E 46 B5
Navahermosa E 46 E4
Navajas E 48 E4
Naval E 42 C4
Navalagamella E 46 D4
Navalcaballo E 41 E6
Navalcán E 45 D10
Navalcarnero E 46 D4
Navalero E 40 E6
Navalmanzano E 46 B4
Navalmoral E 46 D3
Navalmoral de la Mata E 45 E9
Navalonguilla E 45 D10
Navalosa E 46 D3
Navalperal de Pinares E 46 C4
Navalpino E 46 F3
Navaluenga E 46 D3
Navalvillar de Ibor E 45 E10
Navalvillar de Pela E 45 F10
Navamorcuende E 46 D3
Navan IRL 7 E9
Navapolatsk BY 133 E5
Navarcles E 43 D7
Navardún E 32 E3
Navarredonda de la Rinconada E 45 C8
Navarrenx F 32 D4
Navarrés E 48 F3
Navarrete E 41 D6
Navarrevisca E 46 D3
Navàs E 43 D7
Navascués E 32 E3
Navas de Estrena E 46 E3
Navas de Jorquera E 47 F9
Navas del Madroño E 45 E7
Navas del Rey E 46 D4
Navas de Oro E 46 B4
Navas de San Juan E 55 C6
Navasfrías E 45 D7
Navata E 43 C9
Navatalgordo E 46 D3
Nave I 69 B9
Nave P 50 E2
Nave de Haver P 45 C7
Nävekvarn S 93 B9
Navelli I 62 C5
Nåverdal N 101 A12
Näverede S 106 E8
Nave Redonda P 50 E3
Näverkärret S 97 C14
Näverrys FIN 119 C15
Naverstad S 91 B10
Navès E 43 D7
Naves F 29 E9
Navezuelas E 45 E10
Navia E 39 A6
Navilly F 31 B7
Navit N 112 D8
Năvodari RO 155 E3
Nävragöl S 89 C9
Nawojowa PL 145 D2
Naxos GR 176 E5
Nay-Bourdettes F 32 D5
Nazaré P 44 E2
Nazelles-Négron F 24 F4
Nazza D 79 D7
Ndroq AL 168 B2
Nea Agathoupoli GR 169 D8
Nea Alikarnassos GR 178 E9
Nea Anchialos GR 169 F8
Nea Apollonia GR 169 C9
Nea Artaki GR 175 B8
Nea Efesos GR 169 D7
Nea Epidavros GR 175 D7
Nea Figaleia GR 174 E4
Nea Filadelfeia GR 175 C8
Nea Fokaia GR 169 D9
Nea Ionia GR 169 F8
Nea Iraklitsa GR 171 C6
Nea Kallikrateia GR 169 D9
Nea Karvali GR 171 C6
Nea Karya GR 171 C7
Nea Kerdylia GR 169 C10
Nea Kios GR 175 D6
Nea Koroni GR 174 F4
Nea Lampsakos GR 175 C8
Neale IRL 6 E4
Nea Liosia GR 175 C8
Nea Madytos GR 169 C10
Nea Makri GR 175 C8
Nea Malgara GR 169 C8
Nea Mesimvria GR 169 C8
Nea Michaniona GR 169 D8
Nea Moudania GR 169 D9
Nea Olynthos GR 169 D9
Nea Pella GR 169 C8
Nea Peramos GR 171 C6
Nea Peramos GR 175 C7
Nea Plagia GR 169 D9
Neapoli GR 168 D5
Neapoli GR 178 B5
Neapoli GR 179 E10
Nea Poteidaia GR 169 D9
Nea Roda GR 170 D5
Nea Santa GR 169 C8
Nea Santa GR 171 B9
Nea Silata GR 169 D9
Nea Styra GR 175 C9
Neath GB 13 B7
Nea Tiryntha GR 175 D6
Nea Triglia GR 169 D9
Neaua RO 152 E5
Nea Vravrona GR 175 D9
Nea Vyssa GR 171 A11
Nea Zichni GR 169 B10
Nebel D 82 A4
Nébias F 33 E10
Nebljusi HR 156 C4
Nebra (Unstrut) D 79 D10
Nebreda E 40 E4
Nechanice CZ 77 B9
Neckarbischofsheim D 187 C6
Neckargemünd D 21 F11
Neckarsteinach D 21 F11
Neckarsulm D 21 F12
Neckartenzlingen D 27 C11
Necșești RO 160 E6
Necton GB 15 B10
Nečujam HR 156 F5
Neda E 38 B3
Nedansjö S 103 B12
Nedašov CZ 146 C6
Neddemin D 84 C4
Neded SK 146 E5
Nedelino BG 171 B8
Nedelišće HR 149 D6
Nederby DK 86 B4
Nederhögen S 102 B7
Nederhorst den Berg NL 183 A6
Neder Hvam DK 86 C4
Nederlangbroek NL 183 A6
Nedervetil FIN 123 C10
Neder Vindinge DK 87 E9
Nederweert NL 16 F5
Nedlitz D 79 B11
Nedožery-Brezany SK 147 D7
Nedrebø N 94 E4
Nedre Saxnäs S 109 F14
Nedre Soppero S 116 B7
Nedstrand N 94 D3
Nedvědice CZ 77 D10
Nedyalsko BG 167 E7
Nędza PL 142 F5
Needham Market GB 15 C11
Neer NL 183 C8
Neerijnen NL 183 B6
Neermoor D 17 B8
Neeroeteren B 183 C7
Neerpelt B 19 B11
Neetze D 83 D9
Nefyn GB 10 F2
Negenborn D 78 C6
Negoi RO 160 F2
Negomir RO 159 D11
Negorci NMK 169 B7
Negoslavci HR 157 B11
Negotin SRB 159 E10
Negotino NMK 163 F10
Negotino NMK 169 B7
Negrar I 66 A2
Negrași RO 160 D6
Negredo E 47 B7
Negreira E 38 C2
Nègrepelisse F 33 B9
Negrești RO 153 D10
Negrești-Oaș RO 145 H7
Negri RO 153 D9
Negru Vodă RO 155 F2
Nehoiu RO 161 C8
Neiden N 114 D6
Neidín IRL 8 E3
Neitaskaite S 116 E8
Neitsuanto S 116 D5
Neittävä FIN 119 E17
Neive I 37 B8
Nejdek CZ 75 B12
Nekézseny H 145 G1
Nekla PL 81 B12
Neksø DK 89 E8
Nelas P 44 C5
Nellim FIN 114 F4
Nellingen D 74 E6
Nelson GB 11 D7
Nemaitonys LT 137 D9
Neman RUS 136 C5
Nemanjica NMK 164 F4
Nemanskoye RUS 136 C5
Nembro I 69 B8
Nemea GR 175 D6
Nemenčinė LT 137 D11
Nemesgulács H 149 C8
Nemesnádudvar H 150 E3
Nemesvámos H 149 B9
Nemesvid H 149 C8
Németkér H 149 C11
Nemėžis LT 137 D11
Nemours F 25 D8
Nemsdorf-Göhrendorf D 79 D10
Nemšová SK 146 D6
Nemunaitis LT 137 E9
Nemunėlio Radviliškis LT 135 D9
Nemyriv UA 144 C7
Nenagh IRL 8 C6
Nendaz CH 31 C11
Nenince SK 147 E8
Nenita GR 177 C7
Nennhausen D 79 A12
Nennslingen D 75 D9
Nenonpelto FIN 124 F8
Nentershausen D 21 D9
Nentershausen D 78 D6
Nenthead GB 5 F12
Nenzing A 71 C9
Neo Agioneri GR 169 C8
Neochoraki GR 175 C7
Neochori GR 169 B9
Neochori GR 169 F6
Neochori GR 171 B10
Neochori GR 174 A3
Neochori GR 174 C3
Neo Erasmio GR 171 C7
Neoi Epivates GR 169 C8
Neo Monastiri GR 169 F7
Neoneli I 64 C2
Neo Petritsi GR 169 B9
Neorić HR 156 E6
Neos Kafkasos GR 168 C5
Neos Marmaras GR 169 D10
Neos Mylotopos GR 169 C7
Neo Souli GR 169 B10
Neos Pagontas GR 175 B8
Neos Pyrgos GR 175 B7
Neos Skopos GR 169 B10
Néoules F 36 E4
Nepi I 62 C2
Nepomuk CZ 76 D5
Nérac F 33 B6
Neratovice CZ 77 B7
Nerău RO 150 F6
Neravai LT 137 E9
Nerchau D 79 D12
Nercillac F 28 D5
Nerdal N 101 A9
Nerde Gärdsjö S 103 E9
Néré F 28 D5
Nereju RO 153 F9
Neresheim D 75 E7
Neresnica SRB 159 E8
Neresnytsya UA 145 G8
Nereta LV 135 D10
Nereto I 62 B5
Nerezine HR 67 C9
Nerežišće HR 156 F6
Néris-les-Bains F 29 C11
Nerja E 53 C9
Nerkoo FIN 124 D8
Nerlia N 108 E7
Nerokouros GR 178 E7
Néronde F 30 D5
Nérondes F 30 B2
Neroth D 21 D7
Nerpio E 55 C8
Nersac F 28 D6
Nersingen D 75 F7
Nerskogen N 101 A11
Nerushay UA 155 B5
Nerva E 51 D6
Nervesa della Battaglia I 72 E5
Nervieux F 30 D5
Nes FO 2 A3
Nes N 95 D9
Nes N 96 A2
Nes N 110 D9
Nes N 111 D10
Nes NL 16 B5
Nesbyen N 101 E10
Neschwitz D 80 D6
Nesebŭr BG 167 D9
Neset N 112 C7
Nes Flaten N 94 C5
Nesgrenda N 90 B4
Nesheim N 94 D3
Nesje N 110 D6
Nesjegjerde N 100 A6
Nesland N 110 D5
Neslandsvatn N 90 B5
Nesle F 18 E6
Nesna N 108 D5
Nesovice CZ 77 D12
Nessa F 37 F9
Nesse D 17 A8
Nesseby N 114 C6
Nesselwang D 71 B11
Nesslau CH 27 F11
Nessodtangen N 95 C13
Nestani GR 175 D5
Nestby N 108 B9
Nesterov RUS 136 D6
Neston GB 10 E5
Nestorio GR 168 D5
Nestoyita UA 154 B4
Nesttun N 94 B2
Nesvady SK 146 F6
Nesvatnstemmen N 90 B3
Nesvik N 94 D4
Nethy Bridge GB 3 L9
Netolice CZ 76 D6
Netphen D 21 C10
Netra (Ringgau) D 79 D7
Netretić HR 148 E4
Netstal CH 71 C8
Nettancourt F 25 C12
Nettersheim D 21 D7
Nettetal D 16 F6
Nettuno I 62 E3
Netvořice CZ 77 C7
Neu-Anspach D 21 D11
Neuberend D 82 A7
Neuberg an der Mürz A 148 A5
Neubeuern D 72 A5
Neubiberg D 75 F10
Neubrandenburg D 84 C4
Neubruchhausen D 17 C11
Neubrunn D 187 B8
Neubukow D 83 B11
Neubulach D 27 C10
Neuburg am Rhein D 187 D5
Neuburg an der Donau D 75 E9
Neuburg-Steinhausen D 83 C11
Neuburxdorf D 80 D4
Neuchâtel CH 31 B10
Neu Darchau D 83 D9
Neudietendorf D 79 E8
Neudorf A 146 F2
Neudrossenfeld D 75 B10
Neuenbürg D 27 C10
Neuendettelsau D 75 D8
Neuenhagen Berlin D 80 A5
Neuenhaus D 17 D7
Neuenhof CH 27 F9
Neuenkirch CH 27 F9
Neuenkirchen D 17 A11
Neuenkirchen D 17 C11
Neuenkirchen D 17 D8
Neuenkirchen D 17 D9
Neuenkirchen D 82 B6
Neuenkirchen D 82 D7
Neuenkirchen D 84 A4
Neuenkirchen D 84 B4
Neuenkirchen (Oldenburg) D 17 C10
Neuenkirchen-Seelscheid D 21 C8
Neuenrade D 185 B8
Neuenstadt am Kocher D 27 B11
Neuenstein D 187 C8
Neuenwalde D 17 A11
Neuerburg D 20 D6
Neufahrn bei Freising D 75 F10
Neufahrn in Niederbayern D 75 E11
Neufchâteau B 19 E11
Neufchâteau F 26 D4
Neufchâtel-en-Bray F 18 E3
Neufchâtel-Hardelot F 15 F12
Neufchâtel-sur-Aisne F 19 F9
Neufeld D 17 A12
Neufeld an der Leitha A 77 G10
Neuffen D 27 C11
Neufmanil F 184 E2
Neufra D 27 D11
Neugersdorf D 81 E7
Neuharlingersiel D 17 A9
Neuhaus A 73 A11
Neuhaus A 73 C10
Neuhaus (Oste) D 17 A12
Neuhaus am Inn D 76 F4
Neuhaus am Klausenbach A 148 C6
Neuhaus am Rennweg D 75 A9
Neuhaus an der Pegnitz D 75 C10
Neuhausen CH 27 E10
Neuhausen D 80 E4
Neuhausen D 187 D6
Neuhausen ob Eck D 27 E10
Neuhof D 74 B6
Neuhof an der Zenn D 75 D8
Neuhofen D 187 C5
Neuhofen an der Krems A 76 F6
Neuillé-Pont-Pierre F 24 E4
Neuilly F 25 F10
Neuilly-en-Thelle F 18 F5
Neuilly-le-Réal F 30 C3
Neuilly-l'Évêque F 26 E3
Neuilly-St-Front F 25 B9
Neu-Isenburg D 187 A6
Neukalen D 83 C13
Neu Kaliß D 83 D10
Neukirch D 80 D6
Neukirchen D 21 C12
Neukirchen D 80 E3
Neukirchen D 83 B10
Neukirchen D 187 D5
Neukirchen am Großvenediger A 72 B5
Neukirchen an der Enknach A 76 F4
Neukirchen an der Vöckla A 76 F5
Neukirchen-Balbini D 75 D11
Neukirchen beim Heiligen Blut D 76 D3
Neukirchen vorm Wald D 76 E4
Neukloster D 83 C11

Neulengbach A 77 F9
Neuler D 75 E7
Neulewin D 84 E6
Neulikko FIN 121 E10
Neulise F 30 D5
Neu Lübbenau D 80 B5
Neum BIH 162 D4
Neumagen D 185 E6
Neumark D 79 E11
Neumarkt am Wallersee A 73 A7
Neumarkt im Mühlkreis A 77 F6
Neumarkt in der Oberpfalz D 75 D9
Neumarkt in Steiermark A 73 B9
Neumarkt-Sankt Veit D 75 F12
Neu Mukran D 84 B5
Neumünster D 83 B7
Neunburg vorm Wald D 75 D11
Neundorf D 75 A11
Neung-sur-Beuvron F 24 E6
Neunkirch CH 27 E10
Neunkirchen A 148 A6
Neunkirchen D 21 C10
Neunkirchen D 21 F8
Neunkirchen am Brand D 75 C9
Neunkirchen am Sand D 75 C9
Neuötting D 75 F12
Neupetershain D 80 C6
Neupölla A 77 E8
Neureichenau D 76 E5
Neuruppin D 83 E13
Neuschönau D 76 E4
Neusiedl am See A 77 G11
Neusorg D 75 C10
Neuss D 21 B7
Neussargues-Moissac F 30 E2
Neustadt D 27 E9
Neustadt D 79 E10
Neustadt D 83 E12
Neustadt (Harz) D 79 C8
Neustadt (Hessen) D 21 C12
Neustadt (Wied) D 21 C8
Neustadt am Kulm D 75 C10
Neustadt am Rübenberge D 78 A5
Neustadt an der Aisch D 75 C8
Neustadt an der Donau D 75 E10
Neustadt an der Waldnaab D 75 C11
Neustadt an der Weinstraße D 21 F10
Neustadt bei Coburg D 75 B9
Neustadt-Glewe D 83 D11
Neustadt in Holstein D 83 B9
Neustadt in Sachsen D 80 D6
Neustift im Stubaital A 72 B3
Neustrelitz D 84 D4
Neutraubling D 75 E11
Neutrebbin D 80 A6
Neu-Ulm D 74 F7
Neuvéglise F 30 F2
Neuves-Maisons F 186 D1
Neuvic F 29 E6
Neuvic F 29 E10
Neuville-aux-Bois F 24 D7
Neuville-de-Poitou F 29 B6
Neuville-les-Dames F 31 C7
Neuville-lès-Dieppe F 18 E3
Neuville-sur-Saône F 30 D6
Neuvilly-en-Argonne F 26 B3
Neuvy-Grandchamp F 30 B4
Neuvy-le-Roi F 24 E4
Neuvy-Pailloux F 29 B9
Neuvy-St-Sépulchre F 29 B9
Neuvy-sur-Barangeon F 25 F7
Neuweiler D 27 C10
Neuwied D 21 D8
Neuwittenbek D 83 B8
Neu Wulmstorf D 83 D7
Neu Zauche D 80 C6
Neuzelle D 81 B7
Neu Zittau D 80 B5
Névache F 31 E10
Nevarėnai LT 134 D4
Neveja LV 130 F4
Neveklov CZ 77 C7
Nevel' RUS 133 D7
Nevele B 19 B8
Neverfjord N 113 C12
Nevernes N 108 F4
Neverness N 110 C9
Neveronys LT 137 D9
Nevers F 30 A3
Nevesinje BIH 157 F9
Nevestino BG 165 E6
Névez F 22 E4
Neviano I 61 C10
Néville F 18 E2
Nevlunghavn N 90 B6
Nevsha BG 167 C8
New Abbey GB 5 F9
New Aberdour GB 3 K12
New Alresford GB 13 C12
Newark-on-Trent GB 11 E10
Newbawn IRL 9 D9
Newbiggin-by-the-Sea GB 5 E13
Newbliss IRL 7 D8
Newborough GB 11 F11
Newbridge GB 13 B8
Newbridge IRL 7 F9
New Buildings GB 4 F2
Newburgh GB 3 L12
Newburgh GB 5 C10
Newbury GB 13 C12
Newby Bridge GB 10 C6
Newcastle GB 7 D11
Newcastle GB 13 A8
Newcastle IRL 7 F10
Newcastle IRL 7 F10
Newcastle Emlyn GB 12 A6
Newcastleton GB 5 E11
Newcastle-under-Lyme GB 11 E7
Newcastle upon Tyne GB 5 F13
Newcastle West IRL 8 D4
New Cumnock GB 5 E8
New Deer GB 3 K12
Newel D 21 E7
Newent GB 13 B10
New Galloway GB 5 E8
New Inn IRL 6 F6
New Inn IRL 7 E8
Newinn IRL 9 D7
New Kildimo IRL 8 C5
Newmarket GB 2 J4
Newmarket GB 15 C9
Newmarket IRL 8 D4
Newmarket IRL 9 D8
Newmarket-on-Fergus IRL 8 C5
Newmill GB 3 K11
New Milton GB 13 D11
Newnham GB 13 B10
New Pitsligo GB 3 K12
Newport GB 3 J10
Newport GB 11 F7
Newport GB 12 A5
Newport GB 13 B9
Newport GB 13 D12
Newport GB 15 D9
Newport IRL 6 E3
Newport IRL 8 C6
Newport-on-Tay GB 5 C11
Newport Pagnell GB 15 C7
Newport Trench GB 4 F3
New Quay GB 12 A6
Newquay GB 12 E4
New Radnor GB 13 A8
New Romney GB 15 F10
New Ross IRL 9 D9
Newry GB 7 D10
Newton GB 4 C6
Newton GB 10 D7
Newton Abbot GB 13 D7
Newton Aycliffe GB 5 F13
Newton Ferrers GB 12 E6
Newtonhill GB 5 A12
Newton-le-Willows GB 10 E6
Newton Mearns GB 5 D8
Newtonmore GB 5 A8
Newton Stewart GB 4 F8
Newtown GB 10 F5
Newtown GB 13 A9
Newtown IRL 6 F6
Newtown IRL 8 D5
Newtown IRL 8 D6
Newtown IRL 9 C8
Newtownabbey GB 4 F5
Newtownards GB 7 C11
Newtownbarry IRL 9 C9
Newtownbutler GB 7 D8
Newtown Crommelin GB 4 F4
Newtown Forbes IRL 7 E7
Newtown Mount Kennedy IRL 7 F10
Newtown St Boswells GB 5 D11
Newtownstewart GB 4 F2
Nexon F 29 D8
Neyland GB 12 B5
Nezamyslice CZ 77 D12
Nezavertailovca MD 154 D5
Nézsa H 147 F8
Nezvěstice CZ 76 C5
Nianfors S 103 C12
Niata GR 175 F6
Nibbiano I 37 B10
Nibe DK 86 B5
Nīca LV 134 D2
Nicastro I 59 B9
Nice F 37 D6
Nīcgale LV 135 D12
Nichelino I 37 A7
Nickelsdorf A 77 G12
Nicolae Bălcescu RO 153 B9
Nicolae Bălcescu RO 153 E9
Nicolae Bălcescu RO 155 D3
Nicolae Bălcescu RO 155 E2
Nicolae Bălcescu RO 160 D4
Nicolae Bălcescu RO 161 E9
Nicolae Titulescu RO 160 E5
Nicolaevca MD 154 B2
Nicolosi I 59 D7
Nicoreni MD 153 B11
Nicorești RO 153 F10
Nicosia I 58 D5
Nicotera I 59 B8
Nicșeni RO 153 B9
Niculești RO 161 D7
Niculițel RO 155 C2
Nida LT 134 F1
Nidau CH 27 F7
Nidda D 21 D12
Nidzica PL 139 D9
Niebla E 51 E6
Nieborów PL 141 F2
Niebüll D 82 A5
Niebylec PL 144 D4
Niechanowo PL 138 F4
Niechcice PL 143 D8
Niechłonin PL 139 D9
Niechlów PL 81 C10
Niechorze PL 85 B8
Niederaichbach D 75 E11
Niederanven L 20 E6
Niederau D 80 D5
Niederaula D 78 E6
Niederbipp CH 27 F8
Niederbrechen D 21 D10
Niederbreitbach D 185 C7
Niederbronn-les-Bains F 27 C8
Niederfinow D 84 E5
Niederfischbach D 185 C8
Niedergörsdorf D 80 C3
Niederkassel D 21 C8
Niederkirchen D 21 E9
Niederkrüchten D 20 B6
Niederndorf A 72 A5
Niederneisen D 21 D10
Niedernhall D 74 D6
Niedernhausen D 21 D10
Niederoderwitz D 81 E7
Nieder-Olm D 185 E9
Nieder-Rodenbach D 21 D12
Niederroßla D 79 D9
Niedersachswerfen D 79 C8
Niederselters D 21 D10
Niederstetten D 74 D6
Niederurnen CH 27 F11
Niederviehbach D 75 E11
Niederwerrn D 75 B7
Niederwörresbach D 186 B3
Niederzissen D 21 D8
Niedrzwica Duża PL 141 H6
Niedźwiada PL 141 G7
Niedźwiadna PL 139 C13
Niefern-Öschelbronn D 27 C10
Niegosław PL 85 E9
Niegosławice PL 81 C9
Niegowa PL 143 E7
Niegripp D 79 B10
Nieheim D 17 E12
Niekerk NL 16 B6
Niekłań Wielki PL 141 H3
Niekursko PL 85 D10
Niel B 182 C4
Nielisz PL 144 B7
Niemberg D 79 C11
Niemce PL 141 H7
Niemcza PL 81 E11
Niemegk D 79 B12
Niemelä FIN 113 C20
Niemelä FIN 115 E5
Niemelänkylä FIN 119 F12
Niemenkylä FIN 122 E7
Niemenkylä FIN 126 C6
Niemenpää FIN 119 B11
Niemis S 119 B11
Niemisel S 118 B7
Niemisjärvi FIN 123 F16
Niemisjärvi FIN 124 E8
Niemiskylä FIN 123 C17
Niemodlin PL 142 E4
Niemysłów PL 142 C6
Nienadówka PL 144 C5
Nienburg (Saale) D 79 C10
Nienburg (Weser) D 17 C12
Niepars D 84 B3
Niepołomice PL 143 F9
Nieporjt PL 139 F11
Nierstein D 21 E10
Niesa FIN 117 D11
Niesi FIN 117 D15
Niesky D 81 D7
Nieświń PL 141 H2
Nieszawa PL 138 E6
Nietsak S 116 D4
Nietulisko Duże PL 143 E11
Nieul F 29 D8
Nieuw-Amsterdam NL 17 C7
Nieuw-Bergen NL 16 E6
Nieuwegein NL 16 D4
Nieuwe-Niedorp NL 16 C3
Nieuwe Pekela NL 17 B7
Nieuwerkerk NL 16 E2
Nieuwerkerk aan de IJssel NL 16 E3
Nieuwerkerken B 19 C11
Nieuwe-Tonge NL 16 E2
Nieuw-Heeten NL 16 D6
Nieuwkoop NL 16 D3
Nieuw-Loosdrecht NL 183 A6
Nieuw-Milligen NL 183 A7
Nieuw-Namen NL 182 C4
Nieuwolda NL 17 B7
Nieuwpoort B 18 B6
Nieuwveen NL 182 A5
Nieuw-Vennep NL 16 D3
Nieuw-Vossemeer NL 182 B4
Nieuw-Weerdinge NL 17 C7
Nievern D 185 D8
Niewjgłosz PL 141 G7
Niezabyszewo PL 85 B12
Nigrán E 38 D2
Nīgrande LV 134 D4
Nigrita GR 169 C10
Nigüelas E 53 C9
Niherne F 29 B9
Niinilahti FIN 123 E15
Niinimaa FIN 123 E10
Niinimäki FIN 125 F10
Niinisalo FIN 126 B8
Niinivaara FIN 125 D11
Niinivesi FIN 123 E16
Niirokumpu FIN 121 B11
Níjar E 55 F8
Nijemci HR 157 B11
Nijkerk NL 16 D4
Nijlen B 19 B10
Nijmegen NL 16 E5
Nijverdal NL 17 D6
Nikaia GR 169 E7
Nikaranperä FIN 123 E14
Nikel' RUS 114 E8
Niki GR 168 C5
Nikisiani GR 170 C6
Nikiti GR 169 D10
Nikkala S 119 C11
Nikkaluokta S 111 E17
Nikkaroinen FIN 127 C14
Nikkeby N 112 C6
Nikodin NMK 169 B6
Nikokleia GR 169 C9
Nikolaevo BG 165 C10
Nikolaevo BG 166 D5
Nikola-Kozlevo BG 161 F10
Nikolovo BG 161 F8
Nikolsdorf A 73 C6
Nikopol BG 160 F5
Nikopoli GR 174 A2
Nīkrāce LV 134 C3
Nikšić MNE 163 D6
Nikyup BG 166 C5
Nilivaara FIN 117 C14
Nilivaara S 116 D7
Nilsiä FIN 125 D10
Nilvange F 20 F6
Nim DK 86 D5
Nîmes F 35 C7
Nimigea RO 152 C4
Nimis I 73 D7
Nimisenkangas FIN 125 C11
Nimisjärvi FIN 119 E17
Nimtofte DK 86 C7
Nin HR 67 D11
Nina EST 131 D14
Nindorf D 82 B6
Ninemile Bar GB 5 E9
Ninemilehouse IRL 9 D8
Ninove B 19 C9
Niort F 28 C5
Nirza LV 133 D3
Niš SRB 164 C4
Nisa P 44 E5
Nisbet GB 5 D11
Niscemi I 58 E5
Niška Banja SRB 164 C5
Niskankorpi FIN 123 C13
Niskanpera FIN 119 B15
Nisko PL 144 B5
Niskos FIN 123 F10
Nismes B 19 D10
Nispen NL 16 F2
Nisporeni MD 154 C2
Nissafors S 91 E14
Nissan-lez-Enserune F 34 D5
Nissilä FIN 123 C17
Nissinvaara FIN 121 B13
Nissoria I 58 D5
Nissumby DK 86 B2
Nissum Seminarieby DK 86 B2
Nistelrode NL 16 E5
Nistorești RO 153 F9
Nītaure LV 135 B10
Nitra SK 146 E6
Nitrianske Hrnčiarovce SK 146 E6
Nitrianske Pravno SK 147 D7
Nitrianske Rudno SK 146 D6
Nitrianske Sučany SK 146 D6
Nitry F 25 E10
Nitta S 91 D13
Nittedal N 95 B13
Nittel D 20 E6
Nittenau D 75 D11
Nittendorf D 75 D10
Nittorp S 91 D14
Niukkala FIN 129 B12
Nivå DK 87 D11
Niva FIN 121 F14
Nivala FIN 123 C13
Nivankylä FIN 117 E15
Nivanpää FIN 117 E11
Nivelles B 19 C9
Nivenskoye RUS 136 D2
Nivillac F 23 E7
Nivillers F 18 F5
Nivnice CZ 146 D5
Nivolas-Vermelle F 31 D7
Nivyanin BG 165 C8
Niwiska PL 143 F12
Nižbor CZ 76 C6
Nižná SK 147 C9
Nižná Slaná SK 145 F1
Nižný Hrabovec SK 145 F4
Nižný Hrušov SK 145 F4
Nižný Šipov SK 145 F4
Nizza di Sicilia I 59 D7
Nizza Monferrato I 37 B8
Njavve S 109 C15
Njegovuđa MNE 163 C7
Një Maj AL 168 C3
Njetjavare S 116 E4
Njivice HR 67 B10
Njurundabommen S 103 B13
Njutånger S 103 C13
No DK 86 C2
Noaillan F 32 B5
Noailles F 18 F5
Noain E 32 E2
Noale I 66 A5
Noalejo E 53 A9
Noasca I 31 E11
Nöbbele S 89 B8
Nobber IRL 7 E9
Nobitz D 79 E11
Noblejas E 46 E6
Noćaj SRB 158 D4
Nocé F 24 D4
Nocera Inferiore I 60 B3
Nocera Terinese I 59 A9
Nocera Umbra I 62 A3
Noceto I 66 C1
Noci I 61 B8
Nociglia I 61 C10
Nociūnai LT 135 F8
Nocrich RO 152 F4
Nødebo DK 87 D10
Nodeland N 90 C2
Nödinge S 91 D11
Nodland N 94 F4
Nods F 26 F5
Noé F 33 D8
Noepoli I 61 C6
Noer D 83 B8
Nœux-les-Mines F 18 D6
Noez E 46 E4
Nofuentes E 40 C5
Nogales E 51 B6
Nogara I 66 B3
Nogaro F 32 C5
Nogent F 26 D3
Nogent-le-Bernard F 24 D3
Nogent-le-Roi F 24 C6
Nogent-le-Rotrou F 24 D4
Nogent-sur-Aube F 25 D11
Nogent-sur-Oise F 18 F5
Nogent-sur-Seine F 25 D10
Nogent-sur-Vernisson F 25 E8
Nogersund S 89 C7
Nógrád H 147 F8
Nógrádmegyer H 147 E9
Nógrádsáp H 147 F8
Nograles E 40 F6
Noguera de Albarracín E 47 D9
Noguères F 32 D4
Nogueruelas E 48 D3
Nohant-Vic F 29 B9
Nohfelden D 21 E8
Nohic F 33 C8
Noia E 38 C2
Noicattaro I 61 A7
Noidans-lès-Vesoul F 26 E5
Noilhan F 33 C7
Noirétable F 30 D4
Noirmoutier-en-l'Île F 28 A1
Noisseville F 26 B5
Noja E 40 B4
Nojorid RO 151 C8
Nokia FIN 127 C10
Nol S 91 D11
Nolay F 30 B6
Noli I 37 C8
Nolimo FIN 121 B11
Nolmyra S 99 B8
Nólsoy FO 2 A3
Nombela E 46 D4
Nomeland N 90 A2
Nomenj SLO 73 D9
Nomeny F 26 C5
Nomexy F 26 D5
Nomia GR 178 B5
Nonancourt F 24 C5
Nonantola I 66 C3
Nonaspe E 42 E4
None I 37 B7
Nonnenweier D 186 E4
Nonnweiler D 21 E7
Nontron F 29 D7
Nonza F 37 F10
Nõo EST 131 E13
Noordwijk aan Zee NL 182 A4
Noordwijk-Binnen NL 16 D2
Noordwijkerhout NL 16 D3
Noordwolde NL 16 C6
Noormarkku FIN 126 B6
Nootdorp NL 182 A4
Nopankylä FIN 122 E8
Noppikoski S 102 D8
Nor S 103 C11
Nora S 97 C13
Nora S 103 A12
Nørager DK 86 B5
Noragugume I 64 C2
Norberg S 97 B14
Norcia I 62 B4
Nordagutu N 95 D10
Nordanå S 103 A13
Nordanås S 107 C14
Nordanås S 109 E16
Nordanås S 109 F11
Nordanede S 103 A11
Nordankäl S 107 D10
Nordannälden S 105 E16
Nordano S 98 B6
Nordborg DK 86 E5
Nordbotn N 112 D9
Nordby DK 86 D7
Nordby DK 86 E2
Norddeich D 17 A8
NorŠdepíl FO 2 A3
Norddorf D 82 A4
Norddyrøy N 104 D5
Nordeide N 100 D3
Nordeidet N 112 D4
Norden D 17 A8
Nordendorf D 75 E8
Nordenham D 17 B10
Nordenskov DK 86 D3
Norderåsen S 106 E7
Norderney D 17 A8
Norderö S 105 E16
Norderstedt D 83 C8
Nordfjord N 114 B8
Nordfjordbotn N 111 B17
Nordfjordeid N 100 C3
Nordfold N 110 E9
Nordhalben D 75 B10
Nordhallen S 105 E13
Nordhastedt D 82 B6
Nordhausen D 79 D8
Nordheim D 27 B11
Nordholz D 17 A11
Nordhorn D 17 D8
Nordhuglo N 94 C3
Nordingrå S 103 A15
Nordkil N 111 D10
Nordkirchen D 17 E9
Nordkisa N 95 B14
Nordkjosbotn N 111 B18
Nordland N 110 E4
Nord-Leirvåg N 114 D7
Nordlenangen N 111 A19
Nordli N 105 C15
Nördlingen D 75 E7
Nordmaling S 107 D17
Nordmannvik N 112 D5
Nordmela N 111 B10
Nordnesøy N 108 C4
Nordøyvågen N 108 D4
NorŠragøta FO 2 A3
Nordråk N 101 E12
Nordsand N 111 C12
Nordsinni N 101 E11
Nordsjö S 103 C12
Nordsjö S 107 D10
Nordsjona N 108 D5
NorŠskáli FO 2 A2
Nordskjør N 104 C8
Nordskot N 110 E8
Nordstemmen D 78 B6
Nord-Værnes N 108 C5
Nordvågen N 113 B17
Nordvik N 108 B9
Nordvik S 103 A14
Nordvika N 104 E4
Nordwalde D 17 D8
Nore S 103 C11
Noreikiškės LT 137 D8
Norem N 105 D10
Noreña E 39 B8
Noresund N 95 B11
Norg NL 17 B6
Norheimsund N 94 B4
Norinkylä FIN 122 E8
Norje S 88 C7
Norma I 62 D3
Norn S 97 B14
Nornäs S 102 D5
Noroy-le-Bourg F 26 E5
Norppa FIN 123 C11
Norra Åsum S 88 D6
Norra Blommaberg S 103 C9
Norra Bredåker S 118 C6
Norra bro S 92 A6
Norra Fjällnäs S 109 E10
Norra Holmnäs S 118 C3
Norråker S 106 C9
Norra Klagshamn S 87 D11
Norra Malånäs S 107 A15
Norra Prästholm S 118 C8
Norra Rödupp S 118 B9
Norra Skärvången S 105 D16
Norra Vallgrund FIN 122 D6
Norra Vi S 92 D6
Norrbäck S 103 B12
Norrbäck S 107 B13
Norrbo S 103 C12
Norrboda S 99 B10
Norrboda S 103 D9
Norrby FIN 122 C9
Norrby S 99 B11
Norrbyberg S 107 B14
Norrbyn S 122 C3
Norrbyskär S 122 C3
Nørre Aaby DK 86 E5
Nørre Alslev DK 84 A1
Nørreballe DK 83 A10
Nørre Bork DK 86 D2
Nørre Broby DK 86 E6
Nørre Felding DK 86 C3
Nørre Halne DK 86 A5
Nørre Kongerslev DK 86 B6
Nørre Nebel DK 86 D2
Norrent-Fontes F 18 C5
Nørre Snede DK 86 D4
Nørresundby DK 86 A5
Nørre Vejrup DK 86 D3
Nørre Vorupør DK 86 B2
Norrfällsviken S 107 F15
Norrfjärden S 103 B13
Norrfjärden S 118 D7
Norrfjärden S 122 C5
Norrflärke S 107 D14
Norrfors S 107 C14
Norrfors S 107 D15
Norrgårdssälen S 102 E6
Norr-Greningen S 106 E8
Norrhult-Klavreström S 89 A8
Norrköping S 93 B8
Norrlångträsk S 118 D5
Norr-Moflo S 107 E11
Norrnäs FIN 122 E6
Norrsjön S 106 B8
Norrskedika S 99 B10
Norrstig S 103 A14
Norrstrand S 109 E16
Norrsundet S 103 E13
Norrtälje S 99 C11
Norrtjärn S 103 E12
Norrvåge S 107 E15
Norrvik S 107 B13
Nors DK 86 A3
Norsholm S 92 B7
Norsjö S 107 B17
Nörten-Hardenberg D 78 C6
Northallerton GB 11 C9
Northam GB 12 C6
Northampton GB 15 C7
North Berwick GB 5 C11
Northborough GB 11 F11
North Cave GB 11 D10
North Dell GB 2 J4
North Duffield GB 11 D10
Northeim D 79 C6
North Ferriby GB 11 D10
North Grimston GB 11 C10
North Hykeham GB 11 E10
North Leigh GB 13 B12
North Shields GB 5 E14
North Somercotes GB 11 E12
North Sunderland GB 5 D13
North Tidworth GB 13 C11
Northton GB 2 K2
North Walsham GB 15 B11
Northwich GB 10 E6
Nortmoor D 17 B9
Norton GB 11 C10
Norton GB 15 C10
Norton Fitzwarren GB 13 C8
Nortorf D 83 B7
Nortrup D 17 C9
Nort-sur-Erdre F 23 F8
Norup DK 86 B6
Norvasalmi FIN 117 E15
Norwich GB 15 B11
Norwick GB 3 D15
Noșlac RO 152 E3
Nøss N 111 B10
Nossa Senhora da Boa Fé P 50 B3
Nossa Senhora da Graça de Póvoa e Meadas P 44 E5
Nossa Senhora da Graça do Divor P 50 B4
Nossa Senhora da Graça dos Degolados P 45 F6
Nossa Senhora das Neves P 50 C4
Nossa Senhora de Machede P 50 B4
Nossebro S 91 C12
Nossen D 80 D4
Nossendorf D 84 C3
Nossentiner Hütte D 83 C12
Noszlop H 149 B8
Noszvaj H 145 H1
Notaresco I 62 B5
Notia GR 169 B7
Nőtincs H 147 F8
Nötö FIN 126 F6
Noto I 59 F7
Notodden N 95 C10
Notre-Dame-de-Bellecombe F 31 D10
Notre-Dame-de-Gravenchon F 18 F2
Notre-Dame-de-Monts F 28 B1
Notre-Dame-d'Oé F 24 F4
Nötsch im Gailtal A 73 C8
Nottensdorf D 82 D7
Nottingham GB 11 F9
Nottuln D 17 E8
Notviken S 118 C8
Nouan-le-Fuzelier F 24 E7
Nouans-les-Fontaines F 24 F5
Nouart F 19 F11
Nõuni EST 131 E13
Nousiainen FIN 126 D7
Nousionmäki FIN 125 D10
Nousu FIN 115 D5
Nouvion F 18 D4
Nouzilly F 24 E4
Nouzonville F 19 E10
Nõva EST 130 C7
Nova H 149 C7
Nová Baňa SK 147 E7
Nova Breznica NMK 164 F3
Nova Bukovica HR 149 E9
Nová Bystřice CZ 77 D8
Nová Cerekev CZ 77 D8
Novachene BG 165 B10
Novachene BG 165 D8
Novaci NMK 168 B5
Novaci RO 160 C3
Nova Crnja SRB 158 B6
Nová Dedina SK 147 E7
Novadnieki LV 134 C4
Nová Dubnica SK 146 D6
Novafeltria I 66 E5
Nova Gorica SLO 73 E8
Nova Gradiška HR 157 B7
Nova Ivanivka UA 154 F4
Novaj H 145 H1
Novajidrány H 145 G3
Nova Kamena BG 161 F10
Nova Kasaba BIH 157 D11
Novaki HR 148 E5
Novakovo BG 166 F4
Nováky SK 147 D7
Novales E 40 B3
Novales E 41 D11
Nova Levante I 72 D4
Novalja HR 67 C10
Novallas E 41 E8
Nová Ľubovňa SK 145 E2
Nova Makhala BG 165 F9
Nova Nadezhda BG 166 E5
Nova Nekrasivka UA 155 C3
Nová Paka CZ 77 B9
Nova Pazova SRB 158 D5
Nova Pokrovka UA 155 B4
Novara I 68 C6
Novara di Sicilia I 59 C7
Nová Role CZ 75 B12
Nova Sela HR 157 F8
Nova Siri I 61 C7
Nova Siri Scalo I 61 C7
Novate Mezzola I 69 A7
Nova Topola BIH 157 B7
Nova Varoš SRB 163 C8
Nova Vas SLO 73 E9
Nová Včelnice CZ 77 D8
Nová Ves CZ 77 B8
Nová Ves nad Šitavou SK 146 E6
Nova Zagora BG 166 E6
Nové Hrady CZ 77 E7
Novelda E 56 E3
Novellara I 66 C2
Nové Město nad Metuj CZ 77 B10
Nové Mesto nad Váhom SK 146 D5
Nové Město na Moravé CZ 77 C10
Nové Město pod Smrkem CZ 81 E8
Nove Misto UA 145 D6
Noventa di Piave I 72 E6
Noventa Vicentina I 66 B4
Novés E 46 D4
Noves F 35 C8
Nové Veselí CZ 77 C9
Nové Zámky SK 146 F6
Novgorodka RUS 133 B5
Novgrad BG 161 F7
Novi Banovci SRB 158 D5
Novi Bečej SRB 158 B5
Novi di Modena I 66 C2
Novi Dojran NMK 169 B8
Noviergas E 41 E7
Novi Grad BIH 157 B9
Novigrad HR 67 B8
Novigrad HR 156 D4
Novigrad Podravski HR 149 D7
Novi Iskŭr BG 165 D7
Novi Karlovci SRB 158 C5
Novi Khan BG 165 D8
Novi Kneževac SRB 150 E5
Novi Kozarci SRB 150 F6
Novi Ligure I 37 B9
Novillars F 26 F5
Noville B 182 D5
Novi Marof HR 149 D6
Novion-Porcien F 19 E9
Novi Pazar BG 167 C8
Novi Pazar SRB 163 C10
Novi Sad SRB 158 C4
Novi Šeher BIH 157 C9
Novi Slankamen SRB 158 C5
Novi Travnik BIH 157 D8
Novi Vinodolski HR 67 B10
Novo Beograd SRB 158 D5
Novoborysivka UA 154 C5
Novočići BIH 157 F9
Novo Delchevo BG 169 B9
Novokhovansk RUS 133 E7
Novo Korito SRB 159 F9
Novo Mesto SLO 73 E11
Novo Miloševo SRB 158 B5
Novomoskovskiy RUS 139 A9
Novomykolayivka UA 155 B5
Novo Orahovo SRB 150 F4
Novo Oryakhovo BG 167 D9
Novopetrivka UA 154 C5
Novorzhev RUS 133 B6
Novosamarka UA 154 B5
Novosedly CZ 77 E11
Novoselë AL 163 F10
Novoselë AL 168 C1
Novoselec HR 149 E7
Novoselets BG 166 E6
Novoselija BIH 157 C7
Novoselivka UA 154 B5
Novoselivka UA 154 D5
Novo Selo BG 159 E10
Novo Selo BG 161 F8
Novo Selo BG 165 E6
Novo Selo BG 166 F6
Novo Selo BIH 157 B8
Novo Selo BIH 157 B9
Novo Selo NMK 169 B8
Novo Selo SRB 159 F6
Novoselovo RUS 139 B9
Novoseltsi BG 167 E8
Novosel'ye RUS 132 E4
Novoselytsya UA 153 A8
Novoselytsya UA 154 A6
Novosil's'ke UA 155 C3
Novostroyevo RUS 136 E4
Novot SK 147 C8
Novo Virje HR 149 D8
Novovolyns'k UA 144 B9
Novoyavorivs'ke UA 144 D8
Novska HR 149 F7
Nový Bor CZ 81 E7
Nový Bydžov CZ 77 B8
Novy-Chevrières F 19 E9
Novy Dvor BY 137 F10
Nový Hrozenkov CZ 146 C6
Nový Jičín CZ 146 B5
Nový Knín CZ 76 C6
Nový Malín CZ 77 C12
Novy Pahost BY 133 F2
Nový Rychnov CZ 77 D8
Novyya Kruki BY 133 E3
Novyy Izborsk RUS 132 F2
Novyy Rozdil UA 145 E9
Nový Šivot SK 146 E4
Nowa Brzeźnica PL 143 D7
Nowa Cerekwia PL 142 F4
Nowa Chodorówka PL 140 C8
Nowa Djba PL 143 F12
Nowa Karczma PL 138 B5
Nowa Ruda PL 81 E11
Nowa Sarzyna PL 144 C5
Nowa Słupia PL 143 E11
Nowa Sól PL 81 C9
Nowa Sucha PL 141 F2
Nowa Wieś Ełcka PL 140 C6
Nowa Wieś Ljborskie PL 85 A13
Nowa Wieś Wielka PL 138 E5
Nowa Wola PL 140 D9
Nowa Wola Gołjbiowska PL 141 H4
Nowe PL 138 C6
Nowe Brusno PL 144 C7
Nowe Brzesko PL 143 F9
Nowe Czarnowo PL 84 D6
Nowe Miasteczko PL 81 C9
Nowe Miasto PL 139 E10
Nowe Miasto Lubawskie PL 139 D8
Nowe Miasto nad Pilicą PL 141 G3
Nowe Miasto nad Wartą PL 81 B12
Nowe Ostrowy PL 143 B7
Nowe Piekuty PL 141 E7
Nowe Skalmierzyce PL 142 C4
Nowe Warpno PL 84 C6
Nowinka PL 136 F6
Nowogard PL 85 C8
Nowogród PL 139 D12
Nowogród Bobrzański PL 81 C8
Nowogródek Pomorski PL 85 E8
Nowogrodziec PL 81 D8
Nowosady PL 141 E9
Nowosielce PL 145 D5
Nowosolna PL 143 C8
Nowotaniec PL 145 D5
Nowowola PL 140 D8
Nowy Bartków PL 141 F7
Nowy Duninów PL 139 E7
Nowy Dwór PL 138 D4
Nowy Dwór PL 140 C9
Nowy Dwór Gdański PL 138 B7
Nowy Dwór Mazowiecki PL 139 F10
Nowy Kawjczyn PL 141 G2
Nowy Korczyn PL 143 F10
Nowy Lubliniec PL 144 C7
Nowy Sącz PL 145 D2
Nowy Staw PL 138 B7
Nowy Targ PL 147 C10
Nowy Tomyśl PL 81 B10
Nowy Wiśnicz PL 144 D1
Nowy Żmigród PL 145 D4
Noyal-Muzillac F 22 E7
Noyalo F 22 E6
Noyal-Pontivy F 22 D6
Noyant F 23 E12

Noyarey *F* 31 E8
Noyen-sur-Sarthe *F* 23 E11
Noyers *F* 25 E10
Noyers-sur-Cher *F* 24 F5
Noyers-sur-Jabron *F* 35 B10
Noyon *F* 18 E6
Nozay *F* 23 E8
Nozdrzec *PL* 144 D5
Nozeroy *F* 31 B9
Nuaillé-d'Aunis *F* 28 C4
Nuasjärvi *FIN* 117 E13
Nubledo *E* 39 A8
Nucet *RO* 151 E10
Nuci *RO* 161 D8
Nucşoara *RO* 160 C5
Nudersdorf *D* 79 C12
Nüdlingen *D* 75 B7
Nudyzhe *UA* 141 H10
Nueil-les-Aubiers *F* 28 B4
Nuenen *NL* 16 F5
Nueno *E* 41 D11
Nueva *E* 39 B10
Nueva-Carteya *E* 53 A8
Nueva Jarilla *E* 52 C4
Nuez de Ebro *E* 41 E10
Nufăru *RO* 155 C3
Nughedu di San Nicolò *I* 64 B3
Nuijamaa *FIN* 129 D10
Nuillé-sur-Vicoin *F* 23 E10
Nuits *F* 25 E11
Nuits-St-Georges *F* 26 F2
Nukari *FIN* 127 D12
Ņukši *LV* 133 D3
Nuland *NL* 16 E4
Nule *I* 64 C3
Nules *E* 48 E4
Nulvi *I* 64 B2
Numana *I* 67 E8
Numansdorp *NL* 16 E2
Nummela *FIN* 127 E11
Nummi *FIN* 127 E10
Nummijärvi *FIN* 122 F8
Nummikoski *FIN* 122 F9
Nünchritz *D* 80 D4
Nuneaton *GB* 11 F9
Nunkirchen *D* 186 C2
Nunnanen *FIN* 117 B12
Nunnanlahti *FIN* 125 D12
Nuñomoral *E* 45 D8
Nunsdorf *D* 80 B4
Nunspeet *NL* 16 D5
Nuojua *FIN* 119 E17
Nuoksujärvi *S* 116 E9
Nuolijärvi *FIN* 125 C11
Nuoramoinen *FIN* 127 C14
Nuorgam *FIN* 113 C20
Nuoritta *FIN* 119 D16
Nuoro *I* 64 C3
Nuorunka *FIN* 120 C9
Nuottavaara *FIN* 117 D12
Nuottikylä *FIN* 121 E12
Nur *PL* 141 E6
Nuragus *I* 64 D3
Nurallao *I* 64 D3
Nuraminis *I* 64 E3
Nureci *I* 64 D2
Nuriye *TR* 177 B10
Nurmaa *FIN* 128 C6
Nurmes *FIN* 125 C12
Nurmesperä *FIN* 123 C15
Nurmijärvi *FIN* 125 C13
Nurmijärvi *FIN* 127 E12
Nurmo *FIN* 123 E9
Nürnberg *D* 75 D9
Nurney *IRL* 7 F9
Nurri *I* 64 D3
Nurste *EST* 130 D4
Nürtingen *D* 27 C11
Nurzec-Stacja *PL* 141 F8
Nus *I* 31 D11
Nusco *I* 60 B4
Nuşeni *RO* 152 C4
Nuşfalău *RO* 151 C10
Nusfjord *N* 110 D5
Nusnäs *S* 102 E8
Nusplingen *D* 27 D10
Nußbach *A* 73 A6
Nußdorf *D* 73 A6
Nußdorf am Inn *D* 72 A5
Nuštar *HR* 149 F11
Nustrup *DK* 86 E4
Nuth *NL* 19 C12
Nutheim *N* 95 C9
Nuttuperä *FIN* 123 C15
Nuuksujärvi *S* 116 C8
Nuupas *FIN* 119 B16
Nuutajärvi *FIN* 127 C9
Nuutila *FIN* 119 F16
Nuutilanmaki *FIN* 128 B8
Nuvsvåg *N* 112 C9
Nuvvus *FIN* 113 D17
Nuxis *I* 64 E2
Nüziders *A* 71 C9
Nya Bastuselet *S* 109 F16
Nyåker *S* 107 D13
Nyåker *S* 107 D16
Nyárád *H* 149 B8
Nyáregyháza *H* 150 C4
Nyárlőrinc *H* 150 D4
Nyársapát *H* 150 C4
Nybble *S* 91 A15
Nybergsund *N* 102 D3
Nyborg *DK* 87 E7
Nyborg *N* 114 C5
Nyborg *S* 119 C10
Nybro *S* 89 B9
Nybrostrand *S* 88 E5
Nyby *FIN* 122 E6
Nyby *N* 113 C15
Nyby *S* 106 E8
Nybyn *S* 103 C9
Nybyn *S* 107 E14
Nybyn *S* 118 D6
Nýdek *CZ* 147 B7
Nydri *GR* 174 B2
Nye *S* 89 A8
Nyékládháza *H* 145 H2
Nyelv *N* 114 C5
Nyergesújfalu *H* 149 A11
Nyhammar *S* 97 B12
Nyhem *S* 103 A10
Nyhem *S* 109 E14
Ny Højen *DK* 86 D5
Nyhus *N* 111 B15
Nyhyttan *S* 97 C12
Nyírábrány *H* 151 B9
Nyíracsád *H* 151 B8
Nyírád *H* 149 B8
Nyíradony *H* 151 B8
Nyírbátor *H* 151 B9
Nyírbéltek *H* 151 B9
Nyírbogát *H* 151 B9
Nyírbogdány *H* 145 G4
Nyíregyháza *H* 145 H4
Nyírgelse *H* 151 B8
Nyírgyulaj *H* 145 H5
Nyíribrony *H* 145 G4
Nyírkáta *H* 145 H5
Nyírmada *H* 145 G5
Nyírmeggyes *H* 145 H5
Nyírmihályi *H* 151 B8
Nyírpazony *H* 145 H4
Nyírtass *H* 145 G5
Nyírtelek *H* 145 G4
Nyírtét *H* 145 G4
Nyírtura *H* 145 G4
Nyírvasvári *H* 151 B9
Nykarleby *FIN* 122 C9
Nyker *DK* 89 E7
Nykil *S* 92 C6
Nykøbing *DK* 83 A11
Nykøbing Mors *DK* 86 B3
Nykøbing Sjælland *DK* 87 D9
Nyköping *S* 93 B10
Nykrogen *S* 98 B6
Nykroppa *S* 97 C11
Nyksund *N* 110 C9
Nykvåg *N* 110 C7
Nykvarn *S* 93 A10
Nykyrke *S* 92 B5
Nyland *S* 107 D16
Nyland *S* 107 E13
Nyland *S* 122 C3
Nylars *DK* 89 E7
Nyliden *S* 107 D15
Nymburk *CZ* 77 B8
Nymfes *GR* 168 E2
Nymindegab *DK* 86 D2
Nymoen *N* 112 C6
Nynäshamn *S* 93 B11
Nyneset *N* 105 C13
Ny Nørup *DK* 86 D4
Nyoiseau *F* 23 E10
Nyon *CH* 31 C9
Nyons *F* 35 B9
Nyråd *DK* 87 E9
Nýřany *CZ* 76 C4
Nýrsko *CZ* 76 D4
Nyrud *N* 114 E6
Nysa *PL* 142 F3
Nysäter *S* 97 D8
Nysätern *S* 102 A5
Nysättra *S* 99 C11
Nysted *DK* 83 A11
Nysted *N* 111 C15
Nystrand *S* 118 C5
Nyträsk *S* 118 E4
Nytrøa *N* 111 B16
Nyúl *H* 149 A9
Nyvoll *N* 113 C11
Nyzhankovychi *UA* 144 D6
Nyzhni Petrivtsi *UA* 153 A7
Nyzhni Vorota *UA* 145 F7
Nyzhniy Bystryy *UA* 145 G8
Nyzhnya Vysots'ke *UA* 145 E7
Nyzhnya Yablun'ka *UA* 145 E6

O

Oadby *GB* 11 F9
Oakengates *GB* 10 F7
Oakham *GB* 11 F10
Oakley *GB* 13 B12
Oakley *GB* 13 C12
Oakley *GB* 15 C7
Oancea *RO* 154 F2
Oandu *EST* 131 C13
Oarja *RO* 160 D5
O Arrabal *E* 38 D2
Oarța de Jos *RO* 151 C11
Obal' *BY* 133 E7
Obal' *BY* 133 F6
Obalj *BIH* 157 F9
Oban *GB* 4 C6
O Barco *E* 39 D6
Obârșia *RO* 160 F4
Obârșia-Cloșani *RO* 159 C10
Obârșia de Câmp *RO* 159 E11
Obbola *S* 122 C4
Obdach *A* 73 B10
Obecnice *CZ* 76 C5
Obedinenie *BG* 166 C5
Obejo *E* 54 C3
Obeliai *LT* 135 E11
Oberaich *A* 73 B11
Oberalm *A* 73 A7
Oberammergau *D* 71 B12
Oberasbach *D* 75 D8
Oberau *D* 72 A3
Oberaudorf *D* 72 A5
Obercunnersdorf *D* 81 D7
Oberderdingen *D* 27 B10
Oberding *D* 75 F10
Oberdorla *D* 79 D7
Oberdrauburg *A* 73 C6
Oberegg *CH* 71 C9
Oberelsbach *D* 75 B7
Oberfell *D* 185 D7
Obergebra *D* 79 D8
Obergösgen *CH* 27 F8
Ober-Grafendorf *A* 77 F9
Obergriesbach *D* 75 F9
Obergünzburg *D* 71 B10
Obergurgl *A* 72 C3
Obergurig *D* 80 D6
Oberhaag *A* 148 C4
Oberhaid *D* 75 C8
Oberharmersbach *D* 27 D9
Oberhausen *D* 17 F7
Oberhausen *D* 75 E9
Oberhausen-Rheinhausen *D* 187 C5
Oberheldrungen *D* 79 D9
Oberhof *D* 79 E8
Oberhofen *CH* 70 D5
Oberhoffen-sur-Moder *F* 186 D4
Oberkirch *D* 27 C9
Oberkochen *D* 75 E7
Oberkotzau *D* 75 B10
Oberlangen *D* 17 C8
Oberlungwitz *D* 79 E12
Obermarchtal *D* 71 A9
Obermaßfeld-Grimmenthal *D* 75 A7
Obermoschel *D* 21 E9
Obernai *F* 27 D7
Obernberg am Inn *A* 76 F4
Obernburg am Main *D* 187 B7
Oberndorf *D* 17 A12
Oberndorf am Lech *D* 75 E8
Oberndorf am Neckar *D* 27 D10
Oberndorf bei Salzburg *A* 73 A6
Oberneukirchen *A* 76 F6
Obernfeld *D* 79 C7
Obernheim *D* 27 D10
Obernheim-Kirchenarnbach *D* 186 C4
Obernkirchen *D* 17 D12
Obernzell *D* 76 E5
Ober-Olm *D* 185 E9
Oberpullendorf *A* 149 A7
Oberried *D* 27 E8
Oberrieden *D* 71 A10
Oberriet *CH* 71 C9
Ober-Roden *D* 21 E11
Oberrot *D* 187 C8
Oberrotweil *D* 27 D8
Oberschneiding *D* 75 E12
Oberschützen *A* 148 B6
Obersiebenbrunn *A* 77 F11
Obersinn *D* 74 B6
Obersontheim *D* 187 C8
Oberspier *D* 79 D8
Oberstadion *D* 71 A9
Oberstaufen *D* 71 B10
Oberstdorf *D* 71 C10
Oberstenfeld *D* 27 B11
Oberthal *D* 21 E8
Oberthulba *D* 187 A8
Obertilliach *A* 73 C6
Obertraubling *D* 75 E11
Obertrubach *D* 75 C9
Obertshausen *D* 21 D11
Oberursel (Taunus) *D* 21 D11
Obervellach *A* 73 C7
Oberviechtach *D* 75 D11
Oberwald *CH* 70 D6
Oberwart *A* 148 B6
Oberwesel *D* 21 D9
Oberwolfach *D* 187 E5
Oberwölz *A* 73 B9
Óbidos *P* 44 F2
Obiliq *RKS* 164 D3
Obing *D* 75 F11
Obinitsa *EST* 132 F1
Obitel *BG* 167 C7
Objat *F* 29 E8
Objazda *PL* 85 A12
Öblarn *A* 73 B8
Oblešēvo *NMK* 164 F5
Oblikë e Madhe *AL* 163 E7
Obnova *BG* 165 C10
Obodivka *UA* 154 A4
Oboga *RO* 160 E4
O Bolo *E* 38 D5
Obón *E* 42 F2
Oborci *BIH* 157 D7
Oborín *SK* 145 F4
Oborishte *BG* 165 D9
Oborniki *PL* 81 A11
Oborniki Śląskie *PL* 81 D11
Obrazów *PL* 143 E12
Obreja *RO* 159 C9
Obrenovac *SRB* 158 D5
Obretenik *BG* 166 B5
Obrež *SRB* 158 D4
Obrež *SRB* 159 F7
Obrigheim *D* 21 F12
Obrigheim (Pfalz) *D* 187 B5
Obrnice *CZ* 76 A5
Obrochishte *BG* 167 C10
Obrov *SLO* 67 A9
Obrovac *HR* 156 D4
Obrovac *SRB* 158 C3
Obrowo *PL* 138 E6
Obrtići *BIH* 157 E10
Obruchishte *BG* 166 E5
Obryte *PL* 139 E11
Obrzycko *PL* 85 E11
Obsza *PL* 144 C6
Obudovac *BIH* 157 C10
Obyce *SK* 146 E6
Obzor *BG* 167 D9
O Cádavo *E* 38 B5
Ocaklar *TR* 173 D8
O Campo da Feira *E* 38 B3
Ocaña *E* 46 E6
Ocana *F* 37 H9
O Carballiño *E* 38 D3
O Castelo *E* 38 D3
O Castro *E* 38 C3
O Castro de Ferreira *E* 38 C4
Occhiobello *I* 66 C4
Occimiano *I* 68 C6
Očevlja *BIH* 157 D9
Ochagavía *E* 32 E3
O Chao *E* 38 B4
Ochiltree *GB* 5 E8
Ochla *PL* 81 C8
Ochodnica *SK* 147 C7
Ocholt *D* 17 B9
Ochsenfurt *D* 75 C7
Ochsenhausen *D* 71 A9
Ochtrup *D* 17 D8
Ocke *S* 105 E15
Ockelbo *S* 103 E12
Öckerö *S* 91 D10
Ockholm *D* 82 A5
Ocksjön *S* 102 A8
Ocland *RO* 152 E6
Ocna de Fier *RO* 159 C8
Ocna Mureș *RO* 152 E3
Ocna Sibiului *RO* 152 F4
Ocna Șugatag *RO* 152 B3
Ocnele Mari *RO* 160 C4
Ocnița *RO* 161 D7
Ocolina *MD* 154 A2
Ocoliș *RO* 151 E11
O Convento *E* 38 D2
O Corgo *E* 38 C5
Ocrkavlje *BIH* 157 E10
Öcsa *H* 150 C3
Öcsény *H* 149 D11
Öcsöd *H* 150 D5
Octeville-sur-Mer *F* 23 A12
Ocypel *PL* 138 C5
Odăile *RO* 161 C9
Ödåkra *S* 87 C11
Odda *N* 94 B5
Odden *N* 112 D5
Oddense *DK* 86 B3
Odder *DK* 86 D6
Oddsta *GB* 3 D15
Ödeborg *S* 91 B10
Odeceixe *P* 50 E2
Odeleite *P* 50 E5
Odelouca *P* 50 E3
Odelzhausen *D* 75 F9
Odemira *P* 50 D2
Ödena *E* 43 D7
Ödensbacken *S* 92 A7
Ödensberg *S* 91 C13
Odense *DK* 86 E6
Odensjö *S* 92 D4
Odensvi *S* 93 D8
Oderberg *D* 84 E6
Oderin *D* 80 B5
Odernheim am Glan *D* 21 E9
Oderzo *I* 72 E5
Ödeshog *S* 92 C5
Odiáxere *P* 50 E2
Odiham *GB* 15 E7
Ødis *DK* 86 E4
Odivelas *P* 50 B1
Odivelas *P* 50 C3
Ödkarby *FIN* 99 B13
Odobești *RO* 153 F10
Odobești *RO* 161 D7
Odolanów *PL* 142 C4
Odolena Voda *CZ* 76 B6
Odón *E* 47 C9
Odoorn *NL* 17 C7
Odorheiu Secuiesc *RO* 152 E6
Odry *CZ* 146 B5
Odrzywół *PL* 141 G3
Ödsmål *S* 91 C10
Ødsted *DK* 86 D4
Odŭrne *BG* 165 C10
Odžaci *BIH* 157 E9
Odžaci *SRB* 158 B3
Odžak *BIH* 157 B9
Odžak *BIH* 157 E6
Odžak *BIH* 157 F9
Odžak *MNE* 163 C7
Odziena *LV* 135 C11
Oebisfelde *D* 79 B8
Oedelem *B* 182 C2
Oedelsheim (Oberweser) *D* 78 C6
Oederan *D* 80 E4
Oeffelt *NL* 16 E5
Oegstgeest *NL* 16 D3
Oeiras *P* 50 B1
Oelde *D* 17 E10
Oelixdorf *D* 82 C7
Oelsnitz *D* 75 B11
Oelsnitz *D* 79 E12
Oene *NL* 183 A8
Oenkerk *NL* 16 B5
Oensingen *CH* 27 F8
Oerel *D* 17 B12
Oering *D* 83 C8
Oerlenbach *D* 75 B7
Oerlinghausen *D* 17 E11
Oestrich-Winkel *D* 21 D9
Oettersdorf *D* 79 E10
Oettingen in Bayern *D* 75 E8
Oetz *A* 71 C11
Oetzen *D* 83 D9
Oeversee *D* 82 A6
Œyreluy *F* 32 C3
Ofatinți *MD* 154 B4
Ofehértó *H* 145 H5
Ofena *I* 62 C5
Offanengo *I* 69 C8
Offemont *F* 27 E6
Offenbach am Main *D* 21 D11
Offenbach an der Queich *D* 187 C5
Offenberg *D* 76 E3
Offenburg *D* 27 D8
Offerdal *S* 105 E16
Offersøy *N* 111 D10
Offida *I* 62 B5
Offingen *D* 75 F7
Offranville *F* 18 E3
O Forte *E* 38 C3
Ofte *N* 95 D8
Ofterdingen *D* 27 D11
Oftersheim *D* 21 F11
Ogenbargen *D* 17 A9
Oger *F* 25 C11
Ogeu-les-Bains *F* 32 D4
Ogéviller *F* 26 C6
Oggevatn *N* 90 C3
Ogliastro *F* 37 F10
Ogliastro Cilento *I* 60 C4
Ogmore *GB* 13 C7
Ognyanovo *BG* 169 A10
Ogonelloe *IRL* 8 C6
Ogoya *BG* 165 D8
Ogra *RO* 152 E4
Ogre *LV* 135 C9
Ogren *AL* 168 D3
Ogresgals *LV* 135 C9
Ogrezeni *RO* 161 E7
Ogrodniki *PL* 139 E12
Ogrodzieniec *PL* 143 F8
Ogrosen *D* 80 C6
O Grove *E* 38 D2
Ogulin *HR* 67 B11
Oğulpaşa *TR* 172 A6
Ohaba *RO* 152 E3
Ohaba Lungă *RO* 151 F8
Ohanes *E* 55 E7
Ohey *B* 19 D11
Ohkola *FIN* 127 D13
Ohlsbach *D* 27 D8
Ohlstadt *D* 72 A3
Ohne *D* 17 D8
Ohorn *D* 80 D6
Ohrady *SK* 146 E5
Ohrdruf *D* 79 E8
Ohrid *NMK* 168 B4
Öhringen *D* 27 B11
Ohtaanniemi *FIN* 125 E11
Ohtanajärvi *S* 116 E10
Ohukotsu *EST* 131 C9
Oia *GR* 179 C9
Oiã *P* 44 C3
Oiartzun *E* 32 D2
Oichalia *GR* 169 E6
Øie *N* 105 B12
Oignies *F* 18 D6
O Igrexario *E* 38 D3
Oijärvi *FIN* 119 C15
Oijen *NL* 183 B6
Oijusluoma *FIN* 121 C13
Oikarainen *FIN* 119 B16
Oileán Ciarraí *IRL* 8 D4
Oilgate *IRL* 9 D9
Oímbra *E* 38 E5
Oinacu *RO* 161 F8
Oinas *FIN* 115 E2
Oinasjärvi *FIN* 124 C9
Oinofyta *GR* 175 C8
Oinoi *GR* 175 C7
Oion *E* 41 C7
O Irixo *E* 38 C3
Oiron *F* 28 B5
Oirschot *NL* 183 B6
Oiselay-et-Grachaux *F* 26 F4
Oisemont *F* 18 E4
Oisseau *F* 23 D10
Oissel *F* 18 F3
Oisterwijk *NL* 183 B6
Oisu *EST* 131 D11
Oisu *EST* 131 E11
Oitti *FIN* 127 D13
Oituz *RO* 153 E9
Oitylo *GR* 178 B3
Oivanki *FIN* 121 B13
Oizon *F* 25 F8
Öja *FIN* 123 C9
Öja *S* 93 E12
Ojakkala *FIN* 127 E11
Ojakylä *FIN* 119 D13
Ojakylä *FIN* 119 D14
Ojakylä *FIN* 119 F15
Ojanperä *FIN* 120 F8
Öjarn *S* 106 D8
Ojdula *RO* 153 F8
Öje *S* 102 E6
Öjebyn *S* 118 D6
Öjeforsen *S* 103 B9
Ojén *E* 53 C7
Öjingsvallen *S* 103 C8
Ojos Negros *E* 47 C10
Ojrzeń *PL* 139 E10
Öjung *S* 103 C10
Okalewo *PL* 139 D8
Okány *H* 151 D7
Okçular *TR* 181 C9
Økdal *N* 101 A12
Okehampton *GB* 12 D6
Okhotnoye *RUS* 136 D4
Oklaj *HR* 156 E5
Oknö *S* 89 A11
Okoč *SK* 146 F5
Okonek *PL* 85 C11
Okopy *PL* 141 H9
Ököritófülpös *H* 145 H6
Okorsh *BG* 161 F10
Okříšky *CZ* 77 D9
Okrouhlice *CZ* 77 C8
Okrúhle *SK* 145 E4
Oksa *PL* 143 E9
Öksajärvi *S* 116 C8
Oksakoski *FIN* 123 D12
Oksava *FIN* 123 C14
Oksbøl *DK* 86 D2
Oksbøl *DK* 86 E5
Øksfjord *N* 112 C9
Øksnes *N* 110 C8
Øksneshamn *N* 110 D9
Oksvoll *N* 104 D7
Oktonia *GR* 175 B9
Okučani *HR* 157 B7
Ola *E* 38 D2
Olague *E* 32 E2
Olaine *LV* 135 C7
Olalhas *P* 44 E4
Oland *N* 90 B3
Olănești *MD* 154 E5
Olanu *RO* 160 D4
Olargues *F* 34 C4
Olari *RO* 151 E8
Olaszliszka *H* 145 G3
Olave *E* 32 E2
Oława *PL* 81 E12
Olazti *E* 32 E1
Olba *E* 48 D3
Olbendorf *A* 148 B6
Olbernhau *D* 80 E4
Olbersdorf *D* 81 E7
Olbersleben *D* 79 D9
Olbia *I* 64 B3
Olbijcin *PL* 144 B5
Olbramovice *CZ* 77 C7
Olcea *RO* 151 D8
Oldcastle *IRL* 7 E8
Old Dailly *GB* 4 E7
Oldebroek *NL* 16 D5
Oldedalen *N* 100 C5
Oldehove *NL* 16 B6
Oldeide *N* 100 C2
Oldemarkt *NL* 16 C5
Olden *N* 100 C5
Olden *S* 105 D15
Oldenbrok *D* 17 B10
Oldenburg *D* 17 B10
Oldenburg in Holstein *D* 83 B9
Oldendorf *D* 17 A12
Oldenswort *D* 82 B5
Oldenzaal *NL* 17 D7
Olderdalen *N* 112 D6
Oldereid *N* 108 B8
Olderfjord *N* 113 C15
Oldernes *N* 113 C13
Oldervik *N* 108 C5
Oldervik *N* 111 A18
Oldervik *N* 113 B13
Oldham *GB* 11 D7
Old Head *IRL* 8 E5
Oldisleben *D* 79 D9
Old Leake *GB* 11 E12
Oldmeldrum *GB* 3 L12
Oldsum *D* 82 A4
Oldtown *IRL* 7 E10
Oleby *S* 97 B9
Olecko *PL* 136 E6
Oleggio *I* 68 B6
Oleiros *P* 44 E5
Oleksandrivka *UA* 154 C6
Olekseyivka *UA* 154 B3
Olemps *F* 33 B11
Olen *B* 19 B10
Ølen *N* 94 C3
Olesa de Montserrat *E* 43 D7
Oleśnica *PL* 142 D3
Oleśnica *PL* 143 F11
Olešnice *CZ* 77 C10
Olesno *PL* 142 E5
Olesno *PL* 143 F10
Oleszyce *PL* 144 C7
Olette *F* 33 E10
Olevano Romano *I* 62 D4
Olfen *D* 17 E8
Olgina *EST* 132 C3
Olginate *I* 69 B7
Ølgod *DK* 86 D3
Olgrinmore *GB* 3 J9
Olhalvo *P* 44 F2
Olhão *P* 50 E4
Olhava *FIN* 119 D14
Ølholm *DK* 86 D5
Olho Marinho *P* 44 F2
Ol'hopil' *UA* 154 A5
Oliana *E* 43 C6
Olías del Rey *E* 46 E5
Oliena *I* 64 C3
Oliete *E* 42 E2
Oligastro Marina *I* 60 C3
Olingé *S* 102 C7
Olingsjövallen *S* 102 C7
Oliola *E* 42 D6
Olite *E* 32 F2
Oliva *E* 56 D4
Oliva de la Frontera *E* 51 C6
Oliva de Mérida *E* 51 B7
Olival *P* 44 E3
Olivares *E* 51 E7
Olivares de Júcar *E* 47 E8
Oliveira de Azeméis *P* 44 C4
Oliveira de Frades *P* 44 C4
Oliveira do Arda *P* 44 B4
Oliveira do Bairro *P* 44 C4
Oliveira do Conde *P* 44 D5
Oliveira do Douro *P* 44 B3
Oliveira do Hospital *P* 44 D5
Olivenza *E* 51 B5
Oliveri *I* 59 C7
Olivet *F* 24 E6
Oliveto Citra *I* 60 B4
Oliveto Lucano *I* 60 B6
Olivone *CH* 71 D7
Ol'ka *SK* 145 E4
Olkijoki *FIN* 119 E13
Olkiluoto *FIN* 126 C5
Olkkajärvi *FIN* 117 E16
Olkusz *PL* 143 F8
Ollaberry *GB* 3 D14
Ollerton *GB* 11 E9
Ollerup *DK* 86 E7
Olliergues *F* 30 D4
Ollila *FIN* 121 B13
Ollila *FIN* 127 D8
Ollilanniemi *FIN* 121 E12
Ollioules *F* 35 D10
Ollo *E* 32 E2
Öllölä *FIN* 125 F15
Ollolai *I* 64 C3
Ollon *CH* 31 C10
Ollsta *S* 106 E8
Ölmbrotorp *S* 97 D13
Ölme *S* 97 D11
Olmedilla de Roa *E* 40 E4
Olmedo *E* 46 B3
Olmedo *I* 64 B1
Olmeta-di-Tuda *F* 37 F10
Olmeto *F* 37 H9
Olmos de Ojeda *E* 40 C3
Olney *GB* 15 C7
Olocau *E* 48 E3
Olocau del Rey *E* 42 F3
Olofsfors *S* 107 D16
Olofstorp *S* 91 D11
Olofström *S* 88 C7
Olombrada *E* 40 F3
Olomouc *CZ* 146 B4
Olonne-sur-Mer *F* 28 B2
Olonzac *F* 34 D4
Oloron-Ste-Marie *F* 32 D4
Olost *E* 43 D8
Olot *E* 43 C8
Olovi *CZ* 75 B12
Olovo *BIH* 157 D10
Olpe *D* 21 B9
Olřišov *CZ* 142 G4
Olšany *CZ* 77 C11
Olšany u Prostějova *CZ* 77 C12
Olsätter *S* 97 C10
Olsbenning *S* 97 B15
Olsberg *D* 17 F10
Olsberg *N* 111 B16
Ölsboda *S* 92 A4
Olsfors *S* 91 D12
Olshammar *S* 92 B5
Olsøy *N* 104 D8
Olst *NL* 16 D6
Ølsted *DK* 86 D5
Ølsted *DK* 87 D10
Ølstykke *DK* 87 D10
Olszanica *PL* 145 E5
Olszanka *PL* 142 E3
Olszany *PL* 144 D6
Olszewo-Borki *PL* 139 D12
Olsztyn *PL* 136 F1
Olsztyn *PL* 143 E7
Olsztynek *PL* 139 C9
Olszyn *PL* 141 F8
Olszyna *PL* 81 D8
Olszyny *PL* 144 D2
Oltedal *N* 94 E4
Olten *CH* 27 F8
Oltenești *RO* 153 D11
Olteni *RO* 160 E6
Oltenița *RO* 161 E9
Oltina *RO* 155 E1
Olula del Río *E* 55 E8
Olustvere *EST* 131 D11
Olvan *E* 43 C7
Olvasjärvi *FIN* 120 D9
Ölvega *E* 41 E8
Olvena *E* 42 C4
Olvera *E* 51 F9
Olympiada *GR* 169 C10
Olympiada *GR* 169 E7
Olympos *GR* 181 E6
Olzai *I* 64 C3
Oma *N* 94 B3
Omagh *GB* 4 F2
Omalos *GR* 178 E6
Omarchevo *BG* 166 E6
Omarska *BIH* 157 C6
Ombersley *GB* 13 A10
Omedu *EST* 131 D14
Omegna *I* 68 B5
Ömerköy *TR* 173 E9
Ömerli *TR* 173 D9
O Mesón do Vento *E* 38 B3
Omessa *F* 37 G10
Omiš *HR* 157 F6
Omišalj *HR* 67 B10
Ommen *NL* 16 C6
Omne *S* 107 F14
Omolio *GR* 169 E8
Omoljica *SRB* 159 D6
Omont *F* 19 E10
Ömossa *FIN* 122 F7
O Mosteiro *E* 38 C2
Omurtag *BG* 167 C6
Omvriaki *GR* 174 A5
Oña *E* 40 C5
Ona *N* 100 A5
Onani *I* 64 C3
Onano *I* 62 B1
Oñati *E* 32 D1
Oncala *E* 41 E7
Oncești *RO* 153 E10
Onchan *GBM* 10 C3
Onda *E* 48 E4
Ondara *E* 56 D5
Ondarroa *E* 32 D1
Ondřejov *CZ* 77 C7
Ondres *F* 32 C3
Oneglia *I* 37 D8
Onesse-et-Laharie *F* 32 B3
Onești *RO* 153 E9
Onet-le-Château *F* 33 B11
Ongles *F* 35 B10
Oniceni *RO* 153 D10
Onich *GB* 4 B6
Onifai *I* 64 C4
Oniferi *I* 64 C3
Onițcani *MD* 154 C4
Onkamaa *FIN* 128 D7
Onkamo *FIN* 115 E6
Onkamo *FIN* 119 D15
Onkamo *FIN* 125 F14
Onkiniemi *FIN* 127 C15
Önnestad *S* 88 C6
Önningby *FIN* 99 B14
Ónod *H* 145 G2
Onøya *N* 108 D4
Onsala *S* 91 E11
Onsbjerg *DK* 86 D7
Ønslev *DK* 83 A11
Onslunda *S* 88 D6
Onstmettingen *D* 27 D10
Onstwedde *NL* 17 B8
Ontiñena *E* 42 D4
Ontinyent *E* 56 D3
Ontojoki *FIN* 125 B11
Ontronvara *RUS* 125 E16
Onttola *FIN* 125 E13
Ontur *E* 55 B10
Onuškis *LT* 135 D11
Onuškis *LT* 137 E10
Onzain *F* 24 E5
Onzonilla *E* 39 C8
Oola *IRL* 8 C6
Ooltgensplaat *NL* 16 E2
Oonurme *EST* 131 C13
Oostakker *B* 19 B8
Oostburg *NL* 19 B7
Oostende *B* 18 B6
Oostendorp *NL* 16 D5
Oosterbeek *NL* 183 B7
Oosterend *NL* 16 B3
Oosterhesselen *NL* 17 C7
Oosterhout *NL* 16 E3
Oosterland *NL* 16 E2
Oosterwolde *NL* 16 C6
Oosterzele *B* 19 C8
Oostham *B* 183 C6
Oosthuizen *NL* 16 C3
Oostkamp *B* 19 B7
Oostkapelle *NL* 16 E1
Oostmalle *B* 182 C5
Oost-Souburg *NL* 16 F1
Oostvleteren *B* 18 C6
Oost-Vlieland *NL* 16 B4
Oostvoorne *NL* 182 B4
Ootmarsum *NL* 17 D7
Opaka *BG* 166 C6
Opalenica *PL* 81 B10
Opalenie *PL* 138 C6
Őpályi *H* 145 H5
Opan *BG* 166 E5
Opařany *CZ* 77 D6
Opatija *HR* 67 B9
Opatov *CZ* 77 C10
Opatovice nad Labem *CZ* 77 B9
Opatów *PL* 142 D5
Opatów *PL* 142 E6
Opatów *PL* 143 E11
Opatówek *PL* 142 C5
Opatowiec *PL* 143 F10
Opava *CZ* 146 B5
O Pazo *E* 38 D3
O Pazo de Irixoa *E* 38 B3
Ope *S* 106 E7
O Pedrouzo *E* 38 C3
Opeinde *NL* 16 B6
Opfenbach *D* 71 B9
Opglabbeek *B* 183 C7
Opheusden *NL* 183 B7
Opi *I* 62 D5
Opitter *B* 183 C7
Oploo *NL* 183 B7
Oplotnica *SLO* 148 D4
Opmeer *NL* 16 C3
Opochka *RUS* 133 C5
Opočno *CZ* 77 B10
Opoczno *PL* 141 H3
Opoeteren *B* 183 C7
Opole *PL* 142 E4
Opole Lubelskie *PL* 141 H5
Oporelu *RO* 160 D4
Oporets' *UA* 145 F7
O Porriño *E* 38 D2
Opoul-Périllos *F* 34 E4
Opovo *SRB* 158 C5
Oppach *D* 81 D7
Oppala *S* 103 E13
Oppdal *N* 101 A11
Oppeano *I* 66 B3
Oppeby *S* 92 C7
Oppedal *N* 100 D3
Oppegard *N* 95 C13
Oppenau *D* 27 D9
Oppenheim *D* 21 E10
Oppenweiler *D* 187 D7
Opphaug *N* 104 D7
Opphus *N* 101 D14
Oppido Lucano *I* 60 B5
Oppido Mamertina *I* 59 C8
Oppin *D* 79 C11
Opponitz *A* 73 A10
Oppurg *D* 79 E10
Oprisavci *HR* 157 B9
Oprișor *RO* 159 E11
Oprtalj *HR* 67 B8
Opsa *BY* 135 E13
Opsaheden *S* 97 B10
Optași-Măgura *RO* 160 D5
Ópusztaszer *H* 150 E5
Opuzen *HR* 157 F8
Opwijk *B* 19 C9
Or *H* 145 H5
Ora *I* 72 D3
Øra *N* 112 C8
Orada *P* 50 B5
Oradea *RO* 151 C8
Oradour-sur-Glane *F* 29 D8
Oradour-sur-Vayres *F* 29 D7
Orah *BIH* 157 F7
Orah *BIH* 162 D5
Orahavičko Polje *BIH* 157 D8
Orahova *BIH* 157 B7
Orahov Do *BIH* 162 D4
Orahovica *HR* 149 E9
Oraio *GR* 171 B7
Oraiokastro *GR* 169 C8
Oraison *F* 35 C10
Orajärvi *FIN* 117 E12
Orakylä *FIN* 115 D1
Orange *F* 35 B8
Orani *I* 64 C3
Oranienburg *D* 84 E4
Orán Mór *IRL* 6 F5
Oranmore *IRL* 6 F5
Orašac *BIH* 156 C5
Orašac *HR* 162 D5
Orašac *SRB* 164 C5
Orašje *BIH* 157 B10
Orăștie *RO* 151 F11
Orăștioara de Sus *RO* 151 F11
Orașu Nou *RO* 145 H7
Orätjärn *S* 103 C10

Orava EST 132 F1
Orava FIN 123 D10
Oravainen FIN 122 D8
Oravais FIN 122 D8
Oravala FIN 128 D6
Öravan S 107 B14
Oravankylä FIN 123 C15
Öravattnet S 106 E9
Oravi FIN 125 F11
Oravikoski FIN 124 E9
Oravisalo FIN 125 F13
Oravița RO 159 C8
Oravivaara FIN 121 E11
Oravská Polhora SK 147 B8
Oravské Veselé SK 147 C8
Oravský Podzámok SK 147 C8
Orba E 56 D4
Orbacém P 38 E2
Örbäck S 97 C15
Orbaden S 103 C11
Ørbæk DK 86 E7
Orbais-l'Abbaye F 25 C10
Orbara E 32 E3
Orbassano I 37 A7
Orbe CH 31 B10
Orbeasca RO 160 E6
Orbec F 24 B3
Orbeni RO 153 E10
Orbetello I 65 C4
Örbyhus S 99 B9
Orca P 44 D6
Orce E 55 D8
Orcera E 55 C7
Orchamps-Vennes F 26 F6
Orchies F 19 D7
Orchomenos GR 175 C6
Orchów PL 143 C7
Orchowo PL 138 E5
Orciano di Pesaro I 67 E6
Orcières F 36 B4
Orcival F 30 D2
Ordan-Larroque F 33 C6
Ordes E 38 B3
Ordizia E 32 D1
Ordona I 60 A5
Ordzhonikidze UA 154 C6
Orea E 47 C9
O Real E 38 B3
Örebäcken S 102 C4
Orebić HR 157 G7
Örebro S 97 D13
Ořechov CZ 77 D11
Öregcsertő H 150 D3
Öreglak H 149 C9
Öregrund S 99 B10
Orehoved DK 87 F9
Oreini GR 169 B10
Orekhovitsa BG 165 B9
Orellana de la Sierra E 51 A9
Orellana la Vieja E 51 A8
Ören TR 177 C10
Ören TR 181 B7
Orenhofen D 185 E6
Oreoi GR 175 B7
Orés E 32 F3
Oresh BG 166 B4
Oreshak BG 165 D10
Orestiada GR 171 B11
Öreström S 107 C16
Öretjändalen S 103 A10
Oreye B 19 C11
Orezu RO 161 D9
Orford GB 15 C12
Organi GR 171 B9
Organyà E 43 C6
Orgaz E 46 E5
Orgelet F 31 B8
Ørgenvika N 95 B11
Orgères-en-Beauce F 24 D6
Orgita EST 131 D8
Orgiva E 53 C10
Orgon F 35 C9
Orgosolo I 64 C3
Orhaneli TR 173 E10
Orhaniye TR 171 C10
Orhaniye TR 181 C8
Orhanlar TR 173 E8
Orhei MD 154 C3
Oria E 55 E8
Oria I 61 C9
O Rial E 38 D2
Origny-Ste-Benoîte F 19 E7
Orihuela E 56 E3
Orihuela del Tremedal E 47 C9
Orikhivka UA 154 F3
Orikum AL 168 D1
Orimattila FIN 127 D14
Oriniemi FIN 127 C9
Orio E 32 D1
Oriola P 50 C4
Oriolo I 61 C6
Oriolo Romano I 62 C2
Oripää FIN 126 D8
Orismala FIN 122 E8
Orissaare EST 130 D6
Oristà E 43 D8
Oristano I 64 D2
Oristown IRL 7 E9
Őriszentpéter H 149 C6
Oriv UA 145 E8
Oriveden asema FIN 127 B11
Orivesi FIN 127 B11
Orizare BG 167 D9
Orizari NMK 164 F5
Ørjavik N 104 F2
Ørje N 96 D6
Orkanger N 104 E7
Örkelljunga S 87 C12
Orkény H 150 C3
Orla PL 141 E8
Orlamünde D 79 E10
Orlat RO 152 F3
Orlea RO 160 F4
Orléans F 24 E6
Orlești RO 160 D4
Orlivka UA 155 C2
Orllan RKS 164 D3
Orlová CZ 146 B6
Orlov Dol BG 166 E6
Orlovets BG 166 C5
Orły PL 144 D6
Orlyak BG 161 F10
Orlyane BG 165 C10
Orma GR 169 C6
Ormanli TR 173 B9
Ormaryd S 92 D5
Ormea I 37 C7
Örményes H 150 C6
Örménykút H 150 D6
Ormos GR 176 D4
Ormos Panormou GR 176 D5
Ormos Prinou GR 171 C7
Ormož SLO 148 D6
Ormskirk GB 10 D6
Ormylia GR 169 D10
Ornaisons F 34 D4
Ornans F 26 F5
Ornäs S 97 A14
Örnäsudden S 109 E13
Ornavasso I 68 B5
Ornbau D 75 D8
Ornes N 105 B15
Ørnes N 108 C6
Orneta PL 139 B9
Ørnhøj DK 86 C3
Ornö S 93 A12
Ornontowice PL 142 F6
Örnsköldsvik S 107 E15
Orodel RO 159 E11
Orolik HR 157 B11
Orom SRB 150 F4
Oron-la-Ville CH 31 B10
Oronoz E 32 D2
Orońsko PL 141 H3
Oropa I 68 B4
Oropesa E 45 E10
Oropesa del Mar E 48 D5
Ororbia E 32 E2
Orosei I 64 C4
Orosháza H 150 D6
Oroslavje HR 148 E5
Oroszlány H 149 B10
Orpierre F 35 B10
Orreaga E 32 D3
Orrefors S 89 B9
Orrios E 42 F2
Orrmo S 102 C7
Orroli I 64 D3
Orrviken S 106 E6
Orsa S 102 D8
Orsara di Puglia I 60 A4
Orsay F 24 C7
Örsbäck S 107 D17
Orsennes F 29 C9
Örserum S 92 C5
Orsières CH 31 C11
Örsjö S 89 B9
Ørslev DK 87 E9
Ørsnes N 100 A5
Orsogna I 63 C6
Orsomarso I 60 D5
Orșova RO 159 D9
Ørsta N 100 B4
Ørsted DK 86 C6
Örsundsbro S 99 C8
Ortaca TR 181 C9
Ortacesus I 64 D3
Ortakent TR 177 E9
Ortaklar TR 177 D9
Ortaköy TR 173 B9
Ortala S 99 C11
Orta Nova I 60 A5
Orte I 62 C2
Orten N 100 A5
Ortenberg D 21 D12
Ortenberg D 27 D8
Ortenburg D 76 E4
Orth an der Donau A 77 F11
Orthez F 32 D4
Ortholmen S 102 B6
Orthovouni GR 168 E5
Ortigosa E 41 D6
Ortigueira E 38 A4
Ørting DK 86 D6
Ortisei I 72 C4
Orțișoara RO 151 F7
Ortnevik N 100 D4
Orton GB 10 C6
Ortona I 63 C6
Ortovera I 37 C8
Ortrand D 80 D5
Örträsk S 107 C15
Ortueri I 64 C2
Örtülüce TR 173 D7
Ørum DK 86 C5
Ørum DK 86 C7
Orune I 64 C3
Orusco E 47 D6
Orval F 29 B10
Orvalho P 44 D5
Orvault F 23 F8
Orvieto I 62 B2
Örviken S 118 E6
Orvinio I 62 C3
Oryakhovo BG 160 F3
Orzesze PL 142 F6
Orzinuovi I 69 C8
Orzyny PL 139 C11
Orzysz PL 136 F4
Os N 101 B14
Osa N 100 E6
Osa de Vega E 47 E7
Ošāni LV 135 D11
Osaonica SRB 163 C9
Osbaldwick GB 11 D9
Os Blancos E 38 D4
Osburg D 186 B2
Øsby DK 86 E5
Osby S 88 C5
Osbyholm S 87 D13
Oščadnica SK 147 C7
Oschatz D 80 D4
Oschersleben (Bode) D 79 B9
Oschiri I 64 B3
Ościsłowo PL 139 E9
Os Dices E 38 C2
Osdorf D 83 B8
Osečina SRB 158 E4
O Seixo E 38 E2
Oseja de Sajambre E 39 B9
Osek CZ 76 C5
Osek CZ 80 E5
Osen N 105 C9
Osen N 108 D6
Osenets BG 166 B6
Ošenieki LV 134 C4
Osera E 41 E10
Oșești RO 153 D10
Oset N 101 D10
Osetno PL 81 C10
Ősi H 149 B10
Osica de Sus RO 160 E4
Osidda I 64 B3
Osie PL 138 C5
Osieciny PL 138 E6
Osieck PL 141 G4
Osieczna PL 81 C11
Osieczna PL 138 C5
Osiecznica PL 81 D8
Osiek PL 138 C5
Osiek PL 139 D7
Osiek PL 143 E11
Osiek PL 147 B8
Osiek Jasielski PL 145 D3
Osiek Mały PL 142 B6
Osiek nad Notecią PL 85 D12
Osielsko PL 138 D5
Osiglia I 37 C8
Osijek HR 149 E11
Osikovitsa BG 165 D9
Osilo I 64 B2
Osimo I 67 F7
Osina PL 85 C8
Osini I 64 D3
Osiny PL 141 H6
Osio Sotto I 69 B8
Osipaonica SRB 159 D7
Osjaków PL 142 D6
Oskar S 89 B9
Oskar-Fredriksborg S 99 D10
Oskarshamn S 93 E8
Oskarström S 87 B11
Oskava CZ 77 C12
Oskořínek CZ 77 B8
Osľany SK 146 D6
Oslättfors S 103 E12
Osli H 149 A8
Oslo N 95 C13
Osloß D 79 B8
Osma E 40 C5
Osma FIN 117 D15
Osmancali TR 177 B9
Osmancik TR 173 A7
Osmangazi TR 173 D11
Osmaniye TR 173 E10
Osmaniye TR 173 F10
Osmanki FIN 123 C16
Osmanli TR 173 A6
Os'mino RUS 132 C5
Ösmo S 93 B11
Osmolin PL 141 F1
Osmoloda UA 145 F9
Osnabrück D 17 D10
Osno Lubuskie PL 81 B7
Osny F 24 B7
Osoblaha CZ 142 F4
Osogna CH 69 A6
Osojnik HR 162 D5
Osoppo I 73 D7
Osor E 43 D9
Osor HR 67 C9
Oșorhei RO 151 C9
Osorno E 40 D3
Osowa PL 136 E6
Osowa Sień PL 81 C10
Osøyri N 94 B2
Ospitaletto I 69 B9
Oss NL 16 E5
Ossa GR 169 C9
Ossa de Montiel E 55 B7
Ossana I 69 A10
Osséja F 33 F9
Ossendrecht NL 182 C4
Ossès F 32 D3
Ossiach A 73 C8
Oßmannstedt D 79 D9
Ossun F 32 D5
Östa S 98 B7
Östanå S 88 C6
Östanfjärden S 119 C10
Östansjö S 92 A5
Östansjö S 109 E16
Östanskär S 103 A13
Östanvik S 103 D9
Oštarije HR 156 B3
Ostaszewo PL 138 B6
Östavall S 103 B9
Ostbevern D 17 D9
Østbirk DK 86 D5
Östbjörka S 103 E9
Østby N 91 A9
Østby N 102 D4
Östby S 107 D13
Østed DK 87 D9
Ostellato I 66 C4
Osten D 17 A12
Ostend B 18 B6
Ostend B 182 C1
Ostenfeld (Husum) D 82 B6
Østengård DK 86 D4
Österås S 107 E12
Øster Assels DK 86 B3
Øster Bjerregrav DK 86 C5
Øster Brønderslev DK 86 A5
Osterburg (Altmark) D 83 E11
Osterburken D 27 B11
Österby D 82 B7
Østerby DK 86 A5
Österbybruk S 99 B9
Österbymo S 92 D6
Österede S 107 E11
Österfärnebo S 98 B7
Osterfeld D 79 D10
Österforse S 107 E12
Östergarn S 93 E13
Östergraninge S 107 F12
Österhankmo FIN 122 D7
Osterhever D 82 B5
Osterhofen D 76 E4
Øster Højst DK 86 E4
Osterholz-Scharmbeck D 17 B11
Øster Hornum DK 86 B5
Øster Hurup DK 86 B6
Østerild DK 86 A3
Øster Jølby DK 86 B3
Österjörn S 118 D4
Østerlars DK 89 E7
Øster Lindet DK 86 E4
Österlisa S 99 C11
Østermarie DK 89 E8
Ostermark FIN 126 E8
Ostermiething A 76 F3
Ostermundigen CH 31 B11
Österoret S 107 C12
Östero FIN 122 D8
Osterode am Harz D 79 C7
Osterrönfeld D 82 B7
Österskucku S 102 A8
Östersund S 106 E7
Östersundom FIN 127 E13
Øster Tørslev DK 86 B6
Øster Ulslev DK 83 A11
Östervåla S 98 B8
Øster Vedsted DK 86 E3
Østervrå DK 90 E7
Øster Vrøgum DK 86 D2
Osterwieck D 79 C8
Östese N 94 B4
Ostfildern D 187 D7
Östhammar S 99 B10
Ostheim vor der Rhön D 75 B7
Osthofen D 21 E10
Ostia I 62 D2
Ostiano I 66 B1
Ostiglia I 66 B3
Ostiz E 32 E2
Östloning S 103 A13
Östmark S 97 B8
Östmarkum S 107 E14
Östnor S 102 D7
Ostojićevo SRB 150 F5
Ostoros H 145 H1
Ostra I 67 E7
Ostra RO 153 C7
Östra Åliden S 118 D4
Ostrach D 27 E11
Östra Ed S 93 C9
Östra Frölunda S 91 E13
Östra Granberg S 118 C4
Östra Grevie S 87 E12
Östra Husby S 93 B9
Östra Ljungby S 87 C12
Östra Löa S 97 C13
Östra Lovsjön S 106 D7
Östra Ormsjö S 107 C10
Östra Ryd S 93 C8
Östra Skråmträsk S 118 E5
Östra Sönnarslöv S 88 D6
Östra Stugusjö S 103 A9
Ostrau D 79 C11
Ostrau D 80 D4
Ostrava CZ 146 B6
Östra Vemmerlöv S 88 D6
Ostravice CZ 146 B6
Östra Yttermark FIN 122 E6
Oštrelj BIH 156 D5
Ostren AL 168 B3
Ostřetín CZ 77 B10
Ostrhauderfehn D 17 B9
Ostricourt F 182 E2
Östringen D 21 F11
Ostritsa BG 166 B5
Ostritz D 81 D7
Ostróda PL 139 C8
Ostrołęka PL 140 D5
Ostromecko PL 138 D5
Ostroměř CZ 77 B9
Ostroróg PL 81 A10
Ostrov BG 160 F4
Ostrov CZ 76 B3
Ostrov RO 155 D2
Ostrov RO 161 E10
Ostrov RUS 133 B4
Ostrov SK 146 D5
Ostroveni RO 160 F3
Ostrovo BG 161 F9
Ostrov u Macochy CZ 77 D11
Ostrów PL 143 F12
Ostrówek PL 141 G7
Ostrówek PL 142 D6
Ostrowice PL 85 C9
Ostrowiec PL 85 B11
Ostrowiec Świętokrzyski PL 143 E11
Ostrowite PL 138 F5
Ostrowite PL 139 D7
Ostrów Lubelski PL 141 H7
Ostrów Mazowiecka PL 139 E12
Ostrowo PL 138 E5
Ostrów Wielkopolski PL 142 C4
Ostrowy nad Okszą PL 143 E7
Ostrožac BIH 156 C4
Ostrožac BIH 157 E8
Ostrożeń PL 141 G5
Østrup DK 86 B4
Ostrzeszów PL 142 D4
Ostuni I 61 B9
Ostvik S 118 E6
Ostwald F 186 D4
Osula EST 131 F13
Osuna E 53 B6
Ošupe LV 135 C13
Osvallen S 102 A4
Osvica BIH 157 C8
Oswaldkirk GB 11 C9
Oswestry GB 10 F5
Oświęcim PL 143 F7
Ota F 37 G9
Otaci MD 154 A1
Otalampi FIN 127 E12
Otaņķi LV 134 D2
Otanmäki FIN 120 F9
Otaslavice CZ 77 D12
Otava FIN 128 B7
Otavice HR 156 E5
Oteiza E 32 E2
Oțeleni RO 153 C10
Oțelu Roșu RO 159 B9
Otepää EST 131 E12
Oteren N 111 B18
Oterma FIN 120 E9
Otero de Bodas E 39 E7
Otervik N 105 A11
Oteșani RO 160 C4
Oteševo NMK 168 C4
Otfinów PL 143 F10
Othem S 93 D13
Ötigheim D 27 C9
Ötisheim D 27 C10
Otišić HR 156 E5
Otívar E 53 C9
Otley GB 11 D8
Otley GB 15 C11
Otmuchów PL 77 B12
Otnes N 101 C14
Otočac HR 156 C3
Otok HR 157 B10
Otok HR 157 E6
Otoka BIH 156 C5
Otopeni RO 161 D8
Otorowo PL 81 A10
O Toural E 38 D2
Otovica NMK 164 F4
Otradnoye RUS 129 F14
Otranto I 61 C10
Otricoli I 62 C2
Otrokovice CZ 146 C5
Otta N 101 C11
Ottana I 64 C3
Ottaviano I 60 B2
Ottenby S 89 C10
Ottendorf-Okrilla D 80 D5
Ottenheim D 186 E4
Ottenhöfen im Schwarzwald D 27 C9
Ottenschlag A 77 F8
Ottensheim A 76 F6
Ottenstein D 78 C5
Otterbach D 186 C4
Otterbäcken S 91 B15
Otterberg D 21 E9
Otterburn GB 5 E12
Otter Ferry GB 4 C6
Otterfing D 72 A4
Otterlo NL 16 D5
Otterndorf D 17 A11
Ottersberg D 17 B12
Otterøy N 105 B10
Otterstad S 91 B13
Otterswier D 27 C9
Otterswick GB 3 D14
Otterup DK 86 D6
Otterwisch D 79 D12
Ottevény H 149 A9
Ottignies B 19 C10
Ottmarsheim F 27 E8
Ottobeuren D 71 B10
Ottobrunn D 75 F10
Öttömös H 150 E4
Ottone I 37 B10
Ottrau D 21 C12
Ottsjö S 105 E14
Ottsjön S 106 D7
Ottweiler D 21 F8
Otwock PL 141 F4
Otxandio E 41 B6
Otyń PL 81 C9
Otzing D 76 E3
Ouanne F 25 E9
Ouarville F 24 D6
Ouca P 44 C3
Oucques F 24 E5
Oud-Beijerland NL 16 E2
Ouddorp NL 182 B3
Oudehaske NL 16 C5
Oudemirdum NL 16 C5
Oudenaarde B 19 C8
Oudenbosch NL 16 E3
Oudenburg B 18 B7
Oudeschild NL 16 B3
Oude-Tonge NL 16 E2
Oudewater NL 182 A5
Oud-Gastel NL 16 E2
Oudon F 23 F9
Oud-Turnhout B 16 F3
Oud-Vossemeer NL 16 E2
Oudzele B 182 C2
Oued Laou MA 53 F6
Ouffet B 19 D11
Oughterard IRL 6 F4
Ougney F 26 F4
Ouguela P 45 F6
Ouistreham F 23 B11
Oulainen FIN 119 F13
Oulanka FIN 115 F5
Oulchy-le-Château F 25 B9
Oulder B 20 D6
Oullins F 30 D6
Oulton GB 15 C12
Oulu FIN 119 D14
Oulunsalo FIN 119 E14
Oulx I 31 E10
Oundle GB 15 C8
Oupeye B 19 C12
Ouranoupoli GR 170 D5
Oure DK 87 E7
Ourém P 44 E3
Ourense E 38 D4
Ourique P 50 D3
Ourol E 38 A4
Ouroux-en-Morvan F 25 F10
Ouroux-sur-Saône F 31 B6
Ourville-en-Caux F 18 E2
Oust F 33 E8
Outakoski FIN 113 D16
Outarville F 24 D7
Outeiro P 38 E2
Outeiro P 39 E6
Outeiro de Rei E 38 B4
Outeiro Seco P 38 E5
Outokumpu FIN 125 E12
Outomuro E 38 D4
Outreau F 15 F12
Outwell GB 11 F12
Ouveillan F 34 D4
Ouzouer-le-Marché F 24 E6
Ouzouer-sur-Loire F 25 E7
Ovada I 37 B9
Ovanåker S 103 D10
Ovanmo S 107 D10
Ovar P 44 C3
Ovaro I 73 D6
Ovča SRB 158 D6
Ovcha Mogila BG 166 C4
Ovcharovo BG 166 E6
Ovchepoltsi BG 165 E9
Ove DK 86 B5
Ovelgönne D 17 B10
Överammer S 107 E9
Överäng S 105 D14
Overås N 100 A8
Overath D 21 C8
Överberg S 102 B7
Overbister GB 3 G11
Øverbygd N 111 C17
Överbyn S 103 C12
Overdinkel NL 183 A10
Over Feldborg DK 86 C3
Øvergard N 111 B18
Overhalla N 105 B11
Överhogdal S 102 B8
Överhörnäs S 107 E15
Over Hornbæk DK 86 C5
Overijse B 19 C10
Överissjö S 107 C13
Over Jerstal DK 86 E4
Överkalix S 119 B9
Overlade DK 86 B4
Överlännäs S 107 E13
Överlida S 91 E12
Overloon NL 183 B7
Övermalax FIN 122 E7
Övermark FIN 122 E6
Övermorjärv S 118 B9
Övernäs S 109 D14
Överö FIN 99 B15
Overøye N 100 B6
Overpelt B 19 B11
Over Simmelkær DK 86 C3
Överstbyn S 118 B7
Övertänger S 103 E10
Overton GB 10 F6
Overton GB 13 C12
Övertorneå S 119 B11
Överturingen S 102 B8
Överum S 93 D8
Ovezande NL 16 F1
O Vicedo E 38 A4
Ovidiu RO 155 E3
Oviedo E 39 B8
Oviglio I 37 B8
Oviken S 105 E16
Ovindoli I 62 C5
Oviši LV 130 F3
Öv Långträsk S 109 E16
Ovodda I 64 C3
Övra S 107 D11
Øvre Alta N 113 D11
Øvre Årdal N 100 D7
Øvre Åstbru N 101 D13
Övre Bredåker S 118 C6
Övre Fläsjön S 118 B7
Øvre Kildal N 112 D7
Övre-Konäs S 105 D14
Øvrella N 95 C10
Øvre Rendal N 101 C14
Övre Soppero S 116 B7
Övre Tväråsel S 118 C5
Ovria GR 174 C4
Övsjöbyn S 107 E9
Ovtrup DK 86 D2
Owen D 27 C11
Owingen D 27 E11
Owińska PL 81 A11
Owschlag D 82 B7
Öxabäck S 91 E12
Oxberg S 102 D7
Oxelösund S 93 B10
Oxenhope GB 11 D8
Oxentea MD 154 C4
Oxford GB 13 B12
Oxhalsö S 99 C11
Oxie S 87 D12
Oxkangar FIN 122 D8
Oxshott GB 15 E8
Oxted GB 15 E9
Oxton GB 5 D11
Oxylithos GR 175 B9
Øyangen N 104 E7
Øydegarden N 104 E4
Øyenkilen N 91 A8
Øyer N 101 D12
Øyeren N 96 B7
Øyjord N 108 B9
Oy-Mittelberg D 71 B10
Øynes N 108 B9
Øynes N 111 C11
Oyonnax F 31 C8
Øyslebø N 90 C2
Oyten D 17 B12
Øyvatnet N 111 C12
Oza E 38 B3
Ozaeta E 41 C7
Ozalj HR 148 E4
Ożarów PL 143 E12
Ożarów Mazowiecki PL 141 F3
Ožbalt SLO 148 C4
Özbaşi TR 177 D9
Özbek TR 177 C8
Ózd H 145 G1
Ožďany SK 147 E9
Özdere TR 177 D9
Ożenna PL 145 E3
Ozersk RUS 136 E5
Ozieri I 64 B3
Ozimek PL 142 E5
Ozimica BIH 157 D9
Özlüce TR 181 B9
Ozoir-la-Ferrière F 25 C8
Ozolaine LV 131 F9
Ozoli LV 131 F9
Ozoli LV 134 B4
Ozoli LV 135 C12
Ozolmuiža LV 133 D2
Ozolnieki LV 134 C7
Ozora H 149 C10
Ozorków PL 143 C7
Ozun RO 153 F7
Ozzano dell'Emilia I 66 D3
Ozzano Monferrato I 68 C5

P

Pääaho FIN 121 D10
Pääjärvi FIN 123 E13
Paakinmäki FIN 121 F11
Paakkila FIN 125 E11
Paakkola FIN 119 C13
Paal B 183 C6
Paalasmaa FIN 125 D12
Paaso FIN 127 C15
Paasvere EST 131 C13
Paatela FIN 129 B9
Paattinen FIN 126 D7
Paatus FIN 113 D17
Paavola FIN 119 E14
Pabaiskas LT 135 F9
Paberžė LT 137 D11
Pabianice PL 143 C7
Pabillonis I 64 D2
Pabiržė LT 135 D9
Pabneukirchen A 77 F7
Pabradė LT 137 D12
Pabu F 22 C5
Pacanów PL 143 F11
Paceco I 58 D2
Pacheia Ammos GR 179 E10
Pachino I 59 F7
Pachni GR 171 B7
Paciano I 62 A2
Pácin H 145 G4
Pačir SRB 150 F3
Pack A 73 C10
Pačlavice CZ 77 D12
Pacos de Ferreira P 38 F3
Pacov CZ 77 D8
Pacsa H 149 C8
Păcureți RO 161 C8
Pacyna PL 143 B8
Pacy-sur-Eure F 24 B5
Paczków PL 77 B12
Padasjoki FIN 127 C13
Padborg DK 82 A6
Padbury GB 14 D7
Padej SRB 150 F5
Pađene HR 156 D5
Paderborn D 17 E11
Paderne P 38 E2
Paderne P 50 E3
Paderne de Allariz E 38 D4
Padeș RO 159 C10
Padesh BG 165 F7
Padew Narodowa PL 143 F12
Padežine BIH 157 F8
Padiham GB 11 D7
Pădina RO 159 E11
Padina RO 161 D10
Padina SRB 159 C6
Padinska Skela SRB 158 D5
Padirac F 29 F9
Padise EST 131 C8
Padoby BY 133 F2
Padoux F 26 D6
Padova I 66 B4
Padria I 64 C2
Padrón E 38 C2
Padru I 64 B4
Padstow GB 12 D5
Padsvillye BY 133 F3
Padul E 53 B9
Padula I 60 C5
Paduli I 60 A3
Padure LV 134 C3
Pădureni RO 153 D12
Paesana I 37 B6
Paese I 72 E5
Pag HR 67 D11
Pagani I 60 B3
Paganica I 62 C4
Paganico I 65 B4
Pagėgiai LT 134 F3
Pagiriai LT 135 F8
Pagiriai LT 137 D11
Paglieta I 63 C6
Pagny-sur-Moselle F 26 C5
Pagondas GR 177 D8
Pagouria GR 171 B8
Pagramantis LT 134 F4
Paharova S 116 E8
Páhi H 150 D3
Pahkakoski FIN 119 D16
Pahkakumpu FIN 115 E3
Pahkakumpu FIN 121 C12
Pahkala FIN 119 F11
Pahkamäki FIN 123 D16
Pähl D 72 A3
Pahlen D 82 B6
Pahranichny BY 140 D9
Pahtaoja FIN 119 C14
Paião P 44 D3
Paide EST 131 D11
Paignton GB 13 E7
Paihola FIN 125 E13
Päijälä FIN 127 B12
Paikuse EST 131 E9
Pailhès F 33 D8
Paillet F 32 A5
Paimbœuf F 23 F7
Paimela FIN 127 C14
Paimio FIN 126 E8
Paimpol F 22 C5
Paimpont F 23 D7
Painswick GB 13 B10
Painten D 75 E9
Paipis FIN 127 E13
Paisley GB 5 D8
Paistu EST 131 E11
Paisua FIN 124 C9
Päiväjoki FIN 115 F2
Pajala S 117 D10
Pajares de la Lampreana E 39 E8
Pajarón E 47 E9
Pajęczno PL 143 D6
Pajukoski FIN 125 C11
Pajukoste FIN 113 C20
Pajūris LT 134 F4
Pajuskylä FIN 124 D7
Pajuvaara FIN 121 D14
Páka H 149 C7
Pakaa FIN 127 D14
Pakalnė LT 134 F2
Pakalniai LT 135 F10
Pakapė LT 134 E6
Pakarila FIN 123 E17
Pakisjärvi FIN 117 E12
Pakkala FIN 127 C11
Pakod H 149 C8
Pakość PL 138 E5
Pakosław PL 81 C12
Pakoštane HR 156 E4
Pákozd H 149 B11
Pakrac HR 149 F8
Pakruojis LT 134 E7
Paks H 149 C11
Paksuniemi S 116 C5
Pala EST 131 D14
Palacios del Sil E 39 C7
Palacios de Sanabria E 39 D6
Palaciosrubios E 45 B10
Palade EST 130 D5
Palafrugell E 43 D10
Palagianello I 61 B7
Palagiano I 61 B8
Palagonia I 59 E6
Palaia I 66 E2
Palaia Fokaia GR 175 D8
Palaikastro GR 179 E11
Palaiochora GR 169 C9
Palaiochora GR 178 E6
Palaiochori GR 169 D6
Palaiochori GR 169 D10
Palaiochori GR 175 C7
Palaiokastritsa GR 168 E2
Palaiokastro GR 177 D9
Palaiokipos GR 177 A7
Palaiokomi GR 170 C5
Palaiomonastiro GR 169 F6
Palaiopoli GR 176 D4
Palaiopyrgos GR 169 E6
Palaiopyrgos GR 169 E8
Palaiopyrgos GR 174 C4
Palaiovracha GR 174 B5
Palairos GR 174 B2
Palaiseau F 25 C7
Palamas GR 169 F7
Palamós E 43 D10
Palamuse EST 131 D13
Palanca RO 153 D8
Palanga LT 134 E2
Pålänge S 119 C9
Palanzano I 66 D1
Palárikovo SK 146 E6
Palas de Rei E 38 C4
Palata BY 133 E6
Palata I 63 D7
Pălatca RO 152 D4
Palau I 64 A3
Palavas-les-Flots F 35 C6
Palazzo Adriano I 58 D3
Palazzolo Acreide I 59 E6
Palazzolo sull'Oglio I 69 B8
Palazzo San Gervasio I 60 B6
Paldiski EST 131 C8
Pale BIH 157 E10
Päle LV 131 F9
Paleičiai LT 134 F2
Palena I 63 D6
Palencia E 40 D2
Palenciana E 53 B7
Palenzuela E 40 D3
Palermo AL 168 D2
Palermo I 58 C3
Paleśnica PL 144 D2
Palestrina I 62 D3
Palėvenėlė LT 135 E10
Palež BIH 158 E3
Palhaça P 44 C3
Pálháza H 145 G4
Palia Kavala GR 171 C6
Paliano I 62 D4
Palić SRB 150 E4
Palinges F 30 B5
Palinuro I 60 C4
Paliouri GR 169 E10
Paliouria GR 169 E6
Palis F 25 D10
Paliseul B 19 E11
Palivere EST 131 D7
Palizzi I 59 D9
Paljakka FIN 121 B14
Paljakka FIN 121 E11

Pälkäne FIN 127 C11
Pålkem S 118 B7
Palkino RUS 132 F3
Palkisoja FIN 115 A2
Palkovice CZ 146 B6
Palladio GR 171 B8
Pallagorio I 61 E7
Pallarés E 51 C7
Pallas Grean New IRL 8 C6
Pallas Green IRL 8 C6
Pälli FIN 119 E16
Palling D 75 F12
Palluau F 28 B2
Palluau-sur-Indre F 29 B8
Palma P 50 C2
Palma Campania I 60 B3
Palma del Río E 51 D9
Palma de Mallorca E 49 E10
Palma di Montechiaro I 58 E4
Palmadula I 64 B1
Palmanova E 49 E10
Palmanova I 73 E7
Palmaz P 44 C4
Palmeira P 38 E3
Palmela P 50 B2
Palmi I 59 C8
Pálmonostora H 150 D4
Palmse EST 131 B11
Palnackie GB 5 F9
Palneca F 37 H10
Palo del Colle I 61 A7
Palohuornas S 116 E6
Palojärvi FIN 115 E2
Palojärvi FIN 117 A10
Palojärvi FIN 117 E14
Palojoensuu FIN 116 B10
Palokki FIN 125 E11
Palomaa FIN 113 E19
Palomäki FIN 125 D11
Palomar de Arroyos E 42 F2
Palomares del Río E 51 E7
Palomas E 51 B7
Palombara Sabina I 62 C3
Palombaro I 63 C6
Palomenė LT 137 D9
Palomera E 47 D8
Palomeras del Campo E 47 E7
Palomonte I 60 B4
Palonoja FIN 115 B2
Palonselkä FIN 117 D13
Palonurmi FIN 125 D10
Paloperä FIN 115 F4
Palos de la Frontera E 51 E6
Palosenjärvi FIN 124 C8
Palotabozsok H 149 D11
Palotáshalom H 150 B4
Palovaara FIN 119 B12
Palovaara FIN 119 B16
Palovaara FIN 121 E13
Palovaara FIN 125 E14
Pals E 43 D10
Pålsboda S 92 A6
Palsmane LV 135 B12
Palsselkä FIN 117 D16
Pålsträsk S 118 C6
Paltamo FIN 121 F10
Paltanen FIN 124 F7
Paltaniemi FIN 121 F10
Paltin RO 153 F9
Păltiniș RO 153 A9
Păltiniș RO 159 C9
Păltinoasa RO 153 B7
Pal'tsevo RUS 129 D10
Paludi I 61 D7
Paluel F 18 E2
Paluknys LT 137 E10
Paluzza I 73 C7
Palyatskishki BY 137 E11
Palyessye BY 135 F12
Palzem D 20 E6
Pambukovica SRB 158 E4
Pameče SLO 73 C11
Pamfylla GR 177 A8
Pamhagen A 149 A7
Pamiers F 33 D9
Pampāļi LV 134 C4
Pamparato I 37 C7
Pampelonne F 33 B10
Pampilhosa P 44 D4
Pampilhosa da Serra P 44 D5
Pampliega E 40 D4
Pamplona E 32 E2
Pampow D 83 C10
Pamproux F 28 C5
Pamukçu TR 173 E8
Panaci RO 152 C6
Panagia GR 171 C7
Panagia GR 171 E8
Panagia GR 178 E9
Panagyurishte BG 165 D9
Panagyurski Kolonii BG 165 D9
Panahor AL 168 C2
Panaitolio GR 174 B3
Panaja AL 168 C1
Pănășești MD 154 C3
Panassac F 33 D7
Pănătău RO 161 C8
Panazol F 29 D8
Pancalieri I 37 B7
Pancar TR 177 C9
Pancarköy TR 173 B7
Păncești RO 153 E10
Pančevo SRB 158 D6
Pancharevo BG 165 D7
Panciu RO 153 F10
Pancorbo E 40 C5
Pâncota RO 151 E8
Pancrudo E 42 F1
Pánd H 150 C4
Pandėlys LT 135 D10
Pandino I 69 C8
Pandrup DK 86 A5
Pandy GB 13 B9
Panelia FIN 126 C6
Panemunė LT 136 C4
Panemunėlis LT 135 E10
Panes E 39 B10
Pănet RO 152 D4
Panevėžys LT 135 E8
Panga EST 130 D4
Pângărați RO 153 D8
Pange F 186 C1
Panicale I 62 A2
Panichkovo BG 166 F4
Panissières F 30 D5
Paniza E 41 F9
Panjas F 32 C5
Panjevac SRB 159 E8
Panjik BIH 157 C9
Panka FIN 124 D7
Pankajärvi FIN 125 D14
Pankakoski FIN 125 D14
Panker D 83 B9
Panki PL 142 E6
Pannarano I 60 A3
Pannes F 25 D8
Panni I 60 A4
Panningen NL 16 F5
Pannonhalma H 149 A9
Panóias P 50 D3
Panorama GR 169 C9
Panormos GR 178 E8
Panschwitz-Kuckau D 80 D6
Pantanassa GR 178 B4
Pantäne FIN 122 F8
Pantelimon RO 155 D2
Pantelimon RO 161 E8
Panticeu RO 152 C3
Panticosa E 32 E5
Pantoja E 46 D5
Panttikylä FIN 122 F8
Panttila FIN 122 E8
Pant-y-dwr GB 13 A8
Paola I 60 E6
Pap H 145 G5
Pápa H 149 B8
Papadianika GR 178 B4
Papasidero I 60 D5
Pápateszér H 149 B9
Papenburg D 17 B8
Papendorf D 83 B12
Papendrecht NL 16 E3
Papilė LT 134 D5
Papilys LT 135 D10
Papín SK 145 E5
Papkeszi H 149 B10
Paplaka LV 134 D2
Papowo Biskupie PL 138 D6
Pappades GR 175 B7
Pappados GR 177 A7
Pappenheim D 75 E8
Papradno SK 146 C6
Paprotnia PL 141 F6
Par GB 12 E5
Parabita I 61 C10
Paraćin SRB 159 F7
Paracuellos E 47 E9
Paracuellos de Jarama E 46 C5
Parád H 147 F10
Parada P 45 C6
Parada de Ester P 44 C4
Parada de Pinhão P 38 F4
Parada de Rubiales E 45 B10
Parada de Sil E 38 D4
Paradas E 51 E9
Paradeisi GR 181 D8
Paradeisia GR 174 E5
Paradeisos GR 171 B7
Paradela E 38 C5
Paradela P 38 E4
Paradela P 44 B5
Paradyż PL 141 H2
Parainen FIN 126 E7
Parakalamos GR 168 E4
Parakka S 116 D7
Parakoila GR 177 A7
Paralepa EST 130 D7
Paralia GR 174 C4
Paralia GR 175 F6
Paralia Avdiron GR 171 C7
Paralia Saranti GR 175 C6
Paralia Tyrou GR 175 E6
Paralio Astros GR 175 E6
Paramé F 23 C8
Parâmio P 39 E6
Páramo del Sil E 39 C7
Paramythia GR 168 F4
Paranesti GR 171 B6
Paranhos P 44 D5
Parantala FIN 123 E15
Parapotamos GR 168 E3
Paras N 111 B19
Părău RO 152 F6
Parava RO 153 E9
Paravola GR 174 B4
Paray-le-Monial F 30 C5
Parcani MD 154 B3
Parcent E 56 D4
Parcé-sur-Sarthe F 23 E11
Parchen D 79 B11
Parchim D 83 D11
Parchovany SK 145 F4
Parchów PL 81 D9
Parchowo PL 85 B13
Parciaki PL 139 D11
Parcoul F 28 E6
Parczew PL 141 G7
Pardais P 50 B5
Pardies F 32 D4
Pardilhó P 44 C3
Pardoși RO 161 C9
Pardubice CZ 77 B9
Parechcha BY 137 F9
Paredes de Coura P 38 E2
Paredes de Nava E 39 D10
Pareja E 47 C7
Parempuyre F 28 F4
Parenti I 61 E6
Parentis-en-Born F 32 B3
Parets del Vallès E 43 D8
Parey D 79 B10
Parga GR 168 F3
Pârgărești RO 153 E9
Pargas FIN 126 E7
Parghelia I 59 B8
Pargny-sur-Saulx F 25 C12
Pargolovo RUS 129 E13
Parhalahti FIN 119 F12
Päri EST 131 E11
Parigné-l'Évêque F 24 E3
Parikkala FIN 129 B12
Parincea RO 153 E10
Paris F 25 C7
Parisot F 33 B9
Parisot F 33 C9
Parissavaara FIN 125 E16
Pärjänsuo FIN 120 C9
Pârjol RO 153 D9
Park GB 4 F2
Parkajoki S 117 C10
Parkalompolo S 116 C9
Parkano FIN 123 F10
Parkkila FIN 121 D11
Parkkila FIN 123 C14
Parkkila FIN 128 B7
Parkkima FIN 123 C15
Parkkuu FIN 127 B10
Parksepa EST 131 F13
Parkstein D 75 C11
Parkua FIN 125 B9
Parkumäki FIN 129 B10
Parla E 46 D5
Parlan F 29 F10
Parma I 66 C1
Parndorf A 77 G11
Pärnu EST 131 E8
Pärnu-Jaagupi EST 131 D9
Paroikia GR 176 E5
Parola FIN 127 C11
Paron F 25 D9
Parowa PL 81 D8
Parrillas E 45 D10
Pärsama EST 130 D5
Parsau D 79 A8
Parsberg D 75 D10
Pârscov RO 161 C9
Pârșcoveni RO 160 E4
Parsęcko PL 85 C11
Parsteinsee D 84 E6
Partakko FIN 113 E20
Partaloa E 55 E8
Partanna I 58 D2
Parteboda S 103 A10
Partenen A 71 D10
Partenstein D 74 B6
Pârteștii de Jos RO 153 B7
Parthenay F 28 B5
Partheni GR 177 E8
Partinello F 37 G9
Partinico I 58 C3
Partizani BG 167 C8
Partizani SRB 158 E5
Partizánska Ľupča SK 147 C8
Partizánske SK 146 D6
Partney GB 11 E12
Parton GB 10 B4
Partry IRL 6 E4
Partsi EST 131 E14
Parudaminys LT 137 D11
Pårup DK 86 C4
Parva RO 152 C5
Parviainen S 119 C11
Påryd S 89 B9
Parysów PL 141 G5
Parzęczew PL 143 C7
Pasai Donibane E 32 D2
Paşaköy TR 171 C10
Paşaköy TR 171 E10
Paşaköy TR 173 E8
Paşaköy TR 177 B10
Pasalankylä FIN 125 D10
Paşayiğit TR 172 C6
Pașcani RO 153 C9
Pasching A 76 F6
Paseka CZ 77 C12
Pas-en-Artois F 18 D5
Pasewalk D 84 C6
Pasi FIN 128 D7
Pasiàn di Prato I 73 D7
Pasiano di Pordenone I 73 E6
Pasieki PL 139 E12
Pasiene LV 133 D4
Pasikovci HR 149 F9
Paskalevets BG 166 C4
Paskalevo BG 155 F1
Påskallavik S 89 A10
Pasłęk PL 139 B8
Pasmajärvi FIN 117 D12
Pašman HR 156 E3
Passage East IRL 9 D9
Passail A 148 B5
Passais F 23 C10
Passau D 76 E4
Passignano sul Trasimeno I 66 F5
Passow D 84 D6
Passy F 31 D10
Pastavy BY 135 F13
Pastende LV 134 B5
Pasto FIN 123 E10
Pastoriza E 38 B5
Pastrana E 47 D7
Păstrăveni RO 153 C9
Pašuliene LV 135 E12
Pasvalys LT 135 D8
Pašvitinys LT 134 D7
Pasym PL 139 C10
Pasytsely UA 154 B5
Paszab H 145 G4
Paszowice PL 81 D10
Pásztó H 147 F9
Pasztowa Wola PL 141 H4
Pata SK 146 E5
Pataias P 44 E3
Patak H 147 E8
Patana FIN 123 D11
Pătârlagele RO 161 C8
Patay F 24 D6
Patchway GB 13 B9
Pateley Bridge GB 11 C8
Pateniemi FIN 119 D14
Patergassen A 73 C8
Paterna E 48 E4
Paterna del Campo E 51 E7
Paterna del Madera E 55 B8
Paterna del Río E 55 E7
Paterna de Rivera E 52 C5
Paternion A 73 C8
Paternò I 59 D6
Paterno I 60 C5
Paternopoli I 60 B4
Patersdorf D 76 D3
Påterud S 96 C7
Patiška Reka NMK 164 F3
Pátka H 149 B11
Patmos GR 177 E8
Patna GB 4 E7
Pątnów PL 142 D6
Patokoski FIN 117 E14
Patoniemi FIN 121 B12
Patoniva FIN 113 D19
Patos AL 168 C2
Patra GR 174 C4
Pătrăuți RO 153 B8
Patrica I 62 D4
Patrick GBM 10 C2
Patrimonio F 37 F10
Patrington GB 11 D11
Pátroha H 145 G4
Pattada I 64 B3
Pattensen D 78 B6
Patterdale GB 10 B6
Patti I 59 C6
Pattijoki FIN 119 E13
Pättikkä FIN 116 A7
Pătulele RO 159 E10
Patumšiai LT 134 E5
Pâturages B 182 E3
Páty H 149 A11
Pau F 32 D5
Păuca RO 152 E3
Paudorf A 77 F9
Pauilhac F 33 C7
Pauillac F 28 E4
Paukarlahti FIN 124 E9
Paukkaja FIN 125 E14
Paukkeri FIN 120 D9
Paul P 44 D5
Paularo I 73 C7
Păuleni-Ciuc RO 153 E7
Paulești MD 154 C2
Păulești RO 151 B10
Paulhac-en-Margeride F 30 F3
Paulhan F 34 C5
Paulilatino I 64 C2
Paulinenaue D 83 E13
Pauliș RO 151 E8
Pauliström S 92 E7
Paüls E 42 F4
Paulx F 28 B2
Păunești RO 153 E10
Pausa D 79 E11
Păușești RO 160 C4
Păușești-Măglași RO 160 C4
Pautråsk S 107 B13
Pauvres F 19 F10
Pavel BG 166 C5
Pavel Banya BG 166 D4
Pavia I 69 C7
Pavia P 50 B3
Pavia di Udine I 73 E7
Pavías E 48 E4
Pavie F 33 C7
Pavilly F 18 E2
Pāvilosta LV 134 C2
Pavlešenci NMK 164 F4
Pavliani GR 174 B5
Pavlikeni BG 166 C4
Pavliš SRB 159 C7
Pavlivka UA 154 C5
Pavlivka UA 154 F4
Pavlos GR 175 B7
Pavlovac HR 149 E9
Pavlovce nad Uhom SK 145 F5
Pavullo nel Frignano I 66 D2
Pavy RUS 132 E6
Päwesin D 79 A12
Pawłosiów PL 144 D6
Pawłówek PL 138 D4
Pawłowice PL 81 C11
Pawłowiczki PL 142 F5
Pawonków PL 142 E6
Paxton GB 5 D12
Payerne CH 31 B10
Paymogo E 51 D5
Payrac F 29 F8
Payrin-Augmontel F 33 C10
Payzac F 29 E8
Pazardzhik BG 165 E9
Pazarič BIH 157 E9
Pazarköy TR 173 E7
Pazin HR 67 B8
Paziols F 34 E4
Pázmánd H 149 B11
Pazos E 38 D2
Pchelarovo BG 166 F4
Pchelin BG 165 E8
Pcim PL 147 B9
Pčinja NMK 164 E4
Peacehaven GB 15 F8
Peal de Becerro E 55 D6
Péaule F 23 E7
Pébrac F 30 E4
Peccia CH 71 E7
Peccioli I 66 E2
Pécel H 150 C3
Peceneaga RO 155 C2
Pečenjevce SRB 164 C4
Pechea RO 155 B1
Pechenga RUS 114 D10
Pechina E 55 F8
Pechory RUS 132 F2
Peći BIH 156 D5
Pecica RO 151 E7
Pećigrad BIH 156 B4
Pečinci SRB 158 D4
Pecineaga RO 155 F2
Peciu Nou RO 159 B7
Pecka CZ 77 B9
Pecka SRB 158 E4
Pečky CZ 77 B8
Pęcław PL 81 C10
Pečovská Nová Ves SK 145 E3
Pecq B 19 C7
Pécs H 149 D10
Pécsvárad H 149 D10
Pečurice MNE 163 E7
Pęczniew PL 142 C6
Pedaso I 62 A5
Pededze LV 133 B2
Pederobba I 72 E4
Pedersker DK 89 E7
Pedersöre FIN 122 C9
Pedino GR 169 C8
Pedrafita do Cebreiro E 38 C5
Pedrajas de San Esteban E 40 F2
Pedralba E 48 E3
Pedralba de la Pradería E 39 D6
Pedraza de Campos E 39 E10
Pedrera E 53 B7
Pedro Abad E 53 A8
Pedro Bernardo E 46 D3
Pedroche E 54 C3
Pedrógão P 44 E3
Pedrógão P 45 D6
Pedrógão P 50 C4
Pedrógão Grande P 44 E4
Pedrógão Pequeno P 44 E4
Pedro-Martínez E 55 D6
Pedro Muñoz E 47 F7
Pedrosa E 40 B4
Pedrosa del Príncipe E 40 D3
Pedrosillo de los Aires E 45 C9
Pedroso E 41 D6
Pedroso P 38 F2
Pedroso P 44 B3
Pedrouzos E 38 C2
Peebles GB 5 D10
Peel GBM 10 C2
Peenemünde D 84 B5
Peer B 19 B11
Peera FIN 112 F7
Peetri EST 131 D11
Pefki GR 175 A7
Pefkofyto GR 168 D4
Pefkoi GR 179 E10
Pefkos GR 178 E9
Pega P 45 D6
Pegalajar E 53 A9
Pegau D 79 D11
Peggau A 148 B4
Pegli I 37 C9
Pegnitz D 75 C10
Pego E 56 D4
Pego P 44 F4
Pegões P 50 B2
Pęgów PL 81 D11
Peguera E 49 E9
Pehčevo NMK 165 F6
Pehkolanlahti FIN 120 F9
Pehlivanköy TR 173 B6
Peillac F 23 E7
Peille F 37 D6
Peine D 79 B7
Peio I 71 E11
Peipin F 35 B10
Peipohja FIN 126 C7
Peïra-Cava F 37 D6
Peiraias GR 175 D8
Peißen D 79 C10
Peißen D 79 C11
Peißenberg D 72 A3
Peiting D 71 B11
Peitz D 80 C6
Peize NL 17 B7
Pejë RKS 163 D9
Pekankylä FIN 121 E13
Pekanpää FIN 119 B11
Pekkala FIN 119 B17
Pelagićevo BIH 157 C10
Pelago I 66 E4
Pelahustán E 46 D3
Pelarrodríguez E 45 C8
Pelasgia GR 175 B6
Pelči LV 134 C3
Pełczyce PL 85 D8
Peleagonzalo E 39 F9
Pelēči LV 135 D13
Pelekas GR 168 E2
Peleta GR 175 E6
Pelhřimov CZ 77 D8
Pelinei MD 154 F2
Pelinia MD 153 B11
Pelishat BG 165 C10
Pélissanne F 35 C9
Pelitköy TR 173 F6
Pelkoperä FIN 119 F15
Pelkosenniemi FIN 115 D2
Pella GR 169 C8
Pellaro I 59 C8
Pellegrino Parmense I 69 D8
Pellegrue F 28 F6
Pellérd H 149 D10
Pellesmäki FIN 124 E9
Pellestrina I 66 B5
Pellevoisin F 29 B8
Pellinki FIN 127 E14
Pellizzano I 69 A10
Pello FIN 117 E11
Pello S 117 E11
Pellosniemi FIN 128 C7
Pelm D 21 D7
Peloche E 45 F10
Pelovo BG 165 C9
Pelplin PL 138 C6
Pelsin D 84 C5
Pelso FIN 119 E16
Peltokangas FIN 123 D12
Peltosalmi FIN 124 C8
Peltovuoma FIN 117 B12
Pélussin F 30 E6
Pelvoux F 31 F9
Pély H 150 C5
Pelynt GB 12 E5
Pembrey GB 12 B6
Pembridge GB 13 A9
Pembroke GB 12 B5
Pembroke Dock GB 12 B5
Pembury GB 15 E9
Pemfling D 75 D12
Pempelijärvi S 116 E8
Peñacerrada E 41 C6
Penacova P 44 D4
Peñafiel E 40 E3
Penafiel P 44 B4
Peñaflor E 51 D9
Peñaflor de Hornija E 39 E10
Penagos E 40 B4
Peñalba E 42 E3
Peñalén E 47 C8
Peñalsordo E 51 B9
Penalva do Castelo P 44 C5
Penamacor P 45 D6
Peñaranda de Bracamonte E 45 C10
Peñaranda de Duero E 40 E5
Peñarroya de Tastavins E 42 F4
Peñarroya-Pueblonuevo E 51 C9
Peñarrubia E 55 C8
Penarth GB 13 C8
Peñascosa E 55 B8
Peñas de San Pedro E 55 B9
Peñausende E 39 F8
Penc H 150 B3
Pencader GB 12 A6
Pěnčín CZ 81 E8
Pendeen GB 12 E3
Pendilhe P 44 C5
Pendine GB 12 B5
Pendlebury GB 11 D7
Penedo Gordo P 50 D4
Penedono P 44 C6
Penela P 44 D4
Pénestin F 22 F7
Penészlek H 151 B9
Pengfors S 107 D17
Pengsjö S 107 D13
Pengsjö S 107 D17
Penha Garcia P 45 D6
Peniche P 44 F2
Penicuik GB 5 D10
Penikkajärvi FIN 121 C14
Peninki FIN 123 D15
Peninver GB 4 E5
Peñíscola E 48 D5
Penistone GB 11 D8
Penkridge GB 11 F7
Penkule LV 134 D6
Penkun D 84 D6
Penly F 18 E3
Penmarch F 22 E3
Pennabilli I 66 E5
Penna in Teverina I 62 C2
Pennapiedimonte I 63 C6
Pennautier F 33 D10
Penne F 33 B9
Penne I 62 C5
Penne-d'Agenais F 33 B7
Pennyghael GB 4 C4
Penrhiw-pâl GB 12 A6
Penrhyn Bay GB 10 E4
Penrith GB 5 F11
Penryn GB 12 E4
Pensala FIN 122 D9
Pentalofo GR 174 C3
Pentalofos GR 168 D5
Pentalofos GR 171 A10
Pentapoli GR 169 B10
Penteoria GR 174 C5
Pentinniemi FIN 119 C16
Pentir GB 10 E3
Pentone I 59 B10
Pentraeth GB 10 E3
Pentre GB 13 B8
Pentrefoelas GB 10 E4
Penttäjä S 117 E11
Penttilänvaara FIN 121 C12
Penvénan F 22 C5
Penybont GB 13 A8
Penybontfawr GB 10 F5
Pen-y-fai GB 13 B7
Penzance GB 12 E3
Penzberg D 72 A3
Penzlin D 84 D4
Péone F 36 C5
Pepelow D 83 B11
Pepeni MD 154 B2
Pepingen B 19 C9
Pepinster B 19 C12
Peplos GR 171 C10
Pępowo PL 81 C12
Pëqin AL 168 B2
Peque E 39 D7
Pér H 149 A9
Pêra P 50 E3
Perabroddzye BY 133 E2
Perachora GR 175 C6
Perafita E 43 C8
Perä-Hyyppä FIN 122 F8
Peraia GR 169 C6
Peraia GR 169 C8
Perais P 44 E5
Perälä FIN 122 F7
Peralada E 43 C10
Peraleda de la Mata E 45 E10
Peraleda del Zaucejo E 51 C8
Peralejos E 42 G1
Peralejos de las Truchas E 47 C9
Perales del Alfambra E 42 F2
Perales del Puerto E 45 D7
Peralta E 32 F2
Peralta de Alcofea E 42 D3
Peralta de la Sal E 42 D4
Peraltilla E 42 C3
Peralva P 50 E4
Peralveche E 47 C8
Perama GR 168 E4
Perama GR 175 D8
Perama GR 178 E8
Perämäki FIN 122 D9
Peramola E 42 C6
Peranka FIN 121 D13
Peränne FIN 123 F11
Perä-Posio FIN 121 B10
Perarolo di Cadore I 72 D5
Peräseinäjoki FIN 123 E10
Perast MNE 163 E6
Perävaara FIN 115 E2
Perbál H 149 A11
Perchtoldsdorf A 77 F10
Percy F 23 C9
Perdasdefogu I 64 D3
Perdaxius I 64 E2
Perdifumo I 60 C4
Perdiguera E 41 E10
Perdika GR 168 F3
Perdika GR 175 D7
Perdiki GR 177 D7
Perdikkas GR 169 C6
Perduhovo Selo BIH 157 D6
Perechyn UA 145 F5
Peredo P 39 F6
Peregu Mare RO 151 E6
Perehins'ke UA 145 F9
Pereiras P 50 E3
Pereiro E 38 A4
Pereiro P 50 E4
Pereiro de Aguiar E 38 D4
Perekhrestove UA 154 C5
Pererîta MD 153 A9
Pereruela E 39 F8
Peresecina MD 154 C3
Peressaare EST 131 C13
Peretu RO 160 E6
Pereyma UA 154 A5
Perfugas I 64 B2
Perg A 77 F7
Pergine Valdarno I 66 F4
Pergine Valsugana I 69 A11
Pergola I 67 E6
Perho FIN 123 D12
Periam RO 151 E6
Periana E 53 C8
Pericei RO 151 C10
Périers F 23 B9
Perieți RO 160 E5
Perieți RO 161 D10
Périgueux F 29 E7
Perikleia GR 169 B7
Perila EST 131 C10
Perilla de Castro E 39 E8
Perín-Chym SK 145 F3
Periprava RO 155 C5
Periș RO 161 D7
Perișani RO 160 C4
Perișor RO 160 E2
Perișoru RO 161 E11
Perissa GR 179 C9
Peristasi GR 169 D8
Peristera GR 169 C9
Peristeri GR 175 C8
Perithori GR 169 B10
Perivoli GR 168 E5
Perivoli GR 168 F3
Perivoli GR 174 A5
Perivoli GR 174 B5
Perivolia GR 178 E7
Perjasica HR 156 B3
Perkáta H 149 B11
Perkiömäki FIN 123 D9
Perl D 20 F6
Perlat AL 163 F8
Perleberg D 83 D11
Perlejewo PL 141 E7
Perlez SRB 158 C5
Perloja LT 137 E9
Perły PL 136 E4
Permani HR 67 B9
Permantokoski FIN 117 F16
Përmet AL 168 D3
Pernå FIN 127 E15
Pernarava LT 134 F7
Pernarec CZ 76 C4
Pernegg an der Mur A 148 B4
Pernersdorf A 77 E10
Pernes P 44 F3
Pernes-les-Fontaines F 35 C9
Perni GR 171 B7
Pernik BG 165 D7
Perniö FIN 127 E9
Perniön asema FIN 127 E9
Pernitz A 77 G9
Pernu FIN 121 B10
Pero I 69 B7
Peroguarda P 50 C3
Pérols F 35 C6
Péron F 31 C8
Perondi AL 168 C2
Péronnas F 31 C7
Péronne F 18 E6
Perosa Argentina I 31 F11
Pero Viseu P 44 D6
Perpignan F 34 E4
Perranporth GB 12 E4
Perrecy-les-Forges F 30 B5
Perreux F 30 C5
Perrigny F 31 B8
Perrogney-les-Fontaines F 26 E3
Perros-Guirec F 22 C5
Perrum-Åbmir FIN 113 E19
Persan F 25 B7
Persåsen S 102 A7
Persberg S 97 C11
Persbo S 97 B13
Persenbeug A 77 F8
Pershagen S 93 A11
Pershamawskaya BY 133 E4
Pershore GB 13 A10
Pershotravneve UA 155 C4
Pershyttan S 97 D13
Persnäs S 89 A11
Persön S 118 C8
Perstorp S 87 C12
Perth GB 5 C10
Perthes F 25 D8
Pertouli GR 168 E5
Perttaus FIN 117 D15
Pertteli FIN 127 E9
Perttula FIN 127 E12
Pertuis F 35 C10
Pertunmaa FIN 127 C15
Pertusa E 42 C3
Peruc CZ 76 B5
Perućac SRB 158 F3
Perucica BIH 157 F10
Perugia I 66 F5
Perukka FIN 119 F17
Perunkajärvi FIN 117 E15
Perushtitsa BG 165 E10
Perušić HR 156 C3
Péruwelz B 19 C8
Pervalka LT 134 F2
Pervenchères F 24 D3
Pervomaisc MD 154 D5
Pervomayskoye RUS 129 E12
Perwez B 19 C10
Pesadas de Burgos E 40 C4
Pesaro I 67 E6
Pescaglia I 66 E1
Pescantina I 66 B2
Pescara I 63 C6
Pescari RO 159 D8
Pescasseroli I 62 D5
Pesceana RO 160 D4
Peschadoires F 30 D3
Peschici I 63 D10
Peschiera del Garda I 66 B2
Pescia I 66 E2
Pescina I 62 C5
Pescocostanzo I 62 D6
Pescolanciano I 63 D6
Pescopennataro I 63 D6
Pescorocchiano I 62 C4
Pesco Sannita I 60 A3
Peseux CH 31 B10
Peshkopi AL 163 F9
Peshtera BG 165 E9
Pesiökylä FIN 121 E12
Pesiönranta FIN 121 E12
Pesmes F 26 F4
Pesnica SLO 148 C5
Pesochnyy RUS 129 E13
Peso da Régua P 44 B5
Pesquera de Duero E 40 E3
Pessac F 28 F4
Pessalompolo FIN 117 F12
Pessan F 33 C7
Pesse NL 17 C6
Pessin D 80 A3
Peštani NMK 168 B4
Peștera RO 155 E3
Peștișani RO 159 C11
Peștișu Mic RO 151 F10
Pesués E 40 B3
Pešurići BIH 157 E11
Petacciato I 63 C7
Petäikkö FIN 119 E16
Petäiskylä FIN 125 C12
Petäjäjärvi FIN 119 C17
Petäjäkangas FIN 119 D17
Petäjäskoski FIN 119 B14
Petäjäskoski FIN 119 F13
Petäjävesi FIN 123 F14
Petalax FIN 122 E6
Petalidi GR 174 F4
Pétange L 20 E5
Petas GR 174 A3
Petelea RO 152 D5
Peteranec HR 149 D7
Peterborough GB 11 F11
Peterculter GB 3 L12
Peterhead GB 3 K13
Péteri H 150 C3
Peterlee GB 5 F14
Petersberg D 74 A6
Petersdorf D 75 E9
Petersdorf auf Fehmarn D 83 B10
Petersfield GB 15 E7
Petershagen D 17 D11
Petershagen D 80 B6
Peterswell IRL 6 F5
Pétervására H 147 E10
Pethelinos GR 169 C10
Petilia Policastro I 59 A10
Petín E 38 D5
Petisträsk S 107 B17
Petite-Rosselle F 186 C2
Petit-Mars F 23 F9
Petitmont F 186 D2
Petit-Noir F 31 B7
Petko Karavelovo BG 166 C5
Petko Slaveykov BG 165 C10
Petkula FIN 115 C1
Petkus D 80 C4
Petlovača SRB 158 D3
Pet Mogili BG 166 E6
Petneháza H 145 G5
Petőfibánya H 150 B4
Petra E 57 B11
Petra GR 171 F10
Petrăchioaia RO 161 D8
Petrades GR 172 B6
Petralia-Soprana I 58 D5
Petran AL 168 D3
Petrana GR 169 D6
Petrella Salto I 62 C4
Petrella Tifernina I 63 D7
Petrer E 56 E3
Petrești RO 151 B9
Petrești RO 160 D6
Petreștii de Jos RO 152 D3

Petreto-Bicchisano F 37 H9
Petriano I 67 E6
Petricani RO 153 C8
Petrich BG 169 B9
Petrijevci HR 149 E11
Petrila RO 160 C2
Petrinja HR 148 F6
Petriş RO 151 E9
Petritoli I 62 A5
Petrivka UA 154 D4
Petrivs'k UA 154 E3
Petrochori GR 174 B4
Petrodvorets RUS 129 F12
Pétrola E 55 B9
Petromäki FIN 125 E9
Petronà I 59 A10
Petroşani RO 160 C2
Petrota GR 166 F6
Petroussa GR 170 B6
Petrov CZ 146 D4
Petrova RO 152 B4
Petrovac MNE 163 E6
Petrovac SRB 159 E7
Petrovany SK 145 F3
Petrovaradin SRB 158 C4
Petrovec NMK 164 F4
Petrovice CZ 76 C6
Petrovice u Karviné CZ 147 B7
Petroviči BIH 157 D10
Petrovići MNE 162 D6
Petrovo BG 169 B9
Petrovo RUS 136 D1
Petrovo Selo SRB 159 D9
Petruma FIN 125 F11
Petru Rareş RO 152 C4
Petruşeni MD 153 B10
Petřvald CZ 146 B6
Petřvald CZ 146 B6
Petsakoi GR 174 C5
Petsmo FIN 122 D7
Petten NL 16 C3
Pettigo GB 7 C7
Pettineo I 58 D5
Petting D 73 A6
Pettneu am Arlberg A 71 C10
Pettorano sul Gizio I 62 D5
Petürch BG 165 D7
Petworth GB 15 F7
Peuerbach A 76 F5
Peujard F 28 E5
Peura FIN 119 B14
Peurajärvi FIN 119 B16
Peurasuvanto FIN 115 C1
Pevensey GB 15 F9
Peveragno I 37 C7
Pewsey GB 13 C11
Pewsum (Krummhörn) D 17 B8
Pexonne F 27 D6
Peymeinade F 36 D5
Peynier F 35 D10
Peypin F 35 D10
Peyrat-le-Château F 29 D9
Peyrehorade F 32 C3
Peyriac-Minervois F 34 D4
Peyrieu F 31 D8
Peyrins F 31 E7
Peyrolles-en-Provence F 35 C10
Peyruis F 35 B10
Pézenas F 34 D5
Pjzino PL 85 D8
Pezinok SK 146 E4
Pezuls F 29 F7
Pfaffenberg D 75 E11
Pfaffendorf D 80 B6
Pfaffenhausen D 71 A10
Pfaffenhofen an der Ilm D 75 E10
Pfaffenhofen an der Roth D 187 E9
Pfaffenhoffen F 27 C8
Pfäffikon CH 27 F10
Pfaffing D 75 F11
Pfalzfeld D 185 D8
Pfalzgrafenweiler D 27 C10
Pfarrkirchen D 76 F3
Pfarrweisach D 75 B8
Pfarrwerfen A 73 B7
Pfedelbach D 27 B11
Pflach A 71 B11
Pfons A 72 B3
Pförring D 75 E10
Pforzen D 71 B11
Pforzheim D 27 C10
Pfreimd D 75 D11
Pfronstetten D 27 D11
Pfronten D 71 B11
Pfullendorf D 27 E11
Pfullingen D 27 D11
Pfunds A 71 D11
Pfungstadt D 21 E11
Pfyn CH 27 E10
Phalsbourg F 27 C7
Philippeville B 19 D10
Philippine NL 182 C3
Philippsburg D 187 C5
Philippsreut D 76 E5
Piacenza I 69 C8
Piadena I 66 B1
Piana F 37 G9
Piana GR 174 D5
Piana Crixia I 37 C8
Piana degli Albanesi I 58 D3
Piancastagnaio I 62 B1
Piandimeleto I 66 E5
Pian di Scò I 66 E4
Pianella I 62 C6
Pianello Val Tidone I 37 B10
Piano del Voglio I 66 D3
Pianoro I 66 D3
Pianosa I 65 B2
Pianotolli-Caldarello F 37 J10
Pians A 71 C11
Piansano I 62 B1
Pianu RO 152 F2
Pias P 50 C5
Piaseczno PL 85 D7
Piaseczno PL 141 F4
Piasek PL 84 E6
Piaski PL 81 C12
Piaski PL 141 H7
Piastów PL 141 F3
Piątek PL 143 B7
Piątnica Poduchowna PL 139 D13
Piatra RO 160 F6
Piatra Neamţ RO 153 D8
Piatra Olt RO 160 E4
Piatra Şoimului RO 153 D8
Piau-Engaly F 33 E6
Piazza al Serchio I 66 D1
Piazza Armerina I 58 E5
Piazza Brembana I 69 B8
Piazzatorre I 69 B8
Piazzola sul Brenta I 66 A4
Pibrac F 33 C8
Pićan HR 67 B9
Picar AL 168 D3
Picassent E 48 F4
Picauville F 23 B9
Picerno I 60 B5
Picher D 83 D10
Pichl bei Wels A 76 F5
Pickering GB 11 C10
Pico I 62 E5
Picón E 54 A4
Picoto P 44 B3
Picquigny F 18 E5
Pidbuzh UA 145 E7
Pidhorodtsi UA 145 E7
Pidlisne UA 153 A7
Piebalgas LV 135 C8
Piechcin PL 138 E5
Piechowice PL 81 E9
Piecki PL 139 C11
Piecnik PL 85 D10
Piedicorte-di-Gaggio F 37 G10
Piedicroce F 37 G10
Piedimonte Etneo I 59 D7
Piedimonte Matese I 60 A2
Piedimulera I 68 A5
Piedrabuena E 54 A4
Piedrafita de Babia E 39 C7
Piedrahita E 45 D10
Piedralaves E 46 D3
Piedras Albas E 45 E7
Piedras Blancas E 39 A8
Piedruja LV 133 E2
Piegaro I 62 B2
Piégut-Pluviers F 29 D7
Piehinki FIN 119 E12
Piekary Śląskie PL 143 F6
Piekielnik PL 147 C9
Piekoszów PL 143 E9
Pieksämäen mlk FIN 124 F8
Pieksämäki FIN 124 F8
Pielavesi FIN 123 D17
Pieleşti RO 160 E3
Pielgrzymka PL 81 D9
Pienava LV 134 C6
Pienijżnica PL 85 C11
Pieniężno PL 139 B9
Pieńkowo PL 85 B11
Piennes F 19 F12
Pieńsk PL 81 D8
Pienza I 62 A1
Piera E 43 D7
Pierowall GB 3 G11
Pierre-Buffière F 29 D8
Pierre-Châtel F 31 F8
Pierre-de-Bresse F 31 B7
Pierrefeu-du-Var F 36 E4
Pierrefitte-Nestalas F 32 E5
Pierrefitte-sur-Aire F 26 C3
Pierrefonds F 18 F6
Pierrefontaine-les-Varans F 26 F6
Pierrefort F 30 F2
Pierrelatte F 35 B8
Pierrepont F 19 F12
Pierres F 24 C6
Pierrevert F 35 C10
Piershil NL 182 B4
Piertinjaure S 109 C17
Pierzchnica PL 143 E10
Piesau D 75 A9
Pieścirogi PL 139 E10
Piesendorf A 73 B6
Pieski PL 81 B8
Piesport D 185 E6
Piešťany SK 146 D5
Pieszkowo PL 136 E2
Pieszyce PL 81 E11
Pietrabbondante I 63 D6
Pietracatella I 63 D7
Pietracorbara F 37 F10
Pietra-di-Verde F 37 G10
Pietragalla I 60 B5
Pietralba F 37 F10
Pietra Ligure I 37 C8
Pietralunga I 66 F5
Pietramelara I 60 A2
Pietramontecorvino I 63 D8
Pietraperzia I 58 E5
Pietraporzio I 36 C6
Pietrari RO 160 C4
Pietrasanta I 66 E1
Pietravairano I 60 A2
Pietroasa RO 151 D10
Pietroasele RO 161 C9
Pietroşani RO 161 F7
Pietrosella F 37 H9
Pietroşiţa RO 161 C6
Pietrowice Wielkie PL 142 F5
Pieve d'Alpago I 72 D5
Pieve del Cairo I 68 C6
Pieve di Bono I 69 B10
Pieve di Cadore I 72 D5
Pieve di Cento I 66 C3
Pieve di Soligo I 72 E5
Pieve di Teco I 37 C7
Pieve Fosciana I 66 D1
Pievepelago I 66 D2
Pieve Santo Stefano I 66 E5
Pieve Torina I 62 A4
Pieve Vergonte I 68 A5
Piffonds F 25 D9
Piges GR 174 E5
Pigi GR 169 E6
Pigi GR 177 A7
Piglio I 62 D4
Pigna I 37 D7
Pignans F 36 E4
Pignataro Interamna I 62 E5
Pignataro Maggiore I 60 A2
Pignola I 60 B5
Pihlajakoski FIN 127 B13
Pihlajalahti FIN 127 B10
Pihlajalahti FIN 129 B9
Pihlajavaara FIN 125 D16
Pihlajavesi FIN 123 F12
Pihlava FIN 126 B6
Pihtipudas FIN 123 D15
Piikkiö FIN 126 E8
Piilijärvi S 116 C6
Piiloperä FIN 121 B12
Piippola FIN 119 F15
Piipsjärvi FIN 119 F13
Piirsalu EST 131 C8
Piispa FIN 125 D11
Piispajärvi FIN 121 D13
Piittisjärvi FIN 119 B17
Pijnacker NL 16 D2
Pikkarala FIN 119 E15
Pikkula FIN 119 D17
Piktupėnai LT 134 F3
Pila I 66 C5
Piła PL 85 D11
Pilar de la Mola E 57 D8
Pilas E 51 E7
Piława PL 141 G5
Piława Górna PL 81 E11
Pilchowice PL 142 F6
Pilda LV 133 D3
Piles E 56 D4
Pilgrimstad S 103 A9
Pili GR 175 B8
Pilica PL 143 F8
Pilis H 150 C4
Piliscsaba H 149 A11
Pilisszántó H 149 A11
Pilisszentiván H 149 A11
Pilisvörösvár H 149 A11
Pill A 72 B4
Pilling GB 10 D6
Pilníkov CZ 77 A9
Pilpala FIN 127 D11
Pilsach D 75 D10
Pilskalns LV 135 B13
Pilsting D 75 E12
Piltene LV 134 B3
Pilträsk S 118 C4
Pilu RO 151 D7
Pilviškiai LT 136 D7
Pilzno PL 143 G11
Pimentel I 64 E3
Pimperne GB 13 D10
Pimpiö S 117 E10
Piña de Campos E 40 D3
Piña de Esgueva E 40 E3
Piñar E 53 B10
Pinarbaşi TR 171 E10
Pinarca TR 173 B9
Pinarejo E 47 E8
Pinarhisar TR 173 A8
Pinarköy TR 181 B7
Pinarlibelen TR 177 E10
Pinasca I 31 F11
Pincehely H 149 C10
Pinchbeck GB 11 F11
Pińczów PL 143 E10
Pindstrup DK 86 C6
Pineda de Cigüela E 47 D7
Pineda de la Sierra E 40 D5
Pineda de Mar E 43 D9
Pinela P 39 E6
Piñel de Abajo E 40 E3
Pinerolo I 31 F11
Pineto I 62 B6
Piney F 25 D11
Pinggau A 148 B6
Pinhal Novo P 50 B2
Pinhanços P 44 D5
Pinhão P 44 B5
Pinheiro P 50 C2
Pinheiro Grande P 44 F4
Pinhel P 45 C6
Pinhoe GB 13 D8
Pinilla de Molina E 47 C9
Pinilla de Toro E 39 E9
Pinkafeld A 148 B6
Pinneberg D 82 C7
Pinnow D 81 C7
Pino E 39 E7
Pino F 37 F10
Pino del Río E 39 C10
Pinofranqueado E 45 D8
Pinols F 30 E3
Piñor E 38 C3
Pinoso E 56 E2
Pinos-Puente E 53 B9
Pinsac F 29 F9
Pinsiö FIN 127 B9
Pinsoro E 41 D9
Pintamo FIN 121 D10
Pintano E 32 E3
Pinto E 46 D5
Pinwherry GB 4 E7
Pinzano al Tagliamento I 73 D6
Pinzio P 45 C6
Pinzolo I 69 A10
Piobbico I 66 E6
Piolenc F 35 B8
Pioltello I 69 C7
Piombino I 65 B3
Piombino Dese I 72 E4
Pionerskiy RUS 139 A9
Pionki PL 141 H4
Pionsat F 29 C11
Pioraco I 67 F6
Piornal E 45 D9
Piossasco I 31 F11
Piotrkowice PL 81 D11
Piotrków Kujawski PL 138 E5
Piotrków Trybunalski PL 143 D8
Piove di Sacco I 66 B5
Piovene Rocchette I 69 B11
Piperskärr S 93 D9
Pipirig RO 153 C8
Pipriac F 23 E8
Piqeras AL 168 D2
Pir RO 151 C9
Piraino I 59 C6
Piran SLO 67 A8
Pirčiupiai LT 137 E10
Pirdop BG 165 D9
Pirg AL 168 C4
Pirgovo BG 161 F7
Piriac-sur-Mer F 22 F6
Piricse H 151 B9
Pirin BG 169 A10
Pirinççi TR 173 B10
Pîrjolteni MD 154 C2
Pirkkala FIN 127 C10
Pîrliţa MD 153 C11
Pîrliţa MD 154 A2
Pirmasens D 21 F9
Pirna D 80 E5
Pirnmill GB 4 D6
Pirot SRB 164 C6
Pirovac HR 156 E4
Pirtó H 150 E3
Pirttijoki FIN 121 E9
Pirttikoski FIN 119 B18
Pirttikoski FIN 119 F12
Pirttikoski FIN 127 C10
Pirttimäki FIN 123 C17
Pirttimäki FIN 124 E7
Pirttimäki FIN 125 C10
Pirttinen FIN 123 D10
Pirttivaara FIN 121 D14
Pirttivuopio S 111 E17
Pisa FIN 119 B14
Pisa I 66 E1
Pisanets BG 161 F8
Pisarovina HR 148 E5
Pisarovo BG 165 C9
Pischelsdorf in der Steiermark A 148 B5
Pişchia RO 151 F7
Pisciotta I 60 C4
Pişcolt RO 151 B9
Piscu RO 155 B1
Piscu Vechi RO 159 F11
Pišece SLO 148 D5
Písečná CZ 77 B12
Písek CZ 76 D6
Písek CZ 147 B7
Pishcha UA 141 G9
Pishchana UA 154 A5
Pishchanka UA 154 A3
Pisisaare EST 131 D11
Piskokefalo GR 179 E11
Piškorevci HR 157 B9
Pisoderi GR 168 C5
Pisogne I 69 B9
Pissonas GR 175 B8
Pissos F 32 B4
Pistiana GR 168 F5
Pisticci I 61 C7
Pisto FIN 121 D13
Pistoia I 66 E2
Pisz PL 139 C12
Piszczac PL 141 G8
Pitagowan GB 5 B9
Pitäjänmäki FIN 123 C15
Pitarque E 42 F2
Piteå S 118 D6
Piteşti RO 160 D5
Pithiviers F 25 D7
Pitigliano I 65 B5
Pitkäjärvi FIN 127 D9
Pitkälä FIN 129 B11
Pitkälahti FIN 124 E9
Pitkäsenkylä FIN 119 F12
Pitkyaranta RUS 129 B15
Pitlochry GB 5 B9
Pitomača HR 149 E8
Pitrags LV 130 F4
Pitres E 55 F6
Pîtres F 18 F3
Pitscottie GB 5 C11
Pitsinaiika GR 174 C4
Pitstone GB 15 D7
Pitsund S 118 D7
Pitt GB 13 C12
Pittem B 19 C7
Pitten A 148 A6
Pittentrail GB 3 K8
Pittenweem GB 5 C11
Pitvaros H 150 E6
Pivašiūnai LT 137 E9
Pivka SLO 73 E9
Pivnice SRB 158 C3
Piwniczna-Zdrój PL 145 E2
Pizarra E 53 C7
Pizzighettone I 69 C8
Pizzo I 59 B9
Pizzoferrato I 63 D6
Pizzoli I 62 C4
Pjedsted DK 86 D5
Pjelax FIN 122 F6
Pjenovac BIH 157 D10
Pjesker S 118 C3
Plaaz D 83 C12
Plabennec F 22 C3
Placencia de las Armas E 32 D1
Plachkovtsi BG 166 D4
Plācis LV 135 B9
Plaffeien CH 31 B11
Plagia GR 169 B8
Plaidt D 21 D8
Plăieşii de Jos RO 153 E8
Plaintel F 22 D6
Plaisance F 33 C6
Plaisance-du-Touch F 33 C8
Plaisir F 24 C6
Plaka GR 168 F5
Plaka GR 171 D8
Plaka GR 175 E6
Plaka GR 179 B7
Plakhtiyivka UA 154 E5
Plakias GR 178 E7
Plakovo BG 166 D5
Plana BIH 157 G9
Planá CZ 75 C12
Plana GR 169 D10
Planá nad Lužnicí CZ 77 D7
Plaňany CZ 77 B8
Plancher-Bas F 27 E6
Plancoët F 23 C7
Plancy-l'Abbaye F 25 C10
Plan-de-Baux F 31 F7
Plan-de-la-Tour F 36 E5
Plandište SRB 159 C7
Plan-d'Orgon F 35 C8
Planegg D 75 F9
Planès F 33 F10
Plāņi LV 131 F11
Plánice CZ 76 D4
Planina SLO 73 E9
Planina SLO 148 D4
Planina SRB 158 E3
Planinica SRB 159 F9
Planjane HR 156 E5
Plankenfels D 75 C9
Planos GR 174 D2
Plasencia E 45 D8
Plasencia del Monte E 41 D10
Plaški HR 156 B3
Plassen N 102 D4
Plášťovce SK 147 E7
Plasy CZ 76 C4
Platajes GR 175 C7
Platamona Lido I 64 B1
Platamonas GR 169 E8
Platamonas GR 171 B7
Platania I 59 A9
Platanias GR 175 A7
Platanistos GR 175 C10
Platanorrevma GR 169 D7
Platanos GR 174 D4
Platanos GR 175 A6
Platanos GR 178 E6
Platanos GR 178 E8
Platanovrysi GR 174 C4
Plătăreşti RO 161 E8
Plataria GR 168 F3
Plate D 83 C11
Plateliai LT 134 D3
Platerów PL 141 F7
Plati GR 171 A10
Platì I 59 C9
Platiana GR 174 D4
Platičevo SRB 158 D4
Platja d'Aro E 43 D10
Platja de Nules E 48 E4
Platone LV 134 C7
Plattling D 76 E3
Platy GR 169 C8
Platykampos GR 169 E8
Platys Gialos GR 176 E5
Platys Gialos GR 176 F4
Plau D 83 D12
Plaue D 79 E8
Plauen D 75 A11
Plav MNE 163 D8
Plavë RKS 163 E10
Plaveč SK 145 E2
Plavecký Štvrtok SK 77 F12
Pļaviņas LV 135 C11
Plavna SRB 159 E9
Plavni UA 155 C3
Plavnica SK 145 E2
Plavno HR 156 D5
Plavy CZ 81 E8
Pławno PL 85 C10
Plaza E 40 B6
Plazac F 29 E8
Płazów PL 144 C7
Pleaux F 29 E10
Plech D 75 C9
Plecka Dąbrowa PL 143 B8
Pleine-Fougères F 23 C8
Pleikšņi LV 133 D2
Plélan-le-Grand F 23 D7
Plélo F 22 C6
Plémet F 22 D6
Plénée-Jugon F 23 D7
Pléneuf-Val-André F 22 C6
Pleniţa RO 159 E11
Plentzia E 40 B6
Plérin F 22 C6
Plescop F 22 E6
Pleşcuţa RO 151 E9
Pleşeni MD 154 E2
Plešivec SK 145 F1
Plesná CZ 75 B11
Pleśna PL 144 D2
Pleşoiu RO 160 E4
Plessa D 80 D5
Plessé F 23 E8
Plestin-les-Grèves F 22 C4
Pleszew PL 142 C4
Pleternica HR 157 B8
Plettenberg D 21 B9
Pleubian F 22 C5
Pleudihen-sur-Rance F 23 C8
Pleumartin F 29 B7
Pleumeur-Bodou F 22 C4
Pleurs F 25 C10
Pleuven F 22 E3
Pleven BG 165 C10
Plevník-Drienové SK 147 C7
Pleyben F 22 D4
Pleyber-Christ F 22 C4
Pliego E 55 D10
Plienciems LV 134 B6
Plieševce SK 147 E8
Pliezhausen D 187 D7
Plikati GR 168 D4
Plisa BY 133 F3
Pliska BG 167 C8
Plitvica HR 156 C4
Pljevlja MNE 163 C7
Pllanejë RKS 163 E10
Ploaghe I 64 B2
Plobannalec F 22 E3
Plobsheim F 186 E4
Ploče HR 157 F7
Ploce LV 134 C2
Plochingen D 187 D7
Pločica SRB 159 D6
Płociczno PL 136 E6
Płock PL 139 E8
Plodovoye RUS 129 D13
Ploegsteert B 182 D1
Ploemeur F 22 E5
Ploeren F 22 E6
Ploërmel F 23 E7
Plœuc-sur-Lié F 22 D6
Plogonnec F 22 D3
Plogshagen D 84 A4
Ploieşti RO 161 D8
Plomari GR 177 B7
Plombières-les-Bains F 26 E5
Plomeur F 22 E3
Plomin HR 67 B9
Plomodiern F 22 D3
Plön D 83 B8
Plonéour-Lanvern F 22 E3
Plonévez-du-Faou F 22 D4
Plonevez-Porzay F 22 D3
Płońsk PL 139 E9
Plop MD 153 A11
Plopana RO 153 D10
Plopeni RO 161 C7
Plopi MD 154 B4
Plopii-Slăviteşti RO 160 F5
Plopşoru RO 160 D2
Plopu RO 161 C8
Plosca RO 160 E6
Ploscoş RO 152 D3
Ploska UA 152 B6
Płoskinia PL 139 B8
Płośnica PL 139 D9
Plößberg D 75 C11
Płoty PL 85 C8
Plötzin D 79 B12
Plötzky D 79 B10
Plou E 42 F2
Plouagat F 22 C6
Plouaret F 22 C5
Plouarzel F 22 D2
Plouay F 22 E5
Ploubalay F 23 C7
Ploubazlanec F 22 C5
Ploubezre F 22 C5
Ploudalmézeau F 22 C2
Ploudiry F 22 D3
Plouescat F 22 C3
Plouézec F 22 C6
Ploufragan F 22 D6
Plougasnou F 22 C4
Plougastel-Daoulas F 22 D3
Plougonven F 22 C4
Plougonver F 22 D5
Plougrescant F 22 C5
Plouguenast F 22 D6
Plouguerneau F 22 C2
Plouguernével F 22 D5
Plouguiel F 22 C5
Plouguin F 22 C2
Plouha F 22 C6
Plouharnel F 22 E5
Plouhinec F 22 D3
Plouhinec F 22 E5
Plouigneau F 22 C4
Ploumagoar F 22 C5
Ploumilliau F 22 C4
Plounévez-Moëdec F 22 C5
Plounévez-Quintin F 22 D5
Plouray F 22 D5
Plouvorn F 22 C3
Plouyé F 22 D4
Plouzané F 22 D2
Plouzévédé F 22 C3
Plovdiv BG 165 E10
Plozévet F 22 E3
Pluck IRL 7 C7
Plüderhausen D 187 D8
Plugari RO 153 C10
Plumbridge GB 4 F2
Plumelec F 22 E6
Pluméliau F 22 E6
Plumergat F 22 E6
Plumlov CZ 77 D12
Pluneret F 22 E6
Plungė LT 134 E3
Pluszkiejmy PL 136 E5
Pluvigner F 22 E5
Plužine BIH 157 F9
Plužine MNE 157 F10
Płużnica PL 138 D6
Pluzunet F 22 C5
Plwmp GB 12 A6
Plymouth GB 12 E6
Plympton GB 12 E6
Plymstock GB 12 E6
Plytra GR 178 B4
Plyussa RUS 132 E5
Plyusy BY 133 E2
Plzeň CZ 76 C4
Pniewo PL 85 D11
Pniewo PL 139 E11
Pniewo PL 143 B8
Pniewy PL 81 A10
Pniewy PL 141 G3
Poarta Albă RO 155 E2
Pobedím SK 146 D5
Pobedino RUS 136 D6
Poběžovice CZ 75 C12
Pobiedno PL 145 D5
Pobiedziska PL 81 B12
Pobierowo PL 85 B7
Pobikry PL 141 E7
Pobladura del Valle E 39 D8
Poblete E 54 B5
Pobłocie PL 85 A13
Poboleda E 42 E5
Poboru RO 160 D5
Pobožje NMK 164 E3
Počátky CZ 77 D8
Poceirão P 50 B2
Pöchlarn A 77 F8
Pociems LV 131 F9
Počitelj BIH 157 F8
Pociumbeni MD 153 B10
Pöcking D 75 G9
Pocking D 76 F4
Pocklington GB 11 D10
Pocola RO 151 D9
Pocrnje BIH 157 F9
Pocsaj H 151 C8
Pócspetri H 145 H4
Poczesna PL 143 E7
Podareš NMK 169 A8
Podari RO 160 E3
Podayva BG 161 F9
Podbiel SK 147 C8
Podbořany CZ 76 B4
Podborov'ye RUS 132 F4
Podbožur MNE 163 D6
Podbrdo BIH 157 D7
Podbrdo SLO 73 D8
Podbrezová SK 147 D9
Podčetrtek SLO 148 D5
Poddębice PL 143 C6
Poděbrady CZ 77 B8
Podedwórze PL 141 G8
Podegrodzie PL 145 D2
Podelzig D 81 B7
Podem BG 165 B10
Podeni RO 159 D10
Podenii Noi RO 161 C8
Podensac F 32 A5
Podenzana I 69 E8
Podenzano I 37 B11
Podersdorf am See A 77 G11
Podgajci Posavski HR 157 C10
Podgaje PL 85 D11
Podgora HR 157 F7
Podgorač HR 149 F10
Podgorac SRB 159 F8
Podgoria RO 161 C10
Podgorica MNE 163 E7
Podgorica SLO 73 D10
Podgorie AL 168 C4
Podgoritsa BG 167 C6
Podgórze PL 139 D13
Podgrab BIH 157 E10
Podgrad SLO 67 A9
Podgrade BIH 157 E8
Podhorod SK 145 F5
Podhum BIH 157 E7
Podil's'k UA 154 B5
Podivín CZ 77 E11
Podkova BG 171 B8
Podkowa Leśna PL 141 F3
Podkrajewo PL 139 D9
Podkrepa BG 166 F5
Podkum SLO 73 D11
Podlapača HR 156 C4
Podlehnik SLO 148 D5
Podles NMK 169 A6
Podlipoglav SLO 73 D10
Podmilečje BIH 157 D7
Podnanos SLO 73 E8
Podnovlje BIH 157 C9
Podochori GR 170 C6
Podogora GR 174 B3
Podoima MD 154 B3
Podoleni RO 153 D9
Podolí CZ 77 D11
Podolie SK 146 D5
Podolínec SK 145 E2
Podorozhnye UA 145 E9
Podosoje BIH 162 D5
Podrašnica BIH 157 D6
Podravske Sesvete HR 149 D8
Podromanija BIH 157 E10
Podsreda SLO 148 D5
Podstrana HR 156 F6
Podtabor SLO 73 E10
Podturen HR 149 D7
Podu Iloaiei RO 153 C10
Podujevë RKS 164 D3
Poduri RO 153 E9
Podu Turcului RO 153 E10
Podvelež BIH 157 F8
Podvrška SRB 159 D9
Podvysoká SK 147 C7
Podwilk PL 147 B9
Poederlee B 182 C5
Poeni RO 160 E6
Poeniţa MD 153 A11
Pofi I 62 D4
Pogăceaua RO 152 D4
Pogana RO 153 E11
Pogar BIH 157 D9
Poggendorf D 84 B4
Poggiardo I 61 C10
Poggibonsi I 66 F3
Poggio Berni I 66 D5
Poggio Bustone I 62 B3
Poggio Catino I 62 C3
Poggiodomo I 62 B3
Poggio Imperiale I 63 D8
Poggio-Mezzana F 37 G10
Poggio Mirteto I 62 C3
Poggio Moiano I 62 C3
Poggio Picenze I 62 C5
Poggio Renatico I 66 C4
Poggiorsini I 60 B6
Poggio Rusco I 66 C3
Pöggstall A 77 F8
Pogny F 25 C11
Pogoanele RO 161 D9
Pogoniani GR 168 E3
Pogorzela PL 81 C12
Pogorzelice PL 85 B13
Pogradec AL 168 C4
Pogrodzie PL 139 B8
Pohja FIN 127 C12
Pohja FIN 127 E10
Pohja-Lankila FIN 129 C11
Pohjasenvaara FIN 117 D11
Pohjaslahti FIN 119 B17
Pohjaslahti FIN 123 F12
Pohjavaara FIN 121 F11
Pohjois-Ii FIN 119 D14
Pohjoisjärvi FIN 123 F13
Pohorelá SK 147 D10
Pohořelice CZ 77 E11
Pohronská Polhora SK 147 D9
Pohronský Ruskov SK 147 F7
Poian RO 153 E8
Poiana RO 161 D7
Poiana Blenchii RO 152 C3
Poiana Câmpina RO 161 C7
Poiana Cristei RO 161 B9
Poiana Lacului RO 160 D5
Poiana Mare RO 159 F11
Poiana Mărului RO 160 B6
Poiana Sibiului RO 152 F3
Poiana Stampei RO 152 C6
Poiana Teiului RO 153 C7
Poiana Vadului RO 151 E10
Poibrene BG 165 E8
Pöide EST 130 D6
Poienari RO 153 D10
Poienarii Burchii RO 161 D8
Poienarii de Argeş RO 160 C5
Poieneşti RO 153 D11
Poieni RO 151 D10
Poienile de Sub Munte RO 152 B4
Poijula FIN 121 D10
Poikajärvi FIN 117 E15
Põikva EST 131 D10
Poinçon-lès-Larrey F 25 E11
Poing D 75 F10
Pointis-Inard F 33 D7
Poirino I 37 B7
Poiseux F 25 F9
Poissons F 26 D3
Poissy F 24 C7
Poitiers F 29 B6
Poix-de-Picardie F 18 E4
Poix-Terron F 19 E10
Pojan AL 168 C4
Pojanluoma FIN 122 E9
Pojatno HR 148 E5
Pojejena RO 159 D8
Pojo FIN 127 E10
Pojorâta RO 152 B6
Pókaszepetk H 149 C7
Poki LV 134 C7
Pokka FIN 117 B15
Poklečani BIH 157 E7
Pokoj BIH 156 C4
Pokój PL 142 E4
Pokrówka PL 141 H8
Pokupsko HR 148 F5
Polac RKS 163 D10
Polača HR 156 D5
Polače HR 162 D3
Pola de Allande E 39 B6
Pola de Laviana E 39 B8
Pola de Lena E 39 B8
Pola de Siero E 39 B8
Pola de Somiedo E 39 B7
Polaincourt-et-Clairefontaine F 26 E5
Połajewo PL 85 E11
Polán E 46 E4
Polanica-Zdrój PL 77 B10
Połaniec PL 143 F11
Polanów PL 85 B11
Polatsk BY 133 F5
Polch D 21 D8
Polcirkeln S 116 E6
Połczyno PL 138 A5
Połczyn Zdrój PL 85 C10
Polegate GB 15 F9
Polena BG 165 F7
Poleñino E 41 E11
Polepy CZ 76 A6
Polesella I 66 C4
Polessk RUS 136 D3
Polgár H 145 H3
Polgárdi H 149 B10
Polgaste EST 131 F13
Polia I 59 B9
Poliçan AL 168 C3
Poliçan AL 168 D3
Police PL 84 C7
Police nad Metují CZ 81 E10
Polichni GR 169 C8
Polichnitos GR 177 A7
Polička CZ 77 C10
Policoro I 61 C7
Policzna PL 141 H5
Polientes E 40 C4
Polignano a Mare I 61 B8
Poligny F 31 B8
Polikrayshte BG 166 C5
Polisot F 25 D11
Polistena I 59 C9
Politika GR 175 B8
Pölitz D 83 C8
Polizzi Generosa I 58 D5
Pōljä FIN 124 D9
Poljana SRB 159 D7
Poljanak HR 156 C4
Poljana Pakračka HR 149 F7
Poljane SLO 73 D9
Poljčane SLO 148 D5
Polje BIH 157 C8
Poljica HR 156 D3
Poljice BIH 157 D10
Poljice-Popovo BIH 162 D5

Polkowice PL 81 D10
Polla I 60 B4
Pölläkkä FIN 125 F11
Pöllau A 148 B5
Pöllauberg A 148 B5
Polle D 78 C5
Pollença E 57 B11
Pollenfeld D 75 E9
Pollenza I 67 F7
Pollfoss N 100 C7
Polliat F 31 C7
Pollica I 60 C4
Pollina I 58 D5
Pollitz D 83 E11
Pollos E 39 F9
Polmak N 113 C20
Polminhac F 29 F11
Polmont GB 5 D9
Polo FIN 121 C12
Polomka SK 147 D9
Polop E 56 D4
Pölöske H 149 C7
Połoski PL 141 G8
Polovragi RO 160 C3
Polperro GB 12 E5
Pöls A 73 B10
Polsbroek NL 182 B5
Polsingen D 75 E8
Polska Cerekiew PL 142 F5
Polski Gradets BG 166 E6
Polski Trŭmbesh BG 166 C5
Polsko Kosovo BG 166 C5
Polso FIN 123 D12
Poltár SK 147 E9
Põltsamaa EST 131 D11
Põlula EST 131 C13
Polumir SRB 163 B10
Połupin PL 81 B8
Põlva EST 131 E14
Polvela FIN 125 D12
Polvenkylä FIN 122 E8
Polverigi I 67 E7
Polvijärvi FIN 125 E12
Polyana UA 145 F6
Polyanets'ke UA 154 A6
Polyantho GR 171 B8
Polyany RUS 129 E11
Polyatsite BG 167 D8
Polydendro GR 169 D7
Polydrosos GR 175 B6
Polygyros GR 169 D9
Polykarpi GR 169 C7
Polykastano GR 168 D5
Polykastro GR 169 C8
Polymylos GR 169 D7
Polyneri GR 168 D5
Polypotamo GR 168 C5
Polzela SLO 73 D11
Pölzig D 79 E11
Pomaluengo E 40 B4
Pomarance I 66 F2
Pomarão P 50 D4
Pomarez F 32 C4
Pomarico I 61 B7
Pomarkku FIN 126 B7
Pomârla RO 153 A8
Pomáz H 150 B3
Pombal P 38 F5
Pombal P 44 E3
Pomer E 41 E8
Pomeroy GB 7 C9
Pomezeu RO 151 D9
Pomezí CZ 77 C10
Pomezia I 62 D3
Pomi RO 151 B11
Pomiechówek PL 139 F10
Pömiö FIN 119 C14
Pommard F 30 A6
Pommelsbrunn D 75 C10
Pommersfelden D 75 C8
Pomol BIH 157 D11
Pomorie BG 167 D9
Pomorsko PL 81 B8
Pompaire F 28 B5
Pompei I 60 B3
Pompey F 26 C5
Pompia GR 178 E8
Pompignan F 35 C6
Pomysk Mały PL 85 B13
Poncin F 31 C7
Ponferrada E 39 C6
Poniatowa PL 141 H6
Poniatowo PL 139 D8
Poniec PL 81 C11
Poniklá CZ 81 E8
Poniky SK 147 D8
Ponoarele RO 159 D10
Ponor RO 151 E11
Ponoshec RKS 163 E9
Pons F 28 D4
Ponsa FIN 127 B11
Ponsacco I 66 E2
Pont-à-Celles B 19 C9
Pontacq F 32 D5
Pontailler-sur-Saône F 26 F3
Pontaix F 31 F7
Pont-à-Marcq F 19 C7
Pont-à-Mousson F 26 C5
Pontardawe GB 13 B7
Pontarion F 29 D9
Pontarlier F 31 B9
Pontassieve I 66 E3
Pontaubault F 23 C9
Pont-Audemer F 18 F2
Pontault-Combault F 25 C8
Pontaumur F 29 D11
Pont-Aven F 22 E4
Pont-Canavese I 68 C4
Pontcharra F 31 E9
Pontchâteau F 23 F7
Pont-Croix F 22 D3
Pont-d'Ain F 31 C7
Pont-de-Buis-lès-Quimerch F 22 D3
Pont-de-Chéruy F 31 D7
Pont-de-Larn F 33 C10
Pont-de-l'Isère F 30 E6
Pont-de-Loup B 182 E5
Pont-de-Poitte F 31 B8
Pont-de-Roide F 27 F6
Pont-de-Salars F 34 B4
Pont de Suert E 33 F7
Pont-de-Vaux F 31 C6
Pont-de-Veyle F 30 C6
Pont-d'Hérault F 35 B6
Pont-d'Ouilly F 23 C11
Pont-du-Casse F 33 B7
Pont-du-Château F 30 D3
Pont-du-Navoy F 31 B8
Ponte I 60 A3
Ponte Aranga E 38 B4
Ponteareas E 38 D3
Pontebba I 73 C7
Pontecagnano Faiano I 60 B3
Ponte Caldelas E 38 D3
Ponteceso E 38 B2
Pontechianale I 36 B6
Pontecorvo I 62 E5
Pontecurone I 37 B9
Ponte da Barca P 38 E3
Pontedassio I 37 D8
Pontedecimo I 37 B9
Ponte de Lima P 38 E2
Ponte dell'Olio I 37 B11
Pontedera I 66 E2
Ponte de Sor P 44 F4
Pontedeume E 38 B3
Ponte di Legno I 69 A10
Ponte di Piave I 72 E5
Ponte do Rol P 44 F2
Pontefract GB 11 D9
Ponte Gardena I 72 C4
Pontelagoscuro I 66 C4
Ponteland GB 5 E13
Pontelandolfo I 60 A3
Ponte-Leccia F 37 G10
Pontelongo I 66 B5
Ponte nelle Alpi I 72 D5
Ponte Nizza I 37 B10
Ponte Nossa I 69 B8
Ponte Nova I 72 D3
Pont-en-Royans F 31 E7
Pontenure I 69 C8
Pontenx-les-Forges F 32 B3
Ponte San Nicolò I 66 B4
Ponte San Pietro I 69 B8
Ponte Valga E 38 C2
Pontevedra E 38 D2
Pontével P 44 F3
Pont-Évêque F 30 D6
Pontevico I 66 B1
Pont-Farcy F 23 C9
Pontfaverger-Moronvilliers F 19 F9
Pontgibaud F 30 D2
Pont-Hébert F 23 B9
Pontinha P 50 B1
Pontinia I 62 E4
Pöntiö FIN 120 F2
Pontivy F 22 D6
Pont-l'Abbé F 22 E3
Pont-la-Ville F 25 D12
Pont-les-Moulins F 26 F5
Pont-l'Évêque F 23 B12
Pontlevoy F 24 F5
Pontoise F 24 B7
Pontokomi GR 169 D6
Pontones E 55 C7
Pontonnyy RUS 129 F14
Pontonx-sur-l'Adour F 32 C4
Pontoon IRL 6 E4
Pontorson F 23 C8
Pontpoint F 18 F6
Pontremoli I 69 E8
Pontresina CH 71 E9
Pontrhydfendigaid GB 13 A7
Pontrieux F 22 C5
Pontrilas GB 13 B9
Ponts E 42 D6
Pöntsö FIN 117 C12
Pont-Ste-Marie F 25 D11
Pont-Ste-Maxence F 18 F6
Pont-St-Esprit F 35 B8
Pont-St-Martin I 68 B4
Pont-sur-Yonne F 25 D9
Pontvallain F 23 E12
Pontyberem GB 12 B6
Pontycymer GB 13 B7
Pontypool GB 13 B8
Pontypridd GB 13 B8
Ponyativka UA 154 D6
Ponza I 62 F3
Ponzone I 37 B8
Poola FIN 122 E7
Poole GB 13 D11
Poolewe GB 2 K5
Pooley Bridge GB 5 F11
Pool of Muckhart GB 5 C9
Pootsi EST 131 E8
Pope LV 134 B3
Popeasca MD 154 D5
Poperinge B 18 C6
Popești RO 151 C9
Popești RO 153 C10
Popești RO 160 C4
Popești RO 160 E6
Popești-Leordeni RO 161 E8
Popielów PL 142 E4
Popina BG 161 E9
Popintsi BG 165 E9
Popitsa BG 165 C8
Poplaca RO 152 F4
Popoli I 62 C5
Popovača HR 149 E7
Popovica SRB 159 E9
Popovitsa BG 166 E4
Popovo BG 166 C6
Popów PL 141 F1
Popów PL 143 D6
Poppenhausen D 75 B7
Poppenricht D 75 D10
Poppi I 66 E4
Poprad SK 145 E1
Popricani RO 153 C11
Poproč SK 145 F2
Popsko BG 171 A9
Pópulo P 38 F5
Populonia I 65 B2
Porąbka PL 147 B8
Poraj PL 143 E7
Porcari I 66 E2
Porcia I 73 E6
Porcsalma H 145 H6
Porcuna E 53 A8
Pordenone I 73 E6
Pordim BG 165 C10
Poręba PL 143 F7
Poręba-Kocęby PL 139 E12
Poreč HR 67 B8
Pori FIN 126 C6
Porice BIH 157 D7
Porjus S 116 E3
Porkhov RUS 132 F6
Porkkala FIN 127 F11
Porkuni EST 131 C12
Porlammi FIN 127 D15
Porlezza I 69 A7
Porlock GB 13 C7
Pornainen FIN 127 E13
Pornassio I 37 C7
Pornic F 23 F7
Pornichet F 23 F7
Poroina Mare RO 159 E10
Poros GR 174 C2
Poros GR 175 D7
Poroschia RO 160 F6
Poroshkove UA 145 F6
Poroszló H 150 B6
Porozina HR 67 B9
Porpi GR 171 B8
Porqueres E 43 C9
Porras FIN 127 D10
Porraskoski FIN 127 C12
Porrentruy CH 27 F7
Porreres E 57 B11
Porretta Terme I 66 D2
Porsangmoen N 113 D14
Pörsänmäki FIN 124 D8
Porsåsen N 102 E3
Porsgrunn N 90 A6
Porsi S 118 B5
Porspoder F 22 C2
Port N 113 D17
Porta F 33 E9
Portadown GB 7 D10
Portaferry GB 7 D11
Portaje E 45 E7
Portakallık TR 181 B8
Portalegre P 44 F6
Portals Vells E 49 F10
Portaria GR 169 D9
Portaria GR 169 F8
Portarlington IRL 7 F8
Port Askaig GB 4 D4
Portavogie GB 7 D12
Portbail F 23 B8
Port-Barcarès F 34 E5
Portbou E 34 F5
Port Brillet F 23 D10
Portchester GB 13 D12
Port d'Andratx E 49 E9
Port-de-Bouc F 35 D8
Port-de-Piles F 29 A7
Port de Pollença E 57 B11
Port-des-Barques F 28 D3
Port de Sóller E 49 E10
Portel P 50 C4
Portel-des-Corbières F 34 D4
Portell de Morella E 42 F3
Port Ellen GB 4 D4
Port-en-Bessin-Huppain F 23 B10
Portencross GB 4 D7
Port Erin GBM 10 C2
Portes-lès-Valence F 30 F6
Portets F 28 F5
Portet-sur-Garonne F 33 C8
Port Eynon GB 12 B6
Port Glasgow GB 4 D7
Porth GB 13 B8
Porthcawl GB 13 C7
Port Henderson GB 2 K5
Porthleven GB 12 E4
Porthmadog GB 10 F3
Porticcio F 37 H9
Portici I 60 B2
Portieux F 26 D5
Portilla E 47 D8
Portilla de la Reina E 39 B10
Portillo E 40 F2
Portillo de Toledo E 46 D4
Portimão P 50 E2
Portimo FIN 119 B16
Portimojärvi FIN 119 B11
Portishead GB 13 C9
Port-Joinville F 28 B1
Portknockie GB 3 K11
Port Láirge IRL 9 D8
Portland IRL 6 F6
Port-la-Nouvelle F 34 D5
Port Laoise IRL 7 F8
Portlaoise IRL 7 F8
Portlethen GB 5 A12
Port-Leucate F 34 E5
Port Logan GB 4 F7
Port-Louis F 22 E5
Portmagee IRL 8 E2
Portmahomack GB 3 K9
Portman E 56 F3
Portmarnock IRL 7 F10
Port Mearnóg IRL 7 F10
Portmuck GB 4 F5
Port-na-Con GB 2 H7
Portnaguran GB 2 J4
Portnahaven GB 4 D3
Portnalong GB 2 L4
Port-Navalo F 22 E6
Porto E 39 D6
Porto F 37 G9
Porto P 44 B3
Porto Alto P 50 B2
Porto Azzurro I 65 B2
Porto Botte I 64 E2
Portobravo E 38 C2
Porto Cervo I 64 A4
Porto Cesareo I 61 C9
Portocheli GR 175 E7
Portocolom E 57 C11
Porto Covo da Bandeira P 50 D2
Porto Cristo E 57 B11
Porto d'Ascoli I 62 B5
Porto de Lagos P 50 E2
Porto de Mós P 44 E3
Porto do Barqueiro E 38 A4
Porto do Son E 38 C1
Porto Empedocle I 58 E4
Porto Ercole I 65 C4
Portoferraio I 65 B2
Portofino I 37 C10
Port of Ness GB 2 J4
Porto Garibaldi I 66 C5
Porto Germeno GR 175 C7
Portogruaro I 73 E6
Porto Koufo GR 170 E5
Porto Levante I 59 C6
Porto Levante I 66 B5
Pörtom FIN 122 E7
Portomaggiore I 66 C4
Portomarin E 38 C4
Port Omna IRL 6 F6
Portopalo di Capo Passero I 59 F7
Porto Petro E 57 C11
Portør N 90 B5
Porto Rafti GR 175 D9
Porto Recanati I 67 F8
Porto Rotondo I 64 A4
Portorož SLO 67 A8
Porto San Giorgio I 67 F8
Porto San Paolo I 64 B4
Porto Sant'Elpidio I 67 F8
Porto Santo Stefano I 65 C4
Portoscuso I 64 E1
Porto Tolle I 66 C5
Porto Torres I 64 B1
Porto-Vecchio F 37 H10
Portovenere I 69 E8
Porto Viro I 66 B5
Portpatrick GB 4 F6
Portrane IRL 7 F10
Port Reachrann IRL 7 F10
Portreath GB 12 E4
Portree GB 2 L4
Portroe IRL 8 C6
Portrush GB 4 E3
Portsalon IRL 4 E1
Portsmouth GB 13 D12
Portsoy GB 3 K11
Port-Ste-Marie F 33 B6
Portstewart GB 4 E3
Port-St-Louis-du-Rhône F 35 D8
Port St Mary GBM 10 C2
Port-St-Père F 23 F8
Port-sur-Saône F 26 E5
Port Talbot GB 13 B7
Portugalete E 40 B5
Portumna IRL 6 F6
Port-Vendres F 34 E5
Port William GB 4 F7
Poruba SK 147 D7
Porubne UA 153 A8
Porumbacu de Jos RO 152 F4
Porvoo FIN 127 E14
Porządzie PL 139 E11
Porzuna E 46 F4
Posada E 39 B8
Posada I 64 B4
Posada de Valdeón E 39 B10
Posadas E 53 A6
Poșaga RO 151 E11
Poschiavo CH 69 A9
Posedarje HR 156 D3
Poseidonia GR 176 E4
Poseritz D 84 B4
Posești RO 161 C8
Pösing D 75 D12
Posio FIN 121 B11
Positano I 60 B2
Possagno I 72 E4
Posseberg S 97 D11
Possendorf D 80 E5
Possesse F 25 C12
Pößneck D 79 E10
Posta I 62 B4
Poșta Câlnău RO 161 C9
Postal I 72 C3
Posta Piana I 60 A5
Postau D 75 E11
Posterholt NL 20 B6
Postiglione I 60 B4
Postojna SLO 73 E9
Postoliska PL 139 F11
Postoloprty CZ 76 B5
Postomino PL 85 B11
Postřelmov CZ 77 C11
Postupice CZ 77 C7
Posušje BIH 157 F7
Poświętne PL 140 E7
Poświętne PL 141 G2
Potamia GR 171 C7
Potamia GR 174 F5
Potamochori GR 171 B8
Potamoi GR 170 B6
Potamos GR 168 E2
Potamos GR 178 C4
Potashnya UA 154 A5
Potcoava RO 160 E5
Potęgowo PL 85 B12
Potenza I 60 B5
Potenza Picena I 67 F8
Potes E 39 B10
Potidania GR 174 C5
Potigny F 23 C11
Potkraj BIH 157 E7
Potku FIN 119 E17
Potlogi RO 161 D7
Potočac SRB 159 F7
Potočani BIH 157 E7
Potoci BIH 156 D6
Potoci BIH 157 F8
Potok Złoty PL 143 E7
Potsdam D 80 B4
Pötsönvaara FIN 125 D16
Potštát CZ 146 B5
Pottendorf A 77 G10
Pottenstein A 77 G10
Pottenstein D 75 C9
Potterne GB 13 C10
Potters Bar GB 15 D8
Pöttmes D 75 E9
Potton GB 15 C8
Pöttsching A 146 F2
Potworów PL 141 G3
Pouancé F 23 E9
Pougny F 25 F9
Pougues-les-Eaux F 30 A3
Pougy F 25 D11
Pouillon F 32 C4
Pouilly-en-Auxois F 25 F12
Pouilly-sous-Charlieu F 30 C5
Pouilly-sur-Loire F 25 F8
Pouilly-sur-Saône F 31 A7
Poulaines F 24 F6
Pouldreuzic F 22 E3
Poulgorm Bridge IRL 8 E4
Pouligny-St-Pierre F 29 B8
Poulithra GR 175 E6
Poullaouen F 22 D4
Poulnamucky IRL 9 D7
Poulstrup DK 90 E7
Poulton-le-Fylde GB 10 D6
Pounta GR 176 E5
Poupas F 33 C7
Pourcieux F 35 D10
Pouri GR 169 F9
Pourrain F 25 E9
Pourrières F 35 C10
Pousada P 45 C6
Pousos P 44 E3
Poussan F 35 D6
Poussay F 26 D5
Poussu FIN 121 C13
Pouxeux F 26 D6
Pouyastruc F 33 D6
Pouydesseaux F 32 C5
Pouzauges F 28 B4
Pouzay F 24 F4
Považská Bystrica SK 146 C6
Povedilla E 55 B7
Poviglio I 66 C2
Povlja HR 157 F6
Póvoa de Lanhoso P 38 E3
Póvoa de São Miguel P 51 C5
Póvoa de Varzim P 38 F2
Póvoa do Concelho P 45 C6
Povoletto I 73 D7
Povrly CZ 80 E6
Powburn GB 5 E13
Power's Cross IRL 6 F6
Powick GB 13 A10
Powidz PL 138 F4
Powmill GB 5 C9
Poyales del Hoyo E 45 D10
Poyatos E 47 D8
Poyntz Pass GB 7 D10
Poyrazcik TR 177 A9
Poysdorf A 77 E11
Pöytyä FIN 126 D8
Poza de la Sal E 40 C5
Pozaldez E 39 F10
Požarevac SRB 159 D7
Požarnica BIH 157 C10
Požega HR 149 F9
Požega SRB 158 F5
Požerė LT 134 E4
Pozezdrze PL 136 E4
Pozharan RKS 164 E3
Pozherevitsy RUS 133 B7
Poznań PL 81 B11
Pozo Alcón E 55 D7
Pozoamargo E 47 F8
Pozoantiguo E 39 E9
Pozoblanco E 54 C3
Pozo Cañada E 55 B9
Pozo de Guadalajara E 47 D6
Pozohondo E 55 B9
Pozo-Lorente E 47 F10
Pozondón E 47 C10
Pozořice CZ 77 D11
Pozorrubio E 47 E7
Poźrzadło Wielkie PL 85 D9
Pozuel del Campo E 47 C10
Pozuelo E 55 B8
Pozuelo de Alarcón E 46 D5
Pozuelo de Aragón E 41 E9
Pozuelo del Páramo E 39 D8
Pozuelo del Rey E 46 D6
Pozuelo de Zarzón E 45 D8
Pozuelos de Calatrava E 54 B4
Pozza di Fassa I 72 D4
Pozzallo I 59 F6
Pozzolo Formigaro I 37 B9
Pozzomaggiore I 64 C2
Pozzuoli I 60 B2
Pozzuolo del Friuli I 73 E7
Prabuty PL 139 C7
Prača BIH 157 E10
Prachatice CZ 76 D6
Pracht D 21 C9
Prackenbach D 76 D3
Prádanos de Ojeda E 40 C3
Pradejón E 32 F1
Pradelles F 30 F4
Prádena E 46 B5
Prades F 33 E9
Prades F 33 E10
Prades-d'Aubrac F 34 A4
Pradillo E 41 D6
Pradines F 33 B8
Prado P 38 E3
Prado de la Guzpeña E 39 C9
Prado del Rey E 53 C5
Pradoluengo E 40 D5
Præstbro DK 86 A6
Præstø DK 87 E10
Pragelato I 31 E10
Pragersko SLO 148 D5
Prägraten A 72 B5
Praha CZ 77 B6
Prahecq F 28 C5
Prahovo SRB 159 E10
Praia a Mare I 60 D5
Praia da Barra P 44 C3
Praia da Rocha P 50 E2
Praia da Tocha P 44 D3
Praia de Esmoriz P 44 C3
Praia de Mira P 44 D3
Praiano I 60 B3
Praid RO 152 D6
Prăjeni RO 153 B10
Prakovce SK 145 F2
Pralognan-la-Vanoise F 31 E10
Pralyetarsk BY 133 E7
Pramanta GR 168 E5
Prambachkirchen A 76 F5
Pranjani SRB 158 E5
Prapatnica HR 156 E5
Prašice SK 146 D6
Praszka PL 142 D5
Prata di Pordenone I 73 E6
Pratau D 79 C12
Prat de Comte E 42 F4
Pratdip E 42 E5
Pratella I 60 A2
Prato I 66 E3
Prato allo Stelvio I 71 D11
Pratola Peligna I 62 C5
Pratovecchio I 66 E4
Prats de Lluçanès E 43 C8
Prats-de-Mollo-la-Preste F 33 F10
Pratteln CH 27 E8
Prauliena LV 135 C12
Prauthoy F 26 E3
Pravda BG 161 F10
Pravdinsk RUS 136 E3
Pravets BG 165 D8
Pravia E 39 B7
Prayssas F 33 B7
Prazaroki BY 133 F4
Praz-sur-Arly F 31 D10
Prebold SLO 73 D11
Préchac F 32 B5
Preci I 62 B4
Précigné F 23 E11
Prečin SK 147 C7
Précy-sous-Thil F 25 F11
Predappio I 66 D4
Predazzo I 72 D4
Predeal RO 161 B7
Predeal-Sărari RO 161 C8
Predejane SRB 164 D5
Predești RO 160 E3
Preding A 148 C4
Predlitz A 73 B8
Predmeja SLO 73 E8
Předměřice nad Labem CZ 77 B9
Predosa I 37 B9
Pré-en-Pail F 23 D11
Prees GB 10 F6
Preetz D 83 B8
Préfailles F 23 F7
Preganziòl I 72 E5
Pregarten A 77 F7
Pregrada HR 148 D5
Preignan F 33 C7
Preiļi LV 135 D13
Preitenegg A 73 C10
Preiviiki FIN 126 C6
Preixan F 33 D10
Prejmer RO 153 F7
Prekaja BIH 156 D6
Preko HR 156 D3
Prekopa HR 148 F6
Preljina SRB 158 F5
Prelog HR 149 D7
Prelošćica HR 149 F6
Přelouč CZ 77 B9
Prem SLO 73 E9
Premantura HR 67 C8
Prémery F 25 F9
Premia I 68 A5
Premià de Mar E 43 E8
Premilcuore I 66 E4
Prémilhat F 29 C11
Premnitz D 79 A11
Premosello Chiovenda I 68 A5
Prenzlau D 84 D5
Préporché F 30 B4
Přerov CZ 146 C4
Prerow D 83 B13
Preselentsi BG 155 F2
Preševo SRB 164 E4
Presicce I 61 D10
Prešov SK 145 F3
Pressac F 29 C7
Pressath D 75 C10
Pressbaum A 77 F10
Presseck D 75 B10
Pressel D 79 C12
Pressig D 75 B9
Prestatyn GB 10 E5
Prestbakken N 111 C15
Prestbury GB 13 B10
Pre-St-Didier I 31 D10
Prestebakke N 91 B10
Presteigne GB 13 A8
Prestfoss N 95 B11
Přeštice CZ 76 C4
Preston GB 5 D12
Preston GB 10 D6
Prestwick GB 4 E7
Prettin D 80 C3
Pretushë AL 168 C4
Pretzfeld D 75 C9
Pretzier D 83 E10
Pretzsch D 79 C12
Pretzschendorf D 80 E5
Preuilly-sur-Claise F 29 B7
Preutești RO 153 C8
Prevalje SLO 73 C10
Prévenchères F 35 A6
Préveranges F 29 C10
Prevešt SRB 159 F7
Preveza GR 174 B2
Prevršac HR 156 B5
Prežganje SLO 73 D10
Prezid HR 73 E10
Prez-sous-Lafauche F 26 D3
Priaranza del Bierzo E 39 C6
Pribelja BIH 157 D6
Pribeta SK 146 F6
Pribinić BIH 157 C8
Pribislavec HR 149 D6
Priboieni RO 160 D6
Priboj BIH 157 C10
Priboj SRB 163 B8
Příbor CZ 146 B6
Priborn D 83 D13
Priboy BG 165 D6
Příbram CZ 76 C6
Pribrezhnoye RUS 136 D1
Pribude HR 156 E5
Pribylina SK 147 C9
Přibyslav CZ 77 C9
Prichaly RUS 134 F2
Prichsenstadt D 75 C7
Pridvorci BIH 157 F9
Priedaine LV 134 C3
Priedes LV 131 F9
Priego E 47 D8
Priego de Córdoba E 53 B8
Priekulė LT 134 E2
Priekule LV 134 D3
Priekuļi LV 135 B10
Prienai LT 137 D8
Prienai LT 137 D12
Prien am Chiemsee D 72 A5
Prieros D 80 B5
Prießnitz D 79 D10
Prießnitz D 79 D12
Priestewitz D 80 D5
Prievidza SK 147 D7
Priežmale LV 133 D2
Prignac-et-Marcamps F 28 E5
Prigor RO 159 D9
Prigoria RO 160 C3
Prigradica HR 162 D2
Prigrevica SRB 158 B3
Prijeboj HR 156 C4
Prijedor BIH 157 C6
Prijepolje SRB 163 C8
Prikuļi LV 135 D13
Priladozhskiy RUS 129 F15
Prilep NMK 169 B6
Prilike SRB 158 F5
Prillimäe EST 131 C9
Priluka BIH 157 E6
Přimda CZ 75 C12
Primišlje HR 156 B3
Primolano I 72 E4
Primorsk RUS 129 E10
Primorsk RUS 139 A9
Primorsko BG 167 E9
Primor'ye RUS 139 A9
Primošten HR 156 E4
Princes Risborough GB 15 D7
Princetown GB 12 D7
Prinos GR 171 C7
Prinsenbeek NL 16 E3
Prinzhöfte D 17 C11
Priolithos GR 174 D5
Priolo Gargallo I 59 E7
Prioro E 39 C10
Priozersk RUS 129 C13
Priponești RO 153 E10
Prirechnyy RUS 114 E8
Prisăcani RO 153 C11
Priseaca RO 160 D4
Priseltsi BG 167 C9
Prishtinë RKS 164 D3
Prisjan SRB 164 C6
Prisoja MNE 163 D8
Prisoje BIH 157 E7
Příšovice CZ 81 E8
Prissac F 29 B8
Prissé F 30 C6
Pristol RO 159 E10
Prittriching D 71 A11
Pritzerbe D 79 B11
Pritzier D 83 D10
Pritzwalk D 83 D12
Privas F 30 F6
Priverno I 62 E4
Privlaka HR 67 D11
Privlaka HR 157 B10
Prizna HR 67 C10
Prizren RKS 163 E10
Prizzi I 58 D3
Prkosi BIH 156 C5
Prnjavor BIH 157 C8
Prnjavor SRB 158 D3
Proaza E 39 B7
Probištip NMK 164 E5
Probota RO 153 C10
Probsteierhagen D 83 B8
Probus GB 12 E5
Proceno I 62 B1
Prochoma GR 169 C8
Prochowice PL 81 D10
Procida I 60 B2
Prodromos GR 175 C6
Produlești RO 161 D7
Proença-a-Nova P 44 E5
Proença-a-Velha P 45 D6
Profen D 79 D11
Profesor-Ishirkovo BG 161 F10
Profilia GR 181 D7
Profitis GR 169 C9
Profitis Ilias GR 178 E9
Profondeville B 19 D10
Progonat AL 168 D2
Prohn D 84 B4
Prokhladnoye RUS 134 F2
Prokopi GR 175 B7
Prokuplje SRB 164 C4
Prolaz BG 167 C6
Prolog BIH 157 E6
Promachoi GR 169 B7
Promachonas GR 169 B9
Promna PL 141 G3
Promyri GR 175 A7
Pronsfeld D 20 D6
Propriano F 37 H9
Proseč CZ 77 C10
Prosek AL 163 F8
Prosenik BG 167 D8
Prosenjakovci SLO 149 C6
Prosetín CZ 77 C9
Proshkava BY 133 F4
Proskynites GR 171 C9
Prosotsani GR 170 B5
Prosperous IRL 7 F9
Prossedi I 62 D4
Prostějov CZ 77 D12
Prostki PL 140 C6
Prostřední Bečva CZ 146 C6
Prószków PL 142 E4
Proszowice PL 143 F9
Proszówki PL 143 F9
Proti GR 170 C5
Protići BIH 157 D6
Protivanov CZ 77 D11
Protivín CZ 76 D6
Protokklisi GR 171 B10
Protoria GR 178 E9
Prötzel D 80 A5
Provadiya BG 167 C8
Provatas GR 169 B9
Provenchères-sur-Fave F 27 D7
Provins F 25 C9
Provo SRB 158 D4
Prozor BIH 157 E8
Prozor HR 156 C3
Prrenjas AL 168 B4
Pruchnik PL 144 D6
Prudhoe GB 5 F13
Prudnik PL 142 F4
Prudzinki BY 133 E4
Prugoc RKS 164 D3
Prügy H 145 G3
Prüm D 20 D6
Pruna E 51 F9
Prundeni RO 160 D4
Prundu RO 161 E8
Prundu Bârgăului RO 152 C5
Prunières F 36 B4
Pruniers-en-Sologne F 24 F6
Prunișor RO 159 D10
Prusac BIH 157 D7
Prušánky CZ 77 E11
Prusice PL 81 D11
Prusinovice CZ 146 C5
Prūšiši LV 135 B13
Pruszcz PL 138 D4
Pruszcz PL 138 D5
Pruszcz Gdański PL 138 B6
Pruszków PL 141 F3
Prutz A 71 C11
Pružina SK 146 C6
Prvačina SLO 73 E8
Pryamobalka UA 154 F4
Prymors'ke UA 155 B5
Prymors'ke UA 155 B5
Pryozerne UA 155 B4
Prypruttya UA 153 A8
Przasnysz PL 139 D10
Przechlewo PL 85 C12
Przeciszów PL 143 F7
Przecław PL 143 F11
Przedbórz PL 143 D8
Przedecz PL 138 F6
Przejazdowo PL 138 B6
Przelewice PL 85 D8
Przemęt PL 81 B10
Przemków PL 81 C9
Przemyśl PL 144 D6
Przerośl PL 136 E6
Przewale PL 144 B8
Przewłoka PL 141 G8
Przeworno PL 81 E12
Przeworsk PL 144 C5
Przewóz PL 81 D7
Przeździatka PL 141 E6
Przeździęk Wielki PL 139 D10
Przezmark PL 139 C7
Przine-Zdralovac BIH 156 D6
Przodkowo PL 138 B5
Przybiernów PL 85 C7
Przyborów PL 81 C9
Przyborowice PL 139 E9
Przybranowo PL 138 E6
Przygodzice PL 142 C4
Przykona PL 142 C6
Przyłęk PL 141 G1
Przylep PL 81 C8
Przylesie PL 142 E3
Przyrów PL 143 E8
Przysieki PL 144 D3
Przystajń PL 142 E6
Przystałowice Duże PL 141 H3
Przysucha PL 141 H3
Przyszów PL 144 C4
Przytoczna PL 81 A9
Przytoczno PL 141 G6
Przytuły PL 140 D6
Przytyk PL 141 H3

Przywidz PL 138 B5
Psača NMK 164 E5
Psachna GR 175 B8
Psara GR 177 B6
Psarades GR 168 C5
Psari GR 174 E4
Psari GR 175 D6
Psathopyrgos GR 174 C4
Psinthos GR 181 D8
Pskov RUS 132 F3
Psychiko GR 169 B10
Psychro GR 178 E9
Pszczew PL 81 B9
Pszczółki PL 138 B6
Pszczonów PL 141 G1
Pszczyna PL 147 B7
Pteleos GR 175 A6
Pteri GR 174 C5
Ptolemaïda GR 169 C6
Ptuj SLO 148 D5
Publier F 31 C10
Puchberg am Schneeberg A 146 F1
Pucheni RO 160 C6
Puchenii Mari RO 161 D8
Puchheim D 75 F9
Púchov SK 146 C6
Pucioasa RO 161 C6
Pučišće HR 157 F6
Puck PL 138 A5
Puckaun IRL 8 C6
Puçol E 48 E4
Pudasjärven kirkko FIN 119 D17
Pudasjärvi FIN 119 D17
Puddletown GB 13 D10
Puderbach D 185 C8
Pudinava LV 133 C3
Pudsey GB 11 D8
Puebla de Albortón E 41 F10
Puebla de Alcocer E 51 B9
Puebla de Alfindén E 41 E10
Puebla de Almenara E 47 E7
Puebla de Beleña E 47 C6
Puebla de Don Fadrique E 55 D8
Puebla de Don Rodrigo E 46 F3
Puebla de Guzmán E 51 D5
Puebla de la Calzada E 51 B6
Puebla de la Reina E 51 B7
Puebla de Lillo E 39 B9
Puebla del Maestre E 51 C7
Puebla del Príncipe E 55 B7
Puebla del Prior E 51 B7
Puebla del Salvador E 47 E9
Puebla de Obando E 45 F7
Puebla de Sanabria E 39 D6
Puebla de Sancho Pérez E 51 C7
Puebla de San Miguel E 47 D10
Puebla de Yeltes E 45 C8
Puente de Domingo Flórez E 39 D6
Puente de Génave E 55 C7
Puente del Congosto E 45 D9
Puente de Montañana E 42 C5
Puente de San Miguel E 40 B3
Puente-Genil E 53 B7
Puente la Reina E 32 E2
Puentenansa E 40 B3
Puente Viesgo E 40 B4
Puerto de Béjar E 45 D9
Puerto de Mazarrón E 56 F2
Puerto de San Vicente E 45 E10
Puerto Lápice E 46 F6
Puertollano E 54 B4
Puerto Lumbreras E 55 D9
Puertomingalvo E 48 D4
Puerto Real E 52 C4
Puerto Seguro E 45 C7
Puerto Serrano E 51 F8
Pueyo E 32 E2
Pueyo de Santa Cruz E 42 D4
Pufești RO 153 E10
Puget-Théniers F 36 D5
Puget-Ville F 36 E4
Pugnochiuso I 63 D10
Puhja EST 131 E12
Puhoi MD 154 D4
Puhos FIN 121 D10
Puhos FIN 125 F13
Puhovac BIH 157 D9
Pui RO 159 B11
Puiatu EST 131 E10
Puiești RO 153 E11
Puiești RO 161 C10
Puig E 48 E4
Puigcerdà E 33 F9
Puigpunyent E 49 E10
Puig-reig E 43 D7
Puikkola FIN 115 E3
Puikule LV 131 F9
Puimoisson F 36 D4
Puiseaux F 25 D7
Puisieux F 18 D6
Puisseguin F 28 F5
Puisserguier F 34 D5
Puivert F 33 E10
Pujaut F 35 B8
Pujols F 28 F5
Pujols F 33 B7
Puka EST 131 E12
Pukanec SK 147 E7
Pukaro FIN 127 D15
Pukavik S 88 C7
Pukë AL 163 E8
Pukiš BIH 157 C10
Pukkila FIN 127 D14
Pula HR 67 C8
Pula I 64 E3
Puławy PL 141 H5
Pulborough GB 15 F7
Pulfero I 73 D7
Pulgar E 46 E4
Pulheim D 21 B7
Pulju FIN 117 B13
Pulkau A 77 E9
Pulkkaviita FIN 115 D5
Pulkkila FIN 119 F15
Pulkkinen FIN 123 D11
Pulkonkoski FIN 124 D8
Pulpí E 55 E9
Pulsa FIN 128 D8
Pulsano I 61 C8
Pulsen D 80 D4
Pulskala FIN 115 D4
Pulsnitz D 80 D6
Pulsujärvi S 116 B6
Pułtusk PL 139 E11
Pulversheim F 27 E7
Pumpėnai LT 135 E8
Pumpuri LV 134 C4
Pumsaint GB 13 A7
Pūņas LV 134 B4
Punat HR 67 B10
Pundsvik N 111 D12
Punduri LV 133 D3
Pungești RO 153 D10
Punghina RO 159 E10
Punia LT 137 D9
Punkaharju FIN 129 B11
Punkalaidun FIN 127 C9
Punkka FIN 128 C7
Punta Ala I 65 B3
Punta Križa HR 67 C9
Punta Sabbioni I 66 B5
Punta Umbría E 51 E6
Puokio FIN 120 E9
Puolakkovaara FIN 115 D1
Puolanka FIN 121 E10
Puoliväli FIN 124 D9
Puoltikasvaara S 116 D6
Puottaure S 118 B4
Pūpoli LV 133 D2
Puraći BIH 157 C8
Puračić BIH 157 C10
Purani RO 161 F6
Puras FIN 121 E14
Purbach am Neusiedler See A 77 G11
Purcari MD 154 D5
Purchena E 55 E8
Pūre LV 134 B5
Purgstall an der Erlauf A 77 F8
Purila EST 131 C9
Purkersdorf A 77 F10
Purkijaur S 109 C18
Pürksi EST 130 C7
Purley GB 15 E8
Purmerend NL 16 C3
Purmo FIN 123 C9
Purmojärvi FIN 123 D10
Purmsāti LV 134 D3
Purnu S 116 E6
Purnumukka FIN 115 B2
Purnuvaara FIN 121 C12
Purnuvaara S 116 D6
Purola FIN 128 E6
Purontaka FIN 123 C12
Purujärvi FIN 129 B12
Purujosa E 41 E8
Purullena E 55 E6
Pŭrvenets BG 165 E10
Purviniškė LT 137 D7
Pŭrvomay BG 166 E4
Pŭrvomay BG 169 B9
Puša LV 133 D2
Pušalotas LT 135 E8
Puschendorf D 75 C8
Pushkinskiye Gory RUS 133 B5
Pušmucova LV 133 C3
Püspökladány H 151 C7
Püssi EST 131 C14
Pusterwald A 73 B9
Pusté Úľany SK 146 E5
Pustków PL 143 F11
Pustomyty UA 144 D8
Pustoshka RUS 133 D6
Pŭstrovo BG 166 E4
Pusula FIN 127 E10
Puszcza Mariańska PL 141 G2
Puszczykowo PL 81 B11
Pusztaföldvár H 150 D6
Pusztakovácsi H 149 C9
Pusztamérges H 150 E4
Pusztamonostor H 150 B4
Pusztaszabolcs H 149 B11
Pusztaszer H 150 D4
Pusztavacs H 150 C4
Pusztavám H 149 B10
Putaja FIN 126 C8
Putanges-Pont-Écrepin F 23 C11
Putbus D 84 B4
Putifigari I 64 B1
Putignano I 61 B8
Putikko FIN 129 B11
Putinci SRB 158 C4
Putineiu RO 160 F5
Putineiu RO 161 F7
Putkivaara FIN 119 B17
Putlitz D 83 D12
Putna RO 153 B7
Putnok H 145 G1
Putte B 19 B10
Putte NL 16 F2
Puttelange-aux-Lacs F 27 B6
Putten NL 16 D5
Puttgarden D 83 A10
Püttlingen D 21 F7
Putula FIN 127 C13
Putyla UA 152 B6
Putzar D 84 C5
Putzkau D 80 D6
Puukari FIN 125 C11
Puukkokumpu FIN 119 C14
Puumala FIN 129 B9
Puurmani EST 131 D12
Puurs B 19 B9
Puurtila FIN 125 F9
Puutossalmi FIN 124 E9
Puutturinjärvi FIN 119 E17
Puybrun F 29 F9
Puycasquier F 33 C7
Puygouzon F 33 C10
Puylaroque F 33 B9
Puylaurens F 33 C10
Puy-l'Évêque F 33 A8
Puymirol F 33 B7
Puymoyen F 29 D6
Puyôo F 32 C4
Pwllheli GB 10 F3
Pyaozerskiy RUS 121 C17
Pyatidorozhnoye RUS 139 B9
Pyatirech'ye RUS 129 D14
Pyelishcha BY 141 F9
Pyershamayski BY 137 F11
Pyhäjärvi FIN 113 F16
Pyhäjärvi FIN 115 D2
Pyhäjoki FIN 119 F12
Pyhäjoki FIN 126 C7
Pyhäkylä FIN 121 D12
Pyhältö FIN 128 D7
Pyhämaa FIN 126 D5
Pyhänkoski FIN 119 F12
Pyhäntä FIN 119 F16
Pyhäntä FIN 121 F11
Pyhäntaka FIN 127 C14
Pyhäranta FIN 126 D5
Pyhäsalmi FIN 123 C15
Pyhäselkä FIN 125 F13
Pyhe FIN 126 D6
Pyhra A 77 F9
Pyhtää FIN 128 E6
Pyle GB 13 B7
Pyles GR 181 E6
Pyli GR 169 F6
Pyli GR 175 C8
Pyli GR 177 F9
Pylkönmäki FIN 123 E13
Pylos GR 174 F4
Pylypets' UA 145 F7
Pyntäinen FIN 126 B6
Pyrbaum D 75 D9
Pyrgetos GR 169 E8
Pyrgi GR 177 C6
Pyrgiotika GR 175 D6
Pyrgoi GR 169 C6
Pyrgoi GR 170 B6
Pyrgos GR 174 D3
Pyrgos GR 176 D5
Pyrgos GR 177 D8
Pyrgos GR 178 E9
Pyrgos Dirou GR 178 B3
Pyrrönperä FIN 123 B15
Pyrsogianni GR 168 D4
Pyrzyce PL 85 D7
Pyšely CZ 77 C7
Pyskowice PL 142 F6
Pyssyperä FIN 121 D10
Pystan' UA 152 A6
Pysznica PL 144 B5
Pytalovo RUS 133 B3
Pythagoreio GR 177 D8
Pythio GR 169 D7
Pythio GR 172 B6
Pyykkölänvaara FIN 121 E12
Pyykköskylä FIN 121 D13
Pyyli FIN 125 F11

Q

Qafzez AL 168 D4
Qelëz AL 163 E8
Qeparo AL 168 D2
Qerret AL 168 B2
Quadrazais P 45 D7
Quadri I 63 D6
Quakenbrück D 17 C9
Qualiano I 60 B2
Quaregnon B 182 E3
Quargnento I 37 B9
Quarona I 68 B5
Quarrata I 66 E2
Quarré-les-Tombes F 25 F10
Quarteira P 50 E3
Quartell E 48 E4
Quarten CH 27 F11
Quartu Sant'Elena I 64 E3
Quatre-Champs F 19 F10
Quatretonda E 56 D4
Quattro Castella I 66 C1
Quedlinburg D 79 C9
Queenborough GB 15 E10
Queensbury GB 11 D8
Queenstown IRL 8 E6
Queidersbach D 21 F9
Queige F 31 D9
Queiriga P 44 C5
Quel E 41 D7
Quelaines-St-Gault F 23 E10
Quellendorf D 79 C11
Queluz P 50 B1
Quemada E 40 E4
Quend F 18 D4
Quendorf D 17 D8
Queralbs E 33 F10
Quercianella I 66 F1
Querenhorst D 79 B8
Querfurt D 79 D10
Quérigut F 33 E10
Quern D 82 A7
Quernheim D 17 D10
Quero E 47 E6
Quero I 72 E4
Querrieu F 18 E5
Quesa E 48 F3
Quesada E 55 D6
Quesnoy-sur-Deûle F 18 C7
Quessoy F 22 D6
Questembert F 22 E7
Quettehou F 23 A9
Quettreville-sur-Sienne F 23 C9
Quevauvillers F 18 E5
Queyrac F 28 E4
Quézac F 29 F10
Quiaios P 44 D3
Quiberon F 22 F5
Quickborn D 83 C7
Quierschied D 21 F8
Quiévrain B 19 D8
Quiévrechain F 182 E3
Quiliano I 37 C8
Quillan F 33 E10
Quillebeuf-sur-Seine F 18 F2
Quimper F 22 E3
Quimperlé F 22 E4
Quin IRL 8 C5
Quincinetto I 68 B4
Quincy-Voisins F 25 C8
Quingey F 26 F4
Quinson F 36 D4
Quinssaines F 29 C11
Quintana de la Serena E 51 B8
Quintana del Castillo E 39 C7
Quintana del Pino E 40 C4
Quintana del Puente E 40 D3
Quintana de Rueda E 39 C9
Quintana-Martín Galíndez E 40 C5
Quintanapalla E 40 D4
Quintanar de la Orden E 47 E6
Quintanar de la Sierra E 40 E5
Quintanar del Rey E 47 F9
Quintana Redonda E 41 E6
Quintanilla de Onésimo E 40 E3
Quintenas F 30 E6
Quintin F 22 D6
Quinto CH 71 D7
Quinto E 41 E11
Quintos P 50 D4
Quinzano d'Oglio I 69 C9
Quiroga E 38 D5
Quiruelas de Vidriales E 39 D8
Quismondo E 46 D4
Quissac F 35 C7
Quittebeuf F 24 B4
Qukës AL 168 B3

R

Raab A 76 F5
Raabs an der Thaya A 77 E8
Raahe FIN 119 E12
Raajärvi FIN 115 E1
Rääkkylä FIN 125 F13
Raalte NL 16 D6
Raamsdonksveer NL 16 E3
Raanujärvi FIN 117 E13
Raappananmäki FIN 121 E10
Raasiku EST 131 C10
Raate FIN 121 E14
Raattama FIN 117 B12
Rab HR 67 C10
Rabac HR 67 B9
Rabaçal P 44 D4
Rabaçal P 45 C6
Rábade E 38 B4
Răbăgani RO 151 D9
Rábahidvég H 149 B7
Rábakecöl H 149 B8
Rabanales E 39 E7
Rábapaty H 149 B7
Rabastens F 33 C9
Rabastens-de-Bigorre F 33 D6
Rábatamási H 149 A8
Raba Wyżna PL 147 B9
Rabbalshede S 91 B9
Rabča SK 147 C8
Rabčice SK 147 B9
Rabe SRB 150 E5
Rabenstein an der Pielach A 77 F8
Raben Steinfeld D 83 C11
Råberg S 107 B13
Rąbino PL 85 C9
Rabisha BG 159 F10
Rabivere EST 131 C9
Rabka PL 147 B9
Räbke D 79 B8
Rabrovo BG 159 E10
Rabrovo SRB 159 D8
Rača SRB 159 E6
Rača SRB 164 D3
Răcăciuni RO 153 E9
Racale I 61 D10
Rácalmás H 149 B11
Racalmuto I 58 E4
Răcari RO 161 D7
Răcășdia RO 159 D8
Racconigi I 37 B7
Rače SLO 148 D5
Rachanie PL 144 B8
Rachecourt-sur-Marne F 26 C3
Raches F 182 E2
Raches GR 175 B6
Raches GR 177 D7
Răchiți RO 153 B9
Răchitoasa RO 153 E10
Răchitova RO 159 B10
Rachoni GR 171 C7
Raciąż PL 138 C4
Raciąż PL 139 E9
Racibórz PL 142 F5
Raciechowice PL 144 D1
Racimierz PL 85 C7
Račinovci HR 157 C10
Račišće HR 162 D3
Răciu RO 152 D4
Răciula MD 154 C2
Ráckeve H 149 B11
Racksätter S 97 D14
Racksund S 109 D14
Racławice PL 143 F9
Răcoasa RO 153 F9
Racoș RO 152 E6
Racova RO 153 D9
Racovița RO 159 B8
Racovița RO 160 B4
Racovița RO 161 C8
Racovițeni RO 161 C9
Raczki PL 136 F6
Rączki PL 139 D9
Rád H 150 B3
Råda S 91 C13
Råda S 97 B9
Råda S 97 B10
Rada de Haro E 47 E7
Radalj SRB 158 E3
Radanovo BG 166 C5
Rădășeni RO 153 C8
Rădăuți RO 153 B7
Rădăuți-Prut RO 153 A9
Raddestorf D 17 D11
Raddi in Chianti I 66 F3
Raddusa I 59 E6
Radë AL 168 B2
Rade N 95 D13
Radeberg D 80 D5
Radebeul D 80 D5
Radeburg D 80 D5
Radeče SLO 73 D11
Radęcin PL 85 D9
Radefeld D 79 D11
Radegast D 79 C11
Rådelsbråten S 102 E3
Radenci SLO 148 C6
Rădeni MD 153 C12
Radensleben D 84 E3
Radenthein A 73 C8
Rădești RO 152 E3
Radevormwald D 21 B8
Radibor D 80 D6
Radići BIH 157 C7
Radicofani I 62 B1
Radicondoli I 66 F3
Radilovo BG 165 E9
Radiměř CZ 77 C10
Radiovce NMK 163 F10
Radis D 79 C12
Radizelj SLO 148 D5
Radko Dimitrievo BG 167 C8
Radków PL 77 A10
Radlje ob Dravi SLO 73 C11
Radłów PL 142 E6
Radłów PL 143 F10
Radnejaur S 109 E15
Radnevo BG 166 E5
Radnice CZ 76 C5
Rădoaia MD 153 B12
Radoč BIH 157 F8
Radohova BIH 157 D8
Rădoiești RO 160 E6
Radojevo SRB 150 F6
Radolfzell am Bodensee D 27 E10
Radom PL 141 H4
Rådom S 107 E11
Radomin PL 139 D7
Radomir BG 165 D6
Radomirești RO 160 E5
Radomirtsi BG 165 C9
Radomsko PL 143 D7
Radomyšl CZ 76 D5
Radomyśl nad Sanem PL 144 B4
Radomyśl Wielki PL 143 F11
Radonice CZ 76 B4
Radopole LV 133 C1
Radošina SK 146 D5
Radošovce SK 146 D4
Radoszyce PL 143 D9
Radoszyn PL 81 B8
Radovan RO 160 E3
Radovanu RO 161 E9
Radovets BG 167 F6
Radovići MNE 163 E6
Radoviš NMK 169 A7
Radovljica SLO 73 D9
Radovnica SRB 164 E5
Radowo Małe PL 85 C8
Radožda NMK 168 B4
Radslavice CZ 146 C5
Radstadt A 73 B7
Radstock GB 13 C10
Răducăneni RO 153 D11
Radučic HR 156 D5
Raduil BG 165 E8
Radujevac SRB 159 E10
Radun' BY 137 E10
Radvanice CZ 81 E10
Radvaň nad Laborcom SK 145 E4
Radviliškis LT 134 E7
Radwanice PL 81 C9
Radymno PL 144 D6
Radzanów PL 139 E9
Radzanów PL 141 G3
Radzanowo PL 139 E8
Radzice Duże PL 141 H2
Radzicz PL 85 D12
Radzieje PL 136 E4
Radziejów PL 138 E6
Radziejowice PL 141 F3
Radziemice PL 143 F9
Radzików PL 81 B7
Radziłów PL 140 D6
Radzymin PL 139 F11
Radzyń Chełminski PL 138 D6
Radzyń Podlaski PL 141 G7
Rær DK 86 A3
Rækker Mølle DK 86 C3
Raeren B 20 C6
Raesfeld D 17 E7
Rafelbunyol E 48 E4
Raffadali I 58 E4
Rafford GB 3 K9
Rafina GR 175 C9
Råforsen S 97 B10
Răfov RO 161 D8
Rafsbotn N 113 C12
Raften N 110 D9
Raftsjöhöjden S 106 D8
Ragaciems LV 134 B6
Ragama E 45 C10
Ragana LV 135 B9
Rageliai LT 135 E11
Rägelin D 83 D13
Raglan GB 13 B9
Råglanda S 91 A13
Ragösen D 79 B12
Raguhn D 79 C11
Ragunda S 107 E10
Ragunda S 107 E10
Ragusa I 59 F6
Raguva LT 135 E9
Rahden D 17 D11
Rahkio FIN 127 D8
Rahkonen FIN 123 C12
Rahman RO 155 D2
Råholt N 95 B14
Rahovec RKS 163 E10
Rahumäe EST 132 E1
Raiano I 62 C5
Raikuu FIN 125 F12
Räimä FIN 124 D9
Rain D 75 E8
Rain D 75 E11
Rainbach im Mühlkreis A 77 E6
Raippo FIN 129 D9
Räisälä FIN 115 E3
Raisdorf D 83 B8
Raisio FIN 126 E7
Raiskio FIN 119 C16
Raiskio FIN 125 B12
Raismes F 19 D7
Raistakka FIN 121 B11
Rait GB 5 C10
Raitajärvi S 119 B10
Raja EST 131 D13
Raja-Jooseppi FIN 115 B4
Rajala FIN 117 C16
Rajamäki FIN 127 D12
Rajastrand S 106 B8
Rajcza PL 147 B8
Rájec CZ 77 D11
Rajec SK 147 C7
Rajecká Lesná SK 147 C7
Rajgród PL 140 C7
Rajhrad CZ 77 D11
Rajince SRB 164 E4
Rajka H 146 E4
Raka EST 131 C9
Raka SLO 148 E4
Rakamaz H 145 G3
Rakek SLO 73 E9
Rakevo BG 165 C7
Rakhiv UA 152 A4
Rakh'ya RUS 129 E14
Rakita BG 165 C9
Rakita BG 165 D6
Rakitna SLO 73 E9
Rakitovec SLO 67 B8
Rakitovo BG 165 F9
Rakke EST 131 D12
Rakkeby DK 90 E6
Rakkestad N 95 D14
Raklitsa BG 167 D7
Rákóczifalva H 150 C5
Rákócziújfalu H 150 C5
Rakoniewice PL 81 B10
Rakoshyn UA 145 G6
Rakova Bara SRB 159 D8
Rakovica HR 156 C4
Rakovinë RKS 163 E10
Rakovitsa BG 159 F9
Rakovník CZ 76 B5
Rakovo BG 165 E6
Rakovski BG 165 E10
Rakow D 84 B4
Raków PL 143 E11
Rakvere EST 131 C12
Ralingen D 21 E7
Ralja SRB 158 D6
Rälla S 89 B11
Ram SRB 159 D7
Ramacca I 59 E6
Rämälä FIN 123 E12
Ramales de la Victoria E 40 B5
Ramalhal P 44 F2
Ramatuelle F 36 E5
Ramberg N 110 D5
Rambervillers F 26 D6
Rambin D 84 B4
Rambouillet F 24 C6
Rambrouch L 19 E12
Rambucourt F 26 C4
Ramelton IRL 7 B7
Râmeț RO 152 E3
Ramillies B 182 D5
Ramingstein A 73 B8
Ramirás E 38 D4
Ramløse DK 87 C10
Rämma S 102 D6
Ramme DK 86 C2
Rammelsbach D 186 B3
Rammingen D 75 E7
Râmna RO 159 C8
Ramnäs S 98 C6
Ramnes N 95 D12
Râmnicelu RO 161 C10
Râmnicelu RO 161 C11
Râmnicu Sărat RO 161 C10
Râmnicu Vâlcea RO 160 C4
Ramonville-St-Agne F 33 C8
Ramosch CH 71 D10
Rämpsänkylä FIN 121 F13
Rampside GB 10 C5
Ramså N 111 B11
Ramsau im Zillertal A 72 B4
Ramsberg S 97 C13
Ramsbottom GB 11 D7
Ramsele S 107 C17
Ramsele S 107 D10
Ramsen CH 27 E10
Ramsey GB 15 C8
Ramsey GBM 10 C3
Ramsey St Mary's GB 15 C8
Ramsgate GB 15 E11
Ramsi EST 131 E11
Ramsing DK 86 B3
Ramsjö S 103 B10
Ramsloh (Saterland) D 17 B9
Ramstadlandet N 105 B10
Ramstein D 21 F9
Ramsund N 111 D12
Ramučiai LT 134 F3
Ramundberget S 102 A3
Ramvik S 103 A14
Ramygala LT 135 E8
Råna N 111 D13
Rånäs S 99 C10
Rånäs S 102 C5
Rånåsfoss N 95 B14
Rance B 19 D9
Randaberg N 94 E3
Randalstown GB 4 F4
Randan F 30 C3
Randaträsk S 118 B6
Randazzo I 59 D6
Rånddalen S 102 B5
Randegg A 77 F7
Randen N 101 C9
Randen N 101 E8
Randers DK 86 C6
Randersacker D 187 B8
Randijaur S 109 C17
Randonnai F 24 C4
Randsjö S 102 B6
Randsverk N 101 C10
Råne N 111 E11
Råneå S 118 C8
Rânes F 23 C11
Rångedala S 91 D13
Rangendingen D 187 E6
Rangersdorf A 73 C6
Rangsby FIN 122 E6
Rangsdorf D 80 B4
Ranhados P 44 C5
Ranilović SRB 158 E6
Ranis D 79 E10
Ranizów PL 144 C4
Ranka LV 135 B12
Ranķi LV 134 C3
Rankinen FIN 119 F14
Rankweil A 71 C9
Ranna EST 131 D14
Rannankylä FIN 123 C15
Rannankylä FIN 123 C16
Rannapungerja EST 131 D14
Rannaväg S 91 D13
Rännelslöv S 87 C12
Rännö S 103 B12
Rannsundet S 102 B5
Rannu EST 131 E12
Ranovac SRB 159 E7
Ransbach-Baumbach D 21 D9
Ransberg S 92 C4
Ransby S 102 E4
Ranskill GB 11 E9
Ranst B 182 C5
Ransta S 98 C7
Ranta FIN 113 F19
Rantajärvi S 117 E11
Rantakangas FIN 123 E11
Rantasalmen asema FIN 125 F10
Rantasalmi FIN 125 F10
Ranta-Töysä FIN 123 E11
Ranten A 73 B9
Rantsila FIN 119 E15
Ranttila FIN 113 E16
Rantum D 82 A4
Rantzausminde DK 86 E7
Ranua FIN 119 C17
Ranum DK 86 B4
Rånvassbotn N 111 D13
Ranxë AL 163 F8
Raon-l'Étape F 27 D6
Raossi I 69 B11
Rapakkojoki FIN 123 C17
Rapallo I 37 C10
Raphoe IRL 4 F1
Rapice PL 81 B7
Räpina EST 132 E1
Rapla EST 131 D9
Rapolano Terme I 66 F4
Rapolla I 60 B5
Rapoltu Mare RO 151 F11
Raposa P 44 F3
Raposeira P 50 E2
Rapotín CZ 77 B12
Rapoula do Côa P 45 D6
Rapperswil CH 27 F10
Räpplinge S 89 B11
Rapsani GR 169 E8
Raron CH 68 A4
Raša HR 67 B9
Räsälä FIN 125 E9
Rasanovci BIH 156 D5
Râșca RO 153 C8
Rascafría E 46 C5
Rascăieți MD 154 D5
Raschau D 75 A12
Rașcov MD 154 B3
Rasdorf D 78 E6
Raseiniai LT 134 F6
Råsele S 107 C11
Rasen N 96 A6
Rasharkin GB 4 F4
Rašica SLO 73 E10
Rasina EST 131 E14
Rășinari RO 160 B4
Rasines E 40 B5
Rasinja HR 149 D7
Rasinkylä FIN 121 E10
Rasinvaara FIN 121 D14
Rasivaara FIN 125 F13
Råsjö S 103 B10
Raška SRB 163 C10
Rask Mølle DK 86 D5
Raškovice CZ 146 B6
Raslavice SK 145 E3
Răsmirești RO 161 F7
Rasno SRB 163 C9
Râșnov RO 161 B6
Rasony BY 133 E5
Rasova RO 155 E1
Rasovo BG 159 F11
Raspenava CZ 81 E8
Rasquera E 42 E5
Rast RO 160 F2
Raštani BIH 157 F8
Rastatt D 27 C9
Rastdorf D 17 C9
Rasteby N 111 B19
Råsted DK 86 B5
Rastede D 17 B10
Rastenfeld A 77 E8
Raštević HR 156 D4
Rasti FIN 117 C14
Rasti FIN 125 G13
Rastinkylä FIN 125 C13
Răstolița RO 152 D5
Rastošnica BIH 157 C10
Rastovac MNE 163 D6
Rastow D 83 D10
Råstrand S 107 A14
Răsuceni RO 161 E7
Rasueros E 45 B10
Rasvåg N 94 F5
Raszków PL 142 C4
Raszyn PL 141 F3
Rataje SRB 164 C3
Rätan S 102 B8
Ratan S 122 C5
Rätansbyn S 102 B8
Ratasjärvi FIN 117 E11
Ratasvuoma FIN 119 B12
Rateče SLO 73 C8
Ratekau D 83 C9
Rătești RO 160 D6
Rathangan IRL 7 F9
Ráth Bhoth IRL 4 F1
Ráth Caola IRL 8 C5
Rathconrath IRL 7 E7
Rathcoole IRL 7 F10
Ráth Cúil IRL 7 F10
Ráth Domhnaigh IRL 9 C7
Rathdowney IRL 9 C7
Ráth Droma IRL 9 C10
Rathdrum IRL 9 C10
Rathenow D 79 A11
Rathfriland GB 7 D10
Rathgormuck IRL 9 D7
Ráth Iomgháin IRL 7 F9
Rathkeale IRL 8 C5
Rathkeevin IRL 9 D7
Rathlee IRL 6 D4
Rathluirc IRL 8 D5
Ráth Mealtain IRL 7 B7
Rathmolyon IRL 7 F9
Rathmore IRL 8 D4
Rathmullan IRL 4 E1
Ráth Naoi IRL 7 G10
Rathnew IRL 7 G10
Rathnure IRL 9 D9
Ratho GB 5 D10
Rathowen IRL 7 E7
Rathstock D 81 A7
Rathumney IRL 9 D9
Rathvilly IRL 9 C9
Ratiboř CZ 146 C5
Ratić BIH 158 D3
Ratingen D 17 F7
Ratíškovice CZ 77 E12
Rátka H 145 G3
Ratkoc RKS 163 E10
Ratkovo SRB 158 C3
Ratnieki LV 133 D2
Ratoath IRL 7 E10
Rattelsdorf D 75 B8
Ratten A 148 B5
Rattenberg A 72 B4
Rattosjärvi FIN 117 E13
Rattray GB 5 B10
Rättsel S 118 C3
Rättvik S 103 E9
Ratvika N 104 D8
Ratzeburg D 83 C9
Rätzlingen D 79 B9
Raubach D 185 C8
Rauda LV 135 E12
Raudåna N 90 B4
Raudanjoki FIN 117 D16
Raudaskylä FIN 123 B13
Raudasmäki FIN 123 B13
Raudeberg N 100 C2
Râu de Mori RO 159 C10
Raudėnai LT 134 D5
Raudondvaris LT 137 D8
Raudonė LT 136 C7
Rauen D 80 B6
Raufoss N 101 E13
Rauha FIN 129 C10
Rauhala FIN 117 C12
Raulhac F 29 F11
Rauma FIN 126 C6
Rauna LV 135 B11
Raunds GB 15 C7
Rauris A 73 B6
Râu Sadului RO 160 B4
Rauschenberg D 21 C11
Raussila FIN 128 D6
Rautajärvi FIN 127 C12
Rautalampi FIN 124 E7
Rautaperä FIN 114 E4
Rautas S 111 D18
Rautavaara FIN 125 C10
Rautenkranz D 75 B11
Rautila FIN 119 F11
Rautila FIN 126 D6
Rautio FIN 120 F3
Rautionmäki FIN 123 E16
Rautjärven kk FIN 129 C11
Rautjärvi FIN 129 C11
Rautuskylä FIN 117 C13
Rauvanniemi FIN 129 B11
Rauzan F 28 F5
Ravadinovo BG 167 E9
Ravanusa I 58 E4
Rava-Rus'ka UA 144 C8
Ravasd H 149 A9
Ravča HR 157 F7
Ravda BG 167 D9
Ravels B 16 F3

Ravelsbach A 77 E9
Rävemåla S 89 B8
Ravenglass GB 10 C5
Ravenna I 66 D5
Ravensburg D 71 B9
Ravenstein NL 16 E5
Ravières F 25 E11
Ravijoki FIN 128 D8
Ravik N 108 B7
Rävlanda S 91 D12
Ravna Dubrava SRB 164 C5
Ravna Gora HR 67 B10
Ravna Reka SRB 159 E8
Ravne SLO 73 D11
Ravne na Koroškem SLO 73 C10
Ravnets BG 167 D8
Ravni BIH 157 F8
Ravnište SRB 164 C3
Ravnje SRB 158 D3
Ravnkilde DK 86 B5
Ravno BIH 157 E7
Ravno BIH 162 D4
Ravnogor BG 165 F9
Ravno Selo SRB 158 C4
Ravnshøj DK 90 E7
Ravnstrup DK 86 C4
Råvsön S 103 A15
Ravsted DK 86 E4
Rawa Mazowiecka PL 141 G2
Rawicz PL 81 C11
Rawmarsh GB 11 E9
Rawtenstall GB 11 D7
Raykovo BG 171 A7
Rayleigh GB 15 D10
Rayol-Canadel-sur-Mer F 36 E4
Räyrinki FIN 123 D11
Ražana SRB 158 E4
Ražanac HR 156 D3
Ražanj SRB 159 F8
Războieni RO 153 C9
Razboj BIH 157 B7
Razbojna SRB 164 C3
Razdelna BG 167 C9
Razdol BG 169 A9
Razdrto SLO 73 E9
Razès F 29 C8
Razgrad BG 160 F2
Razgrad BG 167 B7
Ražljevo BIH 157 C10
Razlog BG 165 F7
Razlovci NMK 165 F6
Ražňany SK 145 E3
Ráztočno SK 147 D7
Răzvad RO 161 D6
Reading GB 14 E7
Reaghstown IRL 7 E9
Real P 38 F3
Réalmont F 33 C10
Realmonte I 58 E3
Réalville F 33 B8
Rear Cross IRL 8 C6
Réaup F 33 B6
Reay GB 3 H9
Rebais F 25 C9
Rebbenesbotn N 112 C2
Rebecq B 19 C9
Rébénacq F 32 D5
Rebild DK 86 B5
Rebollosa de Jadraque E 47 B7
Reboly RUS 125 C15
Rebordelo E 38 B3
Rebordelo P 38 E5
Rebra RO 152 C4
Rebricea RO 153 D11
Rebrișoara RO 152 C4
Rebrovo BG 165 D7
Rebŭrkovo BG 165 C8
Reca SK 146 E4
Reçan RKS 163 E10
Recanati I 67 F8
Recaș RO 151 F8
Recco I 37 C10
Recea MD 153 B11
Recea MD 154 C3
Recea RO 151 B12
Recea RO 152 F5
Recea RO 160 D6
Recea-Cristur RO 152 C3
Recess IRL 6 F3
Recey-sur-Ource F 25 E12
Réchicourt-le-Château F 27 C6
Rechlin D 83 D13
Rechnitz A 149 B6
Recht B 20 D6
Rechtenbach D 74 C6
Reci RO 153 F7
Rečica SLO 73 D11
Rečice BIH 157 F8
Recke D 17 D9
Reckingen CH 70 E6
Recklinghausen D 17 E8
Recoaro Terme I 69 B11
Recoubeau-Jansac F 35 A9
Recsk H 147 F10
Recuerda E 40 F6
Recz PL 85 D9
Rjczno PL 141 H1
Reda PL 138 A5
Redalen N 101 E13
Redange L 20 E5
Redcar GB 11 B9
Redcastle IRL 4 E2
Redcross IRL 9 C10
Reddelich D 83 B11
Redditch GB 13 A11
Réde H 149 B9
Redea RO 160 E4
Redefin D 83 D10
Redhill GB 15 E8
Rédics H 149 C6
Réding F 27 C7
Redinha P 44 D3
Rediu RO 153 C11
Rediu RO 153 D9
Rediu RO 153 F11
Rediul Mare MD 153 A11
Rednitzhembach D 75 D9
Redon F 23 E7
Redondela E 38 D2
Redondelo P 38 E4
Redondo P 50 B4
Redován E 56 E3
Red Point GB 2 K5
Redruth GB 12 E4
Redsted DK 86 B3
Reduzum NL 16 B5
Rjdzikowo PL 85 B12
Rjdziny PL 143 E7
Reen IRL 8 E3
Reens IRL 8 C5
Reepham GB 15 B11
Rees D 16 E6
Reeßum D 17 B12
Reetz D 79 B11
Reetz D 83 D11
Reftele S 87 A13
Regalbuto I 59 D6
Regen D 76 E4
Regensburg D 75 D11
Regensdorf CH 27 F9
Regenstauf D 75 D11
Reggello I 66 E4
Reggio di Calabria I 59 C8
Reggiolo I 66 C2
Reggio nell'Emilia I 66 C2
Reghin RO 152 D5
Reghiu RO 153 F9
Regna S 92 B7
Regnitzlosau D 75 B11
Régny F 30 D5
Regöly H 149 C10
Regozero RUS 121 D17
Regstrup DK 87 D9
Reguengo E 38 D2
Reguengos de Monsaraz P 50 C4
Rehau D 75 B11
Rehburg (Rehburg-Loccum) D 17 D12
Rehden D 17 C10
Rehling D 75 F8
Rehlingen-Siersburg D 21 F7
Řehlovice CZ 80 E5
Rehmsdorf D 79 D11
Rehna D 83 C10
Rehula FIN 129 C9
Reibitz D 79 C11
Reichelsheim (Odenwald) D 187 B6
Reichenau an der Rax A 148 A5
Reichenbach CH 70 D5
Reichenbach D 79 E11
Reichenbach D 187 B6
Reichenberg D 74 C6
Reichenfels A 73 B10
Reichenthal A 76 E6
Reichertsheim D 75 F11
Reichia GR 178 B5
Reichling D 71 B11
Reichmannsdorf D 75 A9
Reicholzheim D 74 C6
Reichraming A 73 A9
Reichshoffen F 27 C8
Reichstett F 186 D4
Reiden CH 27 F8
Reigada P 45 C7
Reigate GB 15 E8
Reignac F 28 E4
Reignier F 31 C9
Reil D 21 D8
Reilingen D 187 C6
Reillanne F 35 C10
Reillo E 47 E9
Reims F 19 F9
Reina E 51 C8
Reinach CH 27 F8
Reinach CH 27 F9
Reinbek D 83 C8
Reinberg D 84 B4
Reine N 110 E5
Reinfeld (Holstein) D 83 C8
Reinheim D 21 E11
Reinosa E 40 C3
Reinøysund N 114 D8
Reinsfeld D 21 E7
Reinskard N 112 D4
Reinskloster N 104 D7
Reinstad N 111 C10
Reinsvik N 104 E3
Reinsvoll N 101 E13
Reipa N 108 C6
Reisbach D 75 E12
Reischach D 75 F12
Reisjärvi FIN 123 C13
Reiskirchen D 21 C11
Reiss GB 3 J10
Reitan N 100 B8
Reitan N 101 A14
Reitano I 58 D5
Reith bei Seefeld A 72 B3
Reit im Winkl D 72 A5
Reittiö FIN 125 D9
Reivyčiai LT 134 D4
Rejmyre S 92 B7
Rejowiec PL 141 H8
Rejsby DK 86 E3
Reka HR 149 D7
Rekava LV 133 B3
Rekavice BIH 157 C7
Reken D 17 E8
Rekijoki FIN 127 E9
Rekken NL 17 D7
Reklynets' UA 144 C9
Rekovac SRB 159 F7
Rekowo PL 85 B12
Rekvik N 111 A15
Rėkyva LT 134 E6
Relíquias P 50 D3
Relletti FIN 119 E13
Relleu E 56 D4
Rellingen D 83 C7
Rém H 150 E3
Remagen D 21 C8
Rémalard F 24 D4
Rembercourt-Sommaisne F 26 C3
Remda D 79 E9
Remels (Uplengen) D 17 B9
Remennikovo RUS 133 C5
Remeskylä FIN 123 C16
Remetea RO 151 D9
Remetea RO 152 D6
Remetea Chioarului RO 152 B3
Remetea Mare RO 151 F7
Remeți RO 145 H8
Remetinec HR 149 D6
Remetské Hámre SK 145 F5
Remich L 20 E6
Remicourt B 183 D6
Remiremont F 26 D6
Remmam S 107 D14
Remmen S 102 B8
Remmet S 102 B7
Remnes N 108 E4
Remolinos E 41 E9
Remouchamps B 183 E7
Remoulins F 35 C8
Remplin D 83 C13
Remptendorf D 75 A10
Remscheid D 21 B8
Remte LV 134 C5
Remungol F 22 E6
Rémuzat F 35 B9
Rena E 45 F9
Rena N 101 D14
Renaison F 30 C4
Renålandet S 106 D8
Renazé F 23 E9
Renceni LV 131 F10
Renchen D 27 C9
Renda LV 134 B4
Rende I 60 E6
Rendsburg D 82 B7
Renedo E 39 E10
Renedo E 40 B4
Renedo de la Vega E 39 D10
Renens CH 31 B10
Renesse NL 16 E1
Renfrew GB 5 D8
Renginio GR 175 B6
Rengsdorf D 21 C8
Rengsjö S 103 D12
Renholmen S 118 D6
Reni UA 155 C2
Renko FIN 127 D11
Renkomäki FIN 127 D14
Renkum NL 183 B7
Renndal N 104 E5
Rennerod D 21 C10
Rennertshofen D 75 E9
Rennes F 23 D8
Rennes-les-Bains F 33 E10
Renningen D 27 C10
Rennweg A 73 B8
Renòn I 72 C3
Rens DK 86 F4
Rensjön S 111 D18
Reńska Wieś PL 142 F5
Renström S 118 E4
Renswoude NL 183 A7
Rentina GR 174 A4
Rentjärn S 107 A15
Rentweinsdorf D 75 B8
Renwez F 19 E10
Renzow D 83 C10
Repbäcken S 97 A13
Répcelak H 149 B8
Repedea RO 152 B4
Repino RUS 129 E12
Repki PL 141 F6
Replot FIN 122 D6
Repojoki FIN 117 B15
Repolka RUS 132 C6
Reposaari FIN 126 B5
Repparfjord N 113 C13
Reppelin D 83 B12
Reppen N 108 C6
Reppenstedt D 83 D8
Reps AL 163 F9
Repton GB 11 F8
Repvåg N 113 B16
Requejo E 39 D6
Requena E 47 F10
Réquista F 33 B11
Rerik D 83 B11
Resana I 72 E4
Resarö S 99 D10
Resavica SRB 159 E8
Resele S 107 E12
Resen BG 166 C5
Resen NMK 168 B5
Resenbro DK 86 C5
Resende P 44 B5
Rešetari HR 157 B7
Reșița RO 159 C8
Resko PL 85 C8
Resna MNE 163 E6
Resolven GB 13 B7
Respenda de la Peña E 39 C10
Resse (Wedemark) D 78 A6
Ressons-sur-Matz F 18 E6
Restelicë RKS 163 F10
Restinga MA 53 E6
Reston GB 5 D12
Resuttano I 58 D5
Retamal E 51 B8
Retford GB 11 E10
Rethel F 19 E9
Rethem (Aller) D 17 C12
Rethymno GR 178 E7
Retie B 16 F4
Retiers F 23 E9
Retje SLO 73 E10
Retortillo E 45 C8
Retortillo de Soria E 40 F6
Retournac F 30 E5
Rétság H 147 F8
Retuerta del Bullaque E 46 F4
Retunen FIN 125 E11
Retz A 77 E9
Reuden D 79 B11
Reuilly F 24 F7
Reurieth D 75 B8
Reus E 42 E6
Reusel NL 16 F4
Reut D 76 F3
Reute D 27 D8
Reuțel MD 153 B11
Reuterstadt Stavenhagen D 84 C3
Reutlingen D 27 D11
Reutte A 71 C11
Reutuaapa FIN 119 B15
Reuver NL 16 F6
Revel F 33 D10
Revello I 37 B6
Revest-du-Bion F 35 B10
Révfülöp H 149 C9
Revholmen N 91 A8
Reviga RO 161 D10
Revigny-sur-Ornain F 26 C2
Revilla de Collazos E 40 C3
Revilla del Campo E 40 D4
Revin F 19 E10
Revine-Lago I 72 E5
Řevnice CZ 76 C6
Řevničov CZ 76 B5
Revò I 72 D3
Revonlahti FIN 119 E13
Revsnes N 100 D6
Revsnes N 111 C11
Revsund S 103 A9
Revúca SK 147 D10
Rewal PL 85 B8
Rexbo S 103 E9
Reyrieux F 30 D6
Rezé F 23 F8
Rēzekne LV 133 C2
Rezi H 149 C8
Rezina MD 154 B3
Rēzna LV 133 D2
Rezovo BG 167 F10
Rezzato I 66 A1
Rezzo I 37 C7
Rezzoaglio I 37 B10
Rgotina SRB 159 E9
Rhade D 17 B12
Rhaunen D 21 E8
Rhayader GB 13 A7
Rheda-Wiedenbrück D 17 E10
Rhede D 17 E7
Rhede (Ems) D 17 B8
Rheden NL 183 A8
Rheinau D 27 C8
Rheinbach D 21 C7
Rheinberg D 17 E7
Rheinböllen D 185 E8
Rheinbreitbach D 21 C8
Rheinbrohl D 185 D7
Rheine D 17 D8
Rheinfelden (Baden) D 27 E8
Rheinsberg D 84 D3
Rheinstetten D 27 C9
Rheinzabern D 187 C5
Rhêmes-Notre-Dame I 31 D11
Rhêmes-St-Georges I 31 D11
Rhenen NL 16 E5
Rhens D 185 D8
Rhiconich GB 2 J7
Rhinau F 27 D8
Rhinow D 83 E12
Rhisnes B 182 D5
Rho I 69 B7
Rhode IRL 7 F8
Rhoden (Diemelstadt) D 17 F12
Rhoon NL 182 B4
Rhoose GB 13 C8
Rhosllanerchrugog GB 10 E5
Rhôs-on-Sea GB 10 E4
Rhossili GB 12 B6
Rhuddlan GB 10 E5
Rhydaman GB 12 B7
Rhyl GB 10 E5
Rhymney GB 13 B8
Riace I 59 C9
Riachos P 44 F3
Riaillé F 23 E9
Rialp E 33 F8
Riaño E 39 C10
Riano I 62 C3
Rians F 35 C10
Riantec F 22 E5
Rianxo E 38 C2
Riaz CH 31 B11
Riba E 40 B4
Ribadavia E 38 D3
Ribadelago E 39 D6
Riba de Mouro P 38 D3
Ribadeo E 38 A5
Riba de Saelices E 47 C8
Ribadesella E 39 B9
Ribaforada E 41 D8
Ribafrecha E 32 F1
Ribarci SRB 164 E6
Ribare SRB 164 C4
Ribari SRB 158 D3
Ribaritsa BG 165 D9
Riba-roja d'Ebre E 42 E4
Riba-roja de Turia E 48 E3
Ribbåsen S 102 D7
Ribchester GB 10 D6
Ribe DK 86 E3
Ribeauvillé F 27 D7
Ribécourt-Dreslincourt F 18 E6
Ribeira E 38 C2
Ribeira P 38 E3
Ribeira de Pena P 38 E4
Ribemont F 19 E7
Ribera I 58 E3
Ribérac F 29 E6
Ribera del Fresno E 51 B7
Ribesalbes E 48 D4
Ribes de Freser E 33 F10
Ribița RO 151 E10
Ribnica BIH 157 D9
Ribnica SLO 73 E10
Ribnica SLO 148 C4
Ribnica SRB 158 F4
Ribnik HR 148 E4
Rîbnița MD 154 B4
Ribnitz-Damgarten D 83 B12
Ribnovo BG 165 F8
Ribota E 40 F5
Ricadi I 59 B8
Říčany CZ 77 C7
Říčany CZ 77 D10
Riccia I 63 E7
Riccio I 66 F5
Riccione I 66 D6
Riccò del Golfo di Spezia I 69 E8
Richardménil F 26 C5
Richelieu F 29 A6
Richhill GB 7 D9
Richka UA 152 A5
Richmond GB 11 C8
Richvald SK 145 E3
Rickebo S 103 D11
Rickenbach D 27 E8
Rickinghall GB 15 C10
Rickling D 83 B8
Rickmansworth GB 15 D8
Ricla E 41 E9
Ricse H 145 G4
Ridasjärvi FIN 127 D13
Riddarhyttan S 97 C14
Ridderkerk NL 16 E3
Riddes CH 31 C11
Riđica SRB 150 F3
Rīdzene LV 135 B10
Riebiņi LV 135 D13
Riebnesluspen S 109 D13
Riec-sur-Belon F 22 E4
Ried CH 68 A5
Riede D 17 C11
Riedenburg D 75 E10
Rieder D 79 C9
Ried im Innkreis A 76 F4
Ried im Oberinntal A 71 C11
Ried im Zillertal A 72 B4
Ried in der Riedmark A 77 F7
Riedlingen D 71 A8
Riegelsberg D 21 F7
Riegersburg A 148 B5
Riego de la Vega E 39 D8
Riehe (Suthfeld) D 78 B5
Riehen CH 27 E8
Rielasingen-Worblingen D 27 E10
Riello E 39 C8
Rielves E 46 E4
Riemst B 19 C12
Rieneck D 187 A8
Rieni RO 151 D9
Rieponlahti FIN 124 E7
Riepsdorf D 83 B9
Riesa D 80 D4
Rieseby D 83 A7
Riesi I 58 E5
Riestedt D 79 D9
Rietavas LT 134 E3
Rietberg D 17 E10
Rieth D 84 C6
Riethoven NL 183 C6
Rieti I 62 C3
Rietschen D 81 D7
Rieumes F 33 D8
Rieupeyroux F 33 B10
Rieutort-de-Randon F 34 A5
Rieux F 23 E7
Rieux F 33 D8
Riez F 36 D4
Rifiano I 72 C3
Rīga LV 135 C8
Rigaio GR 169 F8
Rigaud F 36 D5
Riggisberg CH 31 B11
Rignac F 33 B10
Rignano Flaminio I 62 C2
Rignano Garganico I 63 D9
Rignano sull'Arno I 66 E3
Rigny-le-Ferron F 25 D10
Rigny-sur-Arroux F 30 B5
Rigny-Ussé F 24 F3
Rigside GB 5 D9
Rihtniemi FIN 126 C5
Riihimäki FIN 127 D12
Riihivaara FIN 125 C14
Riikonkumpu FIN 117 C14
Riipi FIN 117 D16
Riippi FIN 122 F7
Riisipere EST 131 C8
Riistavesi FIN 125 E10
Riitiala FIN 127 B8
Riječa BIH 157 E10
Rijeka BIH 157 D9
Rijeka BIH 157 F11
Rijeka HR 67 B9
Rijeka Crnojevića MNE 163 E7
Rijen NL 16 E3
Rijkevorsel B 16 F3
Rijnsburg NL 16 D2
Rijsbergen NL 16 E3
Rijsel F 19 C7
Rijssen NL 17 D7
Rijswijk NL 16 D2
Rikava LV 133 C2
Riksgränsen S 111 D15
Rila BG 165 E7
Rilhac-Rancon F 29 D8
Rilland NL 182 C4
Rillé F 23 F12
Rillieux-la-Pape F 30 D6
Rillo E 42 F2
Rillo de Gallo E 47 C9
Rimavská Baňa SK 147 D9
Rimavská Seč SK 145 G1
Rimavská Sobota SK 147 E10
Rimavské Janovce SK 147 E10
Rimbach D 76 D3
Rimbach D 187 B6
Rimbo S 99 C10
Rimetea RO 152 E3
Rimforsa S 92 C7
Rimicāni LV 135 D12
Rimini I 66 D6
Rimjokk S 118 B5
Rimmilä FIN 127 D11
Rimóc H 147 E9
Rimogne F 184 E2
Rimont F 33 E8
Rimpar D 74 C6
Rimsbo S 103 D11
Rimšė LT 135 E12
Rimšėnai LT 135 F12
Rimske Toplice SLO 73 D11
Rimsting D 72 A5
Rinchnach D 76 E4
Rincón de la Victoria E 53 C8
Rincón de Soto E 41 D8
Rinda LV 134 A3
Rindal N 104 E6
Rindsholm DK 86 C4
Rineia GR 176 E5
Rinella I 59 B6
Ringarum S 93 C8
Ringaudai LT 137 D8
Ringe D 17 C7
Ringe DK 86 E6
Ringebu N 101 C12
Ringelia N 101 E12
Ringen N 95 B12
Ringford GB 5 F8
Ringhals S 87 A10
Ringkøbing DK 86 C2
Ringleben D 79 D9
Ringsend GB 4 E3
Ringsta S 106 E7
Ringsted DK 87 E9
Ringvattnet S 106 C8
Ringville IRL 9 D7
Ringwood GB 13 D11
Rinkaby S 88 D6
Rinkabyholm S 89 B10
Rinkenæs DK 86 F5
Rinkilä FIN 129 B10
Rinloan GB 5 A10
Rinn S 97 B9
Rinneen IRL 8 C4
Rinøyvåg N 111 D10
Rintala FIN 123 D10
Rinteln D 17 D12
Rio GR 174 C4
Rio Caldo P 38 E3
Rio de Mel P 44 C6
Rio de Moinhos P 50 B4
Rio de Moinhos P 50 C3
Rio de Moinhos P 50 D3
Rio de Onor P 39 E6
Rio di Pusteria I 72 C4
Riofrío E 46 C3
Riofrío de Aliste E 39 E7
Riogordo E 53 C8
Rioja E 55 F8
Riola Sardo I 64 D2
Riolobos E 45 E8
Riolo Terme I 66 D4
Riols F 34 C4
Riom F 30 D3
Riomaggiore I 69 E8
Rio Maior P 44 F3
Rio Marina I 65 B2
Riom-ès-Montagnes F 29 E11
Rion-des-Landes F 32 C4
Rionegro del Puente E 39 D7
Rio nell'Elba I 65 B2
Rionero in Vulture I 60 B5
Rionero Sannitico I 63 D6
Rions F 32 A5
Riorges F 30 C5
Rios E 38 E5
Rioseco de Tapia E 39 C8
Rio Tinto P 44 B3
Rio Torto P 38 E5
Rioz F 26 F5
Ripač BIH 156 C4
Ripacandida I 60 B5
Ripalimosano I 63 D7
Ripanj SRB 158 D6
Riparbella I 66 F2
Ripatransone I 62 B5
Ripe I 67 E7
Ripi I 62 D4
Ripiceni RO 153 B10
Ripley GB 11 C8
Ripley GB 11 E9
Ripoll E 43 C8
Ripon GB 11 C8
Riposto I 59 D7
Rips NL 183 B7
Riquewihr F 27 D7
Risan MNE 163 D6
Risarven S 103 C10
Risbäck S 106 B9
Risberg S 102 D6
Risca GB 13 B8
Rișca RO 151 D11
Rîșcani MD 153 B11
Riscle F 32 C5
Risdal N 90 B3
Risede S 106 C8
Rish BG 167 D7
Risinge S 92 B7
Risliden S 107 B16
Risnabben S 118 D3
Risnes N 94 E5
Risør N 90 B5
Risøyhamn N 111 C10
Rissa N 104 D7
Rissna S 106 E8
Rissnaben S 118 D4
Riste FIN 126 C7
Risteli FIN 125 B12
Risti EST 131 D8
Ristiina FIN 128 B7
Ristijärvi FIN 121 F11
Ristilä FIN 121 B11
Ristilampi FIN 117 E17
Ristinen FIN 124 D7
Ristinkylä FIN 125 E12
Ristioja FIN 117 E13
Ristonmännikkö FIN 117 D16
Ristråsk S 107 B12
Risudden S 119 B11
Risum-Lindholm D 82 A5
Rītausmas LV 135 D8
Rite LV 135 D10
Rīteri LV 135 C11
Ritini GR 169 D7
Ritola FIN 123 E11
Ritterhude D 17 B11
Rittersdorf D 185 D5
Rittersgrün D 75 B12
Riudarenes E 43 D9
Riudecols E 42 E5
Riudoms E 42 E6
Riutta FIN 123 C12
Riutula FIN 113 F18
Rīva LV 134 C2
Riva del Garda I 69 B10
Riva di Solto I 69 B9
Riva di Tures I 72 C5
Rivanazzano I 37 B10
Rivardo Ligure I 37 C9
Rivarolo Canavese I 68 C4
Rivarolo Mantovano I 66 B1
Rivas-Vaciamadrid E 46 D6
Rive-de-Gier F 30 D6
Rivedoux-Plage F 28 C3
Rivello I 60 C5
Riverchapel IRL 9 C10
Rivergaro I 37 B11
Rivero E 40 B3
Riverstown IRL 7 F7
Riverstown IRL 8 E6
Rivery F 18 E5
Rives F 31 E8
Rivesaltes F 34 E4
Rivière-sur-Tarn F 34 B5
Rivignano I 73 E7
Rivinperä FIN 119 F16
Rivodutri I 62 B3
Rivoli I 68 C4
Rivolta d'Adda I 69 C8
Rixensart B 19 C10
Rixheim F 27 E7
Rixö S 91 C9
Riza GR 175 C6
Rizes GR 174 E5
Rizia GR 171 A10
Rizomata GR 169 D7
Rizomylos GR 169 F8
Rizziconi I 59 C8
Rjånes N 100 B3
Rjukan N 95 C9
Rø DK 89 E7
Ro I 66 C4
Rö S 103 A14
Roa E 40 E4
Roa N 95 B13
Roade GB 15 C7
Roadside GB 3 H10
Roadside of Kinneff GB 5 B12
Roager DK 86 E3
Roaillan F 32 B5
Roald N 100 A4
Roan N 104 C8
Roanne F 30 C5
Roata de Jos RO 161 E7
Roath GB 13 C8
Röbäck S 122 C4
Robănești RO 160 E4
Robbio I 68 C6
Robeasca RO 161 C10
Robecco d'Oglio I 69 C9
Röbel D 83 D13
Robella I 68 C5
Robert-Espagne F 26 C3
Roberton GB 5 D9
Roberton GB 5 E11
Robertsfors S 118 F5
Robežnieki LV 133 E3
Robiac-Rochessadoule F 35 B7
Robilante I 37 C6
Robin Hood's Bay GB 11 C10
Robion F 35 C9
Robledo E 55 B8
Robledo de Chavela E 46 C4
Robledo del Mazo E 46 E3
Robledollano E 45 E9
Robles de la Valcueva E 39 C9
Robliza de Cojos E 45 C9
Robøle N 101 E11
Robregordo E 46 B5
Robres E 41 E11
Robres del Castillo E 32 F1
Roč HR 67 B9
Rocafort de Queralt E 43 E6
Rocamadour F 29 F9
Roca Vecchia I 61 C10
Roccabianca I 66 B1
Roccadaspide I 60 C4
Rocca d'Evandro I 60 A1
Rocca di Cambio I 62 C4
Rocca di Mezzo I 62 C5
Rocca di Neto I 61 E7
Rocca di Papa I 62 D3
Roccafranca I 69 C8
Roccagloriosa I 60 C4
Roccagorga I 62 D4
Rocca Grimalda I 37 B9
Rocca Imperiale I 61 C7
Roccalbegna I 65 B5
Roccalumera I 59 D7
Roccamandolfi I 63 D6
Rocca Massima I 62 D3
Roccamena I 58 D3
Roccamonfina I 60 A1
Roccamontepiano I 62 C6
Roccanova I 60 C6
Roccapalumba I 58 D4
Rocca Pia I 62 D5
Roccaraso I 62 D6
Rocca San Casciano I 66 D4
Rocca San Giovanni I 63 C6
Roccasecca I 62 D5
Roccasecca dei Volsci I 62 E4
Rocca Sinibalda I 62 C3
Roccastrada I 65 A4
Roccavione I 37 C6
Roccella Ionica I 59 C9
Rocchetta Sant'Antonio I 60 A4
Rochdale GB 11 D7
Roche GB 12 E5
Rochechouart F 29 D7
Rochefort B 19 D11
Rochefort F 28 D4
Rochefort-en-Terre F 23 E7
Rochefort-Montagne F 30 D2
Rochefort-sur-Nenon F 26 F4
Rochehaut B 184 E3
Roche-la-Molière F 30 E5
Rochemaure F 35 A8
Roches-Bettaincourt F 26 D3
Rocheservière F 28 B2
Rochester GB 5 E12
Rochester GB 15 E10
Rochetaillée F 26 E3
Rochford GB 15 D10
Rochfortbridge IRL 7 F8
Rochin F 19 C7
Rochlitz D 79 D12
Rociana del Condado E 51 E6
Ročinj SLO 73 D8
Rociu RO 160 D6
Rockanje NL 182 B4
Rockchapel IRL 8 D4
Rockcliffe GB 5 F9
Rockcorry IRL 7 D8
Rockenhausen D 21 E9
Rockesholm S 97 C12
Rockhammar S 97 C13
Rockhill IRL 8 D5
Rockingham GB 11 F10
Rockmills IRL 8 D6
Rockneby S 89 B10
Röcknitz D 79 D12
Rocourt-St-Martin F 25 B9
Rocroi F 19 E10
Roda de Bara E 43 E6
Roda de Ter E 43 D8
Rodalben D 21 F9
Rodaljice HR 156 D4
Rödåsel S 118 F3
Rodberg N 95 B9
Rødbergshamn N 111 B15
Rødby DK 83 A10
Rødbyhavn DK 83 A10
Rødding DK 86 B3
Rødding DK 86 C5
Rødding DK 86 E4
Rödeby S 89 C9
Rodeiro E 38 C4
Rødekro DK 86 E4
Rodel GB 2 K3
Rodellar E 32 F5
Rodelle F 34 A4
Roden NL 17 B6
Ródenas E 47 C10
Rodenkirchen (Stadland) D 17 B10
Rödental D 75 B9
Rodewald D 82 E6
Rodewisch D 75 A11
Rodez F 33 B11
Rodi Garganico I 63 D9
Roding D 75 D12
Rodingträsk S 107 C14
Rödjebro S 98 B8
Rødkærsbro DK 86 C4
Rodleben D 79 C11
Rødlia N 108 E7
Rödmyra S 103 C11
Rodna RO 152 C5
Rododafni GR 174 C5
Rodolivos GR 170 C5
Rödön S 105 E16
Rodopoli GR 169 B9
Rodopos GR 178 D6
Rodos GR 181 D8
Rødovre DK 87 D10
Rødsand N 111 B13
Rødsand N 114 D8
Rødseidet N 105 B11
Rödvattnet S 107 D13
Rødvig DK 87 E10
Roela EST 131 C13
Roermond NL 20 B5
Roeselare B 19 C7
Roești RO 160 D4
Roetgen D 20 C6
Röfors S 92 B5
Rofrano I 60 C4
Rogač HR 156 F5
Rogačica SRB 158 E4
Rogaška Slatina SLO 148 D5
Rogaszyce PL 142 D4
Rogate GB 15 E7
Rogatec SLO 148 D5
Rogatica BIH 157 E11
Rogätz D 79 B10
Roggel NL 16 F5
Roggenburg D 75 F7
Roggendorf D 83 C10
Roggentin D 84 D3
Roggiano Gravina I 60 D6
Roghudi I 59 C8
Rogienice Wielkie PL 139 D13
Rogil P 50 E2
Rogliano F 37 F10
Rogliano I 61 E6
Rognac F 35 D9

Rognan N 108 B9
Rognes F 35 C9
Rognes N 104 E8
Rognonas F 35 C8
Rogova RO 159 E10
Rogovë RKS 163 E10
Rogovka LV 133 C2
Rogów PL 141 G1
Rogowo PL 138 E4
Rogowo PL 139 E7
Rogozen BG 165 B8
Rogoznica HR 156 E4
Rogoźnica PL 81 D10
Rogoźniczka PL 141 F7
Rogoźno PL 85 E12
Rogslösa S 92 C5
Rogsta S 102 A8
Rogsta S 103 C13
Roguszyn PL 139 F12
Rohan F 22 D6
Röhlingen D 75 E7
Rohlsdorf D 83 D11
Rohlsdorf D 83 D12
Rohod H 145 G5
Rohovce SK 146 E4
Rohožník SK 77 F12
Rohr D 79 E8
Rohrau A 77 F11
Rohrbach D 75 E10
Rohrbach in Oberösterreich A 76 E5
Rohrbach-lès-Bitche F 27 B7
Rohrberg D 83 E10
Rohr in Niederbayern D 75 E10
Röhrmoos D 75 F9
Röhrnbach D 76 E5
Rohrsen D 17 C12
Rohuküla EST 130 D6
Roiffieux F 30 E6
Roisel F 19 E7
Roismala FIN 127 C8
Roivainen FIN 115 B2
Roiz E 40 B3
Roja LV 134 A5
Rojales E 56 E3
Röjan S 102 B7
Röjdåfors S 97 B8
Rojewo PL 138 E5
Rökå S 107 A15
Rokai LT 137 D8
Rokiciny PL 143 C8
Rokietnica PL 81 A11
Rokietnica PL 144 D6
Rokiškis LT 135 E11
Rokitno PL 141 F8
Rokkøy N 111 C10
Røkkum N 101 A8
Røkland N 108 C9
Roklum D 79 B8
Roknäs S 118 D6
Rokycany CZ 76 C5
Rokytnice CZ 146 C4
Rokytnice v Orlických Horách CZ 77 B10
Rolampont F 26 E3
Rold DK 86 B5
Røldal N 94 C5
Rolde NL 17 C7
Rolfs S 119 C10
Rolfstorp S 87 A10
Rollag N 95 B10
Rollán E 45 C9
Rolle CH 31 C9
Rolsted DK 86 E7
Rolvåg N 108 D3
Rolvsnes N 94 C2
Rolvsøy N 95 D14
Rom D 83 D11
Rom F 29 C6
Roma I 62 D3
Roma RO 153 B9
Roma S 93 D12
Romagnano Sesia I 68 B5
Romagné F 23 D9
Romainmôtier CH 31 B9
Romakkajärvi FIN 117 E13
Roman BG 165 C8
Roman RO 153 D9
Romana I 64 C2
Românaşi RO 151 C11
Româneşti RO 153 B10
Români RO 153 D9
Romanija BIH 157 E10
Romano d'Ezzelino I 72 E4
Romano di Lombardia I 69 B8
Romanones E 47 C7
Romanovce NMK 164 E4
Romanovo RUS 136 D1
Romanowo PL 85 E11
Romanshorn CH 27 E11
Romans-sur-Isère F 31 E7
Romanu RO 155 C1
Romazy F 23 D9
Rombas F 20 F6
Rombiolo I 59 B9
Romeira P 44 F3
Rometta I 59 C7
Romeu P 38 E5
Romford GB 15 D9
Romhány H 147 F8
Römhild D 75 B8
Romillé F 23 D8
Romilly-sur-Seine F 25 C10
Rommerskirchen D 21 B7
Romont CH 31 B10
Rømonysæter N 102 C3
Romorantin-Lanthenay F 24 F6
Romos RO 151 F11
Romppala FIN 125 E13
Romrod D 21 C12
Romsey GB 13 D12
Rømskog N 96 C6
Romsley GB 13 A10
Romstad N 105 C11
Romuli RO 152 B4
Rona de Jos RO 145 H9
Rona de Sus RO 145 H9
Rönäs S 108 E8
Rønbjerg DK 86 B3
Roncade I 72 E5
Roncadelle I 66 A1
Roncal E 32 E4
Roncegno I 69 A11
Ronce-les-Bains F 28 D3
Ronchamp F 26 E6
Ronchi dei Legionari I 73 E7
Ronciglione I 62 C2
Ronco Canavese I 68 C4
Roncone I 69 B10
Ronco Scrivia I 37 B9
Ronda E 53 C6
Rønde DK 86 C6
Rondissone I 68 C4
Rone S 93 E12
Ronehamn S 93 E12
Rong N 94 A1
Rõngu EST 131 E12
Rönnäng S 91 D10
Rönnäs S 107 B10
Rönnbacken S 103 E11
Rönnberg S 109 E17
Rönnberget S 118 D6
Rønne DK 88 E7
Rønnebæk DK 87 E9
Ronneburg D 79 E11
Ronneby S 89 C8
Ronnebyhamn S 89 C8
Rønnede DK 87 E10
Ronnenberg D 78 B6
Rönneshytta S 92 B6
Rönnholm S 107 D16
Rønningen N 111 C15
Rönnliden S 109 F17
Rönnöfors S 105 D15
Rönö S 93 C9
Ronov nad Doubravou CZ 77 C9
Ronsberg D 71 B10
Ronse B 19 C8
Ronshausen D 78 E6
Ronvik N 108 B7
Rooaun IRL 6 F6
Roodeschool NL 17 B7
Rookchapel IRL 8 D4
Roosendaal NL 16 E2
Roosinpohja FIN 123 F13
Roosky IRL 7 E7
Roosna-Alliku EST 131 C11
Ropa PL 145 D3
Ropaži LV 135 C9
Ropcha UA 153 A7
Ropczyce PL 143 F12
Ropeid N 94 D4
Roperuelos del Páramo E 39 D8
Ropienka PL 145 D5
Ropinsalmi FIN 116 A7
Ropotovo NMK 168 B5
Roquebillière F 37 C6
Roquebrun F 34 C5
Roquebrune-Cap-Martin F 37 D6
Roquebrune-sur-Argens F 36 E5
Roquecor F 33 B7
Roquecourbe F 33 C10
Roquefort F 32 B5
Roquemaure F 35 B8
Roquesteron F 36 D6
Roquetas E 42 F5
Roquetas de Mar E 55 F7
Roquevaire F 35 D10
Rørbakken N 111 C14
Rörberg S 103 E12
Rørby DK 87 D8
Rore BIH 157 D6
Røros N 101 A14
Rorschach CH 71 C9
Rörvattnet S 105 D16
Rørvig DK 87 D9
Rørvik N 94 F5
Rørvik N 105 B10
Rørvik N 110 D7
Rörvik S 88 A7
Rosà I 72 E4
Rosala FIN 126 F7
Rosal de la Frontera E 51 D5
Rosans F 35 B9
Rosapenna IRL 7 B7
Rosário P 50 D3
Rosarno I 59 C8
Rosavci BIH 157 C6
Rosbach vor der Höhe D 21 D11
Roscanvel F 22 D2
Ros Cathail IRL 6 F4
Rosche D 83 E9
Roscigno I 60 C4
Rościszewo PL 139 E8
Roscoff F 22 C4
Ros Comáin IRL 6 E6
Roscommon IRL 6 E6
Ros Cré IRL 9 C7
Roscrea IRL 9 C7
Rosdorf D 78 D6
Rose I 60 E6
Rose MNE 162 E6
Rosée B 184 D2
Rosehearty GB 3 K12
Rosemarkie GB 3 K8
Rosen BG 167 E9
Rosenallis IRL 7 F8
Rosendal N 94 C4
Rosenfeld D 27 D10
Rosenfors S 92 E7
Rosengarten D 83 D7
Rosenheim D 72 A5
Rosenlund S 91 D13
Rosenow D 84 C4
Rosenthal D 21 C11
Roserberg S 99 C9
Roses E 43 C10
Roseţi RO 161 E10
Roseto Capo Spulico I 61 D7
Roseto degli Abruzzi I 62 B6
Roseto Valfortore I 60 A4
Roshchino RUS 129 E12
Rosheim F 27 C7
Roshven GB 4 B5
Roşia RO 151 D9
Roşia RO 152 F4
Roşia de Amaradia RO 160 C3
Roşia de Secaş RO 152 E3
Roşia Montană RO 151 E11
Rosica LV 133 D3
Rosice CZ 77 C9
Rosice CZ 77 D10
Rosières F 30 E4
Rosières-en-Santerre F 18 E6
Roşieşti RO 153 E11
Rosignano Marittimo I 66 F1
Roşiile RO 160 D3
Roşiori RO 153 D10
Roşiori RO 161 D10
Roşiori de Vede RO 160 E6
Rositsa BG 155 F1
Rositsa BY 133 E3
Rositz D 79 D11
Rosiyanivka UA 154 C5
Roskhill GB 2 L3
Roskilde DK 87 D10
Rosko PL 85 E10
Roskovec AL 168 C2
Roskow D 79 B12
Röslau D 75 B10
Roslev DK 86 B3
Rosmalen NL 16 E4
Rosmaninhal P 45 E6
Ros Mhic Thriúin IRL 9 D9
Rosnowo PL 85 B10
Rosolina I 66 B5
Rosolina Mare I 66 B5
Rosolini I 59 F6
Rosoman NMK 169 A6
Rosoy F 25 D9
Rosporden F 22 E4
Rösrath D 21 C8
Rossano I 61 D7
Rossano Veneto I 72 E4
Roßbach D 76 E3
Rossbol S 106 E7
Rosscahill IRL 6 F4
Ross Carbery IRL 8 E4
Rosscarbery IRL 8 E4
Rosscor GB 6 D6
Roßdorf D 21 E11
Rossell E 42 F4
Rosselló E 42 D5
Rosses Point IRL 6 D5
Rossett GB 10 E6
Rossfjord N 111 B15
Roßhaupten D 71 B11
Rossiglione I 37 B9
Rossignol B 19 E11
Rössing (Nordstemmen) D 78 B6
Rossington GB 11 E9
Rossio ao Sul do Tejo P 44 F4
Roßla D 79 D9
Rosslare IRL 9 D10
Rosslare Harbour IRL 9 D10
Roßlau D 79 C11
Rosslea GB 7 D8
Roßleithen A 73 A9
Rossnowlagh IRL 6 C6
Rossön S 107 D10
Ross-on-Wye GB 13 B9
Rossosz PL 141 G8
Rossoszyca PL 142 C6
Rossow D 83 D13
Roßtal D 75 D8
Rossum NL 183 B6
Røssvassbukta N 108 E7
Rossvik N 105 A11
Rossvoll N 104 E4
Rossvoll N 111 B15
Roßwein D 80 D4
Røst N 108 A3
Röstabo S 103 D11
Röstånga S 87 C12
Rostarzewo PL 81 B10
Röste S 103 D11
Rostellan IRL 8 E6
Rostock D 83 B12
Rostrenen F 22 D5
Rostrevor GB 7 D10
Röström S 107 C10
Rostrup DK 86 B5
Rostundelva N 112 D6
Rosturk IRL 6 E3
Rostuša NMK 168 A4
Røstvollen N 102 B3
Røsvik N 109 B9
Rosvik S 118 D7
Röszke H 150 E5
Rot S 102 D7
Rota E 52 C4
Rota N 111 E10
Rota Greca I 60 E6
Rot am See D 74 D7
Rot an der Rot D 71 A10
Rotava CZ 75 B12
Rotberget N 97 A8
Roteberg S 103 D10
Rotello I 63 D7
Rotenburg (Wümme) D 17 B12
Rotenburg an der Fulda D 78 D6
Rötgesbüttel D 79 B8
Rotgülden A 73 B7
Roth D 75 D9
Rothbury GB 5 E13
Röthenbach an der Pegnitz D 75 D9
Rothenberg D 21 E11
Rothenbuch D 74 C5
Rothenburg (Oberlausitz) D 81 D7
Rothenburg ob der Tauber D 75 D7
Rothéneuf F 23 C8
Rothenfels D 74 C6
Rothenschirmbach D 79 D10
Rothenstein D 79 E10
Rotherham GB 11 E9
Rothes GB 3 K10
Rothesay GB 4 D6
Rotheux-Rimière B 19 C11
Rothiesholm GB 3 G11
Rothley GB 11 F9
Rothrist CH 27 F8
Rothwell GB 11 D9
Rothwell GB 15 C7
Rothwesten (Fuldatal) D 78 D6
Rotimlja BIH 157 F8
Rotimojoki FIN 123 C17
Rotnäset S 106 C9
Rotonda I 60 D6
Rotondella I 61 C7
Rotselaar B 19 C10
Rotsjö S 103 A10
Rotsjön S 118 F4
Rotsund N 112 D6
Rott D 71 B11
Rottach-Egern D 72 A4
Rott am Inn D 75 G11
Røttangen N 111 E10
Rottenacker D 71 A9
Röttenbach D 75 D9
Rottenbach D 79 E9
Rottenbuch D 71 B11
Rottenburg am Neckar D 27 D10
Rottenburg an der Laaber D 75 E11
Rottendorf D 74 C7
Rottenmann A 73 A9
Rotterdam NL 16 E3
Rotthalmünster D 76 F4
Röttingen D 74 C6
Rottleberode D 79 C8
Rottne S 89 A7
Rottnemon S 96 B8
Rottneros S 97 C9
Rottofreno I 69 C8
Rottweil D 27 D10
Rötunda RO 160 F4
Rötviken S 105 D16
Rötz D 75 D12
Rouans F 23 F8
Roubaix F 19 C7
Rouchovany CZ 77 D10
Rõude EST 131 D7
Roudnice nad Labem CZ 76 B6
Rouen F 18 F3
Rouffach F 27 E7
Rouffignac F 29 E7
Rõuge EST 131 F13
Rougé F 23 E9
Rougemont F 26 F5
Rougemont-le-Château F 27 E6
Roughton GB 15 B11
Rougnac F 29 D6
Rouillac F 28 D5
Rouillé F 28 C6
Roujan F 34 C5
Roukala FIN 119 F11
Roukalahti FIN 125 F13
Roulans F 26 F5
Roulers B 19 C7
Roulers B 182 D2
Roumazières-Loubert F 29 D7
Roumoules F 36 D4
Roundstone IRL 6 F3
Roundway GB 13 C11
Roundwood IRL 7 F10
Rouravaara FIN 117 C14
Roure I 31 E11
Rousínov CZ 77 D11
Rousky GB 4 F2
Rousset F 35 D10
Roussillon F 30 E6
Roussillon F 35 C9
Rousson F 35 B7
Routot F 18 F2
Rouvroy F 182 E1
Rouvroy-sur-Audry F 19 E10
Rouy F 30 A4
Rovala FIN 115 C5
Rovala FIN 115 E1
Rovaniemi FIN 117 F15
Rovanpää FIN 117 C15
Rovanpää FIN 117 E12
Rovapää FIN 115 D2
Rovastinaho FIN 119 C16
Rovato I 69 B9
Rovegno I 37 B10
Roverbella I 66 B2
Roveredo CH 69 A7
Rovereto I 69 B11
Rövershagen D 83 B12
Roverud N 96 B7
Roviano I 62 C3
Rovies GR 175 B7
Rovigo I 66 B4
Rovinari RO 159 D11
Rovine BIH 157 B7
Rovinj HR 67 B8
Rovinka SK 146 E4
Rovišće HR 149 E7
Rovisuvanto FIN 113 E16
Rovsättra S 99 B10
Rów PL 85 E7
Rowde GB 13 C10
Równa PL 142 C6
Rownaye BY 133 F6
Roxmo S 93 A8
Roxton GB 15 C8
Royal Wootton Bassett GB 13 B11
Royan F 28 D3
Royat F 30 D3
Roybon F 31 E7
Roybridge GB 4 B7
Roydon GB 15 C11
Roye F 18 E6
Royère-de-Vassivière F 29 D9
Røyken N 95 C12
Røykenes N 111 C10
Röykkä FIN 127 E12
Roylyanka UA 154 E5
Røyrvik N 105 B15
Røyse N 95 B12
Royston GB 15 C8
Royton GB 11 D7
Röyttä FIN 119 C12
Roytvollen N 105 A12
Royuela E 47 D10
Roza BG 166 E6
Rožaje MNE 163 D9
Rozalén del Monte E 47 E7
Rozalimas LT 134 E7
Różan PL 139 E11
Różanki PL 85 E8
Rozavlea RO 152 B4
Rozay-en-Brie F 25 C8
Rožďalovice CZ 77 B8
Rozdil UA 145 E9
Rozdil'na UA 154 D6
Rozdrażew PL 142 C4
Rozenburg NL 182 B4
Rozendaal NL 183 A7
Roženica HR 148 E5
Rozes LV 135 B11
Rozhniv UA 152 A6
Rozhnyativ UA 145 F9
Rozino BG 165 D10
Rožmitál pod Třemšínem CZ 76 C5
Rožňava SK 145 F2
Rożniatów PL 142 B6
Roznov RO 153 D9
Rožnov pod Radhoštěm CZ 146 C6
Roznowo PL 85 E11
Rozogi PL 139 D11
Rozovets BG 166 E4
Rozoy-sur-Serre F 19 E9
Rozprza PL 143 D8
Roztoka Wielka PL 145 E2
Roztoky CZ 76 B5
Roztoky UA 152 A6
Rozula LV 135 B9
Rožupe LV 135 D12
Rożwienica PL 144 D6
Rozzano I 69 C7
Rrëshen AL 163 F8
Rrogozhinë AL 168 B2
Rromanat AL 168 B2
Rtkovo SRB 159 D10
Rtyně v Podkrkonoší CZ 77 B10
Ru E 38 B3
Rua P 44 C5
Ruabon GB 10 F5
Ruaudin F 23 E12
Ruba LV 134 D5
Rúbaň SK 146 F6
Rubano I 66 B4
Rubashki BY 133 F3
Rubayo E 40 B4
Rubbestadneset N 94 C2
Rubena E 40 D4
Rübenau D 80 E4
Rubene LV 135 B10
Rubeņi LV 135 D11
Rubí E 43 E8
Rubiá E 39 D6
Rubí de Bracamonte E 40 F2
Rubielos de la Cérida E 47 C10
Rubielos de Mora E 48 D3
Rubiera I 66 C2
Rubik AL 163 F8
Rublacedo de Abajo E 40 C5
Rucăr RO 160 C6
Rucava LV 134 D2
Ruciane-Nida PL 139 C12
Rückersdorf D 80 C5
Ruda PL 142 D6
Ruda S 89 A10
Rudabánya H 145 G2
Ruda Maleniecka PL 141 H2
Rudamina LT 137 D11
Rudamina LT 137 E7
Ruda Różaniecka PL 144 C7
Rudartsi BG 165 D7
Ruda Śląska PL 142 F6
Rudbārži LV 134 C3
Ruddervoorde B 182 C2
Rude LV 134 B5
Rude LV 134 D2
Rudelzhausen D 75 E10
Rudersberg D 74 E6
Rudersdorf A 148 B6
Rüdersdorf Berlin D 80 B5
Rüdesheim D 185 E8
Rudice BIH 156 C5
Rudina SK 147 C7
Rūdiškės LT 137 D10
Rudka PL 141 E7
Rudkøbing DK 87 F7
Rudky UA 145 D7
Rudná CZ 76 B6
Rudna PL 81 C10
Rudna Glava SRB 159 E9
Rudňany SK 145 F2
Rudna Wielka PL 81 C11
Rudne UA 144 D8
Rudnica PL 81 A8
Rudnica SRB 163 C10
Rudnik BG 167 D9
Rudnik PL 142 F5
Rudnik SRB 158 E5
Rudniki PL 142 D6
Rudnik nad Sadem PL 144 C5
Rüdnitz D 84 E5
Rudno PL 141 G6
Rudno SRB 163 C9
Rudnyky UA 145 E8
Rudnytsya UA 154 A3
Rudo BIH 158 F3
Rudolfov CZ 77 E7
Rudolstadt D 79 E9
Rudozem BG 171 B7
Rudsgrendi N 95 C9
Rudsjön S 107 D10
Rudston GB 11 C11
Ruds Vedby DK 87 D8
Rudzāti LV 135 D13
Rudziczka PL 142 F4
Rudziniec PL 142 F5
Rue F 18 D4
Rueda E 39 F10
Rueda de Jalón E 41 E9
Rueil-Malmaison F 24 C7
Ruelle-sur-Touvre F 29 D6
Ruen BG 167 D8
Ruente E 40 B3
Ruffano I 61 D10
Ruffec F 29 B8
Ruffec F 29 C6
Ruffey-lès-Echirey F 26 F3
Ruffiac F 23 E7
Ruffieu F 31 C8
Ruffieux F 31 D8
Rufford GB 10 D6
Rufina I 66 E3
Rugāji LV 133 B2
Rugby GB 13 A12
Rugeley GB 11 F8
Rugge N 110 C8
Rugince NMK 164 E4
Rugineşti RO 153 E10
Ruginoasa RO 153 C9
Rügland D 75 D8
Rugles F 24 C4
Rugvica HR 148 E6
Ruha FIN 123 E9
Ruhala FIN 124 G2
Ruhla D 79 E7
Ruhland D 80 D5
Ruhmannsfelden D 76 E3
Rühn D 83 C11
Ruhpolding D 73 A6
Ruhstorf an der Rott D 76 F4
Ruidera E 55 B7
Ruikka FIN 119 B14
Ruinas I 64 D2
Ruinen NL 16 C6
Ruinerwold NL 16 C6
Ruiselede B 19 B7
Ruismäki FIN 123 E10
Ruivães P 38 E3
Ruja PL 81 D10
Rūjiena LV 131 F10
Rujišta BIH 157 F8
Ruka FIN 121 B13
Rukajärvi FIN 121 B13
Rukkisperä FIN 119 E14
Rulbo S 102 C8
Rullbo S 102 E7
Rullnäs S 107 D15
Rully F 30 B6
Rülzheim D 27 B9
Rum A 72 B3
Rum BY 133 E5
Rum H 149 B7
Ruma SRB 158 C4
Rumboci BIH 157 E7
Rumburk CZ 81 E7
Rumelange L 20 F6
Rumelifeneri TR 173 B11
Rumenka SRB 158 C4
Rumes B 19 C7
Rumia PL 138 A5
Rumigny F 19 E9
Rumilly F 31 D8
Rummu EST 131 C8
Rummukkala FIN 125 F12
Rumo FIN 125 C11
Rumont F 26 C3
Rumšiškės LT 137 D9
Rumskulla S 92 D7
Rumst B 19 B9
Rumyantsevo BG 165 C9
Runaberg S 107 E11
Runcorn GB 10 E6
Runcu RO 155 D2
Runcu RO 160 C4
Runcu RO 160 C6
Runděni LV 133 D3
Rundfloen N 102 D4
Rundhaug N 111 B16
Rundmoen N 108 D8
Rundvik S 107 D16
Rungsted DK 87 D11
Runhällen S 98 B7
Runik RKS 163 D10
Runkel D 185 D9
Runni FIN 124 C7
Runović HR 157 F7
Runsten S 89 B11
Runtuna S 93 B10
Ruohokangas FIN 115 A3
Ruohola FIN 119 C15
Ruokojärvi FIN 117 D12
Ruokojärvi FIN 129 B11
Ruokojärvi S 117 E10
Ruokolahti FIN 129 C10
Ruokoniemi FIN 129 B10
Ruokotaipale FIN 128 C8
Ruolahti FIN 127 B13
Ruoms F 35 B7
Ruona FIN 119 B17
Ruona FIN 123 E11
Ruonajärvi FIN 117 D13
Ruopsa FIN 115 E2
Ruorasmäki FIN 127 B15
Ruotaanmäki FIN 124 D7
Ruoti I 60 B5
Ruotsalo FIN 123 C10
Ruotsinkylä FIN 127 D15
Ruotsinpyhtää FIN 127 D15
Ruottisenharju FIN 120 D9
Ruovesi FIN 123 G12
Rupa HR 67 B9
Rupea RO 152 E6
Ruppovaara FIN 125 F14
Rupt-sur-Moselle F 26 E6
Rus E 55 C6
Rus RO 152 C3
Rusånes N 108 C9
Rusăneşti RO 160 F5
Rusca Montană RO 159 B9
Ruscova RO 152 B4
Rusdal N 94 E4
Ruse BG 161 F7
Ruše SLO 148 C5
Rusele S 107 B14
Ruseni MD 153 A10
Ruşeţu RO 161 D10
Ruševo HR 149 F9
Rush IRL 7 E10
Rushden GB 15 C7
Rusiec PL 143 D6
Ruşii-Munţi RO 152 D5
Rusinovo NMK 165 F6
Rusinów PL 141 H3
Rusinowo PL 85 D10
Ruskeala RUS 129 B14
Ruskele S 107 B15
Ruski Krstur SRB 158 B3
Rusko FIN 126 D7
Rusko Selo SRB 150 F6
Ruskov SK 145 F3
Rusksträsk S 107 B15
Rusnė LT 134 F2
Rusokastro BG 167 E8
Rušona LV 133 D1
Rüsselsheim D 21 D10
Russelsheim?

Sachsenberg (Lichtenfels) D 21 B11
Sachsenbrunn D 75 B8
Sachsenburg A 73 C7
Sachsenhagen D 17 D12
Sachsenhausen (Waldeck) D 17 F12
Sachsenheim D 27 C11
Sacile I 72 E5
Sacoşu Turcesc RO 159 B7
Sacović BIH 156 E6
Sacquenay F 26 E3
Sacramenia E 40 E4
Sacu RO 159 B9
Săcueni RO 151 C9
Săcuieu RO 151 D10
Sačurov SK 145 F4
Sada E 38 B3
Sádaba E 32 F3
Sadala EST 131 D13
Sadali I 64 D3
Saddell GB 4 D5
Sadina BG 166 C6
Sadki PL 85 D12
Sadkowice PL 141 G3
Sadkowo PL 85 C10
Sadlinki PL 138 C6
Sadova MD 154 C2
Sadova RO 152 B6
Sadova RO 160 F3
Sadove UA 154 E4
Sadovets BG 165 C9
Sadovo BG 165 E10
Sadowie PL 143 E11
Sadowne PL 139 E12
Sadská CZ 77 B7
Sadu RO 160 B4
Sädvaluspen S 109 D12
Sæbo N 94 B6
Sæbø N 100 B4
Sæbøvik N 94 C3
Sæby DK 87 D8
Sæby DK 90 E8
Sæd DK 86 F3
Saelices E 47 E7
Saelices de la Sal E 47 C8
Saelices del Rio E 39 C9
Saelices de Mayorga E 39 D9
Saerbeck D 17 D9
Særslev DK 86 D6
Sæter N 104 C8
Sætra N 104 E6
Sætre N 95 C13
Saeul L 20 E5
Sævareid N 94 B3
Safaalan TR 173 B9
Safara P 51 C5
Säffle S 91 A12
Saffré F 23 E8
Saffron Walden GB 15 C9
Sâg RO 151 C10
Sâg RO 159 B7
Sagama I 64 C2
Sagard D 84 A5
Sage D 17 C10
Săgeata RO 161 C9
Sågen S 97 B11
Sagiada GR 168 E3
Sağırlar TR 173 F9
Sağlamtaş TR 173 C7
Sågmyra S 103 E9
Sagna RO 153 D10
Sagone F 37 G9
Sagres P 50 E2
Sagstua N 95 B15
Sâgu RO 151 E7
Sagunto E 48 E4
Sagvåg N 94 C2
Ságvár H 149 C10
Sagy F 31 B7
Sahagún E 39 D9
Sahaidac MD 154 D3
Sahalahti FIN 127 C11
Sahankylä FIN 122 F8
Saharna Nouă MD 154 B3
Săhăteni RO 161 C8
Şahin TR 173 B6
Şahinli TR 172 D6
Sahl DK 86 C5
Sahrajärvi FIN 123 F14
Sahun E 33 E6
Sahune F 35 B9
Šahy SK 147 E7
Saiakopli EST 131 C12
Saighdinis GB 2 K2
Saija FIN 115 D5
Säijä FIN 127 C10
Saikari FIN 124 E7
Saillagouse F 33 F10
Saillans F 35 A9
Sail-sous-Couzan F 30 D4
Saimaanharju FIN 129 C9
Säimen FIN 125 F12
Sains-Richaumont F 19 E8
St Abbs GB 5 D12
St-Affrique F 34 C4
St-Agnan F 30 B4
St-Agnan-en-Vercors F 31 F7
St-Agnant F 28 D4
St-Agnant-de-Versillat F 29 C9
St Agnes GB 12 E4
St-Agrève F 30 E5
St-Aignan F 24 F5
St-Aignan-sur-Roë F 23 E9
St-Aigulin F 28 E5
St-Albain F 30 C6
St-Alban F 22 C6
St-Alban-Leysse F 31 D8
St Albans GB 15 D8
St-Alban-sur-Limagnole F 30 F3
St-Amand-en-Puisaye F 25 E9
St-Amand-les-Eaux F 19 D7
St-Amand-Longpré F 24 E5
St-Amand-Montrond F 29 B11
St-Amand-sur-Fion F 25 C12
St-Amans F 34 A5
St-Amans-des-Cots F 30 F2
St-Amans-Soult F 33 D10
St-Amant-de-Boixe F 29 D6
St-Amant-Roche-Savine F 30 D4
St-Amant-Tallende F 30 D3
St-Amarin F 27 E7
St-Ambroix F 35 B7
St-Amour F 31 C7
St-Andiol F 35 C8
St-André F 34 E4
St-André-de-Corcy F 31 D6
St-André-de-Cruzières F 35 B7
St-André-de-Cubzac F 28 F5
St-André-de-l'Eure F 24 C5
St-André-de-Sangonis F 34 C6
St-André-de-Valborgne F 35 B6
St-André-le-Gaz F 31 D8
St-André-les-Alpes F 36 D5
St-André-les-Vergers F 25 D11
St Andrews GB 5 C11
St-Angel F 29 D10
St Anne GBG 23 A7
St-Anthème F 30 D4
St-Antonin-Noble-Val F 33 B9
St-Août F 29 B9
St-Apollinaire F 26 F3
St-Arcons-d'Allier F 30 E4
St-Arnoult-en-Yvelines F 24 C6
St Asaph GB 10 E5
St-Astier F 29 E7
St-Astier F 29 F6
St Athan GB 13 C8
St-Auban F 36 D5
St-Auban-sur-l'Ouvèze F 35 B9
St-Aubin F 31 A7
St-Aubin-Château-Neuf F 25 E9
St-Aubin-d'Aubigné F 23 D8
St-Aubin-de-Blaye F 28 E4
St-Aubin-du-Cormier F 23 D9
St-Aubin-lès-Elbeuf F 18 F3
St-Aubin-sur-Mer F 23 B11
St-Aulaye F 29 E6
St Austell GB 12 E5
St-Avé F 22 E6
St-Avertin F 24 F4
St-Avold F 26 B6
St-Ay F 24 E6
St-Aygulf F 36 E5
St-Barthélemy-d'Agenais F 33 A6
St-Barthélemy-de-Vals F 30 E6
St-Bauzille-de-Putois F 35 C6
St-Béat F 33 E7
St-Beauzély F 34 B4
St Bees GB 10 C4
St-Benin-d'Azy F 30 A3
St-Benoît F 29 B6
St-Benoît F 33 D10
St-Benoît-du-Sault F 29 C8
St-Benoît-sur-Loire F 25 E7
St-Béron F 31 D8
St-Berthevin F 23 D10
St-Bertrand-de-Comminges F 33 D7
St-Blaise CH 31 A10
St-Blaise-la-Roche F 27 D7
St-Blin-Semilly F 26 D3
St-Boil F 30 B6
St-Bonnet-de-Bellac F 29 C7
St-Bonnet-de-Joux F 30 C5
St-Bonnet-en-Bresse F 31 B7
St-Bonnet-en-Champsaur F 36 B4
St-Bonnet-le-Château F 30 E5
St-Bonnet-le-Froid F 30 E5
St-Bonnet-sur-Gironde F 28 E4
St-Branchs F 24 F4
St Brelade GBJ 23 B7
St-Brevin-les-Pins F 23 F7
St-Briac-sur-Mer F 23 C7
St-Brice-en-Coglès F 23 D9
St Brides Major GB 13 C7
St-Brieuc F 22 C6
St-Bris-le-Vineux F 25 E10
St-Brisson F 25 F11
St-Broing-les-Moines F 25 E12
St Buryan GB 12 E3
St-Calais F 24 E4
St-Cannat F 35 C9
St-Céré F 29 F9
St-Cergue CH 31 C9
St-Cergues F 31 C9
St-Cernin F 29 E10
St-Chaffrey F 31 F10
St-Chamarand F 33 A8
St-Chamas F 35 C9
St-Chamond F 30 E6
St-Chaptes F 35 C7
St-Chef F 31 D7
St-Chély-d'Apcher F 30 F3
St-Chély-d'Aubrac F 34 A4
St-Chinian F 34 D4
St-Christol F 35 B9
St-Christol-lès-Alès F 35 B7
St-Christoly-Médoc F 28 E4
St-Christophe I 31 D11
St-Christophe-en-Bazelle F 24 F6
St-Christophe-en-Brionnais F 30 C5
St-Ciers-sur-Gironde F 28 E4
St-Cirq-Lapopie F 33 B9
St-Clair-du-Rhône F 30 E6
St-Clar F 33 C7
St-Claud F 29 D6
St-Claude F 31 C8
St Clears GB 12 B6
St-Clément F 25 D9
St-Clément F 26 C6
St-Clément F 29 E9
St Clement GBJ 23 B7
St-Clément-de-Rivière F 35 C6
St Columb Major GB 12 E5
St Combs GB 3 K13
St-Constant F 29 F10
St-Cosme-en-Vairais F 24 D3
St-Cricq-Chalosse F 32 C4
St-Cyprien F 29 F8
St-Cyprien F 33 B8
St-Cyprien F 34 E5
St-Cyr-sur-Loire F 24 F4
St-Cyr-sur-Mer F 35 D10
St Cyrus GB 5 B12
St David's GB 9 E12
St Day GB 12 E4
St-Denis F 25 C7
St-Denis-d'Anjou F 23 E11
St-Denis-de-Gastines F 23 D10
St-Denis-de-Jouhet F 29 B9
St-Denis-de-Pile F 28 F5
St-Denis-d'Oléron F 28 C3
St-Denis-en-Bugey F 31 D7
St-Denis-lès-Bourg F 31 C7
St Dennis GB 12 E5
St-Désert F 30 B6
St-Didier-en-Velay F 30 E5
St-Didier-sur-Chalaronne F 30 C6
St-Dié F 27 D6
St-Dier-d'Auvergne F 30 D3
St-Dizier F 25 C12
St-Dizier-Leyrenne F 29 C9
St-Dolay F 23 E7
St-Donat-sur-l'Herbasse F 31 E6
St-Doulchard F 25 F7
Ste-Adresse F 23 A12
Ste-Alvère F 29 F7
Ste-Bazeille F 33 A6
Ste-Cécile-les-Vignes F 35 B8
Ste-Croix CH 31 B10
Ste-Croix F 31 B7
Ste-Croix F 31 F7
Ste-Croix-Volvestre F 33 D8
Ste-Engrâce F 32 D4
Ste-Énimie F 34 B5
Ste-Eulalie d'Olt F 34 B4
Ste-Eulalie-en-Born F 32 B3
Ste-Feyre F 29 C9
Ste-Foy-de-Peyrolières F 33 D8
Ste-Foy-la-Grande F 29 F6
Ste-Foy-l'Argentière F 30 D5
Ste-Foy-lès-Lyon F 30 D6
Ste-Foy-Tarentaise F 31 D10
Ste-Geneviève F 18 F5
Ste-Geneviève-sur-Argence F 30 F2
St-Égrève F 31 E8
Ste-Hélène F 28 F4
Ste-Hermine F 28 B3
Ste-Livrade-sur-Lot F 33 B7
St-Élix-le-Château F 33 D8
St-Élix-Theux F 33 D6
Ste-Lizaigne F 29 A10
St-Éloy-les-Mines F 30 C2
Ste-Lucie-de-Tallano F 37 H10
Ste-Marguerite F 186 E2
Ste-Marie F 34 E5
Ste-Marie-aux-Mines F 27 D7
Ste-Maure-de-Peyriac F 33 B6
Ste-Maure-de-Touraine F 24 F4
Ste-Maxime F 36 E5
Ste-Menehould F 25 B12
Ste-Mère-Église F 23 B9
St-Émiland F 30 B5
St Endellion GB 12 D5
St Enoder GB 12 E5
Ste-Orse F 29 E8
Ste-Pazanne F 23 F8
Ste-Radegonde F 28 B5
St-Erme-Outre-et-Ramecourt F 19 E8
St Erth GB 12 E4
Saintes F 28 D4
Ste-Sabine F 25 F12
Ste-Savine F 25 D11
Ste-Sévère-sur-Indre F 29 C10
St-Esteben F 32 D3
St-Estèphe F 28 E4
St-Estève F 34 E4
Ste-Suzanne F 23 D11
St-Étienne F 30 E5
St-Étienne-de-Baïgorry F 32 D3
St-Étienne-de-Fontbellon F 35 A7
St-Étienne-de-Fursac F 29 C9
St-Étienne-de-Montluc F 23 F8
St-Étienne-de-St-Geoirs F 31 E7
St-Étienne-de-Tinée F 36 C5
St-Étienne-du-Bois F 31 C7
St-Étienne-du-Rouvray F 18 F3
St-Étienne-en-Dévoluy F 35 A10
St-Étienne-les-Orgues F 35 B10
St-Étienne-lès-Remiremont F 26 D6
St-Étienne-Vallée-Française F 35 B6
Ste-Tulle F 35 C10
Ste-Vertu F 25 E10
St-Fargeau F 25 E9
St-Félicien F 30 E6
St-Félix-Lauragais F 33 D9
St Fergus GB 3 K13
St-Ferme F 28 F6
Saintfield GB 7 D11
St Fillans GB 5 C8
St-Firmin F 26 D5
St-Firmin F 31 F9
St-Flavy F 25 D10
St-Florent F 37 F10
St-Florent-des-Bois F 28 B3
St-Florentin F 25 D10
St-Florent-le-Vieil F 23 F9
St-Florent-sur-Cher F 29 B10
St-Flour F 30 E3
St-Flovier F 29 B8
St-Fons F 30 D6
St-Fort-sur-Gironde F 28 E4
St-Frajou F 33 D7
St-François-Longchamp F 31 E9
St-Front-de-Pradoux F 29 E6
St-Fulgent F 28 B3
St-Galmier F 30 D5
St-Gaudens F 33 D7
St-Gaultier F 29 B8
St-Gein F 32 C5
St-Gély-du-Fesc F 35 C6
St-Genest-Malifaux F 30 E5
St-Geniez F 36 C4
St-Geniez-d'Olt F 34 B4
St-Genis-de-Saintonge F 28 E4
St-Genis-Laval F 30 D6
St-Genis-Pouilly F 31 C9
St-Genix-sur-Guiers F 31 D8
St-Genou F 29 B8
St-Geoire-en-Valdaine F 31 E8
St-Georges-Buttavent F 23 D10
St-Georges-d'Aurac F 30 E4
St-Georges-de-Commiers F 31 E8
St-Georges-de-Didonne F 28 D4
St-Georges-de-Luzençon F 34 B4
St-Georges-de-Mons F 30 D2
St-Georges-de-Reneins F 30 C6
St-Georges-des-Groseillers F 23 C10
St-Georges-d'Oléron F 28 D3
St-Georges-du-Vièvre F 18 F2
St-Georges-en-Couzan F 30 D4
St-Georges-lès-Baillargeaux F 29 B6
St-Georges-sur-Baulche F 25 E10
St-Georges-sur-Cher F 24 F5
St-Georges-sur-Loire F 23 F10
St-Geours-de-Maremne F 32 C3
St-Gérand-le-Puy F 30 C4
St-Germain-Chassenay F 30 B3
St-Germain-de-Calberte F 35 B6
St-Germain-de-la-Coudre F 24 D4
St-Germain-des-Fossés F 30 C3
St-Germain-d'Esteuil F 28 E4
St-Germain-du-Bel-Air F 33 A8
St-Germain-du-Bois F 31 B7
St-Germain-du-Corbéis F 23 D12
St-Germain-du-Plain F 31 B6
St-Germain-du-Puy F 25 F7
St-Germain-du-Teil F 34 B5
St-Germain-en-Laye F 24 C7
St-Germain-Laval F 30 D5
St-Germain-Lembron F 30 E3
St-Germain-les-Belles F 29 D8
St-Germain-les-Vergnes F 29 E9
St-Germain-l'Herm F 30 E4
St Germans GB 12 E6
St-Germé F 32 C5
St-Gervais F 28 B1
St-Gervais F 31 E7
St-Gervais-d'Auvergne F 30 C2
St-Gervais-la-Forêt F 24 E5
St-Gervais-les-Bains F 31 D10
St-Gervais-les-Trois-Clochers F 29 B6
St-Gervais-sur-Mare F 34 C5
St-Géry F 33 B9
St-Ghislain B 19 D8
St-Gildas-de-Rhuys F 22 E6
St-Gildas-des-Bois F 23 E7
St-Gilles F 35 C7
St-Gilles-Croix-de-Vie F 28 B2
St-Gingolph F 31 C10
St-Girons F 33 E8
St-Girons-Plage F 32 C3
St-Gobain F 19 E7
St-Guénolé F 22 E3
St-Guilhem-le-Désert F 35 C6
St-Haon-le-Châtel F 30 C4
St-Héand F 30 D5
St Helens GB 10 E6
St Helier GBJ 23 B7
St-Herblain F 23 F8
St-Hilaire F 33 D10
St-Hilaire-de-Brethmas F 35 B7
St-Hilaire-de-Riez F 28 B2
St-Hilaire-des-Loges F 28 C4
St-Hilaire-de-Villefranche F 28 D4
St-Hilaire-du-Harcouët F 23 C9
St-Hilaire-du-Rosier F 31 E7
St-Hilaire-Fontaine F 30 B4
St-Hilaire-le-Grand F 25 B11
St-Hilaire-St-Florent F 23 F11
St-Hippolyte F 27 D7
St-Hippolyte F 27 F6
St-Hippolyte-du-Fort F 35 C6
St-Honoré-les-Bains F 30 B4
St-Hostien F 30 E5
St-Hubert B 19 D11
St-Imier CH 27 F6
St-Ismier F 31 E8
St Ive GB 12 E6
St Ives GB 12 E4
St Ives GB 15 C8
St-Izaire F 34 C4
St-Jacques-de-la-Lande F 23 D8
St-James F 23 C9
St-Jean F 33 C8
St-Jean-Bonnefonds F 30 E5
St-Jean-Brévelay F 22 E6
St-Jean-d'Angély F 28 D4
St-Jean-d'Assé F 23 D12
St-Jean-de-Bournay F 31 D7
St-Jean-de-Braye F 24 E6
St-Jean-de-Daye F 23 B9
St-Jean-de-la-Ruelle F 24 E6
St-Jean-de-Losne F 26 F3
St-Jean-de-Luz F 32 D2
St-Jean-de-Marsacq F 32 C3
St-Jean-de-Maurejols-et-Avéjan F 35 B7
St-Jean-de-Maurienne F 31 E9
St-Jean-de-Monts F 28 B1
St-Jean-de-Sixt F 31 D9
St-Jean-de-Védas F 35 C6
St-Jean-d'Illac F 28 F4
St-Jean-du-Bruel F 34 B5
St-Jean-du-Falga F 33 D9
St-Jean-du-Gard F 35 B6
St-Jean-le-Centenier F 35 A8
St-Jean-Pied-de-Port F 32 D3
St-Jean-Poutge F 33 C6
St-Jean-sur-Erve F 23 D11
St-Jeoire F 31 C9
St-Jeure-d'Ay F 30 E6
St-Jeures F 30 E5
St-Joachim F 23 F7
St John GBJ 23 B7
St John's Chapel GB 5 F12
St John's Town of Dalry GB 5 E8
St-Jores F 23 B9
St-Jorioz F 31 D9
St-Jory F 33 C8
St-Jouan-des-Guérets F 23 C8
St-Jouin-Bruneval F 23 A12
St-Jouin-de-Marnes F 28 B5
St-Julien F 31 C7
St-Julien F 33 D8
St-Julien-Beychevelle F 28 E4
St-Julien-Boutières F 30 F5
St-Julien-Chapteuil F 30 E5
St-Julien-de-Concelles F 23 F9
St-Julien-de-Vouvantes F 23 E9
St-Julien-du-Sault F 25 D9
St-Julien-du-Verdon F 36 D5
St-Julien-en-Beauchêne F 35 A10
St-Julien-en-Born F 32 B3
St-Julien-en-Genevois F 31 C9
St-Julien-l'Ars F 29 B7
St-Junien F 29 D7
St-Just F 35 B8
St Just GB 12 E3
St-Just-en-Chaussée F 18 E5
St-Just-en-Chevalet F 30 D4
St-Just-Ibarre F 32 D3
St-Justin F 32 C5
St Just in Roseland GB 12 E4
St-Just-la-Pendue F 30 D5
St-Just-Luzac F 28 D3
St-Just-Sauvage F 25 C10
St-Just-St-Rambert F 30 E5
St Keverne GB 12 E4
St-Lambert-des-Levées F 23 F11
St-Lary-Soulan F 33 E6
St-Laurent F 36 C5
St-Laurent-Bretagne F 32 D5
St-Laurent-d'Aigouze F 35 C7
St-Laurent-de-Carnols F 35 B8
St-Laurent-de-Cerdans F 34 F4
St-Laurent-de-Chamousset F 30 D5
St-Laurent-de-la-Cabrerisse F 34 D4
St-Laurent-de-la-Salanque F 34 E4
St-Laurent-de-Neste F 33 D6
St-Laurent-des-Autels F 23 F9
St-Laurent-du-Pont F 31 E8
St-Laurent-du-Var F 37 D6
St-Laurent-en-Caux F 18 E2
St-Laurent-en-Grandvaux F 31 B8
St-Laurent-les-Bains F 35 A6
St-Laurent-Médoc F 28 E4
St-Laurent-Nouan F 24 E6
St-Laurent-sur-Gorre F 29 D7
St-Laurent-sur-Sèvre F 28 B4
St-Léger B 19 E12
St-Léger-des-Vignes F 30 B3
St-Léger-en-Yvelines F 24 C6
St-Léger-sous-Beuvray F 30 B5
St-Léonard F 27 D6
St-Léonard-de-Noblat F 29 D8
St Leonards GB 13 D11
St-Lizier F 33 D8
St-Lô F 23 B9
St-Lon-les-Mines F 32 C3
St-Loubès F 28 F5
St-Louis-lès-Bitche F 186 D3
St-Loup-Géanges F 30 B6
St-Loup-Lamairé F 28 B5
St-Loup-sur-Semouse F 26 E5
St-Lubin-des-Joncherets F 24 C5
St-Lunaire F 23 C7
St-Lupicin F 31 C8
St-Lyé F 25 D11
St-Lys F 33 C8
St-Macaire F 32 A5
St-Macaire-en-Mauges F 23 F10
St-Magne F 32 A4
St-Magne-de-Castillon F 28 F5
St-Maime F 35 C10
St-Maixent-l'École F 28 C5
St-Malo F 23 C7
St-Malo-de-la-Lande F 23 B8
St-Mamert-du-Gard F 35 C7
St-Marcel F 24 B5
St-Marcel F 29 B9
St-Marcel F 30 B6
St-Marcel-d'Ardèche F 35 B8
St-Marcel-lès-Annonay F 30 E6
St-Marcel-lès-Sauzet F 35 A8
St-Marcel-lès-Valence F 31 F6
St-Marcellin F 31 E7
St-Marc-sur-Seine F 25 E12
St-Mards-en-Othe F 25 D10
St Margaret's Hope GB 3 H11
St-Marsal F 34 E4
St-Mars-d'Outillé F 24 E3
St-Mars-du-Désert F 23 F9
St-Mars-la-Brière F 24 D3
St-Mars-la-Jaille F 23 E9
St-Martial F 35 B6
St-Martial-de-Nabirat F 29 F8
St-Martial-de-Valette F 29 D7
St-Martin F 35 C10
St Martin GBG 22 B6
St Martin GBJ 23 B7
St-Martin-Boulogne F 15 F12
St-Martin-d'Ablois F 25 B10
St-Martin-d'Arrossa F 32 D3
St-Martin-d'Auxigny F 25 F7
St-Martin-de-Belleville F 31 E10
St-Martin-de-Castillon F 35 C10
St-Martin-de-Crau F 35 C8
St-Martin-de-Landelles F 23 C9
St-Martin-de-Londres F 35 C6
St-Martin-d'Entraunes F 36 C5
St-Martin-de-Ré F 28 C3
St-Martin-des-Besaces F 23 B10
St-Martin-des-Champs F 22 C4
St-Martin-de-Seignanx F 32 C3
St-Martin-de-Valamas F 30 F5
St-Martin-de-Valgalgues F 35 B7
St-Martin-d'Hères F 31 E8
St-Martin-d'Oney F 32 C4
St-Martin-du-Mont F 31 C7
St-Martin-du-Var F 37 D6
St-Martin-en-Bresse F 31 B7
St-Martin-le-Beau F 24 F4
St-Martin-sur-Ouanne F 25 E9
St-Martin-Valmeroux F 29 E10
St-Martin-Vésubie F 37 C6
St-Martory F 33 D7
St Mary's GB 3 H11
St-Mathieu F 29 D7
St-Mathurin F 28 B2
St-Maur F 29 B9
St-Maurice CH 31 C10
St-Maurice-de-Lignon F 30 E5
St-Maurice-des-Lions F 29 D7
St-Maurice-la-Souterraine F 29 C8
St-Maurice-l'Exil F 30 E6
St-Maurice-Navacelles F 35 C6
St-Maurin F 33 B7
St Mawes GB 12 E4
St-Max F 26 C5
St-Maximin-la-Ste-Baume F 35 D10
St-Médard-en-Jalles F 28 F4
St-Méen-le-Grand F 23 D7
St-Méloir-des-Ondes F 23 C8
St-Memmie F 25 C11
St-Menoux F 30 B3
St Merryn GB 12 D5
St-Mesmin F 25 D10
St-Mesmin F 29 E8
St-Michel F 19 E9
St-Michel F 28 D6
St-Michel F 33 D6
St-Michel-Chef-Chef F 23 F7
St-Michel-de-Castelnau F 32 B5
St-Michel-de-Maurienne F 31 E9
St-Michel-en-l'Herm F 28 C3
St-Michel-sur-Meurthe F 27 D6
St-Mihiel F 26 C4
St Monans GB 5 C11
St-Montant F 35 B8
St-Nabord F 26 D6
St-Nauphary F 33 C8
St-Nazaire F 23 F7
St-Nazaire-le-Désert F 35 A9
St-Nectaire F 30 D2
St Neots GB 15 C8
St-Nicolas B 183 D7
St-Nicolas F 18 D6
St-Nicolas-d'Aliermont F 18 E3
St-Nicolas-de-la-Grave F 33 B8
St-Nicolas-de-Port F 26 C5
St-Nicolas-de-Redon F 23 E7
St-Nicolas-du-Pélem F 22 D5
St-Oedenrode NL 16 E4
St-Omer F 18 C5
St-Orens-de-Gameville F 33 C9
St-Ost F 33 D6
St Osyth GB 15 D11
St-Ouen F 18 D5
St-Ouen F 24 E5
St Ouen GBJ 23 B7
St-Ouen-des-Toits F 23 D10
St-Pair-sur-Mer F 23 C8
St-Palais F 32 D3
St-Palais-sur-Mer F 28 D3
St-Pal-de-Chalancon F 30 E4
St-Pal-de-Mons F 30 E5
St-Pantaléon F 30 B5
St-Pantaléon F 33 B8
St-Papoul F 33 D10
St-Pardoux-Isaac F 33 A6
St-Pardoux-la-Rivière F 29 E7
St-Parize-le-Châtel F 30 B3
St-Parres-lès-Vaudes F 25 D11
St-Paterne F 23 D12
St-Paterne-Racan F 24 E3
St-Paul F 36 B5
St-Paul-Cap-de-Joux F 33 C9
St-Paul-de-Fenouillet F 33 E11
St-Paul-de-Jarrat F 33 E9
St-Paul-en-Born F 32 B3
St-Paul-en-Forêt F 36 D5
St-Paul-et-Valmalle F 35 C6
St-Paulien F 30 E4
St-Paul-le-Jeune F 35 B7
St-Paul-lès-Dax F 32 C3
St-Paul-lès-Durance F 35 C10
St-Paul-Trois-Châteaux F 35 B8
St-Pé-de-Bigorre F 32 D5
St-Pée-sur-Nivelle F 32 D2
St-Péray F 30 F6
St-Père F 25 F10
St-Père-en-Retz F 23 F7
St Peter in the Wood GBG 22 B6
St Peter Port GBG 22 B6
St-Phal F 25 D10
St-Philbert-de-Bouaine F 28 B2
St-Philbert-de-Grand-Lieu F 28 A2
St-Pierre I 31 D11
St-Pierre-d'Albigny F 31 D9
St-Pierre-de-Chignac F 29 E7
St-Pierre-de-Côle F 29 E7
St-Pierre-de-la-Fage F 34 C5
St-Pierre-de-Maillé F 29 B7
St-Pierre-de-Plesguen F 23 D8
St-Pierre-des-Champs F 34 D4
St-Pierre-des-Corps F 24 F4
St-Pierre-des-Échaubrognes F 28 A4
St-Pierre-des-Landes F 23 D9
St-Pierre-des-Nids F 23 D11
St-Pierre-de-Trivisy F 33 C10
St-Pierre-d'Irube F 32 D3
St-Pierre-d'Oléron F 28 D3
St-Pierre-du-Chemin F 28 B4
St-Pierre-du-Mont F 32 C4
St-Pierre-Église F 23 A9
St-Pierre-en-Faucigny F 31 C9
St-Pierre-en-Port F 18 E1
St-Pierre-le-Moûtier F 30 B3
St-Pierre-lès-Elbeuf F 18 F3
St-Pierre-lès-Nemours F 25 D8
St-Pierre-Montlimart F 23 F9
St-Pierre-Quiberon F 22 E5
St-Pierre-sur-Dives F 23 B11
St-Plancard F 33 D7
St-Pois F 23 C9
St-Poix F 23 E9
St-Pol-de-Léon F 22 C4
St-Pol-sur-Mer F 18 B5
St-Pol-sur-Ternoise F 18 D5
St-Pompont F 29 F8
St-Pons F 36 C5
St-Pons-de-Thomières F 34 D4
St-Porchaire F 28 D4
St-Pourçain-sur-Sioule F 30 C3
St-Prex CH 31 C9
St-Priest F 30 D6
St-Priest-de-Champs F 30 D2
St-Priest-Laprugne F 30 D4
St-Priest-Taurion F 29 D8
St-Privat F 29 E10
St-Privat-d'Allier F 30 F4
St-Prix F 30 C4
St-Projet F 33 B9
St-Puy F 33 C6
St-Quentin F 19 E7
St-Quentin-la-Poterie F 35 B7
St-Quirin F 27 C7
St-Rambert-d'Albon F 30 E6
St-Rambert-en-Bugey F 31 D7
St-Raphaël F 36 E5
St-Remèze F 35 B7
St-Rémy F 30 B6
St-Rémy-de-Provence F 35 C8
St-Remy-en-Bouzemont-St-Genest-et-Isson F 25 C12
St-Rémy-sur-Avre F 24 C5
St-Rémy-sur-Durolle F 30 D4
St-Renan F 22 D2
St-Révérien F 25 F10
St-Rhemy I 31 D11
St-Riquier F 18 D4
St-Romain-en-Gal F 30 D6
St-Romain-sur-Cher F 24 F5
St-Romans F 31 E7
St-Rome-de-Cernon F 34 B4
St-Rome-de-Tarn F 34 B4
St-Saëns F 18 E3
St Sampson GBG 22 B6
St-Saturnin-lès-Apt F 35 C9
St-Saud-Lacoussière F 29 D7
St-Saulge F 25 F10
St-Sauves-d'Auvergne F 29 D11
St-Sauveur F 22 D3
St-Sauveur F 26 E5
St-Sauveur-de-Montagut F 30 F6
St-Sauveur-en-Puisaye F 25 E9
St-Sauveur-Gouvernet F 35 B9
St-Sauveur-Lendelin F 23 B9
St-Sauveur-le-Vicomte F 23 B8
St-Sauveur-sur-Tinée F 36 C6
St-Sauvy F 33 C7
St-Savin F 28 E5
St-Savin F 29 B7
St-Savinien F 28 D4
St Saviour GBJ 23 B7
St-Sébastien-de-Morsent F 24 B5
St-Sébastien-sur-Loire F 23 F8
St-Seine-l'Abbaye F 25 F12
St-Sernin F 35 A7
St-Sernin-sur-Rance F 34 C4
St-Seurin-sur-l'Isle F 28 E5
St-Sever F 32 C4
St-Sever-Calvados F 23 C9
St-Siméon-de-Bressieux F 31 E7
St-Simon F 19 E7
St-Simon F 29 F11
St-Sorlin-d'Arves F 31 E9
St-Soupplets F 25 B8
St-Sulpice F 33 C9
St-Sulpice-Laurière F 29 C8
St-Sulpice-les-Champs F 29 D10
St-Sulpice-les-Feuilles F 29 C8
St-Sulpice-sur-Lèze F 33 D8
St-Sulpice-sur-Risle F 24 C4
St-Sylvain F 23 B11
St-Symphorien F 30 F4
St-Symphorien F 32 B5
St-Symphorien-de-Lay F 30 D5
St-Symphorien-sur-Coise F 30 D5
St Teath GB 12 D5
St-Thégonnec F 22 C4
St-Thibéry F 34 D5
St-Thiébault F 26 D4
St-Thurien F 22 E4
St-Trivier-de-Courtes F 31 C7
St-Trivier-sur-Moignans F 30 C6
St-Trojan-les-Bains F 28 D3
St-Tropez F 36 E5
St-Uze F 30 E6
St-Valérien F 25 D9
St-Valery-en-Caux F 18 E2
St-Valery-sur-Somme F 18 D4
St-Vallier F 30 B5
St-Vallier F 30 E6
St-Vallier-de-Thiey F 36 D5
St-Varent F 28 B5
St-Vaury F 29 C9
St-Victor F 30 E6
St-Victor-de-Cessieu F 31 D7
St-Victoret F 35 D9
St-Victor-la-Coste F 35 B8
St Vigeans GB 5 B11
St-Vigor-le-Grand F 23 B10
St-Vincent I 68 B4
St-Vincent-de-Connezac F 29 E6
St-Vincent-de-Paul F 32 C4
St-Vincent-les-Forts F 36 C4
St-Vit F 26 F4
St-Vite F 33 B7
St-Vith B 20 D6
St-Vivien-de-Médoc F 28 E3
St-Xandre F 28 C3
St-Yan F 30 C5
St-Ybars F 33 D8
St-Yorre F 30 C3
St-Yrieix-la-Perche F 29 D8
St-Yrieix-sur-Charente F 29 D6
St-Yvy F 22 E4
St-Zacharie F 35 D10
Sainville F 24 D6
Saissac F 33 D10
Saittarova S 116 D8
Saivomuotka S 116 B10
Saïx F 33 C10
Sajaniemi FIN 127 D11
Šahyajince SRB 164 E5
Šajkaš SRB 158 C5
Sajóbábony H 145 G2
Sajókaza H 145 G2
Sajókeresztúr H 145 G2
Sajólád H 145 G2
Sajószentpéter H 145 G2
Sajószöged H 145 H3
Sajóvámos H 145 G2
Säjvis S 119 C11
Saka LV 134 C2
Sakajärvi S 116 D5
Sakalishcha BY 133 E5
Sakaravaara FIN 121 E12
Šakiai LT 136 D7
Säkinmäki FIN 123 F16
Sakizköy TR 173 B7
Säkkilä FIN 121 B13
Sakshaug N 105 D10
Saksild DK 86 D6
Sakskøbing DK 83 A11
Saksun FO 2 A2
Saku EST 131 C9
Sakule SRB 158 C6
Säkylä FIN 126 C7
Šakyna LT 134 D6
Sala LV 134 C7
Sala LV 135 C11
Sala S 98 C7
Šaľa SK 146 E5
Salaca LV 131 F10
Sălacea RO 151 C9
Salacgrīva LV 131 F8
Sala Consilina I 60 C5
Salagnac F 29 E8
Salahmi FIN 124 C7
Salaise-sur-Sanne F 30 E6
Salakas LT 135 E12
Salakos GR 181 D7
Salakovac BIH 157 F8
Salamajärvi FIN 123 D13
Salamanca E 45 C9
Salamina GR 175 D7
Salandra I 61 B6
Salanki FIN 117 B13
Salantai LT 134 D3
Salar E 53 B8
Sălard RO 151 C9
Salardu E 33 E7
Salarli TR 172 B6
Salas E 39 B7
Salaš SRB 159 E9
Salas de los Infantes E 40 D5
Salash BG 164 B6
Salaspils LV 135 C8
Sălașu de Sus RO 159 C10
Sălățig RO 151 C11
Sălătrucel RO 160 C4
Sălătrucu RO 160 C5
Salaunes F 28 F4
Salberg S 107 D16
Salbertrand I 31 E10
Sälboda S 97 C8
Salbohed S 98 C6
Salbris F 24 F7
Salbu N 100 D2
Salcea RO 153 B8
Salching D 75 E12
Salcia RO 159 E10
Salcia RO 160 F5
Salcia RO 161 C8
Salcia Tudor RO 161 C10
Sălciile RO 161 D8
Šalčininkai LT 137 E11
Šalčininkėliai LT 137 E11
Sălciua RO 151 E11
Salcombe GB 13 E7
Sălcuța MD 154 D4
Sălcuța RO 160 E2
Saldaña E 39 C10
Saldenburg D 76 E4
Saldón E 47 D10
Salduero E 40 E6
Saldus LV 134 C4
Sale GB 11 E7
Sale I 37 B9
Saleby S 91 C13
Salem D 27 E11
Salem D 83 C9
Salemi I 58 D2

Salen GB 4 B5
Salen GB 4 B5
Sälen S 102 D5
Salernes F 36 D4
Salerno I 60 B3
Salers F 29 E10
Salettes F 30 F4
Saleux F 18 E5
Salford GB 11 E7
Şalgamli TR 173 B6
Salgótarján H 147 E9
Salgueiro P 44 E5
Salhus N 94 A2
Sali HR 156 E3
Salice Salentino I 61 C9
Saliceto I 37 C8
Saliena LV 135 C7
Saliena LV 135 E13
Salies-de-Béarn F 32 D4
Salies-du-Salat F 33 D7
Salignac-Eyvignes F 29 F8
Salillas de Jalón E 41 E9
Salinas E 39 A8
Salinas E 56 D3
Salinas del Manzano E 47 D9
Salinas de Pamplona E 32 E2
Salinas de Pisuerga E 40 C3
Salin-de-Giraud F 35 D8
Saline di Volterra I 66 F2
Sälinkää FIN 127 D13
Salins F 29 E10
Salins-les-Bains F 31 B8
Salir P 50 E3
Salisbury GB 13 C11
Sălişte RO 152 F3
Săliştea RO 151 F11
Săliştea de Sus RO 152 B4
Salka SK 147 F7
Sal'kove UA 154 A5
Sall DK 86 C5
Salla EST 131 D12
Salla FIN 115 E5
Sallanches F 31 D10
Sallent E 43 D7
Sallent de Gállego E 32 E5
Salles F 32 A4
Salles-Curan F 34 B4
Salles-d'Angles F 28 D5
Salles-la-Source F 33 B11
Salles-sur-l'Hers F 33 D9
Sallgast D 80 C5
Sälliku EST 131 C14
Sallingberg A 77 F8
Sallins IRL 7 F9
Sällsjö S 105 E15
Sallypark IRL 8 C6
Salme EST 130 E4
Salmerón E 47 C8
Salmeroncillos de Abajo E 47 C7
Salmi FIN 123 E10
Salmi S 119 B10
Salmijärvi FIN 121 D10
Salminen FIN 121 B12
Salminen FIN 124 E8
Salmivaara FIN 115 E4
Salmiyarvi RUS 114 E8
Salmoral E 45 C10
Salmtal D 21 E7
Salnava LV 133 C3
Salnö S 99 C11
Salo FIN 127 E9
Salò I 69 B10
Salobre E 55 B7
Salobreña E 53 C9
Saločiai LT 135 D8
Saloinen FIN 119 E12
Salon F 25 C11
Salon-de-Provence F 35 C9
Salonkylä FIN 123 C11
Salonpää FIN 119 E14
Salonta RO 151 D8
Salorino E 45 F6
Salornay-sur-Guye F 30 B6
Salorno I 69 A11
Salou E 42 E6
Salouël F 18 E5
Šalovci SLO 148 C6
Salsåker S 107 F14
Salsbruket N 105 B11
Salsburgh GB 5 D9
Salses-le-Château F 34 E4
Sălsig RO 151 B11
Salsomaggiore Terme I 69 D8
Salt E 43 D9
Saltara I 67 E6
Saltash GB 12 E6
Saltburn-by-the-Sea GB 11 B10
Saltcoats GB 4 D7
Salteras E 51 E7
Salthill IRL 6 F4
Salto P 38 E4
Saltoniškės LT 137 D11
Saltrød N 90 C4
Saltsjöbaden S 99 D10
Saltum DK 90 E6
Saltvik FIN 99 B14
Saltvik S 103 C13
Saludecio I 67 E6
Saluggia I 68 C5
Salur TR 173 D8
Salussola I 68 C5
Salutaguse EST 131 C9
Saluzzo I 37 B6
Salva RO 152 C4
Salvacañete E 47 D10
Salvagnac F 33 C9
Salvaleón E 51 B6
Salvaterra de Magos P 50 A2
Salvaterra do Extremo P 45 E7
Salvatierra E 32 E1
Salvatierra de los Barros E 51 C6
Salvatierra de Santiago E 45 F8
Salve I 61 D10
Salviac F 33 A8
Sály H 145 H2
Salzburg A 73 A7
Salzgitter D 79 B7
Salzhausen D 83 D8
Salzhemmendorf D 78 B6
Salzkotten D 17 E11
Salzmünde D 79 C10
Salzwedel D 83 E10
Salzweg D 76 E4
Samadet F 32 C5
Samaila SRB 158 F6
Samarate I 68 B6
Samarica HR 149 E7
Samarina GR 168 D5
Samarineşti RO 159 D11
Samassi I 64 E2
Samatan F 33 D7
Sambade P 39 F6
Sâmbăta RO 151 D9
Sambiase I 59 B9
Sambir UA 145 D7
Samboal E 40 F3
Samborzec PL 143 E12
Sambuca di Sicilia I 58 D3
Sambuca Pistoiese I 66 D3
Sambuco I 36 C6
Sâmbureşti RO 160 D4
Samedan CH 71 D9
Sameiro P 44 D6
Samer F 15 F12
Sames E 39 B9
Sami GR 174 C2
Samil P 39 E6
Samir de los Caños E 39 E7
Şamli TR 173 E8
Sammakko S 116 E7
Sammakkola FIN 125 C10
Sammaljoki FIN 127 C9
Sammatti FIN 127 E10
Sammichele di Bari I 61 B7
Samnaun CH 71 D10
Samobor HR 148 E5
Samoëns F 31 C10
Samões P 38 F5
Samokov BG 165 E8
Samokov NMK 164 F3
Samolaco I 69 A7
Samora Correia P 50 B2
Šamorín SK 146 E4
Samos E 38 C5
Samos GR 177 D8
Samoš SRB 159 C6
Samothraki GR 171 D9
Samovodene BG 166 C5
Samper de Calanda E 42 E3
Sampeyre I 37 B6
Sampierdarena I 37 C9
Sampieri I 59 F6
Sampigny F 26 C4
amşud RO 151 C10
Samswegen D 79 B10
Samtens D 84 B4
Samuelsberg N 112 D6
Samugheo I 64 D2
Samuil BG 167 B7
Samuilovo BG 166 E5
San Adrián E 32 F2
San Agustín de Guadalix E 46 C5
Sanaigmore GB 4 D4
San Amaro E 38 D3
Sânandrei RO 151 F7
San Andrés del Rabanedo E 39 C8
San Antolín E 39 B6
San Antonio E 47 E10
Sanary-sur-Mer F 35 D10
San Asensio E 40 C6
San Bartolomé de las Abiertas E 46 E3
San Bartolomé de la Torre E 51 E5
San Bartolomé de Pinares E 46 C3
San Bartolomeo al Mare I 37 D8
San Bartolomeo in Galdo I 60 A4
San Basilio I 64 D3
San Benedetto dei Marsi I 62 C5
San Benedetto del Tronto I 62 B5
San Benedetto Po I 66 B2
San Benito E 54 B3
San Benito de la Contienda E 51 B5
San Biagio di Callalta I 72 E5
San Biago Platani I 58 D4
San Bonifacio I 66 B3
San Buono I 63 D7
San Candido I 72 C5
San Carlos del Valle E 55 B6
San Casciano dei Bagni I 62 B1
San Casciano in Val di Pesa I 66 E3
San Cataldo I 58 E4
San Cataldo I 61 C10
San Cebrián de Castro E 39 E8
Sâncel RO 152 E3
Sancergues F 25 F8
Sancerre F 25 F8
San Cesario sul Panaro I 66 C3
Sancey-le-Grand F 26 F6
Sancheville F 24 D6
Sanchidrián E 46 C3
San Chirico Nuovo I 60 B6
San Chirico Raparo I 60 C6
San Cibrão das Viñas E 38 D4
San Cipirello I 58 D3
San Cipriano d'Aversa I 60 B2
San Clemente E 47 F8
San Clodio E 38 D5
Sancoins F 30 B2
San Colombano al Lambro I 69 C7
San Cosme E 38 A5
San Costantino Albanese I 61 C6
San Costanzo I 67 E7
Sâncrăieni RO 153 E7
Sâncraiu RO 151 D10
Sâncraiu de Mureş RO 152 D5
San Cristóbal de Entreviñas E 39 D8
San Cristóbal de la Vega E 46 B3
Sancti-Spíritus E 45 C8
Sancti-Spíritus E 51 B9
Sand N 94 D4
Sand N 95 B15
Sand N 110 D5
Sand (Bad Emstal) D 17 F12
Sanda S 93 E12
Sandager DK 86 E5
Sandamendi E 40 B5
San Damiano d'Asti I 37 B8
San Damiano Macra I 37 C6
Sandane N 100 C4
San Daniele del Friuli I 73 D7
San Daniele Po I 66 B1
Sandanski BG 169 A9
Sandared S 91 D12
Sandarne S 103 D13
Sandau D 83 E12
Sandbach GB 11 E7
Sandberg D 74 B7
Sandby DK 87 F8
Sande D 17 B10
Sande N 95 C12
Sande N 100 D3
Sande P 44 B4
Sandefjord N 90 A7
Sandeggen N 111 A17
Sandeid N 94 C3
Sandelva N 112 D7
San Demetrio Corone I 61 D6
San Demetrio ne Vestini I 62 C5
Sander N 96 B6
Sandersdorf D 79 C11
Sandershausen (Niestetal) D 78 D6
Sandersleben D 79 C10
Sandes N 110 C8
Sandes N 110 C9
Sandfjord N 114 B9
Sandfors S 118 E5
Sandgarth GB 3 G11
Sandhausen D 21 F11
Sandhead GB 4 F7
Sandhem S 91 D14
Sandhult S 91 D12
Sandhurst GB 15 E7
Sandiás E 38 D4
Sandillon F 24 E7
Sandkrug D 84 E5
Sandl A 77 E7
Sandland N 112 C8
Sandnäset S 102 A8
Sandnes N 90 A5
Sandnes N 94 E3
Sandnes N 105 C12
Sandneshamn N 111 A15
Sandness N 111 C11
Sandnessjøen N 108 D4
Sando E 45 C8
Sandomierz PL 143 E12
Sândominic RO 153 D7
San Donaci I 61 C9
San Donà di Piave I 72 E6
San Donato di Lecce I 61 C10
San Donato di Ninea I 60 D6
San Donato Milanese I 69 C7
San Donato Val di Comino I 62 D5
Sándorfalva H 150 E5
Sandown GB 13 D12
Sandøy N 100 A5
Sandplace GB 12 E6
Šandrovac HR 149 E8
Sandsele S 107 A13
Sandsend GB 11 B10
Sandsjö S 102 C8
Sandsjöfors S 92 E5
Sandsjönäs S 107 A13
Sandslån S 107 E13
Sandstad N 104 D6
Sandstedt D 17 B11
Sandstrak N 108 D3
Sandstrand N 111 C12
Sandtangen N 114 D7
Sandtorg N 111 C12
Sandträsk S 118 B6
Sânduleni RO 153 E9
Sânduleşti RO 152 D3
Sandur FO 2 B3
Sandvatn N 94 F5
Sandved DK 87 E9
Sandvik FO 2 B3
Sandvik N 101 D15
Sandvik N 108 B7
Sandvik N 111 A16
Sandvik N 111 B14
Sandvik N 113 B16
Sandvik S 103 C11
Sandvika N 95 C13
Sandvika N 105 D12
Sandviken S 103 E12
Sandviken S 107 E15
Sandviken S 107 F13
Sandviksjön S 106 D7
Sandvikvåg N 94 C2
Sandwich GB 15 E11
Sandwick GB 3 F14
Sandy GB 15 C8
Sanem L 20 E5
San Emiliano E 39 C8
San Esteban de Gormaz E 40 E5
San Esteban de la Sierra E 45 C9
San Esteban de Litera E 42 D4
San Esteban del Molar E 39 E8
San Esteban del Valle E 46 D3
San Fele I 60 B5
San Felice a Cancello I 60 A2
San Felice Circeo I 62 E4
San Felices de los Gallegos E 45 C7
San Felice sul Panaro I 66 C3
San Ferdinando I 59 C8
San Ferdinando di Puglia I 60 A6
San Fernando E 52 D4
San Fernando de Henares E 46 D5
San Fili I 60 E6
San Filippo del Mela I 59 C7
Sanfins do Douro P 38 F5
San Francisco Javier E 57 D7
San Fratello I 59 C6
Sanfront I 37 B6
Sånga S 107 E13
Sangarcía E 46 C4
Sangaste EST 131 F12
Sangatte F 15 F12
San Gavino Monreale I 64 D2
Sångbäcken S 102 B7
San Gemini I 62 B3
Sângeorgiu de Mureş RO 152 D5
Sângeorgiu de Pădure RO 152 E5
Sângeorz-Băi RO 152 C5
Sânger RO 152 D4
Sangerhausen D 79 D9
San Germano Chisone I 31 F11
Sângeru RO 161 C8
Sangijän S 119 C11
San Gimignano I 66 F3
San Ginesio I 62 A4
Sanginjoki FIN 119 E16
Sanginkylä FIN 119 E17
San Giorgio a Liri I 62 E5
San Giorgio della Richinvelda I 73 D6
San Giorgio del Sannio I 60 A3
San Giorgio di Lomellina I 68 C6
San Giorgio di Nogaro I 73 E7
San Giorgio di Piano I 66 C3
San Giorgio Ionico I 61 C8
San Giorgio la Molara I 60 A3
San Giorgio Lucano I 61 C6
San Giovanni a Piro I 60 C4
San Giovanni Bianco I 69 B8
San Giovanni d'Asso I 66 F4
San Giovanni Gemini I 58 D4
San Giovanni Incarico I 62 D4
San Giovanni in Croce I 66 B1
San Giovanni in Fiore I 61 E7
San Giovanni in Persiceto I 66 C3
San Giovanni Lupatoto I 66 B3
San Giovanni Rotondo I 63 D9
San Giovanni Suegiu I 64 E2
San Giovanni Teatino I 63 C6
San Giovanni Valdarno I 66 E4
Sangis S 119 C10
San Giuliano Terme I 66 E1
San Giuseppe Jato I 58 D3
San Giuseppe Vesuviano I 60 B3
San Giustino I 66 E5
San Godenzo I 66 E4
San Gregorio I 59 C8
San Gregorio Magno I 60 B4
San Gregorio Matese I 60 A2
Sangüesa E 32 E3
San Guiliano Milanese I 69 C7
San Guim de Freixenet E 43 D6
Sanguinet F 32 B3
Sanguinetto I 66 B3
Sani GR 169 D9
San Ildefonso E 46 C5
Sanislău RO 151 B9
Sanitz D 83 B12
San Javier E 56 F3
San Jordi E 42 F4
San Jorge de Alor E 51 B5
San José E 55 F8
San José del Valle E 52 C5
San José de Malcocinado E 52 D5
San Juan E 41 B6
San Juan de Alicante E 56 E4
San Juan de Aznalfarache E 51 E7
San Juan de la Nava E 46 D3
San Juan del Puerto E 51 E6
San Justo de la Vega E 39 D7
Sankt Aegyd am Neuwalde A 77 G9
Sankt Andrä A 73 C10
Sankt Andrä am Zicksee A 149 A7
Sankt Andreasberg D 79 C8
Sankt Anna S 93 C9
Sankt Anna am Aigen A 148 C5
Sankt Anton an der Jeßnitz A 77 G8
Sankt Augustin D 21 C8
Sankt Gallen A 73 A10
Sankt Gallen CH 27 F11
Sankt Gallenkirch A 71 C9
Sankt Gangloff D 79 E10
Sankt Georgen am Walde A 77 F7
Sankt Georgen im Schwarzwald D 27 D9
Sankt Gilgen A 73 A7
Sankt Goar D 21 D9
Sankt Goarshausen D 21 D9
Sankt Ingbert D 21 F8
Sankt Jakob im Rosental A 73 C9
Sankt Jakob im Walde A 148 B5
Sankt Jakob in Defereggen A 72 C5
Sankt Johann am Tauern A 73 B9
Sankt Johann im Pongau A 73 B7
Sankt Johann im Walde A 73 C6
Sankt Johann in Tirol A 72 A5
Sankt Julian D 21 E9
Sankt Katharinen D 185 C7
Sankt Lambrecht A 73 B9
Sankt Leonhard am Forst A 77 F8
Sankt Leonhard am Hornerwald A 77 E9
Sankt Leonhard im Pitztal A 71 C11
Sankt Lorenz A 73 A7
Sankt Lorenzen im Gitschtal A 73 C7
Sankt Lorenzen im Lesachtal A 73 C6
Sankt Lorenzen im Mürztal A 148 B4
Sankt Lorenzen ob Murau A 73 B9
Sankt Marein im Mürztal A 148 B4
Sankt Margarethen D 17 A12
Sankt Margarethen an der Raab A 148 B5
Sankt Margarethen bei Knittelfeld A 73 B10
Sankt Margarethen im Burgenland A 77 G11
Sankt Märgen D 27 D9
Sankt Martin A 73 B7
Sankt Martin A 77 E7
Sankt Martin im Mühlkreis A 76 F6
Sankt Michael im Burgenland A 148 B6
Sankt Michael im Lungau A 73 B8
Sankt Michael in Obersteiermark A 73 B11
Sankt Michaelisdonn D 82 C6
Sankt Moritz CH 71 D9
Sankt Nikolai im Saustal A 148 C4
Sankt Nikolai im Sölktal A 73 B9
Sankt Olof S 88 D6
Sankt Oswald bei Freistadt A 77 E7
Sankt Oswald ob Eibiswald A 73 C11
Sankt Pankraz A 73 A9
Sankt Paul im Lavanttal A 73 C10
Sankt Peter am Kammersberg A 73 B9
Sankt Peter am Ottersbach A 148 C5
Sankt-Peterburg RUS 129 F13
Sankt Peter-Freienstein A 73 B11
Sankt Peter in der Au A 77 F7
Sankt Peter-Ording D 82 B5
Sankt Pölten A 77 F9
Sankt Radegund A 76 F3
Sankt Ruprecht an der Raab A 148 B5
Sankt Stefan im Gailtal A 73 C8
Sankt Stefan ob Leoben A 73 B10
Sankt Stefan ob Stainz A 148 C4
Sankt Ulrich bei Steyr A 76 F6
Sankt Valentin A 77 F7
Sankt Veit am Vogau A 148 C5
Sankt Veit an der Glan A 73 C9
Sankt Veit an der Gölsen A 77 F9
Sankt Veit im Pongau A 73 B7
Sankt Veit in Defereggen A 72 C5
Sankt Wendel D 21 F8
Sankt Wolfgang D 75 F11
Sankt Wolfgang im Salzkammergut A 73 A7
San Lazzaro di Savena I 66 D3
San Leo I 66 E5
San Leonardo de Yagüe E 40 E5
San Leonardo in Passiria I 72 C3
San Lorenzo I 59 D8
San Lorenzo al Mare I 37 D7
San Lorenzo Bellizzi I 61 D6
San Lorenzo de Calatrava E 54 C5
San Lorenzo de El Escorial E 46 C4
San Lorenzo de la Parrilla E 47 E8
San Lorenzo di Sebato I 72 C4
San Lorenzo in Campo I 67 E6
San Lorenzo Nuovo I 62 B1
San Luca I 59 C9
Sanlúcar de Barrameda E 52 C4
Sanlúcar de Guadiana E 50 E5
Sanlúcar la Mayor E 51 E7
San Lucido I 60 E6
Sanluri I 64 D2
San Maddalena Vallalta I 72 C5
San Mamés de Campos E 40 D2
San Marcello I 67 E7
San Marcello Pistoiese I 66 D2
San Marco Argentano I 60 D6
San Marco dei Cavoti I 60 A3
San Marco in Lamis I 63 D9
San Marcos E 38 B3
San Marino RSM 66 E5
San Martin E 32 D1
San Martín E 41 B6
Sânmartin RO 151 C8
Sânmartin RO 152 C4
Sânmartin RO 153 E7
San Martín de la Vega E 46 D5
San Martín de la Vega del Alberche E 45 D10
San Martin del Pimpollar E 45 D10
San Martín de Montalbán E 46 E4
San Martín de Pusa E 46 E3
San Martin de Unx E 32 E2
San Martín de Valdeiglesias E 46 D4
San Martino Buon Albergo I 66 B3
San Martino di Castrozza I 72 D4
San Martino di Lupari I 72 E4
San Martino di Venezze I 66 B4
San Martino in Badia I 72 C4
San Martino in Passiria I 72 C3
San Martino in Pensilis I 63 D8
San Mateo de Gállego E 41 E10
San Mauro Castelverde I 58 D5
San Mauro Forte I 60 C6
San Mauro Marchesato I 61 E7
San Mauro Pascoli I 66 D5
San Mauro Torinese I 68 C4
San Menaio I 63 D9
San Michele al Tagliamento I 73 E6
San Michele Mondovì I 37 C7
San Michele Salentino I 61 B9
San Miguel de Arroyo E 40 F3
San Miguel de Bernuy E 40 F4
San Miguel de Salinas E 56 F3
Sânmihaiu Almaşului RO 151 C11
Sânmihaiu de Câmpie RO 152 D4
Sânmihaiu Român RO 159 B7
San Millán de la Cogolla E 40 D6
San Miniato I 66 E2
Sänna S 92 B5
Sannahed S 92 A6
Sannazzaro de'Burgondi I 69 C6
Sannicandro di Bari I 61 B7
Sannicandro Garganico I 63 D9
Sannicola I 61 C10
San Nicola dell'Alto I 61 E7
San-Nicolao F 37 G10
San Nicolás del Puerto E 51 C8
Sânnicolau Mare RO 150 E6
San Nicolò I 66 C4
San Nicolò d'Arcidano I 64 D2
San Nicolò Gerrei I 64 E3
Sanniki PL 139 F8
Sanok PL 145 D5
San Pablo de los Montes E 46 E4
San Pancrazio I 72 C3
San Pancrazio Salentino I 61 C9
San Paolo di Civitate I 63 D8
Sânpaul RO 151 D11
Sânpaul RO 152 E4
San Pedro E 55 B8
San Pedro de Alcántara E 53 D7
San Pedro de Ceque E 39 D7
San Pedro del Arroyo E 46 C3
San Pedro de Latarce E 39 E9
San Pedro del Pinatar E 56 F3
San Pedro del Romeral E 40 B4
San Pedro de Rozados E 45 C9
San Pedro Manrique E 41 D7
San Pedro Palmiches E 47 D8
San Pellegrino Terme I 69 B8
Sânpetru RO 153 F7
Sânpetru de Câmpie RO 152 D4
Sânpetru Mare RO 150 E6
San Piero a Sieve I 66 E3
San Piero Patti I 59 C6
San Pietro I 59 B7
San Pietro di Cadore I 73 C6
San Pietro in Cariano I 66 A2
San Pietro in Casale I 66 C3
San Pietro in Guarano I 61 E6
San Pietro Vernotico I 61 C10
San Polo d'Enza I 66 C1
San Prospero I 66 C3
Sanquhar GB 5 E9
San Quirico d'Orcia I 65 A5
San Rafael del Río E 42 F4
San Remo I 37 D7
San Román E 38 C5
San Román de Cameros E 41 D7
San Román de la Cuba E 39 D10
San Román de los Montes E 46 D3
San Roque E 38 B2
San Roque E 38 D3
San Roque E 53 D6
San Rufo I 60 C4
Sansac-de-Marmiesse F 29 F10
San Salvador de Cantamunda E 40 C3
San Salvatore I 64 D1
San Salvatore Monferrato I 37 B9
San Salvatore Telesino I 60 A2
San Salvo I 63 C7
San Sebastián E 32 D2
San Sebastián de los Ballesteros E 53 A7
San Sebastián de los Reyes E 46 C5
San Secondo Parmense I 66 C1
Sansepolcro I 66 E5
San Severa I 62 C1
San Severino Lucano I 60 C6
San Severino Marche I 67 F7
San Severo I 63 D8
San Silvestre de Guzmán E 51 E5
Sânsimion RO 153 E7
Sanski Most BIH 157 C6
Sansol E 32 E1
San Sosti I 60 D6
San Sperate I 64 E3
San Spirito I 61 A7
Şanţ RO 152 C5
Santa Amalia E 51 A7
Santa Ana E 55 B9
Santa Ana de Pusa E 46 E3
Santa Ana la Real E 51 D6
Santa Bàrbara E 42 F5
Santa Bárbara de Casa E 51 D5
Santacara E 32 F2
Santa Cataliña de Armada E 38 B2
Santa Catarina P 50 C3
Santa Catarina da Fonte do Bispo P 50 E4
Santa Caterina dello Ionio I 59 B10
Santa Caterina di Pittinuri I 64 C2
Santa Caterina Villarmosa I 58 D5
Santa Cesarea Terme I 61 C10
Santa Cilia de Jaca E 32 E4
Santa Clara-a-Nova P 50 E3
Santa Clara-a-Velha P 50 D3
Santa Clara de Louredo P 50 D4
Santa Coloma de Farners E 43 D9
Santa Coloma de Queralt E 43 D6
Santa Colomba de Somoza E 39 D7
Santa Columba de Curueño E 39 C9
Santa Comba Dão P 44 D4
Santa Comba de Rossas P 39 E6
Santa Cristina d'Aro E 43 D9
Santa Cristina de la Polvorosa E 39 D8
Santa Croce Camerina I 59 F6
Santa Croce del Sannio I 60 A3
Santa Croce di Magliano I 63 D8
Santa Croce sull'Arno I 66 E2
Santa Cruz P 50 C2
Santa Cruz da Tapa P 44 C4
Santa Cruz de Bezana E 40 B4
Santa Cruz de Campézo E 32 E1
Santa Cruz de la Serós E 32 E4
Santa Cruz de la Sierra E 45 F9
Santa Cruz de la Zarza E 47 E6
Santa Cruz de los Cáñamos E 55 B7
Santa Cruz del Retamar E 46 D4
Santa Cruz de Moya E 47 E10
Santa Cruz de Mudela E 55 B6
Santadi I 64 E2
Santa Domenica Talao I 60 D5
Santa Domenica Vittoria I 59 D6
Santa Elena E 55 C5
Santa Elena de Jamuz E 39 D8
Santa Elisabetta I 58 E4
Santaella E 53 A7
Santa Engracia E 32 F1
Santa Eufemia E 54 B3
Santa Eugèni E 49 E10
Santa Eulalia E 39 B8
Santa Eulalia E 39 B9
Santa Eulalia E 47 C10
Santa Eulália P 51 A5
Santa Eulalia del Río E 57 D8
Santa Eulalia de Oscos E 38 B5
Santa Eulàlia de Riuprimer E 43 D8
Santa Fé E 53 B9
Santa Fiora I 65 B5
Sant'Agata de'Goti I 60 A3
Sant'Agata del Bianco I 59 C9
Sant'Agata di Esaro I 60 D5
Sant'Agata di Militello I 59 C6
Sant'Agata di Puglia I 60 A4
Sant'Agata Feltria I 66 E5
Santa Giusta I 64 D2
Santa Giustina I 72 D5
Sant'Agostino I 66 C3
Sant Agustí de Lluçanès E 43 C8
Santahamina FIN 127 E13
Santa Iria P 50 D4
Santa Justa P 50 A3
Sant'Alberto I 66 C5
Santalha P 38 E5
Santa Liestra y San Quílez E 33 F6
Santa Luce I 66 F2
Santa Lucia I 64 B4
Santa Lucia del Mela I 59 C7
Santa Lucía de Moraña E 38 C2
Santa Luzia P 50 D3
Santa Magdalena de Pulpís E 48 D5
Santa Mare RO 153 B10
Santa Margalida E 57 B11
Santa Margarida da Serra P 50 C2
Santa Margarida de Montbui E 43 D7
Santa Margarida do Sádão P 50 C3
Santa Margherita di Belice I 58 D3
Santa Margherita Ligure I 37 C10
Santa Maria CH 71 D10
Santa María E 32 F4
Santa Maria Capua Vetere I 60 A2
Santa Maria da Feira P 44 C3
Santa María de Cayón E 40 B4
Santa María de Corcó E 43 C8
Santa María de Huertas E 41 F7
Santa María del Berrocal E 45 C10
Santa María del Camí E 49 E10
Santa María del Campo E 40 D4
Santa María del Campo Rus E 47 E8
Santa María del Cedro I 60 D5
Santa Maria della Versa I 37 B10
Santa María de los Llanos E 47 F7
Santa María del Páramo E 39 D8
Santa María del Val E 47 C8
Santa María de Nieva E 55 E9
Santa María de Palautordera E 43 D8
Santa Maria di Castellabate I 60 C3
Santa Maria di Sala I 66 A5
Santa María la Real de Nieva E 46 B4
Santa Maria Maggiore I 68 A5
Santa Maria Navarrese I 64 D4
Santa Maria Nuova I 67 F7
Sântămăria-Orlea RO 159 B10
Santa Maria Rezzonico I 69 A7
Santa-Maria-Siché F 37 H9
Santa Marina I 60 C5
Santa Marina del Rey E 39 C8
Santa Marina Salina I 59 B6
Santa Marinella I 62 C1
Santa Marta E 47 F8
Santa Marta E 51 B6
Santa Marta de Penaguião P 44 B5
Santa Marta de Tormes E 45 C9
Sant'Ambroggio F 37 F9
Santana P 44 D3
Santana P 50 C1
Sântana RO 151 E8
Santana da Serra P 50 D3
Santana de Cambas P 50 D4
Santana do Mato P 50 B3
Sant'Anastasia I 60 B2
Sant'Anatolia di Narco I 62 B3
Santander E 40 B4
Sant'Andrea Apostolo dello Ionio I 59 B10
Sant'Andrea Frius I 64 E3
Sântandrei RO 151 C8
Sant'Angelo I 59 B9
Sant'Angelo a Fasanella I 60 C4
Sant'Angelo dei Lombardi I 60 B4
Sant'Angelo di Brolo I 59 C6
Sant'Angelo in Lizzola I 67 E6
Sant'Angelo in Vado I 66 E5
Sant'Angelo Lodigiano I 69 C7
Sant'Angelo Muxaro I 58 E4
Santa Ninfa I 58 D2
Sant'Anna Arresi I 64 E2
Sant'Antimo I 60 B2
Sant'Antioco I 64 E1
Sant Antoni de Portmany E 57 D7
Sant'Antonio Abate I 60 B3
Sant'Antonio di Gallura I 64 B3
Sant'Antonio di Santadi I 64 D1
Santanyí E 57 C11
Santa Olalla E 46 D4
Santa Oliva E 43 E7
Santa Ollala del Cala E 51 D7
Santa Pau E 43 C9
Santa Pola E 56 E3
Santar P 44 C5
Sant'Arcangelo I 60 C6
Santarcangelo di Romagna I 66 D5
Santarém P 44 F3
Sant'Arsenio I 60 C4
Santa Severina I 61 E7
Santas Martas E 39 D9
Santa Sofia I 66 E4
Santa Sofia P 50 B3
Santa Sofia d'Epiro I 61 D6
Santa Susana P 50 B4
Santa Susana P 50 C3
Santa Teresa di Gallura I 64 A3
Santa Teresa di Riva I 59 D7
Santău RO 151 C10
Santa Uxía E 38 C2
Santa Venerina I 59 D7
Santa Vitória P 50 D3
Santa Vitória do Ameixial P 50 B4
Sant Boi de Llobregat E 43 E8
Sant Carles de la Ràpita E 42 F5
Sant Celoni E 43 D8
Sant Cugat del Vallès E 43 E8
Sant'Egidio alla Vibrata I 62 B5
Sant'Elia a Pianisi I 63 D7
Sant Elia Fiumerapido I 62 D5
Sant Elm E 49 E9
San Telmo E 51 D6
Sant'Elpidio a Mare I 67 F8
San Teodoro I 64 B4
Santeramo in Colle I 61 B7
Santervás de la Vega E 39 C10
Santes Creus E 43 E6
Santhià I 68 C5
Sant Feliu de Guíxols E 43 D10
Sant Feliu de Pallerols E 43 C9
Sant Feliu Sasserra E 43 D8
Sant Hilari Sacalm E 43 D9
Sant Hipòlit de Voltregà E 43 C8
Santiago de Alcántara E 45 E6
Santiago de Calatrava E 53 A8
Santiago de Compostela E 38 C2
Santiago de Covelo E 38 D3
Santiago de la Espada E 55 C7
Santiago de la Ribera E 56 F3
Santiago del Campo E 45 E8
Santiago do Cacém P 50 C2
Santiago do Escoural P 50 B3
Santiagomillas E 39 D7
Santibáñez de Béjar E 45 D9
Santibáñez de la Peña E 39 C10
Santibáñez de la Sierra E 45 C9
Santibáñez de Tera E 39 E8
Santibáñez de Vidriales E 39 D7
Santibáñez el Bajo E 45 D8
Santibáñez Zarzaguda E 40 D4
Sant'Ilario d'Enza I 66 C1
Santillana E 40 B3
Sântimbru RO 152 E3

Santiponce E 51 E7
Santisteban del Puerto E 55 C6
Santiuste de San Juan Bautista E 46 B3
Santiz E 45 B9
Sant Jaime Mediterráneo E 57 B13
Sant Jaume d'Enveja E 42 F5
Sant Joan de Labritja E 49 F8
Sant Joan de les Abadesses E 43 C8
Sant Joan de Vilatorrada E 43 D7
Sant Joan les Fonts E 43 C9
Sant Josep de sa Talaia E 57 D7
Sant Julià de Lòria AND 33 F9
Sant Llorenç de Morunys E 43 C7
Sant Llorenç des Cardassar E 57 B11
Sant Lluís E 57 B13
Sant Martí de Tous E 43 D7
Sant Martí Sarroca E 43 E7
Sant Mateu E 42 G4
Sant Miquel de Balansat E 57 C7
Santo Aleixo P 50 B5
Santo Aleixo da Restauração P 51 C5
Santo Amador P 51 C5
Santo André P 50 C2
Santo Antoniño E 38 C2
Santo António dos Cavaleiros P 50 B1
Santo Domingo de la Calzada E 40 D6
Santo Domingo de Silos E 40 E5
Santo Estêvão P 50 B2
Santo Estêvão P 50 E4
Santo Isidro de Pegões P 50 B2
Santok PL 85 E8
Santomera E 56 E2
Sant Omero I 62 B5
Santoña E 40 B5
Santo Pietro I 58 E6
Santo-Pietro-di-Tenda F 37 F10
Santo-Pietro-di-Venaco F 37 G10
Santo Stefano al Mare I 37 D7
Santo Stefano Belbo I 37 B8
Santo Stefano d'Aveto I 37 B10
Santo Stefano di Cadore I 72 C6
Santo Stefano di Camastra I 58 C5
Santo Stefano di Magra I 69 E8
Santo Stefano Quisquina I 58 D3
Santo Stino di Livenza I 73 E6
Santo Tirso P 38 F3
Santo Tomé E 55 C6
Santovenia E 39 E8
Santpedor E 43 D7
Sant Pere de Ribes E 43 E7
Sant Pere de Torelló E 43 C8
Sant Pere Pescador E 43 C10
Sant Pol de Mar E 43 D9
Santpoort NL 182 A5
Sant Privat d'en Bas E 43 C8
Sant Quintí de Mediona E 43 E7
Sant Quirze de Besora E 43 C8
Sant Sadurní d'Anoia E 43 E7
Santullano E 39 B8
Santu Lussurgiu I 64 C2
Santurtzi E 40 B5
Sant Vicenç dels Horts E 43 E8
Sant Vincenç de Castellet E 43 D7
San Venanzo I 62 B2
San Vendemiano I 72 E5
San Vero Milis I 64 C2
San Vicente de Alcántara E 45 F6
San Vicente de Arana E 32 E1
San Vicente de la Barquera E 40 B3
San Vicente de la Sonsierra E 40 C6
San Vicente del Raspeig E 56 E3
San Vicente de Palacio E 46 B3
San Vicente de Toranzo E 40 B4
San Vicenzo E 38 C2
San Vincenzo I 59 B7
San Vincenzo I 65 A3
San Vincenzo Valle Roveto I 62 D5
San Vitero E 39 E7
San Vito I 64 E4
San Vito al Tagliamento I 73 E6
San Vito Chietino I 63 C6
San Vito dei Normanni I 61 B9
San Vito di Cadore I 72 D5
San Vito lo Capo I 58 C2
San Vito Romano I 62 D3
San Vito sullo Ionio I 59 B9
San Vittoria in Matenano I 62 A4
Sanxenxo E 38 D2
Sanxhax AL 168 A2
Sanza I 60 C5
Sânzieni RO 153 E8
Sanzoles E 39 F8
São Barnabé P 50 E3
São Bartolomeu P 44 F5
São Bartolomeu da Serra P 50 C2
São Bartolomeu de Messines P 50 E3
São Bento do Cortiço P 50 B4
São Brás P 50 D4
São Brás de Alportel P 50 E4
São Brás do Regedouro P 50 C3
São Brissos P 50 C4
São Cosmado P 44 B5
São Domingos P 50 D2
São Facundo P 44 F4
São Francisco da Serra P 50 C2
São Geraldo P 50 B3
São Gregório P 50 B4
São Jacinto P 44 C3
São João da Madeira P 44 C4
São João da Pesqueira P 44 B6
São João da Venda P 50 E4
São João do Campo P 44 D4
São João dos Caldeireiros P 50 D4
São José da Lamarosa P 44 F4
São Lourenço de Mamporcão P 50 B4
São Luís P 50 D2
São Manços P 50 C4
São Marcos da Ataboeira P 50 D4
São Marcos da Serra P 50 E3
São Marcos do Campo P 50 C4
São Martinho da Cortiça P 44 D4
São Martinho das Amoreiras P 50 D3
São Martinho de Angueira P 39 E7
São Martinho do Porto P 44 E2
São Matias P 50 C4
São Miguel de Acha P 45 D6
São Miguel de Machede P 50 B4
São Miguel de Rio Torto P 44 F4
São Miguel do Outeiro P 44 C4
São Miguel do Pinheiro P 50 D4
Saône F 26 F5
São Pedro da Cadeira P 44 F2
São Pedro de Muel P 44 E2
São Pedro de Solis P 50 E4
São Pedro do Sul P 44 C4
Saorge F 37 D7
São Romão P 51 B5
São Romão do Sado P 50 C3
São Sebastião dos Carros P 50 D4
São Teotónio P 50 D2
Saou F 35 A9
São Vicente P 38 E5
São Vicente da Beira P 44 D5
Sáp H 151 C7
Sapanca TR 171 E10
Săpânța RO 145 H8
Sapareva Banya BG 165 E7
Saparevo BG 165 E7
Săpata RO 160 D5
Sapes GR 171 B9
Sapna BIH 157 C11
Sa Pobla E 57 B11
Săpoca RO 161 C9
Sapotskin BY 137 F8
Sappada I 73 C6
Sap'parjåkka N 113 D17
Sappee FIN 127 C11
Sappen N 112 D7
Sappetavan S 107 A13
Sappetsele S 107 A13
Sappisaasi S 116 C7
Sapri I 60 C5
Sapsalampi FIN 123 F11
Sapsoperä FIN 125 B11
Sara FIN 122 F9
Saraby N 113 C12
Saracena I 60 D6
Saračinec HR 148 D6
Sarafovo BG 167 D9
Saraikļ LV 134 C2
Säräisniemi FIN 119 F17
Saraiu RO 155 D2
Sarajärvi FIN 120 C9
Sarajärvi FIN 129 B11
Sarajevo BIH 157 E9
Saramo FIN 125 C12
Saramon F 33 C7
Saran F 24 E6
Sáránd H 151 C8
Sarandë AL 168 E3
Sarantaporo GR 169 D7
Sarantsi BG 165 D8
Sa Ràpita E 57 C10
Sarasău RO 145 H8
Sarata UA 154 E5
Sărata Galbenă MD 154 D2
Sărata-Monteoru RO 161 C9
Sărata Nouă MD 154 E2
Sărăteni MD 154 D2
Sărătenii Vechi MD 154 B3
Saray TR 173 B8
Sarayakpinar TR 167 F7
Saraylar TR 173 C8
Šarbanovac SRB 159 F9
Sârbeni RO 161 E6
Sárbogárd H 149 C11
Sarcelles F 25 C7
Sarconi I 60 C5
Sardara I 64 D2
Šardice CZ 77 E12
Sardinia GR 174 B3
Sardoal P 44 E4
Sare F 32 D2
S'Arenal E 49 E10
Šarengrad HR 158 C3
Sarentino I 72 C3
Särevere EST 131 D10
Sarezzo I 69 B9
Sargans CH 71 C8
Sariai LT 137 C13
Saribeyler TR 173 F8
Saricaali TR 171 C10
Sariçam TR 177 B9
Sarichioi RO 155 D3
Saridanişment TR 167 F7
Sariegos E 39 C8
Sarikemer TR 177 D9
Sariköy TR 173 D8
Sariñena E 42 D3
Šarišské Michal'any SK 145 E3
Sariyer TR 173 B11
Sarjankylä FIN 123 B14
Sarkad H 151 D7
Sarkadkeresztúr H 151 D7
Särkelä FIN 121 C12
Sárkeresztúr H 149 B11
Särkijärvi FIN 117 C11
Särkijärvi FIN 119 C15
Särkijärvi FIN 120 E9
Särkikorpi FIN 125 D12
Särkikylä FIN 123 D11
Särkilahti FIN 127 B14
Särkilahti FIN 129 B11
Särkiluoma FIN 121 B14
Särkimo FIN 122 D8
Särkisalmi FIN 129 B11
Särkisalo FIN 123 E16
Särkisalo FIN 127 E8
Şarköy TR 173 C7
Sarlat-la-Canéda F 29 F8
Sarliac-sur-l'Isle F 29 E7
Sărmaș RO 152 D6
Şărmăşag RO 151 C10
Sărmașu RO 152 D4
Sármellék H 149 C8
Sarmijärvi FIN 114 F4
Sarmizegetusa RO 159 B10
Särna S 102 C5
Sarnadas do Ródão P 44 E5
Sarnaki PL 141 F7
Sarnano I 62 A4
Sārnate LV 134 B2
Sarnen CH 70 D6
Sarniç TR 177 C9
Sarnico I 69 B8
Sarno I 60 B3
Sarnowa PL 81 C11
Särnstugan S 102 C5
Särö S 91 D10
Sarochyna BY 133 F5
Saronno I 69 B7
Sárosd H 149 B11
Sárospatak H 145 G4
Šarovce SK 147 E7
Sarow D 84 C4
Sarpsborg N 95 D14
Sarracín E 40 D4
Sarral E 42 E6
Sarralbe F 27 C7
Sarrance F 32 D4
Sarrancolin F 33 E6
Sarraquinhos P 38 E4
Sarras F 30 E6
Sarre GB 15 E11
Sarre I 31 D11
Sarreaus E 38 D4
Sarrebourg F 27 C7
Sarreguemines F 27 B7
Sárrétudvari H 151 C7
Sarre-Union F 27 C7
Sarria E 38 C5
Sarrià de Ter E 43 C9
Sarrians F 35 B8
Sarrión E 48 D3
Sarroca de Lleida E 42 E5
Sarròch I 64 E3
Sarród H 149 A7
Sarrola-Carcopino F 37 G9
Sarron F 32 C5
Sarry F 25 C11
Sarsina I 66 E5
Sarstedt D 78 B6
Sárszentágota H 149 C11
Sárszentlőrinc H 149 C11
Sart B 183 D7
Sartaguda E 32 F1
Sarteano I 62 B1
Sartène F 37 H9
Sarti GR 170 D5
Sartilly F 23 C9
Sartininkai LT 134 F3
Sarud H 150 B6
Şaru Dornei RO 152 C6
Şaruhanli TR 177 B10
Sarule I 64 C3
Sărulești RO 161 C9
Sărulești RO 161 E9
Sárvár H 149 B7
Sarvela FIN 122 F9
Sarvijoki FIN 122 E7
Sarvikumpu FIN 125 F12
Sarviluoma FIN 122 F8
Sarvinki FIN 125 E14
Sarvisé E 32 E5
Sarvisvaara S 116 E6
Särvsjön S 102 A5
Sar"ya BY 133 E3
Sarzana I 69 E8
Sarzeau F 22 E6
Sarzedas P 44 E5
Sarzedo P 44 B5
Sasa NMK 164 E6
Sasalli TR 177 C8
Sasamón E 40 D3
Sasbach D 27 C9
Sasbachwalden D 186 D5
Sasca Montană RO 159 D8
Saschiz RO 152 E5
Săsciori RO 152 F3
Sascut RO 153 E10
Sásd H 149 D10
Sasina BIH 157 C6
Sasnava LT 137 D7
Sassali FIN 117 D15
Sassano I 60 C5
Sassari I 64 B2
Sassello I 37 C8
Sassen D 84 B4
Sassenage F 31 E8
Sassenberg D 17 E10
Sassenheim NL 16 D3
Sassetta I 65 A3
Sassnitz D 84 A5
Sassocorvaro I 66 E5
Sassoferrato I 67 F6
Sasso Marconi I 66 D3
Sassuolo I 66 C2
Sástago E 41 F11
Šaštín-Stráže SK 77 E12
Sas Van Gent NL 16 F1
Sáta H 145 G1
Satão P 44 C5
Satchinez RO 151 F7
Šateikiai LT 134 E3
Såtenäs villastad S 91 C12
Säter S 97 B14
Sätervallen S 102 A5
Sāti LV 134 C5
Satikļ LV 134 C5
Sätila S 91 D11
Satillieu F 30 E6
Satkūnai LT 134 D7
Satnica Đakovačka HR 149 F10
Sätofta S 87 D13
Sátoraljaújhely H 145 G4
Satovcha BG 170 A5
Satow D 83 C11
Sätra brunn S 98 C6
Satriano di Lucania I 60 B5
Satrup D 82 A7
Sattajärvi FIN 119 B12
Sattajärvi S 117 D10
Sattanen FIN 117 D17
Satteins A 71 C9
Satteldorf D 75 D7
Satter S 116 E7
Sattledt A 76 F6
Satulung RO 151 B11
Satu Mare RO 151 B10
Saubusse F 32 C3
Saúca E 47 B7
Sauca MD 154 A1
Săuca RO 151 C9
Saucats F 32 A4
Săucești RO 153 D9
Sauclières F 34 C5
Sauda N 94 C4
Saue EST 131 C9
Sauerlach D 75 G10
Sauga EST 131 E8
Saugnacq-et-Muret F 32 B4
Saugos LT 134 F2
Saugues F 30 F4
Saujon F 28 D4
Sauk AL 168 B2
Sauka LV 135 D10
Šaukėnai LT 134 E5
Saukko FIN 125 C11
Saukkoaapa FIN 115 D2
Saukkojärvi FIN 119 B16
Saukkola FIN 127 E10
Saukkoriipi FIN 117 E12
Saukonkylä FIN 123 E11
Sauland N 95 C9
Saulce-sur-Rhône F 35 A8
Sauldorf D 27 E11
Saulepi EST 130 E7
Săulești RO 160 D2
Saulgau D 71 A9
Saulgrub D 71 B12
Saulheim D 21 E10
Şăulia RO 152 D4
Saulieu F 25 F11
Saulkalne LV 135 C8
Saulkrasti LV 135 B8
Sault F 35 B9
Sault-de-Navailles F 32 C4
Sault-lès-Rethel F 19 F9
Saulx F 26 E5
Saulxures-sur-Moselotte F 27 E6
Saulzais-le-Potier F 29 B11
Saumos F 28 F3
Saumur F 23 F11
Saunajärvi FIN 125 C13
Saunakylä FIN 123 D13
Saunavaara FIN 115 D3
Saundersfoot GB 12 B5
Saurat F 33 E9
Sauriešl LV 135 C8
Sauris I 73 D6
Saursfjord N 110 E9
Sausnēja LV 135 C11
Sausset-les-Pins F 35 D9
Saussy F 26 F2
Sautens A 71 C11
Sautiņl LV 135 B8
Sautron F 23 F8
Sautso Kraftverk N 113 D12
Sauvagnon F 32 D5
Sauve F 35 C6
Sauveterre-de-Béarn F 32 D4
Sauveterre-de-Guyenne F 28 F5
Sauveterre-la-Lémance F 33 A8
Sauviat-sur-Vige F 29 D9
Sauvo FIN 126 E8
Sauxillanges F 30 D3
Sauzet F 33 B8
Sauzé-Vaussais F 29 C6
Sauzon F 22 F5
Sava I 61 C9
Sava SLO 73 D10
Săvădisla RO 151 D11
Savalia GR 174 D3
Savaloja FIN 119 E15
Sävar S 122 C5
Săvârșin RO 151 E9
Sävast S 118 C7
Savaştepe TR 173 F8
Säve S 91 D10
Savelli I 61 E7
Savenay F 23 F8
Săveni RO 153 B9
Săveni RO 161 D11
Saverdun F 33 D9
Saverna EST 131 E13
Saverne F 27 C7
Sävi FIN 126 B8
Säviä FIN 123 D17
Saviaho FIN 125 C10
Savières F 25 D10
Savigliano I 37 B7
Savignac-les-Églises F 29 E7
Savignano Irpino I 60 A4
Savignano sul Rubicone I 66 D5
Savigné-l'Évêque F 23 D12
Savigneux F 30 D5
Savigny-en-Sancerre F 25 F8
Savigny-lès-Beaune F 25 F12
Savigny-sur-Braye F 24 E4
Savijärvi FIN 125 C13
Savikylä FIN 125 C11
Savilahti FIN 129 C10
Savimäki FIN 124 C7
Savines-le-Lac F 36 B4
Săvinești RO 153 D8
Savino Selo SRB 158 B4
Saviranta FIN 121 F10
Saviselkä FIN 123 B16
Savitaipale FIN 128 C8
Sävja S 99 C9
Šavnik MNE 157 G11
Savognin CH 71 D9
Savoisy F 25 E11
Savona I 37 C8
Savonlinna FIN 129 B10
Savonranta FIN 125 F12
Savran' UA 154 A6
Sävsjö S 92 E5
Sävsjön S 97 C12
Savudrija HR 67 B7
Savukoski FIN 115 D4
Sawin PL 141 H8
Sawston GB 15 C9
Sax E 56 D3
Saxdalen S 97 B12
Saxen A 77 F7
Saxhyttan S 97 C11
Saxilby GB 11 E10
Saxmundham GB 15 C11
Saxnäs S 106 B8
Saxon CH 31 C11
Saxthorpe GB 15 B11
Saxvallen S 105 D12
Sayalonga E 53 C8
Sayatón E 47 D7
Sayda D 80 E4
Säynäjä FIN 121 B13
Säynätsalo FIN 123 F15
Säyneinen FIN 125 D10
Sázava CZ 77 C7
Sazli TR 171 E10
Sazli TR 177 D9
Sazoba TR 173 D7
Sazoba TR 177 B10
Scaër F 22 D4
Scăești RO 160 E3
Scafa I 62 C6
Scalasaig GB 4 C4
Scalby GB 11 C11
Scalea I 60 D5
Scaletta Zanclea I 59 C7
Scalloway GB 3 E14
Scandale I 61 E7
Scandiano I 66 C2
Scandicci I 66 E3
Scandriglia I 62 C3
Scanno I 62 D5
Scano di Montiferro I 64 C2
Scansano I 65 B4
Scânteia RO 153 D11
Scânteia RO 161 D10
Scânteiești RO 153 F12
Scanzano Jonico I 61 C7
Scapa GB 3 H11
Scarborough GB 11 C11
Scardovari I 66 C5
Scarinish GB 4 B3
Scario I 60 C4
Scărișoara RO 160 F5
Scarlino I 65 B3
Scarperia I 66 E3
Scartaglen IRL 8 D4
Scartaglin IRL 8 D4
Šćenica-Bobani BIH 162 D5
Scerni I 63 C7
Scey-sur-Saône-et-St-Albin F 26 E4
Schaafheim D 187 B7
Schaan FL 71 C9
Schaarsbergen NL 183 A7
Schaerbeek B 19 C9
Schaesberg NL 20 C6
Schaffhausen CH 27 E10
Schafflund D 82 A6
Schafstädt D 79 D10
Schafstedt D 82 B6
Schäftlarn D 75 G9
Schagen NL 16 C3
Schaijk NL 183 B7
Schalchen A 76 F4
Schalkau D 75 B9
Schalkhaar NL 183 A8
Schalksmühle D 17 F9
Schänis CH 27 F11
Schapen D 17 D9
Schaprode D 84 A4
Scharbeutz D 83 B9
Schardenberg A 76 E4
Schärding A 76 F4
Scharendijke NL 16 E1
Scharnebeck D 83 D9
Scharnitz A 72 B3
Scharnstein A 73 A8
Scharrel (Oldenburg) D 17 B9
Scharwoude NL 16 C4
Schashagen D 83 B9
Schattendorf A 149 A7
Schebheim D 75 C7
Scheemda NL 17 B7
Scheer D 27 D11
Scheeßel D 82 D6
Schefflenz D 21 F12
Scheggia e Pascelupo I 67 F6
Scheggino I 62 B3
Şcheia RO 153 B8
Şcheia RO 153 D11
Scheibbs A 77 F8
Scheiblingkirchen A 148 A6
Scheidegg D 71 B9
Scheifling A 73 B9
Scheinfeld D 75 C7
Schela RO 155 B1
Schela RO 160 C2
Schelklingen D 74 F6
Schellerten D 79 B7
Schemmerhofen D 71 A9
Schenefeld D 82 B6
Schenefeld D 83 C7
Schenkenfelden A 76 E6
Schenkenzell D 187 E5
Schenklengsfeld D 78 E6
Schermbeck D 17 E7
Schermen D 79 B10
Schermerhorn NL 16 C3
Scherpenheuvel B 19 C10
Scherpenzeel NL 16 D4
Scherwiller F 27 D7
Scherzingen CH 27 E11
Scheßlitz D 75 C9
Schiavi di Abruzzo I 63 D6
Schiedam NL 16 E2
Schieder-Schwalenberg D 17 E12
Schieren L 20 E6
Schierling D 75 E11
Schiermonnikoog NL 16 B6
Schiers CH 71 D9
Schiffdorf D 17 A11
Schifferstadt D 21 F10
Schifflange L 20 E6
Schiffweiler D 186 C3
Schijndel NL 16 E4
Schilde B 16 F3
Schillingen D 186 B2
Schillingsfürst D 75 D7
Schilpario I 69 A9
Schiltach D 27 D9
Schiltigheim F 27 C8
Schimatari GR 175 C8
Schinnen NL 183 D7
Schinos GR 174 B3
Schinveld NL 20 C5
Schio I 69 B11
Schipkau D 80 C5
Schipluiden NL 182 B4
Schirmeck F 27 D7
Schirmitz D 75 C11
Schitu RO 160 E5
Schitu RO 161 E7
Schitu Duca RO 153 C11
Schitu Golești RO 160 C6
Schkeuditz D 79 D11
Schkölen D 79 D10
Schköna D 79 C12
Schkopau D 79 D10
Schlabendorf D 80 C5
Schladen D 79 B8
Schlangen D 17 E11
Schlangenbad D 21 D10
Schleching D 72 A5
Schleiden D 20 C6
Schleife D 81 C7
Schleinbach A 77 F10
Schleitheim CH 27 E9
Schleiz D 79 E10
Schlema D 79 E12
Schlepzig D 80 B5
Schleswig D 82 A7
Schleusingen D 75 A8
Schlieben D 80 C4
Schliengen D 27 E8
Schlier D 71 B9
Schlierbach A 73 A9
Schlieren CH 27 F9
Schliersee D 72 A4
Schlitters A 72 B4
Schlitz D 78 E6
Schlossberg A 148 C4
Schloss Holte-Stukenbrock D 17 E11
Schlossvippach D 79 D9
Schlosswil CH 70 D5
Schlotheim D 79 D8
Schluchsee D 27 E9
Schlüchtern D 74 B6
Schlüsselfeld D 75 C8
Schmallenberg D 21 B10
Schmelz D 21 F7
Schmidgaden D 75 D11
Schmidmühlen D 75 D10
Schmiedeberg D 80 E5
Schmölln D 79 E11
Schmölln D 84 D6
Schnabelwaid D 75 C10
Schnackenburg D 83 D11
Schnaittach D 75 C9
Schneeberg D 79 E12
Schneidlingen D 79 C9
Schneizlreuth D 73 A6
Schnelldorf D 187 C9
Schnellmannshausen D 79 D7
Schneverdingen D 82 D7
Schnürpflingen D 187 E8
Schobüll D 82 A6
Schodnia PL 142 E5
Schoenberg B 20 D6
Scholen D 17 C11
Schollene D 83 E12
Schöllkrippen D 187 A7
Schöllnach D 76 E4
Schömberg D 27 D10
Schömberg D 187 D6
Schönaich D 187 D7
Schönau D 76 F3
Schönau im Schwarzwald D 27 E8
Schönbach A 77 F8
Schönberg D 83 C9
Schönberg D 84 E3
Schönberg (Holstein) D 83 B8
Schönberg am Kamp A 77 E9
Schönberg im Stubaital A 72 B3
Schönborn D 80 C5
Schondra D 74 B6
Schönebeck D 83 D12
Schönebeck (Elbe) D 79 B10
Schöneck D 75 B11
Schönecken D 20 D6
Schönenberg-Kübelberg D 186 C3
Schönermark D 84 D5
Schönewalde D 80 C4
Schönewörde D 79 A8
Schongau D 71 B11
Schönhausen D 79 A11
Schöningen D 79 B8
Schönkirchen D 83 B8
Schönow D 84 E5
Schönsee D 75 C12
Schöntal D 74 D6
Schönthal D 75 D12
Schönwalde D 80 C5
Schönwalde am Bungsberg D 83 B9
Schönwies A 71 C11
Schoondijke NL 16 F1
Schoonebeek NL 17 C7
Schoonhoven NL 16 E3
Schoorl NL 16 C3
Schopfheim D 27 E8
Schopfloch D 75 D7
Schöppenstedt D 79 B8
Schoppernau A 71 C10
Schöppingen D 17 D8
Schörfling am Attersee A 73 A8
Schorndorf D 74 E6
Schorndorf D 75 D12
Schortens D 17 A9
Schoten B 16 F2
Schotten D 21 D12
Schramberg D 27 D9
Schrecksbach D 21 C12
Schrems A 77 E8
Schrepkow D 83 E12
Schriesheim D 21 F11
Schrobenhausen D 75 E9
Schröder A 73 B9
Schrozberg D 74 D6
Schruns A 71 C9
Schübelbach CH 27 F10
Schuby D 82 A6
Schulenberg im Oberharz D 79 C7
Schull IRL 8 E3
Schulzendorf D 84 E6
Schüpfheim CH 70 D6
Schuttertal D 186 E4
Schutterwald D 186 E4
Schüttorf D 17 D8
Schwaan D 83 C12
Schwabach D 75 D9
Schwäbisch Gmünd D 74 E6
Schwäbisch Hall D 74 D6
Schwabmünchen D 71 A11
Schwabstedt D 82 B6
Schwaförden D 17 C11
Schwaigern D 27 B11
Schwalbach D 21 F7
Schwalmstadt-Treysa D 21 C12
Schwalmstadt-Ziegenhain D 21 C12
Schwanberg A 73 C11
Schwanden CH 71 C8
Schwandorf D 75 D11
Schwanebeck D 79 C9
Schwanenstadt A 76 F5
Schwanewede D 17 B11
Schwangau D 71 B11
Schwanstetten D 75 D9
Schwarme D 17 C12
Schwarmstedt D 82 E7
Schwarz D 83 D13
Schwarza D 79 E8
Schwarzach D 76 E3
Schwarzau im Gebirge A 148 A5
Schwarzenau A 77 E8
Schwarzenbach A 149 A6
Schwarzenbach am Wald D 75 B10
Schwarzenbek D 83 C8
Schwarzenberg D 79 E12
Schwarzenborn D 78 E5
Schwarzenburg CH 31 B11
Schwarzenfeld D 75 D11
Schwarzheide D 80 D5
Schwaz A 72 B4
Schwechat A 77 F10
Schwedeneck D 83 B8
Schwedt an der Oder D 84 D6
Schwegenheim D 187 C5
Schwei (Stadland) D 17 B10
Schweiburg D 17 B10
Schweich D 21 E7
Schweigen-Rechtenbach D 27 B8
Schweighouse-sur-Moder F 186 D4
Schweinfurt D 75 B7
Schweinitz D 80 C4
Schweinrich D 83 D13
Schwelm D 17 F8
Schwendau A 72 B4
Schwendi D 71 A9
Schwenningen D 27 D10
Schwepnitz D 80 D5
Schwerin D 83 C10
Schweringen D 17 C12
Schwerte D 17 F9
Schwichtenberg D 84 C5
Schwieberdingen D 27 C11
Schwiesau D 79 A9
Schwindegg D 75 F11
Schwinkendorf D 83 C13
Schwoich A 72 A5
Schwyz CH 71 C7
Sciacca I 58 D3
Sciara I 58 D4
Scicli I 59 F6
Sciez F 31 C9
Scigliano I 61 E6
Scilla I 59 C8
Ścinawa PL 81 D10
Scionzier F 31 C10
Scoarța RO 160 C2
Scobinţl RO 153 C9
Scoglitti I 58 F5
Scolaticci I 59 C6
Scole GB 15 C11
Scone GB 5 C10
Sconser GB 2 L4
Scopello I 68 B5
Scoppito I 62 C4
Scorbé-Clairvaux F 29 B6
Scordia I 59 E6
Scornicești RO 160 D5
Scorrano I 61 C10
Scorțaru Nou RO 161 C11
Scorțeni MD 154 C3
Scorțeni RO 153 D9
Scorțeni RO 161 C7
Scorțoasa RO 161 C9
Scorton GB 11 C8
Scorzè I 66 A5
Scotch Corner GB 11 C8
Scotch Corner IRL 7 D9
Scotshouse IRL 7 D8
Scourie GB 2 J6
Scousburgh GB 3 F14
Scrabster GB 3 H9
Screeb IRL 6 F3
Screggan IRL 7 F7
Scremerston GB 5 D13
Scribbagh GB 6 D6
Scrioaștea RO 160 E5
Scriob IRL 6 F3
Sculeni MD 153 C11
Scundu RO 160 D4
Scunthorpe GB 11 D10
Scuol CH 71 D10
Scurcola Marsicana I 62 C4
Scurtu Mare RO 160 E6
Scutelnici RO 161 D9
Seaca RO 160 E5
Seaca RO 160 F6
Seaca de Pădure RO 160 E2
Seaford GB 15 F9
Seaham GB 5 F14
Seahouses GB 5 D13
Seamer GB 11 C11
Seapatrick GB 7 D10
Seara P 38 E2
Seascale GB 10 C5
Seaton GB 5 F9
Seaton GB 13 D8
Seaton Delaval GB 5 E13
Seaton Sluice GB 5 E14
Seaview GB 13 D12
Sebal P 44 D3
Sébazac-Concourès F 34 B4
Sebbersund DK 86 B5
Sebechleby SK 147 E7
Sebedražie SK 147 D7
Sebeș RO 152 F3
Šebetov CZ 77 C11
Sebezh RUS 133 D4
Sebiș RO 151 E9
Sebnitz D 80 E6
Seč CZ 77 C9
Sečanj SRB 159 C6
Seča Reka SRB 158 E4
Secăria RO 161 C7
Secaș RO 151 F8
Sece LV 135 C10
Secemin PL 143 E8
Seckach D 27 B11
Seckau A 73 B10
Seclin F 19 C7
Secondigny F 28 B5
Sečovce SK 145 F4
Sečovská Polianka SK 145 F4
Secu RO 160 E2
Secuieni RO 152 E5
Secuieni RO 153 D9
Secuieni RO 153 D10
Secusigiu RO 151 E6
Seda LT 134 D4
Seda LV 131 F11
Sedan F 19 E10
Sedano E 40 C4
Sedbergh GB 10 C6
Seddülbahir TR 171 D10
Seden DK 86 E6
Šēdere LV 135 E12
Séderon F 35 B10
Sedgefield GB 5 F14
Sedico I 72 D5
Sedilo I 64 C2
Sedini I 64 B2
Sedlarica HR 149 E8
Sedlčany CZ 77 C6
Sedlec Prčice CZ 77 C7
Sedlice CZ 76 D5
Sedlice SK 145 F3
Sedliská SK 145 F4
Sedlnice CZ 146 B6
Sedrina I 69 B8
Šeduva LT 134 E7
Sįdziejowice PL 143 C7
Sįdzin PL 138 E6
Sįdziszów PL 143 E9
Sįdziszów Małopolski PL 143 F12
See A 71 C10
See A 73 B7
Seebach D 79 E7
Seebach D 187 D5
Seebergen D 79 E8
Seeboden A 73 C8
Seebruck D 72 A5
Seeburg D 79 C7
Seedorf D 83 C9
Seefeld D 75 F9
Seefeld D 80 A5
Seefeld (Stadland) D 17 B10

Seefeld in Tirol *A* 72 B3
Seeg *D* 71 B11
Seehausen *D* 79 B9
Seehausen *D* 84 D5
Seehausen (Altmark) *D* 83 E11
Seeheim-Jugenheim *D* 21 E11
Seekirchen am Wallersee *A* 73 A7
Seelow *D* 80 A6
Seelze *D* 78 B6
Seend *GB* 13 C10
Seeon *D* 72 A5
Sées *F* 23 C12
Seesen *D* 79 C7
Seeshaupt *D* 72 A3
Seethal *A* 73 B8
Seevetal *D* 83 D8
Seewiesen *A* 148 A4
Séez *F* 31 D10
Seferihisar *TR* 177 C8
Sefkerin *SRB* 158 C6
Sefrivatn *N* 105 A14
Seftigen *CH* 31 B12
Segalstad *N* 101 D12
Şegarcea *RO* 160 E3
Şegarcea-Vale *RO* 160 F5
Segeletz *D* 83 E13
Segersäng *S* 93 A11
Segersta *S* 103 D12
Segerstad *S* 89 C11
Segesd *H* 149 D8
Seggiano *I* 65 B5
Séglien *F* 22 D5
Seglinge *FIN* 99 B15
Seglingsberg *S* 98 C6
Seglodden *N* 114 C9
Seglvik *N* 112 C7
Segmon *S* 97 D9
Segni *I* 62 D4
Segonzac *F* 28 D5
Segorbe *E* 48 E4
Segovia *E* 46 C4
Segré *F* 23 E10
Ségrie *F* 23 D12
Ségur *F* 34 B4
Segura *P* 45 E7
Segura de la Sierra *E* 55 C7
Segura de León *E* 51 C6
Segura de los Baños *E* 42 F2
Segurilla *E* 46 D3
Sehlde *D* 79 B7
Sehma *D* 76 A3
Sehnde *D* 79 B6
Seia *P* 44 D5
Şeica Mare *RO* 152 E4
Şeica Mică *RO* 152 E4
Seiches-sur-le-Loir *F* 23 E11
Seiersberg *A* 148 B4
Seierstad *N* 105 B10
Seifhennersdorf *D* 81 E7
Seignelay *F* 25 E10
Seignelégier *CH* 27 F6
Seilhac *F* 29 E9
Seillans *F* 36 D5
Seilles *B* 183 E6
Seimeni *RO* 155 E2
Seinäjoki *FIN* 122 E9
Seini *RO* 151 B11
Seinsheim *D* 75 C7
Seipäjärvi *FIN* 117 D16
Seirijai *LT* 137 E8
Seissan *F* 33 D7
Seitajärvi *FIN* 115 C3
Şeitin *RO* 150 E6
Seix *F* 33 E8
Seixal *P* 50 B1
Sejerby *DK* 87 D8
Sejerslev *DK* 86 B3
Sejet *DK* 86 D5
Sejny *PL* 136 E7
Sekkemo *N* 112 D8
Šekovići *BIH* 157 D10
Sjkowa *PL* 145 D3
Sjkowo *PL* 81 A10
Sel *S* 107 E10
Sel *S* 107 E13
Sela *HR* 149 E6
Selånger *S* 103 B13
Selanovtsi *BG* 160 F3
Selänpää *FIN* 128 C6
Selargius *I* 64 E3
Şelaru *RO* 160 E6
Selattyn *GB* 10 F5
Selaya *E* 40 B4
Selb *D* 75 B11
Selbekken *N* 104 E7
Selbitz *D* 75 B10
Selbu *N* 105 E10
Selbustrand *N* 105 E9
Selby *GB* 11 D9
Selcë *AL* 163 D8
Selce *HR* 67 B10
Selce *SK* 147 D8
Selci Đakovački *HR* 149 F10
Selçuk *TR* 177 D9
Selde *DK* 86 B4
Selegas *I* 64 D3
Selenicë *AL* 168 C2
Selent *D* 83 B8
Selero *GR* 171 B7
Sélestat *F* 27 D7
Selet *S* 118 C7
Selet *S* 122 B3
Seleuş *RO* 151 E8
Seleuš *SRB* 159 C6
Selevac *SRB* 159 E6
Seleznevo *RUS* 129 D10
Selfjord *N* 110 D5
Sēļi *LV* 131 F10
Selice *SK* 146 E5
Seligenstadt *D* 187 A6
Şelimbăr *RO* 152 F4
Selimiye *TR* 177 E10
Selimpaşa *TR* 173 B9
Selimşahlar *TR* 177 B9
Selishtë *AL* 168 A3
Selishte *BG* 165 E7
Selište *SRB* 159 F9
Selitë *AL* 168 C2
Selja *S* 102 D7
Selje *N* 100 B2
Seljeli *N* 108 D6
Seljelynes *N* 111 B17
Seljenes *N* 113 B15
Seljord *N* 95 D9
Selkäjärvi *S* 116 E8
Selkälä *FIN* 115 E6
Selkirk *GB* 5 D11
Selkopp *N* 113 B14
Selkoskylä *FIN* 121 D13
Sella *E* 56 D4
Sellano *I* 62 B3
Sellasia *GR* 174 E5
Selles-St-Denis *F* 24 F6
Selles-sur-Cher *F* 24 F6
Sellia *GR* 178 E7
Sellia Marina *I* 59 B10
Sellières *F* 31 B8
Sellin *D* 84 B5
Sellindge *GB* 15 E10
Selling *DK* 86 C6
Sellingen *NL* 17 C8
Sellrain *A* 72 B3
Sellye *H* 149 E9
Selm *D* 17 E8
Selmes *P* 50 C4
Selmsdorf *D* 83 C9
Selnes *N* 104 D7
Selnes *N* 111 B17
Selnes *N* 111 C13
Selo *BIH* 157 D10
Selommes *F* 24 E5
Selongey *F* 26 E3
Selonnet *F* 36 C4
Selow *D* 83 C11
Seløy *N* 108 D3
Selsey *GB* 15 F7
Selsingen *D* 17 B12
Selsjön *S* 107 E12
Selsøyvika *N* 108 C4
Selters (Westerwald) *D* 21 C9
Seltjäm *S* 107 D13
Seltz *F* 27 C9
Selva *E* 57 B10
Selva *I* 61 B8
Selva *N* 104 D7
Selva dei Molini *I* 72 C4
Selva di Progno *I* 69 B11
Selva di Val Gardena *I* 72 C4
Selvær *N* 108 C3
Selvåg *N* 104 D6
Selvazzano Dentro *I* 66 B4
Selvino *I* 69 B8
Selyatyn *UA* 152 B6
Selzthal *A* 73 A9
Sem *N* 95 D12
Seman *AL* 168 C1
Sembadel *F* 30 E4
Sembrancher *CH* 31 C11
Sēme *LV* 134 B6
Séméac *F* 33 D6
Sémelay *F* 30 B4
Semeliškės *LT* 137 D10
Semeljci *HR* 149 F11
Semeni *MD* 153 C11
Semenivka *UA* 154 E6
Semerovo *SK* 146 E6
Semič *SLO* 73 E11
Semide *P* 44 D4
Semily *CZ* 81 E8
Seminara *I* 59 C8
Semizovac *BIH* 157 E9
Semlac *RO* 151 E6
Semlow *D* 83 B13
Semmenstedt *D* 79 B8
Semoutiers-Montsaon *F* 26 D3
Sempach *CH* 27 F9
Šempeter *SLO* 73 E8
Semproniano *I* 65 B5
Semriach *A* 148 B4
Šemša *SK* 145 F3
Šemševo *NMK* 164 E3
Semur-en-Auxois *F* 25 F11
Semur-en-Brionnais *F* 30 C5
Semussac *F* 28 D4
Sena *E* 42 D3
Seňa *SK* 145 F3
Senales *I* 71 D11
Senarpont *F* 18 E4
Sénas *F* 35 C9
Sencelles *E* 57 B10
Senčur *SLO* 73 D9
Send *GB* 15 E7
Senden *D* 75 F7
Sendenhorst *D* 17 E9
Sendets *F* 32 D5
Sendim *P* 38 F3
Sendim *P* 39 F7
Şendreni *RO* 155 C1
Şendriceni *RO* 153 B8
Senec *SK* 146 E4
Seneffe *B* 19 C9
Seneghe *I* 64 C2
Senes *E* 55 E8
Senez *F* 36 D4
Senftenberg *A* 77 F9
Senftenberg *D* 80 C6
Sengouagnet *F* 33 E7
Senhora do Rosário *P* 45 F6
Senica *SK* 146 D4
Senice na Hané *CZ* 77 C12
Senigallia *I* 67 E7
Senis *I* 64 D2
Senise *I* 60 C6
Senj *HR* 67 C10
Senje *SRB* 159 F7
Senjehesten *N* 111 B12
Senjehopen *N* 111 B13
Senjski Rudnik *SRB* 159 F8
Sen'kava *BY* 133 D3
Šenkvice *SK* 146 E4
Senlis *F* 25 B8
Sennan *S* 87 B11
Sennariolo *I* 64 C2
Sennecey-le-Grand *F* 30 B6
Sennels *DK* 86 B3
Sennen *GB* 12 E3
Sennik *BG* 165 D11
Sennori *I* 64 B2
Sennwald *CH* 71 C8
Sennybridge *GB* 13 B7
Senohrad *SK* 147 E8
Senokos *BG* 167 B10
Senonches *F* 24 C5
Senones *F* 27 D6
Senorbì *I* 64 D3
Senouillac *F* 33 C9
Senovo *BG* 161 F8
Senožeče *SLO* 73 E9
Sens *F* 25 D9
Sens-de-Bretagne *F* 23 D8
Senta *SRB* 150 F5
Sentein *F* 33 E7
Senterada *E* 33 F7
Šentilj *SLO* 148 C5
Šentjernej *SLO* 148 E4
Šentjur pri Celju *SLO* 148 D4
Senuc *F* 19 F10
Seon *CH* 27 F9
Šepak *BIH* 157 C11
Sepekov *CZ* 77 D6
Sepino *I* 60 A3
Sjpólno Krajeńskie *PL* 85 D13
Sjpolno Wielkie *PL* 85 C11
Seppois-le-Bas *F* 27 E7
Şepreuş *RO* 151 D8
Septèmes-les-Vallons *F* 35 D9
Septemvri *BG* 165 E9
Septemvriytsi *BG* 160 F2
Septeuil *F* 24 C6
Septfonds *F* 33 B9
Septmoncel *F* 31 C8
Sepulcro-Hilario *E* 45 C8
Sepúlveda *E* 40 F4
Sequals *I* 73 D6
Sequeros *E* 45 C8
Seraincourt *F* 19 E9
Seraing *B* 19 C12
Séranon *F* 36 D5
Seravezza *I* 66 E1
Şerbăneşti *RO* 160 E5
Şerbettar *TR* 173 B6
Sërboc *RKS* 163 D10
Şercaia *RO* 152 F6
Serdiana *I* 64 E3
Sereď *SK* 146 E5
Seredka *RUS* 132 E3
Seredyne *UA* 145 F6
Seredžius *LT* 137 C7
Seregélyes *H* 149 B11
Seregno *I* 69 B7
Séreilhac *F* 29 D8
Sērene *LV* 135 C10
Sérent *F* 22 E6
Serényfalva *H* 145 G1
Serfaus *A* 71 C11
Sergen *TR* 167 F9
Sergines *F* 25 D9
Sergnano *I* 69 C8
Serhat *TR* 172 E6
Serhiyivka *UA* 154 B6
Seriate *I* 69 B8
Sérifontaine *F* 18 F4
Serifos *GR* 175 E10
Sérignan *F* 34 D5
Sérignan-du-Comtat *F* 35 B8
Serina *I* 69 B8
Serino *I* 60 B3
Serinyà *E* 43 C9
Sermaises *F* 25 D7
Sermano *F* 37 G10
Sermenin *NMK* 169 B7
Sermide *I* 66 C3
Sermite *LV* 134 C3
Sermoneta *I* 62 D4
Sermoyer *F* 31 B6
Sērmūkši *LV* 135 B11
Sernancelhe *P* 44 C6
Serno *D* 79 C11
Serock *PL* 138 D5
Serock *PL* 139 E11
Serokomla *PL* 141 G6
Serón *E* 55 E8
Serón de Nájima *E* 41 F7
Serooskerke *NL* 182 B3
Seròs *E* 42 E4
Serpa *P* 50 D4
Serpins *P* 44 D4
Serpneve *UA* 154 E4
Serqueux *F* 26 E4
Serquigny *F* 24 B4
Serra *E* 48 E4
Serracapriola *I* 63 D8
Serrada *E* 39 F10
Serra de'Conti *I* 67 E7
Serradifalco *I* 58 E4
Serra-di-Ferro *F* 37 H9
Serradilla *E* 45 E8
Serradilla del Arroyo *E* 45 C8
Serra-di-Scopamène *F* 37 H10
Serramanna *I* 64 E2
Serramazzoni *I* 66 D2
Serranillos *E* 46 D3
Serra Riccò *I* 37 B9
Serra San Bruno *I* 59 B9
Serrastretta *I* 59 A9
Serravalle *RSM* 66 E5
Serravalle di Chienti *I* 62 A3
Serravalle Scrivia *I* 37 B9
Serre *I* 60 B4
Serrejón *E* 45 E9
Serrenti *I* 64 E2
Serres *F* 35 B10
Serres *GR* 169 B10
Serres-Castet *F* 32 D5
Serri *I* 64 D3
Serriera *F* 37 G9
Serrière-de-Briord *F* 31 D7
Serrières *F* 30 E6
Serrig *D* 21 E7
Serritslev *DK* 90 E6
Serrungarina *I* 67 E6
Sers *F* 29 D6
Sersale *I* 59 A10
Sertã *P* 44 E4
Sertolovo *RUS* 129 E13
Servance *F* 26 E6
Serverette *F* 30 F3
Servia *GR* 169 D7
Servian *F* 34 D5
Serviana *GR* 168 E4
Servigliano *I* 62 A4
Servon-sur-Vilaine *F* 23 D9
Servoz *F* 31 D10
Sery *F* 19 E9
Serzedo *P* 44 B3
Sesa *E* 42 D3
Sesava *LV* 134 D7
Seseña *E* 46 D5
Seskarö *S* 119 C11
Seskinore *GB* 7 C8
Sesma *E* 32 F1
Sessa Aurunca *I* 60 A1
Sessa Cilento *I* 60 C4
Ses Salines *E* 57 C11
Seßlach *D* 75 B8
Sesta Godano *I* 69 E8
Šestanovac *HR* 157 F6
S'Estanyol de Migjorn *E* 57 C10
Sestao *E* 40 B6
Sestino *I* 66 E5
Sesto *I* 72 C5
Sesto al Reghena *I* 73 E6
Sesto Calende *I* 68 B6
Sesto Campano *I* 60 A2
Sesto Fiorentino *I* 66 E3
Šeštokai *LT* 137 E7
Sestola *I* 66 D2
Sesto San Giovanni *I* 69 B7
Sestriere *I* 31 F10
Sestri Levante *I* 37 C10
Sestrimo *BG* 165 E8
Sestroretsk *RUS* 129 E12
Sestu *I* 64 E3
Šešuoliai *LT* 135 F9
Sesvete *HR* 148 E6
Seta *GR* 175 B8
Šeta *LT* 135 F8
Sète *F* 35 D6
Setenil *E* 51 F9
Setermoen *N* 111 C15
Seternes *N* 100 A6
Setiles *E* 47 C9
Setivoho *BIH* 158 F3
Šetonje *SRB* 159 E7
Setter *GB* 3 E14
Settimo San Pietro *I* 64 E3
Settimo Torinese *I* 68 C4
Settimo Vittone *I* 68 B4
Settle *GB* 11 C7
Setúbal *P* 50 B2
Seubersdorf in der Oberpfalz *D* 75 D10
Seui *I* 64 D3
Seuil-d'Argonne *F* 26 C3
Seulo *I* 64 D3
Seurre *F* 31 A7
Seva *E* 43 D8
Sevar *BG* 161 F9
Sevaster *AL* 168 D2
Sevel *DK* 86 C3
Sevenoaks *GB* 15 E9
Sevenum *NL* 16 F6
Sévérac-le-Château *F* 34 B5
Sever do Vouga *P* 44 C4
Severin *HR* 149 E7
Severinovca *MD* 154 A3
Severnyak *BG* 155 F1
Seveso *I* 69 B7
Ševětín *CZ* 77 D7
Sevettijärvi *FIN* 114 E5
Sevid *HR* 156 E5
Sévignacq *F* 32 D5
Sevilla *E* 51 E8
Sevilla la Nueva *E* 46 D4
Sevilleja de la Jara *E* 46 E3
Şevketiye *TR* 173 D8
Sevlievo *BG* 166 C4
Sevnica *SLO* 148 D4
Sevojno *SRB* 158 F4
Sévrier *F* 31 D9
Sexdrega *S* 91 D13
Seyches *F* 33 A6
Seyda *D* 79 C12
Seymen *TR* 173 B8
Seymen *TR* 173 B9
Seyne *F* 36 C4
Seynes *F* 35 B7
Seynod *F* 31 D9
Seyrek *TR* 177 B8
Seyssel *F* 31 D8
Seysses *F* 33 C8
Sežana *SLO* 73 E8
Sézanne *F* 25 C10
Sezemice *CZ* 77 B9
Sezimovo Ústí *CZ* 77 D7
Sezze *I* 62 E4
Sfaka *GR* 179 E10
Sfântu Gheorghe *RO* 153 F7
Sfântu Gheorghe *RO* 161 D9
Sfendami *GR* 169 D8
Sfinţeşti *RO* 160 E6
Sgiogarstaigh *GB* 2 J4
's-Gravendeel *NL* 16 E3
's-Gravenhage *NL* 16 D2
's-Gravenmoer *NL* 182 B5
's-Gravenpolder *NL* 16 F1
's-Gravenvoeren *B* 183 D7
's-Gravenzande *NL* 16 E2
Sgurgola *I* 62 D4
Shabla *BG* 155 F3
Shaftesbury *GB* 13 C10
Shalfleet *GB* 13 D12
Shalwy *IRL* 6 C5
Shanacrane *IRL* 8 E4
Shanagolden *IRL* 8 C4
Shanavogh *IRL* 8 C4
Shankill *IRL* 7 F10
Shanklin *GB* 13 D12
Shanlaragh *IRL* 8 E4
Shantonagh *IRL* 7 D9
Shanvus *IRL* 6 D6
Shap *GB* 10 B6
Sharashova *BY* 141 E10
Sharavogue *IRL* 7 F7
Sharkawshchyna *BY* 133 F2
Sharkovo *BG* 167 E7
Shatilava *BY* 133 F6
Shats'k *UA* 141 H9
Shaverki *RUS* 125 D17
Shawbost *GB* 2 J3
Shchyrets' *UA* 145 D8
's-Heerenberg *NL* 16 E6
's-Heerenhoek *NL* 182 C3
Sheerness *GB* 15 E10
Sheffield *GB* 11 E9
Shefford *GB* 15 C8
Shelekhove *UA* 154 B6
Shëmri *AL* 163 E9
Shëngjergj *AL* 168 B3
Shëngjin *AL* 163 F8
Shepit *UA* 152 B6
Shepshed *GB* 11 F9
Shepton Mallet *GB* 13 C9
Sherborne *GB* 13 D9
Sherborne St John *GB* 13 C12
Sherburn in Elmet *GB* 11 D9
Shercock *IRL* 7 E9
Sheringham *GB* 15 B11
Sherston *GB* 13 B10
's-Hertogenbosch *NL* 16 E4
Shetaj *AL* 168 A2
Shevchenkove *UA* 155 B4
Shieldaig *GB* 2 K5
Shifnal *GB* 11 F7
Shijak *AL* 168 B2
Shildon *GB* 5 F13
Shillelagh *IRL* 9 C9
Shinfield *GB* 15 E7
Shinness Lodge *GB* 2 J8
Shinrone *IRL* 7 G7
Shipka *BG* 166 D4
Shipkovo *BG* 165 D10
Shipley *GB* 11 D8
Shipston on Stour *GB* 13 A11
Shipton *GB* 10 F6
Shiroka Lŭka *BG* 165 F10
Shirokë *AL* 163 E7
Shivachevo *BG* 166 D6
Shkodër *AL* 163 E8
Shkorpilovtsi *BG* 167 D9
Shlissel'burg *RUS* 129 F15
Shmoylovo *RUS* 132 F4
Sho *BY* 133 F4
Shoreham-by-Sea *GB* 15 F8
Shotts *GB* 5 D9
Shrewsbury *GB* 10 F6
Shrewton *GB* 13 C11
Shrigley *GB* 7 D11
Shrivenham *GB* 13 B11
Shrule *IRL* 6 E4
Shtëpaj *AL* 168 C3
Shtërmen *AL* 168 C3
Shtërpcë *RKS* 164 E3
Shtime *RKS* 164 E3
Shtiqën *AL* 163 E9
Shtit *BG* 166 F6
Shtrŭklevo *BG* 161 F8
Shumen *BG* 167 C7
Shumilina *BY* 133 F7
Shushicë *AL* 168 B3
Shymkove *UA* 154 B6
Shyroke *UA* 145 G7
Shyroke *UA* 154 F6
Shyryayeve *UA* 154 C6
Siamanna *I* 64 D2
Sianów *PL* 85 B10
Siatista *GR* 169 D6
Šiaulėnai *LT* 134 E6
Šiauliai *LT* 134 E6
Sibari *I* 61 D6
Sibbhult *S* 88 C6
Sibbo *FIN* 127 E13
Šibenik *HR* 156 E4
Sibinj *HR* 157 B8
Sibiu *RO* 152 F4
Sible Hedingham *GB* 15 D10
Sibnica *SRB* 158 E5
Sibo *S* 103 D12
Şibot *RO* 151 F11
Sibsey *GB* 11 E12
Sic *RO* 152 D3
Sićevo *SRB* 164 C5
Sicheviţa *RO* 159 D8
Sicienko *PL* 138 D4
Siciny *PL* 81 C10
Sickte *D* 79 B8
Şicula *RO* 151 E8
Şiculeni *RO* 153 E7
Siculiana *I* 58 E3
Šid *SK* 147 E9
Šid *SRB* 158 C3
Sidari *GR* 168 E2
Sidbury *GB* 13 D8
Sidcup *GB* 15 E9
Siddeburen *NL* 17 B7
Siddi *I* 64 D2
Sideby *FIN* 122 F6
Sidensjö *S* 107 E14
Siderno *I* 59 C9
Sidgunda *LV* 135 C9
Sidirokastro *GR* 169 B9
Sidirokastro *GR* 174 E4
Sidironero *GR* 171 B6
Sidmouth *GB* 13 D8
Sidrabiņi *LV* 135 C11
Sidsjö *S* 103 A9
Sidskogen *S* 103 C10
Sidzina *PL* 142 E3
Siebe *N* 112 F11
Siebengewald *NL* 183 B8
Siebenlehn *D* 80 D4
Siecieborzyce *PL* 81 C9
Sieciechów *PL* 141 G5
Siedlanka *PL* 143 F12
Siedlce *PL* 141 F6
Siedlec *PL* 81 B10
Siedlice *PL* 85 C8
Siedliska *PL* 144 D3
Siedlisko *PL* 81 C9
Siedlisko *PL* 85 E10
Siedliszcze *PL* 141 H8
Siedliszcze *PL* 144 A8
Siegburg *D* 21 C8
Siegen *D* 21 C10
Siegenburg *D* 75 E10
Sieggraben *A* 149 A6
Sieghartskirchen *A* 77 F10
Siegsdorf *D* 73 A6
Sieima *N* 112 E8
Siek *D* 83 C8
Siekasjärvi *S* 117 E10
Siekkinen *FIN* 121 C11
Sielec *PL* 144 A8
Sielnica *SK* 147 D8
Siemianowice Śląskie *PL* 143 F7
Siemianówka *PL* 141 E9
Siemiatycze *PL* 141 F7
Siemień *PL* 141 G7
Siemkowice *PL* 143 D6
Siemyśl *PL* 85 B9
Siena *I* 66 F3
Sieniawa *PL* 144 C6
Sieniec *PL* 142 D6
Siennica *PL* 141 F5
Siennica Różana *PL* 144 A7
Sienno *PL* 143 D11
Sieppijärvi *FIN* 117 D11
Siepraw *PL* 147 B9
Sieradz *PL* 142 C6
Sieraków *PL* 81 A10
Sieraków *PL* 142 E6
Sierakówek *PL* 139 F7
Sierakowice *PL* 138 B4
Sierck-les-Bains *F* 20 F6
Sierentz *F* 27 E7
Sierksdorf *D* 83 B9
Sierniczyno *PL* 85 C10
Sierndorf *A* 77 F10
Sierning *A* 76 F6
Sieroszewice *PL* 142 C4
Sierpc *PL* 139 E8
Sierra de Fuentes *E* 45 F8
Sierra de Luna *E* 41 D10
Sierra de Yeguas *E* 53 B7
Sierra Engarcerán *E* 48 D5
Sierre *CH* 31 C12
Sierro *E* 55 E8
Siershahn *D* 185 D8
Siersleben *D* 79 C10
Siete Iglesias de Trabancos *E* 39 F9
Sietow *D* 83 D13
Şieu *RO* 152 C5
Şieu-Măgheruş *RO* 152 C4
Şieu-Odorhei *RO* 152 C4
Şieuţ *RO* 152 D5
Sieversdorf *D* 83 E12
Sieverstedt *D* 82 A6
Sievi *FIN* 123 C13
Sievin asema eli Korhoskylä *FIN* 123 C12
Siewierz *PL* 143 F7
Sifferbo *S* 97 A13
Sifjord *N* 111 B13
Sig *DK* 86 D3
Sigean *F* 34 D4
Sigerfjord *N* 111 C10
Siggelkow *D* 83 D11
Siggerud *N* 95 C13
Sigglesthorne *GB* 11 D11
Sighetu Marmaţiei *RO* 145 H8
Sighişoara *RO* 152 E5
Sigillo *I* 67 F6
Sigmaringen *D* 27 D11
Sigmaringendorf *D* 27 D11
Sigmen *BG* 167 D7
Sigmundsherberg *A* 77 E9
Signa *I* 66 E3
Signau *CH* 70 D5
Signes *F* 35 D10
Signy-l'Abbaye *F* 19 E9
Signy-le-Petit *F* 19 E9
Sigogne *F* 28 D5
Sigoulès *F* 29 F6
Sigri *GR* 177 A6
Sigtuna *S* 99 C9
Sigüeiro *E* 38 C3
Sigüenza *E* 47 B7
Sigües *E* 32 E3
Sigulda *LV* 135 B9
Sihelné *SK* 147 B8
Sihtuuna *FIN* 119 B13
Sihva *EST* 131 E12
Siikainen *FIN* 126 B6
Siikajoki *FIN* 119 E13
Siika-Kämä *FIN* 119 B16
Siikakoski *FIN* 128 B8
Siilinjärvi *FIN* 124 D9
Siimusti *EST* 131 D12
Siironen *FIN* 119 F11
Siivikko *FIN* 121 D10
Sijarinska Banja *SRB* 164 D4
Sijekovac *BIH* 157 B8
Sijsele *B* 182 C2
Sikås *S* 106 D8
Sikeå *S* 118 F5
Sikfors *S* 118 C6
Sikirevci *HR* 157 B9
Siklós *H* 149 E10
Siknäs *S* 118 C9
Sikole *SRB* 159 E9
Sikórz *PL* 139 E8
Sikovuono *FIN* 113 F18
Sīkrags *LV* 130 F4
Siksele *S* 107 B16
Sikšjö *S* 107 B12
Siksjö *S* 107 C13
Siksjön *S* 102 C8
Siksjönäs *S* 107 B10
Sikšņi *LV* 134 D2
Sil *S* 107 D10
Silajāņi *LV* 133 D1
Šilalė *LT* 134 F4
Silandro *I* 71 D11
Silanus *I* 64 C2
Silavēveri *LV* 135 D10
Šilavotas *LT* 137 D8
Silba *HR* 67 D10
Silbaš *SRB* 158 C3
Silene *LV* 135 E13
Silenen *CH* 71 D7
Silenrieux *B* 19 D9
Siles *E* 55 C7
Silfiac *F* 22 D5
Siligo *I* 64 B2
Şilindia *RO* 151 E8
Šiliqua *I* 64 E2
Siliştea *RO* 155 C1
Siliştea *RO* 155 E2
Siliştea *RO* 160 E6
Siliştea Crucii *RO* 160 E2
Siliştea Nouă *RO* 160 E5
Silistra *BG* 161 E10
Silivaşu de Câmpie *RO* 152 D4
Silivri *TR* 173 B9
Siljan *N* 95 D11
Siljansnäs *S* 102 E8
Siljeåsen *S* 106 C9
Siljeborg *DK* 86 C5
Silla *E* 48 F4
Sillamäe *EST* 132 C2
Sillano *I* 66 D1
Sillanpää *FIN* 123 D11
Sillans-la-Cascade *F* 36 D4
Sillebotten *S* 96 D7
Silleda *E* 38 C3
Sillé-le-Guillaume *F* 23 D11
Sillerö *S* 97 A10
Sillian *A* 72 C5
Silloth *GB* 5 F10
Sillre *S* 103 A12
Silnowo *PL* 85 C10
Silo *HR* 67 B10
Sils *CH* 71 E9
Sils *E* 43 D9
Silsjönäs *S* 107 D10
Siltaharju *FIN* 115 C1
Siltakylä *FIN* 128 E6
Silte *S* 93 E12
Šilukalns *LV* 135 C13
Šilutė *LT* 134 F2
Šiluva *LT* 134 E6
Silva *LV* 135 B11
Silvalen *N* 108 E3
Silvaplana *CH* 71 E9
Silvares *P* 44 D5
Silveiras *P* 50 B3
Silverdalen *S* 92 D7
Silvermines *IRL* 8 C6
Silverstone *GB* 13 A12
Silverton *GB* 13 D8
Silvi *I* 62 B6
Silz *A* 71 C11
Simala *I* 64 D2
Simancas *E* 39 E10
Şimand *RO* 151 E7
Simandre *F* 31 B6
Šimanovci *SRB* 158 D5
Simantra *GR* 169 D9
Simat de la Valdigna *E* 56 C4
Simaxis *I* 64 D2
Simbach *D* 75 E12
Simbach am Inn *D* 76 F4
Simbario *I* 59 B9
Simeå *S* 103 C11
Simeonovgrad *BG* 166 E5
Simeria *RO* 151 F11
Simeri-Crichi *I* 59 B10
Simested *DK* 86 B5
Şimian *RO* 151 C9
Şimian *RO* 159 D10
Simiane-la-Rotonde *F* 35 C10
Simićevo *SRB* 159 E7
Siminicea *RO* 153 B8
Simitli *BG* 165 F7
Simlångsdalen *S* 87 B12
Şimleu Silvaniei *RO* 151 C10
Simmelsdorf *D* 75 C9
Simmerath *D* 20 C6
Simmerberg *D* 71 B9
Simmern (Hunsrück) *D* 21 E9
Simnas *LT* 137 E8
Simnicu de Sus *RO* 160 E3
Simo *FIN* 119 C14
Simola *FIN* 129 D9
Şimoneşti *RO* 152 E6
Simoniemi *FIN* 119 C13
Simonkangas *FIN* 119 C17
Simonkylä *FIN* 119 C14
Simonsberg *D* 82 B5
Simonstorp *S* 93 B8
Simontornya *H* 149 C11
Šimonys *LT* 135 E10
Simopoulo *GR* 174 D4
Simorre *F* 33 D7
Simos *GR* 174 C4
Simpelveld *NL* 20 C5
Simplon *CH* 68 A5
Simrishamn *S* 88 D6
Simskardet *N* 106 A5
Simuna *EST* 131 C12
Sinabelkirchen *A* 148 B5
Sinaia *RO* 161 C7
Sinalepa *EST* 130 D7
Sinalunga *I* 66 F4
Sinanli *TR* 173 B7
Sinarades *GR* 168 E2
Sinarcas *E* 47 E10
Şinca *RO* 152 F6
Sindal *DK* 90 E7
Sindel *BG* 167 C9
Sindelfingen *D* 27 C10
Sindi *EST* 131 E9
Sindia *I* 64 C2
Sindos *GR* 169 C8
Sinekçi *TR* 173 D7
Sinekli *TR* 173 B9
Sinemorets *BG* 167 E9
Sines *P* 50 D2
Sineşti *RO* 153 C10
Sineşti *RO* 160 D3
Sineşti *RO* 161 D8
Sinetänsalmi *FIN* 117 E14
Sinettä *FIN* 117 E14
Sineu *E* 57 B11
Singen (Hohentwiel) *D* 27 E10
Sîngera *MD* 154 D3
Sîngerei *MD* 153 B12
Singhofen *D* 21 D9
Singsjön *S* 106 E8
Singureni *RO* 161 E7
Singusdal *N* 90 A4
Sinimäe *EST* 132 C2
Siniscola *I* 64 B4
Sinj *HR* 157 E6
Sinlabajos *E* 46 B3
Sin-le-Noble *F* 19 D7
Sinn *D* 21 C10
Sinnai *I* 64 E3
Sinnes *N* 94 E5
Sinoie *RO* 155 D3
Sinole *LV* 135 B12
Sinopoli *I* 59 C8
Sins *CH* 27 F9
Sinsheim *D* 21 F11
Sint Annaland *NL* 16 E2
Sint Annaparochie *NL* 16 B5
Sint Anthonis *NL* 16 E5
Sintautai *LT* 136 D7
Şintava *SK* 146 E5
Sintea Mare *RO* 151 D8
Şintereag *RO* 152 C4
Şinteu *RO* 151 C10
Sint-Genesius-Rode *B* 182 D4
Sint-Gillis-Waas *B* 16 F2
Sint-Huibrechts-Lille *B* 183 C6
Sint Jansteen *NL* 182 C4
Sint-Katelijne-Waver *B* 19 B10
Sint-Laureins *B* 182 C3
Sint-Lenaarts *B* 182 C5
Sint Maartensdijk *NL* 16 E2
Sint-Margriete *B* 182 C3
Sint-Maria-Lierde *B* 19 C8
Sint-Martens-Latem *B* 19 B8
Sint Michielsgestel *NL* 183 B6
Sint Nicolaasga *NL* 16 C5
Sint-Niklaas *B* 19 B9
Sint Odilienberg *NL* 183 C8
Sint-Pauwels *B* 182 C4
Sint Philipsland *NL* 16 E2
Sint-Pieters-Leeuw *B* 19 C9
Sintra *P* 50 B1
Sint-Truiden *B* 19 C11
Sint Willebrord *NL* 16 E3
Sinzheim *D* 27 C9
Sinzig *D* 21 C8
Siógárd *H* 149 D11
Siófok *H* 149 C10
Sion *CH* 31 C11
Sion *RO* 161 C8
Sion Mills *GB* 4 F2
Şipca *MD* 154 C5
Sipinen *FIN* 121 F12
Šipkovica *NMK* 163 E10
Sipola *FIN* 119 F15
Şipote *RO* 153 C10
Şipotina *MD* 154 C2
Šipovo *BIH* 157 D7
Sipplingen *D* 27 E11
Sippola *FIN* 128 D7
Sira *N* 94 F5
Sirač *HR* 149 E8
Siracusa *I* 59 E7
Siran *F* 29 F10
Sirbmá *N* 113 C19
Siret *RO* 153 B8
Sireţel *RO* 153 C9
Sirevåg *N* 94 F3
Sirgala *EST* 132 C2
Şiria *RO* 151 E8
Širig *SRB* 158 C4
Şirineasa *RO* 160 D4
Širitovci *HR* 156 E5
Siriu *RO* 161 C8
Sirkka *FIN* 117 C13
Sirkkakoski *FIN* 117 E12
Sirkkamäki *FIN* 123 E16
Sirmione *I* 66 B2
Şirna *RO* 161 D7
Širnach *CH* 27 F11
Sirniö *FIN* 121 C11
Sirnitz *A* 73 C9
Sirod *F* 31 B9
Sirogojno *SRB* 158 F4
Sirok *H* 145 H1
Široki Brijeg *BIH* 157 F8
Sirolo *I* 67 E8
Siròr *I* 72 D4
Sirotsina *BY* 133 F7
Siruela *E* 54 B2
Sirutiškis *LT* 135 F7
Širvintos *LT* 137 C10
Sisak *HR* 149 F6
Sisante *E* 47 F8
Şişcani *MD* 154 D2
Sisco *F* 37 F10
Şişeşti *RO* 152 B3
Şişeşti *RO* 159 D10
Şişli *TR* 173 B10
Sissa *I* 66 C1

Sissach CH 27 F8
Sisses GR 178 E8
Sissonne F 19 E8
Şiştarovăţ RO 151 E8
Sisteron F 35 B10
Sistranda N 104 D5
Sistrans A 72 B3
Sita Buzăului RO 161 B8
Sitaniec PL 144 B7
Siteia GR 179 E11
Sitges E 43 E7
Sitkówka-Nowiny PL 143 E10
Sitnica BIH 157 C7
Sitochori GR 169 C10
Sitovo BG 161 E10
Sitsyenyets BY 133 E6
Sittard NL 19 C12
Sittensen D 82 D7
Sittersdorf A 73 C10
Sittingbourne GB 15 E10
Sitzendorf an der Schmida A 77 E9
Sitzenroda D 80 D3
Siulaisiadar GB 2 J4
Siuntio FIN 127 E11
Siuro FIN 127 C9
Siurua FIN 119 D16
Siurunmaa FIN 115 D1
Sivac SRB 158 B3
Sivakka FIN 125 C13
Sivakkajoki FIN 119 B13
Sivakkavaara FIN 125 E11
Siverić HR 156 E5
Siverskiy RUS 132 C7
Sivertgården N 108 E7
Sivry B 19 D9
Sivry-sur-Meuse F 19 F11
Sixarby S 99 B9
Six-Fours-les-Plages F 35 D10
Sixmilebridge IRL 8 C5
Sixmilecross GB 7 C8
Six Road Ends GB 4 F5
Sixt-Fer-à-Cheval F 31 C10
Sizun F 22 D3
Sjemeć BIH 158 F3
Sjenica SRB 163 C9
Sjetlina BIH 157 E10
Sjoa N 101 C11
Sjøåsen N 105 C10
Sjöbo S 87 D13
Sjöbotten S 118 E6
Sjöbrånet S 107 C17
Sjøholt N 100 B5
Sjølund DK 86 E5
Sjömarken S 91 D12
Sjonbotn N 108 D6
Sjørring DK 86 B3
Sjørslev DK 86 C4
Sjørup DK 86 C4
Sjösa S 93 B10
Sjösäter S 99 B11
Sjötofta S 91 E13
Sjötorp S 91 B14
Sjoutnäset S 106 B7
Sjøvassbotn N 111 B17
Sjøvegan N 111 C14
Sjövik S 91 D11
Sjulsåsen S 106 C7
Sjulsmark S 118 C7
Sjunnen S 92 E6
Sjuntorp S 91 C11
Sjursvik N 111 B12
Skademark S 107 E16
Skælsør DK 87 E8
Skærbæk DK 86 E3
Skævinge DK 87 D10
Skaftung FIN 122 F6
Skagen DK 90 D8
Skagersvik S 91 B15
Skäggebyn S 91 A12
Skagshamn S 107 E16
Skaidi N 113 C13
Skaidiškės LT 137 D11
Skaill GB 3 H11
Skaista LV 133 E2
Skaistgiriai LT 135 E8
Skaistgirys LT 134 D6
Skaistkalne LV 135 D9
Skala GR 174 C2
Skala GR 175 B7
Skala GR 175 F6
Skala GR 177 E8
Skała PL 143 F8
Skala Eresou GR 177 A6
Skala Kallonis GR 177 A7
Skala Marion GR 171 C7
Skålan S 102 A7
Skaland N 111 B13
Skala Oropou GR 175 C8
Skálavík FO 2 B3
Skalbmierz PL 143 F9
Skåle N 105 C15
Skålevik N 90 C3
Skälgården S 103 A12
Skáli FO 2 A3
Skalica SK 146 D4
Skalice CZ 81 E7
Skalité SK 147 C7
Skalitsa BG 166 E6
Skallelv N 114 C8
Skällinge S 87 A10
Skallvik S 93 C9
Skalmodal S 108 F8
Skalmsjö S 107 D13
Skalná CZ 75 B11
Skålö S 97 A11
Skaloti GR 171 B6
Skals DK 86 B4
Skålsjön S 103 D10
Skalstugan S 105 D12
Skålsvik N 108 B7
Skålvallen S 103 C10
Skån S 103 B11
Skanderåsen S 102 A7
Skanderborg DK 86 C5
Skånes-Fagerhult S 87 C12
Skåne-Tranås S 88 D5
Skånevik N 94 C3
Skåningen N 112 C4
Skaņkalne LV 131 F10
Skänninge S 92 C6
Skanör med Falsterbo S 87 E11
Skansbacken S 97 B11
Skansen N 105 D9
Skansholm S 107 B10
Skansnäs S 107 A10
Skansnäs S 109 E13
Skansnäset S 106 C9
Skåpafors S 91 A11
Skape PL 81 B8
Skapiškis LT 135 E10
Skår N 94 D4
Skara S 91 C13
Skäran S 118 F6
Skarberget N 111 D11
Skärblacka S 92 B7
Skarda S 107 C15
Skardmodalen N 108 F7
Skardmunken N 111 A18
Skardstein N 111 B11
Skardsvåg N 113 A16
Skare N 94 C5
Skåre S 97 D9
Skärhamn S 91 D10
Skarkdalen S 102 A4
Skärkind S 92 C7
Skarnes N 96 B6
Skärplinge S 99 B9
Skarp Salling DK 86 B4
Skarrild DK 86 D3
Skärså S 103 D13
Skarsfjord N 112 D2
Skärsjövålen S 102 B5
Skarstad N 111 D11
Skärstad S 92 D4
Skarsvåg N 111 B15
Skarszewy PL 138 B5
Skårup DK 86 E7
Skarv N 112 C11
Skärvången S 105 D16
Skarvfjordhamn N 112 B11
Skarvsjöby S 107 B12
Skaryszew PL 141 H4
Skarżysko-Kamienna PL 141 H3
Skasenden N 96 B7
Skästra S 103 C11
Skatamark S 118 C7
Skatan S 103 B13
Skattkärr S 97 D10
Skattungbyn S 102 D8
Skatvik N 111 B14
Skaudvilė LT 134 F5
Skaugvoll N 108 C7
Skaulo S 116 D6
Skaune LV 133 D3
Skavdal N 111 B10
Skave DK 86 C3
Skavnakk N 112 C7
Skawina PL 143 G8
Skebobruk S 99 C11
Skebokvarn S 93 A9
Skeda udde S 92 C7
Šķēde LV 134 C4
Skede S 92 E6
Skedevi S 92 B7
Skedsmokorset N 95 B14
Skee S 91 B9
Skegness GB 11 E12
Skegrie S 87 E12
Skei N 100 C4
Skei N 105 A11
Skela SRB 158 D5
Skelby DK 87 E9
Skelde DK 82 A7
Skelhøje DK 86 C4
Skellefteå S 118 E5
Skelleftehamn S 118 E6
Skelmersdale GB 10 D6
Skelton GB 11 B10
Šķeltova LV 133 D2
Skelund DK 86 B6
Skelwick GB 3 G11
Skėmiai LT 134 E7
Skenderaj RKS 163 D10
Skender Vakuf BIH 157 D7
Skenfrith GB 13 B9
Skepasto GR 174 C5
Skjpe PL 139 E7
Skepplanda S 91 D11
Skeppshamn S 103 B14
Skeppshult S 87 A12
Skeppsmalen S 107 E16
Skerries IRL 7 E10
Skhidnytsya UA 145 E7
Ski N 95 C13
Skiathos GR 175 A7
Skibbereen IRL 8 E4
Skibbild DK 86 C3
Skibby DK 87 D9
Šķibe LV 134 C6
Skibinge DK 87 E10
Skibotn N 111 B19
Skidal' BY 140 C10
Skiemonys LT 135 F10
Skien N 90 A6
Šķieneri LV 135 B13
Skierbieszów PL 144 B7
Skierniewice PL 141 G2
Skiippagurra N 114 C4
Šķilbēni LV 133 B3
Skillebotn N 108 F3
Skillefjordnes N 113 C11
Skillingaryd S 92 E4
Skillinge S 88 E6
Skillvassbakk N 111 D10
Skinias GR 178 E9
Skinnarud N 101 E12
Skinnskatteberg S 97 C14
Skipmannvik N 109 B9
Skipness GB 4 D6
Skipsea GB 11 D11
Skipton GB 11 D7
Skiptvet N 95 D14
Skirlaugh GB 11 D11
Skitenelv N 111 A17
Skiti GR 169 E8
Skivarp S 87 E13
Skive DK 86 B4
Skivjan RKS 163 E9
Skivsjön S 107 C16
Skiwy Duże PL 141 F7
Skjærhalden N 91 A9
Skjåholmen N 113 B12
Skjånes N 113 B18
Skjånes N 113 B21
Skjåvika N 108 E6
Skjeberg N 91 A9
Skjeggedal N 90 B3
Skjelelv N 111 C13
Skjellbreid N 105 C14
Skjelman N 111 A17
Skjelnes N 111 A18
Skjelstad N 105 D10
Skjelvik N 108 B7
Skjern DK 86 D3
Skjern N 105 C9
Skjerstad N 108 B9
Skjervøy N 112 C6
Skjød DK 86 C5
Skjold N 111 B17
Skjoldastraumen N 94 D3
Skjolden N 100 D7
Skjombotn N 111 D13
Skjøtningberg N 113 A19
Sklithro GR 169 E8
Skobelevo BG 166 D4
Skoby S 99 B10
Skočivir NMK 169 C6
Škocjan SLO 148 E4
Skoczów PL 147 B7
Skodborg DK 86 E4
Skodje N 100 A5
Skøelv N 111 B15
Škofja Loka SLO 73 D9
Škofljica SLO 73 E10
Skog S 103 D12
Skogaholm S 92 A6
Skoganvarri N 113 D15
Skoger N 95 C12
Skogfoss N 114 E7
Skoghall S 97 D9
Skogly N 114 E6
Skogmo N 105 B12
Skogn N 105 D10
Skogså S 118 C7
Skogsby S 89 B11
Skogsfjord N 112 C3
Skogshöjden S 91 C11
Skogstorp S 87 B10
Skogstorp S 98 D6
Skogstue N 112 D11
Skogum N 114 E6
Skoki PL 85 E12
Sköldinge S 93 A8
Skole UA 145 E8
Skollenborg N 95 C11
Sköllersta S 92 A6
Skoltenes N 110 C8
Skoltevatn N 114 E7
Skołyszyn PL 144 D3
Skomlin PL 142 D5
Skonseng N 108 D7
Skönvik S 103 E12
Skopelos GR 175 A8
Skopelos GR 177 A7
Skopi GR 179 E11
Skopje NMK 164 F3
Skopos GR 169 C6
Skopos GR 171 B7
Skopun FO 2 B3
Skórcz PL 138 C6
Skorica SRB 159 F8
Skorild N 104 E6
Skorogoszcz PL 142 E4
Skoroszyce PL 142 E3
Skorovatn N 105 B14
Skorped S 107 E13
Skorpetorp S 89 A10
Skørping DK 86 B5
Skorstad N 105 B10
Skórzec PL 141 F6
Skoteini GR 174 D5
Skotfoss N 90 A6
Skotina GR 169 D8
Skotoussa GR 169 B9
Skotselv N 95 C11
Skotterud N 96 C7
Skottsund S 103 B13
Skoura GR 175 E5
Skourta GR 175 C8
Skoutari GR 169 B10
Skoutari GR 178 B4
Skoutaros GR 171 F10
Skovby DK 86 C5
Skövde S 91 C14
Skoved S 107 E14
Skovlund DK 86 D3
Skovsgård DK 86 A4
Skra GR 169 B7
Skräddrabo S 103 D10
Skradin HR 156 E4
Skråmestø N 100 E1
Skranstad N 110 E9
Skravena BG 165 D8
Skrea S 87 B11
Skreia N 101 E13
Skriaudžiai LT 137 D8
Skrinyano BG 165 E6
Skřipov CZ 146 B5
Skrīveri LV 135 C10
Skröven S 116 E7
Skrøytnes N 111 E7
Skrudaliena LV 135 E13
Skrunda LV 134 C4
Skruv S 89 B8
Skrwilno PL 139 D8
Skrzatusz PL 85 D11
Skrzyńsko PL 141 H3
Skrzyszów PL 143 G11
Skucani BIH 157 E6
Skudeneshavn N 94 D2
Skuhrov nad Bělou CZ 77 B10
Skujene LV 135 B10
Skujetnieki LV 133 C2
Skuķi LV 133 E3
Skuldelev DK 87 D10
Skule S 107 E14
Skulerud N 95 C15
Skulgammen N 111 A17
Skulsfjord N 111 A16
Skulsk PL 138 F5
Skulte LV 135 B8
Skulte LV 135 C7
Skultorp S 91 C14
Skultuna S 98 C6
Skuodas LT 134 D3
Skurträsk S 107 C16
Skurup S 87 E13
Skuteč CZ 77 C9
Skutskär S 103 E13
Skutvik N 110 D9
Skutvik N 111 B16
Skwierzyna PL 81 A9
Skýcov SK 146 D6
Skydra GR 169 C7
Skyllberg S 92 B6
Skylnäs S 103 A9
Skyros GR 175 B10
Skyttmon S 106 E9
Skyttorp S 99 B9
Slabodka BY 133 E2
Słaboszów PL 143 F9
Sládkovičovo SK 146 E5
Slagavallen S 102 B5
Slagelse DK 87 E8
Slagnäs S 109 E15
Slaidburn GB 10 D7
Slaka S 92 C7
Slampe LV 134 C6
Slane IRL 7 E9
Slanec SK 145 F3
Slangerup DK 87 D10
Slănic RO 161 C7
Slănic Moldova RO 153 E8
Slano HR 162 D4
Slantsy RUS 132 C3
Slaný CZ 76 B6
Slap BIH 158 F3
Slap MNE 163 D7
Slap SLO 73 D8
Šlapaberžė LT 135 F7
Šlapanice CZ 77 D11
Släppträsk S 107 A15
Slate LV 135 D12
Slatina BIH 157 C7
Slatina BIH 157 C8
Slatina BIH 157 E8
Slatina BIH 157 E10
Slatina HR 149 E9
Slatina RO 153 C8
Slatina RO 160 E4
Slatina SRB 158 E4
Slatiňany CZ 77 C9
Slatina-Timiş RO 159 C9
Slatino NMK 168 B4
Slatinski Drenovac HR 149 E9
Slătioara RO 160 C3
Slătioara RO 160 E4
Slato BIH 157 F9
Slättberg S 102 D8
Slåttholmen N 110 D8
Slättmon S 103 A13
Slattum N 95 C13
Slava Cercheză RO 155 D3
Slava Rusă RO 155 D3
Slaveino BG 165 F10
Slavičín CZ 146 C5
Slavinja SRB 165 C6
Slavkov CZ 146 B5
Slavkovichi RUS 132 F5
Slavkov u Brna CZ 77 D11
Slavonice CZ 77 E8
Slavonski Brod HR 157 B9
Slavošovce SK 145 F1
Slavotin BG 165 B7
Slavovitsa BG 160 F4
Slavovitsa BG 165 E9
Slavsk RUS 136 C4
Slavs'ke UA 145 F7
Slavsko Polje HR 148 F5
Slavyani BG 165 C10
Slavyanovo BG 165 C10
Slavyanovo BG 166 C6
Slavyanovo BG 166 F5
Sława PL 81 C10
Sławatycze PL 141 G9
Sławjcin PL 85 C13
Sławków PL 143 F7
Sławno PL 85 B11
Sławoborze PL 85 C9
Sławsko PL 85 B11
Sleaford GB 11 F11
Sledmere GB 11 C10
Sleen NL 17 C7
Sleidinge B 182 C3
Sleights GB 11 C10
Slemmestad N 95 C12
Ślesin PL 138 D4
Ślesin PL 138 F5
Sletta N 112 C9
Slevik N 91 A8
Sliač SK 147 D8
Slidre N 101 D9
Sliedrecht NL 16 E3
Šlienava LT 137 D9
Sligachan GB 2 L4
Sligeach IRL 6 D6
Sligo IRL 6 D6
Slimminge DK 87 E9
Slimnic RO 152 F4
Slinfold GB 15 E8
Slipra N 105 D9
Slišane SRB 164 D4
Slite S 93 D13
Sliven BG 166 D6
Slivileşti RO 159 D11
Slivnitsa BG 165 D7
Slivo Pole BG 161 F8
Śliwice PL 138 C5
Sllatinë e Madhe RKS 164 D3
Slobidka UA 154 B4
Slobozia MD 154 D5
Slobozia RO 160 D6
Slobozia RO 161 D10
Slobozia RO 161 F7
Slobozia Bradului RO 161 C10
Slobozia Ciorăşti RO 161 B10
Slobozia Conachi RO 155 B1
Slobozia Mândra RO 160 F5
Slobozia Mare MD 155 B2
Slobozia Moară RO 161 D7
Slochteren NL 17 B7
Slöinge S 87 B11
Słomniki PL 143 F9
Słonowice PL 85 C9
Słońsk PL 81 A7
Slootdorp NL 16 C3
Slottsskogen S 99 C9
Slough GB 15 D7
Sloupnice CZ 77 C10
Sløvåg N 100 E2
Slovenj Gradec SLO 73 C11
Slovenska Bistrica SLO 148 D5
Slovenská Ľupča SK 147 D8
Slovenská Ves SK 145 E1
Slovenske Konjice SLO 148 D4
Slovenské Nové Mesto SK 145 G4
Slovenský Grob SK 146 E4
Slovinci HR 157 B6
Slovinky SK 145 F2
Sløvra N 110 D8
Slov"yanoserbka UA 154 D5
Słowik PL 143 C7
Słubice PL 81 B7
Słubice PL 139 F8
Sluderno I 71 D11
Sluis NL 19 B7
Sluiskil NL 16 F1
Šluknov CZ 81 D6
Slunj HR 156 B4
Słupca PL 142 B4
Słupcza PL 144 B4
Słupia PL 141 G1
Słupia PL 143 D9
Słupia PL 143 E8
Słupno PL 139 E8
Słupsk PL 85 B12
Slušovice CZ 146 C5
Slussfors S 109 F11
Słuszków PL 142 C5
Slyuda RUS 115 D8
Smailholm GB 5 D11
Smålandsstenar S 87 A12
Smalåsen N 105 A14
Smalfjord N 113 C21
Smalininkai LT 136 C6
Smalvos LT 135 E12
Smârdan RO 155 C1
Smârdan RO 155 C2
Smārde LV 134 C6
Smârdioasa RO 161 F6
Smardzewice PL 141 H2
Smardzewo PL 81 B9
Smardzko PL 85 C9
Smarhon' BY 137 E13
Šmarje pri Jelšah SLO 148 D5
Šmarjeta SLO 148 E4
Šmartno SLO 73 D10
Šmartno SLO 73 D11
Smarves F 29 B6
Smedby S 89 B10
Smederevo SRB 159 D6
Smederevska Palanka SRB 159 E6
Smedjebacken S 97 B13
Smedsbyn S 118 C8
Smedvik N 110 D6
Smeeni RO 161 C9
Smjgorzów PL 143 F11
Smelror N 114 C10
Smelteri LV 135 D13
Smjtowo Graniczne PL 138 C6
Smidary CZ 77 B8
Smidstrup DK 86 D5
Smidstrup DK 87 C10
Śmigiel PL 81 B11
Smilčić HR 156 D4
Smilde NL 17 C6
Smilets BG 165 E9
Smilevo NMK 168 B5
Smilgiai LT 135 D9
Smilgiai LT 135 E8
Smilgiai LT 137 D8
Smilgynai LT 134 E2
Smilovci SRB 165 C6
Śmiłowice PL 138 E7
Śmiłowo PL 85 D11
Smiltene LV 135 B11
Smiltynė LT 134 E2
Smilyan BG 171 A7
Smines N 110 C8
Smiřice CZ 77 B9
Smirnenski BG 159 F11
Smirnenski BG 161 F8
Smiugard N 101 D11
Smižany SK 145 F2
Smögen S 91 C9
Smokvica HR 162 D2
Smokvica NMK 169 B7
Smołdzino PL 85 A12
Smolenice SK 146 D4
Smolice PL 81 C12
Smolmark S 96 C7
Smolnica PL 84 E7
Smolník SK 145 F2
Smolyan BG 171 A7
Smolyanovtsi BG 165 C6
Smørfjord N 113 B15
Smulţi RO 153 F11
Smyadovo BG 167 C8
Smygehamn S 87 E12
Smyków PL 143 D9
Snagov RO 161 D8
Snainton GB 11 C10
Snaith GB 11 D9
Snålroa N 102 E2
Snappertuna FIN 127 E10
Snaptun DK 86 D6
Snarby N 111 A18
Snåre FIN 123 C10
Snartemo N 94 F6
Snåsa N 105 C12
Snave Bridge IRL 8 E4
Snedsted DK 86 B3
Sneek NL 16 B5
Sneem IRL 8 E3
Snejbjerg DK 86 C3
Snēpele LV 134 C3
Snerta N 101 C15
Snertinge DK 87 D8
Snesslinge S 99 B10
Snesudden S 118 B4
Snettisham GB 11 F13
Śniadowo PL 139 D12
Snikere LV 134 D6
Snina SK 145 F5
Šnjegotina Velika BIH 157 C8
Snøde DK 87 E7
Snøfjord N 113 B14
Snogebæk DK 89 E8
Snoghøj DK 86 D5
Snoldelev DK 87 D10
Soajo P 38 E3
Şoarş RO 152 F6
Soave I 66 B3
Søberg N 110 C7
Soběslav CZ 77 D7
Sobienie-Jeziory PL 141 G4
Sobolew PL 141 G5
Sobota PL 143 B8
Soboth A 73 C11
Sobotín CZ 77 B12
Sobotište SK 146 D4
Sobotka CZ 77 B8
Sobótka PL 81 E11
Sobótka PL 142 C4
Sobótka PL 143 E12
Sobowidz PL 138 B6
Sobra HR 162 D4
Sobradelo E 39 D6
Sobradiel E 41 E9
Sobrado E 38 B3
Sobrado E 38 D3
Sobral da Adiça P 51 C5
Sobral de Monte Agraço P 50 A1
Sobrance SK 145 F5
Sobreira Formosa P 44 E5
Søby DK 86 F6
Soča SLO 73 D8
Sočanica RKS 163 C10
Soçanicë RKS 163 C10
Socchieve I 73 D6
Sočerga SLO 67 B8
Sochaczew PL 141 F2
Sochaux F 27 E6
Sochocin PL 139 E9
Sochos GR 169 C9
Socodor RO 151 D7
Socol RO 159 D7
Socond RO 151 B10
Socovos E 55 C9
Socuéllamos E 47 F7
Sodankylä FIN 117 D17
Söderåkra S 89 C10
Söderala S 103 D12
Söderås S 103 E9
Söderbärke S 97 B14
Söderboda S 99 B10
Söderby-Karl S 99 C11
Söderfors S 98 B8
Söderhamn S 103 D13
Söderköping S 93 C8
Söderkulla FIN 127 E13
Södersvik S 99 C11
Södertälje S 93 A11
Södra Åbyn S 118 E5
Södra Brännträsk S 118 C4
Södra Drängsmark S 118 E5
Södra Harads S 118 B5
Södra Johannisberg S 109 F15
Södra Löten S 102 E4
Södra Sandby S 87 D12
Södra Sandträsk S 107 A16
Södra Sunderbyn S 118 C7
Södra Tresund S 107 B11
Södra Vallgrund FIN 122 D6
Södra Vi S 92 D7
Sodražica SLO 73 E10
Soerendonk NL 16 F5
Soest D 17 E10
Soest NL 16 D4
Soesterberg NL 183 A6
Sofades GR 169 F7
Sofia BG 165 D7
Sofia MD 153 B11
Sofiko GR 171 B11
Sofiko GR 175 D7
Sofporog RUS 121 C17
Şofrîncani MD 153 A10
Şofronea RO 151 E7
Sofronievo BG 160 F3
Søften DK 86 C6
Søftestad N 90 A4
Sofular TR 181 A9
Sögel D 17 C9
Sogndalsfjøra N 100 D6
Søgne N 90 C2
Soğucak TR 173 A8
Soğucak TR 173 F8
Soğucak TR 177 D9
Soğukoluk TR 181 A7
Söğüt TR 181 C8
Söğütalan TR 173 D10
Soham GB 15 C9
Sohatu RO 161 E9
Soheit-Tinlot B 19 D11
Sohland D 80 D6
Sohodol RO 151 E11
Sohren D 21 E8
Soidinkumpu FIN 121 B12
Soidinvaara FIN 121 F12
Soignies B 19 C9
Soikko FIN 119 C14
Şoimari RO 161 C8
Şoimi RO 151 D9
Şoimuş RO 151 F10
Soing F 26 E4
Soings-en-Sologne F 24 F6
Soini FIN 123 E12
Soinilansalmi FIN 125 F10
Soinlahti FIN 124 C8
Soissons F 19 F7
Soivio FIN 121 C13
Soizy-aux-Bois F 25 C10
Sójkowa PL 144 C5
Söjtör H 149 C7
Sokal' UA 144 C9
Söke TR 177 D9
Soklot FIN 122 C9
Sokna N 95 B11
Soknedal N 104 F8
Sokobanja SRB 159 F8
Sokojärvi FIN 125 D14
Sokolac BIH 157 E10
Sokolany PL 140 D8
Sokolce SK 146 F5
Sokolivka UA 154 A3
Sokółka PL 140 D9
Sokółki PL 136 E5
Sokolnice CZ 77 D11
Sokolniki PL 142 D5
Sokolov CZ 75 B12
Sokolovac HR 149 D7
Sokolovce SK 146 D5
Sokolovici BIH 157 E10
Sokolovo BG 166 C5
Sokolovo BG 167 C10
Sokolovo BIH 157 C6
Sokołów Małopolski PL 144 C5
Sokołów Podlaski PL 141 F6
Sokoły PL 140 E7
Sokorópátka H 149 B9
Sokyrnytsya UA 145 G7
Sól PL 144 B6
Soľ SK 145 F4
Sola N 94 E3
Solacolu RO 161 E9
Solana de los Barros E 51 B6
Solana del Pino E 54 C4
Solana de Rioalmar E 45 C11
Søland N 95 B10
Solarino I 59 E7
Solaro F 37 H10
Solberg N 101 E15
Solberg N 111 B14
Solberg S 107 D11
Solberg S 107 D13
Solberga S 92 D5
Solbjerg DK 86 C6
Solca RO 153 B7
Solčava SLO 73 D10
Solda I 71 D11
Şoldăneşti MD 154 B3
Şoldanu RO 161 E9
Soldatnes N 113 D14
Sölden A 71 D12
Soldeu AND 33 E9
Solec Kujawski PL 138 D5
Solec-Zdrój PL 143 F10
Solenzara F 37 H10
Solesino I 66 B4
Solesmes F 19 D7
Solesmes F 23 E11
Soleşti RO 153 D11
Soleto I 61 C10
Solf FIN 122 D7
Solférino F 32 B4
Solferino I 66 B2
Solfjellsjøen N 108 D4
Soliera I 66 C2
Solignano I 69 D8
Solihull GB 13 A11
Solin HR 156 E5
Solina PL 145 E5
Solingen D 21 B8
Solivella E 42 E6
Soljani HR 157 C10
Sölje S 97 D8
Solkei FIN 128 C8
Söll A 72 A5
Sollacaro F 37 H9
Sollas GB 2 K2
Sollebrunn S 91 C12
Sollefteå S 107 E12
Sollenau A 77 G10
Sollenkroka S 99 D11
Sollentuna S 99 D9
Sóller E 49 E10
Sollerön S 102 E8
Søllested DK 83 A10
Söllichau D 79 C12
Solliès-Pont F 36 E4
Solliès-Toucas F 36 E4
Sollihøgda N 95 C12
Söllingen D 79 B8
Sollstedt D 79 D8
Solmaz TR 181 B9
Solms D 21 C10
Solnice CZ 77 B10
Solnik BG 167 D9
Solofra I 60 B3
Solojärvi FIN 113 F18
Solomiac F 33 C7
Solomos GR 175 D6
Solopaca I 60 A3
Solórzano E 40 B4
Solosancho E 46 C3
Sološnica SK 146 E4
Solothurn CH 27 F8
Solotvyna UA 145 H8
Soløy N 111 C14
Solre-le-Château F 19 D9
Solrød Strand DK 87 D10
Solsem N 105 A11
Solskjela N 104 E4
Sølsnes N 100 A6
Solsona E 43 D7
Solsvik N 94 B1
Solt H 150 D3
Soltau D 83 E7
Soltendieck D 83 E9
Sol'tsy RUS 132 E7
Soltszentimre H 150 D3
Soltvadkert H 150 D3
Solumshamn S 103 A14
Solva GB 9 E12
Solvalla S 99 C10
Solvarbo S 97 B14
Sölvesborg S 88 C7
Solvorn N 100 D6
Solymár H 149 A11
Soma TR 177 A10
Somain F 19 D7
Somberek H 149 D11
Sombernon F 25 F12
Sombor SRB 150 F3
Sombreffe B 19 C10
Şomcuţa Mare RO 151 B11
Somercotes GB 11 E9
Someren NL 16 F5
Somerniemi FIN 127 D10
Somero FIN 127 D10
Someronkylä FIN 119 F12
Somerovaara FIN 119 D16
Sõmerpalu EST 131 F13
Somerton GB 13 C9
Sõmeru EST 131 C12
Someş-Odorhei RO 151 C11
Somianka PL 139 E11
Sominy PL 85 B13
Somlóvásárhely H 149 B8
Sommacampagna I 66 B2
Somma Lombardo I 68 B6
Sommariva del Bosco I 37 B7
Sommarøy N 110 C9
Sommarøy N 111 A15
Sommarset N 109 A10
Sommatino I 58 E4
Somme-Leuze B 19 D11
Sommen S 92 C5
Sommepy-Tahure F 19 F10
Sömmerda D 79 D9
Sommerfeld D 84 E4
Sommersted DK 86 E4
Sommesous F 25 C11
Somme-Suippe F 25 B12
Sommevoire F 25 D12
Sommières F 35 C7
Sommières-du-Clain F 29 C6
Somogyapáti H 149 D9
Somogyjád H 149 D9
Somogyszob H 149 D8
Somogyudvarhely H 149 D8
Somogyvár H 149 C9
Somonino PL 138 B5
Somontín E 55 E8
Somotor SK 145 G4
Somova RO 155 C3
Somovit BG 160 F5
Sompa EST 131 C14
Sompolno PL 138 F6
Sompujärvi FIN 119 C14
Somzée B 19 D9
Son N 95 C13
Son NL 16 E4
Sona I 66 B2
Sona N 105 E10
Şona RO 152 E4
Sonceboz CH 27 F7
Soncillo E 40 C4
Soncino I 69 C8
Sonda EST 131 C13
Sondalo I 69 A9
Søndeled N 90 B5
Sønder Balling DK 86 B3
Sønder Bjerre DK 86 D5
Sønder Bjert DK 86 E5
Sønderborg DK 86 F5
Sønderby DK 87 D10
Sønder Dråby DK 86 B3
Sønder Felding DK 86 D3
Sønderho DK 86 E2
Sønderholm DK 86 A5
Sønder Hygum DK 86 E3
Sønder Nissum DK 86 C2
Sønder Omme DK 86 D3
Sønder Onsild DK 86 B5
Sønder Rubjerg DK 90 E6
Sondershausen D 79 D8
Søndersø DK 86 E6
Sønder Stenderup DK 86 E5
Sønder Vilstrup DK 86 E5
Sønder Vissing DK 86 C5
Sønder Vium DK 86 D2
Sondori LV 133 C2
Sondrio I 69 A8
Soneja E 48 E4
Songe N 90 B5
Songeons F 18 E4
Sonim P 38 E5
Sonka FIN 117 E14
Sonkajärvi FIN 124 C9
Sonkakoski FIN 124 C9
Sonkamuotka FIN 117 B10
Sonneberg D 75 B9
Sonneborn D 79 E8
Sonnefeld D 75 B9
Sonnewalde D 80 C5
Sonnino I 62 E4
Sonntag A 71 C9

Sonntagberg A 77 G7
Sonseca E 46 E5
Son Servera E 57 B11
Sońsk PL 139 E10
Sonstorp S 92 B7
Sonta SRB 157 A11
Sontheim an der Brenz D 75 E7
Sonthofen D 71 B10
Sontra D 78 D6
Soodla EST 131 C10
Söörmarkku FIN 126 B6
Soorts-Hossegor F 32 C3
Sopeira E 33 F7
Sopelana E 40 B6
Sopilja BIH 157 F9
Sopište NMK 164 F3
Soponya H 149 B10
Šoporňa SK 146 E5
Sopot BG 165 C9
Sopot BG 165 D10
Sopot PL 138 B6
Sopot RO 160 E3
Sopot SRB 158 D6
Sopotnica NMK 168 B5
Şopotu Nou RO 159 D8
Soppela FIN 115 E3
Sopron H 149 A7
Sopronkövesd H 149 A7
Sora I 62 D5
Soraga I 72 D4
Soragna I 66 C1
Söråker S 103 A14
Söräng S 103 D11
Sorano I 62 B1
Sørarnøy N 108 B6
Sør-Audnedal N 90 C1
Sorbas E 55 E8
Sorbie GB 5 F8
Sorbiers F 30 E5
Sörbo S 103 D11
Sörböle S 103 B13
Sorbolo I 66 C1
Sörby S 97 C9
Sörbygden S 103 A11
Sørbymagle DK 87 E8
Sörbyn S 118 B7
Sörbyn S 118 E4
Sorcy-St-Martin F 26 C4
Sord IRL 7 F10
Sørdal N 109 C10
Sorde-l'Abbaye F 32 C3
Sore F 32 B4
Sørebo N 100 D3
Sören S 118 C9
Søreng N 111 B19
Soresina I 69 C8
Sorèze F 33 D10
Sörfjärden S 103 B13
Sørfjord N 108 D5
Sørfjord N 111 C14
Sørfjorden N 111 C10
Sørfjordmoen N 109 A10
Sörflärke S 107 E13
Sörfors S 103 B13
Sörfors S 122 C4
Sörforsa S 103 C12
Sorge D 79 C8
Sorges F 29 E7
Sorgono I 64 C3
Sorgues F 35 B8
Sørheim N 100 D6
Soria E 41 E7
Soriano Calabro I 59 B9
Soriano nel Cimino I 62 C2
Sorihuela E 45 D9
Sorihuela del Gaudalimar E 55 C6
Sorisdale GB 4 B4
Sørkjosen N 112 D6
Sørkjosen N 112 D6
Sorkwity PL 136 F3
Sørland N 110 E4
Sørlenangen N 111 A19
Sørli N 105 C15
Sørli N 111 B14
Sörmark S 97 B8
Sörmjöle S 122 C4
Sørmo N 111 C16
Sorn GB 5 D8
Sornac F 29 D10
Sörnoret S 107 C12
Sorø DK 87 E9
Soroca MD 154 A2
Sorokino RUS 133 B7
Soroni GR 181 D7
Sorradile I 64 C2
Sørreisa N 111 B15
Sorrento I 60 B2
Sorring DK 86 C5
Sørrollnes N 111 C12
Sorsakoski FIN 124 F9
Sorsele S 109 E14
Sörsjön S 102 D5
Sorso I 64 B2
Sörstafors S 98 C6
Sørstraumen N 112 D8
Sort E 33 F8
Sortavala RUS 129 B14
Sortelha P 45 D6
Sortino I 59 E7
Sörtjärn S 102 B8
Sortland N 110 C9
Sør-Tverrfjord N 112 C8
Sõru EST 130 D5
Sørum N 101 E11
Sorumsand N 95 C14
Sorunda S 93 A11
Sörup D 82 A7
Sørvad DK 86 C3
Sørvær N 112 B8
Sörvåge S 107 E15
Sørvågen N 110 E5
Sørvágur FO 2 A2
Sörvattnet S 102 B4
Sørvik N 111 C13
Sörvik S 97 B13
Sørvika N 101 B15
Sörviken S 107 D9
Sorvilán E 55 F6
Sos F 33 B6
Sosandra GR 169 C7
Sösdala S 87 C13
Sos del Rey Católico E 32 E3
Sosedno RUS 132 E4
Soses E 42 D4
Soshe-Ostrivs'ke UA 154 C5
Sösjö S 103 A9
Sóskút H 149 B11
Sośnica PL 85 D10
Sośnie PL 142 D4
Sośno PL 138 D4
Sosnovka RUS 136 D3
Sosnovo RUS 129 D13
Sosnovyy Bor RUS 129 F11
Sosnowica PL 141 G8
Sosnowiec PL 143 F7
Sosnówka PL 141 G8
Soso FIN 119 E15
Sospel F 37 D6
Sossonniemi FIN 121 C14
Sost F 33 E7
Šoštanj SLO 73 D11
Sostis GR 171 B8
Sot N 96 C6
Şotânga RO 160 D6
Sótés E 41 D6
Sotiel Coronada E 51 D6
Sotillo de la Adrada E 46 D3
Sotillo del Rincón E 41 E6
Sotin HR 157 B11
Sotkajärvi FIN 119 E16
Sotkamo FIN 121 F11
Soto E 39 A7
Soto de la Vega E 39 D8
Soto del Real E 46 C5
Soto de Ribera E 39 B8
Soto en Cameros E 41 D7
Sotopalacios E 40 D4
Sotos E 47 D8
Sotoserrano E 45 D8
Soto y Amío E 39 C8
Sotres E 39 B10
Sotresgudo E 40 C3
Şotrile RO 161 C7
Sotrondio E 39 B8
Sotta F 37 H10
Sotteville-lès-Rouen F 18 F3
Sottomarina I 66 B5
Sottrum D 17 B12
Sottunga FIN 99 B15
Sotuélamos E 55 A7
Soual F 33 C10
Soubès F 34 C5
Soucy F 25 D9
Souda GR 178 E7
Soudan F 23 E9
Soueix F 33 E8
Souesmes F 24 F7
Soufflenheim F 27 C8
Soufli GR 171 B10
Sougia GR 178 E6
Souillac F 29 F8
Souilly F 26 B3
Souk el Had el Rharbia MA 52 E5
Souk-Khémis-des-Anjra MA 53 E5
Soukolojärvi S 119 B11
Souk Tleta Taghramet MA 53 E6
Soulac-sur-Mer F 28 D3
Soulaines-Dhuys F 25 D12
Soulatgé F 33 E11
Souli GR 175 D6
Soullans F 28 B2
Soulom F 32 E5
Soultz-Haut-Rhin F 27 E7
Soultz-sous-Forêts F 27 C8
Soumagne B 19 C12
Soumoulou F 32 D5
Souppes-sur-Loing F 25 D8
Souprosse F 32 C4
Sourdeval F 23 C10
Soure P 44 D3
Sournia F 33 E10
Souro Pires P 45 C6
Sourpi GR 175 A6
Sours F 24 D6
Sourzac F 29 E6
Sousceyrac F 29 F10
Sousel P 50 B4
Soustons F 32 C3
Southam GB 13 A12
Southampton GB 13 D12
South Anston GB 11 E9
South Bank GB 11 B9
Southborough GB 15 E9
South Cave GB 11 D10
South Chard GB 13 D9
Southend GB 4 E5
Southend-on-Sea GB 15 D10
Southery GB 11 F12
Southgate GB 15 D8
South Harting GB 15 F7
South Kelsey GB 11 E11
South Kirkby GB 11 D9
Southminster GB 15 D10
South Molton GB 13 C7
South Ockendon GB 15 D9
Southport GB 10 D5
South Queensferry GB 5 D10
South Shields GB 5 F14
Southwell GB 11 E10
Southwold GB 15 C12
South Woodham Ferrers GB 15 D10
Souto E 38 C4
Souto P 38 E2
Souto P 44 E4
Souto P 45 D7
Souto da Casa P 44 D5
Soutuperä FIN 123 B14
Souvala GR 175 D8
Souvigny F 30 B3
Şovarna RO 159 D10
Søvassli N 104 E6
Sovata RO 152 D6
Soveja RO 153 E9
Soverato I 59 B10
Soveria F 37 G10
Soveria Mannelli I 59 A9
Sovetsk RUS 136 C4
Sovetskiy RUS 129 D10
Sovići BIH 157 F7
Sovicille I 66 F3
Søvik N 100 A4
Søvind DK 86 D5
Sowno PL 85 B11
Sowno PL 85 D7
Soyaux F 29 D6
Soye F 26 F5
Soylu TR 173 B7
Soymy UA 145 F7
Soyons F 30 F6
Sozopol BG 167 E9
Spa B 19 D12
Spa IRL 8 D3
Spabrücken D 21 E9
Špačince SK 146 E5
Spačva HR 157 B10
Spadafora I 59 C7
Spaichingen D 27 D10
Spalding GB 11 F11
Spálené Poříčí CZ 76 C5
Spalt D 75 D8
Spangenberg D 78 D6
Spanish Point IRL 8 C4
Spantekow D 84 C5
Spanţov RO 161 E9
Sparanise I 60 A2
Sparbu N 105 D10
Spāre LV 134 B4
Sparreholm S 93 A9
Spartà I 59 C8
Sparti GR 174 E5
Sparto GR 174 B3
Spartylas GR 168 E2
Spasovo BG 155 F2
Spata GR 175 D8
Spay D 185 D8
Spean Bridge GB 4 B7
Specchia I 61 D10
Speen GB 13 C12
Speia MD 154 D4
Speicher D 21 E7
Speichersdorf D 75 C10
Spello I 62 B3
Spenge D 17 D10
Spennymoor GB 5 F13
Spentrup DK 86 B6
Spercheiada GR 174 B5
Sperlinga I 58 D5
Sperlonga I 62 E4
Spermezeu RO 152 C4
Spersboda S 99 C11
Spetalen N 95 D13
Spetses GR 175 E7
Spey Bay GB 3 K10
Speyer D 21 F10
Spezzano Albanese I 61 D6
Spiczyn PL 141 H7
Spiddal IRL 6 F4
Spielberg bei Knittelfeld A 73 B10
Spiere B 182 D2
Spiesen-Elversberg D 21 F8
Spiez CH 70 D5
Spigno Monferrato I 37 B8
Spigno Saturnia I 62 E5
Spiiniigied'di N 113 E15
Spijk NL 17 B7
Spijkenisse NL 16 E2
Spikberg S 118 B5
Spilamberto I 66 C3
Spili GR 178 E8
Spilimbergo I 73 D6
Spilinga I 59 B8
Spillersboda S 99 C11
Spillum N 105 C11
Spilsby GB 11 E12
Spinazzola I 60 B6
Spincourt F 19 F12
Špindlerův Mlýn CZ 81 E9
Spinea I 66 B5
Spineni RO 160 D5
Spinetoli I 62 B5
Spink IRL 9 C8
Spinuş RO 151 C9
Špionica BIH 157 C10
Špišić-Bukovica HR 149 E8
Spiss A 71 D10
Spišská Belá SK 145 E1
Spišská Nová Ves SK 145 F2
Spišská Stará Ves SK 145 E1
Spišská Teplica SK 145 E1
Spišské Bystré SK 145 F1
Spišské Podhradie SK 145 F2
Spišské Vlachy SK 145 F2
Spišský Hrušov SK 145 F2
Spital am Pyhrn A 73 A9
Spital am Semmering A 148 A5
Spitsyno RUS 132 D2
Spittal GB 3 J10
Spittal an der Drau A 73 C7
Spittal of Glenshee GB 5 B10
Spitz A 77 F8
Spjald DK 86 C3
Spjelkavik N 100 B4
Spjutsbygd S 89 C9
Spjutsund FIN 127 E14
Split HR 156 E5
Splügen CH 71 D8
Spodnja Idrija SLO 73 D9
Spodnje Hoče SLO 148 C5
Spodsbjerg DK 87 F7
Spofforth GB 11 D9
Spoleto I 62 B3
Spoltore I 63 C6
Spondigna I 71 D11
Spontin B 19 D11
Spornitz D 83 D11
Spotorno I 37 C8
Spraitbach D 74 E6
Sprakensehl D 83 E9
Sprâncenata RO 160 E5
Sprängsviken S 103 A14
Spreenhagen D 80 B5
Spremberg D 80 C6
Sprendlingen D 185 E8
Spresiano I 72 E5
Spriana I 69 A8
Sprimont B 19 C12
Şpring RO 152 F3
Springe D 78 B6
Springholm GB 5 E9
Springliden S 107 A16
Sproatley GB 11 D11
Sprockhövel D 17 F8
Sproge S 93 E12
Sprogi LV 135 D10
Sprova N 105 C10
Sprowston GB 15 B11
Sproxton GB 11 C9
Spungēni LV 135 C11
Spuž MNE 163 D7
Spychowo PL 139 C11
Spydeberg N 95 C14
Spytihněv CZ 146 C5
Spytkowice PL 143 G7
Spytkowice PL 147 B9
Squillace I 59 B10
Squinzano I 61 C10
Sráid an Mhuilinn IRL 8 D4
Sraith Salach IRL 6 F3
Sranea IRL 6 D6
Srath an Urláir IRL 7 C7
Srbac BIH 157 B8
Srbobran SRB 158 B4
Srbovac RKS 163 D10
Srdevići BIH 157 E6
Srebrenica BIH 158 E3
Srebrenik BIH 157 C10
Srebŭrna BG 161 E10
Sredets BG 166 E5
Sredets BG 167 E8
Središče SLO 148 D6
Sredishte BG 161 F10
Srednje BIH 157 D9
Srednjevo SRB 159 D8
Sredno Gradishte BG 166 E4
Śrem PL 81 B12
Sremčica SRB 158 D5
Sremska Kamenica SRB 158 C4
Sremska Mitrovica SRB 158 D4
Sremski Karlovci SRB 158 C4
Srenica BIH 156 D6
Srnice BIH 157 C9
Srockowo PL 136 E4
Środa Śląska PL 81 D11
Środa Wielkopolska PL 81 B12
Srpska Crnja SRB 158 B6
Srpski Itebej SRB 159 B6
Srpski Miletić SRB 157 A11
Sta S 105 E13
Staatz A 77 E10
Stabbfors S 108 E8
Stabbursnes N 113 C14
Stabroek B 16 F2
Stabulnieki LV 135 D13
Staburags LV 135 C11
Staburnaäs S 107 B11
Staby DK 86 C2
Stachy CZ 76 D5
Stade D 17 A12
Staden B 18 C7
Stadl-Paura A 76 F5
Stadra S 97 C12
Stadsbygd N 104 E7
Stadskanaal NL 17 C7
Stadtallendorf D 21 C12
Stadtbergen D 75 F8
Stadthagen D 17 D12
Stadtilm D 79 E9
Stadtkyll D 21 D7
Stadtlauringen D 75 B7
Stadtlohn D 17 E7
Stadtroda D 79 E10
Stadtschlaining A 148 B6
Stadum D 82 A6
Stäfa CH 27 F10
Staffanstorp S 87 D12
Staffin GB 2 K4
Staffolo I 67 F7
Stafford GB 11 F7
Stahovica SLO 73 D10
Stai N 101 D14
Staicele LV 131 F9
Staig D 74 F6
Stainach A 73 A9
Staindrop GB 11 B8
Staines-upon-Thames GB 15 E7
Stainforth GB 11 C7
Stainforth GB 11 D9
Staintondale GB 11 C11
Stainville F 26 C3
Stainz A 148 C4
Staiti I 59 D9
Stakčín SK 145 F5
Stakevtsi BG 164 B6
Stāķi LV 135 B13
Stakiai LT 134 F6
Stakkvik N 112 D4
Stakliškės LT 137 D9
Stakroge DK 86 D3
Stalać SRB 159 F7
Stalbe LV 135 B10
Stålbo S 98 B7
Stalbridge GB 13 D10
Stalden CH 68 A4
Staldzene LV 134 B3
Stalgėnai LT 134 E3
Stalģene LV 135 C7
Stalham GB 15 B12
Stalheim N 100 E5
Stalidzāni LV 135 C13
Staliogargo N 113 B12
Stall A 73 C7
Stallarholmen S 98 D8
Ställberg S 97 C12
Ställdalen S 97 C12
Stallwang D 75 D12
Stalon S 107 B9
Stalowa Wola PL 144 B5
Stâlpeni RO 160 C5
Stâlpu RO 161 C9
Stamboliyski BG 165 E10
Stambulčić BIH 157 E10
Stamford GB 11 F11
Stamford Bridge GB 11 D10
Stamfordham GB 5 E13
Stammham D 75 E9
Stamna GR 174 B3
Stamovo BG 166 E5
Stams A 71 C11
Stamstik N 110 E9
Stamsund N 110 D6
Stânceni RO 152 D6
Stăncuţa RO 155 D1
Standdaarbuiten NL 182 B5
Standish GB 10 D6
Stăneşti RO 159 C11
Stăneşti RO 161 F7
Stånga S 93 E12
Stângăceaua RO 160 D2
Stangnes N 111 B13
Stångviken S 105 D16
Stanhoe GB 15 B10
Stanhope GB 5 F12
Stănileşti RO 154 D2
Stanin PL 141 G6
Stănişeşti RO 153 E10
Stanišić SRB 150 F3
Stanišinci SRB 163 B10
Stanisławów PL 141 F5
Stăniţa RO 153 C10
Štanjel SLO 73 E8
Staňkov CZ 76 C4
Stankovany SK 147 C8
Stanley GB 5 C10
Stanley GB 5 F13
Stanley GB 11 D9
Stannington GB 5 E13
Stanomino PL 85 C9
Stanos GR 169 C10
Stanos GR 174 B3
Stan'ovsti BG 165 D6
Stans CH 71 D6
Stansted Mountfitchet GB 15 D9
Stantër RKS 163 D10
Stanton GB 15 C10
Stanzach A 71 C11
Stanz im Mürztal A 148 B5
Stapar SRB 158 B3
Stapel D 83 D9
Stapelburg D 79 C8
Stapelfeld D 83 C8
Staphorst NL 16 C6
Staplehurst GB 15 E10
Stąporków PL 141 H3
Stara Błotnica PL 141 G3
Stará Bystrica SK 147 C7
Starachowice PL 143 D11
Stara Gradina HR 149 E9
Stará Huť CZ 76 C6
Stara Kamienica PL 81 E9
Stara Kamionka PL 140 D9
Stara Kiszewa PL 138 C5
Stara Kornica PL 141 F7
Stara Kul'na UA 154 B4
Stara Łubianka PL 85 D11
Stará Ľubovňa SK 145 E2
Stara Moravica SRB 150 F3
Stara Novalja HR 67 C10
Stara Pazova SRB 158 D5
Stara Ploščica HR 149 E7
Stara Reka BG 166 D6
Stara Rudnica PL 84 E6
Stara Sil' UA 145 E6
Stara Tsarychanka UA 154 E5
Stará Turá SK 146 D5
Stara vas-Bizeljsko SLO 148 E5
Stará Ves nad Ondřejnicí CZ 146 B6
Staravina NMK 169 B6
Stara Wieś PL 144 B6
Stara Zagora BG 166 E5
Stara Zhadova UA 153 A7
Starčevo SRB 158 D6
Starchiojd RO 161 C8
Starcross GB 13 D8
Stare Babice PL 141 F3
Stare-Bogaczowice PL 81 E10
Stare Budkowice PL 142 E5
Stařeč CZ 77 D9
Stare Czarnowo PL 85 D7
Stare Dąbrowa PL 85 D8
Stare Dolistowo PL 140 C7
Stare Hołowczyce PL 141 F7
Stare Kurowo PL 85 E9
Staré Město CZ 77 B11
Staré Město u Uherského Hradiště CZ 146 C4
Stare Miasto PL 142 B5
Stare Pole PL 139 B7
Stare Puchały PL 141 E7
Stare Selo UA 144 D9
Stare Strącze PL 81 C10
Stargard Szczeciński PL 85 D8
Star Huta SK 147 E8
Stari LV 135 B13
Stari Banovci SRB 158 D5
Staříč CZ 146 B6
Stari Dulići BIH 157 F10
Starigrad HR 67 C10
Starigrad HR 156 D3
Starigrad HR 156 F6
Stari Gradac HR 149 E8
Stari Kuty UA 152 A6
Stari Log SLO 73 E10
Stari Majdan BIH 156 C6
Stari Mikanovci HR 157 B10
Stari Trg SLO 67 B11
Stari Trg SLO 73 E9
Stari Troyany UA 155 B4
Starkenberg D 79 E11
Stärkesmark S 122 B3
Starnberg D 75 G9
Starogard PL 85 C9
Starogard Gdański PL 138 C6
Staroglavice BIH 158 E3
Starokozache UA 154 E5
Staro Oryakhovo BG 167 D9
Staropatitsa BG 159 F9
Staro Petrovo Selo HR 157 B8
Starosel BG 165 E10
Staro Selo BG 161 F9
Staro Selo BIH 157 D7
Staro Selo SRB 159 E7
Staroseltsi BG 165 B9
Starosiedle PL 81 C7
Starowa Góra PL 143 C7
Staroye Syalo BY 133 F7
Staro Zhelezare BG 165 E10
Starożreby PL 139 E8
Startforth GB 11 B8
Starup DK 86 E5
Stary Brus PL 141 H8
Stary Cykarzew PL 143 E7
Stary Dzierzgoń PL 139 C7
Stary Dzikowiec PL 144 C4
Stary Kisielin PL 81 C9
Stary Kobrzyniec PL 139 E7
Starý Kolín CZ 77 B8
Stary Majdan PL 144 C6
Starynovichy BY 133 F6
Stary Pahost BY 133 F3
Starý Plzenec CZ 76 C4
Stary Sącz PL 145 D2
StarýStarý SK 145 E1
Stary Szelków PL 139 E11
Stary Targ PL 139 C7
Stary Uścimów PL 141 H7
Staryy Sambir UA 145 E6
Stary Zamość PL 144 B7
Starzyno PL 138 A5
Staškov SK 147 C7
Staßfurt D 79 C10
Staszów PL 143 E11
Stathelle N 90 A6
Statland N 105 C10
Statsås S 107 B11
Statzendorf A 77 F9
Stăuceni MD 154 C3
Stăuceni RO 153 B9
Stauchitz D 80 D4
Staufenberg D 21 C11
Staupitz D 80 C5
Štavalj SRB 163 C9
Stavang N 100 C2
Stavanger N 94 E3
Stavaträsk S 118 D4
Stavchany UA 153 A8
Stave N 111 B10
Staveley GB 11 E9
Stavelot B 20 D5
Stavenisse NL 16 E2
Stavern N 90 B7
Stavertsi BG 165 B9
Stavky UA 144 A9
Stavne UA 145 F6
Stavning DK 86 D2
Stavoren NL 16 C4
Stavre S 103 A9
Stavre S 105 E16
Stavreviken S 103 A13
Stavrodromi GR 174 D4
Stavros GR 169 C7
Stavros GR 169 C10
Stavros GR 169 F7
Stavros GR 174 C2
Stavroupoli GR 171 B7
Stavrove UA 154 B5
Stavsätra S 103 C10
Stavsnäs S 99 D11
Stavtrup DK 86 C6
Staw PL 85 E7
Stawiguda PL 139 C9
Stawiski PL 139 D13
Stawiszyn PL 142 C5
Stębark PL 139 C9
Steblevë AL 168 B3
Stebnyk UA 145 E8
Steccato I 61 F7
Štěchovice CZ 76 C6
Stechow D 79 A11
Steckborn CH 27 E10
Stedesdorf D 17 A9
Stedten D 79 D10
Steeg A 71 C10
Steenbergen NL 16 E2
Steenderen NL 183 A8
Steenvoorde F 18 C6
Steenwijk NL 16 C6
Steeton GB 11 D8
Stefanaconi I 59 B9
Ştefan cel Mare RO 153 D9
Ştefan cel Mare RO 153 D11
Ştefan cel Mare RO 153 E9
Ştefan cel Mare RO 155 E1
Ştefan cel Mare RO 160 D6
Ştefan cel Mare RO 160 F4
Ştefăneşti MD 154 E5
Ştefăneşti RO 153 B10
Ştefăneşti RO 160 D5
Ştefăneşti RO 161 D9
Ştefăneştii de Jos RO 161 D8
Stefani GR 175 C8
Štefanje HR 149 E7
Stefan Karadzha BG 167 C8
Stefan-Karadzhovo BG 167 E7
Štefanov SK 146 D4
Stefanovikeio GR 169 F8
Stefanovo BG 167 C9
Stefanovouno GR 169 E7
Ştefan Vodă MD 154 D5
Ştefan Vodă RO 161 E10
Ştefeşti RO 161 C7
Steffisburg CH 70 D5
Stegaurath D 75 C8
Stege DK 87 F10
Stegelitz D 79 B10
Stegersbach A 148 B6
Stegna PL 138 B7
Stegny PL 139 B8
Stehag S 87 D12
Ştei RO 151 D9
Steigen N 110 E8
Steigra D 79 D10
Steimbke D 17 C12
Stein D 75 D9
Stein NL 19 C12
Steinach D 75 B9
Steinach D 75 E12
Steinach D 186 E5
Steinach am Brenner A 72 B3
Stein am Rhein CH 27 E10
Steinau D 17 A11
Steinau an der Straße D 74 B5
Steinbach D 21 C11
Steinbach D 80 E4
Steinbach am Attersee A 73 A8
Steinbach am Wald D 75 B9
Steinbakk N 114 E7
Steinberg D 75 D11
Steinberg D 82 A7
Steine N 105 D11
Steine N 110 C7
Steinen D 27 E8
Steinfeld A 73 C7
Steinfeld D 186 C5
Steinfeld D 187 B8
Steinfeld (Oldenburg) D 17 C10
Steinfjord N 111 B13
Steinfort L 20 E5
Steinfurt D 17 D8
Steingaden D 71 B11
Steinhagen D 17 D10
Steinhagen D 84 B3
Steinheim D 17 E12
Steinheim N 111 B15
Steinheim am Albuch D 187 D9
Steinheim an der Murr D 187 D7
Steinhöring D 75 F11
Steinhorst D 83 E8
Steinigtwolmsdorf D 80 D6
Steinkirchen D 82 C7
Steinkjer N 105 C11
Steinland N 110 C9
Steinløysa N 100 A7
Steinsdorf D 81 B7
Steinsfeld D 75 D7
Steinshamn N 100 A5
Steinsholt N 95 D11
Steinskjærnes N 114 D7
Steinsland N 94 B2
Steinsvik N 100 C3
Steinwenden D 186 C4
Steinwiesen D 75 B9
Stejaru RO 155 D3
Stejaru RO 160 E5
Stekene B 19 B9
Stelle D 83 D8
Stellendam NL 16 E2
Stelnica RO 155 E1
Stelpe LV 135 C9
Stemland N 108 B9
Stemmen D 82 D7
Stemnes N 111 D13
Stemnitsa GR 174 D5
Stemshorn D 17 D10
Stenåsa S 89 B11
Stenay F 19 F11
Stenbacken S 111 D17
Stenbjerg DK 86 B2
Stenbo S 93 E8
Stendal D 79 A10
Stende LV 134 B5
Stenderup DK 86 D3
Steneset N 108 D4
Stengelse N 113 D11
Stenhammar S 91 B13
Stenhamra S 99 D9
Stenhousemuir GB 5 C9
Stenico I 69 A10
Steninge S 87 B11
Stenis S 102 E7
Stenkumla S 93 D12
Stenkyrka S 93 D13
Stenlille DK 87 D9
Stenløse DK 87 D10
Stennäs S 107 D14
Stenness GB 3 E13
Steno GR 174 D5
Steno GR 175 E5
Stensån S 103 B9
Stensele S 107 A12
Stensjö S 107 E10
Stensjön S 92 D5
Stenskär S 99 B10
Stenstorp S 91 C14
Stensträsk S 107 A17
Stenstrup DK 86 E6
Stensund S 109 D15
Stensund S 109 F13
Stensved DK 87 F10
Stenton GB 5 D11
Stenträsk S 118 B3
Stenudden S 109 C14
Stenum DK 90 E6
Stenungsund S 91 C10
Stenvad DK 86 C7
Stenzharychi UA 144 B9
Stepanci NMK 169 B6
Stepanivka UA 154 D5
Štěpánov CZ 77 C12
Stepen BIH 157 F10
Stepnica PL 84 C7
Stepojevac SRB 158 D5
Stepping DK 86 E4
Sterdyń-Osada PL 141 E6
Sterławki-Wielkie PL 136 E4
Sterna GR 171 A10
Sterna GR 175 D6
Sterna HR 67 B8
Sternberg D 83 C11
Šternberk CZ 146 B4
Sternes GR 178 D7
Stes-Maries-de-la-Mer F 35 D7
Stjszew PL 81 B11
Štětí CZ 76 B6
Stetten am kalten Markt D 27 D11
Steuerberg A 73 C9
Steutz D 79 C11
Stevenage GB 15 D8
Stevenston GB 4 D7
Stevensweert NL 183 C7
Stevnstrup DK 86 C5
Stewarton GB 4 D7
Stewartstown GB 7 C9
Steyerberg D 17 C12
Steyning GB 15 F8
Steyr A 76 F6
Steyregg A 76 F6
Stěžery CZ 77 B9
Stezherovo BG 166 C4
Stężyca PL 138 B4
Stężyca PL 141 G5
Stia I 66 E4
Stibb Cross GB 12 D6
Stickney GB 11 E12
Stidsvig S 87 C12
Stiege D 79 C8
Stiens NL 16 B5
Stienta I 66 C4
Stigen S 91 B11
Stigliano I 60 C6
Stignano I 59 C9
Stigsjö S 103 A14
Stigtomta S 93 B9
Stijena BIH 156 C5
Stikli LV 134 B4
Stilligarry GB 2 L2
Stilling DK 86 C5
Stillington GB 11 C9
Stillorgan IRL 7 F10
Stilo I 59 C9
Stilton GB 11 G11
Stimpfach D 75 D7
Stintino I 64 B1
Stio I 60 C4
Štip NMK 164 F5
Stirfaka GR 174 B5
Stiring-Wendel F 21 F7
Stirling GB 5 C9
Štitar HR 157 B10
Štitar SRB 158 D4
Štítina CZ 146 B6
Štítnik SK 145 F1
Štíty CZ 77 C11
Ştiubieni RO 153 B9
Ştiuca RO 159 B8
Stivan HR 67 C9
Stjær DK 86 C5
Stjärnfors S 97 C13
Stjärnhov S 93 A9
Stjärnorp S 92 B7
Stjørdalshalsen N 105 E9
Støa N 101 E14
Støa N 102 D4
Stobiecko Miejskie PL 143 D7
Stobreć HR 156 E6
Stoby S 87 C13
Stochov CZ 76 B5
Stocka S 103 C13
Stockach D 27 E11
Stockamöllan S 87 D12
Stockaryd S 88 A7
Stöcke S 122 C4
Stockelsdorf D 83 C9
Stockenboi A 73 C8
Stockerau A 77 F10
Stockheim D 75 B9
Stockholm S 99 D10
Stocking A 148 C5
Stockport GB 11 E7
Stocksfield GB 5 F13
Stockstadt am Rhein D 21 E10
Stockton-on-Tees GB 11 B9
Stockvik S 103 B13
Stoczek PL 139 E12
Stoczek Łukowski PL 141 G5
Stod CZ 76 C4
Stöde S 103 B12
Stoeneşti RO 160 C4
Stoeneşti RO 160 C6
Stoeneşti RO 160 E5
Stoeneşti RO 161 E7
Stoer GB 2 J6
Stoholm DK 86 C4
Stoianovca MD 154 E2
Stoicăneşti RO 160 E5
Stoileşti RO 160 D4
Stoina RO 160 D3
Stojakovo NMK 169 B8
Stojdraga HR 148 E5
Stojnci SLO 148 D5
Stoke Ash GB 15 C11
Stoke-on-Trent GB 11 E7
Stokesay GB 13 A9
Stokesley GB 11 C9
Stokite BG 166 D4
Stokka N 108 E3
Stokkasjøen N 108 E4
Stokkdal N 111 D12
Stokke N 90 A7
Stokkemarke DK 83 A10
Stokkvågen N 108 D5
Stokmarknes N 110 C8
Štoky CZ 77 D9

Stolac BIH 157 F8
Stolberg (Harz) Kurort D 79 C8
Stolberg (Rheinland) D 20 C6
Stołczno PL 85 C12
Stolerova LV 133 D3
Stollberg D 79 E12
Stöllet S 97 B9
Stolmen N 94 B2
Stolniceni MD 154 D3
Stolniceni-Prăjescu RO 153 C9
Stolnici RO 160 D5
Stolnik BG 165 D8
Stolno PL 138 D6
Stolpe D 83 B8
Stolpe D 84 E6
Stolpen D 80 D6
Stolzenau D 17 C12
Stomio GR 169 E8
Stömne S 97 D8
Ston HR 162 D4
Stone GB 11 F7
Stone GB 13 B10
Stonehaven GB 5 B12
Stonehouse GB 5 D9
Stong N 94 D3
Stongfjorden N 100 D2
Stonglandseidet N 111 B13
Stonybreck GB 3 F13
Stoob A 149 A7
Stöpen S 91 C14
Stopiče SLO 148 E4
Stopki PL 136 E3
Stopnica PL 143 F10
Storå N 111 D11
Storå S 97 C13
Stora Åby S 92 C5
Storåbränna S 106 D7
Stora Höga S 91 C10
Stora Levene S 91 C12
Stora Melby S 91 C12
Stora Mellösa S 92 A6
Storarmsjö S 107 C16
Storås N 104 E7
Storåsen S 103 A10
Storåsen S 106 D7
Stora Skedvi S 97 B14
Stora Tallberg S 109 E17
Stora Vika S 93 B11
Storbäck S 106 B9
Storbacka FIN 123 D10
Storbäcken S 102 C4
Storberg S 109 E16
Stor-Blåsjön S 105 B16
Storbo S 102 C3
Storbogaren S 107 D14
Storbränna S 106 D7
Storbrännan S 118 E4
Storbukt N 113 B12
Storby FIN 99 B13
Stordal N 100 B6
Štore SLO 148 D4
Storebø N 94 B2
Storebro S 92 D7
Storebru N 100 C3
Store Damme DK 84 A2
Store Darum DK 86 E3
Store Heddinge DK 87 E10
Storeidet N 111 E10
Storekorsnes N 112 C11
Storelv N 112 B10
Store Merløse DK 87 D9
Store Molvik N 114 B5
Støren N 104 E8
Storenga N 112 D7
Store Rise DK 83 A8
Store Rørbæk DK 86 B5
Storfjäten S 102 C5
Storfjord N 111 B18
Storfjordbotn N 113 C18
Storfors S 97 C11
Storforshei N 108 D8
Storhågna S 102 A7
Storhallaren N 104 D5
Stor-Hallen S 102 A7
Storhogen S 106 E8
Stor-Hullsjön S 103 A12
Štorje SLO 73 E8
Storjola S 106 B7
Storjord N 109 C9
Storjorda N 108 C6
Storjorda N 111 C11
Storkow D 80 B5
Storli N 101 A10
Storlien S 105 E12
Stormi FIN 127 C9
Stornara I 60 A5
Stornarella I 60 A5
Stornäs S 106 A8
Stornäs S 107 A11
Stornäset S 107 C10
Stornes N 111 C11
Storneshamn N 112 D7
Stornoway GB 2 J4
Storo I 69 B10
Storobăneasa RO 161 F6
Storodden N 104 E6
Storöhamn S 119 C10
Storozhynets' UA 153 A7
Storrington GB 15 F8
Storrøsta N 101 B13
Storsand S 103 C13
Storsand S 118 B5
Storsandsjö S 107 C17
Storsätern S 102 B3
Storsävarträsk S 118 F3
Storsele S 107 D14
Storseleby S 107 B11
Storseløy N 108 C4
Storsjö S 102 A5
Storskog S 109 E10
Storslett N 112 D7
Storsletta N 112 D6
Storsteinnes N 111 A18
Storsteinnes N 111 B17
Storsund S 118 C5
Storuman S 107 A12
Storvik N 108 C6
Storvik N 110 C9
Storvik N 112 C9
Storvik N 112 D7
Storvik S 103 E12
Storvorde DK 86 A6
Storvreta S 99 C9
Štós SK 145 F2
Stößen D 79 D10
Stössing A 77 F9
Stoszowice PL 81 E11
Støtt N 108 C5
Stötten am Auerberg D 71 B11
Stotternheim D 79 D9
Stouby DK 86 D5
Stoumont B 19 D12
Stourbridge GB 13 A10
Stourport-on-Severn GB 13 A10
Støvran N 108 B8
Støvring DK 86 B5
Støvset N 108 B8
Stow GB 5 D11
Stowięcino PL 85 A12
Stowmarket GB 15 C10
Stow-on-the-Wold GB 13 B11
Stoyan Mikhaylovski BG 167 C8
Stoyanovo BG 165 C10
Stoykite BG 165 F10
Stozher BG 167 C9
Stożne PL 136 E5
Stra I 66 B5
Straach D 79 C12
Strabane GB 4 F2
Strabla PL 141 E8
Strachan GB 5 A11
Strachówka PL 139 F12
Strachur GB 4 C6
Stracin NMK 164 E5
Stračiūnai LT 137 E9
Strackholt (Großefehn) D 17 B9
Strączno PL 85 D10
Stradalovo BG 165 E6
Stradbally IRL 7 F8
Stradbroke GB 15 C11
Stradella I 69 C7
Stradi LV 135 B13
Stradishall GB 15 C10
Stradone IRL 7 E8
Stradsett GB 11 F12
Straelen D 16 F6
Stragari SRB 158 E6
Strai N 90 C2
Straimont B 19 E11
Straja RO 153 B7
Strakhilovo BG 166 C5
Strakonice CZ 76 D5
Straldzha BG 167 D7
Stralki BY 133 E4
Straloch GB 5 B9
Strålsnäs S 92 C6
Stralsund D 84 B4
Strambino I 68 C4
Stramproy NL 19 B12
Strâmtura RO 152 B4
Stráňavy SK 147 C7
Strančice CZ 77 C7
Strand N 101 D15
Strand N 110 C9
Strand S 106 D9
Stranda N 100 B5
Strandå N 108 A8
Strandby DK 86 B4
Strandby DK 90 E8
Strande D 83 B8
Strandnorum S 91 C10
Strandvål N 105 B10
Strangford GB 7 D11
Stranghele N 100 E3
Strängnäs S 98 D8
Strangolagalli I 62 D4
Strångsjö S 93 B8
Strání CZ 146 D5
Stranocum GB 4 E4
Stranorlar IRL 7 C7
Stranraer GB 4 F6
Străoane RO 153 F10
Strasatti I 58 D2
Strasbourg F 27 C8
Strasburg D 84 D5
Strășeni MD 154 C3
Strašice CZ 76 C5
Stråssa S 97 C13
Straßberg D 27 D11
Straßberg D 79 C9
Straßburg A 73 C9
Strassen L 20 E6
Straßengel A 148 B4
Straßenhaus D 21 C9
Strasshof an der Nordbahn
A 77 F11
Straßkirchen D 75 E12
Straßwalchen A 76 G4
Stratford IRL 7 G9
Stratford-upon-Avon GB 13 A11
Strathaven GB 5 D8
Strathblane GB 5 D8
Strathpeffer GB 2 K7
Strathy GB 3 H9
Strathyre GB 5 C8
Stratinska BIH 157 C6
Stratiyivka UA 154 A4
Stratoni GR 169 C10
Stratoniki GR 169 C10
Stratos GR 174 B3
Stratton GB 12 D5
Stratton St Margaret GB 13 B11
Straubing D 75 E12
Straum N 104 D5
Straum N 108 E5
Straume N 90 A2
Straume N 110 C7
Straumen N 104 E4
Straumen N 105 D10
Straumen N 108 B8
Straumen N 109 B10
Straumen N 111 A19
Straumen N 111 C11
Straumen N 114 B7
Straumfjord N 110 C9
Straumgjerde N 100 B5
Straumnes N 110 D7
Straumsnes N 108 B9
Straumsnes N 110 C8
Straumsnes N 111 B13
Straumstad N 111 B17
Straunen N 111 B15
Straupe LV 135 B9
Straupitz D 80 C6
Strausberg D 80 A5
Straußfurt D 79 D8
Stravaj AL 168 C3
Strawczyn PL 143 E9
Straža SRB 159 D7
Strazhitsa BG 166 C5
Stráž nad Nežárkou CZ 77 D7
Stráž nad Nisou CZ 81 E8
Strážnice CZ 146 D4
Stráž pod Ralskem CZ 81 E7
Strážske SK 145 F4
Štrba SK 147 C10
Streatley GB 13 B12
Strečno SK 147 C7
Streda nad Bodrogom SK
145 G4
Streek D 17 B10
Street GB 13 C9
Strehaia RO 159 D11
Strehla D 80 D4
Strejești RO 160 D4
Strekov SK 146 F6
Strelac SRB 164 D5
Strelcë AL 168 C4
Strelcha BG 165 D9
Strellc i Epërm RKS 163 D9
Strēlnieki LV 135 C8
Strem A 149 B6
Strembo I 69 A10
Stremț RO 152 E3
Strenči LV 131 F11
Strendur FO 2 A3
Strengberg A 77 F7
Strengelvåg N 110 C9
Strengen A 71 C10
Strengen N 95 D9
Stresa I 68 B6
Stretford GB 11 E7
Stretham GB 15 C9
Streufdorf D 75 B8
Strezimirovtsi BG 164 D5
Strib DK 86 D5
Striberg S 97 C12
Stříbro CZ 76 C3
Strichen GB 3 K12
Strigno I 72 D4
Štrigova HR 148 C6
Strijen NL 16 E3
Strimasund S 108 D8
Strimoniko GR 169 B9
Strinda N 111 E10
Strittjomvare S 109 E16
Strizivojna HR 157 B9
Strmec HR 148 E5
Strmen HR 149 F7
Strmica BIH 156 D5
Strmica HR 156 D5
Ströbeck D 79 C8
Strobl A 73 A7
Strøby DK 87 E10
Strøby Egede DK 87 E10
Stroești RO 160 C3
Stroevo BG 165 E10
Strofylia GR 175 B7
Ströhen D 17 C11
Stroiești RO 153 B8
Strokestown IRL 6 E6
Ström S 108 E8
Strömbäck S 122 C4
Strömbacka S 103 C12
Stromberg D 185 E8
Stromeferry GB 2 L5
Strömfors S 118 E4
Strömholm S 109 E15
Stromiec PL 141 G4
Strommen N 95 C13
Strömmer S 96 C6
Strömnäs S 107 B10
Strömnäs S 118 D5
Stromness GB 3 H10
Strömsberg S 99 B9
Strömsbro S 103 E13
Strömsbruk S 103 C13
Strömsholden S 98 C6
Strømsmoen N 111 C16
Strömsnäs S 107 E9
Strömsnäsbruk S 87 B13
Strömstad S 91 B9
Strömsund S 106 D9
Strömsund S 107 A11
Stronachlachar GB 4 C7
Stroncone I 62 C3
Strongoli I 61 E8
Stronie Śląskie PL 77 B11
Stronsdorf A 77 E10
Strontian GB 4 B5
Stropi LV 135 E13
Stropkov SK 145 E4
Stroppiana I 68 C5
Stroppo I 36 B6
Stroud GB 13 B10
Strövelstorp S 87 C11
Strovija NMK 168 A5
Stróża PL 147 B9
Štrpce RKS 164 E3
Strücklingen (Saterland) D 17 B9
Struer DK 86 C3
Struga NMK 168 B4
Strugi-Krasnyye RUS 132 E5
Strullendorf D 75 C8
Strumë AL 168 C2
Strumica NMK 169 B8
Strumień PL 147 B7
Strumkivka UA 145 G5
Strumok UA 155 B4
Strumyani BG 169 A9
Strunkovice nad Blanicí
CZ 76 D6
Strupļi LV 133 C1
Struth D 79 D7
Strūžāni LV 133 C2
Stružec HR 149 E7
Stryama BG 165 E10
Stryków PL 143 C8
Stryksele S 107 C16
Stryn N 100 C5
Stryy UA 145 E8
Strzała PL 141 F6
Strzałkowo PL 142 B4
Strzebień PL 143 E6
Strzegocin PL 139 E10
Strzegom PL 81 E10
Strzegowo PL 139 E9
Strzelce PL 143 B7
Strzelce Krajeńskie PL 85 E9
Strzelce Opolskie PL 142 E5
Strzelce Wielkie PL 143 D7
Strzeleczki PL 142 F4
Strzelin PL 81 E12
Strzelno PL 138 E5
Strzepcz PL 138 B5
Strzyżewice PL 144 A5
Strzyżów PL 144 D4
Sts-Geosmes F 26 E3
Stubbæk DK 86 F4
Stubbekøbing DK 84 A2
Stubben D 17 B11
Stubel BG 165 C7
Stubenberg A 148 B5
Stubica SRB 159 F7
Štubik SRB 159 E9
Stubline SRB 158 D5
Stubno PL 144 D6
Stuchowo PL 85 C8
Studena BG 165 D7
Studena BG 166 F6
Studená CZ 77 D8
Studena UA 154 A3
Studençan RKS 163 E10
Studenci HR 157 E7
Studenec CZ 81 E9
Stüdenitz D 83 E12
Studénka CZ 146 B6
Studienka SK 77 E12
Studina RO 160 F4
Studley GB 13 A11
Studsvik S 93 B10
Studsviken S 107 D14
Studzienice PL 85 B13
Studzieniec PL 81 C9
Stugubacken S 103 D11
Stuguflåten N 100 B8
Stugun S 106 E9
Stühlingen D 27 E9
Stuhr D 17 B11
Stukmaņi LV 135 C11
Stülpe D 80 B4
Stulpicani RO 153 C7
Stumm A 72 B4
Stumsnäs S 102 E8
Stuorajavrre N 112 E10
Stuorragâr'žl N 113 E16
Stupari BIH 157 D10
Stupava SK 77 F12
Stupsk PL 139 D9
Stupurai LT 134 D7
Sturefors S 92 C7
Stūri LV 134 C5
Sturkö S 89 C9
Šturlić BIH 156 B4
Šturmai LT 134 F2
Sturminster Newton GB 13 D10
Šturovo NMK 164 F5
Štúrovo SK 149 A11
Sturry GB 15 E11
Sturzelbronn F 27 B8
Stuttgart D 27 C11
Stützerbach D 79 E8
Styggedalen N 111 B19
Stylida GR 175 B6
Stypsi GR 171 F10
Styra GR 175 C9
Styrkesnes N 109 A9
Styrnäs S 107 E13
Styrmanstø N 111 A18
Suances E 40 B3
Suaningi S 117 E10
Suatu RO 152 D3
Subačius LT 135 E9
Subaşi TR 171 B10
Subaşi TR 173 B9
Subaşi TR 177 C9
Subate LV 135 D11
Subbiano I 66 E4
Suben A 76 F4
Subiaco I 62 D4
Subkowy PL 138 B6
Subotica SRB 150 E4
Subotište SRB 158 D4
Subotniki BY 137 E12
Sučany SK 147 C7
Suceava RO 153 B8
Suceveni RO 153 E12
Sučevići HR 156 D5
Sucevița RO 153 B7
Sucha Beskidzka PL 147 B9
Suchacz PL 139 B7
Suchá Hora SK 147 C9
Suchá Loz CZ 146 D5
Suchań PL 85 D8
Suchá nad Parnou SK 146 E4
Suchdol CZ 77 C8
Suchdol nad Lužnicí CZ 77 E7
Suchdol nad Odrou CZ 146 B5
Suchedniów PL 143 D10
Suchowola PL 140 C8
Suchożebry PL 141 F6
Suchy Dąb PL 138 B6
Suchy Las PL 81 B11
Sucina E 56 F3
Suciu de Sus RO 152 C4
Suckow D 83 D11
Sucleia MD 154 D5
Sućuraj HR 157 F7
Sudanell E 42 D5
Sudargas LT 136 C6
Sudbury GB 15 C10
Suddendorf D 183 A10
Suddesjaur S 109 E17
Süden D 82 B5
Süderbrarup D 82 A7
Süderhastedt D 82 B6
Süderlügum D 86 F3
Süderstapel D 82 B6
Sudervė LT 137 D11
Sudiți RO 161 D11
Sudkov CZ 77 C11
Südlohn D 17 E7
Sudok S 118 B4
Sudoměřice CZ 146 D4
Sudova Vyshnya UA 144 D7
Sudovec HR 149 D6
Sudrabkalns LV 135 D12
Suđurađ HR 162 D4
Sudwalde D 17 C11
Sueca E 48 F4
Suedinenie BG 165 E10
Suelli I 64 D3
Suèvres F 24 E5
Şugag RO 152 F3
Suha BIH 157 D9
Suha BIH 157 F10
Suhaia RO 160 F6
Suharău RO 153 A8
Suharekë RKS 163 E10
Suhl D 79 E8
Suhlendorf D 83 E9
Suhmura FIN 125 F13
Suho Polje BIH 157 C11
Suhopolje HR 149 E8
Šuica BIH 157 E7
Şuici RO 160 C5
Šuijavaara S 116 B9
Suilly-la-Tour F 25 F9
Suinula FIN 127 B11
Suinula FIN 127 B12
Suippes F 25 B12
Sukeva FIN 124 C8
Sukhindol BG 166 C4
Sukhodil UA 145 D9
Sukhodil UA 145 F9
Sukošan HR 156 D3
Sükösd H 150 E2
Sukovo SRB 165 C6
Sukow D 83 C11
Sul N 105 D12
Suldrup DK 86 B5
Sulechów PL 81 B9
Sulęcin PL 81 B8
Sulęcin Szlachecki PL 139 E12
Sulęczyno PL 138 B4
Sulejów PL 141 H1
Sulejówek PL 141 F4
Suleskar N 94 D5
Sulesund N 100 B4
Suletea RO 153 E11
Süleymaniye TR 173 B6
Süleymaniye TR 173 C6
Süleymanli TR 177 B10
Sulików PL 81 D8
Sulingen D 17 C11
Suliszewo PL 85 D9
Sulița RO 153 B9
Sulitjelma N 109 B11
Sulkava FIN 123 D17
Sulkava FIN 129 B9
Sulkavanjärvi FIN 123 D16
Sulkavanjärvi FIN 123 D17
Sulkavankylä FIN 123 F11
Sułkowice PL 147 B9
Sullington GB 15 F8
Sully F 30 A5
Sully GB 13 C8
Sully-sur-Loire F 25 E7
Sulmierzyce PL 142 C4
Sulmierzyce PL 143 D7
Sulmona I 62 C5
Sulniac F 22 E6
Süloğlu TR 167 F7
Sułoszowa PL 143 F8
Sułów PL 81 D12
Sułów PL 144 B6
Sulsted DK 86 A5
Sultanıça TR 171 C10
Sultaniye TR 173 D9
Sultanköy TR 171 C10
Sultanköy TR 173 B8
Suluca TR 171 C10
Suluca TR 172 D6
Sulvik S 96 C7
Sulviken S 105 D14
Sulz A 71 C9
Sulz am Neckar D 27 D10
Sulzbach am Main D 21 E12
Sulzbach an der Murr D 27 B11
Sulzbach-Laufen D 74 E6
Sulzbach-Rosenberg D 75 C10
Sulzbach/Saar D 186 C3
Sulzdorf an der Lederhecke
D 75 B8
Sulzemoos D 75 F9
Sulzfeld D 75 B7
Sulzfeld D 187 C6
Sulzheim D 75 C7
Sulzthal D 75 B7
Sumartin HR 157 F6
Sumba FO 2 C3
Sumburgh GB 3 F14
Šumećani HR 149 E6
Sümeg H 149 C8
Sumène F 35 C6
Šumiac SK 145 F1
Sumiainen FIN 123 E16
Šumice CZ 146 C5
Sumiswald CH 70 C5
Summer Bridge GB 11 C8
Summerhill IRL 7 F9
Šumperk CZ 77 C11
Sumsa FIN 121 F14
Šumvald CZ 77 C12
Sumvitg CH 71 D7
Sunākste LV 135 D11
Suňava SK 147 C10
Sunbilla E 32 D2
Şuncuiuș RO 151 D10
Sund FIN 99 B14
Sund N 108 B7
Sund N 110 D5
Sund N 110 D5
Sund S 92 D6
Sund S 103 B10
Sund S 107 E14
Sundborn S 103 E10
Sundby DK 86 B3
Sundby DK 86 B3
Sundby FIN 122 C9
Sundby N 108 B9
Sunde N 94 C3
Sunde N 104 E6
Sunderland GB 5 F14
Sundern (Sauerland) D 17 F10
Sundet S 105 D13
Sundklakk N 110 D7
Sundnäs S 109 D14
Sundom FIN 122 D7
Sundom S 118 C8
Sundre S 93 F12
Sunds DK 86 C4
Sundsbruk S 103 B13
Sundsjö S 103 A9
Sundsli N 90 A3
Sundsvall S 103 B13
Sundvollen N 95 B12
Sungurlare BG 167 D7
Sunhultsbrunn S 92 D5
Suni I 64 C2
Sunja HR 149 F7
Sünna D 79 E7
Sunnan N 105 C11
Sunnanfors S 97 C14
Sunnansjö S 97 B12
Sunnansjö S 107 E14
Sunnås S 103 A12
Sunndal N 94 B4
Sunndalsøra N 101 A9
Sunne S 97 C9
Sunne S 103 A14
Sunne S 106 E6
Sunnemo S 97 C10
Sunnersta S 107 D12
Sunningen S 91 C10
Suntaži LV 135 C9
Suodenniemi FIN 126 B8
Suojanperä FIN 114 E4
Suojoki FIN 122 F7
Suolahti FIN 123 E15
Suolijärvi FIN 121 D11
Suolijoki FIN 119 B14
Suoluvuobmi N 113 D12
Suomela FIN 119 C15
Suomenniemi FIN 128 C7
Suomijärvi FIN 122 F9
Suommu FIN 115 E4
Suomusjärvi FIN 127 E10
Suomussalmi FIN 121 E12
Suonenjoki FIN 124 E8
Suoniemi FIN 127 C9
Suonnankylä FIN 121 B11
Suontee FIN 124 F8
Suopajärvi FIN 117 E15
Suorajärvi FIN 121 B13
Suorsa FIN 120 B9
Šuosjav'ri N 113 E13
Suostola FIN 115 D2
Suovaara FIN 121 F11
Suovanlahti FIN 123 D16
Superdévoluy F 35 A10
Supersano I 61 C10
Supertarska Draga HR 67 C10
Supetar HR 156 F6
Supino I 62 D4
Suplac RO 152 E5
Suplacu de Barcău RO 151 C10
Suplai RO 152 C4
Supraśl PL 140 D8
Supru FIN 114 E4
Supur RO 151 C10
Súr H 149 B10
Surahammar S 98 C6
Suraia RO 153 F10
Șura Mare RO 152 F4
Șura Mică RO 152 F4
Șurani RO 161 C8
Šurany SK 146 E6
Suraż PL 140 E7
Surbo I 61 C10
Surčin SRB 158 D5
Surdegis LT 135 E9
Surdila-Găiseanca RO 161 C10
Surdila-Greci RO 161 C10
Surduc RO 151 C11
Surdulica SRB 164 D5
Surfleet GB 11 F11
Surgères F 28 C4
Surhuisterveen NL 16 B6
Súria E 43 D7
Surier I 31 D11
Surnadalsøra N 104 F5
Sûrnevets BG 166 E4
Sûrnevo BG 166 E5
Sûrnitsa BG 165 F9
Šurovce SK 146 E5
Sursee CH 27 F9
Surte S 91 D11
Surviliškis LT 135 F8
Surwold D 17 C9
Sury-le-Comtal F 30 D5
Surzur F 22 E6
Susa I 31 E11
Șușani RO 160 D4
Šušara SRB 159 D7
Susch CH 71 D10
Susegana I 72 E5
Susek SRB 158 C4
Süsel D 83 B9
Suseni RO 152 D5
Suseni RO 153 D7
Suseni RO 160 D5
Sushitsa BG 166 C5
Sušice CZ 76 D5
Susiec PL 144 C7
Suškova LV 133 D4
Susleni MD 154 C3
Susort N 94 D2
Susteren NL 19 B12
Sustinente I 66 B3
Sustrum D 17 C8
Susurluk TR 173 E9
Susuzmüsellim TR 173 B7
Susz PL 139 C7
Sutera I 58 D4
Sutești RO 160 D4
Șutești RO 161 C10
Šutina BIH 157 E7
Sutivan HR 156 F5
Sutjeska SRB 158 C6
Sütlüce TR 173 A8
Sutri I 62 C2
Sutri LV 135 D12
Sutterton GB 11 F11
Süttő H 149 A10
Sutton GB 15 C9
Sutton Bridge GB 11 F12
Sutton Coldfield GB 11 F8
Sutton in Ashfield GB 11 E9
Sutton-on-the-Forest GB 11 C9
Suure-Jaani EST 131 D10
Suurejõe EST 131 D10
Suuremõisa EST 130 D5
Suurimäki FIN 124 D9
Suurmäki FIN 125 E11
Suur-Miehikkälä FIN 128 D8
Suurpea EST 131 B11
Suutarinkylä FIN 119 E15
Suutarinkylä FIN 119 F17
Suvainiškis LT 135 D10
Suvanto FIN 115 D2
Suvantokumpu FIN 117 C15
Suvereto I 65 A3
Suviekas LT 135 E12
Suvodol NMK 168 A5
Suvodol NMK 169 B6
Suvorov MD 155 B2
Suvorove UA 155 B3
Suvorovo BG 167 C9
Suwałki PL 136 E6
Suystamo RUS 129 B15
Suze-la-Rousse F 35 B8
Suzzara I 66 C2
Svabensverk S 103 D10
Svalboviken S 93 A8
Svalenik BG 166 B6
Svallerup DK 87 D8
Svalöv S 87 D12
Svalsta S 93 B9
Svalyava UA 145 F6
Svanå S 98 C6
Svanabyn S 107 C11
Svanberga S 99 C11
Svaneke DK 89 E8
Svanesund S 91 C10
Svängsta S 89 C7
Svaningen S 106 C8
Svannäs S 107 B11
Svannäs S 109 D15
Svansele S 106 B8
Svansele S 107 B17
Svanskog S 91 A12
Svanstein S 117 E11
Svanström S 118 E5
Svantjärnåsen S 102 B7
Svanträsk S 118 D3
Svanvik N 114 E8
Svanvik S 91 C10
Svappavaara S 116 C6
Svardal N 101 A12
Svärdsjö S 103 E10
Svarinci LV 133 D3
Svarstad N 95 D11
Svartå FIN 127 E10
Svartå S 92 A5
Svartbo S 103 D11
Svartbyn S 119 B9
Svarte S 87 E13
Svartemyr N 100 D3
Svärtinge S 92 B8
Svartisdalhytta N 108 D7
Svartlå S 118 B6
Svartnes N 108 B8
Svartnes N 111 B17
Svartnes N 114 C10
Svartöstaden S 118 C8
Svartträsk S 107 A12
Svartvik S 103 A14
Svartvik S 103 B13
Svartvik S 103 D13
Svatava CZ 75 B12
Svätuše SK 145 G4
Svätý Jur SK 146 E4
Svätý Peter SK 146 F6
Svebølle DK 87 D8
Svedala S 87 D12
Svėdasai LT 135 E10
Svedja S 103 C12
Svedje S 106 C9
Svedje S 107 D15
Svedjebo S 103 C12
Švedlár SK 145 F2
Sveg S 102 B7
Sveggesundet N 104 E3
Sveicarija LT 137 C9
Sveindal N 90 C1
Sveio N 94 C2
Svejbæk DK 86 C5
Sveķi LV 135 B13
Švėkšna LT 134 E3
Svelgen N 100 C2
Svellingen N 104 D5
Svelvik N 95 C12
Švenčionėliai LT 135 F11
Švenčionys LT 135 F12
Svendborg DK 86 E7
Svene N 95 C11
Svenes N 90 B3
Svenljunga S 91 E13
Svenningdal N 108 F5
Svensbu N 111 A18
Svensbyn S 118 D6
Svenshögen S 91 C10
Svenstavik S 102 A7
Svenstrup DK 86 B5
Svenstrup DK 86 E5
Svenstrup DK 87 E8
Svente LV 135 E12
Šventežeris LT 137 E8
Šventoji LT 134 D2
Sverepec SK 146 C6
Sveta Marija HR 149 D7
Svētciems LV 131 F8
Svēte LV 134 C7
Sveti Nikola BG 167 C10
Sveti Nikola MNE 163 F7
Sveti Nikole NMK 164 F4
Sveti Rok HR 156 D4
Sveti Stefan MNE 163 E6
Světlá Hora CZ 142 F3
Světlá nad Sázavou CZ 77 C8
Svetlen BG 166 C6
Svetlogorsk RUS 139 A9
Svetlyy RUS 139 A9
Svetogorsk RUS 129 C10
Svetozar Miletić SRB 150 F3
Svetvinčenat HR 67 B8
Svezhen BG 165 D11
Švica HR 67 C11
Svidník SK 145 E4
Švihov CZ 76 D4
Sviibi EST 130 D6
Svilajnac SRB 159 E7
Svilengrad BG 166 F6
Svindinge DK 86 E7
Svinesund S 91 A9
Svingen N 111 A18
Svingstad N 101 E12
Svingvoll N 101 D12
Svinhult S 92 D6
Svinia SK 145 E3
Svinița RO 159 D9
Svinná SK 146 D6
Svinnersta S 92 B5
Svinninge DK 87 D8
Svinninge DK 87 D9
Svinninge S 99 D10
Svínoy FO 2 A4
Svinvika N 104 E4
Svir BY 137 D13
Svirkos LT 135 F12
Svishtov BG 160 F6
Svislach BY 140 D10
Svit SK 145 E1
Svitávka CZ 77 C11
Svitavy CZ 77 C10
Svitene LV 135 D7
Svitlodolyns'ke UA 154 E5
Svityaz' UA 141 H9
Svoboda BG 155 F1
Svoboda BG 166 E4
Svoboda RUS 136 D4
Svoboda nad Úpou CZ 81 E9
Svobodinovo BG 166 F4
Svođe SRB 164 D5
Svodín SK 146 F6
Svodna BIH 156 B6
Svoge BG 165 D7
Svogerslev DK 87 D10
Svolvær N 110 D8
Svorkmo N 104 E7
Svratka CZ 77 C10
Svrčinovec SK 147 C7
Svrljig SRB 164 C5
Svullrya N 96 B7
Swadlincote GB 11 F8
Swaffham GB 15 B10
Swalmen NL 20 B6
Swan IRL 9 C8
Swanage GB 13 D11
Swanley GB 15 E9
Swanlinbar IRL 7 D7
Swansea GB 13 B7
Swanton Morley GB 15 B10
Swarożyn PL 138 B6
Swarzędz PL 81 B12
Swatragh GB 4 F3
Sway GB 13 D11
Świątki PL 139 C9
Świbno PL 138 B6
Świderki PL 141 G6
Świdnica PL 81 C8
Świdnica PL 81 E10
Świdnik PL 141 H7
Świdwin PL 85 C9
Świebodzice PL 81 E10
Świebodzin PL 81 B9
Świecie PL 138 D5
Święciechowa PL 81 C11
Świeciechów-Duży PL 144 B4
Świedziebnia PL 139 D8
Świekatowo PL 138 D5
Świeradów-Zdrój PL 81 E8
Świercze PL 139 E10
Świerczów PL 142 E4
Świerklaniec PL 143 F6
Świerklany Górne PL 142 F6
Świerzawa PL 81 D9
Świerże PL 141 H9
Świerzenko PL 85 B11
Świerzno PL 85 C7

Świeszyno PL 85 B10
Świątajno PL 136 E5
Świątajno PL 139 C11
Świętochłowice PL 143 F6
Świątoszów PL 81 D8
Swifterbant NL 16 C5
Świlcza PL 144 C4
Swindon GB 13 B11
Swineshead GB 11 F11
Swinford IRL 6 E5
Świnna PL 147 B8
Świnoujście PL 84 C6
Swinton GB 5 D12
Swinton GB 11 D7
Swobnica PL 84 D7
Swords IRL 7 F10
Swornegacie PL 85 C13
Syalyawshchyna BY 133 E5
Sycewice PL 85 B11
Syców PL 142 D4
Sydalen N 110 D7
Sydänmaa FIN 123 E10
Sydänmaankylä FIN 123 C16
Sydnes N 94 C3
Syelishcha BY 133 F4
Syfteland N 94 B2
Sykaminia GR 171 F10
Sykäräinen FIN 123 C12
Syke D 17 C11
Sykea GR 178 B4
Syki GR 169 F9
Sykia GR 169 E7
Sykia GR 170 D5
Sykies GR 169 F7
Sykkylven N 100 B5
Sykorrachi GR 171 C9
Sykourio GR 169 E8
Sylling N 95 C12
Sylte N 100 B6
Symbister GB 3 E14
Symi GR 181 C7
Synej AL 168 B2
Synevyr UA 145 G8
Synevyrs'ka Polyana UA 145 F8
Synod Inn GB 12 A6
Synsiö FIN 123 F17
Synyak UA 145 F6
Syötekylä FIN 121 C10
Sypniewo PL 85 D11
Sypniewo PL 139 D11
Syrau D 75 A11
Syre GB 3 J8
Syrgenstein D 75 E7
Syri FIN 123 C13
Syrjä FIN 125 F10
Sysmä FIN 127 B14
Sysslebäck S 102 E4
Syston GB 11 F9
Syväjärvi FIN 117 D15
Syvänniemi FIN 124 E8
Syvärinpää FIN 125 D9
Syvde N 100 B3
Syvdsnes N 100 B3
Syvota GR 168 F3
Syvros GR 174 B2
Syvsten DK 90 E7
Syyspohja FIN 129 C10
Szabadegyháza H 149 B11
Szabadhidvég H 149 C10
Szabadkígyós H 151 D7
Szabadszállás H 150 D3
Szabolcsbáka H 145 G5
Szada H 150 B3
Szadek PL 143 C6
Szaflary PL 147 C10
Szajol H 150 C5
Szakály H 149 C10
Szakcs H 149 C10
Szakmár H 150 D3
Szakoly H 151 B8
Szákszend H 149 A10
Szalánta H 149 E10
Szalaszend H 145 G3
Szalkszentmárton H 150 D3
Szalonna H 145 G2
Szamocin PL 85 D12
Szamosszeg H 145 G5
Szamotuły PL 81 A11
Szank H 150 D4
Szany H 149 B8
Szár H 149 B11
Szarvas H 150 D6
Szászberek H 150 C5
Szatmárcseke H 145 G6
Szatymaz H 150 E5
Százhalombatta H 149 B11
Szczaniec PL 81 B9
Szczawin Kościelny PL 139 F8
Szczawne PL 145 E5
Szczawnica PL 145 E2
Szczawno-Zdrój PL 81 E10
Szczebrzeszyn PL 144 B6
Szczecin PL 84 D7
Szczecinek PL 85 C11
Szczekociny PL 143 E8
Szczepankowo PL 139 D12
Szczepanowo PL 138 E4
Szczerców PL 143 D7
Szczucin PL 143 F11
Szczuczyn PL 140 C6
Szczurkowo PL 136 E2
Szczurowa PL 143 F10
Szczutowo PL 139 E8
Szczyrk PL 147 B8
Szczytna PL 77 B10
Szczytniki PL 142 C5
Szczytno PL 139 C10
Szécsény H 147 E9
Szederkény H 149 D10
Szedres H 149 D11
Szeged H 150 E5
Szeghalom H 151 C7
Szegi H 145 G3
Szegvár H 150 D5
Székely H 145 G4
Székesfehérvár H 149 B10
Székkutas H 150 D6
Szekszárd H 149 D11
Szemud PL 138 B5
Szendehely H 147 F8
Szendrő H 145 G2
Szendrőlád H 145 G2
Szentendre H 150 B3
Szentes H 150 D5
Szentgál H 149 B9
Szentgotthárd H 148 C6
Szentistván H 150 B6
Szentkirály H 150 D4
Szentlászló H 149 D9
Szentőrinc H 149 D9
Szentpéterfa H 149 B6
Szepetnek H 149 D7
Szepietowo PL 141 E7
Szerecseny H 149 B9
Szeremle H 149 D11
Szerencs H 145 G3
Szerep H 151 C7
Szerzyny PL 144 D3
Szestno PL 136 F3
Szigetbecse H 149 B11
Szigetcsép H 149 B11
Szigethalom H 150 C2
Szigetszentmiklós H 150 C3
Szigetvár H 149 D9
Szigliget H 149 C8
Szihalom H 150 B5
Szikszó H 145 G2
Szil H 149 A8
Szilvásvárad H 145 G1
Szirák H 147 F9
Szirmabesenyő H 145 G2
Szkaradowo PL 81 C12
Szklarska Poręba PL 81 E9
Szklary Górne PL 81 D10
Szlichtyngowa PL 81 C10
Szob H 147 F7
Sződ H 150 B3
Szögliget H 145 F2
Szokolya H 147 F8
Szolnok H 150 C5
Szőlősgyörök H 149 C9
Szombathely H 149 B7
Szomód H 149 A10
Szomolya H 145 H1
Szówsko PL 144 C6
Szpetal Górny PL 138 E7
Szprotawa PL 81 C9
Szreńsk PL 139 D9
Szropy PL 139 C7
Sztabin PL 140 C8
Sztum PL 138 C7
Sztutowo PL 139 B7
Szubin PL 138 D4
Szőcsi H 150 B4
Szudziałowo PL 140 D9
Szügy H 147 E8
Szuhogy H 145 G2
Szulborze Wielkie PL 141 E6
Szumowo PL 139 E13
Szurdokpüspöki H 147 F9
Szydłów PL 143 E11
Szydłowiec PL 141 H3
Szydłowo PL 85 D11
Szydłowo PL 139 D9
Szymanów PL 141 F2
Szymonka PL 136 F4
Szynkielów PL 142 D6
Szypliszki PL 136 E7

T

Taagepera EST 131 F11
Taalintehdas FIN 126 E8
Taapajärvi FIN 117 D13
Taastrup DK 87 D10
Tab H 149 C10
Tabajd H 149 B11
Tabaky UA 155 B3
Tabanera de Cerrato E 40 D3
Tábara E 39 E8
Tabarz D 79 E8
Tabasalu EST 131 C9
Tabdi H 150 D3
Taberg S 91 D15
Tabernas E 55 E8
Taberno E 55 E8
Tabivere EST 131 D13
Taboada E 38 C4
Taboadela E 38 D4
Tábor CZ 77 D7
Táborfalva H 150 C3
Tábua P 44 D4
Tabuaço P 44 B5
Tabuenca E 41 E8
Täby S 99 D10
Tác H 149 B10
Tacen SLO 73 D9
Tacherting D 75 F12
Tachov CZ 75 C12
Tackåsen S 103 C9
Tăcuta RO 153 D11
Tadasuni I 64 C2
Tadcaster GB 11 D9
Tadley GB 13 C12
Taebla EST 130 D7
Tælavåg N 94 B1
Taevaskoja EST 131 E14
Tafalla E 32 E2
Tafers CH 31 B11
Taff's Well GB 13 B8
Tafjord N 100 B6
Täfteå S 107 E15
Täfteå S 122 C4
Țaga RO 152 D4
Tagaranna EST 130 D4
Taggia I 37 D7
Taghmon IRL 9 D9
Tagliacozzo I 62 C4
Taglio di Po I 66 B5
Taglio-Isolaccio F 37 G10
Tagnon F 19 F9
Tågsjöberg S 107 D11
Tahal E 55 E8
Tähemaa EST 131 E14
Tahilla IRL 8 E3
Tahitótfalu H 150 B3
Tähtelä FIN 117 D17
Taibòn Agordino I 72 D5
Taíde P 38 E3
Tain GB 3 K8
Tainiemi FIN 119 C15
Tainijoki FIN 119 C15
Tain-l'Hermitage F 30 E6
Taintrux F 27 D6
Taio I 72 D3
Taipale FIN 119 B15
Taipale FIN 119 C14
Taipale FIN 123 D17
Taipale FIN 124 D8
Taipale FIN 126 B8
Taipaleenharju FIN 119 D17
Taipalsaari FIN 129 C9
Taipalus FIN 123 E10
Taivalkoski FIN 121 C11
Taivassalo FIN 126 D6
Taizé F 30 B6
Tajmište NMK 168 A4
Tajno Łanowe PL 140 C7
Takácsi H 149 B8
Takamaa FIN 127 B10
Takeley GB 15 D9
Takene S 97 C9
Takene S 97 D10
Taklax FIN 122 E6
Taksony H 150 C3
Taktakenéz H 145 G3
Taktaszada H 145 G3
Talais F 28 E3
Talamantes E 41 E8
Talamona I 69 A8
Talamone I 65 B4
Talange F 186 C1
Talant F 26 F3
Talarrubias E 51 A9
Talaván E 45 E8
Talavera de la Reina E 46 E3
Talavera la Real E 51 B6
Talayuela E 45 E9
Talayuelas E 47 E10
Talea RO 161 C7
Talence F 28 F4
Talensac F 23 D8
Tales E 48 E4
Taleža BIH 162 D5
Talgarreg GB 12 A6
Talgarth GB 13 B8
Talhadas P 44 C4
Tali EST 131 E9
Taliard F 36 C4
Taliesin GB 10 F4
Táliga E 51 B5
Tälje S 103 A10
Talla I 66 E4
Tallås S 103 E11
Tallås S 109 E14
Tallåsen S 103 C11
Tällberg S 103 E8
Tallberg S 118 B8
Taller F 32 C3
Tallinn EST 131 C9
Talljärv S 118 B8
Talloires F 31 D9
Tallone F 37 G11
Tallós E 38 C2
Tallow IRL 8 D6
Tallsjö S 107 C14
Talluskylä FIN 124 D7
Tallvik S 119 B9
Tállya H 145 G3
Tălmaciu RO 160 B4
Talmay F 26 F3
Talmaz MD 154 D5
Talmont F 28 D4
Talmont-St-Hilaire F 28 C2
Talpa RO 160 E6
Talsano I 61 C8
Talsi LV 134 B5
Taluskylä FIN 119 F12
Talviainen FIN 127 B12
Talvik N 112 C10
Tama E 39 B10
Tămădău Mare RO 161 E9
Tamajón E 47 B6
Tamames E 45 C8
Tamarë AL 163 E8
Tamarino BG 167 E7
Tamarite de Litera E 42 D4
Tamashowka BY 141 G9
Tamási H 149 C10
Tamași RO 153 D10
Tambach-Dietharz D 79 E8
Tâmboești RO 161 B10
Tåme S 118 E4
Tamins CH 71 D8
Tamiş TR 171 E10
Tamm D 27 C11
Tammela FIN 121 C15
Tammela FIN 127 D10
Tammensiel D 82 A5
Tammijärvi FIN 127 B14
Tammiku EST 131 C12
Tammisaari FIN 127 F9
Tammispää EST 131 D14
Tâmna RO 159 D11
Tamnay-en-Bazois F 30 A4
Tamnes N 101 A15
Tamnič SRB 159 E9
Tampere FIN 127 C10
Tamsalu EST 131 C12
Tamsweg A 73 B8
Tamurejo E 54 B3
Tamworth GB 11 F8
Tana Bru N 113 C21
Tanacu RO 153 D11
Tanaji LV 135 E13
Tananes N 114 B4
Tananger N 94 E3
Tănăsoaia RO 153 E10
Tanaunella I 64 B4
Tancarville F 18 F1
Tandådalen S 102 D4
Țăndărei RO 161 D11
Tandö S 102 B5
Tandragee GB 7 D10
Tandsbyn S 106 E7
Tandsjöborg S 102 C8
Tang IRL 7 E7
Tångaberg S 87 A10
Tangaveane IRL 6 C6
Tångböle S 105 E13
Tange DK 86 C5
Tangen N 95 A12
Tangen N 101 E14
Tangen N 111 B14
Tanger MA 52 E5
Tångeråsen S 105 D15
Tangerhütte D 79 B10
Tangermünde D 79 A10
Tångstamon S 107 E11
Tangstedt D 83 C8
Tängvattnet S 108 E8
Tanhua FIN 115 C3
Taninges F 31 C10
Tankapirtti FIN 115 B2
Tankavaara FIN 115 B2
Tanlay F 25 E11
Tann D 76 F3
Tann (Rhön) D 79 E7
Tanna D 75 B10
Tannadice GB 5 B11
Tännäs S 102 B4
Tannay F 19 E10
Tannay F 25 F10
Tänndalen S 102 A3
Tanne D 79 C8
Tannenbergsthal D 75 B11
Tännesberg D 75 C11
Tannhausen D 75 E7
Tannheim A 71 C11
Tannila FIN 119 D15
Tånnö S 88 A6
Tannroda D 79 E9
Tannsjön S 106 D9
Tanowo PL 84 C6
Tansa RO 153 D10
Țânțăreni RO 160 D2
Tantonville F 26 D5
Tanumshede S 91 B9
Tanvald CZ 81 E8
Taormina I 59 D7
Tapa EST 131 C11
Tapanikylä FIN 121 F13
Tapfheim D 75 E8
Tapia de Casariego E 39 A6
Tápióbicske H 150 C4
Tápiógyörgye H 150 C4
Tapionkylä FIN 117 E14
Tapionniemi FIN 115 E2
Tápiószág H 150 C4
Tápiószecső H 150 C4
Tápiószele H 150 C4
Tápiószentmárton H 150 C4
Tápiószőlős H 150 C4
Táplánszentkereszt H 149 B7
Tapojärvi FIN 117 C11
Tapolca H 149 C8
Tappeluft N 112 C9
Tappenbeck D 79 B8
Tappernøje DK 87 E9
Taps DK 86 E4
Tapsony H 149 D8
Tar H 147 F9
Taracena E 47 C6
Taraclia MD 154 D4
Taraclia MD 154 F3
Taradeau F 36 E4
Taradell E 43 D8
Taramundi E 38 B5
Tarancón E 47 D6
Tarano I 62 C3
Taranto I 61 C8
Tarany H 149 D8
Tarare F 30 D5
Tarascon F 35 C8
Tarascon-sur-Ariège F 33 E9
Tarashany UA 153 A8
Tarazona E 41 E8
Tarazona de la Mancha E 47 F9
Tárbena E 56 D4
Tarbert GB 2 K3
Tarbert GB 4 D5
Tarbert GB 4 D6
Tarbert IRL 8 C4
Tarbes F 33 D6
Tarbja EST 131 D11
Tarbolton GB 4 D8
Tărcaia RO 151 D9
Tarcal H 145 G3
Tarcău RO 153 D8
Tarcea RO 151 C9
Tarcento I 73 D7
Tarčin BIH 157 E9
Tarczyn PL 141 G3
Tard H 145 H2
Tardajos E 40 D4
Tardelcuende E 41 E6
Tardets-Sorholus F 32 D4
Tardienta E 41 E10
Tardona H 145 G2
Tärendö S 116 D9
Țareuca MD 154 B3
Tārgale LV 134 B3
Targon F 28 F5
Târgoviște RO 161 D6
Targowa Górka PL 85 F12
Târgu Bujor RO 153 F11
Târgu Cărbunești RO 160 D3
Târgu Frumos RO 153 C9
Târgu Jiu RO 159 C11
Târgu Lăpuș RO 152 C3
Târgu Mureș RO 152 D5
Târgu Neamț RO 153 C8
Târgu Ocna RO 153 E9
Târgu Secuiesc RO 153 E8
Târgușor RO 155 E2
Târgu Trotuș RO 153 E9
Tarhos H 151 D7
Tarifa E 53 D5
Țarigrad MD 153 A11
Tarján H 149 A11
Tárkány H 149 A9
Tarleton GB 10 D6
Tărlișua RO 152 C4
Tarłów PL 143 D12
Tărlungeni RO 161 B7
Tarm DK 86 D3
Tarmstedt D 17 B12
Tärnaby S 108 E9
Tärnafors S 108 E9
Tarnala FIN 129 B12
Tarnalelesz H 145 G1
Tarna Mare RO 145 G7
Tarnaméra H 150 B5
Tärnamo S 108 E9
Tarnaörs H 150 B5
Tarnaszentmiklós H 150 B5
Târnăveni RO 152 E4
Tarnawa Duża PL 144 B6
Tarnawatka PL 144 B7
Tarnazsadány H 150 B5
Tårnelv N 111 B15
Tårnes N 104 D7
Tårnet N 114 D8
Tarnobrzeg PL 143 E12
Tarnogród PL 144 C6
Tárnok H 149 B11
Tarnos F 32 C3
Tarnoszyn PL 144 C8
Târnova RO 151 E8
Târnova RO 159 C8
Tarnow D 83 C12
Tarnów PL 85 E7
Tarnów PL 143 F10
Tarnowiec PL 144 D4
Tarnówka PL 85 D11
Tarnówko PL 85 E11
Tarnowo Podgórne PL 81 B11
Tarnów Opolski PL 142 E5
Tarnowskie Góry PL 142 F6
Tärnsjö S 98 B7
Tårnvik N 108 A9
Tårnvik N 113 C18
Taron-Sadirac-Viellenave F 32 C5
Tarouca P 44 B5
Tarp D 82 A6
Tarp DK 86 D2
Tarpa H 145 G6
Tarprubežiai LT 136 E7
Tarquinia I 62 C1
Tarquinia Lido I 62 C1
Tarragona E 42 E6
Tàrrega E 42 D6
Tarrel GB 3 K9
Tarrenz A 71 C11
Tarrio E 38 B3
Tarroja de Segarra E 42 D6
Tårs DK 87 F8
Tårs DK 90 E7
Tarsele S 107 D11
Tarsia I 60 D6
Tărșolț RO 145 H7
Tårstad N 111 D12
Tartas F 32 C4
Tărtășești RO 161 D7
Tartu EST 131 E13
Tårup DK 87 E7
Tarutyne UA 154 E4
Tarvaala FIN 123 E14
Tarvasjoki FIN 126 D8
Tarves GB 3 L12
Tarvisio I 73 C8
Tarvola FIN 123 D11
Taşağıl TR 173 A7
Tașca RO 153 D8
Tåsjö S 107 C9
Taşlîc MD 154 C4
Tășnad RO 151 C10
Tass H 150 C3
Tassagh GB 7 D9
Tassin-la-Demi-Lune F 30 D6
Taszár H 149 D9
Tát H 149 A11
Tata H 149 A10
Tatabánya H 149 A10
Tataháza H 150 E3
Tătărani RO 153 D11
Tătărani RO 160 D6
Tătăranu RO 161 B10
Tătărăști RO 153 E10
Tătărăștii de Jos RO 160 E6
Tătărăștii de Sus RO 160 E6
Tătărăuca MD 153 A12
Tatarbunary UA 154 F5
Tătărești MD 154 E2
Tatarevo BG 166 E4
Tatarköy TR 173 B7
Tatarlar TR 167 F7
Tatárszentgyörgy H 150 C3
Tating D 82 B5
Tatlisu TR 173 D8
Tatranská Javorina SK 145 E1
Tattershall GB 11 E11
Tătulești RO 160 D5
Tau N 94 D3
Tauberbischofsheim D 74 C6
Taucha D 79 D11
Tauche D 80 B6
Tauer D 81 C6
Taufkirchen D 75 F10
Taufkirchen D 75 F11
Taufkirchen (Vils) D 75 F11
Taujėnai LT 135 F9
Țaul MD 153 A11
Taulé F 22 C4
Taulignan F 35 B8
Taunton GB 13 C8
Tauplitz A 73 A9
Tauragė LT 134 F4
Tauragnai LT 135 F11
Tauralaukis LT 134 E2
Taurasi I 60 A3
Taurene LV 135 B11
Taureni RO 152 D4
Taurianova I 59 C9
Taurisano I 61 D10
Taurupe LV 135 C10
Tauste E 41 E9
Țăuț RO 151 E8
Tăuteu RO 151 C9
Tăuții-Măgherăuș RO 151 B12
Tauves F 29 D11
Tauvo FIN 119 E13
Tauzhne UA 154 A6
Tavaco F 37 G9
Tavagnacco I 73 D7
Tavakli TR 171 E10
Tavankut SRB 150 E4
Tavannes CH 27 F7
Tavant F 24 F3
Tavarnelle Val di Pesa I 66 E3
Tavastila FIN 128 D6
Tavastkenkä FIN 119 F16
Tavaux F 31 A7
Taveiro P 44 D4
Tavel F 35 B8
Tavelsjö S 122 B4
Tavera F 37 G9
Taverham GB 15 B11
Taverna I 59 A10
Tavernay F 30 A5
Tavernelle I 62 A2
Tavernes F 36 D4
Tavernes de la Valldigna E 56 C4
Tavernspite GB 12 B5
Taverny F 25 B7
Tavertet E 43 D8
Taviano I 61 D10
Tavira P 50 E4
Tavistock GB 12 D6
Tavullia I 67 E6
Tawern D 186 B2
Taxenbach A 73 B6
Taxiarchis GR 169 D10
Taxobeni MD 153 C11
Tayfur TR 171 D10
Tayinloan GB 4 D5
Taylor's Cross IRL 7 F7
Taynuilt GB 4 C6
Tayport GB 5 C11
Tayvallich GB 4 C5
Tázlár H 150 D4
Tazlău RO 153 D8
Tazones E 39 A9
Tczew PL 138 B6
Tczów PL 141 H4
Teaca RO 152 D5
Teano I 60 A2
Tearce NMK 164 E3
Teasc RO 160 E3
Teba E 53 C7
Tebar E 47 E8
Tebay GB 10 C6
Tebstrup DK 86 D5
Techendorf A 73 C7
Techirghiol RO 155 E3
Tecuci RO 153 F10
Tedavnet IRL 7 D8
Teeriranta FIN 121 C14
Teerivaara FIN 120 B9
Tefeli GR 178 E9
Tegelen NL 16 F6
Tegelträsk S 107 D13
Teggiano I 60 C5
Téglás H 151 B8
Teglio I 69 A9
Tegnäset S 107 C16
Teichwolframsdorf D 79 E11
Teignmouth GB 13 D8
Teijo FIN 127 E8
Teikosuvanto FIN 117 E11
Teillay F 23 E8
Teillet F 33 C10
Teișani RO 161 C8
Teisendorf D 73 A6
Teisko FIN 127 B10
Teisnach D 76 D4
Teistungen D 79 D7
Teiu RO 160 D6
Teiuș RO 152 E3
Teixeiro E 38 B3
Teixoso P 44 D6
Tejadillos E 47 D9
Tejado E 41 E7
Tejeda de Tiétar E 45 D9
Tejn DK 89 E7
Tekeler TR 181 A7
Tekeli TR 177 C9
Tekeriš SRB 158 D4
Tekija BIH 157 D11
Tekija SRB 159 D9
Tekirdağ TR 173 C7
Tekovské Lužany SK 147 E7
Teksdal N 104 D7
Telaki PL 141 E6
Telatyn PL 144 B8
Telč CZ 77 D8
Telciu RO 152 C4
Teldau D 83 D9
Telečka SRB 150 F3
Telega RO 161 C7
Telekgerendás H 151 D6
Telenești MD 154 B2
Telerig BG 161 F11
Telese I 60 A3
Telești RO 159 C11
Telford GB 10 F7
Telfs A 72 B3
Telgárt SK 145 F1
Telgte D 17 E9
Telhado P 44 D5
Telish BG 165 C9
Teliu RO 153 F7
Teliucu Inferior RO 159 B10
Teljo FIN 125 C13
Telkkälä FIN 119 C17
Tellancourt F 19 E12
Tellejåkk S 118 B3
Tellin B 19 D11
Tellingstedt D 82 B6
Telneset N 101 B13
Telnice CZ 77 D11
Telões P 38 F4
Telšiai LT 134 E4
Telti I 64 B3
Teltow D 80 B4
Tembleque E 46 E6
Temeleuți MD 153 C12
Temeni GR 174 C5
Temerin SRB 158 C4
Temmes FIN 119 E15
Tempi GR 169 E8
Tempio Pausania I 64 B3
Temple Bar GB 12 A6
Templeboy IRL 6 D5
Temple Ewell GB 15 E11
Templemore IRL 9 C7
Templepatrick GB 4 F4
Temple Sowerby GB 5 F11
Templeton GB 12 B5
Templetuohy IRL 9 C7
Templeuve F 182 D2
Templin D 84 D5
Tempo GB 7 D8
Temse B 19 B9
Temska SRB 164 C6
Temù I 69 A9
Tenala FIN 127 E9
Tenay F 31 D8
Ten Boer NL 17 B7
Tenbury Wells GB 13 A9
Tenby GB 12 B5
Tence F 30 E5
Tende F 37 C7
Tendilla E 47 C7
Tendu F 29 B9
Teneniai LT 134 F3
Tenevo BG 167 E7
Tengelic H 149 C11
Tengen D 27 E10
Tengesdal N 94 C4
Tenhult S 92 D4
Teningen D 27 D8
Tenja HR 149 F11
Tenk H 150 B5
Tennänget S 102 D6
Tennenbronn D 27 D9
Tennevik N 111 C12
Tenneville B 19 D12
Tennevoll N 111 C14
Tennilä FIN 119 B16
Tennilä FIN 127 D13
Tennskjer N 111 B15
Tennstrand N 110 D9
Tenterden GB 15 E10
Tentúgal P 44 D3
Teora I 60 B4
Teovo NMK 169 A6
Tepasto FIN 117 C13
Tépe H 151 C8
Tepeboz TR 177 B7
Tepecik TR 173 B10
Tepecik TR 173 E10
Tepelenë AL 168 D3
Teplá CZ 76 C3
Teplice CZ 80 E5
Teplice nad Metují CZ 81 E10
Teplička SK 145 F2
Teplička nad Váhom SK 147 C7
Tepsa FIN 117 C15
Țepu RO 153 F10
Ter Aar NL 182 A5
Teramo I 62 B5
Tērande LV 134 B3
Ter Apel NL 17 C8
Teratyn PL 144 B8
Tërbaç AL 168 D2
Terborg-Silvolde NL 16 E6
Terchová SK 147 C8
Terebești RO 151 B10
Tereblya UA 145 G8
Teregova RO 159 C9
Teremia Mare RO 150 F6
Terena P 50 B5
Teresa E 48 E3
Teresa de Cofrentes E 47 F10
Teresin PL 141 F2
Terespol PL 141 F9
Teresva UA 145 G8
Terezín CZ 76 A6
Terezino Polje HR 149 E8
Tergnier F 19 E7
Tergu I 64 B2
Terheijden NL 182 B5
Terikeste EST 131 E14
Terjärv FIN 123 C11
Terka PL 145 E5
Terlano I 72 C3
Těrlicko CZ 146 B6
Terlizzi I 61 A7
Terme Luigiane I 60 E5
Térmens E 42 D5
Termignon F 31 E10
Terminiers F 24 D6
Termini Imerese I 58 D4
Termoli I 63 D7
Termon IRL 7 B7
Termonfeckin IRL 7 E10
Ternaard NL 16 B5
Ternavka UA 153 A8
Ternberg A 76 G6
Terndrup DK 86 B6
Terneuzen NL 16 F1
Terni I 62 B3
Ternitz A 148 A6
Ternove UA 145 G8
Terovo GR 168 F4
Terpeziţa RO 160 E3
Terpni GR 169 C9
Terpsithea GR 169 E7
Terpyllos GR 169 B8
Terracina I 62 E4
Terrades E 34 F4
Terråk N 105 A12
Terralba I 64 D2
Terranova da Sibari I 61 D6
Terranova di Pollino I 60 D6
Terranuova Bracciolini I 66 E4
Terrasini I 58 C3
Terrassa E 43 D8
Terrasson-Lavilledieu F 29 E8
Terraube F 33 C7
Terravecchia I 61 E7
Terricciola I 66 E2
Terriente E 47 D10
Terrin IRL 7 E8
Terrinches E 55 B7
Terrou F 29 F9
Terrugem P 50 B1
Terrugem P 51 B5
Terryglass IRL 6 F6
Terslev DK 87 E9
Tërstenik RKS 164 D2
Tertenia I 64 D4
Teruel E 47 D10
Tervajoki FIN 122 D8
Tervakoski FIN 127 D12
Tervavaara FIN 121 D11
Tervel BG 161 F10
Terves F 28 B4
Tērvete LV 134 D6
Tervo FIN 123 E17
Tervola FIN 119 B13
Tervolan asema FIN 119 B13
Tervuren B 19 C10
Tés H 149 B10
Tešanj BIH 157 C8
Těšany CZ 77 D11
Tešedíkovo SK 146 E5
Tesero I 72 D4
Tešica SRB 164 C4
Tesimo I 72 C3
Tesjoki FIN 127 E15
Teslić BIH 157 C8
Teslui RO 160 D3
Teslui RO 160 E4
Tespe D 83 D8
Tessenderlo B 19 B11
Tessin D 83 B12
Tesson F 28 D4
Tessy-sur-Vire F 23 C9
Testa del Gargano I 63 D10
Testa dell'Acqua I 59 F6
Testelt B 182 C5
Teşvikiye TR 173 C11
Tét H 149 A9
Tetbury GB 13 B10
Teţcani MD 153 A9
Teţchea RO 151 C9
Teteringen NL 182 B5
Teterow D 83 C13
Tetétlen H 151 C7
Teteven BG 165 D9
Teti I 64 C3
Tetney GB 11 E11
Tetoiu RO 160 D3
Tétouan MA 53 E6
Tetovo BG 161 F8
Tetovo NMK 163 E10
Tettens D 17 A9
Tettnang D 71 B9
Tetyń PL 85 D7
Teublitz D 75 D11
Teuchern D 79 D11
Teufen CH 27 F11
Teufenbach A 73 B9
Teulada E 56 D5
Teulada I 64 F2
Teunz D 75 D11
Teupitz D 80 B5
Teurajärvi FIN 117 D11
Teurajärvi S 116 E9
Teuro FIN 127 D10
Teuschnitz D 75 B9
Teutschenthal D 79 D10
Teuva FIN 122 F7
Tevaniemi FIN 127 B9
Tevansjö S 103 B9
Tevel H 149 D10
Tēvenāni LV 133 C1
Tevfikiye TR 171 E10
Teviothead GB 5 E11
Tewkesbury GB 13 B10
Teyssieu F 29 F9
Thal D 79 E7
Thale (Harz) D 79 C9
Thaleischweiler-Fröschen D 186 C4
Thalfang D 21 E7
Thalheim D 79 C11
Thalheim bei Wels A 76 F6
Thaljina BIH 157 F7
Thalmässing D 75 D9
Thalwil CH 27 F10
Thame GB 14 D7
Thann F 27 E7
Thannhausen D 75 F7
Thaon-les-Vosges F 26 D5
Tharandt D 80 E5
't Harde NL 16 D5
Tharsis E 51 D5
Thasos GR 171 C7
Thatcham GB 13 C12
Thaumiers F 29 B11
Thaxted GB 15 D9
Thaya A 77 E8
Thayngen CH 27 E10
Theale GB 13 C12
Thedinghausen D 17 C12
Theillay F 24 F7
Theißen D 79 D11

Theix F 22 E6
Them DK 86 C5
Themar D 75 A8
The Mumbles GB 12 B6
Thenay F 29 B8
Thénezay F 28 B5
Thenon F 29 E8
Theologos GR 171 C7
Théoule-sur-Mer F 36 D5
The Pike IRL 9 D7
Therma GR 171 D9
Thermi GR 169 C9
Thermisia GR 175 E7
Thermo GR 174 B4
Thermopyles GR 175 B6
Thérouanne F 18 C5
The Sheddings GB 4 F4
Thespies GR 175 C7
Thesprotiko GR 168 F4
Thessaloniki GR 169 C8
The Stocks GB 15 E10
Thetford GB 15 C10
Theth AL 163 E8
Theux B 19 C12
Thèze F 32 D5
Thèze F 35 B10
Thiaucourt-Regniéville F 26 C4
Thiberville F 24 B3
Thibie F 25 C11
Thiéblemont-Farémont F 25 C12
Thiendorf D 80 D5
Thiene I 72 E3
Thierhaupten D 75 E8
Thierrens CH 31 B10
Thiers F 30 D4
Thiersee A 72 A5
Thiersheim D 75 B11
Thiesi I 64 B2
Thießow D 84 B5
Thiézac F 29 E11
Thimert-Gâtelles F 24 C5
Thin-le-Moutier F 19 E10
Thionville F 20 F6
Thiron Gardais F 24 D4
Thirsk GB 11 C9
Thisted DK 86 B3
Thisvi GR 175 C6
Thiva GR 175 C7
Thivars F 24 D5
Thiviers F 29 E7
Thizy F 30 C5
Thoirette F 31 C8
Thoiry F 24 C6
Thoissey F 30 C6
Tholen NL 16 E2
Tholey D 21 F8
Thomastown IRL 9 C8
Thommen B 20 D6
Thônes F 31 D9
Thonnance-lès-Joinville F 26 D3
Thonon-les-Bains F 31 C9
Thorame-Haute F 36 C5
Thoras F 30 F4
Thoré-la-Rochette F 24 E4
Thorenc F 36 D5
Thorigny-sur-Oreuse F 25 D9
Thörl A 73 A11
Thorn NL 19 B12
Thornaby-on-Tees GB 11 B9
Thornbury GB 13 B9
Thorne GB 11 D10
Thorney GB 11 F11
Thornhill GB 5 E9
Thorning DK 86 C4
Thornton GB 10 D5
Thorpe-le-Soken GB 15 D11
Thorpe Market GB 15 B11
Thorpeness GB 15 C12
Thorsager DK 86 C6
Thorshøj DK 90 E7
Thorsø DK 86 C5
Thouarcé F 23 F11
Thouaré-sur-Loire F 23 F9
Thouars F 28 B5
Thouria GR 174 E5
Thourotte F 18 F6
Thrapston GB 15 C7
Threshfield GB 11 C7
Thropton GB 5 E13
Thrumster GB 3 J10
Thuès-entre-Valls F 33 E10
Thueyts F 35 A7
Thuin B 19 D9
Thuine D 17 D9
Thuir F 34 E4
Thum D 80 E3
Thun CH 70 D5
Thundersley GB 15 D10
Thüngen D 74 C6
Thüngersheim D 74 C6
Thuré F 29 B6
Thuret F 30 D3
Thurey F 31 B7
Thüringen A 71 C9
Thurins F 30 D6
Thürkow D 83 C13
Thurlby GB 11 F11
Thurles IRL 9 C7
Thurnau D 75 B9
Thursby GB 5 F10
Thurso GB 3 H9
Thury-Harcourt F 23 C11
Thusis CH 71 D8
Thwaite GB 11 C7
Thyborøn DK 86 B2
Thyez F 31 C10
Thymiana GR 177 C7
Thyregod DK 86 D4
Thyrnau D 76 E5
Tia Mare RO 160 F5
Tiana I 64 C3
Ţibana RO 153 D10
Ţibănești RO 153 D10
Tibble S 99 D9
Tiberget S 102 D6
Tibi E 56 D3
Tibolddaróc H 145 H2
Tibro S 92 C4
Ţibucani RO 153 C9
Tice BIH 156 D6
Ticehurst GB 15 E9
Ticha BG 167 D6
Tichá CZ 146 B6
Tichilești RO 155 C1
Tičići BIH 157 D9
Ticknall GB 11 F9
Ţicleni RO 160 D2
Ţicușu RO 152 F6
Ticvaniu Mare RO 159 C8
Tidaholm S 91 C14
Tidan S 91 B15
Tiddische D 79 A8
Tidenham GB 13 B9
Tidersrum S 92 D7
Tiebas E 32 E2
Tiedra E 39 E9
Tiefenbach D 75 D12
Tiefenbach D 76 E4
Tiefenbronn D 27 C10
Tiefencastel CH 71 D9
Tiefensee D 84 E5
Tiel NL 16 E4
Tielen B 182 C5
Tielt B 19 C7
Tiemassaari FIN 125 F10
Tienen B 19 C10
Tiengen D 27 E9
Tiercé F 23 E11
Tierga E 41 E8
Tierp S 99 B9
Tierzo E 47 C9
Ţifești RO 153 F10
Ţigănași RO 153 C10
Ţigănești RO 160 F6
Tigare BIH 158 E3
Ţighina MD 154 D4
Ţighira MD 153 C11
Tighnabruaich GB 4 D6
Tignale I 69 B10
Tignes F 31 E10
Tigveni RO 160 C5
Tigy F 25 E7
Tiha Bârgăului RO 152 C5
Tihany H 149 C9
Tihemetsa EST 131 E10
Tihilä FIN 123 C16
Tihusniemi FIN 124 F9
Tiistenjoki FIN 123 E10
Tiitilänkylä FIN 123 E17
Tijesno HR 156 E4
Tijnje NL 16 B5
Tíjola E 55 E8
Tikkakoski FIN 123 F15
Tikkala FIN 123 F14
Tikkala FIN 125 F14
Tikkurila FIN 127 E13
Tikob DK 87 C10
Tilburg NL 16 E4
Tilbury GB 15 E9
Til-Châtel F 26 E3
Tildarg GB 4 F4
Tileagd RO 151 C9
Tilehurst GB 13 C12
Tilh F 32 C4
Tilișca RO 152 F3
Tillac F 33 D6
Tillberga S 98 C7
Tillicoultry GB 5 C9
Tillières-sur-Avre F 24 C5
Tilloy-et-Bellay F 25 B12
Tillyfourie GB 3 L11
Tilly-sur-Seulles F 23 B10
Tilvikai LT 134 E3
Tilža LV 133 C2
Tim DK 86 C2
Timahoe IRL 7 G8
Timár H 145 G3
Timau I 73 C7
Timelkam A 76 F5
Timiryazevo RUS 136 C4
Timișești RO 153 C9
Timișoara RO 151 F7
Timmele S 91 D13
Timmendorfer Strand D 83 C9
Timmernabben S 89 B10
Timmersdala S 91 B14
Timola FIN 125 F9
Timoleague IRL 8 E5
Timolin IRL 7 G9
Timoniemi FIN 121 F13
Timovaara FIN 125 D12
Timrå S 103 A13
Timring DK 86 C3
Timsgearraidh GB 2 J2
Tinahely IRL 9 C10
Tinajas E 47 D7
Tinalhas P 44 E5
Tinca RO 151 D8
Tinchebray F 23 C10
Tineo E 39 B7
Tiņģere LV 134 B5
Tinglev DK 86 F4
Tingsryd S 89 B7
Tingstad S 93 B8
Tingstäde S 93 D13
Tingvatn N 94 F6
Tingvoll N 100 A8
Tingwall GB 3 G10
Tinja BIH 157 C10
Tinjan HR 67 B8
Tinn N 95 C9
Tinnoset N 95 C10
Tinos GR 176 D5
Tiñosillos E 46 C3
Tinosu RO 161 D8
Tinqueux F 19 F8
Tintagel GB 12 D5
Tinténiac F 23 D8
Tintern Parva GB 13 B9
Ţintești RO 161 C9
Tintigny B 19 E12
Tīnūži LV 135 C9
Tiobraid Árann IRL 8 D6
Tione di Trento I 69 A10
Tipasoja FIN 125 B11
Tipperary IRL 8 D6
Tiptree GB 15 D10
Tipu EST 131 E10
Tîra MD 154 B2
Tiranë AL 168 B2
Tiranges F 30 E4
Tirano I 69 A9
Tiraspol MD 154 D5
Tiraspolul Nou MD 154 D5
Tire TR 177 C10
Tiream RO 151 B9
Tīreļi LV 134 C7
Tirgo E 40 C6
Tiriez E 55 B8
Tírig E 48 D5
Tiriolo I 59 B10
Tirkšliai LT 134 D4
Tîrnova MD 153 A11
Tirrenia I 66 E1
Tirro FIN 113 F18
Tirschenreuth D 75 C11
Tirstrup DK 86 C7
Tirteafuera E 54 B4
Tirza LV 135 B12
Tisău RO 161 C9
Tišća BIH 157 D10
Tishevitsa BG 165 C8
Tishono RUS 136 E2
Tišice CZ 77 B7
Tismana RO 159 C10
Tišnov CZ 77 D10
Tisovec SK 147 D9
Tistrup Stationsby DK 86 D3
Tisvilde DK 87 C10
Tiszaalpár H 150 D4
Tiszabecs H 145 G6
Tiszabezdéd H 145 G5
Tiszabő H 150 C5
Tiszabura H 150 C5
Tiszacsege H 151 B7
Tiszadada H 145 G3
Tiszaderzs H 150 B6
Tiszadob H 145 G3
Tiszaeszlár H 145 G3
Tiszaföldvár H 150 D5
Tiszafüred H 150 B6
Tiszagyenda H 150 C6
Tiszaigar H 150 B6
Tiszajenő H 150 C5
Tiszakanyár H 145 G4
Tiszakarád H 145 G4
Tiszakécske H 150 D5
Tiszakerecseny H 145 G5
Tiszakeszi H 151 B6
Tiszakürt H 150 D5
Tiszalök H 145 G3
Tiszalúc H 145 G3
Tiszanagyfalu H 145 G3
Tiszanána H 150 B6
Tiszaörs H 150 B6
Tiszapalkonya H 145 H3
Tiszapüspöki H 150 C5
Tiszaroff H 150 C5
Tiszasas H 150 D5
Tiszasüly H 150 C5
Tiszaszalka H 145 G5
Tiszaszentimre H 150 C6
Tiszasziget H 150 E5
Tiszatarján H 147 F12
Tiszatelek H 145 G4
Tiszatenyő H 150 C5
Tiszaug H 150 D5
Tiszaújváros H 145 H3
Tiszavárkony H 150 C5
Tiszavasvári H 145 H3
Titaguas E 47 E10
Titel SRB 158 C5
Ţitești RO 160 C6
Tithorea GR 175 B6
Tito I 60 B5
Titova Korenica HR 156 C4
Titov Drvar BIH 156 D5
Titran N 104 D4
Tittelsnes N 94 C3
Titting D 75 E9
Tittmoning D 76 F3
Titu RO 161 D7
Titulcia E 46 D5
Tiukuvaara FIN 117 C13
Tiurajärvi FIN 117 C12
Tivat MNE 163 E6
Tivenys E 42 F5
Tiverton GB 13 D8
Tivissa E 42 E5
Tivoli I 62 D3
Tizzano F 37 H9
Tjæreborg DK 86 E3
Tjäkkjokk S 109 E15
Tjällmo S 92 B6
Tjåmotis S 109 C16
Tjappsåive S 109 E17
Tjärmyrberget S 106 C9
Tjärn S 107 D13
Tjärnäs S 98 A6
Tjärnberg S 107 A15
Tjärstad S 92 C7
Tjärutträsk S 118 B8
Tjautas S 116 D5
Tjeldnes N 111 D11
Tjeldstø N 100 E1
Tjelle N 100 A7
Tjentište BIH 157 F10
Tjöck FIN 122 F6
Tjøme N 90 A7
Tjønnefoss N 90 B4
Tjorhom N 94 E5
Tjörnarp S 87 D13
Tjøtta N 108 E3
Tjuda FIN 126 E8
Tjuvskjær N 111 C13
Tkon HR 156 E3
Tleń PL 138 C5
Tlmače SK 147 E7
Tłuchowo PL 139 E7
Tlumačov CZ 146 C5
Tłuszcz PL 139 F11
Toab GB 3 F14
Toaca RO 152 D5
Tóalmás H 150 C4
Toano I 66 D2
Tobar an Choire IRL 6 D5
Tobarra E 55 B9
Tobercurry IRL 6 D5
Tobermore GB 4 F3
Tobermory GB 4 B4
Tobo S 99 B9
Tobyn S 97 C8
Tocane-St-Apre F 29 E6
Tocco da Casauria I 62 C5
Tocha P 44 D3
Töcksfors S 96 C6
Tocón E 53 B9
Todal N 104 E5
Toddington GB 13 B11
Todi I 62 B2
Todireni RO 153 B10
Todirești RO 153 B8
Todirești RO 153 C9
Todirești RO 153 D10
Todmorden GB 11 D7
Todolella E 42 F3
Todorići BIH 157 D7
Todor-Ikonomovo BG 161 F10
Todorovo BG 161 F9
Todtmoos D 27 E8
Todtnau D 27 E8
Toén E 38 D4
Toft GB 3 E14
Toft N 108 F3
Tofta S 87 A10
Tofta S 93 D12
Tofte N 95 C13
Töftedal S 91 B10
Tofterup DK 86 D3
Toftir FO 2 A3
Toftlund DK 86 E4
Tofyeli BY 133 E5
Togher IRL 7 E10
Togher IRL 7 F7
Togher IRL 8 E4
Togston GB 5 E13
Tohmajärvi FIN 125 F14
Tohmo FIN 115 E2
Toholampi FIN 123 C12
Toija FIN 127 E9
Toijala FIN 127 C10
Toila EST 132 C2
Toirano I 37 C8
Toivakka FIN 119 B17
Toivakka FIN 123 F16
Toivala FIN 124 E9
Toivola FIN 128 C6
Tojaci NMK 169 B6
Töjby FIN 122 E6
Tök H 149 A11
Tokachka BG 171 B9
Tokaj H 145 G3
Tokarnia PL 143 E9
Tokarnia PL 147 B9
Tokod H 149 A11
Tököl H 149 B11
Tokrajärvi FIN 125 E15
Toksovo RUS 129 E14
Tolastadh Úr GB 2 J4
Tolbaños E 46 C3
Tolbert NL 16 B6
Tolcsva H 145 G3
Toledo E 46 E4
Tolentino I 67 F7
Tolfa I 62 C1
Tolga N 101 B14
Toliejai LT 135 F10
Tolja FIN 119 B17
Tolk D 82 A7
Tolkmicko PL 139 B8
Tollarp S 88 D5
Tollered S 91 D11
Tollesbury GB 15 D10
Tollo I 63 C6
Tølløse DK 87 D9
Töllsjö S 91 D12
Tolmachevo RUS 132 D6
Tolmezzo I 73 D7
Tolmin SLO 73 D8
Tolna H 149 D11
Tolnanémedi H 149 C10
Tolne DK 90 E7
Tolo GR 175 D6
Tolocănești MD 153 A11
Tolonen FIN 117 E14
Tolosa E 32 D1
Tolosa P 44 F5
Tolosenmäki FIN 125 F14
Tolox E 53 C7
Tolšići BIH 157 D10
Tolva E 42 C5
Tolva FIN 121 B12
Tolvayarvi RUS 125 F16
Tolve I 60 B6
Tomai MD 154 D2
Tomai MD 154 E3
Tomar P 44 E4
Tomares E 51 E7
Tomaševac SRB 158 C6
Tomaševo MNE 163 C8
Tomašica BIH 157 C6
Tomášikovo SK 146 E5
Tomášovce SK 147 E9
Tomaszów Lubelski PL 144 C7
Tomaszów Mazowiecki PL 141 G2
Tomatin GB 3 L9
Tombebœf F 33 A6
Tomelilla S 88 D5
Tomelloso E 47 F6
Tomești RO 151 E10
Tomești RO 151 F9
Tomești RO 153 C11
Tomice PL 147 B8
Tomiño E 38 E2
Tomintoul GB 3 L10
Tomislavgrad BIH 157 E7
Tømmerneset N 111 E10
Tommerup DK 86 E6
Tomnavoulin GB 3 L10
Tömörkény H 150 D5
Tompa H 150 E4
Tomra N 100 A5
Tomșani RO 161 D8
Tona E 43 D8
Tonara I 64 C3
Tonbridge GB 15 E9
Tondela P 44 C4
Tønder DK 86 F3
Tonezza del Cimone I 69 B11
Tongeren B 19 C11
Tongland GB 5 F8
Tongue GB 2 J8
Tönisvorst D 183 C8
Tonkopuro FIN 115 E4
Tonna GB 13 B7
Tonnay-Boutonne F 28 D4
Tonnay-Charente F 28 D4
Tonneins F 33 B6
Tonnerre F 25 E10
Tonnes N 108 C5
Tönning D 82 B5
Tønsberg N 95 D12
Tönsen S 103 D12
Tonstad N 94 E5
Tonsvik N 111 A17
Toombeola IRL 6 F3
Toomebridge GB 4 F4
Tootsi EST 131 D9
Topana RO 160 D5
Topares E 55 D8
Toparlar TR 181 C9
Topchii BG 161 F9
Topchin D 80 B5
Topčic-Polje BIH 157 D8
Topcliffe GB 11 C9
Töpen D 75 B10
Topeno FIN 127 D11
Tophisar TR 173 D9
Toplet RO 159 D9
Topliceni RO 161 C10
Topli Do SRB 165 C6
Toplița RO 152 D6
Toplița RO 159 B10
Töplitz D 79 B12
Topojë AL 168 C1
Topola SRB 158 E6
Topolčani NMK 168 B5
Topoľčany SK 146 D6
Topoľčianky SK 146 E6
Topolia GR 178 E6
Topólka PL 138 E6
Topolnica SRB 159 E9
Topoľníky SK 146 F5
Topolog RO 155 D2
Topolovac HR 149 F6
Topolovățu Mare RO 151 F8
Topoloveni RO 160 D6
Topolovgrad BG 166 E6
Topolovnik SRB 159 D7
Topolovo BG 166 F4
Topolšica SLO 73 D11
Toponica SRB 158 F6
Toporec SK 145 E1
Toporivtsi UA 153 A8
Toporów PL 81 B8
Toporu RO 161 E7
Toporzyk PL 85 C10
Toppenstedt D 83 D8
Topraisar RO 155 E2
Topsham GB 13 D8
Topusko HR 156 B4
Torà E 43 D6
Toral de los Guzmanes E 39 D8
Toral de los Vados E 39 C6
Torano Castello I 60 E6
Torasalo FIN 125 F10
Toras-Sieppi FIN 117 C11
Torbali TR 177 C9
Torbjörntorp S 91 C14
Torbygget S 102 A4
Torchiara I 60 C4
Torchiarolo I 61 C10
Torcy F 30 B5
Torda SRB 158 B5
Tordas H 149 B11
Tordehumos E 39 E9
Tordera E 43 D9
Tordesillas E 39 E10
Tordesilos E 47 C9
Töre S 118 C9
Töreboda S 91 B15
Toreby DK 83 A11
Torekov S 87 C11
Torella del Sannio I 63 D7
Torellano E 56 E3
Torelló E 43 C8
Toreno E 39 C6
Torestorp S 91 E12
Torgau D 80 C3
Torgelow D 84 C6
Torgiano I 62 A2
Torhamn S 89 C9
Torhout B 19 B7
Tori EST 131 E9
Torigni-sur-Vire F 23 B10
Torija E 47 C6
Torino I 68 C4
Toritto I 61 B7
Torkanivka UA 154 A4
Torkovichi RUS 132 D7
Torla E 32 E5
Torma EST 131 D13
Tormac RO 159 B7
Törmänen FIN 113 E19
Törmänen FIN 115 A2
Törmänki FIN 117 E13
Törmänmäki FIN 121 E10
Törmäsenvaara FIN 121 C13
Törmäsjärvi FIN 119 B12
Tormestorp S 87 C13
Tormón E 47 D10
Tormore GB 4 D6
Tornadizos de Ávila E 46 C3
Tornaľa SK 145 G1
Tornavacas E 45 D9
Tornby DK 90 D6
Tornemark DK 87 E9
Tornes N 100 A6
Tørnes N 111 D11
Tornesch D 82 C7
Torneträsk S 111 D18
Tornimäe EST 130 D6
Tornio FIN 119 C12
Tornjoš SRB 150 F4
Torno I 69 B7
Tornos E 47 C10
Tornow D 84 D4
Toro E 39 E9
Torö S 93 B11
Törökbálint H 149 B11
Törökszentmiklós H 150 C5
Torony H 149 B7
Toros BG 165 C9
Toroshino RUS 132 F4
Torp FIN 99 B13
Torpa S 92 D6
Torphins GB 3 L11
Torpo N 101 E9
Torpoint GB 12 E6
Torpsbruk S 88 A7
Torpshammar S 103 B11
Torquay GB 13 E7
Torquemada E 40 D3
Torralba de Calatrava E 54 A5
Torralba E 47 D8
Torralba I 64 B2
Torralba de Aragón E 41 E10
Torralba de El Burgo E 40 E6
Torralba de los Sisones E 47 C10
Torralba de Oropesa E 45 E10
Torrão P 50 C3
Torrböle S 107 D17
Torre-Alháquime E 51 F9
Torre Annunziata I 60 B2
Torrebaja E 47 D10
Torreblanca E 48 D5
Torreblascopedro E 53 A9
Torrebruna I 63 D7
Torrecaballeros E 46 C4
Torrecampo E 54 C3
Torre Canne I 61 B8
Torre-Cardela E 55 D6
Torrecilla de Alcañiz E 42 F3
Torrecilla de la Jara E 46 E3
Torrecilla de la Orden E 45 B10
Torrecilla del Rebollar E 42 F1
Torrecillas de la Tiesa E 45 E9
Torrecuso I 60 A3
Torre da Gadanha P 50 B3
Torre das Vargens P 44 F5
Torre de Coelheiros P 50 C4
Torre de Dona Chama P 38 E5
Torre de Embesora E 48 D4
Torredeita P 44 C4
Torre de Juan Abad E 55 B6
Torre del Bierzo E 39 C7
Torre del Burgo E 47 C6
Torre del Campo E 53 A9
Torre del Greco I 60 B2
Torre del Mar E 53 C8
Torredembarra E 43 E6
Torre de Miguel Sesmero E 51 B6
Torre de Moncorvo P 45 B6
Torre de'Passeri I 62 C5
Torre de Santa María E 45 F8
Torredonjimeno E 53 A9
Torre do Terrenho P 44 C6
Torrefarrera E 42 D5
Torregamones E 39 F7
Torregrossa E 42 D5
Torreiglesias E 46 B4
Torreira P 44 C3
Torrejoncillo E 45 E8
Torrejoncillo del Rey E 47 D7
Torrejón de Ardoz E 46 D6
Torrejón del Rey E 46 C6
Torrejón el Rubio E 45 E9
Torrelacarcel E 47 C10
Torrelaguna E 46 C5
Torrelapaja E 41 E8
Torrelavega E 40 B3
Torrellas E 41 E8
Torrelles de Foix E 43 E7
Torrelobatón E 39 E9
Torrelodones E 46 C5
Torremaggiore I 63 D8
Torremanzanas-La Torre de les Macanes E 56 D4
Torremayor E 51 B6
Torremegía E 51 B7
Torre Mileto I 63 D9
Torremocha E 45 F8
Torremocha de Jiloca E 47 C10
Torremolinos E 53 C7
Torrenostra E 48 D5
Torrent E 48 F4
Torrente del Cinca E 42 E4
Torrenueva E 55 B6
Torreorgaz E 45 F8
Torre Orsaia I 60 C4
Torre-Pacheco E 56 F3
Torre Pellice I 31 F11
Torreperogil E 55 C6
Torres E 53 A9
Torresandino E 40 E4
Torre San Giovanni I 61 D10
Torre Santa Susanna I 61 C9
Torres de Albánchez E 55 C7
Torres de Berrellén E 41 E9
Torres de la Alameda E 46 D6
Torres del Carrizal E 39 E8
Torresmenudas E 45 B9
Torres Novas P 44 F3
Torres Vedras P 44 F2
Torrevelilla E 42 F3
Torrevieja E 56 F3
Torrice I 62 D4
Torricella I 61 C9
Torricella in Sabina I 62 C3
Torricella Peligna I 63 C6
Torricella Sicura I 62 B5
Torricella Taverne CH 69 A6
Torrico E 45 E10
Torri del Benaco I 69 B10
Torridon GB 2 K5
Torriglia I 37 B10
Torrijas E 48 D3
Torrijo E 41 F8
Torrijo del Campo E 47 C10
Torrijos E 46 E4
Torrin GB 2 L4
Tørring DK 86 D4
Tørring N 105 C10
Torrita di Siena I 66 F4
Torroal P 50 C2
Torroella de Montgrí E 43 C10
Torrox E 53 C9
Torrubia del Campo E 47 E7
Torrubia de Soria E 41 E7
Tørrvika N 104 C7
Torsåker S 98 A6
Torsång S 97 B14
Torsås S 89 C10
Torsbøl DK 86 F4
Törsbole S 107 E15
Torsborg S 102 A5
Torsby S 97 B9
Torsby S 97 C9
Torsebro S 88 C6
Torshälla S 98 D6
Tórshavn FO 2 A3
Torsholma FIN 126 E5
Torsken N 111 B13
Torslanda S 91 D10
Torsminde DK 86 C2
Torsö S 91 B14
Torsvåg N 112 C4
Törtel H 150 C4
Tortellà E 43 C9
Torteval GBG 22 B6
Torthorwald GB 5 E9
Tortinmäki FIN 126 D7
Tórtola de Henares E 47 C6
Tórtoles de Esgueva E 40 E3
Tortolì I 64 D4
Tortomanu RO 155 E2
Tortona I 37 B9
Tortora I 60 D5
Tortoreto I 62 B5
Tortorici I 59 C6
Tortosa E 42 F5
Tortozendo P 44 D5
Tortuera E 47 C9
Tortuna S 98 C7
Toruń PL 138 D6
Torun' UA 145 F8
Torup S 87 B12
Tõrva EST 131 E11
Tor Vaianica I 62 D2
Tõrvandi EST 131 E13
Torvenkylä FIN 119 F11
Torvik N 100 B3
Torvik N 104 F4
Torvikbukt N 104 F3
Tørvikbygd N 94 B4
Torvinen FIN 117 D17
Torvizcón E 55 F6
Torvsjö S 107 C12
Torysa SK 145 E2
Torzym PL 81 B8
Tosbotn N 108 F4
Toscolano-Maderno I 69 B10
Tossa E 43 D9
Tossåsen S 102 A5
Tossåsen S 102 A7
Tossavanlahti FIN 123 D16
Tosse F 32 C3
Tösse S 91 B12
Tossicia I 62 B5
Tosside GB 11 C7
Töstamaa EST 131 E7
Tostedt D 82 D7
Tószeg H 150 C5
Toszek PL 142 F6
Totana E 55 D10
Totebo S 93 D8
Tôtes F 18 E3
Totești RO 159 B10
Tótkomlós H 150 E6
Totland GB 13 D11
Totnes GB 13 E7
Totra S 103 E13
Tótszerdahely H 149 D7
Tøttdal N 105 C10
Tottijärvi FIN 127 C9
Totton GB 13 D12
Tótvázsony H 149 B9
Touça P 45 B6
Toucy F 25 E9
Touffailles F 33 B8
Touget F 33 C7
Toul F 26 C4
Toulon F 35 D10
Toulon-sur-Allier F 30 B3
Toulon-sur-Arroux F 30 B5
Toulouges F 34 E4
Toulouse F 33 C8
Tounj HR 156 B3
Touques F 23 B12
Tourch F 22 D4
Tourcoing F 19 C7
Tourlaville F 23 A8
Tournai B 19 C7
Tournan-en-Brie F 25 C8
Tournay F 33 D6
Tournecoupe F 33 C7
Tournefeuille F 33 C8
Tournon-d'Agenais F 33 B7
Tournon-St-Martin F 29 B7
Tournon-sur-Rhône F 30 E6
Tournus F 30 B6
Tourny F 24 B6
Tourouvre F 24 C4
Tours F 24 F4
Tourteron F 19 E10
Tourtoirac F 29 E8
Toury F 24 D6
Tous E 48 F3
Tõusi EST 131 D7
Touvois F 28 B2
Toužim CZ 76 B3
Tovačov CZ 146 C4
Tovariševo SRB 158 C3
Tovarné SK 145 F4
Tovarnik HR 157 B11
Toven N 108 D5
Tovrljane SRB 164 C3
Towcester GB 14 C7
Tower IRL 8 E5
Toymskardlia N 106 A5
Töysä FIN 123 E11
Traar D 183 C9
Trabada E 38 B5
Trabanca E 45 B8
Trabazos E 39 E7
Traben D 21 E8
Trąbki PL 144 D1
Trąbki Wielkie PL 138 B6
Traboch A 73 B10
Trabotivište NMK 165 F6
Traby BY 137 E12
Trachili GR 175 B9
Tradate I 69 B6
Trädet S 91 D14
Trædal N 111 D14
Trafrask IRL 8 E3
Tragacete E 47 D9
Tragana GR 175 B7
Tragano GR 174 D3
Tragjas AL 168 D2
Tragwein A 77 F7
Traian RO 153 D10
Traian RO 155 C1
Traian RO 155 C2
Traian RO 160 E4
Traian RO 160 F6
Traian Vuia RO 151 F9
Traid E 47 C9
Traiguera E 42 F4
Train D 75 E10
Traînel F 25 D9
Traînou F 24 E7
Traisen A 77 F9
Traiskirchen A 77 F10
Traismauer A 77 F9
Traitsching D 75 D12
Trakai LT 137 D10
Trakovice SK 146 E5
Trakšėdžiai LT 134 F2
Tralee IRL 8 D3
Trá Li IRL 8 D3
Tramacastilla E 47 D9
Tramagal P 44 F4
Tramariglio I 64 B1
Tramatza I 64 C2
Tramayes F 30 C6
Tramelan CH 27 F7
Trá Mhór IRL 9 D8
Tramonti di Sopra I 73 D6
Tramonti di Sotto I 73 D6
Tramore IRL 9 D8
Tramutola I 60 C5
Tranås S 92 C5
Tranbjerg DK 86 C6
Trancoso P 44 C6
Tranebjerg DK 86 D7
Tranemo S 91 E13
Trängen S 105 D15
Trånghalla S 92 D4
Trängslet S 102 D6
Trångsviken S 105 E16
Trani I 61 A6
Trannes F 25 D12
Tranovalto GR 169 D6
Tranøy N 111 D10
Trans F 23 D8
Trans-en-Provence F 36 D4
Transtrand S 102 D5
Transtrand S 102 E5
Tranum DK 86 A4
Tranvik S 99 D11
Trapani I 58 C2
Trapene LV 135 B13
Traplice CZ 146 C4
Trappes F 24 C7
Trarbach D 185 E7
Traryd S 87 B13
Trasacco I 62 D5
Träskvik FIN 122 F7
Trasmiras E 38 D4
Trasobares E 41 E8
Tratalias I 64 E2
Traun A 76 F6
Traunreut D 73 A6
Traunstein A 77 F8
Traunstein D 73 A6
Traupis LT 135 E9
Trava SLO 73 E10
Trävad S 91 C13
Travagliato I 66 A1
Travanca do Mondego P 44 D4
Travassô P 44 C4
Travemünde D 83 C9
Travenbrück D 83 C8
Travers CH 31 B10
Traversetolo I 66 C1
Trávnica SK 146 E6
Travnik BIH 157 D8
Travo I 37 B11

Trawniki PL 141 H8
Trawsfynydd GB 10 F4
Trbovlje SLO 73 D11
Trbuk BIH 157 C9
Trebaseleghe I 72 E5
Trebatice SK 146 D5
Trebatsch D 80 B6
Trebbin D 80 B4
Třebechovice pod Orebem CZ 77 B9
Trebel D 83 E10
Treben D 79 D11
Třebenice CZ 76 B5
Trebenow D 84 D5
Trèbes F 33 D10
Trébeurden F 22 C4
Třebíč CZ 77 D9
Trebinje BIH 162 D5
Trebisacce I 61 D7
Trebišov SK 145 F4
Trebnje SLO 73 E11
Trebolle E 38 C4
Třeboň CZ 77 D7
Trebsen D 79 D12
Trebujena E 51 F7
Trebur D 21 E10
Trecastagni I 59 D7
Trecate I 68 C6
Trecchina I 60 C5
Trecenta I 66 B3
Tredegar GB 13 B8
Tredington GB 13 A11
Tredozio I 66 D4
Treehoo IRL 7 D8
Trefaldwyn GB 10 F5
Trefeglwys GB 10 F4
Treffen A 73 C8
Treffort-Cuisiat F 31 C7
Treffurt D 79 D7
Trefriw GB 10 E4
Trefynwy GB 13 B9
Tregaron GB 13 A7
Trégastel F 22 C4
Tregde N 90 C2
Tregnago I 66 A3
Tregony GB 12 E5
Trégueux F 22 D6
Tréguier F 22 C5
Trégunc F 22 E4
Tregynon GB 10 F5
Trehörna S 92 C5
Trehörningsjö S 107 D15
Treia D 82 A6
Treia I 67 F7
Treignac F 29 D9
Treigny F 25 E9
Treimani EST 131 F8
Treis D 185 D7
Trekanten S 89 B10
Treklyano BG 165 D6
Trélazé F 23 F11
Trelech GB 12 B6
Trélissac F 29 E7
Trelleborg S 87 E12
Trelleck GB 13 B9
Trélon F 19 D9
Tremadog GB 10 F3
Tremblay-les-Villages F 24 C5
Tremedal de Tormes E 45 B8
Tremelo B 19 C10
Trémentines F 23 F10
Tremês P 44 F3
Tréméven F 22 E4
Tremezzo I 69 B7
Trémolat F 29 F7
Třemošná CZ 76 C4
Trémouilles F 34 B4
Tremp E 42 C5
Trenance GB 12 E4
Trenčianska Turná SK 146 D6
Trenčianske Jastrabie SK 146 D6
Trenčianske Stankovce SK 146 D5
Trenčianske Teplice SK 146 D6
Trenčín SK 146 D6
Trendelburg D 21 A12
Trengereid N 94 B3
Trensacq F 32 B4
Trent D 84 A4
Trenta SLO 73 D8
Trentels F 33 B7
Trento I 69 A11
Tréon F 24 C5
Treorchy GB 13 B7
Trepča HR 148 F5
Treppeln D 81 B7
Trept F 31 D7
Trepuzzi I 61 C10
Trequanda I 66 F4
Tres Cantos E 46 C5
Trescléoux F 35 B10
Trescore Balneario I 69 B8
Tresenda I 69 A9
Tresfjord N 100 A6
Tresigallo I 66 C4
Tresjuncos E 47 E7
Treski EST 132 F2
Treskog S 97 C8
Trešnjevica SRB 158 F5
Tresnuraghes I 64 C2
Trespaderne E 40 C5
Tressait GB 5 B9
Třešť CZ 77 D8
Tretower GB 13 B8
Trets F 35 D10
Tretten N 101 D12
Treuchtlingen D 75 E8
Treuenbrietzen D 79 B12
Treungen N 90 A4
Trévé F 22 D6
Trevélez E 55 F6
Tréveray F 26 C3
Trèves F 34 B5
Trevi I 62 B3
Treviana E 40 C5
Trévières F 23 B10
Treviglio I 69 B8
Trevignano Romano I 62 C2
Trévillers F 27 F6
Treviño E 40 C6
Treviso I 72 E5
Trevllazër AL 168 C2
Trevões P 44 B6
Trévoux F 30 D6
Trézelles F 30 C4
Trezzo sull'Adda I 69 B8
Trgovište SRB 164 E5
Trhová Hradská SK 146 F5
Trhové Sviny CZ 77 E7
Trhovište SK 145 F4
Trhový Štěpánov CZ 77 C8
Triacastela E 38 C5
Triaize F 28 C3
Trianta GR 181 D8
Triantaros GR 176 D5
Tribalj HR 67 B10
Tribanj-Krušćica HR 156 D3
Tribehou F 23 B9
Tribsees D 83 B13
Tribunj HR 156 E4
Tricarico I 60 B6
Tricase I 61 D10
Tricesimo I 73 D7
Trichiana I 72 D5
Tricot F 18 E6
Trieben A 73 A9
Triebes D 79 E11
Trie-Château F 18 F4
Trier D 21 E7
Trierweiler D 186 B2
Trieste I 73 E8
Trie-sur-Baïse F 33 D6
Trieux F 20 F5
Trifeşti RO 153 C11
Trifeşti RO 153 D9
Triftern D 76 F4
Trigaches P 50 C4
Trigance F 36 D4
Triggiano I 61 A7
Triglitz D 83 D12
Trignac F 23 F7
Trigrad BG 165 F9
Triguères F 25 E8
Trigueros E 51 E6
Trigueros del Valle E 39 E10
Triigi EST 130 D5
Trikala GR 169 E6
Trikāta LV 131 F11
Trikeri GR 175 A7
Trilj HR 157 E6
Trillevallen S 105 E14
Trillick GB 7 D8
Trillo E 47 C7
Trilofo GR 174 E5
Trilofos GR 169 D8
Trilport F 25 C8
Trim IRL 7 E9
Trimdon GB 5 F14
Trimley St Mary GB 15 D11
Trimmis CH 71 D9
Trimsaran GB 12 B6
Trindade P 38 F5
Trindade P 50 D4
Třinec CZ 147 B7
Tring GB 15 D7
Trinità d'Agultu I 64 B2
Trinitapoli I 60 A6
Trino I 68 C5
Trins A 72 B3
Trinta P 45 C6
Trinwillershagen D 83 B13
Triollo E 39 C10
Triora I 37 D7
Tripkau D 83 D10
Tripoli GR 174 D5
Tripotama GR 174 D4
Tripotamos GR 169 C7
Trippstadt D 21 F9
Triptis D 79 E10
Tritenii de Jos RO 152 D4
Trittau D 83 C8
Trittenheim D 21 E7
Trivalea-Moşteni RO 160 E6
Trivento I 63 D7
Trivero I 68 B5
Trivigno I 60 B5
Trizac F 29 E11
Trnakovac HR 157 B7
Trnava CZ 146 C5
Trnava SK 146 E5
Trnava SRB 158 F5
Trnavá Hora SK 147 D7
Trnjani BIH 157 C6
Trnovci NMK 168 B5
Trnovec Bartolovečki HR 149 D6
Trnovec nad Váhom SK 146 E5
Trnovica BIH 157 F9
Trnovo BIH 157 E9
Tro N 108 E4
Troarn F 23 B11
Tröbitz D 80 C4
Trochtelfingen D 27 D11
Trödje S 103 E13
Troense DK 86 E7
Trofa P 38 F2
Trofaiach A 73 B11
Trofors N 108 E5
Trogir HR 156 E5
Trøgstad N 95 C14
Troia I 60 A4
Tróia P 50 C2
Troianul RO 160 F6
Troina I 59 D6
Troisdorf D 21 C8
Troisfontaines F 186 D3
Trois-Ponts B 19 D12
Troissereux F 18 F5
Trois-Vèvres F 30 B3
Troisvierges L 20 D6
Troiţsoe MD 154 D4
Trojane SLO 73 D10
Trojanów PL 141 G5
Troldhede DK 86 D3
Trollbukta N 113 C19
Trollhättan S 91 C11
Trollvik N 112 D6
Tromello I 69 C6
Tromsdalen N 111 A16
Tromsø N 111 A16
Tromvik N 111 A15
Tronco P 38 E5
Trondenes N 111 C12
Trondheim N 104 E8
Trones N 105 B13
Trongisvágur FO 2 B3
Tronnes N 108 C8
Trönninge S 87 B11
Trönningeby S 87 A10
Trönö S 103 D12
Trontano I 68 A5
Tronvik N 105 D9
Tronville-en-Barrois F 26 C3
Tronzano Vercellese I 68 C5
Troo F 24 E4
Troon GB 4 D7
Trooz B 183 D7
Tropaia GR 174 D4
Tropea I 59 B8
Trory GB 7 D7
Trosa S 93 B11
Troshan AL 163 F8
Trösken S 98 B7
Troškūnai LT 135 E9
Trošmarija HR 148 F4
Trossin D 79 C12
Trossingen D 27 D10
Tröstau D 75 B10
Trostberg D 75 F12
Trostyanets' UA 145 E9
Trostyanets' UA 153 A12
Troszyn PL 139 D12
Troubky CZ 146 C4
Troubsko CZ 77 D10
Troutbeck GB 10 C6
Trouville-sur-Mer F 23 B12
Trouy F 29 A10
Troviscal P 44 E4
Trowbridge GB 13 C10
Troyan BG 165 D10
Troyanovo BG 167 D8
Troyes F 25 D11
Troyits'ke UA 154 B6
Troyits'ke UA 154 D6
Troyon F 26 B3
Trpanj HR 157 F7
Trpejca NMK 168 C4
Trpezi MNE 163 D9
Trpinja HR 157 B10
Trsa MNE 157 F10
Trstená SK 147 C9
Trstené pri Hornáde SK 145 F3
Trstenik HR 162 D3
Trstenik SRB 163 B11
Trstice SK 146 E5
Trstín SK 146 D4
Trubar BIH 156 D5
Trubia E 39 B8
Truchas E 39 D7
Truchtersheim F 27 C8
Trud BG 165 E10
Trudovets BG 165 D8
Trudy BY 133 E6
Trujillanos E 51 B7
Trujillo E 45 F9
Trulben D 27 B8
Trŭn BG 165 D6
Trun CH 71 D7
Trun F 23 C12
Trŭnchovitsa BG 165 C11
Truro GB 12 E4
Truşeşti RO 153 B10
Trusetal D 79 E7
Trush AL 163 F7
Truskava LT 135 F8
Truskavets' UA 145 E8
Trŭstenik BG 161 F7
Trŭstenik BG 165 C9
Trustrup DK 87 C7
Trutnov CZ 81 E9
Try N 90 C2
Tryavna BG 166 D4
Trybusivka UA 154 A3
Tryfos GR 174 B3
Tryggelev DK 83 A9
Trygona GR 168 E5
Tryńcza PL 144 C6
Trysserum S 93 C9
Trysil N 102 D3
Tryškiai LT 134 D5
Trysunda S 107 E15
Tržac BIH 156 C4
Trzcianka PL 85 D10
Trzcianka PL 139 E12
Trzcianne PL 140 D7
Trzciel PL 81 B9
Trzebiatów PL 85 B8
Trzebiechów PL 81 B9
Trzebiel PL 81 C7
Trzebielino PL 85 B12
Trzebień PL 81 D9
Trzebieszów PL 141 G7
Trzebieszowice PL 77 B11
Trzebież PL 84 C7
Trzebinia PL 143 F7
Trzebiszewo PL 81 A8
Trzebnica PL 81 D12
Trzebnice PL 81 D10
Trzebownisko PL 144 C5
Trzeciewiec PL 138 D5
Trzemeszno PL 138 E4
Trzemeszno Lubuskie PL 81 B8
Trześcianka PL 140 E8
Trześniów PL 145 D4
Trzeszczany Pierwsze PL 144 B8
Tržič SLO 73 D9
Trzcińsko-Zdrój PL 84 E7
Trzyciąż PL 143 F8
Trzydnik Duży PL 144 B5
Tsagkarada GR 169 F9
Tsakarisianos GR 174 C2
Tsalapitsa BG 165 E10
Tsamantas GR 168 E3
Tsaparevo BG 169 A9
Tsareva Livada BG 166 D4
Tsarev Brod BG 167 C8
Tsarevo BG 167 E9
Tsarimir BG 165 E10
Tsaritsani GR 169 E7
Tsar Kaloyan BG 161 F8
Tsar-Petrovo BG 159 F10
Tschagguns A 71 C9
Tschernitz D 81 C7
Tsebrykove UA 154 C6
Tselina BG 166 E4
Tsenovo BG 166 B5
Tserovo BG 165 C7
Tserovo BG 165 E9
Tsiistre EST 131 F14
Tsirguliina EST 131 F12
Tsivaras GR 178 E7
Tsooru EST 131 F13
Tsotili GR 168 D5
Tsoukalades GR 174 B2
Tsŭrvaritsa BG 165 E6
Tsvetino BG 165 F8
Tsyatsyerki BY 133 E2
Tua N 105 D9
Tuaim IRL 6 E5
Tuaim Beola IRL 6 F3
Tuam IRL 6 E5
Tuamgraney IRL 8 C5
Tubbercurry IRL 6 D5
Tubbergen NL 17 D7
Tubilla del Agua E 40 C4
Tübingen D 27 C11
Tubize B 19 C9
Tubre I 71 D10
Tučepi HR 157 F7
Tuchan F 34 E4
Tüchen D 83 D12
Tuchheim D 79 B11
Tuchola PL 138 C4
Tuchomie PL 85 B12
Tuchów PL 144 D3
Tuchowicz PL 141 G6
Tuckur FIN 122 D8
Tuczna PL 141 G8
Tuczno PL 85 D10
Tudela E 41 D8
Tudela de Duero E 40 E2
Tudora RO 153 B9
Tudor Vladimirescu RO 155 B1
Tudu EST 131 C13
Tudulinna EST 131 C14
Tudweiliog GB 10 F2
Tuéjar E 47 E10
Tuenno I 72 D3
Tufeni RO 160 E5
Tufeşti RO 155 D1
Tuffé F 24 D4
Tufjord N 113 A12
Tuhkakylä FIN 125 B10
Tui E 38 D2
Tuili I 64 D2
Tuin NMK 168 A5
Tuiskula FIN 122 E8
Tūja LV 135 B8
Tukhkala RUS 121 C16
Tukhol'ka UA 145 F7
Tukums LV 134 C6
Tula I 64 B2
Tulach Mhór IRL 7 F8
Tulare SRB 164 D3
Tuławki PL 136 F2
Tulbing A 77 F10
Tulca RO 151 D8
Tulce PL 81 B12
Tulcea RO 155 C3
Tulčík SK 145 E3
Tulette F 35 B8
Tulgheş RO 153 D7
Tuli BIH 162 D5
Tuliszków PL 142 B5
Tulje BIH 162 D5
Tulka S 99 B11
Tulla IRL 8 C5
Tullaghan IRL 6 D6
Tullamore IRL 7 F8
Tulle F 29 E9
Tullebølle DK 87 F7
Tulleng N 111 A15
Tulleråsen S 105 E16
Tullingsås S 106 D9
Tullins F 31 E7
Tulln A 77 F10
Tullow IRL 9 C9
Tully GB 7 D7
Tully GB 7 D8
Tullyallen IRL 7 E10
Tullyvin IRL 7 D8
Tulnici RO 153 F9
Tulos RUS 125 C14
Tulovo BG 166 D5
Tułowice PL 139 F9
Tułowice PL 142 E4
Tulppio FIN 115 C6
Tulsk IRL 6 E6
Tulstrup DK 87 D10
Tulucești RO 155 B2
Tumba S 93 A11
Tumbo S 98 D6
Tume LV 134 C6
Tummel Bridge GB 5 B8
Tumšupe LV 135 B9
Tun S 91 C12
Tunadal S 103 B13
Tuna-Hästberg S 97 B13
Tunari RO 161 D8
Tunbridge Wells, Royal GB 15 E9
Tunga GB 2 J4
Tungozero RUS 121 C17
Tunnerstad S 92 C4
Tunnhovd N 95 B9
Tunnsjø-Røyrvika N 105 B14
Tunsjön S 107 E12
Tunstall GB 15 C11
Tuntenhausen D 72 A5
Tunvågen S 102 A8
Tuohikotti FIN 128 C7
Tuohikylä FIN 115 E5
Tuolluvaara S 116 C4
Tuomikylä FIN 122 E9
Tuomioja FIN 119 E14
Tuorila FIN 126 B6
Tuoro sul Trasimeno I 66 F5
Tuovilanlahti FIN 124 D8
Tupilaţi RO 153 C9
Tuplice PL 81 C7
Tuppurinmäki FIN 125 E10
Tura H 150 B4
Turanlar TR 177 D10
Turany SK 147 C8
Turawa PL 142 E5
Turba EST 131 C8
Turbe BIH 157 D8
Turbenthal CH 27 F10
Turburea RO 160 D3
Turceni RO 160 D2
Turcia E 39 C8
Turčianske Teplice SK 147 D7
Turcifal P 44 F2
Turcinești RO 160 C2
Turcoaia RO 155 C2
Turda RO 152 D3
Turdaş RO 151 F11
Turégano E 46 B4
Turek PL 142 B6
Tureni RO 152 D3
Turenki FIN 127 D12
Turew PL 81 B11
Turgeliai LT 137 E12
Tŭrgovishte BG 167 C7
Turgut TR 181 B8
Turgutalp TR 177 A10
Turgutbey TR 173 B7
Turgutlu TR 177 C10
Turgutreis TR 177 F9
Türi EST 131 D10
Turi I 61 B8
Turia RO 153 E8
Turić BIH 157 C10
Turie SK 147 C7
Turija BIH 157 C9
Turija SRB 158 B4
Turija SRB 159 D8
Turís E 48 F3
Turiya BG 166 D4
Türje H 149 C8
Turka UA 145 E7
Türkeve H 150 C6
Türkgücü TR 173 B8
Türkheim D 71 A11
Turki LV 135 D12
Türkmenli TR 171 E10
Turkova BY 133 E4
Turkovići BIH 162 D4
Turku FIN 126 E7
Turlava LV 134 C3
Turleque E 46 E5
Turmantas LT 135 E12
Turmenti BIH 162 D5
Turna LV 131 F11
Tŭrnak BG 165 C9
Turňa nad Bodvou SK 145 F2
Turnau A 148 A4
Tŭrnava BG 165 B8
Turnberry GB 4 E6
Turners Hill GB 15 E8
Turnhout B 16 F3
Turnišče SLO 149 C6
Türnitz A 77 G9
Turnov CZ 81 E8
Turnu Măgurele RO 160 F5
Turnu Roşu RO 160 B4
Turnu Ruieni RO 159 C9
Turobin PL 144 B6
Turośl PL 139 C12
Turośl PL 139 D12
Turów PL 141 G7
Turowo PL 85 C11
Turquel P 44 F3
Turrach A 73 C8
Turre E 55 E9
Turri I 64 D2
Turriff GB 3 K12
Tursi I 61 C6
Turţ RO 145 H7
Turtel NMK 164 F5
Turtola FIN 117 E11
Turulung RO 145 H7
Turup DK 86 E5
Tur"ya-Bystra UA 145 F6
Tur"ya-Polyana UA 145 F6
Turyatka UA 153 A8
Tur"ye UA 145 E7
Tur"yi Remety UA 145 F6
Turynka UA 144 C9
Turza Wielka PL 139 D9
Turzovka SK 147 C7
Tusa I 58 D5
Tuscania I 62 C1
Tuse DK 87 D9
Tuset N 105 E10
Tušilović HR 148 F5
Tuşnad RO 153 E7
Tussenhausen D 71 A11
Tüßling D 75 F12
Tuszów Narodowy PL 143 F11
Tuszyma PL 143 F12
Tuszyn PL 143 C8
Tutbury GB 11 F8
Tutjunniemi FIN 125 F13
Tutora RO 153 C11
Tutova RO 153 E11
Tutow D 84 C4
Tutrakan BG 161 E9
Tuttlingen D 27 E10
Tütüncü TR 173 D8
Tutzing D 72 A3
Tützpatz D 84 C4
Tuudi EST 130 D7
Tuukkala FIN 127 B16
Tuuliharju FIN 117 D13
Tuulimäki FIN 121 F11
Tuulos FIN 127 C12
Tuupovaara FIN 125 F15
Tuuri FIN 123 E11
Tuusjärvi FIN 125 E10
Tuusniemi FIN 125 E10
Tuusula FIN 127 E12
Tuv N 101 E8
Tuv N 108 B8
Tuvattnett S 106 D7
Tuve S 91 D10
Tuvnes N 104 D5
Tuvträsk S 107 B15
Tuxford GB 11 E10
Tuzburgazi TR 177 D9
Tuzculu TR 177 B8
Tŭzha BG 166 D4
Tuzi MNE 163 E7
Tužina SK 147 D7
Tuzla BIH 157 C10
Tuzla RO 155 E3
Tuzla TR 171 E10
Tužno HR 148 D6
Tuzora MD 154 C2
Tuzsér H 145 G5
Tvååker S 87 A10
Tvärålund S 107 C17
Tvärån S 118 C6
Tväråträsk S 107 A13
Tvardiţa MD 154 E3
Tvärsele S 106 B8
Tvärskog S 89 B10
Tvede DK 86 B6
Tvedestrand N 90 B4
Tveit N 90 C3
Tveit N 94 D4
Tverai LT 134 E4
Tverečius LT 135 F13
Tverråga N 108 D7
Tverråmo N 109 B10
Tverrelmo N 111 C18
Tversted DK 90 D7
Tving S 89 C8
Tvis DK 86 C3
Tvøroyri FO 2 B3
Tvorozhkovo RUS 132 E4
Tvrdošín SK 147 C9
Tvrdošovce SK 146 E6
Tvŭrditsa BG 166 D5
Twardogóra PL 142 D3
Twatt GB 3 G10
Tweedmouth GB 5 D12
Tweedsmuir GB 5 D10
Twello NL 16 D6
Twist D 17 C8
Twiste (Twistetal) D 17 F11
Twistringen D 17 C11
Two Mile Borris IRL 9 C7
Twomileborris IRL 9 C7
Two Mile Bridge IRL 7 F8
Tworóg PL 142 E6
Twyford GB 13 C12
Twyford GB 15 E7
Twyning GB 13 A10
Tyachiv UA 145 G8
Tychero GR 171 B10
Tychówko PL 85 C10
Tychowo PL 85 C10
Tychy PL 143 F6
Tyczyn PL 144 D5
Tydal N 105 E11
Tydavnet IRL 7 D8
Tyfors S 97 B11
Tygelsjö S 87 D11
Tyinkrysset N 101 D8
Tykocin PL 140 D7
Tylawa PL 145 E4
Tylissos GR 178 E9
Tyllinge S 93 C8
Tylmanowa PL 145 D1
Tylösand S 87 B11
Tylstrup DK 86 A5
Tymbark PL 144 D1
Tymień PL 85 B9
Tymowa PL 81 D10
Tympaki GR 178 E8
Tynderö S 103 B14
Tyndrum GB 4 C7
Týnec nad Labem CZ 77 B8
Týnec nad Sázavou CZ 77 C7
Tynemouth GB 5 E14
Tyngsjö S 97 B10
Tyniewicze Małe PL 141 E8
Týniště nad Orlicí CZ 77 B10
Tynkä FIN 119 F12
Týn nad Vltavou CZ 77 D6
Tynset N 101 B13
Typpö FIN 119 F12
Typpyrä FIN 117 E14
Tyrämäki FIN 121 D12
Tyrävaara FIN 121 D12
Tyrawa Wołoska PL 145 D5
Tyresö S 99 D10
Tyringe S 87 C13
Tyristrand N 95 B12
Tyrjänsaari FIN 125 E15
Tyrnävä FIN 119 E15
Tyrnavos GR 169 E7
Tyrrellspass IRL 7 F8
Tyrväntö FIN 127 C11
Tysnes N 111 D10
Tysse N 94 B3
Tysse N 100 D2
Tyssebotnen N 100 E3
Tyssedal N 94 B5
Tystberga S 93 B10
Tyszowce PL 144 B8
Tytuvėnai LT 134 E6
Tyukod H 145 H6
Tyulenovo BG 167 B11
Tywyn GB 10 F3
Tyykiluoto FIN 119 D14
Tzermiado GR 178 E9
Tzummarum NL 16 B5

U

Uachdar GB 2 L2
Uachtar Ard IRL 6 F4
Ub SRB 158 E5
Übach-Palenberg D 183 D8
Ubby DK 87 D8
Úbeda E 53 A10
Überherrn D 21 F7
Überlingen D 27 E11
Übersee D 72 A5
Ubli HR 162 D2
Ubli MNE 163 D6
Ubli MNE 163 D7
Ubrique E 53 C6
Ubstadt-Weiher D 21 F11
Ucciani F 37 G9
Uccle B 19 C9
Ucea RO 152 F5
Uceda E 46 C6
Ucel F 35 A7
Ucero E 40 E5
Ucha P 38 E2
Uchanie PL 144 B8
Uchaux F 35 B8
Uchizy F 30 B6
Uchte D 17 D11
Üchtelhausen D 75 B7
Uchtspringe D 79 A10
Uckange F 186 C1
Uckfield GB 15 F9
Uckro D 80 C5
Uclés E 47 E7
Üçpınar TR 177 B9
Uda RO 160 D5
Udanin PL 81 D10
Udavské SK 145 F4
Udbina HR 156 C4
Udby DK 87 D9
Uddebo S 91 E13
Uddeholm S 97 B10
Uddel NL 183 A7
Uddevalla S 91 C10
Uddheden S 97 C8
Uddington GB 5 D9
Uden NL 16 E5
Udenhout NL 16 E4
Udenisht AL 168 C4
Uderns A 72 B4
Üdersdorf D 21 D7
Udeşti RO 153 B8
Udiča SK 146 C6
Udine I 73 D7
Udorpie PL 85 B13
Üdruma EST 131 D8
Udrycze PL 144 B7
Uebigau D 80 C4
Ueckermünde D 84 C6
Uehlfeld D 75 C8
Uelsen D 17 D7
Uelzen D 83 E9
Uetendorf CH 31 B12
Uetersen D 82 C7
Uettingen D 74 C6
Uetze D 79 B7
Uffculme GB 13 D8
Uffenheim D 75 C7
Uffing am Staffelsee D 72 A3
Uftrungen D 79 C8
Ugāle LV 134 B4
Ugao SRB 163 C9
Ugarana E 40 B6
Uge DK 86 F4
Ugelbølle DK 86 C6
Ugento I 61 D10
Ugerløse DK 87 D9
Uggdal N 94 B2
Uggelheden S 102 E3
Uggelhuse DK 86 C6
Uggerby DK 90 D7
Uggerslev DK 86 D6
Uggiano la Chiesa I 61 C10
Ugíjar E 55 F6
Ugine F 31 D9
Üglen BG 165 C9
Uglev DK 86 B3
Ugljan HR 67 D11
Ugljane HR 157 E6
Ugljevik BIH 157 C11
Ugod H 149 B9
Ugŭrchin BG 165 C9
Uğurlu TR 171 D9
Uharte-Arakil E 32 E2
Uherské Hradiště CZ 146 C4
Uherský Brod CZ 146 C5
Uhingen D 74 E6
Uhldingen D 27 E11
Uhlířské Janovice CZ 77 C8
Uhlstädt D 79 E9
Uhniv UA 144 C8
Uhtna EST 131 C13
Uhyst D 81 D7
Uig GB 2 K4
Uimaharju FIN 125 E14
Uimila FIN 127 C15
Uitgeest NL 16 C3
Uithoorn NL 16 D3
Uithuizen NL 17 B7
Uivar RO 159 B6
Ujazd PL 141 G1
Ujazd PL 142 F5
Újezd CZ 77 C12
Újezd CZ 146 C5
Újfehértó H 151 B8
Újhartyán H 150 C3
Újkér H 149 B7
Újkígyós H 151 D7
Újléta H 151 C8
Újpetre H 149 E10
Ujście PL 85 D11
Ujsoły PL 147 C8
Újszalonta H 151 D7
Újszász H 150 C5
Újszentiván H 150 E5
Újszentmargita H 151 B7
Újszilvás H 150 C4
Újtikos H 145 H3
Újudvar H 149 C7
Ukhozhany UA 154 A5
Ukkola FIN 125 E14
Ukmergė LT 135 F9
Ukri LV 134 D6
Ula BY 133 F6
Ula TR 181 B8
Ulamiş TR 177 C8
Uland S 103 A14
Ulan-Majorat PL 141 G6
Ulanów PL 144 C5
Ulaş TR 173 B8
Ulassai I 64 D4
Ula Tirso I 64 C2
Ulbjerg DK 86 B4
Ulbroka LV 135 C8
Ulbster GB 3 J10
Ulcinj MNE 163 F7
Uldum DK 86 D5
Ulefoss N 95 D10
Uleila del Campo E 55 E8
Ülenurme EST 131 E13
Ulëz AL 163 F8
Ulfborg DK 86 C2
Ulft NL 16 E6
Ulhówek PL 144 C8
Ulič SK 145 F5
Ulicoten NL 182 C5
Ulieş RO 152 E6
Ulieşti RO 161 D6
Ulila EST 131 E12
Uljanik HR 149 E8
Uljma SRB 159 C7
Ullånger S 107 E14
Ullapool GB 2 K6
Ullared S 87 A11
Ullatti S 116 D7
Ullava FIN 123 C11
Ullbergsträsk S 107 A17
Ulldecona E 42 F4
Ulldemolins E 42 E5
Ullerslev DK 86 E7
Ullervad S 91 B14
Üllés H 150 E4
Ulleskelf GB 11 D9
Ullisjaur S 107 A10
Ullits DK 86 B4
Üllő H 150 C3
Ullsfjord N 111 A18
Ulm D 74 F6
Ulma RO 152 B6
Ulmbach D 74 B5
Ulme P 44 F4
Ulmen D 21 D7
Ulmeni RO 151 C11
Ulmeni RO 161 C9
Ulmeni RO 161 E9
Ulmi RO 161 D6
Ulmu RO 161 D10
Ulmu RO 161 E9
Ulog BIH 157 F9
Uløybukta N 112 D6
Ulricehamn S 91 D13
Ulrichsberg A 76 E5
Ulrichstein D 21 C12
Ulrika S 92 C6
Ulriksberg S 97 B12
Ulriksfors S 106 D9
Ulrum NL 16 B6
Ulsberg N 101 A11
Ulsta GB 3 D14
Ulsted DK 86 A6
Ulsteinvik N 100 B3
Ulstrup DK 86 C5
Ulstrup DK 87 D7
Ulsvåg N 111 D10
Ultrå S 107 E16
Uluabat TR 173 D9
Ulucak TR 177 B9
Ulucak TR 177 C9
Ulukonak TR 181 A7
Ulvåker S 91 C14
Ulvenhout NL 16 E3
Ulverston GB 10 C5
Ulvik N 100 E5
Ulvila FIN 126 C6
Ulvöhamn S 107 E15
Ulvsjön S 102 C7
Ulvsjön S 103 B11
Ulvvik S 103 A14
Ul'yanovka UA 154 A6
Ul'yanovo RUS 136 D5
Umag HR 67 B8
Umberleigh GB 12 D7
Umbertide I 66 F5
Umbrăreşti RO 153 F10
Umbriatico I 61 E7
Umbukta N 108 D8
Umčari SRB 158 D6
Umeå S 122 C4
Umfors S 108 E9
Umgransele S 107 B14
Umhausen A 71 C11
Umin Dol NMK 164 E4
Umka SRB 158 D5
Umkirch D 27 D8
Umljanović HR 156 E5
Ummeljoki FIN 128 D6
Ummern D 79 A7
Umnäs S 109 F11
Ümraniye TR 173 B11
Umurbey TR 172 D6
Umurga LV 135 A9
Uña E 47 D9
Uña de Quintana E 39 D7

Unaja FIN 126 C6
Únanov CZ 77 E10
Unapool GB 2 J6
Unari FIN 117 D15
Unbyn S 118 C7
Uncastillo E 32 F3
Undenäs S 92 B4
Undereidet N 112 D9
Underfossen N 113 C18
Undersåker S 105 E14
Undingen D 27 D11
Undløse DK 87 D9
Undva EST 130 D3
Undy GB 13 B9
Unelanperä FIN 120 F9
Ungerhausen D 71 A10
Ungheni MD 153 C11
Ungheni RO 152 E4
Ungheni RO 160 E5
Ungra RO 152 F6
Unguraș RO 152 C4
Ungureni RO 153 B9
Ungureni RO 153 D10
Ungurpils LV 131 F9
Unhais da Serra P 44 D5
Unhais-o-Velho P 44 D5
Unhošť CZ 76 B6
Uničov CZ 77 C12
Uniejów PL 142 C6
Unieux F 30 E5
Unín SK 146 D4
Unirea RO 152 E3
Unirea RO 155 C1
Unirea RO 155 F3
Unirea RO 159 B10
Unirea RO 159 E11
Unirea RO 161 E11
Unisław PL 138 D5
Unkel D 21 C8
Unken A 73 A6
Unlingen D 71 A9
Unna D 17 E9
Unnaryd S 87 B13
Unnau D 185 C8
Unntorp S 102 D7
Unset N 101 C14
Unsholtet N 101 A14
Unstad N 110 D6
Untamala FIN 122 D9
Untamala FIN 126 D6
Unțeni RO 153 B9
Unterägeri CH 27 F10
Unterammergau D 71 B12
Unterdießen D 71 B11
Untergriesbach D 76 E5
Unterhaching D 75 F10
Unterkulm CH 27 F9
Unterlüß D 83 E8
Untermaßfeld D 75 A7
Untermerzbach D 75 B8
Untermünkheim D 74 D6
Unterneukirchen D 75 F12
Unterpleichfeld D 75 C7
Unterreit D 75 F11
Unterschächen CH 71 D7
Unterschleißheim D 75 F10
Untersiemau D 75 B8
Untersteinach D 75 B10
Unterweißenbach A 77 F7
Unterwössen D 72 A5
Unverre F 24 D5
Upavon GB 13 C11
Upenieki LV 134 C5
Upenieki LV 135 D12
Upesgrīva LV 134 B6
Upgant-Schott D 17 A8
Úpice CZ 77 A10
Upinniemi FIN 127 E11
Uplyme GB 13 D9
Upninkai LT 137 C10
Upper Knockando GB 3 L10
Upperlands GB 4 F3
Upphärad S 91 C11
Uppingham GB 11 F10
Upplanda S 99 B9
Upplands-Väsby S 99 C9
Uppsala S 99 C9
Uppsälje S 97 A11
Uppsete N 100 E5
Uppsjö S 103 C12
Upton upon Severn GB 13 A10
Upyna LT 134 E5
Upyna LT 134 F4
Upytė LT 135 E8
Urafirth GB 3 E14
Urago d'Oglio I 69 B8
Uraiújfalu H 149 B7
Uras I 64 D2
Ura Vajgurore AL 168 C2
Uraz PL 81 D11
Urbach D 21 C9
Urbania I 66 E6
Urbar D 185 D8
Urbe I 37 C9
Urberach D 187 B6
Urbino I 66 E6
Urbisaglia I 67 F7
Urbise F 30 C4
Určice CZ 77 D12
Urda E 46 F5
Urdari RO 160 D2
Urdax-Urdazuli E 32 D2
Urdorf CH 27 F9
Urdos F 32 E4
Urduña E 40 C6
Ure N 110 D6
Urecheni RO 153 C9
Urechești RO 153 E10
Urechești RO 161 B10
Urë e Shtrenjtë AL 163 E8
Urepel F 32 D3
Ureterp NL 16 B6
Urga LV 131 F9
Úrhida H 149 B10
Úri H 150 C4
Uri I 64 B2
Uricani RO 159 C11
Uriménil F 26 D5
Uringe S 93 A11
Uriu RO 152 C4
Urjala FIN 127 C10
Urk NL 16 C5
Ürkmez TR 177 C8
Úrkút H 149 B9
Urla TR 177 C8
Urlați RO 161 D8
Urlingford IRL 9 C7
Urmeniș RO 152 D4
Urmince SK 146 D6
Urnäsch CH 27 F11
Urnieta E 32 D2
Üröm H 150 B3
Urovica SRB 159 E9
Urrea de Gaén E 42 E3
Urrea de Jalón E 41 E9
Urretxu E 32 D1
Urriés E 32 E3
Urros P 45 B6
Urroz E 32 E3
Urrugne F 32 D2
Ursberg D 71 A10
Ursensollen D 75 D10
Urshult S 89 B7
Ursviken S 118 E6
Urszulin PL 141 H8
Urt F 32 D3
Urtenen CH 31 A11
Urtimjaur S 116 E5
Urueña E 39 E9
Ururi I 63 D8
Urville Nacqueville F 23 A8
Urzędów PL 144 B5
Urzica RO 160 F4
Urziceni RO 151 B9
Urziceni RO 161 D9
Urzicuța RO 160 E3
Urzulei I 64 C4
Urzy F 30 A3
Usagre E 51 C7
Ušari BIH 157 C7
Ušće SRB 163 C10
Uschlag (Staufenberg) D 78 D6
Uście Gorlickie PL 145 D3
Uście Solne PL 143 F10
Uscio I 37 C10
Usedom D 84 C5
Usellus I 64 D2
Useras E 48 D4
Ushachy BY 133 F5
Uši LV 130 F5
Usingen D 21 D11
Usini I 64 B2
Usk GB 13 B9
Uskali FIN 125 F14
Uskedal N 94 C3
Üsküdar TR 173 B11
Üsküp TR 167 F8
Uslar D 78 C6
Usma LV 134 B4
Úsov CZ 77 C12
Uspenivka UA 154 E5
Usquert NL 17 B7
Ussana I 64 E3
Ussassai I 64 D3
Usseglio I 31 E11
Ussel F 29 D10
Ussel F 30 E2
Usson-du-Poitou F 29 C7
Usson-en-Forez F 30 E4
Ustaoset N 95 B8
Ustaritz F 32 D3
Ust'-Chorna UA 145 G8
Ust'-Dolyssy RUS 133 D7
Úštěk CZ 80 E6
Uster CH 27 F10
Ustibar BIH 163 B7
Ustica I 58 B3
Ustikolina BIH 157 E10
Ústí nad Labem CZ 80 E6
Ústí nad Orlicí CZ 77 C10
Ustiprača BIH 157 E11
Ustirama BIH 157 E8
Ustka PL 85 A11
Ust'-Luga RUS 132 B3
Ustou F 33 E8
Ustovo BG 171 A7
Ustrem BG 167 E6
Ustroń PL 147 B7
Ustronie Morskie PL 85 B9
Ustrzyki Dolne PL 145 E6
Ustya UA 154 A5
Ustyluh UA 144 B9
Usurbil E 32 D1
Uszew PL 144 D2
Uszód H 149 C11
Utajärvi FIN 119 E16
Utåker N 94 C3
Utakleiv N 110 D6
Utanede S 103 A12
Utanen FIN 119 E16
Utansjö S 103 A14
Utanskog S 107 E14
Utarp D 17 A8
Utbjoa N 94 C3
Utebo E 41 E10
Utelle F 37 D6
Utena LT 135 F11
Utersum D 82 A4
Uthaug N 104 D7
Uthleben D 79 D8
Uthlede D 17 B11
Utiel E 47 E10
Utne N 94 B5
Utö S 93 B12
Utoropy UA 152 A6
Utrecht NL 16 D4
Utrera E 51 E8
Utrillas E 42 F2
Utrine SRB 150 F4
Utro N 104 C8
Utsjoki FIN 113 D18
Utskor N 110 C8
Uttendorf A 72 B6
Uttendorf A 76 F4
Uttenweiler D 71 A9
Utterbyn S 97 B9
Utterliden S 109 F17
Uttersberg S 97 C14
Uttersjö S 107 D14
Utterslev DK 87 F8
Utti FIN 128 D6
Utting am Ammersee D 71 A12
Uttoxeter GB 11 F8
Utula FIN 129 C9
Utvalnäs S 103 E13
Utvik N 100 C5
Utvorda N 105 B9
Utzedel D 84 C4
Uuemõisa EST 130 D7
Uukuniemi FIN 129 B13
Uulu EST 131 E9
Uura FIN 121 F10
Uurainen FIN 123 E14
Uuro FIN 122 F8
Uusikaarlepyy FIN 122 C9
Uusikartano FIN 126 D7
Uusikaupunki FIN 126 D5
Uusikylä FIN 123 D12
Uusikylä FIN 127 D15
Uusi-Värtsilä FIN 125 F14
Uva FIN 121 E11
Uvac BIH 158 F4
Uvåg N 110 C8
Úvaly CZ 77 B7
Uvanå S 97 B10
Uvdal N 95 B9
Üvecik TR 171 E10
Uvernet-Fours F 36 C5
Uv'jarátto N 113 D12
Uxbridge GB 15 D8
Uxeau F 30 B5
Üxheim D 21 D7
Uyeasound GB 3 D15
Uza F 32 B3
Užava LV 134 B2
Uzdin SRB 158 C6
Uzel F 22 D6
Uzer F 35 A7
Uzerche F 29 E9
Uzès F 35 B7
Uzhhorod UA 145 F5
Uzhok UA 145 F6
Užice SRB 158 F4
Uzlovoye RUS 136 D5
Uznovë AL 168 C2
Užpaliai LT 135 E11
Uzrechcha BY 133 F3
Uzundzhovo BG 166 F5
Uzunköprü TR 172 B6
Uzunkuyu TR 177 C8
Užventis LT 134 E5

V

Vaadinselkä FIN 115 E5
Vaajakoski FIN 123 F15
Vaajasalmi FIN 124 E7
Vääkiö FIN 121 D12
Vaala FIN 119 E17
Vaalajärvi FIN 117 D16
Vaale D 82 C6
Vaalimaa FIN 128 D8
Vaals NL 20 C6
Vaarakylä FIN 121 C11
Vaarankylä FIN 121 F10
Vaaranniva FIN 121 D11
Vaaraperä FIN 121 C13
Vaaraslahti FIN 123 D17
Väärinmaja FIN 124 G2
Vaas F 24 E3
Vaasa FIN 122 D7
Vaassen NL 16 D5
Väätäiskylä FIN 123 E13
Väätsa EST 131 D10
Vaattojärvi FIN 117 D12
Vabalninkas LT 135 E9
Vabole LV 135 D12
Vabre F 33 C10
Vabres-l'Abbaye F 34 C4
Vác H 150 B3
Văcărești RO 161 D6
Vaccarizzo Albanese I 61 D6
Váchartyán H 150 B3
Vacheresse F 31 C10
Vachlia GR 174 D4
Väckelsång S 89 B7
Vacov CZ 76 D5
Vacqueyras F 35 B8
Vácrátót H 150 B3
Văculești RO 153 B8
Vad RO 152 C3
Vad S 97 B14
Vadakste LV 134 D5
Vadaktai LT 135 E7
Vădastra RO 160 F4
Vădăstrița RO 160 F4
Vaddas gruver N 112 D8
Vădeni RO 155 C1
Väderstad S 92 C5
Vad Foss N 90 B5
Vadheim N 100 D3
Vadla N 94 D4
Vadocondes E 40 E4
Vadokliai LT 135 F8
Vado Ligure I 37 C8
Vadskinn N 111 C11
Vadsø N 114 C7
Vadstena S 92 C5
Vadu Crișului RO 151 D10
Vadu lui Isac MD 155 B2
Vadu Izei RO 145 H8
Vadul lui Vodă MD 154 C4
Vadul Turcului MD 154 B3
Vadum DK 86 A5
Vadu Moldovei RO 153 C8
Vadu Moților RO 151 E10
Vadu Pașii RO 161 C9
Vaduz FL 71 C9
Vadžgirys LT 134 F5
Væggerløse DK 83 A11
Vafaika GR 171 B7
Vafiochori GR 169 B8
Våg N 94 D2
Vågaholmen N 108 C5
Vågåmo N 101 C10
Vagan BIH 157 D6
Vågan N 111 B14
Vågdalen S 106 D9
Våge N 94 B3
Våge N 94 C6
Vaggatem N 114 E6
Vaggeryd S 92 E4
Vågholmane N 100 A4
Vagia GR 175 C7
Văgiulești RO 159 D11
Vaglia I 66 E3
Vaglio Basilicata I 60 B5
Vagli Sotto I 66 D1
Vagney F 26 D6
Vagnhärad S 93 B11
Vagnsunda S 99 C11
Vagos P 44 C3
Vågseidet N 100 E2
Vägsele S 107 B14
Vågsodden N 108 E3
Vágur FO 2 C3
Vähäjoki FIN 119 B14
Vähäkangas FIN 123 B13
Vähäkyrö FIN 122 D8
Vähäniva FIN 116 B9
Vahanka FIN 123 E13
Vahastu EST 131 D10
Vahenurme EST 131 D8
Vähikkälä FIN 127 D12
Vahojärvi FIN 127 B9
Váhovce SK 146 E5
Vahterpää FIN 127 E15
Vahto FIN 126 D7
Vaiamonte P 44 F6
Vaiano I 66 E3
Vaickūniškės LT 137 D10
Vaida EST 131 C9
Vaidava LV 135 B10
Vaideeni RO 160 C3
Vaidotai LT 137 D11
Vaiges F 23 D11
Vaiguva LT 134 E5
Väike-Maarja EST 131 C12
Väike-Pungerja EST 131 C14
Vaikijaur S 116 E3
Vaikko FIN 125 D11
Vailly-sur-Aisne F 19 F8
Vailly-sur-Sauldre F 25 F8
Vaimastvere EST 131 D12
Väimela EST 131 F14
Vaimõisa EST 131 D8
Vainikkala FIN 129 D9
Vaiņode LV 134 D3
Vainotiškiai LT 134 F7
Vainupea EST 131 B12
Vairano Patenora I 60 A2
Vairano Scalo I 60 A2
Väisälä FIN 121 E11
Vaison-la-Romaine F 35 B9
Vaïssac F 33 B9
Vaišvydava LT 137 D9
Vaivio FIN 125 E12
Vaivre-et-Montoille F 26 E5
Vaja H 145 H5
Vajangu EST 131 C12
Vajdácska H 145 G4
Våje N 90 B4
Våje N 110 D5
Vajkal AL 168 A3
Vajmat S 109 C18
Vajska SRB 157 B11
Vajszló H 149 E9
Vajta H 149 C11
Vakarel BG 165 D8
Vakern S 97 B11
Vakıflar TR 173 B8
Vaklino BG 155 F2
Vaksdal N 94 B3
Vaksevo BG 165 E6
Vaksince NMK 164 E4
Vál H 149 B11
Valada P 44 F3
Vålådalen S 105 E13
Valadares P 38 D3
Valajanaapa FIN 119 C15
Valajaskoski FIN 119 B14
Valaliky SK 145 F3
Valand N 90 C2
Valandovo NMK 169 B8
Vålånger S 103 A14
Valanida GR 169 E7
Valanjou F 23 F10
Valareña E 41 D9
Vålåsjø N 101 B10
Valaská SK 147 D9
Valaská Belá SK 146 D6
Valašská Bystřice CZ 146 C6
Valašská Polanka CZ 146 C5
Valašské Klobouky CZ 146 C6
Valašské Meziříčí CZ 146 C5
Välax FIN 127 E14
Valberg F 36 C5
Valberg N 110 D6
Vålberg S 97 D9
Valbiska HR 67 B9
Valbo S 103 E13
Valbom P 44 B3
Valbona E 48 D3
Valbondione I 69 A9
Valbonë AL 163 E8
Valbonnais F 31 F8
Valbonne F 36 D6
Valbuena de Duero E 40 E3
Valča SK 147 C7
Valcabrère F 33 D7
Valcău de Jos RO 151 C10
Vâlcele RO 153 F7
Vâlcele RO 160 E5
Vâlcelele RO 161 C10
Vâlcelele RO 161 E10
Valdagno I 69 B11
Valdahon F 26 F5
Valdaora I 72 C5
Valddak N 113 C14
Valdealgorfa E 42 E3
Valdeblore F 37 C6
Valdecaballeros E 45 F10
Valdecañas de Tajo E 45 E9
Valdecarros E 45 C10
Valdecilla E 40 B4
Valdecuenca E 47 D10
Valdefuentes E 45 F8
Valdeganga E 47 F9
Valdekļi LV 134 C5
Valdelacasa E 45 C9
Valdelacasa de Tajo E 45 E10
Valdelamusa E 51 D6
Valdelinares E 48 D3
Valdemanco del Esteras E 54 B3
Valdemārpils LV 134 B5
Valdemarsvik S 93 C9
Valdemeca E 47 D9
Valdemorillo E 46 C4
Valdemoro E 46 D5
Valdemoro-Sierra E 47 D9
Valdenoches E 47 C6
Valdeobispo E 45 D8
Valdeolivas E 47 C8
Valdepeñas E 55 B6
Valdepeñas de Jaén E 53 A9
Valderas E 39 D9
Val-de-Reuil F 18 F3
Valderice I 58 C2
Valderiès F 33 B10
Valderøy N 100 A4
Valderrobres E 42 F4
Val de Santo Domingo E 46 D4
Valdestillas E 39 F10
Valdetormo E 42 F4
Valdetorres E 51 B7
Valdeverdeja E 45 E10
Valdevimbre E 39 D8
Valdgale LV 134 B5
Valdice CZ 77 B8
Valdidentro I 71 E10
Valdilecha E 47 D6
Val-d'Isère F 31 E10
Valdisotto I 71 E10
Valdivienne F 29 B7
Val-d'Izé F 23 D9
Valdobbiadene I 72 E4
Valdoie F 27 E6
Valdunquillo E 39 D9
Vale GBG 22 B6
Vale N 95 D12
Våle S 103 A8
Valea Adîncă MD 154 A3
Valea Argovei RO 161 E9
Valea Călugărească RO 161 D8
Valea Chioarului RO 151 C11
Valea Ciorii RO 161 D11
Valea Crișului RO 153 F7
Valea Danului RO 160 C5
Valea Doftanei RO 161 C7
Valea Dragului RO 161 E8
Valea Ierii RO 151 D11
Valea Largă RO 152 D4
Valea lui Mihai RO 151 B9
Valea Lungă RO 152 E4
Valea Lungă RO 161 C7
Valea Măcrișului RO 161 D9
Valea Mare MD 153 C11
Valea Mare RO 160 D3
Valea Mare RO 160 D6
Valea Mare RO 160 E4
Valea Mare-Pravăț RO 160 C6
Valea Mărului RO 153 F11
Valea Moldovei RO 153 C8
Valea Nucarilor RO 155 C3
Valea Râmnicului RO 161 C10
Valea Salciei RO 161 C9
Valea Sării RO 153 F9
Valea Seacă RO 153 C9
Valea Seacă RO 153 E10
Valea Stanciului RO 160 F3
Valea Teilor RO 155 C3
Valea Ursului RO 153 D10
Valea Viilor RO 152 E4
Valea Vinului RO 151 B11
Vale da Rosa P 50 E4
Vale das Mós P 44 F4
Vale de Açor P 44 F5
Vale de Açor P 50 D4
Vale de Cambra P 44 C4
Vale de Cavalos P 44 F3
Vale de Espinho P 45 D7
Vale de Estrela P 45 C6
Vale de Figueira P 44 F3
Vale de Lobo P 50 E3
Vale de Prazeres P 44 D6
Vale de Reis P 50 C3
Vale de Salgueiro P 38 E5
Vale de Santarém P 44 F3
Vale do Peso P 44 F5
Válega P 44 C3
Valeggio sul Mincio I 66 B2
Valen N 94 C3
Valença P 38 D2
Valença do Douro P 44 B5
Valençay F 24 F6
Valence F 30 F6
Valence F 33 B7
Valence-d'Albigeois F 33 B10
Valence-sur-Baïse F 33 C6
Valencia E 48 F4
Valencia de Alcántara E 45 F6
Valencia de Don Juan E 39 D8
Valencia de las Torres E 51 C7
Valencia del Mombuey E 51 C5
Valencia del Ventoso E 51 C7
Valenciennes F 19 D8
Văleni RO 153 D11
Văleni RO 160 E5
Vălenii de Munte RO 161 C8
Valensole F 35 C10
Valentano I 62 B1
Valentigney F 27 F6
Valenza I 37 A9
Valenzano I 61 A7
Valenzuela E 53 A8
Valenzuela de Calatrava E 54 B5
Våler N 95 D13
Våler N 101 E15
Valera de Arriba E 47 E8
Valernes F 35 B10
Vales Mortos P 50 D5
Valestrand N 94 A2
Valevåg N 94 C2
Valfabbrica I 66 F6
Valfarta E 42 D3
Valfroicourt F 26 D5
Valfurva I 71 E10
Valga EST 131 F12
Valgalciems LV 134 B5
Valgale LV 134 B4
Valgrisenche I 31 D11
Valgu EST 131 D9
Valguarnera Caropepe I 58 E5
Valgunde LV 134 C7
Valhelhas P 44 D6
Valhermoso E 47 C9
Vålhovd N 101 E12
Välijoki FIN 119 B15
Välikangas FIN 119 B16
Väli-Kannus FIN 123 C11
Valikardhë AL 168 A3
Välikylä FIN 123 C11
Valimi GR 174 C5
Välitalo FIN 117 C16
Văliug RO 159 C9
Väli-Viirre FIN 123 C11
Valjala EST 130 E5
Valjevo SRB 158 E4
Valjok N 113 D16
Valjunquera E 42 F4
Valka LV 131 F12
Valkeajärvi FIN 123 F12
Valkeakoski FIN 127 C11
Valkeakoski S 117 E11
Valkeala FIN 128 D6
Valkeiskylä FIN 124 C8
Valkeiskylä FIN 125 D10
Valkenburg NL 19 C12
Valkenswaard NL 16 F4
Valkininkai LT 137 E10
Valkla EST 131 C10
Valko FIN 127 E15
Valkó H 150 B4
Valla S 93 A8
Valla S 107 E10
Valladolid E 39 E10
Valladolises E 56 F2
Vállaj H 151 B9
Vallåkra S 87 D11
Vallargärdet S 97 D10
Vallata I 60 A4
Vallauris F 36 D6
Vallberga S 87 C12
Vallbo S 105 E14
Vallbona d'Anoia E 43 D7
Vallda S 91 E10
Valldal N 100 B6
Vall d'Alba E 48 D4
Valldemossa E 49 E10
Valle E 40 B3
Valle LV 135 C9
Valle N 90 A2
Valle N 90 B6
Valle N 110 D9
Valle Castellana I 62 B5
Vallecorsa I 62 E4
Valle de Abdalajís E 53 C7
Valle de la Serena E 51 B8
Valle de Matamoros E 51 C6
Valle de Santa Ana E 51 C6
Valle di Cadore I 72 D5
Valledolmo I 58 D4
Valledoria I 64 B2
Valleiry F 31 C8
Vallelunga Pratameno I 58 D4
Valle Mosso I 68 B5
Vallen S 107 D11
Vallen S 118 F6
Vallenca E 47 D10
Vallendar D 185 D8
Vallentuna S 99 C10
Vallerås S 102 E6
Valleraugue F 35 B6
Vallermosa I 64 E2
Vallerotonda I 62 D5
Vallersund N 104 D7
Vallervatnet N 105 B15
Vallet F 23 F9
Valley D 72 A4
Valley GB 10 E2
Vallfogona de Riucorb E 42 D6
Vallières F 29 D10
Vallioniemi FIN 121 B12
Vallmoll E 42 E6
Valløby DK 87 E10
Vallo della Lucania I 60 C4
Vallo di Nera I 62 B3
Valloire F 31 E9
Vallombrosa I 66 E4
Vallon-en-Sully F 29 B11
Vallon-Pont-d'Arc F 35 B7
Vallorbe CH 31 B9
Vallorcine F 31 C10
Vallouise F 31 F9
Vallrun S 105 D16
Valls E 42 E6
Vallsbo S 103 E12
Vallsjön S 103 A11
Vallsta S 103 C11
Vallstena S 93 D13
Vallvik S 103 D13
Valmadrera I 69 B7
Valmadrid E 41 F10
Valmen N 101 D15
Valmiera LV 131 F10
Valmiermuiža LV 131 F10
Valmojado E 46 D4
Valmont F 18 E2
Valmontone I 62 D3
Valmorel F 31 E9
Valmy F 25 B12
Valnes N 108 B7
Valognes F 23 A9
Valongo P 44 B4
Valongo P 44 F5
Válor E 55 F6
Valoria la Buena E 40 E2
Valøy N 105 B9
Valøy N 105 C11
Valpaços P 38 E5
Valpalmas E 41 D10
Valpelline I 31 D11
Valperga I 68 C4
Valpovo HR 149 E10
Valpperi FIN 126 D7
Valras-Plage F 34 D5
Valréas F 35 B8
Valros F 34 D5
Vals CH 71 D8
Valsavarenche I 31 D11
Vålse DK 87 F9
Valseca E 46 B4
Valsequillo E 51 C9
Valsgård DK 86 B5
Valsgarth GB 3 D15
Valshed S 103 E9
Valsinni I 61 C6
Valsjöbyn S 105 C16
Valsjön S 103 B11
Valška SRB 158 E6
Valskog S 97 D14
Vals-les-Bains F 35 A7
Valsøybotn N 104 E5
Välsta S 103 C13
Valstagna I 72 E4
Val-Suzon F 26 F2
Valtablado del Río E 47 C8
Valtero GR 169 B9
Valtesiniko GR 174 D5
Valtice CZ 77 E11
Valtiendas E 40 F4
Valtierra E 41 D8
Valtimo FIN 125 C11
Valtola FIN 128 C7
Valtopina I 62 A3
Valtos GR 171 A10
Valtotopi GR 169 C10
Valtournenche I 68 B4
Valtura HR 67 C8
Valu lui Traian RO 155 E2
Valun HR 67 C9
Väluste EST 131 E11
Valverde de Burguillos E 51 C6
Valverde de Júcar E 47 E8
Valverde de la Virgen E 39 C8
Valverde del Camino E 51 D6
Valverde de Leganés E 51 B6
Valverde del Fresno E 45 D7
Valverde de Llerena E 51 C8
Valverde del Majano E 46 C4
Valverde de Mérida E 51 B7
Valvika N 108 B8
Valvträsk S 118 B7
Valyra GR 174 E4
Vama RO 145 H7
Vama RO 153 B7
Vama Buzăului RO 161 B7
Vamberk CZ 77 B10
Vamdrup DK 86 E4
Våmhus S 102 D7
Vamlingbo S 93 F12
Vammala FIN 127 C8
Vammen DK 86 B5
Vamos GR 178 E7
Vámosmikola H 147 F7
Vámospércs H 151 B8
Vámosújfalu H 145 G3
Vampula FIN 126 C8
Vamvakofyto GR 169 B9
Vamvakou GR 169 F7
Vanaja FIN 127 D12
Vana-Koiola EST 131 F14
Vânători RO 152 E5
Vânători RO 153 C9
Vânători RO 153 F10
Vânători RO 155 B2
Vânători RO 159 E10
Vânătorii Mici RO 161 E7
Vânători-Neamț RO 153 C8
Vanault-les-Dames F 25 C12
Vana-Vigala EST 131 D8
Vana-Võidu EST 131 E11
Váncsod H 151 C8
Vanda FIN 127 E12
Vandel DK 86 D4
Vandellós E 42 E5
Vandenesse F 30 B4
Vandenesse-en-Auxois F 25 F12
Vandœuvre-lès-Nancy F 186 D1
Vandoies I 72 C4
Vändra EST 131 D10
Vändträsk S 118 C6
Vandzene LV 134 B5
Vandžiogala LT 135 F7
Vāne LV 134 C5
Väne-Åsaka S 91 C11
Vänersborg S 91 C11
Vañes E 40 C3
Vang N 101 D9
Vånga S 92 B7
Vangaži LV 135 B9
Vänge S 93 E13
Vängel S 107 D10
Vangshamn N 111 B15
Vangshylla N 105 D10
Vangsnes N 100 D5
Vangsvik N 111 B14
Vanha-Kihlanki FIN 117 C10
Vanhakylä FIN 122 F7
Vänjaurbäck S 107 C15
Vänjaurträsk S 107 C15
Vânjuleț RO 159 E10
Vânju Mare RO 159 E10
Vannareid N 112 C4
Vännäs S 122 C3
Vännäsberget S 118 B9
Vännäsby S 122 C3
Vannavalen N 112 C4
Vånne N 90 B2
Vannes F 22 E6
Vannvåg N 112 C4
Vannvikan N 104 D8
Vänö FIN 126 F7
Vansbro S 97 A11
Vanse N 94 F5
Vänsjö S 103 C9
Vantaa FIN 127 E12
Vanttausjärvi FIN 119 B17
Vanttauskoski FIN 119 B17
Vanvey F 25 E12
Vanyarc H 147 F8
Vanzone I 68 B5
Vaour F 33 B9
Vápenná CZ 77 B12
Vaplan S 105 E16
Vaqueiros P 50 E4
Vara EST 131 D13
Vara S 91 C12
Vara del Rey E 47 F8
Varades F 23 F9
Vărădia RO 159 C8
Vărădia de Mureș RO 151 E9
Varages F 35 C10
Varaire F 33 B9
Varajärvi FIN 119 B13
Varajoki FIN 121 F14
Varakļāni LV 135 C13
Varallo I 68 B5
Varangerbotn N 114 C5
Varano de'Melegari I 69 D8
Varapayeva BY 133 F2
Varapodio I 59 C8
Vărăști RO 161 E8
Vărătec RO 153 C8
Varaždin HR 149 D6
Varaždinske Toplice HR 149 D6
Varazze I 37 C9
Varberg S 87 A10
Vărbilău RO 161 C7
Varbla EST 130 E7
Varbó H 145 G2
Varbola EST 131 C8
Varces-Allières-et-Risset F 31 E8
Vârciorog RO 151 D9
Varda GR 174 C3
Vardali GR 174 A5
Varde DK 86 D2
Vardim BG 161 F6
Vardište BIH 158 F3
Vårdö FIN 99 B14
Vardø N 114 C10
Várdomb H 149 D11
Varejoki FIN 119 B13
Varekil S 91 D10
Varel D 17 B10
Varėna LT 137 E10
Varengeville-sur-Mer F 18 E2
Varenna I 69 A7
Varennes-en-Argonne F 19 F11
Varennes-St-Sauveur F 31 C7
Varennes-sur-Allier F 30 C3
Varennes-Vauzelles F 30 A3
Vareš BIH 157 D9
Varese I 69 B6
Varese Ligure I 37 C11
Varetz F 29 E8
Vârfu Câmpului RO 153 B8
Vârfuri RO 161 C7
Vârfurile RO 151 E10
Vårgårda S 91 C12
Vărgata RO 152 D5
Vârghiș RO 153 E7
Vargön S 91 C11
Vargträsk S 107 C15
Varhaug N 94 E3
Vari GR 175 D8
Vari GR 176 E4
Variaș RO 151 E6
Varik NL 183 B6
Variku EST 130 C7
Varilhes F 33 D9
Varimbombi GR 175 C8
Varín SK 147 C7
Väring S 91 B14
Variņi LV 135 B12
Variskylä FIN 121 F9
Varislahti FIN 125 E11
Varistaipale FIN 125 E11
Varjakka FIN 119 E14
Varjisträsk S 109 D18
Varkaliai LT 134 E3
Varkaus FIN 125 F9
Varkava LV 135 D13
Varkhi BY 133 E7
Vârlezi RO 153 F11
Varlosen (Niemetal) D 78 D6
Vārme LV 134 C4
Värmlandsbro S 91 A13
Varna BG 167 C9
Varna I 72 C4
Varna SRB 158 D4
Värnamo S 88 A6
Värnäs S 97 B9
Varnavas GR 175 C8
Varnhem S 91 C14
Varniai LT 134 E4
Varnja EST 131 E14
Varnsdorf CZ 81 E7
Varntresken N 108 E7
Varnyany BY 137 D13
Väröbacka S 87 A10

Varonichy BY 133 F5
Varonka BY 133 F2
Városföld H 150 D4
Varoška Rijeka BIH 156 B5
Városlőd H 149 B9
Varpaisjärvi FIN 124 D9
Várpalota H 149 B10
Varpanen FIN 128 C6
Varparanta FIN 125 G11
Varpasalo FIN 125 F12
Varpsjö S 107 C11
Varpuselkä FIN 115 E5
Varpuvaara FIN 115 E4
Värriö FIN 115 D3
Varrio FIN 115 E2
Vars F 29 D6
Vars F 36 B5
Vârşand RO 151 D7
Varsány H 147 E8
Värsås S 91 C15
Varsi I 69 D8
Värska EST 132 F2
Vârşolţ RO 151 C10
Varsseveld NL 17 E6
Värst DK 86 B6
Vårsta S 93 A11
Varstu EST 131 F13
Varteig N 95 D14
Vartemyagi RUS 129 E13
Vârteşcoiu RO 153 F10
Vartholomio GR 174 D3
Vartius FIN 121 E14
Vârtoape RO 160 E6
Vartofta S 91 C14
Vârtop RO 160 E2
Värtsilä FIN 125 F15
Varuträsk S 118 E5
Varvara BG 165 E9
Varvara BG 167 E9
Varvara GR 169 C10
Varvarin SRB 159 F7
Varvasaina GR 174 D4
Värve LV 134 B3
Varvikko FIN 115 E4
Várvölgy H 149 C8
Vârvoru de Jos RO 160 E3
Varyazh UA 144 B9
Vărzăreşti MD 154 C2
Varzi I 37 B10
Varzo I 68 A5
Varzy F 25 F9
Vasa FIN 122 D7
Vasalemma EST 131 C8
Vasanello I 62 C2
Vasaniemi FIN 115 D2
Vasankari FIN 119 F11
Vasaraperä FIN 121 B12
Vásárosdombó H 149 D10
Vásárosnamény H 145 G5
Vaşcău RO 151 E10
Väse S 97 D10
Vashkivtsi UA 153 A7
Vashtëmi AL 168 C4
Vasilaţi RO 161 E8
Vasilika GR 169 D9
Vasilika GR 177 A7
Vasiliki GR 174 B2
Vasiliko GR 175 C8
Vasilikos GR 174 D2
Vasilis GR 169 F7
Vasilitsi GR 178 B2
Vasil Kolarov BG 165 F10
Vasil Levski BG 166 E5
Vasilopoulo GR 174 B3
Vasilovtsi BG 159 F11
Vasil'yevo RUS 132 F2
Vaškai LT 135 D8
Vaski LV 134 C6
Vaškiai LT 134 E2
Väskinde S 93 D12
Vaskio FIN 127 E9
Vaskivesi FIN 123 F11
Vasknarva EST 132 C2
Vaskút H 150 E2
Vaskuu FIN 123 F11
Vasles F 28 B5
Vaslui RO 153 D11
Vasmegyer H 145 G4
Vassaras GR 175 E6
Vassbo S 102 C4
Vassbotn N 111 C13
Vassbygdi N 100 E6
Vassdalen N 111 C14
Vassdalsvik N 108 C6
Vassenden N 100 D4
Vassieux-en-Vercors F 31 F7
Vassmolösa S 89 B10
Vassnäs S 105 D14
Vassor FIN 122 D8
Vasstrand N 111 A15
Vassy F 23 C10
Vasszécseny H 149 B7
Västana S 103 A12
Västanå S 103 B13
Västanå S 107 E16
Västanbäck S 107 D12
Västanfjärd FIN 126 E8
Västannäs S 118 B9
Västansjö S 103 A12
Västansjö S 103 C12
Västansjö S 107 A9
Västansjö S 107 C13
Västansjö S 107 E12
Västansjö S 108 E9
Västansjön S 103 B12
Västanvik S 103 E8
Vastemõisa EST 131 E10
Västerås S 98 C7
Västeråsen S 107 F11
Västerberg S 103 E12
Västerby S 97 B14
Västerbyn S 99 B10
Västerfärnebo S 98 C6
Västerhållan S 102 A5
Västerhaninge S 93 A12
Västerhejde S 93 D12
Västerhus S 107 E15
Västerlandsjö S 107 E15
Västerljung S 93 B10
Västermyckeläng S 102 D7
Västerottna S 97 C8
Västerträsjö S 103 C11
Västervik S 93 D9
Västilä FIN 127 B12
Vastinki FIN 123 E13
Västinniemi FIN 125 E10
Vasto I 63 C7
Vastorf D 83 D9
Västra Åmtervik S 97 C9
Västra Bodarna S 91 D11
Västra Eneby S 92 C7
Västra Fagelberget S 105 C17
Västra Harg S 92 C6
Västra Hjäggböle S 118 E5
Västra Husby S 93 C8
Västra Karup S 87 C11
Västra Kiilisjärvi S 119 B10
Västra Lainejaure S 107 A15
Västra Ormsjö S 107 C10
Västra Sjulsmark S 118 F5
Västra Stugusjö S 103 A9
Västra Tåsjö S 106 C9
Västra Torup S 87 C13
Västra Yttermark FIN 122 E6
Vastse-Kuuste EST 131 E13
Vastseliina EST 132 F1
Vasvár H 149 B7
Vasylivka UA 155 B3
Vasylivka UA 155 B4
Vaszar H 149 B9
Vatan F 29 A9
Vătava RO 152 D5
Väte S 93 E12
Vatera GR 177 A7
Vaterholmsbru N 105 D11
Vatero GR 169 D6
Vaterstetten D 75 F10
Vatheia GR 178 C3
Vathy GR 175 C8
Vathy GR 177 D8
Vathylakkos GR 169 C8
Vathylakkos GR 169 D6
Vathys GR 177 F9
Vati GR 181 D7
Vatican City E 62 D2
Vatici MD 154 C3
Vatjusjärvi FIN 123 B14
Vatla EST 130 D7
Vatland N 94 F6
Vatnahalsen N 100 E6
Vătnas S 103 C13
Vatne N 94 E3
Vatne N 100 A5
Vatolakkos GR 169 D5
Vatoussa GR 177 A7
Vatra Dornei RO 152 C6
Vatra Moldoviţei RO 153 B7
Vats N 101 E8
Vatta H 145 H2
Vattholma S 99 B9
Vattjom S 103 B13
Vattlång S 103 C13
Vattrång S 103 C13
Vattukylä FIN 119 F14
Vatula FIN 127 B8
Våtvoll N 111 C10
Vaubadon F 23 B10
Vaubecourt F 26 C3
Vauchassis F 25 D10
Vauclaix F 25 F10
Vauconcourt-Nervezain F 26 E4
Vaucouleurs F 26 C4
Vaudémont F 26 D5
Vaugneray F 30 D6
Vauldalen N 101 A16
Vaulx-en-Velin F 30 D6
Vaulx-Milieu F 31 D7
Vauvenargues F 35 C10
Vauvert F 35 C7
Vauvillers F 26 E5
Vaux-le-Pénil F 25 C8
Vaux-sur-Mer F 28 D3
Vaux-sur-Sûre B 19 E12
Vavdos GR 169 D9
Växbo S 103 D12
Vaxholm S 99 D10
Växjö S 89 B7
Växtorp S 87 C12
Väylä FIN 113 E20
Väylänpää FIN 117 D11
Vayrac F 29 F9
Vayres F 29 D7
Väyrylä FIN 121 E10
Vaysal TR 167 F7
Väystäjä FIN 119 B12
Včelná CZ 77 E6
Veäskoonjarga FIN 113 F20
Veauche F 30 D5
Veavågen N 94 D2
Vebbestrup DK 86 B5
Veberöd S 87 D13
Veblungsnes N 100 A7
Vebomark S 118 F6
Vebron F 35 B6
Vecate LV 131 F10
Vecauce LV 134 D5
Vecbebri LV 135 C10
Vecchiano I 66 E1
Vechelde D 79 B7
Vechta D 17 C10
Vecinos E 45 C9
Veckerhagen (Reinhardshagen) D 78 D6
Veckrape LV 135 C10
Veclaicene LV 131 F14
Vecmikeļi LV 134 D6
Vecpiebalga LV 135 B11
Vecpils LV 134 C2
Vecsaikava LV 135 C12
Vecsalaca LV 131 F8
Vecsaule LV 135 D8
Vecsés H 150 C3
Vecskulte LV 135 B8
Vecslabada LV 133 D3
Vecumnieki LV 135 C9
Veda S 103 A14
Vedde DK 87 D9
Veddelev DK 87 D10
Veddige S 88 A2
Veddum DK 86 B6
Vēde LV 134 B3
Vedea RO 160 D5
Vedea RO 161 F7
Vedelago I 72 E5
Vedevåg S 97 C13
Vedjeön S 106 C8
Vedra E 38 C3
Védrines-St-Loup F 30 E3
Vedro Polje BIH 156 D5
Vedsted DK 86 E4
Vedum S 91 C13
Veendam NL 17 B7
Veenendaal NL 16 D5
Veenhusen D 17 B8
Veensgarth GB 3 E14
Veere NL 182 B3
Veerle B 182 C5
Veflinge DK 86 E6
Vegacervera E 39 C8
Vega de Espinareda E 39 C6
Vegadeo E 38 B5
Vega de Pas E 40 B4
Vega de Tirados E 45 B9
Vega de Valcarce E 39 C6
Vega de Valdetronco E 39 E9
Veganzones E 46 B5
Vegaquemada E 39 C9
Vegarienza E 39 C7
Vegarshei N 90 B4
Vegas del Condado E 39 C9
Vegas de Matute E 46 C4
Vegby S 91 D13
Végegyháza H 151 E6
Veggen N 111 D13
Vegger DK 86 B5
Veghel NL 16 E5
Veģi LV 134 B4
Veglie I 61 C9
Vegset N 105 C12
Vehkajärvi FIN 127 B12
Vehkalahti FIN 127 B15
Vehkalahti FIN 128 D7
Vehkataipale FIN 129 C9
Vehlow D 83 D12
Vehmaa FIN 126 D6
Vehmaa FIN 128 B8
Vehmasjärvi FIN 125 C9
Vehmersalmi FIN 125 E10
Vehniä FIN 123 F15
Vehu FIN 123 E12
Vehvilä FIN 124 E8
Veidholmen N 104 D3
Veidneset N 113 B18
Veigy-Foncenex F 31 C9
Veihtivaara FIN 121 E14
Veikkola FIN 127 E11
Veimo N 105 D11
Veinge S 87 B12
Veiros P 50 B4
Veisiejai LT 137 E8
Veitastrond N 100 D6
Veitsbronn D 75 C8
Veitsch A 148 A5
Veitservasa FIN 117 C13
Veiveriai LT 137 D8
Veivirženai LT 134 E3
Vejano I 62 C2
Vejby DK 87 C10
Vejbystrand S 87 C11
Vejen DK 86 E4
Vejer de la Frontera E 52 D5
Vejle DK 86 D5
Vejle DK 86 E6
Vejprnice CZ 76 C4
Vejrum DK 86 C5
Vejstrup DK 87 E7
Vekilski BG 161 F10
Vela RO 160 E2
Velagići BIH 157 C6
Vela Luka HR 162 D2
Velamazán E 41 F6
Velanda S 91 C11
Velanidia GR 178 C5
Veľaty SK 145 F4
Velaux F 35 C9
VelbastaŠur FO 2 B3
Velbert D 17 F8
Velburg D 75 D10
Velçë AL 168 D2
Veldegem B 182 C2
Velden D 75 F11
Velden NL 183 C8
Velden am Wörther See A 73 C9
Veldhoven NL 16 F4
Velefique E 55 E8
Velehrad CZ 146 C4
Velen D 17 E7
Velence H 149 B11
Velenje SLO 73 D11
Veles NMK 164 F4
Veleševec HR 148 E6
Velešín CZ 77 E6
Velešta NMK 168 B4
Velestino GR 169 F8
Vélez-Blanco E 55 D8
Vélez de Benaudalla E 53 C10
Vélez-Málaga E 53 C8
Vélez-Rubio E 55 D8
Velgast D 83 B13
Velika HR 149 F9
Velika Brijesnica BIH 157 C9
Velika Drenova SRB 159 F7
Velika Gorica HR 148 E6
Velika Greda SRB 159 C7
Velika Ilova BIH 157 C8
Velika Ivanča SRB 158 E6
Velika Kladuša BIH 156 B4
Velika Kopanica HR 157 B9
Velika Krsna SRB 159 E6
Velika Mlaka HR 148 E6
Velika Obarska BIH 157 C11
Velika Pisanica HR 149 E8
Velika Plana SRB 159 E7
Velika Plana SRB 164 C3
Velika Račna SLO 73 E10
Velika Trnovitica HR 149 E7
Velike Lašče SLO 73 E10
Veliki Crljeni SRB 158 E5
Veliki Drvenik HR 156 F5
Veliki Gaj SRB 159 C7
Veliki Grđevac HR 149 E8
Veliki Kupci SRB 164 C3
Veliki Preslav BG 167 C7
Veliki Prolog HR 157 F7
Veliki Radinci SRB 158 C4
Veliki Šiljegovac SRB 164 B4
Veliki Troyany UA 154 A6
Velikiy Lyubin' UA 144 D8
Veliki Zdenci HR 149 E8
Veliko Gradište SRB 159 D8
Veliko Laole SRB 159 E7
Veliko Središte SRB 159 C7
Veliko Trojstvo HR 149 E7
Veliko Tŭrnovo BG 166 C5
Veliköy TR 173 B8
Velilla de Cinca E 42 D4
Velilla del Río Carrión E 39 C10
Veli Lošinj HR 67 C9
Velimeşe TR 173 B8
Velimlje MNE 163 D6
Vélines F 28 F6
Velingrad BG 165 E9
Velipojë AL 163 F7
Velise EST 131 D9
Veliuona LT 136 C7
Velje Duboko MNE 163 D7
Veljun HR 156 B4
Velká Bíteš CZ 77 D10
Velká Bystřice CZ 146 B4
Velká Dobrá CZ 76 B6
Velká Hleďsebe CZ 75 C12
Veľká Ida SK 145 F3
Velká Lomnica SK 145 E1
Veľká Mača SK 146 E5
Veľká nad Ipľom SK 147 E9
Velká nad Veličkou CZ 146 D5
Velká Polom CZ 146 B6
Velké Bílovice CZ 77 E11
Velké Březno CZ 80 E6
Velké Heraltice CZ 146 B5
Veľké Kapušany SK 145 F5
Velké Karlovice CZ 146 C6
Veľké Leváre SK 77 E12
Velké Losiny CZ 77 B12
Veľké Lovce SK 146 E6
Veľké Ludince SK 147 F6
Velké Meziříčí CZ 77 D10
Velké Němčice CZ 77 E11
Velké Opatovice CZ 77 C11
Velké Pavlovice CZ 77 E11
Veľké Rípňany SK 146 E5
Velké Svatoňovice CZ 81 E10
Veľké Uherce SK 146 D6
Veľké Úľany SK 146 E5
Velký Beranov CZ 77 D9
Veľký Blh SK 147 E10
Veľký Cetín SK 146 E6
Veľký Ďur SK 146 E6
Veľký Krtíš SK 147 E8
Veľký Kýr SK 146 E6
Veľký Lapáš SK 146 E6
Veľký Meder SK 146 F5
Velký Osek CZ 77 B8
Velký Šenov CZ 80 D6
Veľký Slavkov SK 145 E1
Velký Týnec CZ 146 B4
Velký Újezd CZ 146 B4
Vellahn D 83 D9
Vellberg D 74 D6
Velletri I 62 D3
Vellevans F 26 F6
Velling DK 86 C2
Vellinge S 87 E12
Vellisca E 47 D7
Vellmar D 78 D6
Velo GR 175 D6
Velosnes F 19 E11
Velp NL 183 B7
Velpke D 79 B8
Velten D 84 E4
Veltruby CZ 77 B8
Veltrusy CZ 76 B6
Velturno I 72 C4
Velušina NMK 168 C5
Velvary CZ 76 B6
Velventos GR 169 D7
Velyatyn UA 145 G7
Velyka Horozhanna UA 145 D8
Velyka Kisnytsya UA 154 A2
Velyka Kopanya UA 145 G7
Velyka Mykhaylivka UA 154 C5
Velyka Tur"ya UA 145 E9
Velyki Kom"yaty UA 145 G6
Velyki Luchky UA 145 G6
Velyki Mosty UA 144 C9
Velykokomarivka UA 154 C5
Velykoploske UA 154 D5
Velykozymenove UA 154 C6
Velykyy Bereznyy UA 145 F5
Velykyy Bychkiv UA 145 H9
Velykyy Rakovets' UA 145 G7
Velžys LT 135 E8
Vemb DK 86 C2
Vemdalen S 102 B6
Vemdalsskalet S 102 B6
Véménd H 149 D11
Vemhån S 102 B7
Vemundvik N 105 B11
Vena S 92 D7
Venaco F 37 G10
Venafro I 62 E6
Venansault F 28 B2
Venarey-les-Laumes F 25 E11
Venaria I 68 C4
Venarotta I 62 B4
Venås S 103 C11
Venasca I 37 B6
Venčane SRB 158 E5
Vence F 36 D6
Venciūnai LT 137 E9
Venda Nova P 38 E4
Vendargues F 35 C6
Vendas Novas P 50 B3
Vendays-Montalivet F 28 E3
Vendenheim F 186 D4
Vendeuvre-du-Poitou F 29 B6
Vendeuvre-sur-Barse F 25 D11
Vendinha P 50 C4
Vendœuvres F 29 B8
Vendôme F 24 E5
Veneheitto FIN 119 F17
Venejärvi FIN 117 D12
Venelles F 35 C9
Vénès F 33 C10
Venesjärvi FIN 126 B7
Veneskoski FIN 123 E10
Venetmäki FIN 124 D7
Venetmäki FIN 124 F7
Venetpalo FIN 123 C15
Venets BG 167 B7
Venets BG 167 D7
Venevere EST 131 C13
Venezia I 66 B5
Vengasaho FIN 119 D16
Vengsoy N 111 A16
Venhuizen NL 16 C4
Venialbo E 39 F8
Vénissieux F 30 D6
Venizel F 19 F7
Venjan S 102 E6
Venlo NL 16 F6
Venna GR 171 B9
Vennesla N 90 C2
Vennesund N 105 A12
Venosa I 60 B5
Venoy F 25 E10
Venray NL 16 E5
Vensac F 28 E3
Venta LT 134 D5
Venta LV 134 C4
Venta de Baños E 40 E3
Venta del Charco E 54 C4
Venta del Moro E 47 F10
Venta de los Santos E 55 C6
Venta las Ranas E 39 A8
Venta Nueva E 39 B6
Ventas de Huelma E 53 B9
Ventas de Zafarraya E 53 C8
Ventava LV 134 B3
Ventavon F 35 B10
Venteuges F 30 F4
Ventimiglia I 37 D7
Ventiseri F 37 H10
Ventnor GB 13 D12
Ventry IRL 8 D2
Ventschow D 83 C11
Ventspils LV 134 B3
Venzone I 73 D7
Vép H 149 B7
Vepriai LT 135 F9
Vepsä FIN 119 E16
Vepsä FIN 125 C12
Vepsä FIN 125 F14
Vera E 55 E9
Vera Cruz P 50 C4
Verbania I 68 B6
Verberie F 18 F6
Verbicaro I 60 D5
Verbier CH 31 C11
Verbiţa RO 159 E11
Verbka UA 154 A4
Verceia I 69 A7
Vercelli I 68 C5
Vercel-Villedieu-le-Camp F 26 F5
Verchen D 84 C3
Verd SLO 73 E9
Verdaches F 36 C4
Verdalen N 94 E3
Verdalsøra N 105 D10
Verden (Aller) D 17 C12
Verdikoussa GR 169 E6
Vërdovë AL 168 C4
Verdun F 26 B3
Verdun-sur-Garonne F 33 C8
Verdun-sur-le-Doubs F 31 B7
Verebiejai LT 137 E8
Veresegyház H 150 B3
Vereşti RO 153 B8
Verfeil F 33 B9
Verfeil F 33 C9
Vērgale LV 134 C2
Vergato I 66 D3
Vergaville F 27 C6
Verges E 43 C10
Vergèze F 35 C7
Verghereto I 66 E5
Vergi EST 131 B12
Vergi GR 169 C9
Vergigny F 25 E10
Vergina GR 169 D7
Vergongheon F 30 E3
Vergt F 29 E7
Verguleasa RO 160 D4
Veriči BIH 157 C6
Verín E 38 E5
Veringenstadt D 27 D11
Veriora EST 132 E1
Verkebro S 98 A8
Verkhivka UA 154 A4
Verkhni Petrivtsi UA 153 A7
Verkhniy Bereziv UA 152 A5
Verkhniy Yaseniv UA 152 A5
Verkhnya Vysots'ke UA 145 F7
Verkhnya Vyznytsya UA 145 F6
Verkhnya Yablun'ka UA 145 E6
Verkhnye Syn'ovydne UA 145 E8
Verkhovyna UA 152 A5
Verl D 17 E11
Verla FIN 128 C6
Verlaine B 19 C11
Verma N 100 B8
Vermand F 19 E7
Vermenton F 25 E10
Vermeş RO 159 B8
Vermiglio I 69 A10
Vermiosa P 45 C7
Vermoil P 44 E3
Vermosh AL 163 D8
Vermuntila FIN 126 C6
Vernante I 37 C7
Vernantes F 23 F12
Vernayaz CH 31 C11
Vern-d'Anjou F 23 E10
Verneřice CZ 80 E6
Verneşti RO 161 C9
Vernet F 33 D8
Vernet-les-Bains F 33 E10
Verneuil-sur-Avre F 24 C4
Verneuil-sur-Vienne F 29 D8
Vernier CH 31 C9
Verningen N 90 A7
Vernio I 66 D3
Verniolle F 33 D9
Vernole I 61 C10
Vernon F 24 B5
Vernouillet F 24 C5
Vernoux-en-Vivarais F 30 F6
Vern-sur-Seiche F 23 D8
Verny F 26 B5
Vero F 37 G9
Verőcemaros H 147 F8
Veroia GR 169 C7
Verolanuova I 69 C9
Veroli I 62 D4
Verona I 66 B2
Verosvres F 30 C5
Verpelét H 145 H1
Verrabotn N 105 D9
Verran N 105 D9
Verres I 68 B4
Verrières F 29 C7
Versailles F 24 C7
Verseg H 150 B4
Vers-en-Montage F 31 B8
Versmold D 17 D10
Versoix CH 31 C9
Versols-et-Lapeyre F 34 C4
Verson F 23 B11
Vers-Pont-du-Gard F 35 C8
Vert F 32 B4
Verteillac F 29 E6
Vértesacsa H 149 B11
Vértesboglár H 149 B11
Vértessomló H 149 A10
Vértesszőlős H 149 A10
Verteuil-d'Agenais F 33 B6
Vertheuil F 28 E4
Verton F 18 D4
Vertou F 23 F9
Vertus F 25 C11
Verucchio I 66 E5
Verviers B 19 C12
Vervins F 19 E8
Verwood GB 13 D11
Verzino I 61 E7
Verzuolo I 37 B6
Verzy F 25 B11
Vesajärvi FIN 126 B8
Vesala FIN 119 D16
Vesamäki FIN 123 E17
Vesanka FIN 123 F15
Vesanto FIN 123 E16
Vescovato I 66 B1
Vése H 149 D8
Vesela Dolyna UA 154 E4
Veselava LV 135 B10
Veselé SK 146 D5
Veselets BG 161 F9
Veselie BG 167 E9
Veselí nad Lužnicí CZ 77 D7
Veselí nad Moravou CZ 146 D4
Veselinovo BG 167 D8
Vesijako FIN 127 C13
Vesijärvi FIN 122 F7
Vesilahti FIN 127 C10
Vesime I 37 B8
Vesivehmaa FIN 127 C14
Vesløs DK 86 A3
Vesnovo RUS 136 D5
Vesoul F 26 E5
Vespolate I 68 C6
Vessa GR 177 C7
Vessem NL 16 F4
Vessigebro S 87 B11
Vestad N 101 C13
Vestbjerg DK 86 A5
Vestby N 95 C13
Vestby N 102 D2
Vestbygd N 111 D10
Vester Åby DK 86 E6
Vesterås N 105 C12
Vesterby DK 87 F8
Vester Hæsinge DK 86 E6
Vester Hassing DK 86 A6
Vester Herborg DK 86 C3
Vester Hjermitslev DK 90 E6
Vester Hornum DK 86 B4
Vestermarie DK 89 E7
Vester Nebel DK 86 D4
Vesterø Havn DK 87 A7
Vestertana N 113 C20
Vester Torup DK 86 A4
Vester Vedsted DK 86 E3
Vestervig DK 86 B2
Vestfossen N 95 C11
Vestiena LV 135 C11
Vestmanna FO 2 A2
Vestnes N 100 A6
Vestone I 69 B9
Vestpollen N 110 D8
Vestre Gausdal N 101 D12
Vestre Jakobselv N 114 C6
Vestvågen N 108 E4
Veszkény H 149 A8
Veszprém H 149 B9
Veszprémvarsány H 149 B9
Vésztő H 151 D7
Veţca RO 152 E5
Veţel RO 151 F10
Veteli FIN 123 D11
Veternik SRB 158 C4
Vetersko NMK 164 F4
Vétheuil F 24 B6
Vetiş RO 151 B10
Vetlanda S 92 E6
Vetlefjorden N 100 D5
Vetovo BG 161 F8
Vetovo HR 149 F9
Vetralla I 62 C2
Vetren BG 165 E9
Vetren BG 166 D5
Vetren BG 167 D8
Vetrino BG 167 C9
Vetrişoaia RO 154 E2
Větřní CZ 76 E6
Vetschau D 80 C6
Vetsikko FIN 113 D19
Vettasjärvi S 116 D7
Vettelschoss D 185 C7
Vettersley DK 87 E9
Vetto I 66 D1
Veulettes-sur-Mer F 18 E2
Veurne B 18 B6
Vevang N 104 E2
Vevčani NMK 168 B4
Veverská Bítýška CZ 77 D10
Vevey CH 31 C10
Vevi GR 169 C6
Vex CH 31 C11
Vexala FIN 122 D8
Veynes F 35 A10
Veyre-Monton F 30 D3
Vėžaičiai LT 134 E2
Vezdemarbán E 39 E9
Vézelay F 25 F10
Vézelise F 26 D5
Vézénobres F 35 B7
Vezins F 23 F10
Vézins-de-Lévézou F 34 B4
Vezza d'Oglio I 69 A9
Vezzani F 37 G10
Vezzano I 69 A11
Viadana I 66 C2
Viala du Tarn F 34 B4
Vialas F 35 B6
Viana E 32 E1
Viana de Cega E 39 E10
Viana do Alentejo P 50 C4
Viana do Bolo E 38 D5
Viana do Castelo P 38 E2
Vianden L 20 E6
Viane F 34 C4
Vianen NL 16 E4
Viannos GR 178 E9
Viaño Pequeno E 38 B3
Vianos E 55 B8
Viantie FIN 119 C13
Viareggio I 66 E1
Viarmes F 25 B7
Vias F 34 D5
Viasvesi FIN 126 C6
Viatodos P 38 F2
Viator E 55 F8
Viazac F 33 A10
Vibble S 93 D12
Vibbyn S 118 C7
Vibonati I 60 C5
Viborg DK 86 C4
Vibo Valentia I 59 B9
Vibraye F 24 D4
Viby DK 87 D10
Viby S 88 C6
Vic E 43 D8
Vícar E 55 F7
Vicari I 58 D4
Vicarstown IRL 7 F8
Vicchio I 66 E3
Vicdessos F 33 E9
Vic-en-Bigorre F 33 D6
Vicenza I 66 A4
Vic-Fezensac F 33 C6
Vichy F 30 C3
Vickan S 91 E11
Vic-le-Comte F 30 D3
Vico F 37 G9
Vico del Gargano I 63 D9
Vico Equense I 60 B2
Vicoforte I 37 C7
Vico nel Lazio I 62 D4
Vicovaro I 62 C3
Vicovu de Jos RO 153 B7
Vicovu de Sus RO 153 B7
Vicq-Exemplet F 29 B10
Vic-sur-Cère F 29 F11
Vic-sur-Seille F 26 C6
Victoria RO 153 C11
Victoria RO 160 B5
Victoria RO 161 D11
Victor Vlad Delamarina RO 159 B8
Vidaga LV 135 B12
Vidago P 38 E4
Vidais P 44 F2
Vīdāle LV 130 F4
Vidamlya BY 141 F9
Vidángoz E 32 E3
ViŠareiŠI FO 2 A3
Vidauban F 36 E4
Vidče CZ 146 C6
Viddal N 100 B5
Viddalba I 64 B2
Videbæk DK 86 C3
Videle RO 161 E7
Videm SLO 73 E10
Videm SLO 148 C6
Videmonte P 44 C6
Videniškiai LT 135 F10
Vidhas AL 168 B3
Vidigueira P 50 C4
Vidin BG 159 F10
Vidiškiai LT 135 F9
Vidlin GB 3 E14
Vidnava CZ 77 B12
Vidovec HR 148 D6
Vidovice BIH 157 C10
Vidra RO 151 E11
Vidra RO 153 F9
Vidra RO 161 E8
Vidrare BG 165 C9
Vidrek N 111 D13
Vidrenjak HR 149 E7
Vidrieres E 43 D9
Vidriži LV 135 B9
Vidsala LV 135 D11
Vidsel S 118 C5
Vidstrup DK 90 D6
Vidukle LT 134 F5
Vidzy BY 135 F13
Viechtach D 76 D3
Vieille-Brioude F 30 E3
Vieira de Leiria P 44 E3
Vieira do Minho P 38 E3
Vieki FIN 125 D13
Viekšniai LT 134 D5
Vielank D 83 D10
Vielha E 33 E7
Vielle-Aure F 33 E6
Vielle-St-Girons F 32 C3
Vielmur-sur-Agout F 33 C10
Vielsalm B 20 D5
Vielverge F 26 F3
Vienenburg D 79 C8
Vienība LV 134 C6
Vienne F 30 D6
Viereck D 84 C6
Vieremä FIN 124 C8
Viereth-Trunstadt D 75 C8
Vierlingsbeek NL 16 E5
Viernau D 79 E8
Viernheim D 21 E11
Vierraden D 84 D6
Viersen D 16 F6
Vierumäki FIN 127 C14
Vierville-sur-Mer F 23 B10
Vierzon F 24 F7
Viesecke D 83 D12
Viesīte LV 135 D11
Vieste I 63 D10
Viešvėnai LT 134 E4
Viešvilė LT 136 C5
Vietas S 109 A15
Vietri di Potenza I 60 B5
Vietri sul Mare I 60 B3
Vieux-Boucau-les-Bains F 32 C3
Vieux-Condé F 182 E3
Vievis LT 137 D10
Vif F 31 E8
Vig DK 87 D9
Vīganti LV 135 D13
Vigarano Mainarda I 66 C3
Vigasio I 66 B2
Vigaun A 73 A7
Vigdenes N 100 D10
Vigeland N 94 F6
Vigeois F 29 E9
Vigevano I 69 C6
Vigge S 102 A7
Vigge S 103 B12
Viggianello F 37 H9
Viggianello I 60 D6
Viggiano I 60 C5
Vígľaš SK 147 D8
Vigliano Biellese I 68 B5
Vignacourt F 18 D5
Vignale Monferrato I 37 A8
Vignanello I 62 C2
Vigneulles-les-Hattonchâtel F 26 C4
Vignola I 66 D3
Vignola Mare l'Agnata I 64 A3
Vignory F 26 D3
Vigny F 24 B6
Vigo E 38 D2
Vigodarzere I 66 B4
Vigo di Cadore I 72 D5
Vigo di Fassa I 72 D4
Vigone I 31 F11
Vigonza I 66 B4
Vigo Rendena I 69 A10
Vigrestad N 94 E3
Viguzzolo I 37 B9
Vigy F 20 F6
Vihalsen N 104 E5
Vihanti FIN 119 F13
Vihiers F 23 F10
Vihtari FIN 125 F11
Vihtasuo FIN 125 D12
Vihtavuori FIN 123 F15
Vihteljärvi FIN 126 B8
Vihti FIN 127 E11
Vihtijärvi FIN 127 D12
Vihula EST 131 B12
Viiala FIN 127 C10
Viiksimo FIN 121 F15
Viile Satu Mare RO 151 B10
Viimsi EST 131 B9
Viinamäki FIN 125 B10
Viinijärvi FIN 125 E12
Viinikka FIN 123 D10
Viinikkala FIN 123 D16
Viinikoski FIN 119 D17
Viiratsi EST 131 E11
Viirinkylä FIN 119 B17
Viirre FIN 119 F12
Viisarimäki FIN 123 F16
Viişoara MD 153 B10
Viişoara RO 151 E7
Viişoara RO 152 D3
Viişoara RO 152 E5

Viişoara RO 153 A9
Viişoara RO 153 D8
Viișoara RO 153 E11
Viișoara RO 160 F6
Viitaila FIN 127 C13
Viitala FIN 123 E10
Viitamäki FIN 123 C16
Viitaniemi FIN 125 D10
Viitapohja FIN 127 B11
Viitaranta FIN 115 D3
Viitaranta FIN 121 B12
Viitasaari FIN 123 D15
Viitavaara FIN 121 E13
Viitavaara FIN 121 F12
Viitka EST 132 F1
Viitna EST 131 C12
Viivikonna EST 132 C2
Vijciems LV 131 F11
Vik N 90 C4
Vik N 94 B2
Vik N 108 B9
Vik N 108 F3
Vik N 110 D7
Vik S 88 D6
Vika FIN 117 E16
Vika N 101 A15
Vika S 97 A14
Vikajärvi FIN 117 E16
Vikan N 104 E5
Vikan N 105 B10
Vikarbyn S 97 B15
Vikarbyn S 103 E9
Vikartovce SK 145 F1
Vikbyn S 97 B15
Vike N 100 E3
Vike S 103 A12
Vikebukt N 100 A6
Vikedal N 94 D3
Viken S 87 C11
Viken S 103 B9
Viken S 103 B11
Vikersund N 95 C11
Vikesâ N 94 E4
Vikevåg N 94 D3
Vikholmen N 108 D4
Viķi LV 131 F9
Vikingstad S 92 C6
Vikmanshyttan S 97 B14
Vikna N 105 B9
Vikoč BIH 157 F10
Vikøyri N 100 D5
Vikran N 111 A16
Vikran N 111 C12
Vikran N 113 A12
Viksberg S 97 B14
Viksjö S 103 A13
Viksjöfors S 103 D10
Viksmon S 107 E12
Vīksna LV 133 B2
Viktarinas LT 137 E8
Vikten N 110 D5
Viktorivka UA 154 C6
Vikýřovice CZ 77 C11
Vila E 38 E3
Vila Boa P 45 D7
Vila Boa do Bispo P 44 B4
Vila Caiz P 38 F3
Vila Chã de Sá P 44 C5
Vila Cova da Lixa P 38 F3
Vilada E 43 C7
Viladamat E 43 C10
Vila da Ponte P 38 E4
Viladecans E 43 E8
Vila de Cruces E 38 C3
Vila de Frades P 50 C4
Vila de Rei P 44 E4
Vila do Bispo P 50 E2
Vila do Conde P 38 F2
Viladrau E 43 D8
Vilafamés E 48 D4
Vilafant E 43 C9
Vila Fernando P 51 B5
Vila Flor P 38 F5
Vila Franca das Naves P 45 C6
Vilafranca de Bonany E 57 B11
Vilafranca del Penedès E 43 E7
Vila Franca de Xira P 50 B2
Vilagarcía de Arousa E 38 C2
Vilajuïga E 34 F5
Viļaka LV 133 B3
Vilalba E 38 B4
Vilallonga E 33 F10
Vilamartín E 38 D5
Vilamarxant E 48 E3
Vilamoura P 50 E3
Viļāni LV 133 C1
Vila Nogueira de Azeitão P 50 B1
Vilanova E 38 B5
Vila Nova da Baronia P 50 C3
Vila Nova da Barquinha P 44 F4
Vilanova d'Alcolea E 48 D5
Vilanova de Arousa E 38 C2
Vila Nova de Cacela P 50 E4
Vila Nova de Famalicão P 38 F2
Vila Nova de Foz Coa P 45 B6
Vila Nova de Gaia P 44 B3
Vilanova de la Barca E 42 D5
Vilanova de L'Aguda E 42 D6
Vilanova de Meià E 42 D6
Vila Nova de Paiva P 44 C5
Vila Nova de Poiares P 44 D4
Vilanova de Prades E 42 E5
Vila Nova de São Bento P 50 D5
Vilanova de Sau E 43 D8
Vilanova i la Geltrú E 43 E7
Vila Pouca da Beira P 44 D5
Vila Pouca de Aguiar P 38 E4
Vila Praia de Âncora P 38 E2
Vilar P 38 E3
Vilar P 44 F2
Vilarandelo P 38 E5
Vilarchao E 38 D4
Vilar da Veiga P 38 E3
Vilar de Andorinho P 44 B3
Vilar de Barrio E 38 D4
Vilar de Santos E 38 D4
Vilardevós E 38 E5
Vila Real P 38 F4
Vila Real de Santo António P 50 E5
Vilarelho da Raia P 38 E5
Vilar Formoso P 45 C7
Vilarinho da Castanheira P 45 B6
Vilarinho do Bairro P 44 D3
Vilariño de Conso E 38 D5
Vila-rodona E 43 E6
Vila Ruiva P 50 C4
Vila Seca P 38 E2
Vilaseca de Solcina E 42 E6
Vilassar de Mar E 43 D8
Vilasund S 108 D8
Vila Velha de Ródão P 44 E5
Vila Verde P 38 E3
Vila Verde P 38 F4
Vila Verde P 44 D3
Vila Verde da Raia P 38 E5
Vila Verde de Ficalho P 51 D5
Vila Viçosa P 50 B5
Vilce LV 134 D7
Vilches E 55 C6
Vildbjerg DK 86 C3
Vilémov CZ 77 C9
Vilgāle LV 134 C3
Vilhelmina S 107 B11
Vilia GR 175 C7
Viljakkala FIN 127 B9
Viljandi EST 131 E11
Viljevo HR 149 E10
Viljolahti FIN 125 F10
Vilkaviškis LT 136 D7
Vilkene LV 131 F9
Vilkija LT 137 C8
Vilkjärvi FIN 128 D8
Vilkyškiai LT 134 F4
Villa Bartolomea I 66 B3
Villabate I 58 C3
Villablanca E 51 E5
Villablino E 39 C7
Villabona E 32 D1
Villabrágima E 39 E9
Villabuena del Puente E 39 F9
Villac F 29 E8
Villacañas E 46 E6
Villa Carcina I 69 B9
Villacarriedo E 40 B4
Villacarrillo E 55 C6
Villa Castelli I 61 B8
Villacastín E 46 C4
Villach A 73 C8
Villacidro I 64 E2
Villaciervos E 41 E6
Villaconejos E 46 D6
Villaconejos de Trabaque E 47 D8
Villada E 39 D10
Villa d'Almè I 69 B8
Villa del Prado E 46 D4
Villa del Río E 53 A8
Villadepera E 39 E7
Villa de Ves E 47 F10
Villadiego E 40 C3
Villadose I 66 B4
Villadossola I 68 A5
Villaeles de Valdavia E 39 C10
Villaescusa de Haro E 47 E7
Villaescusa la Sombría E 40 D5
Villafáfila E 39 E8
Villafeliche E 47 B10
Villaflores E 45 B10
Villafranca d'Asti I 37 B8
Villafranca de Córdoba E 53 A7
Villafranca de Ebro E 41 E10
Villafranca del Bierzo E 39 C6
Villafranca del Campo E 47 C10
Villafranca del Cid E 48 D4
Villafranca de los Barros E 51 B7
Villafranca de los Caballeros E 46 F6
Villafranca di Verona I 66 B2
Villafranca in Lunigiana I 69 E8
Villafranca-Montes de Oca E 40 D5
Villafranca Tirrena I 59 C7
Villafranco del Guadalquivir E 51 E7
Villafrati I 58 D3
Villafrechós E 39 E9
Villafruela E 40 E4
Villafuerte E 40 E3
Villagarcía de Campos E 39 E9
Villagarcía de la Torre E 51 C7
Villagarcía del Llano E 47 F9
Villagio Mancuso I 59 A10
Villagonzalo E 51 B7
Villagrande Strisaili I 64 D4
Villaharta E 54 C3
Villähde FIN 127 D14
Villahermosa E 55 B7
Villahermosa del Campo E 47 B10
Villahermosa del Río E 48 D4
Villaherreros E 40 D3
Villahizán E 40 D4
Villahoz E 40 D4
Villaines-en-Duesmois F 25 E12
Villaines-la-Juhel F 23 D11
Villajoyosa E 56 D4
Villala FIN 125 F13
Villala FIN 129 D9
Villa Lagarina I 69 B11
Villalago I 62 D5
Villalar de los Comuneros E 39 E9
Villa Latina I 62 D5
Villalba I 58 D4
Villalba de Duero E 40 E4
Villalba de Guardo E 39 C10
Villalba del Alcor E 51 E7
Villalba de la Sierra E 47 D8
Villalba de los Alcores E 39 E10
Villalba de los Barros E 51 B6
Villalba del Rey E 47 D7
Villalba dels Arcs E 42 E4
Villalba de Rioja E 40 C6
Villalcampo E 39 E7
Villalcázar de Sirga E 40 D2
Villalengua E 41 F8
Villalgordo del Júcar E 47 F8
Villa Literno I 60 A2
Villalobos E 39 E9
Villalón de Campos E 39 D9
Villalonga E 56 D4
Villalpando E 39 E9
Villalpardo E 47 F9
Villaluenga de la Sagra E 46 D5
Villalumbroso E 39 D10
Villamalea E 47 F9
Villamañán E 39 D8
Villamandos E 39 D8
Villamanrique E 55 B7
Villamanrique de la Condesa E 51 E7
Villamanta E 46 D4
Villamar I 64 D2
Villamartín E 51 F8
Villamartín de Campos E 39 D10
Villamassargia I 64 E2
Villamayor E 45 C9
Villamayor de Calatrava E 54 B4
Villamayor de Campos E 39 E9
Villamayor de Santiago E 47 E7
Villamayor de Treviño E 40 D3
Villamblard F 29 E7
Villamediana E 40 D3
Villamediana de Iregua E 32 F1
Villamejil E 39 C7
Villamesías E 45 F9
Villamiel E 45 D7
Villa Minozzo I 66 D1
Villamo FIN 122 F7
Villamor de los Escuderos E 39 F8
Villamuelas E 46 E5
Villamuriel de Cerrato E 40 E3
Villandraut F 32 B5
Villanova I 61 B9
Villanova d'Albenga I 37 C8
Villanova d'Asti I 37 B7
Villanova del Battista I 60 A4
Villanovafranca I 64 D3
Villanova Monferrato I 68 C5
Villanova Monteleone I 64 B1
Villanova Truschedu I 64 D2
Villanova Tulo I 64 D3
Villanterio I 69 C7
Villanúa E 32 E4
Villanubla E 39 E10
Villanueva de Alcardete E 47 E6
Villanueva de Alcorón E 47 C8
Villanueva de Algaidas E 53 B8
Villanueva de Argaño E 40 D4
Villanueva de Bogas E 46 E5
Villanueva de Cameros E 41 D6
Villanueva de Castellón E 56 C4
Villanueva de Córdoba E 54 C3
Villanueva de Gállego E 41 E10
Villanueva de Gómez E 46 C3
Villanueva de la Cañada E 46 D5
Villanueva de la Concepción E 53 C7
Villanueva de la Fuente E 55 B7
Villanueva de la Jara E 47 F9
Villanueva de la Reina E 53 A9
Villanueva del Arzobispo E 55 C6
Villanueva de las Cruces E 51 D5
Villanueva de la Serena E 51 B8
Villanueva de la Sierra E 45 D8
Villanueva de las Torres E 55 D6
Villanueva de la Vera E 45 D10
Villanueva del Campo E 39 E9
Villanueva del Duque E 54 C3
Villanueva del Fresno E 51 C5
Villanueva de los Castillejos E 51 D5
Villanueva de los Infantes E 55 B7
Villanueva del Rey E 51 C9
Villanueva del Río Segura E 55 C10
Villanueva del Río y Minas E 51 D8
Villanueva del Rosario E 53 C8
Villanueva del Trabuco E 53 B8
Villanueva de Mesía E 53 B8
Villanueva de San Carlos E 54 B5
Villanueva de San Juan E 51 E9
Villanueva de Tapia E 53 B8
Villanueva de Valdegovia E 40 C5
Villanuño de Valdavia E 40 C2
Villány H 149 E10
Villa Opicina I 73 E8
Villapalacios E 55 B7
Villaperuccio I 64 E2
Villapiana I 61 D6
Villapiana Lido I 61 D6
Villa Poma I 66 C3
Villapourçon F 30 B4
Villaputzu I 64 E4
Villaquejida E 39 D8
Villaquilambre E 39 C8
Villaralbo E 39 F8
Villaralto E 54 C3
Villarcayo E 40 C4
Villard-Bonnot F 31 E8
Villard-de-Lans F 31 E8
Villar de Cañas E 47 E7
Villar de Chinchilla E 55 B9
Villar de Ciervo E 45 C7
Villardeciervos E 39 E7
Villardefrades E 39 E9
Villar del Arzobispo E 48 E3
Villar de la Yegua E 45 C7
Villar del Buey E 39 F7
Villar del Cobo E 47 D9
Villar del Humo E 47 E9
Villar de los Barrios E 39 C6
Villar de los Navarros E 42 E1
Villar del Pedroso E 45 E10
Villar del Rey E 45 F7
Villar del Salz E 47 C10
Villar de Olalla E 47 D8
Villar de Peralonso E 45 B8
Villar de Rena E 45 F9
Villar de Torre E 40 D6
Villardompardo E 53 A8
Villareal E 48 E4
Villarejo de Fuentes E 47 E7
Villarejo de Montalbán E 46 E3
Villarejo de Orbigo E 39 D8
Villarejo de Salvanés E 47 D6
Villa Rendena I 69 A10
Villarente E 39 C9
Villares de la Reina E 45 B9
Villargordo E 53 A9
Villargordo del Cabriel E 47 E10
Villarino de los Aires E 39 F7
Villarluengo E 42 F2
Villarosa I 58 D5
Villarquemado E 47 C10
Villarramiel E 39 D10
Villarrasa E 51 E6
Villarreal de Huerva E 47 B10
Villarrín de Campos E 39 E8
Villarrobledo E 47 F7
Villarrodrigo E 55 C7
Villarroya de la Sierra E 41 F8
Villarroya de los Pinares E 42 F2
Villarrubia de los Ojos E 46 F5
Villarrubia de Santiago E 46 E6
Villarrubio E 47 E7
Villars F 29 E7
Villars F 30 E5
Villars-Colmars F 36 C5
Villars del Saz E 47 E8
Villars-les-Dombes F 31 D7
Villars-sur-Var F 36 D6
Villar-St-Pancrace F 31 F10
Villarta E 47 F9
Villarta de los Montes E 46 F3
Villarta de San Juan E 46 F6
Villasalto I 64 E3
Villasana de Mena E 40 B5
Villasandino E 40 D3
Villa San Giovanni I 59 C8
Villa San Pietro I 64 E3
Villa Santa Maria I 63 D6
Villasante de Montija E 40 B5
Villa Santina I 73 D6
Villasarracino E 40 D3
Villasavary F 33 D10
Villasayas E 41 F6
Villasbuenas E 45 B7
Villasdardo E 45 B8
Villaseca de Laciana E 39 C7
Villaseca de la Sagra E 46 E5
Villaseco de los Gamitos E 45 B8
Villaseco de los Reyes E 45 B8
Villaseco del Pan E 39 F8
Villasequilla de Yepes E 46 E5
Villasimius I 64 E4
Villasmundo I 59 E7
Villasor I 64 E2
Villaspeciosa I 64 E2
Villasrubias E 45 D7
Villastar E 47 D10
Villasur de Herreros E 40 D5
Villatobas E 46 E6
Villatoro E 45 C10
Villatoya E 47 F10
Villatuerta E 32 E2
Villaturiel E 39 C9
Villaumbrales E 39 D10
Villaurbana I 64 D2
Villava E 32 E2
Villavallelonga I 62 D5
Villavelayo E 40 D6
Villaverde de Guadalimar E 55 C7
Villaverde del Río E 51 D8
Villaverde y Pasaconsol E 47 E8
Villavernia I 37 B9
Villaviciosa E 39 B9
Villaviciosa de Córdoba E 54 C2
Villaviciosa de Odón E 46 D5
Villavieja E 48 E4
Villavieja de Yeltes E 45 C8
Villaviudas E 40 E3
Villayón E 39 B6
Villazanzo de Valderaduey E 39 C10
Villé F 27 D7
Villebois-Lavalette F 29 E6
Villebrumier F 33 C8
Villecomtal-sur-Arros F 33 D6
Villecomte F 26 E3
Villecroze F 36 D4
Villedaigne F 34 D4
Villedieu-la-Blouère F 23 F9
Villedieu-les-Poêles F 23 C9
Villedieu-sur-Indre F 29 B9
Ville-en-Tardenois F 20 F1
Villefagnan F 28 C6
Villefontaine F 31 D7
Villefort F 35 B6
Villefranche-d'Albigeois F 33 C10
Villefranche-d'Allier F 30 C2
Villefranche-de-Lauragais F 33 D9
Villefranche-de-Lonchat F 28 F6
Villefranche-de-Panat F 34 B4
Villefranche-de-Rouergue F 33 B10
Villefranche-du-Périgord F 33 A8
Villefranche-sur-Cher F 24 F6
Villefranche-sur-Mer F 37 D6
Villefranche-sur-Saône F 30 D6
Villefranque F 32 D3
Villegas E 40 D3
Villel E 47 D10
Villelaure F 35 C9
Villemandeur F 25 E8
Villemorien F 25 D11
Villemoustaussou F 33 D10
Villemur-sur-Tarn F 33 C9
Villena E 56 D3
Villenauxe-la-Grande F 25 C10
Villeneuve CH 31 C10
Villeneuve F 33 B10
Villeneuve F 35 C10
Villeneuve-au-Chemin F 25 D10
Villeneuve-d'Allier F 30 E3
Villeneuve-d'Ascq F 19 C7
Villeneuve-de-Berg F 35 A8
Villeneuve-de-Marsan F 32 C5
Villeneuve-de-Rivière F 33 D7
Villeneuve-la-Guyard F 25 D9
Villeneuve-l'Archevêque F 25 D10
Villeneuve-lès-Avignon F 35 C8
Villeneuve-lès-Béziers F 34 D5
Villeneuve-Loubet F 36 D6
Villeneuve-sur-Allier F 30 B3
Villeneuve-sur-Lot F 33 B7
Villeneuve-sur-Yonne F 25 D9
Villeneuve-Tolosane F 33 C8
Villepinte F 33 D10
Villercomtal F 33 A11
Villeréal F 33 A7
Villerest F 30 D5
Villerías E 39 E10
Villerouge-Termenès F 34 D4
Villers-Bocage F 18 E5
Villers-Bocage F 23 B10
Villers-Bretonneux F 18 E6
Villers-Carbonnel F 18 E6
Villers-Cotterêts F 19 F7
Villers-Écalles F 18 E2
Villers-en-Argonne F 25 B12
Villersexel F 26 E5
Villers-Farlay F 31 A8
Villers-le-Bouillet B 183 D6
Villers-le-lac F 31 A10
Villers-lès-Nancy F 26 C5
Villers-Outréaux F 19 D7
Villers-Semeuse F 19 E10
Villers-sur-Glâne CH 31 B11
Villers-sur-Mer F 23 B11
Villerville F 23 B12
Villery F 25 D11
Villeseneux F 25 C11
Ville-sur-Tourbe F 20 F3
Villetta Barrea I 62 D5
Villeurbanne F 30 D6
Villeveyrac F 35 C6
Villevocance F 30 E6
Villié-Morgon F 30 C6
Villiers-Charlemagne F 23 E10
Villiers-en-Lieu F 25 C12
Villiers-en-Plaine F 28 C4
Villiers-le-Sec F 26 D3
Villiers-St-Benoît F 25 E9
Villiers-St-Georges F 25 C9
Villieu-Loyes-Mollon F 31 D7
Villikkala FIN 128 D6
Villingen D 27 D9
Villingsberg S 97 D12
Villmar D 185 D9
Villoldo E 39 D10
Villora E 47 E9
Villorba I 72 E5
Villoria E 45 C10
Villoruela E 45 B10
Villotte-sur-Aire F 26 C3
Villshärad S 87 B11
Villvattnet S 118 E4
Vilmány H 145 G3
Vilnius LT 137 D11
Vilovi d'Onyar E 43 D9
Vilppula FIN 123 F12
Vilpulka LV 131 F10
Vils A 71 B11
Vils DK 86 B3
Vilsbiburg D 75 F11
Vilseck D 75 C10
Vil'shanka UA 154 A3
Vilshofen D 76 E4
Vilshult S 88 C7
Vilslev DK 86 E3
Vilsted DK 86 B4
Vilsund Vest DK 86 B3
Vilusi BIH 157 C7
Vilusi MNE 162 D6
Viluste EST 132 F1
Vilvestre E 45 B7
Vilvoorde B 19 C9
Vilzēni LV 131 F10
Vima Mică RO 152 C3
Vimbodí E 42 E6
Vimeiro P 44 F2
Vimercate I 69 B7
Vimianzo E 38 B1
Vimieiro P 50 B4
Vimioso P 39 E6
Vimmarvattnet S 107 D9
Vimmerby S 92 D7
Vimory F 25 E8
Vimoutiers F 23 C12
Vimpeli FIN 123 D11
Vimperk CZ 76 D5
Vimy F 18 D6
Vinac BIH 157 D7
Vinadio I 37 C6
Vinaixa E 42 E5
Vinařice CZ 76 B6
Vinaròs E 42 G4
Vinarsko BG 167 D8
Vinäs S 102 E8
Vinassan F 34 D5
Vinay F 31 E7
Vinberg S 87 B11
Vinça F 34 E4
Vinča SRB 158 D6
Vincey F 26 D5
Vinchiaturo I 63 E7
Vinci I 66 E2
Vind DK 86 C3
Vindblæs DK 86 B4
Vindeballe DK 86 F6
Vindeby DK 86 E7
Vindel-Ånäset S 118 F3
Vindelgransele S 107 A14
Vindeln S 107 C17
Vinderei RO 153 E11
Vinderslev DK 86 C4
Vinderup DK 86 C3
Vindhella N 100 D7
Vindinge DK 87 D10
Vindinge DK 87 E7
Vindsvik N 94 D4
Vinebre E 42 E5
Vineuil F 24 E5
Vineuil F 29 B9
Vinga RO 151 E7
Vingåker S 92 A7
Vingäng S 102 E4
Vingrau F 34 E4
Vingrom N 101 D12
Vingsand N 104 C8
Vinhais P 39 E6
Vinhas P 39 E6
Vinica HR 148 D6
Vinica NMK 164 F5
Vinica SK 147 E8
Vinica SLO 67 B11
Viničné SK 146 E4
Viniegra de Arriba E 40 D6
Vinine BIH 157 G8
Vinišće HR 156 F5
Vinje N 94 C7
Vinje N 100 E4
Vinjeøra N 104 E5
Vinkovci HR 149 F11
Vinkt B 182 C2
Vinliden S 107 B13
Vinné SK 145 F4
Vinnes N 94 B3
Vinnesvåg N 94 B2
Vinni EST 131 C12
Vinninga S 91 C13
Vinningen D 27 B8
Vinodol SK 146 E6
Vinograd BG 166 C5
Vinogradets BG 165 E9
Vinon-sur-Verdon F 35 C10
Vinsa S 116 E9
Vinslöv S 87 C13
Vinsobres F 35 B9
Vinsternes N 104 E4
Vinstra N 101 C11
Vintervollen N 114 D8
Vintilă Vodă RO 161 C9
Vintjärn S 103 E11
Vintrosa S 97 D12
Vintturi FIN 123 C11
Vințu de Jos RO 152 E2
Viñuelas E 46 C6
Vinuesa E 40 E6
Vinzelberg D 79 A10
Viöl D 82 A6
Violay F 30 D5
Violès F 35 B8
Vipava SLO 73 E8
Vīpe LV 135 D12
Viperești RO 161 C8
Vipiteno I 72 C3
Vipperød DK 87 D9
Vipperow D 83 D13
Vir BIH 157 E7
Vir HR 67 D11
Vir SLO 73 D10
Vira S 93 B8
Virawlya BY 133 E7
Virazeil F 33 A6
Virbalis LT 136 D6
Virbi LV 134 B5
Virče NMK 165 F6
Vire F 23 C10
Virešl LV 135 B12
Vireux-Molhain F 184 D2
Vireux-Wallerand F 19 D10
Virey-sous-Bar F 25 D11
Virgen A 72 B5
Virginia IRL 7 E8
Viriat F 31 C7
Virieu-le-Grand F 31 D8
Virigneux F 30 D5
Virignin F 31 D8
Viriville F 31 E7
Virķēni LV 131 F10
Virkkala FIN 127 E11
Virkkula FIN 121 B13
Virkkunen FIN 121 C10
Virklund DK 86 C5
Virmaanpää FIN 124 E8
Virmaila FIN 127 C13
Virmutjoki FIN 129 C10
Virolahden kk FIN 128 D8
Virolahti FIN 128 D8
Virovitica HR 149 E8
Virpazar MNE 163 E7
Virpe LV 134 B4
Virrat FIN 123 F11
Virsbo S 97 C15
Virserum S 89 A9
Virtaniemi FIN 114 F4
Virtasalmi FIN 124 F8
Virton B 19 E12
Virtsu EST 130 D7
Virttaa FIN 126 D8
Viru-Jaagupi EST 131 C12
Viru-Nigula EST 131 C13
Viry F 31 C9
Vis HR 63 A10
Visaginas LT 135 E12
Višakio Rūda LT 137 D7
Visan F 35 B8
Vişani RO 161 C10
Visåsen S 103 A13
Visbek D 17 C10
Visborg DK 86 B6
Visby DK 86 E3
Visby S 93 D12
Visé B 19 C12
Višegrad BIH 158 F3
Visegrád H 149 A11
Viserba I 66 D6
Viseu P 44 C5
Vișeu de Jos RO 152 B4
Vișeu de Sus RO 152 B4
Vishnyeva BY 137 E13
Vishovgrad BG 166 C4
Visiedo E 42 F1
Visikums LV 133 B2
Vișina RO 160 D6
Vișina RO 160 F4
Vișinești MD 154 E2
Vișinești RO 161 C7
Visingsö S 92 C5
Visjövalen S 105 E12
Viskafors S 91 D12
Viskan S 103 B11
Viškī LV 135 D13
Visланda S 88 B6
Visnes N 94 D2
Višnja Gora SLO 73 E10
Višnjićevo SRB 158 D3
Višňová CZ 81 E8
Višňové CZ 77 E10
Višňové SK 147 C7
Visoca MD 153 A11
Viso del Marqués E 55 B5
Visokë AL 168 C2
Visoko BIH 157 E9
Visone I 37 B9
Visonta H 150 B5
Visp CH 68 A4
Vissac-Auteyrac F 30 E4
Vissani GR 168 E4
Visselfjärda S 89 B9
Visselhövede D 82 E7
Vissenbjerg DK 86 E6
Visso I 62 B4
Vissoie CH 68 A4
Vist N 105 D10
Vistabella del Maestrazgo E 48 D4
Vistbäcken S 118 C5
Viștea RO 152 F5
Vistheden S 118 C5
Visthus N 108 E4
Vištytis LT 136 E6
Visuvesi FIN 123 F11
Visznek H 150 B5
Vita I 58 D2
Vitå S 118 C8
Vitaby S 88 D6
Vitåfors S 118 C8
Vitanová SK 147 C9
Vitanovac SRB 159 F6
Vitanovac SRB 164 C5
Víťaz SK 145 F2
Vitberget S 118 C4
Viterbo I 62 C2
Viterne F 26 C5
Vitez BIH 157 D8
Vítězná CZ 77 B9
Viti RKS 164 E3
Vitigudino E 45 B8
Vitina BIH 157 F8
Vītiņi LV 134 D5
Vitis A 77 E8
Vítkov CZ 146 B5
Vitkovići BIH 157 E10
Vītoliņi LV 134 C7
Vitolište NMK 169 B6
Vitomirești RO 160 D4
Vitomiricë RKS 163 D9
Vitorchiano I 62 C2
Vitoria-Gasteiz E 41 C6
Vitoševac SRB 159 F8
Vitovlje BIH 157 D8
Vitré F 23 D9
Vitrey-sur-Mance F 26 E4
Vitrolles F 35 D9
Vitry-en-Artois F 18 D6
Vitry-en-Perthois F 25 C12
Vitry-le-François F 25 C12
Vitry-sur-Loire F 30 B4
Vittangi S 116 C7
Vittaryd S 87 B13
Vitteaux F 25 F12
Vittel F 26 D4
Vittikko FIN 115 E4
Vittikko FIN 119 B13
Vittikkovuoma FIN 117 E12
Vittinge S 98 C8
Vittjärv S 118 C7
Vittoria I 59 F6
Vittorio Veneto I 72 E5
Vittsjö S 87 C13
Vitulano I 60 A3
Vitulazio I 60 A2
Vitvattnet S 102 B8
Vitvattnet S 107 D16
Vitvattnet S 119 B10
Vitzenburg D 79 D10
Viuruniemi FIN 125 E11
Vivario F 37 G10
Vivastbo S 98 B7
Viveiro E 38 A4
Vivel del Río Martín E 42 F2
Viver E 48 E3
Viverols F 30 E4
Viveros E 55 B7
Vivier-au-Court F 19 E10
Viviers F 35 B8
Viviez F 33 A10
Vivild DK 86 C6
Viv-le-Fesq F 35 C7
Vivonne F 29 C6
Vix F 25 E12
Vix F 28 C4
Vizantea-Livezi RO 153 F9
Vize TR 173 A8
Vizille F 31 E8
Vižinada HR 67 B8
Viziru RO 155 C1
Vizitsa BG 167 E9
Vizovice CZ 146 C5
Vizslás H 147 E9
Vizsoly H 145 G3
Vizzini I 59 E6
Vlaardingen NL 16 E2
Vlachata GR 174 C2
Vlacherna GR 174 D5
Vlachia GR 175 B8
Vlachiotis GR 175 F6
Vlachokerasia GR 174 E5
Vlachovice CZ 146 C5
Vlădaia RO 159 E11
Vladaya BG 165 D7
Vlădeni RO 153 B9
Vlădeni RO 153 C10
Vlădeni RO 155 D1
Vlădești RO 154 F2
Vlădești RO 160 C4
Vlădești RO 160 C5
Vladičin Han SRB 164 D5
Vlădila RO 160 E4
Vladimir MNE 163 E7
Vladimir RO 160 D3
Vladimirci SRB 158 D4
Vladimirescu RO 151 E7
Vladimirovac SRB 159 C6
Vladimirovo BG 161 F11
Vladimirovo BG 165 B7
Vladinya BG 165 C10
Vladislav CZ 77 D9
Vlad Țepeș RO 161 E10
Vladychen' UA 155 B3
Vlăhița RO 153 E7
Vlahovići BIH 157 F9
Vlanduk BIH 157 D8
Vlaole SRB 159 E8
Vlase SRB 164 D4
Vlasenica BIH 157 D10
Vlašići HR 156 D3
Vlašim CZ 77 C7
Vlasina Okruglica SRB 164 D5
Vlăsinești RO 153 B9
Vlasotince SRB 164 D5
Vlatkovići BIH 157 D7
Vlčany SK 146 E5
Vlčnov CZ 146 D5
Vledder NL 16 C6
Vleuten NL 16 D4
Vlijmen NL 16 E4
Vlissingen NL 16 F1
Vlochos GR 169 E7
Vlorë AL 168 D1
Vlotho D 17 D11
Vlycho GR 174 B2
Vnanje Gorice SLO 73 D9
Vnorovy CZ 146 D4
Vočin HR 149 E9
Vöcklabruck A 76 F5
Vöcklamarkt A 76 F4
Voden BG 161 F9
Voden BG 167 E7
Voderady SK 146 E5
Vodica BIH 157 D7
Vodice HR 67 B9
Vodice HR 156 E4
Vodinci HR 157 B10
Voditsa BG 166 C6
Vodjenica BIH 156 C5
Vodňany CZ 76 D6
Vodnjan HR 67 C8
Vodskov DK 86 A6
Vodstrup DK 86 B3
Voe GB 3 E14
Voel DK 86 C5
Voerde (Niederrhein) D 17 E7
Voerendaal NL 183 D7
Voerladegård DK 86 C5
Voersâ DK 86 A6
Vogatsiko GR 168 D5
Vogelenzang NL 182 A5
Vogelgrun F 27 D8
Vogelsang D 84 D4
Vogelsdorf D 80 B5
Vogelweh D 21 F9
Voghera I 37 B10
Voghiera I 66 C4
Vognill N 101 A11
Vognsild DK 86 B4
Vogošća BIH 157 E9
Vogt D 71 B9
Vogtareuth D 72 A5
Vogüé F 35 A7
Vohburg an der Donau D 75 E10
Vohenstrauß D 75 C11
Vöhl D 21 B11
Võhma EST 130 D4
Võhma EST 131 D11
Vohonjoki FIN 120 B9
Vöhringen D 27 D10
Vöhringen D 75 F7
Voicești RO 160 D4
Void-Vacon F 26 C4
Voikkaa FIN 128 D6
Voikoski FIN 128 C6
Voila RO 152 F5
Voillecomte F 25 C12
Voineasa RO 160 C3
Voinești RO 153 C10
Voinești RO 160 C6
Voiron F 31 E8
Võiste EST 131 E8
Voiteg RO 159 C7
Voiteur F 31 B8
Voitsberg A 73 B11
Voivodeni RO 152 D5

Vojakkala FIN 119 C12
Vojakkala FIN 127 D11
Vojčice SK 145 F4
Vojens DK 86 E4
Vojka SRB 158 D5
Vojkovic BIH 157 E9
Vojnić HR 148 F5
Vojnik NMK 164 E4
Vojnik SLO 148 D4
Vojtjajaure S 108 E9
Voka EST 132 C2
Vokány H 149 E10
Vokil BG 161 F10
Voknavolok RUS 121 E16
Voksa N 100 B2
Volakas GR 170 B5
Volary CZ 76 E5
Volda N 100 B4
Voldby DK 86 C5
Voldby DK 87 C7
Voldum DK 86 C6
Volendam NL 16 D4
Volgsele S 107 B11
Volimes GR 174 D2
Volintiri MD 154 E5
Volissos GR 177 C6
Voljevac BIH 157 E8
Voljice BIH 157 E8
Volkach D 75 C7
Volkel NL 183 B7
Völkermarkt A 73 C10
Volketswil CH 27 F10
Völklingen D 21 F7
Volkmarsen D 17 F12
Volkovija NMK 163 F10
Voll N 101 E13
Völlen D 17 B8
Vollenhove NL 16 C5
Vollersode D 17 B11
Vollsjö S 87 D13
Volmunster F 27 B7
Voloiac RO 159 D11
Voloka UA 153 A7
Volonne F 35 B11
Volos GR 169 F8
Voloshcha UA 145 D8
Volosovo RUS 132 C5
Volosyanka UA 145 F6
Volovăț RO 153 B7
Volovets' UA 145 F7
Volovo BG 166 B5
Volpago del Montello I 72 E5
Volpedo I 37 B9
Volpiano I 68 C4
Völs A 72 B3
Völschow D 84 C4
Voltaggio I 37 B9
Volta Mantovana I 66 B2
Volterra I 66 F2
Voltlage D 17 D9
Voltri I 37 C9
Voltti FIN 122 D9
Volturara Appula I 63 E8
Volturara Irpina I 60 B3
Volturino I 63 E8
Voluntari RO 161 E8
Volvic F 30 D3
Volx F 35 C10
Volya Arlamivs'ka UA 144 D7
Volyně CZ 76 D5
Vomp A 72 B4
Voneshta Voda BG 166 D5
Vonge DK 86 D4
Vonges F 26 F3
Voni GR 178 E9
Vonitsa GR 174 B2
Võnnu EST 131 E14
Võõpste EST 131 E14
Võõpsu EST 132 E2
Voorburg NL 16 D2
Voore EST 131 D13
Voorhout NL 182 A4
Voorschoten NL 16 D2
Voorst NL 16 D6
Voorthuizen NL 183 A7
Voose EST 131 C10
Vörå FIN 122 D8
Voranava BY 137 E11
Vorau A 148 B5
Vorbasse DK 86 D4
Vorchdorf A 76 F5
Vorden NL 16 D6
Vordernberg A 73 A10
Vordingborg DK 87 E9
Vordorf D 79 B8
Vorë AL 168 B2
Voreppe F 31 E8
Vorey F 30 E4
Vorgod DK 86 C3
Vormsele S 107 B15
Vormstad N 104 E7
Vormsund N 95 B14
Vormträsk S 107 B15
Vorna FIN 119 F15
Vorniceni RO 153 B9
Voroi GR 178 E8
Vorokhta UA 152 A5
Vorona RO 153 B9
Vorra D 75 C9
Vorst B 19 B11
Vorța RO 151 E10
Võru EST 131 F14
Vorwerk D 17 B12
Voskopojë AL 168 C4
Voșlăbeni RO 153 D7
Voss N 100 E4
Vosselaar B 16 F3
Voštane HR 157 E6
Võsu EST 131 B11
Votice CZ 77 C7
Votonosi GR 168 E5
Voudia GR 179 B8
Vougeot F 26 F2
Vouillé F 28 C5
Vouillé F 29 B6
Voukolies GR 178 E6
Voula GR 175 D8
Voulaines-les-Templiers F 25 E12
Vouliagmeni GR 175 D8
Voulpi GR 174 A4
Voulx F 25 D8
Vouneuil-sous-Biard F 29 B6
Vouneuil-sur-Vienne F 29 B7
Vourgareli GR 168 F5
Vourvourou GR 169 D10
Voutenay-sur-Cure F 25 E10
Voutezac F 29 E8
Voutianoi GR 174 E5
Vouvant F 28 B4
Vouvray F 24 F4
Vouvry CH 31 C10
Vouzela P 44 C4
Vouzi GR 174 A5
Vouziers F 19 F10
Vouzon F 24 E7
Voves F 24 D6
Vowchyn BY 141 F8
Vowkawshchyna BY 133 E2
Voxna S 103 D10
Voynika BG 167 E7
Voynitsa RUS 121 D15
Voynovo BG 161 F10
Voynyagovo BG 165 D10
Vozmediano E 41 E8
Voznesenka-Persha UA 154 E4
Vrå DK 90 E6
Vrabevo BG 165 D10
Vráble SK 146 E6
Vračev Gaj SRB 159 D7
Vraćevšnica SRB 158 E6
Vrachasi GR 179 E10
Vrachati GR 175 D6
Vrachesh BG 165 D8
Vrachnaiika GR 174 C4
Vrachos GR 168 D5
Vracov CZ 146 D4
Vrådal N 95 D8
Vrakúň SK 146 F5
Vrané nad Vltavou CZ 76 C6
Vrani RO 159 C8
Vranino BG 167 B10
Vranisht AL 163 E9
Vranisht AL 168 D2
Vranjak BIH 157 C9
Vranje SRB 164 D4
Vranjska Banja SRB 164 D5
Vranovice CZ 77 E11
Vranov nad Topľou SK 145 F4
Vransko SLO 73 D10
Vrapčište NMK 163 F10
Vrapčići BIH 157 F8
Vrasene B 182 C4
Vrasna GR 169 C10
Vratarnica SRB 159 F9
Vratimov CZ 146 B6
Vratnica NMK 164 E3
Vratsa BG 165 C8
Vrattsa BG 165 E6
Vražogrnac SRB 159 F9
Vrbanja BIH 157 C7
Vrbanja HR 157 C10
Vrbanjci BIH 157 C7
Vrbas SRB 158 B4
Vrbaška BIH 157 B7
Vrbica SRB 150 E5
Vrbice CZ 77 E11
Vrbnik HR 67 B10
Vrbnik HR 156 D5
Vrbno pod Pradědem CZ 142 F3
Vrbovac SRB 159 F9
Vrbovce SK 146 D4
Vrbové SK 146 D5
Vrbovec HR 149 E6
Vrbovsko HR 67 B11
Vrchlabí CZ 81 E9
Vrčin SRB 158 D6
Vrdy CZ 77 C8
Vrebac HR 156 C4
Vrécourt F 26 D4
Vreden D 17 D7
Vreeland NL 183 A6
Vrees D 17 C9
Vrellë RKS 163 D9
Vrelo SRB 164 C4
Vrena S 93 B9
Vrensted DK 90 E6
Vřesina CZ 146 B6
Vresse B 19 E10
Vresthena GR 175 E6
Vretstorp S 92 A5
Vrgorac HR 157 F7
Vrhnika SLO 73 E9
Vrhopolje BIH 157 C6
Vrhovine HR 156 C3
Vridsted DK 86 C4
Vries NL 17 B7
Vriezenveen NL 17 D7
Vrigstad S 92 E4
Vrinners DK 86 C6
Vrisa GR 177 A7
Vrizy F 19 F10
Vrlika HR 156 E5
Vrnjačka Banja SRB 163 B10
Vrnograč BIH 156 B4
Vron F 18 D4
Vrontados GR 177 C7
Vrontero GR 168 C5
Vrontou GR 169 D7
Vroomshoop NL 17 D7
Vrosina GR 168 E4
Vrouchas GR 179 E10
Vroutek CZ 76 B4
Vrouwenpolder NL 16 E1
Vrpolje HR 156 E5
Vrpolje HR 157 B9
Vrrin AL 168 B1
Vršac SRB 159 C7
Vršani BIH 157 C11
Vrsar HR 67 B8
Vrsi HR 156 D3
Vrtoče BIH 156 C5
Vrtojba SLO 73 E8
Vrulja MNE 163 C7
Vrútky SK 147 C7
Vrutok NMK 163 F10
Vrŭv BG 159 E10
Vrysia GR 169 F7
Vrysoula GR 168 F4
Všemina CZ 146 C5
Všeruby CZ 76 C4
Všetaty CZ 77 B7
Vsetín CZ 146 C5
Vsevolozhsk RUS 129 E14
Vŭbel BG 160 F5
Vučijak BIH 157 C8
Vučja Lokva SRB 163 C10
Vučje SRB 164 D4
Vught NL 16 E4
Vŭglevtsi BG 166 D5
Vuka HR 149 F10
Vukova Gorica HR 148 F4
Vukovar HR 157 B11
Vuku N 105 D11
Vulcan RO 159 C11
Vulcan RO 160 B6
Vulcana-Băi RO 160 C6
Vulcănești MD 155 B2
Vŭlchedrŭm BG 160 F2
Vŭlchidol BG 167 C9
Vulpeni RO 160 E3
Vultureni RO 152 D3
Vultureni RO 153 E10
Vulturești RO 153 B8
Vulturești RO 153 D11
Vulturești RO 160 D4
Vulturu RO 155 D2
Vulturu RO 161 B10
Vuobmaved FIN 113 E16
Vuohijärvi FIN 128 C6
Vuohtomäki FIN 123 C16
Vuojärvi FIN 117 D17
Vuokatti FIN 121 F11
Vuokko FIN 125 D12
Vuolenkoski FIN 127 C15
Vuolijoki FIN 120 F8
Vuolle FIN 123 C11
Vuollerim S 118 B5
Vuonisjärvi FIN 125 D14
Vuonislahti FIN 125 D13
Vuonos FIN 125 E12
Vuontisjärvi FIN 117 B11
Vuorenmaa FIN 124 G9
Vuorenmaa FIN 126 C8
Vuoreslahti FIN 121 F9
Vuorimäki FIN 123 E11
Vuorimäki FIN 124 C9
Vuoriniemi FIN 129 B11
Vuosaari FIN 127 E13
Vuosanka FIN 121 F13
Vuostimo FIN 115 E2
Vuostimojärvi FIN 115 E2
Vuotner S 118 C3
Vuotso FIN 115 B2
Vuottas S 118 B7
Vuottolahti FIN 120 F9
Vuotunki FIN 121 B14
Vŭrbitsa BG 166 E4
Vŭrbitsa BG 167 D7
Vurpăr RO 152 F4
Vŭrshets BG 165 C7
Vushtrri RKS 164 D2
Vustsye BY 133 E3
Vutcani RO 153 E11
Vuzenica SLO 73 C11
Vuzlove UA 145 G5
Vvedenka UA 154 E5
Vyalets BY 133 F3
Vyalikaya Byerastavitsa BY 140 D10
Vyalikaya Stayki BY 133 F7
Vyalikaye Syalo BY 133 F3
Vyarkhovichy BY 141 F8
Vyartsilya RUS 125 F15
Vyaz RUS 133 C7
Vyborg RUS 129 D10
Výčapy-Opatovce SK 146 E6
Východná SK 147 C9
Vydeniai LT 137 E10
Vydrany SK 146 E5
Vyerkhnyadzvinsk BY 133 E3
Vyetryna BY 133 F4
Vyhne SK 147 D7
Vyhoda UA 145 F8
Vy-lès-Lure F 26 E5
Vylkove UA 155 C5
Vylok UA 145 G6
Vynnyky UA 144 D9
Vynohradiv UA 145 G7
Vynohradivka UA 154 F4
Vyritsa RUS 132 C7
Vyronas GR 175 D8
Vyroneia GR 169 B9
Vyshgorodok RUS 133 B3
Vyshka UA 145 F6
Vyshkiv UA 145 F8
Vyshkove UA 145 G7
Vyshneve UA 154 F5
Vyshniv UA 141 H10
Vyskod' RUS 132 F7
Vyškov CZ 77 D12
Vyšné Ružbachy SK 145 E2
Vyšný Mirošov SK 145 E3
Vyšný Orlík SK 145 E4
Vyšný Šipov SK 145 F4
Vysoká nad Kysucou SK 147 C7
Vysokaye BY 141 F8
Vysoké Mýto CZ 77 C10
Vysokoye RUS 136 D4
Vysotsk RUS 129 D10
Vyšší Brod CZ 76 E6
Vyssinia GR 168 C5
Vytina GR 174 D5
Vyzhnytsya UA 152 A6
Vyžuonos LT 135 E11
Vzmor'ye RUS 139 A9

W

Waabs D 83 A7
Waal D 71 B11
Waalre NL 16 F4
Waalwijk NL 16 E4
Waarschoot B 19 B8
Wabern D 21 B12
Wąbrzeźno PL 138 D6
Wachenheim an der Weinstraße D 187 C5
Wąchock PL 143 D11
Wachow D 79 A12
Wachtebeke B 19 B8
Wächtersbach D 21 D12
Wacken D 82 B6
Wackersdorf D 75 D11
Waddeweitz D 83 D9
Waddington GB 11 E10
Waddinxveen NL 16 D3
Wadebridge GB 12 D5
Wädenswil CH 27 F10
Wadern D 21 E7
Wadersloh D 17 E10
Wadgassen D 21 F7
Wadhurst GB 15 E9
Wadlew PL 143 C7
Wadowice PL 147 B9
Wadowice Górne PL 143 F11
Wądroże Wielkie PL 81 D10
Waganiec PL 138 E6
Wagenfeld D 17 C11
Wagenhoff D 79 A8
Wageningen NL 16 E5
Waghäusel D 21 F11
Waging am See D 73 A6
Wagna A 148 C5
Wagrain A 73 B7
Wągrowiec PL 85 E12
Wahlhausen D 79 D6
Wahlsdorf D 80 C4
Wahlstedt D 83 C8
Wahrenholz D 79 A8
Waiblingen D 27 C11
Waibstadt D 187 C6
Waidhofen an der Thaya A 77 E8
Waidhofen an der Ybbs A 77 G7
Waigolshausen D 75 C7
Waimes B 20 D6
Wain D 71 A10
Wainfleet All Saints GB 11 E12
Wainhouse Corner GB 12 D5
Waischenfeld D 75 C9
Waizenkirchen A 76 F5
Wakefield GB 11 D8
Wakendorf II D 83 C8
Walberswick GB 15 C12
Wałbrzych PL 81 E10
Walburg D 78 D6
Walchum D 17 C8
Walcourt B 19 D9
Wałcz PL 85 D10
Wald CH 27 F10
Wald D 27 E11
Wald D 75 D11
Waldachtal D 27 D10
Waldböckelheim D 185 E8
Waldbreitbach D 185 C7
Waldbröl D 21 C9
Waldbrunn-Lahr D 21 C10
Waldburg D 71 B9
Waldbüttelbrunn D 74 C6
Walddrehna D 80 C5
Waldegg A 77 G10
Waldenbuch D 27 C11
Waldenburg CH 27 F8
Waldenburg D 74 D6
Walderbach D 75 D11
Waldershof D 75 C11
Waldesch D 185 D8
Waldfischbach-Burgalben D 21 F9
Waldhausen A 77 E8
Waldhausen im Strudengau A 77 F7
Waldheim D 80 D4
Walding A 76 F6
Waldkappel D 78 D6
Waldkirch D 27 D8
Waldkirchen D 76 E5
Waldkraiburg D 75 F11
Wald-Michelbach D 187 B6
Waldmohr D 21 F8
Waldmünchen D 75 D12
Wałdowo-Szlacheckie PL 138 D6
Waldrach D 21 E7
Waldsassen D 75 B11
Waldsee D 187 C5
Waldshut D 27 E9
Waldstatt CH 27 F11
Waldstetten D 75 F7
Waldstetten D 187 D8
Walenstadt CH 27 F11
Walferdange L 20 E6
Walim PL 81 E10
Walkendorf D 83 C13
Wallasey GB 10 E5
Walldorf D 21 D11
Walldorf D 21 F11
Walldorf D 79 E7
Walldürn D 27 A11
Wallenfels D 75 B9
Wallerfing D 76 E3
Wallern im Burgenland A 149 A7
Wallersdorf D 75 E12
Wallerstein D 75 E7
Wallgau D 72 A3
Wallhausen D 75 D7
Wallhausen D 185 E8
Wallisellen CH 27 F10
Walls GB 3 E13
Wallsbüll D 82 A6
Wallstawe D 83 E10
Walmer GB 15 E11
Wałowice PL 81 C7
Wals A 73 A6
Walsall GB 11 F8
Walschleben D 79 D8
Walsleben D 83 E13
Walsoken GB 11 F12
Walsrode D 82 E7
Waltenhofen D 71 B10
Waltershausen D 79 E8
Waltham on the Wolds GB 11 F10
Walton-on-Thames GB 15 E8
Walton on the Naze GB 15 D11
Wamba E 39 E10
Wamel NL 183 B6
Wanderup D 82 A6
Wandlitz D 84 E4
Wandre B 183 D7
Wang A 77 F8
Wangen CH 27 F8
Wangen im Allgäu D 71 B9
Wängi CH 27 E10
Wankendorf D 83 B8
Wanna D 17 A11
Wanne-Eikel D 183 B10
Wanroij NL 183 B7
Wanssum NL 183 B8
Wantage GB 13 B12
Wanze B 19 C11
Wanzleben D 79 B9
Wapenveld NL 16 D6
Wąpiersk PL 139 D8
Waplewo PL 139 C9
Wąpnica PL 85 D8
Wapno PL 85 E12
Warberg D 79 B8
Warboys GB 15 C8
Warburg D 17 F12
Warcop GB 11 B7
Warcq F 20 F5
Wardenburg D 17 B10
Wardington GB 13 A12
Ware GB 15 D8
Waregem B 19 C7
Wareham GB 13 D10
Waremme B 19 C11
Waren D 83 C13
Warendorf D 17 E9
Warffum NL 17 B7
Warin D 83 C11
Waringstown GB 7 D10
Wark GB 5 E12
Warka PL 141 G4
Warkworth GB 5 E13
Warlingham GB 15 E8
Warloy-Baillon F 18 D6
Warlubie PL 138 C6
Warmeriville F 19 F9
Warmington GB 13 A12
Warminster GB 13 C10
Warmond NL 182 A5
Warmsen D 17 D11
Warnemünde D 83 B12
Warngau D 72 A4
Warnice PL 85 D7
Warnice PL 85 E7
Warnino PL 85 C10
Warnow D 83 C11
Warnsveld NL 16 D6
Warrenpoint GB 7 D10
Warrington GB 10 E6
Warsingsfehn D 17 B8
Warslow GB 11 E8
Warstein D 17 F10
Warszawa PL 141 F4
Warszkowo PL 85 B11
Warta PL 142 C6
Warta Bolesławiecka PL 81 D9
Wartberg an der Krems A 76 G6
Wartenberg D 75 F10
Wartenberg-Angersbach D 78 E5
Warth A 71 C10
Wartin D 84 D6
Wartkowice PL 143 C7
Wartmannsroth D 74 B6
Warwick GB 13 A11
Warwick Bridge GB 5 F11
Warzyce PL 144 D4
Wasbek D 83 B7
Wasbister GB 3 G10
Wäschenbeuren D 74 E6
Wąsewo PL 139 E12
Washington GB 5 F13
Wasigny F 19 E9
Wasilków PL 140 D8
Waśniów PL 143 E11
Wąsosz PL 81 C11
Wąsosz PL 140 C6
Wąsowo PL 81 B10
Waspik NL 16 E3
Wasseiges B 183 D6
Wasselonne F 27 C7
Wassen CH 71 D7
Wassenaar NL 16 D2
Wassenberg D 20 B6
Wasseralfingen D 75 E7
Wasserbillig D 186 B2
Wasserburg am Inn D 75 F11
Wasserliesch D 186 B2
Wasserlosen D 74 B7
Wassertrüdingen D 75 D8
Wassigny F 19 D8
Wassy F 26 C2
Wasungen D 79 E7
Watchet GB 13 C8
Watchgate GB 10 C6
Waterbeck GB 5 E10
Waterford IRL 9 D8
Watergrasshill IRL 8 D6
Wateringen NL 182 A4
Waterland-Oudeman B 182 C3
Waterloo B 19 C9
Waterlooville GB 14 F6
Waterville IRL 8 E2
Watford GB 15 D8
Wathlingen D 79 A7
Watlington GB 14 D6
Watten F 18 C5
Watten GB 3 J10
Wattenbek D 83 B8
Wattens A 72 B4
Watten-Scheid D 183 C10
Wattenwil CH 31 B12
Wattlebridge GB 7 D8
Watton GB 15 B10
Wattwil CH 27 F11
Wavre B 19 C10
Wavrin F 18 C6
Wąwelno PL 85 D13
Wąwelno PL 142 E4
Wąwolnica PL 141 H6
Wawrów PL 85 E8
Wawrzeńczyce PL 143 F9
Waxweiler D 20 D6
Waziers F 182 E2
Weaverham GB 10 E6
Wechmar D 79 E8
Wechselburg D 79 D12
Wedde NL 17 B8
Weddingstedt D 82 B6
Wedel (Holstein) D 82 C7
Wedmore GB 13 C9
Wednesbury GB 11 F7
Weede D 83 C8
Weedon Bec GB 13 A12
Weelde B 182 C5
Weem GB 5 B9
Weener D 17 B8
Weerberg A 72 B4
Weerselo NL 17 D7
Weert NL 16 F5
Weesen CH 27 F11
Weesp NL 16 D4
Weeze D 16 E6
Weferlingen D 79 B9
Wegberg D 20 B6
Wegenstedt D 79 B9
Weggis CH 71 C6
Wegscheid A 148 A4
Wegscheid D 76 E5
Wehdel D 17 A11
Wehl NL 16 E6
Wehr D 27 E8
Wehrbleck D 17 C11
Wehringen D 71 A11
Weibern D 183 E10
Weibersbrunn D 74 C5
Weichering D 75 E9
Weichs D 75 F9
Weida D 79 E11
Weidenberg D 75 C10
Weiden in der Oberpfalz D 75 C11
Weidenstetten D 187 D8
Weidenthal D 21 F9
Weiding D 75 D12
Weiersbach D 186 B3
Weigersdorf D 81 D7
Weihmichl D 75 E11
Weikersheim D 74 D6
Weil D 71 A11
Weil am Rhein D 27 E8
Weilbach D 21 E12
Weilburg D 21 D10
Weil der Stadt D 27 C10
Weilerbach D 186 C4
Weilerswist D 21 C7
Weilheim an der Teck D 74 E6
Weilheim in Oberbayern D 72 A3
Weilmünster D 21 D10
Weimar D 79 E9
Weinbach D 185 D9
Weinböhla D 80 D5
Weinfelden CH 27 E11
Weingarten D 71 B9
Weingarten (Baden) D 187 C6
Weinheim D 21 E11
Weinsberg D 21 F12
Weinsheim D 20 D6
Weinsheim D 21 E9
Weinstadt D 27 C11
Weischlitz D 75 B11
Weisen D 83 D11
Weiskirchen D 21 E7
Weismain D 75 B9
Weissach D 27 C10
Weißbriach A 73 C7
Weißenbach am Lech A 71 C11
Weißenberg D 81 D7
Weißenbrunn D 75 B9
Weißenburg in Bayern D 75 D8
Weißenfels D 79 D10
Weißenhorn D 75 F7
Weißensee D 79 D9
Weißenstadt D 75 B10
Weißenstein A 73 C8
Weißenthurm D 185 D7
Weißig D 80 D5
Weißkeißel D 81 D7
Weißkirchen in Steiermark A 73 B10
Weißkollm D 80 D6
Weißwasser D 81 C7
Weistrach A 77 F7
Weiswampach L 20 D6
Weisweil D 27 D8
Weitbruch F 186 D4
Weitefeld D 185 C8
Weiten A 77 F8
Weitensfeld A 73 C9
Weitersfeld A 77 E9
Weiterstadt D 187 B6
Weitra A 77 E7
Weixdorf D 80 D5
Weiz A 148 B5
Wejherowo PL 138 A5
Wekerom NL 16 D5
Welkenraedt B 20 C5
Well NL 16 E6
Wellaune D 79 C12
Welle D 82 D7
Wellen B 183 D6
Wellesbourne GB 13 A11
Wellheim D 75 E9
Wellin B 19 D11
Welling D 21 D8
Wellingborough GB 15 C7
Wellington GB 10 F6
Wellington GB 13 D8
Wellingtonbridge IRL 9 D9
Wellington Bridge IRL 9 D9
Wells GB 13 C9
Wells-next-the-Sea GB 15 B10
Welney GB 11 F12
Wels A 76 F6
Welschbillig D 21 E7
Welshpool GB 10 F5
Welsickendorf D 80 C4
Welsleben D 79 C10
Welver D 17 E9
Welwyn GB 15 D8
Welwyn Garden City GB 15 D8
Welzheim D 74 E6
Welzow D 80 C6
Wem GB 10 F6
Wembdon GB 13 C8
Wemding D 75 E8
Wemeldinge NL 182 B4
Wemyss Bay GB 4 D7
Wendeburg D 79 B7
Wendelsheim D 21 E10
Wendelstein D 75 D9
Wenden D 21 C9
Wendens Ambo GB 15 C9
Wendisch Priborn D 83 D12
Wendisch Rietz D 80 B6
Wendlingen am Neckar D 27 C11
Wendover GB 15 D7
Wenduine B 182 C2
Wengen CH 70 D5
Wengsel (Isterberg) D 17 D8
Wennigsen (Deister) D 78 B6
Wenningstedt D 86 F2
Wenns A 71 C11
Wentorf D 83 C8
Wentorf bei Hamburg D 83 D8
Wenzenbach D 75 D11
Wenzlow D 79 B11
Wépion B 182 E5
Werbach D 74 C6
Werbellin D 84 E5
Werben D 80 C6
Werben (Elbe) D 83 E11
Werbig D 80 C4
Werbkowice PL 144 B8
Werbomont B 19 D12
Werdau D 79 E11
Werder D 79 B12
Werder D 84 C4
Werdohl D 17 F9
Werfen A 73 B7
Werkendam NL 182 B5
Werl D 17 E9
Werlte D 17 C9
Wermelskirchen D 185 B7
Wermsdorf D 80 D3
Wernau D 27 C11
Wernberg-Köblitz D 75 C11
Werndorf A 148 C5
Werne D 17 E9
Werneck D 75 C7
Werneuchen D 80 A5
Wernigerode D 79 C8
Wernshausen D 79 E7
Werpeloh D 17 C9
Wertach D 71 B10
Wertheim D 74 C6
Werthenstein CH 70 C6
Werther D 79 D8
Werther (Westfalen) D 17 D10
Wertingen D 75 E8
Wervershoof NL 16 C4
Wervik B 19 C7
Wesel D 17 E7
Wesenberg D 84 D3
Wesendorf D 79 A8
Wesepe NL 183 A8
Wesoła PL 141 F4
Wesselburen D 82 B5
Wesseling D 21 C7
Wesseln D 82 B6
Wessem NL 183 C7
Weßling D 75 F9
Wessobrunn D 71 B12
West Auckland GB 5 F13
West Bridgford GB 11 F9
West Bromwich GB 11 F8
Westbury GB 13 C10
Westendorf A 72 B5
Westensee D 83 B7
Westerbeck (Sassenburg) D 79 A8
Westerbork NL 17 C7
Westerburg D 21 C9
Westerdale GB 3 J10
Westeregeln D 79 C9
Westerende-Kirchloog (Ihlow) D 17 B8
Westergate GB 15 F7
Westergellersen D 83 D8
Westerhaar NL 17 D7
Westerheim D 187 D8
Westerholt D 17 A8
Westerhorn D 82 C7
Westerhoven NL 183 C6
Westerland D 86 F2
Westerlo B 19 B10
Westerrönfeld D 82 B7
Westerstede D 17 B9
Westerstetten D 74 E6
Westervoort NL 16 E5
Westgate GB 5 F12
West Grinstead GB 15 F8
West Haddon GB 13 A12
Westhausen D 75 E7
Westhill GB 3 L12
Westhofen D 187 B5
Westhoffen F 186 D3
Westkapelle NL 19 A7
West Kilbride GB 4 D7
West Kirby GB 10 E5
West Knapton GB 11 C10
West Lavington GB 13 C11
Westleton GB 15 C12
West Linton GB 5 D10
West Looe GB 12 E6
West Lulworth GB 13 D10
Westmalle B 16 F3
West Malling GB 15 E9
West Meon Hut GB 13 C12
West Mersea GB 15 D10
West Moors GB 13 D11
Westness GB 3 G10
Westnewton GB 5 F10
Weston GB 11 F7
Weston GB 13 D10
Weston-super-Mare GB 13 C9
Westonzoyland GB 13 C9
Westport IRL 6 E3
Westport Quay IRL 6 E3
West Somerton GB 15 B12
West Tarbert GB 4 D6
West-Terschelling NL 16 B4
Westward Ho! GB 12 C6
West Wellow GB 13 D11
West Winch GB 11 F12
Wethau D 79 D10
Wetheral GB 5 F11
Wetherby GB 11 D9
Wetlina PL 145 E5
Wetter (Hessen) D 21 C11
Wetter (Ruhr) D 185 B7
Wetteren B 19 B8
Wetterzeube D 79 D11
Wettin D 79 C10
Wettingen CH 27 F9
Wettrup D 17 C9
Wetzikon CH 27 F10
Wetzlar D 21 C11
Wevelgem B 19 C7
Wewelsfleth D 17 A12
Wexford IRL 9 D10
Weyarn D 72 A4
Weybridge GB 15 E8
Weyerbusch D 21 C9
Weyer Markt A 73 A10
Weyersheim F 27 C8
Weyhausen D 79 B8
Weyhe D 17 C11
Weymouth GB 13 D10
Whalton GB 5 E13
Whauphill GB 4 F8
Wheddon Cross GB 13 C7
Wherwell GB 13 C12
Whiddon Down GB 13 D7
Whitburn GB 5 D9
Whitby GB 11 C10
Whitchurch GB 10 F6
Whitchurch GB 13 B8
Whitchurch GB 15 D7
Whitecross GB 7 D10
Whitegate IRL 8 C6
Whitegate IRL 8 E6
Whitehall GB 3 G11
Whitehall IRL 9 C8
Whitehaven GB 10 B4
Whitehead GB 4 F5
Whitehill GB 15 E7
Whitehills GB 3 K11
Whitfield GB 15 E11
Whithorn GB 5 F8
Whiting Bay GB 4 E6
Whitland GB 12 B5
Whitley Bay GB 5 E14
Whitstable GB 15 E11
Whittington GB 10 F5
Whittlesey GB 11 F11
Wiartel PL 139 C12
Wiatrowo PL 85 E12
Wiązów PL 81 E12
Wiązowna PL 141 F4
Wiązownica PL 144 C6
Wichelen B 19 B8
Wick GB 3 J10
Wick GB 13 C7
Wick GB 15 F7
Wickede (Ruhr) D 185 B8
Wickenrode (Helsa) D 78 D6
Wickford GB 15 D10
Wickham GB 13 D12
Wickham Market GB 15 C11
Wicklow IRL 7 G10
Wicko PL 85 A13
Widawa PL 143 D6
Widecombe in the Moor GB 13 D7
Widnau CH 71 C9
Widnes GB 10 E6
Widuchowa PL 84 D6
Więcbork PL 85 D12
Wieck am Darß D 83 B13
Wieczfnia Kościelna PL 139 D9
Wieda D 79 C8
Wiedensahl D 17 D12
Wiederau D 80 E3
Wiednitz D 80 D6
Wiefelstede D 17 B10
Wiehe D 79 D9
Wiehl D 21 C9
Wiek D 84 A4
Większyce PL 142 F5
Wielbark PL 139 D10
Wieleń PL 85 E10
Wielenbach D 72 A3
Wielgie PL 139 E7
Wielgomłyny PL 143 D8

Wielichowo PL 81 B10
Wieliczka PL 143 G9
Wieliczki PL 136 F6
Wielka Wieś PL 143 F8
Wielkie Oczy PL 144 C7
Wielki Klincz PL 138 B5
Wielopole Skrzyńskie PL 143 G12
Wielowieś PL 142 E6
Wielsbeke B 182 D2
Wieluń PL 142 D6
Wiemersdorf D 83 C7
Wien A 77 F10
Wienerbruck A 77 G8
Wiener Neustadt A 77 G10
Wieniawa PL 141 H3
Wieniec PL 138 E6
Wienrode D 79 C8
Wiepke D 79 A9
Wieprz PL 147 B8
Wieprz PL 147 B8
Wiercień Duży PL 141 F7
Wierden NL 17 D7
Wieren D 83 E9
Wieringerwerf NL 16 C4
Wiernsheim D 187 D6
Wieruszów PL 142 D5
Wierzawice PL 144 C5
Wierzbica PL 141 H4
Wierzbica PL 141 H8
Wierzbica Górna PL 142 D4
Wierzbijcin PL 85 C8
Wierzbinek PL 138 F6
Wierzbnik PL 142 E3
Wierzbno PL 139 F12
Wierzbowa PL 81 D9
Wierzchlas PL 142 D6
Wierzchosławice PL 138 E5
Wierzchosławice PL 143 F10
Wierzchowo PL 85 C11
Wierzchowo PL 85 D10
Wierzchucino PL 138 A5
Wies A 148 C4
Wiesa D 80 E3
Wiesau D 75 C11
Wiesbaden D 21 D10
Wieselburg A 77 F8
Wiesen A 149 A6
Wiesen CH 71 D9
Wiesen D 74 B5
Wiesenau D 81 B7
Wiesenburg D 79 B11
Wiesenfelden D 75 D12
Wiesensteig D 187 D8
Wiesent D 75 D11
Wiesenthau D 75 C9
Wiesentheid D 75 C7
Wiesloch D 21 F11
Wiesmath A 148 A6
Wiesmoor D 17 B9
Wieszowa PL 142 F6
Wietmarschen D 17 C8
Wietze D 78 A6
Wietzen D 17 C12
Wietzendorf D 83 E7
Wiewiórczyn PL 143 C7
Wigan GB 10 D6
Wiggensbach D 71 B10
Węgierska Górka PL 147 B8
Węgliniec PL 81 D8
Wigmore GB 13 A9
Węgorzewo PL 136 E4
Węgorzyno PL 85 C9
Węgrów PL 139 F13
Węgrzynice PL 81 B8
Węgrzynowo PL 139 F9
Wigston GB 11 F9
Wigton GB 5 F10
Wigtown GB 5 F8
Wijchen NL 16 E5
Wijewo PL 81 C10
Wijhe NL 183 A8
Wijk aan Zee NL 16 D3
Wijk bij Duurstede NL 16 E4
Wijk en Aalburg NL 183 B6
Wil CH 27 F11
Wilamowice PL 147 B8
Wilczęta PL 139 B8
Wilczogóra PL 138 F5
Wilczyn PL 138 F5
Wildalpen A 73 A10
Wildau D 80 B5
Wildberg D 27 C10
Wildberg D 83 E13
Wildberg D 84 C4
Wildeck-Richelsdorf D 79 E7
Wildendürnbach A 77 E10
Wildenfels D 79 E12
Wildeshausen D 17 C10
Wildflecken D 74 B6
Wildon A 148 C5
Wildpoldsried D 71 B10
Wildshut A 76 F3
Wilga PL 141 G4
Wilhelminadorp NL 183 C6
Wilhelmsburg A 77 F9
Wilhelmsburg D 84 C5
Wilhelmsdorf D 27 E11
Wilhelmshaven D 17 A10
Wilkau-Haßlau D 79 E12
Wilkinstown IRL 7 E9
Wilkołaz Pierwszy PL 144 A5
Wilków PL 141 H5
Wilków PL 142 D4
Wilkowice PL 147 B8
Wilkowo PL 81 B8
Willand GB 13 D8
Willebadessen D 17 E12
Willebroek B 19 B9
Willemstad NL 16 E2
Willich D 17 F7
Willingdon GB 15 F9
Willingen (Upland) D 17 F11
Willingshausen D 21 C12
Willisau CH 27 F9
Williton GB 13 C8
Willstätt D 27 C8
Wilmersdorf D 84 D5
Wilmslow GB 11 E7
Wilnis NL 182 A5
Wilnsdorf D 21 C10
Wilp NL 183 A8
Wilsdruff D 80 D5
Wilsickow D 84 D5
Wilster D 82 C6
Wilsum D 17 C7
Wiltersdorf A 77 E11
Wiltingen D 21 E7
Wilton GB 13 C11
Wiltz L 20 E5
Wimblington GB 11 F12
Wimborne Minster GB 13 D11
Wimereux F 15 F12
Wimmelburg D 79 C10
Wimmis CH 70 D5
Wimpassing A 148 A6
Wincanton GB 13 C10
Winchburgh GB 5 D10
Winchelsea GB 15 F10
Wincheringen D 186 B1
Winchester GB 13 C12
Wincrange L 20 D5
Winda PL 136 E3
Windach D 71 A12
Windeby D 83 B7
Windermere GB 10 C6
Windesheim D 21 E9
Windhagen D 21 C8
Windigsteig A 77 E8
Windischeschenbach D 75 C11
Windischgarsten A 73 A9
Windorf D 76 E4
Windsbach D 75 D8
Windsor GB 15 E7
Wingate GB 5 F14
Wingene B 19 B7
Wingen-sur-Moder F 27 C7
Winklarn D 75 D11
Winkleigh GB 13 D7
Winklern A 73 C6
Winklern bei Oberwölz A 73 B9
Winnenden D 27 C11
Winnert D 82 B6
Winnica PL 139 E10
Winningen D 79 C9
Winningen D 185 D8
Winnweiler D 186 B4
Winschoten NL 17 B8
Winsen (Aller) D 83 E7
Winsen (Luhe) D 83 D8
Winsford GB 10 E6
Wińsko PL 81 D11
Winslow GB 15 D7
Winssen NL 183 B7
Winston GB 11 B8
Winsum NL 16 B5
Winterberg D 21 B11
Winterbourne Abbas GB 13 D9
Winterfeld D 83 E10
Winterswijk NL 17 E7
Winterthur CH 27 E10
Winterton GB 11 D10
Winton GB 11 C7
Wintrich D 185 E6
Wintzenheim F 27 D7
Winwick GB 15 C8
Winzenburg D 78 C6
Winzer D 76 E4
Wipperdorf D 79 D8
Wipperfürth D 21 B8
Wippra Kurort D 79 C9
Wirdumer (Wirdum) D 17 B8
Wirges D 185 D8
Wirksworth GB 11 E8
Wirsberg D 75 B10
Wisbech GB 11 F12
Wischhafen D 17 A12
Wishaw GB 5 D9
Wiskitki PL 141 F2
Wisła PL 147 B7
Wiślica PL 143 F10
Wismar D 83 C10
Wiśniew PL 141 F6
Wiśniewo PL 139 D9
Wiśniowa PL 144 D1
Wiśniowa PL 144 D4
Wissant F 15 F12
Wissembourg F 27 B8
Wissen D 21 C9
Wissenkerke NL 16 E1
Wistedt D 82 D7
Wisznia Mała PL 81 D12
Wisznice PL 141 G8
Witaszyce PL 142 C4
Witham GB 15 D10
Witheridge GB 13 D7
Withernsea GB 11 D12
Witkowo PL 85 D8
Witkowo PL 138 F4
Witley GB 15 E7
Witmarsum NL 16 B4
Witney GB 13 B12
Witnica PL 84 E6
Witnica PL 85 E7
Witonia PL 143 B7
Witosław PL 85 D12
Witry-lès-Reims F 19 F9
Wittdün D 82 A4
Witten D 17 F8
Wittenbach CH 27 F11
Wittenberge D 83 E11
Wittenburg D 83 C10
Wittenförden D 83 C10
Wittenhagen D 84 B4
Wittenheim F 27 E7
Wittibreut D 76 F3
Wittichenau D 80 D6
Wittighausen D 74 C6
Wittingen D 83 E9
Wittlich D 21 E7
Wittmar D 79 B8
Wittmund D 17 A9
Wittstock D 83 D12
Witzenhausen D 78 D6
Witzin D 83 C11
Witzwort D 82 B5
Wiveliscombe GB 13 C8
Wivenhoe GB 15 D10
Wiżajny PL 136 E6
Wizernes F 18 C5
Wizna PL 140 D6
Władysławów PL 142 B5
Władysławowo PL 138 A5
Wleń PL 81 D9
Włocławek PL 138 E7
Włodawa PL 141 G9
Włodzienin PL 142 F4
Włodzimierzów PL 143 D8
Włostów PL 143 E11
Włoszakowice PL 81 C10
Włoszczowa PL 143 E8
Wöbbelin D 83 D11
Woburn GB 15 D7
Wodynie PL 141 F5
Wodzierady PL 143 C7
Wodzisław PL 143 E9
Wodzisław Śląski PL 142 F5
Woensdrecht NL 182 C4
Woerden NL 16 D3
Wœrth F 27 C8
Wohlen CH 27 F9
Wohlen CH 31 B11
Wohlmirstedt D 79 D9
Wohltorf D 83 C8
Wöhrden D 82 B6
Wohyń PL 141 G7
Woippy F 26 B5
Wojaszówka PL 144 D4
Wojcieszków PL 141 G6
Wojcieszów PL 81 E9
Wójcin PL 138 E5
Wojkowice PL 143 F7
Wojnicz PL 143 G10
Wojnowo PL 138 D4
Wojsławice PL 144 B8
Woking GB 15 E7
Wokingham GB 15 E7
Wola PL 138 E7
Wola Mołodycka PL 144 C6
Wola Mysłowska PL 141 G5
Wolanów PL 141 H3
Wola-Rębkowska PL 141 G5
Wola Uhruska PL 141 H9
Wola Wierzbowska PL 139 E10
Wolbórz PL 141 H1
Wolbrom PL 143 F8
Wołczyn PL 142 D5
Woldegk D 84 D5
Woldendorp NL 17 B8
Wolfach D 27 D9
Wolfegg D 71 B9
Wolfen D 79 C11
Wolfenbüttel D 79 B8
Wolfenschiessen CH 71 D6
Wölfersheim D 21 D11
Wolfhagen D 17 F12
Wölfis D 79 E8
Wolfpassing A 77 F8
Wolfratshausen D 72 A3
Wolfsberg A 73 C10
Wolfsburg D 79 B8
Wolfstein D 21 E9
Wolfurt A 71 C9
Wolgast D 84 B5
Wolhusen CH 70 C6
Wolin PL 84 C7
Wólka PL 139 E7
Wólka PL 141 H7
Wólka Dobryńska PL 141 F8
Wolkersdorf A 77 F11
Wollbach D 75 B7
Wollerau CH 27 F10
Wolmirstedt D 79 B10
Wolnzach D 75 E10
Wołomin PL 139 F11
Woloskowola PL 141 H8
Wołów PL 81 D11
Wolpertshausen D 74 D6
Wolpertswende D 71 B9
Wolphaartsdijk NL 182 B3
Wölpinghausen D 17 D12
Wolsingham GB 5 F13
Wolsztyn PL 81 B10
Woltersdorf D 80 B4
Woltersdorf D 83 E10
Wolvega NL 16 C6
Wolverhampton GB 11 F7
Wombwell GB 11 D9
Wommelgem B 19 B10
Wommels NL 16 B5
Wonfurt D 75 B7
Wonsees D 75 C9
Woodbridge GB 15 C11
Woodcote GB 13 B12
Woodford IRL 6 F6
Woodhall Spa GB 11 E11
Woodland GB 5 F13
Woodley GB 15 E7
Woodstock GB 13 B12
Woodton GB 15 C11
Woodtown IRL 7 E9
Wool GB 13 D10
Wooler GB 5 D12
Wootton Bassett GB 13 B11
Worb CH 31 B12
Worbis D 79 D7
Worcester GB 13 A10
Wördern A 77 F10
Worfield GB 11 F7
Wörgl A 72 B5
Workington GB 5 F9
Worksop GB 11 E9
Workum NL 16 C4
Wörlitz D 79 C11
Wormeldange L 20 E6
Wormerveer NL 16 D3
Wormhout F 18 C5
Worms D 21 E10
Worpswede D 17 B11
Wörrstadt D 21 E10
Wörschach A 73 A9
Wortel B 182 C5
Wörth A 73 B6
Worth GB 15 E8
Wörth am Main D 187 B7
Wörth am Rhein D 27 B9
Worthing GB 15 F8
Woudenberg NL 183 A6
Woudrichem NL 16 E3
Woudsend NL 16 C5
Woustviller F 27 B7
Wouw NL 16 E2
Woźniki PL 143 E7
Wragby GB 11 E11
Wrangle GB 11 E12
Wrecsam GB 10 E6
Wręczyca Wielka PL 143 E6
Wredenhagen D 83 D13
Wrelton GB 11 C10
Wremen D 17 A11
Wrestedt D 83 E9
Wrexham GB 10 E6
Wriedel D 83 D8
Wriezen D 84 E6
Wrist D 82 C7
Wróblew PL 142 C6
Wrocław PL 81 D12
Wrohm D 82 B6
Wronki PL 85 E10
Wronki PL 136 E5
Wrotnów PL 139 E13
Wrzącielka PL 142 B6
Wrzelowiec PL 144 A4
Wrzeście PL 85 A12
Września PL 85 F13
Wrzosowo PL 85 B9
Wschowa PL 81 C10
Wulfen D 79 C10
Wulfersdorf D 83 D12
Wülfershausen an der Saale D 75 B7
Wulfsen D 83 D8
Wulften D 79 C7
Wulkau D 83 E12
Wullersdorf A 77 E10
Wundschuh A 148 C4
Wünnenberg D 17 E11
Wünsdorf D 80 B4
Wunsiedel D 75 B11
Wunstorf D 78 B5
Wuppertal D 17 F8
Wurmlingen D 27 D10
Würselen D 20 C6
Wurzbach D 75 B10
Würzburg D 74 C6
Wurzen D 79 D12
Wüstenrot D 27 B11
Wusterhausen D 83 E12
Wusterhusen D 84 B5
Wustermark D 79 A12
Wusterwitz D 79 B11
Wustrau-Altfriesack D 84 E3
Wustrow D 83 E10
Wustrow D 84 D3
Wustrow D 83 B12
Wutha D 79 E7
Wutöschingen D 27 E9
Wuustwezel B 16 F3
Wyczechy PL 85 C12
Wydminy PL 136 F5
Wye GB 15 E10
Wygoda PL 143 E7
Wygon PL 85 D9
Wyhl D 27 D8
Wyk auf Föhr D 82 A5
Wyłatowo PL 138 E4
Wylye GB 13 C11
Wymondham GB 15 B11
Wyre Piddle GB 13 A10
Wyrozęby-Konaty PL 141 F6
Wyry PL 143 F6
Wyryki-Połód PL 141 G8
Wyrzysk PL 85 D12
Wyśmierzyce PL 141 G3
Wysoka PL 85 D12
Wysoka PL 85 E8
Wysoka Kamieńska PL 85 C7
Wysokie PL 136 F6
Wysokie PL 144 B6
Wysokie Mazowieckie PL 141 E7
Wysowa PL 145 E3
Wyszanów PL 142 D5
Wyszki PL 141 E7
Wyszków PL 139 E11
Wyszogród PL 139 F9
Wyszyny PL 85 E11
Wythall GB 13 A11
Wytyczno PL 141 H8

X

Xanceda E 38 B3
Xanten D 17 E6
Xanthi GR 171 B7
Xarrë AL 168 E3
Xátiva E 56 D3
Xeraco E 56 C4
Xeresa E 56 C4
Xermade E 38 B4
Xerta E 42 F5
Xertigny F 26 D5
Xifiani GR 169 C7
Xino Nero GR 169 C6
Xinzo de Limia E 38 D4
Xirivella E 48 F4
Xirochori GR 174 D4
Xirokampi GR 174 F5
Xirokampo GR 177 E8
Xiropotamos GR 170 B6
Xixón E 39 A8
Xonrupt-Longemer F 27 D6
Xove E 38 A4
Xunqueira de Ambía E 38 D4
Xylagani GR 171 C8
Xylokastro GR 175 C6
Xyloupoli GR 169 C9

Y

Yablanitsa BG 165 C9
Yablanovo BG 167 D7
Yabluniv UA 152 A5
Yabŭlchevo BG 167 D8
Yabŭlkovo BG 166 E4
Yağci TR 173 C7
Yağcılar TR 173 F9
Yağcılı TR 173 F8
Yagoda BG 166 D5
Yakimovo BG 160 F2
Yakoruda BG 165 E8
Yakovo BG 169 A9
Yalıçiftlik TR 173 D10
Yalıkavak TR 177 E9
Yalıköy TR 173 B9
Yalova TR 171 D10
Yambol BG 167 E7
Yamkino RUS 132 F5
Yamm RUS 132 E3
Yampil' UA 154 A2
Yangi TR 181 C9
Yanguas E 41 D7
Yanıkağıl TR 173 B8
Yaniskoski RUS 114 F5
Yankavichy BY 133 E5
Yankovo BG 167 C8
Yantarnyy RUS 139 A8
Yapıldak TR 172 D6
Yaraş TR 181 B8
Yareva BY 135 F13
Yarlovo BG 165 E7
Yarm GB 11 B9
Yarmouth GB 13 D12
Yarnton GB 13 B12
Yarove UA 154 E4
Yarrow GB 5 D10
Yasen BG 165 C10
Yasen' UA 145 F9
Yasenkovo BG 167 B7
Yasenovets BG 161 F9
Yasinya UA 152 A4
Yas'ky UA 154 D6
Yasna Polyana BG 167 E9
Yasnoye RUS 134 F3
Yassıören TR 173 B10
Yasski RUS 132 F7
Yatağan TR 181 B8
Yate GB 13 B10
Yatova E 48 F3
Yatton GB 13 C9
Yavora UA 145 E7
Yavoriv UA 144 D7
Yavoriv UA 152 A5
Yaxley GB 11 F11
Yaylagöne TR 172 C6
Yazıbaşı TR 177 C9
Yazıköy TR 181 C6
Yazna BY 133 F4
Yazvina BY 133 F7
Ybbs an der Donau A 77 F8
Ybbsitz A 77 G7
Ychoux F 32 B4
Ydby DK 86 B2
Ydes F 29 E10
Ydra GR 175 E7
Ydrefors S 92 D7
Y Drenewydd GB 10 F5
Yeadon GB 11 D8
Yealmpton GB 12 E7
Yebra E 47 D7
Yebra de Basa E 32 F5
Yecla E 56 D2
Yecla de Yeltes E 45 C8
Yedy BY 133 F2
Yémeda E 47 E9
Yemişendere TR 181 B9
Yenice TR 171 C10
Yenice TR 173 D7
Yenice TR 173 D9
Yenice TR 181 B8
Yeniçiftlik TR 173 B8
Yeniçiftlik TR 173 D7
Yeniçiftlik TR 177 C9
Yenifoça TR 177 B8
Yenihisar TR 177 E9
Yeniköy TR 172 D6
Yeniköy TR 173 B6
Yeniköy TR 173 E8
Yeniköy TR 177 B9
Yeniköy TR 177 B10
Yeniköy TR 177 C9
Yeniköy TR 177 D10
Yeniköy TR 177 E9
Yeniköy TR 181 B8
Yenimuhacirköy TR 172 C6
Yenişakran TR 177 B9
Yenne F 31 D8
Yeovil GB 13 D9
Yepes E 46 E5
Yerkesik TR 181 B8
Yerseke NL 16 F2
Yershovo RUS 132 F3
Yerville F 18 E2
Yesa E 32 E3
Yeşilsirt TR 173 B7
Yeşilyurt TR 181 B8
Yeste E 55 C8
Yevtodiya UA 154 B4
Yezyaryshcha BY 133 E7
Y Fenni GB 13 B8
Ygos-St-Saturnin F 32 C4
Ygrande F 30 B2
Ykspihlaja FIN 123 C10
Ylakiai LT 134 D3
Yläköngäs FIN 113 D17
Ylä-Luosta FIN 125 D11
Ylämaa FIN 129 D9
Ylämylly FIN 125 E13
Yläne FIN 126 D7
Ylä-Valtimo FIN 125 C11
Ylihärmä FIN 122 D9
Yli-Ii FIN 119 D15
Ylijärvi FIN 128 D8
Yli-Kärppä FIN 119 C15
Ylikiiminki FIN 119 D16
Yli-Körkkö FIN 119 B16
Ylikulma FIN 127 E9
Yli-Kurki FIN 121 D10
Ylikylä FIN 115 E2
Ylikylä FIN 117 E15
Ylikylä FIN 123 D12
Ylikylä FIN 123 E10
Ylikylä FIN 125 C12
Yli-Kyrö FIN 117 B12
Yli-Lesti FIN 123 D13
Yli-Liakka FIN 119 C12
Yli-Livo FIN 120 C9
Yli-Muonio FIN 117 B10
Yli-Nampa FIN 117 E16
Ylinenjärvi S 117 E10
Yli-Olhava FIN 119 C15
Ylipää FIN 119 E12
Ylipää FIN 119 E13
Ylipää FIN 119 E13
Ylipää FIN 119 E14
Ylipää FIN 119 E16
Ylipää FIN 119 F13
Ylipää FIN 123 C14
Ylipää FIN 123 D11
Yli-Paakkola FIN 119 B13
Yli-Siurua FIN 119 C17
Ylistaro FIN 122 E9
Yli-Tannila FIN 119 D16
Ylitornio FIN 119 B11
Yli-Utos FIN 120 E8
Yli-Valli FIN 123 F9
Ylivieska FIN 123 B13
Yli-Vuotto FIN 119 E17
Ylläsjärvi FIN 117 C12
Ylöjärvi FIN 127 B10
Ylönkylä FIN 127 E9
Ylvingen N 108 E3
Ymonville F 24 D6
Yngsjö S 88 D6
Yoğuntaş TR 167 F8
Yolageldi TR 173 A6
Yonkovo BG 161 F9
York GB 11 D9
Youghal IRL 9 E7
Yovkovo BG 155 F2
Yoxford GB 15 C12
Ypäjä FIN 127 D9
Ypäjänkylä FIN 127 D9
Ypati GR 174 B5
Yport F 18 E1
Yppäri FIN 119 F12
Ypsos GR 168 E2
Ypyä FIN 123 C13
Yrittäperä FIN 121 D10
Yrttivaara S 116 E7
Ysane S 88 C7
Ysbyty Ystwyth GB 13 A7
Yset N 101 A12
Ysselsteyn NL 183 C7
Yssingeaux F 30 E5
Ystad S 87 E13
Ystalyfera GB 13 B7
Ytre Arna N 94 B2
Ytre Årnes N 111 B15
Ytre Billefjord N 113 C15
Ytre Kjæs N 113 B16
Ytre Sandvik N 113 C15
Ytterån S 105 E16
Ytteräng S 105 D14
Ytterberg S 102 B7
Ytter-Busjö S 107 B15
Ytteresse FIN 123 C9
Ytterhogdal S 102 B8
Ytterjeppo FIN 122 D9
Yttermalung S 102 E6
Yttersta S 118 D6
Ytterträsk S 118 F4
Ytterturingen S 103 B9
Yttervik S 109 E10
Yttre Lansjärv S 116 E8
Yukaribey TR 177 A9
Yukarıkızılca TR 177 C9
Yukhavichy BY 133 D5
Yuncler E 46 D5
Yuncos E 46 D5
Yundola BG 165 E8
Yunquera E 53 C7
Yunquera de Henares E 47 C6
Yuper BG 161 F8
Yuratsishki BY 137 E12
Yuravichy BY 133 E5
Yürücekler TR 173 E10
Yürük TR 173 C7
Yutz F 20 F6
Yuzhnyy RUS 136 D2
Yverdon CH 31 B10
Yvetot F 18 E2
Yvignac F 23 D7
Yvoir B 19 D10
Yvoire F 31 C9
Yvonand CH 31 B10
Yxnerum S 93 C8
Yxsjö S 107 C13
Yxsjöberg S 97 B12
Yxskaftkälen S 106 D8
Yzeure F 30 B3
Yzeures-sur-Creuse F 29 B7

Z

Zaamslag NL 182 C3
Zaandam NL 16 D3
Zaazyer"ye BY 133 F5
Zăbala RO 153 F8
Žabalj SRB 158 C5
Žabari SRB 159 E7
Zabeltitz-Treugeböhla D 80 D5
Żabia Wola PL 141 F3
Zabica BIH 162 D5
Zabiče SLO 67 A9
Zabiele PL 139 D12
Zabierzów PL 143 F8
Ząbki PL 141 F4
Ząbkowice Śląskie PL 81 E11
Zablaće SRB 158 D4
Zablaće SRB 158 F5
Zableće BIH 157 D6
Žabljak MNE 163 C7
Zabłudów PL 140 D8
Žabno HR 149 E7
Żabno PL 143 F10
Żabno PL 144 B6
Zabok HR 148 D5
Žabokreky SK 147 C7
Žabokreky nad Nitrou SK 146 D6
Zabolova LV 133 A2
Zabór PL 81 C9
Zabor"ye BY 133 E6
Żabów PL 85 D7
Żabowo PL 85 C8
Zăbrani RO 151 E8
Zabrđe BIH 157 C10
Zábřeh CZ 77 C11
Zăbriceni MD 153 A10
Zabrze PL 142 F6
Zabŭrdo BG 165 F10
Zabuzhzhya UA 141 H9
Zacharo GR 174 E4
Zaclău RO 155 C2
Žacléř CZ 81 E9
Zaczopki PL 141 F8
Zadar HR 156 D3
Zadunayivka UA 154 F4
Zádveřice CZ 146 C5
Zadzim PL 142 C6
Zadzyezhzha BY 133 E4
Zafarraya E 53 C8
Zafferana Etnea I 59 D7
Zafirovo BG 161 F9
Zafra E 51 C7
Zafra de Záncara E 47 E7
Zafrilla E 47 D9
Žaga SLO 73 D7
Żagań PL 81 C8
Zagăr RO 152 E5
Zagarë LT 134 D6
Zagarise I 59 A10
Zagkliveri GR 169 C9
Žaglav HR 67 E11
Zagnańsk PL 143 E10
Zagon RO 153 F8
Zagora GR 169 F9
Zagorë AL 163 E8
Zagorje SLO 73 E9
Zagorje ob Savi SLO 73 D10
Zagórów PL 142 B4
Zagortsi BG 167 E8
Zagórz PL 145 D5
Zagra E 53 B8
Zagra RO 152 C4
Zagrazhden BG 160 F5
Zagrazhden BG 166 F3
Zagreb HR 148 E5
Zagrodno PL 81 D9
Žagrović HR 156 D5
Žagubica SRB 159 E8
Zagvodz HR 157 F7
Zagyvarékas H 150 C5
Zahara E 51 F9
Zahara de los Atunes E 52 D5
Zahinos E 51 C6
Zahna D 79 C12
Zahnitkiv UA 154 A3
Záhony H 145 G5
Záhorská Ves SK 77 F11
Zahor"ye BY 133 F5
Zăicani MD 153 B10
Zaiceva LV 133 B2
Zaidín E 42 D4
Žaiginys LT 134 F6
Zaim MD 154 D4
Zajas NMK 168 A4
Zaječar SRB 159 F9
Zaječí CZ 77 E11
Zaječov CZ 76 C5
Zajezierze PL 85 C9
Zákamenné SK 147 C8
Zákány H 149 D7
Zákányszek H 150 E4
Zakharnichy BY 133 E5
Zakliczyn PL 144 D2
Zaklików PL 144 B5
Zaklopača BIH 157 D11
Zakoma BIH 157 E10
Zakopane PL 147 C9
Zakros GR 179 E11
Zakrzew PL 141 H4
Zakrzewo PL 85 D12
Zakrzewo PL 138 E6
Zakrzówek-Wieś PL 144 B5
Zákupy CZ 81 E7
Zakynthos GR 174 D2
Zalaapáti H 149 C8
Zalaegerszeg H 149 C7
Zalakaros H 149 C8
Zalakomár H 149 C8
Zalalövő H 149 C7
Zalamea de la Serena E 51 B8
Zalamea la Real E 51 D6
Zalaszántó H 149 C8
Zalaszentbalázs H 149 C7
Zalaszentgrót H 149 C8
Zalaszentiván H 149 C7
Zalău RO 151 C11
Zalavár H 149 C8
Zalavas LT 137 D13
Załazy PL 141 H5
Zaldibar E 41 B6
Žalec SLO 73 D11
Zalenieki LV 134 C7
Zalesie PL 85 E13
Zalesie PL 141 F8
Zalesie Śląskie PL 142 F5
Zalesje LV 133 D4
Zales'ye RUS 136 D4
Zaleszany PL 144 B4
Zalewo PL 139 C8
Zalha RO 152 C3
Zālīte LV 135 C8
Zalivnoye RUS 136 D2
Zall-Dardhë AL 163 F9
Żalno PL 138 C4
Zalogovac SRB 159 F7
Zaltbommel NL 16 E4
Załuski PL 139 E10
Zalužje BIH 158 E3
Zalužnica HR 156 C3
Zalve LV 135 D10
Zalyessye BY 133 F3
Zalyessye BY 137 E13
Zam RO 151 E9
Zamárdi H 149 C9
Zamarte PL 85 C12
Žamberk CZ 77 B10
Zambrana E 40 C6
Zâmbreasca RO 160 E6
Zambrów PL 140 E6
Zambujal de Cima P 50 C1
Zambujeira do Mar P 50 D2
Zamęcin PL 85 D8
Zamfirovo BG 165 C7
Zamogil'ye RUS 132 D2
Zámoly H 149 B10
Zamora E 39 E8
Zamość PL 139 D12
Zamość PL 144 B7
Zamoshsha BY 133 F2
Zamostea RO 153 B8
Zams A 71 C11
Zámutov SK 145 F4
Zandhoven B 19 B10
Žandov CZ 80 E6
Zandvliet B 16 F2
Zandvoort NL 16 D3
Zănești RO 153 D9
Zaniemyśl PL 81 B12
Zante LV 134 C5
Zaorejas E 47 C8
Zaovine SRB 158 F3
Zapałów PL 144 C6
Zaplanik BIH 162 D5
Zaplyus'ye RUS 132 E6
Zăpodeni RO 153 D11
Zapolice PL 142 C6
Zapolyarnyy RUS 114 E9
Zapol'ye RUS 132 E6
Zaporozhskoye RUS 129 D14
Zappeio GR 169 F7
Zapponeta I 60 A5
Zaprešić HR 148 E5
Zapruddzye BY 133 F3
Zapytiv UA 144 D9
Zaragoza E 41 E10
Zărand RO 151 E8
Zarańsko PL 85 C9
Zarasai LT 135 E12
Zaratamo E 40 B6
Zaratán E 39 E10
Zarautz E 32 D1
Zarcilla de Ramos E 55 D9
Zaręby PL 139 D11
Zaręby-Kościelne PL 139 E13
Zarechcha BY 133 E7
Žarėnai LT 134 E4
Zaricheve UA 145 F6
Żarki PL 143 E7
Żarki Wielkie PL 81 C7
Zărnești RO 160 B6
Zărnești RO 161 C9
Žarnovica SK 147 D7
Żarnów PL 141 H2
Żarnowiec PL 143 F8
Zaronava BY 133 F7
Zaros GR 178 E8
Žarošice CZ 77 D11
Żarów PL 81 E10
Zarpen D 83 C9
Zarra E 47 F10
Zarren B 182 C1
Zarrentin D 83 C9
Zarszyn PL 145 D5
Żary PL 81 C8
Zarza Capilla E 51 B9
Zarza de Alange E 51 B7
Zarza de Granadilla E 45 D8
Zarza de Tajo E 47 D6
Zarzadilla de Totana E 55 D9
Zarza la Mayor E 45 E7
Zarzecze PL 144 D6
Zarzuela del Monte E 46 C4
Zarzuela del Pinar E 40 F3
Zas E 38 B2
Zasa LV 135 D11
Zaskarki BY 133 F5
Zaškov SK 147 C8
Žasliai LT 137 D10
Zásmuky CZ 77 C8
Zasów PL 143 F11
Zastražišće HR 157 F6
Žatec CZ 76 B5
Zaton HR 156 E4
Zaton HR 162 D5
Zátor CZ 142 F4
Zator PL 143 G7
Zatory PL 139 E11
Zătreni RO 160 D3
Zatyshshya UA 154 C5
Zaube LV 135 C10
Zau de Câmpie RO 152 D4
Zavadka UA 145 E7
Zavadka nad Hronom SK 147 D9
Zavala BIH 162 D4
Zavala HR 157 F6
Zavalje BIH 156 C4
Zavallya UA 153 A7
Zavallya UA 154 A6
Zavattarello I 37 B10

Závažná Poruba SK 147 C9
Zaventem B 19 C9
Zavet BG 161 F9
Zavidovići BIH 157 D9
Zavlaka SRB 158 E3
Závoaia RO 161 D10
Závod SK 77 E12
Závoi RO 159 B9
Zavoj SRB 165 C6
Zavutstsye BY 133 F4
Zavyachellye BY 133 F5
Zavydovychi UA 144 D8
Zawada PL 81 C9
Zawada PL 141 G1
Zawada PL 142 E4
Zawada PL 143 E7
Zawada PL 144 B7
Zawady PL 140 D7
Zawadzkie PL 142 E5
Zawichost PL 144 B4
Zawidów PL 81 D8
Zawidz Kościelny PL 139 E8
Zawiercie PL 143 F7
Zawoja PL 147 B9
Zawonia PL 81 D12
Zaytsevo RUS 132 F4
Žažina HR 148 E6
Zázrivá SK 147 C8
Žažvić HR 156 E4
Zbąszyn PL 81 B9
Zbąszynek PL 81 B9
Zbehy SK 146 E6
Zberoaia MD 153 D12
Zbiczno PL 139 D7
Zbiersk PL 142 C5
Zbiroh CZ 76 C5
Zblewo PL 138 C5
Zbludowice PL 143 F10
Zbójna PL 139 D12
Zbójno PL 139 D7
Zborov SK 145 E3
Zborovice CZ 146 C4
Zborov nad Bystricou SK 147 C7
Zbraslav CZ 77 D10
Zbraslavice CZ 77 C8
Zbrzeźnica PL 140 D6
Zbuczyn Poduchowny PL 141 F6
Ždala HR 149 D8
Ždánice CZ 77 D12
Žďár CZ 77 A8
Žďár nad Sázavou CZ 77 C9
Zdenci HR 149 E9
Ždiar SK 145 E1
Zdice CZ 76 C5
Zdihovo HR 67 B11
Zdíkov CZ 76 D5
Zdírec nad Doubravou CZ 77 C9
Zdounky CZ 146 C4
Ždralovac BIH 157 E6
Zdravets BG 167 C9
Zdravinje SRB 164 C3
Ždrelac HR 156 D3
Ždrelo SRB 159 E8
Zdunje NMK 164 F3
Zduńska Wola PL 143 C6
Zduny PL 81 C12
Zduny PL 141 F1
Zdynia PL 145 E3
Zdziarzec PL 143 F11
Zdziechowa PL 85 E13
Zdzieszowice PL 142 F5
Zdziłowice PL 144 B6
Zębowice PL 142 E5
Žebrák CZ 76 C5
Zebreira P 45 E6
Zebrene LV 134 C5
Zebrzydowa PL 81 D8
Zechlinerhütte D 84 D3
Zeddam NL 183 B8
Zeddiani I 64 D2
Zedelgem B 19 B7
Zederhaus A 73 B8
Žednik SRB 150 F4
Zędowice PL 142 E6
Zeebrugge B 19 B7
Zeeland NL 16 E5
Zeewolde NL 183 A7
Zegama E 32 E1
Żegiestów PL 145 E2
Žegljane NMK 164 E4
Żegocina PL 144 D1
Zehdenick D 84 E4
Zehna D 83 C12
Žehra SK 145 F2
Zehren D 80 D4
Zeilarn D 76 F3
Žeimelis LT 135 D8
Žeimiai LT 135 F8
Zeiselmauer A 77 F10
Zeiskam D 187 C5
Zeist NL 16 D4
Zeithain D 80 D4
Zeitlofs D 74 B6
Zeitz D 79 D11
Zejmen AL 163 F8
Żelazków PL 142 C5
Zele B 19 B9
Żelechlinek PL 141 G2
Żelechów PL 141 G5
Zelena UA 152 A5
Zelena UA 152 B5
Zelena UA 153 A9
Zeleneč SK 146 E5
Zeleni Jadar BIH 158 E3
Zelenikovo BG 166 E4
Zelenikovo NMK 164 F4
Zelenogorsk RUS 129 E12
Zelenogradsk RUS 136 D1
Zelenohirs'ke UA 154 B6
Želetava CZ 77 D9
Železná Ruda CZ 76 D4
Železné SK 147 D8
Železnice CZ 77 B8
Železniki SLO 73 D9
Železný Brod CZ 81 E8
Zelhem NL 16 D6
Želiezovce SK 147 E7
Zelina HR 148 E6
Zelinja BIH 157 C9
Želino NMK 164 F3
Želiv CZ 77 C8
Željuša BIH 157 F8
Zelków-Kolonia PL 141 F6
Zell D 75 B10
Zell (Mosel) D 21 D8
Zella-Mehlis D 79 E8
Zell am Harmersbach D 27 D9
Zell am Main D 187 B8
Zell am See A 73 B6
Zell am Ziller A 72 B4
Zell im Wiesental D 27 E8
Zellingen D 74 C6
Zell-Pfarre A 73 D9
Zelmeņi LV 134 D6
Želovce SK 147 E8
Zelów PL 143 D7
Zeltingen-Rachtig D 21 E8
Zeltiņi LV 135 B13
Zeltweg A 73 B10
Želva LT 135 F10
Zelzate B 19 B8
Žemaičių Naumiestis LT 134 F3
Žemberovce SK 147 E7
Zemblak AL 168 C4
Zembrów PL 141 E6
Zembrzyce PL 147 B9
Zemen BG 165 E6
Zemeno GR 175 C6
Zemeș RO 153 D8
Zemianska Oľča SK 146 F5
Zemīte LV 134 C5
Zemitz D 84 C5
Zemmer D 21 E7
Zemné SK 146 F6
Zemplénagárd H 145 G5
Zemplínske Hámre SK 145 F5
Zemst B 19 C9
Zemun SRB 158 D5
Zenica BIH 157 D8
Zennor GB 12 E3
Zentene LV 134 B5
Žepa BIH 157 E11
Žepče BIH 157 D9
Žeravice CZ 146 C4
Zerbst D 79 C11
Zerf D 21 E7
Zerind RO 151 D8
Żerków PL 142 B4
Zernez CH 71 D10
Zernien D 83 D9
Zernitz D 83 E12
Zero Branco I 72 E5
Zerpenschleuse D 84 E5
Zerrenthin D 84 D6
Zestoa E 32 D1
Žetale SLO 148 D5
Zetea RO 152 E6
Zetel D 17 B9
Zet'ovo BG 166 E4
Zeulenroda D 79 E10
Zeven D 17 B12
Zevenaar NL 16 E6
Zevenbergen NL 16 E3
Zevgolatio GR 175 D6
Zevio I 66 B3
Zeytinalani TR 181 C9
Zeytinbağı TR 173 D10
Zeytindağ TR 177 B9
Zeytineli TR 177 C8
Zeytinli TR 173 E6
Zeytinliova TR 177 B10
Zgierz PL 143 C7
Zgłobice PL 143 G10
Zgornje Bitnje SLO 73 D9
Zgornje Jezersko SLO 73 D9
Zgornji Duplek SLO 148 C5
Zgorzelec PL 81 D8
Zgropolci NMK 169 A6
Zgurița MD 153 A11
Zhabinka BY 141 F10
Zhabokrychka UA 154 A3
Zhdeniyevo UA 145 F7
Zhegër RKS 164 E3
Zheleznodorozhnyy RUS 136 E3
Zhelyazkovo BG 167 E8
Zhelyu Voyvoda BG 167 D6
Zheravna BG 167 D6
Zhilino RUS 136 D4
Zhitkovo RUS 129 D11
Zhitnitsa BG 167 C9
Zhitom AL 168 C2
Zhodzishki BY 137 D13
Zhorany UA 141 H9
Zhovkva UA 144 C8
Zhovtantsi UA 144 D9
Zhovtneve UA 144 B9
Zhovtneve UA 155 B3
Zhovtyy Yar UA 154 F5
Zhuprany BY 137 E13
Zhur RKS 164 E2
Zhvyrka UA 144 C9
Zhydachiv UA 145 E9
Zhyrmuny BY 137 E11
Žiar nad Hronom SK 147 D7
Zibalai LT 137 C10
Zibello I 66 B1
Zibreira P 44 F3
Zicavo F 37 H10
Žichovice CZ 76 D5
Zickhusen D 83 C10
Zidani Most SLO 73 D11
Zidarovo BG 167 E8
Židikai LT 134 D4
Židlochovice CZ 77 D11
Ziduri RO 161 C10
Ziębice PL 81 E12
Ziedkalne LV 134 D6
Ziegelroda D 79 D9
Ziegendorf D 83 D11
Ziegenrück D 79 E10
Ziegra D 80 D4
Zieleniewo PL 85 B9
Zieleniewo PL 85 D9
Zielitz D 79 B10
Zielkowice PL 141 F2
Zielona PL 139 D8
Zielona Chocina PL 85 C12
Zielona Góra PL 81 C9
Zielona Góra PL 85 E11
Zielonka PL 139 F11
Zielonki PL 143 F8
Zieluń PL 139 D8
Ziemeri LV 131 F14
Ziemnice Wielkie PL 142 E4
Ziemupe LV 134 C2
Zierenberg D 17 F12
Zierikzee NL 16 E1
Ziersdorf A 77 E9
Zierzow D 83 D11
Ziesar D 79 B11
Žiežmariai LT 137 D9
Žigljen HR 67 C10
Zīguri LV 133 B3
Žihárec SK 146 E5
Žihle CZ 76 B4
Zilaiskalns LV 131 F10
Žilina SK 147 C7
Žilinai LT 137 E10
Zillis CH 71 D8
Ziltendorf D 81 B7
Zilupe LV 133 D4
Zimandu Nou RO 151 E7
Zimbor RO 151 C11
Zimmersrode (Neuental) D 21 B12
Zimnicea RO 160 F6
Zimnitsa BG 167 D7
Žindaičiai LT 134 F5
Zingst D 83 B13
Zinkgruvan S 92 B6
Zinnowitz D 84 B5
Ziras LV 134 B3
Zirc H 149 B9
Zirchow D 84 C6
Žiri SLO 73 D9
Zirndorf D 75 D8
Zîrnești MD 154 E2
Zirņi LV 134 C4
Zirós GR 179 E11
Žirovnice CZ 77 D8
Zistersdorf A 77 E11
Žitište SRB 158 C6
Žitkovac SRB 164 B4
Žitni Potok SRB 164 C4
Žitomislići BIH 157 F8
Žitorađa SRB 164 C4
Žitoše NMK 168 B5
Zitsa GR 168 E4
Zittau D 81 E7
Zitz D 79 B11
Živaja HR 157 B6
Živinice BIH 157 D10
Živogošće HR 157 F7
Žiželice CZ 77 B8
Zizers CH 71 D9
Zizurkil E 32 D1
Zlarin HR 156 E4
Zlata SRB 164 C4
Zlatar BG 167 C7
Zlatar HR 148 D6
Zlatar-Bistrica HR 148 D6
Zlataritsa BG 166 C5
Zlaté Hory CZ 142 F3
Zlaté Klasy SK 146 E4
Zlaté Moravce SK 146 E6
Zlaten Rog BG 159 E10
Zlatitsa BG 165 D9
Zlatna RO 151 E11
Zlatna Panega BG 165 C9
Zlatograd BG 171 B8
Zlatokop SRB 164 D4
Zławieś Wielka PL 138 D5
Žlebič SLO 73 E10
Žleby CZ 77 C8
Zlēkas LV 134 B3
Zletovo NMK 164 F5
Žlibinai LT 134 E4
Zlín CZ 146 C5
Zliv CZ 76 D6
Žljebovi BIH 157 D10
Zllakuqan RKS 164 D2
Złocieniec PL 85 C10
Złoczew PL 142 D6
Zlokuchene BG 165 E8
Zlonice CZ 76 B6
Złota PL 141 G2
Złota PL 143 F10
Złotniki Kujawskie PL 138 E5
Złotoryja PL 81 D9
Złotów PL 85 D12
Złoty Stok PL 77 B11
Zlozela BIH 157 D7
Žlutice CZ 76 B4
Zmajevac BIH 156 C5
Zmajevac HR 149 E11
Zmajevo SRB 158 C4
Zmeyovo BG 166 E5
Żmigród PL 81 D11
Zmijavci HR 157 F7
Žminj HR 67 B8
Żmudź PL 144 A8
Znamensk RUS 136 D3
Żnin PL 138 E4
Znojmo CZ 77 E10
Zoagli I 37 C10
Zöblitz D 80 E4
Zoelen NL 183 B6
Zoersel B 16 F3
Zoetermeer NL 16 D2
Zofingen CH 27 F8
Zogno I 69 B8
Zografou GR 175 D8
Zola Predosa I 66 C3
Zolder B 19 B11
Zoldo Alto I 72 D5
Żółkiewka-Osada PL 144 B6
Zölkow D 83 C11
Zollikofen CH 31 A11
Zollikon CH 27 F10
Zolotkovychi UA 144 D6
Żółtnica PL 85 C11
Żołynia PL 144 C5
Zomba H 149 D11
Zomergem B 19 B8
Zonhoven B 19 C11
Zoni GR 171 A10
Zoniana GR 178 E8
Zonnebeke B 18 C6
Zonza F 37 H10
Żórawina PL 81 E12
Zörbig D 79 C11
Zorita E 45 F9
Zorita del Maestrazgo E 42 F3
Zorleni RO 153 E11
Zorlențu Mare RO 159 C8
Zorneding D 75 F10
Zornheim D 21 E10
Zörnigal D 79 C12
Zornitsa BG 167 C9
Zornitsa BG 167 E7
Żory PL 142 F6
Zossen D 80 B4
Zottegem B 19 C8
Zoutkamp NL 16 B6
Zoutleeuw B 183 D6
Zovi Do BIH 157 F9
Zovka RUS 132 E4
Zreče SLO 148 D4
Zrenjanin SRB 158 C5
Zrin HR 156 B5
Zrinski Topolovac HR 149 D7
Zrmanja Vrelo HR 156 D5
Zrnovci NMK 164 F5
Zruč CZ 76 C4
Zruč nad Sázavou CZ 77 C8
Zsadány H 151 D7
Zsáka H 151 C7
Zsámbék H 149 A11
Zsámbok H 150 B4
Zsana H 150 E4
Zschaitz D 80 D4
Zscherben D 79 D10
Zschopau D 80 E4
Zschortau D 79 D11
Zsombó H 150 E4
Zuberec SK 147 C9
Zubia E 53 B9
Zubiaur E 40 B6
Zubiči BIH 157 D8
Zubiena I 68 C5
Zubieta E 32 D1
Zubieta E 32 D2
Zubin Potok RKS 164 D2
Zubiri E 32 E2
Zubří CZ 146 C6
Zubrohlava SK 147 C9
Zubrów PL 81 B8
Žuć SRB 164 C3
Zucaina E 48 D4
Zuchwil CH 27 F8
Zudaire E 32 E1
Zudar D 84 B4
Zuera E 41 E10
Zufre E 51 D7
Zug CH 27 F10
Zuhatzu-Kuartango E 40 C6
Zuheros E 53 A8
Zuid-Beijerland NL 182 B4
Zuidhorn NL 16 B6
Zuidland NL 182 B4
Zuidlaren NL 17 B7
Zuidwolde NL 17 C6
Zuienkerke B 182 C2
Zújar E 55 D7
Żuków PL 141 F2
Żuków PL 141 G8
Żukowice PL 81 C9
Żukowo PL 138 B5
Žuljana HR 162 D3
Žulová CZ 77 B12
Zülpich D 21 C7
Zulte B 19 C7
Zumaia E 32 D1
Zumarraga E 32 D1
Zundert NL 16 F3
Zungri I 59 B8
Zunzarren E 32 E3
Zuoz CH 71 D9
Županja HR 157 B10
Zūras LV 134 B3
Zúrgena E 55 E8
Zürich CH 27 F10
Zurndorf A 77 G12
Zŭrnevo BG 161 F10
Żuromin PL 139 D8
Zurow D 83 C11
Zusmarshausen D 75 F8
Züsow D 83 C11
Züssow D 84 C5
Žuta Lokva HR 67 C11
Žutautai LT 134 E2
Zutendaal B 19 C12
Zutphen NL 16 D6
Žužemberk SLO 73 E10
Zveçan RKS 164 D2
Zvejniekciems LV 135 B8
Zverino BG 165 C8
Zvezdë AL 168 C4
Zvezdel BG 171 B8
Zvezdets BG 167 E8
Zvolen SK 147 D8
Zvolenská Slatina SK 147 D8
Zvonce SRB 164 D6
Zvoriștea RO 153 B8
Zvornik BIH 157 D11
Zwartemeer NL 17 C8
Zwartsluis NL 16 C6
Zweeloo NL 17 C7
Zweibrücken D 21 F8
Zweisimmen CH 31 B11
Zwenkau D 79 D11
Zwethau D 80 C4
Zwettl A 77 E8
Zwevegem B 19 C7
Zwevezele B 182 C2
Zwickau D 79 E12
Zwiefalten D 27 D11
Zwierzyn PL 85 E9
Zwierzyniec PL 144 B6
Zwiesel D 76 D4
Zwijndrecht B 19 B9
Zwijndrecht NL 16 E3
Zwinge D 79 C7
Zwingen CH 27 F8
Zwingenberg D 21 E11
Zwochau D 79 D11
Zwoleń PL 141 H5
Zwolle NL 16 C6
Zwönitz D 79 E12
Zwota D 75 B11
Zyabki BY 133 F4
Zyal'ki BY 133 E4
Zyalyonka BY 133 E5
Żychlin PL 143 B8
Żydowo PL 85 B11
Żydowo PL 85 F13
Žygaičiai LT 134 F4
Zygos GR 171 B6
Zygry PL 143 C6
Žyniai LT 134 F2
Żyraków PL 143 F11
Żyrardów PL 141 F2
Żyrzyn PL 141 H6
Żytkiejmy PL 136 E6
Żytniów PL 142 D6
Żytno PL 143 E8
Żywiec PL 147 B8
Żywocice PL 142 F4

Æ

Ærøskøbing DK 86 F6

Ø

Ødis DK 86 E4
Ødsted DK 86 D4
Øie N 105 B12
Økdal N 101 A12
Øksfjord N 112 C9
Øksnes N 110 C8
Øksneshamn N 110 D9
Ølen N 94 C3
Ølgod DK 86 D3
Ølholm DK 86 D5
Ølsted DK 86 D5
Ølsted DK 87 D10
Ølstykke DK 87 D10
Ønslev DK 83 A11
Øra N 112 C8
Ørbæk DK 86 E7
Ørgenvika N 95 B11
Ørjavik N 104 F2
Ørje N 96 D6
Ørnes N 108 C6
Ørnhøj DK 86 C3
Ørslev DK 87 E9
Ørsnes N 100 A5
Ørsta N 100 B4
Ørsted DK 86 C6
Ørting DK 86 D6
Ørum DK 86 C5
Ørum DK 86 C7
Øsby DK 86 E5
Østbirk DK 86 D5
Østby N 91 A9
Østby N 102 D4
Østengård DK 86 D4
Øster Assels DK 86 B3
Øster Bjerregrav DK 86 C5
Øster Brønderslev DK 86 A5
Østerby DK 86 A5
Øster Hornum DK 86 B5
Øster Hurup DK 86 B6
Øster Højst DK 86 E4
Østerild DK 86 A3
Øster Jølby DK 86 B3
Østerlars DK 89 E7
Øster Lindet DK 86 E4
Østermarie DK 89 E8
Øster Tørslev DK 86 B6
Øster Ulslev DK 83 A11
Øster Vedsted DK 86 E3
Østervrå DK 90 E7
Øster Vrøgum DK 86 D2
Østese N 94 B4
Østrup DK 86 B4
Øverbygd N 111 C17
Øvergard N 111 B18
Øvre Alta N 113 D11
Øvre Kildal N 112 D7
Øvrella N 95 C10
Øvre Rendal N 101 C14
Øvre Årdal N 100 D7
Øvre Åstbru N 101 D13
Øyangen N 104 E7
Øydegarden N 104 E4
Øyenkilen N 91 A8
Øyer N 101 D12
Øyeren N 96 B7
Øyjord N 108 B9
Øynes N 108 B9
Øynes N 111 C11
Øyslebø N 90 C2
Øyvatnet N 111 C12

Å

Å N 104 F7
Å N 110 E4
Å N 111 B12
Å N 111 C13
Åberget S 109 E18
Åbo S 103 C10
Åbodarna S 107 E14
Åbogen N 96 B7
Åbosjö S 107 D13
Åby S 89 A7
Åby S 93 B8
Åbyen DK 90 D7
Åbyggeby S 103 E13
Åbyn S 118 D6
Åbytorp S 92 A6
Ådalsliden S 107 E11
Ådum DK 86 D3
Åfarnes N 100 A7
Åfjord N 104 D8
Åfoss N 90 A6
Ågerup DK 87 D10
Ågotnes N 94 B2
Ågskaret N 108 C5
Åheim N 100 B3
Åhus S 88 D6
Åkarp S 87 D12
Åkerbränna S 107 D11
Åkerby S 99 B9
Åkerholmen S 118 C6
Åkersberga S 99 D10
Åkers styckebruk S 98 D8
Åkerstrømmen N 101 C14
Åknes N 110 C9
Åkran N 105 D12
Åkrehamn N 94 D2
Åkullsjön S 118 F5
Åkvisslan S 107 E13
Ål N 101 E9
Ålberga S 93 B9
Ålbo S 98 B7
Ålbæk DK 90 D7
Åle DK 86 D5
Åled S 87 B11
Ålem S 89 B10
Ålen N 101 A14
Ålesund N 100 B4
Ålgnäs S 103 D12
Ålgård N 94 E3
Ålhult S 92 D7
Ålloluokta S 109 B17
Ålmo N 104 E4
Ålsrode DK 87 C7
Ålstad N 110 E9
Ålund S 118 D6
Ålvik N 94 B4
Ålvund N 101 A9
Ålvundeid N 101 A9
Ålåsen S 106 D7
Åmdals Verk N 95 D8
Åminne FIN 122 E7
Åminne S 87 A14
Åmland N 94 F5
Åmli N 90 A3
Åmli N 90 B3
Åmmeberg S 92 B6
Åmot N 94 C7
Åmot N 95 B11
Åmot N 95 C8
Åmot N 95 C11
Åmot S 103 E11
Åmotfors S 96 C7
Åmsele S 107 B16
Åmsosen N 94 D3
Åmynnet S 107 E15
Åmål S 91 A12
Åmål S 91 B12
Åmøyhamn N 108 C5
Åna-Sira N 94 F4
Åndalsnes N 100 A7
Åneby N 95 B13
Ånes N 104 E4
Ånge S 103 A10
Ånge S 109 E14
Ångelsberg S 97 C15
Ångersjö S 102 C8
Ånn S 105 E13
Ånstad N 110 C8
Ånsvik N 109 B9
Ånäset S 118 F6
Årbostad N 111 C13
Årby DK 87 D8
Årbyn S 118 C8
Årdal N 100 C4
Årdalstangen N 100 D7
Åre S 105 E14
Årfor N 105 B11
Årgård N 105 C10
Århult S 89 A10
Årjäng S 96 D7
Årnes N 95 B14
Årnes N 104 F5
Årnes N 111 B15
Årnäs S 91 B14
Åros N 95 C12
Årosjåkk S 111 E17
Årre DK 86 D3
Årrenjarka S 109 C15
Årsandøy N 105 A12
Årsdale DK 89 E8
Årset N 105 A11
Årslev DK 86 E6
Årstein N 111 C14
Årsunda S 98 A7
Årvik N 100 B3
Årviksand N 112 C6
Årvågen N 104 E5
Åryd S 89 B7
Åryd S 89 C8
Årøybukta N 111 A19
Årøysund N 90 A7
Ås N 95 C13
Ås N 105 E11
Ås S 96 C7
Ås S 97 C12
Ås S 106 E7
Ås S 107 E11
Åsa N 95 B12
Åsa S 91 E11
Åsan N 105 B12
Åsarna S 102 A7
Åsby S 87 A10
Åse N 111 B10
Åsebyn S 96 D7
Åseda S 89 A8
Åsegg N 105 C9
Åsele S 107 C12
Åselet S 118 D4
Åsen N 105 D10
Åsen S 102 C7
Åsen S 102 D6
Åsen S 106 E7
Åsen S 109 E16
Åsenbruk S 91 B11
Åseral N 90 B1
Åshammar S 103 E12
Åskilje S 107 B13
Åskogen S 118 C7
Åsli N 101 E11
Åsljunga S 87 C12
Åsmansbo S 97 B13
Åsmarka N 101 D13
Åsskard N 104 E5
Åsta N 101 D14
Åstan N 104 E7
Åsteby S 97 B9
Åstorp S 87 C11
Åstrand S 97 B9
Återvänningen S 103 A13
Åtorp S 92 A4
Åträsk S 118 B7
Åträsk S 118 D5
Åttonträsk S 107 C14
Åtvidaberg S 92 C7
Åva FIN 126 E5
Åvestbo S 97 C14
Åvist FIN 122 D9

Ä

Äetsä FIN 126 C8
Ähtäri FIN 123 E12
Ähtärinranta FIN 123 E12
Äijäjoki FIN 116 B10
Äijälä FIN 123 E16
Äkäsjokisuu FIN 117 D11
Äkäslompolo FIN 117 C12
Älandsbro S 103 A14
Älgarås S 92 B4
Älgered S 103 B12
Älghult S 89 A9
Älmestad S 91 D13
Älmhult S 88 B6
Älmsta S 99 C11
Älta S 99 D10
Älvdalen S 102 D7
Älvho S 102 D8
Älvkarleby S 103 E13
Älvkarleö S 99 A8
Älvros S 102 B8
Älvsbyn S 118 C6
Älvsered S 87 A11
Älvängen S 91 D11
Ämmälänkylä FIN 123 E9
Ämmänsaari FIN 121 E12
Ämådalen S 102 D8
Äng S 92 D5
Änge S 105 E16
Ängebo S 103 C11
Ängelholm S 87 C11
Ängersjö S 122 C3
Ängeslevä FIN 119 E15
Ängesträsk S 118 B8
Ängesån S 116 E8
Ängom S 103 B13
Äppelbo S 97 B11
Ärla S 98 D7
Ärnäs S 102 D5
Ärnäs S 102 E5
Ärtled S 103 E9
Ärtrik S 107 E11
Äsarp S 91 C14
Äsbacka S 103 D11
Äsköping S 92 A8
Ässjö S 103 B12
Ätran S 87 A11
Äyskoski FIN 123 D17
Äystö FIN 122 F7
Äänekoski FIN 123 E15

Ö

Öckerö S 91 D10
Ödeborg S 91 B10
Ödeshog S 92 C5
Ödkarby FIN 99 B13
Ödsmål S 91 C10
Ödåkra S 87 C11
Öja FIN 123 C9
Öja S 93 E12
Öjarn S 106 D8
Öje S 102 E6
Öjebyn S 118 D6
Öjeforsen S 103 B9
Öjingsvallen S 103 C8
Öjung S 103 C10
Öksajärvi S 116 C8
Öllölä FIN 125 F15
Ölmbrotorp S 97 D13
Ölme S 97 D11
Ölsboda S 92 A4
Ömossa FIN 122 F7
Önnestad S 88 C6
Önningby FIN 99 B14
Öratjärn S 103 C10
Öravan S 107 B14
Öravattnet S 106 E9
Örbyhus S 99 B9
Örbäck S 97 C15
Örebro S 97 D13
Örebäcken S 102 C4
Öregrund S 99 B10
Öreström S 107 C16
Öretjändalen S 103 A10
Örkelljunga S 87 C12
Örnsköldsvik S 107 E15
Örnäsudden S 109 E13
Örsbäck S 107 D17
Örserum S 92 C5
Örsjö S 89 B9
Örsundsbro S 99 C8
Örträsk S 107 C15
Örviken S 118 E6
Ösmo S 93 B11
Östa S 98 B7
Östanfjärden S 119 C10
Östansjö S 92 A5
Östansjö S 109 E16
Östanskär S 103 A13
Östanvik S 103 D9
Östanå S 88 C6
Östavall S 103 B9
Östbjörka S 103 E9
Östby S 107 D13
Österbybruk S 99 B9
Österbymo S 92 D6
Österede S 107 E11
Österforse S 107 E12
Österfärnebo S 98 B7
Östergarn S 93 E13
Östergraninge S 107 F12
Österhankmo FIN 122 D7
Österjörn S 118 D4
Österlisa S 99 C11
Östermark FIN 126 E8
Östernoret S 107 C12
Östero FIN 122 D8
Österskucku S 102 A8
Östersund S 106 E7
Östersundom FIN 127 E13
Östervåla S 98 B8
Österås S 107 E12
Östhammar S 99 B10
Östloning S 103 A13
Östmark S 97 B8
Östmarkum S 107 E14
Östnor S 102 D7
Östra Ed S 93 C9
Östra Frölunda S 91 E13
Östra Granberg S 118 C4
Östra Grevie S 87 E12
Östra Husby S 93 B9
Östra Ljungby S 87 C12
Östra Lovsjön S 106 D7
Östra Löa S 97 C13
Östra Ormsjö S 107 C10
Östra Ryd S 93 C8
Östra Skrämträsk S 118 E5
Östra Stugusjö S 103 A9
Östra Sönnarslöv S 88 D6
Östra Vemmerlöv S 88 D6
Östra Yttermark FIN 122 E6
Östra Åliden S 118 D4
Överammer S 107 E9
Överberg S 102 B7
Överbyn S 103 C12
Överhogdal S 102 B8
Överhörnäs S 107 E15
Överissjö S 107 C13
Överkalix S 119 B9
Överlida S 91 E12
Överlännäs S 107 E13
Övermalax FIN 122 E7
Övermark FIN 122 E6
Övermorjärv S 118 B9
Övernäs S 109 D14
Överstbyn S 118 B9
Övertorneå S 119 B11
Överturingen S 102 B8
Övertänger S 103 E10
Överum S 93 D8
Överäng S 105 D14
Överö FIN 99 B15
Öv Långträsk S 109 E16
Övra S 107 D11
Övre Bredåker S 118 C6
Övre Flåsjön S 118 B7
Övre-Konäs S 105 D14
Övre Soppero S 116 B7
Övre Tväråsel S 118 C5
Övsjöbyn S 107 E9
Öxabäck S 91 E12

Collins Language Learning on the go
Collins easy learning
French Audio Course
THE EASIEST WAY TO LEARN A LANGUAGE
Collins easy learning
Greek Audio Course
THE EASIEST WAY TO LEARN A LANGUAGE
Download on the App Store
audible
an amazon company
Collins easy learning
Japanese Audio Course
THE EASIEST WAY TO LEARN A LANGUAGE
Collins easy learning
Mandarin Chinese Audio Course
THE EASIEST WAY TO LEARN A LANGUAGE
Collins easy learning
Polish Audio Course
THE EASIEST WAY TO LEARN A LANGUAGE
Collins easy learning
Spanish Audio Course
THE EASIEST WAY TO LEARN A LANGUAGE
Ideal for beginners | from £14.99 collins.co.uk/languagelearning
@collinsdictionary
facebook.com/collinsdictionary

Unlocking languages with Paul Noble
Unlocking FRENCH with Paul Noble
Unlocking SPANISH with Paul Noble
Unlocking ITALIAN with Paul Noble
Unlocking GERMAN with Paul Noble
YOUR KEY TO LANGUAGE SUCCESS
ESSENTIAL ITALIAN in 2 HOURS with Paul Noble
ESSENTIAL SPANISH in 2 HOURS with Paul Noble
ESSENTIAL MANDARIN CHINESE in 2 HOURS with Paul Noble
LEARN FRENCH with Paul Noble
Discover the Paul Noble method -
your key to language learning success
LEARN SPANISH with Paul Noble
LEARN ITALIAN with Paul Noble
LEARN GERMAN with Paul Noble
• Keeps things simple
• A fun, jargon-free way to learn
• Easy-to-understand French pronunciation
• Thousands of satisfied customers
http://books.harpercollins.co.uk/paulnoble/
books.harpercollins.co.uk